D1596158

THE DISCOURSE OF LEGITIMACY
IN EARLY MODERN ENGLAND

The Discourse of Legitimacy
in Early Modern England

ROBERT ZALLER

Stanford University Press
Stanford, California
2007

Stanford University Press
Stanford, California
© 2007 by the Board of Trustees of the
Leland Stanford Junior University.
All rights reserved.

Printed in the United States of America on acid-free, archival-
quality paper

Library of Congress Cataloging-in-Publication Data
Zaller, Robert.
The discourse of legitimacy in early modern England / Robert Zaller.
p. cm.
Includes bibliographical references and index.
ISBN 978-0-8047-5504-7 (cloth : alk. paper)
1. Legitimacy of governments — Great Britain — History — 17th century.
2. Monarchy — Great Britain — History — 17th century. 3. Great Britain —
Politics and government — 17th century. 4. Great Britain — History —
Stuarts, 1603-1714.   I. Title.
JN191.Z35 2007
320.941'09032 — dc22   2006035446

Original printing 2007

*To the memory of Richard Lee Greaves
and Philip Steven Rethis.*

Contents

Preface

This book began life under another title and with a different subject, but, as all authors know, books write themselves as they wish, and the names that appear on their title pages are only their secondary instruments. This is particularly the case with books of history, which are by their nature multivocal and transgenerational, a dialogue with the dead and a conversation with the living. In such a discourse, no word—even one as long as this is— can be the final one, but its best use is to further discussion. I hope this book will do so.

Many colleagues, institutions, and libraries have assisted me. I am grateful to the John Simon Guggenheim Foundation for the grant that enabled me to begin my initial research, to the University of Miami and Drexel University for sabbatical leaves that furthered it, and to Dean Donna Murasko of Drexel's College of Arts and Sciences for a timely subvention. Conrad Russell, John Morrill, and Peter Lake kindly permitted me to try out ideas in their seminars, as did Linda Levy Peck at the Folger Institute. These colleagues have all stimulated my own thinking, as subsequent pages will attest. Maija Jansson of the Yale Center for Parliamentary History provided help and encouragement over many years. Paul Seaver, my reader at Stanford, has long been a model of patient, insightful, and dedicated scholarship to me, and he applied those same qualities to the present work. It is certainly the better for it. I am indebted to the staffs of many libraries, including those of Miami and Drexel; the British Library; the Cambridge University Library; the University of Pennsylvania Libraries; the Folger Shakespeare Library; the Henry E. Huntington Library; the Washington University Library; and the Library of Bryn Mawr College. The staff of the Korman Computer Center at Drexel helped me through technical quandaries, as did Reid Addis, Amy

Gagas, Richard Greaves, and, especially, Kimon Rethis. Long ago, Jack Hexter taught me to think through every idea critically, especially my own. I hope I have remembered that counsel. A section of this book appeared in *Albion* 34 (2002): 371-390, as "King, Commons, and Commonweal in Holinshed's *Chronicles.*" I thank its editor, Michael Moore, for that hospitality, and for many years of professional association and friendship.

Norris Pope, my editor at Stanford University Press, has been an unfailing supporter of this book. He has my thanks and gratitude, as does Janet Gardiner, who has saved it as far as humanly possible from error while indulging an American author's idea of the English language. The defects that remain are mine alone.

My son Kimon, my daughter-in-law Theresa Storm, and my granddaughter Athena Marie Rethis have cheered and inspired me in more ways than they can know. I will always owe a debt to Michele Franco Rethis. Barbara Radin and Robin Radin, too, have their place in these pages, as only friends can.

Lili Bita, my companion and love, has been the dedicatee, and certainly the source, of almost everything I have ever written. It is with her generous permission that I substitute the two names at the head of this book for hers. Richard Greaves was my colleague, collaborator, and friend for nearly thirty years. He was the first reader of this book, and his characteristically thorough and penetrating comments have made it a far better one. That he devoted such time and care to it in the last months of his life was a more generous gift than any man can deserve, and certainly the most generous one I have ever received. With him I must thank his wife, Judith R. Greaves, who sustained him with her love and care, and who was a copartner in all of his, and our, work.

Philip Steven Rethis was my son. He was the bravest man I ever knew. I take courage from him every day, and bless his memory.

Robert Zaller
Bala Cynwyd, Pennsylvania
June 11, 2006

THE DISCOURSE OF LEGITIMACY
IN EARLY MODERN ENGLAND

Introduction

It was Lawrence Stone who, in his *The Causes of the English Revolution, 1529–1642*, staked out the era between the onset of the English Reformation and the outbreak of the English civil war as the period that generated England's bloodiest domestic conflict, its last royal execution, and its lone experiment in republican government.[1] Stone's book was seen as a late, perhaps belated product of the Whig tradition that saw modern English history in terms of a progressive constitutionalism whose first great crisis occurred between 1640 and 1660 and whose final triumph was modern representative democracy. This paradigm, long challenged ideologically if not structurally by Marxism, was newly under attack by a generation of functionalist historians generically referred to as revisionists. The revisionists taxed Whigs and Marxists alike with misreading the early modern era. Neither incipiently democratic nor capitalist, it was, they contended, a period to be understood in its own right, and one whose operational assumptions were rooted in the feudal and chivalric past. Accordingly, the great Revolution—seedbed of liberal democracy or bourgeois dominion, according to taste—was demoted to a civil war with an untidy aftermath. No longer tied to the grand narrative of modernity, it could be seen as the result of contingent circumstances, a misfortune that might well have been avoided with greater prudence, skill, or luck. Put another way, whereas weighty and unitary events seem to require great and long-matured causes, less cohesive and consequential ones, even if on a large scale, do not. As Conrad Russell puts it in his *The Causes of the English Civil War*, a work whose title deliberately echoes Stone's while purposefully deflating its argument:

A large part of the confusion on this subject results from taking the coming of the English Civil War as a single event, whereas in fact it was a somewhat unpredictable sequence of events and non-events. Since the war was the result, not merely of these events and non-events, but of the fact that they came in the order they did, it is hard to build up an orderly sequence of long-term causes for the King's raising his standard at Nottingham.[2]

It is to Russell's credit that, having declared his subject well-nigh incoherent at the outset, he proceeds to say many useful and perceptive things about it. His uncertainty nonetheless remains; as he says toward the end, "England in 1637 was, no doubt, a country with plenty of discontents, some of them potentially serious, but it was still a very stable and peaceful one, and one which does not show many visible signs of being on the verge of a major upheaval."[3] I share what I take to be one part of his concern, namely that causes can be neatly fitted to events in human affairs, and even that the concept of "cause," as commonly understood, is one ill-suited to historical explanation in general. It is not in any event the purpose of this book to account for what I still think is best referred to as the English Revolution. Nevertheless, it seems to me impossible to speak intelligibly of the period from 1529 to 1642 without reference to the events of 1642 themselves, at least if one wishes to construe the period as a whole. If I were writing a different sort of book, I might indeed wish to contend that the entire span of English history between 1529 and 1689 constituted a single revolutionary arc, on one side of which was a polity still communitarian in its outlook, and on the other one deeply infused with the principle of personal interest. My aims, however, are more limited. What I do wish is to describe a highly dynamic society over a period of slightly more than one hundred years in terms of the changing and often conflicting self-perceptions of its elite; in short, to describe its political languages as expressed in sacred, legal, constitutional, and dramatic discourse, as well as in those of counsel and command. This is only one sort of possible description, and not necessarily the most profound. It pays little direct attention to the great economic and demographic changes that shaped these languages. My excuse for this is that I must say what I think I can say best. Others will make good my deficiencies, and many already have.

All political languages express legitimacy, the cluster of ideas, assumptions, and significations by which men explain, enact, and contest authority. Singly and collectively, these languages constitute a discourse. The discourse of legitimacy will be understood, in its broadest sense, as the sum total of articulated statements from, to, or about power and its instruments. Such statements may be intentional (a command, a petition), ritualized (bowing, kneeling, and other forms of ceremonial address; the wearing and doffing of certain articles of clothing; the taking of oaths and the recitation of prescribed texts), representational (the likeness of a ruler on his coinage; his personification in pageantry; the depiction of his predecessors on the stage), or expressive (toasts and jests; lighting bonfires; ringing bells). The forms of discourse inevitably overlap; they are all to a greater or lesser degree expressive; they frequently carry multiple significations. Their sum is the currency of legitimacy, the form in which the daily transaction of power occurs and the shape in which it is ultimately constituted; the content of the civil culture.

Early modern England was a society in transition, and its modes of discourse were in flux, not to say turmoil. The focal point of change, and in appearance at least its most visible source, was the state and its central organ, the monarchy. The degree to which the state concentrated its authority and assimilated functions previously exercised by other power centers was revolutionary in itself—the Tudor revolution in government, as Geoffrey Elton phrased it—and also the precondition of modern revolution as such. Before the Tudors, the monarchy was a dynastic prize whose capture had, to be sure, profound civic repercussions, but did not necessarily involve the whole of society. By 1640, a successful coup or rebellion against the crown was a totalizing event that affected the religious no less than the secular allegiance of English men and women, and their livelihoods as well. In that sense, the "cause" of the English Revolution was the enlarged state itself. A breakdown in its functions or a slippage in its controls was a general catastrophe.

The expansion of the state both created and reflected an expansion of the civil public to which it was accountable. Thus, the greater claims of centralized government were matched by the greater demands made on it. It was more powerful, but also more vulnerable. This in turn made legitimation more critical to it, and more contestable. The result was that the polity itself became increasingly fissile. The fact that the official rhetoric of legitimation construed dissent as faction or disobedience complicated matters further. By the early seventeenth century, the constitutional consensus had effectively broken down, and, with it, the legal responsibilities of the subject—the terms of obedience itself—had become uncertain. At the same time, the state church, never wholly accepted by all, began to appear apostate to a significant minority. For many, political breakdown and religious disorder were entwined in the vision of a conspiracy to deprive English men and women of their civil and spiritual liberty. This was the crisis of legitimacy.

From this perspective, a series of faultlines had opened up beneath the seemingly placid surface of English life described by Russell. These faultlines were reflected in the increasingly contested discourses of legitimacy, the official discourse of the monarchy itself, the sacred discourse of the pulpit, the professional discourse of the law, the institutional discourse of Parliament, and the self-mirroring discourses of the realm at large and of its unique epitome, the stage. They gradually widened and deepened, until a chasm had opened beneath church and state. Thus, the breakdown of 1640 was overdetermined — not the product of any mechanical sequence of causes, but an event made cumulatively more probable by systemic stress, and finally precipitated by contingent but not unforeseeable circumstances.

The English Revolution may thus be seen as the endpoint of a complex process whose initial impulse was the profound alteration in the relationship between church and state introduced by the Reformation. If the Revolution is the climax of the story, however, it is far from the whole of it. It is a safe axiom in human affairs that nothing has to happen until it actually does, and only then does the search for process begin. The Revolution might not have occurred as it did if indeed at all, and in that case we might be telling the tale of how the English commonwealth successfully negotiated the difficult passage of the Reformation and rose to the other challenges of early modernity without a general crisis. The process, in short, is well worth investigating in its own right, and that is what for the most part this book aims to do.

Because the Revolution did in fact occur, however, the antecedent facts look differently, and bear a different signification. This is, then, a story about how early modern England deployed the languages of legitimacy, some of them common to other Reformed commonwealths, some of them unique, and all of them colored by a distinct historical background. It is simultaneously the story of how those languages came to bear increasing strain, how that strain spread across the entire discursive field as political and religious division widened, and how, finally, the legitimated order broke down.

As the governing consensus began to unravel, the story became more complex and the languages more intertwined, and Parliament took center stage as the site of conflict. It is, indeed, in Parliament that the several lines of discourse fuse into a compelling narrative of conspiracy and betrayal in which the people and their representatives stand on one side, and the forces of tyranny and sedition on the other. This narrative will find its ultimate expression in the Grand Remonstrance of the Long Parliament, but its essential framework is already fully developed in the parliamentary sessions of 1628–1629.

It is fitting, then, that our story climaxes with the great events of the Parliament of 1628, the Petition of Right and the Protestation of the House of Commons on March 2, 1629, just as it had begun with the convening of the Reformation Parliament exactly a century before. In the intervening years, the central state had both aggrandized power and lost cohesion, for its critical elements, crown and Parliament, had become radically polarized. Recent historiography has seen the matter differently. The old Whig paradigm of liberty-loving country gentlemen resisting monarchical encroachment has been gradually replaced with a view of Parliament as a dependent and declining institution that was in danger of functional obsolescence. Not by accident, it has also become more difficult to explain the breakdown of 1640–1642, or to conceptualize the English Revolution as such.

I believe this view to be mistaken. Nor is the older one it replaced sufficient. Rather, it seems to me that both crown and Parliament expanded in scope and (assumed) authority in the century after the Reformation, and that what happened in 1640 was a migration of legitimacy from the former to the latter, a revolution *within* the state. It is with that moment that our story will end, although with it the English Revolution was just begun.

CHAPTER 1

The Discourse of Monarchy

High authoritie is alwaye in perylle.[1]

The society of early modern England was both hierarchical and dynamic, and its modes of discourse reflected this instability. In part this resulted from groups that claimed greater inclusion for themselves (or demanded the exclusion of others), but in part it was the effect of pressure from the state for more and more elaborate tokens of acknowledgment and respect and the imposition of ever-wider and more prescriptive codes of conduct. The notion of a Tudor despotism has long gone by the boards, and Tudor government is now seen as resting on the cooperation of elites. It is worth recalling, however, the extent to which the Tudors and their parliaments felt justified in ordering the most intimate aspects of their subjects' lives. The wearing of a silk or velvet bonnet, of a proscribed hide on one's shoulders or hose on one's legs, could result in fines, imprisonment, or a trip to the stocks. Diet, work, and wages were regulated no less than dress, as well as a host of activities ranging from the length of wood one could cut to the size of horses one could breed.[2] Such regulations tended to fall more heavily as one descended the social scale, but the extraordinary mortality rate among the leading families of the realm—the Staffords, Seymours, Courtenays, Howards, and Greys—suggested the singular disadvantages of proximity to the royal bloodline or to royal favor; only under James I did it become the norm to lose one's place without forfeiting one's head.

Altogether, the range and scope of the Tudor state's intrusion into everyday life and the zest for control which it exhibited toward the most mundane social functions and activities would have made all but the severest of present-day authoritarian regimes blush. Had its reach equaled its grasp, it would have been a truly Orwellian commonwealth, Elizabeth I's famous remark about not making windows into men's souls notwithstanding. Of course, the Tudors were not notably more obtrusive than other comparably developed sixteenth-century monarchies; the tendency they represented was a general one. It is true as well that sumptuary laws and labor controls had a long late-medieval history. What was novel in the Tudors was their assiduity, and their success in suppressing sources of countervailing power and incorporating them into the state apparatus. The chivalric tradition—to which Henry VIII alone of the Tudor sovereigns was anachronistically attached— had been, as practiced in the days of Edward III and Henry V, a camaraderie of freebooters led by the sovereign as *primus inter pares*, both reflecting and perpetuating a rough-and-ready power sharing between the crown and the baronial elite. If this tradition affirmed the majesty of the crown it also limited it, and the quite deliberate glorification of majesty, its identification with a fixed (although frequently peripatetic) Court, its elevation above the peerage (partly accomplished by leveling down: for fifty years England had no dukes), and its vigorous exercise through proclamation and statute, was the hallmark of the Tudor experiment. At the same time the Tudors reduced their chief rivals in the peerage, they promoted the gentry, making them the custodians of local government and linking them through county magnates with a Court-based system of patronage policed by justices dispatched from Westminster and by the slow, studied royal progresses by which the Tudors personally surveyed their realm.

The most important authority annexed by the Tudor state was that of ecclesiastical governance. By disavowing the church of Rome, Henry VIII at once removed what remained of a major rival and possessed himself of its temporal wealth—a process not unlike his father's policy of attainder, but on a vastly larger scale. At the same time he incorporated its sacerdotal power as Supreme Head of his own creation, the Church of England, thus becoming the first monarch in Christendom to reign supreme over both the temporal and spiritual dimensions of his realm. This was an incalculable gain to monarchy, imparting to it not only control over an activity that vitally penetrated all aspects of English life but enhancing and in a crucial sense transforming its institutional charisma. As with other areas of government, the crown did not entirely monopolize the church; as it shared the monastic endowment with gentry purchasers so too it did lay patronage, while the Anglican bishops, capitalizing on the Elizabethan compromise, were able to assert doctrinal controls and *jure divino* claims. Nonetheless, the episcopal bench was a bulwark of the throne, a counterweight to the peerage in the House of Lords, and the enforcing arm of a disciplinary apparatus that reached into every parish in the land.

Control of the church gave the crown direct access to the most important medium of information and propaganda in early modern England, the pulpit. By law, every Englishman and woman was required to attend an Anglican service each Sunday, there to receive such instruction and guidance as was good for the soul and expedient to the state. Travelers, merchants, itinerant peddlers, strolling players, publicans, priests in mufti, country correspondents, and others with access to informal networks had alternative means of information, and Dame Rumor, as ever, traveled wide; but until the development of newsletters in the seventeenth century there was no comparable avenue of news. Understandably, the Tudors were anxious both to exploit this potent medium and—rather more difficult than anticipated—to control it. A malleable pulpit was only one aspect of the crown's effort to manage discourse, a problem greatly complicated by the rise of print literature and the popular stage. Through licensing, censorship, and by hireling pens of its own, the state took up the Sisyphean task of shaping discourse in the midst of an unfolding communications revolution. Its right to do so was sometimes sharply contested. Godly ministers claimed the warrant of Scripture for their prophesyings, scholastic disputants guarded their privileges in the universities, and members of Parliament asserted their right to speak freely on public matters in high terms. Often they did so under the sponsorship and protection of great men. Often as well, censorship and repression produced a backlash of sympathy and defiance. Foxe's *Book of Martyrs*, which achieved canonical status in Elizabethan England, was a work that celebrated heroic acts of resistance against the state; such a message, even if useful and necessary in clearing the ground for the restored Anglican church, was double-edged at best. A subtler problem, entwined with the Reformation in general and the divagations of Tudor religious policy in particular, was the rise of skepticism. Like a great deal of repressed speech, it crept out in the portrayal of stage villains, and tainted the reputation of playwrights such as Marlowe.

The Tudor regime, like any expansionist state, was in fact embarked upon an inherently ambiguous enterprise. As it widened the scope of governmental activities and therefore of legitimacy claims, it enlarged the boundaries of discourse it was seeking to contain. As it demanded more of loyalty and obedience, so more was demanded of it by way of performance. If the number of justices of the peace increased, so too did the expectation that they would keep order, relieve dearth, and reconcile conflicting interests. Petitions for services ranging from repair of the roads to the suppression of pirates streamed up toward Whitehall and Westminster, particularly in time of Parliament. Merchants, too, drawn into the web of franchises, concessions, and monopolies by which the crown sought to promote, regulate, and skim revenue from trade, made vigorous claims on the state, competing for favor (which meant gaining access to Court through the increasingly elaborate system of patronage) or protesting the advantages of those who had already gained it, and demanding secure coasts and an aggressive policy toward foreign competitors, a stable coinage, and an expanded money supply. Many of these claims spilled over into the law courts, which were already strained beyond capacity in the sixteenth century.

The Tudors were not in any case dealing with a static society. The population of England more than doubled between 1500 and 1640, raising it to the highest levels in its history.[3] This put great pressure on land and food supply, both of which were further affected by enclosure and other devices to ensure elite resource control. Proprietors strove to break customary leases which, in an age of rising prices, inhibited the growth of land value. Even the condemnation of relatively unexploited church lands provided only a temporary sop, and by the seventeenth century the acuteness of the land crisis was evident in the Irish and New World plantations, the pace of deforestation, and the draining of the fens. All of these expedients involved the displacement of existing populations, which led to protest and sometimes insurrection, as in the case of Kett's Rebellion in 1549 and the West Country risings of 1629–1631. The most severe—and unfortunately timed—of these rebellions came in Ireland in 1641, creating a wave of political reaction that helped topple England itself into revolution in 1642.[4]

The challenge of these demographic changes—which were compounded by climatic ones beginning in the late sixteenth century that made for less temperate weather over most of the next century, and after 1618, by the economic dislocations of the Thirty Years War—have had too little attention from many recent historians, who have been at pains to construct static paradigms that have made it exceedingly difficult for them to address even gross upheavals in the political order, let alone to gauge the subtler strains and divisions in the fabric of English society.[5] These strains were becoming acute in the late Tudor and early Stuart periods. For the five hundred years between the Norman Conquest and the accession of Elizabeth, the proportion of English peasants working in whole or part for wage hire fluctuated between a range of two and twelve per cent; by the first decade of Stuart rule that proportion had risen to more than one-third (including those subsisting on relief), and by the end of the seventeenth century it exceeded one-half.[6] Concomitantly, there was a significant rise in vagrancy and begging.[7] The enhanced powers of local justices and the succession of acts dealing with vagrancy and apprenticeship may be seen in large part as a response to this radically new situation. Its consequences included a drastic shrinkage in crown income that, coupled with the rising costs of government and especially of armament and the tight control over extraordinary revenues exercised by Parliament, had made the definitive activity of the state—waging war—an almost prohibitively expensive one for the English monarchy by the 1620s. When those plain facts of the case collided with ideological imperatives to ride to the rescue of international Calvinism in the period between 1620 and 1640, intense strains arose at the local and national political levels.

A good deal of the nostalgia for order that pervaded the Court of Charles I, including the new Arminian piety whose adoption helped relieve the pressure to assist a beleaguered Christendom, can be seen as a retreat by the crown from demands that had become systemically unanswerable.

The early modern English **state** was thus both a locus of power and a focus of aspiration and demand. If from one perspective the Tudor regime seemed aggressively intrusive, from another it was only responding to the exigent needs of an emerging market economy, itself the product of demographic and monetary pressures. There is no simple answer to the chicken-and-egg question of whether the state was opportunistically expanding its powers or anxiously servicing increased social demand; no doubt both propositions were variably correct at any given time. As the crown appropriated new functions or discharged old ones with greater zeal, its internal bureaucracy developed and expanded, its ties to local elites became more ramified, and its claims to general authority waxed broader and more autocratic. Divine right absolutism was the logical (if not necessary) culmination of this process, with its claim of final and ultimately unquestionable responsibility for the general welfare. As the career of the Long Parliament was to show, such a claim could be reversed with devastating effect.

Whether considered as aggrandizing or reactive, the early modern English state sought in a great variety of ways to shape and control the discourse of legitimacy. As the state's predicament worsened, as the gap between demand and performance widened in a society subjected to increased demographic and social strain, the control of symbolic or ideologically weighted discourse became all the more urgent. Elizabeth managed this problem with legendary skill if not always assured results; James I, more waywardly attentive, projected a less consistent image; Charles I compounded his very real problems with a public style so disastrous that it brought monarchy itself into disrepute. Under Charles, the range of warrantable opinion was steadily narrowed and dissent was zealously suppressed; at the same time, as the crown disengaged itself more and more from the political community, the articulation of command became hollow and peremptory. As the Caroline monarchy was increasingly isolated, it retreated into a self-validating world of fantasy that collapsed abruptly in 1640.

Ritual and Ceremony

The natural focus of monarchy was the prince's own person. As Ernst Kantorowicz noted, the royal person was both corporal and corporate, a dual entity that was simultaneously the most public of property and the most forbidden of objects.[8] The royal person was in short sacred. Formally, the sacralization of the royal person occurred in the act of anointment during the coronation ceremony, but popular sentiment held the ruler to be sacred from the moment of his accession, if not before. A widespread belief in royal stigmata dated back to the thirteenth century, and it was believed that James I had borne on his body since infancy the insignia of a lion, a crown, and in some versions a sword as well.[9]

The nature and significance of the coronation process was a continually evolving one. A long medieval tradition held that the anointment of the monarch conferred on him a share in the *sacerdotium* of the priesthood, though whether beside or beneath the papacy was a subject of protracted controversy. It was in any case unwise for the ruler to lay too much emphasis on the point, for it not only invited clerical pretension to powers of investiture but raised uncomfortable questions about the status of an uncrowned king. A similar consideration arose with regard to the communal aspects of investiture, particularly the coronation oath. In the ceremony devolved from the fourteenth century, the king offered promises to the community through answers to set questions, a form which signified election rather than mere approbation. At Henry VII's coronation, which followed as speedily on Bosworth Field as decorum and adequate preparation would allow, he was acknowledged by right of conquest, heredity, and election—"elected, chosen and required by all three estates of this same land," as the formula had it. Henry VIII was also represented as king by inheritance and election, but that passionate reviser undertook a number of emendations to the oath in his own hand to reflect his conception of the subordinate role of church and Parliament. These revisions were incorporated in spirit if not in letter into Edward VI's coronation oath, probably by Thomas Cranmer. Edward assumed the crown by inheritance alone, and promised only to maintain the laws according to their right meaning, of which he was the final interpreter. Cranmer, who of course performed the ceremony and preached the sermon of investiture, glossed it in a manner that eviscerated both its consensual and sacerdotal elements:

> The solemn rites of coronation have their ends and utility, yet neither direct force nor necessity. They be good admonitions to put kings in mind of their dignity; for they be God's anointed, not in respect of the oil which the bishop useth, but in consideration of their power, which is ordained, of their sword, which is authorised, of their persons, which are elected by God, and indued with the gifts of his Spirit for the better ruling and guiding of this people. The oil, if added, is but a ceremony; if it be wanting, that king is yet a perfect monarch notwithstanding, and God's anointed, as well as if he was inoiled.[10]

Cranmer's monarch fits the Henrician description of kingship perfectly. "Elected" by God rather than the people, he has no need of approbation from the vulgar. Similarly, the function of the coronation is to put him in mind of his dignity rather than his duty. He receives no addition to his power by the ceremony, for it is already complete; he makes no compact with the people by his oath, for they can only give him what they already owe: loyalty and obedience. We have here all the lineaments of absolute monarchy, and are not far from the precincts of Hobbes. The function of the coronation is not to exalt the king but to show him already exalted.

Cranmer's chief concern was not to remove the crown from commerce with the multitude, however, but from the claims of papal authorization. His coronation sermon was specifically addressed to this, and his denial of efficacy to the ritual of anointment was designed to underline it. One suspects he would have been just as happy to have been able to dispense with it altogether ("the oil, *if* added"). If, however, both oath and anointment were to be stripped of their traditional significance—the assumption of real powers, civil and sacerdotal, conferred as a trust by the laity and clergy—then the coronation was no longer a ceremony in any meaningful sense, but a pageant, a scene at which power was not conveyed but displayed.

The power thus exhibited was, in time, to be fully secularized, a process which in modern society would require its symbolic reconnection to a civil public in the uneasy fiction of popular sovereignty. At first, however, absolutist monarchy would exalt itself above both its lay and clerical publics, identifying itself with and deriving its powers solely from divinity. The result was both an emphasis on the inherent sacerdotal powers of kingship and a cult of royalty that tapped into the revival of antiquity to embellish the crown with a repertoire of classical and biblical personae, exemplary and allegorical, regal and divine. Absolute monarchy was, in its first instance and its fundamental character, sacred.

The most immediate and demonstrable attribute of sacred monarchy was the efficacy of the royal touch. Since the time of Edward the Confessor, English kings had touched to heal the King's Evil (scrofula) and other ailments. Henry VII, true to the bureaucratizing instincts of the Tudors, had codified the ceremonial connected to the event, and claimed by rubbing gold and silver rings together to produce a charm against epilepsy. Touching could not have been among the most pleasant of royal duties, but it was one of the severest charges laid to Charles I's debit that he shied from the practice. Charles II practiced it in exile and made it a cornerstone of the restored monarchy, touching an estimated 100,000 sufferers during his reign. The curve of his healing rose in times of uncertainty and crisis, notably in the early years of the reign and during the crackdown that followed the Exclusion crisis.[11]

The royal touch was the most immediate and symbolically intimate connection between king and commonwealth. Access to the royal presence was ordinarily limited to courtiers, emissaries, and ambassadors, and even the most familiar exchanges with members of the household entourage were bound by protocol; it was not the Earl of Essex's military blunders, his unbridled ambition, or his tasteless sexual conquests that destroyed him, but his temerity in bursting in unannounced on Elizabeth after his recall from Ireland in 1599, an act of lèse-majesté even the fond queen could not excuse. At no other time and under no other circumstances, except for coronations, formal civic entrances, and chance encounters during royal travels, could the ordinary subject come into close proximity to the monarch, let alone physical contact. One recalls that amongst the charges of praemunire against Cardinal Wolsey was one which accused him of exposing Henry VIII to foul and pestilential vapors by his excessively close personal attendance on the King. The tubercular sufferers who were admitted during the touching ceremony, and who crowded about in their scores and hundreds while waiting their turn, were surely more of a danger; but clearly the intended message was that divinity hedged a king while he performed his sacerdotal function and that, unlike the ordinary physician, the royal healer was immune, at least in that space, from contagion. The more precisian of Anglican bishops could scarcely have been comfortable with this relic of medieval practice and the priestly magic it suggested, but although some were ready enough to take issue with a cross in the royal chapel they dared not object to so direct (and popular) a manifestation of regal charisma.

The aura of the royal person was extended by tokens and amulets; each of those touched by the monarch received a gold piece minted for the occasion and worn about the neck as a charm, as Henry VII distributed his cramping-rings as a specific for epilepsy. Elizabeth exploited her chivalric cult by giving lockets to those in her favor; these too were often worn about the neck. At a further remove were objects not directly connected with the physical person of the monarch but charged with symbolic association, such as staffs, orbs, and keys. The portraits of Elizabeth almost invariably depict her as touching or holding something: a globe, a fan, the arc of a rainbow. Significantly, only one extant picture, Nicholas Hilliard's portrait of the Queen playing a lute, shows her doing something. In use, an object is consumed in its activity; in being touched or held (as in much other Renaissance portraiture) it is marked as a symbol or possession; but in being touched by a royal hand it is invested with majesty itself.

The reverse of this process was to identify the ruler with deities or heroes. Often, investiture was combined with association: thus, in the 1569 portrait of Elizabeth and the Judgment of Paris, Elizabeth confronts the three goddesses with a jewel-encrusted globe surmounted by a cross (the apple of discord turned into the apple of concord), confounding Hera and Athena; only Aphrodite sits with a calm, untroubled gaze, her posture representing not only submission to but identification with the conquering monarch and her nudity a suggestive counterimage to the stiffly brocaded Virgin Queen.

Elizabeth's iconography was richly variegated, but the tensions between virgin modesty, favor sublimated, and triumphant love became her distinctive regnal theme. These circumlocutions in turn reflected an ambiguous relationship with the ultimate symbol of chastity. Mariolatry was the vice of Romanism, and the happenstance that both Elizabeth's immediate predecessor and her chief rival were both named Mary made any direct attempt at association with the Virgin awkward, as the desire to court Catholic forbearance diplomatically made it, at least until Pius V's bull of excommunication, impolitic. Elizabeth, as usual, turned this liability to advantage. Her iconography evoked virtually every classical, literary, and imagistic association with virginity known to tradition; she was Cynthia, the moon goddess, Diana, goddess of the hunt, the chaste Laura of Petrarch's *I Trionfi*, and above all Astraea, the just virgin of Virgil's Fourth Eclogue, whose return to earth would restore the golden age. These associations enabled Elizabeth to exploit the strong liminal feelings still bound up with the cult of Mary without invoking the specter of popery or the scorn of iconoclasts. Elizabeth had been born on the eve of the Virgin's Nativity, and when she died on the eve of Mary's Assumption, the association was fixed for posterity; as one panegyrist had it, she was second in paradise only to the Queen of Heaven.[12]

Elizabeth's circumspect approach to the figure of the Virgin contrasts with Queen Mary's direct appropriation of it; thus, Mary's deliverance of the Catholic church was likened to the Virgin's deliverance of Christ through the flight to Egypt, and Cardinal Pole even greeted her on returning from his own exile with the words "Hail Mary, full of grace." The persons of the trinity were appropriated as well by Henry VII, who with Arthur, the Prince of Wales, was likened in pageant to the Father and the Son. James I's penchant for likening kings to gods thus had a long iconographic precedent before the first Stuart mounted the throne. Other biblical figures were used to frame specific royal virtues or to stress particular themes of governance: Henry VIII was variously apostrophized as Moses, Solomon, David, and even Judith. With the Reformation, these associations took on an imperial significance as well.[13]

Books (especially bibles), prints, and broadsides carried royal images and iconography into the humblest home, as well as taverns, alehouses, and inns. The representation of Elizabeth was a cottage industry employing pattern portraits under the Queen's own close scrutiny, and large poster portraits depicting royal genealogies and topical events such as princely weddings were evidently popular.[14] But no other mode of display amplified and projected the monarch's person more brilliantly and multifariously and engaged the subject so directly as pageantry. Henry VII was the first English king to fully grasp the importance of representation and spectacle. He appointed the first Court painter and commissioned the first Tudor history cycle, a series of panels depicting the great events of his reign. He employed three troupes of players and two minstrel companies to perform in the Chapel Royal and by 1501 had built the first pageant cars. The King's Glazier, no longer an artisan but a titled functionary, adorned Henry's buildings and chapels with stained glass on the Burgundian model; Flemish weavers provided him with sumptuous tapestries; illuminators were employed to embellish royal proclamations and even to touch some up retroactively. This patronage paid off handsomely at the royal competition between Henry VIII and Francis I of France on the Field of the Cloth of Gold, where Henry's glittering tents and pavilions marked the Tudors' entry on the stage of Renaissance monarchy and provided a spectacle "si belle et singulière," as one observer remarked, "que l'on n'en a point veu de pareille."[15]

A display before one's fellow sovereigns was a bid for acknowledgment or supremacy among one's peers, but a procession before subjects was a spectacle in which the monarch was simultaneously exalted and exposed, a theatricalization of majesty in which, however carefully prepared the scene and controlled the show, the groundlings always had the last word. The most important pageant of a reign was the one that accompanied the coronation. Each of the Tudors staged their coronations with great care. It was the single spectacle which, above all, proclaimed, celebrated, and certified legitimacy; it was the one occasion on which the monarch's claim to and display of sovereign authority was seen in its purest and most generalized state, and in which the response of the realm was most immediate and affirming, if not enabling. It was also the occasion on which the monarch, by a suitable deployment of imagery, could best signal the personal style, political agenda, and ideological orientation of the new regime.

Although the coronation was regarded as a single event, however, it was composed of two distinct elements, the rite and the oath proper, and the attendant celebration. As we have seen, the early Tudors regarded the oath and investiture as symbolic, an attestation of power already possessed in full rather than a transfer of authority, let alone an election. Thus the distinction between ritual and pageantry was blurred, and the ritual itself tended to become only a formality, albeit a solemn one, between procession and celebration—the "crowning event," to use modern parlance, rather than an actual conveyance of authority. But this trend was strikingly reversed under Mary, who used her coronation to publicly reembrace the Catholic church. Mary's coronation service and ceremony, separated by four days from her entry procession, was nearly seven hours in length. She was anointed with chrism imported from Flanders whose sacred efficacy had been vouched for by the Pope. Not a jot of the traditional ceremony was omitted or abridged. As Mary donned each of her three crowns a trumpet fanfare sounded, and a Te Deum capped the whole. A vast banquet followed. Nothing could have dramatized the coronation ritual more emphatically or more grandly affirmed its function as the vessel of a sanctified authority.

Elizabeth's coronation thus presented her with the unwelcome choice of submitting to the ministrations of her Catholic bishops and thereby affirming the papal regime in England, or signaling, prematurely at best, her intention to recover her father's imperial powers in church and state. Her solution to the problem was a decisive moment in the evolution of the British monarchy. Elizabeth made a splendid entrance into London and "was of the people received merveylous entierly," returning her own goodwill to the multitude in the first of the many such enactments of legitimacy that characterized her reign. She rode in an open litter from the Tower to Westminster through a series of triumphal arches and past an elaborately festooned *tableau vivant* depicting the united houses of Lancaster and York, including Henry VII and his queen, Elizabeth, Henry VIII and Anne Boleyn—the latter daringly restored as an affirmation of the new Queen's literal as well as figurative legitimacy—with an effigy of Elizabeth herself enthroned above the rest. At the Little Conduit in Cheapside the Queen stopped to receive an English Bible, raising it high and dramatically pressing it to her breast in a movement that affirmed her assumption of both the truth and the protection of the Word into her keeping. With this gesture, the Anglican church was symbolically reborn.

The coronation ceremony, in contrast, was as far muted as possible. Precisely what occurred in Westminster Abbey remains obscure. According to one tradition, Elizabeth withdrew before the elevation of the host, perhaps into a private closet; according to another, she veiled her face with a handkerchief at the moment of elevation; according to a third, she ordered that the ritual be omitted. We are not even sure whether the officiating minister was Carew of Windsor or Oglethorpe of Carlisle; nor (as in the case of Mary) do we have the text of the oath taken. Either Elizabeth's conduct was a masterpiece of evasion or her control of its reporting was very tight.[16]

The tacit signal given to the London crowds to do away with "the dregges of Papistry" not only by the symbolism of the coronation pageant but by the Aesopian Twelfth Night entertainments that had preceded it had swift results. Scores of religious monuments were defaced and toppled in London during January 1559. When a statue of St. Thomas was beheaded and cast down, its place was taken by a stucco image of a little girl, one of the prominent symbols of Elizabeth in the pageant. Thus did pageant and carnival—the validating gesture of authority, the obediently "lawless" response of the crowd—begin anew the work of the English Reformation, and the identification of ruler and church that was its particular stamp.[17] In contrast, the relative isolation of the coronation ceremony, the blurring of its symbolism, and the confusion of its personnel, relegated it to the margins of the royal investiture. Cranmer's view had been vindicated. Spectacle had triumphed over ceremony, and the contested dialogue between church and state that had been the essence of the medieval process of legitimation would be replaced by the dialogue between the imperial church and state and loyal subject, with the former represented by the indivisible person of the monarch as Christian emperor and the latter, ultimately, by the personified subject in Parliament.

This process was still in its formative stages when Elizabeth assumed the throne, and Parliament was only one of the many stages on which the Queen performed. The specular nature of Renaissance monarchy has been often commented on.[18] Early modern rulers were on display to an extraordinary degree as royal entries and progresses made monarchy a moveable feast. The trope of the mirror was of course of respectable medieval lineage. Whereas the medieval speculum had been a pattern, however—the godly prince conforming to the maxims of virtue that pleased heaven, served the realm, and were in turn a pattern for pious imitation—the Renaissance mirror was brazen, a surface on which self-fashioning monarchs simultaneously invented and projected themselves. It could not be otherwise, as the processes of secularization left rulers in control of churches, and centralized authority as the final locus of power and arbiter of value.

The Renaissance speculum thus no longer offered the static image of virtue but the dynamic one of policy; it was, that is to say, mobilized, theatricalized. Elizabeth grasped this point intuitively; "We princes," as she said famously, "are set on stages, in the sight and view of all the world duly observed."[19] The pageantry of the coronation was echoed, renewed, and reinforced by the summer progresses that marked the reign. Again and again, in Coventry, in Warwick, in Sandwich, in Bristol, Elizabeth symbolically renewed her marriage vows to the realm. While her last suitor was still negotiating for her hand, Elizabeth was appearing again as Deborah in Norwich under a garland of red and white roses, watching Chastity and Philosophy put Cupid to rout. Elizabeth did not need pageantry to create a stage, however, and she could work a crowd anytime. Godfrey Goodman has left us an account of the excitement caused by her passage through the streets of Westminster in December 1588, where the populace had gathered spontaneously to catch a glimpse of her leaving Somerset House. Elizabeth stopped to chat, and used her well-worn line that although her subjects might have a greater prince they would never have a more loving one. It was a small occasion of devotion; there were many others like it. "And so the queen and the crowd there," Goodman noted, "looking upon one another awhile, her Majesty departed. This wrought such an impression upon us . . . that all the way long we did nothing but talk what an admirable queen she was and how we would adventure our lives in her service." Of such casual episodes no less than formal pageantry and occasions of state was the myth of Gloriana woven.

Not everyone thought such performances quite compatible with the royal dignity, however. The Stuart courtier Sir Robert Naunton commented that there was "no prince living . . . that was so great a courter of her people, yea, of the commons, that stooped and descended lower in presenting her person to the public view as she passed in her perambulations and in the ejaculations of her prayers upon the people." Naunton acknowledged that Elizabeth was also appropriately "tender of her honor" and insistent upon her sovereignty, but, looking back from the safety of a succeeding reign, he taxed her with the lack of "magnanimity" in stooping to the vulgar. Elizabeth herself disclaimed the virtue of magnanimity as a trait beyond her sex; but her feminine ones served her well enough.[20]

James I established his own iconographic themes early: *rex pacificus* and Solomonic prince. Acknowledging the Senecan fashion as well as staking his own claims to the British imperium, he had commemorative coins struck that depicted him in Roman dress and insignia, and the imperial idiom remained a leitmotif of his reign. Of James as royal author we shall have more to say. Gregarious among cronies but uncomfortable in crowds, his progresses, though important among narrower elite circles, were essentially private touring parties. Elizabeth's real successor, in this sense, was the short-lived Prince Henry, James' eldest son.

The young Henry was invested as Prince of Wales in June 1610, a ceremony that marked his political coming-of-age. Several months earlier, he had sponsored an elaborate pageant that emphasized England's role as the leader of Protestant Europe and his own image as a champion of the Reformed cause. His investiture was marked by a series of festivities that eclipsed any previous spectacle at his father's Court, including a river triumph and an aquatic battle, a masque, a tourney, a fireworks display, and the creation of knights.[21] He was also responsible for the dazzling spectacle that welcomed the Elector Palatine Frederick V to England in 1612 as the fiancé of his sister Elizabeth. With drums beating, trumpets sounding, and guns firing from the Tower, a procession of 150 ships accompanied the Elector up the Thames. Henry's martial displays were clearly at variance with the Augustan themes of peace and prosperity sounded by James, nor could the King have been pleased by the evident kinship in arms between his son and his prospective son-in-law and the immense enthusiasm shown for them both by the London populace. Still not halfway into his reign, he was faced with the prospect of a serious reversionary interest from an impetuous, headstrong heir determined to project an image of kingship independent of and in some respects contradictory to his own.

Henry's sudden death in November 1612 was in many ways the turning point of James' reign. Neither the Spanish match nor the ascendancy of the Duke of Buckingham as both royal favorite and chief minister would likely have occurred had the Prince lived, and his "lost" reign haunted the popular imagination. When James in his grief told Frederick that he must fill the place in his affection left vacant by Henry he laid a heavier charge than he knew, for Frederick's attempts to live up to the role of surrogate Protestant champion were to have disastrous effects for all concerned. In some sense Frederick remained heir to the succession Henry had represented and that never passed whole to Charles. After the Elector's death that spectral inheritance belonged to his son Charles Lewis, who was seriously considered as an alternative to Charles in some quarters during the 1640s.[22]

Divinely marked by the insignia of orb and scepter, reconsecrated in the holy oils of coronation, resplendent on thrones, stamped on healing coins and rings, depicted in the form and virtue of the patriarchs, paraded in show, prayed for in church and closet, the royal person was the living icon of legitimacy, whose breath was law, whose voice command, and whose mortal flesh was the token of immortal authority. In the most favored representation of medieval and early modern monarchy, the sovereign was incorporate in the body politic and vice versa, an indissoluble unity displayed in Elizabethan and Jacobean chorography and perhaps most imperially asserted in the Ditchley portrait of an Elizabeth bestriding the map of her kingdom. The royal body was the realm; the realm the body.

The Discourse of the Court

The immediate extension of the sovereign presence, the theater and market of its activity, the locus of power and the focus of aspiration, was the Court. The Court was neither a settled abode nor a settled concept; like the *majestas* it was meant to body forth, it was simultaneously an ideal and a working political instrument. In an age in which power was both more centralized and less accountable, and in which the once countervailing forces of clergy and nobility were being slowly but inexorably reduced to subaltern status, the play of sovereignty was at once more brilliant and more diffuse, more promising and more threatening, more august and more familiar. The boundaries of new monarchy were still undefined, and the space into which its powers were both directly and mediately projected were, in the widest sense, the "Court."

In the most concrete terms, the Court consisted of the royal abodes and the business transacted there. The Tudors built, bought, inherited, and confiscated some 71 residences. Many of them fell into disrepair and ruin despite spasmodic attempts at renovation; others were alienated or deeded to courtiers; one, Bridewell, which had housed the Emperor Charles V on his state visit in 1522, became a workhouse.[23] The records of the acquisition, exchange, and transfer of these domiciles offer rich insight into the shifting relations between crown, church, and nobility in the sixteenth century; for our purposes they provide the image of a restless, peregrinative dynasty imprinting itself on the landscape of England. If the cartographic surveys of William Saxton and John Speed laid out, as it were, the chessboard of the royal demesne, then the palaces and lodges of the crown were its shifting pieces. Each sovereign had his or her favored abodes—for Henry VII it was Richmond and Woodstock; for Henry VIII Whitehall, Hampton Court, and Nonsuch; for Elizabeth, Greenwich; while the Stuarts, as befitted a new dynasty, had their own special resorts as well, notably St. James' Palace and Somerset House, as well as extensive building and decorating projects. Castles were an expensive indulgence, and as much as one-third of the crown's revenue was devoted to the general maintenance of the Court.[24]

The roll-call of royal residences is in many ways misleading, not merely because many of them were seldom if ever used but because the Court so frequently took hospitality with the principal courtiers and nobility, a means both of conferring honor and of spreading expense. In this sense as well as others the Court was not so much a place or even an idea as a process of negotiation. At its most precise it was a jurisdictional liberty bounded by a verge, commonly interpreted as twelve miles; but precision, legal or otherwise, meant little in an experimental monarchy that was constantly on the move. The Court could also detach pieces of itself as quasi-autonomous bureaucratic and institutional entities, as the law courts were detached in the fifteenth century and the Great Wardrobe in the sixteenth. Sometimes this process was purely adventitious, as when Henry VIII vacated Westminster after the great fire of 1512, leaving it wholly to the Exchequer and the law courts.[25] It might be said that modern bureaucracy sprang up in the abandoned tenements of royalty; at any rate, it represented that part of the Renaissance Court that was less portable, less discursive, and less quickened by charisma. This did not mean that it was in any genuine sense independent or even less immediately amenable to the royal will. Such an idea would have made no sense to any of the Tudors, nor was it countenanced by the Stuarts, as the great jurist Sir Edward Coke would learn to his cost in 1616.

The Court's travels were not confined to its residences, of course. As it wound its cumbered way through the countryside, it both stimulated and burdened local economies, requisitioning extensive goods and services which it paid for tardily, if ever. The costs of hospitality could lie heavily on the nobleman or magnate whose estate sustained a royal visit. But the gate swung both ways; regal favor meant bounty in the form of grants, patents, and forfeitures, as well as less tangible but no less coveted benefits. The taming of the nobility—simultaneously the Tudor regime's greatest triumph and its most destabilizing legacy—was accomplished by redefining the nature and locus of honor. The Tudor Court, at rest or in motion, required attendance and service. Some of it was personal and ceremonial; the young sons of Henry VIII's nobility sat at his table as carvers and cupbearers. Some of it was honorific, such as the representation of the monarch in embassies. Most of it, however, was administrative. The dominion exercised by feudal magnates through their armed retainers was converted into county lieutenancies based on musters, while the gentry took up the civilian tasks of ordinary peacekeeping, law enforcement, and provision for dearth and penury in the justiceships of the peace and at the county assizes. These were traditional functions, but now integrated into a bureaucratic structure that transformed power based on landed wealth and the capacity for mayhem into authority conferred (and revocable) by writs of commission.

The processes by which baronial power were tamed and disciplined was gradual, and the interests they served were reciprocal. Local wealth and standing determined the range of choices open to the crown in recruiting its agents, if not the actual selection. Unpaid or at any rate irregularly compensated service, as well as the requirements of domestic tranquility, assured that it would generally confirm rather than disturb the nexuses of power in the countryside. Nonetheless, officeholding as such transformed the relations between the crown and the elite. A single, acknowledged site of command replaced a polyvalent system that had given lip service but often little more to the idea of an authoritative center. Political conflict in the countryside turned more on intra-elite competition for favor and reward than on the assertion of any genuine independence of the center; as the abortive revolts of 1536 and 1569 made clear, there was no longer any possibility of achieving it. More to the point, the specific grievances that had led to these episodes aside, there was no longer any effective will to resist the crown. Centralization was the only viable response to the surge in population and inflation and its accompanying dislocations, the demand for a legal and political framework for an increasingly commercialized economy, and the ideological crisis of the Reformation, which, whether England had remained Catholic or not, would have profoundly altered church-state relations and required the active engagement of the crown. The question was not whether sixteenth-century English monarchy would expand but what the character and competence of its expansion would be. That was still the question before the country in 1640.

If the boundaries of the Court were uncertain, however, its center was not. The Court radiated outward from the throne, and as Henry VIII reminded Parliament the ruler was embodied both personally and corporatively in all his institutions, and wherever his writ ran. Nonetheless he was most solemnly present in the act of formal command, the royal proclamation. The proclamation, as Paul Hughes and James Larkin have shown, had become by Tudor times a complex enactment that passed through distinct and pre-scribed stages, each attested by seal or warrant, and authenticated both by the royal signature and the Great Seal—the stamp of the king's two bodies.[26] Here was sovereignty at its most direct, whether speaking to great matters or small—the announcement of war and peace, of pardon or condemnation, of licensing or prohibiting—but here, too, was the sovereign act most clearly and painstakingly related to law and statute and advised of counsel, that is, legitimated as an act of process and merely set forth, as an enabling form, by will. Proclamations were carefully researched. Where possible they were set forth as under the authority of statute as well as prerogative (a good number of them, of course, concerned the enforcement of statute), or other-wise as under the law of God, of custom, or of the bench. Frequently they were signed as well by members of the Privy Council. Invariably they ap-pealed to good order and the common welfare.

Proclamations were addressed to the realm at large but communicated di-rectly to the officers responsible for their enforcement: deputy lieutenants, justices of the peace, town councils, subsidy commissioners. These were the agents of local government, and in the sense that we can draw a line of ad-ministrative demarcation between the Court and the commonwealth it is no doubt here, in what has been called the county community. But this line can easily be a misleading one, for the crown was deeply dependent on the un-paid servants in the shires on whom it relied for the collection of revenues, the maintenance of order, and the execution of government (and whose co-optation in this service was the most signal achievement of the Tudor dy-nasty). This relation between center and periphery was mediated by a com-plex network of patronage whose focus was the Court. If the hierarchy of of-ficialdom was the formal instrument of government, the patronage network was the efficient one. The former was a matter of places, which grew with the demands of a burgeoning population, a market-oriented economy, and the ambitions of the Tudors themselves; the latter was a matter of persons, of traditions of lordship and dependency transferred from manor to Court (and transformed en route, as sworn fealty gave place to the subtler negotiations and occasional caprices of favor), of service and reward, of all the tangible and intangible fruits of power and esteem that gave one a purchase on the world's stage. The "courtier," that quintessential creature of Renaissance monarchy, was simultaneously servant and bureaucrat, place-hunter and place-dispenser, a shifting point on a diagram of power. He was also, in the Court of England, a man of many local connections, often a county leader and occasionally a spokesman. In Parliament time he might represent the lo-cal interest formally as a member, although of course he was the crown's ser-vant too. This could give rise to confusion, not to say conflict of interest; in

1621, Serjeant Ashley, attempting to assure the House of Commons of his bona fides, protested that "My gown and knighting shall not carry me against my conscience."[27] The tension among these multifarious roles could not easily be sustained, and the rhetoric of harmony that was such a pervasive feature of the Tudor and early Stuart idiom may be seen in good part as an attempt to reconcile interests that were simultaneously divergent and hopelessly intertwined.[28]

In such a system, where all political appeal ultimately rested with the ruler, the representation of interests was crucial. It was vitally important that interests not only be represented—that no significant element of the political community (including, unofficially, even such proscribed groups as recusants) be without access to the fount of power—but that they be seen to be represented. Hence the critical importance of the Privy Council as the apex of the patronage system and the final court of appeal before the crown, and hence the significance of its inclusion in acts of proclamation. The Council's seal meant that the monarch had consulted not only the law of the realm but its interest and opinion as well.

The Discourse of Counsel

The question of counsel was one of the prime indices of legitimacy for the early modern state. What distinguished the good ruler from the tyrant was that he act advisedly, with the concurrence of learned and experienced opinion. Sir Francis Bacon noted "the incorporation, and inseparable conjunction, of counsel with kings," concluding that majesty was not diminished but "exalted" by it.[29] In contrast, an uncounseled king—which was to say, an unrestrained one—would inevitably succumb to whim and pleasure. Such a ruler would be harsh and despotic if his will was strong, or fond and susceptible if it was weak. In either case the essence of his rule was caprice. The fascination of early modern culture with the figure of the tyrant bespeaks the anxiety that attended the centralization of authority and the fear of the untrammeled power that might be exercised by monarchs freed from the feudal bond. Where barons could no longer beard a king and estates as yet lacked the power to do so (or had already lost it), counsel was the sole bulwark against arbitrary rule. Yet counsel itself was inherently bound up with the pleasure of the ruler. His command summoned it, his necessity determined it, his will concluded it, whether in privy council or before the estates of the realm. If it was prudent to make a show of consulting the privy council or the bench, it was, as Bacon also observed, easy to ventriloquize through them; a nod or an inflection could be sufficient to indicate, and so obtain, the desired result. Bacon's reflections were the culmination of a lengthy European debate on the function of counsel, whose poles were represented by Machiavelli and Erasmus and whose English participants included such figures as Sir Thomas More, Sir Thomas Elyot, Thomas Starkey, Sir Thomas Wyatt, John Hales, Roger Ascham, and Sir Philip Sidney. All English commentators agreed on the vital importance of conscientious counsel; all experienced the frustrations, not to say far worse, of trying to deliver it.

What was most striking in this debate was the conviction of each interlocutor that his particular counsel was both worthy and necessitous. To a certain extent this was a function of his eagerness to impart it; Thomas Starkey conceded that life outside Court service was "both tedyouse and displesant." With wit readily for hire, however, the humanist courtiers had to offer something more: and that something was, assertedly, a disinterested concern for the commonweal.

The validity of such a claim was less significant than the fact of its being made. Erasmus spoke on behalf of a *respublica Christiana* that by the end of his life had ceased to exist, and whose crisis his career attested. The humanist debate was both a harbinger and a consequence of that crisis, which shook the traditional authority of Christendom, and, in the lands of Reform, permanently redefined it. If political power had remained by and large firmly in the hands of Europe's rulers, the purposes of that power were often contested and the moral and institutional constraints within which it operated weakened, reconfigured, or overthrown. Humanist counsel addressed itself to this situation, proposing to bind power with conscience.

The difficulty was that honest counsel had no means but rhetoric and no guerdon but virtue in the face of temptation and flattery. The humanist in politics, as More's Raphael Hytholoday had pointed out, was often obliged to support decisions he not only opposed but reviled. Worse, he might be unable to rebut wicked counsel at all, for a councillor's duty, as Elyot noted, lay in "holding thy tonge when it behoueth the[e], and spekying in tyme that which is conuenient."[30] Scarce wonder that the Dorus of Sidney's *Arcadia* might prefer to be "private/ In sorrow's torments" than reduced to the "whisp'ring note" of the courtier.[31] Could conscience and integrity survive under such circumstances, and if so to what purpose other than self-laceration and self-contempt? More had tipped the balance in favor of service by suggesting that if policy could not be made to embrace the good, yet counsel might at least mitigate the worst effects of the bad. His own career proved the best refutation of the argument.

The humanist counselor was of course presented as an ideal type, a servant of the commonwealth who advanced no private interest and sought no personal gain. This accorded with more general convention. Sixteenth-century political discourse presupposed harmony as the only acceptable goal of the social order. In the realm of harmony, all things properly tended toward reconciliation and order, and discord could arise only from faction or malice from below or vaunting arrogance — *superbia* — from above. The role of the humanist counselor was, then, to serve as a voice of conscience, tempering prudence and reproaching pride.

This happy representation was not only severely at odds with the realities of the council board but with the practical status of the humanist courtier as well. Lacking title or estate he was obliged to curry patronage and favor; as a friend noted, no one said good morning to Cardinal Wolsey earlier than Sir Thomas More.[32] But powerful family connections were no guarantee of access or influence, as Sidney discovered, and even a chancellor's robes were no shield against disgrace, as More and Bacon found as well. At best, the Tudors and Stuarts appropriated humanist learning as an ornament of their prestige; at worst, they suborned it. Their advice they took from the men of prudence, the Cromwells and Pagets and Cecils.

The "problem of counsel" as posed by the humanists might be dismissed as the power seeking of frustrated intellectuals who sought to substitute their own judgment for that of seasoned professionals and to occupy a moral position to which their own opinion alone entitled them. But the humanist critique pointed up a genuine dilemma. To the extent the monarch could shape the counsel he received to his own predilection, he robbed it of its implied but critical function of representing opinion (and interest). The idea of a humanist ombudsman who would represent the interest of the commonwealth at large might be untenable if not illusory, but in the absence of such a check what could restrain arbitrary and tyrannical government?

This concern was not merely a theoretical one. Henry VIII had considerably streamlined and reorganized his Privy Council, beginning with the Eltham Ordinance of 1526. The effect of this reorganization was to convert the Council from a body in which appointment reflected recognized status in the community to one in which it conferred a status dependent on, and often confined to, court favor. The issue at stake was not the overt exercise of power, for membership in the old, unwieldy Council was frequently ceremonial, but representation. A broadly inclusive Council reflective of prevailing hierarchy and interest was, at least residually, a guarantor of the king's incorporation in the realm; a narrowly based one, stripped for efficiency and serving a constituency of one, was inapt if not incapable of discharging such a function. When at the same time the King's powers were formidably augmented by his investiture as Supreme Head of the church, there was apprehension that the Henrician state might become virtually unaccountable.

Thomas Starkey, contemplating this problem in the early 1530s, offered a radical solution. He suggested that in the absence of Parliament a permanent council, empowered with the complete authority of the two houses and of convocation, sit in London to "defend the liberty of the whole body of the people *at all such time as the king or his counsel tended to anything hurtful or prejudicial to the same*" (emphasis added). This council would, like Parliament, hear grievances upon petition, but it would also have the power to "repress seditions," a function which suggested a broad executive mandate. Its members would consist of four temporal lords, "two bishops, as of London and Canterbury," four of the chief judges of the realm, and four citizens of London, thus encompassing not only the estates but the bench as well. This "little parliament," as Starkey called it, would in turn choose the members of the king's own Council, "for this," he wrote, "may in no case be committed to the arbitrament of the prince." The royal council, consisting of six members learned in divine, civil, and common law, and four noblemen expert in "policy," would in turn make all major civil and ecclesiastical appointments, confer all dignities, and in general govern and rule "all things pertaining to the princely state." The king himself would serve merely as the "head and president" of this council. The permanent council would be chaired by a Constable, who with the council would be empowered to call Parliament "whensoever they see any peril of the loss of the liberty" [of the realm].[33]

Starkey's concerns paralleled those of More and Elyot, and they found echo in the demands of the Pilgrimage of Grace, the most serious rebellion of Henry's reign. The scheme he proposed was rooted in the conciliarist visions of the fourteenth and fifteenth centuries, with their close suspicion of both clerical and monarchical power; his reliance on elites, expanded to include the legal and merchant classes, was traditional as well.[34] In reviving the Constable's office, a position left vacant after the execution of the Duke of Buckingham in 1521, Starkey blended conciliarism and medieval precedent to produce a balance at once novel and conservative. By tying the Constable to his council, he would avoid the "sedition and debate" that his unchecked authority had given rise to in feudal times, while the council's prestige would be augmented by a figure traditionally associated with the restraint of monarchic power.[35]

Starkey was not the only one interested in the revival of feudal dignities. The Earl of Essex hoped to combine the office of Constable with that of the Earl Marshal as a vehicle of power in the 1590s, and fifty years later his son, as Captain-General of the parliamentary army, would seek a similar authority. It was not a Devereaux but a Howard, however, the Earl of Arundel, on whom the staff (though not the title) of Constable was finally bestowed by James I in 1622. The practical inconsequence of this step was in part evidence of James' shrewdness in judging character—Arundel was a courtier, not a warrior—and in part an indication of the dependent nature of the nobility, for whom proximity to the royal closet, not independence of it, was now the final measure of power. The Constable's staff gave Arundel formal precedence at the Privy Council under the King and Prince Charles (and over Buckingham, at whom the stroke appears to have been intended),[36] rather than the active headship of an independent body such as Starkey had contemplated. If for Starkey the problem had been to contain the overweening authority of a Constable within the framework of a representative body, a century later the authority of the office had so dwindled that apart from such a body its functions were largely honorific.

In the event, the narrowing of conciliar representation was neither as extreme nor as exclusive as men such as Starkey feared, while the enactment of the Reformation by statute affirmed the connection between the authority of the crown and the consent of the realm. As the almost skeletonized Elizabethan council demonstrated, moreover, the effect of representation could be achieved even with a drastic economy of personnel, particularly where administration was perceived as responsive and the monarch as accessible.[37]

The council expanded in size even as it decreased in significance under James I, whose politics of entourage, while apparently a retrograde step, was expedient to the absorption of Scots courtiers into the English system. By the time of Charles I the anglicizing of the Stuart Court was more or less complete, but the return to tradition was not accompanied by a revival of confidence.[38] The Stuarts might acquire the trappings of an English monarchy, but they never achieved—at least to popular satisfaction—an English perspective. This made the function of counsel all the more critical. Bacon, the Earl of Salisbury, and the Earl of Strafford all envisioned themselves as chief councillors who would mediate between the Stuarts and their subjects, but the only person to whom a genuinely ministerial role was confided, the Duke of Buckingham, was the one most supremely unfit for it. James ruled in a wash of faction, Charles by fiat. Neither method was intrinsically unworkable—James, at least, was generally successful in balancing complex civil and religious constituencies through most of his reign—but neither was designed to allay anxieties about a new foreign dynasty. This situation was compounded by fears of renewed Spanish, French, and papal influence at the Stuart Court. These fears, themselves intensified by the beleaguered fortunes of Continental Protestants and the growing climate of apocalyptic expectation, mounted steadily through the latter part of James' reign and became well-nigh obsessional during the decade of Personal Rule by Charles I.

Concern about the effect of foreign precepts of rule on the English constitution was also heightened by the advent of a royal author in the person of James I. Because the king was, as James liked to put it, *lex loquens*, royal speech was customarily circumspect and formal. Sovereigns spoke in their regal capacity before Parliament and in proclamations, but in the first case their words were mediated by the occasion and the body, and in the second by avowal of counsel. Where they expressed themselves directly to a noninstitutional audience, they tended to confine themselves to subjects that lent themselves to homily or platitude. The one polemical work to bear a royal signature in Tudor times, Henry VIII's *Assertion of the Seven Sacraments*, was in the main the work of Court scholars, including Sir Thomas More; the King's name on the title page was largely in the nature of an honorific, and would have been so understood by its intended audience.[39] James' penchant for discourse and his appetite for controversy were therefore both novel and alarming, particularly as his preferred theme was the power of kings and the duty of subjects.

The cultural significance of James' career as an author has only recently received due attention.[40] It marks strikingly the transition between the declamatory culture of image and oration, with its fixed representations, and the print culture of self-definition, excogitated role-playing, and public controversy. Whereas Elizabeth signified herself primarily through the visual emblems of pageant and portraiture whose supporting verbal structure — biblical or mythical — was a more or less conventional prop for display, James expressed (and exposed) himself primarily in the contestatory medium of prose. This was not only a matter of personal preference; as her letters show, Elizabeth was no less eloquent an author than James, and certainly a pithier one. Rather, it reflected a profound shift in the legitimation of secular and religious authority in sixteenth-and seventeenth-century Europe. Put simply, that shift was from one of display to one of appeal. The power of an image is its reflection of the known, its reinforcement of the given. The decay of an image-system is, correspondingly, a token of disturbance and transition, and the outbreak of iconoclasm is often the signal for revolution.[41] That great iconoclast, Henry VIII, in putting the seal of royal power where that of the papacy had been and making spoil of its lands and monuments, had made profane what had been consecrated.[42] Elizabeth, essentially conservative and recuperative in her outlook, had continued the Henrician imperium, but, rebuilding the *Ecclesia Anglicana* against the blasts of post-tridentine Rome, had balked at completing the reformation of images that her father and brother had begun. This was the half-Reformed church at which the godly railed, a church not only defaced by the images and ceremonies of idolatry but all too often unvisited by the Word.

James had grown up in the severer discipline of Presbyterian Scotland, and though he had no use for "rash-headie" preachers, he was fond of disputation. Words were his medium; ceremony was something he endured. For James, though, bundled through childhood and early kingship by such fierce mentors as George Buchanan and Andrew Melville, writing was far more than the pleasurable display of a natural skill. Although he cautioned his son Henry not to write at the expense of ruling, it is clear that James' earliest authorial exercises — particularly the *Basilikon Doron* and *The Trew Law of Free Monarchies* — were autobiographical acts in which the king defined the space of monarchy in highly, not to say tendentiously personal terms. Given the facts of his biography, such an effort was not surprising.[43] What James sought was an absolute source for his authority and an inviolable zone for both his person and his sovereignty. He found it in divine right theory, which, together with Roman law, he sought to plant after 1603 in the unaccommodating soil of England. It was doubly disconcerting for the English to find themselves with a king who claimed, after Roman law fashion, to be *lex loquens*, when he spoke as he did to Parliament in 1610:

> The State of MONARCHIE is the supremest thing vpon earth: For Kings are not onely GODS Lieutenants vpon earth, and sit vpon GODS throne, but euen by GOD himselfe they are called Gods. . . . Kings are iustly called Gods, for they that exercise a manner or resemblance of Diuine power vpon earth: For if you will consider the Attributes to God, you shall see how they agree with the person of a King. God hath power to create, or destroy, make, or vnmake at his pleasure, to giue life, or send death, to iudge all, and to be iudged nor accomptable to none: To raise low things, and to make high things low at his pleasure, and to God are both soule and body due. And the like power haue Kings: they make and vnmake their subiects: they haue power of raising, and casting downe: of life, and of death: Iudges ouer all their subiects, and in all causes, and yet accomptable to none but God onely.[44]

It was one thing for Elizabeth to put on fancy mythological dress as Astraea or Gloriana, or James to bill himself as Solomon, and quite another for the first king of a foreign dynasty to claim divine powers and demand unconditional submission. It did not help sufficiently for James to reassure his subjects that he had no intention of governing arbitrarily, however he might. Englishmen heard a direct threat to established property rights in his words, and Parliament men to their control of the taxing power. The latter responded at once, in 1604 with the Apology and Satisfaction[45] and in 1610 with the Petition of Right. Alarm at the King's rhetoric and suspicion at the purposes it concealed helped lead to the rejection of his project for Anglo-Scottish union and to the failure of the Great Contract, the only serious attempt to rationalize Stuart finances before 1640.

The war of words between James and his parliaments climaxed in the bitter exchanges of December 1621, in which the House of Commons finally claimed as sweeping an interest in the general welfare as James had asserted for the powers of the crown. The discourse of the crown as embodied in proclamations and other acts of power took the form of commands requiring specific performance. They might be controversial, as James' prohibition of Sunday sports had been, or catastrophic, as Charles' Forced Loan was to be, but they engaged determinate processes of law and legitimation, and could be responded to in appropriate forms. James' ex cathedra pronouncements on monarchy occurred not within but outside this normative framework,

and while explicitly challenging that framework as most Englishmen understood it, they admitted of no response. For this reason they were deeply unsettling. When Sir Edward Coke declared during the parliamentary crisis of
December 1621, "I will not dispute with my Maister for his words," he expressed the frustration of a jurist confronted with an arbitrament beyond the
law. He then of course proceeded to dispute the King very firmly.[46] But such
defiance could occur only within the unique confines of a Parliament, if even
there. In any other venue, Coke's words could have been construed as high
treason.[47]

Charles inherited neither James' gift nor his penchant for authorship. The
sins of the father were visited upon the son nonetheless. Royal utterances of
any sort were scrutinized much more diligently, and relations between
crown and Parliament took on an adversarial cast. If James offended less by
what he did than by what he said, it must be remembered that royal words,
especially words uttered not merely by the legal but by the actual person of
the king, were deeds themselves in the strongest sense: they set the context
within which all action was to be interpreted, all commands obeyed. When
Charles put into effect what James had merely spoken, the suspicions that
the Stuart dynasty had aroused from the beginning were confirmed.

The Discourse of Courtesy

The command of the sovereign was simultaneously the terminus of a
given discourse and the starting-point of a fresh cycle of response; thus, the
chain of discourse was perpetual, its continuity unbroken even by the death
of the prince. We have focused thus far on the praxis of command in its efficient, symbolic, and performative aspects, but if command demanded compliance, it was shaped in turn by address and mediated by comment. The
process of address involved more than the articulation of need or the representation of interest. It was also exhortative, whether in the general sense of
urging appropriate values to the ruler (valor, magnanimity, etc.) or in the
specific one of entreating public policy (the marriage of Queen Elizabeth,
military intervention in the Netherlands or the Palatinate). Where this form
of address took place in the presence of the ruler (as entertainment or display) or was offered, less immediately, as compliment or allegory, we shall
call it *courtesy*.

Because of its privileged status as discourse addressed to or enacted before the ruler, courtesy was particularly conventionalized. It began with a
formal acknowledgment—disclaimer or salute—and ended with a formal
submission. Its principal literary mode was allegory, which permitted both
graceful compliment without the reproach of flattery, and oblique criticism
without the risk of lèse-majesté. Needless to say, the success of the occasion
depended on the discretion and skill of the allegorist as well as on the tem-

per of the monarch, whose response—an immediate and definitive act of criticism—capped the performance. The disastrous failures of George Gascoigne's Kenilworth pageant in 1575 and Francis Bacon's masque for the Accession Day tilts of 1595 demonstrated how Elizabeth could use her entertainments to rebuke courtiers (Leicester in the first case, Essex in the second) through their spokesmen. The Queen's reported response on the latter occasion, that "if she had thought their had bene so moch said of her, she wold not haue bene their that Night," castigated both patron and poet, the former for transparency of motive as the latter for transparency of art.[48]

As the preceding cases suggest, courtesy was not simply a means of communicating with the ruler, but an occasion for sovereign discourse as well. The response to courtesy enabled the ruler to indicate his own disposition to the realm, to dispense or deny favor to individuals, and to articulate public values. In its broadest sense, courtesy was the conversation of the Court, the dialectic through which the early modern state defined itself. It epitomized the rituals of petition, response, and submission that formally constituted the political process; it dramatized sovereignty; it made power visible while keeping it ceremonially aloof. Ritual and power are at all times indivisible, the display of authority essential to its exercise, but at few times in European history have the two been as purposively entwined as in the early modern moment. Courtesy was the language through which Renaissance monarchy most comprehensively defined and represented itself. It incorporated the Roman theme of empire and the Arcadian ideal of harmony (itself already an appeal to nostalgic visions of order in a rapidly commercializing society), fashionable Neoplatonism and the "chemical" theater of magic and romance. All these modes of power and imagination—the sum and substance of Renaissance discourse—were laid as tribute before the royal throne, and all were reflected back, after symbolic appropriation, in the refulgence of majesty. This totalizing discourse absorbed all competing power centers into itself, reconstituting them as authorized and therefore subordinate.

A prime example of this process was the domestication of the nobility. When Henry VIII jousted with his peers he descended among them as a *primus inter pares*; yet the very act of descent, the construal of lawless tumult as chivalric competition, affirmed the supremacy of the crown. Perhaps the most overtly symbolic of the Henrician tournaments was the assault on the Castle of Loyalty staged at Greenwich in 1524, which reenacted the archetypal act of civil war (the siege of a royal castle) as an assertion of duty and obedience. The already notable Tudor appetite for castles and manors, acquired by forced sale and attainder, could not but have added a somewhat uncomfortable piquancy to the event.[49]

By the time of Elizabeth's Accession Day tilts, royal patronage of chivalry had assumed a retrospective if not mannerist air, in which panoply had become more important than prowess. As George Puttenham noted, brave armor, sumptuous trappings, "apt posies, and wittie inventions," in short, display, had become the chief raison d'être of the occasion: knightly valor had given way to courtiership. This shift reflected long-term processes of centralization and bureaucratization, and complex recalibrations of "noble" and "gentle" values in a world in which status-hungry but decidedly nonmartial landowners, "the common sort of nobility" as Camden called them, clamored for recognition. It also reflected the dispute within Court culture between humanism and chivalry.[50] If "courtesy," as I have used the term, denotes the full range of literature and spectacle devised as royal address, it encompassed the contested field of elite values as well. The courtier was ideally a man of equal facility in letters and arms, but in practice the two skills were rarely met and still more rarely accommodated together, as the career of Sidney and the verse of Spenser attested. *The Faerie Queene* interrogates the premise that a courtly chivalry can still be relevant as a code of conduct and a style of life in the late sixteenth-century world, without settling its terms or reconciling its inherent contradictions except in the idyllic world of pastoral. If the regime of bureaucracy had triumphed over the humanist vision of counsel, it was still more emphatically victorious over knight-errantry. In the long battle between Essex and the Cecils, the outcome could never have been in doubt.

For most Elizabethans, however, the ideals of humanism, courtesy, and chivalry existed along a single if conflicted continuum of value, and if they could not be embodied simultaneously they could, at least in theory, be served in turn. The struggle to embrace the code of the courtier in each of its disparate (not to say opposed) aspects demanded a further application, panache. To perform with skill that which is difficult requires grace, but to perform successively, uninterruptedly, and without apparent contradiction roles that are in continual tension if not in conflict requires dexterity, aplomb, self-mastery, and wit; in a word—Castiglione's word—*sprezzatura*. Such a performance, in an arena of fierce competition for material advancement and status reward, could not be rendered indefinitely without cost. So brilliant a gamesman as Raleigh could not keep it up without disgust, and the bitterest dissections of the Court's "rotten wood" came not from country moralists but within chambers. The pastoral idiom deployed by Sidney and Spenser offered not only a foil to the vices of the Court (simplicity versus sophistry, sincerity versus tergiversation) but the illusion of an idyllic retreat, an internal rustication for the role-wearied self. In the end, however, there was no escape from the round. "Tell Potentates they live/ Acting by others' action," Raleigh wrote, affirming the dependence of his sovereign on her dependents, the circularity of a self-legitimized discourse.

Courtesy, then, was the self-conscious creation of a centralized Court whose participants were simultaneously actors and instruments. No doubt the ground-level experience of the participants themselves was often if not persistently alienating, a process brilliantly described by Stephen Greenblatt and others in the recent scholarly revival of the theme of Renaissance individualism.[51] Viewed as a whole, however, the mature Tudor Court was the nexus of a widely ramified web of patronage in which no single act or career stood alone, and through which all power and status relations were mediated from crown level to that of the lowest dogsbody constable. For this reason no utterance, however distinctive, was ever solitary, and no discursive performance was ever the act of a single agent. The patron was implicated in the behavior of his client, where his needs and interests did not dictate it. A sonnet—much less a suit—was not merely a mode of expression but a move in an intricate game of status and political maneuver in which the nominal author was often understood as the secondary agent of his noble "authorizer." Wit and eloquence were prized in themselves, of course, as the oil that made ambition keen and flattery tolerable, and among the later Elizabethans there was a discernible tendency to make large claims for stylistic finesse; but no Elizabethan or Jacobean would have conceived of literary address as an autonomous activity.

The ultimate ideological function of courtesy, as of patronage itself, was to reinforce a hierarchical social order that culminated in the throne. Whatever values it might espouse, whatever tensions it incorporated, courtesy literature exalted the institution of monarchy and the person of the monarch: as its existence was premised on the one, so its subsistence was on the other. As Frank Whigham points out, Elizabeth's courtier-poets, in creating the cult of Gloriana, inscribed themselves in the closed circle of her devotees. When Spenser, for example, prefaces his compliment to the Queen with an elaborate apology for daring to address her at all, he sets monarchy upon terms so awful and reverent that vulgar praise is tantamount to lèse-majesté while at the same time asserting a privileged access based upon genre and validated by favor. The Elizabethan defense of "poesie," in these terms, valorized literature as a hierophantic code which laid claim—beyond the rival discourses of law, counsel, and even theology—to constitute the most fitting address to majesty.

This rhetorical claim of intimacy, buttressed by the platonic love-conceits that surrounded the aging queen, offered almost vertiginous attenuations of erotic approach, the most rarefied filaments of desire reaching for the most gossamer threads of favor. Elizabeth's success in manipulating this courtly code—her eroticization of politics—was her supreme achievement. It rationalized penury (virtuously identified with chastity), and made what by Continental standards was an almost laughably impecunious Court into a "bower" of grace and glamour. Had Elizabeth been less adroit, the game could hardly have been kept up. But as she escaped her literary suitors (and sidetracked her royal ones) by becoming the bride of the nation, so too they sought to escape her by redefining the nation itself. As Richard Helgerson has persuasively argued, the generation bounded by Spenser and Hooker at one end and Shakespeare and Marlowe at the other was engaged in the massive collective project he has called "the Elizabethan writing of England."[52] The dimensions of this project far transcended the conventions of courtesy, yet courtesy remained in an essential sense its master trope and ultimate frame. To extend "England" was to extend monarchy, for the Tudors had made the throne coterminous with the realm, and under Elizabeth ubiquitous as well, the avowed source and embodiment—in her person and her power—of the nation as such. The celebrated Ditchley Portrait, which depicted the Queen poised on a cartographic image of the realm beneath a sky of lightnings, the unmoved mover and unshaken center, the virgin progenitor of all that was England, is perhaps the most triumphant representation of this vision. The great Elizabethans were both empowered and contained by that vision, and their labors only served to enlarge its dominion. This fruitful tension produced a Court culture like no other. Yet it was a self-consciously belated one, not only in its stylized evocation of medieval chivalry and Arthurian romance but in its sense of evanescence and "mutabilitie," in the certainty that the Virgin Queen would be the end of the tenuous Tudor line. As such, it was an unrepeatable, and in significant ways an unextendable performance. The Jacobean Court was necessarily another affair. When James I declared that kings were as gods, he rang an altogether different and harsher note from the conceits of Elizabethan courtesy; when he commissioned his lawyers rather than his poets to extol his powers, he provoked dispute rather than celebration; and when he attempted to unite the realms of England and Scotland, he evoked not imperial pride but ethnic animosity.

James lacked not only his predecessor's personal touch but the remarkable plasticity of her regnal theme. The Virgin Queen was simultaneously available and remote, nubile and chaste, an object of cultural fantasy in a way obviously unavailable to the new king, a mature male with a wife and heirs. After an unprecedented half century of female rule, James might have offered the realm a martial image, but neither his own inclination nor the circumstances of his accession made it feasible. It was not his lot to wage a glorious war but, after a long and debilitating struggle, to make a pragmatic peace, and by the time bellicosity was again in favor, Prince Henry had appropriated the hero's role. Neither Gloriana nor Mars, James was the worthy but uninspiring part of Solomon.

The passing of Elizabeth also meant the passing of the courtier ideal. Spenser had died in 1599, Essex was beheaded in 1601, and only the imprisoned Raleigh survived into the new reign as a symbol, pathetically caged, of the poet-adventurer. The pragmatic Cecils were contested now only by their own likes, the Bacons and Northamptons. A similar shift was apparent in the Jacobean patronage of spectacle and drama. James took his entertainments indoors, and although the Court continued to have vigorous commerce with the public theater of London, a clear ideological as well as dramatic division emerged between palace spectacles, with their self-conscious "studie of magnificence," and the popular stage with its brisk satire and its saga of urban mobility.

A good deal of this had to do with the codification of royal genres. Elizabeth's entertainments, however elaborate, had an improvisatory air; they were tableaux threaded with narrative conceits rather than true dramatic performances. The Stuart masque, as we have come to appreciate, was a much more sophisticated undertaking, a complex integration of text, music, and décor whose theme was not the rustication but the amplitude of majesty. In the fully developed masque, with its intricate machinery and revolving stage, majesty could be not merely represented as in the *tableau vivant* but projected dynamically in a manner hitherto associated only with divine worship. The similitude was not accidental. Majesty, like divinity, could be uniquely "revealed" by the devices of controlled spectacle, where sight, sound, and motion were coordinated to produce a sublime effect; and surely this was a desirable association, where majesty was conceived as the effulgence of divinity on earth. As Graham Parry notes, "Given James's conviction of the divine right of his tenure . . . the masque provided an eminently appropriate form for demonstrating the numinous powers of majesty in a setting of the utmost splendour."[53]

The relationship between theatricality and power was more than metaphoric; as Frances Yates has pointed out, the elaborate machinery employed in stage productions on the Continent and introduced to England by Inigo Jones in 1605 may have marked the first instance in which state funds were deployed on a large scale to produce mechanical devices of a nonmilitary nature.[54] If war, however, was a mode of display, the mechanized Jacobean theater, even as its texts celebrated the virtues of peace, carried a subtext of martial prowess. Prince Henry's entertainments were clearly rehearsals for battle; James', at any rate, were at least in part a sublimation of it.

The mechanization of the masque had obvious consequences for production as well. Frugal Elizabeth had left it to her hosts to provide entertainments on her progresses, which though suitably lavish were not prodigious. With the advent of Inigo Jones' "Mighty Showes," however, the cost and complexity of staging a full-blown masque exceeded any private resources, and the Court itself, specifically the Banqueting Hall, became the only feasible site of performance. Spectacle was thenceforward a major preoccupation of the Court, and a not inconsiderable drain on revenues as well; a single masque cost £4,000 to produce in 1618, more than the cost of a state embassy.

The ideological implications of the mechanized masque were no less significant. The rise of the Elizabethan public theater had produced a strong backlash among commentators who feared the effects of representing tyranny, paganism, and vice, and were scandalized by the sight of strolling players in royal robes. The Court's relations with this theater were complex, but with the erection of a more or less permanent theater in Whitehall the Court itself was the chief cynosure of the stage, with all the suspicion if not scandal this gave to antitheatrical sentiment. The secluded nature of royal performances, their concealed and mysterious arts, and their dramaturgical and illusionistic focus upon the person of the monarch, all tended to reinforce suspicions as to their true import. The theater was closely associated with magical and demonic forces, where — as in plays such as *The Tragical History of Dr. Faustus*, *The Tempest*, and *The Alchemist* (the latter of course the product of Ben Jonson, the scenarist of the Jacobean masques) — they were not overtly its subject; but, as Yates reminds us, machinery as such was associated with hellish devices in Renaissance culture as well, an association that would persist into the days of Luddism and beyond.[55]

What blunted criticism of the Jacobean masque was the incontrovertible and oft-displayed religious orthodoxy of James himself. There seemed little likelihood of his Court being transformed into a den of sorcery like that of Rudolf II. With the advent of Charles, however, the masque took on an altogether more suspect air. The new King's modest bearing and chaste demeanor at first augured well, but as he seemed to fall under the spell of his Catholic Queen and her entourage, his quondam virtues appeared increasingly as weakness, gullibility, and uxorious submission. To be sure, Charles' promotion of Arminian bishops and his reception of a papal envoy were of far more substantive concern than the style of his Court theatricals, but it would be a mistake to ignore their reciprocal impact. The pagan entertainments of the King's private theater, in which the Queen was not only a chief sponsor and participant but a principal object of celebration, and the popish devotions of the Queen's closet, were easily interpreted as aspects of a single ominous imposture. The long-term consequences of this were dire. When Charles was denounced at his trial in 1649 as "a tyrant, traitor, murderer, and a public and implacable enemy to the Commonwealth of England," the charge of tyranny derived not merely from the King's political acts on the public stage but from the image of the doting, inconstant, idolatrous despot of theatrical tradition that, at least for the godly party, had become inextricably associated with his patronage and performance on the private stage of the masque and with the popish aspect of his Court and church generally. Milton's *Eikonoklastes* would ridicule the image of a prayerful Charles grasp-

ing a martyr's crown of thorns that his supporters put out in the aftermath of
the regicide as "a Masking Scene . . . to catch fools and silly gazers . . . [with]
quaint Emblems and devices begg'd from the Pageantry of some Twelft-
nights entertainment." In the end, as he would remark elsewhere, such
strategems would backfire, "For a tyrant, just like a player king indeed," was
"only the ghost and mask" of a true king.[56]

The *techne* of the masque would come in time to seem part of the wall that
had separated Court and Country, crown and subject. It would have no less
adverse an impact on the discourse of courtesy itself. Jonson's celebrated
complaint about the displacement of text in the masque by artifice and
"show" expressed a more general sense of the decline of royal pageantry as a
means of articulating values, airing policy questions, and knitting the throne
to the country by hospitality and display. David Norbrook has faulted Jonson himself for setting a pattern of complacent "courtly classicism" in his
own texts, but Jonson's own career, with its repeated brushes with censorship, suggests a far more complex case in which trimming at Court was balanced by the assumption of a more independent stance on the public stage.[57]
The evolution of the masque text itself, with its counterpoint between the
hieratic mise-en-scène of the masque proper and the violent, popular elements of the anti-masque, suggests too the polarization of attitude between
the Court and the rude multitude.

If the supremacy of spectacle in the masque and the more rigidly controlled and conventionalized nature of the masque texts themselves signaled
the decline of courtesy, so too did the increasing professionalization of the
theater both at Court and on the London stage. No longer would a lawyer
like Bacon be expected (or indulged) to devise texts for Court entertainments; these were now the province of a handful of poets, specifically patronized for the purpose, whose expertise guaranteed not only the polish of
the product but its conformity to thematic and ideological prescription.
Kevin Sharpe has shown how the masque texts of Davenant and Carew reflected subtler currents of faction and debate at Court in the 1630s, and incorporated a certain degree of criticism as well; but the closed, self-
referential nature of this theater and its audience contained it within a system of congratulation that remained impervious to feeling in the country
and incapable of formulating a genuine dissent.[58] At the same time, those
playwrights who earned their livelihood on the commercial stage set themselves off scornfully from the hireling pens at Court: Brome's scathing attack
on Sir John Suckling in *The Court Beggar* (1639-1640) showed that the rift between Court and Country had divided the stage as well.[59]

In the hands of a Spenser or a Sidney, the discourse of courtesy proposed
to mediate between prince and subject, virtue and prudence; in those of
Suckling and his fellow wits, it was an ornament of power. Between a satiric

stage and a sequestered Court, the Caroline poets had no platform for a mediatory discourse. It is highly doubtful, of course, that any amount of rhetorical agility or theatrical display could have reconciled broad sections of the English (and Scots) public to the policies of Charles I. As it was, the seclusion of Stuart Court entertainments added the suspicion of secret ritual and license to the visible tokens of prerogative rule. What was acted and danced under the tapers of the Banqueting Hall was less to the point than what might be inferred about it in godly conventicles and distant shires. Graham Parry has observed, in an extraordinarily damning comment, that Charles I's "major public appearances really began on the battlefields of the 1640s."[60] The Court masques of the 1630s compounded the psychological distance between a deeply isolated King and his subjects.

The Discourse of History

"Farewell, good and honest Lambarde," said the elderly Elizabeth to her famous antiquary after a talk about his researches in the Tower of London.[61] Not all such conversations ended amicably. In a culture ruled by custom and precedent, control of the past was the key to governing the present.

In this as in so many other respects, Henry VII was alert to his opportunities. A king by conquest, he had more need to rewrite history than most; a peer of his brother monarchs by aspiration, he imported a young Continental humanist, Polydore Vergil, to tell his tale. This was a decisive moment in English letters. Lancastrian England, like the contemporary Balkans, had produced more history than it could assimilate, much less record; with an uncertain throne and declining ecclesiastical patronage, English historiography had fallen on hard times. Vergil's *Anglica Historia*, with its sophisticated techniques, skeptical address, and official sponsorship, was a powerful stimulus in all directions to Richard Helgerson's "writing of England." It inspired the next several generations of historians, antiquaries, and chorographers; chroniclers and playwrights quarried from it; and succeeding Tudors themselves found in its imperial theme both inspiration and rationale for a policy of expansion.[62]

But Tudor history, too, outraced its encomiasts. The Henrician Reformation, the Marian reaction, and the Elizabethan settlement left fissures in English life that no account could reconcile; more fundamentally, they left irreconcilable audiences which no master narrative could satisfy. Vergil himself, a collector of papal taxes, opposed the breach with Rome, and the general division it caused among the Erasmian humanists, sealed by the martyrdom of More and Fisher and bonded by recusancy, left a permanently alienated confessional interest. If Foxe's *Book of Martyrs* came closest to an authoritative Protestant narrative (albeit one in which the Tudors played an equivocal role), it evoked a potentially subversive authority of conscience, and, despite its canonical status, underscored the fault lines within the Anglican polity.

Vergil's position as royal historiographer thus proved unique; there no longer could be, even in theory, a single prescriptive interpretation of England's past. England might be seen in providential terms (with Elizabeth as deliverer), a vision best pursued in sermon and homily, or in pastoral and idealizing ones, the genre preferred by Elizabeth herself; but its secular history resisted ideological closure. At the same time, however, the very travails of that history and the pressures of unprecedented social and demographic change stimulated the enterprise of national self-definition. The imperial theme sounded by Vergil would work itself out in the metahistorical discourse of the godly emperor and the subhistorical ones of the antiquary and the chorographer, whose labors provided an immensely detailed and cumulative tapestry of the nation from which only the royal pattern (though not the royal stamp) was missing.

The discourse of scholarship was thus an extension, continuous if not wholly seamless, of the humanist discourse of counsel and the Elizabethan discourse of courtesy. It connected in turn with the discourse of law adumbrated in Coke's *Institutes* and *Reports* and the grand, historicizing enterprise of the popular theater, culminating in the overreaching, syncretic vision of Bacon's *Novum Organum*. Each separate discourse, while having its own function and audience, was tributary to the whole, and that whole was finally the self-definition of the nation. England—an England timeless but not static, an imperializing England, isolate but conquering—was the object of this collective discourse. Its warp was the act of boundary-making in an age when "the Borders" still connoted a physically insecure and culturally indistinct frontier—*The Description of England*, the *Survey of London*, the *Perambulation of Kent*.[63] Its weft was a contested historical and cultural formation, whose often bloodied ground belied any simple, hortatory appeal to unity and discipline. Elizabethan and Jacobean Englishmen evoked "England" so repeatedly and multifariously not because of any settled consensus about what the term meant, but precisely because of the lack of it.

Because this discourse, for all its variety, had a common theme and focus, and because as well of the courtier ideal of the cultivated polymath, it was easy to cross what we would now call disciplinary boundaries. Thus, as the humanist, lawyer, and courtier Sir Thomas More had begun his career with a cautionary tale about England's past, the *History of King Richard the Third*, so Sir Francis Bacon, scientist, jurist, philosopher, and sometime deviser of Court entertainments, would end his with *The History of the Reign of King Henry the Seventh*. Increasingly, however, the professionalization we have already observed on the stage was also evident in scholarly pursuits. Lambarde, Camden, Selden, and Cotton were no dilettantes, but men of national and, in the latter two cases, international reputation.

Patronage tied these men to the crown as it had the earlier generations of humanist courtiers—William Lambarde as Keeper of the Rolls, William Camden as Clarenceaux King at Arms in the College of Heralds, John Selden and Sir Robert Cotton as clients of the Howards—but their common interests linked them to one another in the Society of Antiquaries, founded by Camden with the young Cotton's help, which Elizabeth viewed with some skepticism and James finally abolished. The gesture was futile; the growing sophistication of English scholarship inexorably extended the network of communication among scholars and sharpened their standards of discourse, and as an authoritative interpretation of the historical record became ever more critical in the tense decades of the 1620s and 1630s, scholars were drawn into the fray not only as consultants but as active participants. Selden and Cotton went into what can not unreasonably be called opposition in the 1620s,[64] and although both tried to maintain their purchase at Court, both suffered spells of imprisonment and other marks of disfavor. The sequestration of Cotton's library after the parliamentary session of 1629, an act amply noted by contemporaries,[65] signified the felt threat that legal and historical scholarship posed to Caroline rule. More than the suppression of a given work or the punishment of a particular author, the closing of Cotton's library deprived all scholars of an invaluable and irreplaceable resource. As for Cotton himself, he wrote pitifully that the "detaining of his books" would be the cause of his death. Whatever the case, he died shortly after.

As with chronicle plays on stage, historical accounts of particular rulers and reigns attracted close attention from the public and scrutiny by the crown. The complexity of this interaction in the context of the decaying codes of courtesy and chivalry can be seen in the reception of three regnal studies. John Hayward's *The First Part of The Life and Raigne of King Henrie IIII*, the story of a usurping king, was published in 1599. It was a moment at which all eyes were turned upon the Elizabethan succession, and references to Richard II, in whatever context, were automatically suspect. Hayward's context was that of a fulsome dedication to the Earl of Essex, lately patron of a volume containing the even more pointedly titled *The Ende of Nero and the Beginning of Galba*.[66] If any further prompting were needed, the association of Essex's name with the comment that Henry "would more happily and more safely go forth among the people" no doubt sufficed. Historical characters were not merely taken for present exemplars by sixteenth century readers, they were, in the Tacitean code of the time, clearly intended to be. If Henry were not Essex, he was certainly what contemporaries called "a lively portrait" of what the Earl might not implausibly become.

Hayward's book was licensed for publication (perhaps somewhat surprisingly)[67] in January, and it appeared the following month. It was eagerly bought; "No book," his satisfied publisher commented, "ever sold better." Doubtless the attractions of Hayward's prose and the scandal of the subject accounted in part for this, but interest centered particularly on the dedication to Essex, then just on the point of departure for a much-heralded campaign against Tyrone's rebellion in Ireland.[68] Hayward had neglected a critical point, however, namely to secure the Earl's permission for the dedication, that is his patronage and endorsement of a book bound to be regarded as controversial if not inflammatory at the most critical juncture of his career. Essex's position was delicate. He could not disavow the book without some loss of face, if not honor; he could not accept it without presumption. He chose a middle course, referring the dedication to Archbishop Whitgift for inquiry without, however, repudiating it.

Whitgift took the hint, and ordered the dedication excised. Hayward prepared an "Epistle Apologeticall" for the new edition. Without mentioning Essex, he denied any intention to draw parallels between Ricardian times and his own, or to question, in depicting them, the prerogative right to lay taxes. Essex departed for Ireland with great fanfare in late March, and Hayward's as-yet unaltered *Life and Raigne* continued to circulate without impediment. If Essex could not embrace the book without antagonizing the Queen, neither could the authorities suppress it without appearing to undermine his mission.

A more general response, however, was in preparation. On June 1, the Council ordered the Stationers to confiscate certain classes of books, and mandated "that noe English historyes be printed except they be allowed of some of her maiesties privie counsell."[69] Hayward's publisher surrendered all 1500 copies of the as-yet undistributed second edition, the working copy of the first edition with Hayward's changes and interlineations, and the manuscript of the "Epistle Apologeticall." The new books were burned at the Bishop of London's house, and the manuscript material was remanded for scrutiny.

Scrutiny it received, particularly in the aftermath of Essex's fall. By that time Hayward's text had become "a seditious pamphlet" and a "treasonable book,"[70] proof positive of the Earl's long-standing design against the government. Lord Chief Justice Popham was assigned to investigate it, together with Attorney-General Coke and Francis Bacon, Essex's former client and Elizabeth's maid-of-all legal work. Hayward was remanded to the Tower, where Elizabeth considered torturing him for information; at the same time (June 1600) she revoked the permission she had given Essex to travel in the country for his health, thus plainly tying the two cases together. Coke asked why:

1. [Hayward] selecteth a story 200 yere olde, and publisheth it this last yere, intendinge the application of it to this tyme 2. maketh choice of that story only, a kinge is taxed for misgovernment, his council for corrupt and covetous for their private [ends], the king censured, for conferring benefits of hateful parasites and favourites, the nobles discontented, the commons groning under continuall taxations.

He concluded: "Hereuppon the king is deposed by an erle and in the ende murdre[d]."[71]

Hayward was examined on these and other points in January 1601, in the tense atmosphere just prior to Essex's final uprising. Immediately after the Earl's execution, a circular advising London preachers about how to discuss his fate referred, without title or attribution, to a certain "history of Henry IV" printed two years previously that had "falsely attributed to these times" the vices of Richard II and insinuated that the Queen might suffer the same fate. The circular went on to say that "This book was no sooner published but the earl, knowing hundreds of them to be dispersed, would needs seem the first that disliked it, where he has confessed that he had the written copy with him to peruse 14 days, plotting, how he might become another Henry IV . . ."[72]

Such was the narrow ground on which Hayward kept his head. His book was condemned as a thinly veiled slander and an incitement to rebellion, but the government was unable to establish that Essex had sponsored it or that he and Hayward had any substantial connection; if anything, the implication of the circular was that the Earl had been naively seduced into imagining himself another Bolingbroke by reading it. Hayward was released from the Tower sometime between December 1602 and June 1603. He promptly produced tracts in favor of the Stuart succession and the union with Scotland, earning in the fullness of time a knighthood and a seat on the High Commission among other preferences. Camden was a friend and defender, and Cotton a close colleague. Hayward never ceased to proclaim the innocence of his work. In the "Epistle Apologeticall" he declared that he had "purposely passed over many imputations . . . which the deepe searchers of our time have rather framed then found," and in 1612 he noted that, in reading histories, the "guiltiness" of malefactors "maketh them apt to conceive, that, whatsoever the words are, the finger pointeth only at them."[73] *Honi soit qui mal y pense.*

Modern commentators have tended to acquit Hayward of anything worse than injudiciousness and opportunism — severe enough offenses in the tense climate of late Elizabethan England[74] — but they may have missed some of the subtler overtones of the affair. Hayward defended himself by citing his sources, but he could hardly have been unaware of the censorship of Holinshed's *Chronicle* or the particular sensitivity of treating Richard II. Nor could he have been ignorant of the Jesuit Robert Persons' inflammatory suggestion that Essex could determine (if not usurp) the succession.[75] In this context, his public bid for Essex's patronage, using the parallel of an abused nobleman vindicating his rights against a tyrannical ruler, seems almost brazen in its effrontery.

The more important issue is not Hayward's judgment, however, but the crown's. The case for Hayward's complicity in treasonable plots or "designs" was circumstantial, but the latitude of Tudor treason statutes was wide. Much turned on the authorship of the critical preface, titled "A. P. to the Reader," which Hayward insisted was his own although many had attributed it to Essex. This perfectly conventional piece of humanistic bluster might appear harmless or sinister, depending on who had actually written it; similarly, the text itself could be read, according to taste, as a chronicle retold or a blueprint for rebellion. Hayward's examiners read his text very assiduously indeed. Coke and Popham questioned him closely about a number of passages and references, but Bacon, though eager enough to implicate Essex, dismissed the question of textual treason with a witticism.[76] So did a disinterested commentator, the Court gossip John Chamberlain, who noted sagely that in such matters "everything is as it is taken."[77]

The decision not to try Hayward for treason thus turned on a number of factors. There is no doubt that Elizabeth, who was very much angered by the book, could have had Hayward's head had she wished it. But there was sufficient ambiguity both about the dedicatory connection to Essex and the intention of the text itself to give pause. Hayward himself was cooperative with his examiners, and gave a plausible defense. In the end, he was a bit player in the tragedy of Essex's fall. To have tried him prior to the Earl's final uprising would have seemed a provocation; to have tried him after, supererogatory.

In another sense, however, Hayward's case posed a special problem in the hermeneutics of legitimacy. The same calculus that would hang a poor man for words uttered in his cups or cut off the right hand of a John Stubbes for questioning the Queen's intended marriage to the Duke of Alençon was also at work in determining Hayward's fate. The state had need of men such as Hayward, a scholar and a civilian whom Archbishop John Whitgift had only a few years before admitted to practice in the Court of Arches. His fault— whether construed as an error or a crime—certainly merited punishment, but the effect of trying him for treason would have been to cast a pall over much of the literature of counsel to which, as a genre specimen, *The Life and Raigne of King Henrie IIII* clearly belonged. On a quite different social level, Shakespeare and his company escaped punishment (and for that matter imprisonment) for their notorious performance of *The Life and Death of King Richard II* on the eve of Essex's rising, although the deposition scene of the play was omitted from all editions of the text published in Shakespeare's lifetime. The task of censorship was to constrain, not to crush. Even when an offending text skirted the precincts of treason, scrupulous criteria had to be applied, and due regard given to invoking a capital penalty upon a literary act. In that sense, Hayward's case required as careful and pondered a consideration as Essex's own.

Hayward's case inevitably invites comparison with the more complex and symbolically richer one of Sir Walter Raleigh. Raleigh was the courtier's courtier; he showed both the merits and the limits of his type. Elizabeth had never trusted him with a seat on the Council, the place that separated the men of business from the boys of valor. As an ornament he was incomparable; as an adventurer he was a splendid failure; as a martyr he was perfected. He gloried in the challenge of disgrace, and that astute observer Dudley Carleton caught him at his ultimate, theatrical best, at his trial for treason in 1603:

> Sir Walter Ralegh served for a whole act, and played all the parts himself. . . . He answered with that temper, wit, learning, courage, and judgment, that, save it went with the hazard of his life, it was the happiest day that ever he spent. And so well he shifted all advantages that were taken against him, that were not *fama malum gravius quam res*, and an ill name half hanged, in the opinion of all men, he had been acquitted.[78]

In the event, Raleigh's head was not yet required; confined to the Tower, he haunted the popular imagination like a fabulous beast, the caged reminder of the Queen's great days and of the "Protestant option" latterly represented by Prince Henry, to whom Raleigh for a time grew close. If Raleigh, even in captivity, was thus still a subversive presence, he had his uses as a foil to James' pacifism and a reminder of its limits; and the first Stuart was never one to squander an asset. Even treason had its political market value.

To understand this, we must consider Raleigh's case a little more closely. There is general consensus that Raleigh was framed at his treason trial in 1603; D. H. Willson describes the evidence against him as "absurdly weak," and Maurice Lee likens Coke's prosecutorial zeal to that of Judge Jeffreys.[79] Allegedly, Raleigh had conspired with his client, Lord Cobham, and the ambassador of the Spanish Netherlands to depose James and place Arabella Stuart on the throne. But the term "framed" must be bracketed. Raleigh's real crime was that he was an overmighty courtier, the late Elizabethan equivalent of the fifteenth century's overmighty subject, the feudal magnate. His political enemies, the bureaucrats Cecil and Howard, characterized him, in Willson's words, as "dangerous, malcontent and warlike,"[80] sufficient warning to a king whose Scottish reign, from Bothwell to Gowrie, had been thick with plot and faction. James himself, who wished Raleigh's post of Captain of the Guard for his own entourage, found these denunciations a suitable pretext for spurning Raleigh's service. Whether or not the Cobham plot was anything more than impolitic grumbling, if that, is beside the point; by one means or another, Raleigh was to be driven to a position where he must either resort to "treason" or be plausibly accused of doing so.

In a larger sense, Raleigh's condemnation was a framing device for the new reign as such. In the dialectic of legitimacy, the obedient subject was contrasted with the traitor, and the high drama of treason's discovery, narration, and exemplary punishment made loyalty an active rather than a passive virtue; indeed, as in the Elizabethan Bond of Association, one that might well border on vigilantism. James' accession, after a decade of alarums, was anticlimactically peaceful, and though most (and most notably the King himself) were profoundly grateful for the fact, the fillip of danger was lacking to give the full measure of drama to England's deliverance from a disputed or Romish succession. The alleged Cobham plot thus filled a void, and it is not to suggest that it simply was manufactured to note that had it not existed something like it must needs have been invented.

At the same time, the Cobham plot was too dubious an episode, and Raleigh too unsatisfactory a scapegoat, to properly dramatize the new reign. That was left to the Gunpowder plot, whose indelibly graphic image of subversion—the twenty barrels laid to blow James and his Parliament to kingdom come—knit the dynasty to the nation in a bond of common peril. At the same time, the terms of Raleigh's imprisonment were mitigated. He was given access to his library, which, if no commission to write, certainly removed a chief impediment; and more active encouragement came from Prince Henry. The result was the massive torso of his *History of the World*.

A man under sentence of death—as the fifty-seven-year-old Raleigh necessarily regarded himself, naturally no less than civilly, when he took up the *History*—must either aim for purposeful brevity or amplitude of vision. Raleigh chose the latter. Unlike his younger contemporaries, Hayward, Samuel Daniel, and Michael Drayton, he eschewed British history; the frontispiece of the 1614 edition, which shows a globe upheld by the figure of Magistra Vitae (History), affords a wedge-shaped England no particular prominence.[81] Yet Raleigh had originally conceived his work as a national, not a world history. As he declared in the Preface, his intention was "to have set together . . . the unjointed and scattered frame of our English Affairs" and "(some sallies excepted) to confine my discourse, within this our renowned Island of Great Britain."[82] Instead, the "sallies" became the 1,500-page text, and the ostensible subject disappeared: the narrative got no further than Rome's conquest of the east, stopping just short of the invasion of Britain with which the national history might properly have begun.

What had induced Raleigh to this *volte-face*; why, having dropped his original plan, did he nonetheless publish it? His own cryptic comment was that his "inmost, and self-piercing wounds," as well as the advice of friends, had led him to write of that to which he was "nothing indebted" rather than of events which "can yield me no . . . profit." In short, Raleigh had forestalled the censor by censoring himself. This was nothing out of the ordinary; indeed, as Annabel Patterson notes, it was the very "condition" of early modern writing. But Raleigh was less concerned to evade the censor than to trump him. In stating his constraints, in noting how direly he had already suffered for his patriotism, he proclaimed not a reluctance to offend but a superiority to persecution. He had lost his liberty; nature, if not man, would soon take his life. He was as far beyond consolation as he was beyond punishment. What better evidence could he give of his bona fides as an historian?

Raleigh's subject, then, was not a safer but a grander one. Nor had he truly abandoned his British history. Not only did he promise subsequent volumes, already "hewn out," but since his theme—the well-worn Renaissance *topos* of fortune and providence in the affairs of men—applied equally to ancient and modern times, on native or foreign soil, he could write British history in the chronicles of biblical and pagan kingdoms, and vice versa. Did the personification of King James as the British Solomon not imply as much?

James himself thought so. He was said to have been particularly irked by the depiction of Ninias, the feeble and effeminate successor of Queen Semiramis, but Raleigh's denunciation of wicked kings was so relentless and his relish in their condign fate so evident as to approach, at least to someone with James' well-documented sensitivities on the subject, a slander against monarchy itself. Nor was Raleigh's censure limited to ancient rulers. He took advantage of his Preface to interpolate a brief but vivid sketch of the Norman line in England. Founded in violence, it had been from the beginning, in his view, a saga of almost unremitting conspiracy, rebellion, and civil war; a generation later, the Levellers would hardly find much worse to say of it. But no king, ancient or modern, had exceeded the cruelty, faithlessness, vanity, and lust of Henry VIII:

> If all the pictures and Patterns of a merciless Prince were lost in the World, they might all again be painted to the life, out of the story of this King. For how many servants did he advance in haste (but for what virtue no man could suspect) and with what change of his fancy ruined again; no man knowing for what offence? To how many others of more desert gave he abundant flowers from whence to gather honey, and in the end of Harvest burnt them in the Hive? How many wives did he cut off, and cast off, as his fancy and affection changed? How many Princes of the blood (whereof some of them for age could hardly crawl towards the block) with a world of others of all degrees (of whom our common Chronicles have kept the account) did he execute? . . .[83]

It was hardly surprising that the *History* was called in upon its initial publication in 1614 "for beeing to sawcie in censuring princes," but James was still unwilling to waste an asset, and the book suffered no worse fate than having its author's name effaced from the title page: a mark of disfavor rather of censorship, since Raleigh's identity was notorious.[84] It went into a second edition in 1614, and when another one appeared in 1616 to coincide with Raleigh's voyage to Guiana, his name was restored, and James himself made confiscated stocks from the first edition available. Nor did Raleigh's subsequent disgrace and execution impede its circulation; it saw three more editions by 1630, and a popular abridgment in 1636.[85]

Raleigh's *History* pointed up not only the limits but the politics of monarchical legitimacy. The violence of his attack upon Henry VIII would obviously have been unthinkable while Elizabeth was alive, and, coming from the author of *Ocean to Cynthia*, it is still rather jarring. An eye to the faults of the Tudor dynasty was not necessarily unwelcome at the Court of the first Stuart, but so unmeasured an assault seemed to cast a jaundiced eye in prospect as well as retrospect over monarchy in England: James was not mistaken in seeing in it an aspersion on his office, if not indeed on his person. At the same time, however, the portrait of Henry fell recognizably into the genre of tyrant literature, in which the evil ruler appeared as the necessary foil of the good one.[86] If the rule of thumb (as well as of law) was that a sitting king could do no wrong, it certainly did not apply to deceased ones, and in a world so generally sinful it was hardly to be wondered that the wicked bore rule with some frequency. Thus the unjust ruler was not a problem for monarchical legitimacy as such, as long as subjects bore in mind that he was merely an instrument of their penance, and that as a wise Providence had appointed chastisement for their good, so a merciful one would both remit it in due course and requite the instrument according to his deserts. Nor did it pose an insuperable difficulty when the same prince appeared successively as good and evil. Henry VIII was a paradigmatic case in this regard, having been praised as the liberator of true religion in England and damned as its fell usurper. Raleigh, it was true, had savaged Henry on purely secular grounds, but it was understood that the lens of history was often adjusted to the perspective of a new reign, and even more so to that of a new dynasty. The wisdom of Providence—or the legitimacy of kings—was open to question only when history was regarded, Orosius-like, as a more or less unrelieved sequence of disasters, and tyranny as the norm rather than the exception to the monarchical office. Raleigh rather did regard it that way, which led to the suspicion of atheism that dogged his career, as well as to the charge of antiroyalism with which James taxed him. But he never renounced Providence, or embraced republicanism. Perhaps he was, in the end, too much the courtier for either.

Sir Robert Cotton's *Short View of the Long Life and Raigne of King Henry the Third, King of England*, was allegedly written in 1614, but was published only in 1627, against the background of the Forced Loan and the failed impeachment of Buckingham. It was linked at once to Hayward's *Henrie IIII*; both were issued in a single volume in 1642, an edition frequently reprinted thereafter. Cotton's brief treatise made no pretense to original scholarship; it was transparently a work of counsel, and freely manipulated the historical record to suit that purpose. His Henry moves from one minion to another while the land waxes corrupt from "the surfeit of long peace" and the King is led by foreign councillors "into an evill opinion of his people," references to James' sexual preferences, his foreign policy, and his Scottish retinue respectively that would have needed no contemporary gloss. But as Henry's reign unfolds, his reliance on a single upstart favorite, Mountford (Simon de Montfort), the resultant envy and anger of the nobility, the incursion of the church into affairs of state, and a succession of turbulent parliaments that challenge a wide range of abuses and royal officers, all suggest with even greater force the travails of the early Caroline monarchy. Worse yet, however, lay ahead. Henry was compelled to reaffirm Magna Carta, to banish his Norman companions, and to submit to humiliating financial constraints at the hands of his commons. This led not to sound reformation but popular usurpation. The result was a "licencious Soveraignty" in which "tribunes" were appointed to oversee the government, and the King, reduced to selling lands and jewels and pillaging shrines, would be compelled finally to yield the prerogative and to reflect on the fatal error of his ways: "Here hee [found] his wastfull hand had beene too quick . . . over the fortunes and blessings of his People, [and by] the griping Avarice of his Civill Ministers and lawless liberty of his Martiall followers, the neglect of grace, and breach of his word, [he had] lost his Nobility at home, and, necessity, his Reputation abroad, by making Merchandize of peace, and warre . . ."[87] It was scarce wonder that the *Short View* should have been reprinted in 1642. From the Petition of Right to the surrender of his coastal waters to the desertion of his nobility at York to the depredations of the Cavaliers, Cotton's Henry III would no doubt have seemed in the first year of the Civil War to have been reborn in the person of Charles I. At the same time, the happy ending Cotton had supplied to Henry's reign—a chastened King once again in command of his throne and ruling with the advice of prudent and nobly born counsel— was clearly intended to suggest a wiser course to Charles. Cotton's perspective in the *Short View* thus appears to be a highly traditional one. The moral of Henry III's reign was that royal weakness was soon translated into social anarchy. The older nobility, deprived of precedence and honor, stooped downward to become "the darlings of the multitude," while the gentry, "Spirits of as much Acrimony and Arrogant spleene" as any, seconded their efforts. Emboldened by the decay of valor, in Cotton's view as well as in that of his contemporaries the linchpin of social order and government, giddy heads arose who, seeming "to decipher every blemish in Government" and "holding certaine imaginary and fantastick forms of commonwealths," proposed to new-fashion the state. Institutions, too, were inevitably corrupted: "Thus Parliaments that before were ever a medicine to heale up any rupture in Princes fortunes, [were] now growne worse than the mallady, sith from thence more malignant humours beganne to raigne in them, then well composed tempers."[88]

Cotton's thought was far more sophisticated than this "rhetorical parable," in Daniel Woolf's phrase, would suggest, and his political loyalties and affiliations were far more complex. His first editor, James Howell, recalled "how in all Parlements, where he served so often, his main endeavours were to assert the public Liberty, and that Prerogative and Privilege might run in their due Channels."[89] By 1627 he had become not only a principal advocate of parliamentary authority but an *éminence grise* of the nascent Caroline opposition. At the same time, he remained a lifelong client of the Howard family, and kept a careful purchase at Court.[90] In short, like most Englishmen of his time he was an advocate of strong monarchy within a balanced polity that included institutional safeguards against arbitrary rule and guarantees for personal liberty and property rights; like some, he was increasingly persuaded that only frequent and vigilant parliaments could curb the absolutistic tendencies of the Stuarts, the arrogance of their favorites, and the pretensions of their clergy. By the same token, he knew that the occasional cudgels of a Parliament were no substitute for the day-to-day discipline of good counsel. His services to Parliament, both political and scholarly, his active involvement with the anti-Buckingham circle around the Earl of Arundel, and his publication of the *Short View* were all efforts toward the same end, but of these the *Short View* was most clearly an act of counsel.

To whom was this counsel addressed? As a preceptive statement wrapped in the form of historical representation, it could speak only by analogy to current issues; as a public comment, it could reach the King's ears only in terms of the most egregious comparison. James I had scorned to be likened to weak and silly kings, and his son was all the less likely to appreciate a similar inference. But Cotton's intended audience was not directly or even principally Charles I, and the object of his counsel was not merely the government but the political nation. If on one side a rash king had provoked his subjects, on the other, covetous lords and ambitious gentry had behaved no less irresponsibly in response. An ancient nobility was the best stay against the corruption of honor, as Parliament was against the traducing of the law. These, too, however, had their proper bounds, and if on the pretext of checking the monarchy they exceeded them, the consequences were certain to be dire. That so much of the *Short View* would read in 1642 as if it had been an act of prophecy, at least from a moderate or neutralist point of view, underscores Cotton's perception of the fault lines in the English polity and their potential for rupture. Where Cotton himself might have stood in 1642 is another matter. Kevin Sharpe's suggestion that he would have joined the King is dubious; the career of Selden, also a client and adviser of the Howards, is perhaps more instructive.[91]

Cotton was called in for questioning over the *Short View*, but his interrogators seem to have accepted his disingenuous claim that the manuscript had been written in the previous reign and that it had been published without his consent.[92] It seems likelier that the crown was more interested in coopting Cotton (and conciliating the Arundel interest) than in seriously rebuking him. In this sense, Cotton's gambit was successful. The Council invited him to comment more directly on the political situation, and the resultant memorandum, published as *The Danger wherein The Kingdome now standeth and the Remedy*, may well have been instrumental in the decision to call a new Parliament in 1628.[93] Charles could not, however, be induced to give up his old ways. Cotton's London home, a frequent resort of the parliamentary leadership, was placed under surveillance, and Cotton was among those arrested in a sweep of the Country opposition in November 1629. Arundel helped to secure his release, but, despite mutual feelers, Cotton's "counsel" was not sought again.

CHAPTER 2

Sacred Discourse

"Is not the government of Ecclesiasticall matters, matter of State, and great matter too?"[1]

The Erastian Church and Its Challenges

No question in sixteenth- and seventeenth-century England was more vehemently contested than that of who could speak for God, the ultimate source of all legitimation in early modern society. Throughout the period before 1640, however, the distinction between the clerical and lay estates had been maintained throughout all shifts of ecclesiastical doctrine and organization. In that sense, the term "Reform" precisely signified the purposes of both Lutheranism and Calvinism, for what both sought was a scriptural church and a purified clergy, not the subjection of either. The horror with which Anabaptists, Familists, and Brownists were regarded by all segments of respectable opinion made clear that a learned, licensed, and disciplined clergy was the *sine qua non* of a Christian polity.

The real political question posed by the Reformation, therefore, was not whether there would be an ordained clergy but what its relation to the civil authority would be. On this subject Henry VIII was unambiguous. He assumed the position of Supreme Head of the Church of England, with full dispositive power over its lands and goods. The decapitation of Cardinal John Fisher ended, at least for the time, any question of how far it might extend to its personnel as well.

The Marian reaction was doubly significant, in marking both the renewed submission of the monarchy to the spiritual authority of Rome on terms of abasement not seen since the early thirteenth century, and the first female reign in England in four hundred years. The connection between gynecocracy and idolatry was forcefully set out in John Knox's *First Blast of the Trumpet against the Monstrous Regiment of Women* (1559), and Elizabeth I's sex was clearly a factor in the more limited title and authority granted her by Parliament as Governor of the restored, or rather refounded Anglican Church. In retrospect, Elizabeth's *via media* seemed a steadfast middle course between the ideological furies of Geneva and Rome, with what was conceded in doctrine to the former being balanced by what was retained in liturgy from the latter. But it was not until Pius V had declared her excommunication and deposition in 1570 that a Gallican reconciliation with the papacy appeared out of the question, and only after the collapse of the Alençon marriage negotiations in 1581 was the possibility of a backstairs rapprochement finally abandoned. If Foxe had hailed Elizabeth as the new Constantine in his *Book of Martyrs*, it was far less because she appeared fully committed to the role in the 1560s than in hopes that with suitable encouragement she would ultimately embrace it; and when John Stubbes voiced two decades of frustration and anxiety with England's Deborah in his attack on the Alençon match in *The discoverie of a gaping gulf*, he was much nearer the mark, though he and his publisher paid for it with their right hands.

From the 1530s to the 1580s, therefore, the Anglican Church owed its existence less to doctrinal consensus than to reasons of state. Henry VIII had left the Church of Rome for dynastic purposes and cemented the breach by distributing its properties to his landed elite; Elizabeth had restored her father's church in good part to reassure that same elite, to recoup the authority and revenue Mary had surrendered to Rome, and to assert her own title and independence. Its first clerical defender, John Jewel, was clearly more concerned to placate Catholic opinion at home and abroad than to define England's place in the Reformed community. Jewel denied that the Anglican Church had fostered faction and heresy, or that it allowed "every man to be a priest, to be a teacher, and to be an interpreter of the Scriptures." Doctrinally, too, it was still within hailing distance of Rome, "For, although we do not touch the body of Christ with teeth and mouth, yet we hold him fast and eat him by faith, by understanding, and by spirit."[2] To characterize this church as but halfly reformed, as the hotter sort of Protestants were wont to do, was perhaps less to state a complaint than to express a hope. Even after the Elizabethan settlement was finally completed by the adoption of the Thirty-Nine Articles in 1563, the battle only shifted ground from doctrine to practice—from formal adherence to the principles of the Reformed faith to the creation of a genuinely Protestant culture.

The turning point in the church's fortunes came with the Catholic counteroffensive of the 1580s: the infiltration of Jesuit priests, who raised the stakes of recusancy; the plots against the Queen that prompted the Bond of Association, the most spontaneous loyalist manifestation of the century; the growing plight of the Huguenots and the Dutch, which drew a reluctant Elizabeth inexorably into the Continental wars of religion; and the descent of the Armada, for subsequent generations the cornerstone of a new providential chronology focused on England and its Christian emperor. Here again, the threat to national independence and the security of the state was the overriding popular concern, and the church was folded into the cause of the realm. Henceforth, Anglicanism was not merely "the church by law established" but part of the nation's patrimony, and its defense, at least for the majority, was inseparable from the defense of English liberty. Conversely, the notion of "popery" became associated not only with the suppression of Christian liberty represented by Rome but with the direct threat of foreign domination, whether by overt invasion or covert subversion.

After 1588, the Church seemed at last to have come to safe harbor. Catholics were no longer to be placated; Puritans had been cast on the defensive. Oxford and Cambridge had begun to produce the learned clergy who had been in such short supply in earlier decades. The Church reaffirmed its creed. John Whitgift gave it efficient administration, and Richard Hooker an intellectual foundation. In James I, it found not merely a ruler but a patron. Perhaps most importantly, it had become a genuinely comprehensive institution, disciplined enough to maintain cohesion, flexible enough to accommodate a considerable range of practice and belief. By most standards, it was a success.

The viability of the Church was nonetheless dependent on a complex set of understandings and arrangements. If the sovereign was Supreme Governor of the Church, the landed elite was in good part its proprietor. A substantial number of church livings were in lay hands, and although ordination and discipline remained with the hierarchy, it was a rash bishop who would challenge a powerful patron. This checkered distribution of power and influence reflected power relations in the secular commonwealth as well, where the practical authority of the crown was dependent on the cooperation of local elites. The bishops were, however, servants of two masters, royal and noble, a fact reflected in the low social status accorded them well into the seventeenth century. More than most institutions of early modern England, the Anglican Church was a tissue of compromise and diffused authority.

The situation of Anglicanism reflected the paradox of the Reformation in an era of state-building and the centralization of power. In an age when the Word of God as revealed in the Bible was passionately affirmed as the immediate warrant and ultimate ground of all authority, interpretive control of the Scriptures was more and more dispersed. This was the tiger princes had chosen to ride when they yielded to the secular charms as well as the redemptive promise of the Reformed faith; this was the spiritual anarchy Bishop Jewel had disavowed, in which "we allow every man to be a priest, to be a teacher, and to be an interpreter of the Scriptures."

The difficulty was twofold. The scarcity of vernacular bibles, the low literacy rate, and the hermeneutic monopoly claimed and enforced by the Roman Church had sustained elite control of the Scriptures, but these conditions were attenuated or reversed in the sixteenth century. The print revolution had exponentially increased the available number and variety of bibles and stimulated the growth of a wide lay reading public, while the Protestant emphasis on a preaching ministry addressed a new and more participatory audience, the godly community (itself consisting of actively pious households, and, ultimately, the individual conscience) that had begun to create a culture in which units of piety were increasingly decentralized and in which clerical performance was scrutinized on a case by case basis. These conditions—complicated by the assumption of material control over the church by secular authority—profoundly altered the terms on which hierarchical controls could be maintained and justified. The result was nothing less than a transformation in the text, reception, and interpretation of the Word of God.

The Vulgate text of the Bible had been under scholarly and political challenge since the days of John Wyclif, but with the advent of Luther the need to take unauthorized versions of Scripture in hand was apparent to Henry VIII and his councillors. As the Henrician Bishop Cuthbert Tunstall noted,

> [M]any children of iniquity . . . wandering from the way of truth and the catholic faith, have craftily translated the New Testament into our English tongue, intermeddling therewith many heretical articles and erroneous opinions, pernicious and offensive, seducing the simple people, attempting by their wicked and perverse interpretations to profane the majesty of the scriptures, which hitherto have remained undefiled, and craftily to abuse the most holy word of God . . .[3]

The problem was more easily described than corrected, however, and for the remainder of the century the Holy Bible—even when it was chained up in churches, an act eloquent of the state's endeavor to contain the energies of the Reformation—remained, in most versions, textually and interpretively the mandate of others. At best, the crown could give these versions the stamp of a royal licensing and preface, but the translation and marginalia were the work of men who were separate if not fugitive from authority, and whose religious and civil views were to a greater or lesser extent at variance with it.

The most widely read and influential version of Scripture, the Geneva Bible (1560), was also the most heavily and radically annotated, with many unflattering glances at the magistrate. The Geneva New Testament went through at least sixty-six editions,[4] with revisions in both the translation and notes, making the Word of God, or at least its presentation, a work in progress. Most of the scholarship, moreover, both in text and annotation, was the work of Continental theologians, notably Beza, Bullinger, and Junius.

Such dependence on foreign sources emphasized both the transnational character of the Reformed project and the belatedness of England's adherence to it. As no English thinker until Richard Hooker made a contribution to Protestant ecclesiology comparable to those of Continental Reformers, so no English divine until William Perkins gave the Anglican Church a theology that freed it, at least directly, from the tutelage of a foreign tongue.[5] While England's size made it the Joshua of the Protestant cause (with a corresponding increase in pressure on the Christian emperor to perform his own role), the junior status and Erastian foundation of its church gave it more the aspect of a Goliath: rude, untutored, provincial, dependent.

This condition changed, but slowly. If in 1624 Joseph Hall could esteem the British clergy as *stupor mundi*, it was only fifty years since Bishop Edwin Sandys had characterized their condition as *excrementum mundi*. The Continental patriarchs had allowed that the governance of bishops was compatible with Scripture, but it had few committed supporters and, especially in the wake of the Vestments controversy, an active opposition that had concluded with John Field and Thomas Wilcox that "their tyrannous Lordshippe [could] not stand wyth Christes kingdome." Elizabeth's demeaning and sometimes degrading treatment of her bishops, while in the familiar style of her father, had not made their service more pleasant or their calling more reputable.[6]

The bishops had not lost sight of Tunstall's point that the circulation of vernacular bibles was the greatest single threat to Christian conscience and clerical authority. They fought a rearguard action in the 1530s against Henry VIII's sensible conclusion that mere suppression would not suffice in the new print age, and, having failed to produce a version of their own, were forced to accede at last to the authorized publication of Miles Coverdale's Bible. Its text was largely the work of William Tyndale, whom the bishops had burned as a heretic; but when Henry countered their objections by asking whether the translation itself promoted heresy, they demurred, and the first Anglican bible was thereupon published. This text became in turn the basis for the so-called Great Bible, to which Archbishop Cranmer contributed a preface. Unauthorized versions of the Tyndale and Coverdale bibles were called in; thus, it became legal to possess their texts with the royal imprimatur but illegal without it.[7]

Archbishop Parker at last provided an official translation in response to the Geneva Bible, but this so-called Bishops' Bible never became popular. It was only with King James that a true Authorized Version was produced, encompassing not only the best of contemporary scholarship but a broad spectrum of Anglican opinion. The King James Bible could not fully compensate the godly party for the church reformation it had failed to win at Hampton Court, but it was a significant gesture of conciliation and inclusion after the long years under Whitgift. It did not, however, replace the Geneva Bible, which remained the most popular English version of Scripture down to 1640, and whose marginalia—to which James had strenuously objected—were incorporated into his own Bible during the Civil War.[8]

If the Bible remained the basis of sacred discourse, it was surrounded by an ancillary literature of devotion, explication, and commentary, which in turn spawned an even wider literature of controversy. From the Henrician Ten Articles of 1536 to the Laudian Canons of 1640, official formularies sought to define the boundaries of faith and worship.[9] Liturgical works such as the Book of Common Prayer were particularly objectionable to tender consciences, since they combined the function of (obligatory) scriptural recitation with contestable interpretation and, to some, detestable practice. To clothe Holy Writ in the garments of popish ceremony was the means by which the Antichrist had kept the Word in thrall for a thousand years. To have such practices continued, confirmed, and extended in a church that claimed to be Reformed meant only that prelacy was still alive, and Antichrist not purged.

But the Prayer Book itself was only the most immediate snare of the Word and the most egregious affront to conscience. Honest preachers and parishioners were caught in an ever-widening web of articles, regulations, licenses, and subscriptions, often contradictory among themselves when not repugnant to God. The result was that:

> although some truth be taught by some preachers, yet no preacher may withoute great danger of the lawes, utter all truthe comprised in the booke of God. It is so circumscribed & wrapt within the compasse of suche statutes, suche penalties, such injunctions, suche advertisements, suche articles, suche canons, suche sober caveats, and suche manifolde pamphlets, that in manner it doth but peepe out from behinde the screene. The lawes of the lande, the booke of common prayer, the Queenes Injunctions, the Commissioners advertisements, the bishops late Canons, Lindwoodes Provincials, every bishops Articles in his diocesse, my Lord of Canterburies sober caveates . . . may not be broken or offended against, but with more daunger then to offende against the Bible. To these subscribing, and subscribing againe, and the third subscribing, are required, for these, Preachers and others are endited, are fined, are prisonned, are excommunicated, are banished, and have worse things threatned them: and the Bible, that must have no further scope, then by these it is assigned. Is this to professe God his worde? is this a reformation?[10]

Thomas Cartwright's plea to free the Gospel and the consciences of those who preached it set the Anglican dilemma in high relief. A comprehensive church—and the Tudors would have and could afford no other—must necessarily be governed centrally and hierarchically. Such governance rested on the twin pillars of conformity and uniformity, set out by the authority of the bishops, prescribed by oath, and enforced by statute.

The goal of this effort was civil tranquility. What Elizabeth wished to see, ideally, was every head in the realm bowed each Sunday before the same page; whether there was much comprehension of what the page contained was of little consequence (the less, perhaps, the better), so long as the appropriate gestures were made and the appropriate rules observed. In a world largely populated by the reprobate, and in a church necessarily so constituted too, this was as much as could be reasonably hoped for, and, no doubt, responsibly aspired to. Elizabeth knew that such perfect compliance could not be, but she was determined to secure as much of it as possible short of provoking worse tumults than those she suppressed.

The bishops had a more complex view of the matter, but their hopes were congruent with Elizabeth's. God's worship had to be provided for in an orderly manner; propriety was an essential aspect of respect. This entailed ceremonies, some of which were necessary or desirable in themselves—a common liturgy, for example—and some of which were theologically indifferent but practically useful in weaning a population still accustomed (as not a few of the bishops were themselves) to popish forms from outright superstition and idolatry to a seemly and becoming worship. That these latter practices, the adiaphora, helped increase respect for the clergy as well as for God was sufficient justification for them. Under such circumstances it did not seem too much to ask the clergy themselves to conform to a regime designed for their benefit.

Here was the crux of the matter. The Anglican hierarchy began, in its institutional capacity at least, with the conception of a House of God, and its godly antagonists with the Book of God. For the former, the church was the divinely appointed means by which God's ordinance was to be carried out on earth, his faithful gathered, his name worshiped, his blessing received, and his Word protected from misappropriation and heresy. Needless to say, the Bible, as the repository of revealed truth, divine law, and sacred history, was the touchstone of the ministry and the basis of all human institutions. But the same virtue that made it infinitely precious in the hands of the just and the wise made it fearfully dangerous in the hands of the wicked and the ignorant. Of these latter, there was more than enough example. On the one hand there was the Luciferian pride of prelacy in the justly reprehended sense of the word. This was the attempt to confound sacred and secular governance in the all-embracing spiritual tyranny of Rome. On the other, there was the equally diabolical anarchy of Münster. In each case, a sound and vital principle—the necessity for orderly worship in the first, and for Christian liberty in the second—had, taken to a false extreme, produced a perverted and damnable result. The answer was a learned and temperate clergy and a church that, proof under a righteous prince against pride and enthusiasm, was the best guarantee of the ordered liberty that was the true portion of the just.

The godly were no less convinced of the vital importance of the church, and their bitterest complaint was not, *pace* Cartwright, for their own part—suffering was, after all, the Christian vocation—but for those whom the church had failed to include in any meaningful sense through the provision of a learned and zealous ministry free to preach the Word. This point needs due emphasis, particularly in view of the Separatist and Congregational destiny of the godly community. The term "Puritan" meant many things in Elizabethan England, but what distinguished the generation of Cartwright, Field, and Wilcox above all was that they took the notion of a comprehensive church with the utmost seriousness. Such a church would necessarily include the reprobate, but if they were incapable of grace, obedience to divine law was still required of them. Where the godly differed from their fellow Anglicans was in their conception of what true inclusion in the church represented. On the minimalist definition that appeared to satisfy Elizabeth, and, often enough, her bishops, mere conformity—more or less regular church attendance and tithing—sufficed to constitute church membership. By that cold token, there would be little to distinguish the Church of England from the Church of Rome, for the latter too required no more than blind submission to authority. A true church, in contrast, was a place of godly fellowship where the Christian life could be lived, examined, and deepened; where the mind and heart could be refreshed by Scripture; where God could be worshiped with the genuine piety that alone was acceptable to him.

For the godly, the establishment of the true church was the end of all Christian endeavor. It was also the only means to purge the darkness of the previous thousand years. The false church, the church of Antichrist so lately and providentially escaped in England and Scotland, and rampant still throughout most of Continental Europe and the Spanish New World, was by no means defeated: it had, in most places and among most Christian souls, barely been contested. The true and the false church did not represent available models along a spectrum of ecclesiastical polity from which one might pick and choose, taking a point of doctrine here and a ceremony there. They were antitheses, as stark and absolute as the antithesis of good and evil. The goal of the Erastian was stability, an orderly worship in an orderly state, and the quickest path to that goal was that of least resistance and therefore of least disturbance. But the true church could not be established without disturbance. The habits of idolatry could not be indulged; they must be broken and cast out. A church but halfly reformed was a church in which the Devil still had a handhold. The Devil would know how to exploit it, and God would not suffer it to prosper. In the depths of the Laudian persecution, when it seemed, in Thomas Gataker's words, that God was going out of England, the godly recalled their long travail in the Anglican Church and their attempts to sanctify a part if not the whole of it. They realized then with utter finality that these efforts had been in vain, that truth could not abide in an unclean vessel, that any compromise with prelacy was tantamount to surrender.

The concept of a true church thus hovered over the reality of the existing one, absolutely real if materially unrealized, as the eternal City of God reigned above the temporal City of Man. It must be emphasized that this Augustinian ideal was shared by all who trafficked with the Anglican Church, and that Archbishop Laud held to it in his own fashion no less than a Cartwright, a Penry, or a Prynne. The point that separated these parties was the question of what constituted an adequate realization of this ideal in a fallen world, and the degree to which they identified this world with the persistence of the false church—that is, of the Antichrist.

For those who constituted the more or less contented majority of the Anglican Church, both clerical and lay—those whom earlier historians were wont to call Anglicans *tout court*—the Elizabethan settlement was a sound basis for a true church. On the unsophisticated level of ordinary parishioners, it provided a place of decent worship, a context of pastoral care, and a nexus of patriotic identification: this was England's church at last, under its own ruler, free of the wars of praemunire and the galling tribute to Rome. Elizabeth herself essentially shared this vision. For its hardworking and chronically underpaid clergy, the church was, paradoxically, a less satisfactory arrangement, at least in material terms. The Henrician confiscations had left it impoverished; and one impetus to godly perfection among the clergy was, certainly, the willingness of devout congregations to pay attractive salaries to learned and painful ministers, and even to compete for them. Obviously such competition was hardly desirable from the viewpoint of the hierarchy, and the *jure divino* case for tithes first made openly by George Carleton in 1606 soon became the quasi-official position of the church.[11] Adequate maintenance for ministers was, of course, only one aspect of the capital requirements of the Anglican establishment. There were churches to be kept up, schools to be maintained, visitations performed. The general penury of the clergy focused continual attention on material questions and forced many bishops into the unseemly role of entrepreneurs if not exploiters of their estates. Felicity Heal has well described the sixteenth-century church as "ground between the upper millstone of inflation and the nether millstone of lay power."[12] The result was that, all too often, the "visible church" of the Anglican clergy was the dangling shingle, the leaking roof, and the tattered prayer book. Laud's program to restore the beauty of holiness, while driven by an aesthetic and spiritual vision, derived as well from his own degrading experience of personal and institutional poverty. The honor of the church was bound up finally with its endowment, and what had begun three generations earlier with a political decision to enforce conformity through a ministerial dress code had become a manifestation of the dignity and sanctity of the clerical estate.

The godly vision of the true church was far otherwise. In its ideal form, it was the communion of saints—the "invisible church" of those predestined to salvation, whose governor was Jesus Christ. The invisible church was both perennial and indestructible, but, since actual election was known only to God, it could never be made fully manifest, and even the godliest congregation would contain its leaven of hypocrites. This was a part not only of God's inscrutability but of his wisdom and grace, since if election could be certainly known the reprobate majority would revenge itself upon the saints as the pagans once had, by fire and sword. By the same token, the saints would wish to shun the world, consigning it to the damned and thereby leaving God's ordinance that it be governed to his glory unfulfilled. Worse yet, it would leave the unredeemed world to the Antichrist, under whose rule the godly had suffered in the centuries of Roman rule. Surely the rebirth of a sanctified church, nourished by the blood of English martyrs, was not only a wonderment and a blessing but a call to spiritual arms.

It was in this light that the godly were prepared to view the Church of England. A comprehensive church, reformed in doctrine and protected from prelacy by the governance of a Christian emperor, was not a true church in the ideal sense, but it *contained* the true church and therefore, providing it ordained nothing repugnant to conscience or the Word of God, it was the best protection for the saints on earth and the fittest instrument for maintaining divine order and worship.

This proviso was a large one, however. A comprehensive church was perpetually in danger of becoming a persecuting and even an anti-Christian one unless the godly maintained stout vigilance and control. At first, it was thought that sound doctrine, right worship, and active propagation of the Word under a godly prince would suffice to keep the church in order. A certain amount of latitude would have to be granted ecclesiastical authorities who had to govern both the godly and the reprobate; of course, those authorities would themselves be godly, learned, and discreet.

The argument for a comprehensive church in 1559 was framed in far starker terms: the alternative to it was not a godly communion but the continued dominion of Rome. The reformers had to rough-hew their church as best they could and leave the refinement of doctrine and practice to later occasions. Major concessions were entailed on liturgy and governance, notably the acceptance of the Prayer Book and episcopacy. The existing bishops were tendered the Oath of Supremacy that accompanied the restoration of the national church, and although such notorious figures as Edmund Bonner of London were expected to decline, Elizabeth had hopes of staffing perhaps a third of her bench with Marian holdovers. In the event only two obscure figures, Kitchin of Llandaff and Stanley of Sodor and Man, accepted the oath and remained at their posts, but the prospect of being governed by former persecutors was a bitter pill for the godly: too bitter for Christopher Goodman, who left for Scotland, leveling an angry blast at the government that had placed again in authority those "upon whom God hath expressly pronounced the sentence of death."[13]

Equally scandalous, and equally unavoidable, were the liturgical injunctions that, to godly consciences, encouraged where they did not openly espouse Romish interpretations of the sacraments. These included kneeling at communion and the crossing of infants during baptism. No matter seemed too small to contest; the lines across which the battle for the soul of the Anglican Church were fought were as fine as the prescribed thickness of the bread at mass. It was little wonder that members of the godly party were soon known by the sobriquet of "precisians," a more properly descriptive if less evocative term than that of its successor, "puritan." To an unsympathetic or indifferent eye, the relentless application of Scripture by the godly to the minutest details of ecclesiastical custom was a species of conformity far narrower and more cramping to conscience than that required by church authorities. Doubtless the severity of episcopal regulation complained of by Cartwright in the *Second Admonition* owed much to issues raised by the godly themselves.

From a godly perspective, however, the forms of divine worship were central to the meaning of the Reformed profession. Gesture, image, and attire were not incidental to doctrine but essential manifestations of it.[14] Popery could not be rooted out of people's hearts while it was still before their eyes. Centuries of idolatry had tarnished virtually every object, intonation, and physical movement of divine service. For this reason, many godly reformers paid more attention to subjects such as clerical vestments and the placement of church furniture in the early years of the Elizabethan regime than to the form of ecclesiastical governance. It was true of course that their Erastian dependence on the royal supremacy left them with little leverage on the latter subject, especially after Elizabeth had made her intentions known. The fact was, however, that the godly did not begin to repudiate episcopacy until it was clear that the church as constituted would permanently frustrate their reforms. If the episcopate included scandalous relics such as Kitchin and Stanley, it also contained stalwarts such as Grindal and Sandys. In the Earl of Leicester, moreover, the reformed party had a patron who promised, not to say boasted of his ability to secure godly preferments, and to protect those whom he preferred. It was doubtless with the sense of such support in high places that Edward Dering, in his famous sermon of February 25, 1570, dared to tax Elizabeth herself with dereliction in her duty to the church:

> I would first leade you to your Benefices, and behold some are defiled with impropriations, some with sequestrations, some loaden with pensions, some robbed of their commodities. And yet behold more abhominations than these. Looke after this upon your Patrons, and loe, some are selling their Benefices, some farming them, some keepe them for their children, some give them to Boyes, some to Servingmen. . . . Looke upon your Ministery . . . some Ruffians, some Hawkers and Hunters, some Dicers and Corders. . . . And yet you in the meane while that all these whordoms are committed, you at whose hands God will require it, you sit still and are carelesse, let men doe as they list . . .[15]

No other sixteenth-century English monarch endured so open a rebuke as this. Catholics contested Elizabeth's legitimacy, and the Pope declared her an outlaw, but no other subject dared to speak such words in Elizabeth's presence. In another reign, Dering's audacity could easily have cost him his head; as it was, it did not even deprive him of patronage. Leicester remained a strong supporter, and Bishop Sandys of London appointed Dering reader of the divinity lecture at St. Paul's Cathedral. Even Burghley, whom Dering had chastised in private as severely as the latter had the Queen in public, appeared reluctant or at least ambivalent about proceeding against him. He was finally ordered to cease preaching, but it is unclear whether the ban was enforced. The offending sermon was not only published but went through three editions in a year and a dozen in Elizabeth's lifetime.

Dering's case illustrates the persistent strength of the godly party in the early Elizabethan church and the extraordinary latitude that a gifted preacher could command in a culture defined and authenticated by Scripture. The quickening of the Word by eloquence produced edification, the uplifting of the individual conscience and the union of hearts and minds that constituted the praxis of a true church. Many other things conduced to edification as well, to be sure. It was the goal of godly conversation, the fellowship of the elect; it derived from pastoral counsel and divine worship. But nothing inspired it more immediately and nurtured it more profoundly than the exposition of the Word.

Certainly the advent of printing had stimulated and facilitated the concentration on textual contemplation and analysis that marked Reformed piety, and whose culminating ritual was the sermon, heard or read. The general dissemination of the word in Reformation Europe conduced to the triumph of the divine Word, of active individual piety over passive communal worship. The sermon was both the natural fulfillment of this process and its most potent stimulus. Particularly when heard, it was an intensely charged experience. Preacher and auditor, mutually exalted, renewed through it the covenant that bound the true congregation together, even as the heightened experience of Holy Writ refreshed the sense of covenant between God and his chosen. In the godly congregation, preacher and laity spurred one another on toward spiritual perfection, so that the sermon became the true act of communion. Because it was thus, in its best sense, a reciprocal act, and because its efficacy was tried anew on each occasion, the sermon was democratic rather than corporate, not a patented miracle like the Eucharist but a trial of the spirit, particular to each case. Such trials, repeated with success, bound individual congregations to their pastors in a manner difficult to recapture in a secular age. The loyalties it built up were both deep and intensely parochial, and the relations it fostered between congregations were those of spiritual equality and fellowship rather than of hierarchy and subordination. Presbyterianism was the natural outgrowth of this experience. If the episcopal order had seemed tolerable and even desirable as a means of providing a godly ministry and planting righteousness in the dark corners of the land, its legitimacy was strictly defined by its diligence and success in promoting these ends. Should it fail to accomplish, or, worse, actually inhibit them, no license and no authority could justify it. Master Dering had not quite said all of this—questioned about Presbyterian leanings, he affirmed his loyalty to the established system of church governance, and when he died in 1576, the Presbyterian challenge was still aborning—but the warning he sounded was unmistakable. The Church of England existed for the faithful, not the other way around. The Queen no less than the bishops would forget that point at her peril.

The elevation of Edmund Grindal to the see of Canterbury in 1575 seemed to justify those who were, with Dering, zealous for reform but not yet willing to abandon hope of achieving it under episcopal auspices. Grindal's predecessor, Matthew Parker, had become even to moderate opinion the very image of the lordly, time serving prelate, and, as Patrick Collinson comments, "It was on the cards that Parker would be succeeded by a metropolitan who would point the Church still more firmly in the direction of conformism and anti-puritan repression."[16] That this did not occur was due in part to Grindal's considerable energy and merit but even more so to a desire to end the intellectual isolation the bench had fallen into under Parker and to avoid schism by reaching out to those he had alienated. In this not only the "Puritan" earls of Huntingdon and Leicester concurred but Burghley, long a sponsor of Grindal, and, more importantly, the Queen's closest adviser.

Grindal and the Crisis of Episcopacy

This promising moment was short-lived. Within a year of his appointment, Grindal had been sequestered from office, and he remained a virtual prisoner in Lambeth House until his death in 1583. The reforms he had begun went unexecuted. The hopes he had aroused for godly governance in the church were dashed.

Grindal's downfall, as is well known, resulted from his refusal to execute a royal command to suppress the popular preaching exercises known as prophesying. Prophesying had begun in Zwinglian churches, and was brought back to England by the Marian exiles. Derived from the Pauline injunction, "Let the Prophets speake two, or three, and let the other[s] iudge" (I Corinthians 14: 29 [Geneva version]), it typically consisted of two or three sermons preached on a set verse before a clerical and lay audience, with ministerial responses. Prophesyings were thus public symposia offered by local clergy to an at-large congregation. They fed the godly appetite for sermon and disputation, and served many of the functions of a modern professional convention: to expound knotty points of doctrine, to give scope to talent, and to bring lesser brethren up to speed.

In a larger sense, the purpose of prophesying was the edification of the church through dialectical exchange, the *discordia concors* that, as Hans Joachim Schoeps has noted, runs through the whole of Pauline ecclesiology.[17] Central to this was the tension between the concept of an absolute truth, embodied in Revelation, and the necessarily provisional formulations of a church that could be "true" only in the sense of a continual aspiration to translate the abiding mystery and inexhaustible grace of Scripture into godly practice and understanding. On a congregational level, the ordinary means of this was the sermon, the lecture, and, less formally, the daily experience of godly conversation and fellowship. Prophesying was, or seemed to be, the logical extension of such exercises into the wider godly neighborhood of the region or county. Prophesying did not merely enlarge ordinary congregational practice, however, but raised it to precisely that dialectical level at which Scripture yielded its most precious fruits, and hearts were most deeply searched. Nor was this merely an optional tool, an educational device among many, but one clearly prescribed by Holy Writ:

> Follow after loue, and couet spiritual *gifts*, and rather that ye may prophecie. [H]e that prophecieth, speaketh vnto men to edifying, and to exhortation, and to comfort. He that speaketh *strange* language, edifieth himselfe: but he that prophecieth, edifieth the Church. Euen so, forasmuch as yee couet spirituall *gifts*, seeke that yee may excell vnto the edifying of the Church. [P]rophecying *serueth* not for them that beleeue not, but for them which beleeue. [I]f all prophecie, and there come in one that beleeueth not, or one vnlearned, he is rebuked of all men, and is iudged of all, And so are the secrets of his heart made manifest, and so hee will fall downe on his face and worship God, and say plainely that God is in you in deede. [Therefore] Let the Prophets speake two, or three, and let the other iudge. And if any thing be reueiled to another that sitteth by, let the first hold his peace.

For yee may all prophecie one by one, that all may learne, and all may haue comfort. And the spirits of the Prophets are subiect to the Prophets. If any man thinke himselfe to be a Prophet, or spirituall, let him acknowledge, that the things I write vnto you, are the commandements of the Lord.

[I Corinthians 14: 1, 3, 4, 12, 22–25, 29–32, 37]

The "prophet" is identified by Paul with the "interpreter" and specifically with him who is able to exercise the functions of edifying, exhortation, and comfort—that is, with the pastoral functions of the minister in settled congregations. Throughout I Corinthians 14, he is contrasted with the inspired speaker in tongues, whose revelation is personal and incommunicable to the congregation without the interpreter ("If any man speake a *strange* tongue, *let it be* by two, or at the most, by three, and that by course, and let one interprete" [v. 27]).

The unpastored congregations which Paul describes and for which he attempts to prescribe order in I Corinthians 14 would have had no counterpart in the Church of England. To conformists such as Parker or Whitgift, this text was a perfect example of those customary usages that, appropriate to apostolic times, had been superseded in mature churches, and a frightening description of the near-anarchy that had often reigned in the primitive congregations as well. The "office" of prophet had been long subsumed under that of the pastor (not to say the beadle and the constable), and to revive it as a kind of suprafunction of the ministry could only be subversive of established hierarchy and of the good order that Paul himself had been trying to bring to the apostolic Church. It would be as well to resuscitate the practice of speaking in tongues, which had no less warrant from Corinthians.

Herein lay the fundamental difference between godly and conformist interpretations of Scripture. For the godly, biblical history read not progressively from disorderly primitive churches to ordered and mature ones, but regressively from churches corrupted by an accretion of usurped authority and idolatrous ceremony to the pure wellhead of offices and practices directly ordained by God. This led in turn to an even deeper hermeneutic division. Conformists tended to read Scripture diachronically, as the record of an unfolding revelation and an evolving church, whose development did not cease with and was not limited to the institutions and practices it described. The godly tended to read it synchronically, as a text whose overt, historical dimension was secondary to the abiding message of revelation that informed the Word, and which could not be negated or diminished by altered temporal circumstances. Thus, while the conformist could regard "prophecy" as a practice superseded by the progress of the church, like the injunctions of the Mosaic law, the godly looked upon it as an office still in force even if requiring new modes of implementation.

At the same time, the godly did not regard the mere existence of a biblically sanctioned office as sufficient ground for its revival. The verse that most emphatically authorized the prophet—I Corinthians 12: 28—authorized as well other offices that could not be regarded as candidates for reinstatement, including healers, miracle-workers, and those who spoke in tongues. What made prophecy specifically relevant to the world of the Anglican parish was its connection with the function of edification in the church.

Edification was the animating principle of Pauline ecclesiology. It meant both the building of the church—the gathering of mankind into the universal congregation of the Word—and the uplifting of its members through acts of piety and testimonies of zeal. Edification was thus a continuous process, forever renewed, forever incomplete. Conformists emphasized the task of edification no less than the godly, but interpreted it in terms of an injunction to corporate decorum ("Let all things bee done honestly, and by order") rather than as a prompting of the individual spirit. For the godly, however, the congregants of a true church were "lively stones," and the church itself an edifice built on the active faith of its members.

The difference between these two approaches was profound and fundamental. For the conformist, the true church was defined by right doctrine; once that doctrine was established, as by general consent it had been with the adoption of the Thirty-Nine Articles in 1563, the subsidiary task of edification was satisfied by the regular exercise of preaching and worship. Where preaching was in short supply—a regrettable but unavoidable circumstance in a church so recently planted—worship alone would suffice, supplemented by homilies. On the conformist view, edification thus tended to flatten toward maintenance and routine. If a sufficient number of parishioners regularly participated in an orderly and decorous service, a reasonable degree of edification, at least by conformist standards, was assumed to be provided. An unreasonable degree—particularly if it entailed unruly enthusiasms that might prove socially as well as ecclesiastically disruptive, or stirred the laity to consider matters best left to the clerical hierarchy and the Supreme Governor—was neither desirable nor, beyond a certain point, tolerable. Thus edification, like other aspects of the spiritual life in an orderly church commonwealth, was subject to the *via media*—that is to say, to governance. Edification could not be reduced to mere order—that way lay idolatry—but, within the uniformity of right doctrine and right worship, order was the best sign of its abiding presence. The Apostle had said so.

Essentially, then, the conformist conceived edification as a spiritual efflux that, like a rising water level, slowly lifted parishioners toward greater consciousness of their blessings and duties. Although there was no theoretical limit to the development of this consciousness, it was clearly not desirable to flood the rafters with enthusiasm or to drown the distinction between clergy and laity. The mysteries of the Christian faith were beyond its wisest doctors; its doctrine had lately been rescued from error and its government from bondage. Certitude of authority and quietude of worship were the prime conditions for maintaining a true church. The chief internal danger to such a church was not from an errant clergy but a curious laity. The key to edification, in short, was discipline.

Implicit in such a view was a conception of the church as fully realized in its doctrine and discipline. Edification might sustain and advance the church, but it was in no way constitutive of it. The godly, in contrast, regarded doctrine and discipline as merely the foundation for a church of living stones that was to be built, as the Pauline text had it, by the free exercise of spiritual gifts. On this view, the true church was not a static entity but a living organism, and Christian liberty not the right to sift among the empty forms of human institutions but to partake, in John Coolidge's phrase, in "a new kind of communal life as the body of Christ."[18]

The question that the Elizabethan church raised for the godly was whether its discipline and governance were finally compatible with Christian liberty. It was a question confronted with reluctance, for a negative answer meant at best a sojourn into a civil and ecclesiastical wilderness, at worst the prospect of exile and death. Most would choose to stay and struggle within the church, or find protected enclaves. A small but significant number chose partial or complete separation. This act was often accompanied by much bitterness, for, as Murray M. Tolmie points out, "[The Separatists'] schism was more painful to the puritans, for whom it represented a rending of meaningful Christian fellowship, than it was to the ecclesiastical authorities, to whom it was merely a wilful defiance of legitimate authority."[19] Living stone was parted from living stone.

The first *crise de conscience* of the godly had come with the Vestments controversy of the mid-1560s, a dispute which had put the difference between the conformist and godly conception of edification in clear perspective. The cap and surplice mandated by Archbishop Parker for all clergy were "adiaphora" to the conformist, things indifferent to be commanded by authority for reasons of polity, but "idolothytes" to the godly, un- and therefore antiscriptural devices that conduced not to God's service but the Devil's. The conformist argument was not distinguished by subtlety. What authority declared lawful in the church was *ipso facto* lawful; what it defined as indifferent was therefore not idolatrous. John Whitgift, then Dean of Lincoln, turned the knife in with particular relish. If, he said, the function of the ministry was to edify and the wearing of cap and surplice was a condition of exercising that function, then the cap and surplice conduced to edification.

A more conciliatory argument was that clerical vestments, by promoting respect for the minister and awe for the service, helped create the proper climate for the preaching and reception of the Word. This argument was not, of course, likely to be convincing to those who believed that Scripture could not be preached in the rags of the Antichrist. Nor did it gain plausibility from the fact that thirty-seven conscientious clergymen had been deprived in the diocese of London for refusing to conform to the new code, thereby depleting an already insufficient preaching ministry. It was a not unreasonable surmise that the true purpose of the vestment ordinance was to snare the godly and therefore deliberately to curtail the preaching of the Word. Such, indeed, could only be the work of the Antichrist. But even if less sinister motives were imputed to the hierarchy, merely to suggest some sequential connection between the awe (presumably) aroused by cap and surplice and the edification attendant upon the preaching of Scripture was to conflate the effect of a material image with the pure sustenance of the Word. This was popery.

For the sterner of the godly, no compromise was possible. Edmund Grindal, then Bishop of London, was not among them. He spoke for many of those who, at that moment and in succeeding decades, would prefer the lesser evil of submitting to an edict that offended conscience than to abandoning what was still in essence a true church:

> We, who are now bishops, on our first return, and before we entered on our ministry, contended long and earnestly for the removal of those things that have occasioned the present dispute; but as we were unable to prevail, either with the queen or the parliament, we judged it best, after a consultation on the subject, not to desert our churches for the sake of a few ceremonies, and those not unlawful in themselves, especially since the pure doctrine of the gospel remained in all its integrity and freedom. . . .[20]

Grindal's statement stakes out what Peter Lake has called the "moderate Puritan" position in the church: that as long as doctrine remains pure, Christian liberty is not infringed nor edification subverted by the provision of ceremonies conformable to Scripture, however objectionable or even (to tender consciences) odious they may be. For such brethren, the abandonment of a true church from a scruple over inessentials was an act of pride rather than of conscience. It was also a sedition for which the full civil penalty was to be exacted. As Grindal declared:

> Some London citizens of the lowest order, together with four or five ministers remarkable neither for their judgement nor their learning, have openly separated from us; and sometimes in private houses, sometimes in the fields, and occasionally even in ships, they have held their meetings and administered the sacraments. . . . The number of this sect is about two hundred, but consisting of more women than men. The privy council have lately committed the heads of this faction to prison, and are using every means to put a timely stop to this sect.[21]

It was significant that Grindal addressed these comments to his Continental colleague Heinrich Bullinger. Bullinger had been involved in the case of John Hooper, who had refused to be consecrated Bishop of Gloucester in traditional vestments under Edward VI. He was a venerated figure to many in the English church, and in addressing him Grindal was profoundly conscious of England's position as the largest and (but for Scotland) the newest of the Reformed congregations. In the battle with Antichrist, no threat was greater than that of schism, and in no church would schism be more consequential to the Reformed cause than in England's. Yet only eight years later Grindal, now himself the metropolitan, would refuse a direct royal command to suppress prophesying, defying the royal supremacy of which he was the most immediate officer.

Grindal's celebrated defiance seems all the more puzzling in its immediate political context. Queen Elizabeth had been induced to suppress the prophesyings in Norwich in 1574. Her action was promoted by conformists and their patrons at Court as part of the backlash to the Admonition controversy and in anticipation of the struggle over the succession to Parker. Prophesyings were not very important in themselves to the conformist party, at least when weighed against the general challenge to episcopacy. True, they were symptoms of indiscipline, and they might plausibly be regarded as stalking-horses for a Presbyterian polity. But their chief attraction as a point of attack, apart from their vulnerability as an unlicensed exercise, was the apparent store the godly put on them.

The transparency of this maneuver should have been obvious to an experienced clerical politician such as Grindal. So should have been the means for evading it. Prophesying could be regarded as a point of doctrine, enjoined by the Pauline texts, and therefore a matter of clerical ordinance. But it could also be seen as a point of discipline, and therefore properly subject to the Supreme Governor. As we have seen, not every church practice described by Paul—for instance, speaking in tongues—was considered meet in a mature congregation. Seemingly, then, it could have squared both with conscience and with professional responsibility for Grindal to have relayed his sovereign's command as an administrative duty, while blunting or mitigating its effects in practice. It would also have been a means of sidestepping an evident trap whose function, at this point, was to frustrate the wider program of consensual reform to which Grindal was committed, and which seemed to offer the best hope of avoiding a tragic polarization between church authority and godly conscience. The choice, for a man as skilled in the art of the possible and as cognizant of the dictates of necessity as Grindal, would have seemed evident.

Grindal's initial approach was cautious. He sent a circular letter asking his provincial bishops to describe prophesyings (if any) in their dioceses, and to comment on their value. Most responded positively, stressing their utility in training ministers, their good effects on the laity, and their patronage by local magistrates. Richard Curtis of Chichester noted that the number of "competent" preaching ministers in his diocese had risen within six years from three to 70 or 80, thanks largely to the exercises. Thomas Bentham of Coventry and Lichfield opined that "here in the contrye" prophesying was "the onely waye both to increase learninge in the symple and ignorant and to continue the same theare in the learned, without ruste or disvse." William Bainbridge of Exeter found that the laity "delighte to heare and gladlye doe resorte" to prophesyings and that "many gentilmen and other zealous desyr the[ir] continewance." There were ancillary benefits, too. John Walker, Archdeacon of Sussex, contrasted the open, public nature of prophesying with the "secret conventicles" of Papists and sectaries. David Kemp, Archdeacon of St. Albans, used the exercises as a means of ferreting out Romish tendencies in the older clergy, compelling them to affirm the royal supremacy and the doctrine and discipline of the church.[22]

On rare occasions, it was reported, the laity had expostulated with the clergy, among whom were sometimes found deprived as well as ordained ministers. But almost all the respondents agreed that the exercises were generally orderly, and genuinely popular. The presence of magistrates assured a reasonable level of decorum, and indicated the support of local magnates. The message was clear. The bishops had their misgivings about an unlicensed practice, particularly one that might involve defrocked ministers. But the benefits of an exercise that linked the entire community in a voluntary devotional praxis, that emphasized learning and the cultivation of rhetorical skills in the clergy and encouraged piety, edification, and admiration for the cloth in the laity, far outweighed the occasional jar or stir it might bring; and in any case it was far better to give it an open forum that could be policed from above than to drive it underground, offending powerful lay interests in the process.

Grindal drafted orders for bringing the exercises under episcopal control. By screening ministers and topics, banning lay commentary, and providing penalties for anyone criticizing the dispensation in church or state, the exercises could be standardized and the objections to them met. Many of them, indeed, already functioned under rules approved by the local bishop. Grindal chose as his model *The Order of the Prophecy at Norwich*, which had been accepted by Bishop Cooper of Lincoln, no friend to enthusiasm. It envisioned a weekly disputation, open to ministers only, whose avowed purpose was "to rip up the [scriptural] text, to show the sense of the Holy Ghost, and briefly, pithily and plainly to observe such things as afterward may be well applied"—in short, to produce better preaching from the pulpit. Presumably the model was not to be prescriptive, particularly where lay participation was customary. As Bishop Sandys of London had warned, "I feare the chaunge of suche profitable exercise as men have been in possession of so manie yeares . . . will breed further vnquietnes than I shall well be able to staye."[23]

Sandys' warning and Grindal's best efforts notwithstanding, Elizabeth was unbudged in her determination to suppress the prophesyings. An audience with the Queen proved disastrous; refusing to hear any argument, she reportedly berated the Archbishop at length.[24] Why was Elizabeth so adamant? A closer look at the Norwich *Order of the Prophecy* may provide a clue. The text begins and ends as follows:

> *It is judged meet by the brethren* that the Prophecy be kept every Monday. . . . The names of such *as shall be judged by the brethren meet to speak* in the Prophecy shall be written in a Table. . . . Let none be suffered to speak in the Prophecy *except he will submit himself to the orders that are or shall be set down hereafter by the consent of the brethren.* New orders are to be set down *by the knowledge and consent of the brethren only, and not by any one man's authority* . . .[25] [Emphases added]

Bishop Cooper's belated imprimatur notwithstanding, this document plainly describes a self-constituted band of ministers meeting privately to perform rigorous and unfettered exegesis on scriptural texts ("rip up the text"). "It shall be free," the Order states, "for any godly-learned brother to lay forth any fruitful matter revealed unto him out of the text." If false doctrine be propounded, "the same is to be confuted and handled with great wisdom," and the raising of manifest heresies must be avoided, "except they be some very pernicious now revived, which must be soundly overthrown by the Scriptures." The warrant for such proceedings *was* of course scriptural, and a prayer was prescribed at the end "for the whole church and all Estates [and] for the Queen's Majesty [and] Council." Nonetheless, it was as close to an exercise of unaccountable free speech, behind closed doors and on the most potentially sensitive subjects, as could well be imagined. It was freer, as a practical matter, than the speech of the Queen's own Council. And it was a freedom neither granted through nor revocable by any authority in church or state. The form and content of the exercise were wholly set by the brethren, and the brethren alone might reprove or discipline erring or offending members. This was not the kind of license Elizabeth was prepared to grant anywhere in her church, even if Bishop Cooper had.

The suppression of the prophesyings underscored the fault line that ran through the reconstituted Anglican church more than any other episode in the early Elizabethan period. That church might not be all its godlier supporters wished. It might be far from the preaching ministry that alone could make the Word efficacious; it might harbor dumb dogs and even concealed Papists, at least until time had winnowed out the remnants of the Henrician

and Marian clergy. It might chafe under the yoke of a secular governance
that while affording it the material and political conditions of existence too
often stinted its body and bridled its spirit. It might be forced to parade in
the swaddlings of popery and to endure a clerical hierarchy of at best dubious scriptural warrant. But as long as it provided an outward bulwark
against the threat of Rome and a haven for the elect, its blessings could outweigh its faults and even its abuses.

The bedrock of this compromise was the commitment to sound doctrine
and edification. Doctrine was the foundation of the true church, but the
church itself was built of the lively stones that made the Word efficacious in
the world; in contrast, the false church was based not only on spurious doctrine but rote performance—the repetition of idolatrous ceremony that sti-
fled Christian liberty. A church that coldly professed the Word but suppressed its vital dynamic—a church that relied on homily and a corrupted
Prayer Book, and under the guise of adiaphora promoted popish images and
mandated popish ceremonies—such a church was, if not a false church in
mufti, then perhaps well on its way to becoming one. Had not the original
true church of the apostles been corrupted in precisely the same way, by the
slow accretion of vain ceremony and usurped powers over conscience? Edification—the unity of zealous teaching and godly practice—was therefore
the ultimate touchstone of a true commitment to the Word. A church but
halfly reformed that sought to complete the task of reformation as rapidly
and diligently as its circumstances would permit was worthy of patient support; only a zeal puffed up with its own pride would demand more. Such a
church content to stand still, however, would soon find itself backsliding
toward popery. From this perspective, the commitment of the godly to a national church might be best described as vigilantly conditional. True allegiance was owed only to the Word.

There was considerable sympathy for this attitude among key members of
Elizabeth's inner circle, if not for the separatist implication it harbored. But
Elizabeth also maintained a strong conformist group centered around Sir
Christopher Hatton, a courtier newly risen to favor. There is little doubt
where her own convictions lay. For Elizabeth, an Erastian *avant la lettre*, her
power in church and state was indivisible, and her duty to keep the peace of
the realm paramount. To that end she required a church as comprehensive
as possible, one not vexed by niceties of doctrine or hemmed by straitness of
practice. She had found an indispensable clerical ally in Archbishop Parker,
as she would later find another in Archbishop Whitgift. In between she had
to endure the grim interregnum of Grindal, who had seemed pliable enough
during the Vestments controversy but now, in the matter of prophesying,
was to do what no sovereign could brook from any subject: not only to defy
an order despite public command and private rebuke, but to challenge the

authority from whence it came. Grindal's famous letter in defense of prophesying, and, more generally, of the autonomy of the elect within the order of the church, was composed in late 1576. It circulated widely and caused a great stir,[26] as did its immediate and in retrospect inevitable consequence, the suspension of Grindal from his archiepiscopal office. As Collinson remarks, "Queen Elizabeth never received such another letter as this, and with good reason."[27] What contemporaries knew as Grindal's "book" to the Queen chalked out the limits of her sovereignty in the church and affirmed the moral guardianship of the bishops over matters of discipline no less than doctrine. It was a pastoral rebuke to Elizabeth by her senior spiritual counselor and a frontal challenge to the Erastian polity she had labored to build. No monarch would hear the like from an English divine until Hugh Peter took it upon himself to admonish Charles I on his way to the scaffold in 1649.

What did Grindal hope to accomplish? The issue as he construed it went to the heart of the church's ministry, while the stakes, as he defined them, were nothing less than Elizabeth's own salvation, for should he fail to perform his duty in a matter of such consequence, "you might fale into perrill towards God and I my selfe into endles damnation." The notion that the fate of the Queen's immortal soul rested upon the discharge of her Archbishop's conscience was not well calculated to sharpen for her the distinction between his sense of office and that of Roman or Genevan prelacy, despite his claim that "We admitte noe man to the office [of minister] that eyther professeth papistrie or puritanism." But Grindal saw his letter as firmly rooted in scriptural and patristic tradition. For Grindal, the covenant line of the true church extended in an unbroken descent from the Old Testament prophets who rebuked the kings of Israel, to Ambrose, who had renewed their office in bringing the Emperor Theodosius to contrition, to those in his own time who, like Latimer, had spoken truth fearlessly to power. To be sure, the godly bishop must honor the royal station even as he admonished the royal person. This was particularly true in light of the scurrilous diatribes delivered by Romish clergy against the Plantagenets—a Satanic inversion of prophetic authority in which the Antichrist harangued the magistrate for upholding the civil powers ordained of God. But past abuse could never be an excuse for quailing before present duty. "Let the preacher . . . never fear to declare the messages of God unto all men," Latimer had said. "If he preach before a king, let his matter be concerning the office of a king."[28] And if God ordained that the preacher should speak, he also commanded that the prince should listen, whatever the civil subjection of the former to the latter.

Thus fortified, Grindal plunged into his subject. That he already knew upon ample personal evidence that Elizabeth would not listen, that his counsel would almost certainly be received as an act of insubordination if not of lèse-majesté, made his letter both a manifesto and a personal testament. This would account for its wide immediate circulation. Grindal was too good a clerical politician not to have reckoned the balance of forces within the Queen's inner circle. If the godly party was to be mobilized at this point, a dramatic stroke was necessary, one which would compel men to take sides. Grindal must not merely have anticipated a violent response from the Queen as a result of his letter. He must have counted on it.

What ailed the church, Grindal declared, was the grievous want of preaching ministers. If Solomon's "materiall" temple had required the labor of six score thousand workmen and overseers, he asked, "how can it be thought that 3 or 4 preachers may suffice" to cultivate the lively stones of Christ's spiritual temple in each shire? Nor should Elizabeth delude herself that prayer and homily could bind and support the church. "The reading of homilies hath his commoditie," Grindal allowed, "but it [is] nothing comparable to the office of preaching." Scripture was not plainer on any point than "then that the gospell of Christ should be plentifully preached. . . . Publike and continuall preaching of Gods word is the ordinarye meanes and instrument of the salvation of mankinde." It was also the principal means of preserving public order, for:

> By preaching also due obedience vnto Christian princes and magistrates is planted in the hartes of subiectes, for obedience proceedeth of conscience, conscience is grounded vppon the worde of God, the worde of God worketh his effect by preaching, so as generally where preaching faileth wanteth obedience. (131–132)

Here in essence is the Puritan doctrine of civil legitimacy, the compact between Christian emperor and godly subject. In upholding God's Word the emperor upholds his own throne. The Word, which both constructs conscience and fortifies it, implants in the subject the only sure guarantor of obedience, that which is grounded in Christian liberty. Laws may direct civil conduct and penalties enforce compliance, but only conscience can ensure the inward consent that distinguishes loyal subjects from suppressed rebels, just as it does true Christians from mere formal professors.

This was a powerful argument. The Tudor regime required frequent tokens of loyalty, a demand that showed the anxious importance it attached to displays of conscientious assent. Was the Anglican Church itself not based on an act of conscience? Had not the royal founder himself declared that "Though the law of every man's conscience be but a private court, yet it is the highest and supreme court for judgment or justice"?[29] An informed conscience was both the immediate foundation and the ultimate bulwark of the civil order.

The key term in this equation was *informed*. If conscience was inherent in humanity, its operation was flawed. No other faculty was more easily abused than an ignorant or misguided conscience, as the reign of popery attested. The proper instruction of conscience was the business of preaching. The ample provision of a preaching ministry was thus the cornerstone of sound polity in church and state. Consequently it was a principal obligation of the Christian emperor upon whom the care of both devolved.

Grindal situated his defense of prophesying in this context. It was bad enough that Elizabeth did not do more for preaching, and seemed to find it suspect ("I cannot marvell enough how this strange opinion should once enter into your minde, that it shoulde be good for the church to have few preachers"). It was intolerable that she should suppress the voluntary efforts of learned ministers to train up their less skillful brethren to expound the Word. "I am well assured," Grindal concluded,

> . . . that the said exercises . . . are both profittable to increase knowledge amongst the ministers and tend to the edifieing of the hearers. I am forced with all humilitie and yet plainely to confesse that I cannot with a safe conscience and without the offence of the majestie of God give my assent to the suppressing of the said exercises; much less can I send out an iniunction for the vtter and universall subvertion of the same. I saie with Paule, I have no power to destroye, but only to edifie, and with the same apostle, I can doe nothing against the truth, but with the truth. (138)

Like Luther and—even more pointedly to the case at issue—like Henry VIII himself, Grindal took his stand with conscience, a conscience that revealed itself to him as "truth." Against this, Elizabeth could offer only the "strange opinion" insinuated into her by false counsel. But Grindal would not rest his case on mere personal conviction. He pointed out that his episcopal colleagues had certified the exercises as both lawful in Scripture and profitable in practice. This corporate determination—informed conscience in the highest sense of the word—must rightly take precedence over any lay judgment, no matter how exalted the source. As the Queen acknowledged her deference to judges in matters of civil law, so she should refer all pronouncements on the doctrine and discipline of the church to her bishops, "according to the example of all godlie Christian emperours and princes of all ages." Indeed, the spiritual authority was even more to be respected than the temporal, for "in Gods causes the will of God and not the will of any earthlie creature is to take place" [i.e., precedence].

Here then was the carrot and the stick of Grindal's "book," his vision of the godly commonwealth. The loyalty and obedience of the Queen's subjects could be secured only by the continuous efforts of a preaching ministry. Such a ministry was no mere passive channel for transmitting royal dicta— the Tudor ideal of the pulpit—but a mediating force that translated secular into sacred discourse, its final if not its efficient form. What was owed to the sovereign, in Grindal's formulation, was not blind submission but "due obe-

dience"—the response of instructed Christian liberty to just command. The
role of the clergy in this was as critical as that of the crown's ministers, if not
more so. As the sovereign command was constructed through counsel and
certified by bench and bar, so its conformity to divine law provided the ultimate seal of its legitimacy.

The function of the ministry was of course not to question royal acts but to
attest the general tenor of their godliness. Implicit in this function, however,
was an irreducible act of judgment. The preaching ministry, as Grindal conceived it, constituted an essential level of mediation between ruler and subject. Ideally, the just command was fortified by this mediation. By placing
the just command in the context of divine purpose it strengthened the subject's sense of conscientious duty, and offered him active participation in that
purpose as well. Grindal contrasted the love and loyalty Elizabeth received
in London with the seditious North:

> Whereof cometh this [love], Madame, but of the continuall preaching of
> Gods word in that Citie, whereby that people hath bin plentifully instructed
> in theire duties towardes God and your Majestie. On the contrary, what
> bread rebellion in the North? Was it not papistrie and ignorance of Gods
> word through want of often preaching? (132)

But there was peril in this process, too. It added a new burden of explication to the secular command and cultivated a new level of introspection in
the subject's response to it; in effect, it imposed new criteria for obedience,
and therefore new obligations for command. Moreover, since such criteria
were applied ex post facto, a double act of judgment was presupposed: in
the parish setting itself, where the minister and congregation translated civil
command into sacred discourse, and in the private arena of conscience
where each parishioner reflected on what had been said to him and what
was expected of him. It was understandable that the Queen should have preferred the risks of simple obedience to the rewards of such an exercise.

Grindal's application of the process to his own case, moreover, provided a
perfect negative paradigm. He was refusing a royal command, conscientiously. And although he offered to resign his post he came extraordinarily
close to threatening Elizabeth with an anathema, or at any rate as close to
one as an Archbishop of Canterbury could get:

> I consider with myself, *quod horrendum est incidere in manus Dei viventis.* I
> consider also, *quod qui facit contra conscientum (deuinus iuribus nixem) edificat
> ad gehenam.* And what should I winne if I gained, I will not saie a bishop-
> ricke, but the whole world, and lose myne owne soule: beare with me, I be-
> seech you, Madame, if I chuse rather to offend your earthlie Majestie then
> to offend the heavenly Majestie of God. . . . Remember, Madame, that you
> are a mortall creature. Remember not only (as was said to Theodosius)
> vppon the purple and princely araye wherewith you are apparelled, but

consider withall what it is that is covered therewith: is it not flesh and
bloud? Is it not dust and ashes? Is it not a corruptible bodie whiche must returne to his earth againe (God knoweth how soone)? . . . Ye have donne
many things well, but except ye persevere to the end ye cannot be blessed.
(138, 140, 141)

It was hardly surprising that Grindal was suspended from his duties after
this disquisition; the wonder was that he not only escaped harsher punishment but that he was able to resume some of his functions and to hope, with
broad Court and clerical backing, for a return to favor.[30] If he died without
achieving it, he had struck a powerful blow not only for the rights of conscience but for the independence and corporate identity of the episcopal
bench. Although Elizabeth would find a successor at Canterbury more to her
liking in John Whitgift, Grindal's defense of the prophetic, Theodosian role
of the bishops would give powerful impetus to the development of a *jure divino* episcopacy. If an Alexander Leighton could claim true descent from
Grindal on the one hand, so too could a William Laud on the other.

At the same time, the campaign to restore Grindal was in many respects
an attempt to forestall a potentially disastrous breach between the crown
and the church. As long as hope of a reconciliation between the Queen and
the Archbishop could be kept alive, Grindal's colleagues—whose opinion he
had directly invoked in his dispute—could avoid choosing between duty
and conscience, or at any rate between loyalty to their metropolitan and to
their sovereign.

In this contretemps, no one's position was more delicate than that of
Archbishop Sandys of York. Sandys had been particularly warm in his defense of prophesying, as we have seen. He had also been outspoken on the
subject of pastoral responsibility. At his institution as Bishop of London in
1570, he described the episcopal office as a perilous one: "For if we preach
things pleasant unto men, we discharge not the duty of the servants of God:
if we preach his truth, we are hated as their deadly enemies to whom we
preach."[31] Conventional as these sentiments were—Sandys himself had suffered imprisonment and exile under Mary—he must have found them awkward indeed when applied to a trial of strength between his Primate and his
Queen. What counsel he may have offered either we do not know, but he
chose not to widen the breach, and took his stand with what he regarded as
the corporate interest of the church. That choice required him to part company with those for whom prophesying to edification was at the core of a
true, Pauline church. The later Sandys denounced Precisians and Papists
alike as engines of the Antichrist.[32] Such rhetoric increasingly characterized
the post-Grindalian church, and James I used the equation between Puritanism and popery as a tag line. This grated on some, such as Matthew Hutton,
Dean (and later Archbishop) of York, who remained close both to Grindal

and to their mutual patron, Leicester. Hutton had accused Sandys of under-mining Grindal, and there was bad blood between them. It spilled over in the examination of one William Whitingham, who had asserted that the Or-der of Geneva was equivalent to that established by the Church of England. The exchange will bear quoting at some length, since it neatly encapsulates the divisions of the mid-Elizabethan church. Sandys asserted that:

> . . . the order [of Geneva] was not according to the ecclesiastical laws and orders of England. The Dean of York said that the order was better than any popish order in the world and, saith he, I dare defend with any papist in Europe that the orders at Geneva are more agreeable to the word of God than popish orders. The Archbishop said to the Dean of York if you defend and like so well those orders leave your own orders and take those. . . . To which words the Dean of York answered no my Lord my orders are better than yours. No, saith the Archbishop, thou liest in so saying. Yes, saith the Dean, I will say it for I was made minister by order of the Queen's Majesty and laws now established and your grace a priest after the order of popery. Which order of this realm is better than your grace's order or any popish order. What, saith the Archbishop, dost thou call me a papist? If I be a pa-pist, thou be puritan.[33]

Behind this exchange lay a sense of the belatedness of the Anglican Church, which although the largest Protestant church in Europe was also among the most junior members of the Reformed community, and a lingering anxiety about the unpurged taint of popery it had absorbed in its Henrician founda-tion and received anew as a result of the Marian apostasy. If even Sandys' archepiscopal dignity and his canonical inclusion among the faithful suffer-ers in Foxe's *Book of Martyrs* could not shield him from Hutton's taunt about his Henrician ordination, what was to be said about the run of dumb dogs and covert Papists who comprised, at least from a godly perspective, so much of its ministry? It was equally telling, however, that Sandys thought the charge of Puritanism a suitable riposte to the imputation of popery. Per-sonal and political differences aside, both he and Hutton were as close to a core as the Anglican Church had. In the year of their quarrel, 1578, the future antipapal polemicist William Whitaker had dedicated his Latin translation of Bishop Jewel's defense of the Anglican creed to Grindal and Sandys among others as nursing fathers of the church, while Hutton's most recent historian describes him as the archetypal representative of the "essential protestant consensus" of the Elizabethan church polity. If two figures who seemed so central to the ecclesiastical establishment both to contemporaries and later observers could see such ideological distance between themselves, it may be fair to ask whether a genuine point of equilibrium existed within the Elizabe-than church, rather than an unresolved tension held in suspension by exter-nal authority.

If the primary elements in the church's discourse were doctrine, praxis, and order, then its first three decades under the Settlement of 1559 were marked by successive crises of all three. The initial crisis of doctrine had no sooner been resolved (or, as it may be better to say once more, suspended) by the promulgation of the Thirty-Nine Articles than it gave way to one of praxis, concentrating first on the external protocols of worship (images, vestments, and other "adiaphora"), and then, via prophesying, on the far more substantive question of preaching to edification. This in turn provoked the crisis of order in which the episcopal regime was itself contested.

Episcopacy in England rested on a combination of ecclesiastical tradition and royal institution. Bishops had been part of the primitive church, although their precise origin and antiquity and the nature of (valid) authority they had exercised were matters of dispute, not to say controversy. Protestants had divided sharply on the issue of their legitimacy and utility; this had been a principal subtext of the clash between Hutton and Sandys. They had entered the English Reformation because Henry VIII had chosen to become in effect pope of his own church, and to retain, at least immediately, the subordinate elements of the preexisting ecclesiastical structure. Cranmer and Latimer had given episcopacy the cachet of martyrdom, but the time-serving of Gardiner and the persecutions of Bonner had largely negated this effect; the former had died, after all, as witnesses to their faith, not their office, while the latter had acted specifically in their episcopal function. The Marian bishops' effort to stonewall the Elizabethan settlement in 1559 further eroded the image of episcopacy, and the mixed feelings of their successors, eloquently expressed in *The Zurich Letters*, reflected skepticism about the validity of orders in the ministry as well as about the direction of the restored Anglican Church. Grindal himself defended his assumption of the bishopric of London, replacing the despised Bonner, as a stay against worse.[34] It was obvious that picking up the bloody miter of the most infamous see in the kingdom could only be justified by a purification of both the office and the church it served.

If the episcopal office was not as theologically controversial as it would become in later decades—even Calvin objected less to its function than its subordination to worldly power—it was at best passively defended in the early Elizabethan church. Episcopacy was, as Elizabeth herself put it, a part of "the ecclesiastical ancient policy of the realm," and in a temporally established and governed church—the only one on offer in 1559—a hierarchy more or less parallel to that of the Queen's secular administration was the most natural option. If the bishops could provide leadership in affirming sound doctrine and practice, asserting discipline, and protecting the church from the spoliation it had endured under Henry VIII, they would justify their place; if not, no amount of pleading could excuse them. In short, the view of episcopacy held by most reformers in the early Elizabethan church, including most of the bishops themselves, was an instrumental one.[35]

Elizabeth also viewed her bishops as a means to an end, but her agenda was one of complaisance and conformity, not further reformation. The widespread clerical poverty of her reign reflected policy as well as penuriousness; a church on short rations was likelier to be quiescent, and less a magnet for active and turbulent spirits. This was true on the parish level, where the not accidental result was a plethora of dumb dogs and time servers, and true at the top, where the straitened revenues of many episcopal sees compelled their occupants to spend a considerable portion of their time and energy in the pursuit of maintenance and favor. Elizabeth had seen enough of clerical pomp and arrogance, and clerical meddling too. She was determined to have no Wolseys or Gardiners in her church, and she would certainly not have brooked a William Laud. No churchman sat on her Council until Whitgift, having proved both his utility and his docility as an ecclesiastical manager, was admitted in 1586. The Court of High Commission, the chief arm of ecclesiastical enforcement, was dominated by lay councillors through much of Elizabeth's reign as well. But nothing more pointedly attested the Queen's attitude toward clerical government than the long episcopal vacancies she permitted to accumulate, in one case nineteen years. If the early Elizabethan bishops were equivocal about the function they had assumed, their royal mistress did not encourage them to take any but the most modest view of it.

In this respect, too, the suspension of Archbishop Grindal was a watershed event. There is ample suggestion of the progressive slackening of church discipline and administration during the six-year primatial hiatus, although Grindal continued to discharge at least some of his functions. With no direction from above the bishops quarreled among themselves, and with no protection from their superior they were increasingly abused by the local gentry, who not surprisingly took their cue from on high. Visitations, it was alleged, lacked rigor; suits for dilapidations multiplied. At the Convocation of Canterbury in 1581 there was lamentation, in Collinson's words, that Grindal's continuing sequestration "was a wound through which the whole Church bled." The contemporary author of "Inconveniences by the sequestration of the archbishop of Canterbury" noted that processes and commissions going out in the Archbishop's name were being challenged. The entire structure of ecclesiastical authority appeared to be in danger of falling into desuetude, if not discredit.

This high-stakes gamble appears to have been the policy of the Queen alone. Grindal did not lack for support at Court; Leicester and Walsingham interceded for him, and Burghley was active behind the scenes on his behalf. Elizabeth tacked evasively, as she usually did under pressure, and showed occasional signs of relenting. But she held fast in the end, and Grindal was in the process of negotiating his resignation when he died.

For the Queen, Grindal was only part of a larger scenario. The years of his sequestration coincided with a worsening situation abroad, Jesuit infiltration at home, and new demands for Protestant solidarity and militancy. The stiff new recusancy fines passed by Parliament in 1581 were a call to arms against the Catholic nobility, while Puritan magnates, increasingly disaffected from the Laodicean course of the church, gave shelter to the godly remnant. In short, the policy of a broadly comprehensive church was under its gravest attack at just the moment when the prestige and morale of the church hierarchy was at its lowest ebb, and its helm stood rudderless. There was an extremely persuasive argument to be made that Elizabeth's refusal to be reconciled with her Primate was putting both church and state at risk.

But Elizabeth knew what she wanted, and saw that she soon might have it. The elder generation of bishops was dying out, and the Queen had carefully filled their places with conformists: Freke, Aylmer, Piers, Young, and above all the able and energetic John Whitgift.[36] It was a policy as deliberately plotted and pursued as the promotion of conformist bishops, the so-called Arminian faction, under Charles I. (Then, too, a godly archbishop, George Abbot, could only look on from the sidelines in disgrace, although the cause of his banishment was not disobedience but accidental homicide.) Elizabeth had only to wait out the death of her ailing archbishop, and control of the episcopal bench would be fully hers at last.

Control of the bench, however, did not mean control of the church, and it was here that Elizabeth's gamble was most calculated. If the original ground of her quarrel with Grindal had been the suppression of the prophesyings, it was evident that crippling the see of Canterbury was hardly the way to produce the desired result. The prophesyings continued, albeit with greater circumspection; more ominously, however, they began to evolve in the direction of a Presbyterian underground that would emerge full-blown in the classical movement of the 1580s. If Elizabeth could not fully have anticipated such a development, it had to be a risk of which she was cognizant, and one she was willing to run. Under Whitgift and Bancroft, she would treat the Presbyterian movement as a police problem, and by and large successfully as such. To do that, however, she had to have the levers of ecclesiastical authority firmly in her grasp, which meant an episcopal bench willing to do her bidding. The alternative was to embrace the activism of the godly reformers and their conciliar allies, with every dire consequence that portended both for a conformist church and a prudent foreign policy.

Elizabeth paid a price for this second reformation of her church. She had to endure an open Protestant challenge to her authority and ultimately the schism of a separatist minority that, while far noisier than numerous, marked the end of the dream of a fully comprehensive church. On the whole, however, she got what she wanted. The great magnates, wherever their religious sympathies lay, were not about to jeopardize the dispensation on which their own fortunes depended. They did not need to: in their private chapels and households, in the colleges they endowed and the benefices they controlled, they could promote and partake of godliness and zeal to their hearts' content. All that was asked of them, in the end, was that they uphold the royal supremacy in the church as represented by the authority of the bishops. If this meant acceptance of the de facto division of the church into a leavened and an unleavened lump, it also meant unity in the face of the greatest foreign threat to England's civil and religious independence in five hundred years. It was the Spanish Armada that finally sealed the Elizabethan settlement.

If Grindal's sequestration was a crisis of conscience for those who hoped for godly reformation within the existing structure of the church, it was no less one for the newly promoted bishops. "Conformism," like "Puritanism," was a complex of ideologically refined responses to the political, liturgical, and theological issues posed by the Elizabethan ecumene, and men such as Sandys, Hutton, Matthew, Aylmer, and Whitgift, however they might tack to the wind, were no mere careerists. These men knew that no church could stand that did not reflect the Queen's will and ultimately do her bidding, but they knew also that no church could deserve the name of Christ's which did that and nothing more. If, so far as the Queen, her Council, and most of the nobility and greater gentry were concerned, they were no more than glorified policemen—in Roger Manning's phrase, "ecclesiastical justices of the peace"—the bishops themselves were bound to take a higher view of their calling: policemen they might be, but the law they enforced was ultimately a divine one. Others might forget or conveniently lose sight of that fact, but they could not. In it lay the difference between the *potestas ordinis* and the commission of the peace.

The new Elizabethan bishops were also more conscious of themselves as the heirs of a tradition. Episcopacy has had a long history in England; it remains the hardiest and most resilient institution of the English Church. Bishops had been fighting the encroachments of royal authority for centuries, and if it was chiefly a rearguard action in which direct confrontation had almost invariably proved disastrous, it had also nurtured powerful instincts of survival. Never had those instincts been more severely tested than in the period between Henry VIII's demand for the Submission of the Clergy and Grindal's sequestration. The fealty of the English church had been sworn variously to the Bishop of Rome, to a Supreme Head, and to a Supreme Governor; its doctrine had been Catholic, semi-Pelagian, Lutheran, Zwinglian, Calvinist, and a host of shades in between; its assets had been plundered and its jurisdictions curtailed; its leaders had been jailed, exiled, beheaded, and sent to the stake. Through all these travails the episcopal governance of the church had remained the only constant. The bishops had stood in the lists. They had disputed with and even persecuted one another, but as a corporate body they represented at any given moment the continuity of Christ's church. Their lands and rents—such as remained—were its endowment; their courts enforced its law. They had withstood visitations and viceregencies; they had survived massive purges and prolonged vacancies; they had endured derision and contempt from their betters and inferiors alike. Now they faced a Presbyterian insurgency that threatened their authority from within. If they were to be nursing fathers of the church or even competent agents of the *potestas ordinis,* they would have to define their role more positively and defend it more forcefully than their immediate predecessors had done.

Such a defense would have to walk a fine line between deference and assertion. Grindal's fate was a grim reminder that the scope of episcopal functions no less than their exercise remained at the Queen's pleasure; the prosecution of recusants following the act of 1581 was left to secular courts, and the jurisdiction of the church as a whole was more seriously compromised than at any time since the Henrician supremacy. Any further challenge to the Erastian polity was clearly out of the question, at least in Elizabeth's lifetime.

Whitgift and Conformity

It was the wisdom of Grindal's successor, John Whitgift, to realize that an Erastian polity was not only the legal framework of the English Church but the only surety for the episcopal regime itself. He won and retained Elizabeth's trust, and, as we have seen, the Queen rewarded him with what she no doubt conceived to be the highest mark of favor and esteem she could confer on a cleric, appointment to the Council.

The core of Whitgift's perception was twofold: that as Elizabeth would not tolerate any challenge to the royal supremacy from within the church, so she would not permit any derogation of it from outside. Elizabeth's protection and patronage of the church stemmed immediately from the fact that ecclesiastical governance was an inseparable aspect of her authority, as intrinsic to the Crown Imperial as her titles to Ireland, Wales, or France. The visible church of Christ in England had no other constitution, and no other security. If James I would reply to those who upon his accession urged him to alter that constitution, "No bishop, no king," it was because Archbishop Whitgift had preached steadily for twenty years on the text, "no king, no bishop."

Whitgift understood that the bishops must make themselves useful as policemen before they could lay claim to any higher function within the church. He imposed a triple subscription oath on the clergy and enjoined strict compliance with the vestments code, forbade all conventicles and unlicensed preaching, and provided strict procedures for dealing with recusancy. To enforce this policy he established a new Commission for Ecclesiastical Causes, empowered to compel testimony upon oath. He made a point of pursuing godly nonconformists as zealously as Papists, and of setting out his new ordinances by the "most gracious consent and allowance" of the Queen.

Whitgift's strategy was risky. In carrying out the royal mandate he ran afoul of powerful lay interests, godly and otherwise. These interests, whose resistance to episcopal controls was evident in both Council and countryside, severely restricted Elizabeth's own freedom of maneuver. It was not only that so many of the church's livings and so much of its wealth were irretrievably in gentry hands but that the entire process of creating a Protestant England depended crucially on the acculturation of a lay elite. No bishop, no king; but, equally, no gentry, no church.

The ecclesiastical polity of England was therefore a complex, shifting cluster of stresses and accommodations within a fluid power grid, the whole framed within a larger process of evolving cultural norms and values. "Conformity" was the effort to impose monarchical-episcopal controls on this dynamic in the interests of order. But the interests of the crown and of the bishops, however entwined they might be, were by no means identical even under the post-Whitgiftian regime of the church. Nor were their respective conceptions of order. For Elizabeth as Erastian prince and for James I in the more activist role of Protestant Solomon, order meant essentially the establishment and maintenance of doctrinal and disciplinary consensus: a viable status quo. For the bishops, or at least some of them, it meant the opportunity to elaborate a more central and independent role for themselves.

Whitgift's goals were essentially administrative. He lived modestly, worked hard, and claimed for episcopacy only a superintendency lawfully ordained by the prince. When the Marprelate tracts called him the second most powerful person in the kingdom—a considerable exaggeration, if pardonable from a Martinate perspective—they paid him the unwitting tribute of acknowledging how well he had served the Erastian church. Ironically, it was this very service that enabled some of his colleagues and successors to claim powers for themselves that far exceeded any he believed himself to possess.

The new clerical activism was manifested in both governance and doctrine. Beginning in 1588 and particularly with Richard Bancroft's Paul's Cross sermon in early 1589, clerics and scholars inched toward the claim that episcopacy was the divinely ordained form of church government, not merely one acceptable scheme among many. This doctrine became fully explicit in Bancroft's own *Survay of the Pretended Holy Discipline* (1593). Neither

Whitgift nor Hutton, now Archbishop of York, ever embraced it, and though James VI was alarmed enough to risk antagonizing Elizabeth by denouncing it, he was sufficiently reconciled with Bancroft in the end to name him Whitgift's successor at Canterbury. If *jure divino* episcopacy was never generally accepted, neither was it decisively rebutted, in part because it emerged in the context of anti-Presbyterian polemics and presented itself as a defense of the established order rather than as a departure from it. As Hugh Trevor-Roper noted, after its initial flourish "it receded back into the . . . Elizabethan amalgam," there to await more propitious circumstances for development.[37] It was not forgotten, however, particularly by James, who as James I of England elaborated a parallel argument for the divine right of kings that must be seen at least in part as a response to the challenge of divine right episcopacy.

Doctrine, too, was in flux during the 1590s. The international crisis of the 1580s had unleashed a flood of antipapal polemics in England and on the Continent, and these had the consequence of hardening theological as well as political differences between the Reformed community and Rome. The consequence was pressure on (and from) Anglican savants to define the doctrine of their church more closely, particularly with regard to the central issue of predestination. The two fundamental texts of the Elizabethan church, the Thirty-Nine Articles of 1563 and the Prayer Book, were neither fully satisfactory to doctrinal purists nor fully consistent with each other. The defects of the Prayer Book, including the retention of patently Roman rites and ceremonies, had precipitated a major rift in the church in the 1570s, the so-called Admonition Controversy. Now the subject matter of the Thirty-Nine Articles, the church's formal credal statement, was to become embroiled in controversy.

The occasion of the dispute was a frontal assault on predestinarian doctrine by two Cambridge divines, Peter Baro and William Barrett. As Peter Lake has stressed, Baro and Barrett were as much reacting to a provocative sermon before an elite audience of peers and gentry by William Whitaker, the Regius Professor of Divinity and a leading antipapal polemicist, as initiating controversy on their own.[38] Nonetheless, the Pelagian views they espoused hardly constituted a merely defensive response. Barrett contended that actual, not imputed sin was the cause of reprobation, and that no person could be sure of the remission of his sins and hence the certainty of his salvation. Baro subsequently affirmed that grace had been given to all men, and that Christ had died for the sins of all.

These views struck at the doctrine of irresistible grace and the notion of an invisible church of the elect. The Heads of the University demanded a retraction from Barrett, and the ensuing controversy produced a challenge to Whitgift's authority in the University. The upshot of this was a gathering of divines at the Archbishop's palace that produced a new formulary, the Lambeth Articles, which affirmed a staunchly Calvinist interpretation of the Thirty-Nine Articles. Whitgift issued it under his own imprimatur and drew a prompt rebuke from Elizabeth, who declared the matter "tender and dangerous." Not wishing to repeat the Grindal affair, she suspended the Articles but not the Archbishop. Her supposed comment to Whitgift that he had committed praemunire by convening a church council without her consent, whether apocryphal or not, suggests the depths of her irritation.

The Cambridge contretemps is instructive on a number of points. Clearly Elizabeth regarded the whole episode as a willful nuisance. Theology was not one of her strong points, and unlike James she did not regard divinity as an evolving science; her preference for homilies over sermons reflected a bias toward serviceable formulas that conveyed truths rather than disputing them. The Thirty-Nine Articles was a text in which she and apparently the vast majority of her subjects could rest their consciences, and that, for her, was as precise as any credal statement needed to be. Although Elizabeth had disavowed any claim to "define, decide or determine any article or point of the Christian faith and religion," she did not cede that authority to anyone else without express license, and that license was, after the first few years of her reign, never granted. There were to be no more prescriptive texts, and no authoritative exegeses. If divinity could not be suppressed as such, it would be kept at the level of disputation, that is, of censorable utterances. This meant, however, that disputed points could never be definitively resolved, and heretical doctrine suppressed. The Lambeth Articles remained in limbo, neither accepted nor repudiated. The theology of grace espoused by Barrett and Baro would soon return.[39]

Four decades of the Elizabethan settlement had produced, from one point of view, a church well defined in governance and creed. The governance was episcopal, under the firm hand of a Christian magistrate, and the creed Calvinist, though not as strictly so as some would have wished it. It was a church not only accepted among its Reformed brethren but looked to for leadership and succor in the struggle against the Romish Antichrist. Its ecclesiology and ceremony were rooted in native tradition, and, if the diffusion of much of its wealth and patronage among lay elites imposed an often oppressive dependency on the clergy, it also provided the broad secular basis of a genuinely national church. The Anglican Church might represent a web of compromise that was in some respects even more frustrating to conformists than to the godly, but it was one that held and ramified itself nonetheless. By the first quarter of the seventeenth century England had acquired a distinctively Protestant culture that had become entwined with social custom and hierarchy, political values, and patriotic expression.[40]

At the same time, however, the inner relation between the ecclesiology and the eschatology of this church, as well as its external relation to the Supreme Governor, was unresolved and in some cases sharply contested. Cal-vinist orthodoxy imposed a polarizing schema in the contrast between the invisible, predestined, spiritual church of the elect and the visible, this-worldly church that encompassed the redeemed and the reprobate alike. Both godly and conformist members of the church accepted this distinc-tion—if, as did all Anglican archbishops until William Laud, they accepted Calvinism itself—but they interpreted the obligation it enjoined differently. For the godly, the nurture of the invisible church and the primacy of its in-fluence within the visible church was the chief priority of ecclesiastical pol-icy, and the governance of the reprobate a secondary consequence of this. For the conformist, the invisible church was beyond both the reach and the need of the visible church, whose task was the governance of the elect and the reprobate alike in a fallen world in which no one was immune from sin.[41]

These visions were, as ideal types, fundamentally incompatible. On the godly view, the true constituency of the church, the active component on be-half of which it existed, was the elect; the reprobate, unlike the members of the political community whose consent if not determination in the governing process was posited by even the most absolutist theories of state, were akin to a conquered population bound to obedience by force (the recusancy stat-utes). Considered as a whole, then, the visible church comprised both wheat and tares joined by the divine command to universal order and worship. This consociation was ontologically separate and distinct, however, just as the governance of the church was (or properly ought to be) distinguished by the subordination of the reprobate mass to a godly presbytery. The visible church was thus to be conceived not as an organic whole but as a construct required by the need to compel the reprobate to offer due submission to their creator. Edification, in this light, was the constant struggle not merely to cul-tivate piety and godly conversation in the elect but to counter the sinful im-pulses of the reprobate majority, to prevent the leaven from being drowned in the lump. Without this struggle, a "true" church—a church not merely faithful in doctrine but meet in ceremony and vigilant in governance—would soon fall prey to Satan, as had the church of the apostles itself under the Romish Antichrist. Should this occur, partial or full separation might be the only choice left to the faithful.

From a conformist perspective, however, the eternal church of those pre-destined for salvation was invisible in the temporal world, and while a com-prehensive, visible church was bound to contain the invisible one (from which followed the argument for conformity as the only guarantee of a true church), the impossibility of making a precise or even proximate census of the latter meant that the leaven must indeed drown in the lump. Given this unavoidable circumstance, the maintenance of external worship and disci-pline was the principal and defining duty of the visible church. Since the elect (if not fallen under the temporary sway of sin) would voluntarily keep discipline and render worship by themselves, the church then existed for the sake of the reprobate. The elect remained crucial to the visible church, of course, for without them there would be no stay against heresy, idolatry, and worse. But the church was for them a civil institution, or more properly a civil responsibility, for their salvation was entirely independent of it. The only benefit it could confer on them, apart from liturgical convenience, was the repression of manifest sin in the reprobate. In that sense the visible church was indeed a mere extension of the state, its objective being the maintenance of spiritual propriety as that of the state was the maintenance of temporal order. It was well to work a sense of repentance in the reprobate, but since according to God's eternal decree this was inefficacious to salvation, external conformity was, first and last, the church's defining function. In a certain sense the comprehensive visible church of the conformists might be said to have no members at all, at least in eschatological terms, for the elect did not need it and the reprobate could not be saved by it. It existed for the sake of order, at the command of Christ.

There might be practical accommodation between these visions — the Anglican church as it existed until 1625 was the consequence of such an accommodation — but intellectually they were irreconcilable. The only common ground they shared was the assumption, explicitly stated by the Presbyterian community and implicitly held by conformist divines, that the governance of the church must rest with the probable elect, for a church fallen into the hands of the reprobate was (as all Presbyterians and many conformists held Rome to be) clearly a church of the Antichrist. The difficulty lay in properly discerning the elect. The Presbyterians looked toward men of godly conversation for lay eldership and skill in preaching for the ministry; the congregational model dispensed with hierarchy (the bait of Satan) and therefore required only rudimentary administrative skills in its pastors and presbyters. Conformists tempered their need for able administrators with an emphasis on the gravitas of clerical office and liturgical solemnity; where the godly made edification the touchstone of a true church, conformists stressed dignity and order. Presbyterians and the godly in general pointed to signs of visible assurance in identifying the elect. Conformists eschewed the overt displays of assurance in part to avoid the charge of prelacy, but also because their hierarchical conception of the church placed more emphasis on its abiding structure than on its transient instruments. No doubt Anglican bishops (at least those of thoroughly Calvinist persuasion) believed themselves to be of the elect, but they did not say so aloud. Modesty in those highly placed was the best claim for sanctity.

The vexed question of election (as well as the older conventions of scholastic debate) enforced a degree of personal restraint on Anglican controversialists. A Cartwright and a Whitgift might cast aspersions on one another's competence, erudition, or motive, but they remained brethren within the church. Even when Cartwright waxed most eloquent in denouncing Whitgift's exercise of episcopal authority as antiscriptural, he did not extend his condemnation of the usurped powers of the office to an implication of reprobation in the man. Similarly, when conformists such as John Bridges and Thomas Cooper accused Presbyterians of succoring popery by sowing dissension in the church, they stopped short of calling them actual agents of the Antichrist. This fine line was crossed when Martin Marprelate — significantly, a lay pamphleteer rather than a cleric — insisted that Whitgift's obdurate persecution of the faithful signified his personal reprobation.[42] Cartwright's disavowal of the Marprelate tracts did not spare him imprisonment in the crackdown that followed, and though the first claims of *de jure* episcopacy had preceded Martin, his rhetorical escalation of the controversy over discipline helped stimulate the more radical formulations that culminated in Bancroft's *Survey*. As long as the disputants could agree on their joint membership in a true church there was ground for debate and room for informal accommodation. That condition removed, the logic of the godly position pushed it toward separation, as the conformist position ultimately dictated a policy of compulsion or exclusion. The imbalance of forces — vulnerable pulpits and hidden printing presses on one side, subscription oaths, pursuivants, courts and gaols, and a determined Queen on the other — was such that, with few though significant exceptions, the godly submitted rather than separated.

If the Presbyterians' defeat was clear, however, it was by no means certain to whom the victory belonged, or what it represented. As Arthur McGrade has noted, the only person fully satisfied by the Elizabethan settlement appears to have been Elizabeth herself.[43] For the Queen the central problematic of Anglican theology, the relationship between the invisible and the visible church, did not exist. She knew only one church, entirely visible, and governed by herself. The mysteries of salvation and reprobation were beyond human ken, and therefore priests' meddling; the clerical task was to instill a proper reverence toward heavenly and earthly majesty as expressed in seemly worship.

Even if Elizabeth had provided adequate material means to support these goals, which she did not, they could hardly have satisfied even the most Erastian of her bishops. The acceptance of a Calvinist soteriology by conformists no less than the godly meant that the invisible church would remain at the heart of any conception of a true church. Whitgift's intervention in the Cambridge disputes of 1595–1596 showed that he and his episcopal colleagues were wedded to Calvinist orthodoxy no less than their severest critics. But if both sides could agree on the invisible church abstractly considered, the godly party had wholly preempted it on the level of praxis. For the conformist, the invisible church was real but latent; for the godly, it was present in a particular church only to the degree to which it could be made manifest. What the latter wished to express, the former sought to repress.

This placed the conformists at a polemical disadvantage, however their control of the church's coercive apparatus gave them the last word in practice. Conformists might show themselves no less doctrinally sound than the godly, and find as much warrant for *de jure* episcopacy as the Presbyterians could claim for lay eldership; what they had failed to do, in thirty years of controversy, was to put forward a positive and energizing conception of their pastoral function that could compete with that of their adversaries. As long as the Erastian church was perceived as the mere handmaiden of the state, replicating the passive ceremonies of submission and obedience required of the political subject in the command mechanisms of homily (authorized injunction) and prayer (formulaic response), it could not capture, let alone contain, the energies of the Reformed faith. Such a church could be seen at best as a static, not to say sterile entity (despite defensive claims that ceremony, too, conduced to edification); at worst, it was a haven for popery and an inlet for the Antichrist. In the end its failure to purge itself of dross and superstition would lead it to persecute the faithful, forcing them to make agonizing choices between conscience and loyalty and thereby depriving the state itself of the natural allegiance of its most devoted and truehearted subjects. Thus the church in subordinating itself to the state (rather than maintaining the watchful parity dictated by the Calvinist doctrine of two coequal regiments)[44] weakened both elements of government. Whether this proceeded from folly, complacency, or the workings of the serpent, the result was the same: the invisible church was marginalized if not extruded from the visible church, leaving a reprobate mass to be indulged in their idolatry by an arrogant and grasping priesthood. Was this not, in fact, a Roman church in all but its profession of allegiance to the Pope? And could that profession be far behind when all else was in place? People with long memories in the 1630s could see in the prelacy of Laud, the crypto-Catholicism of Arminianism, and the open reception of a papal emissary at the Court of Charles I the natural consequence of the Whitgift and Bancroft regimes.

The *via media* of Richard Hooker

The work of Richard Hooker was an attempt to vindicate the ecclesiological dignity of the Anglican Church. Hooker's rhetorical strategy was important to, and indeed inseparable from, the substance of his argument. His irenic stance, reflecting in part the political if not the polemical victory of the conformist party, suggested not only that the godly might yet be welcome in the bosom of the church but that in a sense they could never truly leave it. In a similar fashion, the argument itself turned upon the hypostatized union of church and state in a divine order in which neither partner could claim priority or preeminence. Hooker's response to the contention that the bishops had subordinated the church to secular interests was to describe church and crown as a joint imperium, and to deny any possible divergence of purpose between them. This was not to say that Hooker was content with the actual state of the Elizabethan church. Few controversialists of the age, indeed, bewailed the lay usurpation of clerical wealth and power and the material desuetude of the church more insistently. Hooker ascribed the ill estate and low esteem of the church to the historical circumstances of the Reformation, with its splintering of churches and excessive lay influence, and the disrepute its godly critics had brought upon it. He persistently characterized the Roman church as a true church fallen into error rather than an antitype that signified the beast, and his work is permeated by regret not only for the divided condition of the Anglican Church but for the schism of the Christian commonwealth.

Hooker thus rejects the trope of binary opposition that was so fundamental to the godly figuration of the world, with its unyielding polarization of good and evil, God and Dagon, the true church and the false, in favor of an ecumenical vision in which conflict is blurred if not elided. This vision is grounded in Hooker's conception of creation as issuing from divine perfection and, in accordance with God's rational will, as perfectly embodying it. The world is simultaneously the objectification of God's purpose and the process by which it is displayed and fulfilled in the temporal continuum. Faith itself, in this context, is nothing more than the world's acknowledgment, through humanity, of its divine constitution and perfection:

> The general end of God's eternal working is the exercise of his most glorious and abundant virtue. Which abundance doth shew itself in variety, and for that cause this variety is oftentimes in Scripture exprest by the name of *riches*. . . . The particular drift of every act proceeding externally from God we are not able to discern, and therefore cannot always give the proper and certain reason of his works. Howbeit undoubtedly a proper and certain reason there is of every finite work of God, inasmuch as there is a law imposed upon it; which if there were not, it should be infinite, even as the worker himself is. They err therefore who think that of the will of God to do this or that there is no reason besides his will. Many times no reason [is] known to us; but that there is no reason thereof I judge it most unreasonable to imagine, inasmuch as he worketh all things *kata tin voulin tou thelimatos afton*, not only according to his own will, but "the Counsel of his own will." And whatsoever is done with counsel or wise resolution hath of necessity some reason why it should be done. . . . The book of this law we are neither able nor worthy to open and look into. That little thereof which we darkly ap-

prehend we admire, the rest with religious ignorance we humbly and meekly adore.[45]

The world is thus the supreme display of God's self-advised rational intentionality, an intentionality which the smaller but correspondent world of the well-counseled ruler reflects in human terms. Even collective human vision—which, in theological terms, is what the church represents—must fall short of a complete understanding of divine reason, as the vision of the individual is inferior to the wisdom of the social whole—but it is always *adequate* to its role in fulfilling the divine purpose, as a single musician in a consort participates in a harmony he may be unable to fully hear. Hooker takes up this image in describing nature itself as "an instrument," a metaphor which, both musical and mechanical, suggests both the determinism of a perfectly contrived artifact and the voluntarism of a cosmic harmony in which the master chord is human praise. All of creation testifies reflexively to the glory of the Creator, and all its elements embody instrumentally the perfection of divine reason, but in humanity's participation alone there is an element of rational will. This will is limited but not imperfect; like everything else in nature, it is attuned to its task. Thus, the rational human intelligence is sufficient to "darkly apprehend" the divine, and that apprehension in turn is sufficient to elicit the adoration of man's "religious ignorance." The limitation of human reason, that is, requires the testimony of faith to complete its task, and the act of worship to crown its comprehension.

As numerous commentators have suggested, this is assuredly a Thomist vision, a theodicy in which the central question of the Judeo-Christian tradition—how can good coexist with evil, and how, if the good is primary, can evil be engendered?—is replaced by the question of how perfection can coexist with imperfection. As we have seen, for Hooker perfection resides in the whole of creation as such, the discrete elements of which participate in that perfection while remaining imperfect considered simply in themselves. "Imperfection" is thus nothing other than partial vision and limited function, an apparent discord which is resolved in the perfect intention of the whole. The irresolution of apparent discord (whose condition implies temporality, as the dissonant musical chord requires duration to resolve itself in harmony) neither contradicts nor derogates from perfection; it is simply the condition of creation itself, as opposed to the pure, self-sufficient Being of divinity.

By refiguring the question of theodicy in terms of a contrast between perfection and imperfection rather than good and evil, Hooker is able to introduce temporality into his system without regarding it is a consequence of and punishment for sin. Indeed, there is little difference in Hooker between pre- and postlapsarian creation, and no sense whatever of creation itself as degraded by the Fall. Sin itself is almost a matter of maladjustment, the result of a pride that derives fundamentally from the overestimation of one's individual capacity. Satan is thus the pattern (rather than the author) of our sins because his sense of his gifts exceeded their actual strength, and correspondingly diminished the sense of gratitude and obedience he owed his Creator. In this sense sin is the unresolved discord of human experience, the salutary reminder of our proper distance from divinity. It, too, serves God's rational purpose.

The Thomist model of reason informed by faith serves as the template for Hooker's concept of ecclesiastical polity as well. Just as the task of reason is completed by faith in relation to divine praxis, so the work of secular government—the unity of the nation under law—is crowned by the ecclesiastical regiment in the unity of the church in faith and worship. The combined unity of these two elements constitutes the corporate life of the English people, and forms a single indivisible whole. Loyal subject and faithful congregant are two halves of the same coin, singly and collectively.

By aligning church conformity with secular allegiance—or rather, by collapsing the distinction between the two—Hooker takes up a strong position. Conformity, he blithely proposes, is as normative a condition in the church as sovereign allegiance is in the realm, not merely because the sovereign, in mandating the clerical order, makes it a part of the law of the land, but because both the clerical and the secular order are subsumed in the higher unity of reverent obedience. Each order thus presupposes the constancy and uniformity of the other, for neither can achieve its ultimate purpose alone. At the same time, each remains autonomous within its proper sphere. The sovereign can ordain the government of the church but not its doctrine or discipline, just as he can erect courts but not give law. What is established within the church by secular command is precisely what is indifferent; what the church itself establishes (and the secular arm merely supports) is what is essential.

In eliding the argument for *jure divino* episcopacy that Bridges and Bancroft had laboriously advanced, Hooker characteristically abandons ground that, in his view, could only be held by sterile contention and would remain vulnerable to charges of self-interest, a move no doubt made easier by the fact that he himself neither occupied nor sought high clerical office at any time in his career. It was sufficient for him that episcopacy had been established by royal authority, was conformable to Scripture, and had demonstrated its efficacy in practice; debates about its antiquity or priority to other forms of clerical government were superfluous. Hooker's pragmatism gives his argument a modern air, but in fact his restrictive view of essentials and his wide definition of adiaphora were traditional. Above all, he had taken to heart the good medieval dictum about not multiplying necessities. In the version of Occam's razor he applied to ecclesiastical legitimacy, the simplest argument that cinched the duty to conform was the one closest to worldly practicality. Divine sanction was not to be invoked without need. It was a mark of weakness, not of strength, to tease out biblical citations in support of mere custom. This applied equally to the divine right defense of kingship. God had commanded his ends; his means he left to the determination of rational creatures.

Hooker's emphasis on the unity of all government dictated his approach to the distribution of secular and ecclesiastical powers. Appropriating Henry VIII's view of the crown as most plenipotent when joined to the estates of the realm in Parliament, he reminded his readers that the clerical estate was represented by the lords spiritual, who comprised almost a fourth of the Upper House, and in Convocation, which he regarded not as a body separate and distinct from the lay chambers of Parliament but as a third and coordinate branch. Though its ordinary function and jurisdiction might be different, its concerns could not be separated from those of the entire realm, nor vice versa:

> The Parliament of England together with the Convocation annexed thereunto is that whereupon the very essence of all government within this kingdom doth depend. It is even the body of the whole Realm, it consisteth of the King and of all that within the Land are subject unto him. . . . The Parliament is a Court not so merely temporal as if it might meddle with nothing but only leather and wool. In matters of God, to set down a form of public prayer, a solemn confession of the Articles of Christian faith, rites and ceremonies meet for the exercise of religion, it were unnatural not to think the Pastors and Bishops of our souls a great deal more fit than men of secular trades and callings. Howbeit when all which the wisdom of all sorts can do is done for devising of laws in the Church it is the general consent of all that giveth them the form and vigor of laws. . . . This taketh not away from Ecclesiastical persons all right of giving voice with others, when Civil Laws are proposed for regiment of that Commonwealth whereof themselves . . . are . . . a part.[46]

Hooker here blandly revises a history that would still have been fresh in the minds of older contemporaries, for although the Henrician bishops had finally been led to endorse the original Anglican dispensation, the Acts of Supremacy and Uniformity that restored the church in 1559 and proclaimed Elizabeth its Supreme Governor had been passed without the voice of a single churchman.[47] The bishops neither had nor would play an active role in Parliament thereafter; indeed, the standard contemporary account of the Elizabethan polity, Sir Thomas Smith's *De Republica Anglorum* (1565), makes no mention of their role in Parliament at all. Against this background—and the absence as well, until Whitgift, of episcopal presence on the Privy Council—Hooker's depiction of a virtual clerical coregency in the state was a utopian stratagem rather than a plausible description of the actual situation of the church.

As to that situation, Hooker could be as indignant as any, and more tellingly so in that the contrast between the exalted station he conceived for the church and its threadbare material condition was so glaring. Here as elsewhere, the "brethren" served as a convenient foil, deflecting attention from the lay spoliation of the church that was the real source of its poverty. Although in the infancy of churches a rough simplicity of worship might suffice—a desert tabernacle, a manger—whenever God had permitted his faithful to prosper, both gratitude for bounty and spontaneous accolade toward divine majesty had expressed itself in splendor: "Temples were erected. No cost was spared, nothing judged too dear which that way should be spent. The whole world did seem to exult, that it had occasion of pouring out gifts to so blessed a purpose."[48] That pagans, too, adorned their temples did not make ornament itself idolatrous; rather, it attested to the universality of the religious instinct, however clouded by error: to abhor the error was not to reject the instinct or even the ceremony. It was only the godly who opined that it was God's delight "to dwell beggarly" and to be worshiped "in poor cottages." So perverse a notion could only be suspect, and the "privy conventicles" where the godly sequestered themselves a cloak for "dangerous practices,"[49] a covert designation for familism. If godly iconoclasts could decry the natural instinct for decency of worship as a mark of the beast and the lawful ordinances of the church as collusion with the Antichrist, their affected righteousness might as easily conceal lust, their abhorrence of images an idolatry of the Word, their certitude of election a Luciferian pride. Hooker's irenic stance and his refusal to take up the gambit of binary opposites precluded him from making such charges directly, but he could justly point out how vulnerable the godly were to them from other quarters.

In contrast, Hooker's own emphasis on the glory of God and the perfection of creation (which included the universality of reason) led him to take not only a tolerant but an accommodating view of pagan practice. Immediate truth was given by revelation, but the intimation of that truth could not be denied even to infidels: "Indeed we condemn not all as unmeet, the like whereunto have been either devised or used haply amongst Idolators. For why should conformity with them in matter of opinion be lawful when they think that which is true, if in action when they do what is meet it be not lawful to be like unto them? Are we to forsake any true opinion because idolators have maintained it? . . . It is no impossible thing but that sometimes they may judge as rightly what is decent about such external affairs of God, as in greater things what is true."[50] Nothing in Hooker more clearly expresses the inclusive nature of his Christian humanism, with its Thomistic emphasis on reason and its Renaissance appeal to the unity of the classical and Christian heritage. Revelation perfected reason, it did not supplant it; and reason alone, though incapable of disclosing divine truth, yet argued for a creator to whom reverence and worship were due. Hooker's broadest conception of a church, the company of all rational creatures who acknowledged divinity, was comprehensive in a sense that far exceeded the ambition of the most zealous conformist or indeed the bounds of any ecclesiastical polity. Obviously, such a church was merely an ideal entity; historically, it had been superseded by the fact of revelation, which enabled one to distinguish true from false belief. But it existed in two important senses: first, as attesting the dignity of reason, and second, as a part of the history of man's acknowledgment of the divine and therefore of the true church itself. The progressive nature of revelation carried with it a salutary caution, namely that the divine purpose always remained largely hidden and finally inscrutable, and that even a true church was defined by adherence to a limited number of essential principles of faith and practice rather than a strict concordance with divine will in every particular.

It was on this point that Hooker was not only able to establish that the Anglican Church was a true church but to specify wherein its godly minority was misled. The gospels had asserted the principles of faith and salvation in terms such that the rudest intelligence could grasp them; in doing so, and at the same time in liberating the Word from Jewish orthodoxy, they had prepared the way for a universal, ecumenical church. By insisting on a prescriptive discipline, the brethren were rejudaizing the church, forcing Christian conscience into the Procrustean bed of their own fancies. This was manifestly contrary to the spirit and intent of the gospels, which was to enlarge rather than narrow the community of the faithful. The adiaphora were in this sense by no means indifferent; they represented the latitude granted to custom and circumstance in the planting of churches. To abridge their scope was to read human reason into divine command: precisely what the godly themselves accused the Anglican establishment of doing.

Behind this analysis lay a profound difference of approach in interpreting the Reformation as an historical event. If one were not to see it merely as a tragic rift in Christendom, only two constructions were possible. Either it was necessary to construe it as a painful but necessary purgation of the Christian body politic which left it divided in discipline and government but still united in essentials (a circumstance the gospels had provided for), or as the recovery of the true church from the clutches of the Antichrist. In the former case, Rome might still be regarded as a true church, however flawed; in the latter, its seeming concurrence with the Reformed churches in point of doctrine was only proof of its diabolical provenance, since the Antichrist deceived most wickedly by plausible resemblance.

Hooker was as clearly on one side of this divide as his godly opponents were on the other, but he alone among his party recognized its full implications for the conformist position. Anglican controversialists had regularly denounced the Roman church as anti-Christian in the 1580s, in part as a response to militant Catholicism but in part as well to preempt their godly critics. In doing so, however, they had left themselves vulnerable to charges of hypocrisy or worse, for if Rome was indeed the Antichrist then how could Romanist survivals in the Anglican liturgy be defended? From a godly perspective, the practices of popery were not only as pernicious as its principles but the more easily grasped as such, for while Rome might speciously affirm some of the tenets of a true church (the divinity of Christ, the efficacy of his sacrifice, etc.), the mark of the beast was fully evident in its discipline and worship. If this perspective were correct the distinction between false doctrine and harmless ceremony, between essence and adiaphora, fell away. There were no matters indifferent between Babylon and new Jerusalem, no practices they could validly share, for what was done faithfully by a true church could only be parodied by a false one. What proper motive could then be attributed to those who denounced the Antichrist while still wearing his garments? The more conformists acquiesced in the ideological denunciation of Rome as a false church, the more untenable their retention of Romish ceremonies became.

Until the crisis of the Armada had passed, there was perhaps no way of addressing this dilemma. Writing in the 1590s, however, Hooker could at last grasp the nettle. He did so with characteristic boldness, acknowledging Rome to be a true if misled church and holding out the prospect of an ultimate reconciliation with it. This move enabled him to reinstate the adiaphora, and freed him to argue for splendor in worship without apology. No longer need vestments and hangings excuse themselves by reference to the residual superstitions of an unreformed multitude; rather, they bespoke the natural urge to glorify the creator that was inherent in the religious sensibility, and an intrinsic element of divine praise.

Hooker's defense of a church that was not merely visible but splendid had profound consequences. Bishop Jewel, reflecting the attitude of many first-generation Elizabethan bishops, had spoken with implicit repugnance of the "scenic apparatus" of worship.[51] Until Hooker, no Anglican apologist had attempted to argue positively for clerical vestments and sacred images; at most, they had been defended as things indifferent that lay within the jurisdiction of the governor of the church. As a result, clerical property had been defaced and public monuments vandalized, sometimes with the connivance of godly magistrates. Ministers themselves had quivered in their robes. Hooker's robust defense not only vindicated images as proper aids to worship; going further, he contended that they were literally indispensable. The very elements of the sacrament, the wine and the wafer, were tokens of the divine substance; if these were lawful in the most solemn act of the church service, why should lesser tokens not be so in their several places as well? That the Roman church had confounded token and substance did not mean that holy communion was to be abandoned; similarly, that pagans and Papists had worshiped objects of human contrivance did not mean that the proper distinction between reality and representation could not be maintained.

Hooker proceeded even more boldly in taking the godly up on their own rhetorical ground. He conceded readily, but in his own way, that edification was the goal of clerical praxis: "The end which is aimed at in setting down the outward form of all religious actions is the edification of the church."[52] From this definition it followed that *all* rites and images subscribed by lawful authority might conduce to edification. This bland assertion—which, when repeated as the "Et Cetera" oath in the Canons of 1640, would help trigger a revolution—swept away a generation of apologetics that appealed to the necessity for gradualism in justifying the retention of traditional ceremonies. The church, Hooker averred, was fully constituted from the moment of its inception and need not stand as if it were on probation, "halfly reformed" until certified by self-anointed prophets who judged it by the canon of whichever Continental reformer was lately in favor. The Reformation was not a single event but a process continuous within the church since apostolic times in which those usages that had survived the test (and change) of times had the best title, and prudence dictated that they were not to be lightly discarded. In any case, no prescriptive standard could ever be set up: "Our end ought always to be the same; our ways and means thereunto not so."[53]

Edification had been so narrowly construed by the godly as to exclude virtually the entire historical practice of the church, as if "There must be no communion nor fellowship with Papists, *neither in doctrine, ceremonies, nor government.*" By this definition of popery virtually everything that had edified and comforted sixty generations of Christians was suspect if not demonic, and only an orthodoxy teased out of the earliest and most conflicting records of the church might be regarded as canonical: a case of "inventing tradition" with a vengeance. Such an attitude had led to the absurd contention that hearing and reciting the Word of God itself was inefficacious without preaching, again as if "God hath no ordinary mean to work faith without sermons." It was the reverse that was more nearly the case, however, for the entirety of human wisdom could not "convey to the mind that truth without addition or diminution, which Scripture hath derived from the Holy Ghost."[54]

In denouncing the cult of sermons Hooker struck at the heart of godly discourse and reform, for if a learned ministry (however desirable as such) were not the indispensable precondition of lay edification then the church was competently provided for by the literate ministry it already had, and those phantom populations allegedly perishing for want of the Word were a myth. Beyond this went a fundamental question as to the nature and function of the church. For Hooker, the invisible church of the elect of which Christ was sole head was irrecoverable from the body of the visible church to which it was temporally bound. Through the visible church, and through the secular commonwealth by which that church was authorized and manifested and to which it was indissolubly united, the members of the invisible church were subjected to human governance. Authority in both church and state thus represented a seamless continuum, divided in function but bent to the mutually dependent tasks of civil peace and divine worship. The *saeculum* was penetrated by God's salvific purpose, whose symbol was the sacrifice of Christ and whose token in each generation was the body of the elect, but that body was knowable neither to itself nor to any other than Him who was its head. Everything could be affirmed in its name, but nothing done in that name.

It followed from this that any group or individual claiming warrant for practices or beliefs apart from those sanctioned by the visible church and its princely governor on behalf of the invisible church of Christ was deluded and schismatic. It followed further that none of the godly could certainly distinguish themselves from so-called false professors, those pious in works but not subscribed among the elect. The effect of this was to eliminate any practical distinction between false professors and the godly, and thus to invalidate both as categories of discourse. For the purpose of constituting an apostolic church, outward profession—conformity—was the only reasonable condition for inclusion. Saints and sinners were equally members of this church. They shared equally in the benefits it offered and in the obligations it imposed. The only name applicable in a Christian church was that of Christian; the only appropriate distinction was between clergy and laity; the only authority was that exercised by the clergy under the aegis of its princely governor.

This was the logic of the position embraced though never enunciated by clerics such as Sandys. From such a position, Archbishop Grindal's defiance of Elizabeth was a misguided act of personal conscience rather than a vindication of the church. Elizabeth had exercised her prerogative in suppressing prophesying, a practice within the scope of the adiaphora, and Grindal had misconstrued the proper distinction between praxis and doctrine in threatening the Queen with peril of her soul. The crisis had been painful, but purgative. Relations between the church and the crown had been clarified to the benefit of both. Sedition had been nipped in the bud, and Presbyterianism exposed. Thenceforth, piety could never be used as an excuse for denying the name of Christian to a fellow communicant, or divinity as a pretext for defying legitimate authority.

From the perspective of the 1590s, with the battle against Presbyterianism won and its aging mentors, like Cartwright, forced to repudiate the excesses they had spawned, the wisdom of the Queen's policy and Whitgift's stewardship could be appreciated. What remained was to challenge the intellectual foundations of the godly position and to express a conformist alternative based not merely on worldly prudence but on a coherent vision of the Christian life. Commentators have debated the success of Richard Hooker's attempt to do so from that day to this. The task of his thought was to square a broadly ecumenical view of religious experience with the political exigencies of Reformed solidarity, and a celebratory vision of divine creation with Calvinist doctrine. The resulting tensions bulked clearly through the fabric of his magisterial rhetoric. Though Hooker took care to affirm his doctrinal orthodoxy, his views on predestination had been long attacked by worthies such as Walter Travers, and they were challenged again with the publication of the first books of the *Laws*.[55] The wry comment of Peter Lake that Hooker had "squeeze[d] rather than force[d] his reading of the English church through the grid of Calvinist orthodoxy" is close to the mark, but it is more to the point, again in Lake's words, that his long-range goal was "the displacement of predestination from the centre of Christian concern and its replacement by [a] sacrament- and prayer-centered piety."[56]

One need not question the sincerity of Hooker's professed Calvinism to suggest that the Arminianism *avant la lettre* of Saravia or Baro would have been much more easily compatible with his ecclesiology. Whatever his personal inclination, there was plainly a limit to the novel directions that could be taken in a work whose polemical goal was the defense of the establishment. His successors were not so constrained, however, and the *Laws* was instrumental in paving the way for the reception of Arminian piety and theology within the Anglican church. The Jacobean church of Lancelot Andrewes, Joseph Hall, and others descended from it directly, distilling its precepts into a new style of practical divinity and a heightened sense of the dignity of church office. But Hooker's most ardent disciple was Archbishop Laud. Laud imbibed Hooker's sense of "outward stateliness" as the natural expression of piety, and, surveying the bare ruined choirs of the Anglican estate, he determined to mend and beautify them. He imbibed no less literally the latter's vision of a commonwealth in which the servants of God sat at the right hand of the prince and counseled of polity as well as divinity. What he failed to note in Hooker was the prudence that earned him the sobriquet of "judicious." It was not a quality anyone would come to associate with William Laud.

Dissenting Communities

In 1580, the Jesuit priest Robert Persons published *A brief discourse*, in which he appealed for toleration among the four religions of England, Catholicism, Protestantism, Puritanism, and Familism. Persons' witty typology scored its rhetorical point: that heresy had already bred multiple schism, that the Anglican church was a house divided if not indeed crumbled, and that Catholics, being least liable to faction, were consequently the most secure and loyal subjects. There were those on the conformist side who found this argument not altogether inapt; the analogy between Puritans and Papists was already a commonplace, and modern scholarship has found it until recently a convenient way to schematize religious dissent in the Elizabethan period.[57] After Hooker, it was even possible to argue that popery was less a threat to the integrity of the Anglican establishment than Puritanism, since Hooker had acknowledged Rome to be a true church while the godly, despite their nominal adherence to credal Anglicanism, in effect constituted a rival sect whose effect if not intent was to subvert and discredit the established church in its own name. On such a reading, the godly occupied a place within the church analogous to the political position of Catholics within the commonwealth: a potential fifth column whose professed allegiance might well mask a seditious intent. Whereas the Catholic community generally and strenuously affirmed its loyalty to the crown, however, the godly made no secret of their contempt for and defiance of church discipline.

The Marprelate episode and the growth of Separatist and semi-Separatist congregations in subsequent years gave some color to this argument. Recently, the singularity and isolation of Catholicism in sixteenth-century England has come under challenge from a different direction. Summing up a generation of research into the processes of Protestant acculturation and Catholic survivalism, Christopher Haigh concludes that:

> The religious changes of sixteenth-century England were far too complex to be bound together as 'the Reformation', too complex even to be 'a Reformation'. England had discontinuous Reformations and parallel Reformations. There were three political Reformations: a Henrician political Reformation between 1530 and 1538, much of it reversed between 1538 and 1546; an Edwardian political Reformation between 1547 and 1553, almost completely reversed between 1553 and 1558; and an Elizabethan political Reformation between 1559 and 1563—which was not reversed. These political Reformations could not make England Protestant; statute by statute, however, they gave England Protestant laws and made popular Protestantism possible. What made English people Protestant—some English people Protestant—was not the three political Reformations, but the parallel evangelical Reformation: the Protestant Reformation of individual conversions by preachers and personal contacts, the Reformation which began in London, Cam-

bridge, and Oxford from about 1520, and was never completed. So England had blundering Reformations, which most did not understand, which few wanted, and which no one knew had come to stay.[58]

Haigh's view of the "Reformations" as a process rather than an event—or rather as a process *and* an event, a series of political convulsions coterminous with an autonomous evangelical impulse—extends Patrick Collinson's picture of the gradual and contestatory emergence of a Protestant culture in Elizabethan and Jacobean England. It makes an indubitable point, namely that the Reformation (to revert to the singular) was a *longue durée* of episodic and conflicted transformation rather than a high road to a signposted destination. It is correct, too, in describing the impact of the Reformation on ordinary parish life as often bewildering, as English men and women who had been taught to obey their superiors were given violently contradictory commands and offered widely disparate models of appropriate behavior. It is the very thesis of this book that the effects of this were permanent, novel, and severe. But Haigh's radical separation of political event from evangelical process ignores the obvious interaction of the two, which far from running on different tracks were inextricably linked. The Whiggery he would rightly dispute—the Reformation(s) seen as a clear narrative issuing in modern civil and religious liberty—is replaced by a clash between autonomous imperatives, thus positing two mystifications instead of one.

There is another problem with Haigh's model that reflects directly on the construction of religious community in Tudor England. While most people were no doubt confused and alarmed by the rapid succession of commands from above and the presence of proselytizers hawking strange goods if not strange gods, they did not rest passively in that condition. They constructed their own narratives, through which they attempted both to make sense of the change around them and to affirm the values and community by which they might hope to live. These narratives, which interacted in complex ways with those of official authority, were often suggested by elite or learned sources.

The most obvious and successful such narrative was Foxe's *Book of Martyrs*, which almost singlehandedly created the story of Protestant England and became the only privately penned book in English history to achieve the status of an official chronicle. Foxe's book conditioned all subsequent narratives. By construing the Reformation as a struggle between good and evil, Christ and Antichrist, holy martyrs and Satanic persecutors, it shaped the model by which all subsequent religious minorities defined their experience and their relation to surrounding communities of worship, whether within or without the established state church. It suggested, too, that just as the quest for edification and righteousness was a sign of election in the godly, so the continuing experience of persecution if not martyrdom was the mark of the true church. Though Foxe himself remained a pillar of the Elizabethan establishment, the fundamental tension in his thought between the holy leaven and the unholy lump could never be resolved.[59] In theory, this tension had been reconciled, or at least contained, in the notion of the invisible church. The emphasis in Foxe on a theater of suffering, however, put a considerable burden on the invisible church not only to manifest its presence within the visible church but in opposition to it. It was precisely in response to this that Hooker had argued that the invisible church could never make its presence directly known in the *saeculum*, and that resistance to lawful command in the visible church must be reckoned as mere insubordination.

From this perspective, Persons' contention that Puritanism constituted in effect a separate religion, or less flippantly a distinct schism, was not wholly idle. Any attempt to manifest the invisible church within the temporal order was fissiparous; more broadly, each dissenting religious community tended powerfully to regard itself as divinely sanctioned, those outside it as deluded and misled, and those opposed to it as minions of the Antichrist. Across borders Reformed churches might regard differences of doctrine and discipline with a tolerant eye, but on the same terrain conformity was both a political and a psychological imperative. Attempts to reconcile divergent national traditions were fraught with difficulty and rarely successful, as the Westminster Assembly would amply demonstrate in the 1640s.

Thus, the unity of the political community, itself far from given, was constantly jeopardized by the fragmentation of the religious community. Unlike the political community, the religious community recognized no single head or even form of government, as Catholics and Presbyterians alike rejected Elizabeth's control of the church (if not the church itself). Unlike the political community, the religious community acknowledged no common order, for whereas the social hierarchy was affirmed even during popular rebellions, the very distinction between clergy and laity was in some quarters rejected. The model of a peaceable if somewhat confused kingdom of religious practice and belief drawn by Professor Haigh and other recent scholars is consequently misleading. While it is true that new custom and old survival often coexisted, and that political communities perforce accommodated themselves to the fact of religious diversity (as well as to the shifting dictates of authority), it is also true, and in the long run more significant, that such diversity could not be reconciled on an ideological level. Far from perceiving a graded spectrum of more or less acceptable religious praxis, sixteenth- and early seventeenth-century Englishmen experienced their diversity as a source of anxiety and mutual suspicion. The elaborate nomenclature that arose in the later sixteenth century to describe lay attitudinal and devotional differences—Papists, recusants, church papists, refusing Papists, statute protestants, carnal protestants, temporizers, adiaphorizers, puritans, Precisians, and the like—suggests what the local record bears out abundantly, that the late Tudor parish was often a field of tension if not contention. These differences could only be regarded and hence experienced as division, however the practical requirements of living might compel toleration of them. There is evidence that the lax (and even more laxly enforced) standards of Elizabethan conformity, designed as they were to ensure the widest compliance with the least demanding definitions of churchgoing, were disturbing to many who, while not necessarily identifying themselves with the godly, were made uncomfortable by the presence of church papists.

Particularly within dissenting groups, therefore, but among conformists as well, people tended to range themselves into mutually exclusive communities of belief. Some of those groupings were actual, some merely imputed. All were polarizing. If a relative degree of civil harmony prevailed in spite of this it was because of the strength of neighborly ties and national sentiment, the example of religious strife abroad and the threat of foreign conquest, and complex negotiations among local elites and between these elites and the crown.

The Catholic Dilemma

Catholics were the most problematic of all the dissenting religious groups in England. "Catholicism" itself was in many respects as diffuse and decentralized a phenomenon in mid-sixteenth century Europe as Protestantism, and its revitalization in Elizabethan England was clearly a post-Tridentine phenomenon. The Queen had hoped that residual folk Catholicism could be coopted into a revived Henrician church. If the simpler sort saw no essential breach in the continuity of their faith between a nominal Protestantism and a notional Catholicism, so much the better; and if this required the toleration of traditional practices or even a de facto incorporation of them into the fabric of worship, such an accommodation might be viewed as less the price than the essence of a settlement. If the theologians got their doctrinal orthodoxy, the people their devotional comfort, and the state its operational control, the Erastian commonwealth would be secured. From a *politique* perspective, what counted was less what the church was than who ran it. To this end, Elizabeth clearly distinguished between the images and practices of folk Catholicism she was prepared to tolerate (and perhaps personally approved) and the symbols of papal authority she would not.

This strategy would certainly have worked; for a great many English men and women it undoubtedly did work. But England was too great a prize for either Spanish or papal diplomacy to forgo, and the presence of a Catholic heir if not alternative in Mary Stuart too obvious a means of retrieval. For their part, Catholic militants—nonconformist clergy and lay exiles in the Spanish Netherlands—were constrained both by Spanish and papal caution and by the corporate stake of the elite in the Elizabethan settlement. Under the circumstances, the militants could do little but snipe at Elizabeth's new church while professing loyalty to Elizabeth herself.

The conflicts in the Catholic position were irresolvable. To leave the Catholic laity unpastored as the old priesthood died out or drifted into conformity was to risk losing it, yet to smuggle new priests into the country was to court charges of sedition. Similarly, to regard Elizabeth herself as a lapsed Catholic who might yet be guided back into the fold might buy time and implicit toleration but at the cost of conceding her legitimacy, while to denounce her as a heretic without the prospect of deposition would force Catholics to choose between church and country. Had Elizabeth created martyrs on a Marian scale she could have given plausible excuse to resistance and duplicity, but she studiously avoided doing so; instead, she asked only minimum conformity to a church in most outward respects indistinguishable from its predecessor. Time was on the Queen's side, not the Pope's.

The intrusion of seminary priests, soon followed by Jesuits, was thus essential if hierarchical Catholicism were to be preserved in England. On an obvious level, the seminarists represented Rome. They galvanized the lay community, reminding it of its duty and obedience and of the Holy See's pastoral care. They challenged it to commitment, their personal heroism demanding response from those who risked life and estate to shelter them. These latter were of necessity a small minority, however, and for practical reasons recruited principally among the elite. The bulk of the laity had no means of demonstrating their fidelity other than by attending illicit services. The Jesuits provided one: recusancy.

Recusancy was to become the touchstone of resistance to the legitimacy of the order in church and state up to the Civil War. As such, it must be distinguished from mere church-avoidance. Many Englishmen did not go to church, but few regarded their presence or absence as a political statement. Some stayed away from idleness or a preference for gaming; others came and were rowdy and destructive. To be sure, such acts were politically significant, for church attendance was the single most overt and regular token of legitimation required of the subject. That which is most regularly required in theory, however, is most frequently remitted in practice, and authorities were ready to distinguish contumacy from principled abstention. Not everyone who failed to appear in church was a Papist or a Separatist, any more than was everyone who broke a chair an iconoclast.

Church-avoidance was therefore, to use modern parlance, a broad signifier. It could mean as little as indolence or as much as rejection, and what it meant depended not only on what was intended but what was construed. In short, recusancy did not become a fact until it became an issue, and Elizabeth was not anxious to make it one. The Catholic laity, insofar as we can speak

with confidence of such an entity in the 1560s, had equally little incentive to
see it become one. To be sure, there were Catholics, who like the doughty
gentlewoman cited by Haigh, minced no words at their presentment: "I was
born in such a time when holy mass was in great reverence. . . . I hold me
still to that wherein I was born and bred; and so by the grace of God I will
live and die in it."[60] For the majority, however, conflicting loyalties, fear of
reprisal, and the constraints of good neighborhood all tended to mute any
overt display of conscience. No doubt good Catholics were chagrined to take
shelter with ordinary sinners who shunned the new church services, just as
others who prudently conformed—the church papists—did so with inner
reservation or abstention from communion. But there was little reason and
no reward for them to make any outward show of defiance.

The papacy itself moved initially with caution on the issue of conformity.
The decrees in conclave that condemned attendance at Anglican services
went unpublished, while Pius IV offered to confirm the Anglican liturgy in
return for an acknowledgment of Rome's suzerainty. Only after 1566 was
recusancy actively encouraged, both as an avoidance of mortal sin and as a
testimony of faith. Eventually it was enjoined as a condition of membership
in the faith itself: the head of the Jesuit mission in England, Henry Garnet,
declared conformists to be ipso facto excommunicate, and a colleague, William Gifford, maintained that the Pope himself could not dispense with the
obligation to recusancy.[61]

For the seminarists and the Jesuits, the injunction to recusancy was both a
measured provocation and a calculated risk. The provocation was to the
Elizabethan authorities, who responded with statutes imposing confiscatory
fines for church nonattendance; the risk was that the Catholic community,
already torn by conflicting loyalties, would find the demand intolerable.
Many had already made their peace with occasional conformity, and many
would have concurred with Haigh's observation that "a man was a member
of the [Elizabethan] catholic community not because he refused to attend
Anglican services but because he felt himself to be a catholic and was accepted as such by other members."[62] Such a definition, as Haigh notes, presupposed that Catholicism was "an idea rather than an act." This was precisely the notion that the Jesuits in particular were determined to refute.
When Protestants made attendance at Anglican services the *signum distincti-
vum* of church membership, Catholics could not contend that the public profession of one faith was canceled by the private practice of another. Of all
sins, Nicodemism was the most universally execrated: as the Catholic controversialist Robert Southwell pointed out, even heretics who suffered martyrdom conscientiously might be praised, because to follow a misled conscience was preferable to ignoring it. Could Catholics do less?

The leaders of the English mission thus made recusancy the test of faith. There were other inducements to recusancy in the 1570s, notably the godly demand to exclude the reprobate, of whom church papists were the most notorious. From the government's point of view the cornerstone of its religious policy, conformity, was thus under attack from both sides: scarce wonder that "Puritans" and "Papists" seemed from that perspective equally subversive.

If the Catholic leadership was determined to raise the stakes of conforming, Whitgift and Elizabeth had little choice but to up the ante in kind. Thus "recusancy" was defined not as mere abstention nor even as a sharply punishable offense but as a politically charged act that defied the legitimacy of the established order. If it could not be classed as treason, the incitement of it could, and the Jesuit mission in particular made the object of an intensive manhunt. This was precisely the desired result. As the hotly pursued Edmund Campion wrote:

> I cannot long escape the heretics, they have so many scouts; I wear ridiculous clothes, often change my name, and so often read news letters that Campion is taken, that I am without fear. . . . They brag no more of their martyrs, since now, for a few apostates and cobblers of theirs turned, we have bishops, lords, knights, the old nobility, flower of the youth, noble matrons, and innumerable of the inferior sort either martyred or dying by imprisonment. In the house where I am, there is no talk but of death, flight, prison, or spoil of friends; yet they proceed with courage.[63]

Campion clearly envisages his mission as one of voluntary martyrdom, an *imitatio Christi*. His flight from his persecutors is a Calvary in which, like Christ scourged, he relinquishes his identity for "ridiculous clothes" and assumed names, embraces his destiny, and even sees beyond his death, comforted by apostolic witnesses who will take up his cross and follow his example. With the Act of 1585 it became readily possible to do so, since the concealment of a priest was thereby made a felony punishable by death.

Campion's flight, capture, and execution were the occasion for a major exchange between Catholic militants and government publicists as both sides sought to define his image. It also coincided with a threefold increase in Catholic propaganda in which the incitement to recusancy and the extolling of martyrdom—themes which became perdurable thereafter in recusant literature—were accompanied by effusions of secular loyalty and even, in the work of Persons, paeans to the virtues of the heretic Elizabeth that could scarcely have been bettered by her most obsequious courtiers.

Once again, this mixed signal produced a mixed effect. On the one hand, recusancy was represented not as an act of defiance but one of loyal submission, since by suffering persecution for conscience's sake even unto death the recusant affirmed his obedience to the sovereign in all things but conscience, an exemplary sacrifice and an affirmation of allegiance such as no merely law-abiding subject, and certainly no time-serving conformist, could make. It resolved the conscience of Catholics who wished to obey their natural rulers in both church and state, and doubled the wickedness of the persecutors themselves, who not only punished true religion but destroyed the Queen's most faithful subjects. At the same time, of course, such arguments rejected the concept of an Erastian church in which the secular as well as the religious legitimacy of the Elizabethan commonwealth was considerably invested, and thus subverted the regime more effectively than any frontal assault could have done—certainly more than *Regnans in Excelsis*, the papal bull of excommunication and deposition, had done. The recusants were pleading not for toleration but truth. The militancy of the mission's pamphleteers was not a strategy for accommodation, but for victory.

To the extent that this became apparent, however, the pamphleteers' argument was necessarily self-liquidating: one could not convincingly profess loyalty to the person of the ruler while denying the substantial basis—the Christian imperium—on which her claim to rule stood. Moreover, the very rigor with which recusant literature separated the civil and religious obligations of Catholic subjects suggested an alternative solution, namely that the act of conformity itself might be similarly divided, and mere attendance at Anglican services as a civil duty distinguished from heretical worship. This argument was presented in a tract attributed to Alban Langdale, the deprived Archdeacon of Chichester and chaplain to Lord Montagu of Sussex. Langdale pointed out that canon law did not prohibit Catholics from attending Protestant services as long as they refrained from participating in them, whereas failure to attend was an offense in English law. Why should the Queen's Catholic subjects be asked to break the civil code if not required to do so by the sacred one? Heroic testimony was an obligation for the ordained, but it was supererogatory for the laity, if not indeed an abdication of familial responsibilities from which the clergy were exempt.[64]

This and similar tracts were immediately rebutted by Jesuit apologists, who continued to maintain an uncompromising line in print on the duty of recusancy. On the confessional level, however, there was considerable latitude in dealing with "timorous consciences," and in the casuistical handbooks drawn up for the guidance of English priests the arguments of Langdale and his colleagues were in effect conceded on grounds both of necessity and prudence. It was particularly important, one such book noted, "to keep noble and rich families in their former positions of honour and dignity" so that they might form a nucleus of resistance to the Anglican order and that their wealth and titles not be conveyed to heretics. As William Allen said succinctly, concessions might be made to human frailty "so that the church discipline be not evidently infringed, nor no acte of schisme or synne plainly committed." This defined precisely the case of church papistry.[65]

What emerged from the English mission, therefore, was a double system of rhetoric, a double code of conduct, a double method of moral book-keeping. In print and for the record, the rhetoric was unyielding, the com-mandments rigid, the penalties condign. In the chapel and the confessional, however, sins might be absolved, lapses condoned, necessity relieved. The resulting strains were severe. The older Marian priests, who with their flocks had perforce made their accommodations with the new order, were now confronted by young seminarians, armed with faculties from Rome but igno-rant of local conditions. The seminary priests, moving perilously from refuge to refuge, dependent upon strangers, and confronted by their own dilemmas of conscience, found it generally impossible to execute the letter of their in-structions. The Jesuits, imposing yet another layer of discipline on this un-wieldy structure, themselves resisted the encroachments of another order, the Benedictines. The inevitable consequence was to create tensions between clergy and laity, seculars and seculars, and seculars and religious that, as in the Archpriest controversy, could explode into open and bitter conflict. These were in turn exploited by the government, which entered into serious if abortive negotiations with the anti-Jesuit party known as the Appellants in 1602–1603. The Catholic community, which it was ostensibly the purpose of the English mission to nurture, preserve, and sustain in the face of the com-mon enemy, was now so divided that a substantial portion of it was pre-pared to contemplate a separate peace.

On the face of it the policies that led to this dénouement seem to have been self-defeating. Closer inspection, however, suggests that the sowing of tension and conflict was not only a risk but a calculated element of the strat-egy for maintaining the English Catholic community. The uncompromising demand for recusancy had a twofold aim: to make it both a duty in the eyes of Catholics and a crime in the eyes of the state. Had the Elizabethan regime continued to turn a blind or at least a selectively inattentive eye on simple nonconformity, principled avoidance of the established church would have remained indistinguishable from casual absence. If, added to this, the godly campaign to discourage if not exclude the reprobate from church attendance had widened the scope of nonconformity, the Catholic remnant would have been even more dispersed in a general sea. By publicly defining recusancy as resistance and imposing resistance as a duty of faith, the spokesmen of the mission posed a challenge the state could not ignore; by linking this, particu-larly in the 1580s, to a civil as well as religious rejection of the Elizabethan regime and an open embrace of the Marian standard, they ensured a suitably draconian response. If the embrace of martyrdom was the definitive testi-mony of the priest and Jesuit, the endurance of persecution was that of the laity. The English mission quite consciously maximized the occasions for both.

At the same time it was clear that this policy, if carried to its logical extreme, would have eradicated the mission and destroyed the Catholic community. Priests, of course, were not to court martyrdom, although like Campion they might glory in it when it came. But recusants were by definition enjoined to place themselves in harm's way: to make their commitment publicly known, and to face the penalties which such commitment entailed. Had they done so rigorously, and had the penalties been applied with corresponding severity, the Catholic gentry on which the mission depended for its safety and sustenance would soon have been devastated. This result was obviously not intended. The assumption was that the laity would beg exception and plead for mitigation, and that the government would not drive its Catholic subjects to the wall. The handbooks and instructions for the seminary priests clearly anticipated the laity's response, and provided for indulgence.

The purpose of this strategy (apart from the obvious one of reasserting Roman discipline) was, then, the exercise of conscience. Church papistry had been the Catholic laity's mode of adaptation to the Anglican order; it would commend itself even more strongly as the penalties for nonconformity increased. At the same time, even nominal participation in a heretical church was problematic, and the Marian clergy, anxious to retain their flocks, had been quick to condemn it without any prodding from Rome. Isolated as they were, of course, they could—and dared—do little to discourage it more actively. Church papistry thus rested on a tacit understanding across both sides of the confessional divide: priests would not press the faithful unduly to resist conforming; ministers would not question too closely the convictions of those who did conform.

The mission's overtly uncompromising demand for recusancy was designed to bring the issue of church papistry to a head. Church papists were threatened with eternal damnation, while Protestant zealots warned Anglicans of traitors and idolators in their midst. The recusant risked civil penalties but saved his soul; the church Papist earned the opprobrium and contempt of all parties and, unless his sin was remitted, suffered the judgment of God. Yet, barring a providential restoration of the faith, occasional conformity remained the only practicable long-term option for the Catholic majority, and therefore the indefeasible condition of a Catholic ministry. The state, little as it wished (and limited as its ability was) to prosecute all recusants with the full rigor of the law, could not have tolerated its wholesale defiance, particularly by a group putatively dedicated to its overthrow. The conformity of the many was, in short, the condition which made possible the recusancy of the few. Without church papists there would ultimately have been no kind of Papists at all.

On the other hand, if recusancy was to be more than the heroic testimony of the few, it had to be presented not as a standard to be encouraged but as a duty imposed. Essentially self-motivated recusants were in the nature of the case rare, and their ranks were bound to diminish with time. No significant number of ordinary Catholics could be persuaded to undertake the risks of an action described as merely exemplary; it had to be presented as a condition of obtaining grace, and the failure to perform it as entailing its withdrawal. If recusancy was a duty, conformity was a sin.

Sins could, of course, be remitted, provided that mitigating circumstances were adduced and appropriate penances performed. Thus the practical necessity for church papistry could be accommodated. The essential point was that it no longer be undertaken at the discretion of the individual Catholic but as an activity authoritatively and conditionally licensed. The licensing of behavior and activity was a prime means by which early modern systems of institutional control were adumbrated. This was obvious on an economic level, most notoriously in sumptuary laws, the granting of patents of monopoly, and the like. The need for such licensing was extended in Tudor times in two critical and related areas. The development of print technology required control over the dissemination of opinion. The Reformation itself, once appropriated by the state, required the certification of appropriate modes of worship and belief. No form of control was more exemplary and more intimate, however, than that exercised by the English mission over the Catholic faithful of England: the licensing of conscience itself.

The licensing of conscience differed from the imposition of other forms of authority because it neither prescribed nor prohibited a given action, but specified the conditions under which it might be performed. To do this it was first necessary to define the act in absolute terms, i.e., terms which rendered it subject to prescriptive authority (and which, in the case of conformity, nullified the contrary command of the state). Catholics, as Englishmen, were enjoined to attend the established church; Englishmen, as Catholics, knew conscientiously that this command was or at least appeared to be incompatible with their former obedience. The government imposed penalties for nonconformity but laxly enforced them, and, where Catholics themselves held local sway, confusion was all the greater. The papacy denounced the new church but continued to woo its head, and, even after excommunicating Elizabeth, it was ambivalent in regard to her subjects' secular allegiance to her. It was by no means clear that either Elizabeth or her church would long survive, and that the old church would not be restored; it was also possible that a Gallican understanding might yet be reached. Where authority was divided and conscience was torn, prudence most often decided: and prudence, as always, dictated compliance with the most immediately enforceable command. Church papistry might thus appear as the most compelling response to a situation in which conflicting authorities, each armed with indubitable claims over a part of one's conscience, sought to command the whole. English Catholics of the 1560s, in short, found themselves faced with the dilemma that would confront all other Englishmen as well in the 1640s.

Church papists rationalized their conduct in a variety of ways. When the penalties for recusancy became severe, they pointed to the necessity of providing for their families and preserving their estates. In some cases the male head of the household conformed while his wife and children remained recusant, thereby avoiding fines while making an indirect profession of faith. The casuistry handbooks defined acceptable modes of conformity, for example when one declared that one's presence in church was solely intended to satisfy the Queen's command to appear in a certain place at a certain time. By remaining mute during prayers or not taking communion one could signify not merely a refusal to participate in the ceremonies of the Anglican church but a purposeful rejection of their significance. By sitting in church as if at a stage play, one inferentially mocked its proceedings, and arguably made a more forceful statement of protest than by simply absenting oneself. Even if social pressure made a token participation in the service necessary, one could equivocate, adding a silent reservation or retraction to whatever one spoke. These were techniques practiced by Jesuits themselves in attempting to evade capture or discovery, and the antirecusant literature testified to the frustration they engendered. If praying or oath-taking, the most solemn avowals of conscience that could be made, might be negated by equivocation, then how could any profession of allegiance truly bind the subject or the Christian?

It was one thing, however, when the individual Catholic received permission to conform or absolution for having conformed, and quite another when he attempted to authorize himself. The uninstructed conscience might make inappropriate concessions to heresy, or be seduced by degrees into confusing true and false belief. The claims of prudence, which were always to be resisted and when yielded to were always to be minimized, might dull or eclipse conscience. Above all, the practice of deceit must be regulated, lest confession itself—the core nexus between the Catholic and his church—be compromised. There was thus every difference between a course of action initiated by the Catholic layman himself and the same action as licensed by his priest. Recusancy, it must be insisted, was and remained the duty of conscience; it could not be dispensed with. Conformity was a sin which, like other sins, might be absolved by one's confessor.

Recusancy and occasional conformity must thus be seen not as opposites—although for rhetorical purposes it was necessary to posit them as such—but as dialectical partners within the English Catholic community. In theory, each excluded the other; in practice, neither was possible without the other. Uncompromising recusancy was the posture of rebellion or martyrdom, not a strategy for survival; universal conformity was a formula for surrender, for without the tension of lay resistance the mission could not have been sustained and pastoring would have died out. What was required, therefore, was a balance between resistance and evasion, testimony and silence, and the crux of the balance was the authority of the priest. Since evasion and silence was the easier choice to make, the scales had to be balanced, and conformity reprehended. This act asserted the authority of the priest, for as we have noted, the critical maneuver was to separate conscience from prudence, and by reclaiming control of the former to discipline the latter.

To accomplish this meant instructing conscience prescriptively, and licensing it to comply with necessity only upon terms. In this way conformity could be turned into a species of resistance, for the lay Catholic, while putatively responding to a royal command, was in fact acting under priestly direction. Insofar as legitimation entailed not mere compliance with an order but the acknowledgment of its validity, the church Papist might still withhold true obedience, and deny imposed authority. By remaining firmly aloof in the presence of heretical services (a difficult posture to maintain of one's own in the face of communal pressures for good neighborhood), it was possible to conceive of oneself as making an oppositional gesture in the very act of conforming. Would one wear or doff one's hat? Greet one's neighbors civilly or coolly, or not at all? Sing with others or remain silent? Stand with them or remain seated? Hear out the service or seek to disrupt it by talking and shuffling? Even more than for the godly, whose objective was not to reject but to purge the church and who regarded their attendance not as compulsory but proprietary, every nuance of the church Papist's conduct and decorum was by definition adversarial, every word or sign might be read as contestatory. At the same time nothing was necessarily conceded, for disruptive behavior in church was hardly confined to church papists, and short of an open declaration (or notoriety as a Catholic) almost any act could be construed ambiguously. In a setting whose specific purpose—conformity of worship—required uniformity of response and univalence of feeling, the subversive potential of the church Papist was subtle and pervasive, a potential limited only by his own powers of invention and the interpretive resources of his fellow parishioners. It was scarce wonder that some considered not the recusant but the church Papist "the most dangerous subject the land hath."[66]

For the conscientious church Papist, therefore, the choices of conduct could be agonizing. Much depended, of course, upon the particular situation—the influence of a local magnate or the connivance of a sympathetic magistrate, the temper of the parish or the predilection of the minister. The circumstances of the Catholic conformist were very different in godly Essex and popish Lancashire. There was a natural tendency, too, for parish communities to reach a modus vivendi that accommodated or tokenized dissent. Nonetheless, the church Papist remained a suspect and troubling figure well into the seventeenth century, who in serving two masters could fully satisfy neither, and perhaps least of all himself. John Earle's well-known description is still worth remembering:

> A Church-Papist Is one that parts his Religion betwixt his conscience and his purse, and comes to Church not to serve God, but the King. The face of the Law makes him weare the maske of the Gospell, which he uses not as a meanes to save his soul, but charges. He loves Popery well, but is loth to lose by it, and though he be something scar'd with the Buls of Rome, yet they are farre off, and he is struck with more terrour at the Apparitor. Once a moneth he presents himselfe at the Church, to keepe off the Church-warden, and brings in his body to save his bayle. He kneels with the Congregation, but prayes by himselfe, and askes God forgivenesse for coming thither. If he be forced to stay out a Sermon, he puls his hat over his eyes, and frownes out the houre, and when hee comes home, thinkes to make amends for this fault by abusing the Preacher. His maine policy is to shift off the Communion, for which he is never unfurnish't of a quarrell, and will bee sure to be out of Charity at Easter. . . . He would make a bad Martyr, and a good traveller, for his conscience is so large, he could never wander out of it. . . . His wife is more zealous, and therefore more costly, and he bates her in tyres, what she stands him in Religion.[67]

Like any "character," Earle's church Papist is a composite, an ideal type. As such, he reveals as much about his author—and the author's public—as about himself. The first thing he tells us is that the church papistry was still a notorious and visibly conflicted confessional stance in the third decade of the seventeenth century, as distinctive to observers as its mirror opposite, "Puritanism." It had not, that is to say, disappeared into the general run of occasional conformity, along with neuters, nullifidians, cold professors, statute Protestants, and the merely profane, but remained oppositional. Whether deliberately or involuntarily, the church Papist was bound to signify himself, and in so doing both to challenge the service of worship and to negate his own participation in it. Earle's theatrical metaphors suggest not only the self-polarizing tension of the church Papist's conduct but the paradoxically delegitimating nature of his conformity: "The face of the Law makes him weare the maske of the Gospell." The church Papist distorts the law he obeys even as he is distorted in being compelled to obey it; in acting for the sake of appearances he reduces all else to appearance, to face and mask. When his conformity is most outwardly feigned, he most inwardly subverts the order it represents; in kneeling with the congregation—an act of communal affirmation and of submission to both human and divine law—he is most self-consciously alienated, praying to disavow the very fellowship he seems to share.

Earle depicts the church Papist's motives as mercenary and his conscience as elastic, but his sympathy and insight are evident beneath the veneer of satire. A man who "comes to Church not to serve God, but the King" and who silently prays God's forgiveness as he does so, is one whose conscience is less flexible than distended, less opportunistic than abused. We cannot know directly what such contortions may have cost, because conscientious church papists could make no public statement of their case, and, unlike the godly, they left no record of their inner struggles. It is possible, however, to glimpse something of their travail in the report of a Manchester recusant who attempted to drown himself after attending Common Prayer, or the remorse of Richard Griffiths, a priest who confessed his imposture to a congregation in Bridewell after attending an Anglican service there.[68]

Catholicism and Resistance

From the moment when the Act of Uniformity reestablished an Erastian church in England and the reinstatement of the Book of Common Prayer defined it as a Reformed one, lay Catholics were confronted with the problem of civil as well as ecclesiastical loyalty. The vast majority had no desire to make their parlous religious situation politically untenable as well. On the contrary, they were anxious to profess their loyalty to the crown, and conscious of the necessity to manifest it publicly. The Northern Rising of 1569, followed in successive years by the papal bull of excommunication, the Ridolfi Plot, and the St. Bartholomew's Day massacre, marked a sea change in the fortunes of the laity. These events, together with the Duke of Alva's ruthless campaign against Protestants in the Netherlands, seemed to herald a new era of confessional struggle in which religious minorities, as much the pawns as the agents of great political forces, were faced with persecution at best and expulsion if not extermination at worst. On a pragmatic level, the best hope of survival for English Catholics was a deeply conservative identification with the crown, including the practice of at least occasional conformity. At the same time the relationship between the Catholics and their queen was obviously conflicted, for the Elizabeth who had proscribed their religion was also their sole protectress.

The arrival of the mission was also a source of conflict, for while it brought authoritative direction and pastoral succor it brought danger, divided loyalty, and the demand for self-exposure as well. The mission priests and Jesuits were bound to be welcomed for renewing faith and hope, but resented too for straining the tenuous links of accommodation between the lay community and the government. They brought the familiar sacraments, but also the demanding new post-Tridentine activism. They saved Catholicism, but risked Catholics. As harbingers of a crusade they embodied the hope of deliverance; as agents of a foreign interest they raised the specter of conquest. In the end, the deliverance English Catholics seemed to welcome most wholeheartedly was that from the Armada. As the prospects for a forcible restoration of Catholicism faded after 1588, the Jesuits increasingly found themselves objects of hostility, and the de facto control of the Catholic community by its gentry was rapidly consolidated.

Under these circumstances the polemical literature of the mission generally counseled lay nonresistance, and depicted the mission itself as merely pastoral in intent. Civil nonresistance was hardly a sufficient stance for a suspect minority, however. It bore, in the general view, the same relation to genuine loyalty as church papistry did to an unfeigned acceptance of the Anglican communion. Catholic loyalism thus had to be *plus royaliste que le roi* to compensate even in part for the perception of religious apostasy. This perception was stoked not only by godly thunderings against the party of Antichrist but by missionary demands for recusancy, which served as a continual reminder of Catholic separatism and of the hypocrisy of church papists.

Loyal addresses and submissions were limited by another factor as well. While individual Catholics frequently made such submissions, pleading for exemption from conformity or relief from duress, the basis on which they did so was strictly personal: a claim of conscience, not of franchise. Collective representations, on the other hand, drew unwelcome attention to the existence of a corporate Catholic interest, including not only the community of believers but the Roman hierarchy vested in it. In the eyes of most other Englishmen, this interest constituted a seditious faction at best, a fifth column at worst. The Catholic community was thus caught in a double bind: it could only profess its allegiance in the dress of an open conspiracy.

Under these circumstances it is not surprising that Catholics seldom petitioned in a body. A notable exception was the plea of leading Catholic nobles and gentry in 1585 against the bill to make sheltering priests a felony. The subscribers professed their unconditional loyalty to the crown, their abhorrence of regicide, and their rejection of all papal claims to absolve subjects of their natural allegiance:

> We . . . utterly deny that either pope or cardinal hath power or authority to command or license any man to consent to mortal sin, or to commit or intend any other act *Contra Jus Divinum*. Much less can this disloyal, wicked and unnatural purpose by any means be made lawful, to wit, that a native born subject may seek the effusion of the sacred blood of his anointed sovereign. Whosoever be he therefore spiritual or temporal, that maintaineth

so apparent sacrilege, we therein do renounce him and his conclusion, as false, devilish, and abominable.[69]

The context of the petition was the recently foiled Parry plot; but the unnamed proponents of sedition may have included William Allen and Robert Persons, respectively authors of *A true sincere and modest defence of English catholiques that suffer for their faith* and *The copy of a letter written by a Master of Art of Cambridge* [*Leicester's* Commonwealth]. These works, as Peter Holmes notes, marked a subtle but unmistakable shift in missionary polemics away from the sedulous counsels of nonresistance espoused in the previous decade and back toward the militance of earlier writers such as Nicholas Sander and John Leslie.

This is not the place to rehearse in detail the arguments of Catholic resistance literature as set out by Allen, Persons, and others in the ensuing decade.[70] In general they tracked those of Reformed authors such as John Ponet and the French monarchomachs, and anticipated many of those offered by the Civil War pamphleteers of the 1640s: resistance theory made many a confessional bedfellow.[71] Persons in particular, moving beyond assertions of papal supremacy, adumbrated a free-standing theory of popular sovereignty that gave full discretion to the people both to choose and depose rulers.[72] Persons' obvious purpose was to appeal beyond his Catholic base to all those who entertained a speculative interest in the regime of the aging Queen and the still-unsettled question of the succession.

Persons laid out a far bolder and more invasive program in his *A Memoriall for the Reformation of Englande* (1596), which sketched the plan of a recatholicized England, including a purge of Parliament, the universities, the bench, and the commission of the peace; the restoration of church lands and the reversal of enclosure; and the replacement of such fundamental common law principles as primogeniture by Roman law. No transformation of English society as radical and thoroughgoing had been proposed since the time of More and Starkey; nothing of comparable scope succeeded it until the Civil War. The outraged rejoinders to Persons' populist assault on the common law (even the great Coke was moved to a retort) showed that he had drawn blood on the one subject that could arouse passions as intense as those evoked by religion itself, at least among the elite. Gone, however, was the republican veneer of the *Conference*. In its place was a benevolent theocratic dictatorship, its power and authority unquestioned and unquestionable, operating through traditional but thoroughly subordinated elites. Here was something for everyone in the political nation to abhor, Catholic and Protestant alike, for though lay Catholics clearly stood to gain from a monopoly of secular office and the presumptive spoil of Protestant estates, their privilege would now rest not on a structure of legal entitlement (which a persecuting government's best efforts had failed to overthrow), but on their service to an ultramontane power. It was an exchange few would be tempted to make.[73]

Persons was the ablest and most protean controversialist of his age; he was also the chief scandal and embarrassment of Catholic loyalists. No Englishman conjured up more vividly the stereotypical Jesuit who could maintain any cause and believe in none. He argued alternately for the duty of submission to Elizabeth and the duty to depose her; denied James' claim to the throne and blandly congratulated him on his accession;[74] upheld popular sovereignty one year and papal supremacy the next. But Persons was only the most egregious example of the opportunism of missionary polemics. Tacking skillfully between the shifts of ultramontane policy and the exigencies of English politics, the Jesuits now fanned and now banked the coals of rebellion, often asserting the obligations of lay Catholics toward their apostate prince but never conceding his legitimacy.

In all of this, the laity could speak with no independent voice, affirm no separate interest. They were bound to those who were their pastors, confessors, guides, and, ultimately, their martyrs. The case of Sir Thomas Tresham is instructive. The scion of a prominent Northamptonshire family, he conformed to the Anglican church but was reconverted to Catholicism, perhaps by Persons himself, and was one of those who sheltered Campion. Tresham suffered heavily for recusancy—he was crushingly fined and repeatedly imprisoned, most gallingly during the Armada campaign, and his lands and goods were distrained—but he never wavered, at least publicly, in his professed loyalty to Elizabeth and his stated abhorrence to all counsels of resistance. His private papers suggest greater complexity, however. There he expressed his devotion to Mary Queen of Scots and his conviction of her unimpeachable claim to Elizabeth's throne. His library also contained resistance literature. Was Tresham's loyalty, too, "Jesuitical"? It may be closer to the mark to suggest that, for a man in his position, a public posture of absolute and unconditional support for the regime that persecuted him was the prerequisite of survival. It is unlikely that he and Elizabeth misunderstood each other. The rhetorical code of loyalty, made fulsome in proportion to the vulnerability of the ruler or the dubiety of the subject and wrought to a febrile pitch by the courtier literature surrounding the Queen, required no less of Tresham than the protestations of fealty and submission he offered. It was not necessary for anyone, least of all Tresham himself, to believe that he would in fact, as he claimed, cheerfully serve as public hangman against anyone who plotted harm to the Queen. But it was an indubitable necessity for him to say so.

Tresham's stance was that it was possible to serve a Catholic conscience and a Protestant ruler together. He saw his position as analogous to a Christian under the pagan emperors, rendering that to Caesar which was his due.

Like such a Christian, his religious duty was to testify to his faith when he could not enjoy it quietly, enduring what persecution he must and saving whatever of worldly position and goods he could. For Tresham personally that meant refusing to present himself at the unclean altar, in short recusancy. Less than that—church papistry, for example—would mean the ultimate disappearance of the faith, just as feigned worship at pagan altars, had none resisted it, would have destroyed the early church: Caesar's devices had not changed with the centuries. Tresham's library contained a treatise refuting Langdale's argument for occasional conformity, suggesting he had pondered the question with some care. At the same time he did not judge his weaker brethren; in 1601 he argued that a conforming husband of a recusant wife (as we have seen, a frequent dodge of church papists) should not be liable for her fines.[75]

Laymen such as Tresham, who exchanged the ease of a squire's life for the hazards of recusancy, priest-sheltering (a felony after 1585), and private masses, made the English mission possible. Tresham's case was all the more remarkable, not merely for the prominence and leadership he assumed among Elizabethan Catholics, but because he had been converted after conforming for more than twenty years and tasting the sweets of office and status: at thirty-six, the scion of a family that had produced two speakers of the House of Commons, he could look forward to an honorable if not a distinguished career. His commitment did not satisfy everyone, however. The Jesuit Henry Tichborne warned a correspondent that "Sir Thomas Tresham as a friend to the state is holden among us for an atheist,"[76] a surpassing example of biting the hand that fed. It was true that Tresham, in serving two masters, may have hoped never to be forced to choose between them, and that insofar as the goal of the mission was not merely to revive and succor a Catholic remnant but to prepare for a general Catholic restoration by any means necessary Tresham and his like were not in the final analysis reliable. During the Armada scare Tresham, remanded to custody with other leading Catholics, complained that he and his coreligionists had been deprived of the opportunity to stand in the front line against the invader and prove their loyalty for all to see.[77] Would Tresham indeed have done so, had the Armada reached English shores with a fair prospect of success? Elizabeth might well be forgiven for preferring to moot the question; as matters turned out, Allen and Persons may well have been glad that she did.

The English mission was, from the beginning, shrouded in deception and mystification. That it should have confused and divided English Catholics even as it rallied them is not very surprising; that it should baffle competent historians, who continue to argue whether its purposes were or were not "political," is somewhat more so.[78] It is true that the seminary priests were forbidden to discuss or engage in political activity, a fairly obvious precaution for fugitives dependent on the kindness and discretion of strangers. When Tresham and the other signatories of the petition of 1585 avowed that they would be the first to surrender any priest who attempted to incite them against civil authority they were speaking in a clearly coded language: both priests and laymen understood perfectly well what was to remain unspoken between them. As foot soldiers of the mission, the priests' function was to administer the sacraments, hear confession, and provide pastoral care; this was the sufficient but not the final goal of their presence in England. What lay beyond it was the responsibility of others, the substance of things hoped for but not yet commanded. Most captured priests to whom the "bloody question" was put—whether or not they would assist a papally authorized invasion of England—refused to answer, a logical extension of the code of silence that governed their pastoral activities though obviously one that carried a different significance for their interrogators. As priests they could maintain that such questions did not concern them; as subjects they could claim that they had broken no law except the one that made their vocation a crime in itself. No doubt many internalized their roles, especially when they found more or less secure protection in great houses, and could regard themselves as private chaplains whose day-to-day functions were not very different from, say, deprived ministers who had found employment in godly households.

In time, many of these ministers came to resent the overweening influence of the Jesuits, who regarded the maintenance of a suitable level of militancy (all the more critical as active hopes for a Catholic restoration faded) as a principal duty. This meant keeping the discomfort, not to say the danger level of the Catholic community high. In the wartime conditions of the 1590s, that was not difficult. For their part, the seminary priests could be forgiven for thinking their degree of endangerment already sufficient; nearly three-fifths of them suffered imprisonment, and more than a fifth of them were executed.[79]

This situation was exacerbated by the absence of clear hierarchical controls. English affairs were overseen for the papacy by a Vice-Protector and Allen had been given a cardinal's hat, but there was no English diocese, no direct oversight of the seminary priests, no general enforcement of clerical standards or conduct. The Jesuits stepped into this vacuum of authority, but, even had their willingness to court martyrdom for others been less pronounced, their assumption of control over seculars was in the long run intolerable. The upshot, after a rudimentary attempt at self-organization that was easily pictured as a populist insurgency against Rome, was the appointment of an Archpriest with close Jesuit ties, George Blackwell, who was given broad supervisory powers over the English clergy. Blackwell's appointment was resisted by a clerical party, the Appellants, who went as far as to dicker with Bancroft and Cecil for support. The Privy Council abetted publication of the Appellants' tracts, thus sponsoring a debate among felons if not traitors.

The Archpriest controversy, as this well-known episode has come to be called, was fraught with irony on all sides. The Appellants professed themselves willing to swear temporal fealty to the crown, thus abandoning their political "neutrality" vis-à-vis Westminster and Rome, joining the loyalist laity, and effectively negating the papal deposing power. In effect, they chose to trust themselves to the mercy of heretics rather than to endure a Jesuit-dominated discipline. Moreover, as members of the only Catholic group hitherto silent on the loyalist issue, their entry into the lists was well worth soliciting from the crown's point of view, even if the bargain they offered (de facto toleration in return for an oath of temporal loyalty) was never an acceptable one. The Jesuits, not to be outmaneuvered, undercut the value of the Appellants' loyalism by proclaiming their commitment to nonresistance anew.[80]

The laity was largely silent throughout this dispute, which offered little profit to them. Superficially, the Appellants' stand resembled that of loyalists such as Tresham, but the spectacle of clerical wrangling was unedifying if not embarrassing, and posed security risks as well. The gentry were not pleased that the Appellants should have spoken for themselves individually when their patrons had already vouched corporatively for them. This necessarily cast suspicion on those priests who did not subscribe with them, and on the lay households that sheltered them. Moreover, even those of the laity most sympathetic to the Appellants' position realized that the controversy could only lend credence to the Jesuits' contention that the English mission was in disarray.

The Appellant literature revealed the paradoxes inherent in the theory of two regiments. The Appellants professed unconditional submission to the heretical government of the Queen in all matters save those of conscience, and declared themselves ready to suffer martyrdom without resistance or complaint. At the same time, they not only rejected the regime of the Archpriest but questioned the legitimacy of any command, even from the pontiff himself, that did not square with conscience. The arguments they adduced were strikingly similar to those employed by godly disputants against Anglican ceremonies, and those offered by parliamentary pamphleteers against the government of Charles I four decades later. In each case, resistance was predicated on the existence of an inalterably valid framework of authority. For the godly it was biblical prescription and for the Appellants canon law, as for the common lawyers in Parliament it was to be the ancient constitution. All innovations were suspect within this framework, whether popish practices, new taxes, or novel jurisdictions. The Appellants professed themselves willing, indeed eager to submit themselves to episcopal jurisdiction; they had long pined for a bishop of their own. In any case, they contended, they had the right by canon law to approve any change in their status. If, instead, a superior were imposed on them without their consent and in violation of the traditional mode of governance, it was reasonable to conclude that his institution had been procured under false pretenses and through malicious representation. Such an appointment, proceeding from an abused will — be it that of the pope himself — was ipso facto invalid.

The Appellants saw themselves as members of two communities, one the natural community of the secular commonwealth, the other the voluntary community of the church. As members of the first they owed unwavering allegiance to their sovereign, who could command them even unto death on all matters except faith. (Lacking worldly goods and estates and any secular status save that of fugitives, the Appellants were understandably less concerned about legal formalities than their lay protectors; blood was the only tangible forfeit they could make.) Some Appellants, such as William Clarke, were even eager to answer the bloody question, asserting that they would be bound to resist an invasion led by the pope himself.[81]

The pope's legitimate powers, on the other hand, though formally acknowledged, were in practice restricted to the enforcement of canon law in matters of church governance and to suasion and example on questions of scruple and conscience. The Appellants were thus as zealous in tying papal authority to a constitutional framework as they were indifferent to similarly restraining their temporal sovereign. It is not difficult, of course, to understand how the legal nullity of the Appellants' position in the secular realm should lead them to emphasize their corporate status in the church. Their willingness to assert loyalty to the crown even against the pope in return for a bare toleration of their priestly function should also not surprise us, for they had no other token to offer and (short of the sovereign's miraculous conversion) no other benefit to hope for. How badly some priests of the mission hungered for that elementary recognition of their existence as Englishmen became clear when the government rejected them; the aforementioned Clarke was one of several who were hanged for their involvement in the Bye plot, an attempt to kidnap James I and compel him to grant toleration.

There was thus an unresolvable tension in Elizabethan and early Stuart Catholicism. The Catholic laity (and many long-resident priests as well) practiced a dual allegiance, balancing loyalty to the crown on a secular level with loyalty to Rome on a religious one. Such a division was unacceptable in principle to both parties, each of which demanded an allegiance that excluded the other. In practice accommodation was made, but at a cost — in fine or penance — that continually bore home to English Catholics that to be both "English" (i.e., the subject of a deposed prince)[82] and "Catholic" (a member of the Antichrist's church) were mutually exclusive terms. Denied a genuinely legitimate status in either community, "the English Catholic of moderate and peaceable disposition," as Elliot Rose remarked, could only "endure and suffer."[83]

Separatists and Sectarians

In December 1604 Matthew Hutton, now Archbishop of York, wrote a worried letter to the Earl of Salisbury:

> I have receyved letteres from your Lordshippe and others of his Maiesties honorable privie Counsell, conteyninge two pointes: . . . I wishe with all my hart yt the like order Were gyven not onlie to all Busshops, but to all Magistrates & Iustices of Peace, to proceede against Papists and Recusantes . . . The Puritans (whose fantasticall zeale I mislike) though they dyffer in Ceremonies and Accidentes, Yet they agree with vs in substance of Religion, and I thinke all, or ye most of them, love his Maiestie & the present State, and I hope will yeelde to conformitye; but the Papistes are opposite & contrarie in many verie Mayne pointes of Religion, & can not but wishe the Popes authoritie & Popishe Religion to be established . . .[84]

That a senior cleric such as Hutton should feel the need to remind the crown's chief minister of the difference between nonconforming Protestants and the legions of Antichrist speaks much of the changed atmosphere of the Jacobean Court. The assumptions he grants, however, tell us much about the changed condition of the church as well. Hutton does not challenge the policy of proceeding against "Puritans" as well as Papists, a policy originating directly with the King. He merely asks for more evenhanded enforcement.

What response Hutton may have had from Salisbury we do not know, but his real reply, perhaps, came from Thomas Rogers, Archbishop Bancroft's chaplain. In 1607 Rogers published an exegetical treatise, *The Faith, Doctrine, and Religion, Professed, & protected in the Realme of England*. By that time, the political landscape had been considerably altered. The purge of nonconforming ministers undertaken after the Hampton Court Conference had abated. The Gunpowder Plot had been foiled, its chief sponsors—including Henry Garnet, head of the Jesuit order in England—had been executed, and a second miraculous deliverance from popery had entered Protestant lore to go beside that of 1588. Catholics had been proferred a new loyalty oath, and James I himself entered the lists against Jesuit controversialists on the Continent, making him for some years the paladin of the Protestant cause. It would have seemed, then, that Hutton's pointedly phrased distinction between the political and confessional loyalties of Puritans and Catholics would have found a more sympathetic echo even within the conformist hierarchy. Yet Rogers continued to view the "Brethren" as the principal threat to the church, despite the apparent rout of the Presbyterian cause. They asserted, in fine, that:

> a true ministery they shall neuer haue, till Archbishops, and Bishops be put downe, and all Ministers made equall: the other also will neuer be brought to passe, till Kings and Queenes doe subiect themselues vnto the Church, and submit their scepters, and throwe downe their Crow[n]es before the Church, and lick vp the dust of the feete of the Church, and willingly abide the censures of the Church, that is, of the Presbyterie.[85]

No compromise would placate and no defeat would discourage the Brethren, who would not rest satisfied until they could "excommunicate" and "anathematize" even "Kings and Princes":

> This they say is the great cause, the holy cause, which they will neuer leaue suing for, though they should be a thousand Parliaments in their daies, vntill either they obtaine it, or bring the Lord in vengeance, and blood against the State, and the whole land . . .

The prelatical church of the Brethren, then, is the wolf of Rome in the sheep's clothing of doctrinal Protestantism—a doctrine, however, to be defined by themselves no less imperiously than Roman dogma by the pope. One would hardly suspect this same Thomas Rogers to be the author of a dialogue "Touching Antichrist and Poperie" and featuring, as Protestant champions, "Godly Conversation" and Timothy and Zelotes, "Two professors of the Gospell." This earlier work, written in the wake of the Armada, begins without preamble:

> That Whore of Babylon in the holie boke of Revelation decyphered by Saint John, hath bin long since, & through the goodnes of Th'Almightie, is [sic] manie waies, and by sundrie meanes in this last age of the world most notablie prooued to bee the church of Rome.[86]

Rogers goes on in this work to describe "the Pope now liuing" as the "verie Antichrist," for he would have his feet kissed "euen of Kinges and Emperours" whereas Christ washed the feet of his disciples, and would free subjects of their natural allegiance to princes, thus imbruing the nations in blood.[87] The same rhetoric, as we have seen, is turned two decades later against the Brethren, who would also have princes "lick vp the dust of the feete of the Church." Lacking the power and resources of the Roman monolith, the Brethren would accomplish the same result by a decentralized discipline, for in the Presbyterian scheme each congregation "must have absolute authoritie, to admonish, to censure, to excommunicate, and to anathematize" all members, "And no Prince but must be of some parish, and vnder one Presbytery or other alwaies."[88]

Rogers would even revise the history of 1588 to include deliverance not only from the Armada but from the Brethren:

Among the things for which the yeare 88. is famous, one, and not of least regard, is, that afore it expired, these bookes of the brethren, by a Proclamation from Q. Elizabeth, were denounced Schismaticall, and seditious; and the doctrine in them contained, erroneous, tending to perswade, and bring in a monstrous, and apparent dangerous Innouation within her dominions, and countries; and to make a change, euen a dangerous change of the forme of doctrine then in vse.[89]

By the Queen's timely act, the "fancies" of the Brethren were "hissed and exploded" out of the kingdom, much, one is left to infer, as the warships of Philip II were exploded by Drake's fireballs.

Rogers' animadversions—coming at a time when the conformist position within the church seemed particularly secure—suggest the depth of fear and animosity created by the Presbyterian challenge of the 1570s and 1580s, and the trauma of separation that had followed it. It may also help explain the intensity with which ceremonial conformism was pushed in the two decades prior to the outbreak of the Civil War. If men like Thomas Cartwright had made their decisions to stay within the established church and to cleave to the elect nation, their commitment remained forever suspect in conformist eyes, their influence required constant vigilance, and their obedience (not to say abasement) continual testing. The impulse toward Separatism among the godly, whether acted upon or not, was matched by one on the part of conformists to harass, marginalize, isolate, and ultimately expel the "brethren" from the bosom of the church. This latter impulse conflicted, of course, with the inherent mandate of the state church to maintain the widest possible comprehension. Perfect conformity, in this sense, was as unattainable an ideal as perfect godliness. The result was the periodic purging of the ministry by subscription and oath, a purging that created a symbolically ostracized minority against which purer conformity could be tested and renewed.

All this may seem to say that if separation had not existed the Anglican establishment would have had to invent it, in the sense that all orthodoxy is measured by the heresy it generates. The truth of the first eighty years of the restored Church of England, however, was more complex. From the moment Elizabeth had brought the divergent streams of exile Protestant thought under unitary civil control the English church comprised two churches within a single framework, and to contain those churches as far as possible within one confession of creed and practice was the task of three generations of ecclesiastical governors. For a centrist such as Hutton the task was to be accomplished by accommodation when possible and discipline when necessary; for one such as Sandys, however, discipline was foundational, and the bitter dispute between the two men showed how difficult it was to strike a balance even among moderates.

The bedrock issue, ultimately, was the willingness to remain within the official church under whatever conditions might be imposed. The vast majority of the godly were willing to yield at least nominal conformity, finding comfort in personal piety, family prayer, and the fellowship of their kind. Some, such as Thomas Cartwright and John Field, developed a compensatory theology based on the notion of a national covenant. Deriving their ideas from the Swiss cleric Heinrich Bullinger, they construed England as a modern Israel, bound by special compact with God. Like Israel, England was composed of the reprobate as well as the elect, but God's covenant embraced the nation as a whole. This meant that, whatever the particular destinies of individual members of the nation, the English people were, in Timothy Dwight Bozeman's description, "an organic entity irreducible to the sum of its parts . . . a sacralized corporate folk."[90] It also meant a valid national church from which one could neither lawfully nor conscientiously secede, however deformed or idolatrous it might become. Israel's priests had also worshiped idolatrously, and yet God had commanded the prophets to chasten, not abandon them. So, too, the godly preachers of Elizabethan England had no commission to forsake the church, however obliged they were to censure it.

The idea of a federal covenant had powerful implications. It suggested that England had a special mission in the world, and underwrote the notion of England's monarch as the Christian emperor. It conferred particular responsibility on the elect to promote godly rule in church and state, without granting exemption from civil obedience or leave to deny constituted authority. In this sense it was as fully Erastian as any conformist could wish, though hardly as conformist as an Erastian might desire.

In the short term, the federal covenant provided men like Cartwright a stay against despair, a rationale against separation, and a means of occupation. From a conformist perspective it was easier to deal with such men outside the church than within, and the periodic purges carried out by subscription and oath—an irreconcilable dilemma for godly ministers, for whom oath-taking was, after martyrdom, the supreme act of Christian witness— were at least partly designed with this end in view. Even in exile, however, many deprived ministers continued to regard themselves as members of the corporate church. However much in a minority they might be, they refused to be marginalized; however persecuted they were, they refused to be separated.

The Presbyterian episode had left godly ministers permanently suspect in the minds of men such as Whitgift and Bancroft, and their response to any sign of renewed activism was preemptive. When James I ascended the throne, both sides maneuvered for position. The godly community petitioned James for church reform, and over stiff conformist opposition the

King granted them a hearing in January 1604. The scene at Hampton Court in which the assembled bishops fell to their knees and begged James not to admit the godly representatives who, carefully vetted for moderation, were awaiting their turn, speaks volumes about the internal polarization of the church. The bishops were naturally fearful that the King might yield some point in a moment that would undermine the work of decades, but what they resisted above all was the legitimacy that a royal invitation conferred upon their adversaries and the degradation of authority implicit in their being forced to stand to debate. For James himself, the conference served to emphasize his own Erastian supremacy over both parties, and in that sense he was its clearest beneficiary.[91]

The conformist response to the godly challenge was embodied in the episcopal canons of 1604, the most significant codification of church law between 1559 and 1640. With a few minor concessions, the canons staked out an unequivocally conformist position. For the most part they were a compendium of ecclesiastical pronouncements going back to Cromwell's Injunctions of 1536 and including such godly bêtes noires as Parker's *Advertisements* on proper vestments and Whitgift's Articles of 1583, which had provided subscription tests for conformity. Newly refurbished as Canon 36, the demand for subscription included acceptance of the royal supremacy, the Prayer Book, and the Thirty-Nine Articles. Whitgift and Bancroft applied it immediately to the clergy, demanding full subscription from curates and lecturers and conformity from ministers. Among those refusing subscription was John Reynolds, president of Corpus Christi College and the leader of the godly delegation at Hampton Court, who wrote to Bancroft that to accept the Prayer Book as containing nothing contrary to the word of God would be to affirm "a known untruth."[92] Reynolds was permitted to conform; as the moving figure on the committee to produce a new authorized version of the Bible (a project approved by James over Bancroft's objections), it would hardly have done to defrock him. Some eighty to ninety ministers were less fortunate, and the number of those deprived would doubtless have been higher had James not restrained the zeal of his Archbishop of Canterbury.

The exposition of the Anglican creed published by Thomas Rogers must be seen in light of Bancroft's campaign. In listing the "adversaries" to Article 7 (which stated that the church could not enforce any belief contrary to the word of God), Rogers heaps together "the Puritanes, and all the speculations of Brown[e], Barrow, Greene, Penrie, Marprelate, T. C. [Thomas Cartwright] E. G.[,] R. H. [Robert Harrison?] A. C. [Anthony Cope?] [and] I. B. with all the new Sabbatarians and their fancies."[93] This omnium-gatherum of dissidents aims plainly to efface any ideological distinction between Separatists and godly nonseparatists.

James I himself drew a far more careful distinction in the *Basilikon Doron*, a work of instruction intended for Prince Henry and composed while James was still waiting to inherit the English throne:

> First then, as to the name of Puritanes, I am not ignorant that the stile thereof doth properly belong only to that vile sect amongst the Anabaptists, called the Familie of Love; because they thinke them selves onely pure, and in a manner, without sinne, the onely true churche, and only worthie to be participant of the Sacraments; and all the rest of the worlde to be but ab-homination in the sight of God. Of this speciall sect I principallie meane, when I speake of Puritanes.[94]

James' definition is not only highly restrictive — the Family of Love, despite its relatively high profile, was a small group, probably not numbering much more than a thousand adherents if that many — but also eccentric. As James was well aware, the term "Puritan" was chiefly employed to designate zealous advocates of Calvinist orthodoxy and strict scripturalism, in short those most fervently opposed to everything the free-willing Familists stood for (see below). The King would not have made such an "error" unintentionally, particularly in an edition prepared for an audience of his prospective subjects; the more plausible assumption is that he was proferring an olive branch to the godly, an inference seconded by his subsequent willingness to receive their petitions on his ascension journey south and their representatives at Hampton Court. Conformists would have been correspondingly alarmed; their subsequent behavior suggests that they were, and that moderates such as Hutton were concerned to rein them in. Until further research tells us more about Bancroft's Canon 36 campaign and the forces that restrained it our conclusions must remain conjectural, but James' ecclesiastical policy at large, at least down to 1618, suggests a conscious effort to accommodate both godly and conformist interests within the church. This was at best a delicate balancing act; as the deprived minister Paul Baynes declared in 1621, there was as much agreement between lordly bishops and godly preachers as "betwixt the light which commeth down from heaven and that thick mist which ariseth from the lowest pit."[95]

The policy James suggested in the *Basilikon Doron* was in effect that those zealous and reform-minded Protestants willing to conform with the national church be distinguished from the Separatists who rejected any form of compromise with their vision of the godly commonwealth. What the King might proffer by way of grace, however, was not to be privately petitioned for. When Josias Nichols, a pastor of Kent previously suspended by Whitgift, restated the case for godly reformation within the church in *The Plea of the Innocents*, he provoked a predictable response and again lost his cure. Nichols' work took up James' point that the term "Puritan" referred properly only to Anabaptists. He traced the origin of this "Puritanism" back to the various

Pelagian heresies of the early church, which asserted human perfectability. From this perspective, Papists too were "puritanes," because they claimed to remit sins, whereas those "vncharitablie and vniustlie" called by that name in the Church of England had always acknowledged themselves "to be great & greeuous sinners . . . reioysing of no other purenes, but that which is by the bloud of Christ."[96] In this manner, and with the authority of the King's own words (if not necessarily his practice), the godly could affirm solidarity with the oft-to-be-stated royal position that neither Papists nor Puritans were to be tolerated in the commonwealth.

The connection between Papist and Separatist suggested by Nichols received more substantial development in Timothy Rogers' *The Roman-Catharist* (1621). Rogers traced the true "Puritans" back to Novatus, the leader of those who refused to accept back the lapsed Christians of the Decian persecutions. Novatus' rejectionism led him at length to schism and thence to heresy. He and his followers would "acknowledge no other meanes to reconcile men to God . . . but Baptisme: they bragged much of their merits, & gloried much of the worthines of their works."[97] Novatus' schism presaged that of the popes, who like him engrossed power and dignity by "vngodly sleights" — allegedly, he held three bishoprics — and asserted doctrinal supremacy over the church. Thus the unity of the primitive church, a unity based not on dogma but on the fraternity of kindred congregations, had been destroyed. Both the Novatians and their Papist disciples had arrogated to themselves the title of "the onely church"; both had boasted of their good works, their freedom from sin, and their perseverance in grace. Spiritual tyranny had been set up in place of Christian liberty, monolithic power in place of voluntary association. Unity had only been restored with the Reformation, whose churches, like those of apostolic times, recognized in one another a free community of the faithful. In this restored community there were only two dissident voices — the old apostasy of Rome, and the new Novatians of Separatism and Anabaptism.[98]

In contrast to both Puritan and Papist, the godly and devout constituted the core membership of all Reformed churches. How were they to be known? They were:

> They which *command their children and houshold to keepe the way of the Lord* as *Abraham* did: they which resolue that they and their *house will serue the Lord*, as *Iosua* did: they which rid their families of disordered persons, as lyers, slanderers and proud persons, as *Dauid* did: they which *refuse to company with vaine persons and euill doers, and to sit with the wicked*, as the same Prophet did: they which refuse to doe wickedly when they are prouoked and entised, saying *How shall wee doe this and sinne against God*, as *Ioseph* sayd: they which pray daily vnto God in their families and by themselues, and sometimes seeke him by fasting . . . they which exercise themselues in

reading the Scriptures . . . they which when they haue heard a Sermon, *search the Scriptures whether those things bee so* . . . they which are zealous . . . for the honour of God against idolatry and superstition . . . they which turne *away their foot from doing their owne pleasure, and their owne wayes, on the Sabbath day* . . . they that will not swear in their common talke by *any oath* . . . they that shun all *surfeting, and drunkenness, and worldly cares* . . . they which *desire to keep a good conscience in all things, willing to liue honestly,* as the Apostles did . . .[99]

Such were the people falsely aspersed as Puritans by the idle and the wicked, although their lives were in every way opposite to those properly so called. Their sincerity was derided as pretension, their piety as hypocrisy, their desire to walk in holiness as schism. Yet no one else was farther from separation from the church in word or thought, accounting "as highly the peace and vnitie thereof, as . . . their owne liues."[100]

Rogers had inadvertently put his finger on the problem. Precisely because the godly walked apart they seemed to constitute a sect within the church, more visible than the actual sectarians who stood outside the congregation, more disturbing than the church papists and Familists who blended in with it. They were a permanent irritant to the unregenerate mass of parishioners, a standing reminder of the official rather than the pastoral theology of the church. If the godly saw themselves as the core of the church, the lively stones on which it must build, others saw them as semi-separated, neither truly within the church nor without it, and therefore a challenge to good order and discipline.

One of the consequences of this was that the godly were largely left to patrol the frontier of conscience between separating and nonseparating brethren, where the covenantal pull toward unity warred with the impulse to flee a church not merely flawed but demonstrably false. Historians who argue from the absence of antimonarchical sentiment before the 1640s to the essential stability of the crown in prewar England but ignore the ongoing schism from the established church have gravely misconstrued the challenge posed by separation to the legitimacy of the Reformation state. It was a mistake that Whitgift, Bancroft, and Laud did not make, although their responses could do little but exacerbate the problem. The actual Separatists themselves, never a large and seldom a cohesive group, were only the most visible aspect of a far wider estrangement whose source was in the very essence of the Erastian church. If the godly embraced the Christian emperor as the only guarantor of the peace and security of the church—if they civilly reverenced their persecuting Deborah even as she smote them—they never accepted the permanence of a hierarchical, prelatical regime. For them, the reestablished church of 1559 was no act of settlement, but a stopgap measure, an emergency action against popery, a starting point for true reformation.

In a sense, the English Reformation must be regarded as a drama in three acts. The first act comprised the establishment of the Henrician church, professedly Catholic and orthodox, which was rejected by Romanists and contested by heretics and reformers until, by 1552, it had been substantially remade in doctrine and liturgy if not in discipline. The second act, begun in 1559, involved the refounding of an Erastian church under Elizabeth, whose reforming bishops gave it a nominally Calvinist creed and whose gentry patrons gave it a broader base and a more diffused power structure. This act ended with the collapse of the Laudian regime in 1640. The third act, that of the Restoration, involved the gradual acceptance of plurality and dissent in the context of a desacralized polity, ultimately secular in all but name. That act, still in play, has latterly involved dialogue between Canterbury and the Vatican, thus reinstating what for some have been the best hopes and for others the worst suspicions about the ultimate significance of the Church of England.

The primary concern of this study has been with the period of the second act, but the continuity of issues and the circularity of debate within a church now the better part of five centuries old suggests the tensions and paradoxes at its core: between a national and a universal church, between tradition affirmed and truth restored, between a legitimacy of order and a legitimacy of revolution. The tensions are as powerful and the paradoxes as intractable as ever; what has changed are the stakes for civil society. It is still possible that the fate of the Church of England and the British monarchy will be entwined; it is not likely that the future of either will require civil war or social upheaval to settle.

The Elizabethan church was in principle a viable compromise. Its bishops were civil bureaucrats but also nursing fathers; not functions easily reconciled but not radically incompatible. Its doctrine was recognizably but not rigidly Calvinist, an orthodoxy that gave structure without stifling theological debate. Its liturgy was reassuringly familiar to lay congregants and expedient for a clergy few of whom were painful or learned and many of whom had suspect enthusiasm for the new regime. Its governance was both centrally coordinated and locally diffused, thus combining firmness of command with flexibility of implementation. There was broad satisfaction in the church for the ordinary parishioner who asked little of his religion beyond comfort, regularity, and hope, and sufficient room in it for the bare conformity of church papists and the tender consciences of the godly. Its credentials were quickly accepted, or better said, revalidated by the Reformed community, and it soon graduated from the tutelage of the *Zurich Letters* to leadership in the Synod of Dort. On all these accounts it was a success, but one which bred in the minds of some the conviction of a larger and far more culpable failure. Had the goal of ecclesiastical polity been stability, continu-

ity, and subordination to the secular command—the goal, in short, of Elizabeth—then the Church of England, by the 1580s, was a very tolerable ap-
proximation of it. But from the beginning there had been those who saw the
true church as dynamic, a temple of lively stones and stirring spirits. For
such, the choice soon boiled down to building a church within a church—the
godly leaven of the elect within the gross body of the visible church—or of
severing oneself from iniquity and corruption.

Those who chose the latter course did so silently at first. Some, where Lollard tradition persisted, had never been more than nominally part of the new
church; others, like the Familists, combined pro forma communion with private devotion and belief. For others, the moment of separation came with the
Vestments controversy, when the first godly ministers were suspended and
deprived for refusing to wear the "idolatrous gear" prescribed in Archbishop
Parker's dress code. Congregations loyal to their ministers continued to meet
in private homes and assemblies in and around London. Such groups included those who had participated in the underground Protestant congregations of the Marian period, and who now reconstituted themselves in the
face of another persecuting church. They took the opportunity as well to
dispense with another popish relic, the Prayer Book prescribed by the Act of
Settlement in 1559, and to adopt the Geneva book and order as more "agreeable to the word of God."[101]

Patrick Collinson rightly calls these dissidents, about a hundred of whom
were arraigned in June 1567 and a further seventy-seven in March 1568, "virtual sectarians."[102] Their loyalty was to their minister and the congregational
unit; together, these sufficed to form a self-validated company of worship, if
not yet a gathered church. Within this company they felt free to dispense
with any aspect of ecclesiastical discipline or liturgy that did not in their
view conform to the word of God. Under examination they professed their
willingness to return to their parish churches when the onerous conditions
imposed on them and their ministers had been lifted; in short, when the established church had conformed itself to them rather than the other way
around. From here it was only a short step to the rejection of the episcopal
regime *tout court*, and the discovery of an authentic, autonomous discipline
of pastors, elders, and ordinary congregants.

It was at the point of discipline that the issue of separatism was genuinely
joined. The Reformation, in establishing itself under a wide variety of circumstances, had in its initial phases been less particular about questions of
governance than of doctrine. Christian liberty was the freedom of the Gospel, not of voluntary association. Under conditions of persecution, however,
the two became inseparable. Thus, church organization had become the
prime issue within English Protestantism by the 1570s, whereas serious dis-

putes about doctrine did not emerge, at least outside the universities, until the 1620s.

For godly dissenters, then, the question confronting them was whether the doctrinal orthodoxy of the established church was sufficient to outweigh its disciplinary shortcomings. Allied to this was the issue of whether all the marks of a true church had to be present for a given church to validly represent the Gospel. Episcopacy per se had never been condemned by the Reformed tradition; Calvin himself had allowed it. Even if one concluded it to be finally contrary to Scripture, at least in the form of a command structure that subordinated individual congregations to a hierarchy of controls, the question remained whether gradual edification (including the edification of the Christian prince) might not devolve greater authority on the congregations, or even lead to abolition. Less patient heads sought to expedite the process by petition and bill in Parliament.

The long, fruitless campaign against episcopacy in the 1570s and 1580s made clear the gulf of misunderstanding that separated the Erastian church from its godly communicants and divided its clergy. For Elizabeth and her successors, the settlement of 1559 was permanent and irrevocable. Its essence was summed up pithily in James' formula, "No bishop, no king." It was the creed for which his son would die.

The Erastian position was so clearly defined and so adamantly defended that one commentator, G. W. Bernard, has characterized the ecclesiastical order of prewar England as a "monarchical church."[103] This was the church created by Henry VIII, restored by Elizabeth, and restored again by Charles II. Its essential characteristics were the royal supremacy and the episcopal bench. The doctrine of this church had often been controverted and remained frequently disputed; its discipline remained unaltered down to 1640, and when change did come, it was in the form of a revolution that swept church and state down together. As James would have recognized, and as Charles I came to learn, the abolition of episcopacy portended the end of monarchy, at least in any form that Charles was willing to exercise it.

The centrality of episcopal governance to this church was in no degree lessened by the practical subordination of the bishops to the crown and, even under Laud, to the aristocracy and the greater gentry. It was the idea of episcopacy, the pedigree it gave the upstart Henrician church, the continuity with an ancient past, that was essential. "No bishop, no king" was the tag line that ultimately expressed the interdependence of the monarchy and the Erastian church; but "no bishop, no church" more accurately reflected the circumstances of its founding, and, (from a crown standpoint) the necessary condition of its maintenance. It was not until the 1580s and 1590s that apologists such as Bilson, Bridge, and Hooker, responding to Presbyterian attacks, began to develop a learned justification for episcopacy based on Scripture and tradition, but the very absence of a prior rationale suggests the degree to which (except perhaps for a brief moment after the Marian debacle) bishops were regarded as part of the natural or at any rate the reasonable order of things. Even among godly reformers, the era of Grindal was remembered as "a golden time, ful of godly fruit, great honour to the Ghospell, great loue and kinde fellowship among all the Ministers, preaching the faith, and the people vnited in the true feare of God, and cheerfull reuerence to her Maiestie."[104] Making due allowance for nostalgic enhancement and rhetorical exaggeration, this clearly suggests that episcopacy as such was not the rub for the disaffected.

The root of controversy in the Anglican church was not its governance by the bishops but its control by the crown. An Erastian church was one ultimately subordinated to secular interests if not values, a church whose lodestar was not edification but prudence. Grindal himself had starkly posed the difference in the dispute over prophesying, when, casting personal prudence to the wind, he insisted on the priority of edification before all other goals. Edification was the final purpose of a church, the mother of all its virtues. Discipline and order derived naturally from it, whereas in themselves they merely conduced to edification without assuring it. Nor was edification incompatible with strictly secular virtues; Grindal's point was that an edified church was stronger and more securely planted than a timeserving one, and therefore could serve as a pillar to the state.

If edification might abet the legitimate ends of prudence, however, the converse was not so. The true church was often persecuted and forever at risk; it was known not by its prelates but its martyrs. A prudential church was a contradiction in terms; carnal prosperity was the mark of Rome. Herein lay the danger of a state church: not that the worldly concerns of the prince would corrupt the church, but that in yielding to them the church would betray the state. It was for this reason that Grindal was such a crucial figure for Nichols and others on the margin of nonconformity, for he had spoken truth to power and thereby vindicated the function of the bishop as a nursing father. One could even make a consoling fable from his fall, for Elizabeth, though constrained to punish Grindal for his temerity, nevertheless refused to deprive him. Might the Queen's relative clemency not be seen as tacitly acknowledging the justness of the Archbishop's cause?[105]

For others, however, Grindal's fall was the signal for a reformation without tarrying. The essential problem for the godly community was how to reconcile the need for Christian liberty—worship according to conscience— with obedience to the prince. By the 1580s a small but significant body of this community had decided that these two imperatives could not be squared within the national church as constituted. The Presbyterian movement, from this perspective, represented a last attempt to "erect discipline" within the

Erastian church. The role of the state, never specified, would presumably have been purely custodial, with the Queen herself as churchwarden-in-chief.

It need hardly be said that the Presbyterian movement had no chance of success. It was as unacceptable to the lay elites whose control of church lands and advowsons it threatened as to the crown. Even among godly parishioners presumably to be empowered by control of their affairs it aroused no significant enthusiasm. Elizabethan Presbyterianism, like its Caroline successor sixty years later, was primarily a ministerial insurgency with few congregational roots. The surviving records of the *classes* show that it was dominated and manipulated from the beginning by a few clerical activists, abetted and advised—as sixty years later—by Scots Presbyterians.

What is of interest is the degree to which the activists assumed support not only from the godly laity but from the Queen herself. Even when the attempt to replace by statute the episcopal regime with a Presbyterian one and the Book of Common Prayer with the Geneva Prayer Book was quashed in Parliament in 1587 and its supporters imprisoned, the image of Elizabeth as a Deborah ultimately devoted to reform could not be entirely dispelled.[106] What such loyalism indicated, however, was not the naïveté or self-delusion of the clerical activists—many, such as Thomas Cartwright, John Field, and Walter Travers, seasoned and oft-disappointed men—but the practical limits of dissent.

Loyalism (as opposed to loyalty, the normative response of the subject to the legitimated order) was legitimacy's last line of defense. Based on the principles of hierarchy and blood title, reinforced by homily and oath, and deeply engrained in the political culture, loyalism was founded on the faith in an ultimately benign patriarchal order whose embodiment was the prince (whether male or female).[107] This faith, assiduously cultivated by ritual, catechism, and sermon, was accepted among the powerless not because it accorded with their actual experience but because it made that experience tolerable. Its most extreme and beleaguered manifestation was the loyalist rebellion, a form of armed petitioning in which the avowed purpose was to bring grievances directly to the attention of the sovereign when other means had failed or proved lacking. We shall note its representation in the urban riot and the peasant jacquerie below, as well as its more sophisticated use by the political elite in the first Civil War. In the case of tumults and risings, loyalist avowals signified tacit acknowledgment of the limits of popular revolt, which could not hope to compel or depose the sovereign without elite support (and cooptation). In a sense, such avowals were the counterpart of the legal maxim that "the king can do no wrong"; the coercive behavior behind them assumed, as did legal process, that the ruler properly informed would rectify the wrongs displayed to him.

A similar process, I would contend, was at work in the Presbyterian movement of the 1580s, when activists moved from petition, propaganda, and argument to the practical implementation of a system of congregation, classis, and synod. Though obviously unarmed and undeclared, this movement functionally merits the title of a rebellion, for it clearly struck at royal authority and governance. At the same time it was a typically loyalist rebellion that culminated in petition through Parliament to the crown, and remained, even in suppression, wedded to the fiction of a *dévot* Queen.

The legalist fiction that the king could do no wrong functioned well enough under the Tudors, whose collective dynastic genius was the recognition that the royal will could be exercised most effectively by the scrupulous observation of legal forms; hence it was that they were able to effect four major changes of religion within a generation (1532–1534; 1549–1552; 1554; 1559) without substantial bloodshed. The ultimate triumph of Tudor legalism was the presentation of the Presbyterian Bill and Book in 1587, for it took a powerfully instilled faith in the appropriateness, not to say the magical efficacy of forms, to believe that Queen Elizabeth would better consent to reversing the settlement of 1559 if it were presented to her in a manner identical with its original institution.

In the case of Presbyterian petitioning the legalist and loyalist fictions dovetailed; an essentially sympathetic prince had only to be approached by the proper channels. Needless to say, a good deal more was involved than that—a lengthy propaganda campaign, a detailed parish survey, the engagement of lay sponsors and the courting of godly elites—but, in the end, all depended on winning royal favor, and that in turn on the assumption of a benign prince amenable to petition in prescribed forms.

The loyalist fiction survived the ensuing debacle because there was no alternative to it. Persuasion was the only mode available to those who continued to hope for reform or at least accommodation within a national church. Whether a refractory prince might be coerced was a moot point among beneficed clergy but a step away from deprivation, imprisonment, or exile; whether a reprobate (but not tyrannical) one might be deposed or assassinated was, apart from the formidable sanctions against such actions in the Reformed tradition, a question best left to papal plotters. Particularly in the atmosphere of the 1580s, loyalism was a psychological and political necessity. The failure of the Presbyterian campaign left only two options for godly militants: quietism or schism.

Separation

The history of the Elizabethan church can be divided into chronologically equal halves: the period during which its fundamental legitimacy was publicly unquestioned in England, and the one during which that legitimacy was openly repudiated by Jesuit infiltrators on the one hand and Protestant Separatists on the other. The former challenge was credible on a level the latter one was not; the Separatists raised no daggers and launched no galleons. Ideologically, however, they posed a more subtle and complex threat, for they attacked the church on the basis of its own essential presuppositions and stated ideals. In responding to that attack, the conformist church—bishops such as Bancroft and Bridges, and scholars such as Hooker and Saravia[108]— were driven not only to defend but also to redefine the church in ways that were to be deeply consequential. At the same time godly clerics, although not part of the official campaign, were moved to defend their own conformity against charges of self-interest and hypocrisy and to answer Separatists who quoted them in defense of their own actions and claimed them as precursors.

The first Separatist tracts coincided with those of Martin Marprelate, and John Penry, who may have had a hand in both, claimed that Martin's first screed, the *Epistle*, was based directly on notes found in John Field's study.[109] Certainly the pedigree of dissent they claimed from the Presbyterian controversialists was incontrovertible. The Martinist moment, however, marked a critical point of departure. There had been Separatist congregations in London two decades earlier, and the battle over church discipline and the lawfulness of episcopacy had long been joined. What made the Marprelate and Separatist tracts distinctive was that they were no longer a debate within the church or a silent withdrawal from it, but a public renunciation. The Marprelate tracts were not Separatist per se, but their scorched earth rhetoric boded no other choice. Separation was entailed from a church so ludicrous and deformed.

Yet there was no straight road from the Presbyterian movement of the 1580s to separation. Not only did most godly ministers (not all of whom, of course, were persuaded of the necessity to abandon the episcopal regime) repine at renouncing their livings, but separation—at least on the terms available—was less conducive to the ultimate goal of a Presbyterian polity than continued conformity to the established church. The Presbyterian schema, despite its emphasis on congregational self-governance, was ultimately closer to the hierarchical model of that church than to the congregational model of the Separatists, as the 1640s were to show. Given the realities of the Separatist condition—persecution or exile—no other model was available; and given the fissiparous experience of the Marian congregations abroad, the prospects of federation among autonomous churches were exceedingly small. Moreover, there was a deep sensitivity to the ramifications of schism, for abandoning the national church meant parting as well with the Foxean ideal of a covenanted nation, the core myth of Elizabethan Protestantism. When the Privy Council demanded the opinion of the Presbyterian

Edward Dering concerning the discipline of the church he could not palliate his conviction that it was contrary to the word of God, yet added that no one for that reason "ought to separate himself from the church' which God has given us in this land."[110] The notion of a providential deliverance from popery died hard.

For these reasons, Separatism was neither a simple nor necessarily an irrevocable decision. Some Separatists left the church never to return, but others haunted its fringes or found their way back. As in the case of the Jesuit pamphleteers, an extensive controversial literature sprang up between opponents and defenders of the church. As by the former, souls were sometimes recovered for the church, and although the propaganda value of a Papist won back to the fold might exceed that of a repentant Separatist the drama of apostasy and redemption was often more intense. The reason for this lay in the finer line that divided Separatist pamphleteers from church spokesmen. The latter were most often godly conformists, many of whom had disputed discipline with their clerical superiors. No few had been tempted by Separatism themselves, and in the case they made for the Erastian church—one which conceded many points of criticism—one can detect echoes of an inner dialogue. Moreover, many of the older godly conformists had been mentors and exemplars to those who ultimately separated, if not even closer. Robert Browne, for example, the first publicly declared Separatist,[111] had been a disciple of Cartwright's at Cambridge, and later shared lodgings with the godly conformist Richard Greenham.[112] Even after his defection from the church, some of Browne's writings were included in the godly (but nonseparating) collection entitled *A parte of a register* (1590). Browne himself may well have been reconsidering his position at that point, for he returned to the church soon after, accepting in September 1591 the ordination he had refused twelve years earlier.

We do not know what brought Browne back into the Elizabethan fold—he lived to die languishing in a Northamptonshire gaol in 1633, a victim of the Laudian regime—but the record is fuller in the case of Henry Jacob, a godly conformist who defected and ultimately founded a church of his own. Jacob may at one point have held a benefice at Cheriton, and in the 1590s he disputed with the Separatist Francis Johnson, himself an ordained priest who, after suffering imprisonment for publicly espousing a Presbyterian polity, became minister to the Merchant Adventurers' congregation at Middleburg in the Netherlands.[113] Jacob's record of their debate shows a man in the process of losing an argument with himself. His adversary's generalizations are sweeping; his rhetoric takes no prisoners. The Church of England, Johnson asserts, lacks a lawful ministry, a lawfully gathered people, and a lawful discipline. Its congregations are "holds of all foule spirits, and cages of euery uncleane and hatefull bird. . . . Atheists, Idolators, Papistes, erronious &

hereticall Sectaries, Witches, Charmers, Sorcerors, Murtherers, Theeves, Adulterers, Lyers, & c." Its ministers lack proper ordination, are subject to usurped authority, and teach profane texts. Its own most "forward Preachers," notably Thomas Cartwright, admit as much.

Jacob's response denies not the essential validity of these points (although of course he defends Anglican ordination) but their necessary application. He concedes that "many errors may be added, & truthes wanting in a visible Church," but that as long as nothing "absolutely necessary" is lacking the want of perfection or even the presence of idolators cannot "abolishe our Sacraments." By that standard of chummy ecumenicism it would be difficult to find a communion to exclude, including the Roman one.[114]

Like many conformist divines, Jacob may have been awaiting relief from Scotland, for at James I's accession in 1603 he actively promoted petitions for godly reform in London and Sussex. Perhaps he had already crossed the line into Separatism, for he was denounced as a schismatic and imprisoned in the Clink, as Johnson had been a decade earlier.[115] The treatise he wrote in confinement, however, *Reasons Taken Out of Gods Word* (1604), was clearly a Separatist document. Whereas Jacob had in his *Defence* against Johnson pointed to the Old Testament church as a true one despite its abominations, he now discovered that the second commandment forbade any practice contrary to Scripture, and therefore any form of church polity save the congregational model of the apostles. Thereafter his writings consistently espoused this view. Thus, he declared, "Christ hath seated the power of ordination and iurisdiction in the whole particular Congregation" and nowhere else, "not in the case of necessitie only, but even alwayes at all seasons . . . . indefinitly and without limitation." It followed that "each Congregation is an intire and independent Body politike Spirituall, and is indued with power in it selfe immediately vnder Christ."[116]

Jacob's formulation neatly encapsulated the Separatist position, and marked it off from the Presbyterian model. It rested squarely, as did other assertions of the congregational ideal, on the verses of Matthew 18: 20 ("Where two or three are gathered in my name there am I") and 2 Corinthians 6: 17, 18 ("Come out from among them, and separate yourselves from them"), texts which had been cited by Richard Fitz's London congregation in the 1570s.[117] Modern scholars have remarked on the influence of a second-generation Calvinist legalism, notably that of Theodore Beza, in enforcing an anxious quest for scriptural justification in all details of discipline and worship. But deciphering the Word, appropriating the proof texts, could be immensely liberating as well. It was a sword that cut through all doubts and leveled all opposition. In this sense Separatism was a working-out of some of the logical implications of the Protestant, and specifically the Foxean tradition. The Reformation itself had been an act of separation on behalf of truth.

Revelation was progressive; the major truths—justification by faith, the pre-destination of the elect to salvation—had been enunciated by Luther and Calvin, but these were merely the foundation of the temple. Purity of doctrine had obtained in apostolic times too, only to be corrupted by human invention and Roman usurpation. Now that the light of the Gospel had begun to shine through again after centuries of Babylonian darkness it must be recovered in all its glory, for whatever was not of faith was of sin.

In the Foxean tradition, the Marian martyrs attested the Gospel and paved the way for the recovery of truth as enshrined in the national church. When the godly too were persecuted by that church they readily assimilated their experience to that of the martyrs, but a question nagged. If the national church were indeed a false one too, had the martyrs' sacrifice been efficacious or deluded? Separatists resolved the issue by a doctrine of limited light; the martyrs, though their conception of the church was still stained with impurities, had nonetheless acted on the degree of truth vouchsafed them. No one could do more; but, by the same token, no one might do less: further light entailed further action. That England's reformation had been partial and imperfect was (until Hooker) conceded by all, but as long as edification and amendment were at least in prospect judgment might be suspended. By the 1580s the signs of apostasy were apparent. It was no longer sufficient for the enlightened to withdraw in silence, as the early Separatist congregations had done; testimony was necessary as well.

It is in this context that we must read Robert Browne's *A Treatise of reformation without tarying for anie* (1582) and the subsequent writings of Robert Harrison, John Greenwood, Henry Barrow, and John Penry. For Browne, the question was no longer merely whether the pace of reformation in the national church was adequate, but whether the church as a whole was a true or a false one.

The distinction between true and false churches was fundamental to Reformed discourse, since it was the principal justification for the Reformers' secession from the church of Rome. It was Luther who had suggested that the true visible church might be known by certain marks (*notae ecclesiae*), as false ones by their absence. The Augsburg Confession of 1530 defined the church as a congregation of the faithful in which the Gospel was preached purely and the sacraments properly administered. Calvin endorsed this definition, and the marks of Word and sacrament became the standard indicators of a true church. A third and more controversial mark, that of discipline, was proposed by Martin Bucer in 1544, taken up by Knox and Beza, and incorporated into several Reformed Confessions. Although initially the concept of discipline was limited to admonishing and correcting the faults of the faithful,[118] it immediately raised issues of pastoral supervision and lay-clerical relationships. This in turn suggested an appeal to Scripture for guidance, and ultimately for an authoritative model of church governance. By 1576 Beza had pronounced on this subject. Divinely ordained governance— *Divinus Episcopatus*—involved the coadministration of pastors and lay elders. Humanly instituted governance—*Humanus Episcopatus*—was without scriptural warrant, and tolerable only insofar as it preserved the *notae ecclesiae* and respected congregational autonomy. All other governance was *Satanus Episcopatus*, the usurped spiritual authority of a false church.[119]

By such a standard, it was clear to Browne that the Church of England was a depraved institution. This was less so because of its episcopal governance—repugnant as that was—than its civil lordship. If the spiritual tyranny of Rome was the very regime of the Antichrist, then the Erastian commixture of the sacred and the secular was scarcely less to be deplored:

> They would make the Magistrates more then Goddes, and yet also worse then beastes. For they teache that a lawefull Pastour must giue ouer his charge at their discharging, and when they withholde the Church gouvernement, it ought for to ceasse, though the Church goe to ruine thereby. Beholde nowe, doeth not the Lordes kingdome giue place vnto theirs? And doe they not pull downe the heade Christe Jesus, to sett vppe the hande of the Magistrate?[120]

The "they" responsible for all this are the lordly prelates who, no longer able to practice popery under the seal of Rome, conceal themselves under the skirts of the magistrate and thereby corrupt temporal as well as spiritual administration. Their true purpose is apparent in the style they arrogate to themselves, "for they first proclaime the names and tytles of wicked Bishoppes and popishe officers, and the Lordes name after." In this way they assert their false authority over "lawfull Preachers, and stoppe their mouthes." At the same time they blame the magistrates for their own temporizing, claiming that they prevent them from reforming the church and even bemoaning their subordination to civil authority. This shameless plea unmasked their hypocrisy, for as in all temporal matters the magistrate's authority was "highest under God," so in spiritual ones all magistrates were under "Pastorall charge" and must submit to Christ's government in the church "if they bee Christians." Thus Erastianism was a formula for corrupting the true authority of minister and magistrate alike.[121]

The radical implications of Browne's analysis were clear. The Erastian church was not only incapable of reform but expressly constructed to thwart it. It was pointless to tarry for "anie" in reforming the church, for the prelates were merely intent on preserving their own usurped authority and the magistrates had no spiritual authority in the church to begin with. In a word, the entire Elizabethan settlement was invalid.

How, then, could a true visible church be constituted in England? It could not be comprehensive, since such a church mingled saints and sinners indiscriminately and was by definition incapable of exerting proper discipline. It could not be large, since the appropriate test for membership—a profession of faith attested by strict life and godly conversation—could be validated only through direct and continuing contact. Clerics such as William Fulke, Laurence Chaderton, Dudley Fenner, and Walter Travers all emphasized the necessity of face-to-face encounter among all church members and direct participation by each in the affairs of the church.[122] This implied if it did not entail a congregational model.

From the Separatist point of view, the efforts of godly conformists to realize a Presbyterian system within the established church was in every respect foredoomed. The prelates were implacably opposed to a reform that would annul their titles; the magistrates, assuming they were willing to relinquish their own false role in the church, had no power to constitute a new one. Even Beza's politic suggestion that a *humanus episcopatus* was not strictly speaking incompatible with a true church and Browne's reluctance to pronounce the Church of England wholly apostate were now abandoned. No mark of a true church could subsist with a false government, and any government was false that deviated by a hairbreadth from Scripture, for in such case:

> Christ is thrown out of his house and antychrist exalted and raineth by his officers and lawes. This the promises and present estate [of the Church of England] declareth.[123]

Henry Barrow's identification of the established church with that of the Antichrist was penned at the height of the church's own campaign to equate the Antichrist with Rome, and on the eve of the Armada's descent on England. It was in short a challenge that could not have been issued at a more inopportune moment. Archbishop Whitgift personally (and none too gently) interrogated Barrow, and Bancroft answered him in a Paul's Cross sermon. Barrow was undeterred, and addressed his flock from prison:

> Behould what a Christ they prech ether in the habit of or in subjection to antichrist! The gospell they prech is withowt lybertye, joyned, and well agreing with idollatry and all the synne of the land. What shall I saye of them, or rather what shall I leave unsayd? I am mor weary and grevyd in reckning the[i]r sinnes than they in comiting them. . . . They see not, and canot enduer to hear, that they are naked and poor and miserable, and near unto destruction.[124]

Barrow was not daunted by a Whitgift or a Bancroft, and, although a layman, did not scruple to criticize Calvin himself; but rejection by Thomas Cartwright, at that time a fellow prisoner in the Fleet, brought him (at least by hostile report) close to despair:

Hath he [not] onely brought me into this brake, and will he now leave me? From him I received my grounds, and, out of his premises, did I inferre, and make conclusion of the positions, which I now holde, and for which I suffer bands.[125]

A year later, close to execution, Barrow again (according to the same source) complained bitterly of Cartwright to a delegation of conformist divines that included Lancelot Andrewes: "You are not the men whom I most dislike in these [present] differences. For although you be out of the way, yet you thinke you are in the right (and walk according to that light which God hath given you). But I cannot but complaine of Maister Cartwright and others of his knowledge . . . who yet utterly, against their consciences, forsake us in our sufferings."[126]

As Patrick Collinson has remarked, the distance between godly conformity and separation was as narrow as a ditch and as wide as the Rubicon. It is not therefore surprising to find both a two-way traffic and a number of pilgrims forever hesitant on the shore. Did Barrow seek confirmation of his martyrdom from Cartwright, or was he perhaps willing to yield a submission to his mentor that pride forbade him to make to his persecutors? Was Cartwright unwilling to participate in silencing a sincere if misguided spirit, or did he repine at confronting a specimen of his handiwork? We cannot know. But the charge of acting against conscience—the severest condemnation known to Reformation Europe—lent particular asperity to the ongoing debate between Separatists and godly conformists. For the latter, to remain within an imperfect church despite the seductions of the conventicle *was* the duty of conscience, and separation a yielding to false temptation. Godly conformists often pointed to their labors in exposing Anabaptists and reconverting Separatists as proof of their loyalty to the national church, and complained of their scant thanks, not to say oppression at the hands of the hierarchy.[127] Petitioning for the right to be heard in the church, Josias Nichols declared that "we are all of one faith, one Babtisme, one bodie, one spirit . . . . We are ministers of the word by one order, we administer praiers and sacraments by one form: we preach one faith and substance of doctrine."[128] To which Separatists would have replied, "Exactly."

Gathering the Churches

At the heart of the dispute between Separatists and conformists, and indeed of Reformed ecclesiology as such, was the question, What is a church? The revolt against Rome had meant a rejection of the idea of a universal visible church, for such a church could be maintained only by a priestly army that suppressed the Christian liberty proclaimed by the New Testament, silenced consciences, and imposed human (not to say Satanic) doctrines and ordinances on the purity of the Gospel. Such a church trampled not only on the Christian liberty of believers but on the civil authority of princes, usurping the powers and functions accorded the magistrate in Scripture. Challenged at length by those who labored to restore the Gospel, driven by God's grace from half of Christendom, the Roman Antichrist now sought to regain its dominion by the sword. Thus the spiritual tyranny of the universal church was made overt in the political tyranny of a universal monarchy headquartered in Spain but governed by Rome.[129]

If the universal church was a false model, or at any rate one not to be realized on a temporal level, what then was the appropriate scale and model of a true church? Luther had defined such a church as a company of believers preaching and worshiping in the purity of the Gospel; Calvin had further refined (but also mystified) this concept with his doctrine of election, which necessitated two churches, one the perfect, eternal, invisible company of the elect, gathered by the Father's inscrutable will, and the other its imperfect temporal counterpart, consisting of those whose testimony of faith and conduct of life might give assurance of sanctification. Calvinism thus strongly ruled out of court any concept of a universal visible church, since such a church could not contain the overtly reprobate. But Luther went even further at one point, declaring that "If I were the only one in the whole world who retained the word, I alone should be the Church and should rightly judge of the whole rest of the world that it was not the Church."[130] As Christ had once been the entirety of his church on earth, so the church could again exist fully in the faith of a single believer.

If a single believer could constitute a true visible church and a universal church was necessarily a false one, was there then an ideal size for a true church? an upper limitation? Such questions entailed others: how was such a church to be organized? how composed? how governed? These latter questions defined the subject of discipline. Finally, how were true churches to recognize and relate to one another? How were they to comport themselves within the social order, and what obedience did they owe the secular magistrate?

These questions were all intricately related. The permissible size of a true church, for example, was inseparable from the question of its institutions. The so-called magisterial reformers, beginning with Luther and Calvin, had recognized the validity of *Landeskirchen*, territorially organized churches typically instituted by secular rulers and notionally embracing all the inhabitants of a given area; the Church of England was one such, and (as conformists regularly pointed out) so recognized by its compeers. By this yardstick, the only upper limit of a true church was its ability to govern itself cohesively and the prince's ability to defend it. In practice, of course, most of the Reformed polity consisted of territorial churches; its continuance was as unthinkable without them as its inception would have been impossible but for them.

The problem of a true church constituted by a secular prince could be finessed with a Constantinian model; as we have seen, the ideal of a Christian emperor was a potent one. Even without such a model, it was possible to argue that God could make use of princes in establishing his church without empowering them over it, or that the faith of the just was constitutive of the church and the sword merely its instrument. It was more difficult, however, to deal with the problem of the reprobate. No visible church, however vigilant, could hope to be or remain wholly free of the reprobate, but the omnium-gatherum of a territorial church was almost by definition a tent of sinners, against which the Bible seemed (at least to the godly) very plainly to speak. It was one thing for hypocrites to deceive the righteous, but quite another to deliberately embrace the manifest "Atheists, Idolators, [and] Papistes" of Francis Johnson's description, not to mention the other "foule" representatives of every sort of crime, vice, and heresy. If such a church could be accounted true, then why should a universal church not only be considered a lawful assembly but a logical goal?

This issue exposed the central dilemma of Reformed theology: in a world radically divided between the church of the faithful and the empire of the profane, how were the latter to be governed? Luther's famous distinction between the spiritual world (inhabited only by the faithful) and the secular world (inhabited by the faithful and the profane alike) only posed the problem more starkly. If God had left the government of the secular world to princes and that of his church to the faithful, to which church did the reprobate belong? The commandments of the first table were no less binding on the profane than on the faithful, but if the former were to be conscientiously excluded from worship, how were these commandments to be executed?

Luther did not answer this question, but simply left two incompatible models—the true visible church, an egalitarian priesthood of believers, and the territorial church, a mixture of saints and sinners. In the first church, God's worship could be performed as commanded, but only by the few; in the second, the letter of his command could be kept, but the spirit was mocked. Even among the faithful the occasional hypocrite could not be excluded, but in the *Landeskirche* hypocrisy was the norm.[131]

Calvin posed the problem even more strongly than Luther in his distinction between the elect and the reprobate; his own solution, a theocratic state armed with powers not only of excommunication but of territorial expulsion, was obviously infeasible in a large commonwealth such as England. Essentially, then, the magisterial reformers could not reconcile their concept of a true church with the practical exigencies of sixteenth-century European society. If it were to be sufficiently comprehensive to meet the general require-

ment to observe the commandments of the first table it could not exclude the
profane multitude that could yield an at best formal obedience, and often
enough not even that. From a godly point of view, the territorial church thus
maintained a spurious order at the expense of true worship, substituting
homilies for preaching, rote formulae for prayer, and prelacy for congregational governance. Its chief concern was to avoid recusancy, whereas a true
church was voluntarily constituted, and its discipline concerned not with
compelling the profane to attend, but insuring that none such partook of the
sacraments.

Godly conformists in England tried to resolve the contradictions of a territorial church by reform and edification, hoping that the influence of a
preaching ministry would gradually instill a proper fear and respect in the
profane even as it kindled zeal in the elect. When these and the more aggressive hopes of Presbyterian insurrection were dashed, they migrated internally, seeking to cultivate self-selected devotional communities on the parish
level and thus to form de facto true churches in the interstices of episcopal
government. At the same time they adopted a federal covenant theology to
justify the overall validity of a national church. This muddled accommodation, implicitly supported by clerics such as Hutton and tolerated to a degree
by James I, was challenged by the Laudian regime in the 1630s.

Separatists scorned such shifts, of course, creating independent churches
in exile and, after 1616, in England itself again.[132] As for the reprobate, they
remanded them wholly to the secular arm. The effect—quite consciously intended—was to return to the primitive, pre-Constantinian condition of the
church, in which a minority of the Christian faithful lived civilly among the
heathen but religiously apart. They thus dealt with the problem of embracing a universal Christian community by denying that one existed. Sebaptists
such as John Smyth and Thomas Helwys took this a step further by denying
the validity of infant baptism, thus limiting the visible Christian community
to those who had demonstrated faith and perseverance. As separating ministers had renounced their ordination in the false Anglican church, so now
baptism as well—the very stipulation of one's membership in a Christian
community—was made conditional on the acceptance by others already received into the faith of one's spiritual commitment. The effect of this was to
sever the last link to the post-Constantinian church that, through baptism at
least, had formed an unbroken chain through the Roman church, its Anglican successor, and even the Separatist churches themselves.[133]

Smyth's and Helwys' fellow Separatists denounced their doctrine, which
required in Smyth's case the scandalous act of a self-baptism.[134] However, all
Separatist churches were agreed on the essential manner and requirement
for constituting a true church in accordance with Scripture and the best
primitive models. John Robinson's prescription is typical:

We . . . judg, that no particular church under the new Testament, ought to consist of more members, then can meet together in one place. . . . Now . . . the church (commonly called visible) is then most truly visible indeed, when it is assembled in one place; and the communion thereof then most full, and intire, when all its members inspired, as it were, with the same presence of the holy ghost, do from the same Pastor, receav the same provocations of grace, at the same time, and in the same place: when they all by the same voice, (*bending as it were together*), do with one accord pour out their prayers unto God: when they all *participate of one*, and the same holy *bread*, and lastly, when they all together consent unanimously, either in the choice of the same officer, or censuring of the same offender . . .[135]

Like his fellow Separatists, Robinson insisted that if all the churches of the world but one fell away, it would still remain "the true, & entire Church of Christ." By the same token, however, this one church could never be a universal one, or aspire to more than its proper boundaries:

If any object, that there is one visible, and catholick Church, comprehending as the parts thereof, all the particular Churches, and severall congregations of divers places; as there is one Ocean, or Sea, diversely called . . . I answer, First, that the Catholick church neither is, nor can be called visible: since onely things singular are visible, and discerned by sence: whereas universals, or things catholick, are either onely in the understanding, or as others think better, *are made such*, to wit universals, *by the understanding abstracting* from them *all circumstantial accidents, considering that the kindes intelligible have their existence in nature*, that is in the Individuals. . . . [Thus] the catholic church, which is said to comprehend al particular congregations in her bosom, is not gathered together into one place, nor ever shall be, before the glorious coming of Christ.[136]

Robinson invokes a radical nominalism to rebut the claim of a "universal" church, to wit one of any dimension that asserts the right of control over particular congregations, or the insufficiency of any such congregation to constitute an entire church. He does not deny the right of particular churches to associate on any mutually agreeable basis, including a territorial one, but only that they can be subject to any "subordination, or coordination, or dependencie spirituall" other than the direct lordship of Christ.[137]

The particular interest of Robinson's formulation lies in his emphasis on the absolute impermeability of the spiritual and temporal realms. In the former, truth exists in the unity of the invisible church, one and indivisible, predestined and immutable; in the latter, it is testified by singular and discrete entities that are "visible, and discerned by sence" alone. Each visible church is a jewel in the crown of Christ's kingdom, but none may see that crown in its splendor, let alone wear it, save Christ himself. This is precisely the seduction the Antichrist offers, and it is to combat it that Christian lib-

erty — the indefeasible right of voluntary spiritual association and the collateral exercise of the rights, privileges, and responsibilities of Christian worship — has been instituted. That liberty is exercised first and individually in
conscience, but collectively and visibly as worship. Robinson insists on the
literalness of this visibility, declaring that "no particular church under the
new Testament, ought to consist of more members, then can meet together in
one place."[138] Thus gathered, united in spirit and with "the same voice . . .
pour[ing] out their prayers unto God," they are a representation of the invisible church, an attestation, however impure and adulterated, of its eternal
grace and glory. What it is not in any sense is an actual part or manifestation
of that church. The spiritual and temporal realms of the church thus remain
wholly distinct, joined only by the common headship of Christ.

Christ's lordship in the church had other consequences in Separatist
thought as well. A true visible church arose when like-minded Christians
gathered together for worship. As they were called by no other power than
the quickening of the holy spirit within them, so they dared acknowledge no
binding ecclesiastical authority beyond the congregation in which that spirit
dwelled. Hence prelacy — the imposition of compulsory spiritual discipline
from any source outside the congregation — was intolerable, both as an infringement of the liberty granted by Christ to the faithful and as a usurpation of the immediate lordship of his spirit. From this it followed that any
prelatical church was a false one. Separatists thereby made the mark of discipline, a relatively late addition to the theological armament of the Reformation, the ultimate test of ecclesiastical legitimacy. One had only to look at
whether a church recognized a binding spiritual authority beyond the congregation to know whether it was false, or at any rate enthralled. A church
that passed this test was not necessarily a true one, for the rejection of external authority alone merely defined a conventicle, and it was necessary to establish the marks of preaching and sacramental administration for full certification. (For Separatist churches before 1640 there was an implicit fourth
mark as well, doctrinal orthodoxy.) But prelacy was the immediate and infallible sign of the beast. It was to no avail for the "forward preachers" of the
Anglican church to point to islands of godliness in the general sea of corruption. Where congregations had no liberty in the ordering of their affairs and
the exercise of their faith, and even the best pastors were hirelings, the best
preachers a step away from silencing or deprivation, how could the Word be
anything but mocked and debased?

The forward preachers were therefore not to be regarded as lights in the
church but as false beacons. They were more to be deplored than the mere
timeservers and worldlings, for by their pious pretenses they misled godly
laymen into believing themselves rightly ministered, and even into imagining themselves part of a spiritual elite elevated above the common level of

the church. This was all the more the case after 1604 when they gave up all serious challenge to the prelacy, and, under the shelter of lay patrons or by shifts such as lectureships and impropriations, they tried to emulate the form of gathered churches without their freedom. Thus, warned Henry Ainsworth, "the present ministerie reteyned & vsed in England . . . are a strange & Antichristian ministerie & offices; & are not that ministerie . . . instituted in Christs Testament, or allowed in or ouer his Church." He enjoined "all that will be saved" to fly the established church "with speed," leaving its offices to be dismantled, its wealth confiscated, and its reprobate remnant dispersed by the magistrate. As for its ministers:

> [B]oth all such as haue receyued or exercised anie of these false Offices or anie pretended function of Ministerie in or to this false and Antichristian constitution, are willingly in Gods feare, to giue over and leaue those vnlawfull Offices, and no longer to minister in this maner to these Assemblies in this estate. And that none also, of what sort or condition soever, doo giue anie part of their Goods, Lands, Money, or money['s] worth to the maintenance of this false Ministerie and worship vpon anie Commandement, or vnder anie colour whatsoeuer.[139]

Ainsworth would thus have the magistrate break up the existing prelatical order just as Henry VIII had broken up the papal one.[140] The seizure of its wealth and the ban on an involuntary maintenance of the ministry would prevent any hierarchical structure from arising again.

The latter question was of particular consequence, because it entailed a complete divorce of the material estate of the church from secular control and thus the impossiblity of a territorial or Erastian church. Reformed doctrine had insisted upon the spiritual autonomy of the church from the beginning, and Elizabeth insisted that the *potestas jurisdictionis* she assumed as supreme governor was in no way a *potestas ordinis* over divine offices. This distinction, however, was regularly and inevitably blurred in practice. Elizabeth penned one of the Thirty-Nine Articles herself and vetoed another; more to the point, her government was intimately involved with every aspect of the church's establishment—if, indeed, the bishops, whose legitimacy as church officers was challenged by Presbyterians within the church no less than by Separatists without, could be considered as anything other than crown agents themselves. The only way to avoid the hopeless confusion of secular and spiritual authority, in the Separatist view, was to cut the cash nexus at its focal point—the clerical tithe. Once the church had been made independent of both state and lay patronage and congregations had assumed their proper, scriptural responsibility for ministerial maintenance, the entire scaffolding of prelacy would collapse and spiritual autonomy would follow.

What relation would then remain between the magistrate and the church? In common with the magisterial reformers, the Separatists accorded the prince full power over temporal affairs, including the bodies and goods of the faithful. This included the repression of civil tumults within the church, the general protection of religion, and the extirpation of heresy and idolatry. Thus, according to Ainsworth:

> [I]t is the Office and duty of Princes and Magistrates . . . to suppress and root out by their authoritie all false ministeries, voluntarie Relligions [i.e., so-called will-worshippers such as the Familists] and counterfeyt worship of God, to abolish and destroy the Idoll Temples, Images, Altares, Vestments, and all other monuments of Idolatrie and superstition. . . . And on the other hand to establish & mayntein by their lawes every part of Gods word and his pure Relligion and true ministerie to cherish and protect all such as are carefull to worship God according to his word, and to leade a godly lyfe in all peace and loyalltie.[141]

The Separatists could then conclude, with the Presbyterian conformists, that a true reformation had been begun in England with the statutory demolition of the Roman church, an act that had restored both the Christian liberty of the faithful and the temporal prerogatives of the magistrate. They could agree as well that the establishment of a new clerical hierarchy had been a fateful error. Where they parted company was over the essential legitimacy of a territorial church. No visible church could aspire to perfection, but a church built on error and incapable of discipline was, in the Separatist view, neither tolerable in itself nor amenable to correction. It could only be renounced and abandoned.

The Separatists were convinced that they were obeying a higher law in refusing to consort with the established church, but they believed as well that they were upholding the rightful powers of magistracy and were therefore the more genuinely loyal to the prince. Far from imagining themselves as corporatively independent of temporal jurisdiction, they looked to the secular arm to "establish & mayntein" their churches, i.e., to recognize their civil status and protect them from the profane and wicked. They claimed no special exemption or privilege, but merely the right of free association such as might be granted to any lawful occupation or assembly. Since they claimed no authority beyond the particular congregation, and since such congregations were ideally no larger and in practice usually smaller than existing parish congregations, they could pose no threat to public order or compulsion to conscience. As Henry Jacob summed the matter up, "The Church government desired is more agreable to the state of a Monarchie, and to the Kings Supremacie in causes Ecclesiasticall, and more easie, and safe both for Church & Common wealth, then is the present government by Prelats."[142]

The Separatist position on magistracy failed to address three major issues, however. It did not explain what if any religious instruction was to be given to the reprobate, and what action (other than civil) was to be taken to repress their wickedness and idolatry. Since the reprobate were enjoined no less than the elect to observe the commandments of the first table, the absence of such instruction, together with the spiritual terrors and sanctions customarily applied to it, left the maintenance of order to the magistrate alone. It was for this reason that the Diet of Speyer had established as early as 1526 the principle of *cuius regio, eius religio* on which the territorial church was based. Manifestly, no godly ruler could tolerate the disorder of an unchurched population, and an ungodly one, not bound to belong to a particular congregation (or perhaps not accepted by one), might well establish heresy or even paganism.

A second issue concerned the suppression of false churches and idolatrous practices. Separatists and conformists alike affirmed the prince's responsibility to put down heresy, but whereas the territorial church had a single standard of orthodoxy promulgated by state authority, particular churches had confessions of faith. Even if a single confession were adopted it was binding only as long as voluntarily adhered to, so that the prince was put in the position of being obliged to enforce a code from which any congregation of his subjects could lawfully exempt itself.

Finally, the magistrate was charged, again in Jacob's words, "to take knowledge of, to punish, and redresse all misgoverning or ill teaching of any Church, or Church officer."[143] This was precisely what the Erastian church of England, with its system of superior orders and regular visitations, was designed to do. How such a charge could be effected without similar apparatus on the extremely decentralized level of congregational churches was far from clear. The exile churches in the Netherlands operated under the loose scrutiny of the secular authorities, but, like the Huguenot churches in England, were essentially left to their own devices as long as they did not disturb the public order.[144] Such an arrangement would seem to have been as close to ideal as a particular church could wish, and an appeal to the Huguenot model was occasionally made. But the Separatists were unable to renounce the godly magistrate any more than Erastian conformists were. As long as they adhered to a doctrinaire Calvinism that divided the world between the embattled warriors of Christ and the reprobate hosts of Antichrist, they could not dispense with the magistrate as the final barrier to apostasy. Only when John Smyth and the General Baptists broke with the concept of election were a small group of them (denounced and isolated by the rest) able to conceive the function of the magistrate in strictly civil terms.[145]

The rejection of external hierarchy and the insistence on congregational autonomy raised the problem of internal self-government for the Separatists, and particularly the relation between the pastor, the elders, and the congregation at large. At first it appeared to Reformers that church government could be assimilated to the Aristotelian model of a mixed polity. Peter Martyr Vermigli describes it in straightforwardly classical terms:

> It is not simple, but it is compounded of monarchy, aristocracy, and democracy. From it must be removed pernicious types of government, I mean tyranny, oligarchy, and corrupt domination of the people. If you respect Christ, it is called a monarchy, for He is our king who acquireth the Church for himself with his own blood. He is now in heaven, yet rules this kingdom of his, not with a visible presence, but by the spirit and word of holy scriptures. And there are in the church to execute this office for Him, Bishops, Presbyters, Doctors, and others who rule, in respect of whom it may justly be called an aristocracy. For they who are preferred to the government of churches, because of excellent gifts of God in doctrine and purity of life, must be promoted to these positions. . . . But because in the Church there are matters of very great weight and importance referred to the people (as appears in the Acts of the Apostles), it has an element of polity. But of the most weight are accounted excommunication, absolution, choice of ministers and the like, so it must be concluded that no man can be excommunicated without the consent of the Church.[146]

Vermigli's account was superficially congruent with Sir Thomas Smith's characterization of England as a mixed civil polity consisting of king, lords, and commons.[147] His analogy glossed over fundamental differences, however. As Paul Avis has noted, the essential achievement of Reformed theology was to reinstate the Christological center of the church. Christ's rule over it was conceived as a direct, immediate, and personal rule over each and every one of the faithful through the continuous mediation of his word and spirit. The legitimating source and activating power of the church was the grace that inhered in individual members and whose collective expression it was; hence the concept of the "lively stones" that composed the temple. In Weberian terms, Christ's lordship in the church represented the absolutization of charisma; no more particular and individual a relation between leader and follower could be imagined, nor any application of power at the same time so exalted and so intimate. This relation was not translatable into the secular bond between ruler and subject. Although rulers were generally acknowledged to possess a life-and-death authority over their subjects in all things within the secular sphere save conscience (including all civil aspects of the church), they possessed this authority only by commission and exercised it through established law and custom. Christ, on the other hand, was the supreme lawgiver, the lord of conscience and searcher of hearts. Princes might be likened to Old Testament figures and even "gods" as in the Psalmist verse, but no one would have dreamt of comparing them to any Gospel figure, let alone to him who was the lord and savior of all. Moreover, though the elements of the mixed Aristotelian polity might degenerate into their "pernicious" antitypes and the best of princes be succeeded by the worst of tyrants, the lordship of Christ was perpetual and incorruptible, the guarantor of the church's perpetual estate on earth as of its eternal presence in heaven.

If Vermigli's analogy between secular monarchy and divine lordship was untenable, that between the subject and the faithful was flawed as well. The subject's role was ideally one of passive submission to authority, garnished with suitable displays of gratitude and loyalty. Such displays, as we have seen, were in fact crucial to sustaining legitimacy, but theory at least required that they be ritualized and conventionalized lest any suggestion of voluntarism be introduced into the established mechanisms of consent. But it was precisely an active consent, not to say a partnership, that was required of the faithful congregant; mere submission, the rote performance of required duties and ceremonies, could never suffice. No figure was more repeatedly pilloried than the formal Christian or the "cold professor," and not in godly sermons alone. If conformity were defined simply as the observance of the prescribed norms of Christian worship and behavior then external compliance might satisfy the magistrate, but no ministry could remain content with such a standard, for that way lay idolatry, salvation through works, and the universalist claims of Rome. "God," said the Oxford minister Sampson Price, ". . . cannot endure a Neuter," admonishing his Paul's Cross audience to "Be eyther a whole Protestant or [a] Papist."[148]

The need for active and reciprocal participation in the work of grace was at the heart of covenant theology. God's promise of salvation was indefeasible, but the elect might know themselves only by the inner experience of faith and the outward expression of a godly and zealous life. Such tokens or assurances of election were, however, indicative rather than prescriptive, since faith, although it could never fail "utterly" in the elect, might be temporarily eclipsed, and sin was ineradicable in the fallen state of humankind. Godliness was therefore a perpetual struggle against doubt and temptation, and since it had pleased God to withhold unshakable assurance (that the elect might not wax proud and the reprobate despair), this struggle was integral to his covenant. Historians have somewhat misleadingly termed the reciprocal interaction between God and man in the work of grace the conditional covenant, for grace itself was unconditional and irrevocable, and the performance of one's duties could neither add to nor detract from it.[149] Rather, the knowledge of grace was communicated in such a way as to entail this performance as a means of signifying to oneself and others its presence and action, and the godly community was composed of those whose significations were accepted as valid. On both a sacramental and social level, the legitimation of the self was thus the first (and continuous) task of the faithful Christian. In contrast, one's status as a political subject was objectively given, and the performance of one's secular duties carried no burden of personal validation.

The "conditional" covenant had particular appeal to the Separatists, linking as it did personal election, the godly community, and the visible church in a chain of praxis. As the godly community was revealed by the mutual signification of its members, so the church was constituted by the free association of that community in worship. The church, then, as the sum of its sanctified members, was collectively in covenant with the Lord as each congregant was individually, and its work—the work of edification and praise—was entailed just as was the individual congregant's personal work of Christian striving and obedience. The reciprocity between congregant and church, symbolized by the increasingly elaborate tests for admission that characterized the Separated churches, mirrored the covenant between God and the individual. One's personal labor of righteousness and one's work for the church became, to all intents and purposes, virtually indistinguishable, the one subsumed in the other. Under such circumstances it was inconceivable that righteous conduct, though voluntary, was not as obligatory as legal observance had been under the Old Testament. Henry Barrow, responding from his prison cell to the conformist cleric George Gifford, regarded it as absurd that "the Lord plights his love to us, and requires not again our faith and obedience unto him in the same covenant. Let Mr. Gifford show one place of Scripture through the whole Bible where the Lord made his covenant unto us without this condition."[150]

In sum, as the analogy between the prince's rule over the civil order and Christ's rule over the church failed, so did that between the subject and the faithful church member. The duty of the subject was passive (a response to command) and limited (by positive law). The duty of the church member was self-activated (by conscience) and unlimited (except by zeal). The ruler who imposed inordinate or extralegal duties was apt to be seen as a tyrant, and though the extent to which (and by whom) he might be resisted remained an open question, his behavior was regarded as damnable by no less an authority than James I. Christ's rule, no matter how demanding, was mild and easy, and obedience brought only benefit and reward.

The unique, personal, and immediate relationship between the individual congregant and Christ made the position of Vermigli's "aristocracy"—the officers of the church—even more problematic. The Elizabethan Homily on Obedience taught that all superiors (including, *qua* civil servants, church officers) were to be reverenced and obeyed, but a gathered church might exist for some time without officers, and even, as some held, administer the sacraments in their absence. More importantly, the ministerial powers of the church resided in the congregation at large, for Christ had delegated these powers to the whole. Again, a secular parallel suggested itself, for according to classical theory political power had originally resided in the people and had only by express grant been vested in rulers. Once more, however, the analogy broke down, for ministerial powers were only delegated, not granted or alienated. Church officers possessed no title or property in office, nor any independent power of discipline; excommunication, the ultimate sanction, could only be applied by the entire congregation.

This brought the Separatists to their central dilemma. The logic of their position compelled them to elevate discipline as the central mark of a true church, for the other marks could be found or at least simulated in false churches, but only discipline could keep them from being corrupted and hence guarantee their validity and efficacy. As Brooks Holifield has pointed out, the gradual attenuation of the Reformed emphasis on word and sacrament was part of a long-range trend in covenantal theology, and as John Cook, the Civil War Independent and prosecutor of the regicide court was ultimately to conclude, "the Word and Sacraments" were not "the constitution of a Church."[151] But no other late sixteenth- or early seventeenth-century group, at least none nominally within the Calvinist fold, simultaneously placed so much emphasis on both discipline and Christian liberty. If discipline were to be exercised through the officers of the church as prescribed in Scripture and yet the congregation were to remain fully empowered, where did actual authority reside, and how was order to be kept? The problem of reconciling the liberty of the godly congregation with the responsibilities of the ministry was common to separating and nonseparating theologians alike, but the latter had grappled with it as a practical matter only during the Presbyterian campaign of the 1580s, and even then from under the shelter of the established church. The one attempt at a unified statement by Cartwright, Travers, and the rest of the Presbyterian leadership, the *Book of Discipline*, was long bruited and in the end so vaguely worded that, as Collinson notes, it was little more than a "flexible constitution which might be variously interpreted by a dictatorial pastor, a determined eldership, a vigorous *classis* or a rebellious congregation."[152]

In contrast, each Separatist congregation faced the necessity for actual accommodation. The travails of the Ancient Church of Amsterdam, as its sobriquet implies the eldest of the exile congregations in that city, are illustrative. Gathered by Francis Johnson in 1592 from the remnants of the London Barrow-Greenwood congregation, it migrated to Amsterdam the following year and lived precariously until Johnson, who had been imprisoned, was able to rejoin it in 1597. The congregation had by then fallen to perhaps as few as forty members, who divided into two factions that excommunicated each other. With Johnson's return the rift was healed, and the reunited church so prospered that its membership had grown to between three and four hundred within a decade, and it was wealthy enough to build its own church. Nonetheless, internal strife continued. Johnson was bitterly opposed by his own brother George, who after his excommunication in 1599 waged a pamphlet war against his former brethren. The Johnsons' father, John, who tried to reconcile the two brothers, was expelled in turn by the congregation for his pains. There were charges of philandering and apostasy against some of the church's officers, and of embezzlement against its deacon.

Henry Ainsworth, the church's well-regarded teacher, was caught in the middle of these unseemly disputes. His appointment by the congregation had preceded Francis Johnson's return in 1597, and Johnson immediately suspended his practice of private catechizing. The two men continued to collaborate, however, despite the increasingly authoritarian cast of Johnson's pastorate and his reliance on a controversial elder of similar views, Daniel Studley, until a final schism occurred late in 1610. Ainsworth and his party formed a new congregation and won control of the church building, whereupon Johnson and his followers relocated in Emden.[153]

While Ainsworth was still in fellowship with Johnson he published his magnum opus, *The Communion of Saincts*, as well as *A Defense of the Holy Scriptures, Worship, and Ministerie* (1609), a treatise against John Smyth. Both works reveal a man searching for middle ground between Johnson's ministerially centered ecclesiology and Smyth's radical populism. Ainsworth affirmed the importance of church officers in ministering to the faithful; they were not only "Lords over Gods heritage, but the administers of his graces and blessings among them, and ensamples to the flock; not having dominion over their faith, but helpers of their joy." *The Communion of Saincts* emphasized that the saints were all spiritual equals though their gifts or station might vary, for even "the governours & great men of the earth," if admitted to fellowship, were to have "no haughty harts nor lofty eyes" but to be taught like "weyned children." The church offices themselves remained a collective possession in which the faithful had "fellowship togither" and which they could still actively exercise even after the choice of particular officers, for all men, Ainsworth declared, "hav not onely libertie, but ar exhortted to desire that they may prophesie."[154]

Ainsworth's practical and philosophical differences with Johnson were stark, for the latter regarded church offices and functions as exclusively devolved upon their particular occupants, a view he expressed clearly after the schism of 1610 in a commentary on Matthew 18: 17.[155] For Ainsworth, on the other hand, Christian liberty was inalienable, and officers were the servants of the congregation:

> As the Saincts have al a right & interest in the covenant of God, & seales of the same, wherein they have and hold communion togither: so have and doe they also, in al other Christian spiritual duties, publick or private. . . . The churches in the Apostles dayes had also the like right & libertie; for the

multitudes of beleevers, wer both beholders & actors in the commune af-
fayres, as at the choise & ordination of church-officers, at the deciding of
questions & controversies; at the excommunication or casting out of im-
penitent synners . . . and generally in the publick communion and fellowship of the Apostles, & of one another.[156]

After being attacked in John Smyth's *Paralleles, Censures, Observations* for
preaching "a new kind of Antichristianisme," however, Ainsworth took a far
more conservative line. Smyth's objection was not to *The Communion of
Saincts* but to Ainsworth's *Counterpoyson*, in which he had proclaimed the
mission of the elders to "teach and rule" the church according to Christ's
laws. This, said Smyth, was mere prelacy, since only Christ could rule the
church. Ainsworth in turn chastised Smyth for attempting to "sophisticate
and dally" with the word "rule," as if every application of discipline were an
exercise in sovereignty. Church officers differed precisely from secular rulers
in that their "ministerial power and authority . . . to feed, rule, govern . . .
and direct" the church was delegated directly from Christ. It was absurd to
suggest that such power was thereby less than fully efficacious, or subject to
the overriding authority of the church body itself: "no scripture intendeth to
teach that eyther minister or member, must yeeld to the voice of the multitude, in every thing they lyst." God "hath caled us in peace" to the church,
Ainsworth declared, and it was therefore a mere "contentious humour, to
obiect, that [the officers] have not power to rule contrary to the peoples liking." Their position was analogous to that of lower magistrates in the temporal order, "For as in civil government we are to obey and submit, not onely
to the King as unto the superior, but also to the governours that are sent of
him: so in government ecclesiastical we are to obey and submit, not onely to
the King Christ, but to the Elders his ministers sent of him."[157]

In returning to the secular analogy of Vermigli and Cartwright under the
pressure of Smyth's attack, Ainsworth implicitly repudiated the notion of a
self-governing congregation. Yet he could not dispense with the cardinal
principle of Separatist ecclesiology—the unqualified right of the congregation in the election and expulsion of officers—without abandoning the chief
point of difference with the established church, and returning to prelacy. The
analogy between church officers and the lesser magistrates raised another
problem as well, for although both derived their ultimate authority from
their respective "kings," the former were popularly elected and hence popularly accountable, while the latter (in general) were not. Ainsworth tried to
finesse this point by suggesting that congregants were inspired by the holy
spirit in electing their officers.[158] This argument made little headway, however, for if congregants were so guided in choosing officers, must they not be
similarly guided in expelling them? In the end, Ainsworth was thrown back
on a conception of congregational authority in which the political equality of

the saints existed only until they had chosen "Elders and shepherds" to govern them, or rather recognized their superiors through the infusion of grace. Authority was thus wholly separated from governance. Ainsworth was, to be sure, aware of the potential for clerical abuse inherent in this position, but he was unable to resolve it:

> Christian liberty (which all have) is one thing, the raynes of government (which some have) is another thing. Now how farr the peoples right and liberty & benefit therby extendeth, would require a large discourse to shew; which is not my purpose here.[159]

Ainsworth never provided such a discourse, needless to say. Like Travers, Cartwright, or for that matter Whitgift, he could not imagine a truly nonhierarchical self-government, "for if the multitude govern, then who shal be governed?"[160]

Grace and Government

Ainsworth was not alone in his perplexity. No Calvinist thinker was able to resolve the tension between the perfect pattern of an eternal, invisible church and the imperfect realization of a temporal, visible one. The certainty that the elect were in the world at any given moment and the task laid upon them to build and attest the church created a distinctive community and government. The fact that the elect could not be indubitably known and that sin remained the universal lot of humankind meant that discipline and authority were essential to the church's constitution. This authority was perpetually derived from the body of the church (and not merely originally, as with the civil authority derived from the body of the commonwealth), exercised on its behalf, and revocable at its pleasure. In short, it required continuous affirmation and consent, a consent that pertained to particular congregants as well as to the entire church. The crux of the problem of Calvinist order was that the individual church member could not be coerced, for free consent was the essence of membership, while authority could not be made dependent on voluntarism. This in turn reflected a conception of the church as a body in part utopian and in part this-worldly. It was utopian in the sense of being an enterprise that aimed through edification toward perfection, and this-worldly in that it remained corrupt in its inevitable portion of reprobation and sin. David Little has captured well this aspect of Calvin's thought:

> The very tension observed [in] Calvin—between the old order (the order of coercion and necessity with its provisional forms of control) and the new order (the harmonious order of free, voluntary obedience)—is also present in the Church, albeit in a modified way. Because Christ reigns in Word, sacrament, and Spirit in the Church, the old order is decisively broken there and the new is beginning. Therefore, the hallmark of the old order, coer-

cion, is by definition excluded from it. But there remain these special and temporary forms of control within the church, because the community of wills cannot yet be trusted: it still has a long way to go.[161]

Little goes on to suggest that the wills of the elect may be regarded as "partially" redeemed or sanctified, and that therefore they may be ruled within the church with only "partial" force, i.e., a force that "stops short of actual coercion."[162] Both of these conditions are a little difficult to imagine. Ideally, the church member would freely reverence the officers for their gifts and station, and by such homage be drawn toward voluntary obedience. The least aspect of compulsion, however, might destroy this relation; thus the godly conformist Edward Dering would affirm that church officers were "worthy of double honour . . . singular love . . . [and] great reverence," while at the same time cautioning that "I dare by no means make them lords in the ministry."[163]

The dispute over the relative authority of officer and congregation thus oscillated between the Scylla of prelacy and the Charybdis of anarchy. The rights and powers of church membership were carefully circumscribed within the body of the entire congregation even by those who most forcefully stressed the inalienability of Christian liberty. Thus, John Smyth:

> Wee say Christs ruling powre is originally & fundamentally in the body of the Church the multitude. . . . We maintaine that the powre of the Eldership is a leading, directing, & overseeing powre, ministery, or service, both in the Kingdom & Preisthood of the Church, & that the negative voice, the last, definitive, determining sentence is in the body of the Church, wherto the Eldership is bound to yeeld: & that the Church may do any lawful act without the Elders: but the Elders can do nothing without the approbation of the body, or contrary to the body.[164]

Smyth's argument is wrapped firmly in the organic analogy; power resides in the body and is inseparable from it. If the officers, for all their "leading, directing & overseeing powre," are still subordinate to the body of the church, then a fortiori the individual congregant must be as well. The practical difficulty this poses is how the "body" is to act without a procedure for initiative (and how far even such a procedure can constrain individual conscience).

The glimmer of a solution—but one that would explode all concept of hierarchy in the church, and the Calvinist theology that encased it—is suggested in Smyth's comment that "the Church may do any lawful act without the Elders." The "lawful" acts of Reformed church polity were, of course, preaching, prophesying, and the administration of the sacraments. Calvinists on the right, whether conformist or Separatist, insisted that these acts could be performed only by a ministry. Ainsworth, as we have seen, was willing to admit prophesying in informal settings, but he was adamant that the seals could only be administered by the minister.[165]

When John Smyth baptized himself, thus acting out Luther's suggestion that even one man could (in both senses of the word) constitute a church, he created a radically different kind of church polity. No Reformed doctrine, other than that of justification by faith, was more critical than that of *extra ecclesiam nulla solus*—no salvation outside the church. The doctrine of election brought this into sharp focus, because although church membership was the prime duty of the elect, election itself was not dependent on it. The bridge between the saint and the church (other than the recognition of his duty and the comfort of fellowship) was the need for assurance. Lest perfect assurance obviate the felt necessity for communion, the saint's consciousness of his unworthiness as a sinner (far keener than in the reprobate) compelled him to seek confirmation in the approbation of others; this mechanism constituted the ground of the church. As the formal seal of admission into the fellowship of a church, baptism was critical for the believer; but as the token of the unbroken continuity of Christ's reign on earth it was no less critical for the church. For this reason most Reformers were insistent on the validity of infant baptism even if performed in false churches, since virtually all baptisms prior to the Reformation had been carried out under one or both of those circumstances. On this point Francis Johnson was no less tenacious than John Whitgift.

In baptizing himself—probably in late 1608 or early 1609—Smyth therefore challenged very fundamental assumptions about the nature of a visible church and the authority of its ministers.[166] Smyth did not deny the validity of believers' baptism even at the hands of a false church, but only because the nature of the ritual was irrelevant; what counted was the believer's profession of faith as a Christian. If that profession could be made under the aegis of a false church, then certainly it could be better made by the believer himself. What resulted was, to be sure, a personal covenant rather than a church, but this only emphasized the fact that a visible church was the sum of the individual covenants that comprised it. When, therefore, Smyth spoke of "the body of the Church the multitude," he was not confusing the distinction Ainsworth and others had made between the church as a corporate body and the multitude as its membership severally considered, but insisting on their inseparability. If the church as a whole contained the "powre of Christ," it was only because each of its believing members possessed that power in propria persona. The church did not and could not enjoy any power separate from that of its members any more than it possessed an existence apart from them—another example of the nominalism at the heart of radical Protestant thought.

Smyth was not, of course, offering himself as the foundation of a church. He was already the leader of a congregation of some 150 souls; what his self-baptism was intended to show was the power of Christ that inhered in each of its members. The result, however, was to divide the congregation, over half of whom defected.

Smyth's smaller flock doubtless made it easier for him to institute changes in the ministry itself. He now believed that the several activities described in Scripture—pastor, teacher, and elder—were not offices but merely functions, which could be combined in a single person or distributed indifferently among several. This meant that formal preaching could be dispensed with in favor of mutual prophesying. The result is well described in the account of two congregants:

> We begin with a prayer; after read some one or two chapters of the Bible, give the sense thereof, and confer upon the same: that done, we lay aside our books, and after a solemn prayer made by the first speaker, he propoundeth some text out of the Scripture, and prophesieth out of the same by the space of one hour or three quarters of an hour. After him standeth up a second speaker, and prophesieth out of the said text, the like time and place, sometimes more, sometimes less. After him the third, the fourth, the fifth, etc., as the time will give leave. Then the first speaker concludeth with prayer as he began with prayer, with an exhortation to contribution to the poor, which collection being made, is also concluded with prayer. This morning exercise beginneth at eight of the clock and continueth unto twelve of the clock. The like course and exercise is observed in the afternoon from two of the clock unto five or six of the clock. Last of all, the execution of the government of the Church is handled.[167]

Smyth's church was now ready for its final break with the Genevan Reformed model: the doctrine of predestination itself. Scholars have conjectured about the possible or probable influence of neighboring Anabaptist congregations on Smyth's group. But much of the polemical energy of the Separatist churches had been spent rebutting conformist charges of Anabaptism, and much of their identity was staked on their faithfulness to the principle of election and the ecclesiological principles it entailed. Like many deviant groups, they justified themselves on the basis of their superior devotion to the core ideology of the larger body from which they derived. Nor is there evidence that Smyth, a wholly orthodox Calvinist up to this point, had been influenced by the proto-Arminian stirrings in the Church of England, or the free grace controversy that was about to break out in the Dutch Reformed Church under the aegis of Arminius himself.[168]

We must search then for the abrupt change in Smyth's views in the particular circumstances of his church. Certainly the impact of his self-baptism and the consequent schism of his congregation must have heightened the sense of a unique mission in the remnant, while at the same time breaking down a significant barrier with the Anabaptists. But when Smyth decided that the Mennonites had after all been a true church and sought to unite with them, a small group led by Thomas Helwys seceded. Both Smyth and Helwys continued to adhere to similar views of free grace, however, suggesting again that the Anabaptists had not been the catalyst for their abandonment of Calvinist dogma.

We are left with ecclesiology. The doctrine of election did not entail a specific order of church government, but Calvin's emphasis on the ministry suggested the powerful affinity between the invisible hierarchy of the elect and the manifest authority of the presbytery. Moreover, the fact that even the most severely winnowed church (let alone territorial ones) inevitably contained the reprobate suggested the perils of an unrestrained populism. The elite in the church kept the order that existed spontaneously in the heavenly company of the elect.

By absorbing the functions of the ministry into the body of the congregation and reconfiguring the service as a communal, egalitarian exercise, the Smyth church created a powerful psychological incentive toward group inclusiveness and cohesion. It tended also to reduce the scriptural fetishism toward which more orthodox godly worship was inclined. The congregants laid aside their bibles after the initial prayers and discussions, and relied upon the motions of the spirit. The freeing of the spirit through the grace of the Word was therefore the goal of divine service. As Smyth had written even in his pre-Baptist phase, "the ceremony of bookworship, or the ministerie of the letter was now exspired, and finished."[169] Edification no longer proceeded downward from the pulpit but upward in the form of inspiration and praise. No gift was to be despised, and no testimony could fail. How, then, was it to be believed that with such evidences of grace ultimate salvation might yet be denied?

Smyth did not live long enough to propound his new beliefs systematically, but Thomas Helwys did. Helwys argued that from the initial "misterie of iniquitie"—the presumption to read the thoughts of God and to make him the author of sin—came all the monstrous errors of predestinarian theology: that infants were damned; that Christ's sacrifice was not efficacious for all; that some might be secure in salvation while others were left to "dispare vtterly." Even "faith in praying for one another is overthrowne," Helwys said, "for how can a man off faith pray for any man, when hee cannot knowe, whether God have decreed him to condemnation, & so he pray against Gods decree."[170]

Helwys and his small band returned to England in about 1612, declaring that they would no longer flee persecution but would sacrifice themselves, if need be, "for Christ and his truth" in their own native land. Perhaps for this reason, Helwys' writings apparently went unanswered in the Netherlands, but when his successor, John Murton, defended the Arminian position at the Synod of Dort in *A Description of What God Hath Predestinated Concerning Man* (1620), he drew stinging rebukes from Henry Ainsworth and John Robinson.[171] In good scholastic fashion, Ainsworth distinguished between "naturall" and "moral" actions; the latter alone reflected God's will, while the former were merely permitted by him. Thus, he concluded, "sinne is suffered of God, not done by him, nor decreed, willed, commanded, much less compelled."[172] Similarly, Christ's sacrifice was intended for all, though not accepted by all.

For orthodox Separatists, the Baptist secession was a cautionary tale of how doctrine was inevitably corrupted once discipline was relaxed.[173] True discipline rejected both prelacy and parity, but sought the golden mean between them. Only by such a mean might the visible church of Christ be preserved. Prelacy, the evil from which the Separatists had fled, led to false churches, but parity, if followed to its logical conclusion, would result in no church at all. This problem was much on the mind of an ailing Henry Ainsworth as he delivered his last sermon to his congregation in 1622. The first duty of a Christian, he told them, was to receive the inward call of the Spirit, but the second was to heed the outward call of the Word preached and to gather together under Christ's government, for it was "not lawfull for Christians to wander in the world or to live alone," thinking to enjoy a private grace or to content themselves with "personall good." Christianity could be fulfilled only in the church.[174]

On the whole, then, what distinguished most of the Separatist congregations from the godly conformists who remained in the Church of England was neither ecclesiology nor soteriology but the fact of separation itself. The description of "English Puritanisme" given by the godly conformist William Bradshaw might well have been taken from the platform of any Separatist church: "that the word of God . . . is the sole Canon and rule of all matters of Religion . . . that every Companie, Congregation or Assemblie of true beleevers, joyning together according to the order of the Gospell . . . is a true *visible Church* . . . that Christ Jesus hath not subjected any Church or Congregation of his, to any other Superiour Ecclesiasticall Jurisdiction then unto that which is within it selfe."[175] Similarly, the mainstream Separatist leaders—Ainsworth, Jacob, Jessey, Johnson, Robinson—remained, as we have seen, as rigorously Calvinist in their soteriology as their conformist brethren, and as vigilant against heresy, if not more so. Arminianism had indeed a fairer field in the Church of England even during the heyday of Calvinism portrayed in Collinson's *The Religion of Protestants* than in the embattled congregations of the Separation. If the rationale for abandoning the national church was to realize a greater purity of godly practice and belief, the stakes of success or failure were vastly higher than for a parish congregation. Only General Baptists left the Calvinist fold, and as Arminianism appeared to gain ascendancy in the Laudian church, the Separatists could taste their vindication at last.

If the Baptists were the exception that proved the Separatist rule, however, they were also of course the harbingers of the Civil War Independents. Once returned to England their numbers grew, perhaps to 150 by the early 1620s, and in addition to their principal church in London they established congregations in Lincoln, Sarum, Coventry, and Tiverton. Here too they worked out the other major positions that were to characterize the Independent model: the complete divorce of church from state and its logical corollary, religious toleration.

These positions did not necessarily flow from a theology of free grace, but certainly they were facilitated by it. If salvific grace were available to all, then one of two consequences followed: either the primary responsibility for receiving that grace must reside in the individual, or corporately in the church. Since the Baptists had rejected the corporate concept of salvation, they were thrown back on a praxis of conscience. This did not mean that Christians were to be "wanderers," but, together with the requirement of adult baptism for church membership, it did mean that they might well sojourn for awhile before finding their community of belief. The Christian was in short no longer defined by his church but by his profession of faith; as Leonard Busher asserted, "all those *that confess*, freely, without compulsion, *that Jesus is the Messiah*, the Lord, *and that he came in the flesh*, are to be esteemed the children of God, and true Christians."[176]

The Baptist emphasis on the individual Christian quest, coupled with the availability of grace for all, militated against any interference with religious practice by the magistrate. As Thomas Helwys and John Murton argued, the ordinances of the New Testament were to be enforced only through faith, for Christ had given "no carnal or worldly weapon . . . to the supportation of his kingdom."[177] The principle of believer's baptism made any notion of universal church membership void; as Busher noted, the mere fact of a state church was "a great sign" that its officers were "none of Christ's bishops and ministers."[178] Since conscience could not be compelled, however conformity might be enforced, the result of a compulsory church was to build Babel, for those who attended it necessarily brought their differing religious conceptions with them "as well as their bodies." Indeed, Busher said, to force tender consciences was "a greater sin" than physical rape.[179] Like consciences alone could worship in truth, and only by voluntary association could they find one another.

In short, the magistrate had no jurisdiction over conscience. But what raised this theological commonplace to a revolutionary principle was the

Baptist notion of conscience as a radically autonomous sphere. Conformist divines too described conscience as the site of encounter between the soul and God, but they emphasized the importance of instruction and guidance by qualified authorities, and the pastoring of conscience was regarded, particularly by the godly, as a critical task of the ministry. The more radical disjunction in Ainsworth between the inner call of faith in the elect and the outer call of preaching to congregational association suggested, however, the separation of the two processes, with the latter wholly dependent on the prior accomplishment of the former.

This had profound implications. The search for justifying faith and personal assurance, raised to such a fine art in godly culture, led necessarily to an intense (and potentially morbid) preoccupation with conscience. The considerable early seventeenth-century literature on the subject, as well as the vivid culinary and medical metaphors applied to various conditions of conscience ("tender," "seared," "burnt," "scarred," etc.) indicate how important a branch of practical divinity it had become. Ministers skilled in resolving cases of conscience were sought far and wide, and their clients, as Richard Baxter attests, included their fellow clergy. Keith Thomas has not exaggerated in calling the period "the Age of Conscience,"[180] and if the revolutionary *années* of 1640–1660 can be considered the crisis of early modern legitimacy they represent no less a crisis of conscience—the moment at which individual conscience was exposed as never before and perhaps never since to the terrible consequences of choice.

The casuistry of conscience was by no means limited to the godly, of course; as we have seen, it was crucial to the retrieval of the Catholic interest in England, and even the most casual reader of Andrewes, Donne, and Herbert will readily appreciate its centrality to Anglican divinity as well. Common to all clerical representatives of established churches was the conviction that conscience was, as it were, far too important to be left to the individual, however final the individual's responsibility for it must be. Without proper management, there was no restraint on the folly, delusion, and wickedness to which a deceived conscience might be led, and no limit to the possible consequences for church and state. Above all, it was essential for all to understand that conscience could never be a license to disobedience; one of the most commonly cited passages in Scripture was Romans 13.5, that obedience was owed to the magistrate "for conscience sake." Since at the same time, however, it was equally the case that conscience could not be forced and that the gravest of all sins was to act against it, a certain latitude was necessarily reserved to it. Among Catholics it was the cognizance of a vocation that might lead to sainthood or the founding of an order; in the Reformed tradition—itself founded on an act of conscience—it was the impulse to special piety and zeal, or even the direct experience of divine revelation. As often as ministers might caution that the apostolic age was past and that miracles or other extraordinary communications might no longer be expected,[181] the possibility of further revelation could not be denied. This made proper examination by competent authorities all the more crucial; thus, as William Perkins remarked, God "may sometime . . . reveal His purpose . . . to some His selected servants: yet provided that the revelation be examined and allowed of the Church."[182]

Perkins' comment underscored the importance of ministerial discipline in the church, a concern that linked Erastians, godly conformists, and the more conservative Separatists, however much they might differ on the precise instrumentality by which that discipline was exercised. It explains as well why these groups also agreed on the ultimate responsibility of the magistrate to maintain order in the church, suppress heresy, and require that the word of God be heard by all, again despite their differences as to when and how the magistrate was to act. As William Ames, a nonseparating congregationalist and the principal early seventeenth-century authority on conscience, noted emphatically:

> [T]here is no thing, person or cause ecclesiastical, but in some respects it may pertain to the jurisdiction of the Magistrates, neither is there any action so secular so it be done by a member of the Church, but so far as it respects obedience to God, it may pertain to the taking notice of by the Church.[183]

Here precisely was where the Baptists parted company with the entire spectrum of organized Reformed opinion. By dissolving ministerial authority in the congregation, they removed pastoral controls over conscience; at the same time, they severed the relationship between minister and magistrate—explicit in the territorial churches, implicit in the gathered ones—which had linked church and state in an ultimate bond of union, a single concept of order. For the Baptists, the two realms were now juridically separate.

The logic of their position moved the Baptists inexorably toward the demand for general toleration. Once religious conviction had become exclusively a matter of adult conscience and given the premise that conscience could not be forced, it followed that secular coercion could not be applied to any matter of doctrine or practice. This meant that the distinction between true churches that the magistrate was bound to uphold and false ones he was obligated to suppress was necessarily abandoned, for although erroneous doctrine and idolatrous practice abounded, no one was licensed to pronounce authoritatively on them. The magistrate's role was simply to maintain the civil peace among rival faiths.

In *Certain Reasons Against Persecution*, Busher replied to the familiar objections that removing the magistrate's hand would lead to heresy and anarchy. Heresy, he argued, was fortified by suppression, since it took refuge in equivocation and hypocrisy, whereas exposure would destroy it. Thus, not only Protestants but Papists and Jews must have full freedom "to write, dispute, confer and reason, print and publish" on any point of religion and "for or against whomsoever,"[184] provided that they support their contentions only by reference to Scripture, the unique source of uncorrupted truth. This was, to be sure, a far narrower gauge than most controversialists employed, since it eliminated patristic and classical sources, not to mention canons and decretals. But *sola Scriptura* was a not unreasonable standard, since it was the only one accepted by all parties (including Jews, at least in part) as unimpeachable. It was also the readiest means to establish the full truth of the Gospel and thus to bring its blessings to fruition. Once that truth prevailed, all oppression and violence would cease: "[T]hen shall neither king, prince, nor people be destroyed for difference in religion. Then treason and rebellion, as well as burning, banishing, hanging, or imprisoning for difference in religion will cease and be laid down. Then shall not men, women, and youth be hanged for theft. Then shall not the poor, stranger, fatherless, and widows, be driven to beg from place to place; neither shall the lame, sick, and weak persons, suffer such misery and be forsaken of their kindred, as they now be. Then shall not murder, whoredom, and adultery, be brought out for money. Then shall not the great defraud and wrong the small; neither the rich oppress the poor by usury and little wages. . . . Then shall all men live in peace under their own vine, lauding and praising God, honouring and obeying the king."[185]

The Baptist plea for general toleration thus went well beyond the Separatist call for toleration of particular churches, or the hope of godly conformists for the unhindered exercise of piety and zeal in parochial congregations. By the same token, it was far closer to populist utopian traditions than to any modern concept of toleration. In post-Reformation Europe toleration could be justified by reason of state, as in the case of the Peace of Augsburg or the Edict of Nantes, or as a means of establishing the truth where human authority had obscured or distorted it; in neither case was it seen as a value in itself or as other than a means to an end. At best it could be viewed, from the latter standpoint, as a condition of truth, a freeing of conscience in its quest for perfect knowledge of God's transcendent will. Modern toleration, though it owes a debt to this Age of Conscience, derives primarily from the Pyrrhonist tradition that leads from Montaigne and the Enlightenment to such postmodern skeptics as Rorty. It stands in the ruins of truth.[186]

Familists and Freewillers

The Baptists were far from the first religious dissidents in England to reject infant baptism and proclaim free grace; they were merely the first secessionists from the Elizabethan church to do so. Much scholarly argument has passed as to whether or to what extent the Baptists were influenced by Anabaptist currents in the Netherlands, but Anabaptism had arrived in England itself long before, where it had joined the rich stream of native Lollardy. Similarly, antinomianism was espoused by a group of so-called Freewillers in the mid-sixteenth century. These and other wayward Protestant tendencies were largely absorbed into the Anglican establishment, though some persisted in underground congregations and other small knots of heresy. The most significant of these post-Elizabethan survivals was the Family of Love.

Recent scholars have emphasized the slow dissemination and incomplete absorption of Reformation principles among the lay population in England, and the point is well taken.[187] But the laity had its own reformation before the Reformation, a broad-based movement centered among weavers, clothiers, and merchants which generated its own biblical translation and commentaries, its own schools, and its own sodality.[188] This movement persisted as a powerful countercurrent to both the Roman and Henrician churches for a century and a half and flowed ultimately (though often by diverted routes) into the Dissenting tradition.[189] If it cannot be accounted the direct source of English Protestantism, it was the bedrock on which it rested, and when what may be called the perennial populist religion—anticlerical and antinomian— erupted again in the middle decades of the seventeenth century, it reestablished at once the basic principles that the Separatists and Baptists had labored to recover over two generations, and challenged yet a third established church.

Early nonconformity was not, of course, solely populist, and Lollardy itself was the product of England's greatest late medieval theologian, John Wyclif. What is striking about the long period from about 1540 to 1580, however, is the absence of any dominant figure, and the pervasive anti-intellectualism of nonconformist expression. The Freewiller Henry Hart, perhaps the closest thing to a spiritual leader mid-Tudor nonconformity had, was alleged to have declared "that his faithe was not grownded upon Lernyd men for all errors were broughte in by Lernyd men." Certainly Hart's own prescription for salvation owed little to any Protestant scholasticism: "Obey to the voyce of god, do iustice and equitie, hate the euill, & chose ye good, so shal ye lyue for euer, for thei that do these thynges are born of god, and are made the belouing sonnes of the highest, of what relygion, tong or nacion soeuer thei be."[190]

The absence of intellectual leadership among such early antinomians does not mean a lack of intellectual influence per se. Dutch Anabaptists spread their doctrines in England in the 1530s, finding ready soil particularly in the Lollard strongholds of Essex and Kent; fourteen of them were executed by Henry VIII in June 1535. The Dutch Melchiorite Jan Matthijsz (executed in

1538), then resident in London, was prominent in the Bocholt Anabaptist conference which took place in Westphalia near Wesel in the summer of 1536 and which was partly financed by an unidentified Englishman. John Lambert, a scholar of Greek and a former fellow of Queen's College, was tried and condemned before Henry VIII himself for espousing a mixture of Lollard and Anabaptist doctrines, which in any case substantially overlapped.[191] However, most educated Henrician nonconformists were attracted by the new Lutheran doctrine rather than the *déclassé* traditions of Lollardy. Among them were men such as Robert Barnes, who had once been in orders, and who readily put their talents at the disposal of Henry's church. When Barnes fell along with his patron, Thomas Cromwell, he was accused of Anabaptist heresies, but denied them with much indignation.[192]

The first two decades of England's Reformation thus presented a scene of much confusion. Lutheran intellectuals were drawn into the Anglican fold in hopes of converting Henry, who after a brief flirtation with the new faith affirmed his orthodoxy, while old Lollard and new Anabaptist currents swirled together. Beneath the Henrician facade yet another Continental influence, Calvinism, made steady headway, even in the royal household. By the time of Edward's accession it had captured the intellectual high ground from Lutheranism, and under Cranmer it became the doctrinal basis of the state church. The Freewillers and their activities must be seen in this context, for they represented most distinctively a populist reaction against the new predestinarian theology that seemed radically alien to the native tradition.[193] As the official Anglican formulary phrased it:

> Predestination to life is the everlasting purpose of God, whereby (before the foundations of the world were laid) he hath constantly decreed, by his own judgment secret to us, to deliver from curse and damnation those whom he hath chosen out of mankind; and to bring them to everlasting salvation by Christ, as vessels made to honour.[194]

Such a doctrine, declared the Freewiller Robert[?] Cole of Faversham, "was meter for divilles then for christian men."[195] As their name suggested, the Freewillers seem to have opposed predestination less because it reflected adversely on God's mercy than for denying the efficacy and responsibility of the will. Independent artisans for the most part, they prized—and exercised—their Christian liberty in a way scarcely intended by Luther, conventing for Scripture reading, discussion, and prayer, applying the Gospel to their lives on such mundane subjects as whether gaming was sinful or not, and in general puzzling out the ethical commitments of a Christian life. Despite John Strype's famous characterization of them as "the first that made separation from the Reformed Church of England,"[196] it is not at all clear that they held themselves aloof from their local congregations, much less that they regarded themselves as making formal schism from the church. It is

more likely that they were occasional conformists in the manner of the Lollards, regarding prescribed ceremonies as indifferent so long as they did not
impinge upon conscience. Living in the time of the great monastic dispossession, they were hostile not so much to a privileged clerical order as to the
"Lernyd" who would impose their doctrine on the freedom and purity of the
Word—particularly a doctrine that seemed to suggest that its full benefit was
not available to all.

The Freewillers were thus less concerned to assert a free grace argument
of their own than to rebut what seemed to them the immoral and stultifying
implications of predestination. Not only did it seek to deprive sincere Christians of access to the Gospel, but it encouraged libertinism in those convinced of their election and desperation in those who believed themselves
damned. Henry Hart did not believe "anye man soo reprobate but that he
mighte kepe goddes Comaundementes," nor any so holy "but that he mighte
dampne hime selfe"—not even Saint Paul.[197]

The Freewillers were not alone in their resistance to predestination. Lollards and other dissidents, grouped by authorities under the rubric of "Anabaptists," similarly opposed the doctrine, in some cases more explicitly and
with greater rigor. Although Hart paid little attention to the issue in his
tracts, *A godly newe short treatyse* (1548) and *A consultorie for all Christians*
(1549),[198] the sometime Anabaptist John Champneys drew fire from Jean Veron, a French refugee and controversialist, who devoted half of his *A fruteful
treatis of predestination* (1561) to attacking Champneys' antinomian views. In
the extraordinarily fluid situation of mid-sixteenth century English Protestantism it is difficult to pin down individual, let alone sectarian views with
any great precision; in this respect it foreshadowed the "seeking" (if not the
ranting) of the mid-seventeenth century. Veron identified Champneys as a
Freewiller, the label by this time being as much a catchall term as Anabaptist, although there is no evidence to connect him with the Hart group.[199]

What made the latter notable was the discovery of a large conventicle—
sixty strong—at Bocking, Essex, around Christmas 1550. The Privy Council
had sent John Hooper, the new Bishop of Gloucester, to preach against heresy in Essex and Kent in the aftermath of Kett's Rebellion; the Bocking group
was dismaying evidence of its organized persistence. The ringleaders were
brought before the Council in January 1551, and gave extensive deposi-
tions.[200] It was this exposure that brought them their notoriety, rather than
any coherence of doctrine or emphasis on free grace. The epithet of "free will
men" subsequently applied to them thus reflected the concern of the authorities with antipredestinarian views rather than the group's own special pro-
clivity.

The Bocking detainees were released, but the government continued to
track them, and with the advent of Mary those still active were imprisoned

in the King's Bench. There they met some of their erstwhile antagonists, notably the Cambridge cleric John Bradford, and engaged in a protracted debate over predestination that acquired particular poignance in light of the impending executions of the participants. Hart, still at large, contributed a treatise on "The Enormities Proceeding of the Opinion that Predestination, Calling, and Election is Absolute in Man as it is in God." Bradford responded with a "Defence of Election," and solicited further help from Cranmer, Latimer, and Ridley, themselves imprisoned at Oxford. Ridley, who had been Bradford's mentor, replied, although Hart's "scribbling," as he termed it, seemed to him unworthy of much attention.[201]

Another active participant in the King's Bench debates was John Trew, a Freewiller who, despite his staunchly antipredestinarian views, attempted at various points to find a basis for joint communion with the Bradford group and left an extensive memorial.[202] This episode is significant on several grounds. It marked the longest period of face-to-face debate between conventionally trained members of a clerical establishment and lay conventiclers during the English Reformation. It was also, as Joseph Martin points out, the only time when two such groups met under conditions of parity, for all Protestant worship had been proscribed by the Marian church, and all Protestants were conventiclers and heretics in the eyes of authority. Bradford and his group might regard themselves as defenders of the true faith, but they could no longer look to the civil sword to uphold them. Rather, that sword had been turned against them.

This meant that the Bradford group had no means of prevailing save by persuasion. In effect, the toleration that Busher and Helwys were to call for sixty years later—free disputation according to the Word—had been realized in the hothouse condition of a Marian prison. But the effect on the Freewillers was equally marked. For the first time they confronted reasoned objections to their own views, views which they had never been obliged to codify or even firmly attach themselves to. It was one thing to dismiss the folly of the "Lernyed," but another to defend themselves against men of obvious piety who could articulate a systematic theology and who were no longer persecutors but fellow-sufferers in the faith. The result was that Trew and his colleagues were obliged to respond in kind. They reduced their own principles to a seven-point confession, duly subscribed.[203] This document conceded the validity of the Edwardian church and its ministry, but continued to insist that all who truly repented would be saved. Henry Hart subsequently produced a thirteen-point confession, subscription to which was allegedly to be a precondition of membership among the Freewillers.

What this process reveals is a sect in the making. The Freewillers had begun as simple, Bible-hungry artisans who found insufficient scope for their piety in parish congregations and who reacted against the newfangled doctrine of predestination being preached from Edwardian pulpits. Like their Lollard and Anabaptist coevals, from whom it would be unwise to distinguish them except circumstantially, they conformed at least in part to the established church, regarding their activities as supplementing rather than replacing it. They expressed their piety in generalities of the sort to be found in Hart's writings, were preoccupied with practical questions of conduct and conscience rather than with issues of theology and ecclesiology, and tended to avoid formulations of doctrine. In all this they did very much as Englishmen of similar mind had been doing for a century and a half, if not longer.

Some of the Freewillers were no doubt overborne by the clergy they debated, men of more disciplined intelligence than their own whose stock in trade was precise doctrinal definition. Trew and his cosignatories nonetheless stood their ground. They produced no fewer than twenty-three objections to predestination, including the sophisticated point (to be reiterated by Helwys sixty years later) that it made grace less efficacious than sin, and Adam more consequential than Christ. In short, they began to sound more like sectarians defending their denial of an established orthodoxy and publishing their own principles and doctrines, and less like pious laymen trying their faith and keeping as best they could out of harm's way. They were not "the first who made separation" but the first who were separated—men and women forced into cohesion by an oppositional orthodoxy and then excluded on the basis of that cohesion.

Why did the Freewillers stick so particularly on the point of predestination? It may have been less because the issue was vitally important to them than because it was so to their clerical adversaries. Free grace, if they had imbibed the notion from Lollard tradition or itinerant Anabaptists, may have seemed a natural assumption of the perennial popular religion. Even in disputation, they showed no inclination to elaborate it. Rather, it was predestination—the arbitrary denial of that grace—that struck them as impious and perverse, a human ordinance contrived to set neighbor against neighbor and to provide a rationale for clerical dominance. Challenged by clerical representatives to define their identity and justify their resistance, they may have found in antipredestinarianism precisely the "mark" of their fellowship.

The Freewillers do not appear to have survived Mary's reign, at least as an organized entity. Henry Hart was reported to have died in 1557. John Trew allegedly escaped from prison in 1556, but is not heard from again. Some Freewillers conformed, including Robert Cole of Faversham, who was one of the few clerics associated with the group. He and another quondam Freewiller, John Ledley, joined with others in putting together a devotional book under Mary. Ledley put out a prayer book of his own after Elizabeth's accession that remained in print to the end of her reign and may be taken, at least indirectly, as the last expression of Freewiller piety.[204]

If Bradford and his fellow clerics impressed and in a sense defined the Freewillers, the latter were not without their effect as well. Deprived of the coercive powers (and responsibilities) of his clerical station, Bradford adopted a pastoral stance, trying to exercise charity even in the midst of controversy. The Freewillers were to be his last flock, and he would say to them in the end that, "Though in some things we agree not, yet let love bear the bell away; and let us pray for one another, and be careful one for another; for I hope we be all Christ's."[205]

The Family of Love was the most anomalous religious sect in pre-Civil War England, and by far the most notorious. The English branch has only recently begun to attract scholarly attention, but the outlines of its story are becoming tolerably clear. The Family's founder, Henrik Niclaes (c. 1502-1580), was a mercer born in Münster who according to hagiographers had believed himself since childhood to be in direct communication with God. While resident in Amsterdam in the 1530s he was associated with the Anabaptist David Joris, but around 1540 he moved to Emden and formed his own circle, variously known as the "Communialtie," Household, or Family of Love (Familia Caritatis, Famille de la Charite, Huis der Liefde, etc.). At the same time he began to produce a stream of rhapsodic religious works and broadsides under the semi-pseudonymous initials "H.N.," which referred not only to Niclaes' given name but evoked the symbolism of the *homo novus*, the prophetic voice of the renewed and inward Christ to come.

Niclaes believed that Jesus' witness, while valid, had not been sufficient, and that the persistence of sin in the world required "another performance" before the faithful could be cleansed and united, or in his striking phrase "godded with God." This was to be accomplished not by an outward incarnation but by a long process of spiritual tempering, withdrawal from the world, and inner illumination among the godly. New initiates would be directed by adepts or "elders," who, having attained illumination, could guide them. "Love," in Niclaes' poetics, was a term for this interactive process as well as a metaphor for the state of illumination itself, and to be "in the Love" was consequently to be involved, whether as elder or initiate, in the work of spiritual rebirth. The "Family" was the inclusive body of all those in the Love and the term for each particular household or unit. Within particular households discipline was strict; initiates owed elders complete obedience and confession of all sins, and elders disposed, at least in theory, of communal property. Elders served as couriers between households, which occasionally met in conferences. At the apex of this hierarchy was "H.N.," whose authority was decisive on all questions. In practice, however, Niclaes expressed himself chiefly in vatic pronouncements susceptible of various interpretations. His visionary and governing style were of a piece; both left much to the imagination.

Niclaes' vision was rooted in Christian revelation, and he spoke of Familist illuminati as bearing the Trinity of God the Father, Christ the Son, and the Holy Ghost within themselves. But he was a genuine heresiarch, in whom Arian, Joachite, and Anabaptist sources were finally subsumed in a transcendent mystical state of the type characterized by Rudolf Otto as "numinous." Such a state, as Otto comments, "is perfectly *sui generis* and irreducible to any other; and therefore, like every primary and elemental datum, while it admits of being discussed, it cannot be strictly defined."[206] The more closely one seeks to approach the core of this experience, the more language distends itself, either in the direction of irreconcilable dualities (paradox) or inseparably graded affinities (nondifferentiation). Niclaes' thought tends toward the latter extreme. "Godded with God" is a good example, as is this pronouncement from a book of "Psalmes and Songes": "The darknesses are departed into the Botomlespitt to the darknesses; the light hath lightened us in the light."[207]

In short, Niclaes' vision was sub- or (depending on one's preference) supratheological, employing the conventional idiom of Christian religious discourse (baptism, salvation, resurrection) connotatively rather than denotatively, as metaphoric rather than categoric speech. Similarly, Niclaes appears to have understood Christian revelation as a coded account of the truths of inner experience and not as a literal description of events past or to come. Thus he could speak of Christ as both an inspired but fully human teacher and as an element of the Trinity, and conceive his disciples (once "godded with God") as walking Christs. There was consequently no need to posit a "second" resurrection since Christ—or the regenerate spirit he represented—was continually resurrected in Niclaes' adepts, nor any heaven beyond the beatific condition of being in the Love. Christ's life, and the cycle of redemption it symbolized—baptism into truth, death unto the sins of the world, ascension into the divine presence—was not an inimitable pattern of perfection or a journey to be accomplished only at the end of time, but a path to be trod in the present. At the same time, however, Niclaes preached a millennial climax to the world, of which he himself was prophet and herald.

The paradoxical nature of Niclaes' teaching was reflected in his attitude toward the unregenerate mass of humankind. On the one hand "H.N." preached a gospel for all men and women, and Familist society was intended as a model for the new and final age; on the other, Familism was not a confessional faith to which one could subscribe but an inward state of enlightenment to be attained only within the community of Love itself, and the world was the source of all evil. The result was that Niclaes alternatively counseled his followers to be "goodwilling" to their fellow men and obedient to lawful authority, and to walk warily among the wicked, even despising them as a "Devels Synagogue" of the damned. In effect, he encouraged them to project an almost Manichaean duality on their neighbors. If they were potential children of light they were also actual sons of darkness; if they were objects of evangelism they were also snares of perdition. In one of his most shocking metaphors Niclaes describes the unconverted as actually dead, an embodiment of hell. Again, however, when one recalls that he regarded both heaven and hell as spiritual states, his terms are not exclusionary. Those who were dead today might yet live tomorrow.

These considerations explain what was to authorities the most subversive aspect of Familism, its thoroughgoing Nicodemism. Familists not only attended regular church services but often disavowed any connection to the Family when examined. Such behavior went far beyond equivocation. Church attendance was justified both as "goodwilling" toward neighbors and as obedience to the magistrate. There could be no spiritual harm, moreover, in partaking of any service or communion, since all rites and doctrines, Roman or Reformed, were to be understood symbolically as expressing the underlying truths revealed fully only by "H.N." The contortions of conscience experienced by church papists were hence unknown to Familists. They owed a truthful account of themselves only to their fellow brethren; under all other circumstances, their obligation was to preserve the sacred community.

Familism appears to have come to England through the efforts of an itinerant joiner and mechanick preacher, Christopher Vitel. The authorities first became cognizant of it when a JP in Guildford, Surrey, William More, deposed two Familists in 1561. More was apparently concerned to draw them out on the subject of equivocation and Nicodemism, for he elicited several responses:

> When a question is demanded of any of them [by others] they do of order stay a great while or they do answer and commonly their first word shall be "surely," or "so."

> They may answer to every demandment not being one of their sect in such sort as they think shall best please him, for they say they are bound to deal truly with no man in word or deed, that is not of their congregation, alleging that he is no neighbor and that therefore they may abuse him at their pleasure.

> They say they may be subtle and lie for the Holy Ghost was subtle. If any of them be convented for his opinions and doth deny the same by open recantation, he takes that to be a glory unto him; as though he hath suffered persecution in this doing, and yet still inwardly maintaining the same opinions.[208]

These statements, together with the companion one that "Whosoever is not of their sect, they account as a beast that hath no soul,"[209] would certainly have raised alarm in any Elizabethan magistrate. The experience of Jesuit equivocation and church papistry was still to come. The memory of the Marian martyrs, already being canonized by Foxe, was fresh. No testimony was more solemn, no discourse of greater import than the witness borne for one's faith or the recantation made for one's errors.

The Familist refusal to respect oaths or testify one's conscience must be seen in this context. In an age when relations based on fealty and custom were giving way to ones based on clientage and contract, many tokens of conventional obligation and allegiance had become hollow. As Stephen Greenblatt suggests in *Renaissance Self-Fashioning*, courtly elites were increasingly detached from the multiplicity of roles they were required to play, a theme echoed abundantly in the cautionary literature and theater of the day. For clerical elites (now courtiers as well), the pressures were even greater. Perhaps nowhere was the tension between seeming and being more exacerbated than in the episcopal careers of men such as Gardiner, Tunstall, and Cranmer, who strove to accommodate themselves to the shifting demands of their mid-Tudor sovereigns and to survive where they could not please. Cranmer's martyrdom had done something to redeem his reputation, but the immense popularity of Foxe's *Book of Martyrs* rested on the stories of humble folk who had died for their faith, and the prevalence of these might be read as a rebuke to the great ones who had survived through policy or flight. In the end, the testimony of conscience in the peril of one's soul was the last pledge of truth, the one unimpeachable act of consent. If that, too, might be feigned on the grounds that truth was owed only within the fellowship of the faithful and not to those who, in their unenlightened condition, might be regarded as 'beasts without souls,' the basis for wider association, not to mention a legitimated social order, was difficult to construe.

The Familists were obviously troubling in a number of other ways as well. Unlike other conventiclers and later sectarians, they did not so much stand in an adversarial relationship to the established church as completely outside any relationship at all, a situation only exacerbated by their ready conformism. Other groups, though also resorting to secrecy, signaled their dissent in ways that engaged the common conversation (recusancy or obstruction in church, public defiance of ordinances and edicts, manifestos and confessions). When apprehended, the leaders of such groups generally felt compelled to attest their beliefs and to stand fast in them even unto death. In so doing they affirmed the value of conscience as the ultimate foundation of sacred discourse; and a Cranmer, a Campion, or a Barrow, by enduring martyrdom, laid claim to the same apostolic tradition. For the Familists, who recognized only H.N. as the valid successor of Christ, such questions were otiose, since in the light of H.N.'s revelations all previous Christian practice and tradition was equally valid and equally superseded. To offer oneself up for judgment based on the old, pre-Familist dispensation of the existing churches was consequently as absurd as submitting oneself to the ceremonial law of Moses had become after the revelation of Christ. This applied as well to the "new" Reformed churches as to the old Roman one, for in H.N.'s view they represented merely the last spasm of the old, collapsing order. If anything, his sympathies tended to be with Rome, on grounds of decorum if nothing else. Thus, although Familism was a phenomenon of the Reformation, it stood aloof from its passions and refused to engage in its controversies. It was willing to proselytize, but not (at least in theory) to debate. From this point of view, it stood apart from the discourse of legitimacy.

The government took no further notice of Familism as such until the mid-1570s, perhaps regarding it as a species of Anabaptism. It may indeed have been incompletely distinguished from it until then, since H.N.'s works were not available in English until 1574 and the Guildford Familists were all described as "unlearned," i.e., unable to read any but their native tongue. Presumably they relied on an interlocutor such as Vitel, who at that point seems to have been a religious eclectic rather than a fully committed disciple of Niclaes'.[210] In any case, it was the sudden appearance of H.N.'s works in the mid-1570s, translated by Vitel and possibly printed by Nicholas Bohmberg in Cologne, that alerted authorities to the presence of a Familist network in England and prompted a vigorous counterattack. This first took the form of a staged recantation of five Familists at the Paul's Cross in June 1575, followed by a number of confessions and a series of print refutations, notably John Rogers' *The displaying of an horrible secte of grosse and wicked heretiques, naming themselves the Family of Love* (1578, 2d ed. 1579), John Knewstub's *A confutation of monstrous and horrible heresies taught by H.N. and embraced of a number, who call themselves the familie of Love* (1579), and William Wilkinson's *A confutation of certaine articles delivered unto the Family of Love* (1579). Wilkinson, a Cambridge schoolmaster and divinity student who knew the local Familist community firsthand and who may have coerced some of his informants,[211] seems to have acted on his own initiative; Rogers and Knewstub, however, had sponsors at the highest level—including Burghley, Walsingham, and Warwick—and they both incorporated material supplied by government sources (in Rogers' case, parts of the Guildford deposition, and in Knewstub's, a chapter attributed by Christopher Marsh to Walsingham's Presbyterian secretary, Laurence Thomson).[212] The direct involvement of the Privy Council may reflect the disgrace of Grindal—and even a partial cause of it[213]—but the use of Knewstub, soon to be presented with the living of Cockfield, Suffolk, and often in trouble for nonconformity himself in years to come, suggests again the special interest of the godly in policing fringe and sectarian religious elements.

Knewstub's *Confutation* exhibits the frustration of a university-trained divine with Niclaes' oracular paradoxes as well as the horror of a Calvinist at the anarchic consequences of free grace:

> H.N. turneth religion vpside downe, and buildeth heauen heere vpon earth, maketh God, man: and man, God: & hel heauen. For venom and poyson which will bring present death, hath he dispersed ouer euery member & article of our beliefe, so vniversall is the poyson of his opinion.[214]

Like most other commentators, Knewstub tried to wrestle H.N.'s utterances into some order at least for purposes of description and refutation, only to throw up his hands at the task. Familism was, in fine, "the pestilentest heresie that euer was in the land . . . it leaueth neuer a peece of the knowledge of GOD whole and vnshaken . . . it is a masse or packe of Poperie, Arianisme, Anabaptisme, and Libertinisme." Everywhere and nowhere at the same time, now mimicking this heresy, now borrowing from that, it was pure farrago, a pandemonium of doctrine. Precisely in this, however, lay its most diabolical cunning, for as its very promiscuity was a snare for the simple, offering an idol to every taste and an excuse to any wickedness, so its absurdity tempted the wise to scorn and the magistrate to complacency. This alone could explain the failure to deal with such an abomination as it deserved. But how could the divine be silent when "the glorie of God" was "troden vnder our feete" by such blasphemies, and the justice supine before those who "maketh no conscience of any dutie to men, their owne brood onely excepted," who affirm "that they may lie to all, so they be true to themselues," and who "thinke euery thing lawfull . . . that their fantasticall spirite telleth them"? Did this not "goe straitly and directly to the ouerthrowe of the commonwealth?" Who, indeed, could say that designs against the state were not even now hatched and ready, "which they smother, vntill such time as they haue gotten an armie to execute them"?[215] Knewstub could not resist a final dig at those who cast aspersions on the godly, denied them the lawful exercise of their consciences, and even questioned their loyalty as subjects: "if you seek after the Puritans, these they bee."

Knewstub writes from the standpoint of rigid orthodoxy, and at an obvious personal remove from his subjects. Both Rogers and Wilkinson, in contrast, cultivated Familist sources and seem to have emerged with at an least grudging respect for their adversaries in spite of themselves. Rogers justified his own contacts on the grounds of better exposing Familist doctrines to the light of day. It was not so much that ministers and magistrates were indifferent to the threat posed by Familism as simply unaware of its nature: "There are many diligent & godly teachers," he noted, "whiche in places conuenient do inuey & impugne the doctrine of ye Family of Loue, & yet are not throughly acquainted therwith." This was in large part because Familists proselytized only covertly and would not enter into public disputation, so that "except one will be pliant to their doctrine and shew good will therto, he shal hardly get any of their bookes, no, nor they will not conferre, nor talke of any points of their doctrine with any, except it be to such as they finde inclined, and (as they tearme it) willingly minded therto."[216] Hence the need to "display" them in all their "lothsome spottes and ougly deformities."

The sense of urgency in exposing Familist doctrines and practices is common to all the anti-Familist tracts of the late 1570s, not merely because the sect "daily" increased, as Wilkinson complained (Rogers estimated its numbers at a thousand), but because it violated the rules of discourse, and its subversion was thus seen as foundational. Both Rogers and Wilkinson were successful in eliciting formal replies to their attacks, which they printed and rebutted in the usual style of the day. Even so, the identity of their respondents remained hidden, and a running theme of the debate was the extent to which candor and probity could be required of those who thereby exposed themselves to persecution. One of Rogers' respondents, who signed himself "Your unknowen friend," defended equivocation as a proper means of protecting Christian liberty. In objecting to it, the "friend" declared, Rogers had forgotten the plight of Protestants in Catholic states, who "holde it good policie to defend them selues & their consciences" against "Tyranny" by evading the Inquisition. Another interlocutor, "E.R.," cleverly citing the case of the Henrician martyr William Tyndale, suggested that compulsion of conscience was the mark of the beast:

> It is not Christian like, that one man should envie, belie, and persecute an other, for any cause touching conscience. William Tindale compareth them to Antichrists disciples, that do breake by into the consciences of men, & compel them either to forsweare themselues by the Almightie God, and by the holy Gospell of his mercifull promises, or to testifie against them selues.[217]

What was at issue here was to a certain extent two differing traditions: that of the Reformed church, with its emphasis on preaching and controversy, and that of Lollardy, with its habits of concealment. For men like Rogers and Wilkinson and especially Knewstub, a faith that refused to avow itself was diabolically inspired, for all true conscience was compelled — not by the rack but by its own inner necessity — to declare itself. The Familist attitude toward outsiders, on the other hand, affirmed that truth was not owed to one's persecutors, and duplicity was permissible toward any of the uninitiate. The more that Familists exhibited outward piety and practiced good neighborhood (as they were wont to do), the more suspect they therefore became to their adversaries. What dark designs and hidden contempt did such affectations conceal?

Knewstub, Rogers, and Wilkinson were all secondary players; certainly the government was not about to dignify the Familists with the kind of attention it devoted to Presbyterians or Papists. But sermons were called for, and no less a figure than Laurence Chaderton preached against them at Paul's Cross. Elizabeth's progress through East Anglia in 1578 galvanized action against the Family. This may have backfired: several members of the Queen's personal entourage, the Yeomen of the Guard, were apparently contaminated by the heresy, and a later commentator would complain that "great Doctors of Divinitie, so called, yea, and some great Peers" had entertained or even embraced Familist doctrine.[218] One must surely be cautious in crediting such reports, especially where no names are attached, but in a Court that patronized John Dee and Giordano Bruno a certain consumption of forbidden fruit is not wholly surprising.

What is clear is that the government treated Familism with new seriousness after the Queen's progress. Several Yeomen of the Guard were interrogated and temporarily suspended from their posts, and directives went out to the bishops of London, Ely, Lincoln, Norwich, Salisbury, Winchester, and Worcester to dig for the new heresy. These were capped by a proclamation in October 1580 commanding that "all . . . officers and ministers temporal" assist the clergy in finding and committing members of the Family and destroying their books. The proclamation took a sterner view of those who imported or disseminated Familist tracts than the "ignorant or simple" seduced by them; the latter were to be detained until they had been cleared of charges or had made satisfactory recantation, but the former were in addition "to receive . . . bodily punishment and other mulct as fautors of damnable heresies."[219]

The proclamation was the occasion of a sizable roundup, for on the day of its publication some threescore Familists of Wisbech were taken into custody and immediately examined by a commission consisting of the Bishop of Ely and his chancellor, and three divines. The divines, William Fulke, Richard Greenham, and Roger Goad, were all zealous, another indication of the particular interest that the godly took in the sect, and the value they had in enabling godly ministers to demonstrate loyalty to the established church and to displace the epithet of "Puritan" onto others.[220]

The examiners were well aware of the difficulties they faced in dealing with practiced equivocators, some of whom had made previous recantations. They began "gently and lovingly," in the Bishop's words, and when that approach yielded no result, proceeded to interrogatories upon oath. These too were unavailing, and at last the examiners harangued their prisoners with denunciations of H.N.'s errors, setting beside them "contrary truths" to which they were ordered to subscribe. The whole suggests a carefully orchestrated performance designed to proceed from pastoral solicitude to judicial sternness, culminating in a crescendo of abuse at once shocking and threatening. Yet it was also a contest in which each side understood the rules of play and in which the appropriate moment of capitulation was clearly signaled. The subscribers posted bond and were instructed to repeat their abjuration the following Sunday in Wisbech church, upon which they were judged reconciled to the community and dined with the minister.[221]

The authorities took more care with John Bourne, a glover and the reputed elder of the Wisbech family. He was isolated from his companions, who were induced to give incriminating evidence against him. Bourne held out stoutly, refusing food and drink and deflecting his questioners with sophistries. Although some ten of H.N.'s works had been found concealed on his premises, Bourne declared himself unable to identify "whether he were a man or not," an Aesopian response that could be taken to suggest either that the initials H.N. were a pseudonym or that the person of Henrik Niclaes was divine. Similarly, he could not deny the doctrines of H.N., for if these initials were no more than alphabetic signs then "he should deny the most part of the scriptures," and if they did refer to an actual person he might in denying what was false in them also deny what, passing his understanding, might be true. Pressed as to whether he considered any part of H.N.'s doctrines to be true, he replied that they would be true insofar as they agreed with the word of God, an answer that returned him to the one safe position to which an accused heretic could repair: the inerrancy of Scripture.[222]

Whether Bourne's answers were part of a formulaic pattern used by others or not, his resourcefulness in evading his learned interrogators is impressive. Of course he too yielded in the end, forgiven in advance by H.N. for the lengthy public recantation written out for him by the guardians of orthodoxy and preserved in the Gonville-Caius College manuscripts:

> I do here in the presence of God, of his angels, and of his people, without canker, cavil, or dissimulation of mine own sure and certain knowledge grounded upon the holy word of God, sincerely from my heart confess that H.N. is a most wicked instrument of Satan . . .[223]

What purpose was this elaborate charade meant to serve? John Bourne was not required to become a martyr by his faith (though he held out long enough to keep face with his disciples), and he gave his examiners no grounds for making him one, since he fully discharged the terms of his recantation. The examiners, for their part, would have understood that the recantation was a sham played out for the benefit of the parish; the fact that they provided it ready-made signified as much to Bourne, just as his refusal to eat signaled his persistence in error. At best, then, they might have hoped to expose the Wisbech Familists, and to assert the authority of the church against an egregious challenge to its hegemony. That was clearly all the government hoped, for there is no record of it having pursued the matter further. With the far more substantive threat of a Jesuit invasion to be dealt with, the Familists were in practical terms a minor irritant.

As for the personal response of the examiners themselves, one can only conjecture. Bishop Cox, in making his report directly to Elizabeth herself, used the figure of Deborah in praising her care for religion and prayed for an "increase" of grace in the Queen and her councillors; do we hear in this, as Christopher Marsh has suggested, not only encouragement but rebuke?[224] (If the Bishop were indeed pleading for greater vigilance against heresy and the resources to combat it, the royal response could not have been more crushing: after Cox's death in 1581, the diocese of Ely was left vacant for the remainder of the reign.) As for the three divines, they must have been the more confirmed in their already well-seasoned belief that only a preaching ministry could keep the most appalling heresies at bay. Greenham, whose care and solicitude for a rather tough and intractable flock is chronicled in Clarke's *Martyrologie*, appears to have been particularly taken by Margaret Colville. The sole gentlewoman among the Wisbech familists, Colville was an elderly widow who had perhaps been attracted to the group by a longing for companionship and spiritual certainty. Though she was but a "novice" among them, she had already imbibed the most atrocious doctrines: "that perfection might be attained unto in this life, that the last trump was blown, that the body did arise again in this life, and that the wicked should not rise again in their bodies unto condemnation." After being brought to contrition she was ministered to privately by Greenham, "who gently and lovingly confuted her errors by the scriptures" until she "freely gave up her [Familist] book, [and] acknowledged her errors, with many tears before sufficient witnesses."[225] If a woman of her rank were so vulnerable and so easily seduced, what of the tens of thousands of souls in places far less favored by the Gospel than Cambridgeshire?

The anti-Familist campaign thus pointed up the tensions between the "monarchical church" and the godly. For the latter, manifestations such as Familism were the direct consequence of the neglect of the church and its ministry. For the crown, they were a police matter to be dealt with on the level of interdiction, censorship, and public recantation. The first two conditions met and the last satisfied in their default, the state (including its clerical arm) had done what it prudently could. Elizabeth had no desire to rekindle the fires of Smithfield, particularly against subjects who willingly professed their loyalty, got on well with their neighbors, and came to church. Conformity, not zeal, was the object of government, and although the followers of H.N. held to doctrines as repugnant to the good order of the commonwealth as to that of the church, they did not disturb the peace or subvert the state as did the minions of Rome — or, for that matter, the conferences of the godly.

These considerations underlie the fate of the bill introduced by unknown hands in the Parliament of 1581 "for punishment of the Hereticks called the Family of Love," which provided "that the professors of the Familye of Love may for the first offence be whipped and for the second branded with this lettre H.N., and the third time adjudged a felon."[226] The sponsors were alleged to be "divers preachers" from Convocation—might one or more of our Wisbech divines have been among their number, or, as Christopher Marsh suggests, the indefatigable Knewstub? The strategy behind the bill was, in any case, transparent: if the Familists were not to be tried and burned for their beliefs, they might be executed as felons, as Henry VIII had burned Anabaptists in the 1530s not for heresy but sedition. The bishops weighed in against the bill, however, and the Commons refused to accept the proferred distinction, debating for two days whether "pains of death might be inflicted on a heretic." The bill was sent to a committee for redrafting, but the Council packed it with its own members—including Christopher Hatton, whose duties included supervision of the Yeomen of the Guard—and it died there. The Family of Love persisted into the seventeenth century, the butt of ballads and stage plays[227] but no longer the object of persecution, perhaps merging again with the broader stream of antinomianism during the Civil War years, when it was defended by John Milton, and possibly persisting in places such as the Isle of Ely down to the time of James II and beyond.[228]

The Familist phenomenon illustrates the dilemma of ideological containment in the Reformation. The printing press, which shaped both the form and the content of the Reformation and was indispensable to its success, facilitated the spread of heresy as well. At the same time it reshaped the relations between literacy and orality. Access to the Bible was mediated through preaching by qualified ministers of the Gospel, which tied truth to obedience and inspiration to doctrine. Effective censorship—the confinement of dialogue within approved norms, of which prophesying was a paradigm case—was essential to this process. But the supply of words, and of ministers to utter them, was never sufficient to meet the stanchless tide of print. Licensing and interdiction could not cut off the circulation of unapproved ideas. The attempt to direct and monitor religious experience in an age of contention merely fed traditional suspicions of the "learned." That this attempt came now from a state church (however divided in itself) in turn fueled resentment of both state and church.

Iconoclasm and Authority

In early 1538, the Rood of Grace at Boxley Abbey, Kent, whose image was famous for the miraculous movement of its features and limbs, was brought "at the Kinges commaundement" to the market at Maidstone. Here it was disassembled so that people might "be shewed . . . the craft of moving the eyes and lipps" and thus see how the monks of the abbey "had gotten great riches" by deceiving them. From Maidstone the Rood was conveyed to London, where before a much larger audience at Paul's Cross the Bishop of Rochester, John Hilsey, repeated the process on February 24. He showed that the image was "made of paper and cloutes from the legges upward; ech legges and arms were of timber; and so the people had bene [d]eluded and caused to doe great idolatrie by the said image, of long contynuance, to the derogation of Godes honor and great blasphemie of the name of God . . . and also how other images in the Church, used for great pilgrimages, hath caused great idolatrie to be used in this realme, and shewed how he thincketh that the idolatrie will neaver be left till the said images be taken awaie . . ." The Bishop concluded by smashing the mechanism of the image in his pulpit, after which he "gave it to the people againe, and then the rude people and boyes brake the said image in peeces, so that they left not one peece whole."[229]

The ignominious procession of the Rood of Grace from the abbey chapel to Paul's Cross, the most public ecclesiastical resort in the kingdom, climaxed by a ceremonious act of royal iconoclasm and a licensed tumult, was more than an elaborate piece of anticlerical propaganda followed by a carefully staged rite of approbation. As a pilgrimage in reverse from shrine to pillory, culminating in an act of desecration instead of reverence, it epitomized the entire campaign to suppress the monasteries and efface the protocols associated with them. But it was also a daring act of unmasking, for coronation processions and other royal pageants relied no less on mechanical devices, which became more elaborate and complex with each succeeding reign. The scene at Paul's Cross was a moment in which power stood naked. It could not remain thus. The rejection of papal authority and the massive destruction of traditional furnishings and iconography that took place between the 1530s and 1570s in England left, literally, a visible deficit of authority. There were two forms of order that could fill this vacuum, diametrically opposed in their implication although ideologically reconcilable in principle: the authority of an imperial crown that assumed the governance of the church along with that of the realm, and whose figure, as we have seen, was the Christian emperor; and the authority of individual conscience, informed and guided by the Word of God.

Normally, the conscience of the subject and the command of the sovereign could not be opposed, since one of the first commands of conscience itself, according to oft-emphasized scriptural texts, was obedience to the ruler. Difficulty ensued only when the ruler issued commands contrary to Scripture itself. Even then, the layman was not authorized to resist other than passively. Between the layman, his conscience, his ruler, and his God, however, another authority had been wont to supervene: the church militant and universal. The political struggle between papacy and monarchy had been long resolved in the latter's favor by the sixteenth century, but the corporate church was still a powerful and immediate presence in the lives of English men and women, and its access to conscience—the wellspring of obedience—was far more direct than the crown's. Wherever practical authority lay in secular terms (and that was by no means a settled matter, even after Bosworth Field), the structure of legitimacy was still duple: the subject under his sovereign was at the same time the layman bound by his priest.

When Henry VIII renounced the authority of the papacy in England, this structure was shattered. The priest would thenceforth be consecrated under the authority if not at the hands of the king, and could not possess powers (as opposed to functions) not inhering in the king himself. This was not quite clear to Henry, nor for that matter to conservative bishops such as Stephen Gardiner or Cuthbert Tunstall. If the parish minister still held the keys to salvation in his hand, then every priest in England was a pope, which was to say an autonomous source of spiritual power independent of the king. This could not be. The Reformed view of baptism, confession, the Eucharist, and the last rites was the only one compatible with an Erastian church: that is to say, a view that converted a priest into a pastor.

Henry's innate conservatism led him to persecute potential allies as well as declared foes: thus, sacramentarians were burned together with Papists. If the King's theology was hazy and his long-term strategic grasp weak, however, his immediate political instinct was neither. He was determined to control (or retard) the pace of change in the church of which he was now Supreme Head in Earth[230]; in either case, this pace was not to exceed that of his own laborious thought processes. Those of quicker wit or less serpentine logic might wish to see their royal Hezekiah become a Josias and purge the true church completely of its idols, but they missed the point of a Christian imperium, at least as understood by Henry. The King had once written that "the law of every man's conscience" was "the highest and most supreme court for judgement or justice," a sentiment at once impeccably conservative and profoundly revolutionary. Diarmaid MacCulloch comments that the Reformation afforded Henry "the luxury of erecting his private conscience into the guiding religious teaching of an entire kingdom, and it was a luxury which he often abused."[231] But of course there would have been no Reformation in England at all without the act of the King's conscience, and the essence of that act—of the Henrician Reformation itself—was to convert this particular, private conscience into a public, corporate one. That Henry might err and often reverse himself was not an embarrassment to the King, for the nature of the "tender" conscience, to use the terminology of a later generation, was to grope patiently, humbly, and in hope of divine enlightenment for the truth.

The King's conscience was not without helpers. Here as elsewhere—here perhaps above all—the problem of counsel was crucial. Archbishop Cranmer was Henry's chief guide, discreet enough to let the headstrong wayfarer take his own path when the occasion demanded; but there were other voices, even in the royal bedchamber,[232] and conscience turned out in the end to be political, too. Politics dictated other considerations as well. Henry moved as rapidly as he could to close the monasteries, not merely because he coveted their spoil but because they were nodes of potential resistance, inextricably connected to the Roman church. They were also associated with the most humiliating moment in the history of the English monarchy, the public chastisement of Henry II over the death of Thomas à Becket. Henry VIII himself had gone on a pilgrimage in 1520 to Becket's shrine in Canterbury Cathedral, the most famous and ornate in all England and one internationally renowned. In November 1538 he ordered its destruction together with that of all other monuments to Becket in the kingdom, the removal of his name from all service books, and the suppression of his feast day because his canonization, as the King's proclamation stated, had been only the reward for maintaining the "usurped authority" of the papacy.[233] Pope Paul III was nettled enough to denounce Henry's action in a bull, but the deconsecration of Becket served another purpose as well: it was a standing reminder to all English clerics of their own subordination to the Supreme Head.

The campaign against Becket—long a bête noire of the Lollards—had been anticipated by the Reformers; in 1536 John Bale had written a play denouncing him. Under the patronage of Thomas Cromwell men such as Bale, Hooper, and Latimer became ardent champions of the royal supremacy, and although they were driven into exile at the Vicar General's fall in 1540 their faith in the Christian imperium as the divinely appointed means for the victory of truth and the vanquishing of the Roman Antichrist did not falter. That faith was seemingly rewarded under Edward. Bale's description of his encounter with the boy king resonates with the sense of being borne, even from death's door, into the presence of a more than earthly majesty:

> Upon the .15. daye of August in the yeare from Christes incarnacion 1552 beynge the first daye of my deliveraunce as God wolde from a mortall ague which had holde me long afore. In rejoyce that hys Majestie was come in progresse to Southampton which was .5. myle from my personage of Bysshoppes Stoke within the same countye, I toke my horse about .10 of the clocke for very weaknesse scant able to sytt hym & so came thydre. Betwixt .2. & .3. of the clocke the same daye I drewe towardes the place where as his Majestie was and stode in the open strete ryght against the gallerye. Anon my frinde Johan Fylpot a gentylman & one of hys previe chambre called unto him .2. more of his companyons which in moving their heades towardes me shewed me most frindely countenaunces. By one of these .3. the

Kynge havynge informacion that I was there in the strete he marveled therof for so much as it had bene tolde hym a lytle afore that I was bothe dead & buried. With that hys grace came to the wyndowe and earnestly behelde me a poor weake creature as though he had had upon me so symple a subject an earnest regarde or rather a very fatherly care.[234]

Bale invests this scene with an almost sacred aura; it is a kind of pilgrim's tale, as the godly minister rises from his sickbed to behold his sovereign, whose affirming gaze sets the seal on his recovery. That Edward soon after made him Bishop of Ossory confirmed his sense of the incident as a providential event: "Thus," he relates, "was I called in a maner from deathe to this office." The Christian emperor was, after all, the appointed mediator between the divine mandate and its earthly fulfillment, a concept embedded in the supremacy itself and symbolized by the erection of the royal coat of arms in churches throughout the kingdom and in the iconographic motif of the king, flanked by prophets, handing the Bible to his bishops.[235] The iconoclasts, purge the temple as they would, could not do without one idol at least.

By its nature, iconoclasm was destructive of one kind of authority, but constitutive of another; it was in this respect that it differed from vandalism. To tear down the image of Christ was not to deny Christ but the falsely assumed authority to represent him; it was also to acknowledge the true authority by virtue of which the proper worship of Christ was to be reinstated. For the Lollards, as later for Protestants, that authority was the Holy Bible, but not the Bible alone. In an age in which, translated or not, the Bible was inaccessible to the vast majority of the laity, the mediation of teachers and preachers was essential; the alternative to a culture of images was, at least initially, not a culture of print but one of orality.

One such preacher in England was Thomas Bilney, who inveighed against pilgrimages and invocations in the late 1520s and early 1530s and whose execution in 1531 was followed by an outbreak of iconoclasm in East Anglia, where he had preached. Attacks were recorded on images and shrines at Gracechurch, near Sudbury, and in the Duke of Norfolk's park at Stoke by Nayland, while in neighboring Essex, the Good Rood of Dovercourt was stolen and burned at the instigation of Bilney's associate, Thomas Rose. One captured iconoclast, a shoemaker of Eye, specifically cited Bilney's preaching as his inspiration.[236]

The interaction between reforming preacher and lay iconoclast was, of course, neither simple nor unidirectional. A great many other elements, largely submerged to the historian's eye, had to be in place to create a suitable climate for iconoclasm: perhaps a Lollard or otherwise dissenting tradition; a grasping clerical establishment (or one perceived as such); the circulation of Reformed or humanist tracts and ideas. Nor does the attack on Nor-folk's estate seem adventitious, as the Duke's conservatism was notorious.

A much clearer view of the process appeared in Zurich and other Swiss cities in the 1520s. In Zurich, Huldrych Zwingli spoke against images in January 1523, and Leo Jud preached against them a week before the first acts of destruction later that year. As the most recent historian of Swiss icono-clasm, Lee Palmer Wandel, notes, "The preaching of the reformers inspired no other actions in Zurich as immediate, as violent, and as widespread as the attacks on the idols." In neighboring Hongg, the preaching of Simon Stumpf had a similar result, while in Strasbourg the pastor Diebold Schwarz gave example to his flock by striking an image in the Dominican churchyard.[237]

The power of the Swiss preachers was greatly magnified by the micro-cosmic stage of the small city-states from which they held forth. Although re-formers such as Martin Bucer insisted that the purging of images could only be properly effected through the magistrate, an aroused citizenry could quickly force a temporizing government to legitimate its actions, as in Basel. In Wittenberg, Luther's quondam colleague Andreas Bodenstein von Karl-stadt acted even more boldly. Having forced the town council to set a date certain for the removal of all images, he and a fellow preacher, Gabriel Zwill-ing, incited the populace to proceed at once. Luther's return and the Elector Frederick's prompt response to this provocation restored order (and some of the images), but not before Karlstadt, who suggested that "die gemeyn" could not only anticipate but preempt the magistrate, had given an early ex-ample of reformation without tarrying.[238]

Such clear-cut examples of ministers and their flocks intimidating local authorities or even assuming their functions cannot be found in England, where Reformation was the creature if not the creation of the monarchy from the beginning. There was no period of confusion in England, as in parts of Switzerland and Germany, during which the authority of the magistrate was not paramount. Iconoclasm was, from the mid-1530s on, a royal instrument, to be exercised or not as expedience dictated. Not all clerics were as supple as John Hilsey, the rood-breaker, who tacked skillfully to the right when the wind shifted; Hooper, Latimer, and other reformers who had served Crom-well soon found themselves in exile, if not worse case.[239]

Such iconoclasm as did occur without official sanction (except during the Marian reaction) tended to reflect divided or uncertain counsels in govern-ment rather than express defiance. Henry VIII's last days were attended with the expectation of a godly succession, and at his death the curate and war-dens of the London church of St. Martin's church in Ironmonger Lane had:

> of their owne heedes and presumption, withoute other autorite, and con-trary to the Kinges Majestes doctrine and order by his Highness established to be observed throughowte this realme . . . taken away owte of the saide

Churche aswel the images and pictures of sainctes as also of the crucifixe, setting uppe in their places and abowte the Churche walles certaine textes of Scripture, whereof summe were perversely translated, and in stede of thimage of the crucifixe the Armes of the Kinges Majeste [were] painted, with divers textes of Scripture abowte the same.[240]

The culprits excused themselves in front of a stern Lord Protector Somerset by claiming that the images and crucifix, being rotted, had crumbled during repairs to the church roof. The tale itself collapsed when they admitted that they had subsequently taken down other images in the chancel "for that summe in that parisshe did (as they toke it) comitte Idolatry to the same." They got away with a mild rebuke and the payment of sureties for restoring the crucifix, or at least a picture of one; no mention of the other images was made. Clearly, they had correctly anticipated the lay of the land, and erred only in acting without warrant.[241]

The actions of the St. Martin iconoclasts were typical. One set of authoritative emblems (roodlofts, statuary, paintings) were replaced by another: the royal coat of arms, symbol of the monarchical church, and scriptural passages, the Word of God itself. What was involved here was more complex than a shift in the locus of authority or in the nature of representation from images to print. The medieval church as such presented an image of unified authority in which no more meaningful a distinction could be made between the church per se and its ornamentation than among the functions of a stained glass window as a source of light, a bearer of images, and a structural part of the church edifice. Each individual church was part of the universal one; by definition, whatever this sacred space contained was itself sacred. To reject any aspect of it was to call into question the whole; thus, Lollard iconoclasm of the late fourteenth and fifteenth centuries was inseparable from the rejection of clerical authority. The Northampton Lollard Anne Palmer thought that "it suffices every Christian to serve God's commandments in his chamber, or to worship God secretly in the field, without call for public prayers *in a material building*" [emphasis added].[242] No image, no church: all that remained was an impertinent summons to "a material building."

Lollards, Hussites, and later Lutherans replaced clerical with scriptural command—still a univocal source of authority, albeit one subject to the hazard of individual interpretation ("Christian liberty"). In the Henrician church, however, authority was bifurcated. Henry appropriated the property, rituals, and canons of the church, and, after a brief flirtation with a "national" Catholicism, began to treat them very much as he did his secular endowments and ordinances. At the same time, he confronted a serious perplexity. Unlike Lutheran princes on the Continent, he never embraced Reformed theology, and although his principal advisers and ecclesiastics were perforce Protestant, he balanced them with others — Bonner, Gardiner — whose Catholic sympathies were known. From every point of view but his own, therefore, Henry might be regarded as a heretic, and his frequent changes of doctrinal course (though often reflective of secular concerns) suggested that that point of view as well remained an unsettled one. Under these circumstances, it could not be surprising that more of Henry's subjects were tempted to seek the truth for themselves in the only place where it could certifiably be found — the Holy Scriptures.

English bibles were not illegal, although their possession appears to have required licensing, which effectively limited permissible ownership to the privileged orders. Henry VIII, who was doubtless familiar with the English bible in his father's library, was not averse to making the Scriptures available in the vernacular, provided that unsupervised reading did not lead simple folk astray. This caveat served as the pretext for suppressing Tyndale's *New Testament* (1525), but the breach with Rome brought a swift change of attitude. By 1535 Cranmer had ordered his bishops to correct the Tyndale version with a view toward official publication, and the following year Cromwell commanded that every parish church acquire a bible in the vernacular by August 1, 1537. The English Reformation was thus indelibly associated from the beginning with the English bible.

Richard Rex notes that "The promotion of the vernacular Bible was not only an integral part of the early strategy for the enforcement of the royal supremacy, but, originally at least, an integral part of the supremacy itself."[243] An English bible was, for the vast majority of Henry's subjects, quite literally a revelation. For the first time the Word of God was accessible to them in the form of their own speech, not merely as reflected in images, digested in the formularies of Latin prayers, glimpsed in the pageantry of miracle plays and devotional processions, or expounded in the parish sermon. The impact of this upon the godly (as upon their Lollard predecessors) was to radically delegitimize all but the last of these devices; hence the iconoclasm and antitheatricality that characterized godly culture. These and the far worse hazards of unmediated exposure to the Word presented by the polygamous and communistic Anabaptists of Münster were obvious enough, but the supremacy had transposed the traditional equation between religious authority and control of the Bible. The Henrician Reformation, doctrinally conservative, required more than the settlement of the King's matrimonial problems to dramatize its appearance and to justify its vast assumption of power. It needed nothing less than a gesture that would demonstrate, in the words of Henry's Bishop of Chichester, Richard Sampson, that "the word of God is, obedience to the king rather than to the pope."[244]

This gesture was immediately to hand in the English bible published by Miles Coverdale in 1535. In the bottom quarter of the title page engraving,

Hans Holbein depicted an enthroned king, scepter in hand, conferring the bible on an attendant circle of kneeling bishops and lords. In the center foreground, beneath the throne and separating the lords temporal and spiritual, was the royal coat of arms; directly above it in the upper quarter was a radiant sun inscribed with the name of God in Hebrew letters. In between were images of Moses receiving the Ten Commandments, Jesus preaching the Gospel, and the apostles disseminating it. The line of descent from divine utterance to the Constantinian ruler is clear.[245]

There could hardly have been a more open invitation to royal patronage than this, and Holbein, although working independently for Coverdale, was Cromwell's client. Subsequent editions of this bible—in 1537, 1550, and 1553—obtained royal licensing, as did the so-called Matthew Bible of 1537. It was not until 1539, however, that a bible directly promulgated by royal authority, the Great Bible, made its appearance. The bishops' reluctance and Henry's zeal to produce it are well known; brushing aside all complaint of error in the translation, he demanded only to know whether it contained actual heresy. The title page engraving of this edition, divided by thirds, placed a figure recognizably that of the enthroned Henry at the top, with a multitude of commoners chanting "Vivat Rex" at the bottom.[246] With the edition of November 1540 the title page text itself was altered to read:

> The Byble in Englyshe of the largest and greatest volume, auctorysed and apoynted by the commaundemente of oure most redoubted Prynce and soueraygne Lorde, Kynge Henrye the viii. supreme heade of this his churche and realme of Englande: to be frequented and vsed in euery churche *within* this his sayd realme . . .

With these words, Henry defined his new church as the abrupt shifts of doctrine that characterized the later 1530s could never do. The Anglican church was the place where the English bible could be found.

It was also the place, however, where it was chained. There is no reason to suspect that the King's personal attitudes had changed from that expressed in his proclamation of May 1530 against "English books," that "the holy scripture in English is not necessary to Christian men" (i.e., to their salvation). For Henry, the potential benefits of edification had to be set against the possible "confusion" to simple souls of untutored bible-reading, and as between order and enlightenment Henry's sights were firmly set on the former.[247] His haste to have an authorized bible published in 1539 should not be read as an eagerness to have it read by the laity: it was an eagerness to have it authorized, to have the Word of God licensed by the King's writ.

The King's Bible went through eight editions by the end of 1541. The second and subsequent editions reflected the temporary ascendancy of Archbishop Cranmer at Court, and are known, misleadingly, as Cranmer's

Bibles. Cranmer's prologue to these editions envisioned (without actually calling for) a bible in every layman's hands:

> Doest thou not marke and consider howe the smyth, mason, or carpenter, or any other handy craftesma*n*, what neade so euer he be in, what other shyfte soeuer he make, wyll not sell or laye to pledge the toles of hys occu-pacyon, for then howe shulde he worke his feate or get hys lyuinge therby? Of lyke mynde an affeccyon ought we to be towardes holye scripture, for as mallettes, hammars, sawes, chesylles, axes, and hatchettes be the tooles of theyr occupaycon[,] so bene the bokes of the prophetes, and apostelles, and all holye wryte inspired by the holy ghost, *ye* instrumentes of oure salua-cyon. Wherfore, let vs not stycke to bye and prouyde vs the Byble, that is to saye, the bookes of holy scripture. And lett vs thinke that to be a better Iuell in our house then eyther golde or syluer.[248]

Cranmer's metaphor of the tool carried a double message: first, that the Bible was the instrument of personal salvation; second, that it belonged in every hand and household, however humble. Henry had never subscribed to the first position, and he soon discountenanced the second. By an act of 1543, private possession of the Bible was restricted to persons of quality, and pub-lic readings of it in churches to ministers. The latter restraint grew out of the disturbance of services created by oracular readings, but its symbolic import was unmistakable: the Bible was royal property, and not to be trusted to the vulgar.

As a corollary, the unauthorized Tyndale and Coverdale bibles were banned in 1543 and 1546, respectively, although the Great Bible was in fact little more than an edited conflation of both. These rival editions were, it is true, objectionable on the grounds of their Protestantizing marginalia, espe-cially in the doctrinally more conservative climate of Henry's last years. Henry himself lamented the debasement of Scripture in the hands of the lower orders, complaining that it was "disputed, rhymed, sung, and jangled in every alehouse and tavern."[249] But the good and sufficient reason for re-moving the Tyndale and Coverdale bibles from circulation was that they in-fringed the royal monopoly of the Word.

In the century between 1540 and 1640 English culture became thoroughly steeped in the stories and cadences of the vernacular Bible; it was not only "The Book of Books," as Christopher Hill put it, but the very touchstone of legitimacy.[250] Here was the model not only for all Christian subjects but for all rulers as well, the pattern both of the righteous Josias and the wicked Herod. As early as Henry's reign, English Reformers had begun to apply these typologies to their kings; thus, Henry was a Hezekiah, a man who had cleared the ground for the temple, but only Edward a Josias, one who had actually built it. The Henrician embrace of the Bible that had tied English monarchs to the Christian imperium had given their subjects a rod not only to measure them by, but, potentially, to chastise them with. The revolutionaries of 1642 would base their case against Charles I no less on divine than on positive law.

Henry's efforts to define his church through an authorized bible and the apparatus of worship that went with it—prayer books, homilies, psalters, and primers—was thus a double-edged sword. There could be no national religion without a national bible, but it was an idle dream to believe that the Bible could be contained within the framework that Henry had designed for it. In any event, the goal of authorization—an exclusive text, the Word of God set forth by the King's command—would remain illusory. The Coverdale Bible returned under Edward, with the new king's features gracing its frontispiece.[251] Mary banned all vernacular bibles, though she spared the Great Bible from confiscation and destruction—perhaps because her father's image adorned it? Elizabeth tried to reinstitute its use, but her efforts were preempted by the Geneva Bible, produced independently by the Marian exiles and incorporating the latest Continental scholarship.

The Geneva Bible was dedicated to Elizabeth, but more in the manner of a challenge than a submission. After noting that the Queen herself had been "pulled out of the mouth of the lions" by God's "wonderful mercies," it looked for her to encompass "some wonderful work" for the Gospel:

> Therefore even above strength you must shew yourself strong and bold in God's matters. . . . This Lord of lords and King of kings who hath ever defended his, strengthen, comfort and preserve Your Majesty, that you may be able to build up the ruins of God's house to his glory, the discharge of your conscience, and to the comfort of all them that love the coming of Christ Jesus our Lord.

This was the authentic note of the godly, on behalf of their stern and impatient God. England had been chastised for its sins by the Marian scourge. The remnant faithful had returned triumphant from their persecution with the Word, purified by immersion in the original Hebrew, fortified by extensive annotations to instruct the pious. This was not a bible meant to dangle from a chain but to be (as Cranmer had intended) the jewel and crown of each household, savored and pondered nightly. Having addressed (and tasked) the Queen, charging her not only with the restoration and good governance of the church but with the call to a higher and as yet undisclosed destiny as Christian emperor, it turned to the reader, explaining its protocols and drawing attention to its soon-to-be-famous notes. These would serve as a minister might, indeed in place of one where the parish was unprovided for or where the incumbent was slack, deficient, or even, as was not infrequently the case, covertly Papist. Thus, the beast in Revelation was definitively identified as the papacy; thus, too, King Asa was not praised for deposing his mother for idolatry, but rebuked for sparing her life.

The Geneva Bible was as far from an authorized text as possible; unlike the Tyndale and Coverdale bibles, it did not crave royal patronage. It obtruded itself as a matter of right and justified itself on grounds of scholarship, and although of course it required licensing for its free circulation it did not depend on favor for its existence: it was printed with private funds and published, until 1575, beyond the censor's reach. In the generous acknowledgment it gave to foreign colleagues and sponsors it underscored its links with the international Reformed movement, including Calvin himself. Intended for an English-speaking audience, it was anything but the product of an insular church.

Archbishop Parker, perhaps making a virtue of necessity, allowed that it was "good to have diversity of translations and readings" of the Bible.[252] The fact was that the old Cranmer and Coverdale bibles were now obsolete, and such copies as had survived the Marian persecutions were largely in private hands. A new authorized version, the Bishops' Bible, was not available until 1568. Until that time the Geneva Bible had the field largely to itself, and by then it was already established as the most popular English bible of the sixteenth century. The Bishops' Bible was dutifully reprinted until it was supplanted by the King James version, but Elizabeth never embraced it, and it remained promulgated by episcopal rather than direct royal decree. The Queen even offered it an implicit rebuke when she licensed an edition of the Geneva New Testament, revised by Laurence Tomson, for publication in England in 1576. This edition contained the notorious annotation in support of prophesying. Tomson's sponsors were his own employer, Secretary Walsingham, and Archbishop Grindal. The Tomson edition, like the Cranmer Bible, showed the difficulty of maintaining a united conformist front on behalf of an authorized and ideologically anodyne version of Scripture, even within the government itself.

The Geneva Bible was of course most offensive to the English Catholic community, whose exiles produced their own translation out of the Vulgate, the Douai Bible. The avowed purpose of this bible, which included summaries and annotations, was "for the better vnderstanding of the text, and specially for the discoueries of the Corrvptions of diuers late translations, and for cleering the Controversies in religion, of these daies."[253] The translation itself was merely an aid to, not a substitute for, the Vulgate, which remained the authoritative text; the notes, too, were a guide to the authoritative interpretation, which rested not (as the Geneva exiles had implied) with the translators, nor on the shifting sands of heresy and schism, but on the sure foundation of the apostolic church. The recusant reader therefore stood in a far different relation to the vernacular Bible than his Reformed counterpart. His hermeneutic task, insofar as one was imposed on him, was far less exigent; it was not so much to receive truth as to be armed, in a hostile environment, against manifest error. The Geneva Bible, like its Tyndale and Coverdale predecessors, existed because without it the Word was accessible only to a handful of scholars, and those scholars themselves could not avail themselves of it without discussion and argument; that is, without translation. The Douai Bible existed because the Geneva Bible (and its other Reformed rivals) did.[254]

Elizabeth I's personal religious conviction is as well kept an historical secret as that of her virginity. Her religious governance was based on an elastic conformity designed to produce obedience and tranquillity in a new-modeled Henrician church. Circumstances cast her in the role of a Christian prince when she was quite satisfied to be an Erastian one; prudence told her that, after the religious upheavals that had attended her own first twenty-five years of life, a comprehensive rather than an imperial church was called for. These considerations, as well as the modesty imposed on her by gender, may account for the fact that her reign produced no bible associated with her name, no iconographic appropriation of Scripture such as her father had made in the Great Bible, and no serious attempt either to curtail the Geneva Bible or to promote the Bishops' Bible in its stead. James I thus leaped at the suggestion that he commission a new authorized translation to drive the Geneva Bible, which he described as "untrue," "seditious," and "traitorous," from the field. The King James Bible, published without interpretive notes, was ultimately triumphant, but it did not replace the Geneva Bible until the Civil War. Most of the English men and women who took up the cause against Charles I had been brought up on the exiles' old bible, and the *Soldiers Pocket Bible* that Cromwell's troopers carried into battle was drawn from it. The godly had failed to prevail in their native church, but in the hundred years' contest over printing and disseminating the Word, the innings were mostly theirs.

Making the vernacular bible available was, however, only the first step toward scriptural truth. A bible not preached, especially where the Word had been withheld for so long, was still a bible penned up. As the authors of the *Second Admonition* complained, it remained under the regime of Archbishop Parker

> so circumscribed and wrapt in the compasse of such statu[t]es, suche penalties, suche injunctions, suche advertisements, suche articles, suche canons, suche sober caveats . . . that in manner it doth peepe out from behinde the screene.[255]

The absence of good preaching, or at times of any preaching at all, was to remain a constant complaint of the godly down to 1640. The unique status of the Bible as the locus of divine truth prescribed a distinctive hermeneutics, however. To have made the Word dependent on its preaching suggested the need for a new priestly elite, a point conformists were not slow to raise.

Godly scholiasts such as Fulke and Whitaker were deeply aware of the dark and riddling passages of Scripture that even the most learned could not fully penetrate. The difficulty in interpreting such passages — and the possibility of misconstruing plain truths as well — was compounded by humanity's fallen nature. If the Devil could quote Scripture to his purpose, unreconstructed human sinfulness was no less apt to distort it.

Virtually every issue that divided godly Englishmen from conformists boiled down to the necessity for the strict and literal interpretation of Scripture in all things pertaining to the church. This bred unyielding assurance in the godly when they reached consensus, but doubt and distress when they could not. For conformists, the extraction of general principles and right doctrine from the Bible was sufficient, both for the faithful and for their church. As Hooker pointed out, the Bible was a compendium that contained God's progressively revealed will and truth, embedded in a vast historical narrative; if none of its details were merely anecdotal, not all of them were of equal weight, much less necessary in themselves for salvation. To scrutinize them excessively was not to reveal but to obscure the truth, just as to seek a foundation in Scripture for matters "mean" or indifferent was to derogate from its inherent dignity.[256] In the worst case, truth sufficiently strained could lead to false imaginings: the charge leveled at "prelates" by the godly reversed.[257] Nor could it be forgotten that Holy Writ, though divinely inspired as a whole and perspicuous in its essence, had itself been transmitted through human vessels. To cast down Dagon but make an idol of every syllable of Scripture was to defeat the operations of the Spirit. As John Dryden was to put it a century later:

> ... the *Scriptures*, though not *every where*
> Free from Corruption, or intire, or clear,
> Are uncorrupt, sufficient, clear, intire,
> In *all* things which our needfull *Faith* require.[258]

The "needfull" points of Scripture — in Hooker's time, the essential doctrine enshrined in the Thirty-Nine Articles — could, accordingly, be inculcated by homily and redacted in the Prayer Book. The Bible, that is, might be simplified for popular consumption with no loss of integrity. Erasmus had done precisely this in his *Paraphrases*, and under Edward VI every parish church had been required to purchase a copy of his book in Nicholas Udall's translation. Even the annotators of the Geneva Bible had not seen fit to publish the Scriptures without guidance and commentary.

The conformist approach to the Bible differed fundamentally from that of the godly. For conformists, the truth of Scripture was something to be culled and predigested, at least for the vulgar; for the godly, the Word, and the Spirit it manifested, was endlessly fructifying. No intelligence could fully penetrate it; no learning could encompass it; no analysis could exhaust it.

Mere reason was simply confounded by it. As the conduit of the Spirit, the Word was inherently dynamic, or in contemporary parlance, "lively." To expound the Gospel was to quicken the Spirit in the Christian heart, and this, the office of preaching, was not ancillary to the service of worship but its essence. Hence the great emphasis the godly put on a preaching ministry, and the enormous valuation they placed on the "gifted" minister who could spin a single phrase of Scripture into a compelling two-hour sermon.

There was little in the foregoing with which conformists would have disagreed in principle, and certainly the sermons of Andrewes, Donne, and Herbert are among the glories of English literature. As government functionaries and as representatives of a comprehensive church, however, their role was to police the wayward and the reprobate rather than to stimulate the elect. The *presumption* of election they confined in practice to themselves and to the other elites who served the Christian imperium; whatever lip service they paid to the ultimate destiny of the meek, it was those who preserved God's order in the here and now who did the manifest work of his church. This was what the godly understood as prelacy. The doctrine of predestination to which all members of the church officially subscribed (and, perhaps no less importantly, the reduced social position of the Elizabethan episcopacy) enforced a greater modesty on the senior conformist clergy than on their Catholic counterparts; even a Laud was not to be compared with Wolsey. But there is no question that church administrators and apologists saw themselves in terms that promoted the distinction between the clergy and the laity. The major disputes of the pre-Caroline church—over vestments and ceremonies, preaching and homilies, and the structure of church government itself—all revolved around this distinction and the secular as well as religious hierarchies it presupposed.

The godly also presumed their own election, although the concept of assurance entailed perpetual anxiety and self-vigilance. Their ranks too were stratified, and their aloofness from the common herd of sinners was often experienced by others as arrogance; Zeal-of-the-Land-Busy was not merely a figment of literary imagination. But the democracy of the Word was real too: its truth was dynamic and experiential, holding no commerce with stale formulae and barren ritual but renewed daily in the hearts of the faithful. Status was no help here and hierarchy an encumbrance. There was no higher title to be sought than that of minister of the Word, and the minister was simply *primus inter pares* among his congregants, distinguished not by his ordination or even his learning but by a continual application to the plenitude of Scripture described by that untranslatable term "painful." In the presence of the Word the faithful were united as equals, but that equality was only enforced by their radical separation as individuals. As a distant but also pre-Weberian commentator remarked:

The great significance of the historical process that began with the Reformation is its having isolated individuals, leaving them to themselves, in order
that they might consciously and freely turn to the divine principle and enter into a perfectly free and deliberate union with it.[259]

The godly elect were a perpetual gathering out of a corrupted church and
a reprobate humanity, never to be perfectly a group until the last trump had
sounded, just as their quest for truth was a continual search for understanding and a constant striving for righteousness. The touchstone of that quest
was the Word, in prayer and meditation, in close study and godly conversation, in prophesying and in preaching, in the fulfilling round of the holy life.
The beginning and the end of that quest was the Bible, not as a bare repository of truth but as a perpetual source of comfort and replenishment, as a
terror to the wicked and a spur to the just; in short, as a constant encounter.
But although the intensity of that encounter was the peculiar mark of the
godly, the Bible was omnipresent in the lives of ordinary folk as well. As
Christopher Hill reminds us:

> We should not think of the Bible just as a book to be read, or to listen to. It
> was everywhere in the lives of men, women and children. Not only in the
> church services they had to attend, but in the ballads they bought and sang,
> and in their daily surroundings. Where today we should expect wallpaper,
> almost all houses had hangings to keep out draughts and to cover the
> rough walls. These often took the form of 'painted cloths', among which
> Biblical scenes seem to have preponderated. In accordance with Deuteron-
> omy XI.20, Biblical texts were very often painted on walls or posts in
> houses. . . . In addition, walls were covered with printed matter—almanacs,
> illustrated ballads and broadsides, again often on Biblical subjects.[260]

There is no more striking testimony to the centrality of the vernacular Bible in sixteenth and seventeenth century England than the final illustration
of Foxe's *Actes and Monuments*, in which Justice holds her scales above the
world. In one of them is set the Word; in the other, the entire material wealth
of the Roman church—of the world itself, profanely conceived—fails to balance it. Yet this final iconoclastic triumph of the Word is itself conveyed by
means of a picture, and it must be remembered that the print revolution disseminated not only more words than ever before but more images as well.
No simple picture of a culture of "orality" replacing a visual one, therefore,
will do. What occurred in Protestant England was less the progressive elimi-
nation of religious imagery than the replacement of a set of images upholding the old popish order with another representing the new Reformed one.
Positive images of the deity, the Virgin, the saints, and the traditional martyrs were replaced by depictions of the papacy and its minions as a Satanic
host bestridden by the beasts and hags of Revelation. Such prints (as well as
secular ones of a satiric nature) had a wide and popular audience, and their

chief student believes a growing one in the early seventeenth century.[261] They were exempt from iconoclastic objections on two grounds. Unlike popish images designed to lure the innocent into submission to a false church, they were meant to repel and appall, and thus by definition to discourage idolatrous worship. Basing themselves on scriptural prophecy, they embodied not error but truth.

Not all Reformed iconography was based on negative exempla, of course. There could be no serious objection to representing Old Testament patriarchs; Moses and Aaron adorned the King James Bible, and various heroic figures, historical and allegorical, were frequently depicted routing the popish host. But the new church had its own genealogy of martyrs, immortalized not only in the text of Foxe's book but in the 170 woodcuts that were integral to its presentation. These illustrations ranged from the stylized and the allegorical to the specific and personal. They showed ranks of martyrs steadfast in the flames, and individual heroes—Hus, Oldcastle, Tyndale, Rogers, Latimer, Ridley, Cranmer—meeting their ends in prayer and equanimity of spirit, fortified by divine grace. As in the text, gruesome and sadistic tortures preceded the triumph of martyrdom, as the flames that consumed the bodies of the victims simultaneously translated them to their heavenly reward. In contrast, the torturers themselves were shown as consumed by fleshly lusts; Bishop Bonner, scourging a saint in his garden, has a visible erection. The irony of the reprobate attempting to inflict the punishments of hell that wait for them on the saints whose faithfulness in the last trial is the seal of their salvation could not but have deeply impressed Foxe's readers—and the nonreaders for whom such images were in fact his book. Similarly, the triumph of the true church over the false one is depicted by patterned reversals of images; thus, Henry IV barefoot in the snows of Canossa is reversed by Elizabeth seated in triumph, and Pope Alexander III treading on the neck of Frederick I by Henry VIII doing likewise to Clement VII. Such representations, indeed, affirmed an identity between the true church and the Constantinian emperor far more emphatically than mere text could have done.[262]

The Discourse of Apocalypse

In demolishing the idols of a false church and restoring the Bible to its rightful position at the center of faith, the Reformation had reopened the question of the dynamic of Christian history itself. As Robin Bruce Barnes points out, the origins of Christianity itself were "intimately bound up" with a period of intense apocalyptic speculation in Judaism that began about 200 B.C.[263] The Reformation, by the mid-sixteenth century clearly the most fundamental alteration in Western Christendom in a thousand years, could not but stir similar speculation about the purposes of Providence in giving light to this latter age. The Reformation had, as John Bale argued in *The Image of bothe churches* (1548), not only revealed anew the truth of the Gospel but had exposed the falsity of the Roman church as the Antichrist. This twin revelation was a singular mark of Providence, for, as William Fulke noted a generation later, the Roman Antichrist had been sent specifically as a punishment for humanity's derogation from the purity of the primitive church and its rejection of the Gospel.[264] It also meant, for the faithful, the commencement of a period of perilous struggle, for the Antichrist would resist with all the cunning and wrath of which hell was capable, and the elect would be called to prove their worthiness and mettle. For godly Elizabethans, the Marian persecutions were the eruption of that wrath, and the second restoration of the true church, purchased with the blood of the martyrs, a signal mark of divine mercy. Foxe's *Actes and Monuments*, in its successive editions cast in an increasingly apocalyptic framework, set an official seal on this interpretation of the Reformation in England, and although conformists might prescind from it, they did not reject it.

Apocalyptic thought in England thus cut across the entire spectrum of church opinion. It gave Anglicanism a theological pedigree to underwrite the formally political acts that had brought it into being under Henry, caused it to perish under Mary, and resurrected it under Elizabeth. What from a legal point of view had been the act of the King in Parliament (or, from a Roman one, that of a heretic and his schismatics) was revealed as the divinely ordained restoration of the true church which, submerged but never eclipsed, was unbroken in historical time from the apostolic age, and, through God's calling of the elect, from all eternity. The Church of England had not been born with the Henrician Act of Supremacy but merely freed from the persecution of Antichrist—and not perfectly freed either, until the blood of the Marian martyrs had purchased the at least relatively secure ground of the Elizabethan settlement.

From this point of view, the church existed both immemorially as a spiritual incarnation (the body of Christ) and temporally in its material estate. That estate might be the scattered witness of its faithful or the full-blown Constantinian *établissement* of a national church. It was neither more nor less in either case (the body of the elect being constant); rather, its material condition at any given moment was an index of God's mercy and favor, and that in turn was linked to his providential order—the hidden narrative of history through which his will was unfolded. God's purpose in history was known; it had been fully revealed in the passion of Christ. What remained problematic was the process through which that purpose was to be realized. The tension between certain ends and uncertain means constituted history as such; God's efficient will was inscrutable that redemption might be preceded by repentance.

Nonetheless, God had left tokens of his providential plan throughout both testaments in the form of prophetic books and utterances. Some of these had been fulfilled, most notably the coming of his Son, and the Word of Jesus itself as declared in the Gospels was a new prophetic order. Jesus had spoken, however, chiefly about the ends of the divine purpose and about the duties of the faithful, rather than discursively about the historical process. For that a separate book of prophecy had been reserved, the Revelation of St. John. Together with chapters and passages in the Books of Ezekiel and Daniel and in Matthew, 2 Thessalonians, 1 Timothy, and 1 and 2 John, this prophecy set out in coded form the providential order in history. The reason for the code —especially in the Book of Revelation, whose imagistic language was in stark contrast to the often simple, declarative tone of the Gospels—was two-fold. First, the code concealed the specifics of God's plan from the wicked and the unrighteous, thereby protecting the just. Second, by revealing enough to arm and comfort the faithful in their struggle with the Antichrist but by concealing enough (at least from human understanding) to keep them in a state of continual vigilance, expectation, and militance, God gave proper scope to the exercise of human freedom. The Book of Revelation thus posed a special problem of interpretation. The Revelation was not partial but full, for not only were the essentials of God's plan contained in it but many of the specifics as well—the nature and duration of the Beast's authority, the marks of the faithful, the signs of Advent and even perhaps the hour. All that was revealed would be known in the fullness of time, but to prepare against that time (which might come at any moment) and to play one's allotted part (which was always the most perfect obedience to God's will combined with the utmost resistance to evil), it was imperative to decipher the text as fully as possible. The task of decipherment, in short, was itself a part of Christian duty.

The felt urgency of this task varied with the times. If the Day of Judgment was the presupposition and goal of the Christian conversation, it came to the fore only at moments of crisis. The Reformation was clearly such a moment. Yet its leading figures were, at least initially, cautious in their approach to the Book of Revelation. Luther was reluctant to comment on it, calling it a book he had never understood and expressing doubts (as did other Reformers) as to its canonicity. Calvin too was guarded in his appraisal, sensing its potential for arousing enthusiasm. By mid-century, however, it had become central to the Reformation hermeneutic. No other text so persuasively portrayed the historical drama of redemption, or enabled the Reformers to understand their own roles in it.

Heinrich Bullinger's long course of sermons on Revelation, delivered in 1555–1556, marked a turning point in the reception of apocalyptic thought in England. The Swiss pastor was, as Richard Bauckham notes, the "unofficial chaplain to the English in Europe" during the Marian exile, and his commentary, published in England in 1561, formed the basis of the Geneva Bible annotations on Revelation.[265] For the Marian exiles, Bullinger's exposition expressed their own sense of being uniquely singled out, even among the elect, to testify in the Lamb's war. England's providential deliverance from Mary, followed by Knox's revolution in Scotland, quickened their sense that the struggle with Antichrist was approaching its climax, and that England would be in the forefront of it. Bale's *Image of both churches*, itself building on Wyclifite prophecies as well as Continental sources, had already provided them with a native framework of apocalyptic interpretation. Foxe and the Spanish Armada sealed it. By the end of the sixteenth century, the conviction that England was not merely the recipient of singular mercies and blessings but, in William Haller's famous phrase, an elect nation, had taken root. The phrase must be used with due caution, for the actual elect in any country were held to be a minority, and England was seen as the leader of the general Protestant crusade rather than as a solitary Israel. Nonetheless, the sense of England's special role in the last days seemed clear; as Thomas Rogers remarked in 1589, "He that seeth not a speciall regard of God towardes us . . . is verie blinde."[266]

The tension in apocalyptic thought between England as a collectively sacralized or "redeemer" nation and the sense of the godly that they were an embattled if not a persecuted minority was unresolved and perhaps unresolvable. "England" was, in the godly imagination, sometimes the righteous themselves, and sometimes the land of the reprobate. Apocalypticism was a way of reconciling this opposition that at the same time intensified it. It projected England onto the larger stage of the Lamb's war, but at the same time focused attention on it as a latter-day Israel, destined perhaps not only to give light to the world as the Old Testament kingdom had done but also to lead the nations in the final struggle with Antichrist. Israel, too, had been a land of prophets and sinners, of the righteous few and the idolatrous many. God's greatest favor had alighted on it, and therefore also his greatest wrath, for those who fell away from the Word were far more culpable than those to whom it had not been vouchsafed.

The situations of England and Israel were not wholly apposite, of course, because the Gospel had gone abroad to many nations. The English church was but one of the true churches, and (albeit the largest) far from the most exemplary. At the same time, however, the connection between England and Israel was deeper than one of mere analogy or historical parallelism. Israel might be taken as the prefigurement of England, its destiny finding resolution in England's. Hezekiah walked again in Henry, Josias in Edward, Deborah in Elizabeth. In courtesy literature, these typologies might remain on the plane of allegory (though allegory itself, in the hands of a Spenser or a

Sidney, was a potent form of religious acknowledgment). In apocalyptic commentary, they were the prophesied fulfillment of the scriptural drama. The identity between Deborah and Elizabeth was far deeper than any mere reincarnation; they played the same role in the historical rejuvenation of the eternal church. The role was what counted, not the particular agent, for in the drama of redemption the only true personhood was that of Christ.

Prophecy and observation went hand in hand in the identification of England as the new Israel. Just as the true church was known by its marks, so the elect nation was gradually revealed by the tasks confided to it. England had not been the first nation to embrace the Reformation, but it had been the only one tried again in the fires of the Antichrist and proved in the blood of its martyrs. Foxe's *Actes and Monuments*, the central text of the Elizabethan era, had established the Smithfield martyrs as prime witnesses to the world's final age, laboriously connecting them with the martyrs not only of England's past but of the primitive church as well.

"England" was in this construction still only its faithful, not the nation as such. The Elizabethan restoration provided the decisive, overarching connection between the two. Not only had God shown his extraordinary favor in rescuing the nation a second time from its thralldom to Rome, but in Elizabeth he had placed a second Constantine on the throne. As Richard Helgerson has pointed out, Foxe realigned apocalyptic history in the *Actes* to conform with the British experience. The thousand-year binding of Satan was dated to the reign of the Briton, Constantine, and his loosing to the persecution of the Lollards. If Elizabeth were Constantine's genuine successor, then Britain, too, was destined to lead the spiritual empire of Christ among the nations. The *Actes* clinches this identification as forcefully as possible. Elizabeth is shown enthroned within the embroidered C that forms the first letter of the word *Constantine* on the dedication page of the first edition, holding an imperial orb and scepter and treading the Roman Antichrist, with the broken key of St. Peter, underfoot. In the 1576 and subsequent editions an even more intimate association is made, the same image being depicted within the initial letter of the name *Christ*.[267] The image itself was nothing new; Edward VI had also been depicted with a scepter (although not an orb) treading down the Pope. What was different was the direct and unqualified identification of Britain's sovereign with Constantine, and thus the linking of the nation's destiny with that of providential history. Edward had been shown vindicating the rights of a national church against the usurpations of Rome, an act the King of Denmark could lay equal claim to, or for that matter the King of France. By connecting the "imperial theme" that Henry VIII had made the leitmotif of the Tudor monarchy with the apocalyptic role of the Constantinian emperor, Foxe had elevated Britain to a position of eschatological leadership among the nations, although he himself worked out the implications of this only gradually.

The emerging secular consciousness of England's nationhood as epitomized in Hakluyt's chronicles and Shakespeare's history plays and the eschatological nationalism adumbrated by Foxe and his successors are to some extent parallel and to some extent intertwined developments. As Henrician imperialism had made an Anglican church possible and as that church in turn had buttressed imperial claims, so the notions of the elect and of the imperial nation underwrote each other. Contemporaries were of course fully capable of distinguishing the two, just as they could distinguish the mundane aspects of Anglo-Spanish commercial rivalry from the apocalyptic dimension of the Anglo-Spanish war; they would simply not have thought to disconnect them since they were, at a deeper level of synthesis, self-evidently unified.

This unity took the form of "universal monarchy," a concept that gained currency in the sixteenth and early seventeenth centuries because it so neatly encapsulated the perceived underlying relationships between mercantile hegemony, political despotism, and spiritual tyranny. On this view, universal monarchy was the pretended dominion of Antichrist as exercised during the (variously defined) period when Rome had held sway over Christian consciences, persecuting the faithful and holding the nations in thrall. The Reformation had commenced the second binding of Satan, but, roused to fury, he sought to restore his shattered empire. Thus, while Rome attempted to regain its control over conscience, Spain sought terrestrial empire, each for itself and both, as limbs of the Antichrist, on Satan's behalf.

Despite the polarized and ideologically charged view of international relations to which these notions gave rise, political distinctions were not entirely clear-cut. States adhering to the Roman church were not necessarily, or at any rate unambiguously, in the camp of the Antichrist. France, with its sizable Huguenot minority and its traditional policy of resistance to Habsburg hegemony, might be regarded as an ally, at least in *politique* terms; so too Venice, whose admired constitution mitigated to some degree its confessional status. But Satan required a civil bastion for his final assault on the true church, and that bastion had become identified with Spain, the principal support of the Counter-Reformation, the instrument of the Marian persecution, and the hell-sprung source of the Armada. This was the basis of the "black legend" of late sixteenth and early seventeenth-century fame.[268] To be sure, it was not necessary to share a fully developed apocalyptic vision to regard Spain as an inveterate enemy, and it was possible to hold to at least the presuppositions of that vision and still do business with Spain, as trading companies were eager to do after the settlement of 1604, or even to seek a political entente, as James I did in spite of his own avowed apocalypticism. But patriotic and apocalyptic duty were always ready to fuse; as the godly minister and pamphleteer Thomas Scott noted in urging renewed war against the Spanish empire in the 1620s, "the Commonwealth and Religion of England have had their glory and propagation by opposing Antichrist, and in plaine terms reputing Spain."[269]

Apocalypticism thus added its fervors to the polarized worldview that characterized the godly *mentalité* in post-Reformation England. In the simplest terms, it provided an answer to the most vexing of theological questions, that of evil, and a response to the ancient cry of *How long, O Lord, how long?* John Foxe, in the last edition of the *Actes* published in his lifetime (1583), reflected on the seemingly unending trials of the faithful: "The Israelites in the captivity of Babylon had seventy years limited unto them; and under Pharaoh they were promised a deliverance out; also under the Syrian tyrants threescore and two weeks were abridged unto them. Only in these persecutions [i.e., those under the Gospel] I could find no end determined, nor limitation set for their deliverance."[270] Foxe could seek an answer only in Revelation, and there he found one—or rather, several, for at various times he calculated that the Last Days would commence in 1564, 1570, 1583, and 1587. Like other apocalypticists, Foxe was unconcerned when these years passed without decisive incident, for it was presumed that the sounding of the seventh trumpet meant not the immediate advent of Christ but the inauguration of the world's final epoch, a period of uncertain but possibly substantial duration. In the later Elizabethan period, three years—1583, 1588, and 1593—were the focus of intense apocalyptic speculation, and the events of 1588, certainly, were dramatic enough to meet expectation. But, as Foxe continued to caution, the will of God could be fully known only after the event, and although he felt duty-bound to decipher it as far as he was able (why else had the Gospels offered humankind a book of prophecy?), inscrutability was, as it were, a condition of the investigation. It was enough to know the truth was written to be compelled to seek it; it was enough to know the truth abided to be unashamed of error.

Most of Foxe's successors adopted a similar prudence, although all sought to provide a chronological framework for what was generally assumed to be the allotted six thousand years of history, and all reckoned that the trumpet for the last age had either sounded or was imminent. Even commentators such as William Perkins, who warned against trying to pry open the secrets of a book God had deliberately sealed, shared the essential presuppositions of apocalypticism: belief in a limited and foreordained temporal span of history now nearing its close; the identification of the Church of Rome with the Antichrist; and the conviction that the Reformation had inaugurated a final period of struggle. This view was common to engaged and worldly laymen such as Sir Walter Raleigh and Sir Francis Bacon no less than to divines; indeed, some of the leading apocalypticists of the late Tudor and early Stuart period, notably the Scots mathematician John Napier and the English *érudit* Joseph Mede, were lay figures. Constantine himself endorsed the apocalyptic worldview: James I published a commentary on Revelation in 1616 that closely tied scriptural prophecy to the events of his day.[271]

Apocalypticism would thus seem to have provided a strong ideological buttress to the Church of England after 1559. The embrace of Foxe's *Actes and Monuments* by the church hierarchy was reciprocal; Foxe supported the Elizabethan settlement down to his death in 1587. But apocalypticism was a two-edged sword for the political order. On the one hand, it envisaged a culminating struggle with the Antichrist proceeding through the agency of the true church, the Constantinian emperor, and, ultimately, the elect nation. This triadic structure represented historical destiny in its final phase, the fulfillment of biblical prophecy. The true church, witnessed by its martyrs, was established by the Constantinian emperor, thereby securing it and exposing the falsity of the Antichrist. The emperor, as the ruler to whom obedience was owed on the political level according to scriptural command and to whom gratitude and thanksgiving were due for the restoration of the church, represented the united body of the realm, transcending in his office the distinction between the individually elect and the reprobate and thus personating the elect nation. The latter was a Christian imperium by virtue of its spiritual mandate and destiny, which was to replace the pretended universal monarchy of Antichrist with the true monarchy of Christ. As apocalyptic thought developed and responded to the pressure of events—of which the repulse of the Armada was particularly emblematic—the historical praxis of salvation seemed increasingly clear. God's will was fulfilled in and through the elect nation, and the elect nation was known in the unity of a Constantinian emperor with the true church.

Because the elements of an elect nation—a godly elite, an obedient people, a true church, and a Christian prince—were mutually reinforcing, and because they progressively unfolded themselves in the realization of historical destiny, they constituted an ordained and indissoluble unity. To be sure, the presence of one or more of these elements did not guarantee the rest; the true church had existed (and did exist) in lands where Christian liberty was suppressed, and pious princes had been destroyed by the power of Babylon. Even where the true church and the Constantinian emperor met as one, the challenge to godliness and the peril of destruction were constant: divine grace could never be taken for granted, nor the divine intention fully known. The experience of mercies and the fulfillment of prophecy could build an at best hesitating confidence, for had Israel itself not proved unworthy and succumbed to judgment? Yet the imminence of the Last Days (and here the apocalyptic framework provided a sense of urgency and hope that a merely eschatological one could not), combined with deliverances such as could only be seen as providential, offered grounds for a belief in the collective destiny of the nation and a determination to persevere in it. The defense of the church was the defense of the realm, and vice versa; and the defense of the ruler embodied both.

It would be difficult, certainly, to imagine a more profoundly rooted basis for commitment to the Tudor monarchy and its church. Yet on the other hand, the assumptions behind this commitment carried conditions as well. Apocalyptic thought bore with it the implication that the Constantinian emperor would lead the true church out of its wilderness not to the secure haven of a state religion but forward against the battlements of Antichrist. The Church of England was, in short, a militant church, and the state that civilly governed it was charged with the task of protecting and promoting the other branches of the universal true church abroad.

Taken to its logical extreme, therefore, English apocalypticism, despite its formal posture of deference to the prince, entailed his ultimate subordination to the mission of the church. Since God's will could not be fully known, the subject's role was to pray for the guidance of the prince. This could and did lead to passivity and even quietism; of the leading apocalypticists, only Hugh Broughton offered any challenge to authority. If as individuals the apocalypticists tended toward political (not clerical) conformity in inverse proportion to the boldness of their speculations, however, apocalypticism itself was inescapably judgmental as an interpretive framework. The Constantinian emperor was the prime agent in the drama of redemption. What he did or failed to do advanced or retarded it; the least of his acts was inseparably linked to it. To the extent that specific historical circumstances or events could be identified with prophecy, the success or failure of the emperor, his intrepidity or backwardness to the cause, was transparent. To say that the subject was not to judge his prince was one thing; to refrain from doing so was another. In fact, the Constantinian emperor was no less bound to the expectation that he would do his duty in the lists with Babylon than the medieval prince was by the obligation to deliver the Holy Land from the infidel.

Apocalyptic thought was therefore governed by a state of acute tension. On the one hand, the Constantinian emperor was a heaven-sent deliverer for whom no thanks was sufficient or praise excessive; on the other, the expectations of his office were correspondingly high. The emperor was the shepherd of his church, devoted to its perfection in form and edification in spirit; the paladin of the Reformed faith, militant in God's cause; the unrelenting foe of popery at home and abroad; the hammer of Antichrist. Being human, he could err and falter, but as God's emissary he could not swerve.

Such expectations made government difficult. In the real world, England's ruler faced a checkerboard of politics in which the forces of the Counter-

Reformation, contained only by a precarious détente, were stronger than those of the Reformed cause; in which religious allies were often commercial rivals; in which the perfection of the church (which different men defined differently) and the repression of popery were limited by prudential considerations. In this world, reasons of state dictated that the representatives of Catholic states were to be received with due honor; that marriage alliances with Catholic powers, whether consummated or not, were a necessary diplomatic option; that Catholic recusants, otherwise loyal and obedient, were to be left unmolested; that practices which even godly bishops privately regarded as popish were to be tolerated in the church. In practice English rulers, like those of any other time or place, dealt with the real world immediately, and with the ideological one as time or opportunity permitted. But the latter imposed constraints upon action; it, too, was a factor of "reality." Balance was often difficult to come by. Elizabeth spent forty years before she mastered her church to her own satisfaction, and then only with the help of a war with Spain that made the appeal to conformity at least temporarily one with that to national unity. James I played the roles of Christian emperor and politic statesman deftly, writing controversial works against Cardinal Bellarmine and entertaining Spain's ambassador, Count Gondomar, with equal aplomb. Yet although James was able to reconcile these roles with no apparent sense of contradiction, his subjects were less flexible. The pursuit of a rapproachement in central Europe by means of a Spanish alliance was deeply suspect if not incomprehensible to many, and the notion of a Spanish match for the royal heir, Prince Charles, was even more so. James' diplomatic conception was in fact a flawed one; but it is also true that his freedom of action was limited by the sense of Spain as an apocalyptic enemy.[272]

The ultimate political issue for apocalyptic thought was not how to prepare the way for judgment—it sufficed to follow the lead of the Constantinian emperor—but what to do if the emperor repined, apostatized, or was replaced by a tyrant. The latter case had of course presented itself during the reign of Mary. An active theory of resistance was developed in response to it, but the more general—and approved—course was the passive resistance of the martyrs. This was devastatingly effective, and accomplished far more than even a successful attempt at deposition could have. It not only delegitimated Mary's regime and created the circumstances for a Protestant restoration, but provided the basis for a profoundly significant reconceptualization of the English nation and its monarchy. Matters might have been quite otherwise, of course, without Mary's timely demise. But that itself was widely seen as a divine judgment, purchased with the martyrs' blood.

Passive resistance was therefore by no means limited; it was resistance *à outrance*, an affirming of God's law against the corrupted will of humankind. In the act of martyrdom, ordinary men and women, bypassing their social superiors and the lesser magistrate, might on the authority of conscience alone defy the command of a prince while remaining obedient to God and free from the taint of anarchy or rebellion. As Helgerson notes, "Martyrdom and imperium, suffering and power, divide apocalyptic" discourse[273] — or perhaps one should say reunite it in a dialectic that enables the martyr to prepare the way for the Christian imperium, and suffering, by negating abused power, to attest its lawful exercise. The legitimacy of Elizabeth's government certainly rested on other grounds, but one has only to remember the challenge posed to it by the bull *Regnans in excelsis* to appreciate the importance of the Marian martyrs in giving it a foundation in eschatology as well as in statute law and constitutional tradition.

As we have seen, this dialectic created a powerful investment in Elizabeth. It undergirded not only her identification as the Constantinian emperor, but, more generally, the image of the salvific Virgin Queen and of an Astraea presiding over a golden age (itself an important precursor of the millennialist turn that the apocalyptic was to take with the new century). It permeated not only the courtesy literature of the Court but the most influential literary work of the reign, Spenser's *The Faerie Queene*.[274] It echoed too in the pronouncements of Elizabethan bishops such as Sandys and Aylmer, who hailed her as "God's own elect" and "God's chosen instrument."[275] It was not necessary to go as far as Edward Hellwis, the courtier who identified the Queen with the Woman of Revelation XII (the Mother of the true church), to see in Elizabeth a figure of eschatological significance.

The foregoing may explain why men such as Foxe and Sandys remained firmly wedded to the Elizabethan church despite its popish trappings and the want of a preaching ministry; it also helps explain why men like Cartwright, however deep their differences with the church, never forsook it. But not all those who survived the Marian persecution embraced the Elizabethan settlement, nor were all those whose vision of the world admitted small gradation between a messianic emperor and a servant of the Antichrist willing to accept the taint of compromise. The Plumbers' Hall conventicle that established itself after the Vestiarian controversy affirmed that there could be "no fellowship between Christ and Belial," and a deprived minister, Master Pattenson, called Bishop Grindal an Antichrist to his face. Such sentiments were not confined to radical artisans and rogue clergymen; Pattenson had no less a protector than the Duchess of Suffolk.[276]

Apocalyptic language permeated godly discourse about the English church as well as that of Rome from the *Admonition* onward. While hope of further reformation in the church was still entertained, a distinction was drawn between the persons of the bishops and the popish offices they exercised, but with the advent of Presbyterianism in the 1580s and Separatism in the 1590s there seemed less and less practical or philosophical point to main-

taining it: there was no longer, at least for those who had turned their backs
on a hierarchical church, any real difference between a Bishop Bonner and a
Bishop Bancroft. The Marprelate tracts may be seen to mark a point of no return in this regard; their purpose was not dialogue but denunciation. Many
Presbyterians and some Separatists did of course return to the fold, or at
least to protected enclaves within it, and others, like the semi-Separatist congregations of London, remained on the borders of the church. But apocalypticism provided the ultimate sanction for the Separatist churches and the
"theology of persecution," in Barrie White's phrase, on which they thrived.[277]

If godly opposition could result in a complete repudiation of the church
and its identification with Babylon, however, it did not lead to a corresponding rejection of the Christian emperor. Despite the patent evidence of Elizabeth's residual popish sympathies, from the notorious cross in her chapel to
the silencing of Grindal and the deprivation of nonconforming ministers, no
one was willing to publicly associate her with the defects, if not the apostasy
of her church. Even so committed a Separatist as Henry Barrow continued to
urge a reform program on Burghley, and to caution against any civil action
save through the prince:

> Yet now if I be asked who ought to abolish this idolatry, to destroy these
> synagogues, to dissolve these fraternities, and to depose these antichristian
> priests: to that I answer, the prince, or state; and that it belongeth not to any
> private men: for we see they were set up and remained in Israel and Judah,
> until God raised up godly princes to pluck them down and destroy them;
> yea it were an intrusion into the magistrate's office and seat, for any private
> man so far to intermeddle.[278]

On only one recorded occasion did a "Prophet of Gods vengeaunce," the
tub preacher William Hacket, challenge the Constantinian emperor during
Elizabeth's reign. In July 1591, having concluded that Elizabeth had forfeited
her crown by her rejection of the Presbyterian program, Hacket and two confederates preached repentance to the London populace. They were swiftly
arrested, and Hacket was executed.

Hacket, a former Papist, was an illiterate artisan who honed his prophetic
gifts in alehouses after imbibing godly sermons. He believed himself to be
Christ's vice-regent and, as emperor of Europe, the apocalyptic successor to
all Christian princes. As a precursor of such Civil War-era prophets as Thomas Tany or Arise Evans he is worthy of note, but of even more interest was
his capacity to attract two men of quality, the Queen's servant Edmund Copinger and the Yorkshire gentleman Henry Arthington; the latter actually
took Hacket for the risen Christ, although he later recanted his delusions.
Copinger was able to bring Hacket to the attention of such sober worthies as
Cartwright, Walter Travers, and Job Throckmorton, and Burghley actually
granted Hacket an interview prior to his street escapade. No person of con-

sequence took Hacket seriously, and Copinger, himself unbalanced, died in prison after refusing food for a week. Nonetheless, the fact that he was able to get a hearing of any kind from politically credible figures underscores the heightened eschatological expectations of the age, while Copinger's presence, like those of Familists in Elizabeth's guard, suggests the susceptibility to enthusiasm even in the Queen's entourage.[279]

The question raised by the solitary episode of Hacket is why no other challenge to Elizabeth's Constantinian authority appears to have occurred. Disillusionment with her church and Separatist impulses toward it set in early, and attempts to radically transform it both from within and by means of statute occupied the middle decades of her reign. Elizabeth's flirtation with a Habsburg marriage was no less alarming to her godly subjects than Charles' Spanish match was to be,[280] and no one could mistake her personal piety or her clearly expressed preferences in liturgy, divinity, or ceremonial style for that of her brother Edward, whom legend had made the paragon of the Constantinian emperor and who cast a long shadow over the reigns of both his siblings. Nor did Elizabeth fit the appropriate mold in another critical respect, one she could do nothing to alter: her gender. John Knox's *First Blast of the Trumpet Against the Monstrous Regiment of Women*, his accession present to the Queen, only stated with particular force and impertinence the general presumption about female rulers, a prejudice that neither Mary Tudor nor Mary Stuart did anything to soften.

There were nonetheless powerful inhibitions against repudiating Elizabeth. The most obvious one was that she had been the instrument of England's deliverance from the popery represented by both Marys, and continued to represent the only stay against its return in the person of her cousin. Whatever her defects—and the Constantinian ruler, like anyone else, had only as much light as he was given, and could play only the part he was assigned—it was impossible to regard her role in England's rescue and her own personal deliverance from repeated Catholic assassination attempts as anything but providential. Whom the Lord chose to protect it was rash to abandon.

The second inhibition followed on the first. Although there was no dearth of Protestant resistance theories under Elizabeth, the Catholic plotting against her, following on the rebellion of the northern earls, rallied all Reformed (and indeed much recusant) opinion to her side. What the Devil would accomplish could not be the Lord's will.

Finally, sixteenth-century apocalyptic thought defined the true church as a church of suffering, triumphant only with the end of days. If Elizabeth was its true deliverer, then that moment was (as Foxe and most other apocalypticists believed) drawing near. If she was not, then its task was to bear further affliction.

The tension in apocalyptic thought between the eschatological expectation vested in the Constantinian emperor and the passivity toward his actual performance was unresolvable within the Foxean tradition. It was reinforced by the fear of being associated with Romanist precepts of rebellion and deposition, and with the need for unity in the face of Spanish attack. Even in the troubled 1590s, apocalypticists such as George Gifford and Christopher Heydon would go no further than to flirt with aristocratic reaction.[281] The Spanish threat receded at least temporarily after 1604, but Jacobean conformists continued to equate Puritan and Papist attitudes toward regicide.[282]

With the seventeenth century, however, English apocalypticism took a fateful turn. Millenarianism—the idea, derived from Revelations 20, of a thousand-year reign of the saints on earth—was reinterpreted by Thomas Brightman, Joseph Mede, and others to refer, not as most sixteenth-century commentators had had it, to the binding of Satan in the postapostolic or post-Constantinian history of the church, but to a future period either preceding or following the second Advent. This suggested not a church of affliction destined to suffer until the hour of deliverance, but a church militant reigning in historical time.

The key figure in this shift was Brightman, a Cambridge-educated divine whose *A Revelation of the Revelation*, published posthumously in Germany in 1609, was in many ways a godly answer to Hooker's *Laws of Ecclesiastical Polity*. Brightman saw the seven apostolic churches of antiquity as not merely offering a pattern of primitive Christianity, conformity with which defined a true Reformed church, but as types and prefigurements of their historical successors, including corrupted churches. Thus, the church of Pergamum was the type of the Roman church, which marked the nadir of the church's corruption; that of Thyatira corresponded to the partly reawakened Wyclifite church of the fourteenth and fifteenth centuries; and that of Philadelphia to the Genevan and Scottish churches, which marked the furthest advance toward the final goal, the restoration of not only apostolic but prelapsarian purity: the fully gathered church of the elect. The Church of England, doctrinally superior to the Lutheran churches with their residual taint of consubstantiation but devotionally inferior to the more purified Genevan churches, was the reembodied church of Laodicea whose "lukewarmness" was rebuked in Revelation 3:15–16.

Brightman's schema made possible a more nuanced reading of ecclesiastical history than Bale's or Foxe's. Instead of the stark and absolute opposition between two churches, one true and incorruptible, the other false and anti-Christian, Brightman saw a continuum in which the eternal and indivisible church, manifested in a historical succession of churches, now cleaving more closely to truth and now falling away from it, represented the dialectic of Providence. On this reading no church in unredeemed time could attain perfection, but neither could any, however great its apostasy, be merely Satan's pawn.

Along this continuum, the Church of England was both true and false. As a type of the Laodicean church, its "lukewarmness" was not an innate characteristic (since tepidity could never be a quality of Christian worship) but the product of conflicting opposites. In the case of the original church this conflict could only be inferred, but:

> In our Realme of England, the matter is more cleare, where such a forme of a Church is established, which is neither cold, nor yet hott, but set in the middest betweene both, and compounded of both. It is not cold, inasmuch as it doth professe the sound, pure and sincere doctrine of saluation, by which we haue renounced that Antichrist of Rome. . . . But hott it is not, as whose outward regiment is yet for the greatest parte Antichristian and Romish.[283]

The Church of England thus presented a "lukewarm" aspect when viewed externally and as a whole; when set, that is, against other Reformed churches. To Hooker, this moderation reflected the achievement of a *via media* between tradition and renovation, and conformity not an unhappy compromise between disparate elements but a synthesis that embodied genuine unity. For Brightman, there was no unity at all in such a church but only a grotesque congeries, an "euill" that "consisteth of certaine contraries strangely tempered and blended together."[284] Yet although the result was to be condemned, the elements had to be judged separately. Though chilled by the remnants of popery, the church was warmed by the zeal of godly preaching and piety. Such zeal was not excessive or "inconsiderate," as its conformist detractors would have it, but "a matter of commendation, as being the onely vertue, from which both coldnes and lukewarmenes swerue."[285]

The Church of England was thus composed of both positive elements (sound doctrine, zeal for the Gospel) and negative ones (ceremonialism and episcopacy). The positive elements constituted the church; the negative ones detracted from it but did not invalidate it. In refusing to be trapped by the binary opposition of true and false churches, Brightman was able to characterize the Church of England as a genuine branch of the Reformed churches, distinctive enough in both its strengths and deformities to constitute a third way alongside the Lutheran and Genevan churches.

Superficially, this description too was compatible with Hooker's view of the Church as a valid but distinctive member of the Reformed community. Brightman diverged sharply from Hooker, however, not only in rejecting the style of worship and government celebrated by him but in viewing the English church as eschatologically foretold. The church was not a valid alternative to the Lutheran and Genevan models, a *via media* in Hooker's terms, but a third incarnation of the revived church of the Gospel. Brightman dated the advent of England's church to Edward's accession in 1547, thus severing it from any association with the Henrician statutes (or Constantinian dependence on subsequent Edwardian and Elizabethan ones), and postdating the foundation of Calvin's church in Geneva. This move was critical. As Laodicea had been the last of the churches of antiquity, so the Church of England was to be the last of the postmillennialist churches that ushered in the final struggle with Babylon and the establishment of New Jerusalem. Extending Foxe's closely historicist reading of Revelation in the *Actes* and especially in the posthumously published *Eicasmi seu meditationes in sacram Apocalypsin* (1587), Brightman identified Thomas Cromwell as the avenging angel with the sickle in his hand (Rev. 14: 14-19)—a valuation of that worthy's career exceeding even that of Sir Geoffrey Elton—and Cranmer with the soul from out of the altar (Rev. 6: 9-11). The seventh angelic trumpet, announcing the Last Days (Rev. 11: 15), was the restoration of England's church under Elizabeth, and the four vials opened (three were reserved for future events) included Elizabeth's dismissal of the Papist clergy and the statute 23 Eliz. I c. 1 making it treasonous to seduce Englishmen from their allegiance (Rev. 15-16).[286]

Brightman's schema had two conspicuous flaws. The Church of England was not, in fact, the last Reformed church to be founded; it had been succeeded by that of Scotland. Brightman could not get around this difficulty even by dating England's church from the Elizabethan settlement, but he argued that the Scottish Kirk should notwithstanding be classified with the second, Genevan church, whose ecclesiology it shared.[287] This solution only cast into sharper relief however the scandal of England's episcopal regime, which from Brightman's own perspective was retrograde at best and anti-Christian at worst. How could a church inferior not only to its Continental but to its insular brethren in so critical a respect take precedence over them in the founding of New Jerusalem? John Knox did not think it possible in the 1560s, nor would Robert Baillie in the 1640s.

Brightman was keenly sensitive to this issue. On the one hand, he felt deep gratitude for the free enjoyment of the Gospel: "God forbid that I should willingly distaine that Church with any the least blot of infamy, which by the mercye of God hath brought me forth, hath brought me vppe, and doth sustaine me." On the other, he was overwhelmed by just such a sense of infamy in contemplating its government: "I could not but poure forth teares and sighes from the bottome of my hart, when I beheld in it Christ himselfe loathinge of vs, and prouoaked extremely to anger against vs."[288] This was the paradox of Laodicea: that, most deserving of chastisement, it was showered instead with blessings. Of old, Laodicea had been "a great and renowmed Citie, aboundinge both with Citizens, and wealth." In the modern Laodicea of England it was likewise: "Cities are gorgeously sett out, riches are increased . . . the feildes abound with corne, the pastures with cattell, the mountaynes with sheepe." Above all, England alone enjoyed peace and security while Antichrist raged abroad; the waves themselves had risen to drive the invader from its shores. It was clear that England had been designed as "a Hauen and a Harbour . . . to such as were exiled for Christs cause," and that this was at present "our cheife if not our onely worke."[289]

The tensions inherent in this account could only be speculatively resolved. England's unique status as the home of the third Reformed church, the prophecies fulfilled in its recent history, and the signal favor it enjoyed in a world of strife and devastation, all pointed toward a singular destiny. At the same time, the impurities of its church and the passivity of its role as a mere "haven" for those struggling in the vanguard suggested that it would be bypassed. One might say that its own days of glory, when its martyrs witnessed for the Gospel and its persecuted flock streamed into foreign ports, were already in the past.

It is noteworthy that Brightman, although writing in the midst of England's war with Spain, makes no attempt to assimilate it to his apocalyptic history except in the context of God's mercies. This omission is all the more striking given the apocalyptic concentration on the Armada in the work of contemporaries such as John Napier and Arthur Dent. While Brightman might mark the founding of the new Laodicean church as an event of epochal significance, he was plainly reluctant to credit it or its Constantinian governor with any active eschatological role while it languished in its imperfectly reformed condition. Elizabeth had, it was true, poured one of the seven vials, and all honor was due her for restoring the Gospel to England. But Brightman was roundly critical of the ecclesiastical polity she had established, and silent on the merits of the latter part of her reign. The first Constantine had also founded true religion, only to see it eclipsed shortly thereafter. The godly prince, too, was not to be made an idol.[290]

England was thus in Brightman's view an elect nation but also an Israel gone astray. Before it could play its destined role in the world's redemption it must first be redeemed itself. As the biblical Laodicea had been spewed out of the Lord's mouth, so too England must cast Antichrist out of its church. Unlike the Separatists who felt obliged to reject a church without the requisite number of marks or the godly clerics who resorted to casuistry to remain in it, Brightman had no compunction about his own conformity. However true piety might be mingled with false government in the English church, the former remained undefiled by the latter, as the invisible church was incorruptible in the visible one. Despite occasional misgivings, Brightman remained confident that the godly leaven would remain to restore what he at one point called its original, Edenic purity when the Papist lump had been expelled.[291] Well might his Root and Branch readers believe they were fulfilling apocalyptic prophecy when in 1641 they set about to dismantle episcopacy.[292]

Brightman's belief in England's destiny thus rested on two pillars: his Foxean, historicist reading of Revelation, fulfilled at crucial points by English figures and events; and his identification of the Anglican church both as the reincarnation of the Laodicean church of antiquity and as the third church of the Reformation, from whose very impurities would spring forth a "Church of Eden" at the appointed hour. This in turn would be linked to the conversion of the Jews and the final overthrow of Antichrist, which Brightman expected in 1695:

> For now is that time begun when Christ shal raigne in all the earth, hauing all his enemies round about subdued vnto him and broken in peeces. . . . we shal see out of those things that followe, that this kingdome among the Gentiles is to bee continually added vnto this that began nowe, til it be increased infinitely by the calling of the Iewes, & be at last translated from thence into heauen.[293]

Here indeed was a dream of English empire: that a purified and transfigured Laodicea, the last of Christ's churches to be established in the temporal order, should extend its dominion over all nations until the universal church had been reunited.[294] Brightman noted that the prophecy extended "no furder," but an indeterminate period of earthly bliss could be expected, the "New Jerusalem." The reign of the elect might begin even earlier in the West, since the destruction of Rome was anticipated by 1650. The saints of the Barebone Parliament who tried to create a Mosaic republic in the 1650s evidently thought so.

The strength of Brightman's position was that it enabled godly Englishmen to accept the flawed, Laodicean church of the Elizabethan settlement as fully theirs without compromising the anti-episcopal sentiments which most of them harbored and the Presbyterian principles to which many of them continued to adhere. By petition and example they might seek to reform what was amiss, but rebellion and separation were equally barred. Like most apocalypticists, Brightman spoke only in generalities about the means by which New Jerusalem was to be established. It was evident that the destruction of Rome and the conquest of Gog and Magog would require actual as well as spiritual warfare, but one could only await the specific deliverers appointed by the Lord. These were not necessarily to be English, despite the primacy Brightman forecast for the Church of England. In a passage as remarkable for its practical vagueness as for its prophetic afflatus, he called upon the rulers of Europe to unite against Rome; given, however, the skepticism he expressed elsewhere about the Constantinian prince, it was not clear from which quarter true magistracy might ultimately arise.[295] In the troubled decades after Brightman's death, people looked successively to England's

Prince Henry, the Elector Palatine Frederick V, and Gustavus Adolphus for apocalyptic leadership, but also, beginning in the 1620s, to Parliament as well.

At the same time, the advent of a postmillennial era implied a transformation of the political order. The need for magistracy would presumably remain, but the scope and terms of its exercise would inevitably be different in a world no longer given over to wickedness or menaced by the Antichrist. Neither Brightman nor any of the other English postmillennialists speculated as to what forms such a polity might assume—a dangerous exercise, and a premature one in any case—but the godly had already made their preferred form of ecclesiology clear, and conformists had accused them of harboring similar aspirations for the renovation of the state.[296] Once again, however, the experience of the 1640s and 1650s was to demonstrate where millennialist expectations might lead. The departing bishops of the Long Parliament were replaced by godly ministers whose sermons became an institutionalized part of the life and practice of both houses, and the Barebone Parliament, which may be regarded on a certain level as an experiment in millennialist government, eroded still further the distinction between lay and clerical spheres.

The call to the magistrate—and not merely the prince—to resist the Antichrist and to further the cause of New Jerusalem was evident in Richard Bernard's *A Key of Knowledge* (1617), a critical apocalyptic text of the late Jacobean era. Although rejecting the characterization of the church as Laodicean, Bernard was even more emphatic than Brightman in identifying England as the Lord's elect nation; the first Christian king (the mythical Lucius), the first Christian emperor, Constantine, and the first deliverer from Antichrist, Wyclif, had all been English, while the repulse of the Armada signaled the final phase of Babylon's fall.[297] Bernard saw the climactic struggle as a war on all fronts, at home as well as abroad, and he addressed separate epistles to the judges, the Inns of Court, the justices, and the militia urging no quarter to popery.

That Bernard saw so broad a lay audience for his work says much about the climate of the late Counter-Reformation. From the initial reserve if not skepticism expressed toward the Book of Revelation by Luther and Calvin, apocalyptic thought had come a long way by the first quarter of the seventeenth century. Throughout Protestant Europe generally but in England and Scotland particularly, it had become central to the perception of human and national destiny, filtering down from the studies of country divines not only to godly congregations but into popular prints and ballads. It was deeply linked to polemical rationalizations of the Reformation, structures of political and ecclesiastical legitimation, and concepts of the *saeculum*. To be sure, not all divines accorded it equal weight and some, including the godly William

Perkins, warned against the rasher prognostications built on it. Moderate Jacobean churchmen, including Thomas Adams, Patrick Forbes, and John
Prideaux, the future Bishop of Worcester, were concerned lest apocalyptic
literature sow civil anarchy among the multitude or become a pretext for sedition. But few within the English church or among the educated laity questioned the overall hermeneutic framework upon which apocalypticism
rested. Even Hooker allowed that Scripture had foretold great events "which
were to come in every age from time to time, til the very last of the latter
days."[298]

The great Counter-Reformation offensive of the 1620s stimulated a fresh
outpouring of millennial speculation. The German theologian Johann Heinrich Alsted asserted in his *Diatribe De Milleannis Apocalyptis* (1627) that the
millennium lay entirely in the future, would commence in 1694, and would
last a full thousand years. His views reached England through the active circle around John Comenius, Samuel Hartlib, and John Dury,[299] and in 1643 his
treatise was translated into English.[300] Working independently, the Cambridge
divine Joseph Mede arrived at a similar conclusion in his *Clavis Apocalyptica*
(1627), translated as *The Key of the Revelation* (1643). For Mede, the millennium constituted a thousand-year day of judgment during which New Jerusalem was to be realized, not as the universal church triumphant or a general
spiritual condition diffused among men but as a specific locale giving light
to the nations.[301] Mede did not identify this locale as England, but his Civil
War audience would have fewer interpretive scruples.

The work of Brightman, Alsted, and Mede reflected a more pessimistic
sense of their time than that of Foxe's generation. Brightman's tome represented an ingenious effort to wrest definitional control of the English church
on behalf of a godly minority that had been defeated and marginalized on
the political level; the cost of it was to portray that church as fundamentally
compromised and divided, and redeemable only in the millennial future. In
our terms, it was only conditionally legitimate, for it required a revolutionary transformation to justify it in the end. This in turn necessitated a revolutionary destiny for the nation as a whole. As long as events tended in this direction or at any rate did not visibly decline from it, the Laodicean captivity
of the church could be tolerated as prophetically ordained, a phase through
which redemption must proceed. This phase was not unattended by peril;
indeed, it was only to be expected that England's Laodicean peace would be
tried in the fires of a mighty struggle before Antichrist was vanquished. Little more than a decade after the first publication of *A Revelation of the Revelation* in England, the ordeal of the church seemed to have arrived.

Despite his sense of Protestantism's embattled condition and England's
coming trial, Brightman believed that the millennium had already begun.
Both Alsted and Mede projected it wholly into the future, thus implying that

the Reformation was to be read not as the decisive break with the regime of Antichrist but merely as a step in a long continuum of struggle whose crisis was yet ahead. Whereas English apocalypticists had pointed to the hand of God in raising the waves against the Armada, Alsted found the cause of Antichrist in his day "under full Sail, wanting no favour of winds."[302] Mede's case is somewhat more complex. As Katharine Firth points out, he encompassed the coming of Christ's kingdom as a single epoch spanning the time between the first and the second Advent, and saw the millennium as a period of gradual illumination.[303] For this reason, he declined to predict a date for its arrival, although as Paul Christianson notes one could be inferred without difficulty from his writings. Mede was also difficult to classify within the continuum of the English church. He was a ceremonial conformist, and was held back from advancement under Laud, in his own view at least, chiefly because he refused to compromise his conviction that the Pope was the Antichrist.[304]

As Mede's case reminds us, apocalypticism was broadly based in the English church, and not confined to the godly. In this sense it could be as much a unifying force as an oppositional one, as in the early days of both the Elizabethan and the Jacobean regimes it often had been, providing a framework for controversy with Rome and a rationale for Erastian control. Nonetheless, there was no gainsaying that apocalypticism was a double-edged sword whose keener blade was turned against the clerical establishment. As a radical specimen of utopian thought, it militated against the status quo in any form; as a system based on binary opposition, it precluded compromise or toleration with the perceived enemy; as an historical imperative, it demanded the fulfillment of prophecy. So long as it retained its own vitality — and in the 1620s and 1630s, despite some tendency to hypertrophy, it still had broad appeal and scope for development — it was a standing commission to holy warfare and a challenge to all who failed to wage it with requisite zeal. It was, in short, inherently dynamic, and tended to blur the line between scholar and prophet. That was certainly true of Brightman, who defended his call to the princes of Europe to take arms against Rome in an extraordinary passage:

> I that am vnknowne to you all, and a man of no reckoning in my owne Cuntry, durst not take vpon me to speake to you and to exhort you that are most mighty and renowmed Princes, the glory of the world, & to geue you notice, of a matter of so great moment, if the confidence that I repose in the Truth of God, and the assurance that this is the truth which I speake . . . had not made me take heart and courage, to doe this errand vnto you from the Lorde of Lords & King of Kings.[305]

If Brightman consciously assumed the role of prophet, it was popularly imputed to other millenarians who laid no claim to it, including Napier, Alsted, Mede, and even Bishop Ussher. His call to arms was to be echoed by others in the 1620s and 1630s, notably Alexander Leighton, Henry Burton, and William Prynne; their exhortation was more and more to deliver the English church from bondage at home no less than to wage war on the Antichrist abroad; and their appeal was increasingly to Parliament (or King-in-Parliament) rather than to the king alone, not as the lesser magistrate but as the Lord's instrument.[306]

Brightman's Laodicean view of the English church, however severe, was essentially reformist; the kernel of Jerusalem lay within it, and the dross had only to be purged. For Alsted and Mede, the millennium was yet to begin and the church of deliverance lay in the future. Despite Mede's own emphasis on the continuity of Christ's church through the ages and his caution that Satan would not be crushed until the end of the millennium, his work, as well as Alsted's, lent itself to calls for a more drastic renovation of the English church and even a refounding of it. From there it was only a short step to the creation of sectarian churches in the 1640s. The very subtlety of the Cambridge divine's distinctions led, for less discriminating intellects, to conclusions he would doubtless have disavowed, but for which he remained at least partly responsible.

As godly reformers tended to appropriate apocalyptic discourse and to find it increasingly pertinent not only to the international situation but to the church at home, conformists began to attack what had become one of its essential presuppositions, the identification of the papacy as Antichrist. Anthony Milton has suggested that this stemmed in part at least from a felt need to ground the church's episcopal succession in the medieval Latin church and thus to avoid a blanket condemnation of it.[307] But this had been a polemical issue for nearly a century, and had been vigorously argued ever since the controversy between Jewel and Harding.[308] By the end of the Jacobean era, the last serious domestic challenge to the church hierarchy was more than a generation in the past, and episcopacy, wedded to the Erastian order by James' "No bishop, no king," was more firmly established than ever.[309] Certainly Mede had no difficulty accepting it.[310]

It seems rather that the fraternization with Rome that became increasingly evident under Laud had its roots in a Hookerian ecumenicism that went back in turn to the Henrician and Marian churches, a shared sense of ceremony and clerical prerogative, and a common repugnance to godly styles of worship. As Milton has documented, references to the Pope as Antichrist significantly declined in the licensed publications of the Laudian period, and where they appeared they were often watered down or purged by the censor. This was a trend rather than a party line, but its direction was clear and its import, at least to the godly, was unmistakable. When Laudians such as John Cosin referred to the "Puritane Antichrist," the transposition of rhetoric was complete.[311] Since the papal Antichrist was understood to be distinguished above all by its false claim to represent the doctrine and apostolic succession of Christ, there could be no clearer evidence of its subversive presence than its slander of the elect by the title that belonged properly to itself.

The doctrine that the Pope was the Antichrist had an all but canonical status in the Church of England, and had in fact been formally incorporated in the Articles of the Church of Ireland.[312] Those who found fault with the established church in any number of ways, from the Presbyterian John Field in the 1580s to the godly pamphleteer Thomas Scott in the 1620s, could at least regard this point as fixed and indisputable. It was scarcely less critical a touchstone of Calvinist orthodoxy than predestination itself, and Christopher Hill's observation that both concepts stood or fell together would have been self-evident to most seventeenth-century Englishmen.[313] If what freed Christians was dependence on Christ alone, what had enslaved them was the papal claim to govern conscience. The pope was thus necessarily Christ's antithesis, and any rejection or even softening of that opposition could only have its source in those deceived by Antichrist or in fealty to him. Not everyone, it is true, hastened to this conclusion. Joseph Mede could uphold the identification of the Pope as Antichrist in his *The Apostasy of the Latter Times* as forcefully as any godly stalwart, yet still regard his difference with the hierarchy on the subject as a matter of opinion. Bishops Abbot, Downame, and Hall all maintained the papal Antichrist in the context of *jure divino* episcopacy, as did other conformist writers.[314] Laud himself never rejected the doctrine as such, although on this as on many other issues his views were slippery. "No man can charge me, that I hold not the Pope to be *Antichrist*," he reputedly said, adding however that "it is a great question even among learned Protestants, whether he be so or not. The *Church of England* hath not positively resolved him to be so."[315] As an invitation to debate a subject widely regarded as settled if not sworn to this was disingenuous, and in the event only the skeptics and naysayers—Richard Montagu, Gilbert Sheldon, Robert Shelford—were heard from. No publications referring to the Pope as Antichrist were licensed between Laud's accession to the see of Canterbury in 1633 and the collapse of censorship in 1640. Even in 1640, when Bishop Hall, who had palliated his views, believed that a reaffirmation of the doctrine was essential to the defense of episcopacy, he could not get Laud's permission to print it.[316]

Laud's views may be contrasted with those of Whitgift. Whitgift accepted (and even defended) the doctrine of the papal Antichrist *pro forma* without placing much ideological weight on it, let alone making it central to his eschatology.[317] He may have regarded the subject as too politically charged or, for a man of practical energies, as too speculative. Perhaps he would have agreed with Laud that it was a matter for debate, if indeed Laud thought so. But he did not encourage such debate, and the books he licensed on the subject reflected prevailing opinion. Moreover, Whitgift's theological orthodoxy was not in doubt, as he had demonstrated during the Cambridge disputations of 1595.[318] The same could hardly be said of Laud. As early as 1608, the future Archbishop of Canterbury was arraigned by the future Bishop of Exeter for hiding his true beliefs—if ascertainable at all—under clouds of evasion:

> Today you are in the tents of the Romanists, tomorrow in our's, the next day betweene both. Our adversaries think you our's, wee their's. Your conscience findes you with both, and neither. . . . This of your's is the worst of all tempers. Heat and cold have their uses. Lukewarmnesse is good for nothing but to trouble the stomach.[319]

This was the very epitome of Brightman's Laodicean church, and when Laud came at last to head it, the godly were not alone in believing that its unrighteous members must be spewed out.

Over a century of development, apocalyptic thought had become part of the deep structure of English Protestant culture. It was simultaneously a powerful buttress to authority and a challenge to it. It created in the Christian emperor a figure of destiny whose role was to transform history, but also demanded of particular rulers conformity to that ideal. It justified an imperial foreign policy and a monarchical church, but yoked them to confessional strife and millennial expectation. It saw the world as a binary system of good and evil that required both active struggle and unceasing vigilance against corruption. Its sense of near-universal contagion was crystallized in the Antichrist, a principle of radical evil that took a bewildering variety of forms but which emanated visibly from the Roman papacy. The Antichrist was distinguished by its perverse semblance to authority; unlike the classical tyrant, it subverted truth and justice not by defying but by mimicking them. Its containment was thus bound up with the continual effort of unmasking, and particularly with the identification of its central embodiment in the papacy. When William Laud questioned this identification, he unmasked himself in the sight of those who patrolled the frontiers of the spirit.

CHAPTER 3

The Discourse of the Realm

We have dealt thus far primarily with official discourse, whether accepted, contested, or rejected. The discourse of the realm designates speech neither originating with nor directly reflecting the state and its organs, including the national church; that is, commands, pronouncements, and propaganda. As we have seen, even official (or officially licensed) discourse was far from univocal. The crown, moreover, was continually reinventing itself on both a practical and theoretical level, especially in the critical years between 1529 and 1559. If at any given moment its discourse might be construed as the content of orders in place and the justification given for them, over time it was fluctuating and even contradictory as it responded to concrete situations, ideological pressures, and the personalities and convictions of individual rulers. To behold Behemoth whole required both familiarity with it and distance from it. That distance included establishing perspective on the proper relation between state and commonwealth, a relation official discourse, with its reductive dialectic of command and obedience, always tended to obscure. In this section, we will consider four general commentaries on the realm itself, two descriptive and two historical. All, of course, reflect elite values and assumptions, but all, to a greater or lesser extent, also supply a corrective to official ideology, and indicate the acceptable limits of authority.

Sir Thomas Smith and the Commonweal

One thing the wars of the fourteenth and fifteenth centuries taught the English ruling orders was that that they were no longer French. Sir John Fortescue had expressed this sentiment vigorously in *De Laudibus Legum An-*

glie. Writing a century later—and similarly inspired by a stay in France as Queen Elizabeth's ambassador—Sir Thomas Smith could take it for granted:

> [B]ecause in my absence I felt a yearning for our commonwealth I have put together three books here at Toulouse describing it, taking as the title *De Republica Anglorum*; and in these I have set forth almost the whole of its form, especially those points in which it differs from the others. But it differs in almost all. . . . I have furnished fruitful argument for those who would debate . . . whether what is held here and in those regions which are administered in accordance with the Roman Law. For all things, almost, are different . . .[1]

The theme of English distinctiveness would be sounded not only in Smith's treatise but in many other secular works of the latter Tudor decades. This was the more remarkable in that much of the intellectual labor of the English clergy during this period was devoted to asserting the close kinship of the Anglican Church with its Continental peers. Even those who saw the church in Joachite terms as the final incarnation of Christ's rule on earth connected it to the climactic struggle against the Antichrist, and hence to the common Reformed cause. For more conformist apologists, its continuity with the primitive episcopal church was critical to its defense.

Smith situates his England at a precise historical and biographical moment, to wit "the xxviij of March *Anno* 1565 in the vij yeare of the raigne and administration thereof by the most vertuous and noble Queene *Elizabeth . . .* and in the one and fifteeth yeere of mine age."[2] By aligning the body politic of the realm with his own mortal being and by pinning both to the specificity of a date, he would appear to stress the contingency of the former, its subjection to change and decay. Nor would this be surprising, for "mutabilitie" was one of the deep *topoi* of Elizabethan culture. But Smith's theme is rather the perdurability of the commonwealth, its continuous identity (like that of the individual self, persisting despite bodily change) through time. England in 1565 is distinguished, as the yearbooks and statute books have it, as the seventh year of Elizabeth's reign, an immemorial commonwealth which, apart from the common Christian calendar, can be temporally designated only by reference to the mortal and politic body of its ruler. That body, itself comprehending in its politic aspect the entirety of the realm, the collective body of all subjects, is thereby immortally assimilated to the idea of an "England" that rises above historicity, and which in the triumph of its institutions—of everything entailed by the word custom—remains unimpeachable at its core, whatever the shortcomings of the individuals who compose it at any given moment (a March day in 1565, for example), and whatever the challenges and vicissitudes of events.

Smith goes on in the passage quoted above to mention not only his age but his employment: "in the one and fifteeth yeere of mine age, *when I was ambassador for her majestie in the court of Fraunce . . ."* [emphasis added]. By this he does not specify or distinguish himself, but rather assimilates his person (as a royal servant) to that of the Queen, who in turn is the personation of the realm itself. Smith speaks, that is, not as a detached observer—despite the distance and leisure his foreign service gives him—but as one who cannot be detached from the unity of the commonwealth, for which and through which alone he can speak.

The commonwealth is, for Smith, "a society or common doing of a multitude of free men collected together and united by common accord and covenauntes among themselves, for the conservation of themselves aswell in peace as in warre" (20). It is distinguished from the natural family in that its aims are political, from the host in that those aims are permanent and collective rather than transitory and individual, and from the master and his bondsmen, between whom "there is no mutuall societie or portion, no law or pleading betweene thone and thother" (21) and hence no community of interest. The commonwealth is, then, a political entity, founded by consent among free individuals, and dedicated to the perpetual end of "conservation." This end is served by striving to keep each commonwealth in its "most perfect estate" (10). Smith understands this as a dynamic process:

> For the nature of man is never to stand still in one maner of estate, but to grow from the lesse to the more, and decay from the more againe to the lesse, till it come to the fatall end and destruction, with many turnes and turmoyles of sicknesse and recovering, seldome standing in a perfect health, neither of a mans bodie it selfe, nor of the politique bodie which is compact of the same. (12–13)

Preservation—the only permanent goal of the commonwealth—thus entailed accommodation, for "in common wealthes which have had long continuance, the diversities of times have made all . . . maners of ruling or government to be seene" (12), and at any given moment the form of the constitution was almost invariably mixed, having merely "the name of that which is more and overruleth the other alwayes or for the most part" (14). Sovereignty was thus mixed as well, and the balance between dominant and subordinate elements not static but subject to negotiation and adjustment; that is, to a degree contestatory.

These general observations must be borne in mind in considering Smith's description of the English mode of government. This begins famously with the declaration that "The most high and absolute power of the realme of Englande, consisteth in the Parliament" (48). The term "absolute" has caused much confusion, although Smith's early twentieth-century editor, Alston, cautioned against conflating it with later notions of absolutism (xxxi–xxxiii), a point elaborated by Glenn Burgess.[3] The preeminence of Parliament con-

sists in the fact that it offers one of the two occasions in which the commonwealth is fully comprehended in action:

> For as in warre where the king himselfe in person, the nobilitie, the rest of
> the gentilitie, and the yeomanrie are, is the force and power of Englande: so
> in peace and consultation where the Prince is to give life, and the last and
> highest commaundement, the Baronie for the nobilitie and higher, the
> knightes, esquiers, gentlemen and commons for the lower part of the com-
> mon wealth, the bishoppes for the clergie bee present to advertise, consult
> and shew what is good and necessarie for the common wealth . . . and upon
> mature deliberation everie bill or lawe being thrise reade and disputed up-
> pon in either house . . . the Prince himselfe in presence of both the parties
> doeth consent unto and alloweth. (48)

In making war and in making law, the commonwealth exercises its two
paradigmatic functions. War is not contrasted with "peace and consultation"; rather, both express the unity and vitality of the nation. In each the entirety of the commonwealth is gathered, both actually and symbolically, and
in each the king is personally and visibly present. (Charles I, absent from his
Parliament but exposed to its gunfire on Edgehill, was to revive the image of
the warrior-king with devastating effect when he became the first English
sovereign in a century to lead his armies in person.) The king has, naturally,
pride of place, for the making of war is solely within his prerogative (58),
and it is his consent that gives "life" to the laws made in Parliament, without
which they are "accounted utterly dashed and of no effect" (ibid.). Nonetheless, the king is at no point dissevered from the commonwealth; the separation of function in the exercise of his prerogative is not to be confused with a
separation of powers. This organic inseparability constitutes the inner unity
of a mixed system, in which each integral element—crown, nobility, commons—has its distinct voice, yet all finally cohere in the vital action. Even in
war, where the king's authority appears most untrammeled,[4] the consent of
the nation is implicit, for "the force and power of Englande" is not in the
power of array but the valor of battle, the willing strength of free men. As for
Parliament, it is the very metaphor of the commonwealth itself, in which the
making of each new law is a symbolically constitutive act that enfolds each
individual in the communal whole, for it "is the Princes and whole realmes
deede: whereupon justlie no man can complaine, but must accommodate
himselfe to finde it good and obey it" (48).

Smith spends a good deal of time describing the particulars of the legislative process. It begins with the Commons' traditional request for free speech,
"that they might franckely and freely saye their mindes in disputing of such
matters as may come in question, and that without offence to his Majestie"
(52). Much scholarly ink has been spilled debating whether the privilege of
free speech was conceived as inhering in Parliament or residing with the

crown, and the question was regularly raised in Parliament itself after 1604. For Smith, however, the issue would have been as otiose as the question of whether Parliament or the king made laws, since the answer was, "both, inseparably." Laws could not be made without free speech, so the king could not initiate the legislative process without providing for it. Parliament could not assemble without the king's command, and the request for free speech was a symbolic acknowledgment of that fact: the king's grant of free speech gave "life" to the legislative process at its inception, just as his assent quickened its issue at the end. Although the king's role was hardly passive in between, the grant of free speech was far more than a permission to address public issues (a function which at all times and in all places required licensing); it was also an act of deference to the legislative process. As the king was present but silent in his other courts, represented by his legal officers and participating only by prescribed form, so in Parliament he was represented by his ministers, themselves sitting by virtue of their election as MPs. Only on the rarest occasions did he appear *in propria persona* during a session other than to open or close it, or attempt to intervene directly in the process of debate.

Smith's detailed account of procedure in the two houses presumes the autonomy of Parliament. He describes the manner of reading, committing, and engrossing bills, and of the coordination of both houses. These procedures, as Smith makes clear, operationally define Parliament, no less than the rules and practices of any other court. His comments on the decorum of debate are particularly appreciative:

> In the disputing is a mervelous good order used in the lower house. He that standeth uppe beareheadded is understood that he will speake to the bill. If moe stande uppe, who that first is judged to arise, is first harde, though the one doe prayse the law, the other diswade it, yet there is no altercation. For everie man speaketh as to the speaker, not as one to an other, for that is against the order of the house. It is also taken against the order, to name him whom ye doe confute, but by circumlocution, as he that speaketh with the bill, or he that spake against the bill, and gave this and this reason. . . . No reviling or nipping wordes must be used. For then the house will crie, it is against the order: and if any speake unreverently or seditiouslie against the Prince or the privie counsell, I have seene them not onely interrupted, but it hath beene moved after to the house, and they have sent them to the tower. So that in such a multitude, and in such diversitie of mindes, and opinions, there is the greatest modestie and temperance of speech that can be used. Neverthelesse with much doulce and gentle termes, they make their reasons as violent and as vehement the one against the other as they may . . . (54–55).

The image here is of a court, in which the adversarial thrust of opinion ("reasons . . . violent and . . . vehement") is constrained by decorum, and the collective voice, judicial as well as judicious, ensures order. We may recall that the leading figures in Elizabethan and early Stuart parliaments were, increasingly, lawyers, and that many of the country gentlemen who populated the back benches had at least a smattering of experience in the Inns of Court. When Parliament defended its privilege of free speech in the Apology of 1604, it did so on the basis of being a court of record. The ultimate rationale for parliamentary self-government was, however, not in any claim of autonomy from the king but rather of unity with him. Parliament was the king's highest court and his highest council precisely because he was, in a quasi-mystical sense, inseparable from it. Henry VIII had himself famously expressed this sense when he declared that "we at no time stand so highly in our estate royal as in the time of Parliament, wherein we as head and you as members are conjoined and knit together into one body politic . . ."[5] The king's continual, politic presence in Parliament, not as represented by his councillors (who acted as mere physical intermediaries) but in the entirety of the body, rendered his personal presence superfluous except on prescribed ceremonial occasions. Because of this, nothing could be spoken to the king's dishonor that would not be immediately censured by the whole House ("I have seene them not onely interrupted, but . . . sent . . . to the tower"). For the king to deny Parliament the right to discipline its own members, especially when the matter touched his honor, would be to suggest a division between the head and the members. Misunderstandings and miscommunications could occur in the natural course of business; individuals could err or fail in their duty; factions could cause temporary mischief. But division in the body politic as such was unthinkable.

Smith's discussion of regal power is conventional. The "Prince," as he terms the sovereign, "hath absolutelie in his power the authoritie of warre and peace, to defie what Prince it shall please him, and to bid him warre, and again to reconcile himselfe . . . at his pleasure or the advice onely of his privie counsell" (58–59). Interstate relations are represented as the affair of sovereigns, who alone can dispose of them, since any prince obliged to defer to or consult with inferior bodies before acting would be disadvantaged among his peers both as a practical matter and in terms of honor. Smith's suggestion that the prince may consult with his Privy Council about issues of war and peace implies that he ought to, but also that he may do so with no derogation of his honor because the nature and extent of this consultation is at his discretion (the prince "keepeth so many ambassades and letters sent unto him secret as he will"), and because the councillors themselves are sworn to secrecy about their deliberations. For this latter reason, presumably, Smith does not consider Parliament as an appropriate consultative body for interstate affairs, although in practice it was impossible for fiscal and other reasons to keep foreign policy issues out of it.

By extension, the prince's power also covered martial law; this, however, was restricted to situations which "do not suffer the tariance of pleading and processe," and might not legitimately be extended to any other occasion. Thus, while martial law had been declared at times in the past "before any open warre in sodden insurrections and rebellions," such courses were "not allowed of wise and grave men" (59). Once again, "absolute power" was checked and tempered by counsel. Similarly, although Smith described the prince's power over coinage too as absolute, it was constrained by self-interest, for a ruler who debased his own coin would eventually be paid back in it. Thus, although unaccountable discretionary power — what would be called absolute prerogative by royal legists in the seventeenth century — was irresistible in theory, it was limited in practice, juridically by the discourse of legitimacy (the opinion of "wise and grave men"), and economically by the law to which Smith's contemporary Sir Thomas Gresham gave his name. Smith does not discuss any right of resistance, understandably in a treatise whose purpose is normative empirical description rather than political theory, but his English sovereign is circumscribed by boundaries that are no less real for being implied rather than stated. There would have been no need to point out to contemporaries the relationship between a prince who abused such "absolute" powers as martial law and the incidence of "sodden insurrections and rebellions."

If the relativity of absolute powers needed further signifying, Smith observed that "the kingdome of Englande is farre more absolute than either the dukedome of Venice is, or the kingdome of the Lacedemonians was" (59). Both states were, of course, oligarchies in which all sovereign decisions were consultative. England differed from them in the greater degree of formally unfettered discretion accorded its prince, but not in the kind of power that discretion ultimately represented: whether popular, aristocratic, or monarchical, all authority presupposed where it did not prescribe some form of consultation.

Smith's treatment of the crown is less than half as long as his discussion of Parliament, and much of it focuses on such idiosyncratic powers as pardon and wardship. The latter, he notes, had originally been "graunted by act of Parliament" (62), and Parliament, too, reserved the right to set all standards of weight and measure save that of coin (60). As for "diverse other rights and preeminences the prince hath which be called prerogatives royalles, or the prerogative of the king" (i.e., what the seventeenth century would call the king's ordinary prerogative), the curious reader might find them "declared particularly in the bookes of the common lawes of England" (62): Smith himself says not a word about them.

"Our lawe which is called of us the common lawe" is the real and triumphant subject of Smith's book, and it receives by far the most detailed and
elaborate discussion—more than half the entire text—of any subject in it. For
Smith, the common law is the most distinctive feature of the English polity,
simultaneously the frame and the fabric of its public life. It begins, institutionally, with the king, for all courts have their "force, power, authoritie, rule
and jurisdiction, from the royall majestie and the crowne of England" (141),
but it rests upon the jury, which gives judgment. Smith's discussion of the
jury (a term he employs only once, using instead the contemporary locution
of "the twelve men" or the older term "enquest") is remarkably elliptical. In
civil cases, he states, after proofs are expressed and the law expounded, the
"issue *facti* is founde by the xij men of whom wee shall speake hereafter"
(74). Smith summarily describes them as "commonly rude and ignorant"
(ibid.); Book II, Chapter 15 ("Of the xij. men") picks up the thread. Smith begins it with the assertion that "Of what manner and order of men in the
common welth the xij men be I have alreadie declared" (78), presumably a
reference to his earlier characterization. After describing the summoning and
empaneling of the jury and the trial procedure, Smith gets down to its work:

> When it is thought that it is enough pleaded before them . . . one of the
> Judges with a briefe and pithie recapitulation reciteth to the xii in summe
> the argumentes of the sergeantes of either side, that which the witnesses
> have declared, and the chiefe pointes of the evidence shewed in writing,
> and once againe putteth them in minde of the issue . . . and biddeth them
> goe together. Then there is a baylife charged with them to keepe them in a
> chamber not farre off without bread, drink, light, or fire untill they be
> agreed, that is, till they all agree upon one verdite concerning the same is-
> sue, and uppon one among them who shall speake for them all when they
> be agreed: for it goeth not by the most part, but each man must agree. They
> returne and in so fewe wordes as may be they give their determination:
> fewe I call vi or vii or viii wordes at the most (for commonly the issue is
> brought so narrow, that such number of words may be ynough to affirme
> or to denie it) which doone they are dismissed to goe whither they will.
> (79–80)

It is a curious passage. The entire structure of the law, which Smith describes elsewhere in such loving detail, rests upon the fulcrum of twelve
anonymous men brought in from the surrounding shire and hundred, sworn
and instructed, and kept under close confinement and duress ("without
bread, drinke, light, or fire") as if they were prisoners themselves from
whom unwilling testimony must be forced. Thus compelled, the twelve are
reduced to a single voice which recites a formulaic phrase of "vi or vii or viii
wordes," the sole utterance permitted it. They are then dismissed without
recompense[6] or (in Smith's account) acknowledgment, "to goe whither they

will," a phrase that indicates they have been freed to return to the obscurity from whence they came, their persons and movements of no further consequence or interest to their erstwhile captors. Yet without those who must if need be deliberate in darkness, the edifice of the law itself remains dark, at least until another twelve replace them.

Smith's shadowed and almost mystifying account of the jury may be explained in part by the fact that he is trying to describe a unique custom of English law to a civilian, Continental audience. There is no gainsaying his embarrassment in doing so, however, despite a perfunctory attempt to give the general form of the inquest a classical pedigree: although the mode of pleading before jurors "may seeme strange to our civilians nowe," he declares, "yet who readeth *Cicero* and *Quintilian* well shall see that there was no other order and maner of examining witnesses or deposing among the Romans in their time" (79). Smith might have enlarged his point by citing another ancient inquest that also gave judgment, the Athenian jury. It is precisely the issue of judgment, however, which he is at pains to elide, for it raises the larger question of the nature of the polity and the distribution of authority in it. In a world that notionally excluded all but the propertied elite from any share in governance, how to explain the persistence of an institution, archaic even in Roman times and abandoned by all civil law communities, by which inferiors might determine the fate of their betters?[7]

Smith begins his treatise with a conventional account of the forms of government, monarchical, aristocratic, and democratic. These, he asserts, are never manifested in a pure state but are "always mixed," given commonwealths bearing only "the name of that which is more and overruleth the other alwayes or for the most part" (14). To these political divisions correspond the social ones between what are called in England "gentlemen, citizens, yeomen, and laborers" (31). The category of "gentlemen" includes everybody from the king and the nobility to knights, squires, and "simple [i.e., titularly unmodified] gentlemen," who "be made good cheape" in England by heralds upon what is essentially a self-presentation of the appropriate "port" and "countenaunce" (39, 40). By "citizens" Smith means those who serve the commonwealth in an elected capacity as town burgesses or as backbenchers in Parliament, and by "yeomen" the forty-shilling freeholders who are the shire electorate and who otherwise discharge political functions without holding office, not "meddl[ing] in publike matters and judgements but when they are called, and gladde when they are delivered thereof" (43–44). As politically passive as the yeomen (ideally) seem to be, however, they exhibit a proto-bourgeois acquisitiveness, for they "commonly live welthilie, keepe good houses, and do their businesse, and travaile to acquire riches" (42), setting their sons up as gentlemen after them if they can.

The category of laborers comprises "day labourers, poore husbandmen, yea marchantes or retailers which have no free lande, copiholders, and all artificers, as Taylers, Shoomakers, Carpenters, Brickemakers, Bricklayers, Masons, & c." (46): in short, the majority of the population. These are, in Smith's lapidary phrase, "the fourth sort of men which doe not rule," and whose political function is "onelie to be ruled, not to rule other[s]." Yet they do "commonly" serve, Smith notes, as churchwardens, almoners, and even constables, an office, he concedes, that "toucheth more the common wealth." In addition, they make up "enquests and Juries" (this is Smith's sole use of the latter term) in default of yeomen—indeed typically, according to Smith's description of jurors as rude and ignorant. Smith is clearly uncomfortable with the idea of citizen activity by non-freeholders, just as Henry Ireton was to be eighty years later at Putney, for he notes that the office of constable was not formerly "imployed uppon such lowe and base persons." In fact, the picture he paints is one of broad-based self-government at the local level.

Smith is entirely silent in *De Republica Anglorum* about the most rapidly increasing sector of the population, the poor. As William Harrison, the only other commentator of Smith's day to attempt a comparable *tour d'horizon* of English society, noted, "There is no commonwealth at this day in Europe wherein there is not great store of poor people," who without assistance "would starve and come to utter confusion."[8] The proliferation of the poor was the most obsessively debated social issue of the sixteenth century; they may have been the most obsessively observed social group as well, for Thomas Harman divided the class of "idle vagabonds" alone into twenty-three separate categories.[9] Smith's omission of them in his discussion indicates both the boundaries of his commonwealth and the difficulty in conceptualizing the poor politically (or even humanly) in terms of a property-based society. With Ireton, he would doubtless have accorded them "air and place and ground" as sentient beings, and charity (when deserved) as Christians.

The omission is nonetheless all the more striking when one considers both the sensitive discussion of poverty and its causes in Smith's earlier tract, *A Discourse of the Commonweal* (written in 1549, published in 1581), and in his definition of the commonwealth in *De Republica Anglorum*:

> A common wealth is called a society or common doing of a multitude of free men collected together and united by common accord and covenauntes among themselves, for the conservation of themselves aswell in peace as in warre. (20)

As Ellen Meiksins Wood and Neal Wood point out, Smith posits the commonwealth as a deliberative association of free individuals rather than the layered aggregate of families, corporate bodies, estates, and orders that one finds, for example, in Bodin.[10] This makes it easier to imagine a primal scene of social contract; it also presupposes a juridical equality among those initially composing and subsequently comprising the commonwealth. What the term "free men" primarily denotes in Smith, however, is self-subsistence and independence of means, for the commonwealth is not contrasted with a state of nature as in Hobbes or Locke but with a primitive host or a society of bondmen. A host is merely a temporary gathering, lacking any purpose to cohere once its specific intention is accomplished; bondmen, by contrast, lack any capacity to do so:

> [For] if one man had as some of the old Romanes had (if it be true that is written) v. thousande or x. thousande bondmen whom he ruled well, though they dwelled all in one citie, or were distributed into diverse villages, yet that were no common wealth: for the bondman hath no communion with his master . . . and there is no mutuall societie or portion, no law or pleading betweene thone and thother. (20–21)

The basis for political capacity is an independent means of subsistence, lacking which the bondman is no more than "the instrument of his Lord, as the axe, the sawe, the chessyll and gowge is of the charpenter" (20). The lord may provide for his bondmen as the carpenter cares for his tools, but the "profit" of his labor never accrues to the bondman, nor can he lay any claim to it. The formation of a commonwealth thus requires two conditions: the will to associate permanently, and the capacity as freemen to do so. The host cannot be prolonged beyond its immediate purpose except by coercion, that is, by being converted into a society of bondmen; a society of bondmen cannot aspire to be other than a host, for the only common purpose bondmen can have is rebellion. Smith goes so far as to deny even contemporary states the status of a commonwealth:

> [For] if the prince of the Turkes (as it is written of him) doe repute all other his bondmen and slaves (him selfe and his sonnes only freemen) a man may doubt whether his administration be to be accompted a common wealth or a kingdome, or rather to be reputed onely as one that hath under him an infinite number of slaves or bondmen among whom there is no right, law nor common wealth compact, but onely the will of the Lorde and segnior. (21)

Several points emerge in this brief but powerfully compressed chapter. The purpose of a commonwealth is simultaneously political and economic, not to say commercial: for if its originary goal is "conservation," Smith's conception of this is not static but dynamic, presupposing growth and "profit." It is apparent that the political and economic conditions for founding a commonwealth are indissolubly and indeed (except for purposes of analysis) indistinguishably united: the "free man" is a freeholder, and vice versa. If not quite a commonwealth for increase in Harrington's sense or one of interest in Sidney's, the Smithian community is voluntary and expansionist, committed to a mutual interest that remains composed of its several parts, and to a prosperity to be sought both in peace and in war.

This definition underscores Smith's awkwardness in dealing with the largest element of England's actual population, the "fourth sort" of copyholders, shopkeepers, artificers, and laborers who do not rule but nevertheless discharge public responsibilities *faute de mieux*, and his complete silence, at least in *De Republica Anglorum*, about the destitute and the dispossessed. Smith's commonwealth has at best a grudging place for the former group, but none at all for the latter, for their presence suggests a condition of anarchy that is antithetical to the very conception of a commonwealth and which invites, as a remedy, the imposition of compulsory labor and thus the creation of a society that is de facto half slave and half free. The England of the sixteenth century was in no position to absorb such surplus labor, and devised the poor laws instead. The England of the nineteenth century would, of course, prove a very different affair.

Smith's *A Discourse of the Commonweal* shows him very worried about such issues, in common with the other writers of the 1540s whom we collectively label the Commonwealthmen. What he does not do is to make the conceptual connection between the schematic commonwealth of *De Republica Anglorum* and the actual situation of England — the connection that is, of course, at the heart of Sir Thomas More's discourse in his *Utopia*. For Smith, political conflict occurs within an Aristotelian context, as a self-regulating system of decay and renewal:

> And if a few would take upon them to usurpe over the rest, the rest conspiring together would soone be master over them, and ruinate them wholly. Whereupon necessarily it came to passe that the common wealth must turne and alter as before from one to a few, so now from a few to many and the most part, ech of these yet willing to save the politicke bodie, to conserve the authoritie of their nation, to defende themselves against all other, their strife being onely for empire and rule, and who should doe best for the common wealth, wherof they would have experience made by bearing office and being magistrates. (27)

The conflict within commonwealths is here perceived simply within political terms, as a contest for "empire and rule," that is, of status. The implications of economic domination so anxiously canvassed in *A Discourse of the Commonweal* are wholly absent here, just as the political dimension of the *lutte des classes* is absent in the *Discourse*. As a result, both forms of domination can be cast in terms of distempers, to be remedied in the case of enclosure and dispossession by politic intervention and moral suasion, and in that of status rivalry by the self-correcting praxis of the polity itself. What is not entertained is the possibility — fatal to Smith's schema — that the commonwealth might actually operate not as a mechanism to promote economic enhancement and status competition within the framework of an ultimate, limitary consensus ("to save the politicke bodie, to conserve the authoritie of their nation, to defende themselves against all other") but as an engine to degrade citizens to the level of bondmen by stripping them of land and livelihood.

Here again a clear dividing line appears between Smith's "fourth sort," who occupy a kind of limbo in the commonwealth, having neither the landed independence required for full citizen status nor the complete dependence of the bondman, and the destitute, vagabond population which appears in Harrison but is wholly elided by Smith. The latter can be accounted for, as Harrison notes, in terms of surplus population ("the great increase of people in these days"), and therefore appears as an exogenous element which, while creating serious practical difficulties, does not threaten the theoretical framework of the commonwealth as such. The degradation of copyhold farmers, small retailers, artisans, wage laborers, and above all yeomen, a class admitted by Smith to citizen status and warmly (if at this point rather anachronistically) praised as the backbone of the militia, had far more serious implications for its viability. A commonwealth not merely burdened by its poor but systematically sapping its citizen base and turning freemen into bondmen was, on Smith's definition, almost a contradiction in terms. Yet that, as it appeared, was precisely what was happening in the troubled 1540s. Smith not only lacked a means to conceptualize this, but, with other Commonwealth writers, he could think only of appealing to the magistrate for remedy. Tyranny, status rivalry, and generalized "distemper" in the commonwealth could be imagined, but a commonwealth whose praxis resulted inexorably in the production of its very antithesis, a society of dependent laborers and ultimately of unfree ones, could not.

William Harrison and the Description of the Realm

William Harrison's *The Description of England*, first published as *The Description of Britain* in 1577 and then under the title by which it has been subsequently known in 1587, is an altogether fuller work than Smith's, nothing less than a comprehensive social and chorographical account of England. It was conceived in turn as the preface to a still larger project, Holinshed's *Chronicles of England* (1577). Chorographical and historical description often went side by side in Tudor England, a custom facilitated by the persistence of the chronicle tradition, with its sense of a perpetually unfolding present. Harrison himself produced both a conventional English history and a *Great English Chronology*, which, although it remained unpublished, was his most ambitious work.

The Description was nonetheless an unprecedented work, and Harrison is correct, if not overly modest, in stating that "I am the first that . . . hath taken upon him so particularly to describe this Isle of Britain."[11] As his modern editor Georges Edelen points out, no fewer than five thousand place names are recorded in *The Description*, and Harrison only laments that he is unable to add a Homeric catalog of seaports to the list. Edelen detects in this not only a characteristic thoroughness (and garrulity), but also anxiety:

> Public change is of course a constant of human existence, but the rate of change is not. In some ages transitions in religious, social, and economic life are so slow, even, and predictable as to be almost imperceptibly absorbed by those affected. At other times the gradient becomes much steeper; not only specific developments but the dominance of change forces itself upon the consciousness. With this heightened realization of transience comes the impulse to describe, to come to terms with the novel by verbal ordering, to weigh against the past, to record the potentially unstable. (xxix)

This is the very Elizabethan theme of "mutabilitie," but one must recall as well the pressure of Harrison's *Chronology* on *The Description*, with its eschatological account of world history and its sense of imminent judgment.[12] England's grand past and its flourishing present, the pride of its chroniclers and antiquarians, was only the prelude to a conclusive future that would simultaneously fulfill and obliterate it. There is, indeed, an almost continuous sense of the pressure of divine favor or judgment upon even the humblest of subjects, as for instance in the eight-page essay on the cultivation of saffron (348–356). As Harrison relates:

> Such . . . was the plenty of saffron about twenty years past that some of the townsmen of Walden gave the one-half of the flowers for the picking of the other, and sent them ten or twelve miles abroad into the country, whilst the rest, not thankful for the abundance of God's blessing bestowed upon them (as wishing rather more scarcity thereof, because of the keeping up of the price), in most contemptuous manner murmured against Him, saying that he did shit saffron, therewith to choke the market. But as they showed themselves no less than ingrate infidels in this behalf, so the Lord considered their unthankfulness and gave them ever since such scarcity as the greatest murmurers have now the least store . . . (352)

This parable of bounty, commerce, and blight suggests a larger pattern. There is obviously an element of chauvinism (and, conversely, of xenophobia) in Harrison's claim of superiority for all things English, from the plenty of its fish and fruit and the salubriousness of its waters to the fidelity of its dogs and the comeliness of its women. Even where other nations appear outwardly to excel England, its inner virtues prevail: thus, while English houses may seem comparatively plain, they are far more commodious and hospitable, and foreign observers like "better of our good fare in such coarse cabins than of their own thin diet in their princelike habitations and palaces" (196). England's superiority is ultimately moral rather than material, and

God's bounty toward it, measured rather than prodigal, is like the good husbandman's aimed at cultivating the hardiness and vigor of its stock and avoiding the excesses of effete abundance.

Harrison's view of England was as thoroughly shaped by his vocation (he was rector of Radwinter, Essex, from 1559, and from 1577 also vicar of Wimbush) as was Smith's by his. The first and longest chapter of the *Description* is an account of "The Ancient and Present Estate of the Church of England." Much of it is a screed against the pre-Reformation church, a Norman usurpation that forced popery down the throats of kings and people alike. Some of its more heated rhetoric ("rakehells of the clergy and puddles of all ungodliness") doubtless reflected a convert's zeal, for Harrison, despite pious instruction by Alexander Nowell, had been briefly won over to Romanism during Mary's reign until preaching by the Oxford martyrs brought him by his account to his senses.[13] Nonetheless, Harrison posits continuity between the pre- and post-Reformed church in a fashion that reflects the "moderate Puritan" wing of the Anglican church identified by Peter Lake, accepting Erastian controls and episcopal government.[14]

On this reading, the Elizabethan church was a restoration of the true church that still existed in England—after monasticism and clerical celibacy had been purged from it for a first time—until its corruption by St. Dunstan, Archbishop of Canterbury, in the late tenth century. The Normans, abetted by the scheming of the Archbishop Robert, overthrew the monarchy a hundred years later, thus sealing a regime of secular and spiritual tyranny. The Normans themselves were promptly abused, so that finally they might rule in their own kingdom "no further than it pleased the Pope to like of," thereby contravening "the express law of God, who commandeth all men to honor and obey their kings and princes, in whom some part of the power of God is manifest and laid open to us" (18, 19).

Reserving a fuller account for his still-projected history (and presumably for Holinshed as well), Harrison bypassed the restoration of true magistracy in church and state by the Tudors, proceeding at once to a description of the Reformed order. The bishops were now no longer "idle in their callings . . . being now exempt from court and council, which is one (and a no small) piece of their felicity" (24). Instead, they and their archdeacons were able to "make diligent inquisition and search, as well for the doctrine and behavior of the ministers as the orderly dealing of the parishioners in resorting to their parish churches and conformity unto religion" (25). Accordingly, "There is nothing read in our churches but the canonical Scriptures, whereby it cometh to pass that the Psalter is said over once in thirty days, the New Testament four times, and the Old Testament once a year." In addition, if the curate "be adjudged . . . sufficiently instructed in the Holy Scriptures," he is permitted "to make some exposition or exhortation in his parish unto amendment of life" (33).[15]

In these passages, Harrison sounds as conformist as one could wish, stressing the importance of episcopal discipline and rote reading, and relegating preaching to a subsidiary and optional position. There is, moreover, no mention of the corruption of doctrine in *The Description*, and none of its restoration as enshrined in the Thirty-Nine Articles. Popery is defined by Harrison solely in terms of the usurpation of secular authority, and the Reformation as its proper restoration. If one attends to such passages alone — what is omitted in them as well as what is stated — we seem to be in the presence of a thoroughgoing Erastian whose views would be entirely congenial to Hooker.

Yet this same Harrison is within the same chapter a bitter critic of the impoverishment of clerical livings, the practice of leaving unfilled vacancies, and the abuses of lay patrons. He is a staunch supporter as well of prophesyings, both for the training of ministers and for the edification of laymen who, "thirsty . . . to hear the Word of God . . . have, as it were, with zealous violence intruded themselves" (25–26). These are clearly notes of the godly, and they remind us of the difficulty of squaring particular cases with general rubrics. As usual in such circumstances, we are better advised to think in terms of a spectrum of practices and attitudes along which a given individual might range himself idiosyncratically. There were many ways to conform (and to dissent) in a church as ecumenically conceived as that of Elizabeth. Had this not been the case — had there not, in short, been men like Harrison, in whom seemingly discordant attitudes cohabited peacefully — there would have been no common ground for the anti-Laudian consensus that emerged in the 1630s, and no basis for the swift assumption of leadership by godly ministers in the Long Parliament.

Two further examples of "spectrum slippage" may be adduced in Harrison. Discussing clerical attire, he notes that:

> The apparel . . . of our clergymen is comely, and in truth more decent than ever it was in the popish church . . . For if you peruse well my Chronology ensuing, you shall find that [priests] went either in diverse colors like players, or in garments of light hue, as yellow, red, green, etc., with their shoes piked, their hair crisped, their girdles armed with silver, their shoes, spurs, bridles, etc., buckled with like metal, their apparel (for the most part) of silk and richly furred, so that to meet a priest in those days was to behold a peacock that spreadeth his tail when he danceth before the hen . . . (37)

Harrison builds his indictment of popish foppery to a crescendo of ridicule, sounding all the stops of godly disdain as he likens it to that of strolling players, effeminate courtiers, and fornicators. Knox in his pulpit could hardly outdo this catalog. Yet Harrison finds his own vestments, anathema to the godly and distressing to such bishops as Grindal and Sandys, "comely" and appropriate.

Similarly, Harrison applauds the removal of idols and barriers from the churches without expressing any urgency about their complete destruction:

> As for our churches themselves, bells and times of Morning and Evening Prayer remain as in times past, saving that all images, shrines, tabernacles, rood lofts, and monuments of idolatry are removed, taken down, and defaced; only the stories in glass windows excepted, which, for want of sufficient store of new stuff and by reason of extreme charge that should grow by the alteration of the same into white panes throughout the realm, are not altogether abolished in most places at once but by little and little suffered to decay, that white glass may be provided and set up in their rooms. Finally, whereas there was wont to be a great partition between the choir and the body of the church, now it is either very small or none at all, and to say the truth, altogether needless . . . (35–36)

Once again, the process of "reform" is for Harrison (aside from the categorical rejection of papal authority as such) more a matter of stripping away superfluous accretions than of casting out abominations, in which the ordinary processes of physical decay are speedy enough to remove what is offensive or "needless." Harrison did his part at Radwinter, eliminating traditional rogation processions and other observances that smacked of popery. He believed, however, that idolatry could be permanently held in check only by pastoral (and princely) vigilance, for the "simple," as he noted in the *Chronology*, were constitutionally prone to it. This was another reason to embrace a hierarchical, Erastian church, for a cynical prince could easily exploit the natural superstition of the vulgar. A godly magistrate and a godly ministry went hand in hand.[16]

A godly ministry was also a learned one. The hope of reform, as Harrison made clear, rested with the universities, whose foundation he placed, following Caius and Stow, in Saxon times. He evidently remembered his student days with fondness, and having taken degrees at both Cambridge and Oxford he likened them to "the body of one well-ordered commonwealth, only divided by distance of place and time," so that "In speaking . . . of the one, I cannot but describe the other" (70). As in passing by the doctrine of the church, Harrison makes no mention of the curricular wars of the sixteenth century, contenting himself with the enumeration, provenance, and description of the various colleges, a survey of their degree programs, and their list of functionaries.

Harrison's idyllic picture of Cambridge and Oxford was not without its shadow. Wealth and influence all too often determined admission to the colleges; indeed, he complained, "such bribage is made that poor men's children are commonly shut out" even from scholarships nominally reserved for them (71). Similarly, the rich, their appetites whetted by the sale of monastic property, sought to encroach on university lands as well. These "greedy gripers" had been spurned by Henry VIII and Protector Somerset, only to renew their suit in Elizabeth's time. Harrison saw in this the same kind of standing threat that beset the church in the form of lay patrons who starved it by keeping their benefices vacant and reaping the income for themselves. The answer was to require such patrons to report vacancies promptly to their bishops, who would in turn call upon the university vice chancellors to provide a suitable minister. This would resolve the problems of both institutions. How this fine solution was to be implemented, Harrison did not say (80–81, 75).

Harrison's account of the church and the universities helped to repair the complete absence of discussion in Smith. For Harrison, the two institutions formed a single instrument that, together, tempered the commonwealth. Without them, wealth and force would prevail from above, and superstition hold sway below. This, he concluded, had been the fate of England under the Goths and the Vandals, "who made laws against learning and would not suffer any skillful man to come into their council house, by means where of those people became savage tyrants and merciless hellhounds" (81).

Harrison, who in the fashion of chronicle tradition borrowed liberally from his sources, cribbed his discussion of Parliament (added to the 1587 edition) almost entirely from Smith. Despite apologies for his lack of legal learning (169), he did, however, append his own discussion of English law. It is a perfect summation of the confusion that reigned before the development of legal antiquarianism. Following Bale,[17] Harrison attributed the foundation of British law to one Samothes, or Dis, the supposed grandson of Noah and the founder of the first Celtic kingdom. Succeeding and equally legendary conquerors imposed their own codes, including Brut, the great-grandson of Aeneas (there is no mention of Rome), until Brut's successor, Molmutius, settled the laws so thoroughly that they remained in effect until the Saxon conquest. Though both the Saxons and the Normans sought to replace the Molmutian code, they came to accept it in time as best suited to the governance of the country. Thus England had had, time out of mind, a fundamental law, although Harrison does not employ the term or even the concept as such, nor does he indicate what the content of that law might be, either in its initial or received form. It is merely to be noted that it was originally authoritative; that is, given as a code, but that it had gradually become a *lex terrae* to which successive conquerors, their own coercive authority notwithstanding, were compelled to return. The only substantive innovations the Saxons and Normans were able to achieve, consequently, were procedural: trial by ordeal in the case of the former, trial by due process in that of the latter.

Having depicted the first three thousand years of English legal history as a series of successive and discontinuous beginnings, Harrison brings his account suddenly into the present, distinguishing the "sundry" laws of the realm—civil, canon, and common—and the courts to which they pertain. There is no explanation of how these complex systems grew up in the shade of Molmutian jurisprudence; nor there can be, since the precepts of Molmutius, as Harrison asserts, have been lost, or (presumably) absorbed into later codes. Legend washes across the ages until, at the shore of the contemporary, it curls back on itself and vanishes into the mist.

The "regiment" of present-day England, Harrison continues, is based upon statute law, common law, and customary law and prescription (170). Statute law is produced by a special court, Parliament, which sits at the pleasure of the king and promulgates particular laws with his consent. Customary law and prescription is local law, limited to specific regions, counties, or shires, and typically pertaining to such matters as inheritance, rights of way and usage, and tithes. The common law is the general law of the land, both criminal and civil, and it would appear, if anything, to be the successor of Molmutius:

> The common law standeth upon sundry maxims or principles . . . which do contain such cases as by great study and solemn argument of the judges, sound practice, confirmed by long experience, fetched even from the course of most ancient laws made far before the Conquest, and thereto the deepest reach and foundations of reason, are ruled and adjudged for law. (171)

Harrison admits that he is no legal scholar, "For what hath the meditation of the law of God to do with any precise knowledge of the law of man?" (173). Despite this Erastian disclaimer, however, his definition neatly encapsulates both the strengths and vagaries of the common law in Tudor thought. It is a set of "maxims and principles" derived—"fetched" in Harrison's suggestive phrase—by learned judges from the "most ancient" (i.e., immemorial) laws. This sounds very much (to a modern ear) like a tradition of constitutional interpretation, or judge-made law, especially as the urtexts themselves (if any) have long since disappeared. But those texts themselves represent a composite or compilation, for wisdom does not reside in the text, but in the long oral chain that begins with the "first" lawgiver ("Molmutius") and continues unbroken, if not undisturbed, through successive ages of argument and case law application. The "maxims and principles" of the law are the distilled essence of this endless, perpetual process, the basis, one might say, of legal contemplation, but the law itself is unutterable: it exceeds interpretation, although it can only be known through it. (Statute law, although Harrison distinguishes it from the common law as such [170], is logically only another form of judicial interpretation, that of the King's "High Court.")

The process described by Harrison is very nearly theological—an exercise in practical divinity in which particular cases "reveal" the common law as cases of conscience reveal the moral law. The first activity is proper to judges, the second to pastoral counselors—"what hath the meditation of the law of God to do with any precise knowledge of the law of man?"—but the process of discovery is analogous: a William Perkins and a Sir Edward Coke are, in their separate and distinct spheres, performing similar operations.

The dependence of the common law on "fetching"—especially in the absence of divinity's single and authoritative text—places a virtually complete reliance on the integrity of judges and juries, and hence on their independence. (Harrison has a kinder word for juries than Smith, describing them as "twelve sober, grave, and wise men," though conceding later that they "very often have neither reason nor judgment to perform the charge they come for" [90, 91].) At the same time, however, judges were (like bishops) councillors to the king, defenders of his authority, and, as the case might require, upholders of his claims. A wise ruler would not press this advantage too far, at least without conciliating his elites, but James I was to prove less than prudent on this point, and Charles I fatally unwise. The Ship Money judges, under immense pressure, gave Charles the law he wanted, and cost him his kingdom.

Harrison's notion of England's law would seem to rest upon tradition rightly interpreted by a learned bench. Rulers, even conquerors, who strayed from this tradition were apt to find great hindrance if not danger, as the Normans did (165). The law, then, gave security to king and subject alike. Like a gyroscope, it always returned the commonwealth to first principles, no matter how pushed.

Yet beneath this seeming confidence lurked a palpable anxiety, not only about the practical operations of the law but about its very nature. As the Romish clergy had once battened on the country, "so now," Harrison declared, "all the wealth of our land doth flow unto our common lawyers," with the result that poor men could get no law at all (173, 174). At the same time, men of all classes, egged on by promoters, had grown so litigious that only the brevity of court terms restrained them from wholly consuming themselves in suits. This salutary check produced its own grievance, however, in the form of proceedings endlessly protracted by adjournments.

But the abuse of the law was less unsettling than the sense of its final uncertainty. If law was ultimately in the hands of the lawyers, if its immemorial principles—however firm in the abstract—were made manifest only through interpretation, then who could say at any moment what it was? Thus it appeared that the laws were always so variable and subject to change that "oft in one age diverse judgments do pass upon one manner of case, whereby the saying of the poet, *Tempora mutantur, et nos mutamur in illis,*[18] may very well be applied unto such as, being urged with these words, 'In such a year of the prince this opinion was taken for sound law,' do answer nothing else but that the judgment of our lawyers is now altered so that they say far otherwise" (170).

If law were nothing more than declared opinion or at any rate indistinguishable from it, then litigiousness was not an abuse of the legal system but its very essence, and the quest for law a struggle for power. If Machiavelli perhaps stood behind this statement then Hobbes stood before it, for *certain* law, in the absence of any means but opinion to declare it, could be asserted only as the act of an absolute and arbitrary authority.

Harrison's England was finally both a paragon and a caution. God had favored it in innumerable respects over other lands, yet made it subject to repeated humiliation and conquest. In this it resembled his church, which embodied his truth yet suffered oppression. Whether English exceptionalism had eschatological implications appears to have been a matter on which Harrison reserved judgment, although the defeat of the Armada, which occurred the year after he published the second edition of the *Description*, doubtless prompted thoughts in that direction as it did for other of his contemporaries. At all events he vigorously disputed the view urged by Reformers such as Melanchthon that the prophecy of the four monarchies assigned a special role to Germany as the heir of Rome.

William Camden and Britain's Book

In 1586, the thirty-five year old Westminster schoolmaster and antiquarian William Camden published what F. J. Levy has described as "a small and rather ugly octavo of around 550 pages, unillustrated . . . emphatically not one of the triumphs of Elizabethan book-making."[19] Appearances notwithstanding, *Britannia*—a book whose ambition was announced in the capacious brevity of its title—was immediately recognized as a major work of modern scholarship, the first by a native Englishman. It was also the first comprehensive English chorography, a feat that William Lambarde had only recently announced to be "beyond the power of one man."[20] *Britannia* was indeed a work with many debts: to John Leland, whose attempts to write a similar book had collapsed but whose notes proved invaluable to Camden; to Abraham Ortelius, the Belgian cartographer whose interest in the historical topography of Britain had spurred him on; to the chronicler of London, John Stow; to the poet Sidney and the diplomat Daniel Rogers and the magus John Dee; to the cartographer Christopher Saxton; and to Lambarde himself. Like all great books, *Britannia* was timely, which is to say it was the product of a collective *mentalité* as well as the effort of its author. It was to become in many ways a collective work as well. By the time of Camden's death in 1623 it had expanded to 860 pages and was copiously illustrated.

Subsequent editors continued to augment it down to the nineteenth century, adding fresh archaeological discoveries and bringing the historical narrative up to date. The *Britannia* was to become, more than any other, Britain's book.

The specific stimulus to the *Britannia* was Ortelius' curiosity about Roman Britain. Harrison, and the earlier chroniclers he had followed, had propagated the insular myth of a wholly indigenous English culture, derived from a pristine source (the supposed Trojan migration) and retaining its essential character through all subsequent invasion and conquest. Rome was simply bypassed, a prolonged encampment that was no more, in the end, than an overlay on native custom and an interregnum in native law. In investigating the Roman occupation from the standpoint of historical geography, however, Camden deliberately sought to uncover the wealth of imperial remains, whose amount and distribution attested to the impress of Roman civilization on Britain. So focused was he on this task that, as Graham Parry observes, he largely ignored the no less abundant evidence of pre-Roman habitation, and, his profession of interest in ancient Britons notwithstanding, "Pre-Roman Britain is a blank" in his book.[21] To all intents and purposes, Tiberius Claudius was the founder of Camden's Britain.

This had profound implications for the national history. If the Roman impact on Britain were no more than a glaze on ancient institutions that returned again to their pristine state with the demise of the empire and reimposed themselves on the subsequent Saxon and Norman conquerors, then the story of Britain was precisely in its ahistoricism, its ultimate invulnerability to change. This notion of an ancient, mythical constitution was, as we shall see, to exert a continuing hold on Englishmen until well into the seventeenth century. Its authority rested with the medieval chroniclers, notably Geoffrey of Monmouth. The mere authority of tradition, however, no longer satisfied the canons of Renaissance scholarship against which Camden measured himself, and which the Italian Polydore Vergil had already brought to England in his *Anglicae historia*. The post-Constantinian history of England had, moreover, already been deeply revised by Bale and Foxe, who had labored to extricate its political and ecclesiastical development from the claims of the Roman church. The need to create a Protestant lineage for the English church coincided with the need to justify the Constantinian imperium that ruled it. Camden's interests were secular, but he was clearly aware of the implication of his researches. If Britain had been a mere military outpost or barbarian colony of Rome, its pedigree among the powers of Europe remained to be established. If on the other hand it had been a fully assimilated part of the empire, it shared in the *translatio imperii* by which its power had devolved upon the successor states of the West. English kings had long maintained, as the preface to the Henrician Act of Appeals put it, that "this realm of England is an empire," and that this claim was buttressed in "sundry old authentic histories and chronicles."[22] In the context of late Renaissance scholarship, however, the old chronicles would no longer do, and a more substantial link with classical tradition was required. The *Britannia* provided this; after Camden, it was impossible to doubt that Britain had been an integral part of the Roman Empire, and hence "imperial" if any state were.

Camden's argument was all the more effective for being indirect: his purpose was not to support royal claims or titles, but simply to reconstruct the history and chorography of Roman Britain on the best available evidence. Nonetheless, as his description in the chapter on "The Degrees of England" demonstrates, the monarchy had firm classical foundations:

> The KING, stiled by our Ancestors *Coning*, and *Cyning* . . . and by us contracted into *King*, has in these kingdoms the supreme power, and a *meer* government. He neither holds his Empire by vassalage nor receives it by Investiture from another, nor owns any superior but God. As that Oracle of the Law [Bracton] has delivered it, *Every one is under him, and himself under none but God.* He has very many Imperial Rights (which the learned in the law term *The Holy of Holies,* and *Individuals,* because they are inseparable, but the common People, *The King's Prerogative;*) and these, they tell us, are denoted by the *flowers* in the King's Crown. Some of these the King enjoys by *written Law,* others by Custom, which without any express Law is established by the tacit consent of the whole body: and surely he deserves them, *since by his watchfulness every man's House, by his labour every man's Ease, by his industry every one's Pleasure, and by his toil every one's Recreation, is secure of him* [Seneca]. But these things are too sublime, to belong properly to our present Subject. (ccxxxiii)

Camden's first derivation, as was his wont, is etymological. The English monarch is not *rex, roi,* or *rey,* but *Cyng,* clearly a Germanic rather than a Latin root. He nonetheless possesses the full Roman *potestas* and *majestas,* for he acknowledges no subordination to any power on earth, either temporal (vassalage) or spiritual (investiture), and exercises "very many Imperial Rights" that are inseparable from his crown. The argument is clinched by the quotation from Seneca, which applies the appropriate classical garnishing.

This passage, and the burden of Camden's entire book, would seem at first blush more than ordinarily welcome to a monarch such as Elizabeth, and even more so to James I, during whose reign the first English translation of *Britannia* (1610) was published. Much of it, indeed, sounds rather like the homilies on kingship that James was fond of preaching to his parliaments. Presumably James would have been particularly pleased by the reference to his prerogative as "The Holy of Holies." Nonetheless, the passage is carefully balanced. The king is declared to be under none but God, but his specific powers are derived from law and custom, which is to say express or tacit consent. The powers so flatteringly described as "The Holy of Holies" thus turn out to be neither of divine institution nor otherwise inherent in the crown, but given by the body of the commonwealth. They are given, more-over, for a purpose: as the quotation from Seneca makes clear, the king *serves* the commonwealth, for it is by his "labour" and "industry" that all others take their "Ease" and "Recreation."

For Camden, then, England's monarchy is clearly bounded by law. If it has the full complement of *potestas* and *majestas* that belongs to any other de-scendant of the Roman imperium, it is because this comports with the dig-nity of the nation. If the monarchy has grown, renouncing any claim of "vas-salage" or "investiture," it is because the nation has grown correspondingly with it. The eminence of one is inseparable from that of the other.

This point was reinforced in the remainder of Camden's chapter. Monar-chy received a single long paragraph in it, and, at the other extreme, com-moners (distinguished as "gentlemen," "citizens" [i.e., burgesses], "yeo-men," and "labourers") only the briefest mention at the end. Almost all the rest was devoted to the description and elucidation of English titles of honor. This preoccupation is not surprising in the man who, from 1599, served as Clarenceaux King of Arms. It is nonetheless worthy of note. The crown, in Camden's universe, shared its dignity with a nobility whose titles were often themselves of Roman provenance. In surveying each county of England, Scotland, and Ireland, he promised to provide not only a general historical and geographical description but an account of "who have been Dukes or Earls of each, since the Norman Conquest" (cclxvii). In a society still preoc-cupied with the Wars of the Roses and in which serious rebellion remained a perennial possibility, Camden's valorization of the nobility carried an im-plicit warning. A haughty or presumptuous king might yet provoke over-mighty subjects. This point received added emphasis in one of the stories Camden told in the *Remains Concerning Britain*, the companion source vol-ume to *Britannia* (1605). In the chapter on "Grave Speeches," he related the reply of the Earl of Surrey when Henry VII "demaunded" of him why he had fought for the "tyranne" Richard III:

> He was my crowned King and if the Parliamentary authority of England sette the Crowne of England uppon a stocke, I will fight for that stocke.[23]

Loyalty to the crown, Surrey was reminding the King, was loyalty to the fig-ure — or figurehead — designated by the elite itself.

Camden, too, was far from an uncritical admirer of the Roman imperium. The Romans had brought civilized culture to Britain, but they had also learned valor from the Britons, so that their victories over them were ac-counted "as the most famous monuments of the Roman bravery" (lix). The British had tutored their masters as well, receiving the Christian faith even as it was being persecuted in Nero's time (lxxiii). Nor had they abandoned their love of liberty, as evidenced in the bold complaint of Clodius Albinus against the maladministration of the emperors (lxxxii). For Camden, British history may have effectively begun with the Romans, but British tradition had not. The Romans had conquered Britain, not created it.

This point had permanent significance. As Harrison had celebrated the perdurability of British laws and customs in the face of change and conquest, so Camden, in acknowledging the unique impact of Rome on Britain, was at pains to assert that the Romans were as much the gainers as the givers in the relationship. Britain, as he wrote in the *Remains*, was "one of the fairest and most glorious Plumes in the triumphant Diademe of the Roman Empire," and its stores among the chief imperial sinews.[24] These two attributes — beauty and strength — were the island's natural endowment, and that of its inhabitants; as Camden proudly noted, the charms of a native daughter, Claudia Rufina, had raised "a noble strife in *Italy* and *Greece*."[25] Rome had merely cultivated this endowment and reaped its profit.

In place of Harrison's myth of primal lawgiving, then, Camden and his fellow chorographers substituted an allegorized Britain whose splendor and fertility, nurturing in its inhabitants the natural virtues of liberty and valor, had produced a core national identity. Successive waves of immigration and conquest had shaped this identity in various ways — it was not necessary to maintain the fiction of primitive custom, immune to all changes — but only in accordance with its own bent. The chorographer's myth was of a land and a people bound in indissoluble harmony. The welter of peoples — Gallic, Roman, Saxon, Danish, Norman — who had merged to form the stock of the island were now all indistinguishably British.

The solution of Camden and his successors to the problem of representing the nation was thus to identify it with the island, to subsume "British" under "Britain." The chorographical method, with its county by county approach, emphasized the natural history of Britain at the expense of its national one. Central to this mode of representation was the use of cartography. Camden's 1607 edition of *Britannia* featured fifty-six maps, based on the atlas published by Christopher Saxton in 1579. The Saxton atlas had been commissioned by the Queen, and bore the marks of its patronage both in the enthroned Elizabeth of its frontispiece and in the royal insignia that adorn and embellish it throughout. Far blunter in its iconographic appropriation of the realm is the Ditchley portrait (c. 1592), already noted, which depicts a titanic Elizabeth standing on England's southwestern coast and towering into a sky laced with the gleams and lightnings of majesty, the fan in her right hand dwarfing the full-masted ship that sails offshore. As Richard Helgerson points out, only eleven of Camden's maps contain royal insignia, although the originals from which they were copied all appear to.[26] This is accounted for in part by the absence of royal patronage in either the *Britannia* or the *Remains*, a point made conspicuous in the dedications of both books. Like Harrison, Camden was an independent scholar and proud of his standing; unlike Harrison, he had access to the Court and knew its principals. Perhaps he was describing something of his own aversion when he spoke of "A Gentleman scholler drawne from the Universitie where he was well liked to the Court, for which in respect of his bashfull modestie, he was not so fit."[27]

It was of course impossible for Camden (or anyone else above the level of a parson or squire) to avoid commerce with the Court. He was drawn into James' controversy with the *politique* historian Jacques-Auguste de Thou, and, in part because of this, the task of writing a history of Elizabeth's reign, originally suggested by his patron Burghley, was imposed on him by the King.[28] The composition of it appears to have been distasteful to him, in part because he had little inclination toward narrative, and in part because of the hazards, long ago noted by Livy, of writing history of contemporary import. Camden responded by adopting an annalistic style that offered as little scope for commentary or analysis as possible. He remained determined to avoid compromising a reputation for integrity and nonpartisanship maintained over a lifetime: "By inveighing against the Enemies of my Countrey, to aim at the Commendation of a good Commonwealths-man, and at the same time get the Repute of a bad Historian, I held a thing ridiculous. This I have been careful of, that, according as Polybius directeth, I might have an Eye to the Truth onely."[29]

Camden's value to us lies precisely in the combination of his robust patriotism, social conservatism, and stubborn personal independence. What he said about Roman Britain that was of practical utility to Tudor assertions of empire or Jacobean ones of absolutism was not uttered with any propaganda effect in mind (and James, who liked to trace his ancestry to Brut, could not have been pleased with the chilling skepticism with which Camden treated the Trojan myths). Cotton and Selden were to be his disciples in this, and the inability of the early Stuarts to co-opt the leading intellectual figures of the period (with the conspicuous exception of Bacon) was to be consequential. That Charles I was forced to rely on the services of a Sibthorpe or a Mainwaring to buttress his claims to prerogative taxation while both Cotton and Selden were placing their resources at the service of the parliamentary resistance should have been fair warning that the Stuart monarchy was on precarious ground.

This is not to say that the Court had lost its ability to influence if not to shape English political discourse in the early seventeenth century. "Aspiring minds," to use Anthony Esler's phrase, were eager to please the new dynasty and to serve its agenda. The poet Samuel Daniel, not content with the sycophantic line "Shake hands with union, O thou mighty Isle" in his *Panegyrike Congratulatory* to James I in 1603, altered it to "Shake hands with Union, O thou mighty State." The lower-case "union" with its matter-of-fact declaration—that England and Scotland had now been brought together under a single ruler—became the upper-case "Union" of James VI and I's project for the political as well as dynastic unification of the two nations. More telling, from our perspective, was the transformation of "Isle" to "State." What Camden had accomplished in *Britannia* was to make "Britain"—both the island itself and the indissoluble unity it represented between a people and a place—the subject of the national discourse. The Elizabeth of the Ditchley portrait was a perhaps acceptable figure of this insofar as Elizabeth herself was taken as the concrete embodiment of her people rather than of the alienated power of the "state" (though Camden's long labor on the history of her reign may be seen as a penance imposed for the amonarchical image of "Britain"). In arriving to take possession of the throne of England, James had forced his new subjects to confront the real implications of a hypostatized and rhetorically exalted "Britain." By rejecting his grand scheme of Union (see below, Chapter VI), they had confronted him with the practical limitations of his rule. The issue of "State" versus "Isle," posed in Daniel's altered verse, was to be the dominant trope of British politics for the next hundred years.[30]

All this was far from any deliberate intention in Camden and his fellow chorographers. For Camden, an "imperial" state both in the Henrician sense of one that owed tribute to no earthly power, sacred or secular, and, in that of his contemporary Richard Hakluyt, as a vehicle for expansion and conquest, was not only compatible with his vision of a blessed isle, but (within the limits of law and liberty) a natural expression of it. Monarchy was the traditional form of this state in Britain, and there was no reason to question it; it was as indigenous to the island, in an historical sense, as its flora and fauna. It was not, however, natural or necessary as such. Richard Helgerson overstates the case, but not entirely, when he observes that "The cartographic [and chorographic] representation of England did have an ideological effect. It strengthened the sense of both local and national identity at the expense of an identity based on dynastic loyalty. . . . Maps let [Englishmen] see in a way never before possible the country—both county and nation—to which they belonged and at the same time showed royal authority—or at least its insignia—to be a merely ornamental adjunct to that country. Maps thus opened a conceptual gap between the land and its ruler, a gap that would eventually span battlefields."[31] The point was even clearer when, as in Camden's maps, those insignia were reduced or absent. Five decades later, the imperial vision of Britain, shorn of monarchy, would continue to animate Cromwellian foreign policy and Harrington's "commonwealth for increase."

Holinshed: The Chronicle of the Realm

Raphael Holinshed's *Chronicles*, for which Harrison's *Description of England* had served as a preface, was the most ambitious English history text of the sixteenth century. It is not an easy work to appreciate from a modern perspective. Compared to newer Renaissance models such as Polydore Vergil's *Anglicae historiae*, it lacked the narrative cogency that characterized the best Continental historiography. As the product of several hands — Reyner Wolfe, the printer-scholar who first conceived it as a universal geography-cum-history;[32] Holinshed himself,[33] his former assistant, who produced the histories of England and Scotland; Richard Stanyhurst, whose history of Ireland was itself based on the work of Edmund Campion;[34] and of course William Harrison, whose "prefatory" *Description* has received far more attention from scholars than the work it ostensibly introduced — it lacked the unity that a single author, such as Camden, could bring to disparate materials. The problem was exacerbated by the fact that the first edition of 1577 was superseded by one revised after Holinshed's death in 1582 by a new consortium including the journalist Abraham Fleming,[35] the jurist John Hooker (alias Vowell)[36] and the antiquarian Francis Thynne (or Boteville),[37] who added to the original text considerably but somewhat eclectically. Their product, in turn, was subjected to censorship before its printing was authorized in 1587.[38] Finally, "Holinshed" — as we will denote the product of this collective enterprise — has labored under the immense shadow of Shakespeare, who, with Spenser, Daniel, and virtually every other literary figure of the time, quarried it liberally for his own work.

It has taken a sympathetic modern reader, Annabel Patterson, to restore Holinshed to its rightful centrality in the cultural discourse of late Elizabethan and early Stuart discourse.[39] As Patterson rightly suggests, this text is characterized by its multivocality; it speaks neither with a single voice nor from a single perspective. (In this as well, Shakespeare, whose own ideological sympathies are often so difficult to locate, was a faithful borrower.) In part this derives from the received texts it incorporates, and in part from the varied perspectives of its author/redactors. At one extreme, William Harrison writes from the perspective of a godly critic of the Elizabethan settlement, although not one as alienated, perhaps, as Professor Patterson suggests; at the other, Richard Stanyhurst was a Catholic convert and conspirator, and thus at least covertly a foe both of that settlement and of the English presence in Ireland. A double tension is inherent in the enterprise: the estrangement of at least some of the authors from core elements of the Elizabethan regime, and, at least ideologically, from each other as well.

Multivocality was also, however, implicit in the structure of the *Chronicles* themselves. The chronicle form as such — of which Holinshed was the last great exemplar — involved, at least notionally, the subordination of author to event within a providential framework. History was perceived as a series of morality plays revolving around stock figures and subjects: just or unjust rulers, loyal or rebellious subjects, wars and tumults, natural and divine visitations, deeds to be praised or reprehended. The chronicler himself was the faithful mirror of the events he recorded, and whatever dialogic or dramatic tension was involved in their telling, their true significance emerged in the end. In this sense, the chronicle was the triumph of truth, but a truth that could only manifest itself in the hearing of all voices and the final, chorus-like assent of the community. The last word, then, was the contemporary community's, for while the providential significance of events might lie hidden or be at best partially revealed, their moral and prudential significance was transparent. This word was expressed through the chronicler and transmitted to posterity, which as the continuous historical community ratified it from generation to generation. The chronicler was in this sense effaced, a medium of transmission in which the immortal community recognized itself.[40]

Ideally, therefore, the chronicle involved the reader's ratification of received authority, to which would be added, in due course, the chronicle of his times, whether written by or on behalf of him. This process was continuous, and in principle seamless. The approaching and perhaps apocalyptic future might be fraught with uncertainty; the past, however, in its repetition of pattern and its humble accretion of detail, gave assurance of order and offered a framework for judgment and action.

This model, like any typology, was less transparent than it seemed. The factual record was often incomplete or unclear; the interpretive one might be contested. The chronicle was not a seamless garment but a palimpsest whose superimposed layers concealed as much as they revealed. The task of reading, accordingly, was not a matter of passive and as it were self-congratulatory reception, but an ever-more complex interpretive act. These issues became far more critical when the hermeneutic paradigm was consciously shifted — an event not contemplated by the model, indeed all but precluded by it. This occurred with the Reformation, which had produced a complete revision of ecclesiastical history in the work of Bale, Foxe, and their Continental counterparts, and thus of the *saeculum* enfolded within it under the order of Providence. The new hermeneutic required a constant interrogation of the chronicle sources virtually up to Holinshed's own time, for whatever of factual integrity remained of them — and that too was problematic — their root assumptions were invalid and their polemical purposes at best suspect. In effect, the chroniclers of England's past, at least up to the time of Holinshed's immediate precursor, Edward Hall, had been turned from candid into deceptive witnesses, whose testimony, even in matters of the smallest detail, had to be treated with the greatest circumspection. It was necessary to regard them, that is, as hostile or adversarial, so that the contemporary chronicler found himself in the position of a trial prosecutor, sifting truth as best he could from tainted evidence. Holinshed's account of the death of Henry IV is exemplary in its depiction of a world in which nothing is any longer quite what it seems. On the point of a crusade to the Holy Land, with all forces and provision in readiness, Henry:

> was eftsoons taken with a sore sicknesse, which was not a leprosie, striken by the hand of God (saith maister Hall) as foolish friers imagined; but a verie apoplexie, of the which he languished till his appointed houre, and had none other greefe nor maladie; so that what man ordeineth, God altereth at his good will and pleasure, not giuing place more to the prince, than to the poorest creature liuing, when he seeth his time to dispose of him this waie or that, as to his omnipotent power and diuine prouidence seemeth expedient. During this his last sicknesse, he caused his crowne (as some write) to be set on a pillow at his beds head, and suddenlie his pangs so sore troubled him, that he laie as though all his vitall spirits had beene from him departed. Such as were about him, thinking verelie that he had beene departed, couered his face with a linnen cloth. The prince his sonne being hereof aduertised, entered into the chamber, tooke awaie the crowne, and departed. The father being suddenlie reuiued out of that trance, quicklie perceiued the lacke of his crowne; and hauing knowledge that the prince his sonne had taken it awaie, caused him to come before his presence, requiring of him what he meant so to misuse himselfe. The prince with a good audacitie answered; "Sir, to mine and all mens iudgements you seemed dead in this world, wherefore I as your next heire apparant tooke that as mine owne, and not as yours." Well faire sonne (said that king with a great sigh) what right I had to it, God knoweth. Well (said the prince) if you die king, I will haue the garland, and trust to keepe it with the sword against all mine enimies as you haue doone. Then said the king, "I commit all to God, and remember you to doo well." With that he turned himselfe in his bed, and shortlie after departed to God . . .[41]

The themes, tropes, and anxieties of late Elizabethan culture are all present here: regnal legitimacy and transition, the "mutabilitie" of all earthly fortunes and the frown of Providence on all who trust to them, the problematic nature of the historical record. The dying king's crusade (itself a belated gesture of medieval piety) is rejected as an act of penitence by a Providence that permits a fleet and an army to be raised (at great public expense) that will never sail. Lest the point be missed, Holinshed observes in a marginal aside that "a guiltie conscience in extremitie of sicknesse pincheth sore" (ibid.). At the same time, however, he follows his source, Edward Hall, in dismissing the legend of Henry's leprosy as a clerical invention, thus emphasizing for the reader the unreliability of scribal evidence and the tendency of monastic chroniclers to assume privileged interpretations of divine will.

The clear focus of the passage, however, is on the usurped crown and the fatal circumstances that follow it—circumstances that had not ceased to haunt the public consciousness of Holinshed's own time. As if fearing to be stripped of it, Henry has placed the crown in his direct line of sight, but is soon so overcome that his eyes are covered. Prince Henry, with no apparent ceremony or reverence, plucks it up, only to have the King awake to find his worst fears realized. This leads to the final colloquy between royal father and son, in which Prince Henry's flippant description of the King's condition ("you seemed dead to this world") suggests the judgment he is destined to suffer in the next one. The King's retort, made before witnesses, all but negates his son's right of inheritance, to which the Prince replies that his claim cannot be impugned unless the King condemn himself as a usurper and expose himself or his corpse to a regicide's fate ("if you die king, I will haue the garland"). King Henry's last words, a pious evasion, leave both the truth and the issue to God; equally, his injunction to the Prince ("doo well") might be interpreted as either an ironic call to valor ("fight bravely, for you will be challenged") or an ethical imperative ("rule justly, for you reign under sin"). Shakespeare himself, who turned this grim encounter into a reconciliation scene in his *Henry IV*, could hardly have limned a more compressed or laconic piece of dramaturgy.

The moment of succession—that moment when the immortal community faces its own contingency in the person of its mortal ruler—is always, in the chronicle tradition, not only the logical caesura of the narrative but the point of highest drama, for it is here that the previous reign receives its definitive stamp and the next one its augury. Sometimes it is the king himself who is prophetic, as when Henry V remarks at the birth of his son that "I Henrie borne at Monmouth, shall small time reigne, & much get; and Henrie borne at Windsore, shall long reigne, and all loose" (3: 129). The prophecy harks back to the circumstances of the Lancastrian succession, for as Henry's son is born in a royal palace, he remembers that he was born in a ducal one. It is the Lancastrian blood-taint—the deposition and murder of Richard II, and the extinction not only of his person but of his line—that casts its shadow over the next century, and that, a hundred years later, in the reign of a childless queen and the year of the first royal execution ever carried out on English soil, that of Mary Stuart, would still have been in the minds of Holinshed's readers.[42]

But who were the *Chronicle*'s intended readers? As Patterson points out, the Holinshed syndicate, like the collaborative ventures that for the most part produced Elizabethan chorography, was an independent enterprise aimed at a literate mass public, no longer simply subjects but increasingly, in Arthur Ferguson's phrase, articulate citizens.[43] These were consumers of sermons rather than receivers of homilies, persons before whom conflicting evidence might be set out and argument weighed. If they were not yet the actors of history, neither were they merely its passive spectators. They were persons before whom appeal might be made.

The tension between this modern readership and the hypostatized community, which is invoked in the *Chronicle* to make the ritual obeisances of legitimacy, to behold omens, to petition loyally, to suffer the consequences of disaster or misgovernment, and, *in extremis*, to rebel, is illustrated in the response of the London crowd to the appeal of the Duke of Buckingham to acclaim the usurping Gloucester as Richard III. The text is taken directly from Sir Thomas More, but its relevance to a late Elizabethan audience is even greater than to its original Henrician one:

> When the duke had said, and looked that the people, whome he hoped the maior had framed before should after this proposition made, haue cried; King Richard, king Richard: all was husht and mute, and not one word answered therevnto. Wherewith the duke was maruellouslie abashed, and taking the maior neerer to him, with other that were about him priuie to that matter, said vnto them softlie, What meaneth this, that the people be so still? Sir (quoth the maior) percase they perceiue you not well. That shall we mend (quoth he) if that will helpe. And by & by somewhat lowder he rehersed to them the same matter againe in other order, and other words, so well and ornatlie, and nathelesse so euidentlie and plaine, with voice, gesture and countenance so comelie, and so conuenient, that euerie man much maruelled that heard him, and thought that they neuer had in their liues heard so euill a tale so well told. . . . But were it for woonder or feare, or that each looked that other should speake first: not one word was there answered of all the people that stood before, but all was as still as the midnight, not somuch as rowning [whispering] amongst them, by which they might seeme to commune what was best to do.[44]

The commons, called upon to offer the most basic gesture of legitimation—the acclamation of a new ruler—remains in an attitude of passive spectatorship, indicating neither assent nor resistance. At the same time, however, we are permitted to understand that each man in his separate judgment perceives the "euill" of the Duke's harangue, made only the more transparent by eloquence. The mayor, temporizing, tells Buckingham that the commons are silent because they are accustomed to being addressed only by the recorder, who is "the mouth of the citie." The recorder duly speaks, but "so temper[ing] his tale, that he shewed euerie thing as the dukes words, and no part his owne." The commons remaining silent, the Duke is constrained to speak again:

> Deere friends, we come to mooue you to that thing, which peraduenture we not so greatlie needed but that the lords of this realme, and the commons of other parties migh[t] haue sufficed, sauing that we such loue beare you,

and so much set by you, that we would not gladlie doo without you, that thing in which to be partners is your weale and honor, which (as it seemeth) either you see not, or weie not. Wherefore we require you giue vs answer one way or other, whether you be minded, as all the nobles of the realme be, to haue this noble prince, now protector, to be your king or not. At these words the people began to whisper among themselues secretly, that the voice was neither lowd nor distinct, but as it were the sound of a swarme of bees, till at the last in the nether end of the hall, an ambushment of the dukes seruants and Nashfields, and other belonging to the protector, with some prentisses and lads that thrust into the hall amongst the prease, began suddenlie at mens backes to crie out, as lowd as their throtes would giue; King Richard, king Richard: and threw vp their caps in token of ioy. And they that stood before, cast backe their heads maruelling therof, but nothing they said. Now when the duke and the maior saw this maner, they wiselie turned it to their purpose, and said it was a goodlie crie, & a ioifull, to heare euerie man with one voice, no man saieng naie. (3: 393–394)

The narrative proceeds here on two distinct levels. On the first, it is a story of failed political theater, in which Buckingham, unable to win acceptance for Richard's seizure of power from the commons, crudely substitutes the clamor of his henchmen. As in Cranmer's interpretation of the coronation ceremony, the Duke explains that the commons' acclaim is "not so greatlie needed" but is an act of condescension and grace. The weakness—and manifest illegitimacy—of Buckingham's position is borne out by his shuffling use of tense; when he says that the approval of "the lords of the realme, and the commons of other parties migh[t] have sufficed" without the concurrence of London, he implies without actually stating that this approval has already been secured. Similarly, in asserting that "we such loue beare you," he uses the royal plural without actually specifying its source, so that neither his audience nor Holinshed's can know whether he speaks as Richard's deputy (in which case his casual appropriation of the royal persona reveals the dubious nature of his own allegiance) or on behalf of an actual group, the usurper and his entourage, who bandy the royal power that none of them is able to assert alone. Finally, the offer of partnership to the commons in the act of usurpation ("that thing in which to be partners is your weale and honor") completes the confession of weakness, for royal authority is indivisible, and cannot be shared like loot. More/Holinshed's careful description thus peals back the layers of dissimulation that reveal the vacuum of authority at the heart of power. When Buckingham's henchmen finally rescue him with their cries, the theatricalization of the event is fully declared: the Duke, who speaks for those who have usurped the crown, is acclaimed by his hirelings, who usurp the voice of the people.

On the second level, however, the narrative reveals the steadfastness of the people in the face of confusion, hazard, and temptation. Everything

Buckingham says is perfidious and false; everything the commons do is loyal and true. Their response to his first speech is utter silence, which Holinshed invites us to interpret variously as "wonder," "feare," or the lack of an appropriate spokesman or leader in the absence of consensus—and which, in turn, is a dramatic reflection of the absence of credible authority in the great lord who addresses them.[45] The commons are, as a rule, spoken for, whether by their rulers, their masters, or their representatives; they are left to speak for themselves only by way of acclamation, that is to say unanimously, and lacking unanimity—their only legitimate cue for action—they are, appropriately, struck dumb. Thus, as Holinshed tells us, "each looked that the other should speak first," but, as none can authorize his neighbor, no one can do so. In this sense, the commons' silence is reverential, an acknowledgment of their subordination to due authority as well as an implicit rejection of the usurped power that bids for their favor. There is, indeed, "not somuch as rowning amongest them, *by which they might seem to commune what was best to do*" [emphasis added]. Their silence is not only self-protective, but an act of perfect submission to due (though absent) authority that declines any initiative above its station, beyond which anarchy lies. Once more, however, the ambiguity in Holinshed's tense construction leaves open the possibility that the commons' silence is not merely submissive but politic. It is not only rulers but subjects—even in the midst of their most loyal professions—who have need of prudence.

The wit of the commons is displayed again at the end of Buckingham's second address, in which, compelled to break silence, they respond by buzzing among themselves ("the sound of a swarme of bees"). This is passive resistance turned up a notch, but still faithful, still irreproachable. It is finally overridden by the rather desperate cries of the henchmen ("as lowd as their throtes would giue"), supplemented by "some prentisses and lads that thrust into the hall amongst the prease." There are thus three distinct voices in the tumult: the commons, whose indistinct murmur is deeply purposive; the retainers, whose clamor falsely encodes this murmur as assent; and the apprentices, whose cries are really mere noise, since they simply mimic what they hear. The apprentices offer a final contrast that put the actions of the commons in their proper perspective, since the former, lacking a true political function and the discretion that accompanies it, can only serve as a chorus that echoes the will of others (as the apprentices who harangued Parliament in the 1640s were to do), whereas the latter, although their acclamation may seem merely a knee-jerk response to the display of the appropriate symbols of legitimacy, in fact act freely, and truly grant (or withhold) their assent.

There are two other significant actors on the scene: the mayor and the recorder. The mayor's task, as the commons' elected representative, is in ordinary circumstances to mediate between crown and people, to speak in the commons' name, and to prime their response. This is indeed what Buckingham counts on him to have done ("he hoped the maior had framed [them] before"). When the commons are silent, he turns to the mayor for an explanation, only to receive the ambiguous reply that "percase they perceive you not well." This utterance neatly slips the question of the mayor's own dereliction and leaves the Duke with a choice of signification, i.e., that the people do not *hear* him well or that they do not *take* him well. Caught in a semantic trap, Buckingham can only amplify his harangue; this too failing, the recorder repeats (while mimetically disavowing) the Duke's words. Thus, the commons do not merely react among themselves to Buckingham's exhortations, but respond to the magistrates' negative cues about them. In this, too, they play their role as good citizens properly, following the lead of immediate superiors of known trust rather than the dubious blandishments of overmighty magnates. For the perceptive Elizabethan reader, the suggestion of the critical function assigned inferior magistrates would have been amplified in the monarchomach theories of resistance just beginning to drift over from the Continent in Holinshed's time.[46]

Only in this full perspective can the wisdom and fidelity of More/Holinshed's commons be appreciated. By taking their cue from the magistrates' behavior, they preserve the hierarchy of authority through which the legitimate order is expressed. At the same time, their response is genuinely their own; unlike the henchmen, who are simply under orders, or the apprentices, whose conduct is otiose, they act as responsible free agents, and it is precisely this quality that resists the theatricalization Buckingham tries to impose on them and transcends the hollow triumph that temporarily overrides them. The scene ends as the mayor, with little alternative, acknowledges the henchmen's clamor as the assent of the commons, who remain silent to the end ("but nothing they said"). There can be little doubt, however, of the ultimate end of Richard's usurpation that their silence portends.

Holinshed's account of this faithful commons may be contrasted with his cautionary tales of the Pilgrimage of Grace and Kett's Rebellion. In the former case, the people, "misliking" Henry VIII's new articles on religion, are "prouoked to mischiefe, and deceiued through ouer light credence" by disaffected monks and priests (3: 798). As the rebellion spreads, it takes the overt form of a crusade, or, in the softer parlance of a "loyal" uprising, a pilgrimage:

> They named this their seditious voiage, an holie and blessed pilgrimage: they had also certeine banners in the field, in which was painted Christ hanging on the crosse on the one side, and a chalice with a painted cake in it on the other side, with diuers other banners of like hypocrisie and feigned

holinesse. The souldiers had also imbrodered on the sleeues of their cotes in steed of a badge, the similitude of the fiue wounds of our sauiour, and in the middest thereof was written the name of our Lord. Thus had the rebels host of sathan . . . set out themselues, onelie to deceiue the simple people in that their wicked and rebellious enterprise against their liege lord and naturall prince. . . (3: 800).

Who the "rebels" are—Holinshed again taking care to distinguish them from the "simple people" they deceive—remains unspecified, although by this time the insurrection has spread across a third of England, with an estimated 40,000 "warlike" men encamped in Yorkshire alone, "well appointed, both with capteins, horsses, armor, and artillerie" (ibid.). It would seem impossible to imagine such a force without elite participation, yet no great lord raised his standard and the government's own intelligence indicated that the Pilgrimage was a purely popular tumult, a judgment echoed more than four centuries later by Henry VIII's modern biographer, J. J. Scarisbrick, who characterized it as "a large-scale, spontaneous, authentic indictment of all that Henry most obviously stood for"—in short, a textbook case of delegitimation, which "passed judgment on him as surely and comprehensively as *Magna Carta* condemned John or the *Grand Remonstrance* the government of Charles I."[47] The reality, as G. R. Elton has shown convincingly, was more complex, with outbreaks of popular agitation in some cases incited and in others exploited by disaffected noble families including the Darcys and the Percys.[48]

We must assume that Holinshed, fifty years after the event, had no better information than Thomas Cromwell's spies and torturers had been able to extract, and that he would therefore have confronted the dilemma of dealing with what presented itself on its face as a genuinely popular insurrection. Holinshed's customary style is to attach names to events, but in his account of the 1536 risings almost all the personages who appear are those who lead the King's armies—the dukes of Norfolk and Suffolk, the earls of Shrewsbury, Huntingdon, Rutland, Derby, and Sussex, Lord Admiral Brian, and Sir John Russell. The rebels are represented chiefly by a Captain Cobler and a monk named Makarell, who turn out to be one and the same individual, namely Makarell. The anonymity of the rebel horde may be contrasted with the precise list of those convicted and executed for the subsequent risings in the East Riding of Yorkshire and in the Lake District in January–February 1537 (3: 804).

Although the rebels had ostensibly taken up arms against religious innovation, suspicion of apostasy soon gives way to fear of general tyranny.[49] This is ascribed merely to "false rumours . . . bruting that the king pretended to haue the gold in the hands of his subiects brought into the tower to be touched" [i.e., adulterated], cattle seized, churches despoiled, and new fines levied (3: 799). The rebels remained apparently leaderless, "such nobles and gentlemen [still unnamed] as at the first fauoured their cause" falling away. Yet when the King advanced upon the rebels in Lincolnshire, he was presented with lengthy petitions regarding the "choise of councellors, suppression of religious houses, maintenance of the seruice of almightie God, the statute of vses, the release of the fifteenth, and receiuing of the first fruits, with such other matters as nothing apperteined to them." Holinshed's phrase, as so often, suggests a double meaning: that the matters contained in the petitions do not concern mere commoners (as the seizure of their cattle or the clipping of their coin might), and that their consideration does not belong to them, as subjects who have no direct determinative right in the making of laws and no right at all in the "choise of councellors" for a king. In fact the petitions are incomprehensible except as the product of elite manipulation, yet once again Holinshed is silent on the very subject about which he raises suspicion. The Pilgrimage of Grace remains a story about the simple commons who are seduced by false priests — the handiest of culprits in Henrician England — and malicious rumor. It is a story, moreover, with a happy ending, for on the eve of "vnnaturall battell . . . betwixt men of one nation, and subiect to one king; there fell a raine not great to speake of, but yet as it were by miracle, the riuer of Dun rose suddenlie on such a height, that seldom had beene seene there the like hugenesse of water." Combat is rendered impossible, and guided "by Gods good prouidence" an agreement is reached, bloodshed averted, "*an manie an innocent mans life preserued*" (3: 802; emphasis added).

This is neither the usual end of rebellions, nor the moral preached about them. The opposition of the King and his commons is so "vnnaturall" that it can only be the product of malign forces "forged of diuelish purpose" (3: 799) to deceive the people, and thwarted, appropriately, by a divine intervention that removes the scales from men's eyes at the last moment. Even when determined to resist the King's arms, the commons remain "innocent," and their loyalty is seamlessly restored. If the king, by legal fiction, can do no wrong, however he may be led astray by evil counsel, so by countermyth the commons, too, can never fail in their true allegiance, however they may be abused by the forces of sedition, or even, as Holinshed suggests in this case, of perdition.

The rebellions of 1549 presented Holinshed with a knottier problem, for here the people appeared to rise without instigation, if not without provocation. The first outbreaks swept across a broad swath of northern and eastern England, with spurs as far as Devon and Cornwall.[50] The occasion, as Holinshed describes it, was a proclamation against enclosures, of which the commons had "greeuouslie complained" and which had been "to the great hinderance and vndooing [of] manie a poore man" (3: 916). This seemed to be a

wholly appropriate assertion of the public interest against the "priuat com-
modities and pleasures" of the gentlemen who had converted common land
to sheep pastures and game parks:

> But how well soeuer the setters foorth of this proclamation meant, thinking
> thereby peraduenture to appease the grudge of the people . . . yet verelie it
> turned not to the wished effect, but rather ministered occasion of a foule
> and dangerous disorder. For whereas there were few that obeied the com-
> mandement, *the vnadvised people* presuming vpon their proclamation, think-
> ing they should be borne out by them that had set it foorth rashlie without
> order, tooke vpon them to redresse the matter: and assembling themselues
> in vnlawfull wise, chose to them capteins and leaders, brake open the inclo-
> sures, cast downe ditches, killed vp the deare which they found in parkes,
> spoiled and made hauocke, *after the maner of an open rebellion* (916-917; em-
> phasis added).

The people who take the new law into their own hands are "vnadvised"
rather than actively misled; they lack appropriate guidance from their betters, such as the London commons had had from the mayor and recorder
during Buckingham's appeal to them. They violate the law by thinking to act
on behalf of it, rather than willfully ignoring it to assert what can only become the public interest by royal decree. They act "after the maner of an
open rebellion," which suggests that they are not in fact rebels but merely, to
this point, "disordered." It is only when enclosure riots break out in Devon
and Cornwall that, once again, "certeine popish priests," prevailing on the
people by "sinister and subtill meanes . . . and vnder the colour of religion,"
drive them into what Holinshed is finally willing to describe as "open rebellion." Even then, however, the people are only persuaded to rise "vnder
Gods name & the Kings," that is, to make what they believe to be loyal dem-
onstrations on behalf of the highest authority. Moreover, the priests do not
merely "stir" the people but in some cases lead them to battle, and they
themselves seem a host, for Holinshed lists not only eight by name who
were subsequently executed but adds that "a multitude of other priests
which ioined with them" were also hanged (917).[51]

Led by these "children of Beliall," the rebels besiege Exeter, hoping to
starve out the city. The citizens, however, led by their magistrates, resolve to
hold out to the end:

> [N]othing was left vndoone which the enimie could imagine to serue his
> purpose for the winning of that citie. And albeit there wanted not lustlie
> stomachs among the citizens to withstand this outward force of the enimie:
> yet in processe of time, such scarsitie of bread and vittels increased, that the
> people waxed wearie & loth to abide such extremitie of famine. Howbeit
> the magistrats (though it greeued them to see the multitude of the citizens
> in such distresse) yet hauing a speciall regard of their dutie toward the

prince, and loue to the common-wealth, left no waies vnsought to quiet the people, & staie them in their dutifull obedience to resist the enimies: so that comforting the people with faire promises, and releeuing their necessities verie liberallie, so farre as their power might extend, did in such sort vse the matter, that euerie of them within resolued with one generall consent to abide the end, in hope of some speedie releefe. (918)

In contrast to the deeply misled rebels, the citizens of Exeter are kept loyal by their magistrates, who, unlike the gentlemen enclosers, relieve rather than despoil the people. The result is the univocal response that signals not only obedience but legitimation, the "one generall consent" that is the authentic voice of the commons in a well-ordered commonwealth. The citizens of Exeter are in far direr straits than the peasant rebels had been when they took up arms. Reminded of their duty, however, and provided for by magistrates zealous for their welfare, they remain united, and "albeit mans nature can scarselie abide to feed vpon anie vnaccustomed food; yet these sillie men were glad to eat horsse flesh, and to hold themselues well content therewith" (ibid.).[52]

This was not, as Holinshed reminded his readers, the first siege that Exeter had withstood. During the "troubles" of 1470, the city was assailed not once but twice. In April, a thousand men entered the city under the banner of Henry VI, while a force loyal to Edward IV camped outside, cutting off food and communication. Both sides demanded the keys to the city's gates from the magistrates, who were understandably loath to bet on the success of either:

In these doubts and perplexities consulting what were best to be doone, they did at length resolue & conclude neither to yeeld to the requests of them which were within the citie: but pacifieng both parties with such good words, and in such good order as they might, did reserue to themselues the keeping and safe custodie of the citie, being the chamber of the king, and parcell of the reuenues of the crowne, to the onlie vse of the king and crowne, as to them in dutie and allegiance did apperteine. And therefore forthwith they rampired vp the citie gates, fortified the walles, appointed souldiers, and did set all things in such good order as in that case was requisit; leauing nothing vndoone which might be for the preseruation of the state & commonwealth of the citie. (938)

Food, as in 1549, was in short supply, and the magistrates, knowing that the commons could not long endure famine, "did their best indeuor euerie waie, aswell by diligence in following, as by counselling, in persuading euerie man to continue firme and true to the publike state, and their owne priuate common-weale." As in 1549, their appeal was successful, the commons having "that respect to their owne truth, faith, and safetie, as euerie man yeelded himselfe contented to abide and indure the time of their deliuerance." This came speedily, as Edward IV put the Earl of Warwick to rout. The city was again put to the test in September by Perkin Warbeck; once more, "the noble courage and valiant stomach of the citizens" prevailed against the invader (938–939).

On these occasions as later, leadership by the magistrates and loyal response by the citizens is the key to the city's salvation. Moreover, in Exeter in 1470 as in London in 1483, the magistrates must deal not with a simple rebellion against royal authority but with rival claims to it. Unable to choose either side without jeopardy, the Exeter magistrates affirm their loyalty to the institution of monarchy as such, for which they hold the city in trust. In doing so, they simultaneously uphold both the "publike state," embracing alike the king's authority and their own, and the "priuate common-weale" of each citizen, which can only be secured within the larger commonwealth. The latter is not to be confused with private interest in our modern sense, which opposes one individual's value to another's; for Holinshed, classes and interests cannot be antagonistic in a properly ordered commonwealth, and each person's particular interest is, in accordance with his station, a microcosm of the social whole. Thus, each person perceiving his own good in that of the commonwealth and vice versa, will freely but necessarily assent to the public good, and the citizen body, rightly understanding that good through its magistrates and representatives, will always be unanimous.

Holinshed's account of Kett's Rebellion skirts a number of issues, however. Whereas the anti-enclosure proclamation is first described as set forth by "the kings maiestie, by the aduise of his vncle the lord protector, and other of the councell," the authors subsequently appear merely as "the setters forth of this proclamation," a subtle disavowal of the boy-king's responsibility for a calamitous policy failure. Holinshed notes in passing that "there were few that obeied the commandement" to restore common lands, but makes nothing of the gentry's defiance of the proclamation and fails to link it to the popular insurrection. By Holinshed's account, the peasantry rise in expectation of support from "them that had set it foorth," but the more obvious interpretation is that they attempted instead to force the Protector's hand, or, in the absence of enforcement, to act his part. What is conspicuously absent from this account is precisely what is so carefully foregrounded elsewhere, the mediation of inferior magistrates. The magistrates in this case are the justices of the peace who are, when not enclosers themselves, their family or social brethren. It is they, responding in turn to cues from local magnates, who fail to enforce the Protector's edict, leaving the commons either to accept gentry nullification or to make rough justice for themselves. This suggestion of class warfare, of fundamentally and irreconcilably opposed interests, is of course incompatible with Holinshed's vision of a naturally harmonious social order; it is not so much suppressed by him as simply not entertained.

In Holinshed's world, the loyalty of the commons to the crown—a far more dynamic praxis than mere deference, involving judgment and affirmation—is the product not only of inculcated duty, but of responsible elite behavior and attention to the general welfare. Where this reciprocity breaks down, loyalty does not cease, but it is apt to exceed the proper boundaries of its expression, or to be vulnerable to those who would abuse it. This was the lesson of Kett's Rebellion.

Holinshed's commons are thus subjects in and not merely objects of the political process. At the same time, however, they remain "subject": their scope of action is carefully circumscribed and its expression limited, with one significant exception, to rituals of assent. The exception is the petition. The origin of the medieval court system, including that very singular court called Parliament, lies largely in the receipt and discharge of petitions, which is to say in the shaping of inchoate public discourse into the articulate vessel of legal appeal and response.[53] The very notion of *grievance* as the stimulus to petition is thus defined by and mediated through the structures of control; it is not merely a discontent, but one framed as part of a process that issues in an appropriate (but discretionary) legal action, the redress.

The grievance is thus the form in which the only recognized act of popular initiative makes its first appearance; what precedes it is precisely that of which civil discourse takes no account unless it expresses itself in riot or rebellion instead, namely unfettered popular discussion. The records of central and local Tudor and Stuart administration are replete with proclamations and legal proceedings (including capital execution) against unauthorized talk about public matters in alehouse and pulpit. The very pervasiveness of these records suggests the prevalence and sharpness of such talk. It was a phenomenon that elite discourse, including Holinshed's, could recognize only by way of negation, and yet its presence was at least tacitly acknowledged and in one place at least, the stage, represented. The "buzzing" of the commons in Holinshed's account of Buckingham's harangue may be considered a coded representation of it as well. Here, as will be recalled, the commons construct a wall of meaningless and impenetrable sound to replace the wall of silence that Buckingham has challenged. At the same time, they are turned toward one another rather than the Duke, so that they cannot be accused of disrespect. What they present, then, is the image of intense intramural debate. This too would be an inappropriate reaction, but since nothing is actually being said, no objection can be taken to it. By miming their dissent without actually speaking it, the commons preserve their own unity; by describing it, Holinshed offers his readers a glimpse of what actually occurs behind the scenes of conventional narrative (including his own), political theory, and the rituals of public assent. As he remarks in another context, "men must sometime for the maners sake, not be aknowen what they know" (3: 396).

Holinshed's accounts of the usurpation of 1483 and the rebellions of 1536-1537 and 1549 each describe legitimation crises within the English polity, although only the first is presented as such. Such crises, according to the code under which Holinshed wrote, could only occur when the succession to the throne was in question. For Holinshed, as for his redactor Shakespeare, the entire fifteenth century was shadowed by a series of such disputes, beginning with Henry IV's seizure of the throne and culminating in Richard of Gloucester's. No such issue, however, obtruded into the two great rebellions of the first half of the sixteenth century. There could be no question of either Henry VIII's or of Edward VI's title, except for those who challenged the validity of Henry's divorce from Catherine of Aragon. The precipitating factor in the Pilgrimage of Grace, as modern historians agree, was Henry's liturgical reform, and, more broadly, the confiscatory policies of the Henrician Reformation. Religious alteration also played a significant, and in certain areas perhaps a determinative role in the risings of 1549. Holinshed, as we have seen, typically ascribed this to the machinations of priests and monks, although Kett's Rebellion in Norfolk involved neither. This absolved the people, and gave point to the Erastian moral that Holinshed is at pains to preach through most of the *Chronicles*. But in one case at least, that of Sampford Courtney, Devon, in June 1549, he describes the commons as rising of their own volition after hearing the newly appointed liturgy:

> [When] they had heard and were present at the diuine service said, and had according to the new reformed order, and could not in anie respect, find fault, or iustlie reprehend the same: yet (as old bottels which would not receiue new wine) would rather wallow in the old dreggs and puddels of old superstition, than to be fed and refreshed with the wholsome and heauenlie manna. Wherefore they confederated themselues, vtterlie to renounce, reiect and cast off the same, not onelie to the great offense of God . . . and to the great displeasure of the king . . . but also to the raising of open rebellion, the cause of the spoile of the whole countrie, and the vndooing of themselues, their wiues, and children . . . (3: 939)

On this occasion at least, Holinshed makes no attempt to palliate the commons' resort to "open rebellion." There is no mention of popish priests, even to suggest their presence in the background. The commons' act is a direct and unmediated defiance of an explicit royal command, and doubly offensive to God: first, as disobedience toward his representative on earth; and secondly, as a rejection of the authentic service of his worship, which, after centuries of idolatry and superstition, he has been gracious enough to vouchsafe through the person of Edward VI.

It would be difficult, in the context of a Reformed, Erastian polity, to imagine a more culpable act. Contrary to his usual custom, however, Holinshed does not excoriate the rebels, but rather places blame on the shortage of faithful and learned ministers—a complaint that would have resonated strongly among his readers, as it was a principal theme in godly criticism of the mid-Elizabethan church: "And here dooth appeare what great detriments doo come and insue to the church of God, and what great trouble to the publike and commonweale: when as learned preachers doo want to instruct the people; and well persuaded magistrats to gouerne the common state" (ibid.).[54] Holinshed thus succeeds in saving the appearances even when it seems that he is most ready to chastise the commons for their contumacy. Just as they may be led into evil courses by those who would deceive them, so too they may wander astray or persist in error if they lack proper, especially divine instruction, and wholesome example. This was the essence of the godly prescription for the commonwealth.

Taken as a whole, the commons in Holinshed are, conceptually, the ultimate repository of virtue, fidelity, and discretion, and so they will prove when put to the test of action, provided only that they are properly guided. When the commonwealth is disordered, a failure of leadership is almost always responsible—unreformed (or, sometimes, too zealously reformed) abuses; elite dissension or a succession crisis; the corruption of religion. Rebellion, therefore, is not the result of pressure by the "giddy" or "many-headed" multitude on the frail ramparts of order, but of confusion sown by misgovernment. If it is never justified, it is readily understood. Holinshed is far, certainly, from a theory of responsible government, but in predicating the people as the source of virtue, he suggests that the public welfare is necessarily the means by which this virtue is maintained and through which it is expressed. Loyalty is not brute submission, but part of an immemorial cycle of reciprocity; if it is always owed, it must also be earned. Legitimation is thus, in Holinshed's understanding, a continual, dynamic process; it is, in fact, the life of the commonwealth itself.

Holinshed's commons, moreover, do not simply belong to Smith's "fourth sort which do not rule." There seem, in fact, to be two overlapping models in his conception of them. The rural commons, lacking formal institutions and means of association, are easily turned by rumor and readily deceived by pretenders, clerical or lay. The urban commons, however, who often exercise a measure of self-government and enjoy a regular interaction with accountable magistrates, display considerable sophistication and discretion. They are far likelier to follow known and trusted authorities than interlopers, however imposing their titles or insistent their claims. When properly appealed to, they show discipline, cohesion, and a remarkable capacity for self-sacrifice. Their loyalty, although expressed to the person of a king, is mediated through a system of devolved authority in which they, too, participate. They are law-abiding because law-sharing.

Holinshed's ultimate model of the commons is, in short, that of a jury. The jury does not give judgment but it is the basis of it; it does not pronounce independently but speaks truly — the *ver-dict* — when its speech is required. In this the commons differs from a mere audience; it registers not approval or disapproval but something solemn, something sworn, *juré*. It speaks, too, like the jury, collectively and with one voice, and this very seamlessness of utterance is the source of its unique privilege, for, from the chronicler's perspective, the people always speak last, and, when not abused, they always speak the truth. It is this perspective that helps explain, at least in part, the difference between Holinshed and Smith, whose account of the commons gives them no active voice, and whose almost embarrassed description of the jury itself confines its members to the pronouncement of a formula. Nonetheless, the very writing of a popular history, particularly one intended for an urban audience, takes Holinshed beyond the representation of the commons as a collective entity. Merely to construct a history is, after all, to subject the historical process to a further stage of appeal: the reader. This reader is himself an historical subject. He both participates in the action of history as a citizen according to his role and status, and, as reader, judges the result.[55] Such a double function is relatively unproblematic for a traditional, elite readership among whom the exercise of civil office and the task of counsel is presupposed. For those whose obligation is merely to respond to legitimation cues and to obey appropriate commands, however, the act of reading creates a new, private space, an appeal not merely to duty or conscience but to a hitherto unexercised faculty of judgment. In Holinshed's day, no public sphere existed in which such a faculty could have scope. It was already being reflected, however, in the new London theater, where great men and groundlings came together to witness the spectacle of a nation unfold, not merely as pageant but as drama. Like reading, play-going involved the suspension, or at any rate the bracketing, of social difference, and applause or derision was both a unifying and a leveling force. The step from Holinshed, with its calculated appeal to an expanding urban public, to the theater that drew so liberally from it, was an eminently natural one.[56] It was also part of the move from a reflexive political culture to a reflective one, in which appropriate political behavior was not merely dictated but meditated. If the political structure did little to accommodate these changes, they made their own room rapidly enough when that structure was shaken.[57] Before we can consider this at more length, however, we must first turn to what was perhaps the most specialized form of reading in the country: reading law.

CHAPTER 4

The Discourse of the Law

The Common Law and the Henrician Crisis

England entered the sixteenth century, in Fortescue's phrase, as a *dominium politicum et regale*. The regal component of this equation was extraordinarily dynamic and expansive under the first two Tudors, particularly in the area of jurisprudence. New courts of prerogative and equity sprang up; the land law was changed "almost beyond recognition," as J. H. Baker notes, by the growth of enclosure, the resuscitation of feudal dues, and the transformation of the use; mercantile and admiralty law developed rapidly; ecclesiastical law was brought under royal control; and statute law was made as never before an instrument of crown policy.[1] The pace of change slowed somewhat in the latter Tudor reigns, but the expanded role of prerogative courts, particularly the Court of High Commission, became a critical issue again under the first two Stuarts.

The importance of the law in English life was second only to that of religion. English society was exceedingly rule-bound, and routine business—contracts, tenures, conveyances, property sales—was transacted through courts. This naturally resulted in a great deal of litigation; the major courts accepted three thousand new suits each year even in pre-Tudor times, and may have rejected many more. Government on both the central and local level was principally executed through courts and legal officers. Virtually all organs of the Tudor state had a judicial origin and exercised administrative and judicial functions interchangeably. Lawyers ran the system, and, increasingly, lawyers, or at least those law-trained, ran the state. Few aspiring gentlemen could afford to be without the rudiments of law, and study at the Inns of Court, England's "third university," became *de rigueur* for all who wished a public career. Further down the social scale, the law's toils were often seen as a snare for simple folk, and the complaint of the Kentish rebels in 1450 that "the law servyth of nowght ellys in these days, but for to do wrong"[2] was echoed continually for the next two centuries. Yet most Englishmen believed in an ancient constitution that guaranteed their rights and liberties, however law as actually practiced might derogate from that ideal. This constitution, it was generally believed, had existed from time immemorial, could never be abrogated, and had only to be enforced by good magistrates for justice to be rendered. When an early sixteenth-century broadside asked "Whether the lawes of the kynges of Englande made before the conquest be the common lawes of this Realme, and myght be reuiued agayne?" the question was clearly meant to be rhetorical. The common law, thus hypostatized, *was* the ancient constitution, a belief that bound the peasant at his plow and Sir Edward Coke alike.[3]

In this sense it might truly be said that law was the Englishman's civil religion. One might go further still, and say that England in the sixteenth century had acquired, by courtesy of the Anglican Reformation, a national Christianity to go with that civil religion, and that what Henry VIII and his successors had done in marginalizing if not extirpating the Roman faith only completed the work that William the Conqueror had begun in superseding the Roman law. Neither Romanism surrendered easily, or remained far to seek. But both would be equally suspect henceforth, and the equation between popery and tyranny, so obvious to contemporaries and so apparently difficult for modern historians to grasp, had its source in an intense nativism. Englishmen had their own law, distinct from any other, and, *pace* Papists and Puritans, by 1625 their own church as well.[4]

Like any religion, moreover, English law had developed its own priestcraft, orthodoxy, and heresies. Common lawyers were a tight community, socialized to their calling in the close quarters of the Inns of Court and supervised minutely by the established practitioners who lived with them. Though young gentlemen wishing to pick up their smattering of law might leave the Inns after a year or two, a pleader was required to spend eight years at his Inn before entering practice, at least in theory; sergeants, who had the sole practice of the Court of Common Pleas, were qualified only after sixteen years. Common lawyers had their own unique formulae and jargon, their own sacred texts and commentaries—the voluminous annual law reports that, as the Elizabethan jurist Sir James Dyer put it, were the "witness of the truth"—and their own impenetrable language, law French, which was taught only at the Inns.[5] Pleas, like prayers, could be lost by the slip of a tongue or pen, for the smallest error might result in the dismissal of a suit.[6]

Common law was land law, and England's land law derived from the feudal principle of the Conquest that all land was held of some lord, and ultimately by the crown. Feudal tenures were common enough elsewhere, but only in England were they supposed as universal. The variety of tenures and the modes of their disposition formed the subject of the common law, which was thus powerfully concentrated on real property. The seigneurial courts that had once adjudicated disputes gave way gradually to centralized courts, and these courts spawned the professional class of common law lawyers and judges. The result was a wholly self-contained, self-validating system from which, by the early fourteenth century, all trace of equity—the mitigation of rule by discretion—had been at least temporarily banished, a triumph of principle over compassion, not to say common sense, enshrined in Justice Bereford's dictum, "You must not allow conscience to prevent your doing law." By the late Yorkist period, as Sir Charles Ogilvie sums it up:

> the Common Law had been administered, developed, and refined by a small group of highly trained professional lawyers, who were determined to make out of a bundle of ancient writs, a handful of statutes, and a heap of precedents, a judicial system which would stand comparison as a monument of legal science with the Law of Rome and the Canon Law. With the best intentions they had sought to render it more efficient by making it progressively more and more complicated. It could not be accepted that the answer ultimately arrived at by strict adherence to the intricate rules of process and procedure, coupled with the skilled interpretation of relevant precedents, would not always be the right one. If it was right legally it did not matter that it was obviously unjust . . .[7]

This no doubt states the case harshly; what common lawyers valued above all was law by rule and therefore rule by law, the opposite of which was not the equitable but the arbitrary. There was, inevitably, a great deal of consideration in identifying and applying the appropriate rule to the particular case, but the hermeneutic task was the appeal from the latter to the former, and not vice versa. Only in this way could the law give certainty, its distinguishing virtue and principal end; only in this way could *meum et tuum* be secure. That the rule was more important than the case was not a concession common lawyers would have made; to the common law mind, the case served to disclose the law by uncovering the appropriate rule that applied to it.

In this quasi-Platonic conception, the law itself was a dark jewel whose splendor could never be beheld in itself. The jewel was revealed indirectly by its facets; these facets were structured by rules; the particular case was illuminated by the diligent search for the governing rule. New rules supplemented the law without altering its essence, according to the principle that Sir Edward Coke was to call artificial reason. This "artificial"—we might less mystifyingly call it "synthetic"—reason was the collective application of learned intelligence to the elaboration of the law. Incompetent interpretations produced absurd and inapplicable results, so that the law itself was its own final arbiter, defeating all attempts to wrest it to purposes contrary to its nature. From this it was manifest that the law could be interpreted only by its adepts, who by long study and practice were alone qualified to enter the transcendent realm of artificial reason. The common law reposed in the shared wisdom of common lawyers.

Complaints that the law as interpreted by the lawyers produced and routinely imposed much that was absurd fell on deaf ears. The closed nature of the legal profession, its vested interest in maintaining an exclusive and self-validating expertise, and its conception of the law as a totality beyond the grasp of any given individual or generation, made all efforts at "change" or "reform" otiose. On its own terms, the common law was unassailable, and the position of its guardian elite impregnable.

What this led to, however, was not a secure monopoly, but the expansion and proliferation of rival courts that dispensed a practical justice, equity. The oldest of these was the Court of Chancery, whose presiding officer was also the king's chief legal and on occasion political adviser. The Chancery encroached steadily on the jurisdiction of common law courts from late Yorkist times on, in part abetted by common lawyers themselves who referred their exasperated clients to it. In Henry VI's time, property claims occupied only five per cent of the court's business; by that of Edward VI, the proportion was nearly half.[8] At the same time, the crown spawned a number of new courts, including the Court of Star Chamber, the Court of Requests, and the Council of the North, much of whose business also dealt with such claims. These were particularly invigorated under Henry VIII, whose reforming minister, Thomas Cromwell, had attracted a circle of aspiring careerists and humanists (not identical categories, but far from wholly disparate) who were eager to further the King's imperial agenda. The result was a short-lived but electric panic, the so-called Henrician terror of the mid-1530s. Henry had no quarrel as such with the common lawyers, though it may fairly be said that his first great minister, Cardinal Wolsey, did.[9] He merely wanted business conducted with dispatch, and his preferred means of doing so was to expand the function of existing prerogative courts or to set up new ones. The looming consequence of this was a derailment of the entire system. As John Guy expresses it:

> The point of controversy in the 1530s was that the development of a 'rival' forum for litigation based on Chancery and [the prerogative courts] raised disturbing questions about competing jurisdictions, both at common law and equity, and between individual courts within the equitable arena. Unregulated competition between parallel royal jurisdictions raised, as it seemed for the first time in English History, the truly awful prospect of perpetual litigation, especially in real property suits.[10]

Beyond this lay the yet worse fear that Henry, in his quest for efficient, untrammeled power, might dispense with the quaint formalities of the common law altogether, raising the specter of a new reception of the Roman law, in which "every fortune in England had been removed from the jurisdiction of the Court of Common Pleas to be placed under some sort of council of state, half chancery, half the Chamber, where doctors from Padua would call Henry *Imperator* and administer civil law through administrative form."[11] This fear was given point by Starkey's *Dialogue between Pole and Lupset*, in which Cardinal Pole is made to extol the civil law, "the most auncyent & nobyl monument of the romaynys prudence (and pollycy)," as a model for England.[12] The eminent Maitland thought the revival of civil law jurisdiction in the 1530s a real possibility, and although more recent commentators have dismissed this as a figment, it may have seemed real enough to lawyers and judges wondering where Henry's willingness to overturn established legal traditions — fully displayed in his assault on ecclesiastical law in the 1530s — might lead.

Perhaps the subtlest threat of all was that common lawyers themselves might lose their heads. They were guardians of a sacred trust; they were also men, like others, ambitious for place and profit. As E. W. Ives reminds us, "The dominant position of the crown, taught by political theory and accepted in daily practice by the courts, was reinforced by what we have seen was the implication of a career in law — that a lawyer would inevitably be drawn into royal service. Because they served the law and the law was the king's law, all lawyers were in a sense the king's men; politics, law and government were one."[13] The position of the king as the fount of justice, his power to create new jurisdictions, and the plasticity of administrative and judicial functions within the day-to-day operations of the crown from the Privy Council to commissions of the peace, all underlined the common-sense fact of life that there was no law apart from the king, and therefore no law against the king. Common lawyers might reify the common law in theory, might cling to their corporate privileges, might regard themselves as the ultimate interpreters of the law as church doctors were of theology, but they were vulnerable as men of words always are to the *force majeure* of a sovereign will.

The issues in play can be seen in what was, for common lawyers, the critical event of the reign, the struggle over uses. The use, a form of trust, had developed as a device for evading royal claims on feudal tenures, but also as a means of supplying the defects of the medieval common law, which made little provision for land settlement and affirmatively prohibited devises of freehold land. It involved the separation of legal title to estates from their beneficial enjoyment through the creation of "uses" administered by one or more feoffees. Disputes over uses were adjudicated by church courts, which had jurisdiction over probate, but gradually devolved on Chancery. The common law courts, which did not recognize the use, were by and large excluded from this lucrative field.[14]

Whatever their practical utility, uses were widely understood as a means of exemption from the crown's feudal rights of wardship, escheat, and mortmain. Henry VII had attempted to restrict uses by statute; Henry VIII finally decided to challenge them broadside. The result was an imbroglio that, for a short space, left Englishmen without any secure means of passing on their estates. The story is an exceedingly tangled one. It begins with a bill of uncertain provenance brought into Parliament in 1529 that required the registration of uses in the Court of Common Pleas. At the same time, Lord Chancellor More arrived at an agreement with some thirty peers that would in essence have exempted the nobility from feudal dues on two-thirds of their estates in return for payment on the remaining third. The House of Commons rejected this compromise as a tax bill in disguise and hence a de facto infringement of its own powers. Henry then convened his judges and other legal officials, who conceded that uses had no standing in the common law and therefore could not be protected in any court, including Chancery. This was followed by a suit against the feoffees of Lord Dacre's estate in the Exchequer in which, after the King's direct intervention, the judges found that Dacre's will had deliberately evaded royal wardship. The result was to leave testamentary succession in England in jeopardy. Parliament, thus outflanked by the crown, capitulated. The Statute of Uses (1536), framed by Thomas Cromwell, reinstated the use and placed it under the jurisdiction of the common law courts, but made its beneficiaries subject to the full panoply of feudal dues, thus defeating its essential purpose.[15]

Henry's success was complete, but in the short term he paid dearly for it. The prospect of an unlimited resumption of antiquated taxes, combined with the legal as well as the religious implications of the break with Rome and the suppression of the monasteries, galvanized the gentry, as a similarly combustible mixture was to do a hundred years later in Charles I's time. The Statute of Uses was condemned in every rebel manifesto of the Pilgrimage of Grace, which asked variously that it be "suppressed," "annulled," and "repellyd,"[16] and that the devising of land by will be recognized. The point was duly though belatedly taken. The Statute of Wills (1540) granted full right of devising to those who held land in socage (nonmilitary) tenure and gave permission to devise two-thirds of all lands held in knight service, thus reinstating the original compromise of 1529.[17]

The struggle over the use may be regarded from a variety of perspectives. In Henry's view, it was a bargaining chip in his effort to regain the lost feudal income of the crown, in its turn an episode in the never-ending campaign of this most rapacious of all English monarchs for revenue by forced loan, fine, selective and mass confiscation, and currency debasement. He tried at first to play the nobility off against the gentry, and when that provoked opposition, the common lawyers off against Chancery. This was more successful. The common lawyers could not resist the opportunity to strip Chancery of its jurisdiction over the use, but in taking the bait they opened the door to a challenge to its legality as such, and after Dacre's case they had no choice but to accept its restitution on whatever grounds were offered. The reaction in the country forced Henry to retreat, but he was left with a substantial if reduced victory. The common lawyers, despite the unholy scare Henry had given them, enjoyed an even more unalloyed triumph. They had put the use and other devises on a secure legal footing, and placed them all under their own jurisdiction. The ecclesiastical courts, whose control of probate had been one of the chief grievances of the profession, were no more, and Chancery had been driven out of the estate settlement business. The cost of all this was a revived royal exaction, whose statutory basis did not make it less onerous, or for that matter less ominous. One would like to know more about the scurryings between the common lawyers in Parliament and their brethren on the bench during the Henrician terror, when talk of a general "reform" was darkly bruited and the legal community was presented with the *fait accompli* of the Statute of Uses. Victory was a narrow escape.

The Henrician terror was most fully displayed, of course, in the spoliation of the church courts that accompanied the Reformation. Under heavy polemical attack by lay guilds, humanists, and common lawyers alike, the collective grievance against these courts was shrewdly focused in the parliament Henry summoned in 1529.[18] First, court fees were limited; next, appeals to Rome were cut off; then, appellate rulings were transferred to Chancery; finally, the courts themselves were subsumed under royal jurisdiction, and their functions, where not appropriated by secular courts, were largely devolved to ecclesiastical commissioners and visitors, and, more informally, to local authorities, self-policing congregations, and the self-appointed godly. It is neither surprising nor accidental that the material wealth and corporate identity of the church suffered steady degradation under this regime. It was not until the formation of the Court of High Commission and the reforms of Whitgift in the 1580s that the Church of England began to develop a vigorous jurisdiction of its own again, and fifty years later Archbishop Laud still found it deeply abused, defective in discipline, and shorn of the power and resources necessary to its proper functions.[19]

The common law courts were ultimately the major beneficiaries of the eclipse of ecclesiastical jurisdiction, at least in terms of secular business, but it was not a passage managed without difficulty. If one conceives of the pre-Reformation legal system as triangulated by three distinct though overlapping power centers—the crown, the legal community, and the church—then the Henrician supremacy involved the subsumption of the last by the first two. This could not be accomplished, however, without exalting the imperial powers of the crown, or at least the Crown-in-Parliament. The danger that entailed was that supremacy over the church might become supremacy over the law itself, a point forcefully made by the common lawyer Sir Thomas More.

Christopher St. German and the Defense of the Common Law

More's defense both of his own court, Chancery, and of his embattled church, brought him into conflict with one of the most astute legal and political observers of his time, Christopher St. German (or Germain). St. German (c. 1460–1541) was a barrister of the Middle Temple who had practiced in both common law and prerogative courts, including Star Chamber and Requests, and whose more interesting career began with his retirement in 1511 or 1512. For the next three decades, St. German produced a spate of legal, historical, and confessional works, including the two dialogues on English law known as *Doctor and Student* (1528, 1530), which have been justly characterized as the most significant work on the subject between Fortescue and Coke.[20] In addition, he served as a confidential adviser to the King in the 1520s and 1530s, assisting him in the proceedings against Catherine of Aragon and in the elaboration of the supremacy. St. German's was thus one of those supple wits that served Henry at the critical juncture of his reign, but he was also a shrewdly critical thinker who pondered the chances of the common law at a moment of extraordinary opportunity.[21]

Doctor and Student is at once a handbook of the common law and its applications and a theoretical defense of its formal integrity in terms derived from the civil law scholiasts. St. German's problematic lay in the fact that the common law rested on no central statement of principles or canonical body of texts; it remained, as it had been in the time of Bracton, a cluster of rules derived from feudal custom, elaborated by precedent and refined by statute. How could such an amorphous entity be defined, bounded, and defended?

As its name implies, *Doctor and Student* is a dialogue between two interlocutors, a doctor of divinity and a student of "the Lawes of Englande," although they are, as often in this genre, merely the divided halves of the authorial persona. The Doctor avers that he has "had great desyre of longe tyme to knowe wherupon the lawe of Englande is grounded" but has been stymied by his ignorance of law French. The Student replies that he would willingly answer the Doctor's query, but that it "wolde aske a great leasure" and is moreover "aboue [his] cunnynge." He begs the Doctor to first show him "somwhat of other lawes," upon which he will endeavor to satisfy him—a transparent device to introduce St. German's treatment of the four scholastic categories, "the lawe eternall," "the lawe of nature," "the lawe of

god," and "the lawe of man."[22] Eternal law is the reason of God directed toward the ends of his creation; natural law (or, in humans, the law of reason)
is the sign or instinct that leads men to their human felicity in society, including right governance and right worship; God's law is the revelation that
leads them to salvation (8–26). The law of man, or positive law, is law devised by humans to accomplish specific ends, and more generally their
"peasyble conuersacyon and necessary sustentacyon" (27). The first three of
these laws were prescriptive, the last descriptive. The law of man (which included the law of England) might take a variety of forms, as long as it did no
violence to the other three, whose common principle was reason. Thus, all
forms of law, divine and human, were grounded in reason.

These stipulations validate the common law as such, because the mere
empirical existence of a legal system—the persistence of a body of written
rules accepted by a given community over time—is self-evident and sufficient proof of its rationality. Thus, the Student says, "The fyrste grounde of
the lawe of Englande is the lawe of reason/ . . . the whiche is kepte in this
realme as it is in all other realmes & as of necessytie it must nedes be" (31).
As the community develops, its rules become more extensive and formalized; every legal system, however, has its limit, because all contingencies
cannot be foreseen, and "It is not possyble to make any generall rewle of the
lawe/ but that it shall fayle in some case" (97). For this reason, equity is instituted, not as an exemption from the law but as an essential element of it,
based on the "constant will rendering to every one his right" that is one of
the prime aspects of the law eternal (9), as well, of course, as the explicit
guiding principle of the *Corpus juris civilis*. Equity is present at all times in
the law as "a [ryghtwysenes] that consideryth all the pertyculer cyrcum-
staunces of the dede" at issue; it "must alway be obseruyd in euery lawe of
man/ and in euery generall rewle thereof" (95). As such it is subsumed under the principle of reason and is, in St. German's reading, essentially an aspect of it. Reason itself is properly called "ryghtwyse" because it is necessarily "conformable to the wyll of god" (85). Equity is therefore a further (not a
broader) application of the reason already present in the law. It may not exceed it at any point.

The mode of equity's application to the law is conscience, the moral faculty which immediately discerns good from evil and assents to the former.
Conscience is the original ground of law and therefore the necessary basis of
its extension; it can under no circumstance, however, replace the law. Law is
in relation to conscience as the collective and deliberative assent to the good
is to the individual apprehension of it, and is therefore necessarily superior
to it, for although conscience per se is inerrant, it is frequently clouded in the
individual by carnal nature. St. German approaches very closely here to
Coke's doctrine of artificial reason, which holds collective wisdom always

superior to individual judgment. Thus, in discussing a complex case of a tenant by courtesy, St. German concludes that:

> yf the law helpe hym not: conscyence can nat helpe hym in this case/ for conscyence must alway be grounded vppon some law and it can not in this case be grounded vppon the law of reason nor vpon the law of god/ for it is not dyrectely by those lawes that a man shall be tenaunt by the curtesy/ but by the custome of the realme. And therfore yf that custome helpe hym not: he can nothynge haue in thys case by conscyence/ for conscyence neuer resysteth the lawe of man nor addeth nothynge to it/ but where the law of man is in it selfe dyrectely agaynst the law of reason or els the lawe of god/ and than properly it can not be called a law but a corrupcyon/ . . . (207; cf. 133, 163; introduction, xxvi).

Conscience may be exercised in the law only when a literal application of the latter would produce an absurd result. Thus, St. German argues, if a law should forbid that a city's gates be opened before dawn on pain of death, it would be absurd to apply it to a man who had done so in order to save fellow citizens trapped outside the gates by an approaching enemy. In such a case one must follow "the intent of the lawe" rather than its literal wording, for the intent is to protect the citizenry and no one can be justly punished for doing so (97, 99). Accordingly, conscience clarifies the law; it can never (where law exists at all) act in its stead.

The same may be said of equity, which is the product of conscience. Equity, St. German asserts, "folowyth the lawe." It is nothing in itself "but an excepcyon of the lawe of god/ or of the lawe of reason/ from the generall rewles of the lawe of man . . . the whiche excepcion is secretely vnderstande in euery generall rewle of euery posytyue lawe" (97). Once again, equity is wholly bounded by the law. Since it is the first principle of human law that it can contain nothing repugnant to the law of God and the law of reason, equity is the law's own device for assuring that it remains true to its own stated purposes and intentions in every case.

Equity's place within the law is secure, but the law's control of equity is paramount. If a law against equity were to be made, St. German asserts, it would be void in conscience.[23] By the same token, however, equity may not usurp the law, nor "weary" it with endless delays so that it "shulde neuer haue ende," and for this purpose the law may justly regulate equity and prohibit frivolous appeals from its ordinary judgments (107). St. German notes that positive law may be based on custom or mere convenience, yet as long as it does not violate conscience it suffices to bind it (125, 129). Equity thus has no positive or declarative content in the law as such, but is solely a means of remedying its defects in particular circumstances.

St. German's extensive discussion of equity in *Doctor and Student* has attracted the attention of commentators, who contrast his willingness to concede it a place in the law with the general hostility of common lawyers to Chancery and all its works. A response to St. German, the *Replication of a Serjeant at the Laws of England*, summed up the conventional view: "And so the commen lawe of the realme is nowe a daies by you that be studentes turnede all ynto conscience, and so ye make my lorde chauncellor juge yn every matier."[24] As has been noted, however, it was common lawyers themselves who often took the initiative to litigate in Chancery, and one, John Orenge of the Middle Temple, tried no fewer than 239 cases there.[25] The attempt to wall Chancery and the other prerogative courts off from the common law had only had the effect of breaching the common law itself. To protect the common law, it was necessary to concede Chancery its place in the legal system and to define its appropriate functions. As St. German put it in replying to the Replicator:

> [Y]f ye therfore followe the lawe trewly, ye cannot do amyss nor offende your conscience, ne ye shall not neade to leve the lawe for conscyence; by which saying, as it semyth, he meanyth that yt is yn vayn yn any caas to sue by sub pena, as thoughe a man shuld never have helpe by conscience where he could have non by the lawe. *And* to this saying yt may be answered thus: that if he take the lawe of the realme as a lawe groundede upon the lawe of reason, and the lawe of God, with the custumes and maxymes of the lawe *ordeynd by the realme*, I thinke well that as he saiethe the lawe of the realme wilbe a sufficiente rule to ordre a man and his conscience, what he shall do, and what he shall not doo; but yet it will not allwaies gyve hym remedie when he hathe righte . . .[26]

By remembering that the purpose of the law is always to give each individual his right, and thereby to incorporate conscience, it will never be necessary "to leve the lawe for conscyence." Properly understood, conscience was the leaven of the law. Without it, justice could not be reliably served; with it, the law remained a living, flexible instrument. By the same token, conscience apart from law was, in a civil society, arbitrary rule, for no particular authority could substitute itself for the collective wisdom that law represented. Courts of equity such as the Chancery were, accordingly, no less courts of the common law than Common Pleas or King's Bench.

St. German's attempt to bring prerogative courts under the common law was a sophisticated claim for the unity and sufficiency of English law. It was also a recognition of the way law was being practiced in his time. As long as the common law was normative and common lawyers themselves its keepers, there was no need to fear for the rights of the subject in any court of England, whether new or long-established. On these terms St. German could embrace and indeed serve the Henrician imperium.

For St. German, the real foe of the common law was not Chancery but the ecclesiastical courts. These courts not only supervised the clergy but exercised wide jurisdiction over lay matters, including perjury and defamation, probate and testamentary disputes, and moral conduct in general. They enforced clerical obligation on the laity in the form of tithes, mortuary fees, and "contempt of clergy," and policed heresy. In these courts alone the writ of an alien law ran. Canon law permitted persons to be apprehended on suspicion or common fame, or on the word of anonymous accusers. Defendants could be compelled to testify under oath; records were kept casually if at all.

Henry's assault on the clergy offered St. German his own opportunity to take on the church courts and, ultimately, the independence of the clerical estate as such. In a series of tracts beginning with *A Treatise Concernynge the Division Betweene the Spirytualtie and Temporaltie* (1532 or 1533) and concluding in the *Answer to a Letter* (1535), he tracked the Henrician campaign that culminated in the Act of Supremacy, arriving at last at a fully Erastian position. He thereby laid the basis for the national church, a generation before Jewel's *An Apology of the Church of England.*[27]

For our present purposes, St. German's attack on the church courts is of special interest. From the first, he couched this attack in the broad terms of a general "division" between the clergy and the laity in which neglect of spiritual duty resulted in the abuse of temporal authority. This corrupting process went by the name of worldliness and unchecked over many generations it had finally infected the church as a whole so that, as St. German noted in the *Treatise Concernynge the Diuision*, "though many spyrytuall men may be founde, that haue ryght many great vertues and great gyftes of god . . ./ yet it wyll be harde to fynde any one spyrytuall man, that is nat enfecte with the sayd desyre and affection to haue the worldely honoure of prestes exalted and preferred."[28] Under such circumstances church courts readily became instruments of oppression, particularly as they enforced a legal code and procedure unique to themselves.

St. German sets out the case against these courts under three headings: abuse of procedure; abuse of charge; and usurpation of authority. The first two were inseparable, because the practice of shielding accusers and compelling testimony from the accused gave clerical prosecutors untrammeled discretion to lay and pursue charges, while the latitude granted them to interpret heresy by the statute *De haeretico comburendo* (2 Henry IV, c. 15) was an open warrant on any man or woman incurring their displeasure or inciting their greed. It was, St. German noted, "very peryllous, that spyrytuall men shulde haue auctorytie to arrest a man for euery lyght suspection," a power which naturally led inquisitors to find heresy under every bush (192). The result was that many faithful subjects had been forced to compound for "great sommes of money" or to perform vexatious penances (189). St. German suggested that heresy charges might be brought into the king's courts by the writ *De excommunicato capiendo*, and asked pointedly who would repress heresy among the clergy themselves, for "yf a metropolytane with all his clergye and people of his dioces fel into herisie: it wolde be harde to redresse it withoute temporal power" (190). Here was a clear adumbration of royal supremacy *avant la lettre.*

If clerical courts belonged under royal supervision and control, what could be said of the "dyuers lawes and constitutyons whiche haue bene made by the churche, sometyme by the Pope, somtyme by Legates/ or by Metropolitanes in theyr prouince," which had "attempted in many thynges agaynste the lawe of the realme"? (197) These touched not only high matters of praemunire but various points of testamentary law, such as the decree, contrary to both common law and common sense, that executors might not administer a will until it had been proved (198). Rather than tolerating such infringements, St. German suggests, the laity ought rather to inquire by what right clerics plead exemption from prosecution in secular courts, a claim supported neither by the law of the kingdom nor that of God (199).

The impasse created by such competing claims could be resolved only in one quarter, by the law-making body of the realm. The clergy appealed in support of its supposed rights not only to papal ordinance but to privileges granted by statute, "some of them at the specyall request and peticion of the spiritualtie." But only one person had the obligation to judge both the jurisdiction of courts and the effects of custom and right on the common weal, namely the king: "For he is sworne to maynteigne the good customes of his realme and to breake the euyll." To this he was bound not only by his oath but by the laws, which directed him "to aduoyde all thynges, that may be a let to his peace." As both spiritual and temporal lords were bound to him "as theyr soueraigne lorde," he therefore had "auctorytie in his parlyamente" to curb any injurious practice or nullify any unjust privilege. What statute had granted or custom tolerated, statute could revoke: the King in Parliament was supreme (200–202).

The *Treatise concernynge the diuision* had set out the general argument for reforming the clergy and for bringing clerical jurisdiction under the common law by means of statute. In an appendix to *Doctor and Student*, the *Newe Addicions* (1531),[29] and in the parliamentary drafts on which he was at work that same year,[30] St. German dealt with specific issues and proposals. The thirteen points in the *Newe Addicions* defended the right of Parliament to regulate mortuaries, mortmain, advowsons, sanctuary, suits arising from the neglect of church property, suits for defamation and slander, the beneficing of minors, clerical literacy, the apportioning of tithes, visitation fines, and other matters. "I suppose also/," St. German's Student comments, "that the parliment may assigne all the trees and gresse in church yardes. . . . For thoughe hit be hallowed grounde, yet the freholde therof, the trees/ and herbes are thynges temporall" (323). Similarly, Parliament might decree that no priest wear vestments made from imported cloth, this too being a "temporall" thing although devoted to a sacred purpose (325). It is perhaps not fanciful to see in these encroachments the germ of Henry's wholesale claim on the material estate of the church a few years later. In fact, as St. German remarked elsewhere, "all goodes/ though they be in the handes of spirituall men, be temporall, concernynge the body and nourysshynge the body as they do to temporal men" (318).

What, then, were the limits of lay control of the church? Was St. German prepared to recognize any indefeasible privilege in the clergy? Certainly he acknowledged their unique custodial and exemplary role in keeping "the trewe catholical feith," administering the sacraments, and promoting piety, zeal, meekness, charity, patience, and obedience.[31] For the exercise of these functions a maintenance by tithes was appropriate, subject to lay regulation; the clergy themselves, however, should despise material goods after the example of the apostles, contenting themselves "with grace and goostly comfortes" rather than worldly ease.[32] St. German thereby turned the question of lay domination of the clergy on its head, for to the extent that church courts and customs concerned themselves with temporal goods, particularly the goods of the laity, they exceeded their proper mandate, and invited rebuke if not statutory reform.

St. German did not merely advocate such reform but was active in drafting it in 1531. His proposals included the appointment of a "great standyng counsayll" consisting of lords spiritual and temporal "and other persons" appointed by "the kyng by auctorytye of his parliament," empowered to nullify all inconvenient ecclesiastical "lawes, uses and custumes" lying under parliamentary authority, and to refer all other grievances to the King and such clergy, including but not limited to members of the council, whom it might be fit to consult. The council was specifically charged to conduct preliminary investigations of all accusations of heresy prior to hearings or action in any clerical court.[33] Here was the foundation of Cromwell's vice-regency, and, as John Guy and his fellow editors note, despite Geoffrey Elton's claim for Cromwell's originality, "it was Christopher St. German who, two years before the Act of Appeals and three before the Act of Supremacy, was the first Englishman to articulate the theory of the sovereignty of the King in Parliament—the theory that grounded the English Reformation and finally prevailed."[34]

St. German's proposal gave the council various other tasks, such as determining whether to translate the Bible into the vernacular and mandating that parish priests and other religious carry out their functions diligently— surely duties pertaining to ordinary ecclesiastical administration. The presence of bishops on the council gave it some sacerdotal color, but there could be no question of its dominance by the King and the laity, nor of the King's capacity to pack whatever other advisory body he might create to deal with matters "that the parliamente may not redresse" with compliant clerics.

St. German was purposively vague about which aspects of church law and governance might fall outside the purview of Parliament. Commenting on the enactment of the Statute of Mortuaries, his Student declared, "I holde it nat best to reason or to make argumentes/ whether they had auctoritie to do that they dydde or nat. For I suppose/ that no man wolde thynke, that they wolde do any thynge, that they hadde nat power to do."[35] This intriguing remark—which might well have served the turn of a John Pym a century later—suggested that Parliament, or more accurately King in Parliament, was the final authority in the realm, and statute its seal of pronouncement. There were very few things of a binding nature that the two houses might do of their own, but nothing they could not accomplish with the king. Similarly, there were matters where the initiative lay more appropriately with the king as the guardian of the public welfare, but where statute was the ultimate remedy.

St. German still recognized the clergy as a separate, spiritual estate— indeed, his calls for it to return to its proper duties and to renounce worldly interest, as well as his rhetorical reliance on scholastic authorities and categories, placed him very much in the mold of the pre-Erasmian reform tradition—and he continued, at this point, to recognize some forms of papal jurisdiction in England, conditional upon royal participation and assent. His very doctrinal conservatism, and the careful grounding of his legal claims in statute and precedent, gave his argument particular weight, a fact acknowledged by the foremost lay defender of church liberties and jurisdictions, Sir Thomas More, who vigorously rebutted St. German and defended his own role in heresy persecutions.[36] In conceding the validity of church courts but defining their scope almost wholly in terms of the temporal jurisdictions they had wrongfully invaded, St. German had shrewdly placed them in a highly defensive and unpopular position. In effect, he turned their strategy of encroachment against them: whereas they had refused to accept any limit on their usurpation of lay jurisdiction, St. German not only insisted on repatriating such jurisdiction to the common law courts (and to Chancery, whose equity functions he deftly appropriated to this purpose), but used the notion of King in parliament as a means to reframe spiritual issues in temporal terms. At the end of the exercise, church courts remained as little more than an adjunct of lay courts and royal commissions.

As in the case of Chancery, St. German was less interested to deny church courts an appropriate role than to bring their procedure and jurisdiction under the common law. Once tamed, there was no reason why they could not continue. In future, however, they would be strictly governed, as St. German remarked in another context, "by the olde customes and maximes of the lawe of the realme."

In the *Newe Addicions* and the parliamentary drafts, St. German still envisioned a complex, three-sided process in which ecclesiastical jurisdiction would be regulated by the King in Parliament (including Convocation), the king acting through ad hoc bodies such as the great standing council (whose warrant, as he carefully specified, was to continue only "unto the later ende of the next parliament" [i.e., session]), and the king dealing directly with the papacy. Clerical reform was, however, a rapidly moving target in the early 1530s, and as the argument for royal supremacy over the church took shape,[37] St. German's Erastianism developed apace. Kings, he asserted in *A treatyse concerninge the power of the clergye and the lawes of the Realme* (1535), received their temporal power directly from God, be they pagan or Christian, and their acceptance of Christianity could in no way diminish it. Although kings, like all other persons, were bound by the law of God, no merely ceremonial or customary practice could restrain them in the exercise of their responsibility for the general welfare. Accordingly, as he had declared in *The Addicions of Salem and Byzance* (1534), it was "ryght expediente, that all constitutions prouincialle and legantines, as haue be made in tyme paste, agaynste the lawes of the realme, and the kynges prerogatiue . . . shall be clerely reuoked and put away." This meant, among other things, that church courts were bound to judge any matters that touched temporal rights solely "by the kynges lawes," that the jurisdiction and decisions of such courts might be appealed to Chancery or other royal courts, and that priests were required to answer all "actions real and personall" in the King's courts "as farforth as any laye men shulde be."[38]

The Act of Supremacy, St. German contended, had appropriately clarified these issues. It represented "no newe graunte" of authority to the King, "but only a declaracyon of his fyrst power by god commytted to kinglye & regall auctorite." This in turn rested upon the fact that the temporal and spiritual bodies of the realm were united in the body of all subjects, clerical and lay, and that the church had no corporate existence separate from the community. Although priests performed certain unique functions, therefore, "the auctoritie of kynges and of the clergy be so lynked togyther in many thinges/ that the one can nat be knowen/ but the other be knowen also." Simply put, the clergy could do nothing outside the king's cognizance, and nothing he could not properly regulate.[39]

The proclamation of Henry's headship over what was now constituted as "the Church of England," and the Act Extinguishing the Authority of the Bishop of Rome (28 Henry VIII, c. 10) which followed as its consequence, made possible St. German's identification of the church with the body of the realm. Although the church could, and in pagan times had consisted of less than the body entire, it had no temporal incorporation beyond it. As St. German had pointed out, pagan kings immediately assumed full jurisdiction over it upon their conversion. In reclaiming usurped powers, he could thus argue, Henry had done no more than to reinstate the authority the English crown had enjoyed *ab ovo*. As St. German put it, "oure lorde neuer intended by his commyng into this world to take any power from princes."[40]

St. German encapsulated his argument for the temporal and spiritual inseparability of the church and the realm and the undivided headship of the king in an extended passage:

> And where some men haue sayd that the clergye haue auctorytie by the gospell to here all causes that shulde be shewed vnto them by any maner of complaynt. . . . To that it maye be answered that by that worde chyrche is not vnderstande only the clergye/ for they vndoutydly make nat the churche/ for the hole congregation of Christes people maketh the chyrche: And bycause the hole people of Christendom can nat be gathered togyder/ so that they may here such matters shewed vnto them all: therfore it can nat be taken that our lorde ment yt it shuld be shewed to all the people/ for he commaunded nothyng but that may well & resonably be obserued: And therfore, whan it is sayd shewe it to the church. It is to be vnderstande therby/ that it shall be shewed vnto them that by the lawe & custome there vsed haue auctorite to correct that offence . . . [i.e. to] the kynge or to his iuges/ or to his iustyces of peace in the countrey/ or other offycers that after the lawe & custome of the realme may reforme it.[41]

In refuting the presumption of the clergy to an unlimited temporal jurisdiction, St. German again silently lumped spiritual and temporal offenses together under a single category over which the crown alone had primary jurisdiction: "shewe it to the church" became "show it to the state." What was left for church courts to determine was at the discretion of the temporal power, according to "lawe & custome." Where law and custom were in need of clarification or reform, Parliament was the appropriate remedy, for, as St. German noted in his last controversial tract, *An Answer to a Letter* (1535), when the king summoned his lords spiritual and temporal, "the parliament so gathered togyther/ representeth the estate of al the people within this realme/ that is to say of the whole catholyque churche therof," and its acts represented "the most noble [i.e., final as well as suitable] power that any prince hath ouer his subiectes."[42] In Parliament, and in Parliament alone, the realm was representatively present in both its temporal and spiritual aspects: the entire commonwealth and the whole church, united by and in the person of the anointed king, supreme ruler on earth under God and supreme head of the church under Christ. What authority, save divinity itself, could exceed it?

In St. German's conception, then, the King in Parliament was the ultimate authority in matters spiritual as well as temporal, beyond which there was no appeal except to the law of God as disclosed by reason and conscience. With this, his rhetorical project to bring church courts and courts of equity under the control of the common law was complete. Power and community rested in the self-reflexive notion of the King in Parliament, in which royal authority and popular assent, each affirming and mirroring the other, produced the most definitive and binding act of which the body politic was capable, statute law, in whose harmonious conjuncture the unity of the nation was made manifest. This in turn was grounded in the common law, the repository of the nation's wisdom and the living expression of its historical experience. In the *Newe Addicions* to *Doctor and Student* and again in *The Power of the Clergy*, St. German had taken up the question of whether Parliament, too, might not exceed the common law's authority or even transgress the law of God. In the former text he had made the implicit argument that Parliament was not to be questioned as a court of final decision; in the latter, more expansively, he suggested that it was "nat to presume that so many noble princes and their counseyle, ne the lordes and nobles of the realme, ne yet the Comons gathered . . . wolde . . . renne in to so great offence of conscyence as the breakynge of the lawe of God."[43] There was, however, a further and yet firmer assurance against error, the law of the land. In following it, Parliament, like all other courts, could draw upon a wisdom coextensive with the nation itself. Human affairs could admit of no greater certainty than that.

A serious weakness, however, not to say a contradiction, lay at the heart of St. German's argument. The common law was presumed to be understood, yet nowhere was it systematically expressed. The closest thing England had to a legal code in the accepted civil law tradition was the laws of the Conqueror — the Norman yoke of subsequent Civil War fame — and these, as we have seen in Camden's treatment, were acceptable only insofar as they could be made to blend in with native custom. As Plucknett points out, Bracton had grappled with the same problem centuries earlier. The appeal to custom elided the absence of a written code, since custom was orally understood and transmitted by definition. The existence of the legal profession itself testified to the inadequacy of such tradition. By its very nature, moreover, custom was local, and without unifying principles a mere congeries.

St. German's response to these objections was twofold. Customs of the realm, he asserts, should be distinguished from local practices; for example, "[the custome of the realme is] that no maner of goodes nor catelles reall nor parsonell shall neuer go to the heyre/ but to the executoures/ [or to the ordynarye or admynystratoures] *save in some localities where there is a special custom otherwise* (*DS* 51).[44] Such customs "haue ben acceptyd and approuyd by our soueraygne lorde the kynge and his progenytours and all theyr subgettes," and, offending neither God's law nor the law of reason, "they haue optayned the strengthe of a lawe/ in so moche that he that doth agaynst them doth agaynst Iustyce *and law*" (45, 47). Thus they are legally enforceable even if not specifically expressed in a rule or a statute. Such customs alone belong properly to the common law.

Customs of the realm were not only certified in the courts, St. German asserted, but were "the verye grounde of dyuers courtes" themselves, including Chancery, King's Bench, and Exchequer. Since the royal courts had no statutory or other written basis, they could indeed have been summoned into existence only to express and defend custom. In that sense they were themselves a product of custom, and fixed in the form that custom had initially given them. Consequently, the custom of the realm was "of so hygh auctorytie that the sayde courtes ne theyr auctoryties may not be alteryd/ ne theyr names chaunged without Parlyament," the ultimate legal authority (47).

With this move, St. German bypassed the role of the crown in establishing the courts, or at best assigned it an instrumental function. Custom was immemorial, and only Parliament, which had to be presumed coeval with it, could pronounce definitively on it. All other institutions were merely the emanation of custom.

This was legal organicism with a vengeance. St. German did not pursue its implications in discussing the political structure, for which he found Fortescue's description of the *dominium politicum et regale* serviceable enough,[45] nor did he address the origins of royal jurisdiction as such. The radical potential in his concept of custom is nonetheless patent. For St. German, it trumps all institutions of authority save Parliament (whose determinations are in any case presumed incapable of contradicting it); it is the living voice of social contract, the source and sustenance of the body politic itself.

Similarly, St. German's "conservative" defense of Chancery and by extension other courts of equity takes on a quite different aspect when viewed from this perspective. As the emanation of custom no less than other royal courts, it is no less than they a creature of the common law. No English court, in fine, whatever its origin, scope, or purpose, could escape that law's jurisdiction.

These considerations did not clear up the mystifications in St. German's argument, however, or save it from a charge of tautology. St. German had distinguished between local custom and the custom of the realm, but he offered no account of how or why the latter might have developed out of (or diverged from) the former. From a fundamental law perspective, this was perhaps otiose; the concept of an immemorial constitution precluded any discrimination among its manifest elements, or any quest for ultimate priority among them. Local customs were "inferior" to customs of the realm in the same sense that local courts were inferior to royal ones, but each was to be respected in its sphere. In declining to discriminate further between them, however, St. German was vulnerable to the charge that custom was defined by the court that claimed jurisdiction over it, and the custom of the realm was merely that custom which the royal courts chose to enforce. By the same token, its content was only what those courts declared it to be. Whatever the Platonic theory of custom might be, the nominalist reality was that customary law was judge-made law.

St. German tried to evade this difficulty by enumerating twenty-two customs of the realm (sometimes denoted as "law and custom"). The first of these was a thoroughly familiar one:

> Also by the olde custome of the realme/ no man shall be *adjudged* {taken imprysonyd dysseasyd nor otherwyse destroyed/ but he be} put to answer by the lawe of the lande: & this custome is confermyd by {the statute of} Magna carta the .xxvi chapytre *where it is said No free man shall be taken, nor imprisoned, nor disseised nor in any other way destroyed, nor will we go upon him nor send upon him, save by the lawful judgement of his peers and by the law of the land.* (49)

St. German represents the codification in Magna Carta as a more precise rendering of the underlying customary principle, but in fact it is the other way around: the statement of the originary "principle" is clearly a paraphrase of Magna Carta. Justinian's codes had been derived in precisely this way from Roman jurisprudence, a written record yielding generalized principles. But St. German could not, except by obfuscation, pretend to derive oral custom from written prescription. At best, the preexistence of custom was an inference, an assumption, but the custom itself could not be stated except in the form that the written law had given it.

In founding the common law on custom, St. German was building on sand, especially in seeking to give a plausible account of it (as *Doctor and Student* does) to a civilian audience. This in turn threatened to undermine his entire project. To prop it up, he had recourse to two further categories, one general and one specific. All law, he contended, including English law, was consonant with the law of reason. "Primary" reason dictated such principles as the right of personal and communal self-defense against those who threatened the peace; these were self-evidently disclosed to all. "Secondary" reason was manifested as universal custom, for example the custom of property, found in all societies (33). As criminal law, the common law conformed to primary reason; as land law, it was an instance of secondary reason. Tautology loomed here too, however, for as St. German was obliged to concede, it was "many tymes very harde and of great dyffycultie to knowe what cases of the lawe of Englande be groundyd vpon the lawe of reason/ and what vpon custome of the realme" (69). All valid law in any case derived ultimately from the law of reason, positive law being merely its application in particular circumstances and in a form of expression best adapted to it. This left the notion of custom no more coherent than before.

St. German also had more hesitant resort to what he called, after Fortescue, maxims. Maxims were "dyuers pryncyples . . . the which haue ben alwayes taken for law in this realme/ so that it is not lawfull for none that is lernyd to denye them." Maxims were judicial rules, specifically rules declared by judges based on the custom of the realm, "And they be of the same strength & effect in law as statutis be" (57, 59). The confusion in yoking maxim to custom paralleled that of deriving custom from reason; as St. German remarked defensively, "it nedyth not to assygne any reason *or consideration* why they were fyrste receyued for maxymes for it suffyseth that they be not agaynst the lawe of reason nor the law of god *in any respect*/ [& that they haue alway be taken for lawe.]" Maxims were thus simultaneously historical and immemorial—"fyrste receyued" in a particular court by particular judges, yet "alway . . . taken for lawe" notwithstanding. These statements would have been theoretically reconcilable if the line from custom to maxim were clear and self-evident, but St. German insisted that maxims were only apparent to the learned, "*to such an extent that it is fruitless to argue with those who deny them*" (59). This came very close to saying that the law was what judges declared it to be.

Maxims had the advantage both of being written and of being backed, as St. German acknowledged all law must be, by an authority capable of enforcing them. They also provided a means of distinguishing custom as the ground of law from law as a developmental body of rules and prescriptions. St. German drew back, however, from the suggestion that any rule of law could go beyond declaring custom. "[M]any of the customes [& maxymes] of the lawes of Englande," his Student asserts, "*can* be knowen by the vse and custome of the realme so apparantly that it nedeth not to haue any lawe wrytten therof," while those "that be not so openly knowen amonge the people may be knowen partly by the lawe of reason: & partly by the bokes of the lawis of Englande called yeres of termes/ & partly by dyuers recordis remaynynge in the kynges courtes & in his tresorye" (69, 71). With this statement, St. German erases the critical distinction between customs and maxims. Maxims need not be written; laymen are fully capable of understanding them through the exercise of ordinary reason; the learned are not the sole judges of their meaning. Faced with the tension between law as principle and law as praxis, St. German retreats from the implications of the jurisprudential view.

As a theoretical defense of the common law, St. German's account leaves much to be desired, especially by comparison with its civil law rival. His common law lacks a classical pedigree, a unified code, and a set of coherent principles. Its maxims, which might be considered principles in the bud, turn out on closer inspection to be mere redactions of custom, to which they bear the same relation as proverbs do to folk wisdom. What St. German falls back on in the end, or at any rate what he is left with, is a commonsense version of the verum factum principle. As Giambattista Vico was later to suggest in *La Nuova Scienza*, a thing is known in the use to which its makers put it; thus, the Italian language is precisely what Italians "make" of it, conceptually and experientially. Grammarians can tease out the implication of what Italian speakers can do, can describe variations and prescribe rules, but in the end Italian will be what Italians find adequate for communication with each other from day to day in the sum total of their occasions. St. German's view is the same. En-glish law is what Englishmen have made to govern their so-cial and commercial relations with each other; its discourse is custom. The custom of the realm is a *lingua franca*; local custom is mere dialect. Lawyers, like grammarians, describe variations and prescribe rules, but they can no more revoke custom than the latter can revoke words. Without custom, there is no speech at all.

For an insular culture like England's, St. German's description was for the time being sufficient. English law did not claim descent from any other tradi-tion; its defenders were if anything insistent that it had no truck with any Continental system, and that if it had endured a passage with the Normans (law French was obviously not a derivative of the English tongue), it had not been contaminated by the experience. As long as Englishmen understood their customs aright, the very difficulty of reducing them to terms compati-ble with other legal systems was suggestive of their uniqueness and authen-ticity. They had only to be consistent with the law of God and the law of rea-son, as long usage demonstrated they were, to be rationally accessible to any "doctor" wishing to make acquaintance with them.

Doctor and Student remained a basic guidebook to the common law and a seminal treatise on equity down to Blackstone's time.[46] The common law it-self, strengthened by the suppression of canon law and confirmed in its su-premacy by the Henrician Reformation, had no serious rival for the remain-der of the sixteenth century. It branched out into copyhold tenure, bringing that last vestige of feudalism under the control of its courts. Even there, however, it did not so much reform as assimilate existing custom, precisely in the manner that St. German said it should. As A. W. B. Simpson notes:

> These rules varied from place to place, and so copyholders were never sub-jected to a uniform system of land law; there never grew up anything which could be called a common law of copyhold. . . . The common-law courts [when they achieved jurisdiction] deliberately adopted the role of protec-tors of local manorial custom, and not destroyers of it, for their intervention in the affairs of copyholders was justified upon the ground that they were

doing for the copyholder what the copyholder's lord was primarily bound to do—respect the ancient custom of the manor.[47]

Nothing could better sum up the practical strength and conceptual incoherence of the common law as a mode of enforcing custom.

The Artificial Reason of Sir Edward Coke

Not, perhaps, until Camden had introduced a more skeptical and sophisticated historicism into the discourse of the past could the issues framed by St. German be fruitfully revisited. Camden's more developmental construction of historical process is evident in Sir John Davies' well-known description of the origin of custom in the preface to his *Irish Reports* (1612):

> For a Custome taketh beginning and groweth to perfection in this manner: When a reasonable act once done is found to be good and beneficiall to the people, and agreeable to their nature and disposition, then they do use it and practise it again and again, and so by often iteration and multiplication of the act it becometh a *Custome*; and being continued without interruption time out of mind, it obtaineth the force of a *Law*. And this *Customary Law* is the most perfect and most excellent, and without comparison the best, to make and preserve a Commonwealth. For the *written Laws* which are made either by the Edicts of Princes, or by Councils of Estates, are imposed upon the Subject before any Triall or Probation made, whether the same be fit and agreeable to the nature and disposition of the people, or whether they will breed any inconvenience or no. But a *Custome* doth never become a Law to bind the people, untill it hath been tried and approved time out of mind, during all which time there did thereby arise no inconvenience: for if it had been found inconvenient at any time, it had been used no longer, but had been interrupted, and consequently it had lost the virtue and force of a Law.[48]

In some ways this description is retrograde, for it elides the process by which custom becomes justiciable, and it opposes customary to positive law in a manner St. German would doubtless have found excessively rigid: statute law, as he perceived it, would never prove "inconvenient" as long as it based itself on the common law, and the common law on a rational elucidation of custom. What Davies does provide is an account of the way in which custom ripens into "law" by long usage and, inferentially, progressive refinement. All custom must meet the basic test of reason, as St. German had noted, but beyond that it must also be responsive to the lessons of experience. Consequently, it can be fully formed only over time. Custom is never born whole, out of an ahistorical continuum; it develops out of a process which, though notionally continuous from time out of mind, is at least in principle subject to historical scrutiny. It is only by means of such a process that it can attain the status of law. That this process is necessarily developmental and not a mere succession of mechanical iterations is manifest in the fact that customs do not automatically become law after a sufficient number of identical tests, but only if after long trial they raise no inconvenience.

As we have seen, St. German had adumbrated a developmental theory of his own in deriving maxims from custom, only to draw back from the suggestion that judicial construction was the end product of folk wisdom. Davies, too, appeared to resist the notion that custom was not its own sufficient interpreter. But his acknowledgment of a historical dimension in custom provided an opening, at least, to a theory of law both anchored in tradition and responsive to changing circumstance.

Part of the difficulty faced by both St. German and Davies lay in the tension between oral custom and written law. Oral custom not only took temporal precedence over written law; it remained superior to it. The wisdom of custom was axiomatic and inarguable; the wisdom of written law was subject to interpretation and debate—it was justiciable. Like the cult of primitive Christianity, the cult of custom presumed unbroken praxis derived from a prescriptive source; redaction was necessarily reduction, if not, as in the case of medieval canon law, corruption. The moment of writing was thus the moment of peril and loss in an oral tradition, which in circumscribing the fullness of custom into the narrow formulae of the *lex scriptorum* necessarily did violence to it. The written law was a vessel for containing the uncontainable.

Law could not, of course, replace or abrogate custom; in sixteenth-century parlance, it merely declared it in a form convenient for certain specific purposes. Declared custom—for example, a maxim or a statute—was no less custom for being law; it was just another way of thinking custom's immemorial thought. This approach saved the phenomena, as it were, but at the cost of stunting any developmental conception of the written law. The process Davies had posited for custom was thus debarred for law; indeed, as we have seen, he declared custom a sufficient law unto itself.

For any theory of law to progress, it had to escape the tyranny of custom. Davies was unable to do so himself, but he suggested a way out, one already hit upon by the man who more than any other reified the common law, Sir Edward Coke.

Coke's long life (1552–1634) spanned the years from the Edwardian Prayer Book—the high tide of Calvinist orthodoxy in Reformation England—to the Ship Money levies that marked the final constitutional crisis before the onset of the Civil War. For fifty-six years he was a member of the bar; for forty of them he was at the center of English public life; for thirty, he exerted an influence on the English legal system that had no parallel before and, perhaps saving Blackstone, no equal after. Of no other commoner might it be said that a king of England felt obliged to tell the House of Lords, as James I did in 1621, that he and his disciples were not the exclusive interpreters of the constitution: "For though Sir Edward Coke be verie busie and be called the father of the Law and the Commons' howse have divers yonge lawyers in it, yet all is not law that they say . . ." As Solicitor General and Attorney General, Chief Justice of the courts of Common Pleas and King's Bench, Speaker of the House of Commons and leader of the Country resistance, he was, as Sir Geoffrey Elton well called him, "the great panjandrum of the common law."[49]

Coke's fame rested on the eleven volumes of his *Reports*, published between 1600 and 1615 (the twelfth and thirteenth volumes were published posthumously), and on the four volumes of his *Institutes*, only the first of which appeared in his lifetime. The *Reports* were the culmination of a long tradition of law reporting, originally in the form of so-called yearbooks which served both to summarize important cases and to provide instruction in pleading. These dated back to the 1280s, coinciding with the emergence of the first Inns of Court, became irregular in the early sixteenth century, and, for reasons still debated, ceased after 1535. Their place was taken—and indeed anticipated—by the practice of private reporting, which arose in the early years of the sixteenth century. Probably the first reporters compiled their cases for their own benefit and possibly that of a narrow circle, but the best of them soon commanded a more general audience. At the risk of oversimplifying and perhaps overstating the differences, the yearbooks were intended as a teaching tool for the legal profession, and had therefore something of the neutral, impersonal character of a textbook, whereas the reports, brisker and more selective, reflected more clearly their authors' point of view. They also came to represent an attempt at codifying the welter of accumulated case law and elucidating fundamental principles. In a sense this represented an intellectual coming-of-age for the law, but it also suggested a mood of crisis; as L. W. Abbott remarked of the last and greatest of Coke's predecessors, Edmund Plowden, the goal of his work was "to bring order to a disordered world."[50]

Coke thus inherited a thriving new genre, and one by its nature highly individualized, since in the absence of a standard format the selection of cases, the narrative of fact, the analysis of decisions, and the application of principles were a matter of personal choice. The fact that most reports remained in manuscript reinforced their idiosyncratic character.[51] Coke lamented this state of affairs. The law could not yield its fruits unless the vines of case law were carefully cultivated and pruned. Yet Coke himself waited until the age of forty-eight before publishing his own first *Report*. By that time he had honed his skills as a practitioner and *rapporteur* for nearly thirty years, and many of his manuscript reports had circulated widely. His account of *Shelley's Case*, presented to his patron Lord Buckhurst in 1582, was clearly in the nature of a debut performance, and an earnest of things to come. That he waited so long to publish may be attributed not only to the exigencies of a busy career and the desire to accumulate a fund of significant cases, but to the labor he expended in polishing his accounts.[52] Coke's *Reports* are intellectual drama at the highest level, just as the *Institutes* were intended as a philosophical *summa* of English law. For Coke, to distill the law was to approach, as closely as anyone could, the very essence of English society, the fountain of practical legitimacy.

Like St. German, Coke planted himself squarely in the natural rights tradition.[53] Law (and hence right) was given to humanity with reason, and was thus coextensive with the creation itself: "The Law of Nature," Coke wrote in his report of *Calvin's Case*, "is that which God at the time of creation of the nature of man infused into his heart, for his preservation and direction." At first, this law was expressed orally, not merely as custom but in the form of royal dicta and judgment; thus, for two thousand years, "Kings did decide causes according to natural equity and were not tied to any rule or formality of Law, but did *dare jura*." Only then did God reveal his will directly to Moses, "who was the first Reporter or Writer of Law in the world." With that, what Coke called the "judicial and municipal" law followed, that is, written positive law in courts of record.[54]

Coke asserts that the law of nature alone suffices to create and maintain civil society ("For whatsoever is necessary and profitable for the preservation of the society of man, is due by the Law of Nature"). This includes "Magistracy"; thus, the natural equity dispensed by early kings was juridically valid. The law of nature, moreover, suffuses all subsequent legal systems, including that of England, for it is "*lex aeterna*" and "immutable." Judicial and municipal law could declare but not create law, and no body, including Parliament, could abrogate a natural right. This last point was reinforced by the famous comment in Coke's account of *Bonham's Case* that "in many cases the common law will controul acts of parliament, and sometimes adjudge them to be utterly void: for when an act of parliament is against common right and reason . . . the common law will . . . adjudge such act to be void."[55]

Thus far, Coke is thoroughly conventional, as are the sources he cites: Aristotle, Bracton, Fortescue, and (on these points at least) St. German. Nonetheless, a fundamental tension in his thought is already discernible. Coke treats both natural law and the common law as hypostatized entities that exist independently of human actors and institutions, rebuking them where necessary. At the same time, however, such law is directly and immediately available even to the unlettered as conscience, custom, and in the dicta of rude kings. If parliaments may err where peasants do not, where can any certainty in the law reside? And who, by the law itself, may set a parliament to rights when it does err?

It is possible to give at least qualified answers to these questions along traditional lines. Custom, as accumulated folk wisdom, provides surety in the law, which is why parliaments and other judicial bodies do well to heed it, and can have indeed no other ultimate basis. Statutes that offend the common law are quickly perceived as "repugnant" or "impossible to be performed," and will therefore soon be ignored or repealed.

What this reasoning does not explain in any compelling way is why parliaments and other courts of law are superior to unlettered intuition, or, more specifically, what they add to it. To be sure, courts serve a specialized function in a complex society as the locus of legal decision: they are the places where people come to get law, although in principle they could get it elsewhere and otherwise among themselves. Coke himself makes this clear throughout the *Fourth Institute*, where he describes the history and function of the judicial system. There was, however, one other place as central and convenient as the established courts to which individuals could repair for law, if not (given the brevity of the traditional legal terms) more so: the royal court itself, and the person of the king. The king was, after all, the fount of justice, his writ was the source of all jurisdiction in the realm, and all law was given in his name. As Coke admitted, kings had dispensed law directly for a good part of human history, and in such matters as the granting of pardons they still did so. If it was not practicable for the king to hear all suits, why did this necessarily mean he should hear none at all?

This question was urgent. James I claimed the right to sit and render judgment in any court at pleasure, for, as he declared, kings were "Iudges ouer all their subiects, and in all causes, and yet accomptable to none but God onely." If Coke had unblushingly traced his legal lineage back to Moses, James likened his relation to the law to that of God over his church. As God had originally spoken "by Oracles, and wrought by Miracles," and only later governed by means of his church, so too the first kings had ruled by fiat before setting down laws and delegating authority to their courts.[56] The inference was plain: as God had not given power to divines to blaspheme in his name, so kings had not empowered judges to pervert the law. Thus, while James assured his subjects that he had no intention of disturbing the ordinary course of justice, he reserved the right to "apply sharpe cures" when particular courts and judges overstepped their bounds or failed to consult his interests. The courts he had in mind most often were those presided over by Sir Edward Coke.

Coke responded by restating the ancient formula of the king's two bodies. In *Calvin's Case* he declared that "by the policy of the Law the King is made a body politique: So as for these special purposes the Law makes him a body politique, immortal, and invisible, whereunto our liegance cannot appertain. . . . Our Liegance is due to our natural liege Soveraign, descended of the blood Royal of the Kings of this Realm."[57] The king's custody of the law was reposed in the law's institutions, from whence his politic body had sprung and from which it was inseparable, as "invisible" — i.e., indistinguishable — as it was "immortal." To this politic body no allegiance as such was due, since in obeying the laws the subject fulfilled his obligations of loyalty and respect. Nor could the king in this aspect have any interest separate from the law, such as in his natural capacity he might. Thus, as Coke argued in the case of impositions, while the king's natural need for maintenance made a claim on his subjects' fealty, it did not authorize him in his politic capacity to reach for their purses.

Coke's argument disposed, at least to his satisfaction, of the threat to the independence of the judiciary. Although the king retained the undoubted right to appoint and remove judges, once they had sworn their oath and as long as they served they could not deal partially in any cause or consult any interest but that of justice, a point they made directly to James at Coke's instance in 1608.

The King's appeal was not only to his unique status as God's representative on earth, however, but also to the ingrained populist prejudice in the common law. If the law's function was to declare custom and custom was the common property of all Englishmen, then the courts were a mere convenience and judges had no particular wisdom denied to others. To the extent, indeed, that the courts came to represent a vested professional interest more concerned to profit by the law than to dispense it — a widespread conviction long before the early seventeenth century — the king had a right if not, arguably, a duty to intervene in their proceedings. And if Everyman had a presumed capacity to interpret the law, then why not the king himself?

James, of course, hardly considered himself an Everyman. When in the King's colloquies with his justices in November 1608 Coke suggested that the law protected him too, James went into a fury, and, according to one account, was kept from blows only by Cecil's intercession. His own comments made it clear that he considered "the King the supreme judge; inferior judges his shadows and ministers . . . and [that] the King may, if he please, sit and judge in Westminster Hall in any Court there, and call theere Judgments in question." Nothing, indeed, could have expressed more pithily the gulf between the first Stuart monarch and the common law tradition than his conclusion that "The King being the author of the Lawe is the interpreter of the Lawe."[58]

Coke's embellished account of his rejoinder to the King's claim of direct judicial authority was printed in his posthumous *Twelfth Report*:

> [T]rue it was that God had endowed his majesty with excellent science and great endowments of nature; but his majesty was not learned in the laws of his realm of England, and causes which concern the life or inheritance, or

goods, or fortunes, of his subjects; they are not to be decided by natural reason, but by the artificial reason and judgment of law, which law is an art which requires long study and experience before a man can attain to the cognisance of it; and that the law was the golden met-wand and measure to try the causes of the subject; and which protected his majesty in safety and peace. With which the King was greatly offended, and said, that then he should be under the law, which was treason to affirm, as he said. To which I said that Bracton saith *Quod rex non debet esse sub homine sed sub Deo et lege*.[59]

Coke's coolness, at least in recollection, is striking: when the King accuses him of making a treasonable statement, he records it with an *as he said*, reminding his prospective readers that monarchs are no more the judges of law than any other layperson, especially in their own causes. Even this, however, leaves the ultimate issue posed by the King unsettled: why should judges be the *sole* interpreters of the law?

Coke provides two answers to this question. The first is a narrowly legal one. Parliament, whose acts bind the king because the king himself assents to them, has confided the royal power of justice exclusively to the courts: "8 H.4. the king hath committed all his power judiciall, some in one court, and some in another, so as if any would render himselfe to the judgement of the king in such case where the king hath committed all his power judiciall to others, such a render should be to no effect. And 8 H.6. the king doth judge by his judges (the king having distributed his powers judiciall to severall courts) and the king hath wholly left matters of judicature according to his lawes to his judges."[60] James would have had an at least partial answer to this; as he said in 1621, "I scorne to be likened to the tymes of some Kings. H[enry] 6 was a sillie weake King."[61] What parliaments had done, well or ill-advisedly, could be revoked or modified by the wisdom of later parliaments (and kings). To secure more firmly what Coke considered to be the very basis of the law—the independence of judicial interpretation by impartial and learned judges—only a resort to fundamental principle would suffice.

That principle was Coke's concept of artificial reason, most cogently stated in the *First Institute*:

> [R]eason is the life of the Law, nay the Common Law it selfe is nothing else but reason, which is to be understood of an artificiall perfection of reason gotten by long studie, obseruation and experience and not every mans naturall reason, for *nemo nascitur artifex* [no one is born skilfull]. This legall reason *est summa ratio* [is the highest reason]. And therefore if all the reason that is dispersed into so many severall heads were united into one, yet could he not make such a Law as the Law of England is, because by many succession of ages it hath beene fined and refined by an infinite number of graue and learned men, and by long experience grown to such a perfection

for the gouernment of this Realme, as the old rule may be iustly verified of it *Neminem oportet esse sapientorum legibus*: No man (out of his owne private reason) ought to be wiser than the Law, which is the perfection of reason.[62]

At first, Coke seems to be affirming the scholastic chestnut that the common law, like all valid jurisprudence, conforms to the law of nature as disclosed by reason. It soon becomes clear, however, that what he has in mind is no simple congruence theory. Law is a collective social product, the "fined and refined" essence of the national experience. It is "nothing else but reason" and "the perfection of reason," and in the multiplicity of its aspects, the subtlety of its internal coherence, and the totality of its wisdom it is necessarily beyond the grasp of any single individual or generation. If St. German anticipates Vico, then, Coke reaches toward Hegel. Like the cunning of reason, the law is a sure and guiding hand; and, as with Scripture on the level of salvation, it provides everything needful for justice and comity. Of course, artificial reason does not have the status of revelation; its ends are proximate, its uses situational, and accordingly it must remain a work in progress. Precisely for that reason, however, it must be left in the hands of its adepts. For Coke, the common law was a seamless garment that perfectly fit the English nation, growing and stretching with it, and new threads could be added only by those who understood its configuration and design. No one, perhaps, could see the pattern whole; but the "graue and learned" judges of the bench, searching precedents and consulting together, were best, indeed uniquely qualified to interpret the intent of past ages in the light of present circumstances. The *Reports* were a reenactment of that process, each pleader and judge adding to the fullness of the case perspective until the law shone forth in the majesty of its appropriate determination. The process was contingent, like all human undertakings; but it was not a game for amateurs.

This, then, was Coke's fuller response to the specter of royal interference in the courts. The king had confided royal justice to his judges, a power that inhered not in his person but in his corporate office (it was James' mistake to have confused the two). This grant, implicit in the very construction of the courts as well as in their ordinary function, had been twice confirmed by statute. Statutes were, of course, revocable, and, as James was to suggest in 1621, not all were to be regarded as of equal validity. Artificial reason, however, the very wisdom of the law, was inseparable from its proper exercise. As the king could not wish that other than justice be done—such was the meaning of the ancient legal dictum that the king could do no wrong—so he could not, as king, tamper with the process by which it was done. James himself had recognized this principle in his speech of 1610 when he declared that "a King gouerning in a setled Kingdome, leaues to be a King, and degenerates into a Tyrant, assoone as he leaues off to rule according to his

Lawes."[63] What James had failed to recognize was that the essential stipulation of his laws precluded him from judging them.

Artificial reason accomplished a great deal more in the history of the common law, however. It broke a tyranny even older than that of kings, namely that of custom. It was an article of faith that law was merely declarative of custom or at most a prudent extension of it; the work of judges and legislators was, accordingly, narrow, modest, and subordinate. As long as custom was elevated above law, not merely as its source and ground but as its ideal representation, the law's development could be seen only as a regression toward origins that, like Zeno's arrow, stopped perpetually short of its target. St. German had come close to suggesting something like artificial reason in defending the praxis of the common law courts, as we have seen, only to draw back from the heretical implication that judges made law. There was indeed no way to say such a thing within the premises of Tudor legal thought, and Coke did not say it either. What he did was to overcome the traditional dichotomy between custom and law by means of a concept that united them in a single, seamless discourse. Artificial reason was simultaneously the common sense of custom and the ratiocination of jurists; it was the way the law was both devised and disclosed. Custom and law interpenetrated each other: there was no first word and no last, but only an immemorial dialogue in which judicial determination represented the best sense of the law's meaning at a given juncture. Law was, in this sense, the perfection of custom, a process by which, as Coke's metaphor of "fining and refining" was meant to signify, dross was purged and the prime ore revealed. Since case law, like custom, turned on the inexhaustible variety of circumstance, no judgment could ever fully disclose it. Fixed in its principles (though these, too, could never be definitively declared), it was protean in its capacity. What we would call legal development was thus, for Coke, the measured unfolding of immemorial wisdom in finite consciousness.

Pocock has remarked that "the idea of judge-made law is only a sophistication and extension of the idea of custom."[64] This is true, but so is the reverse: that case law is the retrospective perfecting of the *jus non scriptum*. Every significant judicial decision—every one important enough to be recorded in the *Reports* of Sir Edward Coke—was both a return to origins and an act of codification that gave the law as a whole a manifest shape and coherence, as each facet of a polished diamond shapes the whole. In the dialectic of artificial reason the law had neither a settled past nor a speculative future, but lived in the affirmation of a perennial present. It was thus Coke's genius to have assimilated case law and custom so that the historical priority of the *jus non scriptum* no longer entailed an ideological priority as well. Rather, the former was completed in the latter in a never-ending process that was the daily life of the law itself. It followed from this that judicial independence was the precondition of a law-governed society, and therefore of legitimacy as such.

The independence of the courts was secured not only by external noninterference but by their orderly functioning as well. Both James and Coke agreed on this point, although for the King, of course, royal intervention could not be construed as interference. Each court, James declared in his speech of 1610, had its own proper business and functioned best when, like a river, it kept to its own banks and channels. The question was how these boundaries were to be policed when the courts sought to usurp each other's rightful authority, "a disease," as the King noted, "very naturall to all Courts and Iurisdictions in the world." Aggrieved courts could stay wrongful proceedings in other courts by issuing writs of prohibition, but this was as likely to exacerbate the problem as to relieve it. Here as elsewhere, it was the responsibility of the king to ensure order, "For," as James commented in a lordly figure, "as God conteins the Sea within his owne bounds and marches (as it is in the *Psalmes*,) So is it my office to make euery Court conteine himselfe within his own limits."[65]

Coke's own metaphor for his self-appointed task in defining the court system in the *Fourth Institute*—he lists seventy-four jurisdictions, several of them embracing multiple courts—is equally revealing: it is, he says, like "the raising of [a] great and honourable building."[66] The palace of the law already exists, of course, but far from being grossly apparent like the sea, its true lineaments are invisible to vulgar sight, and may be discerned only by the learned. This is another way of restating the objection to royal intervention; as the king in his natural capacity is incompetent to rule in judicial causes, so by extension he cannot determine in which court given causes belong. Coke indeed affirms that "if one court should usurp, or incroach upon another, it would introduce incertainty, subvert justice, and bring all things in the end to confusion."[67] Appeal, however, cannot rest beyond the judges themselves.

For both James and Coke, the flaw in the system was not in its design but its performance. In Coke's view, the courts, like the laws themselves, were ideally the products of artificial reason; in James', of the king's dispensation of justice. Both, in short, saw the structure of the law as indefeasible, and only its operation as limited by human imperfection. For James, the politico-legal order was validated by its connection to divine will in the person of the ruler. Coke saw the law where James saw himself, as the mediating element between the cosmic order and the human one. The difference was a profound one, although James conceded that kings must rule by law and Coke that prerogative could not be directly fettered by it. What united them was their mutual conviction of a providence reflected in the just commonwealth. Divine reason was continuous and universal, artificial reason a long and arduous travail. But the latter was instant with the former, possessed of it even as it groped toward it. Through law, humanity made contact with the divine.

The dispute between James and Coke was not merely on the plane of theory, however. The victory over civil and ecclesiastical law in the 1530s had left the common law without a serious rival for several decades. By the end of the sixteenth century, though, the expansion of popular prerogative and provincial courts and the recovery of ecclesiastical jurisdiction through High Commission and its allied courts once again posed a challenge to its supremacy. The issues and stakes were essentially the same. If the king could create courts at pleasure, and those courts could then determine the law, procedure, and jurisdiction applicable to them, there was no surety for the common law and the rights it protected.

The response of common lawyers and common law judges to this new threat was both practical and theoretical. Kings had been the original founts of justice, and in their politic capacity they still were; but as they now exercised this power through established courts, they could not unilaterally alter their function either by infringing on them directly, or, what amounted to the same thing, by creating new courts that usurped their jurisdiction or introduced alien law. The touchstones of legitimacy for a given court were two: that it was immemorial, and that its status had been confirmed or recognized by act of Parliament. Thus Coke, like St. German, upheld the antiquity and authority of Chancery as a common law court:

> Certain it is, that both the British and the Saxon kings had their chancelors and court of chancery, the only court out of which originall writs doe issue. . . . The officers and ministers of this court of common law doe principally attend and doe their service to the great seal, as the twelve masters of chancery . . . who by their originall institution . . . should be expert in the common law, to see the forming and framing of originall writs according to law. . . . The processe in this court is under the great seal according to the course of the common law.[68]

On the other hand, Coke denied Chancery any equitable jurisdiction as a court of record: "there is no statute," he declared, "that gives the party grieved remedy in equity," nor was there any mention of such jurisdiction in "our ancient authors, the Mirror, Glanvill, Bracton, Britton and Fleta." As a "court of conscience" it could deal only with covin (fraud), accident, and breach of confidence, and only when there was "no remedy by the ordinary course of law." Nor could it distrain a defendant's lands, chattels, or other property: in short, lay civil penalties. It existed, as it were, in the interstices of the common law; in no case could it be regarded as a substitute for or an alternative to it.[69]

In Coke's insistence on statutory warrant for the powers of a court, especially a new one, one can see the basis of his subsequent claim for the direct exercise of parliamentary judicature not only over the courts themselves but over royal officials. Simply put, although the king could create new courts, he could not endow their judgments with the force of law except by act of Parliament; such courts, attempting to exercise warrantless authority, could be restrained and limited by Parliament; and the persons responsible for such usurpations, or more generally for soliciting, participating in, or countenancing violations of the common law, including but not limited to breaches of statute, could be held accountable judicially by Parliament, their status as crown servants notwithstanding.

Coke would promote this view from within Parliament itself, where, after his dismissal from the bench by James in 1616, he sat in the House of Commons as one of the most influential figures in parliamentary history. It was implicit, however, in his long-standing insistence on the primacy of statute in defining jurisdiction, a theme that echoed St. German's campaign to bring Chancery and the ecclesiastical courts under the common law. As the law itself had emerged from popular custom, so the estates of the realm would settle the question of where justice lay.

Parliament was, however, too blunt an instrument to deal with specific acts of judicial trespass. Its size was unwieldy, its business diverse, and its sittings problematic—it was summoned, prorogued, and dissolved at the pleasure of the monarch, and even in Elizabeth's day it had gone for extended periods without being convened. The common law judges thus relied on writs of prohibition to police the system on a regular basis. These writs were injunctions from superior to lesser courts to cease and desist from improper proceedings. Their numbers rose exponentially from the 1580s on, and culminated during Coke's time on the bench. The judges might prohibit specific cases from being heard, or challenge a general exercise of jurisdiction; thus, in 1598, Common Pleas (which Coke had not yet joined) declared the prerogative Court of Requests a *coram non judice*, a court without the right to enforce its judgments.[70] Similar campaigns were waged against the jurisdiction of the Court of Admiralty, the Council of Wales and the Marches, the Council of the North, and especially the Court of High Commission. These courts made strenuous efforts to defend themselves, but only with the accession of Richard Bancroft as Archbishop of Canterbury in 1604 was a serious counterattack launched.

The Court of High Commission had originally been a body of examiners, licensed first by Mary and then by Elizabeth, to investigate a broad range of religious and ecclesiastical offenses. By 1580, the commissioners for the Province of Canterbury had turned themselves into a court, not only making inquest but trying cases between party and party. Like the old heresy courts that had preceded them, they compelled testimony through the administration of the oath *ex officio*. This made them noxious to the godly, and seemed to give the lie to Elizabeth's promise not to make a window into men's souls.[71] They were suspect as well to the judges at Westminster, who believed they had exceeded the statutory warrant given them by the Elizabethan Act of Supremacy, and who looked askance, as always, at any procedure at variance with common law practice. The stage was thus set at the accession of James for a confrontation involving major interests. The godly had renewed their attack on church policy generally and High Commission in particular. The clerical authorities were no less determined to defend their position, to enforce conformity, and to strengthen their ties to the new king. And Sir Edward Coke was just about to become Chief Justice of the Court of Common Pleas.

Whitgift had forged High Commission into a powerful instrument of conformist policy, and he defended its jurisdiction with vigor. Bancroft, however, was determined to force a showdown with the court's common law tormentors. Armed with the new and radically conformist Canons of 1604, themselves a response to the godly stirrings at James' accession, he sought and obtained the support of the King and Council, and in October 1605 he exhibited twenty-five "Articles of Abuses" concerning prohibitions to the Council.[72] These *Articuli Cleri* protested the "frequent and undue granting of prohibitions," and the "new devised suggestion in the Temporall Courts . . . whereby they may at their will and pleasure draw any cause whatsoever from the Ecclesiasticall Court" (Articles 1, 12). They concluded that the King's powers of ecclesiastical jurisdiction were "greatly impugned by Prohibitions" if not "in effect . . . almost extinguished" (Article 22).

Bancroft's position was a strong one. In *Cawdrey's Case* (1591), which involved the appeal of a godly minister deprived for nonconformity by High Commission, the Queen's Bench had affirmed High Commission's status as a court and declared the enabling Act of 1559 only declaratory of patents which, by virtue of the royal power to dispense spiritual as well as temporal justice, had given the Commission broad latitude to deal with matters of "blasphemy, apostasy from Christianity, heresies, schisms, ordering admissions, institutions of clerks, celebration of divine service, rights of matrimony, divorces, general bastardy, subtraction and right of tithes, oblations, obventions, dilapidations, reparations of churches, probate of testaments, administrations and accounts upon the same, simony, incests, fornications, adulteries, solicitation of chastity, pensions, procurations, appeals in ecclesiastical causes, commutation of penance, and others (the conusance whereof belong not to the common laws of England) . . ."[73] This was a powerful concession. Coke, still as Attorney General a crown spokesman in 1605, wrote cautiously that "It seemeth to me very necessarie that some thing were published manifesting (without any interference or bombasting) the very words of the Auncient Laws and statutes of England . . . whereby it shall appeare, what Jurisdiction Ecclesiasticall by the auncient Laws of England, appertaine to the Crown."[74]

This "some thing" was the text and commentary posthumously published in the second volume of the *Institutes*. It included the text of Bancroft's articles with the responses of the twelve judges at Westminster, followed by the medieval statutes with Coke's commentary. The modern reader can still feel the asperity of the exchange between the ecclesiastical commissioners and the common law judges, now led by Coke himself. In protesting the granting of multiple prohibitions in the same case, the commissioners suggested sarcastically that "if we mistake any thing in the premises, we desire . . . that the Judges, for the justification of their courses, may better enform us," to which the judges as tartly replied, "It shall be good, the Ecclesiastical Judges do better enform themselves . . . and thereupon . . . find their own errour."[75] Here was battle joined in which no quarter was to be given.

The commissioners acknowledged that prohibitions had a valid place in the legal system, but complained that their indiscriminate use had the effect, if not the design, of crippling the ecclesiastical courts. They cited not only the granting of multiple prohibitions in a given case but their issuance even after judgment had been rendered; their granting upon "frivolous suggestions" not only on petition from the principals but from parties wholly outside the case; and their unwarranted deployment against settled forms of ecclesiastical jurisdiction, writ, and procedure (Articles 3, 9, 21, 23). The judges rebutted each charge in turn. Judgments in cases where proper jurisdiction was lacking were invalid; information upon such usurped authority or other material issues might be received at any time and from any source; all forms of proceeding were subject to judicial review.

A telling if humble example of the turf wars between the commissioners and the judges appears in Article 9. The ecclesiastical courts had arrested a woman "for adultery committed with one that suspiciously resorted to her house in the night time," but the temporal judges assumed jurisdiction on the grounds that nothing had been shown "but night walking," which suggested burglary or theft instead. The commissioners accused the judges of attempting to usurp all cases not pertaining to matrimonial or testamentary matters, thereby "to strike away at one blow the whole Ecclesiastical Jurisdiction" (Article 13). Disputes over tithes were particularly vexed. The judges conceded that tithes lay originally under ecclesiastical jurisdiction, but that once sold or converted they became chattels subject to the common law. As ecclesiastical properties and revenues alike declined and more and more livings passed under lay control, actions over tithes multiplied, heightening the stakes over muddied definitions of spiritual and temporal goods.[76] Nor were matters eased when George Carleton, a rising star in the Jacobean church, published his *Tithes examined and proved to be due to the clergy by Di-*

vine Right in 1606. It was a short step from the King's insistence that his divine right authority was exempt from all temporal jurisdiction to a similar claim on behalf of clerical fruits.

The common law judges responded that by statute and precedent they had an unassailable right to grant prohibitions *de modo decimandi*, a position Coke strongly supported in his analysis of clerical legislation.[77] The commissioners attacked this position on three fronts. The precedent cited from Edward IV's time was grounded in "a quirk and false suggestion" and could not "with any sound reason" be maintained. The general assertion that temporal courts had jurisdiction over ecclesiastical causes because the church had been established by an Act of Parliament was absurd; one might argue by the same token that they could judge "all causes of Faith and Religion" because the Book of Common Prayer and the Articles of Religion had also been ratified by statute. Finally, where the meaning of a statute was at issue, it was best referred to the impartial wisdom of the Chancellor, as were jurisdictional disputes in general. For good measure, the commissioners suggested that all prohibitions "upon surmise" should be issued through the Chancellor's court as well.[78]

The commissioners' tactical maneuver in appealing to the Chancellor was not only a bid to establish his office as an arbiter in all disputes between the two branches of the King's justice, but an open solicitation to James himself to intervene personally. If, after all, the godly backers of the Millenary Petition could get a royal audience by appealing directly to the King, forcing the bishops to defend their just authority before the adversaries they had so lately brought to heel, then why could the common law judges not be brought to account for their outrageous claims? It was, of course, necessary for government officials to appeal through proper channels, and it was politic as well for Archbishop Bancroft to enlist his good friend Thomas Egerton, who as Attorney General had enforced the conformist crackdown on godly dissenters and Separatists in the mid-1590s, and who now as Baron Ellesmere and Lord Chancellor had moved to expand the business of his court and to reassert its preeminence. Ellesmere could not only be counted on to endorse the notion that prohibitions should henceforth originate in Chancery; he had already signaled his view that it could hear appeals from the judgments of common law courts, the judges' ruling to the contrary in the case of *Finch v. Throgmorton* (1598) notwithstanding. Nor was the Chancellor Bancroft's only ally. Sir Francis Bacon, the King's Counsel and Ellesmere's eventual successor as Lord Chancellor, held the chancellor to be above all common law judges, singly or collectively, and his jurisdiction in civil and criminal causes superior. The prerogative court justices, notably the Master of Requests, Sir Julius Caesar, were chafing at the restraints placed on them by the judges at Westminster. The civil lawyers who practiced in these courts

had already submitted petitions both to James and to Bancroft begging relief
from the "swarm" of prohibitions that, as they contended, were ruining their
practice. Legists such as Edward Hake provided ideological support for regarding equity, rather than the common law, as the true law of conscience.[79]
Despite the high tone taken by the judges in their response to Bancroft's Articles, their position was far from invulnerable.

The judges' case rested on their undoubted right to regulate the proceedings of all inferior courts through the writ of prohibition, a task they were
sworn to and could only be relieved of by statute. As they noted in response
to the suggestion that such writs should originate in Chancery, it was:

> A strange presumption in the Ecclesiasticall Judges, to require that the
> Kings Courts should not doe that which by law they ought to doe, and al-
> wayes have done, and which by oath they are bound to doe! And if this
> shall be holden inconvenient, and they can in discharge of us obtain some
> Act of Parliament to take [prohibitions] from all other Courts then the
> Chancery, they shall doe us a great ease: but the law of the Realm cannot be
> changed, but by Act of Parliament.[80]

The judges picked no quarrel with the Chancellor, but only pointed out
that he lacked power to accept, as they to decline, a jurisdiction that could be
altered only by Parliament. Absent such action, the judges themselves were,
as Coke commented, "for matters of law of highest Authority next unto the
Court of Parliament," and thus *a fortiori* the sole arbiters of their own powers
and prerogatives. Moreover, the judges remained the final interpreters of all
laws, whether old or new, since, as they declared, "we never heard it excepted unto heretofore, that any statute should be expounded by any other
then the Judges of the land."[81]

Such an argument presupposed, though it dared not state, that the King
could act only in his politic capacity with respect to the laws. As the source
of justice, he was present in all his courts, but what was acted in his name
could be done only according to established forms and procedures. James
himself had allowed that kings in "settled" states should rule by ordinary legal process. What he would not concede, however, was that they could not
suspend or supersede such process at their discretion. James was not alone
in this belief. Sir Julius Caesar, in defending the right of the sovereign to create new jurisdictions against the finding of the Common Pleas judges that
the Court of Requests was a *coram non judice*, declared that the power to set
aside even statutes was "grounded upon that most certaine observation that
every prince imperially raigning is at free libertie for all lawes possitive to
annihilate the same."[82] This was of course a reference to the Henrician acts
declaring England's Crown Imperial to be fully sovereign and independent,
and by extension as freely dispositive of its laws as any other Christian monarchy. The claim that the king could unilaterally revoke statutes, particularly

those that trenched on his authority, went back to Edward III, who asserted that acts of Parliament restraining the royal prerogative were void. In this the crown had the apparent support of Bracton, who stated that its powers could not be legally alienated, and of Parliament itself in the Statute of York (1322). This tradition, which characterized what James liked to call "free" monarchies and what in the parlance of the early seventeenth century would be called "absolute" ones, was summed up in Seneca's dictum, that "To kings belong authority over all men, to subjects ownership" (*Ad reges enim potestas omnium pertinet, ad singulos proprietas*). The implication was that the public sphere was the sole possession of the sovereign, and that what concerned the subject was limited to private questions of *meum et tuum*. The sovereign might take counsel of his estates and act in concert with them, but their will could never conclude his, nor their acts have force without him.

Such a doctrine was designed to preclude the argument that the judges were to make in their response to Bancroft's Articles. The law, they contended, was secure as long as it rested with corporate bodies such as the common law judges, who represented its accumulated wisdom, and the houses of Parliament, in which the body of the realm was gathered. Parliament alone could give definitive statement to the law through statute, and the judges alone could declare what statutory acts meant in the context of previous statutes and judicial decisions. There was thus a necessary and indissoluble connection between the common law courts and the High Court of Parliament. The king's will was comprehended in theirs, directly in the assent he gave to parliamentary bills, indirectly in the justice done in his name. For him to participate or to intervene in person was to slip from his politic into his private capacity, in which he became, precisely, the private individual of imperial theory whose personal *meum et tuum* was not for him to judge. It was, moreover, only a short step from the claim that the king could annul statutes (his power to override them in time of emergency was conceded even by Coke) to asserting, as Henry VIII had done, that his own pronouncements had the force of law, and that statutes were merely royal proclamations endorsed by the estates of the realm.

These matters came to a head after 1607, when James in conference with the judges asserted his right to decide cases and to set jurisdictional limits personally. It was on this occasion that Coke enunciated his doctrine of artificial reason, which at one stroke expressed the rationale for the judges' counterclaim to be the sole interpreters of the law and, by confining the King's interest to his politic capacity, to comprehend his own judgment in it. It would be difficult to overstate the importance of this doctrine in its political context, and those commentators who complain of its reification of the common law or who criticize it from the point of view of later, positivistic assumptions about lawmaking quite miss the point of its significance. It erected an ideological barrier to the concept of personal rule, later further developed through the allied notions of fundamental law and the subject's inalienable political right, and if it did not wholly restrain James or keep his successor from putting his own version of personal rule into effect, it provided the basis for the parliamentary resistance of the 1620s, for the recuperation of constitutional government in the early years of the Long Parliament, and finally for the incorporation of the king's politic capacity into the autonomous Parliament of the Civil War. If Coke's construction looked backward not only to medieval precedent but to medieval premises about the law rather than to the positivism espoused by his brilliant young contemporary John Selden or the even more radical critique of his great adversary Thomas Hobbes, it was its very conservatism that commended it to a broad seventeenth-century audience.

The further story of the struggle over prohibitions has been frequently told, and needs no detailed rehearsal. The common law judges, under Coke's aggressive leadership, answered the challenge to their authority by redoubling their grants of the writ, virtually crippling not only the ecclesiastical courts but the Court of Admiralty as well. When in 1611 Coke himself issued a prohibition in the case of one Cheekitt, a parishioner of St. Botolphe in London accused of heresy and schism, an exasperated High Commission once again asked for a royal conference. For Coke, the issue was Cheekitt's refusal to take the *ex officio* oath until presented with the charges against him; for High Commission, it was an invasion of its most fundamental responsibility, the preservation of church doctrine and governance.

In authorizing what he called "a lovinge and friendly Conference" between the temporal and ecclesiastical judges, James cloaked the renewed threat of his own direct intervention in characteristically pacifist rhetoric, warning that "if noe other peaceable course could be taken amongst themselues, he might at length sett downe *some further or finall order* therein as to Justice . . . houldinge it noe small infortunitie to himselfe that fyndinge all thinges at peace att his cominge hether, and being himselfe soe much addicted to peace . . . he should finde these great differences to arise."[83] At the same time, Ellesmere sought to promote an acceptable compromise.[84] The issues, however, were fundamental, and Coke stood upon them. The ecclesiastical courts, he asserted, not only routinely exceeded their jurisdiction, which was in his view limited to heresy, schism, incest, polygamy, and recusancy, and not only employed procedures such as the *ex officio* oath that were repugnant to the common law, but their refusal to accept prohibitions amounted to a claim of exemption from all judicial review. Judgments in Common Pleas were reversible in the King's Bench; judgments in the King's Bench were reversible in the House of Lords; Acts of Parliament were expounded by the judges; all statutes and decisions were finally subject to the immemorial sense of the common law itself, against which no act or judgment could stand. This process of review, flowing upwards to the High Court of Parliament from all lesser courts and thence back again, was the very pulse of artificial reason. To stand outside it, as the church courts claimed to do, acknowledging no superior but the "Kings authority ecclesiasticall" itself, was to stand outside the law.[85]

The commissioners were not the only ones to reject this reasoning. Chancellor Ellesmere acknowledged that prohibitions were valid in some cases, but he argued that once suits had begun they should in general be allowed to proceed in the courts in which they had been filed, lest entire jurisdictions be usurped. This was the clear direction in which prohibitions in the case of tithes tended: "And if such Actions shall bee continued," he went on, "it will, in tyme, fall out, that all suites for Tythes, will be drawne into ye Temporall Courts, and soe they will determine of ye right of Tythes in all Cases." This was a palpable absurdity. As to the argument that ecclesiastical commissioners should not be judges in their own causes, Ellesmere replied tartly that "The like may bee obiected against all Temporall Iudges, and with more reason and probabilitye, for they haue large possessions, for which they and their Tenants (which are many and wealthie) ought to pay Tithes." Like the commissioners, he argued that prohibitions were to be granted only upon fact and not upon mere allegation ("suggestions"), and were to be issued only under the Great Seal in Chancery in the name of the king, not by judges themselves and "vnder the subordinate seale of the[ir] Court[s]." His concurrence with the commissioners on virtually every point in debate, and with the arguments raised previously in Bancroft's Articles, strongly supports the conclusion that Ellesmere had been in close consultation if not in league with the Archbishop (and now in 1611 with his successor, George Abbot) from the inception of the controversy. Certainly there was no love lost between Ellesmere and Coke. In his "Observacions vpon ye Lord Cookes Reportes" (1615) he accused him of misrepresenting cases, some of which he had been a party to, and of having "purposely Laboured to derogate much from the Rights of the Church and dignity of churchmen, and to disesteeme and weaken the power of ye King in the ancient vse of his Prorogatiue." The Jacobean theme of "no bishop, no king" was plainly in evidence here.[86]

Not surprisingly, Ellesmere rejected as well the contention that the common law judges were the final arbiters of all law in the realm of whatever provenance, including statute. This claim was particularly vexed in relation to royal proclamations. Henry VIII's 1539 Statute of Proclamations had been, from one perspective, an attempt to place the King in Council (by whose authority proclamations were issued) on an equal footing with the authority of the King in Parliament and in his other courts. Since the authority of the King in Council had actually been prior to the legislative power of Parliament (although Coke and other commentators regarded the latter, to all intents and purposes, as immemorial), Henry could in a sense claim that he was only restoring the *lex coronae* to its proper place beside the *lex parliamenti*. The king's power to give justice under his seal was indefeasible; in whichever forum it issued, it was absolute and complete.[87]

The hasty repeal of the Statute by Edward VI's first parliament seemed to reaffirm the preeminence of the King in Parliament. Mary and Elizabeth, however, had continued to use proclamations in ways that encroached on legislative authority, for example the decreeing of capital penalties for idlers and vagabonds, or the limitation of freehold by forbidding the erection of new buildings in London. Elizabeth and James had both used proclamations to enforce conformity and to deprive recalcitrant ministers, thereby offending both the law of God and the law of the land in the eyes of godly parliamentarians. James had rather vauntingly issued a Book of Proclamations, suggesting that even proclamations of a temporary and limited character had a place in the permanent legal record as expressions of the king's will, a suspicion deepened by the almost simultaneous publication of *The Interpreter*, a book by the civilian John Cowell that suggested the King's right to rule by decree. By 1610, complaints against specific proclamations were so numerous that the parliamentary catalog of them filled four folio pages. James was compelled to agree to refer the question of proclamations to the judges, and even to issue a proclamation against *The Interpreter*, which was burned by the common hangman.[88]

The King's consultation with the judges began with a preemptive strike. On September 20, 1611, he called Coke into conference with his councillors. Salisbury launched into a defense of James' proclamations against the erection of new buildings and the adulteration of wheat, responses, as he reminded Coke, to matters presented to him as grievances. Coke protested that he had not been informed of the subject of discussion until that very morning, and asked leave to consult his fellow judges in order to "make an advised answer according to law and reason." Ellesmere then dropped the hammer. Proclamations, backed by penalties, should be regarded as having the force of law, and if a clear precedent for this was lacking, the moment had come to create one:

> The Lord Chancellor said, that every President had a first commencement, and that he would advise the Judges to maintain the power and Prerogative of the King to order in it according to his wisdome, and for the good of his Subjects, or otherwise the King would be no more than the Duke of Venice.[89]

The King's power to issue necessary decrees based on his responsibility for the welfare of his subjects was the very essence of the royal prerogative. As Ellesmere had argued in *Calvin's Case*, the acts of the King in Council had been accepted as law as far back as the medieval Statutes of Merton, subject only (like all laws and customs) to the subsequent judgment of the King in Parliament. The royal will was thus seamless and continuous, the *lex coronae* being perfected by the *lex parliamenti*. This left, however, a considerable question: what of the role of the judges? Their ordinary task was to rule in cases of party against party according to "knowne Principles and Maximes, and ancient Customs, against which there never hath been, nor ought to bee any dispute," or by established precedent, or in the absence of both by consultation and collective judgment, but in all cases by and under "the Kings authoritie." The judges were upon request to give their opinions on disputed points before the Council and in Parliament. In no sphere did they operate as independent agents, although their judgments, as such, stood for law, subject always to the King in Parliament.[90]

In a narrow sense, there was nothing in this view that Coke could have disputed, and many passages in the *Institutes* and the *Reports* could be found to support it. In spirit, however, it was clearly antithetical to the position Coke had staked out for the judges as the sworn defenders of a common law whose strict enforcement and precise interpretation "protected" royal authority no less than the subject's right. Ellesmere certainly thought so. In his "Observacions" on Coke, begun two years later after Coke had become Chief Justice of the King's Bench, he noted that "Whether they be in point of Estate or in point of power, in all his reports he hath stood so much in phrase vpon the King <<s>> honour, as in his Resolucions he hath had no respect to the Kings profitt," charging that in every case he had ruled or commented on as a judge "every Pattent is made good whereby the King parteth with his Inheritance, and every Pattent is made void by which his Maiestie would expresse his Power in dispencing with thinges forbidden, or grant his power in doeing such thinges as formerly had beene done by the like Pattent." His purpose, Ellesmere said, was to engross the King's authority into the Court of King's Bench both by circumscribing the royal prerogative and by curbing the jurisdiction of other courts:

> Werein in giueinge excesse of authoritye to the Kings Bench he doth as much as insinuate that this Court is all sufficient in it selfe to manage the state. For if the Kings Bench may reforme any manner of Misgovernement (as the Words are),[91] it seemeth that their is little or noe vse either of the Kings Royall Care and authoritye exercised in his person and by his proclamacions, ordinances and imediate direccions, nor of the Councell Table, which vnder the King is ye cheife watchtower for all misgovernement, nor of the Star chamber, which hath ever been esteemed the highest Court for extinguishment of all riotts and publike disorders and enormities. And besides, the words do import as if the Kings bench had a superinterdepen-

dency over the governement it selfe, and to iudge wherein any of theym doe misgoverne.[92]

Coke, according to his posthumously published account, stood his ground before the Council, made a general demurrer, and insisted on being permitted to consult with his colleagues. The attempt to surprise or browbeat him into a concession having (predictably) failed, he rallied the judges to declare:

> that the King by his Proclamation cannot create any Offence which was not an Offence before, for then he may alter the Law of the Land by his Proclamation in a high point, for if he may create an Offence where none is, upon that ensues fine and imprisonment: Also the Law of England is divided into three parts, Common Law, Statute Law, and Custom; But the Kings Proclamation is none of them . . . Also it was resolved, that the King hath no prerogative, but that which the Law of the Land allows him. But the King for prevention of Offences, may by Proclamation admonish his Subjects that they keep the Lawes, and do not offend them; upon punishment to be inflicted by the Law, &c. Lastly, if the offence be not punishable in the Star Chamber, the Prohibition of it by Proclamation cannot make it punishable there.

Coke (or his editors) added that "after this resolution, no Proclamation imposing Fine and Imprisonment, was afterwards made."[93] Technically, this was correct; but proclamations continued to create, as the judges had put it, offenses where none had been before, and to impose both civil and ecclesiastical penalties through Star Chamber and High Commission. An example of this was the series of proclamations, first issued by Elizabeth in 1596 and repeated at intervals by James and Charles, enjoining the gentry to quit London and take up residence on their estates. There is at least one instance of a prosecution in Star Chamber under the Elizabethan proclamation, and there were a great many of them in the 1630s under Charles, one of which, that of William Palmer, resulted in a fine of £1,000. If widespread elite social patterns could be turned into punishable offenses, new burdens and obligations could be imposed by fiat as well; when the Caroline Book of Orders mandated the employment of pauper apprentices, one resister protested that such acts were not "compellable . . . by law" and that "the Lords of the Council could not impose any such thing upon them."[94] Ordinary Englishmen had learned the lessons that Coke taught them, and even if the crown continued to legislate in effect through the Council, they knew that "the Law of England is divided into three parts . . . But the Kings Proclamation is none of them." Sir John Eliot refused to recognize the jurisdiction of the Star Chamber that imprisoned him after the Parliament of 1628–1629, John Lilburne rejected its attempt to administer an oath to him, and the lawyer William Prynne, together with his godly colleagues Leighton, Bastwick, and Burton, defied the High Commission. Coke's removal from the bench was already bruited by 1611, when Sir Thomas Lake, the King's Secretary, reported that unless he could defend his most recent prohibitions, "the King will dismiss him, and no longer be vexed with him."[95] The ensuing conference, and the subsequent one on proclamations, may have been designed in part to provide a pretext for just that purpose, but if so Coke shrewdly slipped the trap, refusing to offer any opinion without the concurrence of his colleagues. The net result was a political debacle for the crown. Stuart Babbage noted that the conference on prohibitions ended "inconclusively,"[96] but this meant simply that the judges had offered no concessions and High Commission had obtained no relief. The conference on proclamations yielded only a sweeping rejection of royal claims to exercise jurisdiction outside the common law. This could not, as the event proved, prevent the King from acting on those claims, but the gratuitous opportunity presented Coke and his colleagues to put on record a challenge to his authority was a serious mistake. James himself was highly sensitive to any attempt to define, let alone constrain his prerogative; yet his own theoretical assertions of it invited precisely such efforts.

The problem of Coke remained. His promotion to the King's Bench two years later was widely interpreted as an attempt to limit his caseload and the scope of his decisions. The running series of hostile commentaries Ellesmere undertook on his rulings was plainly designed not only to monitor his performance but to support a case for dismissal. Bacon, who was angling for the now-moribund Ellesmere's place, and Abbot, who had openly sought Coke's removal since 1612, also joined the hunt.[97]

Suitable grounds for action were not long in presenting themselves. The proximate causes of Coke's fall were his refusal to yield to the crown's demand for a pretrial conference with individual judges in the case of Edmond Peacham, a Somerset rector among whose papers had been found speculations about the King's death, and his rejection of a writ for a stay of proceedings in the case of *Commendams*, which concerned the disputed grant of a benefice to Richard Neile, Bishop of Lichfield, until a similar consultation could be held. James was certainly wroth about the issues involved in these cases; he even wrote a brief in his own hand against Peacham. Coke was equally adamant about the "auricular taking of opinions, single and apart" prior to the commencement of trial.[98] Their uncompromising stances laid bare the fundamental incompatibility between a conception of judges as royal officers bound to consult the king's interest, as James put it, in all matters of "honor and profit" to him, and one which saw them as servants of the law whose oaths precluded them from partiality in any cause.

The issue between king and jurist, however, was finally one about the constitutional division of authority. In *Bagg's Case*, which had particularly incensed Ellesmere, Coke laid down a doctrine so sweeping that it seemed to erect a parallel government in the judiciary, and particularly in Coke's own court:

> That Authority doth belong to the Kings Bench, not only to correct errors in judicial proceedings, but othet [sic] errors and misdemeanors extrajudicial tending to the breach of peace, or the oppression of the subjects, or to the raising of faction, controversies or debate, or to any manner of misgovernment; so that no wrong or injury, either publick or private can be done, but that the same shall be reformed or punished by the due course of the Law.[99]

In his commentary on *Darcy v. Allen* (1602) and in the *Earl of Devonshire's Case*, Coke seemed to suggest that the courts could void royal patents or any other commands going out under the privy seal if they were founded upon "false suggestion," an offense also cited in issuing prohibitions.[100] If the cumulative effect of Coke's rulings were not, as James complained, to turn the king into a doge of Venice, they were certainly far from James' conception of a "free" monarchy. The wonder is not that the King's patience finally exhausted itself, but that it had lasted so long.

James R. Stoner Jr. comments on Coke's conception of the law that "His question . . . is always first and foremost, what is law?—not, who rules? . . . The priority of law itself over the particular bodies that enforce it appears a fixed principle in Coke's understanding. It is implied in his defining jurisdiction by law, rather than defining law by its source. It is consistent with his stress on the importance of learning in law: Not where one sits, but what one knows ultimately counts most."[101] For Coke, however, the power to know the law was inseparable from the right to exercise it. In his mature thought, this meant that the judiciary was the centerpiece of constitutional government, not merely interpreting the law but actively superintending its exercise. As his contemporary critics pointed out, though, Coke had espoused a much more unfettered view of the royal prerogative in his days as the King's Attorney, just as, in the final phase of his career as the oracle of the House of Commons, he was to locate preeminent authority in the High Court of Parliament.[102] A consideration of that subject must await our general discussion of Parliament. But the impression that Coke's sense of the locus of constitutional authority tended to gravitate with the particular office and function he exercised is a powerful one. As Stoner notes, apropos of Coke's parliamentary career, "If authority follows wisdom, and if Coke thought himself the most learned lawyer in England . . . then a Parliament filled with lawyers of the stamp of Edward Coke, John Eliot, William Prynne, and others surely was a more reliable source of knowing what the law was than a judiciary packed with Stuart courtiers."[103] We need not imagine that Coke would have placed himself on the level of Eliot (no lawyer at all) or Prynne to take the point that the artificial reason of the law was best embodied in its most artful reasoner, and that, in consequence, the seat of the law was where Sir Edward

Coke sat. Coke therefore succeeded in two almost antithetical projects: to reify the common law as a mystical entity beyond the reach and ken of any mortal, and at the same time to personify it in himself. It was no matter that minds nearly as good as his own, such as Ellesmere's, or even better, such as Bacon's, had very different notions of the common law, seeing it in the broad context of the civil law tradition as one rather idiosyncratic system among many, and even in England as only *primus inter pares*. Coke's uncanny ability to position himself at the center of every juridico-political controversy in a generation that debated the fundamentals of authority as never before, and to pronounce the most authoritative if not the final word on most of them, gave him an influence such as no private subject had enjoyed since the accession of the Tudors. That in itself, in a man who had neither broad acres nor ancient title, and who deployed no other weapon than the power of argument, marked a sea change in the English polity. Before King Pym, the sovereignty of law had been exalted by King Coke.

The Ancient Constitution and the Quest for Legal Origins

The idea that England possessed an "ancient constitution" is perhaps one more sharply delineated in the minds of modern historians than it was in those of early Stuart Englishmen.[104] It seems to have been a missing term in Coke's thought, which, framed as it was between immemorial custom (the ahistorical accretion of folk wisdom) and judicial interpretation (the case-specific wisdom of judges), had little room for constitutional speculation as such. Even Coke's general discussion of the English judiciary in the *Fourth Institute* focuses on each court as a separate entity rather than on the systemic unity of the whole. Nor was Coke atypical, let alone unique in this regard. England was, for most Englishmen, a mosaic of rights, privileges, franchises, and liberties. Some of these, such as those guaranteed in the general clauses of Magna Carta, were common to all Englishmen; the vast majority, such as those spelled out in the far more numerous specific clauses of the Charter, were the property of particular groups or individuals. English law was singularly devoted to giving each man his own.

Law served the general welfare, of course, but it did so by preserving individual right. This was theme of all of Coke's great judicial decisions and glosses, in *Bonham*, in *Calvin*, and in *Darcy v. Allen*. "Power" was simply the scope allotted to each individual or institution by the law. This included the king. James had objected to the suggestion that the king was "under" the law, but what Coke meant was that the royal function was inseparable from the law, indeed inconceivable apart from it. This comprehended the king's discretion, or what was fashionably called his "absolute" prerogative, as well;[105] the king could never act outside or against the law, to which he was bound (as James himself had conceded) by his coronation oath. Subjects, corporations, and magistrates were all children of the law: when they acted within their proper compass, both their own legitimate interests and the general welfare were served; when they exceeded them, the law would return them to their bounds. This atomistic structure was held fast, of course, by a hierarchy of authority, just as the law itself was contained within the discourses of reason and revelation, but all agents, high or low, operated within prescribed limits. Law alone, in Coke's universe, was sovereign; and sovereignty never meant for him what it did for Bodin and Hobbes, unaccountable power. It was, rather, the system by which all power was accounted for.

Coke's system was coherent in its own terms, but it excluded a great deal. It had no discourse of origins, and no theory of distributive authority. Customs or institutions were just as they happened to be, and in essence if not in every particular as they had always been: thus, for example, Stuart parliaments were continuous with Saxon ones. Coke relied for such assertions on a selective and sometimes tendentious reading of ancient records such as the *Modus Tenendi Parliamentum*, the allegedly fourteenth-century treatise that purported to describe the pre-Conquest parliaments of Edward the Confessor. The authenticity of these documents was not of ultimate concern, since if one were discredited another could be found, and if none could be found the general predicate was true that all surviving custom was both immemorial and immortal (though obviously the problem of verification was of greater moment in dealing with legal precedents as such).

While Coke's methodology might suffice in the arena of jurisprudence — and even here, as we have seen, it was not without its critics — it was vulnerable to Continental standards of scholarship represented by resident aliens such as the Italians Marcantonio De Dominis and Alberico Gentili, Regius Professor of Civil Law at Oxford, and the Fleming Hadrian Saravia, like De Dominis a defender of divine right episcopacy.[106] Continental political theorists, adhering to Aristotelian and civilian tradition, tended to emphasize the nature and origins of polities in a far more disjunctive fashion than their English counterparts, and, since Machiavelli and Bodin, to concentrate far more narrowly on the locus and operation of power. To such thinkers, a nation's identity was bound up with its formal political constitution, from which its governing institutions and legal system were derived, and which confirmed or disallowed all custom. That the particular or "municipal" laws of a commonwealth should generate its political institutions rather than the other way around would have seemed to them a perverse if not a preposterous idea. Law, for Continental theorists, was a rational means adopted to a political end through appropriate constitutional processes.

There was one significant native commentator who thought along such lines in England, Sir Francis Bacon. Bacon was a trained common lawyer; he spent his last years in residence at Gray's Inn, and was for ten years its treasurer. At the same time he was thoroughly conversant with the civil law tradition, urging its study and, where appropriate, its application. Bacon's view of both the common and the civil law was instrumental. In his *Reading Upon the Statute of Uses*, delivered as a course of lectures at Gray's Inn in 1600, he derived the use from "common reason" employed in the protection of estates. The devising of ad hoc practices to this end was an entry upon the domain of common law, for, as Bacon asserted, "common reason is common law." He then made a rather breathtaking leap:

> [C]ommon law is common reason, . . . but common reason doth define that uses should be remedied in conscience and not in Courts of law, and ordered by rules in conscience and not by strait cases of law; for the common law hath a kind of rule and survey over the chancery . . .[107]

With that elegant bit of logic-chopping, Bacon removed uses entirely from the cognizance of the common law courts, transferring them to Chancery because, as he blandly noted, it too was part of the common law system. This neatly stood St. German's effort to integrate Chancery with the common law courts on its head. In part, Bacon was responding to the loopholes created by common lawyers to avoid the formal registration of uses contemplated in the Statute of 1536, thereby perpetuating the evasion of taxes that had been the chief attraction of the practice. But his point was more general and radical. Coke interpreted the Statute as requiring all uses to submit themselves *de novo* to common law rules (adjudicated, of course, in common law courts); Bacon, however, argued that the Statute itself spelled out the determining factor in all legal uses, namely the creation of a taxable entity, and provided sufficient direction for devising them. As before the Statute, so after, equitable disputes about uses could be referred to Chancery, and the pettifogging tricks of common lawyers that had made the Statute necessary need no longer trouble either crown or commonwealth.

In contrast, then, to Coke's conception of the law as residing ultimately in the wisdom of common law justices, Bacon regarded lawmaking as a constitutional act neither bound by custom nor subject to review, and requiring only full and perspicuous statement to make its meaning clear. The Statute of Uses, he believed, was an excellent example of such a law. The preamble of the Act set out its occasion and intent; the body, its specific prescriptions and remedies; and its ancillary clauses—what Bacon called its "savings and provisoes"—anticipated any difficulties in application. To parse the Statute properly required only native wit and the application of the rules governing common law procedure. These rules were not, as in St. German, laboriously derived from custom and precedent—*regulae positivae*—but from the application of principles governed ultimately by reason and equity to a body of law, or *regulae rationales*. Bacon culled twenty-five such principles in *A Collection*

of Some Principal Rules and Maximes of the Common Lawes (1596–1597; published 1631).[108] He made it clear that when *regulae positivae* conflicted with
regulae rationales, the latter were to prevail:

> The law hath many grounds and positive learnings, which are not of the
> highest rules of reason, which are *legum leges*, such as we have here col-
> lected, but yet are learnings received, which the law hath set down and will
> not have called into question: these may be rather called *placita iuris* than
> *regulae juris*. With such maxims the law will dispense, rather than crimes
> and wrongs should be unpunished; *quia salus populi suprema lex*, and *salus
> populi* is contained in the repressing offences by punishment.[109]

Nothing could better demonstrate the rationalist, civilian temper of Bacon's
thought than this passage. Mere "learnings received," even if "set down" by
the law, were necessarily subordinate to the *regulae rationales* that were *legum
leges* and served the fixed ends of justice. These alone were in truth the
"Maximes of the Common Lawes," in the sense that they governed all municipal laws. As St. German had assimilated equity to the common law, denying it any scope beyond its bounds, so Bacon now defined the common
law in a manner that subsumed it under a broader civil law tradition that
took precedence over it not only in historical terms but as a matter of actual
practice. This was what Bacon had in mind when he made the odd-seeming
comment that disputes over uses could be referred to Chancery because it
was governed by common law rules. In Bacon's conception, such rules were
rules of reason, and the "common law" itself just the local expression of that
greater commonalty to which all municipal laws belonged. To be sure,
Coke's common law was rational too, but it was a rationality embedded in
custom and inseparable from it. What for Coke was the essence of the law —
the unbroken chain of artificial reason that linked custom, precedent, and
statute through judicial declaration — was for Bacon a husk to be discarded
when it produced an absurd (or inconvenient) result, whether in terms of
justice, equity, or — a short step further — reason of state.[110] Bacon may be said
to have taken that step in an unpublished text, the *Aphorismi de Jure gentium
maiore, sive de fontibus Justiciae et Juris* [*Aphorism on the Greater Law of Nations,
or the Fountains of Justice and Law*]:

> Certainly it partakes of a higher science to comprehend the force of equity
> that has suffused and penetrated the very nature of human society. And it
> should not be concealed that both philosophers and lawyers seem little
> suited or proper for this work. Philosophers, who wander the pleasant by-
> ways of contemplation, ornament civil activities more than they improve
> them; and lawyers, bound by their rules and formulae, do not employ a free
> and higher judgment. Truly this work and endeavor belongs chiefly to
> statesmen and those skilled in public affairs who have learned about hu-

man dispositions, compulsions and habits by much practice and attentive reading, listening, and observation.[111]

It would have taken little imagination for contemporaries to identify this ideal statesman-scholar with their own British Solomon. James I had told his justices that he was not only perfectly capable of judging the laws for himself but better suited to do so than anyone else; his Attorney General and future Lord Chancellor apparently agreed.

"One Kingdom, Intirely Governed": The Anglo-Scottish Union and the Challenge of Absolutism

The relation of English law to that of foreign nations was not merely a theoretical question. The unification of crowns that occurred in 1603 with the accession of James VI of Scotland as James I of England raised at once the question of a broader political and legal rapprochement between the two nations. James' comprehensive call for a "perfect union" of both realms set in motion a debate that dominated the first five years of his reign in England, and a process that eventuated in their mutual incorporation a century later.

At first blush, the union of the realms seemed a natural fulfillment of the vision of a single, imperial rule embracing the whole island of Britain that stretched back to the Roman conquest. It was implicit in the military campaigns of Edward I, Henry VIII, and Protector Somerset, and in the treaties of Greenwich (1543), which projected the union of the English and Scottish crowns through the marriage of Prince Edward and Mary Stuart. What had not been contemplated was a union between juridical equals in which rude and barbarous Scotland was, by virtue of James' accession to the English throne, the senior partner. While, therefore, James' journey southward in 1603 was greeted with predictable encomiums in sermon and verse on the union of the two crowns, there was great anxiety, not to say foreboding, about its effect on the integrity of English institutions. England and Scotland were countries with differing languages, differing civil and ecclesiastical polities, and differing legal systems. In sum, they were, their common habitation of an island notwithstanding, arguably as dissimilar as Normandy and Saxon England had been in 1066. Not a few Englishmen regarded a "perfect union" as the greatest threat to English institutions since the Norman invasion.

James made clear his hopes for the scope of the union in 1604 when he told Parliament that "His wish, above all things, was at his death to leave: one worship to God: one kingdom, intirely governed: one uniformity in laws."[112] On the first point, James had already reassured the English clergy. His acute distaste for the Scottish Kirk was notorious, and he devoted much of the English period of his reign to replacing it with an Anglican-style episcopacy, a process brought to ruinous fruition by his son. On the second point, England and Scotland were to remain a dual monarchy, their crowns and political administrations separate and distinct although united in one person. The third point, however, presented a tangle of difficulties, as even such an enthusiast of union as Bacon appreciated. The slightest alteration in juridical status between either nation beyond the bare fact that they now shared the same ruler could have cataclysmic effects on their legal and constitutional integrity, and such alterations were in the course of time inevitable.

The implications of union, then, were such that a member of the Lower House could remark without exaggeration that it was "the weightiest cause" ever brought before a Parliament, a phrase repeated by Coke on behalf of the Court of Common Pleas when *Calvin's Case*, which involved the legal status of the so-called post-nati, children born in Scotland after 1603, came before him. It might indeed be said that the Jacobean Long Parliament of 1604–1610 was as important for its success in deflecting the King's proposals for Union as Henry VIII's Reformation Parliament had been in legislating the break with Rome and establishing the Church of England. Negative accomplishments are, of course, less easy to appreciate than positive ones, which may be one reason why the significance of the early Stuart parliaments has been so extraordinarily undervalued in some recent historiography.

The mere issue of a common name for the two realms aroused the deepest fears in the House of Commons. James asked Parliament to approve the name of Great Britain to embrace England and Scotland. As antiquarians and unionist pamphleteers pointed out, "Britain" had been the ancient name of the island, and "England" an appellation imposed on it by its Saxon conquerors. To add the flattering style of "Great" could only enhance the new union's imperial preeminence.[113]

The Commons did not agree. Sir Edwin Sandys, MP for Stockbridge, suggested that acceding to a change of royal style would effect the union in and of itself, confounding the constitutions of both countries, for "The name urgeth and inwrappeth the Matter."[114] Bacon, who served as parliamentary floor manager for the union,[115] recorded a long list of objections to the name change. It would "inevitably and infallibly" erect a new kingdom, extinguishing the old ones. It would invalidate the King's coronation oath; reciprocally, it would overturn all oaths of "Allegiance, Homage, and Obedience" made by his subjects, thus dissolving the commonwealth. It would throw into question all acts, records, writs, and pleadings; all laws, customs, liberties, and privileges; and all leagues, treaties, and compacts, thereby sowing legal chaos at home and jeopardizing England's relations with other nations. It could lead to the extinction of the crown of England and its subsumption under the crown of Scotland; it would immediately remove the "priority or precedence" of England to Scotland in the royal style; and it would cast both names into "oblivion." Finally, it was an act without historical precedent except "in the case of conquest," that is, subjection to utter and arbitrary power.[116]

In response, James asked the judges to rule whether Parliament might alter the royal style without abrogating the laws of England. They replied that a union of laws must precede a union of crowns. The King, with the advice of Bacon, fell back on the expedient of issuing a proclamation in October assuming the style of "KING OF GREAT BRITTAINE, FRANCE, [and] IRELAND . . ." for purposes of all "Proclamations, Missives forreine and Domesticall, Treaties, Leagues, Dedications, Impressions, and in all other cases of like nature." In addition, he ordered it used on all new coinage. These jurisdictions were within the King's prerogative, but James went further to declare that they rested on his "Imperiall Power." Bacon had counseled James to avoid using the style on legal documents, but, once again, the language of the proclamation ("Forbearing onely for the present time that any thing herein conteined doe extend to any Legall proceeding, Instrument, or Assurance, untill fuller order be taken in that behalfe") implied that these matters, too, might lie within royal discretion, and with them the whole gravamen of the union. To be sure, James noted that he had left some "particulars" of the union to be determined by the English and Scottish parliaments, and he asserted that the proclamation was meant only as "a first stone" of the great edifice, "a signifier of that, which is in part already done, and a significant Prefiguration of that, which is to be done hereafter."[117] These soothing words suggested that the proclamation was only part of an ongoing public process whose progress it reflected; in fact, what it attested was precisely the lack of such progress. Nor did James specify which particulars had been left to his parliaments, or how "that, which is to be done hereafter" would be accomplished. He did, however, couple the proclamation with the announcement of a royal commission whose task was to smooth the path of union.[118]

The Privy Council seems to have expressed some reservations about the proclamation.[119] Perhaps James saw it as a means of asserting his dignity and of regaining the initiative on the issue which, he hoped, would define his reign. What he had done, however, was to create a constitutional anomaly. In describing his crown as an "imperial" one and acting on its presumed powers to preempt an ongoing parliamentary debate, he introduced an ambiguous term that in civil law tradition implied not only a rule over multiple dominions but independence of all external control. The common law had not recognized such a term until Henry VIII defined the English crown as imperial in the context of the breach with Rome, although English kings had long styled themselves rulers of multiple dominions. But while Henry had embedded the notion of an imperial kingship in the common law by statute, James, by altering the royal style without parliamentary consent, had created an implicit fissure between the monarchy and its prerogatives and the law of the land. His crown was "British," at least in his own estimation, but his laws were still English and Scottish. The new style was widely ridiculed on both sides of the border, and few adopted it outside official circles, John Speed's *Theatre of the Empire of Great Britaine* being a notable exception.[120] When Coke and the judges reminded the King in 1611 that proclamations could create no laws or obligations legally binding on the subject, the proclamation on the royal style was surely one of the examples they had in mind. Coke firmly believed that the powers of the crown were part of the *lex terrae*, but if James were going to assert or imply otherwise by proclamation, then it would be necessary to erect a firewall between the King's statements and the common law.

However styled, the thorniest and most pressing issue of James' rule was the legal status of Scots under English law. His commission proposed that all persons born in Scotland after his accession in England, the so-called post-nati, be regarded as natural subjects in both realms, and that all other Scots, the ante-nati, be naturalized by Act of Parliament. Without such an accommodation, a unified kingdom was impossible.

The proposal ran into a storm of criticism when it was presented in the parliamentary session of 1606–1607. Sandys, again leading the opposition, declared that while subjection "may remain in general to one head . . . the manner of it is locally circumscribed to the places whereof they are brought forth, and those of one place do not, nor should partake of the discipline, privileges and birthright of the other."[121] The crux of the issue was whether subjects in different dominions owed their allegiance to the body personal or to the body politic of their sovereign. If it were to the former, they were fully naturalized in any part of his dominions; if to the latter, then only, as Sandys had put it, "to the places whereof they [were] brought forth."

Despite offering to exclude the ante-nati from all crown and judicial offices and from qualification for England's Parliament, and despite testimony from the judges (including Coke) that the naturalization of subjects from the several dominions of an English crown was the constant practice of ages, James could not persuade Parliament, more specifically the House of Commons, to grant legal rights to either post-nati or ante-nati Scots. The Commons' opposition was at several levels: simple prejudice founded on centuries of enmity and cultural deprecation; skepticism of James' promise (for it was only that, and formed no part of the draft legislation) not to employ Scots in offices of state, and resentment of the Scottish retainers who had already thronged the English Court; and fear of confirming what many regarded as a dangerous extension of the royal prerogative in the steps toward union already taken unilaterally by the King. What was lacking was a legal basis for resistance. The Commons' leaders—including, besides Sandys, Sir Roger Owen and Thomas Wentworth[122]—resorted to the civilian distinction between the king's two bodies. Wentworth laid out the "Difference between the Person Natural and Royal . . . Not Rex Angliae et Scotiae; but, Rex Angliae, et Rex Scotiae."[123] Not only did he thereby suggest that the subject's allegiance pertain-ed to the king as constitutional representative of a given domain rather than as an "imperial" sovereign over all the dominions he might possess, but he pointedly ignored, not to say rejected, James' claim to have forged the imperial union he had styled "Great Brittaine." The King might, in effect, give himself what titles he liked, but he could not create any legal entity corresponding to them, nor any obligation on the part of his subjects that did not exist without them. To the case in point, he could not declare Scottish subjects to be English citizens.

This was precisely what James proposed to do with the post-nati, asking only that Parliament "declare" their status as English subjects by statute, i.e., recognize their preexisting, *de jure* right. The ante-nati, in contrast, required the creation of a new status by Act of Parliament, though it was implicit in the King's concept of union that all his subjects belonged to a common jurisdiction as well as a common bond of allegiance; the king's two bodies could not be separated. For a municipal law in one part of his dominions to exclude the subjects of another part was to do just that.

When James could not persuade Parliament to pass either act, he turned to the courts, whose favorable inclination to the post-nati had already been stated. A test case was arranged involving one "Robert Calvin" (actually Colville), the three-year-old son of Robert Colville, Master of Culross. Two properties in London were conveyed to young Robert for the purpose of having his claim to them contested in separate courts on the grounds that he was an alien. The cases were then adjourned to the Exchequer Chamber for joint resolution, where fourteen judges (five apiece from the King's Bench and Common Pleas, three from the Exchequer, and Lord Chancellor Ellesmere) deliberated them. Even in such a collusive environment, there were two dissenters at the end to the judgment for the plaintiff, Thomas Foster and Sir Arthur Walmesley, both of Coke's Court of Common Pleas.

Calvin's Case was the climactic event of the union in James' reign (it made little further progress after that, except in the Scottish church), and, together with the parliamentary debates on impositions in 1610, the crucial constitutional event of the early Jacobean period. Coke's acquiescence, indeed leadership in what was widely regarded as a rigged verdict left a tarnish on his reputation that did not easily fade; Arthur Wilson, the historian of James' reign, remembered him scornfully as "fit metal for any stamp Royal" in this episode, and the other concurring judges as well.[124] But Coke's argument in *Calvin's Case*, though at variance with that of the parliamentary opposition, was in fact aimed at confining rather than extending royal power, especially when compared with those made by Ellesmere and by Bacon, who served as counsel to the plaintiff.

As Louis Knafla notes, Ellesmere considered the basis of royal sovereignty to be "the allegiance owed by communities who formed a society or commonwealth . . . vested in the private person of the monarch."[125] Such allegiance was, therefore, both personal and corporate, embracing the individual subjects of the ruler's several dominions and the laws and constitutions they lived by. Accordingly, there was no aspect of the subject's legal being or right that did not fall within the royal jurisdiction and no way to divide the king's natural and politic bodies, which in Ellesmere's view constituted a seamless whole:

> [I]n [the] new learning, there is one part so strange, and of so dangerous consequent, as I may not let it passe, viz. that the king is as a king divided in himselfe; and so as two kinges of two severall allegeances, and several subjections due unto him respectively in regarde of his severall kingdomes, the one not participating with the other.[126]

Ellesmere attributed this "dangerous distinction betweene the King and the Crowne" to "traitors," "treasonable Papists," and "seditious Sectaries and Puritans," but of course it was also the argument that had been made by the parliamentary opposition in the naturalization debates. As to the regal power itself, Ellesmere continued, "I make no doubt, but that as God ordained kings, and hath given Lawes to kings themselves, so hee hath authorized and given power to kings to give Lawes to their subjects; and so kings did first make lawes, and then ruled by their lawes, and altered and changed their Lawes from time to time, as they sawe occasion, for the good of themselves, and their subjects." Accordingly, there could be no contradiction between regal authority and the laws it created, for the one necessarily mirrored the other: "So I may not wrong the Judges of the common Lawe of England so much as to suffer an imputation to bee cast upon them, That they, or the Common lawe doe not attribute as great power and authoritie to their Soveraignes the kinges of England, as the Romane lawes did to their Emperours."[127]

This was a tolerable exposition of contemporary absolutism, a term about which much ink has been spilled. Absolutism implied not arbitrary, but indivisible rule. The subject's natural and politic allegiance belonged to the king, this double aspect binding it to the king's two bodies[128]; similarly, all law issued from the king, directly or mediately, thus reflecting both his particular will and general authority. The law could have no independence from the king, still less the people any title reserved from him, since both "law" and "people" derived their existence from him as all natural entities derived their being from God. When the king took his coronation oath he voluntarily accepted the laws of his predecessors, thus affirming the continuity of the immortal body politic of the crown in his natural one.[129]

There remained only the question of interpreting the laws. Here, too, the final authority lay with the king:

> So as now if [a] question seem difficult, that neither direct law, nor Examples and Precedents, nor application of like Cases, nor discourse of reason, nor the grave opinion of the learned and reverend Judges, can resolve it, here is a true and certen Rule, how both by the Civile Lawe, and the ancient Common lawe of England it may and ought to be decided: That is, by the sentence of the most religious, learned, and judicious king that ever this kingdom or Iland had.[130]

Fortunately, Ellesmere added, *Calvin's Case* was so "cleare" and its proper determination so evident that the King's wisdom was supererogatory. Coke, in his own account of *Calvin*, ignored this contention, which we may suspect was made at least partly for political and rhetorical effect. Nonetheless, the Chancellor had directly supported James' own claim to decide the law at his pleasure,[131] and he flatly disputed the concept of artificial reason as enunciated here and elsewhere by Coke. The law could not lack a final locus of determination, and that locus could not be elsewhere than in the king.

Bacon agreed with Ellesmere that the case was a simple matter at law, but that its significance, touching as it did fundamental questions of allegiance and obligation, required fuller disquisition:

> [G]ive me leave in a case of this quality, first to visit and open the foundations and fountains of reason, and not begin with the positions and eruditions of a municipal law. . . . And this doth not detract from the sufficiency of our laws, as incompetent to decide their own cases, but rather addeth a dignity unto them.[132]

Natural law and reason, not the mere citing of common law precedent, was the appropriate mode of addressing the issues in *Calvin*. Indeed, it was the superior dignity and preeminence of monarchy as such that made its connection to natural law transparent. All other commonwealths, Bacon declared, necessarily "subsist by a law precedent" that specifies the rotation of their offices. Only in hereditary monarchies is the object of allegiance naturally, directly, and immediately known, just as is the object of divine reverence.

The resemblance between divine and human monarchy was more than a matter of parallel governance. The king was ruler over his people on the same "pattern" as a father was over his children; as the one was "the author unto them of [natural] being," so the other was the author of their civil being, and both, inferentially, thus shared a privileged participation in the divine creative act. The king was the shepherd of his flock as well, for David had been directly "translated from a shepherd" by God to govern Israel, and all subsequent kings partook of the same commission to guide and protect the people on behalf of God, who was their "sole owner." Finally, the unique relationship of divine and human monarchy was indicated by the fact that monarchy was universally acknowledged to be "sacred," an attribute never predicated of "a senate or people." Bacon cannily referred his auditors to "lord *Coke's* reports" for confirmation of this point.[133]

The natural right of kings to rule was paralleled by the natural obligation of subjects to obey. The grounds of submission might be wholly voluntary (acknowledgment of patriarchal authority or "admiration of virtue" and "gratitude towards merit"), partly voluntary and partly involuntary (the acknowledgment of being under "protection," whether desired or not), or, in the case of conquest, "enforced." However instituted, all forms of monarchy were equally valid, since the king in establishing the polity created the framework through which rights might be bestowed on his subjects, or, by conquering it, abolished all rights under the former dispensation. This Hobbesian-sounding view rested not on force and necessity as such, but on the precedence of monarchy over all other political forms. Since monarchy alone was "natural," so was submission, whether it was founded on force or consent.

The consequence was that power preceded law. It was "evident," said Bacon, that "All these four submissions . . . are more ancient than [any] law. . . . [and] therefore you shall find the observation true, and almost general in all states, that their lawgivers were long after their first kings, who governed for a time by natural equity without law." When kings decided to fix their rules of governance, law was established. The subject's "right" was thus the by-product of the king's convenience rather than of any pre-existing entitlement, natural or politic. "Law," Bacon observed, ". . . is the great organ by which the sovereign power doth move," and therefore not, *pace* Coke, the means by which it was limited. It was true that as the laws without their animating authority were "dead," so too "the king's power, except the laws be corroborated, will never move constantly, but be full of staggering and trepidation." This implied no defect in the royal power itself, however; in particular, the law could not "evacuate or frustrate the original submission" of subject to sovereign. Whether ruled by natural equity or law, and whether that law was properly enforced or not, the subject's allegiance was entailed.[134]

The basis of monarchical rule, then, was the act in which the king's assertion of authority was met by the subject's obedience. That authority might be amplified or regulated by law, as when the king provided for his succession. Such laws then became part of the crown and therefore of the subject's allegiance, but no law, however the king might voluntarily bind his will in governing the commonwealth, could limit or derogate from his absolute authority and the subject's unconditional duty of submission.

Such a form of government could not be described as contractual because it was not necessarily instituted by voluntary consent and because, once established, it was irrevocable. Accordingly, "allegiance cannot be applied to the law or kingdom, but to the person of the king; because the allegiance of the subject is more large and spacious, and hath a greater latitude and comprehension than the law of the kingdom. And therefore it cannot be a dependency of that without the which it may of itself subsist." Similarly, "allegiance is of a greater extent and dimension than laws or kingdom, and cannot consist by the laws merely; because it began before laws, it continueth after laws, and it is in vigour where laws are suspended and have not their force." Thus, "whosoever speaketh of laws, and the king's power by laws, and the subject's obedience or allegiance to laws, speak but of one half of the crown."[135]

The laws themselves, Bacon noted, spoke of the king not merely as "our rightful sovereign, or our lawful sovereign, but our natural liege sovereign." They merely confirmed, however, what reason commanded, "for as the common law is more worthy than the statute law; so the law of nature is more worthy then them both."[136] One might wonder why, on Bacon's premises, the common law *should* be superior to statute law; perhaps we should take it as a politic gesture toward the justices, Coke among them, who were hearing his case. On the other hand, it was a riposte to the Cokean doctrine that the king was "protected" by the common law to remind his auditors that the natural law was supreme above all. On one level this was a commonplace, and as such unobjectionable; but when natural law was taken to state that kings had an absolute right to their subjects' obedience while the rights of subjects were derived from and conditional upon the will of the prince, it acquired a far more tendentious significance. It was in part to placate those alarmed by these and similar statements, some by the King himself, that James would draw the distinction "betweene a Kings gouernment in a setled State, and what Kings in their originall power might doe in *Indiuiduo vago*" in his oft-quoted speech to Parliament in March 1610.[137]

Bacon's comments on the Norman Conquest, that perennial touchstone of constitutional debate, were ambiguous. He credited Edward the Confessor with being "the first lawgiver, who enacting some laws, and collecting others, brought the law to some perfection." William was spoken of as having "refounded" the kingdom when the laws "were in some confusion," thus suggesting an interregnum rather than a conquest in which the Duke of Normandy had asserted a justifiable claim. The continuity of Anglo-Saxon institutions was of course the linchpin of Coke's common law constitutionalism, but Bacon, while agreeing with his elder rival in minimizing the rupture of the Norman accession, turned the event to royalist purposes. The law that had been preserved in essence across the divide of 1066 was not immemorial custom but England's first legal code, given to it by the Lycurgean figure of the Confessor. Edward and William were not, respectively, the last of one dynastic epoch and the first of another, but jointly the founders of the modern English polity.[138]

Altogether, the great debate over the Union in pamphlet, Parliament, and the courts of Westminster had focused attention on the nature and origins of monarchical government in England, and of the rights of monarchy in general, as had no other issue since the Reformation. Whereas the Reformation had entailed the assertion of an "imperial" monarchy acting on behalf of common law rights and procedures against a foreign potentate, however, the Union debate involved an alien prince seeking to submerge critical elements of the national identity in a forced political marriage while making radical claims on the personal allegiance of his new subjects. To be sure, James, like Henry VIII, had submitted his great project to Parliament for ratification, thus tacitly acknowledging its authority; unlike Henry, however, he had not even the beginnings of a consensus on which to build. Henry had made Parliament a partner in his imperial monarchy and the spoliation of the church, but James could offer it neither power nor profit: rather, both seemed likely to suffer serious impairment should the crowns of England and Scotland be united other than in the person of their joint ruler.

The wider significance of the Union debate was the attention it focused on the nature of the English polity. Earlier commentators such as Fortescue or Smith could describe it in functionalist terms as a set of smoothly interlocking parts, each performing its allotted function, without worrying overmuch about how those functions had been distributed and in whose gift they ultimately were; Coke, very much the Elizabethan in this respect, could wave away questions of origin with the fiction of an immemorial constitution and dismiss issues of power with the construction of an artificial reason that "spoke" oracularly through the medium of learned judges. But, as a younger generation was becoming uncomfortably aware, such rationalizations of England's happy *dominium politicum et regale* would no longer suffice. New methods and standards of critical scholarship had made it possible to trace and hence impossible to ignore concrete historical origins; the reception of Bodinian and Machiavellian modes of analysis had sharpened the debate over the distribution of political authority. This scholarship, which Camden had exemplified and whose influence had begun to diffuse itself across a wide cultural spectrum, was loosely linked to aristocratic patrons such as the earls of Pembroke and Arundel but only indirectly to the Court. Its fulcrum was the Society of Antiquaries, which, founded in 1584, gathered together scores of "gentleman-scholars" (the term is Arthur Ferguson's) around London to exchange the results of their research into English records and institutions, and whose products ranged from Camden's *Annales* and *Britannia* to Sir Henry Spelman's *Archaeologus* and John Stow's *Survay of London*. The antiquarians' efforts remained distinct from conventional humanist historiography, with its emphasis on moral exhortation and counsel, but the Union debate inevitably politicized all discourse about national origins. Such recondite subjects as the dispersion of Roman remains in Britain or the customary law of the Anglo-Saxons suddenly acquired intense significance, and little as the gentleman scholars wished to be drawn into controversy they could not avoid the appearance of being *parti pris*. James, the generous patron of so much learning, forced the antiquaries to disband, although their more informal networks remained intact and their researches continued unabated.[139] The King himself attempted to float an Academy Royal in the 1620s as a means of bringing the antiquarians more closely under control, and even invited the Union oppositionist Sir Edwin Sandys to join it, but the project was stillborn.[140] By this time such prominent younger antiquarians as Sir Robert Cotton and John Selden had placed their considerable talents at the service of Parliament, to which the focus of constitutional debate had now shifted.

Jacobean royalism, whether in the sophisticated form espoused by Bacon and James himself or reflected by such lesser lights as Edward Forsett and John Cowell,[141] trumped both "immemorialists" such as Coke and antiquarians such as Camden by asserting that monarchy was divinely ordained and historically unconditioned. Much of its argument, with appropriate scholarly apparatus, was developed in controversy with cardinals Bellarmine and Du Perron over the pope's alleged right to depose princes, a debate which in turn stemmed from the Gunpowder Plot and the new Oath of Allegiance subsequently demanded of the King's subjects.[142] For our purposes, however, the most striking aspect of the royalist claim was its essentially prescriptive character. Monarchy was the model of nature itself, as exemplified in the divine government of the world. Under whatever circumstances it arose, whether by conquest or consent, it was absolute; that is, without equal or superior. Kings might rule as justly by fiat as by laws; indeed, there was no essential distinction between them except as different modes by which the monarch expressed his will. Absolute authority did not mean arbitrary rule; kings were bound by the laws of God and Nature to govern in their subjects' interest and to keep their promises. As divine law alone bound them, however, so they were only subject to divine judgment. No king could be questioned against his will, let alone forcibly resisted. Accordingly, it was vain to plead any municipal law, such as England's common law, against the sovereignty of the crown. Even were it to be shown that such a law was older than the monarchy that inherited it, it was necessarily inferior. No temporal precedence of any law, custom, or institution could derogate from the power of a king.

For defenders of the *dominium politicum et regale,* or in more modern (though not precisely equivalent) terms mixed monarchy, Jacobean absolutism posed awkward difficulties. In the more guarded terms expressed in James' speech to Parliament in 1610, which was quoted approvingly, if selectively, by moderates for much of the remainder of the century, it might be read as a fable of how untrammeled power had been guided safely into legal channels, retaining its force but domesticating its terrors into the more diffuse aura of majesty. As such it could be taken as a left-handed confirmation of the English constitution. But the King's speech was itself the result of a long process of resistance to his more extreme claims, preeminently in the Union debate but also with regard to privilege, impositions, and proclamations, matters which were far from resolved. Moreover, the royal fable was itself problematic. The concept of England as a *dominium politicum et regale* implied not a dual system of authority but a single one composed of distinct but inseparable parts, immemorially related. The fable told a different story, of a self-limiting power that exercised itself through the laws but always retained the capacity to act beyond them. In Fortescue's vision of the constitution, including the amended version put forward by Coke, the question of origins was otiose, since the harmony of its laws and institutions was coextensive with the commonwealth itself; in James' view, the question was irrelevant, since the rightful powers of monarchy stood outside the temporal order altogether. There was no way to reconcile these visions and, since neither appealed to a temporal process, no way to judge historically between them; in effect, James and his supporters had mythologized monarchy just as Coke had mythologized the law. For those who wished to save the *dominium politicum* from royal absolutism, however, it was necessary to reject both mythologies, and to construct an historical account of the constitution based on the latest canons of critical scholarship. So overt a challenge to the King's fable, however, could not be mounted frontally. What was required was something more indirect.

John Selden and the Social Construction of Law

It was Coke's younger colleague John Selden who grasped this nettle. Selden was humbly born; his father was registered as a "minstrell" in the parish records of West Tarring, Sussex, and although his mother was of minor gentry stock, his biographer, David Berkowitz, aptly describes him as a self-made man.[143] He matriculated at Hart Hall, Oxford, and proceeded (without degree) to Clifford's Inn and then to the Inner Temple, whence he was called to the bar in 1612. Unlike Coke, Selden was not primarily interested in a legal career, although he practiced his trade perforce and did well at it. His true bent was scholarly, and he was soon introduced to Sir Robert Cotton and his capacious library. His chief patron was Arundel, whose own interests were reflected in some of Selden's research, but he had wide contacts at all levels: with such noblemen as the earls of Kent, Leicester, and Northampton; with such poets as Drayton, for whose *Poly-Olbion* he supplied a commentary, and such dramatists as Jonson, with whom he exchanged commendatory verses (Jonson's for his *Titles of Honor*; he for Jonson's *Volpone*); with most of the leading Continental scholars of his time and virtually all of the English ones; and with the Court, where he maintained a friendship with Bacon that survived both disagreements about the nature of the law and the latter's banishment from Whitehall following his impeachment in the Parliament of 1621.

Selden's *Jani Anglorum Facies Altera*, which appeared (with a politic dedication to the Earl of Salisbury) in 1610, was a preliminary sketch for the history of the common law he never wrote. There was not much comfort in it for partisans on either side of the constitutional debate. Selden ridiculed the still widely accepted myth of an ur-British state founded by the legendary Brut as a fable deliberately propagated "to raise the *British* name out of *Trojan* ashes."[144] This of course undercut the royal claim to reincarnate an originally unified England and Scotland in the Jacobean Great Britain. Selden's analysis of the pre-Conquest common law suggested that it had borrowed considerably from Gallic and Germanic practice, and, if he did not go as far as the maverick Catholic antiquarian Richard Verstegan in deriving the common law from Anglo-Saxon custom, his account was incompatible with a law code imposed by centralized monarchy. Since, then, there was no evidence that Britain had ever been governed by a single indigenous lawgiver before the Conquest—Selden would later disparage the importance of King Alfred in unifying the country—it followed that the British commonwealth owed more to common custom and religion than to commandment. It was difficult indeed to reconcile this with the supposed natural law preference for monarchy in royalist thought, or with Aristotelian models of state formation in general. Ancient Britons, like ancient Romans, seemed to have gotten along for many centuries without strong or effective kings; nor was there any Tarquinian expulsion to account for this, but only, as far as could be determined, simple preference for an evolving mixture of popular and aristocratic institutions combined with a Druidical judiciary: loosely, the matrix to which first Christianity and then Norman kingship had been joined. One could well argue from this that Britons, rather than Romans or Greeks, were the true republicans of the ancient world, at least insofar as the term was used to represent a commitment to free institutions and elective leadership.[145] This fit in well with Tacitus' account of the vigorously popular institutions of Germanic tribes, and helped explain the ready assimilation of Anglo-Saxon customs to British norms. Selden did not describe the Britons as republicans, nor did any other contemporary author, but the commentators who invented a "free" Anglo-Saxon commonwealth that had languished under the Norman yoke during the Civil War would owe much to his account of the *longue durée* of decentralized British government.[146]

If Selden had stripped British monarchy of much of its ancient pedigree, however, he had also demystified the common law. To say that England's law was immemorial, he suggested, was to say no more than that it was coterminous with its society. Since all traditions of municipal law had a similar origin, deriving their basic principles from the law of nature and adapting them to local circumstances, this was merely to utter a commonplace. The common law, moreover, was not insular, but had demonstrable ties to Continental custom, with which it had been substantively admixed by the Saxon and Norman conquests.

Unlike Coke, who reified the law into an entity that stood above society, prescribing its limits, Selden saw it as a social instrument often repaired and refurbished, as in his famous image of the ship that retained none of its original timbers yet remained the same. On these terms, it was perhaps questionable whether the law could be construed as an historical subject in and of itself at all; that is to say, whether a history of law would not be a history of society. Certainly Selden suggested this in the *Jani Anglorum*. As social need and political will had created the law, so it was, at any given moment of its existence, the formal expression of social content. This was particularly evident at moments of political crisis. Selden initially dismissed the Roman centuries as having left little residue in English laws or institutions, but the Saxon and Norman conquests were another matter. Whether the Saxons and the Normans had fundamentally altered English society or had gradually acclimated themselves to it was a subject on which Selden was ambivalent, both in the *Jani Anglorum* and in subsequent works. It was idle, however, to pretend that events so politically traumatic, especially when accompanied (as the Roman conquest had not been) with the importation of transpontine monarchs and their nobility, would not have far-reaching effects. If it was, as Selden said in the *Jani Anglorum*, "a huge mistake" to imagine a complete overthrow of the existing laws,[147] it was no less erroneous to assume their untroubled continuity.

Whether the law was conceived as the product of social evolution or as subject to catastrophic political change, it was clear that Coke's notion of it as a constant "met-wand" preserving individual right in a perdurable constitutional order would not withstand close historical scrutiny. Yet Selden was not willing to surrender to a purely nominalist construction of the law. In a late work, the *Ad Fletam Dissertatio* (1647), he spoke in almost Cokean terms of "the remarkable esteem in which the English or common law was held, and our constant faithfulness to it as something immemorially fitted (*antiqui-tate adaptata*) to the genius of the nation."[148] Such rhetorical ploys, however — "remarkable esteem," "constant faithfulness," "immemorially adapted," "genius of the nation" — begged every question that could be asked about the actual historical record, as Selden himself was well aware. Even in the *Ad Fletam*, he took the position that the Saxons had replaced the ancient British law with their own customs, and that this had become "the English or com-mon law." England's continuous legal tradition was therefore, on his own reckoning, 740 years old — not a thing of yesterday, but scarcely "immemo-rial."

What Selden's conception of the law needed, then, was a binding agent, analogous to Coke's artificial reason but more responsive to the historical re-cord, which could provide structural coherence amid the continual pressure of change. In the new Bodinian climate, with its constant search for a locus of power, there were two possibilities on offer. The first, grasped by royal abso-lutists, was that kings were the makers, enforcers, and ultimate interpreters of law. As we have seen, this did not require a continuous monarchical tradi-tion, so that even if the English crown were no older than the Norman Con-quest or for that matter than James I himself, the king's law was effectively as "historical" as if it went back to Brut. The second required the conception of a fundamental framework of law, separate from the law of nature and particular to each nation, which continually guided the laws back to their (historically tempered) first principles, a framework beyond positive law or sovereign discretion; in short, a constitution. As Selden pointed out in his edition of Fortescue (1616), the notion of a perpetually balanced *dominium politicum et regale* derived from the laws could give no serious account of the Roman, Saxon, and Norman conquests, nor could it offer a theory of origins. If England's laws really represented so happy and uncontentious a balance between monarchical and popular elements, which of them had preceded and prescribed limits to the other? It was not, after all, very probable that two such distinct modes of governance should have arisen simultaneously and adjusted themselves in the same polity without dispute.

Selden had in fact sketched out the answer to his own question in the first chapter of his *Titles of Honor* (1614), the book that secured his international reputation. On the surface, *Titles of Honor* was an historical account, pursued with much scholarly diligence across an impressive range of European and non-European sources, of the derivation of contemporary aristocratic and armigerous distinctions. But Selden made a radical move by including royal styles among other titles of honor. This enabled him to treat monarchy not as the preordinate political institution, derived immediately from the law of na-ture and incorporating all other honor and distinction as their source and fountain, but as a social construct, neither logically nor historically prior to other modes of social power and status, conditioned by specific circumstances of time and place, limited by other forms of authority, and, at times, inferior or beholden to them. The mere fact of placing royal titles on a plane with other dignities and demonstrating how the former might derive from the latter as well as vice versa gave Selden's analysis a distinctly "republican" bias in the classical sense, making kings *primus inter pares* rather than *primus post deum*.

For Selden, it was axiomatic that society preceded government. In this pre-political state, society was constituted by the "Oeconomique rule" of "particular Families," each of which had its "Husband, Father and Master, *as King*." Far from leading directly to monarchy as in royalist theory, however, this patriarchal authority took the prototypical form of a "Popular state," since "all men" were "equally free and equally possest of superioritie" in relation to each other. Through demonstrated virtue or prowess, a particular individual might commend himself sufficiently to his fellows to be entrusted with supreme authority, and thus "by its owne iudgment," and perhaps by slow degrees, the popular state might be "conuerted into a *Monarchie*."[149]

Selden laid great stress on the distinction between patriarchal rule in families and the strict egalitarianism of the earliest state. Political society resulted not from a struggle between patriarchs or clan leaders in which the strongest prevailed — that is, out of a crucible of anarchy — but from the recognition of a sovereign equality among "all men." It is significant that Selden does not use the terms "patriarch" or "heads of families" to designate the parties to this act of recognition, for such men — patriarchs though they continue to be with respect to their own households — have no authority over each other, and can meet only as equals. There is thus an absolute gulf fixed in Selden's thought between pre-political, patriarchal society and the emergence of political relations among men, which can only occur on a plane of equality. The primordial act of recognition among such men is, indeed, the very birth of politic society itself:

> I know the vsuall assertion, that makes the *first* of those three kindes of States a *Monarchie*. Great Philosophers dare affirm so. . . . But that cannot, in my vnderstanding, be conceiued as truth, otherwise then with a presupposition of a Democracie, out of which . . . a Monarchie might haue originall: no more then can bee imagined how an Aristocracie should be before the Multitude; out of which, such, as make in their less number the Optimacie, must be chosen. . . . Well I allow, that a Family, being in nature before a publique societie or common-welth, was an exemplary Monarchie, and, in that regard, a Monarchie is ancienter then any State: but as it is applied to a common societie of many families and to what we now call a Kingdome, it cannot but presuppose a popular state or Democracie.[149]

Selden shows some hesitation about the historical application of his schema. By a sophisticated analysis of chronology and a rigorous comparison of pagan and scriptural sources he concludes that Nimrod was the first recorded king in history, although "it is not to be doubted that before him and the Floud" there were others. Selden allows for the evolution both of states and of the monarchical institution itself, for it is not merely the primacy of a single individual over a politic society that makes a king, "But the large and supreme Gouernment of a Nation." States and sovereigns, then, develop together, presumably within the context of evolving law and custom. What Selden rejects categorically is the supposition of an "age of Kings in the Heroique times," the so-called Golden Age when forms of government existed in their pure and unmixed state. Neither "absolute power" nor "vnlimited libertie," which such pure forms entailed, could exist except for the briefest periods. All government known to history was mixed, save for moments of extreme crisis such as anarchy or conquest, and the longer established a polity was, the less likely even catastrophic change was to fundamentally alter it; thus, the Norman Conquest, even though far more immediate and decisive in its impact than the Saxon one, had less effect on established law and governance than its predecessor.[150] Each settled polity had, in short, a constitution.

Selden did not use the term "constitution" in describing what we would now understand as the legal charter of a state, but rather the traditional and more inclusive one of "commonwealth." The commonwealth was both polity and nation. Its essence was located not in any blueprint or document but in the temper, and, as Selden put it, the "genius" of a people. It might be expressed, in part, by fundamental laws, such as the Twelve Tables among the Romans or the Great Charter of the English; it might be summarized by law codes or in the eloquence of a great jurisconsult. It was best described by Selden himself in his figure of the ship or house "that's so often repaired, *ut nihil ex pristina materia supersit*, which yet (by the Civill law) is to be accounted the same still" — as an entity dynamic yet enduring, and coextensive with the nation itself.[151]

For this reason, the notion of a truly absolute monarch in the Jacobean sense, of a ruler unlimited by the customs or laws of his people except insofar as he chose to be, was incoherent in Selden's thought. Such a power could never have been derived from the commonwealth itself, since it would have been self-annulling, nor could it have been exercised in practice unless in the aftermath of conquest or under emergency circumstances, as by the tyrants of ancient Greece or the dictator in Rome. James' radical revision of Fortescue, namely that the *dominium politicum* existed at the sufferance of the *dominium regale*, was incompatible with the commonwealth as Selden understood it. That commonwealth was at once the sum total of the national experience, its distillation in laws, and its crystallization in institutions: a living, continuous, collective entity. That it could be subject for any considerable length of time to the unconditioned will of a single person, or a chain of such persons, was as inconceivable as the idea that it could be reinvented at any moment, or that its history was, formally, a succession of such moments.

In Selden's conception, then, the chief characteristic of a commonwealth was its resilience. The proof of its nature was not in its imperviousness to change but in its ability to withstand and adapt to it. What mattered to it at any given moment was less how power was exercised than whether it tended to flow into known and familiar channels, even if these were disrupted for awhile. Thus, the survival of traditional Saxon titles of honor in Norman England was evidence of constitutional continuity, as was the revival of the Saxon Witenagemot in baronial parliaments. Selden could not deny that William had introduced the feudal tenures of Normandy into England, but even these were not without precedent, for "In *England,* before the Normans, plainly [there] were military Fiefs."[152] The Norman Conquest, while undoubtedly far-reaching in its effects, appeared more traumatic than it was only to those who failed to appreciate how much of the Carolingian law had already been incorporated into the English system by the Saxons.

The advantage of Selden's method in establishing a constitutional pedigree for laws and institutions was that it did not require unbroken continuity through the ages. A rupture of decades or generations between Saxon assemblies and Norman parliaments, for example, or a substantive alteration in their modes of recruitment and procedure, posed none of the problems for Selden's interpretive schema that it did for Coke's. Selden could even play with the idea that the Norman Conquest had brought fundamental and lasting changes to English law without challenging his basic conception of it. Commonwealths, like other natural environments, were designed to withstand severe weather and to adapt to shifts in climate.

Selden's hermeneutics, however, were not without their own difficulties. If he expressed confidence that in the long run the commonwealth would always restore itself, he provided little guidance in facing immediate challenges. Since no single law or institution defined the commonwealth, it could turn nowhere for the kind of arbitrament offered by Coke's learned judges and the artificial reason they construed. Moreover, Selden did not so much offer a theory of origins as vacate the question. If the English commonwealth was coterminous with the Saxons, then what of the long ages that had preceded them? If the ancient British tradition had materially survived, then when and how had it arisen and what was its essential character? It was one thing to say that the Druids were a priestly caste who exercised judicial functions; it was another thing to liken them to the Church of England or the courts of Westminster. Selden had chosen the up-to-date model of the historical method, with its attendant requirements of clear evidence and causal sequence; he could not submit mere analogy to validate his argument.

No less than Coke, then, Selden was driven back on axiomatic definitions and an ultimately tendentious reading of history to vindicate his picture of an abiding commonwealth. Chief among those axioms was the assumption of a radical equality in the original polity, an equality that nonetheless gave rise to its polar opposite, monarchy. Such an assumption was perfectly compatible with absolutist thought, which in its more sophisticated versions began not with the instinctive recognition of patriarchal authority as the basis of political association but with a deliberate act of popular elevation. The difference between populist and royalist conceptions of the commonwealth, on this view, lay in whether the recognition of sovereign "merit" and "virtue" in a particular individual was an act of choice or necessity—a passive acknowledgment that pure democracy was inherently untenable or the active consent of a robust citizenry to a *primus inter pares*.

As we have seen, Selden had acknowledged that no pure democracy could long subsist. He also conceded that monarchies could be established by force rather than consent; indeed, the recognition of merit and virtue (including valor) was already shaded in that direction. Even external conquest could confer a valid title: Selden gave short shrift to William the Conqueror's pretended claim to the Saxon throne. All of this appeared to make his originative democracy a theoretical construct rather than a permanent element in the commonwealth, and to bring him close to the royalist contention that popular consent to monarchy entailed an irrevocable and unconditional transfer of authority.

This was not where Selden wanted to be. A commonwealth in the mature sense of the term—that is, a nation voluntarily governed by its laws—could not be the product of a single will, nor of a succession of such wills. The very richness and complexity of its political development (and *Titles of Honor* was, in essence, a history of the changing modes of distributive authority in Europe) argued for a dispersion of power based on an underlying constitution that partook, in most cases, of regal, aristocratic, and at least representatively popular elements. The royalist conception of the commonwealth failed, then, for precisely the same reason that the Cokean one did. Both presumed a fixed, continuous order that could not withstand scholarly scrutiny; both placed a single, reified will—that of an absolute monarch or of disembodied reason—above the historical process.

Selden's own problem, however, was that he could not find sufficient basis himself in the national record for the kind of mixed constitution he wished to describe. It was evident enough that the English commonwealth was composed of three estates that participated jointly in making law, but whether this arrangement reflected the evolved consensus of the commonwealth or existed at the sufferance of the monarch was precisely the issue in debate. Accordingly, Selden attempted to show that monarchy itself represented an historically evolved process, conditioned by law and consent and continually subject to it. There were plentiful examples of baronial rebellion in English history to support this view, but prudence alone precluded resort to such an argument. Selden was acutely conscious of his humble condition, knowing, as he put it, how "Envie *or* Ignorance [might] *question how I, bred from the bottom of Obscuritie . . . should dare at these Honors* (i.e., to describe them).[153]

Selden's recourse, like that of many another native or Continental humanist, was to appeal to Roman history, which could serve as a template for raising constitutional issues without engaging sensitive national episodes. The Roman example was particularly useful to proponents of mixed government, since it provided a well-documented case study of republican experiment over a period of several centuries, followed by an imperial regime that incorporated representative elements. The success of Rome as both a republic and an empire—a success that had overshadowed a thousand years of Western history—was a demonstration of the efficacy of representative institutions and a standing rebuke to those who argued that popular government was at best a holding action for the supposedly natural solution of monarchy. This "ancient prudence," reflected in Aristotelian political philosophy as well as in Roman practice, was contrasted with the "modern" prudence of absolutism, which deformed the commonwealth by exalting the king above it, thereby posing the private interest of the monarch against the general interest of the realm, impoverishing public discourse, and in effect returning society to the pre-political state of patriarchal rule over household or clan structures. Ancient prudence was not incompatible with mixed monarchy, that is with a royal power bound, or, in Coke's nimble phrase, protected by the laws, but absolutism tended inevitably toward despotism, and despotism toward tyranny. The history of imperial Rome bore this out, and the renewed prestige of Tacitus and Seneca in the Renaissance suggests that this warning was being pondered by many in the age of "new monarchy." From Bruni to Machiavelli to Grotius, the alarm over despotism had been sounded, and the example of Rome invoked. John Selden now joined this company.[154]

Selden's approach to the Roman example was a characteristic piece of scholarly deconstruction. There was no greater dignity in Renaissance Europe than the imperial one, and when Henry VIII had wished to express the fullness of his power he had Parliament declare through the Act in Restraint of Appeals that the realm of England was an empire. The title of emperor implied both supreme rule over multiple dominions and the plenipotent majesty associated with such rule. As Selden pointed out, however, the term empire was originally associated with the Republic, and the titles of *princeps* and later *imperator* were a shift adopted by the early emperors to avoid the imputation of monarchy:

> In the infancie of their Empire they abstained from the name of *Rex* or *King*, being a word grown odious to Roman libertie after *Brutus* his plucking it out of *Tarquin's* hands. . . . And to palliat som part of his ambitions *I. Caesar* himselfe being saluted *King* by the multitude, but, withall perceiuing it very distastfull to the State, by the Tribun's pulling off the white fillet from his Lawrell, answered *Caesarem se non Regem esse*; refusing vtterly also, and consecrating the Diadem, which *Antony* would have put on his head, to *Iupiter*. For the same reason, did *Octavian* abstain from the name of *Romulus* which yet he much affected. Alike was the dissimulation of the next [ruler] *Tiberius*. . . . The more proper name of them and their Greatnes, was *Princeps* and *Principatus*; and, one of their own Writers, of *Caligula* thus. *Nec multum abfuit quim statium Diadema sumeret speciema, Principatus in Regni formam conuertet.*[155]

Not until Aurelian, Selden declared, did the imperial ruler take on the visible trappings of a monarch. Neither he nor his successors "long after him, Vsed the title of *King* in their Letters, Commissions, [or] Embassyes, nor otherwise but alwaies *Emperor*," the term bearing even after a lapse of centuries the connotation of a less than royal style. Only with Ulpian (actually a predecessor of Aurelian) did the jurisconsults begin to speak of a *Lex Regia*, an act which finally marked the transfer of "the peoples power to the Emperor. . . . So that at length the name of *Emperor* and *King* grew to bee as one."[156]

In Selden's reading of Roman history, then, a presumably original democracy, subjected by conquest to a foreign dynasty that made the name of king "odious," recovered and perfected its liberty, creating not only the longest-lived of all ancient republics but the greatest of all historic empires as well. Plunged finally into civil war and succumbing at length to what would be later described in England as rule by a "single person," it kept nonetheless, *pace* Tacitus, enough of its ancient constitution and its antimonarchical tradition to retain its identity as a commonwealth.

No previous English interpretation of Rome had stressed the essentially republican character of its polity to such an extent, and, even among Continental humanists, few had seen so lengthy and vigorous a survival of republican institutions in what was conventionally regarded as the imperial era. In Selden's analysis, Rome had retained a genuinely mixed constitution nearly up to its final eclipse; without explicitly commenting on it, he left the reader to speculate on the connection between the decline of republican institutions and the collapse of the state. Thomas Farnaby, in dedicating his translation of Lucan's explicitly republican *Pharsalia* to Selden, was doubtless one such reader.[157]

The axis of Roman history, then, spanned an original democracy (the common foundation of all states); a usurping, alien monarchy imposed on this; a republican revolution that was in some respects creative and in some (presumably) restorative; an imperial devolution that combined republican and monarchical elements, though without any formal recognition of kingship; and a final, overtly monarchical phase that was coincident with Rome's fall and the destruction of its polity. Implicit in this was the assumption of a continuous commonwealth, republican in character, which periodically purged and renewed itself until it lost its vigor, fell into monarchical senescence, and suffered final disintegration. The Roman paradigm was thus applicable to all mixed commonwealths, and offered prescriptive lessons for the conduct of states generally. This was a commonplace of humanist historiography, but in tracing the actual descent of Roman titles, functions, and offices in the successor states of the empire, Selden showed the direct institutional connection between the mother commonwealth of antiquity and its modern descendants. The Greek republics, too, received their due; Selden noted that "divers of the chiefest states of the old *Grecians* . . . were in their most flourishing times *Democracies* or *Optimacies*."[158] But their histories were mere exempla. Rome was the living link.

The influence of Rome was evident in most Continental states, but it created a substantial problem for historians of Britain. Even as Camden and his fellow antiquaries were uncovering the full extent of Rome's occupation of the island, legal scholars (a few civilians aside) continued to insist on the wholly indigenous character of its laws and customs. Why had Rome failed to shape ancient Britain as it had, say, Gaul and Spain? Why had four hundred years of rule left no more than walls, inscriptions, and coins? Milton was to answer this question unflatteringly in his *History of Britain* by suggesting that the British race, although valiant, was too "impolitic[,] . . . crude, . . . headstrong and intractable" to develop the arts necessary to "true civil government."[159] Earlier historians had finessed the problem by giving Britain and Rome a coeval Trojan descent. As the Roman commonwealth had no priority to Britain's, so it had no intrinsic superiority, having derived from the same stock. Indeed, it might well be argued that the Britons, in maintaining their traditions and resisting cultural assimilation, had been more faithful to their commonwealth than had the Rome of the Caesars to theirs.

Selden, as we have seen, had thoroughly rejected the myth of Brut, and the fiction of an immemorially indigenous common law as well. Nor could he contrast the rude virtue of the Britons in preserving their ancient liberties with the decadence of imperial Rome, since for him republican institutions had retained their vigor under the empire. Instead, he bypassed the whole issue of the ancient British polity by deriving England's modern laws and in-stitutions from its Saxon conquerors. By doing so, he linked England firmly to the Continent and, at least derivatively, to the Roman tradition. What the ancient Britons had failed or refused—it did not much matter which—to im-bibe from their Roman masters, they took at second but sufficient hand from Romanized Europe. With Selden, British history had come full circle. From being the remotest heir of legendary Troy, proudly and distinctively aloof from the Continental main, unique in its long-preserved liberties, Britain had become the outermost province of Europe, gradually but firmly linked to its destinies. As readers of the early third millennium will note, the "Trojan" debate has hardly subsided yet in British politics, and in that context John Selden perhaps deserves to be remembered as the first British European.[160]

Selden had not only disavowed the legend of Brut and his successors, however. By dating England's modern institutions to the Saxon conquest, he had relegated the ancient Britons to a constitutional prehistory. This radical reduction cut off many a sterile controversy about the nature of their society and the congruence of their customs with those of post-Saxon times for which the historical record had no definitive answer. More importantly, it aligned England with the cultural tradition of Western Europe and more particularly with its Roman heritage. To the extent that this heritage was a republican one, England shared it too. Modern European monarchies, in-cluding England's, were thus best construed as mixed polities derived from the Roman model and adapted to local circumstances. The relatively weak force of Roman civil law in England was compensated by the larger matrix of Roman constitutionalism in which the successor states of the West were embedded.

For Selden, then, the primary political act in each commonwealth was the establishment of a constitution. Municipal laws followed, as the civil dis-course of the constitution. In this sense, Selden concurred with royalists who regarded the laws as derived from the sovereign will rather than with Coke, for whom the laws embodied the rational will of the community without proceeding from a fixed or ultimate source. Both Coke's essentialist view and Selden's foundationalist one, however, begged a myth of origins. Whether proceeding from an act in the remote past (Selden) or the immemo-rial one (Coke), law was bound to a primal act of will that, while governing the present, was inaccessible to it. In contrast, the royalist position always lo-cated the sovereign act in the immediate will of the king; however voluntar-ily hedged by constitutional processes, law was always affirmed in the pre-sent tense: *le roy le veult.*

The tension in Selden's thought between a foundationalist view of the constitution and a historicist one of the laws was particularly pronounced. The historicist Selden saw laws as a constant process of adaptation to cir-

cumstances, including the radical one of conquest. For this Selden, laws lived
in the present, and the idea of permanent fidelity to a fixed order was a fiction. The foundationalist Selden not only saw law as bound by constitutional
prescription, but derived all modern constitutions, at least among West
European states, from the Roman model. For this Selden, law as a sovereign
activity existed only in the context of first principles and the institutions they
shaped.

Both Seldens were seemingly reconciled in the figure of the ship of the
laws that, containing none of its original timbers, nonetheless retained its
shape and identity. Without continual renovation, Selden had argued, the
ship could not stay afloat; yet, by fidelity to its design, it remained the same.
The problem with this figure, however, was that it assumed a passive element, the sea. To be sure, the sea determined the ship's rate of decay by its
relative calmness or turbulence. It might even, in a storm, threaten to sink it.
But wise mariners would trim their sails to the wind or even, in case of
shipwreck, rebuild the vessel from scratch.

History, however, unlike the open sea that silently figured it in Selden's
image, presented not the challenge of random hazard but that of agency.
What threatened the commonwealth, and sometimes overturned it, was deliberate intention, whether from civil usurpation or foreign invasion. Particularly in the case of a conqueror, the ship of the laws was at the mercy of an
alien helmsman. Selden had finessed the Roman conquest of Britain by assuming that the social foundation of the ancient Britons had lain submerged
under Roman rule; that is, that the Britons had remained a subject rather
than a governed people, incapable of either sustained resistance to the Roman regime or creative assimilation of it. Lacking a genuine commonwealth,
they had fallen back on what remained of ancient custom when the Romans
left, modified by the eventual influence of Christianity. The Saxons had
made a deeper impress because their more primitive culture, though molded
by Rome's, was closer to the Britons' own, and because their settlement was
a permanent one. For the first time, the genuine signs of a commonwealth
had appeared, including a public assembly and law codes. In this sense, the
Norman conquest had at last presented a genuine confrontation of equals in
England, and, as we have seen, Selden had been of various minds about the
extent of the Norman impact before finally settling on a theory of Saxon survivalism based partly on the common Roman foundation of both commonwealths, and partly on the perceived continuity of the Saxon-derived common law. The ship of laws analogy was quite inadequate at this point, however, at least in terms of the English constitution, for the interaction between
Norman and Saxon was far too complex to be accounted for by it.

What Selden's vision of the commonwealth needed was a third term that
would link the notion of a perdurable constitution with the continual and

sometimes violent processes of social transformation; in short, a dynamic of change. Such a term was available in Machiavelli's concept of a periodic reduction to first principles (*ridurre ai principii*). Machiavelli embraced change as normative in society, and, going far beyond Selden's image of passive repairs to an ongoing vessel, he adumbrated a theory of social process involving both the constructive clash of public interests (Lucan's notion of the *concordia discors*) and degenerative change or corruption (typically, the supercession of public interests by private faction).[161] Social interaction was thus a continual process of change that undermined old institutions and created new ones, and corruption was not only endemic to it but functional. Faction provoked *virtù*, the sense of dedication kindled by a felt danger to the public weal in the breast of the honorable man and institutionalized by the Romans in the office of dictator. Whether acting by public consent or on private initiative, the honorable man purged corruption and carried out the reduction, often by supralegal means. As Machiavelli declared in the *Discourse on Remodeling the Government of Florence*, "no man is so much exalted by any act of his as are those men who have with laws and institutions remodeled republics and kingdoms."[162] The legitimate violence of competing interests and the illegitimate violence of contending factions were thus capped by the exemplary violence of the reduction, which, by transcending the laws, paradoxically restored them.

Selden was well acquainted with Machiavelli,[163] but for obvious enough reasons he chose not to avail himself of the concept of reduction. There was clearly no place in the English polity for the virtuous citizen who took it upon himself to suspend the laws, an act that notionally could belong only to the king himself. The concept of social process as a cycle of controlled violence was utterly alien to the rhetoric of harmony that pervaded English political discourse as well. Yet the commonwealth had undergone salutary restoration before, sometimes by its monarch (Henry VII reconciling the houses of Lancaster and York; Elizabeth restoring the true church), but sometimes against him. On those latter occasions, the agent of change had most frequently been Parliament, as in the reigns of Edward III and Richard II, and even when the monarch had been the prime mover, the consent of the realm in Parliament had sealed his act, as in the Henrician Reformation. It was to Parliament, which Selden served as a member and as a confidential adviser from the 1620s to the 1640s, that the realm would turn again in the mounting constitutional crisis of the late Jacobean and Caroline decades. Only when Parliament, too, fell short in the eyes of godly and secular reformers would the stage be set for the emergence of the Machiavellian citizen—and providential hero—in the person of Oliver Cromwell.

In contrast to the condensed and elliptical argument of *Titles of Honor*, Selden's other major contribution to the Jacobean constitutional debate, *The His-*

torie of Tithes (1618), was far more directly an assault on a major prop of establishment politics. Tithes were, in the Anglican as in the Catholic church, the chief source of clerical revenue. The Henrician Reformation had transferred many tithes along with other ecclesiastical property to lay hands, and the consequent loss of income had severely impacted church livings. The eclipse of church courts in the post-Henrician decades compounded the difficulty, and it was only under Archbishop Whitgift that the Anglican clergy had recovered a measure of power and confidence. At the same time, the episcopal regime had yoked itself firmly to the defense of the throne, cementing the mutual interest that James had summarized pithily as "no bishop, no king."

Despite the parity that this formula suggested, however, the bishops had, until Whitgift's time, been little more than middling civil servants; as we have noted, Whitgift himself was the first Anglican cleric to sit on the Privy Council. The Erastian gale in which the Henrician church was formed had continued (the Marian interregnum apart) to blow for fifty years, and its bishops had dutifully acknowledged their politic derivation and sustenance at the hands of the state: as Convocation had declared in the 1530s, "The clergy have submitted to the King, from whom they have immediately jurisdiction and goods . . . and have acknowledged that without his assent and confirmation they could pretend none other."[164] Only the godly community had dissented from this, insisting on a strict scriptural warrant for any rite, practice, or form of church government, and finally deriving a Presbyterian polity from the New Testament.

The bishops had the tools of discipline at their command in deprivation, suspension, and silencing (the last two of which were also used by Elizabeth against one of their own, Grindal), but the Presbyterians had the polemical advantage of making a prescriptive case from Scripture, whereas the bishops could offer only compatibilist arguments for episcopacy. This changed when Elizabeth, alarmed by the spread of a Presbyterian underground and confident in the unswerving loyalty of Whitgift, finally freed the supporters of episcopacy to make a defense of their position not narrowly circumscribed by Erastian politics.

The first phase of this defense, inaugurated by John Bridges and elaborated by Thomas Bilson and Richard Bancroft, was a scripturally based defense of episcopacy as divinely instituted for the governance of the church. Addressing the same texts as their Presbyterian antagonists, they found evidence not only for the presence and primacy of bishops among Christian congregations, but for the close cooperation between church hierarchies and the Constantinian emperor. Divine right episcopacy had become Anglican orthodoxy by the end of Elizabeth's reign, embraced even by moderates such as Hooker and Sutcliffe. The bishops had established, at least to their own satisfaction, that they were in a direct line of apostolic succession, and that their institution at the hands of the secular power was also in accordance with the practice of the primitive church.[165]

If episcopal government could be established by imperial fiat, and if secular authority itself were enjoined by Scripture, the door was clearly open to a claim of *jure divino* monarchy. Just as episcopacy, though not the only acceptable ecclesiastical polity, was demonstrably that of the mature apostolic church, so monarchy was the most excellent and venerable form of secular government, particularly if one subscribed to a theory of patriarchal derivation from Adam. The historical conjuncture of episcopacy and monarchy in the Constantinian church establishment strongly suggested their connection in the divine scheme of things as well. If divine right episcopacy did not demand divine right monarchy, it was powerfully reinforced by it. It was at least arguable that the reverse was true as well.[166]

Elizabeth seems not to have greatly worried about the intellectual pedigree of her church or her state, but James pushed the divine right agenda vigorously on both fronts. The intended consequences were practical as well as theoretical. For James, the *jure divino* authority of kings "in *Abstracto*" meant that "their Subiects bodies & goods are due for their defence and maintenance," and, however they might voluntarily constrain themselves to receive such provision as a free gift, it was no less a sacred obligation.[167] At the same time, and not by coincidence, the clergy openly declared their maintenance by tithes to be due by divine right as well. Such claims had been tentatively put forward during Elizabeth's last decade, but with the publication of George Carleton's *Tithes examined and proved to bee due to the Clergie by a divine right* (1605), a full-blown polemical campaign was launched that included not only clerical advocates but civil lawyers and antiquarians. James tolerated and even encouraged this campaign—Carleton was promoted to the episcopal bench as Bishop of Llandaff and later translated Bishop of Chichester—not to challenge lay impropriations as such, but rather as part of the attempt, already remarked, to pare down the jurisdiction of the common law courts. The confluence of these elements—the divine right claims of both crown and church, their rather bald application to the collection of revenues, and their combination against the restraining power of the courts—was alarming to lawyers, gentry titheholders, and godly moderates alike. By 1613, Henry Spelman would suggest that not only tithes but all spiritual property was inalienable as such, a position that effectively delegitimized the Henrician confiscation and sale of church lands, the largest property transfer since the Conquest. It was hardly likely that even the most die-hard conformists thought matters could be pressed to the point of restitution, but by 1618 "at the latest," as Peter Lake observes, the divine right claim to tithes had become unchallenged orthodoxy, and Spelman was promising a massive tome that would be the last word on the subject. Going still further, the Norwich divine Foulke Robarts warned lay impropriators that they risked eternal damnation, a position that was echoed in the notorious claims of the clerics Robert Sibthorpe and Roger Mainwaring to the same effect against Caroline loan resisters in 1627–1628. What had begun as a campaign to enforce clerical conformity in the 1580s might easily be seen, three or four decades on, as a conspiracy against the property of the subject in general.[168]

This was the climate into which Selden launched *The Historie of Tithes*. If his deconstruction of monarchy in *Titles of Honor* had been at least partially occluded by the general discussion of honor, there was no masking the polemical drift of a lay dissection of tithes. Selden blandly protested that he had "not written *to prove that Tythes are not due by the Law of God,* nor to prove *that the Laity may detain them* . . . ; in sum, not at all *against the maintenance of the* Clergie." As a layman he would not even presume to discuss *jure divino,* "which Divines must determine of," but only, as a lawyer and scholar, to examine the dispositive arrangements made for them in civil societies from the ancient Hebrews to the present. This was not only a legitimate but a necessary line of inquiry, "For what State in all Christendom wherein Tithes are paid *de facto,* [permits it] otherwise than according to humane laws positive?" Such laws could not affect the divine status of tithes one way or another, and their analysis was in fact a necessary adjunct of any *jure divino* argument, because "who-ever disputes it and relyes only on *Jus Divinum,* or the holy Scripture for the right of Tithes, doth but make way for him, whom he cannot perswade that they are due by the law of God, to think that they are no way due."[169] Selden was more dismissive of those who relied only on canon law to deduce the norms of tithing: "To argue . . . from affirmative Canons only to Practice, is equal in not a few things (and especially in this of Tithing) to the proving of the practice of a Custom from some consonant Law of *Plato's* Common-wealth, of *Lucian's* men in the Moon, or of *Aristophanes* his City of Cuckoes in the Clouds."[170] It was difficult for him to conceal his contempt for his adversaries for long.

Selden acknowledged the universality of priestly maintenance among pagan as well as Hebrew and Christian communities. Actual tithes proved voluntary and customary in origin, however, as indicated by their wide variation in practice, and regulated rather than enjoined by positive law. Even among the Hebrews there had been no prescriptive pattern, and the New Testament, as Selden noted, contained no injunction to tithes whatever. No tithing, he asserted, could be demonstrated among primitive Christians, and it was not until the late fourth century that Ambrose and Augustine demanded tithes of their congregations. This did not mean that early ministers had gone in want or had been obliged to support themselves; rather, as "the whole Church, both Lay and Clergie, then liud in common," there was no need for separate clerical maintenance, and the "Bounty" of the church "farre exceeded what the Tenth could haue been."[171] The clear implication was that tithing was required only as the ardor of the early congregations had cooled, and as the clergy had separated themselves (or been separated) as an estate from those to whom they ministered. It thus appeared more than ever as a civil institution dictated by the division of society into lay and clerical components—a distinction the worldly Selden was far from regretting, but whose irony from the standpoint of his adversaries' case he could not help relishing. Tithes were the product not of an active religious enthusiasm but of its waning, and if they were in fact due by divine right, it suggested the awkward claim that the Deity had enjoined them from the prudential care that backsliders not wholly neglect his worship.

Selden relentlessly demolished the claims of medieval canonists to establish a patrimony for tithes in the acts of early church councils; again and again he dismissed the alleged *scripta* as of "no credit," a term that virtually tolls through his pages with its double implication of the literally incredible and the commercially specious. The historical record of tithes was thus "stufft with [the] falshoods" of "idle Monks," a tissue of "fained" documents, a "Hobgoblin storie," a "moniment of ignorance."[172] Their actual exaction, regularized even to some degree only with the utmost exertion by the papalist church of the high Middle Ages, remained a hodgepodge of disparate payments from, to, and for a plethora of sources for a multitude of purposes. There were lay tithes paid both to laymen and clergy, clerical tithes paid between ecclesiastical establishments, and nominally clerical tithes paid to the laity in which "the Incumbent hath not for himselfe aboue a small part of the Tithes, at the arbitrarie disposition of some spirituall Patron who takes the rest . . . to his own vse."[173] The apparent anomaly of clerical tithes being diverted into lay hands was explained by the prevalence of lay infeudation, and by the fact that parish churches in the more settled parts of Europe had typically been founded by laymen, who retained not only proprietary rights in them but the right to appoint ministers directly, often not only without the approval of local bishops but even without their cognizance. Thus was explained the heated protests of laity against papal exemptions from tithing that affected their own infeudations. Viewed globally, the proprietary arrangements of the medieval church were an inextricable tangle of lay and clerical interests in which lay initiative and design had more often than not determined the pattern of revenue extraction and transfer. The Erastian restructuring of the English church under Henry VIII was therefore best seen as a reassertion of lay interest against the encroachments and pretensions of the late medieval papacy.

Even at the height of papal power, Selden noted, the debate over whether tithes were *jus divinum* or merely *jus ecclesiasticum* continued. Scholastics and canonists differed, the former concluding with Luke that "Spirituall Laborers" were, like all other workers, worthy of their hire, but not entitled to any specific proportion of "temporall bountie." Dominicans and Franciscans contended that all clerical maintenance was "meere Almes," a position embraced by Wyclif and others "that otherwise were opposit to the whole Nation of Friers." The scramble for money between priests and mendicants led to an even further inflation of claims, as the former pressed the most "ridiculous falshoods (in the termes wherof they would not spare to abuse the holiest Name)" upon the laity to safeguard their income. As for the laity itself, Selden gleefully quoted anticlerical passages from Chaucer, and summed up with "the great *Erasmus* [who] gaue the common exacting of Tithes by the Clergie of his time, no better name than Tyrannie."[174]

Although forswearing any intention to dispute *jure divino* claims as such, Selden offered what was in effect an inductive test for them. The chief issue to determine, he asserted, was "*by what immediat Law Tithes are payable.* For how euer very many other questions, about the dutie of them, are vsually disputed, yet resolue but this, one way or the other, and most of the rest that follow, about *Customes, Appropriations, Exemptions,* and much more, will soone haue little doubt."[175] Implicit in this was the injunction to heed not what people said, but what they did. If tithes were divinely mandated, the necessity of exacting and paying them would be transparent to natural reason, and this would be clearly and consistently reflected in actual law and practice. If, on the other hand, no such pattern could be detected, but instead only the most disparate custom, then the defenders of divine right were left to explain why heaven's command had been so widely flouted for thousands of years. It was extremely unlikely that they could do so, Selden suggested, because, as he observed, "no reason is, that a custome should take away what God had immediately, and by his Morall law, established."[176] In effect, God could not propose that which man did not actually dispose, because that would either render the divine will inefficacious, or natural reason incapable.

Selden further suggested that apologists for tithes, rather than tackling the historical record, had done their best to obscure it. Thus, in summarizing his lengthy argument for the prevalence of "arbitrarie" (i.e., discretionary) consecrations of tithes by lay proprietors in Norman England (pp. 297–353), he concluded that "By the practiced Law, cleerly euery man gaue the perpetuall right of his Tithes to what Church he would, although the Canon Law were against it . . . and whateuer the Pope wrote from *Rome*, we know the truth by a cloud of home-bred witnesses" (359). In the end, the *jure divino* party had only scriptural texts to fall back on, texts whose conformist interpretation was belied by the historic practice of both Jewish and Christian communities. In declining on grounds of professional incompetence to deal with these texts, Selden effectively removed them from civil discussion. It was a brilliantly Erastian move.

Selden's final chapter was a review of the regulation of tithes in English courts. In Saxon times, he found, jurisdiction had been shared between the local bishop and the sheriff or alderman of the hundred. The clergy had briefly gained the upper hand after the Conquest, but from the time of Henry II "the determination of the right and payment of Tithes hath been subiect to the temporall Courts" (422), a practice confirmed by statute both under Henry VIII and Edward VI. Without glancing at the recent controversy, Selden strongly affirmed the authority of writs of prohibition, a Parthian dart that, in the aftermath of Coke's dismissal from the bench, was particularly well placed.

It was hardly surprising under these circumstances that the *Historie of Tithes* was controversial even in manuscript. In his preface, Selden spoke of those who had "in great numbers already misconceived it," and later of the "distemper'd Malice, Ignorance, or Jealousie" that had condemned it (xv). Publication only provoked further attack, and Selden was obliged to "humbly acknowledge" his fault in disputing matters of theological concern, although he hotly denied Richard Tillesley's claim that he had submitted himself personally before the Court of High Commission — the ultimate indignity for a common lawyer — and continued to defend his book in private.[177]

James I was indulgent at first toward Selden, but then, prodded by his bishops, he personally forbade him to reply to the barrage of refutations that appeared from clerical pens in the next several years. As Selden proceeded to become first as an adviser to the parliamentary opposition of the 1620s and then a leader of it, the royal hand came down more heavily on him. He was arrested after the first session of the Parliament of 1621, and was jailed for sedition and conspiracy at the breakup of the 1629 session, a charge that hung over him for several years.[178]

Selden was still under the custody of the King's Bench when the second edition of *Titles of Honor* appeared in 1631. These circumstances no doubt accounted for the very altered account he now gave of monarchy, as well as for his dedicating his *De Successionibus in Bona Defuncti ad Leges Hebraorum*, published that same year, to Archbishop Laud. Having given short shrift to theories of antediluvian monarchy and having ridiculed the idea of an Adamic kingship, he now allowed that Cain's city "seeme[d] to haue a character of a Kingdome in it," and that even the claim that Adam had been "the first King and Gouernour . . . [had] reason enough." More to the point, it now appeared from ancient testimony that Monarchie hath continually been and, to this day, is not lesse generally admitted and established in all Nations, then as if it were deriued out of the Law of Nature, which doubtlesse was not lesse followed in those many Ages before *Nimrod*, then it hath been since him. And thence is it that diuers good Autors haue without question supposed the Monarchique gouernment, both to haue been presently vpon the first times, and also that, in the frame of Nature it selfe, Man as a ciuill Creature was directed to this forme of subiection.[179]

Selden's seeming retraction of his previous position is, on closer inspection, of a piece with his earlier apology for offending the bishops with his discussion of tithes, in which he had acknowledged not the error of his views but his indiscretion in publishing them. He admits a fact—the prevalence of monarchy as an institution—and relates it to a supposition ("as if it were deriued out of the Law of Nature"), upon which he cites other authors who "without question" (i.e., without questioning) have accepted the link and argued circularly either from its necessity to its antiquity, or vice versa. In all this, Selden at no point accepts the claims he summarizes, although the casual reader might well infer it. His real views were expressed with the pungency and directness that characterized his private conversation[180] in the comment that "A King is a thing men have made for their owne sakes for quietness sake."[181] Monarchy was a *thing*, that is an artificial and not a natural object, rather like the Hobbesian sovereign, and made for a purpose (civil order) that, while perhaps suggestive of an underlying necessity, was achievable—as Hobbes too noted—by other means as well. Selden believed that certain principles, notably the sanctity of contracts, were given by the natural law. These principles governed all social relations, but did not produce them. The whole notion of contract implied an original and radical freedom to voluntarily order civil society, and a like freedom to reorder it should the contract be broken. This would be the basis of Selden's adherence to the parliamentary cause against the King in 1642. Those who believed that natural law compelled what the historical evidence revealed to be discretionary—for example, that the necessity to reward spiritual labor entailed a compulsory system of tithes, or that the ends of government could be fulfilled only by the institution of monarchy—abused the freedom that God had given humankind, and whose exercise he required. Humans were free to be everything except unfree,[182] and those who would constrain freedom must themselves be constrained. Thus it was that Selden could compare Erastus, who had freed civil society from its thralldom to the clerical interest, to Copernicus, who had enabled humanity to see the cosmos.[183]

What Selden saw by Erastus' light was that while God had prescribed the ends of his law and his worship, he had left the means of it to human discretion. Thus it was true both that "All things are held by Jus Divinum either

immediately or mediately" and that "There's no such thing as Spirituall Ju-
risdiccon, all is Civill."[184] As David Berkowitz pointed out, Selden developed
the distinction Bacon had suggested between sacred and profane discourse,
effectively marginalizing the former. God's will, so far as it was known, prescribed a framework for human activity, but nothing more: "Christ himself,"
Selden noted, "was a great Observer of the civill power."[185] Popery—and Puritanism, too—was simply the unwarranted intrusion of the ecclesiastical
upon the civil under the pretext of the sacred. Once it was properly understood that all power exercised within society was subject to positive law,
such abuses were exposed and the claims they made collapsed. The pope at
the height of his power was subject to the civil power of the king,[186] and the
king in turn was subject to the power of the laws, for "Never any King
drop'd out of the Clouds," and "If the prince be *servus Natura*, of a servile
base spirit, & the subjects *liberi* & ingenious, often times they depose their
prince & governe themselves."[187]

Selden remained part of the natural law tradition, although like Hooker
he reduced its scope to a small number of precepts that admitted a wide variety of dispensations. These precepts were known through revelation or by
natural reason, but, as Richard Tuck points out, Selden was skeptical about
the capacity of historically unmediated reason to grasp truth.[188] This would
seem, at least superficially, to align him with Coke's concept of artificial reason, and the two men were closely allied in the 1620s in defense of the subject's rights and liberties. Selden, however, was far too alert to the chances of
history to subscribe to Coke's immemorial constitution, and he had a far
more mundane view of the legal profession as the guardian of the law; it is
difficult to imagine Coke remarking, even in jest, that "There could bee no
mischeife done in the Comon Wealth without a Judge."[189] Selden's own intellectual temperament was far closer to Bacon's, and suggests the basis of their
mutual admiration and friendship; indeed, the *Table Talk* is arguably the
work closest to the worldliness and esprit of Bacon's *Essays* in the English literary tradition.

The difference between Bacon's approach to the law and that of Selden
was not so much the difference between two lawyers as that between the
politician and the scholar, the minister of state and the private subject. Bacon
believed in a law that was flexible, tidy, and crisp, and whose principle of
change was executive initiative based on periodic review rather than on the
tortuous, archaic, runic modalities of case law interpretation favored, as he
saw it, by Coke. Selden, who appreciated the work of the jurisconsults but
recognized the sovereignty of the digests, not to mention the legal catastro-
phism of conquest, was closer in this sense to Bacon's positivism. It was one
thing, however, to gloss the changing and uncertain fortunes of law and custom in episodes five hundred or a thousand years past, and another to con-

template sudden alterations by royal or administrative fiat in the present. What from a Lord Chancellor's perspective might seem a rational or equitable adjustment could well seem arbitrary and threatening from that of a subject. Historically viewed, the law was as vulnerable to change as any other temporal artifact, but certainty in the day-to-day present was its greatest boon, not to say the practical condition of its existence. Some principle beyond expediency or convenience was necessary to bind it, however it might be tested in times of crisis.

Selden found such a principle in what he called in his *Mare Clausum* "the *Universal Obligatorie Law,* which provides for the due observation of Compacts and Covenants." This passage, which Tuck cites,[190] can be construed from a natural law point of view as well as from the one of the rational, egotistic calculator contemplating a Hobbesian social contract for which Tuck ingeniously argues. Divinity instills in us the notion of the sanctity of contracts, because without them no one could be kept to his word against his perceived interest save by force. Civil society thus rests upon it, not only in the sense of the original constitutional contract adumbrated by Selden in his discussion of the origins of monarchy in the 1614 edition of *Titles of Honor,* but in the multitude of personal agreements between individuals which it was the principal task of the law to enforce. The fabric of connection between constitutional first principles and the everyday commerce of life was pithily captured in a passage of the *Table Talk*:

> If our ffathers have lost their libertye—whether may wee not labour to re-
> gaine it. Ans[wer]: wee must looke to ye contract; if that be rightly made
> wee must stand to it. If once wee grant [we may recede] from contracts
> upon any inconvenyence may afterwards happen wee shall have noe bar-
> gain keept. If I sell you A horse and afterwards doe not like my bargain I
> will have my horse again.[191]

Once again it should be noted that the 'fathers' are posited as having an original liberty which is theirs to dispose of, and once again the importance of that original disposition—the constitutional foundation—is emphasized. The people may choose a king for their quietness' sake, but having done so they are not free to unilaterally alter the terms of their allegiance, however irksome those may subsequently appear; in this sense an original compact, like original sin, is a condition that has to be lived with. In the worst of all social orders a man may still sell a horse, and it is only by means of that order that he may.

Selden would seem here to approach the position urged by the first two Stuarts that only passive resistance may be offered against perceived oppression or even tyranny. But the social contract is subject to two conditions: it cannot be enforced against necessity, or where one party has broken the terms. Thus, Selden asks, "If I promise to goe to Oxford to morrow & mean it when I say it & afterward it appears to me that twill bee my undoeing, will you say I have broke my promise, if I stay att home? certainly I must not goe."[192] Similarly, the relation between sovereign and subject depends on the reciprocal keeping of the obligations specified between them:

> To know what obedience is due to the prince you must looke into ye contract betwixt him & his people, as if you would know what Rent is due to the Landlord from the Tenant, You must looke into the Lease. Where the Contract is broken, & there is no Third p[er]son to judge, then the division is by Armes, & this is the Case [i.e., as of 1642] betwixt the prince & the subject.[193]

Selden's comparison of the relationship of sovereign and subject with that of landlord and tenant is striking on several counts. It starkly emphasizes the contractarian nature of his later thought. It suggests, as does the example of the horse trade, that political contracts are not essentially dissimilar from commercial ones, in which a service is provided in return for a mutually agreed consideration. (From this perspective we can better appreciate Selden's antipathy to tithes, which violate the essence of contract by imposing the consumption of a service at a price set wholly by the provider.) Finally, it stipulates a formal equality between the parties, since the relation of landlord and tenant exists only in terms of the contract that binds them both, and can rightfully be enforced by either.

Disputes between subject and sovereign were resolved in the Court of King's Bench, whose judges, as Coke had so frequently insisted, were sworn to provide impartial justice according to the law without reference to the interest of either party. Though the king was entrusted to appoint and dismiss judges, this power could not be exercised arbitrarily, as the elaborate preparations for Coke's own dismissal made clear. Once elevated, the judges were, in Selden's phrase, "third persons" poised indifferently between party and party, especially when one of those parties was the king himself. The proper judge of all judges was Parliament, the highest court in the land. This court, too, was summoned and dismissed at the king's discretion, but the king was not free to govern indefinitely in its absence, as Charles I was to discover. When, indeed, the court system broke down—the mechanism for adjudicating "betwixt the prince & the subject"—then there was no recourse but to arms, for neither party could claim the peremptory right to interpret the contract.

The paradox in Selden's argument was that while it presupposed an original contract, it could not demonstrate the existence of one except by inference. There was no single document that defined the relations between sovereign and subject in a way that corresponded to the lease between landlord and tenant. Selden even admitted that few if any subjects understood the reciprocal rights and obligations of prince and people. "There is no oath scarcely," he declared,

> but wee sweare to things wee are ignorant of, ffor Example, The Oath of Supremacy, How many know how the King is King, what are his rights & his prerogatives? So how many knowe what are the priviledges of the Parliamt. & the liberty of the subject when they take the protestacon [i.e., the oath introduced in 1641 in defense of the Long Parliament], But the meaning is, they will defend them when they doe knowe them.[194]

The practical meaning of the ancient constitution was, therefore, no more than the agreed-upon process for making laws in the present; in short, the rule of custom. Ordinary subjects might not be able to stipulate precisely what that process was, but they sensed when it was being violated, and acted justly in attempting to vindicate it. They knew the principle of contract as they knew the price of a horse or the terms of a lease, and from that they understood that "Every Law is a Contract betwixt the Prince & the people & therefore to bee kept." The right of resistance sprang from the same quarter, for "Though there bee no written Law for it yet there is Custome w[hi]ch is the best Law of the Kingdome; for in England they have allwayes done it."[195]

So starkly reductive a view of the ancient constitution—a view imposed, to be sure, by the circumstances of civil war and in the absence of normal procedures of adjudication—very nearly identified it with the principle of contract as such. Nonetheless, an original compact, even if explicitly stated in no surviving statute or decree, even if simply the shorthand description for an undocumented process embedded in custom, was a necessary stipulation, for it alone could give form to a particular political order, and shape to the chain of obligation to which its history attested.

This rather casual view would not have seemed sufficient to the embattled defenders of the ancient constitution (including the younger Selden himself) who sought a more formal pedigree for it in the parliaments of the first two Stuarts. For such men, Jacobean and Caroline absolutism—the assertion of an unconditioned original authority voluntarily limited by acts of grace—was a dire threat to the mixed polity as described by Fortescue and Smith which they understood as their birthright. Both by reference to older authorities and documents and by counter-assertions of their own, they would seek to demonstrate not only an original covenant that had restrained monarchy, but the historic continuity of its observance. Under James, they simply attempted to restate this covenant, but under Charles, they sought its formal renewal. At last they would feel obliged to take up arms on its behalf as well. Looking back from the vantage point of the Civil War at the Petition of Right, the judicial persecutions of the 1630s, and the Ship Money case, Selden would conclude bluntly:

The Kings oath is not security enough for our prop[erty] for hee sweares to Governe according to Lawe, Now the Judges they interprett the Law, and what Judges cann bee made to doe wee all knowe.[196]

Conclusion

St. German, Coke, and Selden, the principal legal commentators of the sixteenth and early seventeenth centuries, all sought to give shape to the omnium-gatherum of statutes, customs, and precedents that constituted the common law. St. German's maxims, Coke's doctrine of artificial reason, and Selden's notion of law as a community of obligation expressed in various ways their shared sense of the common law as a constitutional system yielding first principles on proper analysis. None of them was himself a systematic thinker, and their general views must be teased for the most part out of prefatory statements or isolated remarks. To a certain extent this reflected the *déformation professionnelle* of common lawyering itself, with its built-in resistances to generalizing; Bacon's proposals for a codification of the laws had no takers, at least before the Civil War. It was not by accident that the one truly philosophic intellect of the period, Thomas Hobbes, had little but contempt for the common law mind.

The discourse of the law in early modern England was largely the discourse of the common law. For the common lawyers, the Reformation represented an opportunity to put to rout their chief rivals, the church courts. Christopher St. German was instrumental in forging a strategy to this end with the Henrician monarchy. There was a price to be paid for victory, however. When ecclesiastical jurisprudence revived at the end of the sixteenth century, it was directly in the service of the crown. Royal servants such as Bacon and Egerton looked to the civil law tradition as well to buttress the royal interest. Despite the eminence of Coke, common lawyers were put increasingly on the defensive in James' time, and found themselves embattled under Charles.

The challenge to the common lawyers had complex roots. Their alliance with the Henrician monarchy was uneasy, as the tempest over the Statute of Uses and the expansion of the prerogative courts demonstrated. The relative conservatism of Elizabeth's regime obscured, for a time, the quite radical innovation (and no less traumatic renovation) that had marked the fifty-year tenure of her father and her two siblings. With the accession of a foreign dynasty in 1603 neither institutionally nor politically committed to the common law, what memory remained of the old Henrician alliance disappeared. Between a king who asserted the right to determine the law personally in his courts—a provocation comparable, for a lawyer like Coke, to that which would have been offered to a churchman by a royal claim to bindingly interpret Scripture—and the renewed competitiveness of church and equity jurisdictions that saw an opportunity to challenge the primacy of the Westminster courts at long last, the common law's defenders were put to their most serious defense of its hegemony in English life since the days, perhaps, of Bracton. At the same time, the impact of Renaissance legal scholarship on someone like Selden suggested the limits of any municipal law in defining a polity. To this must further be added the objective need, in an increasingly commercial society, for speedier, more flexible, and more specialized forms of legal dispensation.

Yet such was the cultural prestige of the common law that, despite the complaints its tortuous procedures and excessive fee-taking aroused, it remained the legal standard for most Englishmen. It was on this basis that the parliaments of the 1620s were to rise to its defense, to assert it as the foundation of the subject's rights and liberties, and to restrain competing jurisdictions. To attack the common law was to attack the law itself. Charles I discovered this to his cost.

Chapter 5

The Discourse of the Stage

From Popular to Professional Theater

All the world's a stage—the Shakespearean tag was no mere professional boast, but a comment on the theatricalization of early modern society. Generally throughout Renaissance Europe, but most famously in England, dramatic representation became not only a principal means of reflecting social action but of expressing, and, in the case of the Caroline masque, substituting for it. As such, it became a prime mode of discourse, and a deeply contested one as well.

Dramatic discourse must be distinguished from the other symbolic occasions in which early modernity was so rich—coronations, triumphal entries, and other civic rituals; royal progresses, episcopal visitations, county musters, the processions of liveried companies, and other forms of perambulation; tournaments, academic debates, and prophesyings; the extensive repertoire of public punishments—whipping, pillorying, branding, boring, amputation, hanging, and beheading—and semi-licensed entertainments such as ducking, tarring, charivari, and festivals of misrule. All of these occasions contained dramatic elements; all were carefully and sometimes elaborately staged and scripted. In none, however, were the spectators and participants intended to lose consciousness of their identities, as all good theatrical performers and audiences must, and in none were they drawn in this beguiled and helpless state into a vortex of conflicting acts and values whose resolution could not, at least for the latter, be foreknown. In a society addicted to risk—gaming, adventuring, exploring—the theater was, in a real sense, the greatest risk of all.

The emergence of the theater as a sphere of cultural activity and civic representation marked off from all others awaited the full development of the

public theater in the last quarter of the sixteenth century, with its professional companies and dedicated, independent performing spaces. Until that
time, actors were itinerant. They performed in the open air as part of fairs
and festivals, competing with minstrels, hawkers, jugglers, and bear-baiters;
in public inns; in churches, where the miracle plays developed from the an-
tiphonal responses of the mass; in Inns of Court, livery companies, and noble
and gentry households; and, of course, at the royal Court. Traveling companies were usually no larger than four to six, and, for guilds and household
performances, members and servants were often recruited. The miracle and
morality plays that made up the bulk of the repertoire were didactic; they reinforced received codes of conduct, extolling the conventional virtues and
excoriating the corresponding vices, and often taught simple liturgical lessons, such as the seven deadly sins or the Lord's Prayer. Human frailty and
the prevalence of wickedness are frequent themes in these dramas, but they
rarely go beyond the flaying of personal vices, and, as F. P. Wilson notes, "Of
any radical criticism of society they are innocent."[1] Of course, aristocratic entertainments were more politically risqué, as in the interlude presented before the French ambassador, Claude la Guische, by the Duke of Norfolk and
the Earl of Wiltshire in January 1531, which showed the recently fallen Cardinal Wolsey descending to hell. The ambassador was not amused by the
scanting reference to Wolsey's pro-French policy that this implied, but the
diplomatic point was doubtless taken.[2]

Recent studies have emphasized the ubiquity and variety of dramatic representation in early sixteenth-century England. Greg Walker observes that
drama, in one form or another, involved a broad cross section of the population as patrons, performers, or spectators. Its purposes were, likewise, polyvalent:

> The Henrician period, unlike our own, was one in which drama 'mattered'.
> It mattered not only to the commonalty and those who made their livings
> by entertaining them, but also to the sophisticated, the rich and the power-
> ful. It mattered to the civic authorities who saw in the Corpus Christi cycles
> both an expression of urban honour, pride and magnificence and a potent
> ritual of communal and spiritual reaffirmation. It mattered to those clerics
> who crafted religious and moral drama as a vehicle for spiritual instruction.
> And . . . it mattered to influential lay men and women who saw in the writ-
> ing, the patronage or commissioning of plays the opportunity, not only for
> diversion, but also for self-expression, advancement and the persuasion of
> others.[3]

Some critics have even lamented the rise of professional theater in the latter part of the sixteenth century, at least to the extent that it usurped the
rough-and-tumble directness and expressiveness of carnival and has, for
later generations of scholars, obscured the historical record. Michael D. Bris-

tol describes the theater of Elizabethan England, in its fullest sense, as existing in an ambiguous, not to say at times adversarial relation to existing power structures, and cautions that "the problem of authority [in this period] cannot be fully elucidated by focusing exclusively on the relationship between what purports to be a monopoly of significant political power and a few individual centers of avant-garde consciousness uneasily balanced between alternatives of affiliation or critical rejection of the imperatives of a ruling elite."[4] Of course, street theater did not simply disappear, nor were "avant-garde" performances in dedicated enclosures greeted without much skepticism and opposition. It is rather the changing dynamic of dramatic representation that concerns us here. While the reasons for the rise of a professional theater are many and complex, the overwhelming motive to control street theater and processional activity in general was the need to Protestantize popular culture. The mystery plays that followed the old sacred calendar, with their invocation of saints and their display of traditional images, were clearly unsuitable to the new order in their existing form, and were to die with the century.[5] At the same time, the theater was the most immediate vehicle, outside the churches themselves, for inculcating Protestant values and doctrine. Despite its hazards, it was too potent and available a tool to pass by.

Reforming the Theater: Bale's King Johan

Thanks to the assiduous John Bale, we know the titles at least of a number of Protestant and antipapal plays written in the 1530s.[6] Some of these were by Bale himself, but the text of only one survives, Bale's own *King Johan* [John], first written around 1531–1534 and apparently performed under the auspices of Cranmer and Cromwell in late 1538 and early 1539.[7] *King Johan* was a play of advocacy rather than propaganda, an intra-Court move in the effort to advance a Protestantizing agenda in the late 1530s. The effort backfired, and David Bevington suggests that Bale, already a suspect figure, might have gone to the stake as a heretic but for Cromwell's intervention.[8]

Bale's play was significant in a number of other respects. As Martha Tuck Rozett points out, his King John was the first quasi-tragic protagonist in English drama, and the first actual monarch to be directly represented on stage. John is a flawed hero who resists but ultimately succumbs to papal tyranny, and whose death unites the nation. The other figures in the play are personifications of the three estates of England and shape-changing Vices such as Sedition, Dissimulation, Usurped Power, and Private Wealth, these latter sometimes appearing in their allegorical dress and sometimes as historical personages such as Innocent III and Stephen Langton. The effect is to sharpen the pathos of John's isolation and ultimate fall, although England is rescued at the end by a figure called Imperial Majesty who rather transpar-

ently represents Henry VIII in the form of the Constantinian emperor. This
deus ex machina brings the story, whose topical allusions would already have
been clear, up to the immediate present and a projected future in which, presumably, Henry would sweep the vestiges of popery from the land.

It is John, however, who remains the focus of the play throughout, and although Bale's purposes are more didactic than dramatic, his beleaguered
king offers us a prototype that leads, ultimately, to *King Lear* and King
Charles the Martyr. In the surviving text, John appears alone at the beginning of the play and sets out his bona fides:

> To shew what I am I thynke yt convenyent.
> Iohn kyng of Ynglond ye cronyclys doth me call.
> My granfather was an emperowre excelent,
> My fathere a kyng by successyon lyneall.
>
> By the wyll of God and his hygh ordynaunce
> In Yerlond and Walys, in Angoye and Normandye,
> In Ynglond also, I haue had the governanunce.
> I haue worne the crown and wrowght vyctoryouslye,
> And now do purpose by practyse and by stodye
> To reforme the lawes and sett men in good order,
> That trew iustyce may be had in euery bordere.
>
> [lines 8–11, 15–21][9]

The John who presents himself here is a sturdy Angevin sovereign who
boasts of the imperial crown that he holds by uncontested claim and divine
right. Having affirmed his imperial claims, as Henry VIII had done at Tour-
nai, he now turns to the second task of royal governance, justice. He is immediately accosted by Widow England, who laments her spoliation by the
pope. John thereupon summons his nobility, clergy, and learned counsel to
advise him on a course of reform, but he is challenged by the pope's
spokesman, Sedition, who tells him that his clergy is unfaithful, his nobility
deceived, and his lawyers corrupt (ll. 237–292). John has only the space of a
single line to reflect dolefully that "this worlde is full of iniquite" before Nobility appears. John tries but fails to detain Sedition (300–312), another sign
of his impotence. Despite Sedition's warning, John upbraids his Clergy in
thoroughly Henrician fashion (348–358), not only alienating Nobility but
leading him to question his sanity ("Yowr grace ys fare gonne; God send
yow a better mynd" [373]). John responds to this with a thinly veiled threat
to confiscate Nobility's wealth ("ye are a lytyll to fatte./ In a whyle, I hope,
ye shall be lener sumwhatte"), and, when Civil Order appears, he too is included in the general censure (398–399).

In rebuking his elites, John points to the despondent figure of England, in
effect asserting his paramount responsibility for the general welfare. This is
momentarily effective, and the elites submit, as rhetorically they must. John

then swears them again "to be of owr hyghe councell" (499–526). He exits—
for the first time in the play—with Civil Order, but as he does so, Sedition
takes the latter's place. In his absence, Clergy soon confounds Nobility again,
and the stage is taken by Sedition, Dissimulation, Usurped Power, and Private Wealth, who celebrate their villainy and pronounce John's coming
doom:

> King Iohan of Englande, bycause he hath rebelled
> Agaynst holy churche, usynge it wurse than a stable,
> To gyue vp hys crowne shall shortly be compelled.
>
> (1005–1007)

John is soon faced with interdict and excommunication. Sedition, in the
person of the Archbishop of Canterbury, Stephen Langton, offers Nobility
"clene remyssyon" of all sin if he will join in deposing the King. Nobility is
tempted by this offer, but mindful as well of the obligations of divine right:

> Yt is clene agenst ye nature of nobelyte
> To subdew his kyng with owt Godes autoryte,
> For his princely estate and powr ys of God.
> I wold gladly do yt, but I fere his ryghtfull rode.
>
> (1176–1179)

The right of resistance, that is, is conditional upon a clear sign of God's
will, for only God can revoke the power he has bestowed. Langton's reply is
to display the Pope's commission, and to remind Nobility that as God's immediate representative on earth he holds the keys of both heaven and hell:

> Godes holy vycare gaue me his whole avtoryte.
> Loo, yt is here, man; beleve yt, I beseche the,
> Or elles thow wylte faulle in danger of damnacyon.
>
> (1180–1182)

Faced with both the carrot and the stick, temptation and condign punishment, Nobility promptly yields. When John refuses a last demand to submit,
rebellion ensues. Taxing Nobility with his unfaithfulness, John wrings from
him the remarkable admission that "I had moche rather do agaynst God,
veryly,/ Than to holy chyrche to do any iniurye" (1455–1456). God, that is to
say, was distant, and his purposes obscure to lay eyes; to obey the church
was the only safe way to acknowledge divine will, and even if the church
should somehow misread or misrepresent that will there was still greater
safety in submitting to it than in substituting private conscience. Bale's own
career—he had been, by his own account, a Carmelite for twenty-four years
prior to his conversion[10]—doubtless enabled him to understand the psychological disposition of the Catholic layman as a later Protestant author could
not. In contrast, the allegorical figure of England vows her allegiance to the
King, blaming Nobility's "blyndnes" toward his true duty to his "lacke of in-

formacyon/ In the word of God." The moral is clear, although of little use to the unfortunate John: where God's word is preached, true obedience to the lawful prince results (1580–1591).

Sedition now demands that John give up his crown, and, despite the pleas of England, he does so to spare the realm bloodshed (1705–1712). England bitterly laments that "Of a fre woman ye haue now mad a bonde mayd/ Yowr selfe and heyres ye haue for euer decayd"; yet still she remains faithful: "Yf yow be plesyd, than I mvst consent gladly" (1767–1768; 1771). John is now taunted by Treason, who is protected by appearing in priestly garb, and the story of Peter Pomfret is recounted (1883–1898). Pomfret, also known as Peter of Wakefield or Peter of York, prophesied that John would no longer be king after Ascension Day 1213 (May 23), and offered to forfeit his life if the prediction were not borne out. John hanged him, presumably demonstrating his continued authority, but since he had in fact resigned his crown to the papacy on May 15, many thought that the prophecy had been fulfilled, and John's act was recorded by chroniclers and historians as late as Polydore Vergil as a prime example of his tyranny. In Bale's version, Peter is a "supersticyouse wretche/ And blasphemouse lyar," an early example of the Protestant revision of chronicle sources to be found later in Foxe and Holinshed.[11]

The penultimate scene in the play rehearses the legend of John's fatal poisoning at Swinehead Abbey in October 1216. In Bale, Dissimulation, assured beforehand of the clergy's prayers for his salvation, shares the poisoned cup with John, whose suspicions are thus allayed. This betrayal caps his martyrdom:

> I haue sore hungred and thirsted ryghteousnesse
> For the oofyce sake that God hath me appoynted;
> But now I perceyue that synne and wyckednesse
> In thys wretched worlde, lyke as Christe prophecyed,
> Haue the ouerhande; in me is it verefyed.
>
> (2167–2171)

With his dying breath John pardons those who have compassed his destruction and prays that God remit their sins. England mourns him and promises to "kepe your bodye for a memoryall" (2183). In the final scene, which follows without pause, Verity enters to certify that "lete men wryte what they wyll,/ Kynge Iohan was a man both valeaunt and godlye" (2193–2194). A colloquy ensues in which Verity upbraids Nobility, the Clergy, and Civil Order, who at last confess their wickedness and unfaithfulness. At this point Imperial Majesty enters, to whom the culprits submit. Verity again points the moral, affirming the king's divine right but skirting the issue of how God will punish those who resist the royal ordinance or person:

> He that condempneth a kynge condempneth God without dought;
> He that harmeth a kynge to harme God goeth abought;

He that a prynce resisteth doth dampne Gods ordynaunce
And resisteth God in withdrawynge hys affyaunce.
All subiectes offendynge are vndre the kynges iudgement;
A kynge is reserued to the lorde omnypotent.

(2350–2355)

Bale suggests no right of resistance here, but he does carefully avoid inti-mating that rebels are necessarily damned, the position that scandalized Par-liament when enunciated by the Caroline clerics Robert Sibthorpe and Roger Mainwaring nearly a century later. It is quite clear throughout *King Johan* that any claim to knowledge of or participation in God's salvific will is a popish usurpation of divine authority, and the genesis of the sedition that the play enacts.

Clergy, Nobility, and Civil Order now urge Imperial Majesty to disavow the authority of the pope and to assume the title of "ye supreme head of ye churche" (2389). Imperial Majesty agrees, but only because their advice ac-cords with Scripture: "I wyll the auctoryte of Gods holy wurde to do it/ And it not to aryse of your vayne slypper wytt" (2397–2398). He observes wryly that their advice is belated ("Knewe ye thys afore and woulde neuer tell?/ Ye shoulde repent it had we not forgyuen ye"), and compels them to for-swear the pope unconditionally, acknowledging his authority alone over the church (2402–2403; 2431–2436).

Sedition makes a last entry at this point. Bale uses him to make a mocking speech that derides Henry VIII's reforms and prophesies the pope's return if the Gospel is not preached:

First of all consydre the prelates do not preache,
But persecute those that the holy scriptures teache;
And marke me thys wele, they neuer poonysh for popery,
But the Gospell readers they handle very coursely,
For on them they laye by hondred poundes of yron
And wyll suffer none with them ones for to common [commune].

In some byshoppes howse ye shall not fynde a testament,
But yche man readye to deuore the innocent.
We lyngar a tyme and loke but for a daye
To sett vp the pope, if the Gospell woulde decaye.

(2540–2545; 2548–2551)

Sedition clearly speaks for Bale here, though in a context—the restitution of papal authority—that permits his quite crushing critique of the Henrician reformation to be disavowed. He is taken out to be hanged after it, although Imperial Majesty has pardoned him on condition that he tell the truth (2497). Sedition reminds him of his promise, but Imperial Majesty, instead of chal-lenging the veracity of his account, sidesteps the point with a witticism:

> *Sed.*   Why, of late dayes ye sayde I shoulde not so be martyred.
>   Where is the pardon that ye ded promyse me?
> *I. Maj.* For [i.e., from] doynge more harme thu shalt sone
>   pardoned be.
>
> (2580–2582)

Bale thus succeeds in striking not only at Henry's lukewarm reformation and the scandal of his time-serving bishops, but at the martyrdom of godly defenders of imperial authority such as William Tyndale.[12] We cannot know exactly what the spoken text of the play performed for Cranmer in late 1538 or early 1539 was. Two versions of the *King Johan* survive, an early A text and a later, fuller B text that includes revisions Bale continued to make as late as the reign of Elizabeth. By that time, Sedition's prediction of the pope's triumphant return had been realized, and England had been vouchsafed the second mercy of a godly queen. It is with the celebration of Elizabeth by Nobility, Clergy, and Civil Order that, after Imperial Majesty has quit the stage, the play in its final version ends:

> England hath a quene — Thankes to the lorde alone —
> Whych maye be a lyghte to other princes all
> For the godly wayes whome she doth dayly moue
> To hir liege people, through Gods wurde specyall.
> She is that Angell, as saynt Iohan doth hym call,
> That with the lordes seale doth marke out hys true seruantes,
> Pryntynge in their hartes hys holy wourdes and Covenauntes.
>
> (2671–2677)[13]

Bale's extant dramatic corpus includes twenty plays. As Thora Blatt notes, they are all concerned with faith as orderly obedience.[14] Sedition is the Devil's companion, or more properly one of his protean guises. The religious/political subject is poised between a God who is merciful and just but also, as in *The Chefe Promyses of God*, given to terrifying wrath,[15] and the ever-gaping toils of Satan. Obedience is the only hope for such a subject, and the chief issue becomes whom to obey. In *King Johan*, the acting, legitimating subject is represented only by the elite, *viz.*, Nobility, Clergy, and Magistracy (Civil Order). This does not mean that the lower orders do not act — the Christian subject is a universal category embracing all souls — but that they are customarily spoken for by the elites, whose instruction and example they must normally follow. Order is thus maintained by hierarchy, and disorder is disseminated in the same way. The problem, in *King Johan*, is that hierarchy has been obscured at the very top, and its praxis consequently inverted. As "The interpretour," a stand-in for Bale inserted in the last version of the play,[16] says at the end of Act I:

> In thys present acte we haue to yow declared,
> As in a myrrour, the begynnynge of kynge Iohan,
> How he was of God a magistrate appoynted

To the goueraunce of thys same noble regyon,
To see maynteyned the true faythe and relygon.
But Satan the Deuyll, whych that tyme was at large,
Had so great a swaye that he coulde it not discharge.

(1086–1092)

John is the true bearer of God's magistracy, but his authority is usurped by Satan's deputy, the pope. The play's tragedy proceeds inexorably from this fatal circumstance. John defends himself with spirit and at times recalls his elites to their true allegiance, but in the end only the crown of martyrdom remains. Like Widow England, who, as the hypostatized image of the commonwealth, helplessly witnesses and suffers all, John is reduced to impotence and passivity. The commons finally makes an appearance in Act II in the person of the Widow's son, "Commynnalte," whom John summons as his last hope. Commonalty is ragged and blind, and, although wishing to serve the King "with all my hart," he is hindered by the "great impedymentes" of ignorance (the spiritual blindness of which his physical want of sight is merely the symbol) and poverty. In this condition he "can but grope" in the dark, his material substance wasted by grasping priests even as they lead him spiritually astray (1544–1567).

Bale's polemical objective in *King Johan* is to expose the false and diabolical claims of the pope and to affirm true authority in the person of Imperial Majesty. The anxiety of this task—the anxiety of the Reformation moment itself—is reflected in the homilies on divine right kingship and imperial autonomy that are repeated throughout the play. These homilies are dramatically trumped by the pope's villainy, however, and it is only with the *deus ex machina* appearance of Verity, upon whom Commonalty vainly calls earlier (1553), that the pope and his minions are put to rout. Even Verity has no easy task, and it requires more than a hundred lines of citation and harangue before Nobility, Clergy, and Civil Order repent the error of their ways (2193–2307). It is only at this point that Imperial Majesty enters to receive his due homage.

Verity appears both as God's agent and as that of Imperial Majesty. He speaks directly in God's name in charging the elites to "gyue to your kynge hys due supremyte/ And exyle the pope thys realme for euermore" (2357–2359), but only leaves after asking Imperial Majesty whether "Your grace is content I shewe your people the same?" (2357–2359; 2362–2363). Even God's messenger spreads the Gospel only by the king's leave; yet implicit in this is that he will and must give such leave, for without it royal authority and due order will again be eclipsed by Satan's wiles, as Sedition suggests. In this sense the preachers of the Gospel, into whose form Verity devolves, are no less ministerial to God than Imperial Majesty, for all that they remain civilly subject to him. No matter how absolute the temporal mandate of the Constantinian emperor may be, including his authority over the church, he can fulfill his divinely appointed role only by promoting the Gospel. It is precisely in this that his legitimate authority is distinguished from the usurped powers of the pope. The pope's tyranny stems not only from his suppression of Christian liberty and his grinding of the poor, but from the fact that he recognizes no authority other than his own. This is the Devil's mark. Antichrist arrogates to himself God's authority while suppressing his Word; conversely, true magistracy is to be known by the fostering of Scripture and the liberty given to its preachers.

By compressing the centuries between John and Henry VIII—a period in which papal power had been considerably attenuated, both in England and elsewhere—Bale threw the drama of the Reformation into high relief. In treating the medieval papacy and early modern monarchy synchronically, that is, as type and antitype, he was able not only to underline the eschatological stakes contested between them, but to argue forcefully that only the maximum authority permitted by Scripture could stand fast against both the visible Antichrist and the equal danger of religious anarchy, represented in *King Johan* by Anabaptism. God's mercies toward England required both the zealous propagation of the Gospel and renewed vigilance against the eternal adversary. The same sentiments were to be echoed a century later in the Long Parliament, when the struggle with Antichrist again seemed to be entering a decisive phase. The due obedience of the Christian subject to the Constantinian emperor was therefore both absolute and conditional. If the emperor was to be judged by God alone, as Bale repeatedly argued, that did not mean God would not make his judgments known, and require the faithful to act upon them. In Bale's own case, the danger of plain speaking and fidelity to conscience was already manifest. He had been examined for heresy in 1536 and ejected from the pulpit in 1537, and at Cromwell's fall in 1540 he fled to Germany, where he remained until 1548. Bishop Bonner of London burned his books at Paul's Cross.[17]

The Marian Reaction

Protestant reformers had urgent need to use the stage as well as the pulpit to propagate the faith. Just as godly sermons were required to inculcate sound doctrine and to purge the memory of popish homilies and practices, so it was necessary to replace the still-popular mystery cycles with their godly equivalents, an attempt Bale himself made. The removal of the familiar images and relics that had carried so much of the instructional and emotional burden of Catholic piety made an acceptable visual substitute all the more imperative, particularly for the unlettered. To some extent this could be accomplished by substituting Protestant tropes for Catholic ones in the existing mystery plays, but for more overtly didactic purposes fresh texts were requisite. Bale provides a vivid glimpse of the battle for the public stage at perhaps its most visible moment of contestation, the accession of Queen Mary. Sallying out into the marketplace, New Testament in hand, to preach on "what reuerence and obedience" were due to worldly powers, he is met by a clerical party:

> In the mean tyme had the prelates gotten .ij. disgysed prestes/ one to beare the myter afore me/ and an other the croser/ makinge .iij procession pageauntes of one. The yonge men in the forenone played a Tragedye of Gods promises in the olde lawe at the market cross/ with organe plainges and songes very aptely. In the afternone agayne they played a Commedie of sanct Johan Baptistes preachinges/ of Christes baptisynge and of his temptacion in the wildernesse/ to the small contentacion of the prestes and other papistes there.[18]

Overtly Protestant sentiments were soon suppressed, and the traditional mystery texts were reinstated. Otherwise, however, there seems to have been little concerted effort to use the stage for polemical purposes under Mary, in part because the restoration of images and processions satisfied the requirements of visual pageantry, and in part because the Reformation was not perceived as having gained a sufficient foothold to necessitate dogmatic refutation. The one extant piece of Marian religious propaganda, the Christmas play *Respublica*, was, like *King Johan*, intended for an elite audience only. Possibly the work of Nicholas Udall, it reads rather like an inversion of Bale's play, with such figures as Avarice, Insolence, Oppression, and Adulation (cloaked, respectively, under the names of Policy, Authority, Reformation, and Honesty) afflicting England (Respublica, a widow) and its People ("the poore Commontie"), the latter in the form of an honest countryman who complains of inflation, enclosure, deforestation, and the debasement of coin.[19] These ills are blamed not upon a grasping clergy, however — the countryman notes that when the old religion held sway, men were "both fedde and cladde" — but on a forty-year crisis of legitimacy that began with the profligate and impious Henry VIII and culminated in the disastrous interregnum of the boy-king Edward VI. The Reformation itself is seen not as a cause but a consequence of this crisis, and Mary as the restorer not of papal authority but of the old English polity, including the old English religion. *Respublica* reminds us that the Marian restoration had quite reasonable prospects of success for awhile, based on a policy of moderation and an appeal to national tradition. It also exposed Mary's greatest challenge. As David Bevington observes, the absence of any royal persona in the first four acts of the play reflects not only a programmatic attack on the "anarchy" of Edward's reign but the very real possibility of a baronial struggle for control of the mid-Tudor state.[20] As a woman, Mary could hardly project the confident image of Imperial Majesty that Bale had devised for Henry VIII (*Respublica's*

Henry is arbitrary, willful, and irresponsible, although the obvious problem
of portraying the royal sire as a tyrant mutes the play's criticism). She appears rather in the traditional garb of "our most wise and worthie Nemesis,"
who, as "goddes of redresse and correction," is sent by Heaven to restore
Respublica "from hir late decay."[21] That Mary's reign eventually came to re-
semble John's more than any other (though without John's excuse) was not
for want of politic advice from the author of *Respublica*.[22]

Dramatizing Conscience

The morality play that pitted Catholic vices against Protestant virtues (or
vice versa), with right triumphing in the Nemesis figure of the sovereign,
passed with the reception of the Elizabethan settlement. Quasi-dramatic religious controversy continued in the form of the literary dialogue, and sacred
drama (controversial or not) remained popular to the end of the century.[23]
But the question of who would rule the English church and what its dogmatic character would be was no longer an overt subject for the stage after
1559 and 1563, however vigorously it might be debated in other quarters. Religious elements and issues remained part of the fabric of secular drama, as
did religious stock figures (the friar, the Puritan).[24] But religious conflict itself was internalized in the protagonists of the new Elizabethan theater, and
increasingly acted out in the arena of private conscience.

The transition between the theater of proselytization and the theater of
conscience is vividly illustrated in Nathaniel Woodes' *A Conflict of Conscience*
(c. 1570–1581). Woodes' play deals with a sensational incident, the conversion of a learned Italian Calvinist, Francis Spira (or Spera), to Catholicism.
Calvin himself took an interest in Spira's abjuration, and commissioned an
account from a supposed eyewitness.[25] Woodes, a minister at Norwich, gives
Spira the Everyman pseudonym of Philologus and surrounds him with such
allegorical figures as Hypocrisy, Sensual Suggestion, Avarice, Tyranny, and
Horror, thus emphasizing the moralizing purposes of the play. As these personifications suggest, Philologus is besieged both by threats and temptations. The threats take the concrete form of a papal inquest into Philologus'
orthodoxy. Philologus spiritedly refutes his interlocutor on points of theology, but capitulates out of concern for his family. His situation here is similar
to that of King Johan, who permits his authority to be usurped to spare
Widow England the consequences of an interdict, but Woodes applies a
coup de grace in the form of a dumbshow depicting the worldly pleasures
that await Philologus as a reward for his submission. The hitherto austere
Philologus joyfully embraces them, thus stepping out of his tragic character
and into that of an Everyman presumably susceptible to such blandishments.

Philologus is appalled when he recovers his wits, and, Faustus-like, experiences the full horror of his reprobation: "I quite from God am whorld:/ My name within the Booke of lyfe, neuer had residence,/ Christ prayeth not, Chhrist suffered not, my sinnes to recompence."[26] His former piety is revealed to him as a sham, for he now knows that he was never one of the elect, and can only await hell with lucid despair. The remonstrances of friends, who instance David and Peter as examples of how even the elect can sin, are of no avail, for Philologus feels an assurance of damnation from which nothing can dissuade him, and he hastens to his end by suicide:

> I would most gladly chuse to lyue, a thousand, thousand yeare
> In all the torments and the griefe that damned soules sustaine,
> So that at length I might haue ease, it would me greatly cheare.
> But I alas, shall in this lyfe, in torments still remaine,
> While Gods iust anger, upon mee, shall be reuealed plaine:
> And I example made to all, of Gods iust indignation,
> Oh that my body were at rest, and soule in condemnation.[27]

Philologus experiences the deepest remorse, but he is unable to achieve repentance, which is possible only through grace. His despair consists in his awareness of the precise measure of the gulf between the two. Unlike the reprobate Machiavels of the later Elizabethan and Jacobean stage, he goes to his doom affirming the Gospel, praising God's mercy, and, much in the style of the medieval morality play, offering himself as a warning to others. But Philologus' horrific example suggests nothing more than that the firmest conviction of salvation may be built on sand, and that the only certain assurance is that of final depravity. The impact of such a message on a godly audience may well be imagined, and it is not surprising that Woodes prepared an alternate version in which the messenger who originally reports Philologus' suicide brings instead the news of his deathbed repentance:

> Oh ioyfull newes, which I report, and bring into your eares,
> Philologus, that would haue hangde himselfe with coard,
> Is nowe converted unto God, with manie bitter teares,
> By godly councell he was won, all prayse be to the Lorde,
> His errours all, he did renounce, his blasphemies he abhorde:
> And being conuerted, left his lyfe, exhorting foe and friend,
> That do professe the fayth of Christ, to be constant to the ende.

The same "godly councell" that fails to console the despairing reprobate in the earlier version of the play now succeeds, and Philologus dies apparently restored to his sense of divine election. But this awkward shift solves nothing, either dramatically or theologically. The remainder of the text remains unchanged, in which Philologus, like Shakespeare's Claudius, vainly attempts to pray ("My prayers turned is to sinne, for God it doth disdaine"), and finally, with a vision of hell before him ("see where Belzabub/ . . . doth invite mee to a feast"), dismisses his comforters ("if you aske ought more of mee, in answer I will be dumbe"). Counsel is therefore unavailing, although Philologus' friends continue to attend him and pray for him. Nor do we hear from Philologus himself at the end, but only from the messenger who announces his "conversion." In fact, however, nothing of what Philologus says to his companions in this condition differs rhetorically from what he had said in his state of despair, for there too he had renounced his errors, abhorred his blasphemies, and commended faith. All that has changed is his restored sense of salvation; that is, his belief in his own belief. Even this is belied by the messenger's description of his end. Philologus refuses all food, and when his friends try to force-feed him broth he locks his teeth together and spits it out. Similarly, he is incapable of rest ("ne sleepe could he attayne"). The best construction one can make of this is that Philologus' faith is so tenuous, his certainty so uncertain, that he hastens his death lest he backslide once more. The picture that emerges from the amended version is, therefore, of a soul suspended between hope and despair, and tormented equally by both. In depicting Philologus clinging to an assurance of salvation literally with his teeth, Woodes subverts the idea that such assurance is real, and suggests instead a ceaseless psychological oscillation in which fear is the only constant. (Calvin scornfully dismissed Spira as a reprobate.)

Like its protagonist, *The Conflict of Conscience* falls between two stools, part morality play and part incipient tragedy. The old morality paradigm, which Woodes still seeks to assert, is unable to accommodate the godly conscience, with its exacerbated sense of inner conflict. The allegorical figures who tempt Philologus are no longer the Devil's surrogates—though the Devil is real enough—but a projection of the hero's own psychological states. Allegory itself, in the accustomed sense of personified forces or dispositions that act from without upon the pilgrim soul, has become inadequate to describe these states. Instead, the soul wanders in a maze of deception in which the stakes alone, salvation or damnation, are given. In this condition it seeks desperately for spiritual instruction, while knowing that the guides upon whom it perforce relies are fallible themselves, and subject to the same confusion. Philologus himself is such a guide, and when his pupil Mathetes seeks his counsel he willingly provides it because, as he says, "it is most chiefly pertinent,/ Unto mine office, to instruct, and teach eche Christian wight,/ True godlynesse, and shew to them, the path that leadeth right,/ Unto Gods kingdome."[28] Philologus' very confidence in his ministerial function is a sign of pride; as his name warns us, he is one who loves to talk. The progress of the play is thus a passage from pride to abjection in which (in the original version) it is Philologus who rejects all godly counsel in his own hour of need.

For the godly, Scripture is the sole repository of saving truth, and prayerful study, assisted by learned and painful ministers, the means of access to it. Sin diverts one from this errand, and the sin of reprobation bars it utterly, for however the hypocrite may master the formulae of righteousness with his tongue, it does not reach his heart. True knowledge is inseparable from saving grace; indeed, they are but two aspects of the same experience. Yet the validation of this experience—the assurance of salvation itself—is the most frustrating quest of all, for doubt is its condition, and perfect assurance is (as in Philologus' case) only the sign of its opposite. The result, for those seeking certainty of election, is a Sisphyean labor in which one forever pushes the stone of faith up the hill of assurance, but can never attain the crest.

This excruciating paradox put an enormous premium on the achievement of secure and efficacious knowledge, a process which, both as desire and quest, was summed up in the volatilized Elizabethan phrase "aspiration."[29] This quest was not confined to the godly alone, but pervaded society on many levels, expressing itself variously as heightened introspection, self-consciousness, and diffused, often worldly ambition. The search for magical wisdom in Elizabethan England associated with figures such as John Dee and Giordano Bruno was the underside of this phenomenon, and its affinity with the stage, with its dependence on illusion and its increasingly sophisticated means of producing it, was obvious.

"All for Mephistophilos": Marlowe's Alienated Subject

The issues reflected in this climate of anxiety came to a head in Christopher Marlowe's *The Tragicall History of the Life and Death of Doctor Faustus*, a play with evident links to *The Conflict of Conscience*.[30] Like *The Conflict of Conscience*, Marlowe's *Faustus* derived (in all probability) from a contemporary German source, the anonymous *Historie of the Damnable Life, and Deserved Death of Doctor John Faustus*, which had been translated into English in 1592. The alteration of the play's title from that of its source is at once striking. Marlowe has replaced the didactic epithets "Damned" and "Deserved," with their bluntly religious and specifically Calvinist connotation, by the modifier "Tragicall." His play is in fact the first fully realized Elizabethan tragedy in that it works out the destiny of a single protagonist who acts freely at a site of moral choice; Thomas Kyd's *The Spanish Tragedy*, which precedes it by several years, is a revenge drama framed by allegorical elements, and Sackville and Norton's *The Tragedie of Gorboduc* (1562) lacks a clearly defined protagonist.[31] Some critics have also fathered a form called "Christian tragedy" on Marlowe, but there has been so much difference of opinion as to the doctrine espoused in *Faustus* that the general effect is discursive, not to say subversive; as John S. Wilks notes, "For some commentators, the play dramatizes the reform doctrines of Wittenberg, or again of Geneva; for others, the informing dogmas are those of Augustine and St. Paul; for still others, the play offers a vague but triumphant vindication of Marlowe's 'unimpeachable' orthodoxy."[32] Notoriously, Marlowe's reputation was haunted by the accusations of atheism made shortly before and after his death. Victorian freethinkers took him up, and a modern critic, G. K. Hunter, suggests him as "the laureate of the atheistical imagination."[33] Certainly Marlowe, like Melville, had a quarrel with God. Divinity was, at least officially, still incontestably the queen of the sciences in his day, but it is precisely sacred knowledge whose adequacy Faustus, the Doctor of Divinity, questions, and which he repudiates as finally inefficacious. The Prologue summarizes his conflict and prefigures the ambiguous nature of its resolution:

> So much he profits in divinity
> That shortly he was grac'd with doctor's name,
> Excelling all, and sweetly can dispute
> In th' heavenly matters of theology —
> Till swoll'n with cunning, of a self-conceit,
> His waxen wings did mount above his reach,
> And melting, Heavens conspir'd his overthrow![34]

Divinity fails in the first instance precisely because it is open to disputation, and therefore not only to uncertainty but to logic-chopping. Faustus, who confesses himself "ravish'd" by Aristotle's *Analytics* (1.6), boasts of how he has:

> with subtle syllogisms
> Gravell'd the pastors of the German church
> And made the flow'ring pride of Wittenberg
> <Swarm> to my problems as th' infernal spirits
> On sweet Musaeus when he came to Hell.

(1.104–107)

Faustus' "sweet" and "subtle" discourse turns divinity on its head; the German pastors find themselves not only abased in their pride but cast, at least in metaphoric terms, as the minions of hell. We are reminded here of Lucifer's fall, and of the proverbial wisdom that the Devil can quote Scripture to his purpose. If in fact the Devil is the supreme theologian, then he is Faustus' only worthy adversary, and in identifying himself with him, Faustus signifies his intention to usurp not only his title but his throne. This is the sense of Faustus' megalomaniacal ambition to control not only the kings of the earth but natural process itself so that "All things that move between the quiet poles/ Shall be at my command" (1.52–53). Faustus covets not the Devil's wit but his power. Divinity, in the last analysis, issues only in piety; that is, in submission to the will of God; that is, in abjection. The Devil sports with Scripture to win humans from rather than to divine power, and thus to constitute his own empire. What Faustus finds intolerable is the human condition as such; toting up his own achievements, he reflects, "Yet art thou still but Faustus and a man" (l.21). If Satan's positive domain is that part of humanity he has wrested from God, for those souls he has seduced, hell's empire is man's to win, and to wield the Devil's own power is the true end of "aspiration."

If theology is the pathway to the divine, the road to Satan lies through conjuration. The equivocal status of magic in the Renaissance derived from belief in a realm of intermediaries through which commerce with the divine and demonic worlds might be negotiated. The Reformation barred access to traditional intermediaries such as saints and guardian angels; henceforth, to call on spirits was to call on hell. This exposed the believer to God directly and immediately, whether as petitioner or as the object of overmastering grace or wrath. In either case, it radically emphasized his utter helplessness and dependence; the final isolation of the soul before God was now the everyday experience of the pious Christian. The temptation of magic, which promised efficacy and control through the manipulation of physical essences or of spirits, was obvious. Belief in such forces was a part of the scientific as well as the theological orthodoxy of the time. For the despairing soul, or the aspiring one—and were they not, perhaps, in the end the same?—the route to God might lead through the Devil.

Faustus' infatuation with magic begins with a rapid surmise of the implications of reprobation: "Why,/ then belike, we must sin, and so consequently die./ Ay, we must die an everlasting death./ What doctrine call you this?" (1: 40–43). He turns at once to his conjuring books ("These metaphysics of magicians/ And necromantic books are heavenly"), and concludes that, after all, "'Tis magic, magic that hath ravished me!" (1: 45–46; 102). The magicians have thus the better of both philosophy and divinity; their necromancy, which raises the dead, is "heavenly" in the dual sense of comforting the soul whose fear of death is paramount, and of exercising divine powers, for heaven to the reprobate is indefinitely prolonged life rather than eternal repose in the deity. As G. K. Hunter points out, the original editions of *Faustus* read "negromantic" for the modern transcription of "necromantic," thus further associating the magicians with the black arts and underlining their ironic association with "heavenly" pursuits.

Faustus, too impatient to peruse his books, summons the assistance of two conjurors, Valdes and Cornelius. Before they can arrive, however, a "Good" and a "Bad" Angel appear (1.1.64), the first to warn and the second to encourage him. The former, evidently a Calvinist emissary, cautions Faustus to avoid "God's heavy wrath" and to "Read, read the Scriptures" instead of books of "blasphemy." The latter, invoking the pagan deity, urges him to be "on earth as Jove is in the sky"—that is, a rival to the sky divinity as the old earth gods were, or, as in the dualist tradition embedded in the rubrics of magic, God and Satan are. Once again, a modern editor's attempted clarification obscures a deliberate ambiguity, for the original text describes Faustus' visitants as an "Angel" and a "Spirit" respectively, the provenance of the latter being left strategically vague. This reflects the ambiguities of magical divination, with its supposition of ethereal intermediaries, as well as the folk belief that nourished it. We are in a world at once Christian and pagan, mirroring (as does Faustus himself) the speculative underside of the Reformation. At the same time, the visitants appear to Faustus alone, thus existing on another plane from traditional allegorical figures such as Virtue and Vice or Conscience and Temptation, which appear not merely as voices but as embodiments visible to and interacting with a variety of characters. Are we, then, to take the Angel and the Spirit as notionally real, or as warring elements within Faustus' soul alone? Marlowe leaves this point unresolved as well.[35] The cumulative effect—which will only be reinforced by the dazzling array of otherworldly images presented to Faustus, culminating in the vision of Helen—is deeply Pyrrhonic. Faustus' Leporello-like servant Wagner and his comic colleagues provide a burlesque counterpart to the action that subverts it on still another level. Showing in the university scholars who have come to remonstrate with Faustus, Wagner mocks their godly carriage:

> I will set my countenance like a precisian and begin to speak thus: Truly, my dear brethren, my master is within at dinner, with Valdes and Cornelius, as this wine, if it could speak, would inform your worships, and so, the Lord bless you, preserve you, and keep you, my dear brethren. (1.2.21–25)

Wagner derides not only the scholars but Faustus, for by extension the pose of the godly servant extends to his master; at the same time, he associates the scholars with the magicians' conference within. Religion and sorcery, he implies, are cut from the same tricksters' cloth, and the wine of the Eucharist is as cheap a conjuring device as the magicians' mumbo jumbo. This coarse skepticism is not the play's dominant tone, of course, but it continually subverts it; in no other major tragedy is tragic argument brought so close to low comedy, and comedy of the most derisive sort. This suggests a still more ironic resolution: that the human comedy itself is, viewed from opposing angles, a solemn game or a sniggering farce.[36] The difference between Wagner and Faust, or between magicians and precisians, is merely one of attitude and style; it is all, to borrow Joel Altman's phrase, a play of mind.

Such a stance provides the dramatic rationale for Faustus' perpetual inconstancy, and his precipitous descent from heaven-storming aspiration to the burlesque episodes with the Emperor's servants and the horse-courser. As Faustus roves from book to book in the play's opening scene, seeking not merely a profession but an identity, so he is reduced to scouting his leg in a ditch by Act IV, as if body as well as soul can no longer be kept together.

This is horrific as well as comedic, for Faustus seems to be disintegrating before our eyes, or, worse yet, turning into an automaton or whirligig, running or hopping as his supply of limbs permits.

Faustus' instability recalls that of the morality play protagonists, with their rapid oscillations between extremes, as well as the sudden shift in Philologos, who after parrying the most sophisticated thrusts of the pope's theologians succumbs suddenly to their crudest blandishments. His japing impersonation of a cardinal at the papal Court in Act III likewise recalls the personifications of the vice figures in *King Johan*, with the roles of course reversed. If Faustus remains the moral center of the play, it is a center incapable of resting in any single identity, since he has renounced the immortal soul that can alone anchor him, and thus remains subject to the unending play of desire.[37] The result is a mutation into a succession of assumed roles and alter egos which constitute both the condition of his damnation and the commentary on it.

The most interesting of these alter egos is Mephistophilos himself, the infernal spirit who accompanies Faustus on his restless wanderings and becomes his Virgilian guide to hell. Faustus conjures him with a farrago of Latin, but as the stage directions make clear he is already attended by Lucifer and an escort of devils; he has no sooner to wish a thing than it appears or is done. For Faustus this is the essence of magic itself, but a more self-conscious age may understand it as fantasized wish-fulfillment, a point underscored by the Freudian trapdoor through which Mephistophilos emerges as a "dragon-head." This is too repellent, i.e., too uncensored an image, and Faustus immediately commands Mephistophilos to come garbed as a friar, a joke the audience is invited to share ("That holy shape becomes a devil best"), and which recalls the shape-changing artifice of the vices in *King Johan* and other morality plays. The interiorization of these previously externalized figures is emphasized by collapsing the geography of heaven and hell, first in Faustus' vaunting boast that he "confound[s] Hell in Elysium" (1.3.56), and then by the famous reply of Mephistophilos that locates hell in the self ("Why this is Hell, nor am I out of it. . . ." [l.3.72]). This latter gambit has strongly Calvinist overtones. If Mephistophilos carries hell within him, then so does reprobate humanity, whether in anticipation, or, in the doctrine of double predestination, as ordained decree. In these terms, Faustus' pact with the Devil merely actualizes his destiny, and Mephistophilos is his familiar not only before he calls on him but perhaps from birth: the visible shape of his damnation.

The nature and provenance of Faustus' damnation is, of course, the theological crux of the play, just as the question of whether or not it is revocable is its dramatic one. In this sense the theme of *Faustus* is identical with that of *The Conflict of Conscience*; the defining difference between them is whether these questions are capable of resolution or merely terroristic—that is, whether assurance is truly possible, or whether it remains a will o' the wisp that is to all intents and purposes a figment of desire alone. This issue—rather than any overtly expressed skepticism—is the corrosive doubt at the heart of *Faustus*, and one that is wholly lacking in *The Conflict of Conscience*. From it flows all the other questions raised in *Faustus*: free will, efficacy, and identity as such. It is because Faustus is a tormented skeptic (but not necessarily a scoffing reprobate) that he will, in the phrase that has long puzzled critics, "tire [his] brains to get a deity" (1.1.58). Faustus is Christian man, wondering whether divinity exists and whether human destiny may be known. He sells his soul to the Devil to discover whether he has one.[38]

The contract scene well illustrates Faustus' perplexities. There is a significant temporal ambiguity in the speech in which Mephistophilos urges him to sign in blood:

> Then, Faustus, stab thy arm courageously
> And bind thy soul that at some certain day
> Great Lucifer may claim it as his own.
> And then be thou as great as Lucifer!

(2.1.48–51)

Will Faustus be at once as great as Lucifer, that is, as potent and glorious, or will he be so only on the "certain day" when the Devil claims his soul "as his own"? If Faustus is immediately possessed of all the Devil's powers, his quest is ended; nothing remains but to try them one by one, though without the Devil's constant goal to "Enlarge his kingdom" (2.1.39). On the other hand, if the Devil retains powers that cannot be exercised by mortals even if, as Faustus demands, he is converted to a spirit "in form and substance" while still alive (2.1.94–95), then Faustus' real reward can only be had in hell when he is, as it were, with the Father. This parodic inversion of the Christian soul's aspiration to dwell with God and of the Son's longing for reunion with the heavenly Father suggests that the twenty-four years' lease on demonic powers for which Faustus bargains is not a limiting contract but an apprenticeship to something far greater; that what Faustus aspires to is to reign equally with if not in place of the Devil. Once again, the implication is that only the Devil possesses certain knowledge of God, which is to say whether he exists. The skeptic's last refuge is the Devil himself.

We are reminded again of the perceived potential of Renaissance magic, which, as Pico della Mirandola puts it, "is nothing other than the highest realization of natural philosophy . . . and, ultimately, the knowledge of the whole of nature," and of Cornelius Agrippa's conviction that the Devil's powers could be subjected to human will.[39] Faustus gambles that he "Will be as cunning as Agrippa was" (1.1.109), and thus able to evade his bargain. At another moment, he reasons that he is only giving up what he can no longer hope to save, "Seeing Faustus hath incurr'd eternal death/ By desperate thoughts against Jove's deity" (1.3.85–86), and that in any case the loss is trivial compared to the prospective gain: "Had I as many souls as there be stars/ I'd give them all for Mephostophilis!" (3.1.99–100). The vaunting confidence of the magician alternates here with the despairing brazenness of the reprobate. It is part of Marlowe's genius to show how the two in fact represent opposite sides of the same coin, and how closely both are linked in turn to the godly *dévot*. The magus, the defiant reprobate, and the churchgoer aggressively pursuing assurance are all part of the same climate of aspiration, and all three inhabit the sprawling, diffuse, mercurial personality of Faustus. Faustus' instability, in short, is that of his age; he is a composite who reveals the deeper unity of his conflicting elements. To be sure, he reflects as well the shifts and incongruities of the morality play personae from whom he is incompletely liberated. One sees gulfs in him rather than, as in Shakespeare, depths. But for that very reason he is a more truly representative figure of his relentlessly self-fashioning age.

If Faustus seems ungrounded — a focus rather than a center for the play — it is because the world around him is equally so. His megalomania betrays the solipsistic anxiety that nothing exists beyond his own fantasy, for in mastering the world he incorporates it and thereby renders it indistinguishable from himself. Faustus seems thus to combine an unbounded, almost infantile ego with the sober and adult terror that he is truly alone. The wager of his soul is in this sense a speculation on the world itself, for in detaching this most intimate and yet hidden part of himself he tests whether its loss is really possible. If the Devil can actually claim his soul, then perhaps God can also rescue it. Without the wager, however, there is no way of knowing certainly whether either God or Devil exists.

These confusions become explicit as the contract scene unfolds. Faustus, who puts great store in visualization (and is therefore particularly susceptible to illusion), points to the effusion of his blood (the most literal transfer of an "inside" to an "outside") as the proof of his deliberate self-alienation: "View here this blood that trickles from mine arm/ And let it be propitious for my wish" (2.1.56–57). No sooner does he do so, however, than the act seems to reverse itself: "My blood congeals and I can write no more!" What follows is a phantasmal sequence in which Faustus seems unable to govern his will:

> What might the staying of my blood portend?
> Is it unwilling I should write this bill?
> Why streams it not that I may write afresh:
> "Faustus gives to thee his soul"? O there it stay'd. . . .

Why shouldst thou not? Is not thy soul thine own?
Then write again: "Faustus gives to thee his soul."

(63–68)

Faustus is doubly alienated, both from body and soul, and it is particularly difficult to posit the identity of the subject at this moment. Syntax itself is strained to the point of unintelligibility, as so often when the multiple layers of Marlowe's intention overlap. "O there it stay'd" may signify either the blood that refuses to flow or the soul that resists being cast away, or of course to both if the soul is construed to reside in the blood. Likewise, the "Why shouldst thou not?" may refer to Faustus' overriding will to complete the pact, but also to the hesitant thought that there is still time to renounce it. The confusion is completed by the fifth question of this brief utterance: "Is not thy soul thine own?" On one level the question is rhetorical—Faustus asserting the possession of that which he intends to give away—but on another it is urgent and fundamental. Is Faustus unable to alienate his soul because it is inseparable from him (yet alien at the same time, since it appears to possess its own will)? Or is he unable to do so because he does not possess it at all in that it belongs to God, and that the will that opposes his is consequently God's?

Mephistophilos helpfully provides fire to restore the flow of blood, and Faustus quickly completes the contract. No sooner has he done so, however, then further wonders appear:

Consummatum est! This bill is ended:
And Faustus hath bequeath'd his soul to Lucifer.
—But what is this inscription on mine arm?
Homo fuge! Whither should I fly?
If unto Heav'n, He'll throw me down to Hell.
—My senses are deceiv'd, here's nothing writ.
—Oh yes, I see it plain! Even here is writ
Homo fuge! Yet shall not Faustus fly.

(73–80)

Instead of questions, this passage gives us contradictory declarations. Faustus' reference to Christ's last words on the cross (made even more blasphemous by its allusion to a tradesman's contract) signifies, in an orthodox context, the utmost stretch of the reprobate will, the rejection of divine mercy and the voluntary act of self-damnation. In the parody of divine aspiration we have been examining, it also represents the assumption of "sonship" (i.e., parity) with the Devil. The cry of *Homo fuge!* is in this sense the physical expression of what Faustus has chosen to do; he will "fly" to Lucifer as Christ rose to the Father. A moment of confusion follows ("Whither should I fly?"), followed by the suggestion that what Faustus must do is flee his act and throw himself upon mercy. This is immediately rejected ("He'll throw me down to Hell"), a sign once again of the unrepentant will. The inscription disappears and reappears, deepening Faustus' sensory confusion, and he concludes with the riddling statement, "Yet Faustus shall not fly."

"Yet Faustus shall not fly": On an orthodox level, this appears to be a despairing response to the inscription, signifying Faustus' acceptance of his condition as one now damned. On another one, however, it may be read as a defiant rejection of submission and a cleaving to his act, an act Faustus still intends to turn to his advantage. The battle, in this sense, is thus fully joined: in spurning a last offer of mercy, or at any rate the last possibility of appeal to a judge whose will is fixed ("He'll send me down to Hell"), Faustus seals his engagement with the Devil.

Faustus' mental confusion in this scene is such, however, that Mephistophilos' aside ("I'll fetch him somewhat to delight his mind") sounds as much like therapeutic intervention as a first installment on the Devil's diversions. Faustus is convinced of the reality of his pact, or at any rate wills his sense of conviction, but how credible is his affirmation? Lucifer never signifies his presence other than through his ostensible proxy, Mephistophilos, and Faustus himself does not interpret the signs and wonders that appear to him as a divine warning, since he regards heaven as foreclosed to him. One is left to infer that they are illusions wrought by his own inner hesitation, an impression reinforced by Faustus' sense of their hallucinatory quality ("My senses are deceiv'd"). We are left with nothing in the scene other than Mephistophilos, and that forces the question of who he finally is.

When Faustus initially conjures Mephistophilos, he gives two contradictory accounts of his appearance:

> *Meph.* I am a servant to great Lucifer
>   And may not follow thee without his leave.
>   No more than he commands must we perform.
> *Fau.* Did not he charge thee to appear to me?
> *Meph.* No, I came now hither of my own accord.
>
>   (1.3.37–41)

Mephistophilos both is and is not an independent agent; and when Faustus asks him whether he did not in fact appear at *his* command, he replies evasively that though "That was the cause, but yet *per accidens*" (43). As with the signs in the contract scene, Mephistophilos' provenance is uncertain, and Faustus is soon able to identify him as the image of his own quest: "Had I as many souls as there be stars/ I'd given them all for Mephostophilis!" (99–100).

The peculiar intimacy between Faustus and Mephistophilos is reinforced when Mephistophilos echoes Faustus' desire and as it were completes his thought:

> But tell me, Faustus, shall I have thy soul—
> And I will be thy slave and wait on thee

And give thee more than thou hast wit to ask.

(2.1.44–46)

Mephistophilos is the efficient will who will translate Faustus' unbounded desire into concrete action, thereby completing Faustus himself as a divine being in whom, like the God whose wrath he tempts by appropriating his powers, thought and action are one. It is of course on behalf of his own master Lucifer that Mephistophilos seeks Faustus' soul, but at the crucial moment he asks it directly and almost amorously for himself ("But tell me, Faustus, shall I have thy soul"), and it is as a lover that Faustus yields: "Lo, Mephostophilis, for love of thee/ Faustus hath cut his arm and with his proper blood/ Assures his soul to be great Lucifer's,/ Chief lord and regent of perpetual night" (51–54).[40] "Lucifer" remains the *tertium quid*, the nominal landlord in this, but, after quizzing Mephistophilos sharply about the infernal regions, Faustus scoffs that "Hell's a fable" (124). Nothing is real for him but what he can perceive directly, and what he perceives he annexes directly to his own ego. Some of this is in the form of the "delights" that Mephistophilos brings him, enabling him to boast that Homer sings for him, that Alexander lies at his feet, and that Helen awaits his pleasure. His constant interrogation of Mephistophilos is, similarly, an attempt to enlarge his own "kingdom," for knowledge is immediately experienced as power by Faustus (the besetting sin of the scholar), and as Mephistophilos reveals to him one by one the secrets of "divine astrology" he swells with his appropriation of the cosmos. At the same time, however, he remains dissatisfied ("These slender questions Wagner can decide," 2.2.47), and presses his demand to know "who made the world" (64). The answer he knows and rejects is that God made it; the reply he wants to hear is that he who commands the world must be regarded as its author, and that Faustus is that commander. When Mephistophilos refuses to provide an answer, Faustus at first coaxes and then reviles him:

> *Fau.* . . . . Now tell me, who made the world?
> *Meph.* I will not.
> *Fau.* Sweet Mephostophilis, tell me.
> *Meph.* Move me not, Faustus!
> *Fau.* Villain, have I not bound thee to tell me anything?
> *Meph.* Ay, that is not against our kingdom. This is. Thou art damn'd.
>   Think thou of Hell!
> *Fau.* Think, Faustus, upon God, that made the world.
> *Meph.* Remember this! [*Exit.*]
> *Fau.* Ay, go accursed spirit to ugly Hell!
>   'Tis thou hast damn'd distressed Faustus' soul. —
>   Is't not too late?

(64–75)

Mephistophilos reminds Faustus of the independent existence of hell ("our kingdom"), and also of its ultimate limits (it will be whatever what is subtracted from heaven "when all the world dissolves," as Mephistophilos tells him at 2.1.118–123; it is what cannot speak the name of God). Hell *requires* heaven, and whatever is not self-subsistent can neither possess nor confer ultimate power. Faustus' fantasy collapses at the realization of this, and he is moved to do the one thing that is within his power but not Lucifer's, namely, to invoke God and affirm his sovereignty. This brings Lucifer himself, who warns him, in effect, not to blaspheme against hell (82–94). On an infantile level, Faustus' dismissal of Mephistophilos is the rejection of the incorporated Other who has failed to realize his fantasies of omnipotence. What is most humiliating, however, is the fact that Mephistophilos has already left the stage, leaving Faustus only to pronounce a futile oath ("go accursed spirit to ugly Hell"). Even that is merely redundant, since, as Mephistophilos has explained, hell is his condition—a condition that, thus far, excludes Faustus. Neither able to call upon heaven nor to command hell, Faustus is left in frustrated impotence: precisely the situation of the infant confronted with a noncompliant reality.

The dramatic suspense that sustains the play is whether Faustus will escape damnation, a question not resolved until its final scene. The very puerility of his desires and the harmlessness of his pranks suggests that he may, after all, still be a child of God, and he periodically expresses the wish to repent. It is Mephistophilos who, with a commercial persistence very like that of Barabas in Marlowe's *The Jew of Malta*, continually reminds him of his bond, and holds him to it with the threat of taking far more than a pound of flesh ("I'll in piecemeal tear thy flesh," 5.1.69). Their relationship is, in this sense, that of an adult charged with minding a particularly wayward child, who is alternately bribed with distractions and threatened with punishments. Insofar as we conceive Mephistophilos as an aspect of Faustus himself, he thus represents his tendency to hardened reprobation; insofar as we see him as a figure apart, he is a surpassing portrait of despairing worldly consciousness. He wins our confidence as one compelled to testify against himself:

> Why this is Hell, nor am I out of it. . . .
> Think'st thou that I who saw the face of God
> And tasted the eternal joys of Heaven
> Am not tormented with ten thousand Hells
> In being depriv'd of everlasting bliss?

> (1.3.73–77)

The image of spiritual torment in these lines would have no equal until Milton; in the peculiarly laconic quality of desolation it projects, it has per-

haps no equal in the Christian literature of the West. And when Mephistophilos, to forestall Faustus' repentance, reverses himself in the lines

> But think'st thou Heaven is such a glorious thing?
> I tell thee, Faustus, it is not half so fair
> As thou or any man that breathe on earth

(2.2.5–7)

we feel he twists the knife far more deeply in himself. Mephistophilos has all
the knowledge Faustus has the wit to seek, but what he knows above all is
what he has lost, which he experiences with an intensity of privation ("ten
thousand Hells") as deep as the joy of the blessed in paradise. Even as we
perceive his duplicity, we share his pathos. Faustus is on one level a gull
waiting to be fooled, but Mephistophilos wants to tell him the truth; he lies
because he must.

The scene of Faustus' damnation is one of the summits of English dramatic poetry. The scholars who attend him clearly recall the attendants at Philologos' deathbed, and Faustus, like his model, struggles to achieve repentance even as hell gapes for him. There is immense pathos in the line, "See,
see where Christ's blood streams in the firmament!", which represents the
only glimpse of heaven's mercy Faustus is vouchsafed, even as it remains
unattainably far from the sinner himself. The image vanishes, and Faustus is
then terrified by the vision of a divine wrath so appalling that, invoking
Scripture, he begs the mountains and hills to fall and cover him (5.2.154–
155)[41] — a reversal of his earlier fantasy-wish to "join the hills that bind the
Afric shore/ And make that country continent to Spain" (1.3.104–105), and
one that emphasizes his complete disempowerment. As Faustus is swept
into hell, the body he has pledged to Lucifer is rent in pieces in grim fulfillment of the premonitory episodes in which he suffers mock decapitation and
the temporary loss of his leg. All that remains of him, as if from a cannibal
repast, are severed limbs, and the scholars' testimony of his bloodcurdling
shrieks (5.3.2–10).

These final scenes would appear to be as orthodox a vision of reprobation
and damnation as one could wish, and one can only imagine their impact on
a contemporary audience. Yet here too a skeptical undercurrent subverts the
apparent message. It is not only that the stage business (chiming clocks, the
roar of thunder, the devils leaping up from the pit) calls attention to itself as
theatrical, but that we are reminded that what Faustus sees is, both literally
and metaphorically, the product of imagination. The blood of Christ that
streams along the firmament reminds us of the blood that flows, congeals,
and flows again on Faustus' arm in the contract scene. Like the migratory inscription *Homo fuge!* that likewise appears on his arm, the image of Christ's
blood disappears ("Where is it now? 'Tis gone!", 5.2.152). Nothing remains
firm or fixed, and the castaway limbs — an image itself compromised by its

association with the mock amputations of Act IV — are all that attest the reality of Faustus' demise. The scholars' solemn burial of his remains and the final chorus, moreover, at least partially rehabilitate Faustus the magus, and vindicate his quest for knowledge:

> Cut is the branch that might have grown full straight
> And burned is Apollo's laurel bough
> That sometime grew within this learned man.
> Faustus is gone. Regard his hellish fall!
> — Whose fiendful fortune may exhort the wise
> Only to wonder at lawful things
> Whose deepness doth entice such forward wits
> To practice more than heavenly power permits.
>
> (5.3.[20–27])

These lines, with their classical allusion, remind us of the occasions on which Marlowe refers to God as "Jove" (1.1.70; 1.3.86; 2.3.[35]). "Jove" is divinity as power, infinitely jealous of his prerogatives and without scruple in crushing all who would aspire to them. He can be approached only in terms of power, that is, of challenge or submission. This is the deity behind the deity that magic invokes, for the currency of magic is power, and whether it is purposed to good ends or bad ("white" or "black") only begs the question of origins. Power is subordinate to will, and the only issue is whether the magician ultimately serves his own ends or those of another, in that case "higher" power. Faustus himself has no particular end in view other than the enjoyment of power for its own sake, either as knowledge or as the more or less idle projects of his fancy (yoking the continents together; bearding the Pope; bringing a duchess a dish of grapes out of season). It has often been noticed that as the play proceeds, Faustus' desires become increasingly trivial, as if tracking the exhaustion of his ego. There is an image of the feminized tyrant in this, whose whims become ever more petty as the dissolution of his character proceeds. In Christian terms, Faustus serves the Devil's ends — the capture of his soul — but he continues to pursue God, though in an increasingly confused and disorganized fashion, by trying his powers this way and that, as if he could discover his own will in them. It is precisely in the conquest of his will, however, that he fails, for it remains trapped in aspiration, and never arrives at the sense of its totality that Elizabethan religious consciousness recognized as divine. Faustus imagines that if he can achieve a virtual simultaneity between wish and act he can approach divinity itself, since for him the immediate enactment of desire is its characteristic. But he never escapes the need for "sweet Mephistophilos" — these words are the last he utters — as the instrument of his desires, and therefore never achieves the true divine simultaneity in which will and power are instant and inseparable.

There is no tincture of mercy in the God Faustus aspires to; he is merely a rival, an adversary.[42] His periodic attempts to repent founder on this rock; he cannot believe in mercy (or, in orthodox terms, experience divine grace). When at the end he sees Christ's blood — the plenitude of God's grace — in the firmament, he begs for the single drop that will save him (5.2.149), only for the image to dissolve before that of an incensed and wrathful deity.[43] From an orthodox perspective, this is simply the sinner's hour of reckoning; but in his "Jovian" aspect, the Calvinist God appears, at least to the reprobate, as a being without mercy, and the fact that his mercy is simply not for *them* makes Faustus' vision not one of justice but of cruelty. Against cruelty one can only revolt. Faustus' reprobation (insofar as we conceive him as reprobate) is thus an act of tragic heroism. As a hopeless striving toward the divine, it is tragic; as a rebellion against the God who veils his face until he is ready to strike, it compels the honor the scholars pay Faustus, albeit under the guise of piety, at the play's end. But we need not, of course, confine Faustus to such narrow antitheses. The questing hero (a variant on the traditional trope of the Christian pilgrim) was more valorized than suspect in the Renaissance world, and Faustus would become the archetypal modern figure of the desire to transcend "natural limitation" that the ancients knew as hubris and that, refashioned by Renaissance Neoplatonism and Calvinist anxiety, appeared among the Elizabethans as aspiration.[44] In this sense Faustus' fall, though depicted through the conventions of the traditional morality play, is tragic in both classic and Christian terms.[45]

C. L. Barber speaks of Marlowe as having created a theater of blasphemy, even a theater *as* blasphemy, which found its perfected form in *Doctor Faustus*. Such a theater was, in its heroic aspects, about transcending limits; it was also, on the religious level, about testing them. The dichotomy between a freethinking and an orthodox Marlowe was, from this perspective, a false opposition; he was both at once and neither exclusively. As Barber observes, "One can have both [Marlowes] precisely because Marlowe was a dramatist. His sensibility was not satisfied by his 'views.' He needed to create a new drama because other forms of expression, adjusted as they were to received attitudes, could not serve his need."[46]

Certainly there were many other reasons for the emergence of the modern drama in England and elsewhere in the late sixteenth century, including, in the English case, the expression of a new civic culture and the interrogation of the country's recent history. But the deepest reason may have been the paradigm shift in Western consciousness of which the Reformation was both source and symbol, a shift that placed all orthodoxies in doubt, and left as its hero not the pilgrim in quest of a grail but a magician who would bring heaven to earth and "confound Hell in Elysium." Onstage, the magician's power was poetry, the mighty Marlovian line that reenchanted the world and, as Barber put it, not only invested "earthly things with divine attributes" but fused "these divine suggestions with [the] tangible values and resources of the secular world."[47] This made the poet himself a kind of "demi-god," as Faustus had described the competent magician (1.1.57), and thus the ultimate protagonist of all his works. With Marlowe, as with Rabelais and Cervantes, the poet-hero steps forward as Author, the overriding intelligence responsible for the text and for the body of work that constituted a career. Collaboration and more or less silent rewrites, such as corrupted the 1604 and 1616 texts of *Faustus*, were still commonplace in Marlowe's time, but the day of the anonymous folkwork was done.[48]

The individuated author presupposed, as Holinshed had not, an atomized audience. As Stephen Greenblatt puts it:

[O]ne of the defining characteristics of the dramaturgy of Shakespeare and Marlowe, as opposed to that of their medieval predecessors, is the startling increase in the level of represented and aroused anxiety. There is, to be sure, fear and trembling in the mysteries and moralities of the fifteenth and early sixteenth centuries, but a dread bound up with the fate of particular situated individuals is largely absent, and the audience shares its grief and joy in a collective experience that serves either to ward off or to absorb private emotions. Marlowe's *Faustus*, by contrast . . . seems like a startling departure from everything that has preceded it precisely because the dramatist has heightened and individuated anxiety to an unprecedented degree and because he has continued to implicate his audience as individuals in that anxiety.[49]

We know that *Faustus* was popular with contemporary audiences, for whom the novel *frisson* of anxiety was perhaps not the least of its attractions.[50] What must the experience have been like? John Melton provides us with a glimpse of the production at the Fortune Theater in Golding Lane in 1592: "There indeed a man may behold shag-hair'd devils run roaring over the stage with squibs in their mouths, while drummers make thunder in the tiring-house, and the twelve-penny hirelings make artificial lightning in their heavens." At another performance, an intruder dressed as a devil interrupted the action.[51] The possibility that representing demons might actually invoke them made Marlowe's audiences complicit in his dramaturgy, if only on a speculative level, and the mixture of credulity and skepticism they brought to such a speculation was itself a further stimulus to doubt. Paradoxically, the psychological verisimilitude of Marlowe's demons, particularly Mephistophilos, made them less plausible as representations of real entities. In the Vice figures of the traditional stage, the distinction between signifier and signified had always been clearly marked; such figures were understood as mere personifications. Mephistophilos, despite his shape-changing, was too realistic a figure to stand for anyone else—unless it were for Faustus himself. He was, in short, that very new thing in the Elizabethan world, a dramatic invention.

Negotiating Discourse: The Theater and Its Critics

Perhaps the remarkable thing about the production history of *The Tragicall History of Doctor Faustus* is that there was one. It is so difficult to credit that a play as subversive of established faith as *Faustus* could have played with relatively minor alteration throughout the Elizabethan and Jacobean periods that a distinguished critic, William Empson, devoted a book to demonstrating the censor's intrusive hand in the presumptive urtext as well as in the published 1604 and 1616 texts.[52] As Richard Dutton points out, Empson's case is purely speculative, and the only revision demonstrably dictated by the authorities was the deletion of certain oaths in conformity with the Act of 1606 in restraint of "Abuses of Players."[53] This does not mean that some of the emendations in the 1616 text were not either in response to orders from above or in anticipation of them. Janet Clare has argued that Elizabeth's censor, Edmund Tilney, may have cut part of the scenes in which Faustus and Mephistophilos beard the papal Court (3.1, 2), and that the alterations in the 1616 text had substantive doctrinal implications.[54] The latter claim is persuasive, but it underlines how belated censorship often was; at this latter point, *Faustus* had already been on the boards for nearly a quarter century.

The relationship of the censor to early modern English literature, more particularly the literature of the stage, has yet to be fully explicated. The Elizabethan Master of the Revels worked within a matrix of political relations in which he had to look not only to his ultimate employer, the Queen, but to various powerful individuals who patronized the theater and sought, as had the Protestantizing circle around Thomas Cromwell in Bale's time, to use it for their own purposes. At the same time, he had to deal with the public theater as an expression of a new urban energy that, while more diffused, was in its own way as difficult to contain. His function, moreover, was negative: not to get certain things said (that was the province of others within the Court), but to decide which things could not be said, or at least had to be said differently. If his powers seemed wide, they could also be frustrated, for his function was to scrutinize texts that by their very nature were allusive and polyvalent. Given the fact that such texts were being produced in unprecedented quantity for publics eager to consume them and that they were often spoken for by powerful patrons, his practical discretion was relatively small. What might seem to playwrights and playing companies a heavy hand from above was, from the censor's point of view, no more than a finger in the dike.

Put differently, the Master of the Revels was only one element in a complex of relationships that simultaneously attempted to govern and to exploit a strikingly new mode of public discourse. Although England had a long and rich history of institutional drama, and although, as we have seen in the case of John Bale, its traditional forms were capable of sophistication, wit, and a wide range of topical allusion, nothing like the theater of Marlowe, Kyd, Shakespeare, Jonson, and their fellows had ever been seen before. Only the discourse of the Reformation itself, from which it so largely derived, had comparable transformative potential. Like Reformed discourse, the new theater was both continuous with an older tradition and violently disruptive of it; like it, too, it refigured an established performative arena, both containing its spectacle in a new, interiorized space and concentrating it in a new illocutionary form—the monologue.

The evolution of Tudor drama and censorship went hand in hand. The Privy Council had regulated dramatic performance extensively between 1529 and 1559, occasionally suppressing it altogether. The church played a lesser role, no doubt reflecting the disarray in which ecclesiastical courts found themselves in the mid-years of the century, although it did gradually resume surveillance of religious drama, and issued all licenses for printing. With Elizabeth, policy shifted. A proclamation prohibiting all unlicensed plays and interludes was issued, vesting authority in local mayors and JPs under the surveillance of the church.[55] The prime purpose of this policy, which reflected the influence of the Marian exiles, was to facilitate the suppression of the mystery plays, which had been purged of elements reflecting Catholic ritual and authority under Henry and Edward but had been tainted again by the Marian restoration and remained, at least to godly perception, inextricably tied to the old order. Within a generation, they had been stamped out. Their suppression was met with resistance, and in York, Chester, Wakefield, and elsewhere the secular authorities, siding with popular sentiment, had to be overborne by the diocesan courts. This chapter of English history has not had the attention it deserves.[56] The mystery plays were not only a source of ethical and religious instruction but of civic pride and festival. They left a vacuum into which touring companies stepped in the 1580s, bringing with them the new repertory of the London stage, and with it the wider, more sophisticated, and more topical interests that stage represented. This was not necessarily a gain in social control.

What emerged in the 1580s was a complex, overlapping system of discourse production and censorship in which the Master of the Revels was only a single point of reference, albeit a focal one. The Privy Council continued to regulate the theater in general, forcing on it frequent interruptions of weeks or months in time of plague (with which the stage was ideologically as well as epidemiologically associated), civic disturbance, national crisis, and regnal succession. In special circumstances, it intervened directly to suppress a particular production, as in the case of the anonymous and now-lost play *Marquis d'Ancre*, which portrayed the recent murder of a French nobleman and presumably gave offense to the ever-sensitive French ambassador, the Count de Tillières:

> Wee are informed that there are certayne players or comedians wee knowe not of what company that goe about to play some enterlude concerning the late Marquesse d'Ancre, which for many respectes wee thincke not fitt to be suffered. Wee doe therefore require you upon your perill to take order that the same be not represented or played in any place about this citty or ellswhere, where you have authoritie. And hereof have you a speciall care.[57]

The addressee of this command was the Master of the Revels himself, Tilney's successor George Buc, and underneath the formulaic language ("upon your perill" was the phrase Buc used in issuing his own instructions) one can sense a degree of irritation; Buc had not done his job. The Master of the Revels had many others to answer to, beginning with the king or queen and descending through a hierarchy of courtiers and notables who might feel themselves the butt of allusion or satire. Particularly under Elizabeth the London City Council was assiduous, sometimes to the point of hysteria, in policing the stage, and in 1595 and 1597 it attempted to suppress it altogether.[58] The City Council was more concerned with order than ideology, for the sense of godly scandal that had latterly arisen about the secular theater had not yet made great inroads among London's elite.[59] The city was a dangerous place in the 1590s, when economic dearth, the Spanish and Irish wars, and the treacherous politics of succession combined to produce an unusually combustible atmosphere. The culminating event of the period, the Essex rising, was notoriously accompanied by a performance of Shakespeare's *Richard II* at the Globe Theater on February 7, 1601, commissioned and with remarkable imprudence attended by the conspirators.

The pressures to curb or even ban the public theater were balanced by the powerful interests that supported it. The Master of the Revels was responsible for producing entertainment as well as censoring it, and, as Janette Dillon points out, hiring professional performers from the London stage was a means of minimizing the expense of Court masques and interludes; the players at King Claudius' Court in Denmark had their counterparts in those of Elizabeth and James. Similarly, members of the Privy Council such as the earls of Leicester, Warwick, and Sussex, Lord Admiral Nottingham, and the two Lords Chamberlain Hunsdon, often formed their own licensed troupes, while Elizabeth herself patronized the Queen's Men, chartered in 1583. James not only kept a playing company, the Chamberlain's Men, but his wife Anna and their son Henry both kept their own stable of actors.[60] Though amateurs such as Bacon still composed royal *divertissements*, professional playwrights such as Jonson were increasingly involved in producing the ever-more elaborate and sophisticated masques that characterized Jacobean and Caroline Court culture. Courtly, aristocratic, and popular theater, though in many ways distinct, were thus symbiotic and deeply entwined. Moreover, if the cost of the theater was tolerating a degree of politico-religious satire and critique, and even the representation of rebellion itself, there were propaganda advantages as well. The Court and the church jointly sponsored a number of satires in response to the Marprelate tracts that de-picted a mock-Martin, composed of various animal parts in human shape, being tossed and spitted on the stage. Public opinion could be manipulated, and foreign governments placed on notice, by the quasi-official sponsorship of such plays as Thomas Middleton's anti-Spanish *A Game at Chess*.[61] The London City Council too had to weigh the political reality of this patronage, and the undoubted economic benefits the public theater brought, against its fear of tumult and contagion.[62]

On a deeper level, the intense theatricality of Elizabethan culture, which Stephen Greenblatt has evocatively described both in terms of personal "self-fashioning" and, collectively, as an expressively competitive circulation of social energy, produced the hothouse climate in which modern theater was born. This theater was profoundly Court-centered, both in terms of the dia-lectical relationship of patronage and censorship that shaped it and in terms of the subject that preoccupied it above all else, what J. W. Lever has called "the tragedy of state."[63] If Elizabeth and her entourage did not engender the public theater, and if the censor's ban on impersonating a living sovereign made it impossible to represent her directly, her own intensely performative style and the innate drama of an aging queen surrounded by male courtiers cast into the dual role of suitors and councilors found natural reflection on the city's stages no less than in the period's major nondramatic works, Sid-ney's *Arcadia* and Spenser's *The Faerie Queene*. The public theater served in this sense as a means of rehearsing and (provisionally) resolving the tensions of Elizabeth's Court, and of testing the nature and limits of Renaissance au-thority generally. As Lever pointed out, the Italian and Spanish settings of much of Elizabethan and Jacobean drama were not merely convenient fic-tions, but ways of incorporating absolutist and republican discourse.[64]

If the English theater embraced much of humanist political discourse, it remained a means of staging the Reformation and, more broadly, a means of pondering the nation's history as well. Both these exercises were combined in a work such as Thomas Heywood's *If You Know Not Me You Know Nobody*, which dealt with Elizabeth's perseverance over the Marian persecution, a triumph attributed, in true Foxean fashion, to the inspiration of the English bible (presumably Coverdale's) continually present at her side. The play's success — it went through eight editions between 1605 and 1639 — doubtless owed more to the cult of Gloriana that was revived at the Queen's death than to its appropriation of her as an icon for godly conventicles.[65] Nonetheless, the theater's unsettling potential for supernatural representation and unlicensed, not to say heretical religious discourse — both of which were abundantly on display in *Doctor Faustus* — made it a frightening and even a diabolic instrument for some. Recent scholarship has given us a far more nuanced view of godly relations with the stage, and has traced the continuity of Reformation theater from its beginnings with Bale and his circle down to the 1570s. As we have seen, these Protestantizing plays were the didactic competitors and successors of the traditional mystery and morality plays, incorporating their dramatic conventions and much of their social piety. Typically, as in the case of Bale, Woodes, and others such as Ulpian Fulwell, William Wager, and Richard Wever, the homiletic playwrights were themselves clergymen. In popularizing the tenets of the Reformation, however, they nurtured an appetite for religious controversy that would be exploited, with no due regard for doctrinal orthodoxy or moral uplift, by the secular, commercial theater. This led, at the end of the 1570s — a crucial moment in Elizabeth's reign, when the failure of the Alençon match ended all lingering hopes for a secure Protestant succession through the Tudor line — to a serious ideological breach. Godly preachers and pamphleteers suddenly denounced the stage as a work of Satan, raking up the denunciations of early church fathers such as Tertullian and Clement of Alexandria to argue that, if their warnings were not heeded, Albion would go the way of Rome. Thus, while the theater continued to reflect on the whole the broadly Reforming agenda of the dominant culture — and even Marlowe's *Faustus* could be read in that vein, as it has been by some modern critics — its godly sponsors abandoned it, abruptly and violently, on the eve of its greatest flowering. What died, then, was the didactic Protestant theater that had flourished from the time of Bale to that of Woodes, and that disappeared, at the same time though for diametrically opposite reasons, with the mystery cycles; and what replaced both, in a word, was tragedy.

What is of particular interest is that the two most vocal opponents of the emerging secular theater, Stephen Gosson and Anthony Munday, were both former playwrights who simultaneously renounced what they denounced. "I confesse," Munday wrote, "that ere this I have bene a great affecter of that vaine art of Plaie-making, insomuch that I haue thought no time so wel bestowed, as when my wits were exercised in the inuention of those follies." Gosson too admitted his former passion for the theater both as patron and playwright, even penning his repudiation of it as a work in "five acts."[66] For Munday, the pleasures of the stage were "but the drifts of Satan":

> What is there which is not abused thereby? Our hartes with idle cogitations, our eies with vaine aspects, gestures, and toies; our eares with filthie speach, unhonest mirth, and rebaldrie; our mouths with cursed speaking;

our heads with wicked imaginations; our whole bodies to uncleanes; our bodies and mindes to the seruice of the Diuel . . .[67]

Munday recoiled viscerally from "that filthie speech, that vile motion, the beastlie gestures," as if quite literally in the presence of evil, and Gosson declared flatly that "stage Plaies" were "the doctrine and inuention of the Devil," and "not to be suffered in a christian common weale." Both Munday and Gosson were appalled by the fact that such spectacles and those who performed them were not only countenanced but protected by the great lords whose livery they wore. Noting that "The warrant which Magistrats haue to forbid plaies is great," Munday urged them "not to shrinke in the Lords cause, or to stand in feare to reforme abuses of the Common-weale, because of some particular men of auctoritie."[68]

As Gosson explained, the drama, based as it was on conflict and suspense, was inherently corrupting, for "The mind of it selfe is simple without mixture or composition, [and] therefore those instructions that are giuen to the minde must bee simple without mingle mangle of fish and flesh, good and bad." Even when good triumphed in the end, the mere presence of any evil not framed by reproof was fatal, for "when both are profred, the hereditarie corruption of our nature taketh ye worst and leaueth the best." This was what made tragedy in particular so dangerous, for "The argument of Tragedies is wrath, crueltie, incest, iniurie, [and] murther eyther violent by sworde, or voluntary by poyson." Comedies, though perhaps less appalling, were only the more insidious as schools of vice, for their ground was "loue, cosenedge, flatterie, bawdrie, [and] slye conveighances of whordome." Neither was to be suffered, for "The best play you can picke out, is but a mixture of good and euill," and the very act of admixture guaranteed that evil alone would be the precipitate. Indeed, it was worse to hear Scripture on the stage than blasphemy, for it was precisely the Devil's art to defile holy writ by lowering it to the level of profane speech and forcing the word of God to consort with the mere word of man. One can only imagine Gosson's reaction to Faustus' concluding his pact with Lucifer with the words, "Consummatum est."[69]

In Gosson, the distinction between a susceptible audience and its sinful entertainment is still maintained, but for Munday the act of attending the theater as such is a choice of evil that makes the spectator complicit with the wickedness he imbibes. By the mere act of witnessing a drama, the audience lends credence and approval to what is performed, and thus "they al by sight and assent be actors" no less than the players on the stage. In the representation of whoredom, for example, "al the people in mind plaie the whores," and by extension they participate equally in every other scene of vice.[70] As the faithful gather for edification and worship, so the wicked as-

semble to pool their lustful imaginations in sin. The theater is the congregation of Satan.

Both Gosson and Munday (and virtually every other contemporary critic
of the theater) shared the same underlying complaint that citizens, particularly the common people who had most need of instruction, had abandoned
the churches in favor of play-going.[71] The preachers themselves were loud in
their reprehension of this: "godlie Preachers," Munday declared, ". . . daie by
daie in al places of greatest resort denounce the vengeance of GOD to them,
be they hie or lowe, that favor plaies, Theaters, or plaiers." Despite this, and
despite repeated edicts against Sunday playing, the theaters remained full:
"So the abhominable practises of plays in *London* haue bene by godly
preachers, both at Paules crosse, and else where, so zealously, so learnedly,
so loudly cried out upon to [such] small redresse, that I may well say of
them, as the Philosophers reporte of the heauens, we neuer heare them, because we euer heare them." Munday summarized: "The temple is despised,
to run vnto Theatres; the Church is emptied, the yeard is filled."[72]

The preachers' diatribes against theatergoers were echoed by conformist
complaints against godly congregants who, forsaking the stale homilies of
their own churches, went gadding after sermons in other parishes. In both
cases, it was claimed, audiences were exposed to seditious doctrine in
church and state by charismatic performers who seduced them from true
reverence and obedience. There was more than superficial truth in the comparison. As Bryan Crockett observes, both the stage and the pulpit offered
similar rhetorical strategies and epistemic services in orienting their respective and—as the cases of Gosson and Munday show—at times overlapping
audiences in a world of competing verities and conflicting ideologies. It has
long been a commonplace, of course, that the visual pomp and imagery extruded from Protestant churches in the sixteenth century (and from godly
ones more than any) migrated to the civic sites of pageant, tiltyard, and
stage. As Crockett points out, however, the Reformed emphasis on the word
placed an emphasis on the corporal presence and rhetorical style of the minister that was inevitably histrionic in nature:

> [The] *newly embodied* word superseded the traditional sacraments, refigur-
> ing in the physical presence of the speaker the Word that had been incar-
> nate in bread and wine. The reformers' impulse to shift the mode of repre-
> sentation from the visual to the aural was checked by the preacher's bodily
> presence, just as the impulse to abolish the priest as mediator resulted in a
> different kind of mediation in the person of the preacher. Rather than be-
> holding a profusion of visually alluring icons and then taking part in a
> communal act of sacrifice . . . the worshipper . . . could watch and listen as
> the preacher performed. Paradoxically, then, the Reformation insistence on
> the centrality of the spoken word reintroduced an element of theater into

the liturgy—albeit theater of a different order from the theatricality of which the medieval liturgy stood accused.[73]

The intense focus on the person of the minister led, then, to the personalization of the ministry, with the best preachers, such as William Perkins, drawing audiences from far and wide. This "gadding," not only after sermons as such,[74] nor even after the most accomplished rhetoricians, but most particularly for those whose evocations of the joys of heaven and the pains of hell were most compelling, all but erased parish boundaries. At the same time, such audiences (no longer, by the same token, "congregations" in the parish sense) became active connoisseurs and even, through endowed lectureships, direct employers of those who ministered to them.[75] Sometimes, as under the charismatic pastorate of John White in early seventeenth-century Dorchester, the symbiotic relationship of minister and public had important social and economic as well as religious consequences[76]; but, in any case, this new audience was, like that of the theater, a self-selected group of voluntary patrons who sought, in the guise of edification, much of the same emotional catharsis as playgoers, and exercised many of the same critical functions. In this, too, they were related to the citizen bodies described by Holinshed who exercised increasing discretion in judging the proffered tokens of legitimacy.

The idea, let alone the fact of competition between ministers of the Gospel and stage players was, of course, a scandal. For the godly, pulpit eloquence was not merely the product of learned study and elocutionary skills but of prophetic gifts, for preachers of the Word were the vessels of divine communication.[77] No matter how gravely and self-effacingly ministers might present themselves they were a cynosure, for, as William Perkins noted, "simple people behold not the ministry, but the person of the minister."[78] The open-air sermons at Paul's Cross, the most prestigious in England, are described by their historian as morality plays in miniature, complete with penitential figures who, though subject to actual chastisement, clearly served a dramatic function as well.[79] Crowds of up to six thousand attended these sermons, twice the number accommodated by London's largest theaters, and keeping such multitudes in order for what amounted to a two-hour monologue was a theatrical challenge few actors would have undertaken. Here as in other respects we are reminded of the extent to which the Elizabethan stage was a child of the Reformation, and that in a culture uniquely conditioned by the power of the spoken word, the clergy had appropriated and theatricalized it before anyone else.

It is in this context that we might consider two exactly contemporaneous phenomena: the suppression of clerical prophesyings by Elizabeth, and the erection of the first public theaters. The performative aspect of prophesyings is evident: clerical disputants ranged on a stage before a large and (on some occasions) actively participatory audience, enacting a discourse that was simultaneously collegial and competitive, illocutionary and hermeneutic. Of course, such exercises were viewed by their proponents as straightforwardly edifying in character and intent, and any comparison to the black arts of the drama would have been deeply offensive. It could nonetheless not have escaped notice that while the theater in all its blasphemy was flourishing under noble and (in short order) royal patronage, the government had forbidden the public expounding of the Scripture beyond the traditional pulpit. The construction of the first enclosed playhouses at the same time (while many churches languished in disrepair) would have been even more galling and provocative. If the stage as such was a temple of Satan, then the Red Lion and the Rose, the Theater and the Curtain, the Swan and the Globe, were his principal synagogues. The celebrated London earthquake of April 10, 1580, was seen in part as a divine punishment for the iniquity of the public stage and the abandonment of the Sabbath it was deemed largely responsible for having caused, as was the fatal collapse of the Paris Gardens, a bearbaiting arena, in January 1583. The destruction of the Globe Theater in 1613 and of the Fortune in 1621 were similarly viewed by godly commentators, and as late as 1653 the collapse of the White Hart Inn in Witney, Oxfordshire, during a stage performance was attributed to providential judgment.[80]

Critics of the stage thus kept up their denunciations until the closing of the theaters in 1642 and beyond. Their chief emphases continued to be on the profanation of the Sabbath and the encouragement of vice. Nonetheless, godly opinion was not univocal. Philip Stubbes, a contemporary of Gosson and Munday, admitted that "when honest & chast playes, tragedies, & interludes, are used . . . for the Godly recreation of the mind, for the good example of life, for the avoyding of that, which is euill, and learning of that which is good, than they are very tollerable exercises."[81] Nor did a didactic Protestant theater entirely disappear with the morality plays; though necessarily more sophisticated and topical, it continued to flourish in the work of Robert Wilson in the 1580s.[82] It is worthy of note too that the godly Earl of Leicester was the first of Elizabeth's courtiers to establish his own playing company, although much to the consternation of anti-theatrical ministers such as John Field who depended on him for protection and support. Protestantizing themes continued to sound on the Jacobean and Caroline stage, particularly at moments of political crisis, and Prince Henry extended Leicester's tradition of godly patronage. In a Court and a world (including the pulpit) as profoundly theatricalized as that of late sixteenth and early seventeenth century England, blanket denunciations of the stage were of little practical consequence except among those whom Ben Jonson referred to sardonically as the "brethren." Even among the fiercest critics, moreover, there were backsliders. Stephen Gosson took holy orders in 1584, but Anthony Munday returned to the stage as an author of comedies and, more surprisingly, of *Sir Thomas More*, a sympathetic account of England's most famously recalcitrant Catholic.[83]

The strands of resistance to the theater were many and complex, as was its dialectical relation to the power centers at whose sufferance it existed and whose purposes (themselves often unstable and conflicting) it both served and subverted. The sudden emergence of godly opposition to the stage is a special case, however, both in the vehemence of its invective and the stubbornness of its persistence. Like the interminable debate between Catholic controversialists and defenders of the Anglican church over the legitimacy of England's secession from Rome, it spanned generations, now flaring in this quarter and now in that. It is true that the stage had always been suspect among those who, like the Lollards, associated it with the idolatry and pomp of the official church.[84] Nonetheless, it had been a chief instrument of the Reformation for forty years, and such men of unimpeachable authority as Bale and Foxe had employed it. The formation of Leicester's company, which included as performer and playwright the godly Robert Wilson,[85] appeared at least in part to have been an extension of this tradition. Why, then, did it suddenly become anathema to godly ministers and critics?

We have canvassed the question of competition between the playing companies and the London clerics, particularly for Sabbath audiences, and taken note of the concurrent suppression of the morality plays in the provinces by ecclesiastical authority. There is clear suggestion in this that the popular religious theater had served its purpose, and that catechizing could now be confined to the more controlled and appropriate forum of the parish pulpit. It was the rise of the new public, commercial theater, however, that presented the greatest threat to a godly commonwealth. This was a theater whose very wares—*As You Like It, What You Will, Believe What You List, A New Way to Pay Old Debts*—proclaimed, as Douglas Bruster observes, its dependence on a marketplace in which consumer satisfaction, construed in terms of base titillation and flattery of the multitude, was the ultimate yardstick.[86] Nothing more adverse to edification could be imagined. It was true that the old morality theater had been popular too, but, tied as it was to traditional, homiletic texts and displays of civic pageantry and rituals of assent, it was a venue for the affirmation and enforcement of dominant values. The public theater, in contrast, no matter how dependent on elite patronage and no matter how often (like that other public performance space, Parliament) a site of elite conflict, was in the last analysis subject to the approbation of an audience whose composition confounded high and low, and whose responses signaled not the completion of a foreordained ritual, but something radically new and contingent: success or failure.

Just as the sternest opposition to the stage came from those who borrowed its techniques in the pulpit, so an intriguing parallel existed between the audiences of the public theater and those of godly conventicles and lecture-ships. Both, in contrast to those at official spectacles such as processions and hangings and those who attended parish churches, were wholly voluntary and self-constituted; both were objects of persuasion whose assent had to be earned rather than invoked, and in whom a merely formulaic response—tepid applause or lukewarm conviction—was more damning than an overtly negative one. Both tended to be, or become, sophisticated critics of the wares offered them, and both shared an even more ineluctable feature of the market: they paid directly and of their own volition for the services they consumed. Both, finally, existed in sequestered pockets or quasi-outlaw borderlands, such as the liberties outside London's municipal authority.[87] Was it this very structural affinity that prompted, at least in part, such ideological revulsion? Christian liberty was at once uncomfortably close to consumer choice and its dialectical opposite, just as virtue was in relation to vice.

The question at issue was not, however, ultimately one between entertainment and edification, which could have been resolved, at least in theory, by vigorously enforced Sabbath legislation. It lay in the very nature of the choices offered by the new theater, the dramatic choice as such. Just as Vice and Virtue were counterposed in the godly sermon, so they might strut together on the morality stage. Vice might even have the best and wittiest lines, as it does in *King Johan*; the rhetorical triumph of Virtue was always assured. The new stage, however, with its complexity of theme and character, suspended and even problematized moral judgment. It was not enough to take home from *Othello* or *Macbeth* or *Doctor Faustus* that jealousy was a vice or ambition a dangerous passion. The corpses that litter the stage of revenge tragedy do not suggest reconstituted order but its intolerable absence—the "Hieronymo's mad againe" that T. S. Eliot plucked from Kyd's *Spanish Tragedy* to describe a world to which violence was the only fitting answer yet in no sense the solution. It was a world in which evil no longer appeared in the form of trapdoor devils or allegorical figures that could be swept from the stage at the end but was embedded in character—Iago's world. In *King Johan* and many another play of the same genre—*Faustus* is a late echo—Vice alone is shape-shifting and duplicitous, and clearly marked as such. The Elizabethan stage Machiavel, in contrast, remains physically and to all appearances morally constant; he corrupts not by offering seductive pleasures but by inspiring confidence. His victims—Desdemona is a paradigmatic example—are those whose real constancy renders them helpless before evil: their virtue no longer protects them (even in martyrdom), but is the very instrument of their downfall. In the City and Italianate comedies, constancy becomes credulity, and those who believe too readily or act too inflexibly become gulls whose misfortune the audience is invited to sneer at, or whose rescue often depends on the resourcefulness of those willing to adopt Machiavellian strategies on their behalf. Such veiled heroes do not always resolve the tensions and ambiguities in their behavior; as in the case of Shakespeare's Duke Vincentio in *Measure for Measure*, they leave us wondering whether a super-Machiavel has not staged a near-tragedy for dubious purposes of his own. Where constancy is finally discarded as a credible source of emplotment, we are left with the theater of Webster and Tourneur, where only Machiavels remain to act out their grim rituals of entrapment and slaughter. We thus return to the starting-point of Elizabethan tragedy, a stage littered with corpses. Such a cul-de-sac is implicit in the dramaturgy of Marlowe, but was Shakespeare's genius to avoid, or, rather, to more deeply problematize. If Marlowe had revealed the instability of character in *Faustus*, Shakespeare suggests its denseness and impenetrability instead. His heroes and villains are alike ultimately fathomless, and the silence in which Iago exits the stage is far more chilling than any number of Revenge corpses.

Calvinist theology had a sufficient framework for characterological evil— reprobation—but it could not subsist without an appeal to the invincibility of grace in the elect. Characters exhibiting virtue and rectitude continued to appear on the English stage, but they were more and more likely to meet untoward ends and less and less likely to prevail without assuming the protean devices of their adversaries. In this rather than in any overtly expressed skepticism lay the basis of the charge of "atheism" that clung to the new theater and whose first targets were Marlowe and Kyd. A conditional good might survive in a world of moral relativism, but invincible grace could hardly be preached in it. For the godly, that was the irremediable flaw of the public stage. It had ceased to be an adjunct of the pulpit; it was worse than a rival to it. Even when it still upheld notionally Protestant values, it had become the mirror of a fallen and abandoned world.

The Play of Sovereignty

The depiction of character on the public stage was nowhere more problematic than in the case of monarchs. It was treason to impersonate a ruler, and no living sovereign could be represented on the stage.[88] It was possible to circumvent this latter restriction by means of allegory, as Jonson had done in *Cynthia's Revels* and Bale in his depiction of the imperial Henry VIII in *King Johan*. Certain sovereigns were taken as coded references for others, as the last Plantagenet had been for Elizabeth long before the famous staging of Shakespeare's *Richard II* on the eve of Essex's rebellion.[89] Topical allusions could be exceedingly risky however, as John Hayward had discovered in writing of Henry IV, and in the riot-torn 1590s the public stage had not only

been intermittently suspended but, at least apparently, had come close to being shut down altogether.[90]

Despite—and perhaps partly because of—these unfavorable auspices, the
English stage saw a plethora of plays about the nation's kings (nine by
Shakespeare alone) in the last decade of the sixteenth century. Nor were
these plays a prop to majesty or nativist pride. As Michael Manheim observes, "The dominant [regal] figure in most plays of the 1590s is a composite of Shakespeare's Henry VI, Richard II, and John"—kings, that is to say,
who suffered the ignominy of domestic rebellion, foreign defeat, and finally
disgrace, deposition, and, in the former two cases, violent death.[91] As a
group, they reflect the profoundly unsettled conditions of the late Elizabethan polity, including divided government, a ruler regarded as increasingly
irrelevant (except as an obstruction), and uncertainty in the succession. They
emerge, moreover, against a deeper literary background that includes the
Senecan reception in English drama; Marlowe's translation of the first book
of Lucan's *Pharsalia*, a republican proof-text for the entire period up to and
including the Civil War;[92] the pessimistic late humanism of Sidney and
Spenser; the controversy over Irish colonization, which, as Markku Peltonen
has shown,[93] concealed an anxious debate over the English commonwealth;
Hayward's *The first part of the life and raigne of king Henrie the IIII*; Samuel
Daniel's *History of the Civil Wars*; and, of course, the Holinshed *Chronicles*,
whose second edition was so heavily subjected to censorship. Even Sir
George Buc, Tilney's successor as Master of the Revels, wrote a *History of the
Life and Reign of Richard III*. This profusion of discourse, unexampled since
the 1530s, could not help but spill over into the new urban theater, which
served both as an extension of courtly debate and as a medium of appeal to
the broader public. Both Richard Dutton and Margot Heinemann are correct
in their very different descriptions of the way this theater functioned. Dutton
writes that "the whole system of a factional Court, supported by a complex
interweaving of patronage, conspired in most circumstances to 'allow' a
wide range of comment on contemporary affairs, so long as this was properly licensed, suitably veiled and not slanted with offensive particularity at a
powerful constituency." Heinemann observes that "From the 1580s the
commercial theatres, together with the pulpits of the popular preachers and
the other great innovation of cheap printing, provided the nearest equivalent
to the modern mass media, helping to create and form something like a secular public opinion far beyond the limits of the recognized 'political nation',
the natural rulers as represented at Court, in parliament, and in central and
local government."[94] By chartering stage companies (and threatening condign punishment for any who attempted to operate outside their confines),
by requiring the licensing of plays for performance and publication, by enmeshing the playwrights themselves in a web of favor and protection, and

by creating overlapping (and sometimes competing) mechanisms of regulation and censorship, the state and its agents created a flexible system of control and accommodation. Performers and productions shuttled between the Court and the city theaters, becoming familiars of both (and of the various quasi-public venues that existed in between). At the same time, the public appetite for comment and satire on city and Court mores, on the play of power itself, created a market whose demands could not be satisfied by mere pomp and pageantry, the increasingly hollow cult of Gloriana. As Catherine Belsey has remarked, power alone, even if unitary, cannot stage itself without becoming mere ceremony; and the late Elizabethan Court was anything but unitary. As that Court played its divisions out, in part upon the public stage, it could not but spur active spirits to press the limits of permissiveness and control—to interrogate, in the unique "liberty" of theatrical space, the nature of authority. In dramatic terms, that meant above all a focus on royalty.

Michael Manheim's reading of the theater of the 1590s posits a progression from the depiction of "weak" kings to the morally ambiguous triumph of Shakespeare's Henry V at the conclusion of his second trilogy. For Manheim, this represents the final supersession of the saintly, ineffectual king whose archetype was Edward the Confessor and whose latter epitome was Henry VI, and the incorporation of the Machiavellian subject in the person of his father, in Hazlitt's phrase the "amiable monster" of modern politics.[95] The weak king image itself was, however, a highly complex one, and met at certain points that of its apparent polar opposite, the strong-willed tyrant whose heroic archetype was Marlowe's Tamburlaine. *Tamburlaine*, though it intersects with traditional notions of the tyrant as the ministerial scourge of God and touches ironically on the concept of the elect ruler,[96] is fundamentally a romance in which Marlowe is concerned, as in *Doctor Faustus*, to push the Renaissance will to power *à outrance*. To explore the anxieties of royal power (and related issues of counsel) on the late Elizabethan and early Jacobean stage, we will examine three plays set closer to home, Marlowe's *Edward II* and Shakespeare's *Richard II*, and Jonson's *Sejanus*. First, however, we will examine the image of King John as it was reworked on the stage of the 1590s.

King John and the Fictions of Legitimacy

No king was as frequently represented in late Elizabethan drama as John. He appears in the anonymous *The Troublesome Raigne of King John*, in *Look About You*, in the popular Robin Hood plays of the period, and of course in Shakespeare's *King John*. This late Tudor John is a very different figure from Bale's saintly martyr. In part this was due to the availability of more recent and positive models of the Confessor archetype in Edward VI and in Eliza-

beth herself, whose resistance to the Marian tyranny was the subject of Thomas Heywood's *If You Know Me Not You Know Nobody* (1603).[97] In part it represented the supersession of that archetype in favor of a more complex dynamic, best exemplified in the figures of Edward II and Richard II. In the
John plays, however, particularly in *The Troublesome Raigne* and *King John*,
the unsettling paradox of a ruler who was at once Constantinian emperor
and tyrant remain unresolved.

John's return to a stage as topical as that of the late sixteenth-century theater reflected the perceived analogies between his reign and Elizabeth's. Like
Elizabeth, he had been confronted by a papally sponsored invasion that
aimed at his deposition. Like her, his legitimacy had been called in question.
Like her, he had overcome baronial insurrection only to face its prospect
anew. Some no doubt saw a more sinister resemblance as well. Elizabeth had
executed her chief rival for the throne, Mary of Scotland, while John had
eliminated his younger brother Arthur. To be sure, there were important differences between these two events. John had done away with an innocent
kinsman whose only offense was the blood they shared, while Elizabeth had
acted publicly and with the support of virtually the entire political nation
against a criminal conspirator. For Catholic polemicists, however, Mary's
execution was the final stamp of a usurper, and Elizabeth's own seeming
equivocation over it the mark of a damned conscience.

Both in *The Troublesome Raigne* and in *King John*, John acts regally in defending his own sovereignty and England's independence from Rome.
Shakespeare's John could not be more the divine right king standing upon
his indefeasible power than in retorting to the papal legate Pandulph:

> What earthly name to interrogatories
> Can task the free breath of a sacred king?
> Thou canst not, cardinal, devise a name
> So slight, unworthy, and ridiculous,
> To charge me to an answer, as the pope.
> Tell him this tale; and from the mouth of England
> Add thus much more,—That no Italian priest
> Shall tithe or toll in our dominions:
> But as we under heaven are supreme head,
> So, under him, that great supremacy,
> Where we do reign, we will alone uphold,
> Without th'assistance of a mortal hand:
> So tell the pope; all reverence set apart
> To him and his usurped authority.

> [III.1.147–160][98]

Bale's petulant John has no such fire in him; this is "the mouth of England" indeed. *The Troublesome Raigne's* author makes him no less defiant: "I

scorne to be subiect to the greatest Prelate in the world . . . and hee that contradicts me in this, Ile make him hoppe headlesse" (I.6.13, 19–20).[99] Yet even at his most regal John reminds us of his fatal handicap, for as heir to the throne only by a contested will his own "usurped authority" is the gravamen of both plays. The punning lines that open *King John* immediately lay the issue before us:

> KING JOHN Now say, Chatillon, what would France with us?
> CHATILLON Thus, after greeting, speaks the King of France
>   In my behaviour to the majesty,
>   The borrowed majesty of England here.
> [Queen] ELEANOR: A strange beginning: 'borrowed majesty'?
> (1.1.1–5)

Eleanor, as it were unwittingly, gives voice to the theme not only of *King John* but of the two Henriads as well, for borrowed majesty is indeed a "strange beginning," both for a reign and for the play that anamorphically represents it. The same phrase invokes as well the bastardy of Philip Falconbridge, who claims to be the son of Richard Coeur de Lion and whom John simultaneously knights and rebaptizes ("Arise Sir Richard and Plantagenet") and whom Eleanor embraces in return for his adherence to John's cause (1.1.162; 168). To "become" a Plantagenet, the Bastard casts off his given name and title, and accepts new legitimacy from a man whose own legitimacy, in the natural as well as regal sense, is challenged (2.1.124–128). John, who is indubitably a queen's son, thus yokes to him the man who claims to be the son of his predecessor, thereby making of their "two bodies" a suppositional regal whole. This makes the Bastard's loyalty to John rather less of a mystery than some commentators have had it, for if he is indeed a self-fashioned Renaissance man who constructs his own identity, he cannot be a self-authorized one. His story must be confirmed, even as part of a cynical bargain, and he must stand by the man who confirms it.

Behind these maneuvers is the perception that legitimacy is ultimately a legal fiction whose keepers are those ordinarily excluded from the political process altogether. As Phyllis Rackin notes, "In a well-ordered patriarchal world, women are silent or invisible. . . . But in *King John*, the fathers and husbands are dead, reduced to the status of names in history books, and the wives and mothers survive on Shakespeare's stage to dispute the fathers' wills and threaten their patriarchal legacies."[100] These dangerous widows are able to make virtual pawns of their sons by the knowledge they threaten to reveal (or invent). In holding the key to the past they hold that of the future as well, for to discredit birth is effectively to castrate. When John declares that he will defend his kingdom by "Our strong possession and our right," Eleanor immediately 'shortens' him: "Your strong possession much more than your right" (1.1.39–40). The shadow of illegitimacy that hangs over him (a double one, involving not only lineage but the dubiety of Richard's will), leads him to command Arthur's death and to crown himself a second time. These actions predictably backfire, and John is forced to accept his crown a third time from Pandulph. This completes his delegitimation, for his one kingly merit was to resist the papacy and to affirm the dependence of his throne on heaven alone. He now enters the Machiavellian world of Richard III, where only the hazard of battle remains and allies must be bought by favor and interest.

If John inhabits this world as a consequence of a weak dynastic claim compounded by his own villainy, the Bastard embraces it openly. When Lady Falconbridge asks whether he has "denied thyself a Falconbridge," he responds with alacrity, "As faithfully as I deny the devil" (1.1.251–252). His conviction of his royal birth—the supposed truth of which he finally wrings from his mother—deprives him of worldly status and estate; as he himself says, "Legitimation, name, and all is gone" (248). What he gains is a quasi-magical faith in his own destiny, based on the sense, still active in Shakespeare's time, of the unique virtue of a king's loins. As another of the play's dubious inheritors, however, he testifies as well to the anxieties of younger males in a world ruled by royal and aristocratic dowagers. In Richard he finds the perfect image of the idealized absent father, who offers him the seal of his identity while leaving his "mounting spirit" (205) scope for fantasy.[101]

What the Bastard gains by mythologizing his origins—for the confession of royal paternity that he bullies out of his mother is no more verifiable than her previous assertions of his lawful birth—is thus the ability to define himself. But to be self-defined in a world maintained by the fictions of legitimacy (1.1.116–129) is simultaneously to be disinherited: to be, as Eleanor neatly puts it, "Lord of thy presence and no land beside" (137). The Bastard's protean, almost Vice-like instability (Michael Manheim identifies four major speaking voices in him, and one might almost say there is a different one for each speech)[102] is the direct outgrowth of this, for apart from John's tacit acceptance of him as the shadowy second body that completes his own, he exists in a social limbo, the lackland adventurer who, on the stage of the 1590s, evokes an elite version of the anxiety stirred by the Elizabethan "sturdy beggar."[103] Such an adventurer is all the more dangerous in the shape of a courtier-Machiavel, and most dangerous of all at the side of a king whom he can personate ("For thus his royalty doth speak in me," 5.2.129). If the Bastard remains a sounding-board for these possibilities rather than a villain himself, it is perhaps because John fills that part so well. Dying, aptly enough, of the same treachery by which he has lived, he experiences a sense of inward reprobation even more terrifying than that of Faustus because beyond the reach of tears or sight:

PRINCE HENRY O that there were some virtue in my tears,
  That might relieve you!
KING JOHN   The salt in them is hot.
  Within me is a hell, and there the poison
  Is, as a fiend, confined to tyrannise
  On unreprievable, condemned blood.

(5.7.43–48)

John's sense of damnation is even more palpable in the deathbed scene of *The Troublesome Raigne*:

Me thinks I see a cattalogue of sinne
Wrote by a fiend in Marble characters,
The least enough to loose my part in heaven.
Me thinks the Deuill whispers in mine eares
And tels me tis in vayne to hope for grace
I must be damnd for *Arthurs* sodaine death,
I see I see a thousand thousand men
Come to accuse me for my wrong on earth,
And there is none so mercifull a God
That will forgiue the number of my sinnes.

(II.13.66–75)

In a dénouement reminiscent of the (revised) *Conflict of Conscience*, the Bastard urges John to seek Christ's mercy, and, remembering David's pardon and prophesying "Babylon's" fall, he dies "in the faith of Jesu" (107, 110).

If *The Troublesome Raigne* ends with a conventional act of piety, Shakespeare's John dies not only unconsoled but with an announcement of catastrophe in his ear—the loss of the Bastard's army in the Lincoln Washes. By this time the condition of John's soul has ceased to matter, at least on Shakespeare's stage, and the play moves briskly to its conclusion, with England's foes discreetly retiring and the Bastard, in a last piece of irony, acknowledging young Prince Henry as the King's legitimate heir.

The flawed protagonist of *The Troublesome Raigne* shows late Elizabethans grappling with the problem of a bad king who represents a good cause. This version of John offers a tyrant redeemed as a martyr, a strategy employed as well in *Edward II* and *Richard II*. Shakespeare's John is in contrast a Machiavellian figure, who even in his finest moment, standing upon his rights as a divine right monarch, acts a role that is arguably not his. Behind this irony is the far more radical suggestion that he who plays the king *is* the king: that every king, whatever his birth, is a successful "pretender."

Herbert Lindenberger has argued that "The action of historical drama is more precisely a struggle for legitimacy than a struggle for power as such."[104] One might reply that the issue is one of establishing identity, for which neither power alone (Eleanor's "strong possession") nor mere titular entitlement suffices. Shakespeare brings this question to a head in the scene before the walls of Angiers in which John and Philip II of France compete (the latter ostensibly on behalf of Arthur) for the acclaim of the townspeople. The people refuse to open their gates to either party, not unlike the burghers of Exeter in Holinshed, and to Philip's sharp command to "Speak, citizens, for England; who's your king?", a spokesman replies, "The King of England, when we know the king" (2.1.362–363). This sly retort draws from the Bastard the suggestion that the two claimants level the town together before resuming their own struggle:

> By heaven, these scroyles of Angiers flout you, kings,
> And stand securely on their battlements
> As in a theatre, whence they gape and point
> At your industrious scenes and acts of death.
> Your royal presences be ruled by me:
> Do like the mutines of Jerusalem,
> Be friends awhile, and both conjointly bend
> Your sharpest deeds of malice on this town.
>
> That done, dissever your united strengths
> And part your mingled colours once again,
> Turn face to face and bloody point to point;
> Then in a moment Fortune shall cull forth
> Out of one side her happy minion,
> To whom in favour she shall give the day,
> And kiss him with a glorious victory.
> How like you this counsel, mighty states?
> Smacks it not something of policy?
>
> (373–380; 388–396)

There are two major points to be observed about the Bastard's speech: first, that he not only leaps in to offer counsel ("Your royal presences be ruled by me") but that he even presumes to "act" the place of both sovereigns; and, second, that what he suggests is the destruction of the very prize for which they contend. This seems absurd on the face of it, but in terms of the Bastard's deliberately theatricalized rhetoric it does, indeed, smack of policy. The townspeople of Angiers, perched on their battlements, are likened to rude spectators at a play who "gape" and "point" at the "scenes" and "acts" performed for their amusement below, i.e., at the clash of arms between John and Philip. This is precisely the privilege that cannot be permitted them, for if subjects become "citizens" in this untoward sense — agents vested with choice, for whose favor rulers contend as actors compete for the applause of an audience — then monarchy itself cannot prevail. Before they fight each other, then, the rival kings must show themselves worthy of a crown by reducing their prospective subjects; otherwise, their combat will only be a spectacle. If the result of this is that neither will have any subjects left to rule, at least in Angiers, they will both have shown their proper mettle, at which point they may hazard themselves before the ultimate, inescapable arbiter, Fortune, who will choose her "happy minion." Power, in this Machiavellian world where appearance and assertion is all, must show its willingness to kill before it can earn the right to rule.

What is conspicuously absent in the Bastard's vision is legitimacy, the legal fiction which is at best the pretext of a claim that can only be vindicated by force, and Providence, which links royal birth to the will of heaven. The Bastard's point of view is, of course, conditioned by the fact that the same lineage that entitles him to the throne also debars him from it, so that to assert his paternal right—the most essential right of a patriarchal society—is simultaneously to relinquish all right, rank, and status. What he sees is that only in so doing can he transcend the profoundest irony of such a society, namely its dependence on the fiction of female virtue. In a play dominated by women, he is the only truly independent male figure, and in that sense the only deserving occupant of a patriarchal throne. It is this that bonds him to John, and vice versa; and this too that accounts for his behavior, in which he simultaneously asserts his loyalty (notionally to John, actually to the throne he regards as rightfully his own) and exercises, not to say usurps the authority of the crown, both in the extraordinary presumption of his Angiers speech ("Your royal presences be ruled by me") and in the scenes in which he acts as John's "deputy" (5.1.77; 5.2.127ff; 5.3.5; 4.4.5).[105] If this is the fate Providence has assigned him he will gladly take his own chances with fortune; and, by inference, all other "mounting spirits" dissatisfied with their lot are likewise encouraged. From there it is a short step, via the Citizen of Angiers who persuades both kings to compromise and thereby saves his city, to the Bastard's famous "commodity" speech (2.1.561–598), and to a world of interest in which all values are negotiable and bravado (as opposed to genuine valor) is the key to success.

The Commodity speech has rightly been taken as the crux of *King John*, and in a sense—coming at the midpoint of a play that stands itself at the center of Shakespeare's traversal of English history—it epitomizes his sense of the shifting ground he saw under his contemporaries' feet. The Bastard's own unstable psyche, itself, in Alexander Leggatt's phrase, an "amalgam"[106] of the conflicting propensities of the age, ranges in the course of this speech from angry moralist to stage Machiavel to the sophistries of the polished Machiavellian courtier. Frustrated in his "wild counsel" for the destruction of Angiers by the politique diplomacy of the Citizen, he lashes out at John for yielding part of his royal claim (which, as John's alter ego, is also his own) in return for a spurious confirmation of the rest, and at Philip for abandoning his "conscience . . . zeal and charity" as "God's own soldier" for a dull bargain. This is the language of honor and crusade, whose ideological obsolescence is a mask for the Bastard's quasi-anarchic spirit and which it-self bespeaks a Machiavellian perception of the unbridled violence at the heart of power (both John and Philip initially agree to level the city before the Citizen intervenes). Shakespeare here demystifies the feudal ethos whose forms survived not only in baronial insurrection and the rituals of Elizabe-than chivalry but had been revived in the Reformed emphasis on conscience and the crusading Constantinian emperor. These pieties soon give way to the description of "tickling Commodity," "that . . . purpose-changer, that sly devil,/ That broker that still breaks the pate of faith" (567–568). Commodity, which the play's editor, L. A. Beaurline, serviceably defines in his interlinear note as "Self-interest at the expense of honour and the general welfare," is thus protean, a Vice figure, and a seller of false goods (the "faith" it breaks can be read as both religious and commercial). Shakespeare then reifies it as a "bias," and a "sway of motion" that displaces all "direction, purpose, course, intent," and unbalances a world "Made to run even upon even ground"—simultaneously an image of an Edenic paradise corrupted by sin and of the celestial dysfunctions of the new astronomy. Along the way it picks up the connotation of a pander as well, becoming finally "This bawd, this broker, this all-changing word," whose only principle is change itself.

It is only after this riptide of descriptive clauses that the Bastard returns to his ostensible subject and blames Commodity for the abandonment of an "honourable" war and the conclusion of a "base" peace. The speaker who concludes this lengthy sentence (561–586) is not the same one who began it, however. In blaming Commodity, the Bastard in effect absolves John and Philip, and thus himself abandons the concept of a moral responsibility cen-tered in the individual—i.e., honor—in favor of an impersonal process. The seventeenth century would recognize this process as interest and the eigh-teenth century as the market, but in the Bastard's speech it is still entangled with Fortune:

> And why rail I on this Commodity?
> But for because he hath not wooed me yet.
> Not that I have the power to clutch my hand
> When his fair angels would salute my palm,
> But for my hand, as unattempted yet,
> Like a poor beggar raileth on the rich.
> Well, whiles I am a beggar I will rail,
> And say there is no sin but to be rich;
> And being rich, my virtue then shall be
> To say there is no vice but beggary.
> Since kings break faith upon commodity,

Gain, be my lord, for I will worship thee.

(587–598)

Commodity's "fair angels" are Fortune's (and heaven's) emissaries, but also the ceremonial coin handed to those touched for the King's Evil and stamped with the intaglio of St. Michael and the Dragon—the image of divine combat and infernal temptation. The Bastard finds himself unable to clasp the angels—that is, to mediate between the conflicting values of traditional loyalty and hireling favor. It is only with the reflection that kings themselves "break faith upon commodity" that the image of the angels is resolved into mere lucre, and the Bastard decides that "Gain" alone will be both liege lord and divinity to him.

At this point, the Bastard steps forward as the compleat Machiavellian. In Act III, when John punningly orders him to shake "imprisoned angels" loose from the monasteries, he replies that "Bell, book, and candle shall not drive me back,/ When gold and silver becks me to come on" (3.3.7–13). The Bastard's condemnation of Hubert de Burgh for Arthur's death does not prevent him from shielding Hubert from Salisbury's wrath (4.3.95–100), nor does his belated perception of Arthur's legitimacy (143–145) turn him from John's service. Whatever residual feelings of pity, compassion, and honor he may have, he too sits among the ravens over "the bare-picked bone of majesty" (148).[107]

The world of *King John* is one in which legitimacy is suspended and the legal fictions on which it rests are rendered transparent. With the accession of Prince Henry, ironically proclaimed by the Bastard, the fictions are restored, but the vision of anarchy (best embodied in the Bastard himself) is not easily dispelled; this, Shakespeare suggests, is what our world is in the "cease of majesty" (*Hamlet* 3.3.16). But if power without legitimacy cannot hold, the abuse of power we have consented to call legitimate is equally problematic. Michael Manheim's study emphasized the dilemma of the weak king on the late Elizabethan stage. Abused power, however, whether it is wielded slackly, arbitrarily, or of wicked purpose, whether in the hands of a weak and vacillating ruler or of a strong and brutal one, is tyranny. Tyranny is identified with usurpation, and refers either to power wrongfully seized or, if legitimately held, then wrongfully exercised. The Citizen of Angiers may swear his fealty to "The King of England, when we know the king," but what if that king, certainly known and duly acclaimed, proves false to his oath and duty? What if the king be not only false to his faith, but if his faith itself be false? Rebecca Bushnell correctly observes that Seneca provided the literary pattern for the theater of tyranny,[108] but Protestant Englishmen would have needed no classical example to find contemporary images of the tyrant. The Antichrist and his Roman minion testified to the constant presence of tyranny in its most explicit form. Papal tyranny was paradoxical in that Catholics accepted Rome's authority as legitimate; thus, the mere reception of a legitimacy claim was not a sufficient title to legitimacy itself. From the perspective of Elizabethan Catholics, of course, it was not a foreign potentate but their native ruler whose religion delegitimated her, and the question was only what obligations a former oath imposed and what forms conscientious resistance might take.

Whether regarded as a legal fiction or as providentially bestowed, therefore, legitimacy was a problematic concept. The restraints on resisting an illegitimate ruler were less, but in Protestant theory any ruler might be resisted, at least passively, for opposing God's word. An impeccable blood title conferred conditional legitimacy only, for a ruler who apostatized might forfeit any claim to be obeyed. By tying legitimacy to the discharge of certain duties, the idea of the Constantinian emperor, despite resting notionally on a divine mandate, was a far weaker basis for obedience than blood, even recognized as a mere legal fiction. The Citizen of Angiers could refuse to decide between John and Arthur, leaving it up to them to vindicate their claims, but the good Protestant could not in the last analysis decline to pass judgment on whether or not he was subject to godly rule.[109]

Against this background, monarchy was interrogated on the late Elizabethan and early Jacobean stage. Kingship had in a sense never been more critical, both in terms of confessional struggle and as the driving mechanism of the new administrative state. For that very reason, the fall of kings acquired the special pathos and anxiety that was the stuff of tragedy itself.

Edward II: To "Be Cruel and Grow Tyrannous"

In Marlowe's *Edward II*, not legitimacy but honor is at stake. The King's obsession with his favorite, Gaveston, alienates the peers of the realm and presages tyranny. Gaveston himself, introduced by two soliloquies and a colloquy with three would-be retainers, reveals his plans to ensnare the king and his contempt for the multitude. His schemes, which include the homoerotic sylvan fantasy that is one of Marlowe's great set-pieces (1.1.54–69) and makes unmistakably clear the nature of the king's affections, are forestalled by Edward himself, who offers him all he can want for the taking:

> Fear'st thou thy person? Thou shalt have a guard.
> Wants thou gold? Go to my treasury.
> Wouldst thou be loved and feared? Receive my seal.
> Save or condemn, and in our name command
> Whatso thy mind affects or fancy likes.
>
> (1.1.165–169)[110]

Edward's rash delegation of his power and his purse is in part a reaction to Lancaster's brutally direct threat of retribution should he persist in honoring Gaveston:

> Adieu, my lord, and either change your mind,
> Or look to see the throne where you should sit
> To float in blood, and at thy wanton head
> The glozing head of thy base minion thrown.
>
> (1.1.129–132)

Such rhetoric, on both sides, already suggests a kingdom on the verge of dissolution. Edward and Gaveston next imprison the Bishop of Coventry, who is seized on his way to officiate at the funeral rites for Edward's father, and who, as we learn, "did incense the parliament" to order Gaveston's initial exile. There is almost everything wrong with this scene. Edward interrupts his father's own exequies, thus not only rejecting his filial duties but scorning the ceremony that confirms and completes his own accession to the throne. The Bishop, for his part, has usurped a secular function in securing Gaveston's exile, and goaded Parliament into exceeding its own bounds of authority. Edward, in turn, lays violent hands on the Bishop and threatens to drown him in the "channel," literally the public sewers but metaphorically the waters that Gaveston had been forced to cross into exile as well. When the King's brother Kent, a shocked witness of the scene, warns him of Rome's reaction, it is Gaveston who answers instead: "Let him complain unto the see of hell;/ I'll be revenged on him for my exile" (1.1.190–191). The Bishop is spared only when Edward decides to convey his lands to Gaveston, appoint him to exercise his office, and compel him to serve the favorite as his chaplain or be used "as thou wilt" (195). There is no suggestion in this of Edward's reasserting his rightful authority or defying the Pope on principle; it is a mere abuse of power that turns the world upside down for the pure sport (or perhaps more accurately spite) of it, and in going beyond the verbal asperities of the first scenes into actual violence it prefigures the descent into anarchy and brutality that will end with Edward's horrific death.

Church and nobility move swiftly to renew Gaveston's banishment. The issue of rebellion is parsed in a swift passage:

> *Lancaster.* What we confirm the king will frustrate.
> *Mortimer Junior.* Then may we lawfully revolt against him.
>
> (1.2.72–73)

For the Archbishop of Canterbury, incensed at Coventry's treatment, it is the King himself who is in revolt:

> *Lancaster.* My lord, will you take arms against the king?
> *Canterbury.* What need I? God himself is up in arms
>   When violence is offered to the Church.
>
> (1.2.39–41)

Even by Marlowe's standards this is uncommonly brusque. Duty, allegiance, the sanctity of crowns—all are dismissed without debate. We are simply in a world of force. When the lords draw their swords in Edward's presence and Kent asks, "Is this the duty that you owe your king?", Warwick replies, "We know our duties; let him know his peers" (1.4.22–23). As Edward resists the demand to banish Gaveston, Mortimer Junior proposes a simple expedient to Canterbury:

> Curse him if he refuse, and then we may
> Depose him and elect another king.
>
> (54–55)

Edward offers not only to confer the highest offices of state on the rebels but to divide the realm: "Make several kingdoms of this monarchy,/ And share it equally amongst you all/ So I may have some nook or corner left/ To frolic with my dearest Gaveston" (70–73). The King reluctantly accedes to them, however, when Canterbury presses his threat to absolve the lords of their allegiance, only to indulge in bitter recrimination when they depart:

> Why should a king be subject to a priest?
> Proud Rome, that hatchest such imperial grooms,
> For these thy superstitious taper-lights,
> Wherewith thy antichristian churches blaze,
> I'll fire thy crazed buildings and enforce
> The papal towers to kiss the lowly ground,
> With slaughtered priests make Tiber's channel swell,
> And banks raised higher with their sepulchres.
> As for the peers that back the clergy thus,
> If I be king, not one of them shall live.
>
> (96–105)

The resemblance of this to the various versions of John's defiant speech to Pandulph is obvious, but the effect here is mere rant. Edward has shown all the classical earmarks of tyranny — effeminacy, profligacy, arbitrary seizures and confiscations, a disregard for honor and law alike, the inability to distinguish between private pleasures and the public weal, and an indifference even to maintaining his own prerogatives and the integrity of the state. His fantasies of revenge are merely that; no one can believe him capable of a single virile act except in "frolic." Even in blaming Canterbury for his woes, he not only ignores the offense he has given but the quite independent disaffection of the lords. The display of impotence is capped, finally, by the fact that the speech is spoken not to lord or legate but in the silence of an unattended throne. The result is not merely that the speech carries no conviction in itself but that it subverts the proud antipapal rhetoric of *King Johan*, *The Troublesome Raigne*, and *King John*.[111] Even the noblest of causes (the overthrow of Babylon) can be reduced to an apologia by the basest of tyrants.

The peers, for their part, admit the essential weakness of their position by their haste to promulgate the decree that banishes Gaveston ("Give it me; I'll have it published in the streets," Lancaster says, literally snatching the paper from Edward's hands [1.4.89]). When Edward's queen, Isabella, persuades Young Mortimer to recall him, the need to cajole popular opinion is again critical:

> For howsoever we have borne it out,
> 'Tis treason to be up against the king.
> So shall we have the people of our side,
>
> And when the commons and the nobles join,
> 'Tis not the king can buckler Gaveston;
> We'll pull him from the strongest hold he hath.
>
> (1.4.280–282; 287–289)

For the peers, Gaveston's offense is not his intimacy with the King as such, nor even the fact that he distracts him from the urgent business of the realm (the soldiers, as Young Mortimer observes, "mutiny for want of pay" [1.4.405]), but that he is baseborn, a "peasant," a "villain," a "lown," and thus that he inverts the social order.[112] To remedy this, however, the peers themselves must stoop to win the favor of the commons, who are Gavestons (and less) many times over.

In Gaveston's absence Edward is seen in mourning for him, thus compounding the offense he has committed in ignoring his father's funeral rites. He thereby completes the image of social inversion, and beneath that of anarchy itself, that Gaveston represents (grief over a living commoner supplanting that for a dead king). For Young Mortimer, Gaveston finally assumes the most threatening of aspects, that of Proteus. In his long speech at the end of Act I, he first protests that it is Gaveston's birth rather than his homosexuality that provokes him ("Uncle, his wanton humour grieves not me"), but he then goes on to paint a portrait that combines social and sexual inversion, Machiavellian deceit, and the deeply anxious sense of self that underlies the Renaissance courtier's display:

> He wears a lord's revénue on his back,
> And, Midas-like, he jets it in the court,
> With base outlandish cullions at his heels,
> Whose proud fantastic liveries make such show
> As if that Proteus, god of shapes, appeared.
> I have not seen a dapper jack so brisk;
> He wears a short Italian hooded cloak
> Larded with pearl, and in his Tuscan cap
> A jewel of more value than the crown.
> Whiles other walk below, the king and he
> From out a window laugh at such as we,
> And flout our train and jest at our attire.

Uncle, 'tis this that makes me impatient.

(1.4.406–418)

Images of profligacy and replenishment, both fiscal and sexual, entwine in this passage; Gaveston "jets" his potency with his "cullions" (base attendants, but also testicles), while at the same time whatever he expends is, "Midas-like," renewed. The king who inexhaustibly turns whatever he touches into gold and the god who, Vice-like, assumes shapes at will, combine in the description of Gaveston's raiment. If the favorite cannot literally change shape or coin gold, his apparel figures this for him. Mortimer's ultimate nightmare is to find himself under a gaze that subjects him to sartorial and, consequently, physical ridicule. Being looked upon by a king elevates one; being stared at by a commoner arbitrarily raised to royal height flattens and degrades. It is that image—of Edward and Gaveston at a window, "jesting" at those who strut below—that is insupportable. It makes Young Mortimer Gaveston's punk.

If anything could be worse in a courtier's universe than to be gazed down upon in ridicule, it is to be ignored altogether, and when Gaveston, returned again from exile, tells the peers that his "mounting thoughts did never creep so low/ As to bestow a look on such as you" (2.2.77–78), "furious Mortimer" wounds him. This act precipitates civil war, as Edward in turn vows to "tread upon their heads/ That think with high looks thus to tread me down" and resolves to "be cruel and grow tyrannous" (96–97; 205). Sensing the realm's weakness, Philip IV of France reclaims Normandy and the clans in Scotland and Ireland revolt, and when Edward refuses to ransom the elder Mortimer from the Scots, he gives the rebel peers a fresh grievance. The elder Mortimer has been distinguished from Young Mortimer by his reluctance to take up arms against Edward, though in resisting the Scots he fights more for England than for the King. The same is true of Kent, whom Edward has now thoroughly alienated (2.2.207–217), and who, though he throws in his lot with young Mortimer, represents a higher patriotism. The rhetoric of patriotism is easily appropriated, however; when the Earl of Warwick spirits Gaveston away to his death under false pretenses, he turns away a rebuke by saying that "it is my country's cause I follow" (2.6.10).[113] Marlowe was well aware of the scoundrel's last refuge long before Dr. Johnson identified it.

With Gaveston's death Edward transfers both his affections and the favorite's titles to young Spenser, who has ingratiated himself with him. The wars are renewed, with Edward at first victorious and then Mortimer, now allied with Isabella and putatively acting on behalf of the young Prince Edward. Kent, meanwhile, laments his defection, understanding at last that the "country's" cause cannot be defended in the abstract, and that those most forward to redress its wrongs are also first to exploit it:

> Edward, alas, my heart relents for thee.
> Proud traitor Mortimer, why dost thou chase
> Thy lawful king, thy sovereign, with thy sword?
> [*Addressing himself*] Vile wretch, and why hast thou, of all
>   unkind
> Borne arms against thy brother and thy king?
> Rain showers of vengeance on my cursèd head,
> Thou God, to whom in justice it belongs
> To punish this unnatural revolt.
>
> (4.6.2–9)

Captured, borne away, and compelled to relinquish his crown, Edward is at last sensible of his royalty, and asks, as Richard II and Lear will, "what are kings when regiment is gone/ But perfect shadows in a summer's day?" (5.1.26–27). Having again and again bandied his crown about while still secure in it, expressly declining his responsibilities, carelessly bestowing his powers, and casually suggesting the division of his kingdom, he holds fast to its first and last symbol, the diadem itself:

> But stay awhile; let me be king till night,
> That I may gaze upon this glittering crown;
> So shall my eyes receive their last content,
> My head, the latest honour due to it
> And jointly yield up their wishèd right.
>
> (5.1.59–63)

There is much pathos in Edward's "let me be king till night," and power in the imagery that equates loss of crown with loss of life; but the focus of the King's concern remains strictly personal. All evidences notwithstanding, he insists upon his "guiltless life," and accordingly sees his persecutors as "Inhuman creatures," "monsters" (71–74).[114] Edward is incapable of taking the counsel of men such as Kent, and the favorites upon whom he dotes are narcissistic projections whom he sees as sources of gratification, erotic or otherwise. What we watch then in his fall is, in essence, the collapse of an infantile ego. This is emphasized in his preoccupation with the crown, which he sees not merely as a symbol but as a thaumaturgic device. When he replaces it on his head and his captors stand unmoved, his first response is that of a baffled magician: "What, fear you not the fury of your king?" (75)

Edward's fall is clearly merited both in Machiavellian and monarchomach terms, for his actions indicate a radical incapacity to govern. He can at times play the king, raising armies and winning battles, and his seeming potential, as the elder Mortimer says, "promiseth as much as we can wish" (1.4.398). Whenever his position seems secure, however (or often when it is not), he reverts to the fantasy world of Arcadian homoeroticism adumbrated by Gaveston (1.1.50–70), and which, in more clinical terms, might be described as psychosexual infantilism ("Sometime a lovely boy in Dian's shape, / With hair that gilds the water as it glides . . ."). Since this fantasy is Marlowe's own, it sets up an undercurrent that has led some critics to see the play as illustrating the conflict between the demands of public and private life.[115] The elder Mortimer points out that even "Great Alexander" had his minion, suggesting that such indulgences are not only permissible but functional to kingship (1.4.390–391). The problem, however, is that Edward's private life precludes, or rather subsumes his public one. When Gaveston is killed, he transfers his emotional dependency at once to young Spenser, along with the titles and offices Gaveston had enjoyed and that had provoked the nobility to rebellion. For Edward, there is no distinction between private and public life; the latter exists solely at and for the pleasure of the former. And that is precisely the definition of tyranny, at least of the "weak king" type, in which the state disappears entirely within a household ruled by passion and caprice.

Ironically, Edward grasps the essence of kingship only in losing it. What he feels, and so vividly conveys in the deposition scene, is the moment at which the king's politic body is stripped away, leaving him only with his naked corporeal one. Yet what Edward does not say is as important as what he does. In contrast to Shakespeare's Richard II or even his John, he invokes neither divine right nor hereditary legitimacy in defense of his right; strictly speaking, he does not defend it at all, but merely bewails its loss in regal metaphors:

> The griefs of private men are soon allayed,
> But not of kings. The forest deer, being struck,
> Runs to an herb that closeth up the wounds;
> But when the imperial lion's flesh is gored,
> He rends and tears it with his wrathful paw,
> And highly scorning that the lowly earth
> Should drink his blood, mounts up into the air.

> (5.1.8–14)

Edward goes on in the same strain to describe a "dauntless mind" that soars to heaven on "the wings of rancor and disdain"; later, in an image that suggests a contrasting, Christological sense of martyrdom, he likens himself to "a lamb, encompassèd by wolves" (15, 20, 41). Both images suggest helpless entrapment, one defiant, the other pathetic, but neither offers a sense of the ideological resistance of which Edward might still be capable, particularly before relatively sympathetic captors such as Leicester and Winchester, in appealing to his indefeasible right. It is as if the political practicalities of kingcraft, of which Shakespeare's John is such a master, are simply beyond, or perhaps beneath him. On the other hand, however, it might be argued that Edward implicitly makes his appeal precisely by *not* articulating it.

What we grasp in Edward's fall is the paradox of regal authority: it is the one power that cannot be defended, at least by its possessor, precisely because it is ineffable and transcendent. Therefore the only proper response of a king to an act of lèse-majesté is silence: the silence with which, in fact, King Charles I greeted the High Court of Justice in 1649.

What comes, though, when unchallengeable power is in fact challenged, and successfully? That is the problem raised by the latter half of *Edward II*. The young Mortimer of the first three acts is proud, ambitious, resolute, and vain; in a word, the "aspiring" sort whose energies a competent monarch must channel productively to achieve successful aristocratic management. Once in power himself, however, he inevitably becomes a tyrant of the "strong" type, whose sole interest is to preserve and consolidate his position. There is no way back for him; having seized the king, he must succeed him, in title or effect, or die.

Mortimer's strategy is to be declared Protector of the heir apparent, Prince Edward, whom he controls through his adulterous alliance with Queen Isabella. Isabella has largely puzzled commentators, yet her role in *Edward II* is as pivotal as that of the widows in *King John*. We meet her in the position of the scorned but patient wife who would rather endure personal misery than brook rebellion against Edward (1.2.64–67). Her grief, nonetheless, is rather showy, and she attracts the attention not only of young Mortimer but of others ("Hard is the heart that injures such a saint," as Pembroke remarks [1.4.190]). Her transformation into Mortimer's paramour and confederate is gradual but complete. By Act III she has become "subtle" (3.2.88); in Act IV, she usurps Edward's power and gives orders for the arrest of Spenser and Baldock; by Act V, "unnatural" and "false," she plots with Mortimer to assassinate Edward and rule through the Prince.

There are, in fact, three distinct Isabellas: the wronged Queen who arouses sympathy but protests too much; the headstrong Amazon whose appetite for battle must be restrained by Mortimer himself ("Nay madam, if you be a warrior/ Ye must not grow so passionate in speeches," 4.4.14–15); and the politic schemer who urges Edward's death while ostentatiously professing her loyalty and concern (5.2.42–45; 67–71). All these Isabellas show energy and capacity; in our first glimpse of her, she is striding across the stage (1.2.46). At the same time, the slow ripening of her affections for Mortimer suggests a maturity that contrasts with Edward's doting, compulsive behavior toward his minions, though her nature is equally passionate. One must make allowances as well for the ways in which Edward virtually drives her into Mortimer's arms. He permits Gaveston to accuse her of infidelity, banishes her from Court, and deliberately undermines the mission she has undertaken on his behalf to France. This latter betrayal is of particular consequence, for without the support of her own kinsmen she has no political purchase, and therefore no choice but to take what refuge she can as civil war approaches.

To this point Isabella retains our sympathies, and Mortimer, though his ambition is manifest from the beginning, is still a positive contrast to the feckless Edward. In many ways Isabella and Mortimer are a natural pair, and Marlowe invites us to glimpse in them what a royal couple might ideally be. But Mortimer is merely a usurper, and Isabella a traitor. There is talk of a Parliament that will "elect" a new king, but it is increasingly clear that Mortimer's co-conspirators are not up to the job of a deposition. This leaves Mortimer with but one option: to remove Edward and to rule as a tyrant in the name of the Prince.

Mortimer's treatment of the captive Edward displays the earmarks of the "strong" tyrant, to wit cruelty and malevolence. Having forced him to yield his crown (a renunciation, but not a deposition), he orders him harried:

> Remove him still from place to place by night,
> Till at the last he come to Killingworth,
> And then from thence to Berkeley back again;
> And by the way to make him fret the more,
> Speak curstly to him; and in any case
> Let no man comfort him if he chance to weep,
> But amplify his grief with bitter words.
>
> (5.2.58–64)

To be destroyed, Edward must first be degraded; he must become neither king nor subject but a thing that can finally be spitted like a side of beef. His face is washed in a puddle and his beard shaved off; he is stood up in a dark cloaca, knee-deep in filth, and kept awake by a pounding drum. In this minuscule kingdom Mortimer, not yet a ruler, tyrannizes over his one subject, who in his patient martyrdom becomes at last a king. By thus radically inverting legitimacy, Mortimer's cause loses all justification, and he emerges as the very embodiment of tyranny:

> The prince I rule, the queen do I command,
> And with a lowly congé to the ground
> The proudest lords salute me as I pass;
> I seal, I cancel, I do what I will.
> Feared am I more than loved; let me be feared,
> And when I frown, make all the court look pale.
>
> Now all is sure; the queen and Mortimer
> Shall rule the realm, the king, and none rule us.
> Mine enemies will I plague, my friends advance,
> And what I list command who dare control?
>
> (5.4.46–51, 65–66]

Mortimer now stands precisely where Gaveston and Spenser had been, except that he not only usurps the honor due his fellow (and senior) nobility but the authority of the crown itself. For this he must fall, as he does in the swift scene that brings the now-crowned Edward III to his majority and sends Mortimer to the block. The play thus concludes on a satisfying if abrupt note of piety, with the legitimate heir executing condign justice, paying filial respects, and restoring general order:

> help me to mourn, my lords.
> Sweet father, here unto thy murdered ghost,
> I offer up this wicked traitor's head,
> And let these tears, distilling from mine eyes,
> Be witness of my grief and innocency.
>
> (5.6.97–101)

Marlowe's Edward III shares much of Hamlet's predicament — a slain father, and a mother implicated in the murder — without his conflicted response. He functions at the end more as an emblem than a character, though his protestation of "innocency" (it is the last word of the play) is not only a plea on behalf of his youth but for the communal amnesia that attends every accession and constitutes a fundamental rite of legitimacy as well. To restore the royal, patriarchal order, Edward must expunge the memory of his father's tyranny and place all blame for the nation's misfortune on Mortimer, whose severed head inaugurates the new reign. He must also publicly sacrifice his mother: "Away with her. Her words enforce these tears,/ And I shall pity her if she speak again" (84–85). Tears are to be shed for the father alone, for the king can do, has done, no wrong. Edward has the makings of a politician already.

While *Edward II* affirms the fictions of legitimacy in the end, however, it lays bare the contradictions they embody as well. The deposed king earns our sympathy only in his fall and as the private individual he has always longed to be, while Mortimer, both the more capable and the more ruthless man, is corrupted by the power that he can exercise only by usurpation. The restoration of majesty requires the suppression of both political and familial history and the reassertion of the patriarchal principle, a principle that Edward II's avowed homosexuality has all but denied and which, as *King John* had demonstrated, is problematic under the best of circumstances. Edward's ruinous career lays bare the fragility of a system which exalts a single person over a narrow elite, a system that was not yet manifestly different in the sixteenth century and that did not fully reveal its obsolescence until 1640.

Richard II: *The Tragedy of Divine Right*

The stakes of rebellion are far higher in Shakespeare's *Richard II*, a play whose affinities to *Edward II* have often been remarked upon but which cannot offer even the pretense of an ideologically satisfactory closure. In Edward's case, a legitimate heir stood in the wings, and the usurpation of Mortimer required the figment of a regency to sustain itself at all. Richard's deposition marked the end of the Plantagenet line, an act followed by the shocking coronation of the rebel Bolingbrooke. No events more traumatic had occurred since the Norman Conquest. The consequence had been nearly a century of civil war, and the loss of Edward III's patrimony in France. The Tudor myth was founded both on Henry VII's reconciliation of the houses of Lancaster and York and on fanciful claims to represent the restoration of a royal blood line originating with Cadwallader, the last British king. The Tudors thus represented themselves both as the agents of a Providence that had finally relented its wrath at the violence done to the Lord's anointed and as the restorers of the pre-Conquest, pre-Saxon succession. The latter element of the myth was not taken seriously, and was perhaps not meant to be apart from the pageantry in which it was invoked, although it lived on even into the seventeenth century in William Warner's popular, multivolume metrical history, *Albion's England* (1586–1606). But the Tudors were far more invested in their role as deliverers, a role which took on not merely providential but eschatological dimensions when they assumed the mantle of Constantinian emperor. The idea that both England and its queen had been "delivered" in 1588 thus had deep roots in the special Tudor interpretation of history.

For this very reason, however, the looming extinction of the dynasty in the 1590s, particularly in the midst of war and economic depression and in the absence of a designated successor, contributed to a sense of crisis that in some ways recalled that of 1399. If the Tudors had indeed been sent by Providence, or had at least embodied its will, why had their line been so unfruitful? The predicament of the childless Richard II was summoned up again in the spinster Elizabeth, just as the proud and headstrong Essex suggested Mortimer and Bolingbrooke,[116] and Elizabeth's famous remark to Lambarde—"Know ye not that I am Richard II?"—reflected a more widespread public perception than is generally acknowledged.

Set in this context, a meditation on the frailties of divine right monarchy had no small implication for the late Tudor scene. As Moody E. Prior observed, "Richard II is the only one of the kings dealt with in Shakespeare's histories who is a king by virtue of natural inheritance in a line established by a long uninterrupted tradition of rule by lineal descent, and whose legitimacy is acknowledged by everyone."[117] This was more than Elizabeth herself could claim. Shakespeare's John was a ruler in whom wickedness was founded on the suspicion of usurpation, but Richard's right is undoubted, and he therefore poses in radical form the question of whether resistance to divine right authority can ever be justified, and what its consequences must be.

The tragic agon of *Edward II* is revisited in *Richard II*, although the protagonists are markedly different in character. Marlowe's Edward becomes a
king only when he ceases to wear the crown, and the same is true in even
more exacerbated form in Richard's case, because the astonishing poetry and
tragic insight wrung from him by his fall seem entirely out of keeping with
his prior behavior and character. Edward's tyrannies are accounted for by a
passive and rather infantile hedonism, but Richard's pleasures are political;
his abuses of power, while not without an element of caprice, are thorough
and systematic, and he manifestly enjoys the more refined cruelties of dominion. Whereas Edward enrages his nobility to no purpose by exalting
Gaveston, Richard cunningly entraps the feuding dukes Hereford (Bolingbroke) and Mowbray in a sham duel by exploiting their sense of honor.
Worse, the very crime of which Hereford has accused Mowbray — the murder of Thomas of Woodstock, the Duke of Gloucester and Richard's uncle —
lies at Richard's own feet, a fact not unknown to Richard's surviving uncles,
John of Gaunt and the Duke of York, and as F. W. Brownlow notes to Hereford as well.[118] Richard's villainy in presiding at a trial of honor over a crime
of which he himself is guilty scarcely needs emphasis, and the loftily detached manner in which he conducts it only further aggravates his offenses.
The audience is as yet unaware of Richard's perfidy, which is revealed only
in the scene that follows between John of Gaunt and Gloucester's widow
(1.2.37–42).[119] But the King's response to Hereford's passionate accusation
("How high a pitch his resolution soars," 1.1.109), may well give pause.
Richard acts as though his role is to reconcile the lords' quarrel with each
other ("Wrath-kindled gentlemen, be rul'd by me") instead of to address the
substance of the charge, the murder of a peer of the realm. His incuriosity
continues even when Mowbray confesses material knowledge of the crime
("I slew him not; but to my own disgrace/ Neglected my sworn duty in that
case," [1.1.133–134]). When we discover that Richard's guilt is common
knowledge, at least among the great nobility, the dumbshow of Hereford's
intended duel with Mowbray becomes a substitute (or rehearsal) for rebellion, and the gage he throws down is revealed as one meant for Richard
himself.

As Hereford suggests, Gloucester's murder is the original sin that has corrupted Richard's reign ("his innocent soul . . ./ . . . like sacrificing Abel's,
cries/ Even from the tongueless caverns of the earth,/ To me for justice and
rough chastisement," 1.1.104–106). Richard deflects the issue, and postpones
the reckoning, by sending Hereford and Mowbray into exile, ostensibly for
disturbing the peace. When John of Gaunt dies, only the aged York remains
to avenge his brother's murder, for without leadership the nobility appears
unwilling to confront the King. The inhibition that silences Gaunt ("God's is
the quarrel. . . . / Let heaven revenge, for I may never lift/ An angry arm

against His minister" [1.2.37, 40–41]), binds the others as well. Even on his
deathbed Gaunt forbears the subject until Richard, enraged by Gaunt's admonitions, threatens to hasten his end. York, too, alludes to it only to swiftly
censor himself:

> I am the last of noble Edward's sons,
> Of whom thy father, Prince of Wales, was first. . . .
> His hands were guilty of no kindred's blood,
> But bloody with the enemies of his kin.
> O Richard! York is too far gone with grief,
> Or else he never would compare between.
>
> (2.1.171–172, 182–185)

What kindles Gaunt's wrath, and York's, is Richard's decision to mulct the
realm. Ostensibly, Richard seeks revenue to quell a rebellion in Ireland, but
the ease with which he slips from merely questionable expedients to blatant-
ly confiscatory ones suggests the tyrant's subjection of law to will:

> We are inforc'd to farm our royal realm,
> The revenue whereof shall furnish us
> For our affairs in hand. If that come short,
> Our substitutes at home shall have blank charters,
> Whereto, when they shall know what men are rich,
> They shall subscribe them for large sums of gold . . .
>
> (1.4.45–50)

Gaunt reproaches the King's resort to tax farming not as illegal but unworthy ("Landlord of England art thou now, not king" [2.1.113]), although
he clearly has in mind the alienation of the royal desmesne to corrupt favorites (97–103). York is shocked by Richard's peremptory seizure of Gaunt's estate, which disinherits Bolingbroke and, by implication, not only every other
subject in the realm but the King himself:

> Take Hereford's rights away, and take from time
> His charters, and his customary rights;
> Let not to-morrow then ensue to-day:
> Be not thyself. For how art thou a king
> But by fair sequence and succession?
>
> (2.1.195–199)

In undoing his subjects Richard undoes himself; in assaulting time itself,
he invokes his own mortality. Shakespeare plays out this theme with tragic
purposiveness. After Gaunt's life is "spent," York exclaims in grief, "Be York
the next that must be bankrout so!" (2.1.151). At this point he does not yet
know of Richard's plan, but the metaphor completes itself a few lines later
when the King announces the seizure of Gaunt's estate. Time takes a man's
life but not his identity; only tyranny can attempt that, and in doing so it

sows the seeds of its own destruction. Richard slowly comes to understand this in his fall, until the full truth of his career is borne home on him: "I wasted time, and now time doth waste me" (5.5.49).

The providential theme, so often invoked by Richard himself, is thus played out in the dialectic between Gloucester's assassination and Richard's usurpations. We may think that bloodshed is the greater crime than theft, and that there is something unworthy in a nobility that will fight to protect its goods but will ignore a murder committed in plain sight. Gloucester's widow makes the point forcibly in begging Gaunt to avenge him, and when the appeal to honor seems to fail she resorts to prudence instead: "In suff'ring thus thy brother to be slaught'red,/ Thou showest the naked path-way to thy life/ Teaching stern murder how to butcher thee" (1.2.30–32). The argument is superficially the same as that which applies to the confiscation of Gaunt's estate; if one man's property may be seized, so may that of all. The clipped brevity of Gaunt's reply is in striking contrast to the Duchess' impassioned speech:

> God's is the quarrel—for God's substitute,
> His deputy anointed in His sight,
> Hath caus'd his death; the which if wrongfully,
> Let heaven revenge, for I may never lift
> An angry arm against his minister.
>
> (1.2.37–41)

Crimes, however heinous, may not be judged by subjects; nor may particular subjects resist them, even if they appear to stand next in harm's way; nor may others do so, even if the acts appear to portend general lawlessness. This almost textbook application of the Elizabethan Homily Against Rebellion would seem to preclude resistance under any circumstances. However, as God may raise up tyrants to chastise the nations, so he may in good time send rebels to mete his (not their) justice on them. Gaunt foresees this in his first speech to the Duchess:

> But since correction lieth in those hands
> Which made the fault that we cannot correct,
> Put we our quarrel to the will of heaven,
> Who, when they see the hours ripe on earth,
> Will rain hot vengeance on offenders' heads.
>
> (1.2.4–8)

The tyrant, in seeming to act his own will, only carries out that of God, as likewise will the rebel. The nice question is when the hours are "ripe on earth," so that the rebel's will is directed by God rather than merely opposed to it. There is no answer to this question, because tyranny and rebellion constitute a cycle of evil in which God's purposes may be fulfilled but which no human reason can justify. In terms of sacred monarchy, there are *no* specifiable conditions under which rebellion is legitimate, and two human wrongs must constitute the mystery of God's right. Only the dramatist can display the dynamic that compels men to take up arms in the teeth of sin.

Gaunt's speech, with its temporal metaphor, again points to the trespass that triggers rebellion. The murder of Gloucester, even though it remains the primal sin that resonates throughout the play, and even though as the un-avenged shedding of kindred blood it lies with particular heaviness on the consciences of both Gaunt and York, is not enough to undo the bonds of allegiance and religion. In the last analysis it remains a private wrong, and on the scales of honor it is not enough to overbear the oath to God's deputy. Gaunt will not even permit himself to speculate on the circumstances of the deed or permit himself to judge whether Richard has acted "wrongfully"; it is for this reason that the Duchess' prudential suggestion that Gaunt's own life is in peril fails to stir him. Only in his deathbed speech to Richard does he vent his true feelings and prophesy Richard's merited fall:

> O, had thy grandsire with a prophet's eye
> Seen how his son's son should destroy his sons,
> From forth thy reach he would have laid thy shame,
> Deposing thee before thou wert possess'd,
> Which art possess'd now to depose thyself.
>
> (2.1.104–108)

Gaunt's prophecy — which by his father's statute of 1352 would have con-stituted treason — is permissible, even obligatory, in the context of death, where humans are compelled to speak the truth. Even here, however, he ob-serves the propriety of a subject and respects the inscrutable will of God. Had Edward III been inspired with prophecy (as he was not), he would have disinherited Richard; but it will now fall to Richard to depose himself (as in-deed he will). The rebels who unseat him are in this sense his own instru-ments as well as God's, even though this cannot absolve them from their own act.

Gaunt's "prophecy" suggests that Richard's impending fall is the moral consequence of Gloucester's death. The efficient cause of it, however, is the King's fiscal policy. Richard's violation of the Decalogue is a personal sin be-fore it is a political one, and thus requires men to wait upon God's judgment. Farming the royal demesne is a direct assault against the welfare of the commonwealth, indeed against a hypostatized "England" itself. The verbal chorography of Gaunt's famous description of England — "This royal throne of kings, this scept'red isle" (2.1.40ff) — rests upon the scornful concluding couplet "Is now leas'd out — I die pronouncing it — / Like to a tenement or pelting farm" (59–60). But Gaunt does not know the worst of it, which will be the confiscation of his estate and the issuing of blank charters. It is left to York to reproach Richard for these acts, and to extend Gaunt's prophecy by warning that if he challenges hereditary succession he liquidates his own temporal right.

Richard's behavior at this point suggests some of the giddiness of Marlowe's Edward II. Almost in the same breath he decides to put down an Irish rebellion in person while furnishing himself by means virtually certain to raise insurrection at home (1.4.42–52). Having heard York all but threaten to rebel himself over the confiscation of Gaunt's estate, he nonetheless appoints him Lord Governor in his absence (2.1.207–208; 219–221). This folly contrasts with the studied craft he displays in exiling Hereford and Mowbray, and while its arrogance is typical enough of him, its heedlessness is not. Some of the awkwardness in this may be ascribed to dramatic foreshortening, but it is perhaps anachronistic to require the kind of consistent character portrayal that the later Shakespeare taught us to expect, or that we find in a more straightforward villain such as Richard III. The stereotypical morality play tyrant on whom Shakespeare draws here self-destructs when heaven's hour is ripe, and the divine purpose has exhausted its need of him.

In spite of provocation old York remains faithful to his commission, even when the dispossessed Bolingbroke lands with a strong force to reclaim his estate. Like the Bastard in *King John* and Kent in *Edward II*, he represents the dilemma of allegiance in a land quartered by tyranny and rebellion, and therefore in a broad sense the commonwealth itself. In one respect, his duty to the King seems clear, though (unlike Gaunt) he does not invoke divine right; in another, he is caught in a civil war between his two nephews, in which the claim of blood is as strong as that of fealty:

> Both are my kinsmen:
> Th'one is my sovereign, whom both my oath
> And duty bids defend; th'other again
> Is my kinsman, whom the king hath wrong'd,
> Whom conscience and my kindred bids do right.
> Well, somewhat we must do.
>
> (2.2.111–115)

The "somewhat" York undertakes is a lukewarm defense of Richard. He rebukes Bolingbroke when he crosses paths with him, but, breaking down, first declares himself neutral and then simply aligns himself with the stronger side:

> Well, well, I see the issue of these arms. / . . . /
>
> be it known to you
> I do remain as neuter. . . . / . . . /
>
> It may be I will go with you; but yet I'll pause;
> For I am loath to break our country's laws.
> Nor friends nor foes, to me welcome you are:

Things past redress are now with me past care.
                                   (2.3.151; 157–158; 167–170)

Inevitably York becomes a go-between, and then an instrument. At first he accepts Bolingbrooke's assurance that he seeks no more than the restoration of his estates, although he is shocked when the Earl of Northumberland refers to Richard without his royal title (3.3.6–8). Later, he conveys Richard's renunciation of his crown and proclaims Bolingbroke as Henry IV (4.1.107–110). This draws a stinging retort from the Bishop of Carlisle, to whose speech—the most forthright defense of divine right authority in Shakespeare—we will return. At this point, York seems not only the herald of the new order but, not to put too fine a point upon it, its flunky. Yet he retains a higher devotion to the crown itself. Watching Richard's surrender to Bolingbroke, he is moved to awe and pity: "Behold, his eye,/ As bright as the eagle's, lightens forth/ Controlling majesty; alack, alack for woe/ That any harm should stain so fair a show" (3.3.68–71). Similarly, but in greater detail, he contrasts Bolingbrooke's triumphant entry into London with Richard's abasement:

> No joyful tongue gave him his welcome home,
> But dust was thrown upon his sacred head;
> Which with such gentle sorrow he shook off,
> His face still combating with tears and smiles,
> The badges of his grief and patience,
> That had not God for some strong purpose steel'd
> The hearts of men, they must perforce have melted,
> And barbarism itself have pitied him.
> But heaven hath a hand in these events,
> To whose high will we bound our calm contents.
> To Bolingbroke are we sworn subjects now,
> Whose state and honour I for aye allow.
>
>   (5.2.29–40)

For York, the now-deposed Richard is still "sacred," still anointed, and his mockingly inverted progress a martyrdom. Richard has already at this point likened himself to a Christ betrayed by Judases and judged by Pilates (4.1.170; 238–241), but it is York's testimony that gives us the image of him as a Man of Sorrows, pelted on his way to Calvary. What nonetheless keeps York at Bolingbroke's side, and willingly sworn to him, is the sense of a divinely ordained tragedy that precludes human judgment. That this tragedy has played itself out partly in York's own divided breast—that he too has been an actor in it—does not invalidate the perception. We may find his defense of his conduct self-serving or even regard him as one of Richard's betrayers, but it is also clear that he is a man torn between his conscience and his oath, and one who in the absence of any practical alternative wishes to

spare the realm useless bloodshed. This is, at least arguably, the higher patriotism of the commonwealthman, for whom the realm itself, "This blessed
plot" that is simultaneously the land of England, its people, and its high,
providential destiny, is the ultimate point of reference.

York's allegiance to Bolingbroke is soon tested by the discovery that his
son, the Duke of Aumerle, has been plotting against him. The scene in which
York demands Aumerle's death for treason while Aumerle and his mother
beg for his life has comical, not to say farcical elements, as Bolingbroke himself notes (5.3.78–79). York's performance may be construed not only as an
attempt to distance himself from Aumerle's plot—he had given surety for
his loyalty—but as an effort to exorcise his own guilty behavior toward
Richard. Certainly there are overtones of Oedipal substitution and sacrifice
in the high strain of his rhetoric:

> Mine honour lives when his dishonour dies,
> Or my sham'd life in his dishonour lies;
> Thou kill'st me in his life—giving him breath,
> The traitor lives, the true man's put to death.
>
> (5.3.78–79)

To whom, we may ask, is this "true man" being true? To Bolingbroke,
whom York had previously disavowed as a kinsman ("I am no traitor's uncle") and denounced for "gross rebellion and detested treason" (2.3.87, 108)?
To himself, having likewise boasted that "in my loyal bosom lies [Richard's]
power" (97)? York indeed cuts a poor figure here. But we would err in thinking him simply to be looking to his own interest. Richard's fall is for York a
divine judgment; it is also a tragedy in which majesty is most resplendent in
the moment of its eclipse. His sympathy and even his loyalty to Richard may
therefore be construed as genuine even as he deserts him, for what he yields
to is not the main chance but his sense of the irresistible tide of affairs and
the underlying divine impulse behind them. It is true that a bolder or perhaps a younger man would have defied adversity ("O . . . how quickly
should this arm of mine,/ Now prisoner to the palsy, chastise thee," he tells
Bolingbroke at their first encounter in the field). One can imagine a Harry
Hotspur or a Prince Hal in his position. But York is not merely infirm of
body. He is torn, as we have seen, between his sense of duty and his sense of
justice. This makes it easier for him to discern the hand of God in Richard's
reverses, and to "content" himself accordingly.

Similarly, there is a better case to be made for York's haste to betray Aumerle's plot than simple expediency. If Bolingbroke is not a divine instrument but simply a rebel, then Carlisle's fearsome prophecy that Richard's
fall "will the woefullest division prove/ That ever fell upon this cursed
earth" (4.1.146–147)—a description that neatly inverts Gaunt's "blessed plot"
speech—will already have borne fruit in York's own household. From a

prudential point of view, Bolingbroke is the best hope of civil peace, and on that basis alone entitled to allegiance; from a providential one, only his success can justify York's conduct. If Bolingbroke fails, the Duke of York stands not only condemned before humanity but at the bar of divine justice. Such a thought might well impel a man to offer up his son's head.

The case of York tells us much about the dilemma of loyalty in a system governed by the presuppositions of divine right. In *King John* those presuppositions had been exposed as resting on the agreed-upon fictions of legitimacy; in the less overtly contested circumstances of Richard's reign, where no birthright was in dispute, Shakespeare could dramatize the issues of tyranny and rebellion far more directly. Richard's tyranny, while less ostentatious than that of some of the stock tyrants who paraded the Elizabethan stage in Oriental dress, is, as we have seen, construed by York as an attack on the temporal order itself, and therefore as a challenge to the divine dispensation. York's comment after Richard repeats his intention to seize Gaunt's estate (and before the King presses him into service) — "I'll not be by the while" (2.1.211) — has interesting temporal resonances of its own. Apart from the inferred pun of by/buy (no property exchanges will be safe while Richard appropriates his subjects' goods at will), what this elliptical statement suggests is that no one can tarry or abide in the new dispensation, King Richard's "while" of arbitrary confiscations.[120] Richard himself has made loyalty impossible by rebelling against God, who enjoins temporal order; he has literally given his subjects no ground to stand upon. Yet stand they must, for the order abides; where then can they seek refuge?

The Bishop of Carlisle does not so much refute this dilemma as restate it:

> What subject can give sentence on his king?
> And who sits here that is not Richard's subject?
> Thieves are not judg'd but they are by to hear,
> Although apparent guilt be seen in them,
> And shall the figure of God's majesty,
> His captain, steward, deputy elect,
> Anointed, crowned, planted many years,
> Be judg'd by subject and inferior breath,
> And he himself not present?

(4.1.121–129)

What subject can give sentence on his king? If a thief must be present to hear his charge, then surely God is entitled to no less when his deputy is arraigned. York's appeal is to the chaos that must ensue when heritable right, the legal frame of temporal order, is abrogated; Carlisle's riposte is to remind him of the procedures in suing for recovery that *he* has abrogated in proclaiming a new king. But though the case be stated by both parties in legal terms, the law as such cannot resolve it, nor any person within its scope.

There is only one individual in the play who fits this requirement — Bolingbroke, the outlaw.

Bolingbroke is without the law because he has twice been civilly slain, first in being denied his right of justice and then exiled, and second in being denied his due inheritance. As an exile, he is without the protection of law in his person, but not in his estate, and his first reaction to exile is to acknowledge his continuing status as a subject: "Your will be done; this must my comfort be,/ That sun that warms you here, shall shine on me/ And those his golden beams to you here lent/ Shall point on me and gild my banishment" (1.3.144–147). This echo of the Lord's Prayer, and the invocation of solar imagery that accompanies it, suggests a perfect submission to divine right authority. At the same time, however, it is a claim to the right of a subject, who no less than the king shares the benefit of that authority; a subtle reminder that, whatever the disparity between king and subject, both are mortal men on whom the sun shines equally; and a warning that Richard's authority, being only "lent," can at God's pleasure "point" and "gild" another. It is a defiant retort wrapped up in the form of an unimpeachable piety, and suggests the supple wit of an instinctive politician.

Bolingbroke uses his enforced condition as an outlaw to claim his rightful status as a subject, and by that means, without ever raising a rebel's banner, he ascends the throne. When York upbraids him as a traitor, he replies with a legal brief: "I am a subject,/ And I challenge law; attorneys are denied me,/ And therefore personally I lay my claim/ To my inheritance of free descent" (2.3.132–135). Shrewdly, Bolingbroke makes the point that "As I was banish'd, I was banish'd as Hereford;/ But as I come, I come for Lancaster" (112–113). He is no longer Hereford; if he is not Lancaster, then he is nothing at all, "A wandering vagabond, my rights and royalties/ Pluck'd from my arms perforce" — in the literal, Middle English signification, *by* force, and not by law. Bolingbroke turns York's own impassioned remonstrance to Richard ("For how art thou a king/ But by fair sequence and succession?") back on him:

> If that my cousin king be King in England,
> It must be granted I am Duke of Lancaster.

> (122–123)

York has no answer to his own argument, and can only upbraid Bolingbroke for pressing his claim by force. Bolingbroke permits his confederate Northumberland to answer for him, but the real reply is implied in his very silence: that if the reciprocal obligation which binds sovereign and subject be broken, the relation itself cannot subsist. Either Bolingbroke is a subject to whom justice is due, or he is an outlaw to whom the use of force cannot be denied — not a rebel, who is a subject wrongly in arms, but a conqueror, who stands out of all relation except that of force.

What Northumberland says ("The noble Duke hath sworn his coming is/ But for his own") affirms that Bolingbroke is still a subject, a fiction he punctiliously observes. His charge to Northumberland to summon Richard from Flint Castle, however, makes clear his altered status:

> Go to the rude ribs of that ancient castle,
> Through brazen trumpet send the breath of parle
> Into his ruin'd ears, and thus deliver:
> Henry Bolingbroke
> On both his knees doth kiss King Richard's hand,
> And sends allegiance and true faith of heart
> To his most royal person; hither come
> Even at his feet to lay my arms and power,
> Provided that my banishment repeal'd
> And lands restor'd again be freely granted;
> If not, I'll use the advantage of my power
> And lay the summer's dust with showers of blood.
>
> (3.3.31–43)

Bolingbroke is already a conqueror although he still speaks in the style of a subject, and what he demands to have "freely granted" is already in his possession, along with the rest of Richard's kingdom. Richard himself compels him to acknowledge this when he offers him the charade of fealty:

> *Bol.* My gracious lord, I come but for mine own.
> *Rich.* Your own is yours, and I am yours, and all.
> *Bol.* So far be mine, my most redoubted lord,
>   As my true service shall deserve your love.
> *Rich.* Well you deserve. They well deserve to have
>   That know the strong'st and surest way to get.
>
>   What you will have, I'll give, and willing too,
>   For do we must what force will have us do.
>   Set on towards London, cousin, is it so?
> *Bol.* Yea, my good lord.
>
> (3.4.196–202, 206–210)

Richard's final act of power, as shrewdly judged as the bite of an adder, is to oblige Bolingbroke to confess that he rules, and will continue to rule, by force alone. In this one instant, Richard's many acts of tyranny are swallowed up in Bolingbroke's single act of usurpation. From this moment, Richard the king steps forward in the robes of Richard the martyr, both in his life and his self-foretold death a standing reproach to everything Bolingbroke now is and anything he can do. It is a remarkable performance, and one that would serve a later king too. "Know ye not that I am Richard?" Elizabeth supposedly asked; but Richard's real successor was Charles I, and Charles' performance in 1649 before the High Court of Justice was his gloss on Richard's deposition scene—a scene the censors forbade on stage while Elizabeth lived.

Bolingbroke is already sitting in state when Richard is brought forward to resign his crown in the presence of Parliament. He quickly signifies his intention to subvert the proceedings:

> God save the king! Will no man say amen?
> Am I both priest and clerk? well then, amen.
> God save the king! although I be not he;
> And yet, amen, if heaven do think him me.
>
> (4.1.172–175)

Richard tauntingly asks Bolingbroke to "seize" the crown from him (181), bandying it back and forth in full view of the assembly. When Bolingbroke asks whether he will willingly surrender it, Richard replies tellingly:

> Ay, no; no, ay; for I must nothing be.
>
> (200)

This anguished line, which begins the long resignation speech (201–221), is in a sense the crux of the play. Richard must resign the crown, yet he cannot, for then in every sense—politically, legally, ontologically—he "must nothing be." If Bolingbroke, deprived of his recourse to justice and stripped of his rightful title and estate, is in the literal sense an outlaw (he calls himself a "vagabond," but a vagabond is still a subject, freely entitled to whatever is lawfully his), Richard without his crown has no status at all, not even a negative one. A deposed king is not the subject of his successor—as Charles I was to remind the High Court, "A king and a subject are two clean different things."[121] He cannot be legally dispossessed, for no mortal authority can judge him, and he cannot dispossess himself, for God alone can release him from the obligation to rule. It is true that a Christian sovereign, the Emperor Charles V, had resigned his titles and entered a monastery at the end of his reign, but no successor, at least in Habsburg Austria, had been crowned in his lifetime, and his last years might in a constitutional sense be regarded as a terminal regency. Even Edward II had only abdicated in favor of his rightful successor. But Richard is asked to do what no king had ever been asked to do before, and what, in a divine right ruler, is the ultimate dereliction: not yield to an heir, not submit to a conqueror, but resign his throne to a usurper. He is asked to embrace a Parmenidian paradox—that he should "nothing be," and with that, that the crown and state he holds should be negated as well:

> Nay, if I turn mine eyes upon myself,
> I find myself a traitor with the rest.
> For I have given here my soul's consent
> T'undeck the pompous body of a king;

Made glory base, and sovereignty a slave;
Proud majesty a subject, state a peasant.

(4.1.246–251)

Bolingbroke and his confederates try to put a plausible face on their acts by forcing Richard to read and confess his crimes "Against the state and profit of this land" — that is, the commonwealth whose laws and welfare he has betrayed. They thereby invoke the ancient doctrine of *salus populi, suprema lex* which was the basis of monarchomach resistance theory and which would serve against Charles I during the Civil War. Richard refuses this until Bolingbroke finally intercedes:

> *Bol.* Urge it no more, my Lord Northumberland.
> *North.* The commons will not then be satisfi'd.
> *Rich.* They shall be satisfi'd. I'll read enough
>   When I do see the very book indeed
>   Where all my sins are writ, and that's myself.

(270–274)

Bolingbroke, ever the *politique*, sees that Richard has been pushed as far as possible, and is reluctant to create a martyr. Northumberland, the stickler for form, knows that a constitutional apology is necessary to convert Bolingbroke's private grievance into a general public wrong. Richard's elliptical "They shall be satisfi'd" refers to the apology he is about to offer in his "mirror" speech, but reflects as well the perennial moral of Shakespeare's source, Holinshed's *Chronicles*: though the commons must suffer the ills visited on them by their betters, the immortal commonwealth will ultimately prevail.

By "reading" his features in a mirror instead of reading the formal charges against him, Richard appeals to the book of conscience, whose verdict is infallible. What Richard wishes to see, however, is not the true image of his guilt or innocence, but the paradox he has become, a royal face that is "bankrupt of [its] majesty" (266). Since this is precisely what may *not* be and therefore what cannot be represented, the image Richard sees is not true but false, a simulacrum that will shatter at last under the pressure of its own contradiction:

>   Was this face the face
> That every day under his household roof
> Did keep ten thousand men? Was this the face
> That like the sun did make beholders wink?
> Is this the face which fac'd so many follies,
> That was at last outfac'd by Bolingbroke?
> A brittle glory shineth in this face;
> As brittle as the glory is the face
> For there it is, crack'd in an hundred shivers.

(280–288)

The image is false, because the true regal image blinds its beholders; its glory is likewise brittle, spurious, and dies with the reflection that bears it. Bolingbroke has "outfac'd" only this simulacrum, because true majesty, being in God's gift alone, is inalienable, and Richard can no more surrender it than Bolingbroke can appropriate it.

Richard is left to ponder the contradiction of the unkinged king as he awaits his assassin. Alone in his cell, he populates his world by fancy, thereby creating another kingdom he cannot rule. The trope of nothingness—the impossibility of being such as he now is—pursues him to the end:

> Thus play I in one person many people,
> And none contented. Sometimes am I a king,
> Then treasons make me wish myself a beggar,
> And so I am. Then crushing penury
> Persuades me I was better when a king;
> Then am I king'd again, and by and by
> Think that I am unking'd by Bolingbroke,
> And straight am nothing. But whate'er I be,
> Nor I, nor any man that but man is,
> With nothing shall be pleas'd, till he be eased
> With being nothing.
>
> (5.5.31–41)

The nothingness Richard plumbs in his cell is akin to that which Lear finds on the heath, but with a difference: whereas Lear embraces all of creation in its final wretchedness of being, Richard shuttles back and forth along the broken string of degree, now commoner and now king, unable to plant his imagination in anything. That is his limit, and his ultimate punishment. Lear goes mad to open the post-Elizabethan imagination to a condition beyond degree, but Richard, condemned to the torment of his sanity, is trapped within it. His tragedy remains political.

There remains only the lean figure of Bolingbroke to consider. He is, presumably, already Henry IV when the play ends, for he orders a hasty coronation in the deposition scene (4.1.318–319) and Northumberland subsequently refers to his "sacred state" (5.6.6). Nonetheless he is mere Bolingbroke from first to last in the printed texts, though occasionally his successive titles are referred to by the characters themselves (1.1.3 and elsewhere, "Hereford"; 4.1.107, "Great Duke of Lancaster"; "Great king," 5.6.30—I omit Richard's ironic designations).[122] For the crowds who hail him on his entry into London he is simply "Bolingbroke," as if in his ascent he retains only a bare given name, just as Richard II becomes plain Richard in his fall (3.3.6; and cf. Richard's comment at 4.1.254–256 that he has been stripped even of his Christian name). It is Shakespeare himself who withholds his regnal name from him, although in *Henry IV, Part I*, he is straightaway "King Henry."

Shakespeare reveals little of the inner Bolingbroke, if there is any; in his way he is as mysterious a figure as Iago. Neither hero nor villain, he is the servant of necessity. Richard notes his vaunting pride early on ("How high a pitch his resolution soars!," 1.1.109), and it certainly breaks out in his speech before Flint Castle. Nonetheless, the nature of his ambition remains unclarified. Though protesting his banishment he is apparently prepared to accept it, and only the forfeiture of his estate brings him back.[123] Once returned, or bent on returning, his only recourse is to seize power, and it is on this basis that his confederates flock to his standard. Since Bolingbroke never lays claim to the throne but only accepts it, Northumberland is left to justify the rebellion that wins it for him:

> we shall shake off our slavish yoke,
> Imp out our drooping country's broken wing,
> Redeem from broking pawn the blemish'd crown,
> Wipe off the dust that hides our sceptre's gilt,
> And make high majesty look like itself   (2.1.291–295)

There seems at first glance little substance to this flight of Shakespearean rhetoric other than the pledge to redeem the crown's estate. What make Bolingbroke's particular cause that of the lords are the blank charters, and presumably the King's exclusion of the senior nobility from his counsel in favor of the upstart trio of Bushy, Bagot, and Greene is also part of their "slavish yoke." The reference to "our sceptre's gilt," however—the feudal, not the royal we—puts us at once outside the dominant divine right frame of discourse. The royal scepter is on this reading a collective, not an individual possession, and the essential presupposition of divine right monarchy, that an anointed king is accountable only to God for the discharge of his office, is thereby rendered null and void. The rebel lords of *Richard II* may not be as casual about disposing of the crown as Mortimer's crew in *Edward II*, but they are no less certain of their right. The "dust" that lies on "our sceptre's gilt" is not only Richard's malfeasance, but, if it comes to that, Richard himself, and if the one must be wiped off with the other, the lords will not shirk the task.

When Northumberland speaks of making "high majesty look like itself," he speaks of that of which crown and scepter—the implements of royalty— are merely the props and symbols. This majesty inheres in nothing less than the realm itself, as Gaunt makes clear in the famous description of England as "This royal throne of kings, this scepter'd isle,/ This earth of majesty . . ." (2.1.40–41). England is "this seat of Mars,/ This other Eden, demi-paradise"; it is a "fortress built by Nature for herself," a "happy breed of men," a "little world," a "blessed plot": only ten lines later do we find it also a "teeming womb of kings," whose virtue and prowess stem from "This land of such dear souls, this dear, dear land," and are finally inseparable from it (51–57). This is not, perhaps, political philosophy, but it represents a profound intuition that sovereignty and nationhood are mutually reflexive, that the former is rooted in the latter, and that it can only be properly exercised and sustained in its service. It is sometimes overlooked that Gaunt's apostrophe is set between two bitter strophes that warn that Richard's "fierce blaze of riot cannot last" (33) and lament that the "dear land" is turned into a "pelting farm" (60).

It is in this light that we must read Northumberland's resolve to make "high majesty look like itself." This image, too, is one of reflexivity, and the mirror in which high majesty will appear is — can be no other than — the realm itself, restored to prosperity and honor. In telling contrast, the fallen Richard seeks majesty's image in the mirror he holds up to his own face, and finds only the "brittle glory" he dashes to the ground. The narcissism Richard shares with Edward II, and which in both cases is at the root of their fall, is never more apparent than here. Both kings alike attempt to absorb majesty wholly into themselves, and, in equating law and will, to emit it as arbitrary power. Richard is genuinely sympathetic — truly a king — only when, returning from Ireland, he "weep[s] for joy" to stand on native earth and bends to touch it (3.2.4–6). Even here, however, he remains trapped in narcissistic fantasy, imagining first that "these stones/ [shall] Prove armed soldiers" and then that "For every man Bolingbroke hath press'd/ . . ./ God for his Richard hath in heavenly pay/ A glorious angel" (24–25; 58, 60–61). Richard is in fact neither of heaven nor earth, and when York rather gently suggests that he disburden himself of his "tired majesty" (4.1.178), he makes fully explicit the idea that authority has migrated from him back to the community that has rallied around Bolingbroke.

Bolingbroke is thus no mere usurper, but the champion of a cause that is, at least in the negative sense, England's itself. There is no doubt that Richard is an unfit king; even his followers chide him for his improvidence and unmanly dejection (3.2.178–185). But though tyranny, however it may reflect the will of heaven, is never warranted, it by no means follows that rebellion is ever justified. Northumberland, like Mortimer, plainly believes so, but Gaunt, Richard's bitterest critic, does not; York, though he is drawn into rebellion, never embraces it; and Carlisle denounces it. The divinity that hedges a king also shields the subject, for it is a barrier between him and the unmediated will of God. That will is so terrible that only the sacred, anointed king is armed to face it. It is a terror beyond terror for the unsanctified subject, laying profane hands on the Lord's anointed, to sinfully face the divine will alone; this too is what Richard means when he speaks of being "out-fac'd" by Bolingbroke and, in breaking the mirror that reflects his own face, symbolically leaving the rebels naked to the wrath they have dared.

Against this, Northumberland has only a few fine phrases about restoring "our sceptre's gilt" (the implied pun making its way to the surface), and the indictment that Richard refuses to read: the appeal to collective majesty, and to the rule of law. When Bolingbroke wearily tells Northumberland to put the indictment aside (4.1.270) and orders a hasty coronation "On Wednesday," he implicitly accepts the brutal facticity of rebellion and the 'cease of majesty' that it entails. It was M. M. Reese who drew attention to this pregnant phrase and its implications for Shakespeare's history cycle.[124] These are nowhere more tellingly exhibited than in the gap that yawns between Richard's deposition and Bolingbroke's assumption of office. The order of these events is actually reversed; York proclaims Bolingbroke before Richard publicly yields the crown (4.1.107–112). The entire deposition scene may, indeed, be read as a protracted attempt by Richard to make the cease of majesty palpable. For Richard, as for Carlisle, the gulf it opens is unbridgeable, a scene of "Disorder, horror, fear, and mutiny" that will embroil the generations and make "future ages groan" (142, 138). Richard is unable to repeat his earlier boast that "Not all the water in the rough rude sea/ Can wash the balm off from an anointed king" (3.2.54–55), but his act of resignation—"With mine own tears I wash away my balm"—restates the point negatively: *if* it were possible for a king to be divested of his sacred authority, it could be only by his own act and consent. But Richard does not, and in his view cannot give such consent. He withholds it even in mouthing the ritual of resignation, for it makes him, as he says, only a "traitor" to himself. Although he has released his subjects from all oaths to him, he immediately taxes Northumberland with violating them, and warns the assembly that "water cannot wash away your sin" (4.1.228–235, 241). He plays again on this figure in imagining himself "a mockery king of snow,/ Standing before the sun of Bolingbroke,/ To melt myself away in water-drops!" (4.1.259–261).[125] The point is clear: though Bolingbroke command enough water to fill the rude sea, though men melt before his brazen scepter, he has mere force, not authority.

The hollowness of Bolingbroke's position is further underscored by Northumberland's indictment. He has appealed to law in claiming justice, yet he will not grant Richard his trial. He is unwilling to have the charges alleged against Richard read except by the King himself, an act which would implicitly make it a confession, and when Richard refuses he abandons the tactic. What remains is the "woeful pageant" of a king's forced abdication, which Richard himself, without contradiction, calls an act of usurpation (316–317, 256). What Richard must renounce is not Bolingbroke's to claim: legitimate authority can be denied, derided, traduced; its seals may be broken and its emblems dragged in the dust; but it cannot be conveyed except by rightful lineal succession. Even as he prepares to surrender the crown, Richard makes the point tellingly in imagery that, in evoking the well-known medieval figure of Fortune's buckets, once again plays on the image cluster of water/tears/balm:

> Now is this golden crown like a deep well
> That owes two buckets, filling one another,
> The emptier ever dancing in the air,
> The other down, unseen, and full of water.
> That bucket down and full of tears am I,
> Drinking my griefs, whilst you mount up on high.
>
> (4.1.183–188)

The tears of a king are precious balm, no less potent for being submerged; the usurper's cup is perpetually empty, cast about on the currents of chance.

Yet Bolingbroke also seizes his Machiavellian moment. The strength of Richard's position lies only in the pathos of his fall; absent that, he is once again the despised tyrant, and Bolingbroke the champion of liberty. The assumption of sovereignty by force is an ungracious act, no matter how justified, and he who performs it will necessarily appear, if only for the naked instant, in the figure of a usurper. Bolingbroke's strategy in the deposition scene is to tacitly acknowledge this predicament, and submit to it while he must. There is no use in jousting with Richard; his pouting and posturing must simply be allowed to run its course. When it does so, it is Richard himself who asks to be led away. In refusing to be baited, Bolingbroke displays the self-command that Richard lacks, and thereby the power to command others. He is the natural politician who in every age knows that this power is the practical basis of all legitimacy, and that where it is firmly exercised, obedience will follow.

Bolingbroke harbors no illusion that the process of legitimation will be a swift or simple one. He assumes the burden of rule knowing that a generation or more must pass before a secure line can be established. He accepts that he will more than likely die without knowing whether he has been the agent or the antagonist of God's will—whether hell awaits him, or merely purgatory. In embracing personal sin in order to restore the communal good, he is arguably the authentic tragic hero of the play.

As the play ends, Bolingbroke's new burdens are already upon him. He faces rebellion on all hands, even before being crowned. As the deposition scene ends a plot is being hatched, and for much of Act V he is preoccupied in dealing with his son Hal, rebellious in his own terms, in the taverns and brothels of London. In contrast to Richard, however, Bolingbroke remains sanguine and meets his challenges with calculation and dispatch. The rebels are swiftly disposed of, and their leaders summarily executed. Bolingbroke spares Aumerle and Carlisle, however, the former as the son of the indispensable York and the latter to avoid shedding clerical blood. We infer these politic reasons, for in both cases he is careful to couch his act in terms of his prerogative of mercy alone, in the one yielding to a mother's plea and in the other acknowledging "High sparks of honour" in an adversary (5.6.29). He shows similar restraint in allowing young Hal to sow his wild oats, despite his obvious embarrassment and concern (5.3.1–22). But he is at his nimblest in disposing of Richard's assassin, Sir Piers Exton, who bursts in on him in full conclave with the King's coffin, and, on being rebuked, protests that he had only carried out Bolingbroke's wish:

> They love not poison that do poison need,
> Nor do I thee. Though I did wish him dead,
> I hate the murtherer, love him murthered.
> The guilt of conscience take thou for thy labour,
> But neither my good word nor princely favour;
> With Cain go wander thorough shades of night,
> And never show thy head by day nor light.
>
> (5.6.38–44)

Bolingbroke simultaneously acknowledges and disavows Exton's act: in admitting that he had "wished" and even "needed" Richard's death he carefully distances it from an actual command, and in calling it a murder he adds further separation, for the king (judicially) can do no wrong and therefore cannot order murder. At the same time, he does not deny that Exton has carried out a perceived act of state whose benefit accrues to Bolingbroke rather than a simple crime. His punishment is ironically couched in the traditional terms of the courtier's reward ("take thou for thy labour"), and it takes the form of bearing communal witness rather than suffering personal retribution. Exton is symbolically sentenced to a guilty conscience, the one punishment that cannot be imposed on an individual, and he is ordered to wander like Cain; that is, under protection of authority. He is, in short, a scapegoat, and what he embodies is the guilt of necessity. The tyranny of an anointed king—his radical threat to the temporal order itself—necessitated his deposition; his deposition entailed his death. These are deeds that (also necessarily) transcend their particular actors; the common interest required them, and their expiation must likewise be a collective one. As the community's scapegoat, Exton is both visible and invisible, banished and present. He is not sent into foreign exile, as Bolingbroke was, but remains with his countrymen, palpable but unacknowledged, a presence among them. In this way he distributes guilt, silently and under cloak of darkness, until the deed that represents the whole has touched the whole.

The one figure this process will ultimately absolve is Bolingbroke himself. In the play's final lines he prescribes the public penance he will lead and perform:

Lords, I protest my soul is full of woe
That blood should sprinkle me to make me grow.
Come mourn with me for what I do lament,
And put on sullen black incontinent.
I'll make a voyage to the Holy Land,
To wash this blood off from my guilty hand.
March sadly after; grace my mournings here
In weeping after this untimely bier.

(45–52)

Bolingbroke expresses "woe" and only secondarily guilt; he also converts Richard's self-styled martyrdom into a sacrifice on his behalf. The blood Richard has spilled becomes, in a breathtaking act of appropriation, his successor's balm, the sacred unction that makes him "grow." When Bolingbroke refers to the pilgrimage that will wash the blood from his "guilty hand," it metaphorically completes the process of this grisly anointment, removing the taint that blood contact, even on a symbolic level, entails. Atonement thus follows anointment, but the guilt Bolingbroke acknowledges, although it attaches to the royal person, is, too, collective rather than individual. Unlike Henry II, who accepts personal responsibility for the murder of Thomas à Becket and submits to corporal chastisement to expiate his sin, Bolingbroke invites the lords to "Come mourn *with me*" (emphasis added) and to "grace my mourning"—that is, to share a common act. In following the dictates of necessity consecrated blood has been shed and divine wrath incurred, but that wrath may be appeased by ritual purgation. Richard's "untimely" bier—the reference once again reminding us of his attempt to deny temporality—is ultimately self-created. The path of purgation was to lead England through prolonged civil war, but not, as Carlisle had prophesied, to leave it a "field of Golgotha" for all ages (4.1.144). The regicide initiated by Henry Bolingbroke achieved closure in the scarcely less dubious accession of Henry Tudor celebrated in *Richard III*.

Shakespeare accepts divine right monarchy in the history cycle as a convention imperfectly ordering the underlying anarchy of human affairs. His view of its capacity is conditioned by his perception of human nature, both among rulers and ruled. The progress of that perception may be gauged in the darkness of the tragedies that followed the history plays, to which his long immersion in the grim weather of England's past doubtless contributed. In the history plays, the civil religion of England itself—the ultimate protagonist of the cycle—serves as a sheet anchor, but in the end it is clear that, for Shakespeare, all men live on islands called the state, which are composed in turn of islands called men.

Roman Auguries: Jonson's Sejanus

Queen Isabel halts her retinue at the beginning of Act V of *Richard II* to await Richard's passage to prison:

> This way the king will come; this is the way
> To Julius Caesar's ill-erected tower

(5.1–2)

Isabel means that the Tower of London, like everything else in England, has been debased by Bolingbroke's usurpation, and that under a tyrant's sway monarchy itself has been momentarily eclipsed. She also means that the brazen monument Bolingbroke has built on the ruins of the ancient constitution cannot stand, and that England, like Rome, is now primed for civil war.

Isabel's analogy would have been fully credible to a sophisticated lay audience of the late sixteenth century that saw Rome as the paradigm of political experience, just as ancient Israel was to godly ones; indeed, much of the controversy of the next hundred years would turn on the rivalry between these two models, culminating in Harrington's *Oceana* and Sidney's *Discourses Concerning Government* on the one hand, and *Paradise Lost* and *The Pilgrim's Progress* on the other. We have seen the reflection of Rome's authority in Selden, among others. The Roman model was particularly prominent on the Elizabethan and Jacobean stage, which provided a privileged ground for assaying republican and monarchical forms of government, their Polybian antitypes of mob rule and tyranny, and the relation of such experience to England's *dominium politicum et regale*.[126] Shakespeare would share in this enterprise directly with his Roman trilogy, *Antony and Cleopatra*, *Julius Caesar*, and *Coriolanus*, but it is perhaps in Ben Jonson's *Sejanus His Fall* (1603), the first major dramatic work to greet the new Stuart dynasty, that the high argument of Rome receives its most self-conscious exposition.[127]

For Tacitean republicanism, the reign of Tiberius was the template for how unaccountable power degenerates into tyranny. The imperial system designed by Augustus had thwarted liberty and reduced the institutions of the republic to a hollow shell, but it was only with the sinister Tiberius that the system displayed its true character, as a regime of favorites. In the aftermath of Essex, this theme had a pointed relevance to the "absolute" monarchy being promoted by James I.

The theme of the play is set in the first act colloquy among the patriots Sabinus, Silius, Cordus, and Arruntius. As Arruntius laments:

> Where is now the soul
> Of god-like Cato? — he, that durst be good
> When Caesar durst be evil; and had power,
> As not to live his slave, to die his master.

> Or where the constant Brutus, that (being proof
> Against all charm of benefits) did strike
> So brave a blow into the monster's heart
> That sought unkindly to captive his country?
> O, they are fled the light. Those mighty spirits
> Lie raked up, with their ashes, in their urns,
> And not a spark of their eternal fire
> Glows in a present bosom: all's but blaze,
> Flashes, and smoke, wherewith we labour so,
> There's nothing Roman in us; nothing good,
> Gallant, or great.

(1.89–103)

In the context of a republic, the rule of a single person—to use the phrase applied by republican opponents of the Cromwellian Protectorate in the 1650s—is the ultimate violation. The loss of virtue in a republican polity is fatal; the commonwealth itself is effectively dissolved, and nothing remains but the rule of a master over his slaves. The title Cromwell chose for himself only emphasized the irregular nature of his regime, for the Lord Protector-ship was a monarchical office used in time of regency, and Cromwell was no one's regent. Similarly, Augustus' self-anointment as princeps or first citizen was meant to suggest continuity with Rome's republican past, but for Jon-son's patriots (as for those of Tacitus) it conveyed only bitter irony. This is not to suggest that Jonson was trying to promote republican sentiments, but rather that, like the legists, he saw each polity as the result of a unique pro-cess of constitutional development that it was fatal to rupture. In England, not even the tyranny of an Edward II or a Richard II could derogate from the essential majesty of the crown or sever its relationship to the commonwealth; in Rome, even the mildest and most benevolent autocracy was destructive of political community. In this sense *Sejanus* was a conservative document, and although Jonson was accused of "popperie and treason" for it by Henry Howard, the future Earl of Northampton, the charge appears to have been a typical piece of Jacobean intrigue, and the play was thought orthodox enough to be performed before James himself by the King's Men.[128]

Nonetheless, the relevance of the Roman example, both as the master trope of Renaissance political discourse in general and as a means of constru-ing the English case in particular, would not have escaped the attention of any sophisticated observer, including England's new king. The differences between Rome and England were marked enough to serve as a disclaimer to any comparison between the two; the resemblances were sufficient to make any play based on Roman history, and particularly one that enacted the ten-sion between monarchical and republican elements, an opportunity for the kind of bracketed discourse that was the only permissible way to approach

questions of political value: as Shakespeare's Hamlet was to say, with perhaps a glance at this device, "the story is extant, and writ in choice Italian"
(*Hamlet*, 3.2.262–263).

The Roman model was indeed arguably more pertinent to the Jacobean
moment than theatrical glosses on the fourteenth-century constitution. "Parliament," both in *Edward II* and *Richard II*, was essentially a conclave of the
nobility, not to say a cabal; the "commons" in these plays are invariably represented as the population at large, whose sole purpose is to reflect the actions of their betters. This was a highly skewed (or let us say dramatically
foreshortened) reading of the late Plantagenet scene; it did scant justice to
the sophisticated publics — electoral, religious, and urban — of late sixteenth-
century England, or to the Parliament that reflected the pressure of their
concerns. The frequency of allusion in Parliament itself to Roman history
and the Roman constitution, which culminated in Sir John Eliot's identification of the Duke of Buckingham with Sejanus in the House of Commons in
1626, suggested the perceived relevance of the Roman model for English
politics. What one favorite had done to destroy an ancient Senate, it was
clearly implied, another might do to a modern one.[129]

When Jonson's Tiberius appears, his affected modesty only serves to emphasize the abasement of Rome's Senate. Rebuking an emissary who presents its letters with excessive deference, he styles himself a mere "servant"
whose "empire [is] to obey/ Where such, so great, so grave, so good, determine" (393; 452–453). The Senate's suit is to erect a temple to the Emperor
and his mother. Tiberius rejects this, ordering instead that Sejanus' statue be
erected in Pompey's theater. The clear implication of this is that imperial
power is above representation and that it will receive honor only through
surrogates.

Tiberius' metaphoric style throughout his first appearance plays on the
contrast between high and low. When an attendant kneels to him, he considers it an offense and orders him to stand: "Take not away our human nature
from us: Look up, on us, and fall before the gods" (377–378). One can, of
course, offer reverence either by looking up or down; Tiberius does not invite the level gaze of equals. When he orders Sejanus' statue erected, he
compels men to look up to one who is inferior to himself, as if putting himself beyond mortal gaze entirely. To the anticipated objection that he himself
"flatters" his own favorite, he replies that "Princes have still their grounds
reared with themselves,/ Above the poor low flats of common men,/ And
who will search the reasons of their acts/ Must stand on equal bases" (537–
540).

Tiberius, then, will not stoop to justify himself, but he does hail Sejanus as
"thou great aid of Rome,/ Associate of our labours, our chief helper" — in
short, as one deserving not only his own thanks, but that of all Romans (528–

529). Since in preceding scenes we have seen Sejanus openly selling offices and plotting the downfall of Tiberius' heir Drusus, we may wonder which services he performs. We discover them when Emperor and favorite plan to destroy the virtuous Agrippina, widow of the slain hero Germanicus, and her three children. Tiberius, revealing his fear of unnamed parties, induces Sejanus to urge their destruction. He then puts him through an elaborately Machiavellian catechism:

> *Tiberius.* That nature, blood, and laws of kind forbid.
> *Sejanus.* Do policy and state forbid it?
> *Tiberius.*   No.
> *Sejanus.* The rest of poor respects, then, let go by;
>   State is enough to make th'act just, them guilty.
> *Tiberius.* Long hate pursues such acts.
> *Sejanus.*   Whom hatred frights,
>   Let him not dream on sov'reignty.
> *Tiberius.*   Are rites
>   Of faith, love, piety, to be trod down?
>   Forgotten, and made vain?
> *Sejanus.*   All for a crown.
>   The prince, who shames a tyrant's name to bear,
>   Shall never dare do anything but fear.
>   All the command of sceptres quite doth perish
>   If it begin religious thoughts to cherish:
>   Whole empires fall, swayed by these nice respects.
>   It is the licence of dark deeds protects
>   Ev'n states most hated, when no laws resist
>   The sword, but that it acteth what it list.
>   (2.170–185)

Tiberius leads Sejanus to the inevitable conclusion that his enemies must be slain, ruefully commenting that:

> We would not kill, if we knew how to save;
> Yet, than a throne, 'tis cheaper give a grave.
>   (270–271)

At the last, Tiberius confesses that "Thy thoughts are ours, in all, and we but proved/ Their voice" (280–281). Sejanus has merely read his master's mind, it seems, and spoken his secret resolve. But much more has actually occurred. Sejanus has counseled murder, not simply become complicit in it. Offered every opportunity to dissuade the Emperor, every moral consideration against so extreme an act, he has put into words what had only been thoughts, and thus taken authorship of the deed upon himself. For More, Elyot, and the other theorists of counsel, the task of the councillor was to help the ruler resist the evil impulses that were a natural temptation of power, not to express and facilitate them. Sejanus not only fails to do this, but by giving voice to these impulses and brushing aside all objections to them, he becomes the agent of their release. Tiberius says that Sejanus has merely "proved" his own preexisting "designs," but he does not say so until Sejanus has stated the case for him and made it the proposition of another that he assents to rather than his own will. The Emperor thereby acquires what in the idiom of a later age would be called deniability; he can truthfully say that Sejanus urged murder upon him and used every black art of rhetoric to defend it. Jonson's scene is a chillingly effective example of a bad man being used by a worse one.

Sejanus, however, has his own plans. As Tiberius moves to use him to complete the removal of the Germanican party, the favorite spins his own plot to poison his mortal enemy Drusus, heir presumptive to the throne, and to turn Agrippina's fall to his advantage. The prince who aims to rule by fear, Sejanus says, will be ruled by it himself, and ambition get the better of power:

> The way to put
> A prince in blood is to present the shapes
> Of dangers greater than they are, like late
> Or early shadows, and, sometimes to feign
> Where there are none, only to make him fear;
> His fear will make him cruel; and once entered,
> He doth not easily learn to stop, or spare
> Where he may doubt. This I have made my rule,
> To thrust Tiberius into tyranny,
> And make him toil to turn aside those blocks
> Which I, alone, could not remove with safety.
>
> (2.383–393)

With both Drusus and the sons of Germanicus disposed of and the aging Emperor isolated and despised, the way will be open for the final stroke:

> Work then, my art, on Caesar's fears, as they
> On those they fear, till all my lets be cleared,
> And he in ruins of his house, and hate
> Of all his subjects, bury his own state;
> When, with my peace and safety, I will rise,
> By making him public sacrifice.
>
> (399–404)

The game is thus set, and the only question is which man will succeed in making "sacrifice" of the other. Much of Act III is taken up with the condemnation of two of the patriots, Silius and Cremutius Cordus, on the floor of the Senate. Both are accused by known agents of Sejanus, Silius of corruption in his military command and Cremutius Cordus of inciting sedition by praising Brutus and Cassius. Silius, after defending his honor and charging Tiberius with tyranny to his face, stabs himself; Cordus, more politic, is remanded for trial. Their cases would have spoken clearly to a Jacobean audience, Silius as a sympathetic stand-in for Essex, and Cordus representing the historians and dramatists who, like Jonson himself, had suffered censorship and imprisonment under Elizabeth.

In the play's counterpoint, the condemnation of Silius and Cordus enables Tiberius to show his dispassion and restraint while compelling Sejanus to demand the harshest penalties; the scene thus reenacts the private colloquy in which Tiberius forces his favorite to call for the blood of Agrippina and her children. The remainder of the act is devoted to Tiberius' rejection of Sejanus' suit to marry Drusus' widow Livia, and the Emperor's engagement of a new minion, Macro, to spy on Sejanus. Macro's own soliloquy paints the classic portrait of the courtier who begins his rise by subordinating all interests to those of his master, and is thus the antitype of the good councillor whose loyalty to the prince is founded on devotion to virtue and justice:

> It is the bliss
> Of courts to be employed, no matter how:
> A prince's power makes all his actions virtue.
> We, whom he works by, are dumb instruments,
> To do, but not enquire: his great intents
> Are to be served, not searched. Yet, as that bow
> Is most in hand whose owner best doth know
> T'affect his aims, so let that statesman hope
> Most use, most price, can hit his prince's scope.
> Nor must he look at what or whom to strike,
> But loose at all; each mark must be alike.
> Were it to plot against the fame, the life
> Of one with whom I twinned; remove a wife
> From my warm side, as loved as is the air;
> Practise away each parent, draw mine heir
> In compass, though but one; work all my kin
> To swift perdition; leave no untrained engine,
> For friendship or for innocence; nay, make
> The gods all guilty: I would undertake
> This, being imposed on me, both with gain and ease.
> The way to rise is to obey and please.
>
> (3: 715–735)

As the catalogue of crimes and betrayals Macro would commit mounts, he seems almost a Vice figure; unlike a direct servant of evil, however, he wishes it not for its own sake but only as a means of advancement. This involves the courtier in a paradox, since to advance himself he must so serve the prince as to merge his interest wholly with his master's. All such ambition is necessarily blind, since it places the courtier at the mercy of a prince in whom not trust but only absolute submission can reside. It is for this reason that the courtier worships Fortune, as Sejanus does at 5.81–93, for only in the one deity more arbitrary than any prince can hope be reposed.[130]

Macro receives a setback when Sejanus saves Tiberius' life at Capreae by courageously interposing himself between the Emperor and the collapsing walls of a grotto (4.47–60), thus ingratiating himself anew. This forces Macro to advance his timetable, for he cannot but assume that Sejanus, his footing regained, will strike first at him:

> Macro, thou art engaged; and what before
> Was public, now must be thy private, more.
>
> (81–82)

Macro means that his will must be his own, not Caesar's, and that, however prematurely, he must separate his interest from his master's. We do not see Tiberius in Act IV, and so have no direct evidence of whether the Emperor has received Sejanus back into favor or has merely altered his own timetable. The beginning of Act V finds Sejanus enjoying an orgiastic sense of power ("Swell, swell, my joys"), and lamenting only the lack of further worlds to conquer. When ill omens presage his fall he sweeps them aside, mocking religion and claiming dominion even over Fortune herself (5.206–210). Like a lamb to the slaughter, he is led to the Senate on the pretext of receiving a new honor, only to be confronted by a letter from Tiberius ordering his arrest and trial. He is seized by Macro, whose innate viciousness promises to make him both a more fitting and more circumspect instrument of tyranny, swiftly condemned and beheaded, and torn to pieces by the Roman mob.

Jonson's Sejanus is, finally, a sacrificial emblem of the new imperial regime, in which the old constitution, based on a polyvalent authority carefully distributed among distinct orders and offices, has been replaced by a two-dimensional system in which absolute power lords itself over ignoble submission. Jonson is not particularly interested in the cause of this change, as Machiavelli was in the *Discourses on Livy*, but only in its consequences. For Jonson, the early empire was a paradigm example of political corruption. With the hindsight denied his sources, he knew that this corruption was irreversible, and, although in his later *Catiline* he showed himself to be thoroughly disabused of the late republic as well, he implicitly aligns himself in *Sejanus* with the Machiavellian republicans who attributed the decadence and fall of Rome to its abandonment of the ancient constitution. As we have noted, no republicanism on Jonson's own part can be inferred from this; rather, it is the derogation from one political order to another that is fatal in a settled state. Lacking the intellectual suppleness of a Selden or Shakespeare's interest in character, Jonson's stance was that of a moralist concerned with the loss of integrity, which in political terms was bound up with the integrity of the commonwealth.

Jonson's fifth act, which begins with Sejanus at the peak of his afflatus and ends with his decapitated corpse so torn and rent as to be beyond burying (5.840–841), would seem to fulfill the classic prescription of the morality play: the would-be tyrant and usurper brought to justice and delivered to the populace he had sought to oppress. What it actually accomplishes is a grim inversion of the paradigm, for Sejanus' punishment, just in itself by the conventions of morality theater, is only the occasion for even worse evil to triumph, and his death symbolizes not the ritual purgation of the commonwealth but its further degradation.

The centerpiece of the act is the long scene in the Senate in which the absent Tiberius' letter of accusation is read out (545–659), punctuated by the sycophantic responses of the Senators and the cynical but impotent asides of Arruntius. As Jonson's editors note, the letter, constructed out of mere hints in the sources, is a "superbly effective piece of studied equivocation."[131] Tiberius ascribes his retirement to Capreae to his confidence in the Senate, thereby alerting it to its responsibility for his as-yet undisclosed complaint. He refers to Sejanus first in terms of the contrast between his low birth ("obscure and almost unknown gentry") and the great honors heaped on him. This, he notes in a Machiavellian turn, is "not without danger," it being a "bold hazard" in a sovereign to prefer one subject over all others. Tiberius here lowers his mask and addresses the Senators not as one citizen to his fellows but as a ruler to subjects. Having done so, he places his implicit self-criticism beyond their comment as well. In the next breath, however, he seems to clear both Sejanus of misconduct and the Senate of resentment, as if both stood on the same level: "we . . . in no way suspect the merit of our Sejanus to make our favours offensive to any" (581–583). The Senate exhales its collective sigh of relief ("O! Good, good!").

From this general gloss on rulers, favorites, and subjects, Tiberius turns to specific criticisms of Sejanus, particularly the zeal with which he has pursued enemies of state, thus preempting the exercise of imperial clemency. "Some" anonymous parties have interpreted these acts as attempts to aggrandize his own power, as likewise the retirement (now described as "unwilling") that he has forced on the Emperor himself; Tiberius, however, while referring the charges to the Senate, dismisses them as "most malicious." The Senators now fall in with the rhythm of this rhetoric ("O, he has restored all, list"), in which each succeeding accusation is accompanied by a ritual disclaimer of belief. When, at length, Tiberius orders Sejanus arrested and tried, he observes only "how grateful a sacrifice to the gods is the life of an ungrateful person" (653–654). The Senate is left in no doubt which "god" is to be satisfied.

The letter scene is thus a ceremonial divestiture of power. In this sense it is parallel to the abdication scene in *Richard II*, except that the source of divestiture is in the latter case from above, in the former from below. Tiberius, his authority all the more potent for his physical absence from the stage, monopolizes the discourse, with Sejanus reduced to virtual silence; his is the sole ability to empower or disempower, to spare or condemn, and the withdrawal of his favor (as its bestowal) is a ritual aspect of its display. In both scenes the ritual requires a fictive premise that underlies a legitimation claim: in Richard's case, that the power he surrenders is still his to renounce; in Sejanus', that the judgment of public crimes still belongs to the Senate. Tiberius "waits" on the Senate in the same sense that Bolingbroke waits on Richard; the acknowledgment of where real power lies rests with those who have been deprived of it. Bolingbroke can rule without Richard's submission, just as Tiberius can destroy Sejanus without the Senate's acquiescence. It is their ability to compel formerly sovereign entities to do their bidding in a public and peculiarly humiliating way, however, that signifies the full transfer of authority. By withholding a direct command, Tiberius forces the Senate to abase itself in trying to divine it: the hollowness of its titular authority affirms the substance of his real one. In Shakespeare's abdication scene, it is Richard who equivocates, a strategy by which he attempts to retain legitimacy even while relinquishing power. As with Tiberius and the Senate, Bolingbroke feigns attendance on his will, but although the scene is in dramatic terms wholly Richard's, Bolingbroke extracts what he requires. His silence, like Tiberius' loquacity, is the speech of actual power.

With *Sejanus*, however, we are on a decidedly Renaissance stage. In *Richard II*, the actors are ultimately the pawns of divine intention—or so Shakespeare invites us to see them—but in Jonson the "god" who will be gratified by the sacrifice of the ungrateful servant is manifestly Tiberius himself, and Sejanus' defiance of augury and demystification of religion at 5:69–93 is merely the symptom of his fatal arrogance rather than a spur to divine retribution. It is true that in Shakespeare's treatment divine right is bracketed rather than affirmed; the characters, rather than the playwright, labor in the belief that God sanctions all authority and forbids all rebellion. But the aggressive skepticism of Jonson, even more than that of Marlowe, places political action within a radically secular world, in which power and justice rest upon the human variables of ambition, virtue, and institutional constraints (or their absence). Political redemption, if it is to come at all, must be through these agencies.

In *Sejanus*, that redemption seems not only farther off by the play's end, but virtually foreclosed. The fall of a wicked minister not only fails to arrest Rome's descent into tyranny, but confirms and accelerates it. The Senate is more impotent and more openly complicit in its own destruction than ever, and the patriot party has been decimated. Tiberius' dominion is so complete that he can rule at a distance through ventriloquism, while indulging the private "lusts" darkly hinted at throughout the play. In Macro, he has found an even more sinister instrument of his will. The morality genre has been wholly inverted, not to say negated: good has not triumphed in the fall of a bad man, but evil in the exemplary sacrifice of one of its own. Cynicism, too, triumphs in the play's last pages, as the unbridled blood lust of Sejanus' dismemberment gives way to his posthumous transformation into a savior figure:

> [*Terentius*] . . . the rude multitude . . .
>
> Run quite transported with their cruelty—
> These mounting at his head, these at his face,
> These digging out his eyes, those with his brain,
> Sprinkling themselves, their houses, and their friends.
> Others are met, have ravished thence an arm,
> And deal small pieces of the flesh for favours;
> These with a thigh; this hath cut off his hands;
> And this his feet; these, fingers, and these, toes;
> That hath his liver; he his heart; there wants
> Nothing but room for wrath, and place for hatred
>
> [*Nuntius*] Part are so stupid, or so flexible,
> As they believe him innocent. All grieve.
> And some, whose hands yet reek with his warm blood,
> And gripe the part which they did tear of him,
> Wish him collected, and created new.
>
> (818, 827–836; 893–897)

What occurs is a mock-Dionysian *sparagmos* in which the sacrificial figure is torn to pieces, his severed parts borne away as talismans, and his person imaginatively reconstituted as a symbol of rebirth. That such a fate should befall the "atheist" Sejanus is, of course, only further grounds for irony. But what is really being worshiped in these barbaric acts is power itself in its most primitive form as identified with the god-king Tiberius and mediated through his surrogate. In this sense, the sacrifice of Sejanus that is proposed from the beginning completes the circuit of power that runs from the body politic to the Emperor and excludes all rival or intermediate authority. On this primal level there remains only the absolute power of the deified emperor and the absolute submission of his subjects. Politics is then reduced to a symbolic spectacle in which the sacrificial surrogate alone mediates between the infinitely exalted ruler and his infinitely abased subjects. His function is to be raised high above his fellows, high enough to illuminate the awful power of the imperium itself, and then to be dashed to pieces ("tread his brains/ Into the earth," says Macro) as a reminder of the terrible and inaccessible splendor of its majesty. Arruntius points the final moral:

> Forbear, you things
> That stand upon the pinnacles of state,
> To boast your slippery height. When you do fall,
> You pash yourselves in pieces, ne'r to rise,
> And he that lends you pity is not wise.
>
> (903–907)

That Arruntius remains to deliver this homily at the end of the play is significant. A minor figure in the sources, Jonson makes him the leader of the republican opposition, a Timonesque figure whose bitter speeches and asides provide a running commentary on the unfolding action and the other characters of the play. The freedom of his tongue, however, is the gauge of his impotence as an actor. In Act II, two of Sejanus' *poursuivants* take note of him while spying on Agrippina's house:

> *Satrius.* They'are grown exceeding circumspect, and wary.
> *Natta.* They have us in the wind. And yet Arruntius
>   Cannot contain himself.
> *Satrias.*   Tut, he's not yet
>   Looked after; there are others more desired,
>   That are more silent.
>
> (405–409)[132]

Arruntius' very loquacity is his protection. He is useful both in leading the henchmen to supposed plotters and in suggesting the "freedom" of citizens to voice their complaints. He need not be removed from the scene until the other members of the opposition have been accounted for. When there is no one left to rail at, he too will disappear, not as the last remaining threat but as a mere redundancy.

There is no actual resistance in *Sejanus*, but only grumbling and pious sentiment. Agrippina is a classic Roman matron who scorns plotting, and, when her danger becomes clear, thinks only of making a suicidal gesture of defiance. Silius, the bluff soldier, commits public suicide in fact. Agrippina counsels her sons finally to "stand upright;/ And though you do not act, yet suffer nobly" (4.73–74); Lepidus commends "the plain and passive fortitude/ To suffer, and be silent" (294–295); and when Sejanus' agent Latiaris tries to entrap another patriot, Sabinus, the latter replies, unimpeachably, that:

> No ill should force the subject undertake
> Against the sovereign, more than hell should make
> The gods do wrong. A good man should and must
> Sit rather down with loss, than rise unjust.
>
> (4.163–166)

This, too, is a paraphrase of the *Homily Against Rebellion*. Jonson wrings drama from the scene by having Latiaris egg Sabinus on until the latter blurts out a treasonable remark (216), at which point he is immediately seized. In this context, "rebellion" is immediately censured, even as the tyrant's greater culpability is affirmed: "The fault's not shameful villainy makes a fault" (232). It is a rare moment indeed in English Renaissance drama when treasonable utterance, though punished, is not reprehended, and rarer still when it is enacted before a royal audience. James I, to be sure, condemned tyranny fulsomely; he was equally insistent, however, that its exercise could be resisted only with the passive reproach of sighs, tears, and prayers. *Sejanus* was in this sense perfectly orthodox, lacking only the familiar morality comeuppance at the end. From another perspective, however, it was profoundly subversive, if we understand this term not as signifying an opposition to the Stuart monarchy (for which there is no evidence in Jonson) nor in the looser sense bandied about by some practitioners of the new historicism, but as a dystopic vision of the nature of power, and as such an anxious reflection on the absolutizing state. The Tacitean moment of *Sejanus*—the exemplary passage at which ascendant, arbitrary power crossed the falling trajectory of republican nostalgia—offered the one acceptable analogue through which such a vision could be projected before the very seat of authority to which Jonson himself was subject. James could behold in Tiberius the tyrant whose depiction only accentuated the contrast with the just, temperate, conscientious, law-abiding rule of England's new king, and in the merely passive resistance of the Germanican and Stoic opposition the appropriate behavior of oppressed but faithful subjects. It was possible to miss (or impossible to fix) the grace note of Machiavellian despair behind the lines, and the even more radical intuition of a political hell without exit.

The dramaturgical problem in *Sejanus* is how to sustain moral tension without the possibility of redemptive action. Jonson is precluded from showing active resistance to tyranny both by his declared fidelity to the historical record[133] and by the ideological constraints on depicting rebellion. Without being able to depict or even foreshadow such resistance, however, he is left only with the unedifying spectacle of a tyrant remorselessly crushing his subjects without the least prospect of justice, vengeance, or the ultimate restoration of a moral order. Jonson's solution, in purely formal terms, is to embrace his difficulty. Instead of a tyrant pursued by avengers, he offers one stalking his subjects, enmeshing them in an ever-more totalized climate of terror. The absence of a climax or of any redemptive reversal (other than the exemplary fall of Sejanus, who from this perspective is just another victim in an open series) is thus not a failure to deliver dramatic resolution, but the resolution itself. As Albert H. Tricomi notes:

From this vantage *Sejanus* dramatizes as a central part of its meaning the means by which the modern state controls the very power of seeing and conceiving. Indeed, the princely practice of overseeing and overhearing everything becomes one of the tragedy's master metaphors. Vaguely described in the opening scenes as devious and subtle, Tiberius appears at first to belong to the tradition of the sleeping prince who nods while his kingdom grows ever more infected. . . . In reality, however, he is Argus-eyed.[134]

Tiberius casts a longer and darker shadow as he withdraws further from the actual scene of the play, and his physical absence from the last two acts only reinforces the sense of his ubiquity and omniscience; nowhere visible, he is everywhere present. This contrasts with the transparency Agrippina promotes as virtue, but which only serves to target her more conspicuously:

> Were all Tiberius' body stuck with eyes,
> And every wall and hanging in my house
> Transparent, as this lawn [linen] I wear, or air;
> Yea, had Sejanus both his ears as long
> As to my inmost closet, I would hate
> To whisper any thought, or change an act,
> To be made Juno's rival. Virtue's forces
> Show ever noblest in conspicuous courses.
>
> (2.450–457)

The image of the Emperor's politic body as all eyes becomes the master trope of the play, and as this body pervades the communal space his natural one is freed to indulge what Sabinus calls its "filthy lusts," thus mirroring in private vice the corruption of the public sphere. The pollution of the Emperor's natural body is simultaneously the degradation of the body politic, and although which of these may be considered as cause and which as effect is functionally irrelevant—they appear at this point to be entailed by each other—it is clear that Tiberius himself is finally a symptom of the deeper decay of the Roman polity that Arruntius laments in his first act speech (86–104) and that Silius attributes to the "riots, pride, and civil hate" of the republic (1.57). Tiberius himself weighs in on the subject when he observes that "Contempt of fame begets contempt of virtue" (502). Fame is properly achieved through the display of virtue, whereas pride, as an end in itself, begets only vanity and strife. The sentiment is thoroughly Machiavellian, as is the ultimate indifference to constitutional forms which a Coke or even a Selden, were they to speak the language of Machiavelli, would regard as the basis of *virtù*. Silius has no nostalgia for the republic, declaring that "Men are deceived who think there can be thrall/ Beneath a virtuous prince," for "Wished liberty/ Ne'er lovelier looks than under such a crown" (1.407–409). Rome's political collapse is ultimately a moral one for the characters of Jonson's play, but its source remains a mystery which talk of Fortune's wheel belabors without illuminating. In dramatic terms, it is perhaps appropriate that these denizens of a fallen world should no longer be able to trace their malady or derive its cause. In the political hell of *Sejanus*, it is part of the punishment its citizen-subjects endure that they only know themselves derogated from a condition of grace they can no longer conceive.

Court Theater: Staging the Royal Sublime

The theater of the mystery and morality plays was an extension of religious ritual. The pre-Reformation church, as the principal site of social narrative, governed the tropes of dramatic representation at a level that enforced ideology without having to assert it, the social mechanism we call tradition. The same stories, featuring the same stock figures, were told over and over at prescribed times on the calendar. This theater collapsed with the transformation of the ritual that had sustained it. Protestantism created a new kind of religious culture whose emphasis on inward self-examination and the attainment of understanding through sermon and exegesis had its theatrical counterparts in character development and soliloquy. It did not, however, create or sponsor its own theater, despite the importance of its appropriation of dramatic form in its earliest decades. In part this was due to its programmatic though ambivalent hostility to spectacle and image (the extended scenes of Roman ritual in *King Johan*, *The Castle of Conscience*, and even *Doctor Faustus* can be read both as satire and nostalgia), and in part to a heightened sense of the opposition between sacred and profane that tended to figure the theater as a rude competitor rather than a potential ally. More important, however, was the replacement of the church (whether Roman or Reformed) as the dominant site of narrative by the Renaissance monarchy. In the English case, this was complicated by the institutional subordination of the church to the crown. In secular terms, at least, the "story" of the English polity was that of its monarchy, and if for instance in Shakespeare's history plays we awaken to a sense of reflective characterization that is distinctively Protestant, the characters so portrayed are royal ones.

The crown's appropriation of the theater as an essential projection of its persona is visible in the reign of Henry VIII; with Elizabeth, the monarchy itself became a species of performance art. As the source, subject, and privileged spectator of the entertainments devised for her both at Court and on progress, Elizabeth herself became the focus of a totalizing discourse in which all terms had ultimate reference to an idealized royal body that, dispersed through representation almost in the manner of a communion, returned always with theurgic intensity to the womanly body of the Queen herself. In this, Elizabeth transcended theater, creating a field in which the mortal and politic bodies of monarchy, like subject and predicate, figured each other in the long romance of her reign.

It was an unrepeatable performance. As spectacle, Elizabeth's entertainments paled before those devised by Inigo Jones for the first two Stuart Courts. By the same token, however, the increasing complexity and mechanical ingenuity of the Jacobean masque—a form that privileged image over text, and subordinated drama to display—tended to dissolve the fruitful tension between the mortal and politic bodies of the monarch that Elizabeth had sought to sustain. A repeated motif of the Elizabethan entertainments (for example, those at Kenilworth, Cowdray, and Elvetham) is the discovery of the Queen's disguised body as the means for recovery of an idealized, Arcadian England. The role of the royal body here is both magical and sexual, as the enthroned Queen liberates various chivalric figures sequestered in hollows or behind bushes. The Queen's body and the land's body become mutually reflective signifiers in which the politic unity of the realm is figured.[135]

James I, who remained James VI not only to his Scottish subjects but to his English ones, never enjoyed the iconic intimacy with his second kingdom that Elizabeth had forged. James' own favorite description of himself as the head and his two realms as the torso of a body now conjoined, now composite ("I am the Husband, and all the whole Isle is my lawfull Wife; I am the Head, and it is my Body"),[136] though a familiar trope of monarchy, had some unfortunate resonances, since his mother had suffered first a symbolic decapitation by her nobility and then a literal one at the hands of Elizabeth. These events were perhaps the latent subtext of his preoccupation with an Anglo-Scottish union, which offered not only a figurative recuperation of Mary's regnal body but an assumptive possession of Elizabeth's, and the ultimate rejection of the Union by Parliament and the public at large was a lingering source of personal as well as political injury.

In one sense, James' uxorious description of his relation to the "Isle" (two historically dissevered realms willfully joined—and feminized—by a royal body asserting prescriptive marital rights) was, in the actual political circumstances of the Union, deeply overbearing, suggesting not a sacramental union but a transgressive contamination. It did not help the King's image when his privately transgressive sexual life became a source of public scandal. James' other favorite trope of governance, that of the head and the body, was, though conventional, rendered similarly problematic not only by the awkward reminder of Mary's fate it contained but by the King's widely observed fear and disdain of crowds. The manifest difference between the King's rhetorical assumption of intimacy with the realm and his actual avoidance of public contact emphasized the separative as opposed to the unifying elements of the head/body metaphor. "Typically," as Jonathan

Goldberg has observed, "James invoked the mystical body [of kingship] as if it were his only one."[137]

James' personal style has been frequently described as Augustan, although Eliot's characterization of Buckingham as Sejanus casts a retrospectively Tiberian shadow over the reign as well.[138] The King himself, as *rex pacificus*, fostered the comparison with Augustus, and made it directly in the proclamation of July 1618 that launched the Jacobean Commission on New Buildings.[139] Like Augustus, James regarded himself as both the founder of a new dynasty and the refounder of the commonwealth; in his conception, "Great Britain," by permanently joining the two halves of Albion's island, would bring its destiny to an ultimate fruition. For many centuries England had sought to realize the goal of insular unity by imposing colonial subjugation on the Scots, a violent solution that could only breed further alienation and whose culminating insult was the execution of Mary Stuart. Only by the peaceful conquest of England through a Scottish dynastic succession—the lesser half, as it were, bringing concord and reconciliation to the greater—could a genuine unity be achieved. That the son of the slain Queen should be tasked with this reconciliation was self-evidently a mark of Providence, no less than the recovery of the Gospel in the two realms itself (the Scottish covenanters of the 1640s would offer a revised version of this narrative at the Westminster Assembly). From this point of view, the most symbolically significant act of the reign was the construction and consecration of Mary's tomb in the Henry VII chapel of Westminster Abbey between 1607 and 1612—dates that, ironically, encompassed the ruin of James' immediate hopes for an Act of Union, and the bitter dynastic check of Prince Henry's death. The act of placing Mary's remains among those of England's sovereigns (apart from being a tart commentary on the legitimacy of Elizabeth's title) was thus an affirmation of the Stuart succession that cast Mary—depicted in a medieval attitude of prayer—in the role of the sacrificial saint whose martyrdom had laid to rest the enmity of the two kingdoms.[140]

The other tutelary figure James chose to emblematize his reign was Solomon—lawgiver, peacemaker, biblical patriarch, and builder of the temple. In performing all of these exemplary roles, at least symbolically, James met resistance from his new subjects: as lawgiver, from the demeaning necessity to deal with Parliament and the impertinent claims of the common lawyers; as peacemaker, from the demands of his position as leader of the Protestant cause and the galling popularity of his bellicose son Henry; as patriarch, from the cult of Elizabethan nostalgia; as the patron of a conformist religious establishment, from godly iconoclasts. There was a certain Oedipal awkwardness too in the choice of a figure whose iconic symbol was a child being held aloft to be cut in two, but for James the reenactment of his own providential escapes from death, beginning in infancy, was the most obsessive ritual of his reign, and the paired image of the threatening but ultimately merciful patriarch and the vulnerable child was his own most intimate self-representation.

In contrast, then, to Elizabeth, who attracted a plethora of biblical, allegorical, and mythological associations, James confined his iconic representation primarily to a pair of regal personages, one representing the religious and the other the imperial dimensions of his crown. Both were images of a royal sublime, serving not, as in the cult of Gloriana, as mediatory figures that enabled Elizabeth's subjects to approach her in the endlessly reinstated courtship that constituted the symbolic politics of her reign, but to exalt the monarch beyond the reach of vulgar desire. To achieve this required not a separation but a conflation of the King's natural and politic bodies, in which the former was enfolded in the latter and was available only through representation. In this quasi-sacramental apotheosis, the King's natural body was transported toward a beatific union with the divine source of his authority, an assumption completed only upon death but continually in process.

As the Reformed church, both as the body of the faithful and as a house of worship, represented the site of Christ's remembered passage from his mortal to his divine body, so the royal apotheosis too required not merely the perfect unity of the king's subjects in fealty and obedience but a specific locus, a sacralized space. Inigo Jones provided this in the rebuilt Royal Banqueting House at Whitehall (1619), which Graham Parry has accurately described as "the Temple of the Stuart kings" and Malcolm Smuts as "a temple of royal divinity."[141] The Banqueting House was the true center of the Jacobean monarchy. Here James sat in state, gave audience and rendered judgment, and, within its protective enclosure, reluctantly dispensed the royal touch that was the irreducible minimum of contact between the natural body of the King and those of his subjects. Jones designed a Roman basilica based on Vitruvian proportions, thus combining both sacerdotal and imperial elements. The King was enthroned in a space corresponding to the apse of the traditional basilica, where he "sat in majesty," as Graham Parry observes, integrated "like a living statue into the architecture of the whole."[142] Parry's apt metaphor captures the quality of the royal presence as simultaneously present and absent. The statue is a token that indifferently represents the living and the dead; it depicts either or both, singly or successively, without altering its own fixed character. The paradox of a living statue is that it is figured as a thing both animate and inanimate at once, sign and object in one. Consequently it points to an ineffable *tertium quid*, a transcendent state in which the simultaneity of representation and reality is reconciled, or in our terms the copresence of the mortal and immortal body of a king. Such an effect is sought by Jones, an effect like that glimpsed by Bolingbroke, York, and Richard himself in the stage monarch's descent, "like glistering Phaethon," from Flint Castle (*Richard II*, 3.3.178). In the temple of the Banqueting Hall, majesty's plenitude is manifest.

The Banqueting House was erected in an astonishingly short time, but its decoration was still unfinished at the time of James' death in 1625. Charles I commissioned Rubens to paint a nine-paneled ceiling whose theme was the apotheosis of his father and, by inference, of the new-founded Stuart dynastic line. Here, at least, James' dream of Union could be realized. The red-robed King, his foot on an orb and an eagle with lightning gripped in its talons beneath it, is presented a child representing the Union as the goddess Minerva hovers above him with the new crown of Great Britain. A splendid tumult of baroque figures and cherubs circles him as the heavens open out, simultaneously illuminating the scene and receiving it into immortal glory. There is something a trifle awkward about the royal pose, and the right leg seems to seek balance. Presumably Rubens intended the dynamism of the effect, and it was perhaps an apt transfiguration for a King who never sat quite securely on any of his thrones.[143]

If the "living statue" of the monarch in state was the ideal iconic reconciliation of the king's two bodies and the Rubens ceiling represented their apotheosis, a third term was yet essential to the enactment of the royal sublime. This term was the masque, which was performed in the Banqueting Hall before the king himself. If Henry VIII could remark that he never sat in higher estate than in Parliament, then for the first two Stuarts the ultimate seat of majesty was Whitehall rather than Westminster. The spectators of the masque were an invited audience, with none of the promiscuity of the commercial theater or the parish church, or, for that matter, a Parliament, where "invited" guests—the numerous seats disposed of by royal and aristocratic patronage—sat with those returned by franchise and containing so-called "popular" or "turbulent spirits." Private entertainments before select audiences in noble households or corporate groups such as the Inns of Court were of course common, but the masque audience was a unique one, chosen not only for quality and decorum but for its suitability to participate in the festive dancing that followed the performance and which affirmed and embodied the harmony between subject and sovereign that was the discourse of the masque. The masque audience thus played a doubly symbolic role, both miming and reflecting the masque itself and mimicking the response of the popular (but excluded) audience whose loyal submission was invoked in the masque action. In this sense the masque performance, encompassing both the stage action and the audience response that completed it, enacted a static progress, a journey to nowhere in which the ritualized display of legitimacy was accompanied by its own assent.

The central actor in the masque was the king himself, whose entry and seating signaled the beginning of the performance. It was not merely that this entry came after all the other spectators had been seated (in careful order of precedence and rank), and was greeted by their rising in unison. The king was neither the last of the spectators nor the first of the performers, but the Archidamian point on which all rested. The performance itself was merely a representation of his presence, and in that sense an anticlimax; what really mattered was the ceremony of the royal entrance and the king's strategic placement as, in Nicoll's phrase, "the cynosure of all eyes."[144] When James was entertained in Christ Church Hall, Oxford, in 1605, the courtiers who canvassed the space objected to the royal vantage, which though calculated by his hosts to provide the King with an optimal view of the stage, obscured the spectators' view of him. The matter was rectified. James complained that he could not hear the play, but the purpose of the occasion was achieved: he was fully visible to all.[145]

Both in the Old Banqueting Hall built for Elizabeth and in the new one designed by Jones, James sat under an "ample canopy" in what was described, simply, as "the state."[146] Since the hall in which masques were performed was the one in which James conducted public business, the transition from reality to fantasy took place in the same space. After the masque performance, which was customarily ended by the entrance of dancers for the ball and followed by the serving of a repast, the festive return to reality completed the arc of ascent from the real to the represented and back again. In a larger sense, however, the performance of monarchy was continuous, and the theatricalization of power meant that no clear distinction between signifier and signified was intended or could be maintained. The king in state, observing his own representation on stage, was a pole in a dynamic circuit of force in which, as it were, he watched the emanation of his own sovereign power, at once the unmoved mover of the action and the emptied vessel of his own authority. This dynamism was the royal sublime itself, in which the king's two bodies could be metaphorically witnessed at once, with the king in state, the living statue, as the authorizing agent of the player king on stage, whose shifting allegorical guises attested the unstable plenitude of representation, the inexhaustibility of power. The masque stopped just short of idolatry and therefore of subversion, for the process of signification—the representational transfer of authority from king to player—remained provisional and incomplete, requiring the continual sovereign assent to sustain the performative fiction. When the circuit of authorization was broken, as by Shakespeare's Claudius during the performance of *The Murder of Gonzago*, disorder ensued. On the other hand, the ball was sometimes incorporated into the Caroline masque, with both the King and Queen entering directly into the ongoing entertainment. Such an incorporation invited the remaining spectators to enter more deeply into fantasy, which was where "reality"— the physical presence of the King—was now to be found.[147] The king's customary two bodies—united in his corporeal presence, signified in his seals, emblems, and representations—thus acquired a third aspect in which it was both present and absent, concealed and revealed; in short, a "new" order of reality.

The progressive mystification of the King's body went hand in hand with the development of the masquing art itself, essentially a visual one in which the textual component was increasingly reduced to the subsidiary role of accompaniment and commentary. As an embittered Ben Jonson, the chief author of Jacobean masque texts, was to remark after his exclusion from Charles' Court:

> O shows! Shows! Mighty shows!
> The eloquence of masques! What need of prose,
> Or verse, or sense, to express immortal you?
> Painting and carpentry are the soul of masque.[148]

One of Jonson's successors at Court, Aurelian Townshend, is largely reduced to describing Jones' scenic effects in his *Albions Triumph*:

The first thing that presented it selfe to the eye, was the Ornament that went about the Scene: in the middest of which, was placed a great Armes of the Kings, with Angels holding an Emperiall Crowne, from which hung a Drapery, of crimson Velvet, fringed with gold, tackt in severall knotts, that on each-side, with many folds, was wound a Pillaster; in the freeze, were festones of severall fruites in their naturall colours, on which, in gratious postures lay Children sleeping; at each end was a double sheild, with a Gorgons head, and at the foot of the pillasters, on each side, stood two Women, the one young, in a watchet Robe looking vpwards, and on her head, a paire of Compasses of gold, the poynte standing towards Heaven: the other more ancient, appareled in a tawney, looking downewards; in the one hand a long ruler, and in the other, a great paire of iron Compasses, one poynt whereof, stood on the ground, and the other touched part of the ruler. Above their heads, were fixt, compertiments of a new composition, and in that over the first, was written *Theorica*, and over the second *Practica*, shewing that by these two, all works of Architecture, and Im[a]gining have their perfection. The Curtaine being suddenly drawne vp, the first Sceane appeared, which represented a *Roman Atrium*, with high Collombs of white Marble, and ornaments of Architecture of a composed maner of great proiecture, enricht with Carving, and betweene every retorne of these Collombs, stood Statues of gold on round predestalls and beyond these, were other peeces of Architecture of a Pallace royall.[149]

As author, Townshend is reduced to admiring spectator, describing in minute detail the theater curtain with its two-dimensional promise of perspectival splendors to come, and only at the end of the passage is the scene onstage disclosed, which itself is merely the premise of "a Pallace royall" whose columns, abutments, and statues point toward an awful and ineffable enthronement beyond the horizon of the spectacle. The reflexivity of the scene, with the royal spectator sitting in the actual splendor of his "state" gazing toward his own withheld image, suggests the ineffability of a deferred representation that can only be realized by the King's own presence on the stage—a realization, however, that comes only in the form of another disguise, that of the masquing or player-king.

The effect of the perspectival enlargement of the masque stage is, consequently, the estrangement of space as both infinitely distended and infinitely collapsed. The tripartite division of the theatrical space—the physical space reserved for the spectators, the illusionistic stage space whose function was to point beyond itself, and the space of the proscenium apron and the dance floor on which the masquers themselves actually performed—corresponded to the tripartite division of the royal persona as the living statue of the king in state, the allegorical or emblematic representation of it in the performance space, and the recessive sublime figured in the vistas of the proscenium perspective.

In this fully encoded space the drama that took place—the essential subject of the masque, endlessly varied but always the same—was the fragmentation and reconstitution of the royal image. This drama, too, had a tripartite structure. The raising of the curtain disclosed the representational space of majesty, whether in the form of monumental architecture or celestial spheres. Allegorical figures represented the king's power, virtue, and benevolence, while in the masques devised for the Queen's Court Anna and Henrietta Maria appeared in mythological guise, both representing themselves and as (incomplete) royal surrogates. In Jonson's *The Masque of Blackness* (1605), one of Anna's earliest entertainments, the Queen and her ladies appeared in blackface as the daughters of "Ethiop," whose transformation into the whiteness of virtue could only be accomplished by their journey to Albion and the sanctifying grace of its ruler. The stately progress of such scenes was interrupted by the antimasque, in which animal, barbarian, or demonic figures suddenly appeared, threatening chaos. In the drama's final movement these figures were tamed, vanquished, or banished by a royal epiphany, and universal harmony restored. The celebratory ball that followed served at once as a seal on the action and as a bridge back to a reality enriched by its representation as sublime. By joining himself in the celebration, the king united his presence as subject with his representation as object, solemnizing and authenticating the ritual and offering it a final, triadic unity.

The Eucharistic elements of the masque-as-ritual are clear. The fatherly king in state, who by his sovereign will authorizes the action of the masque, benevolently observes the allegorical son who, representing him on stage, restores order to a distempered world. The triumph is capped by the king's descent to the stage, symbolically joining heaven and earth in a hypostatized unity that embraces both father and son, eternity and temporality. The theatrical space of the masque itself, embracing the spectators as "parishioners" who not only observe the ritual but participate in it according to prescribed formulas, thus figuratively becomes a church in which the king in state, centrally placed like the Host, is elevated and "offered" by means of the masque, and finally circulates among his worshiper/subjects in the ball like the elements of the Host within the body of the congregation.

What keeps these analogies within the bounds of permissible representation (at least for the participants) is the figurative elements governing the whole, for in the master trope of divine right the king exercises Christ's mandate on earth, and the king's two bodies, at once distinct and conjoined, are an image of the divine unity. Another essential framing device, however, is the use of pagan mythological forms and the general avoidance of overt Christian symbols or Scriptural reference. The masque thus falls back inevitably on the Neoplatonic subtext of Christian doctrine as a means of enacting a Eucharistic rite (itself of course a sublimated form of the Dionysian *sparagmos*), while avoiding the imputation of blasphemy.

The uses of Neoplatonism in the discourse of the masque are well illustrated in the passage between "Publius" and "Platonicus" in *Albions Triumph*. Publius describes the magnificent pageant of King Albanactus (Charles), and the following colloquy ensues:

> *Pub.* Where stood you?
> *Pla.* I stood not.
> *Pub.* You had the better friends sir, I pray where sate you?
> *Pla.* In my studdy.
> *Pub.* Is not your studdy backward? with a shop-light in it,
>   where one can see nothing but the skye?
> *Pla.* I confesse it, what of that?
> *Pub.* Why then you saw no Triumph.
> *Pla.* But I did, and a trew one, thine was but a shew.[150]

Platonicus, his eyes fixed on the heavens, discerns the final essence that the triumph of Albanactus can only represent. Yet the distinction he draws is not merely that between appearance and reality, but between a proximate and an ultimate glory. The triumph is an emblem, a true pattern of the ineffable; it is also an act of homage, by subjects to their sovereign and by the sovereign to the divine authority he embodies. Platonicus sees the entirety of this golden chain with the eye of the visionary, whereas to vulgar sight only the earthly pageant is visible. As a figure, he points toward a transcendent reality just as the receding vistas of the proscenium do, not to negate spectacle but to complete it.

Even within the Court, Neoplatonism was not universally popular. Ben Jonson, the Aristophanes of his time, poked fun at it in a late Jacobean masque, *The Fortunate Isles*. When the simpleton Mere-Foole asks the "aery spirit" Jophiel to reveal to him the magus-figures of Zoroaster, Pythagoras, and Hermes Trismegistus, as well as the Neoplatonists Iamblichus, Porphyry, and Proclus, the latter mockingly replies:

> What would you wish to be now? or what to see?
> Without the fortunate purse to beare your charges,
> Or wishing hat? I will but touch your temples,
> The corners of your eyes, and tinct the tip,
> The very tip o' your nose, with his *Cellyrium*,
> And you shall see i' the aire all the *Ideas*,
> This way, and that way, and are rather admirable,
> Then any way intelligible.
>
> (184–192)

Jonson's audience would doubtless have caught the allusions to Faust and Mephistopholis in this colloquy. What is "admirable" here is not that which is worthy of regard but that which provokes empty wonder, behind which lies not the intelligible, i.e. the real, but the snares of illusion. Some lines later Jophiel espies Plato himself, who, like Inigo Jones, is busily "framing some *Ideas*" which are "bespoken at a groat a dozen,/ Three grosse at least" (253–255). Spawned promiscuously, these cheap inventions suggest not an underlying unity but the vulgar multiplicity of the marketplace. *The Fortunate Isles* is Jonson's protest at the mystification of the masque, its subjection to an increasingly sterile and self-congratulatory royalism.

The problem of proliferating signs, the overdetermination of meaning they represent, and the ultimate instability they portend, is apparent in the preface to one of the very first Jacobean masques, Samuel Daniel's *The Vision of the Twelve Goddesses* (1604), in which the author complains of "the best Mytheologers, who will make somwhat to seeme any thing, are so vnfaithfull to themselues, as they haue left vs no certeine way at all, but a tract of confusion, to take our course at aduenture."[151] In this light, the antimasquers come to represent not the negation but the inversion of the royal surrogates of the masque, for when meaning is constrained but symbols multiply, difference erodes, and representation is pulled toward a black hole of signification in which it finally disappears. Daniel concedes the quandary in his preface to *The Qveenes Arcadia*, acted for Anna in 1605:

> And therefore in the view of state t'have show'd
> A counterfeit of state, had beene to light
> A candle to the Sunne, and so bestow'd
> Our paines to bring our dimnesse unto light.
> For maiesty, and power, can nothing see
> Without it selfe, that can sight-worthy be.[152]

When the royal spectator is (in this case) herself not merely the patron but the signified object of the performance, nothing remains but to offer praise, a task that begins and ends with a confession of ontological inadequacy. The "counterfeit" representation is a mere "dimnesse" that is offered its fleeting existence only by the presence of the authorizing power that confers occasion and value on it. This is far indeed from the stage on which a Richard II is abjured and slain or the cul-de-sac of the Tiberian state exposed.

The point of course is that, in James' case at least, both kinds of theater were on view at Court, and, in Jonson's, that a single sensibility was able to negotiate both genres with artistically gratifying results. The literature of compliment has always faced the problem of flattery; mild degrees of distancing, whether through irony, satire, or reflexive self-consciousness, have been the prescribed antidotes. The increasing importance and growing elaborateness of the masque as a site of royal self-representation — the Privy Council complained about its expense as early as 1604 — suggested another agent of control as well. A discourse as hegemonic as the Stuart masque must reflect the internal divisions of its source (or, in some cases, labor to repress them). As is well known, the politics of Henrietta Maria's retinue had an at least moderately different cast from that of Charles',[153] and the reversionary interest of Prince Henry's Court created tension with that of James. Jonson's *Oberon* has been seen as an effort to create an allegorical catchment for Henry's ambitions, which of necessity expressed while attempting to contain them.[154] On the other hand, his *Neptune's Triumph*, composed to celebrate Charles' return from Madrid, strives, in the words of Martin Butler, to refigure the transparent conflict between James and his son over his trip to the Spanish Court as a "myth of reunion,"[155] and to recast the Duke of Buckingham ("Hippius") as the symbol of royal amity. "Neptune," the ruler of the waves, is James, and the masque takes the covert form of an Odyssean voyage whose hero, Albion (Charles), undertakes an unspecified adventure at the behest of the god, whose powers, together with the guidance of his surrogate, Hippius, ensure Albion's safe return after many trials. It is not the adventure itself, however, but the hero's return that is the subject of the masque, for the tragicomic narrative of Charles' journey (tragic as the final ruin of James' efforts to avert a general European war, comic in its diplomatic fiasco and — in a different sense — as Charles' emergence from the shadows of his minority as the sovereign-in-waiting) is too sensitive even for allegory. What remains is mere celebration:

> Where, what the arts were, vsde to make him stay,
> And how the *Syrens* woo'd him, by the way,
> What Monsters he encountred on the coast,
> How neare our generall Ioy was to be lost,

Is not our subiect now: though all these make
The present gladnesse greater, for their sake.

(144–149)

The scope of *Neptune's Triumph* is, in short, contracted to its title, with the hero's journey undramatized and the antimasque, an element Jonson had made particularly his own, suppressed.[156] Since the "triumph" of Neptune was in actuality James' culminating defeat—the collapse of his policy, the defection of his favorite, the supersession of his reign—what it represented was not merely fantastic but false. The gleeful bonfires that greeted Charles' return were a popular repudiation of the Spanish match, and what they celebrated was the failure of his journey. In turning this political calamity into a festive celebration, *Neptune's Triumph* offers, finally, not a mythic translation of reality but its inversion and antithesis. To be sure, it might have performed an in-house function at Court in providing an allegorical reconciliation between James and Charles, and thereby providing a degree of cover for the anti-Spanish policy subsequently pursued by Charles and Buckingham. It might, too, have been a means of capitalizing on the popular sense of Charles' return from Spain as a providential rescue from the jaws of the Antichrist. Doubtless, however, it would have been as painful for James to watch as for the Spanish ambassador, whose protests were the apparent reason for its nonproduction.[157]

Jonson took care to include *Neptune's Triumph* among his published masques, thus ensuring its survival. Despite the fact that it was never performed, it marks a watershed in the evolution of the masque form. Jennifer Chibnell remarks that Jonson expanded the antimasque to anchor the cloistered entertainments of the Court in the "disorder and vitality" of rude popular culture, which, even when perceived as threatening and offensive, was incorporated in the courtly revel and thereby acknowledged.[158] By omitting it from *Neptune's Triumph* as well as by misrepresenting the journey to Madrid as transacting the will of James, he substituted the comforts of illusion for the hard challenges of fact. Sara Pearl contends that Jonson's late Jacobean masques attempt to mediate "between false mysteries and true ones."[159] But in *Neptune's Triumph* what is on offer is not the sublimation of reality but a mystification that twists the circumstances of a divided Court and nation into a consoling image of effortless control and preordained harmony. In this sense, though its intended performance predated James' demise by sixteen months, it may be regarded as the first Caroline masque.

Jonson himself notoriously failed to please the new king. The reasons for this are complex and to a degree obscure, but his Falstaffian figure was clearly out of place in Charles' fastidious Court, where favor depended increasingly on acceptance within the royal entourage, and the stately decorum of Inigo Jones' spectacles tamed the ruder energies of Jonson's earlier

entertainments.[160] The antimasque, to be sure, continued to feature prominently in the Caroline masque, and Kevin Sharpe has argued that it was
used to balance compliment with criticism.[161] There is little evidence to support this in the texts themselves, however, and some directly belie it. In
Thomas Carew's *Coelum Britannicum* (1633), for example, in which antimasque elements are given particular prominence, the anarchic figure of
Momus offers himself not in the traditional pose of bestiality, barbarism, or
generalized anarchy, but as the patron of Peeping Toms, pettifogging lawyers, and parliamentarians:

> My privileges are an uniquitary, circumabulatory, speculatory, interroga-
> tory, redargutory immunity over all the privy lodgings, behind hangings,
> dores, curtaines, through keyholes, chinkes, windowes, about all Veneriall
> Lobbies, Skonces or Redoubts . . . and at all Courts of civill and criminall
> judicature, all Counsels, Consultations, and Parliamentary Assemblies,
> where though I am but a Woollsacke god, and have no vote in the sanction
> of new lawes, I have yet a Praerogative of wrestling the old to whatsoever
> interpretation, whether it be to the behoofe, or prejudice, of *Iupiter* his
> Crowne and Dignity, for, or against the Rights of either house of Patrician
> or Plebeian gods.[162]

This broad sneer at the legal profession is the royal riposte to Coke's challenge to prerogative government, renewed in alliance with Selden and others
in the parliaments of the 1620s. Momus' reference to himself as a "Woolsacke
god" centers him as a presence in Parliament itself, for by tradition the Lord
Chancellor's seat in the House of Lords contained a sack of wool in token of
the commodity on which England's trade and wealth rested. Although Momus does not have an actual vote in the "sanction" of laws (a careful phrase
that preserves the royal preeminence in making statutes), he infects them as
a spirit of mischief that distorts their meaning through legal mumbo jumbo
and sets itself up as the arbiter of constitutional authority. The connection
between this arrant sprite and the "turbulent and ill-affected spirits" cited by
Charles in dissolving Parliament in 1629[163] would have been unmistakable to
Carew's audience. When Momus warns that he can as easily exalt the royal
prerogative and overturn parliamentary liberties as the reverse he reveals his
fundamental absurdity, because monarchical power is (from a royalist perspective) incommensurable and indisputable. At the same time, the Olym-
pian jest at "plebeian gods" suggests the levity of any comparison between
Jupiter's powers and those of an assembly that exists at his sufferance.

Far from employing the antimasque as a device for admitting excluded
elements of public discourse and offering an even oblique criticism of royal
policies, Carew thus uses it as a means of mocking the constitutional challenge to Caroline absolutism. Momus continues in a similar vein throughout
the seven antimasque scenes. The enforced flight of godly ministers and

congregations is glanced at in the suggestion to "embarque them all together in that good Ship call'd the Argo, and send them to the plantation in *New-England*, which hath purg'd more virulent humors from the politique body, then *Guacum* and all the West-Indian druggs have from the naturall bodies of this kingdome" (386–390). When Poverty enters with what seems at first a sharp rebuke to privilege ("I could pretend,/ Even in these rags, a larger Soverainty/ Then gaudy Wealth in all his pompe can boast;/ For marke how few they are that share the World", 594–597), Mercury rejects her claims as resting upon mere want of industry, and extols "Such vertues onely as admit excesse,/ Brave bounteous Acts, Regall Magnificence, All-seeing Prudence, Magnanimity/ That knowes no bound" (660–663) — in short, the prodigal expense and aristocratic self-congratulation of the masque itself. A last trace of anxiety appears in the figure of Fortune ("her head bald behind, and one great locke before . . . her upper parts naked"), who declares:

> The revolutions of Empires, States,
> Scepters, and Crownes, are but my game and sport,
> Which as they hang on the events of Warre,
> So they depend upon my turning wheele.
>   You warlike Squadrons, who in battels joyn'd,
> Dispute the Right of Kings, which I decide,
> Present the modell of that martiall frame,
> By which, when Crownes are stak'd, I rule the game.
>   (709–716)

Fortune is simply another version of Momus himself, who provides not reasons for disputing "the Right of Kings" (there can be none), but asserts instead the dominion of caprice. Mercury rejects this renewed vision of anarchic misrule, for to "the piercing eye of Providence," which rules all, "thou dost disappeare,/ Losest thy being, and art not at all" (734, 736–737). To the extent, then, that *Coelum Britannicum* acknowledges the existence of dissent from the Caroline program, it is only to banish it to the nether regions of allegory, or (what is substantively the same thing) to those of the New World.[164]

As Stephen Orgel points out, *Coelum Britannicum* "was the greatest theatrical expression of the Caroline autocracy,"[165] in which, after the long parade of false gods and vices, order and virtue triumph in a succession of scenic "reformations" in which a ruined and decadent city is transformed first into a sylvan Arcadia and then by degrees rebuilt and revealed in its temporal majesty as the triune perfection of Charles' three kingdoms. This vision is then transcended by the disclosure of eternity itself, whose "patterne" Charles and his posterity immortally bear:

> [I]n the midst suspended in the Ayre, sate Eternity on a Globe, his Garment was long of a light blue, wrought all over with Stars of gold, and bearing in

his hand a Serpent bent into a circle, with his taile in his mouth. In the firmament about him, was a troope of fifteene starres, expressing the stellifying of our British Heroes; but one more great and eminent than the rest, which was over his head, figured his Majesty. (1077–1084)

Charles' depiction as the godhead, enshrined above the figure of eternity itself and beheld by "the Kings Majesty seated under the State by the Queene" (1051–1052), was the ultimate vision of the royal sublime, the king's two bodies held in focus in a dazzling penumbra of glory ("beames of light" breaking forth from a "great Cloud"). Here is the promise of an "Endlesse Succession," the place in which, as "Eternitie" sings, "faire Desert, and Honour meet, [and]/ . . . / Secure from all disturbing Evill,/ For ever in my Temple revell" (1117, 1119–1120).

Charles' Platonic Arcadia lacked only one element to its perfection: the submission of loyal and contented subjects. The King's irritation with the legal community lingered in the aftermath of the dissolution of Parliament in 1629. Some of Charles' abler parliamentary critics, such as William Noy and Sir Thomas Wentworth, were coopted soon after, Noy to serve as Attorney General and Wentworth as the architect of the coercive fiscal policies known simply as "Thorough." Prison or confiscation had silenced dissenters; so had rustication or voluntary exile. The latter course, as *Coelum Britannicum* had made clear, was particularly recommended for critics of the ceremonial Caroline church. Charles had none of his father's sense of a comprehensive church as a balance of interests, or of orthodoxy as a dynamic process that could entertain and even contain a considerable diversity of opinion. His personal aesthetic, moreover, was too far removed from the godly style to permit him the least sense of how offensive, not to say idolatrous, it might appear to others.

The case of William Prynne brought these matters into sharp focus. Prynne, a Lincoln's Inn barrister already noted for godly stridency, had deeply embarrassed the legal community with his *Histrio-Mastix* (1632), a catchall jeremiad against such abominations as "effeminate mixt Dancing . . . Stage-playes . . . wanton Fashions . . . amorous Pastoralls . . . [and] Mummeries."[166] These categories amply included the Court masque, with particular reference to the scandal of female performers (indexed by Prynne under the famous heading of "Women actors, notorious whores"), and, by extension, both the person of Henrietta Maria and the entire fabric of Platonic romance so integral to Caroline Court culture. Prynne had already suffered his punishment, including imprisonment, the pillory, and a heavy fine, but Charles wanted, and got, a public penance from the profession he represented. This took the form of James Shirley's masque, *The Triumph of Peace*, which, staged in February 1634, was a command performance for the Court devised at ruinous expense by the Inns of Court.[167] The entertainment commenced ("quite unusually," as Sharpe remarks) from Ely and Hatton Houses in Holborn, as three hundred masquers, musicians, and attendants proceeded slowly through the West End to Whitehall in a carnivalesque version of the journey to Canossa. This gaudy humiliation was plainly intended for public consumption, while, in the Banqueting Hall, Charles and Henrietta Maria awaited the submission of the lawyers with "a great assembly of lords and ladies, and other persons of quality."[168]

The procession of *The Triumph of Peace* toward Whitehall was the cynosure of the decade; in the absence of a coronation, a royal wedding, or a meeting of Parliament, it was the only public pageant in which the rituals of authority were extensively displayed, and its staging, by Inigo Jones, was designed to convey the narrative of absolutism to the vulgar. The antimasquers went first, including allegorical figures in motley representing the various "characters" of popular discourse (Opinion, Confidence, Fancy, Jollity, Laughter, Novelty, Admiration); a series of projectors, likewise dressed; and an array of beggars pursued by mastiffs. These were followed by bird-figures whose discordant voices were mimed by a musical accompaniment; assorted satyrs; and finally a Don Quixote and Sancho Panza pair, tilting absurdly at a windmill. The entire procession, as Shirley commented, moved forward "in ridiculous show and posture," thus accentuating the frenzy and disorder of untamed nature and an ungoverned people.

A line of fourteen trumpeters, led by a drummer, put discord to rout, and introduced a Marshal, attended by ten horse and forty foot, who served not only as a bulwark between the antic figures before them and the line of gentlemen behind, "gloriously furnished and gallantly mounted," but also as a means of policing the excited multitude that were "in such triumphs . . . wont to be insolent, and tumultuary" (43). The crowd, in short, had its assigned role as well, confirming by its own disorder the need for overawing regiment and splendor. The splendor was manifested in a cavalcade of chariots bearing priestly and sybilline figures, the "sons and daughters of harmony"; a new set of allegorical figures representing peace, law, and justice; and a final line of Grand Masquers, mounted above everyone else and accompanied by magnificent flourishes.

The presiding figures of the masque, whose symbols were represented on the proscenium stage opposite the state, were Peace (Irene), Law (Eunomia), and Justice (Dichē). Their colloquy represents the heart of the scenario, and much has been made of the discourse between Peace and Law. Irene calls out to Eunomia, suggesting that her glory is incomplete without her sister and indeed rests upon her: "Like dew that falls/ Into a stream/ I'm lost without them that know not how to order me." To Eunomia she protests that

> I am but wild without thee, thou abhorrest
> What is rude, or apt to wound,

> Canst throw proud trees to the ground,
> And make a temple of a forest.

The temple of the law in the clearing of the forest suggests the civilizing process; Arcadia represents the conquest of the savage in which the elements of the scene remain natural, but are informed throughout by order. Both sisters, embracing in song, declare that:

> The world shall give prerogative to neither;
> We cannot flourish but together.

> (539–540)

The use of "prerogative" in this context, where "precedence" might have seemed more suitable, has been seen as a reminder to the King that the law's prerogatives must be respected no less than royal ones.[169] But this isolated legalism may perhaps serve no more exalted a function than to remind Charles that it is, on this occasion, the law that has come to make peace with the monarch. Dichē soon joins her sisters in a chorus of praise to the royal pair, whose dazzling sublimity is seen as their common source and ultimate reference:

> *Dichē.* Am I in earth or Heaven?
> *Irene.* What throne is that,
>   On which so many stars do wait?
> *Dichē.* My eyes are blest again, and now I see
>   The parents of us three:
>   'Tis Jove and Themis; forward move,
>   And sing to Themis, and to Jove.

The stars themselves attend the unity of divine power and love in the persons of Charles and Henrietta Maria. If this represents "criticism," it would be hard to imagine praise. Rather, it follows the example of Townshend's *Albions Triumph*, in which, as Stephen Kogan points out, "For the first time in the history of the seventeenth-century masque, the court is [seen as] even purer and more attractive than the heavens."[170]

Two other sections of *The Triumph of Peace* have been singled out as sites of oppositional and even subversive gestures: the antimasque of the projectors and the sudden, eruptive appearance of rude craftsmen and their spouses.[171] As Martin Butler points out, the former scene was "the brainchild" of Attorney General Noy, himself the licenser of patents of monopoly.[172] Was it, however, intended as an oblique criticism of the licensing program, or at any rate as a warning about its permissible limits? The entrance of the projectors follows a tavern scene in which, after a dance of wenches and gamesters, cripples beg alms and then throw away their crutches. Opinion wonders, pointedly, whether such antics are "the effects of peace?" and concludes, "Corruption rather."

Opinion's comment might be seen as a criticism not only of vagrants and projectors but of the Caroline peace itself, which in suppressing the martial virtues through which aristocratic merit displayed itself had permitted such rogues to flourish. It is more naturally read, however, as a rejection of this suggestion: *not* the Caroline peace, but the corruption it seeks to root out, is responsible for the superflux of "base and sordid persons," and the appropriate remedy is more of the vigorous action the Privy Council had already undertaken to regulate the kind of tavern depicted.[173] The projectors, moreover, are presented as fantastic swindlers promoting various kinds of perpetual motion machines, rather than as well-connected sharpsters seeking to monopolize items of everyday consumption, a type already immortalized on the popular stage in the figure of Sir Giles Overreach (Sir Giles Mompesson).[174] As such, they are dismissed as charlatans who differ from sturdy beggars only in the refinement of their schemes, and who gull only the foolish. Far from being an attack on the patentees, then, let alone a criticism of his own licensing practices, Noy's projectors inhabit a depoliticized cloud-cuckoo-land, providing a harmless diversion for an elite audience. If, as Bulstrode Whitelocke intimated, the commoners who watched the projectors in their outlandish procession construed them as conveying "an information . . . to the King of the unfitness and ridiculousness of [such] projects against the law" (and the legal community may well have been trying to offer such a construction to the public), the masque as *acted* in the Banqueting Hall, against the backdrop of the tavern and the beggars and in the context of Shirley's mocking dialogue, expressed only lofty disdain for figures associated with the conceits of the mob itself. In short, the projectors may have intentionally signified one thing in carnival, and quite another in the precincts of Whitehall. That would explain the fact, puzzling to Sharpe and others, that Charles, who was by all reports highly pleased with *The Triumph of Peace*, absorbed its "praise" while ignoring its "counsel."[175]

While Opinion, Fancy, and the rest represent figures of the common (and corrupted) understanding, the sudden entrance of the craftsmen following the principal masque dance, accompanied by "*a great noise*" and "*a crack in the works, as if there were some danger of some piece of the machines falling,*" introduces a group of humble subjects. They are not quite ordinary, for they work in the palace, and have indeed erected the set and sewn the costumes of the masque itself. Barred (like the spectators outside) from the masque performance, they break through to "challenge a privilege" and witness their own handiwork in operation. Shirley is, unquestionably, reminding his elite audience of the material substratum on which the Court's Platonic fantasy rests, and by extension perhaps of the labor on which the political nation itself subsists. The craftsmen remain intruders nonetheless, and though, as the Embroiderer's Wife says, "we are Christians in these clothes, and the king's

subjects," they have no place in the masque either as spectators or participants. "The masquers will do no feats as long as we are here," the Tailor observes, and, hearing derisive laughter, suggests that his cohorts feign being
part of the antimasque and dance themselves off the stage.

By acknowledging themselves as interlopers the craftsmen confess that,
while their labor has made the masque possible, they have no part in its
fruits. They are both literally present and figuratively absent, since they cannot enter the text although they appear through it. If the popular playwright
Shirley might be thought to have meant the episode of the craftsman as a
"subversive" reminder of the presence of the commons outside the charmed
circle of the masque, the masque writer Shirley brings them onstage only to
chase them off, thereby reinforcing his elite audience's sense of exclusivity:
the craftsmen may "challenge" a privilege, but they do not obtain it. In the
masque world, the commons have neither the price of their labor nor even
the recognition that they have performed it; they exist only as buffoons in
the spectacle of the antimasque, and it is as buffoons that Shirley's honest artificers must seek to disguise themselves.

Both as text and performance, *The Triumph of Peace* was a polysemous
event. It functioned both as a popular spectacle and a privileged rite. For
Charles, it was at once a means of chastening the legal community and of offering it the opportunity for submission and reconciliation. For the lawyers,
it was simultaneously an act of humble contrition and of stubborn defiance.
The defiance lay not in Shirley's ultimately obsequious text but in the very
magnificence of the lawyers' display, which went so far beyond the necessary opulence as to beggar the royal purse by comparison. This point was
noted by the royalist George Garrard, who spoke bitterly of the contrast between the private wealth displayed in staging *The Triumph of Peace* and the
penury of the Crown.[176] Surely it would not have been lost on Charles himself, and the second performance he commanded was a mark of "favor" that
doubled as another levy on the Inns of Court.

In the end, at least on this occasion, appearances were saved. Lawyers and
courtiers danced together in Shirley's masque in a visible display of fraternity. Charles fêted the lawyers afterwards, and invited them to attend a performance of Carew's *Coelum Britannicum*. Each side could interpret these
events to its advantage, and both could acclaim the restoration of harmony.
Like the painted fictions of the masque, that harmony was to prove a brittle
illusion.

The division between the street procession of *The Triumph of Peace* and its
enactment in the Banqueting House mirrored the more general one between
the Court's self-image and the often scathing depiction of Court mores in the
public theater, and particularly of the masque itself. Marlowe's Piers Gaveston seeks to entrap Edward II with "Italian masks," but in Tourneur's *The*

Revenger's Tragedy the Court itself is a trap, and the masque the evil jewel at its heart. Little more than a decade separates the vicious Lussorioso and his pander Vindice from Faustus, but already theirs is a closed world—"O accursed palace!" (1.1.30)[177]—that the Devil rules directly and which virtue cannot enter, as if the humanist dreams of Elyot and Starkey had turned to nightmare. Here councillors have become mere procurers, each an expendable tool in a process by which, as if on some infernal machine, "The falling of one head lifts up another" (3.3.27). The only initiative left the courtiers is rebellion, the very act that eternally constitutes hell. Appropriately, it is to be carried out under cover of the masque:

> Revels are toward,
> And those few nobles that have long suppressed you
> Are busied to the furnishing of a masque,
> And do affect to make a pleasant tale on't.
> The masquing suits are fashioning—now comes in
> That which must glad us all: we to take pattern
> Of all those suits, the colour, trimming, fashion,
> E'en to an undistinguished hair almost.
> Then, ent'ring first, observing the true form,
> Within a strain or two we shall find leisure
> To steal our swords out handsomely,
> And when they think their pleasure sweet and good,
> In midst of all their joys they shall sigh blood.
> (5.10–22)

The masque, in which lust is enjoyed in concealment, thus becomes the instrument of a revenge in which, by a further concealment, the courtiers usurp the place of the nobles, not to offer virtue in their stead but to succeed them in their vices. This, too, is the principle of hell, repetition, and it stands the Stuart masque, with its quest for transformation and sublimity, on its head.

Tourneur's male-centered Court world yields to Thomas Middleton's misogynistic one in *Women Beware Women* (c. 1621). Though its female principals are as much sinned against as sinning, they collectively represent the crowning of lust where virtue should sit and thus the reign of the Whore of Babylon, a figure bitterly evoked by the cuckolded Leantio: "Once again/ I'll see that glitt'ring whore, shines like a serpent/ Now the court's sun's upon her" (4.2.20–22).[178] Here, too, the multiple vengeance plots climax in a deadly masque in which "Juno," ostensibly descending to arbitrate a love triangle, kills her rival with a shower of "flaming gold," only to succumb herself to the poisoned incense prepared for her by the latter (5.2.98–133). Not only the masque performers but the Duke of Florence and the ill-gotten bride who sits with him in state are swept away in death as well.

The masques in Tourneur and Middleton reflect the scandals of the Jacobean Court, but they look forward, too, to the effeminized Court of Charles, whose Catholic queen and retinue were for many the cloak of a Jesuit conspiracy to undermine both church and state.[179] As belated products of the morality play genre they are sweeping in their indictments, and lack the nuanced topicality of satire. Accuracy and refinement of observation are not the issue in these texts, however. As the Stuart masque offered an ideal typology of wise governance as the reflection if not the actual source of order, harmony, and virtue, so Tourneur and Middleton present us with the antitype of a lawless and unrestrained power given over to license and corruption. One might say that the assertion of one provoked the denial of the other. This binary opposition reflected in turn the perennial tendency within Reformation culture to see the world in terms of an apocalyptic contest between good and evil. Such a view is fully adumbrated in *King Johan*, but whereas the locus of evil in Bale's play is the papacy and the Satanic forces it transparently represents, in Tourneur and Middleton it is the secular Court with its skeptical, prudential values in whose de facto atheism the Antichrist shows forth. That the only figure who remains standing at the end of *Women Beware Women* is the Cardinal is doubly ironic, for he appears not as the traditional embodiment of evil but as a hapless bystander whose pious homilies are powerless to deflect the action.

Tourneur, Middleton, and perhaps even more luridly John Webster represent an extreme position in what Albert H. Tricomi has called the tradition of anti-Court drama. The Court simply bulked too large as an institution in the life of the country and in the popular imagination to be reduced to any single or stable image. For good or ill it was irreducibly there, and even when it provoked conscience or threatened the constitutional balance it remained for most, at least in practical terms, the final arbiter of public life. Criticism of the Court, that is, could not transcend the Court, and in this sense it remained conservative; as Martin Butler notes, even Prynne appealed to that "religious vertuous Christian Prince and Magistrate," Charles I, to suppress the very theater that so idolatrously reflected him.[180] Only when sovereign authority and virtuous magistracy were perceived as inhering in another institution—Parliament—was the subversive potential of anti-Court drama realized.

What the popular theater did provide was an arena of resistance to the absolutizing culture of the Stuart Court and a focus of criticism for its policies, both foreign and domestic.[181] To the extent that this criticism was intended to provoke debate and stimulate reform it involved social negotiation, a function the theater has of course always performed.[182] Insofar as it demonstrated starkly opposed conceptions of value, however, it reflected a far deeper impasse. Jonson's *Sejanus* had shown the destruction of public virtue through tyranny, whose means and consequence was a corrupted Court of favorites. Middleton, Tourneur, and Webster had depicted the terminal debauchery of such a Court once all men of honor had been removed or coopted. It is true that the anti-Court paradigm was not new, and that some of the Court's bitterest critics, such as Raleigh and Donne, had come from within. In a sense it was a literary conceit, although Raleigh's fate, which remained in the forefront of public consciousness in the 1620s and beyond, served as a reminder of the reality that underlay it. What kept the antitype current, however, was the Court's own mode of self-presentation. The magnificence of the Stuart Court was not objectionable to most Englishmen as such; it was a mark of their nation's standing among the great monarchies of Europe in an age when display was not merely the signification but in considerable degree the presentation of power. When that magnificence came at the perceived cost of abandoning vital strategic and ideological interests abroad and essential military preparedness at home, however—when, in short, the illusion of power seemed to flourish at the expense of its rightful exercise—it appeared in a far more dubious light. This perception was deepened by the eclipse of Parliament in the decade of the Personal Rule, prerogative taxation, the attempt to yoke the Court system to absolutist principles, and the ascendancy of a new Court Catholicism.

The masque epitomized all these discontents. Its expense was a galling reminder of the purposes to which unpopular taxes were put, and those, such as coastal defense, to which they were not. Its frivolity would have been appalling—as under the vast rodomontade of Prynne's tract it was—to anyone with a sense of England's providential responsibilities and the desperate straits to which Continental Protestantism had been reduced. The prominence given Henrietta Maria and her Catholic retinue would have appeared alarming if not sinister. Beyond this, moreover, the masques projected a conception of English history that was starkly at variance with the mainstream view of a *dominium politicum et regale* descended from Fortescue through St. Germain, Smith, Harrison, Holinshed, Coke, Selden, and even Bacon. As Malcolm Smuts summarizes it:

> The masques . . . reflect the Stuart assumption that the political order is the *product* of the king's power. In the beginnings of time, Englishmen did not live under a free constitution. They roamed wild through the forests, preying on each other, until heroic rulers brought them together and taught them the benefits of civilization. Even in historic times the savagery Caesar encountered in Britain and the endemic warfare of the Middle Ages revealed the inability of Britons to live at peace, except under strong kings.[183]

Smuts reminds us that the Caroline administration, still dependent on local elites, had neither the will nor the capacity to transform its Arcadian dreams of absolutism into any sort of rigorous practice. It is something else, however, to suggest that contemporaries could afford to take such a halcyon view. In the absence of any other state occasion in the 1630s, the masque was the chosen ideological vehicle of Charles' regime. Its message was veiled in Neoplatonic allegory, and, as typified this most reclusive of all monarchs, reserved for the delectation of an elite. Nonetheless, the masques were widely disseminated in print, and reported as gossip. They were revealed, that is to say, as arcana, sublime mysteries impenetrable to the uninitiated and intended not for comprehension but awe. When Charles, pressed by circumstances to embrace the royal constitutionalism of Falkland and Hyde a few years later, spoke of the Upper House of Parliament as providing "an excellent screen and bank between the prince and people,"[184] the theatrical metaphor may have unwittingly reminded some of the exclusionary barriers that had separated the privileged transports of the masque from the rude grotesquerie of the antimasque, the Banqueting Hall from Bishopsgate.

In a sense, the Stuart masque was simply an extension of the Court-centered theater that had grown up in the reign of Henry VIII, and which in its origins—as *King Johan* suggests—had better served the thesis of criticism *cum* compliment than in its latter phases. What separated Henrician from Caroline Court theater, however, was the emergence of the urban, Protestantized opinion that Holinshed had appealed to, and the public theater that served it. If the links between that theater and the Court were many and intricate, they were not univocal, a fact attested to by the resort of disaffected noble patrons such as the Earl of Pembroke to the public stage in works such as Middleton's anti-Spanish *A Game at Chess*. The kind of political lobbying for a militantly Protestant foreign policy that had gone on discreetly in the Court in *King Johan* was now aired publicly. To be sure, the nine-days'-wonder of *A Game at Chess*, which attracted more notoriety than any other theatrical event of the period, was the product of the exceptional and temporary convergence of interest between Charles and Buckingham and the anti-Catholic opposition that followed the collapse of the Spanish match, and as such might well be construed as propaganda no less than as dissent. But the popular Caroline theater remained vigorous in its critique of popery, monopoly, nonparliamentary taxation, and the Scottish wars during the interregnum of the Personal Rule. In this sense, as I have suggested, it served as a place-holder for Parliament; but if it was obviously no substitute for a meeting of the estates themselves, it was in certain respects a freer and more daring forum, and the marked independence and lack of deference with which the Short and Long Parliaments took up the political crisis of 1640 may have owed something to the irreverence of the public stage. As Martin Butler remarks:

> The development of the gentry's political unity is bound up with its development as a discrete social group and the theatres were a prime medium

through which its group consciousness was established. They offered a sort of continuity between the meetings of gentlemen at Westminster in 1629 and 1640, and it is not fanciful to suppose that some of the matters which were under discussion in the parliaments of the 1620s would have come up again in personal interchange in the following decade in the theatres. Obviously, such political dialogue as the theatres could sustain could at best be only sporadic. . . . But the theatres were places where free association and interaction might take place, and which were much more open to radically opposed points of view than is generally allowed.[185]

One thing the public theater offered was the dramatic encapsulation of conflict. On the stage, virtue might be rewarded, tyranny punished, and errant rulers recalled to their duty. These happy outcomes did not always occur: in the plays we have considered resolution was ambiguous at best, and *Sejanus* was as bleak in its own terms as *King Lear*. Nonetheless, the theater was more satisfying on the whole, at least on the level of fantasy, than the broken parliaments of the 1620s. Butler has traced the association of leading gentry families, including former and future MPs, with the theater.[186] While there were obviously many other points of contact for such families, none provided the uniquely privileged space in which their deepest hopes and fears could be enacted in a public setting among their fellow citizens.

Too much should not be made of the distinction between the public theater of the 1630s and that of the Court, since as in former decades there was continual interchange between them. Yet it is fair, I think, to detect a sea change in the courtly spectacles of the Personal Rule. Early modern England was characterized generally by the theatricalization of power, in which displays of authority, both performative and symbolic, deployed increasingly complex levels of meaning and association. What was new in the Caroline period was the aestheticization of power as such in the courtly ritual of the masque, and the resultant division between public command and private representation. Dissent was repressed, whether in Parliament, pulpit, or pamphlet, and ideologically negated in the antimasque, whose function was to trigger the assertion of a sublime in which all contrariety was reconciled in the perfect, all-embracing gesture of the royal act. Thus processed, dissent was dissociated from actual citizen response and refigured as an antitype to wise and benign governance; in short, as an aspect of the demonic. The practical detachment of the King from his subjects, and thus from the semiotic exchange on which legitimation was based, was soon to exact its price.

CHAPTER 6

The Discourse of Parliament:
The Reformation of Parliament

High Court and Great Council: Parliament as Universal Signifier

The ultimate theater of discourse in early modern England was Parliament. Here as nowhere else the unity of the realm was symbolized in the co-presence of the monarch and of the three estates that comprised the realm. The quasi-sacerdotal implications of this unity were underlined by the participation of the bishops in their formal attire in the House of Lords and by the concurrent meeting of the convocation of Canterbury. Even when the bishops had become state functionaries, they were a standing reminder that God's business as well as that of the realm was being transacted in Parliament, and that the two were in a final sense inseparable. Indeed, in the most important parliaments of the period—those of 1529-1536, of November 1554, of 1559, of 1604-1610, of the ideologically charged 1620s, and finally of 1640—God's business was either at the forefront of debate or constituted its immediate background and ultimate goal. By 1640, of course, the bishops themselves had become for many the principal issue, and their expulsion from the Lords in February 1642 marked, perhaps more than anything else, the sacralization of Parliament itself that was the most startling outcome of the long train of events set in motion by Henry VIII's decision to reform the church by statute.

The Henrician Act of Supremacy had made Parliament the final arbiter of the church's fate. It had also affirmed the supremacy of statute itself as the declarative law of the realm. The evolution of statute, and with it of the legislative power as such, had been in process since the distinction between the statute as an act in perpetuity and other parliamentary decrees had first been made in 1327, and although the form of making statutes by reading, debate, amendment, and passage was not fixed until the end of the sixteenth century and royal claims to suspend or dispense with statutes persisted to the end of the seventeenth, the primacy of statute law was generally acknowledged by Court and crown alike. As David L. Smith comments, "After the 1530s, the supremacy of parliamentary statute became an accepted principle that survived until the process of European integration during the closing years of the twentieth century."[1]

At the same time, Parliament remained what it had been from its earliest days, the High Court of the realm. Petitions received by it and presented from it went directly to the king, and although he might refer specific pleas to lower courts for remedy, he remained himself the interlocutor of first instance and the final judge in all cases. Parliament recognized no other authority, and, since its petition together with the king's response constituted the original form of statute, the petition was merely the initial step of a coordinate act. The formula of King in Parliament thus represented the fullness of judgment, and if the king's will could not be constrained by Parliament (any more than the will of either of its houses could be by the other), neither was it separate from it, the statute enclosing a seamless process of petition and assent. This process was nothing less than the will of the realm itself, than which no higher or more authoritative act could be construed. For this reason, and because of the ingrained notion that law was declared rather than created, the notion of "legislation" as a function distinct from judgment was slow to develop. Such a notion would have been superfluous, not to say incongruous prior to the development of the idea of governance as the articulation of independent power centers; in a state conceived as an organic whole, harmonious interaction based on a community of interest and a common interpretation of the law, judgment was both the most appropriate and the most expressive means of conceiving sovereign action.

At the same time, the making of statute law came to be seen as the distinctive function of the estates; as John Pym declared in 1621, "Bills are the end of a Parliament."[2] All acts receiving royal approval were enrolled as statutes, but not all — indeed, significantly fewer than half — were of national import. So-called public bills applied to the realm as a whole, notable examples in our period being the acts dissolving (and later reestablishing) the ecclesiastical ties to Rome; creating (and subsequently restoring) the Anglican church and declaring the royal supremacy; setting the royal succession; defining treason; establishing and disestablishing courts and jurisdictions; regulating trade and conditions of apprenticeship; dealing with vagabondage and providing poor relief; and regulating monopolies. Private bills were of local import — in theory, pertaining to no more than three counties — or personal, such as bills for private restitution or naturalization. By definition, these latter were sought almost entirely by the parties directly concerned, whether individuals, interest groups, or corporate entities. Public bills often but not invariably proceeded from the crown, and royal planning for Parliament increasingly focused on them. A particularly impressive example of this are the legislative drafts produced for the last session of the Reformation Parliament, when the institution of the Anglican church necessitated detailed plans for a new ecclesiastical regime. Among the issues canvassed were means to revise church laws, root out heresy, and provide for an authoritative English bible, as well as such miscellaneous matters as grants in mortmain, clerical charity, and the forced commitment of children to the religious life. The same papers also contain drafts of laws dealing with vagabondage, the decay of husbandry, and cloth manufacture.[3] Not all parliaments produced such levels of activity, of course, and not all parliamentary managers regarded a preemptive legislative agenda as critical. Nor can we determine the provenance of many bills with certainty. As G. R. Elton remarked a generation ago:

> [T]he statute books pose some extremely difficult problems concerning initiative and influence. . . . Nothing, in fact, could be further from the truth than A. F. Pollard's confident assertion . . . that after 1461 the 'new monarchy' dominated legislative activity until in the reign of Elizabeth private members are found promoting bills.[4]

Statute creation appears rather to have been a compound process in which public and private interests were routinely intermixed, and factional contention on the king's Council or different jurisdictional interests both in and out of government might advance or retard a given bill. The notional difference between public and private bills enabled Englishmen to maintain the distinction between those acts intended to benefit the commonweal as a whole (or to clarify the wise customs that already served it) and those intended to relieve particular burdens, inconveniences, or grievances. Since all acts arose from petitioning the king, all partook of the common fount of justice. In this sense the grievance of the whole land might be construed as that of a single individual multiplied many times over. Justice was divided among many but indivisible in itself. And since the king was inseparably united with Parliament, the justice done there was the act of the whole land even when it was extended to only a single individual.

It was thus not only possible but essential to represent particular interests in Parliament as public and universal ones. Other courts existed to settle individual claims and disputes, and by artificial reason the great principles of the common law might be discerned in them, but the High Court of Parliament served to redress the ills of the commonwealth as such. Nothing was more alien to it than the spirit of faction or the espousal of merely private interests. These phantoms were often espied but never, of course, acknowledged. By common consent, matters introduced into Parliament, whatever their provenance, had a public bearing. In this way, the negotiation of interests that was the day-to-day life of legitimation could be conducted under the flag of *salus populi*. Legislation proceeded from crown councillors and their legal advisers, but also from municipalities, corporations, trading companies, and guilds, and from weavers, fishmongers, and brewers. Lobbying efforts became increasingly systematic and sophisticated, a subject that has only recently drawn detailed scholarly attention.[5] The great value of statute was the recognition, finally established by the sixteenth century, that it was the ultimate and definitive statement of positive law. This was so because, as Sir Thomas Smith had put it, an act of Parliament was the act of the "whole realm," from the king whose approval gave it life to the lowliest commoner whose consent was included in the direct or indirect representatives who spoke in his or her name. The fact that legislation could and did derive from the plaints of the humble no less (if rather less often) than from the interests of the great, from the community of the realm as well as from the crown, made it a collective and uniquely comprehensive expression of the will of all. In this sense, the process of making statute was analogous to custom formation itself, with the formal deliberation of the houses and the emergence of consensus through testimony and debate paralleling the slow accretion of wisdom and consent that had shaped the common law. No other kind of law could have the same symbolic legitimation value, and accordingly the same pleadability. It was no surprise that more and more private interests sought shelter in it.

The acknowledgment of the legal supremacy of statute brought with it a subtle shift in the relationship between king and Parliament. As we have noted, statute had begun through acts of petition to the crown, that is as a species of judicial redress. Because the petitioners represented the realm and the redress was, at least for public acts, intended as general, the crown bound itself to its obligations under statute in the interests of orderly justice. One statute could be revoked only by another. The crown possessed recognized discretion to dispense with or suspend the operation of statutes in particular, limited circumstances, although the scope and nature of those limits was, like much of the prerogative, indeterminate.[6] It also possessed the inherent discretion of enforcement. But it could not nullify or otherwise alter the legal terms of a statute. James I contended that this forbearance was voluntary, and that the king retained an inherent, unfettered capacity to override any law. This view constituted the core of royal absolutism. As we have seen, however, James qualified this claim by conceding that "euery iust King in a setled Kingdome is bound to obserue that paction made to his people by his Lawes"[7] — an obligation no less binding for being voluntary.

The relation of the king to the making of statute law was, then, inherently ambiguous. Everyone agreed that neither king nor Parliament could make or unmake statute law alone, at least under "setled" circumstances. James' view that "in the first originall" of monarchy "Kings set downe their minds by Lawes" that could, presumably, do what statute law did, namely bind their subjects' conduct, exact their treasure, create felonies, and extend to the taking of life and limb, suggested that the authority of statute lay ultimately in the crown, and might in time of crisis be reclaimed by the king. Parliaments were, accordingly, a derived and secondary institution, a mode of access to the king granted for the purpose of petition: thus, as James explained, laws "are properly made by the King onely; but at the rogation of the people, the Kings grant being obteined thereunto."[8] The king could not be bound to wait upon the petition of the people to make laws necessary to their welfare; hence his power to act by proclamation, a power restricted (again voluntarily) to specified times and purposes and with limited penalties, but no less law for that. Nor, of course, was the king limited in his lawmaking capacity to what the people might petition him to do in Parliament. The king through his Privy Council might refer laws to the advice of his Great Council of Parliament, which being prepared by them (with the assistance of the king's judges and attorneys) for his final consideration might then become statute law by the ancient formula of *le roi le veult*, the king wills it. No devolution or suspension of the king's lawmaking authority was implied by this process, for he was present in every phase of it, just as he was present at all times in his other courts and councils. Indeed, as Parliament was at once his highest court and council, his presence in it was the highest incarnation of his authority: as Henry VIII had famously put it, "we at no time stand so highly in our estate royal, as in time of Parliament, wherein we as head, and you as members, are conjoined and knit together into one body politic."[9]

The organic analogy served here, as so often, to emphasize the indefeasibility of royal power. As the head could never be severed from the body, so Parliament could never act independently of the authority that animated it. At the same time, the analogy between patriarchy and divinity also served to reinforce the idea of the king as present in all the institutions that served as emanations of his authority. As James put it, God at first "spake by Oracles, and wrought by Miracles,"[10] that is, acted visibly and immediately, and only later circumscribed himself "within the limits of his reueiled will" for church and state. In the same way, kings who at first ruled by direct command voluntarily restrained themselves within a civil and politic order without surrendering their original and inherent authority. The king was ineffably present in the institutions of his justice as God was present in his church, and as God upheld the order of creation by the continuous operation of his will, so the king upheld the frame of the commonwealth by his.

Parliament thus represented the ideal stage, apart from the coronation ceremony itself, for a plenary display of the king's authority. As both his

High Court and Great Council, it combined the functions of petition and counsel. It mobilized not only the three estates of the realm, lords, clergy, and commons, but the senior members of the bench and the Privy Council. The Lord Chancellor (or Lord Keeper) presided over the House of Lords, and the Lord Treasurer, the Lord President of the Council, and the Lord Privy Seal (typically of course noblemen themselves) attended not only in their capacity as peers but as officers of state. The judges of the King's Bench and Common Pleas, the Chief Baron of the Exchequer, the Masters in Chancery, the Master of the Rolls, the king's Attorney and Solicitor, and the royal serjeants-at-law formed another phalanx. If Parliament were the High Court of the realm, supreme above all other courts, it was in part because it was attended by the chief justices and legal officers of the crown, a *magna curia* to go with the *magnum consilium*. They directly faced the king when he addressed the houses, and only dukes had precedence over them in seating. Non-noble councillors and legal officers were detached for service in the House of Commons, where they were obliged to go through the formality of an election, but also sat as a group on the front bench, directly facing the Speaker. Some of those behind them would have owed their seats to their patronage.[11]

The Speaker too was in effect a royal appointee, although formally nominated by the Commons. The Privy Council canvassed likely candidates before the opening of Parliament, and one of the councillors proposed a candidate to the House, where he was confirmed by acclamation. The designee then made a ritual address or "disabling speech," professing his unworthiness, at which the House would insist again upon ratifying the royal choice. As with so much parliamentary ritual, this piece of theater functioned ambiguously, affirming both the Commons' right of "choice" and the king's actual power of selection. Challenges to the royal candidate were exceedingly rare: Richard Onslow in 1566, Sir Edward Seymour in 1673. When the Commons actually rejected a nominee, in 1695, it marked a critical moment in the assumption of modern parliamentary sovereignty; no crown nominee was thereafter submitted.

The Speaker was presented to the king after his acclamation in the House, again rehearsing his faults, and, upon royal acknowledgment, making the customary request for the privileges of the House—freedom of speech, freedom of access to the king, and freedom from arrest for the members and their servants, with concurrent authority to punish members' offenses in the House itself.[12] The Speaker was a feed royal official, receiving £100 from the king for his services and an additional £15 for each private bill passed into law—not a trivial consideration, although Speakers, like most MPs, grumbled about their expenses. Other representatives, in contrast, were paid by their constituencies, although boroughs sometimes expressed their gratitude to the Speaker (as well as to councillors who had eased the passage of their bills) with gifts.

From the royal perspective, then, Parliament was the supreme staging-ground of monarchy. If in a mature commonwealth the monarch always acted advisedly, that is, with the concurrence of his council or other relevant officers of state, and if such concurrence served to certify that he was acting both within his prerogative and within the law, thereby asserting the full deliberative majesty of his act, then for him to act upon the petition and advice of the entire kingdom as represented (and, in the persons of the lords spiritual and temporal, manifest) in Parliament, was to stand in "highest estate" indeed. Statute law, properly understood, was the act of the king upon the motion of the realm, and thus the supreme expression of the unity of each in the other. If the tyrant was defined as one who acted alone on the basis of his private interest or appetite, then the King in Parliament was his polar opposite, the ruler who by his act consummated the will of the entire community.

The dependence of the estates on the pleasure of the monarch was evident not only in the granting of privileges or the making of statutes but in the power to summon and dissolve Parliament, which was wholly at his discretion until 1641. In a sense this dependence was a mark of distinction and honor, since other courts and councils sat routinely or by calendrical term whereas parliaments were summoned individually, in the traditional words of the writ of summons, "to treat and consent about arduous and urgent affairs concerning the state and defense of the kingdom and the Church of England."[13] The irregularity of parliaments testified to the "urgency" of the matters that called them into being—war and peace, the preservation and reformation of religion, the relief of general abuses and grievances. It heightened the sense of drama that surrounded them; unlike the other agencies of state, their histories did not blend into the bureaucratic anonymity of quotidian governance, but remained discrete events, occasionally fixed in memory by the sobriquets that attested their character or fate: "Good," "Merciless," "Addled."

The decreasing frequency of parliaments in the early modern period has often been noted by modern historians. David L. Smith has counted nearly 200 in the 127 years between 1272 and 1399, or an average of about one every eight months. Between 1399 and 1485 the average was roughly one in twenty months, and with the advent of the Tudors parliaments became, except for the mid-period years, decidedly occasional. Henry VII convened four of them in the first six years of his reign but only three in the last eighteen and one in the last twelve. Henry VIII called no parliament between 1515 and 1523, and none again until 1529. Thereafter his parliaments sat more frequently; although only five were called in the last eighteen years of his reign, they sat for a total of fifteen sessions, and in only six of those years (1530,

1535, 1537, 1538, 1541, and 1546) was none sitting. The turbulent reigns of Edward VI and Mary were crowded again with parliaments, but during Elizabeth's long reign their frequency thinned out once more, and it has been calculated that her ten parliaments sat for a grand total of only three years out of her nearly forty-five on the throne.[14]

The early seventeenth century told a similar tale. The reign of James began with the mini-Long Parliament of 1604–1610, the most extended since the Reformation Parliament and one which, as we have noted, was preoccupied like its predecessor with a major royal initiative. A four- and then a seven-year interval followed between the succeeding parliaments of 1614 and 1621, and the brevity of the former — April 5-June 7 — meant that Parliament sat for only two months in the span of a decade. Five parliaments, beginning with that of 1621, sat in the following eight years. This was succeeded by an eleven-year interregnum, the longest in parliamentary history, until the summoning of the Short Parliament in 1640.

For the present we shall concern ourselves with the institutional rather than the political significance of these patterns. Medieval England was a more compact entity than its Tudor and Stuart successor, both geographically and institutionally. The king was more frequently attended by his barons, and both the central and local arms of his government were less developed. It was not until the fourteenth century that the summoning of the commons to Parliament was regarded as obligatory and the clergy began to sit apart from them. Thus, Parliament developed its bicameral character only slowly, and with it fixed institutional procedures for each house. Sittings, moreover, tended to be brief, and it was rare for a parliament to extend beyond a single session. The crown could thus regard Parliament as a flexible extension of itself, serving conciliar and judicial functions that were broader and more comprehensive but not essentially different from those of other governmental bodies. To a degree, this attitude persisted. As James I put it:

> [A]s to the nature of this high Court of Parliament, It is nothing else but the Kings great Councell, which the King doeth assemble either vpon occasion of interpreting, or abrogating old Lawes, or making of new. . . . You are heere assembled by your lawfull King to giue him your best aduises, in the matters proposed by him vnto you.[15]

James allowed that it was also the duty of the two houses "to propone any thing that you can after mature deliberation iudge to be needefull, either for these ends already spoken of, or otherwise for the discouery of any latent euill in the Kingdome, which peraduenture may not haue commen to the Kings eare."[16] This was a far cry from granting the houses any independent initiative or coordinate position in the state. They were to do the king's business first, and petition him on their own only afterwards and upon "mature deliberation." He was the "Head," and they the "Body." It was natural for all impulsion to come from him, and all determination to rest with him.

James' views, although pungently stated, were scarcely novel; John Hooker, in his classic Elizabethan description of Parliament, was equally explicit about its dependence on the sovereign:

> The King who is Gods anoynted beeing the hed and cheef of the whole Realme and upon whome the government and estates therof doo wholy and onely depend: hath the power and authoritie to call and assemble his Parlement, and therin to seek & aske the advise, councel and assistance of his whole Realme, and without this his authoritie: no parlement can properly be summoned or assembled.[17]

His Parliament: this older style was still current, as in the petition against annates to Henry VIII from "this his Grace's high coort of Parliament."[18] It followed from this not only that Parliament could meet at the sovereign's command alone, but that that command should be charily bestowed; Parliament was to be summoned, Hooker said, only "for weightie & great causes."[19] The relative infrequency of Tudor and early Stuart parliaments as compared with their predecessors was an accepted fact, though one that modern historians have tended to misinterpret. If great causes alone should require parliaments, then by definition they were great events. The eagerness of men to obtain place in the Commons, particularly in the prestigious shire seats, led to heated and often bitter contests. This in turn increased the value of patronage.[20] It is hard to imagine why competition would have been so keen to serve in the embattled and declining institution that some have described, or why so many boroughs without representation would have clamored to gain it.[21]

There were practical reasons for the greater rarity of parliaments as well. The Tudor state was a far more articulated, and, by Elizabeth's time, a far more ramified bureaucracy than its Lancastrian and Plantagenet predecessors. This meant not only that its ordinary business was more routinized, but that such business would suffer serious interruption if senior crown servants, including the king's bishops and judges, were detached too frequently from their ordinary work. It is true that both the Lords' and Commons' chambers were located within the precincts that housed the principal offices of state, which made it possible for councillors to shuttle back and forth between their regular duties and their parliamentary ones. Disentangling those duties from each other was not always as simple, however, especially given the oft-breached rule that matters pending in the two houses were not to be discussed outside them. Doing two jobs was one thing; serving two masters was another.

From the members' point of view as well, frequent (or excessively prolonged) parliaments could present a serious inconvenience. They, too, had affairs to attend to, and the expense of several months' residence in London could be a daunting prospect. Boroughs provided their representatives with stipends but they were seldom sufficient and often in arrears; a lengthy session could entail a considerable drain on the municipal purse. The capital was dangerous, too, in time of plague. In 1532 the Commons actually petitioned Henry VIII for a dissolution, considering "what payne, charge and cost his humble subjectes" had borne since its beginning, to which the King made unsympathetic reply:

> For you requyre to have the Parlyament dissolved and to departe into your countreys, and yet you woulde have a reformacion of your griefes with all diligence. Although that your payne have ben great in tariyng, I assure you mine hath ben no lesse then yours, and yet all the payne that I take for your wealthes is to me a pleasure; therefore if you wyll have profyte of your complaynte, you must tary the tyme, or els to be without remedy.[22]

The Reformation Parliament, then in its third session, had another four years to run, and within two weeks of its dismissal in April 1536 another was summoned to deal with a fresh turn in the King's matrimonial saga, his desire to legitimize the issue of his intended third wife, Jane Seymour. Returning members must barely have had time to settle their accounts and reach their estates before the new writs caught up with them.

Summonings and dissolutions were less unpredictable than adjournments and prorogations, however. The only date certain for a given parliament was the one expressed in the writ of summons, which directed temporal and spiritual peers to attend and boroughs and shires to present their representatives at a specified time and place. Sufficient if not commodious time had to be allowed for this, normally between two and three months; the six weeks allotted in calling Parliament in 1536 would probably have represented a bare minimum. Only the Long Parliament was summoned as curtly, and, as Clarendon noted, it met at less than full strength.[23] Dissolutions might be at least anticipated when the work of a parliament was done (or at an impasse), although the abrupt terminations that characterized most of those between 1614 and 1640 must have been personally disruptive as well as politically traumatic. Adjournments for Easter or other short periods could likewise be anticipated; longer adjournments and prorogations left members in suspense, however, for although a return date was normally specified, it might be postponed, at times repeatedly, on short notice. The House of Commons asserted the right to adjourn itself in 1585, and did so in June 1621 when Lord Chief Baron Tanfield brought the King's commission of adjournment into the House, returning it to him unread and declaring itself adjourned on its own authority.[24] More was at issue than a nicety; the Commons were attempting to affirm Parliament's status as a court with its own powers of adjournment and continuance. In 1629, the Lower House famously refused the

King's command to adjourn until it had passed a protestation, whose significance will be considered below. The houses preferred adjournments to prorogations because the latter, like dissolutions, terminated all business, but Parliament claimed no power to control them, and when the King's powers over the frequency and length of parliaments were curbed in 1641, it required his statutory consent.[25]

The fact that throughout our period the life of parliaments (unlike that of other courts and councils) remained at the day-to-day mercy of the royal will was a constant reminder to members that they were there to do the king's business as he defined it and for as long as he required them; the bringing of grievances, petitions, private bills, and the like were matters of grace, to be considered when and as the crown's own purposes were satisfied. Nonetheless, the abiding assumption remained that Parliament was an integral and indispensable part of the constitution, the *dominium politicum* that complemented and in some sort circumscribed the *dominium regale*. No doubt those with specific agendas such as godly reformers or more general concerns such as the royal succession were frustrated by the infrequency of Elizabethan parliaments, but no one expressed the fear that they were likely to disappear. A sea change is apparent, however, with the coming of the Stuart dynasty. Members began to speak of the tradition of annual parliaments, and even of them as a thing required (although neglected) by law. This was part of a wider anxiety. James I was an unknown quantity, a foreigner who confessed his ignorance of English laws and institutions (and gave no greater confidence when he professed to have mastered them). When James expressed the hope that he would learn to be "in love with parliaments," he also voiced the threat of what might occur if he did not do so. Unlike his predecessors, he spoke of his powers as unlimited under God except by his voluntary consent. Above all, he gave alarm by the vague scope of the proposed Scottish Union. Addressing his first Parliament in 1604 he suggested both a union of laws and of parliaments between the two nations. This, as the MP Sir Edwin Sandys grasped, was a means to undo both:

> [W]e can give no laws to Brittaine because we are but parcel: Scotland cannot, because it is another part. Together we cannot: severall corporations. By this our Parliament dissolved.[26]

Here indeed was the dissolution of dissolutions: all former statutes undone, all future ones forestalled. Conrad Russell observes that James' aims "were probably far more limited than they have been taken to be."[27] We can deduce this from the fact that he scaled back the scope of the Union in the face of criticism, offered reassurances and concessions, and finally abandoned the project if not his hope to achieve it. It is possible that he had simply not thought through the implications of his original plan. That in itself would have been alarming, but no one could have known whether this was the case or whether instead the plan had been all too well prepared. "The prerogatives of princes may easily and do daily grow," as the Commons' Apology and Satisfaction of 1604 declared; "the privileges of the subject are for the most part at an everlasting stand."[28] It is not hard to imagine the pressure of the Union and its imponderable consequences behind these words.

The Anglo-Scottish Union was not the first time that a Parliament had felt its character if not its survival to be threatened. The story of the Reformation Parliament has been told in terms of the triumph of common law values and the supremacy of statute. By electing to stage his "divorce" and affirm his headship of the church through Parliament, Henry VIII had made it a copartner in the spiritual governance of the realm; by linking the sovereignty of the crown itself to the triad of King, Lords, and Commons, he had exalted its status. If the King in Parliament represented monarchy itself at its furthest stretch, then the vital importance and permanent standing of Parliament was assured. Henry of course would not have been one to suggest that his powers as *rex solus* were anywise lacking outside of Parliament. But to state that it provided the ultimate dimension of his regality was to bind King and Parliament in a singularly intimate nexus.

This story is not so much incorrect as incomplete. The experience of riding the Henrician juggernaut from divorcing Catherine to the divorce from Rome, with its long periods of idling and its sudden lurches, was a deeply unpredictable and at times an unsettling one. Whether Parliament emerged from it with augmented powers and status—and the Marian parliaments would have to insist anew on their right to participate in the restructuring of the church—was not Henry's concern. No powers could be argued against those of the king, and no status could be acknowledged except by the king. What Henry did aim at was to increase, or at any rate to affirm the power of the monarchy by means of Parliament. It was that augmentation that was perceptible to contemporaries; Parliament's was not. If, indeed, any calculus was made, the King would appear to have gained in authority at the expense of other institutions. Convocation, once a formidable assembly, had been reduced to a pliant instrument of the crown where not bypassed altogether,[29] and the bishops in the House of Lords had been brought to heel. Henry even claimed the right to exercise spiritual as well as temporal jurisdiction over the church, as James would later claim the right to judge both by and beyond the common law.

What the Henrician government really intended by the notion of King in Parliament can best be parsed in the prefaces to the great Reformation statutes. The Act in Restraint of Appeals (1533) declared that:

> Whereby by divers sundry old authentic histories and chronicles it is manifestly declared and expressed that this realm of England is an empire, and so hath been accepted in the world, governed by one supreme head and

king having the dignity and royal estate of the imperial crown of the same, unto whom a body politic, compact of all sorts of people divided in terms and by names of spiritualty and temporalty, be bounden and owe to bear next to God a natural and humble obedience; he being also institute and furnished by the goodness and sufferance of Almighty God with plenary, whole and entire power, preeminence, authority, prerogative and jurisdiction to render and yield justice and final determination to all manner of folk resiants or subjects within this realm, in all causes, matters, debates and contentions happening to occur, insurge or begin within the limits thereof, without restraint or provocation to any foreign powers or potentates of the world . . .[30]

As Elton has noted, this thundering preface was the preamble to a rather modest if significant extension of the laws of praemunire. Rather than citing previous statutes, however, it based its sweeping constitutional assertion on the account of histories and chronicles, and, as Elton wryly observed, "to this day, that act of 1533 remains the only one to call for the testimony of historians as the foundations of a political theory."[31] The theory, as John Guy notes, was based on the assertions that the crown of England entailed secular imperium, spiritual supremacy, and provincial independence within the body of the church.[32] These assertions, as Guy suggests, were not novel, and they should be linked both to earlier conciliar doctrine and to the contemporary development of the Gallican church in France. What made them controversial was that they were part of a process by which England severed its relationship with the papacy, a process completed and summarized by the Act Extinguishing the Authority of the Bishop of Rome (1536; 28 Henry VIII, c. 10). "Sundry old authentic histories and chronicles" — in themselves disputable, of course, despite Henry's considerable efforts to collect and publicize them — could only warrant, not effect the changes he sought in the exercise of spiritual jurisdiction in England. The declarative act itself was perforce a sovereign one, and the ultimate sovereign act in England, as well as the appropriate means for altering jurisdiction, was the King's will as declared by Act of Parliament. Not only had praemunire been spelled out in such acts, but secular jurisdictions were created or clarified in them as well, as the Act in Restraint of Appeals itself noted ("And whereas the King his most noble progenitors, and the Nobility and Commons of this said realm, at divers and sundry Parliaments . . . made sundry ordinances, laws, statutes and provisions for the entire and sure conservation of the prerogatives, liberties and preeminences of the said imperial crown of this realm, *and of the jurisdictions spiritual and temporal of the same* . . . [emphasis added]).[33] If England were what the Act said it was, an empire whose ruler was answerable to no other power under heaven, then the King in Parliament was the proper and definitive authority by which to affirm it.

The Act Against Peter's Pence (1534; 25 Henry VIII, c. 21), which begins in the form of a petition ("Most humbly beseech your most Royal Majesty your obedient and faithful subjects the Commons of this your present Parliament assembled by your dread commandment"), once again asserts the preeminent power of the King in Parliament to order the realm:

> It may therefore please your most noble Majesty for the honour of Almighty God and for the tender love, zeal and affection that you bear and always have borne to the wealth of this realm and subjects of the same, forasmuch as your Majesty is supreme head of the Church of England, as the prelates and clergy of your realm representing the said Church in their synods and Convocations have recognised, in whom consisteth full power and authority upon all such laws as have been made and used within this realm, to ordain and enact by the assent of your Lords spiritual and temporal and the Commons in this your present Parliament assembled and by authority of the same . . .[34]

The King "ordain[s] and enact[s]" not with but *by* the assent and *by* the authority of the Lords and Commons, a small preposition on which much turns. The King enacts, but he cannot do so without the assent and authority, not of Parliament as such (which inferentially contains him), but of the Lords and Commons severally and specifically. What the Commons "petition" for is what in fact cannot be granted without them. Lest we read too much into this, however, Clause XXI of the Act provides for enactment "by authority of this present Parliament," and the Act of Supremacy (1534; 26 Henry VIII, c. 1) declares Henry's headship of the church in similar terms: "Be it enacted by authority of this present Parliament that the King our sovereign lord, his heirs and successors kings of this realm, shall be taken, accepted and reputed the only supreme head in earth of the Church of England called *Anglicana Ecclesia* . . ."[35] "Parliament" here must be clearly understood as containing the King.

The preambles to the Reformation statutes were largely the work of two very careful lawyers, Thomas Cromwell and Thomas Audley. They went through numerous drafts before reaching a final version, and I think we may assume they contain no careless formulations. The discrepancies we have noted must therefore be attributed to the fundamental indeterminacy of Parliament's constitutional position, and thus to its uniqueness as an institution of English government. The king was, from a certain perspective, above Parliament, but from another an indivisible part of it. His sovereignty did not exceed it, as might be said of any other court or council in the realm, but was contained in it. It existed at his pleasure, but there were certain things he could not do without it and which circumscribed his authority in the highest points of sovereignty. He could issue decrees but not make laws; he could collect taxes but not (without dispute) levy them. His subjects' bodies were at his disposal, but he could not deprive the least of them of life or limb without statutory warrant. And, although parliamentary sittings were determined at his discretion, it was understood that this discretion was not arbitrary: as Hooker put it, "WHen any breach, difficultie of dout, or defuse cause of warre or peace dooth appeer within the Realme or without, the cace ought to be declared in writing in the ful Parlement, there to be treated and disputed among the Peeres of the Parlement."[36] Though it was understood that a king's prerogative should not be exercised unadvisedly, only in the case of Parliament were the issues to be referred to it so stipulated.

Parliament, therefore, was not simply a point of contact between center and locality or a cockpit for conciliar wranglings and disputes; it was the great theater and universal signifier of the realm, whose participants often played multiple and not always clearly distinguishable roles but whose discourse, above the Babel of competing interests, ambitions, and policies that found voice in its debates, was the constitution in action. It was the place where the king sat in highest estate because the estates of the realm were not merely representatively but in the communion of its discourse really present, at least in the view of its members. For this reason the official rhetoric of that discourse was always one of harmony or the quest for harmony, and discord—the presence of insurmountable friction or irreducible dissent—was always condemned. For this reason, too, efforts by the crown to aggrandize its powers at parliamentary expense, whether by extending the range of its own authority or by curbing the legislative or consultative function of the two houses, met with resistance.

Statute and Proclamation

The much-discussed Act of Proclamations (1539; 31 Henry VIII, c. 8) is a case in point. There can be no dispute that the Reformation statutes had enlarged the powers of the crown, but in so doing they had acknowledged a shared responsibility with Parliament for the church as well. The acts that had also passed the Reformation Parliament for incorporating Wales and Calais into the English body politic likewise increased the scope of royal authority while creating new shire and borough members for these constituencies.[37] That Henry had used coercive and even terroristic tactics to get his way is undeniable, as with the Statute of Uses or at the remarkable juncture when he threatened the Commons as well as the clergy with praemunire, but the result was a sharing of the spoils of the church that satisfied all parties except the recusant clergy and laity. The Statute of Proclamations was another matter, however. The power being shared here was that which was most distinctively Parliament's own, the power of statute itself.

The statute was apparently the brainchild of Thomas Cromwell. As Cromwell recounted it, Chancellor Audley summoned the chief justices to confer on means to restrain the conveyance of coin from the realm, and upon inquiry from Cromwell received the gratifying answer:

> that the Kyng*es* hyghnes by the advyse of his Cownsayll myght make proc-
> lamations and vse all other polecyes at his pleasure as well in this Case as
> in Any other lyke For the avoyding of any such daungers, and that the sayd
> proclamcyons and polyces so devysyd . . . sholde be of as good effect as
> Any law made by parlyament or otherwyse . . .[38]

As in the case of the Statute of Uses, then—and extending the technique already used to ground the Reformation statutes in learned opinion—Henry had preacquired a judgment that effectively ceded the ground he would later ask Parliament to ratify. The fact that the chief justices, who were advisory to the House of Lords, had declared themselves in advance, might have been expected to smooth passage of the bill or at any rate to blunt opposition when it was introduced four years later in Henry's seventh parliament. Such, however, was not the case. The bill generated a fierce antagonism in both houses that was remembered for many years afterward, passed only with significant amendments and reservations, and when revised four years later was specifically limited to the life of Henry. No subsequent ruler attempted to revive it, and even James I, whose own proclamations stirred controversy, commended those who had spoken "with boldness against [the Act] for the king's seeking in that point was tyrannical."[39] James may have been politic here, but he was not one to praise resistance to the will of kings or to speak lightly of tyranny in his royal predecessors.

What was the intention of the bill? Early commentators descried in it a prime example of Tudor despotism, contained and finally repulsed by liberty-loving subjects.[40] Later ones have seen it as an attempt at bureaucratic convenience with few if any constitutional implications. As Edward Adair put it, "neither the enactment of the statute of proclamations nor its repeal altered the nature or force of royal proclamations in the slightest degree"; more briefly, Elton stated that the Act "left [proclamations] in fact as they were at common law." For Stanford E. Lehmberg, the Act in fact "reveals reverence for statute and desire to ground proclamations upon parliamentary authority rather than any intent to legislate autocratically by proclamation instead of statute."[41]

These sanguine remarks beg the question of the original purpose of the statute as opposed to its final and much modified form. We know that Cromwell jumped at the justices' declaration in 1535 ("which oppy*ny*on, I assure y*our* grace I was veray gladde to here")[42] as if at found gold, although it was gold he had been shrewdly prospecting. We know, too, that when the bill was introduced into the House of Lords in May 1539—where the justices' opinion and persons might be more readily invoked on its behalf—it encountered sharp resistance, and that this resistance was equally acute, not to say tumultuous, in the Commons. As Adair summarizes it, the bill in the Lords, despite the crown's presumed interest in its passage, did not have a second reading for a month. It was then rushed through to a third reading the following day, only to be returned for amendment to the two chief justices, the Master of the Rolls, the Attorney General, and the Solicitor. This occasioned a highly unusual fourth reading before passage in the Lords on June 14. Meanwhile, the Commons gave the bill even rougher welcome. The original bill, though already engrossed, was rejected outright in the Lower House, and a new one substituted for it. Far from trying to salvage their own handiwork, the Lords agreed to consider the Commons' new bill, suggested changes to which the Commons assented, and passed the revised version.[43] All this was accomplished with great haste in the forty-eight hours between June 24 and 26, a performance all the more remarkable in view of the fact that the houses were simultaneously considering the equally contentious act for the King's Six Articles of religion. That the two bills were linked is apparent in the preface of the Statute of Proclamations, which declares as its primary purpose the enforcement of "divers and sundry articles of Christ's religion." The haste is explained by the impending end of the session, only two days away. The crown obviously made a full-court press to achieve its capital goals, in the process abandoning a host of lesser bills.[44] Henry appeared in person to assent to the legislative harvest of the session on June 28.

Our ability to interpret these events is hampered by the absence of the original and intermediate drafts of the Statute of Proclamations, and the lack of any record of the parliamentary debates. While we do possess a late draft with amendments from both houses, it can tell us little about the original form and intent of the bill. A contemporary participant in the Lords' debate, Stephen Gardiner, states that it was designed to remedy a ruling by justices that voided a proclamation against the export of corn on the grounds that it violated statute, and the Act as finally passed was invoked primarily on behalf of proclamations dealing with economic matters.[45] This does not help us very much in divining its first purposes, however. Gardiner's recollection was penned while he was confined in the Fleet in 1547, after the statute had expired, and may reflect many things—ancillary justifications given by royal spokesmen in the parliamentary debates, the actual use to which the Statute was finally put, or even, as R. B. Merriman suggests, a misrendering of "coin" as "corn."

The likelier context for the Statute of Proclamations was a religious one. In his assumed role as Supreme Head of the church, Henry VIII had asserted his rights not only as pastor but as priest, a position he had ceased to insist on but that, like James I's claim to his residual right and capacity to judge the common law, he never abandoned. The growth of Protestant heresy in the wake of the break with Rome, no less than the Catholic challenge to his authority in the Pilgrimage of Grace, greatly troubled him, and after a series of false starts he was determined to impose a final doctrinal unity on the realm. The product of this was the Six Articles, embodied in the statute significantly entitled An Act Abolishing Diversity of Opinions (1539; 31 Henry VIII, c. 14), and passed only after heated debate both in Convocation and in both houses.[46]

The Act of Six Articles not only reinstated much of Catholic doctrine but resurrected the episcopal courts that had formerly dealt with heresy and re-voked the requirement that such trials proceed only after indictment in a common law court. Since these courts were now, like the rest of the church, under state control, the augmentation of the crown's powers was consider-able. Their revival, however, would take time—as we have noted, it was only with the Court of High Commission that ecclesiastical jurisdiction was effectively resumed in general—and the Statute of Proclamations filled the gap by establishing a conciliar tribunal authorized to deal with heresy by proclamation. This same tribunal was also empowered to issue proclama-tions with the force of statute on secular matters, enforceable in common law courts. In the final text of the act, the tribunal's power as set forth was care-fully circumscribed:

> Provided always that the words, meaning and intent of this act be not un-derstood, interpreted, construed or extended that by virtue of it any of the king's liege people, of what estate, degree or condition soever he or they be, bodies politic or corporate, their heirs or successors, should have any of his or their inheritances, lawful possessions, offices, liberties, privileges, fran-chises, goods or chattels taken away from him or any of them, nor by virtue of the said act suffer any pains of death other than shall be hereafter *in this act* declared, nor that by any proclamation *to be made by virtue of this act,* any acts, common laws standing at this present time in strength and force, nor yet any lawful or laudable customs of this realm *or other his dominions,* nor any of them, shall be infringed, broken or subverted, and specially all those acts, standing this hour in force which have been made in the king's high-ness' time; but that every such person or persons, bodies politic and corpo-rate, their heirs and successors of every of them, their inheritance, lawful possessions, offices, liberties, privilege, franchises, goods and chattels shall stand and be in the same condition, to every respect and purpose, as if this act or proviso had never been made; except such forfeitures, pains and pen-alties as in this act *and in every proclamation which hereafter shall be set forth by authority of the same* shall be declared and expressed; and except *such persons which* shall offend any proclamation to be made by the king's highness, his heirs or successors, for and concerning any kind of heresies against chris-tian religion.[47]

This passage has been quoted at length and in all its numbing repetition to demonstrate its authors' concern to restrict the scope of the proclamations authorized by the act, and to confine them within the act; the italicized passages represent the Lords' amendments. Such proclamations, it is declared, cannot create felonies or confiscate life, limb, property, or privilege beyond the specifications of existing statute; their power and commission, insofar as they draw warrant from the Statute of Proclamations, is contained within its parameters. We may liken the powers granted by the act to the royal practice of securing extraparliamentary "loans" on the tacit understanding that such loans would be retroactively authorized in the next session of Parliament and compounded for or forgiven. The king was given latitude to raise money in time of emergency, but the ultimate authorization and supervision of all extraordinary revenues lay with Parliament. Similarly, the decrees authorized in the Statute of Proclamations were to be understood as temporary measures reviewable by Parliament—or, more specifically, by the ultimate authority of the King in Parliament.

One exception to these constraints remained, however: proclamations against schism and heresy. Here, the King's discretion to punish offenders was unfettered. It is this exemption that strongly ties the Statute of Proclamations to the Act of Six Articles, and suggests that the real occasion of the act was not, after all, to regulate corn exports or to penalize the theft of hawks' eggs—subjects for which it was later invoked—but to give the King extraordinary powers to extirpate heresy. Given the outcry in the Reformation Parliament over presentments for heresy in the old church courts, this apparent volte-face is very striking. It can be explained only by the troubled circumstances of the late 1530s. The Pilgrimage of Grace, whose shock waves still resonated, had demonstrated the residual strength of Romanist allegiance in the north, while the Protestant heresy, in all its hydra-headed forms, had penetrated the Court itself, partly through Anne Boleyn's entourage. The King's insistence on a firm and prescriptive statement of doctrine, embodied in statute and backed by savage penalties, was thus a perceived necessity. In the event, the bill was the occasion of a climactic struggle for the soul of the new church, played out in Convocation and the two houses. The winner, as usual, was Henry's conscience, which came down heavily on the side of the conservatives; in the words of one observer, after long debate "finally his Highness confounded them all with God's learning."[48]

The Act of Six Articles, as we have noted, proceeded concurrently with the Statute of Proclamations, the two sometimes being debated on the same day. If the foregoing analysis is correct, however, the former drove the latter, and the penalties it prescribed—death at the stake as a heretic for anyone professing or holding any opinion contrary to the doctrine of the Sacrament as prescribed in the first Article, death as a felon for anyone teaching or persisting in any opinion contrary to the five other articles—would have made supplementary enforcement by proclamation a logical consequence, since the very "diversity" of opinions aimed at made a definitive enumeration impossible. At the same time, the limitations placed on secular proclamations suggest a tradeoff in which the crown conceded at least part of the discretion it had sought for proclamations in general for greater latitude in dealing with religious affairs. By defining the offenses against all but one of the articles as felonies, moreover, the Act of Six Articles had placed most of the new crimes it had established under the rubric of the common law. As a whole, then, Henry VIII had gotten most of what he wanted out of the two major pieces of legislation he sought—a code of uniformity that represented a viable credal center for the Anglican church, at least in the short run, and broad new powers of enforcement—but not without difficulty, and not without compromise.

The question historians have posed about these two acts, particularly the Statute of Proclamations, is whether the crown gained or lost strength by them in relation to Parliament and the common law. Adair and Elton, as we have seen, argue that the status of proclamations at law was left unchanged by the Statute. For M. L. Bush, as for the earlier Whig writers, the crown's authority was clearly augmented by making proclamations enforceable in common law courts, a distinction previously reserved for statutes. But Bush goes on to argue, *per contra*, that in placing a hitherto unconstrained aspect of the prerogative under statutory authority the crown limited its discretion, and that such may actually have been Cromwell's intention.[49]

Henry VIII would certainly not have understood what he was doing by either act in these terms. In his as in James I's later view, the regal power could neither be enlarged nor diminished by any constitutional process, since it could not lack sufficiency in itself nor alienate itself in any of its judicial aspects. This was the meaning of the phrase in the preamble that arraigned those "wilful and obstinate persons" who defied royal edicts, "not considering what a King by his regal power may do, and for lack of a statute and law to coarct offenders to obey." Henry was asserting *both* a general power to take any action necessary for "the advancement of the commonwealth and good quiet of his people" *and* the utility of giving certain proclamations a statutory authority enforceable in common law courts to that end. The King, that is, was not proposing to give himself a new power (for regal authority, like the matter of classical physics, could neither be created nor destroyed), but only to apply an already existing one in a new way.

From the Henrician standpoint, proclamation and statute were different ways of achieving the same end, the provision of royal justice and the enforcement of the royal will. Had his own chief justice not told him so? For the two houses, however, an erosion of the distinction between proclamation and statute was cause for alarm. Bush contends that "there is no good reason to believe that the government sought a replacement to statute for amending the common law," and that what it wanted was simply "an instrument to deal with crises."[50] But to undermine the unique status of statute by raising an executive act to parity with it was indeed to open the door to rule by decree, whether purposely or not. This in any case was apparently the way the two houses took it, for after "many liberall wordes . . . a playne promes" was exacted "that, by autority of the Act for Proclamationes, nothing should be made contrary to an act of Parliament or Common Law."[51] These saving clauses, which by inference were not part of the original bill, reserved to statute alone the power to alter law.

The resistance to the crown's bill was remarked by observers. Lord Lisle's man in London wrote him that the Commons had sat on the bill for fifteen days, and Charles de Marillac, the French ambassador, offered a garbled account of opposition to an act to impose taxation "sans aucune excuse ni delay."[52] We know of no attempt to promote such an act, although Cromwell had supply in mind for the session and the government may have introduced a regular subsidy bill.[53] What the ambassador's confusion does suggest is a link between the Statute of Proclamations and a perceived plan to use it to levy taxes by conciliar authority—not "loans," "benevolences," or "amicable grants," but subsidies themselves, or their legal equivalent. Marillac may have heard rumors to this effect from people outside Parliament, and perhaps even from or through members themselves. The precision of the phrase *sans aucune excuse ni delay* suggests, at any rate, that the supposition was not his alone. Whether the rumors had any foundation or not is less to the point than that some people at least were prepared to assume or conjecture that Henry intended to use the Statute to normalize extraparliamentary taxation. This would help explain why the Statute was amended in 1543 to limit it to Henry's lifetime, why Protector Somerset did not attempt to renew it after the King's death, and why the Statute retained its notoriety even after its expiration. Looking back on the reign, John Aylmer, the future Bishop of London, remarked that "those that in King Henry the viii dais, would not grant him that his proclamations should have the force of statute, were good fathers of the countri, and worthy commendation in defending their liberty."[54] James I's comment half a century later, already noted, suggests that the memory of a constitutional crisis—and the orthodox interpretation of it as a struggle between a usurping crown and steadfast subjects—lingered into the next century.

There is another way of reading the story, however. M. L. Bush ultimately rejects what he calls "the bogey of tyranny" that has surrounded the Statute, attributing the furor it caused to "indiscretion" in the government's initial draft rather than any "despotic" intentions on its part. Elton goes further. The Statute, as he notes, "embodied a definition of, and therefore a limitation upon, a function of the prerogative." The result was to place a restriction on monarchy itself: "By the very fact of introducing a statute on which to rest proclamations, the Crown accepted the principle that the king in Parliament was superior as a legislator to the king in Council."[55] In light of this, Henry's declaration three years later that he never stood so high in his dignity as when in Parliament might plausibly be read as a concession speech.

Elton's argument sounds rather like Whiggism through another door, and, indeed, his position has a nineteenth-century provenance in R. W. Dixon's suggestion that the Statute was a deliberate if hesitant effort to place prerogative under the aegis of statute.[56] Such may have been the outcome of the bill, but it was obviously not the initial intention of the two houses, which grappled to contain what seemed a direct threat to the autonomy of statute law. Nor did the houses think whatever gain had been wrested in imposing new procedures and restraints on proclamations issued through the Statute worth the powers conceded to those proclamations themselves, since they tied the Statute's life to that of the King.

Yet the Statute was not without lasting consequences. The definition of prerogative through statute was in the end a losing game for the crown, and the doctrine of King in Parliament was as likely to exalt the status of Parliament as of the monarch. If the King in Parliament could do anything the law of God allowed then by inference *rex solus* was tied to existing positive law except in emergency, for even the areas left to the king's discretion were bounded by such law. This was spelled out with great concreteness in the Statute of Proclamations, which reminded Henry not only of the inviolability of past acts and acknowledged customs but of his obligation to respect "specially all those acts, standing this hour in force which have been made in the king's highness' time." The King, once having assented to an Act of Parliament, had no discretion to act contrary to it; his will, as *rex solus*, was tied.

The difference at issue was between the conception that all power flowed from the crown and was limited only voluntarily and conditionally—the view espoused by James I—and one which exalted the law (and therefore the supreme lawmaking body) above all particular institutions. These conceptions were entangled, however, since the king was no less present in his *dominium politicum* than in his *dominium regale*, and as King in Parliament he was quintessentially so. The "strong" royal position, then, suggested that the crown could only augment its powers by exercising them through subordinate jurisdictions, including Parliament. The corollary of this was that the king simultaneously authorized and participated in all acts of governance, thus being both *of* and *above* them at once. On this reading, the King in Parliament was simply an extension of *rex solus*, the secondary (if supereminent) manifestation of a primary indefeasible power. This was implicit in Henry's warning of "what a King by his regal power may do," even if the context was an agreement as to what, at least in part, he would forbear to do.

If it was natural, in a system which described the sovereign as the head of the body politic, the father and bridegroom of the commonwealth, and a being sacralized by anointment and answerable only to God, for kings to regard themselves as the source of all justice and authority, it was equally natural for the members of the political elite to regard themselves as the partakers of that authority, and the institution that uniquely embodied not only their own rights and privileges but those of every subject in England as a participant in and not merely an instrument of the royal supremacy. Recent scholarship has emphasized the role of crown servants and so-called men of business in Tudor and early Stuart parliaments, the deference shown to councillors, and the reinforcement of hierarchical dominance in the relations between King, Lords, and Commons.[57] This work has given us a more nuanced view of parliamentary dynamics and the ways in which particular policies (and careers) were shaped, tested, and advanced, but it has come in many cases at the expense of a top-down, consensual view of authority that is implicitly "royalist" in its perspective.[58] As Michael Graves reminds us however, apropos the later sixteenth century, "parliaments were a microcosm of an Elizabethan governing class of independent-tempered men who wore authority easily and naturally and who were themselves accustomed to giving orders."[59] Such men often played a variety of overlapping and sometimes contradictory roles which they strove, not always successfully, to balance. Graves' exemplary man of business, Thomas Norton, spent time in the Tower for expressing views that offended Elizabeth; the crown spokesman James Morice wrecked his career by attacking Archbishop Whitgift in 1593; most notoriously, Sir Edward Coke, rehabilitated as a councillor after judicial disgrace, brought the government to a virtual standstill in the Parliament of 1621 and continued to plague the crown for the rest of the decade.[60] Office and interest were not always a reliable predictor of behavior in the storm of debate, and excessive fidelity to either could be perceived as sycophancy. When Serjeant John Hele declared in the subsidy debate of 1601 that the Queen had "as much right to all our Lands and Goods as to any Revenue of her Crown," he was roundly rebuked by his Exeter colleague, the freshman MP Richard Martin, and shouted down by the House. Twenty years later another serjeant, Sir Francis Ashley, sought to vindicate himself from the imputation that he spoke for the crown rather than for the commonwealth by protesting that "My gown and knighting shall not carry me against my conscience."[61] The view, most notably advanced by Conrad Russell, that Parliament was a cockpit in which conciliar struggles over policy were enacted by proxy, needs serious revision. If such contests did spill over into parliamentary debate, it was not merely to reflect but to prosecute them. Parliament was a place of real power where issues were settled, and not always on the prince's terms. Henry VIII got his Act of Proclamations in 1539 and

Elizabeth I a revived Anglican church twenty years later, but neither exactly as they wished it. James I did not get his Scottish Union in 1604 or security for his finances in 1610 or support for his foreign policy in 1621. Charles I saw his policies repudiated and his powers eroded by a Parliament that finally warred against him and made him a prisoner. In the end, as the Levellers were to complain, the divine right of a sanctified king was replaced by the usurped powers of a self-perpetuating Parliament.

The debate over representation in the Parliament of 1571 offers a particularly instructive view of the way members of the Commons viewed their function and responsibility.[62] The matter at hand was a bill to repeal the acts of 1 Henry V, c. 1 and 23 Henry VI, c. 14 on residential requirements for MPs. Should boroughs be permitted to elect nonresidents? A member for Hereford warned that if boroughs were not confined to their own, "this may touch and over-reach their whole liberties, as not havinge whereunto to stay, but that lordes' letters shall from henceforth bear all the sway." Thomas Norton spoke to retrieve the bill, which he may have had a hand in drafting. He pointed out that, as matters stood, boroughs in fact typically sent "strangers" to Parliament, "whereas by the possitive lawe noe man ought to bee chosen for burgesses but very resientes and inhabitantes." It was precisely this flexibility, however, that served the commonwealth, for "the whole body of the realme and good service of the same was rather to bee respected then the private regard of place or priviledge of any person." The best man was not always the local man, and the interests of the nation were to be preferred before any particular or parochial one.

Norton's argument appeared to carry the day until an anonymous member, who has been identified as Thomas Atkins, Town Clerk of Gloucester, rose.[63] The member began with a disquisition on the three estates of the realm, which, he said, "all are to bee in one knott conioyned and as members of one body in one to be used." This unity, in which every occupation and condition found its perfected meaning as part of the whole, could only be preserved on the foundation of a truly, locally representative Parliament. It was Parliament's high responsibility "to consider of all and, as occasion may serve, to alter, constitute or reform all thinges." To do this, it needed (as both Francis Alford and John Hooker stressed)[64] men of learning, gravity, and experience, but above all it needed men intimately connected with their constituencies. For, our member asked:

> Howe may her Majestie or howe may this court knowe the state of her frontiers, or who shall make report of her portes, or how every quarter, shiere, or country is in state? Wee who nether have seene Barwicke or St Michaelli's Mount can but blindlie guesse at them, albeit wee looke on the mapps that come from thence, or letters of instruccions sent from thence: some one whom observacion, experience and due consideracion of that

countrey hath taught can more perfectly open what shall in question thereof growe, and more effectually reason thereuppon, then the skillfullest otherwise whatsoever.

From this chorographical standpoint, England's organic unity was the product of the multiplicity of its local perspectives. As no accurate map could be produced by mere report but depended on a painstaking survey of the actual ground, so an appraisal of the state of the commonwealth rested on the direct knowledge of the representatives of each borough and shire. Were the defenses of the realm in good or ill repair? Was order kept in all parts, conformity upheld, and the service of God maintained? Did trade and husbandry prosper or flag? What charge were the commons able to bear if the crown's necessity warranted a grant of subsidy? No system of virtual representation by "strangers" and "foreigners," as nonresidents were typically called, could provide the detailed information from which alone a view of the nation could emerge. On such a view, in turn, rested the successful exercise of Parliament's constitutional functions of petition, counsel, judgment, and legislation.

The consequence of this was that only a local resident could truly serve as a national representative, and that, therefore, each member served not only for a particular community but, by specific virtue of that fact, for the kingdom as a whole. This was the very "knott" of unity itself, and the essence of England's unique constitutional stability and perfection. In contrast, our member looked shudderingly at the deformities of Continental states. In Castile and Portugal, he noted, kings ruled by "theire own absolute discretions." In Denmark the king consulted his nobility alone, "and nothing of his com-ons." Where mere popularity held sway matters were even worse, as in the "monstrous governments of the comon people in some parts of Germany": a sally, no doubt, at the late horrors of Münster. Finally, there were "the mangled commonwealthes of the apes" in Italy, the land of the Antichrist. Only by holding fast to ancient custom, liberty, and privilege could tyranny and anarchy alike be kept at bay, and no privilege was as important as that of Parliament: "Wee stand and have stood of late uppon the notorious manifestation of the authoritie of the parliament; except withall you keep the auncient usage of the same, and withall endeavour the freedome thereof, in effect you doe nothing."

The bill was derailed by this address, and another member, Mr. Bill, rose to propose a fine of £40 for every borough returning members at the instance of a nobleman. This would have emptied many a purse. Crown nominees, younger sons of noblemen, and the clients of great magnates were liberally salted throughout the House of Commons. This was the way the system of parliamentary selection worked, at least in good part, and the debate over nonresidency may seem to savor of much the same affectation that hovers over contemporary debates on campaign finance reform in the United States Congress. Nonetheless, it was by no means a mere rhetorical exercise, nor was the defeat of the government's bill without significance. Professor Graves' "independent-minded" gentlemen of the Commons were not so only by inclination or the habit of command; they were intellectually committed, at least, to the connection between electoral independence and public service. That this was honored more in the breach than in the observance — that members were actually enmeshed in an elaborate web of hierarchical kinship and patronage affiliations, and that many in fact owed their places to the recommendation or nomination of a great man — did not blunt its force as an ideological imperative. A Thomas Norton, too, could on occasion challenge the system he served, and could uphold the ideal of an independent commonwealthsman even while proudly professing himself the Queen's servant. A Parliament man was more than the sum of his parts.[65]

Whether or not the Statute of Proclamations be seen as augmenting parliamentary power in the long run by opening the royal prerogative to statutory definition and control, the Act of Six Articles certainly broke new ground. The Reformation Parliament had legislated a shift in the *potestas jurisdictionis* of the church from pope to king, but the Act of Six Articles declared doctrine itself. For the first time, the content of Christian belief had been set forth by the authority of a Parliament. From the Henrician standpoint there was no constitutional significance in this; the King was simply doing in his Great Council what he had done in previous doctrinal pronouncements through his lesser ones. Nonetheless, as in the case of the Reformation statutes, a precedent had been set: the King would enact subsequent changes of doctrine, as any change of ecclesiastical organization, through his High Court of Parliament, or at least with its cognizance.[66] This proved broadly the case in the doctrinal and liturgical reforms of Edward VI, in the Marian restoration of the Roman church, and in the reestablishment of the Anglican church and the promulgation of the Thirty-Nine Articles that served as the basis of its faith. Prescribed oaths and penalties for recusancy (which included fines, extraordinary taxation, and confiscation of property) were also set forth by authority of statute. Moreover, the initiative for ecclesiastical and liturgical reform passed under Elizabeth to Parliament itself, fed by a vigorous pamphlet literature, which, employing the same sophisticated lobbying techniques used to promote secular legislation, culminated in the attempt to abolish episcopacy and to establish a Presbyterian order in the church. These well-known events — the first and second *Admonition to the Parliament* of 1572, the godly census of the realm in 1581, the sabbatarian bill introduced by Sir Walter Mildmay in 1584 and the Presbyterian bills of 1584 and 1587 — all reinforced the sense of Parliament as a participant in the governance of the church, if not a sharer in the powers of the Supreme Governor herself. It also widened the sense of the church as a public sphere, and public opinion as a legitimate element in defining and reforming it. As Michael Graves notes, such documents as the Admonitions were intended not merely or even perhaps primarily for Parliament, but for the public at large.[67] Indeed, the novelty of the Admonitions was in using the form of a parliamentary petition to reach the public directly while avoiding the imputation of "popularity" — the direct address to the public at large that was permitted only in the regulated confines of the pulpit or the theater. In the classic scenario of dutiful address, opinion determined grievance, grievance generated petition, and petition resulted in action by responsible governors. By adopting the form of a petition, the Admonitions subsumed the first two stages, giving the public a packaged view of its own opinion formation. In short, it offered propaganda, a device hitherto the monopoly of the crown (in prefaces to statutes, proclamations, homilies, addresses at the quarter sessions, etc.), but now originating from below. The government was properly alarmed by this,[68] as well as by the associated phenomenon of prophesying, which subjected the mechanism of elite discourse to popular scrutiny; but it was only in the general crackdown following the Marprelate tracts that it was able to take it in hand.

The Elizabethan clerical reaction, which confined itself to repressing popular discourse and policing the universities and pulpits, was reinforced by James, under whom the first extraparliamentary ecclesiastical regimen since the Reformation was issued in the Canons of 1604 and 1606. James was careful to cite his authority by statute as Supreme Governor in ratifying the Canons, but protest against them was swift, and in 1607 the Commons passed a bill (blocked in the Lords by the bishops)[69] against implementing them without parliamentary consent. In the controversy that followed, both sides appealed to statute, the Commons to 13 Elizabeth, c. 12 enforcing subscription to the Thirty-Nine Articles and Archbishop Bancroft to an act of 18 Henry VIII. The issue joined, however, was essentially the one that had arisen over the proclamations: could any royal pronouncement alter the legal and property relations confirmed or established by statute? Bancroft, responding at a joint conference in the Lords to a new bill in 1610 to require all ecclesiastical ordinances to be confirmed by Parliament, pointed out that canons promulgated by Convocation "have no power in themselves unless they have the King's royal assent. As your Lordships are called by writ into the higher House of parliament, so are we summoned by the like power derived from the same fountain your Lordships receive authority." This seemed a curt, perhaps even monitory reminder of the dependence of all subordinate jurisdictions on the will of the King, but Bancroft continued by noting that "that power which his Majesty gives us was conferred unto him by act of parliament, for 18[o] H. Octavi there is power given to the King and his successors forever by act of parliament that what canons the King shall ratify under his great seal of England shall be as good as though they were made in parliament."[70] The King's own authority, then, derived from statute, and the statute itself, as Bancroft noted, declared that any canon made contrary to the prerogative or to the laws, statutes, and customs of the realm was "absolutely naught."[71]

Bancroft's argument extended to the clerical sphere the same power afforded by the Statute of Proclamations, namely the right to issue an indefinite series of ordinances enforceable in courts with powers over life, limb, and property on the basis of a single statutory authorization. This would not do in Henry VIII's day—the authority was restricted to his own lifetime, in 1543 prospectively brief—and it was no more welcome in 1610. The godly Welsh MP Sir Roger Owen brushed aside the question of statutory justification: parliaments had decreed such matters as Sunday observances and holidays "before the pope usurped in this and other kingdoms," and kings had never given their assent to canons before Henry VIII's time. The question was not in any case how the new ordinances had been promulgated but whether they had any scriptural basis, "for your canons are but a heap of ceremonies and where they are but apocrypha you would make them canonical."

Succeeding speakers seconded Owen, dissecting various canons and pointing out how the laity no less than clerics were made subject to them contrary to the common law. Thomas Wentworth, Recorder of Oxford and the son of the great Elizabethan radical Peter Wentworth, underscored the folly of granting bishops the exclusive statutory power to determine schism and heresy, for "if they declare a man to be an heretic . . . he may be burned and we have had too great experience of this in Queen Mary's time." Bancroft was taken aback by the blunt hostility of these responses: "I did not think to have heard the canon law to have been ripped up with such bitterness." Seventy-five years after the Reformation Parliament, anticlericalism was clearly alive and well in the Jacobean House of Commons.[72]

Directly related to the issue of the canons was that of proclamations. These had already fanned controversy in the courts, where Coke was shortly to make his famous pronouncement that they were no part of the common law (see above, p. 310). Parliament was no less concerned with their proliferation in the new reign, and the Commons' Petition of Right in 1610 against, among other things, "Proclamations in prejudice of your subjects' right and liberty," was part of the general anxiety that permeated the halls of Westminster about their increasing scope and number. The enforcement of proclamations in Star Chamber had quietly but significantly expanded under Elizabeth by the device of finding factitious breaches of the peace in their violation—a method not dissimilar to those used by ecclesiastical courts that had brought business to themselves before the Reformation, and appeared to be doing so again—and proclamations had been both a matter of dispute in the Parliaments of 1576 and 1586 and a collateral issue in the Commons' uprising against monopolies in 1601.[73]

In truth, proclamations and statutes were essential both to public order, and to each other. Proclamations at once enforced statutes and anticipated them, providing stopgap orders and penalties for such matters as the control of vagrants and recusants, the improvident export of ordnance and bullion, and the regulation of manufacture. When statutes produced undesirable results, proclamations were used to mitigate them until they could be reconsidered; on the other hand, statutes themselves might specify how proclamations were to be deployed, as in the Act of 1589 concerning proclamations of outlawry (31 Elizabeth, c. 3), which stipulated where and when they were to be read.[74] From the crown's point of view, particularly, the interaction between proclamation and statute was the very pulse of government,[75] and if the primacy of statutory authority was recognized, it was only natural to temper it now and then in the interests of administrative practicality and efficiency. The consequence of this, and of the Henrician position that *rex solus* and King in Parliament were simply two facets of the same authority, was a tendency among working bureaucrats to blur the distinction between the two kinds of pronouncement. Robert Beale, the clerk of the Privy Council, opined in 1592 that "As new evills require new remedies, so if no provic[i]on hath bine heretofore made that may be enforced by Lawe, then her Ma[jes]tie by her prerogative may take order in mannie thinges by proclamac[i]on." As legal acts, Beale thought, proclamations should cite not only relevant statutes but former proclamations as well, and to this end he suggested that the book of proclamations issued under Edward VI be kept to hand, as well as "the bookes of the Edicts and ordinances in France and of the Pragmaticaes in Spayne."[76]

Beale's argument was part of the more assertive royalism of the 1590s, a royalism that reflected both the anticipation of a new, masculine reign and anxiety about the possibility of a disputed succession. The subsumption of proclamation under the prerogative as a species of autonomous lawmaking that created its own body of precedent and with which alien custom and civil law might be promiscuously admixed, bespoke an attitude that was to be, as we have seen, reformulated at higher levels in the Jacobean monarchy. James, far more accustomed to ruling by decree in Scotland, promulgated his new royal style in 1604 before any of the issues of the Union had been settled "by force of our royal prerogative."[77] His Lord Chancellor declared that "All that law which is positive consisteth either in proclamations or in Acts of Parliament," placing both on an equal footing and giving proclamations pride of place.[78] James had actually hoped to unite his kingdoms by proclamation before his English judges disabused him of the idea, and he made so free a use of proclamations in the first years of his reign that the Earl of Salisbury was obliged to deny in 1610 that the crown intended "to burn all the old records" and "to make the power of proclamations equal to the laws."[79]

The House of Commons had contested James' use of proclamations as early as 1604, rejecting the assignment of jurisdiction to Chancery in the disputed electoral case of *Goodwin v. Fortescue* by royal warrant and quashing a bill which, as in 1576, seemed to give excessive enforcement powers to proclamations. In 1607, proclamations were at issue again in the debates over the Union.[80] But it was James' use of proclamation to impose new customs rates in 1608 and the publication under royal imprimatur of a new collection of proclamations early in 1610[81] that raised the subject to the status of a major grievance. Impositions cut to the heart of the taxing power, as the crown's intercession in *Goodwin v. Fortescue* had challenged the Commons' corporate identity and therefore its power to legislate independently. These matters would spill over into the Addled Parliament of 1614 and beyond, but their common thread was "proclamation law."[82]

The debate in 1610 eventuated in a petition of right. This debate challenged the King on a broadly rhetorical as well as a constitutional level. As if in answer to James' image of the kingdom as a "spouse" lying under his virile power, Thomas Hedley declared that "the ports are the king's no otherwise nor to other purpose than the highways and the navigable rivers and streams are, that is, for the freer passage of his people without charge or interruption of any." Heneage Finch added stingingly that he would as soon believe that the crown had an unconditioned power over the ports of the kingdom as that "the king may by his prerogative turn an island into a continent."[83] The retort to the organic analogy of the realm as a body at the disposal of its kingly head was thus, as in *Richard II*, the chorographical figure of the seagirt isle whose customs and interests were no more alterable or assimilable to "continental" notions of monarchy than its physical features and dimensions. In a similar way, the organic analogy could be reversed to show the dependence of the king's power on the provision of the realm, and that in turn on the liberty of the subject. "[A]s the law is the life of the politic body of the kingdom," Hedley said, "so wealth and riches are the blood of that body." Power itself, even of the most exalted kind, derived from the commerce of freeborn Englishmen, for a nation of "bondmen" could never have protected England from its covetous neighbors. Thus it was, he concluded, "that this ancient liberty of the subject is that which doth and always hath maintained and upholden the sovereignty of the king" and made him "so to be an absolute king which dependeth immediately upon God."[84] Even divine right rhetoric could, in supple hands, be made to serve the ideological supremacy of the law.

If the King in Parliament was the highest source of authority in the realm, then a petition of right—a statement declarative of law—was Parliament's means of reading the King's own mind back to him. The Petition of Right of 1610, which in fact consisted of two separate petitions, one for ecclesiastical and the other for temporal grievances, was, as James remarked with asperity, large enough to hang a room.[85] The section on proclamations expressed the gravamen of both:

> [I]t is apparent both that proclamations have been made of late years much more frequent than heretofore, and that they are extended not only to the liberty, but also to the goods, inheritances, and livelihood of men, some of them tending to alter some points of the law, and make a new, other some made shortly after a session of parliament for matter directly rejected in the same session, other appointing punishments to be inflicted before lawful trial and conviction; some containing penalties in form of penal statutes; some referring the punishment of offenders to courts of arbitrary discretion, which have laid heavy and grievous censures upon the delinquents; some, as the proclamation for starch, accompanied with letters commanding the inquiry to be made against the transgressors at the quarter sessions; and some vouching former proclamations, to countenance and warrant the latter, as by a catalogue hereunder more particularly appeareth. By reason whereof there is a general fear conceived and spread amongst your Majesty's people, that proclamations will by degrees grow up and increase to the strength and nature of laws, whereby not only that ancient happiness and freedom will be much blemished, if not quite taken away, which their ancestors have so long enjoyed, but the same may also in process of time bring a new form of arbitrary government upon the realm.[86]

The Petition went on to note "certain books lately published which ascribe a greater power to proclamations than heretofore hath been conceived to belong unto them, as also of the care taken to reduce all the proclamations made since your Majesty's reign into one volume, and to print them in such form as acts of parliament formerly have been, and still are used to be, which seemeth to imply a purpose to give them more reputation and more establishment than heretofore they have had."[87] It asked that James impose no civil or criminal penalties contrary to statute except upon "urgent necessity" and until "other order may be taken by course of law," thereby suggesting what Coke would affirm—that law in England meant common law and statute, and that *rex solus* could neither create nor alter either.[88]

James' reply, made in the Lords on July 23, seemed to grant in principle the distinction between proclamations and laws, though with less specificity than might have been wished: "Although we know well that, by the Constitution of the frame and policy of this kingdom proclamations are not [of] equal force and in like degree as laws; yet nevertheless, we think it a duty appertaining to us and inseparably annexed to our Crown and royal authority to restrain and prevent such mischiefs and inconveniences as we see growing in the common weal, against which no certain law is extant, and which may tend to the great grief and prejudice of our subjects, if there should be no remedy provided until a Parliament; which prerogative our progenitors have as well in ancient as latter times used and enjoyed."[89] James had neatly turned a concession into the form of an affirmation, as was his wont; what he had failed to provide was an assurance that proclamations would no longer institute penal liabilities. The Commons were apparently considering a further remedy for this, for among the papers generated after the summer recess was a sheet of "Resolutions" concerning proclamations that included the statement that "His Majesty by the laws of this realm cannot by his proclamation create any thing to be an offense which was not an offense before against the laws of this realm."[90] The debate was aborted by the swift dissolution of Parliament after the failure of the Great Contract in the fall, and the issue shifted to the courts, where, as we have seen, Coke delivered what at least subsequently appeared to be one of his most ringing obiter dicta.

The frequency of proclamations declined sharply in the next few years, but rose again after 1618. The upturn coincided with the ascendancy of Buckingham and the issuance by proclamation of new patents of monopoly to the royal favorite, his clients, and his grasping kin. The legality of the patents was certified by the Lord Chancellor, an infringement of common law prerogative that brought to mind the proclamation of 1604 placing disputed parliamentary elections under Chancery jurisdiction. Matters came to a head again in 1621 when James issued two proclamations to restrain "lavish," "excessive," and "licentious" speech on matters of state, prompting concerns about the freedom of parliamentary debate which the detention of Sir Edwin Sandys, one of the most prominent critics of "proclamation law," only exacerbated. An even more vociferous critic, Edward Alford, complained gloomily of "Eyes over him to observe," and warned that "if proclamations may committ a man for the least matters of state unknown, pereat Resp[ublica] and let us all be villaines."[91] Alford was making an important discursive point, one which as he perceived pertained to subjects and their representatives alike. The term "matters of state" had an ominous elasticity; it could be applied indiscriminately to public questions great and small. Who, moreover, was to define what such matters were? Grievances were given formal charge by the two houses, but if citizens could not vent their complaints how was Parliament to take cognizance of them? The parliamentary privilege of free speech and petition was meaningless if the channels which fed it were stopped. Secretary Calvert, the King's point man in the lower house, chided members for taking alarm at a proclamation aimed merely at talk in "taverns and alehouses," and sarcastically expressed the hope that the House of Commons was neither. But it was precisely talk in taverns that, suitably shaped by the rituals of deference, became the substance of speeches in Parliament. To cut off one was to choke the other, and reduce all men to "villaines." Nor could even the most careful circumspection protect one. Alford's phrase, "the least matters of state *unknown*," carried a particular chill. If any person's remark, however innocuous, might be retrospectively interpreted as touching on a forbidden topic, who could speak at all? The role of proclamations was to enforce statutes, not to replace them: "We sit here in Parliament to make laws," Alford said, "where our ancestors have sat who have made laws that we are governed by and not by proclamations."[92] The "we" of his reference was distinctly not the royal one.

The right of grievance and petition, the sanctity of the law and the supremacy of statute, the independence of the courts and the autonomy of Parliament as the court of courts, were all bound up in the issue of proclamations. They were, unquestionably, a part of the king's prerogative, an indispensable tool of government, and a chief means for the immediate redress of grievances. By 1610, however, they had become a grievance in themselves. There were too many of them, they too often crossed common law and statute, and they were too frequently granted for private purposes and even enforced by private individuals. By 1621, they were perceived as a threat to the legislative process itself; Alford warned against eliminating grievances by proclamation as "dangerous in precedent."[93] By 1628, they were denounced for bringing about "innovation" and "alteration" in government, words synonymous with subversion in the political discourse of the 1620s. Worse yet, suggested the Cornish MP William Coryton, they boded arbitrary government, the code word for tyranny itself:

> It is better to live under the hardest law than under any man's discretion; yet it is better to live under discretion than to have laws and either not have them executed or else have some commands come that hinder or contract the execution of those laws. I offer to your consideration proclamations that notwithstanding the laws the proclamations contradict them upon a great penalty.[94]

The MP and sometime diplomat Sir Francis Nethersole worried in 1628 that the Henrician Statute of Proclamations had opened the door to the imprisonment of loan resisters, for if "the Council should have power in sudden occasions to make proclamations when the parliament could not assemble, then for the same reasons of state there may be a power in the King to commit any one man for reason of state." Nethersole wanted the preamble to the statute read aloud, and it was done. But Coke reminded the House that the statute had been repealed (actually, it had been permitted to lapse), and that it had exempted all "lands, goods, or franchises" from seizure.[95]

The issue returned in the great debates of June over a remonstrance on the state of the realm and the excessive power of the Duke of Buckingham. Alford once again raised it. New proclamations for Lent, he noted, "do alter the government," crossing statutes and erecting penalties. If such derogations of Parliament's authority and the subject's right could stand, he concluded, "then what need we be here?" Selden, sitting for Ludgershall, Wilts., agreed: "Nothing changes government more than proclamations." Sir Robert Phelips, the leader of the Somerset delegation, remembered the Commons' petition and James' promise in 1610 that "no proclamations should go out contrary to the laws," and John Bankes recalled Coke's dictum that proclamations could neither make nor declare laws. Coke himself, who had taken a relatively moderate position in 1621, agreed that "Proclamations come too high." It was a bald attack on the legislative power when proclamations contravened statutes directly, but, as Bankes warned, a more insidious one when they "supplemented" them with penalties that "extend to a man's freehold . . . [and] take away our propriety." Selden observed that the proclamation requiring the gentry to return to their estates for Christmas was in itself a punishment, since it was "in the nature of a confinement." It was particularly dispiriting when proclamations complained of in one reign, such as those for the erection of houses, should return in the next. As Coke observed, though, "what greater fear can there be than when a general law is made . . . and this is altered by proclamations?" Proclamation law, backed by prerogative courts, was the very essence of arbitrary government. The problem by 1628, however, lay not in identifying the grievance but in removing the evil counselors who persisted in misusing the King's powers. That was why the House finally decided to leave the subject of proclamations out of the remonstrance and to concentrate directly and narrowly on the Duke of Buckingham.[96] Two months later, the Duke was dead, but the Commons' grievances were unredressed.

Parliament, Religion, and the Regiment of Women

The Proclamation for Lent stirred the Commons not only because it contravened statute but because it dealt with a matter of religion. The acts that laid out the statutory basis of the Reformation and culminated in the Act of Six Articles had made Parliament a copartner in the governance and confession of the church. The Church of England existed by virtue of statute; its supremacy was vested in the crown through statute; its creed and its directory of worship had at various times been set forth by authority of statute. It was true that, as in the case of other statutes, those of the Reformation were held to have declared an existing state of affairs, namely an apostolic national church led by the king, a point that church apologetics belabored for decades and that James I and his bishops were still affirming against Catholic controversialists into the next century. Nonetheless, statute defined the national church and its imperial head in terms binding on the body and conscience of every Englishman, and declarative to the entire world.

Of course, matters were never so simple. The Reformation had been a dialectical process involving negotiation between the crown and its elites, in which the initiative lay with the crown. As Diarmaid McCulloch has observed, Henry VIII exercised a "personal headship" of the church he constructed, the more corporate notion of the King in Parliament notwithstanding. The doctrinal shifts of Edward's reign, the return to Rome under Mary, and the new founding of a Reformed church under Elizabeth were all the result of direct decisions by those monarchs or the influence of those who exercised authority in their name. Parliament itself, like the country at large, was divided over religion, with the Lords, stiffened by the bishops, tending to be more conservative than the Commons but, as the Marian parliaments showed, with no more than a minority in either house strongly committed to Reform. Few members were deeply versed in doctrinal matters or eager to debate them. When Thomas Broke of Calais spoke against transubstantiation in the debate on the Six Articles in 1539, the Comptroller of the King's Household threatened to bring "faggots" for him. The fate of Tyndale, Robert Barnes, and others was sufficiently at hand to make this threat no idle one, and Broke was in fact subsequently jailed for heresy.[97] Credal wars occasionally spilled over into Parliament, as in the case of the four-day debate over the Eucharist in the Lords in December 1548, but Parliament was no more suited to play priest than Henry VIII had been.[98]

It was quite otherwise, however, where the properties and jurisdictions of the church were concerned, and of the crown authority with which they were now entwined. Mary was obliged to affirm her supreme headship in the first months of her reign, a personally and politically awkward position for one whose most ardent desire was to relinquish her father's usurped authority and lay a penitent England at the feet of Rome. The Queen got her wish, but only with the consent of Parliament and on the proviso that the Henrician land settlement be confirmed. In this the two houses showed an admirable ability to discriminate between base and superstructure, and on other matters, such as returning first fruits and tenths to the papacy and designating the Marian exiles as heretics, they drove a hard bargain. The ingrained anticlericalism that had been exhibited by the Reformation Parliament was clearly in evidence. Whatever form of church polity emerged—and, even in Catholic states, the constitution of the ecclesiastical order and its relation to Rome displayed considerable variation—the Marian parliaments had plainly little wish to see the kind of regime epitomized by Wolsey return. The best way to avoid this was to keep the church penurious, and the chief means to that end was to keep in lay hands the wealth of which it had been despoiled. The self-interest of gratified gentry purchasers of church lands and emoluments thus coincided with Erastian impulses to confine the church as narrowly as possible to its spiritual function. In essence, this attitude was not to change for the next hundred years. It was the irreversible, bedrock legacy of the Henrician Reformation itself.[99]

The return to Rome thus strengthened the corporate interest of Parliament in religious affairs and as the final arbiter of property rights. If Henry VIII's use of Parliament as the vehicle of his Reformation had been an act of choice (albeit one heavily conditioned by circumstance and precedent), Mary's resort to it to undo that Reformation was one of necessity. This in turn entailed upon Elizabeth the necessity of turning to Parliament again as she attempted to restore her father's church.

More than legal formalities were involved in the mid-Tudor merry-go-round over the English church, however.[100] Edward VI had been a minor; Mary and Elizabeth were female rulers. None, as such, was an acceptable head of the church. The legend of the pious boy-king Edward so zealously promoted by Protestant apologists was in part an attempt to compensate for this, as was the characterization of Elizabeth as a Deborah. The general anxiety over the failure of the male Tudor line, whose roots went back to the death of Prince Arthur in 1502, had particular impact on the question of negotiating the headship of the church.

For these reasons the maintenance of the religious status quo had considerable political appeal in 1559, at least in the abstract. Protestantism was not yet ingrained in the mass of the population, a process that (as the godly would complain) had scarcely begun and would take decades to complete. A Catholic queen would raise none of the Pauline issues about women in the church. Subservient to the papacy, acceptably married, and appropriately counseled, such a ruler could be constrained within patriarchal codes, and the crown thereby protected. A Catholic regime would also have circumscribed Parliament, removing from its purview the three issues that defined it for the next four decades and beyond: religion, marriage, and the succession. The more difficult choice that Elizabeth made to resuscitate her father's church and imperium as a virgin queen, while thus ensuring her personal independence and (as she saw it) defending her monarchical right, problematized the throne and complicated its legitimacy in ways that would haunt her successors.

These issues, and their implications for parliamentary speech, can perhaps best be seen through the prism of John Knox's scandalous tract against female rule, the *First Blast of the Trumpet Against the Monstruous Regiment of Women*,[101] and John Aylmer's substantial rejoinder, *An Harborowe for Faithfull and Trewe Subjects.*[102] Writing in 1558, Knox's avowed purpose was the deposition of Mary, and in his subsequent *Defence*, addressed to Elizabeth, he denied any aspersion against her title as such. The *First Blast* itself, however, makes no distinction among the "monstriferouse empire of women" (7). Knox declares flatly that:

> To promote a woman to beare rule, superioritie, dominion or empire aboue any realme, nation, or citie, is repugnant to nature, contumelie to God, a thing contrarious to his reueled will and approued ordinance, and finallie it is the subuersion of good order, of all equitie and iustice. (11)

Knox proceeded to marshal all of scholastic logic, biblical citation, and historical precedent that could support his thesis. It was an impressive moment in the history of invective, but it created serious embarrassment for godly reformers who could look only to Mary's sister for hope of restoring the true faith. Knox, a figure of international stature, could neither be dismissed, nor, given the gynophobia of the age, easily refuted. A number of Elizabethan apologists replied, but the response of John Aylmer, the Cambridge divine and future Bishop of London, was at once the most important and the most revealing.[103]

Aylmer's strategy was, firstly, to associate Knox's position with the heresies of Anabaptists, Freewillers, and other products of the "forge and shop of Sathan . . . in these our latter daies" (*Harborowe,* sig. A2v–A3). Knox's own argument, however, though admittedly it "hath . . . almost cracked the dutie of true Obedience," was imputed to "zele" rather than "malice," let alone demonic error. As a reaction to Mary's reign it was understandable and perhaps justified, but as a general principle it erred (sig. B–B2).

Aylmer was left with the problem of defending the legitimacy of female rule in church and state as such. Gynocracy could never be desirable in itself, as woman was the weaker vessel and made to bear subjection; all the more, then, was it providential when sent in the form of an undisputed succession and in the context of restored religion. Government in general was God's ordinance and provision, and if he clearly anointed a woman it was "a plain argument, that for some secret purpose he myndeth the female should reigne and gouerne" (B3). The problem was, of course, that Elizabeth's claim to the throne had been almost continuously contested for a quarter of a century. Disinherited after her mother's execution, reinstated by Act of Parliament in 1543, bypassed in the nine-day's reign of Lady Jane Grey, confined by Mary and reluctantly acknowledged at the last as her successor, she owed it, arguably, to the vagaries of a tyrant's will (as not a few of the godly, Aylmer included, regarded Henry VIII), the election of the estates, or the appointment of "a traiteresse and bastard," as Knox had characterized Mary (*First Blast,* 3).

One might argue that these very circumstances were the sign of God's guiding hand, bringing England and its new Queen home through trial and temptation. What it could not be evidence of was an undisputed succession. Nor was it yet clear that England's troubles were over. Aylmer noted that "disturbed and maymed common wealthes are sone ouerturned and cast vnder foote, by soden and straung mutations," and conceded that England was "of late both in honour and possessions, not a little maymed (B3)."[104] For these reasons, he concluded, "All occasions must be cut of, wherby the euyll may be encoraged to cast of the yocke of obedience, and the simple brought into doubt what thei ought to folow" (ibid.). This suggestion was more politique than providentialist, and it demonstrated the difficulty of straight-forwardly supporting Elizabeth, even though she represented the only pos-sibility of a Reformed restoration in England.

Aylmer's strategy was three-pronged. The first element consisted of re-minding his readers not of Elizabeth's paternal lineage—the basis both of her hereditary claim and its parliamentary confirmation—but of her descent from Anne Boleyn, the leader of the Protestant party at Henry's Court and thus by courtesy the patron saint of the English Reformation. "Was not," he wrote, "Quene Anne the mother of this blessed woman, the chief, first, and only cause of the banyshing of the beast of Rome, with all his beggerly bag-gage?" (B3v) It was through Anne that the seeds of godliness had first been planted, and if they had not taken root in Henry's own heart then his in-fatuation with Anne, like that of Nebuchadnezzar for Hester, was the in-strument through which they had borne fruit.[105]

Secondly, Aylmer figured Elizabeth herself as Deborah, the champion raised by God to defend the faith. Her piety, virtue, and learning were be-yond reproach, and she had very nearly suffered her mother's martyrdom: "For there was no more behind, to make a very Iphigenia of her, but her of-fring vp, vpon the altare of the Scaffolde" (N3). Her royal birth, indeed, qualified her less for the throne than her constancy, to which it was ancillary. Mere blood constituted only a claim to the throne, and not, in the absence of fidelity to God's command, an entitlement, for otherwise the rule of Mary had been legitimate.

The strongest argument for tolerating female rule, however, was that it was constitutionally limited by the institution of Parliament:

> The regiment of Englande is not a mere Monarchie, as some for lacke of
> consideracion thinke, nor a meere Oligarchie, nor Democratie, but a rule
> mixte of all these, wherein ech one of them haue or should haue like au-
> thoritie. Thimage whereof, and not the image but the thinge in dede, is to
> be sene in the parliame[n]t hous, wherin you shal find these. 3. estats. The
> King or Quene, which representeth the Monarche. The noble men, which be
> the Aristocratie. And the Burgesses and Knights the democratie. (H3–3v).

England's commonwealth thus exhibited the Aristotelian perfection of Lacedaemon, "the noblest a[n]d best city gouerned that euer was." As the Spartan kings could never act alone, "In like maner, if the parliament vse their priuileges: the King can ordain nothing without them. If he do it is his fault in vsurping it, and their follye in permitting it" (H3v). It was at this point that Aylmer commended Parliament for having resisted Henry VIII's effort to give proclamations the force of statute (above, p. 493). Had Mary's parliaments followed this worthy example and "not . . . stouped contrary to their othes and alledgiances to the crowne," thereby violating their own privileges, they would not have received "the Deuels blessinge" in restoring the Church of Rome (ibid.).

In Aylmer's version of the commonwealth, the tensions inherent in the Fortescuan copulative of *dominium politicum et regale* and the Henrician one of King in Parliament are at once stretched to the breaking-point and re-solved in favor of a conception of Parliament that, by embracing the estates of the realm and the monarchy as an included part of them, becomes su-pereminently the embodiment of the nation, both its final representative and its final representation. Aylmer further separates the person of the ruler from the monarchical office, thus anticipating the argument that would be made during the Civil War that Parliament could act on the crown's behalf in the king's absence or default. "The King or Quene," as Aylmer puts it, "repre-senteth the Monarche," the mortal personification of an institution that was itself a subtended aspect of the commonwealth. As such, he or she had no more than parity with the nobility and the knights and burgesses, who rep-resented, respectively, the "aristocracy" and the "democracy." In a sense, the ruler was, as a single person, less than these parties, for the king could prop-erly "ordein nothing" without the consent of the other estates. Nor did the intermittent nature of parliaments leave the king an independent agent in their absence. Parliament was continually present in its laws, whose due maintenance and enforcement was the king's obligation, and whose altera-tion required its summoning and consent. For this reason, and because kings were prone as single persons (particularly when uncounseled or ill-counseled) to encroach on the estates' prerogative and the subject's liberty, Parliament's refusal to grant Henry VIII "that his proclamacions shuld haue the force of a statute" was an exemplary constitutional moment. The Lords and Commons had been then "good fathers" of the country, a pointed re-minder that while the monarch could be either king or queen, the estates were exclusively represented by males. Aylmer came close to suggesting that a female ruler was not only inferior in capacity but authority to a male: "it is not she that ruleth but the lawes" (H3ii). This provided another occasion to emphasize the consensual nature of the English polity and its ultimate grounding in patriarchal right: "if to be short she [Elizabeth] wer a mere [i.e., absolute] monark, and not a mixte ruler, you might peradue[n]ture make to me to feare the matter the more, and the less to defend the cause." It spoke volumes to the legitimacy of female rule that a peaceful accession based on hereditary descent and confirmed by Act of Parliament should need defense as a "cause," and one problematic even to the defender.

The importance of the precedent of Deborah was particularly to the fore here. As Aylmer pointed out, "Deborah iudged and that lawfully, which cam not to it by enheritaunce, but by extraordinarye callinge. Muche more [therefore] may she that to Gods callinge hathe ioyned thordinarie meanes of enheritaunce, her commons consent, and confirmacio[n] of lawes" (H3ii-ii[v]). This left the problem of Elizabeth's governance of the church still at issue, however. Here Paul's injunction against women speaking in church seemed to bar any female in authority. At one point Aylmer had tried to explain the text away by interpreting it as specific to a particular occasion rather than as binding in general (G4v). He urged that "wee should not . . . grate vpon the woordes [of Paul] so sore," and pointed to the Woman of Samaria as an example of biblically sanctioned edification. To gloss over Scripture was not, however, a winning hand, and Aylmer was compelled at last to resort to Erastian prudence: "But if this [argument] be vtterly taken [away] . . . what maketh it against their gouernement in a politike weale, where neither the woman nor the man ruleth . . . but the lawes." Had not the kings of Israel lived under "the pollycie appoynted by Moyses"? Kings and queens alike were under a higher obedience, for "They be but ministers, obeyed for the lawes sake, and not for their owne" (H2).

Aylmer is still fudging here, for the "pollycie" of Moses is in fact the ordinance of God, not the secular law which princes did not merely administer but even in "mixte" monarchies positively determined. Moreover, even if the question of female governance of the church was disposed of, the issue of matrimonial subordination remained. Here Aylmer could not gainsay the plain words of Scripture: the wife was necessarily "subiecte" to her husband. Because a woman owed obedience to her husband, however, did not mean that she was subject to other men, or that she might not rule them within a commonwealth. Even within marriage, Aylmer suggested, the wife was subordinate by virtue of her "office" and not per se as a woman (C4v–D). This distinction was clearly applicable at the royal level vis-à-vis subject and sovereign, and particularly apt in the case of a female ruler. King (or Queen) in Parliament was really crown in Parliament, a single estate subordinated to the whole and in the last analysis inferior to and if need be separable from it.

In Aylmer's conception, then, the crown was a trust reposed in the monarch by the commonwealth, whose security rested ultimately with Parliament. The suggestion was clear that this trust was revocable in the case of tyranny, a reflection of the resistance theory generated by the Marian opposition. As Aylmer's fellow clergyman John Ponet had put it, the common-wealth was a "degree" above the monarch, who was comprehended in it and to whom obedience was owed only after that due to God and country. Ponet's colleague Christopher Goodman had stressed the responsibility of the individual subject to resist tyranny, if need be without tarrying for the magistrate.[106] John Knox had of course gone further, and called openly for Mary Stuart's deposition in the *First Blast*. When Knox grudgingly conceded that Elizabeth's rule might be justified, he did so with the reservation "that ye be not found vngrate vnto God" (Arber, 59). This went far beyond the standard disclaimer that princes might not act contrary to God's word, and left significantly undefined who might be the judge of whether the Queen was "vngrate" or not.

When one considers that Aylmer's tract was intended as a *defense* of Eliza-beth and that he made a successful career under her that culminated in the bishopric of London, one may well appreciate how parlous the Queen's situation was in the first months of her reign, and how deep the suspicion of female rule remained. In many respects the crisis of 1553–1559 was analo-gous to that presented by James' determination to unite England and Scot-land fifty years later. The curious Act for the Queen's Regal Power passed by Parliament in 1554[107] was on its face a measure designed to assert Mary's right to her father's imperial authority, but it seems to have been to at least one observer a plot to institute arbitrary government. The Dean of Durham, Ralph Skinner, reportedly contended that "If we by a Lawe doe allowe vnto her majestie all such preheminences and authorities in all thinges, as any of her most nobie progenitours kinges of England euer had, enioyed, or vsed: then doo we giue to her majestie the same power that her most noble pro-genitor William the Conqueror had, who seised the Landes of the Englishe people, and did giue the same vnto straingers." Another speaker asserted that the bill was rather an attempt to limit the Queen's unfettered authority, for some had asserted that "there is not any statute extant, made either with or against the Prince of this Realme, wherin the name of a Queene is once expressed," and that without statutory limitation Mary would therefore be in the de novo position of a conqueror who might "aduance her friendes . . . suppresse her enemies, establish the Religion, And doe what she list."[108]

Had Mary received such advice? Did the bill represent an attempted coup d'état, or an effort to prevent one? Historians have differed about the signifi-cance of this episode; the most recent commentator, James Alsop, observes that "The absolutist conspiracy is internally consistent, but unverifiable to date."[109] For our purposes, what is striking is the confusion and anxiety about the legal status of a female sovereign, particularly in the context of impending religious change. Was a queen constitutionally equivalent to a king, or a novelty unforeseen by the law? Could she rule other than tyrannically, whether from passion or weakness of will or a combination of both? Female rule was a perilous experiment, and that of Mary had not gone well — foreign domination, military setback, the shocking fires at Smithfield. Elizabeth was an unknown quantity, ignored and bypassed by her father, sequestered by her sister. A Franco-Scottish invasion was a distinct possibility. The year 1559 was not more promising than 1554 had been.

Aylmer's argument for the purely administrative role of a female sovereign in the church (it offered scarcely more scope for her command of the state) seemed to rule out Elizabeth's resumption of the supreme headship. The only decision in her hands, albeit a crucial one, was whether to continue the Catholic restoration. There was enormous pressure on her to declare a religious preference, and when she did so by walking out of mass in her chapel at the elevation of the host on Christmas Day 1558, it became essential for her to settle religion and acquire statutory authority over the church as quickly as possible.

Sir Nicholas Bacon, Elizabeth's newly appointed Lord Keeper, opened a hastily summoned Parliament in January 1559 with a speech remarkable for the task it assigned the two houses. That task was "the well making of lawes for the accordinge and unitinge of the people of this realme into an uniforme order of religion to the honor and glorie of God, the establishment of his Church and tranquilitie of the realme." This, Bacon said, was "the suer and infallible foundacion whereupon the pollicie of every good publique weale is to be erected and builte, and as the straite lyne whereby it is wholly to be directed and gouerned, and as the chiefe pillar and buttreuxe wherewith it is continually to be sustayned and maynteyned." Accordingly, Parliament was charged to use its "whole indeavor and diligence by law and ordinaunce to establish that which by your learning and wisdomes shalbe thought most meete for the well perfourminge of this godlie purpose; and this without respect of honour, rule or soveraignetie. . . ."[110]

This was an astonishing mandate. Parliament was told that it was its responsibility to decide the religious settlement of the realm without any parameters other than "the honor and glorie of God" and the public weal. The mere tender of such a choice was, of course, a strong indication of the Queen's personal preference. So, too, was her choice of councillors and her overt patronage of Reformed ministers. The fact that she was unable to state this preference openly, however, either in person or through privy councillors, attests to the extraordinary weakness of her position. Had she been able to count on a moderate Protestant interest in both houses directed by the Council, it might have served her purpose to use Parliament to shape a national consensus. Needless to say, there was no way to predict, let alone prepare such an interest. Elizabeth was unable even to account for her bishops, who stubbornly resisted her in the Lords and in the event rejected the settlement almost to a man. Nor did she have better success, at least initially, in trying to recruit approved clerics of a moderate bent such as Matthew Parker.[111]

Did Elizabeth, then, really risk having her religious settlement determined by the luck of a parliamentary draw? To some degree, the answer appears to be yes. If any systematic planning for the Parliament went on, the evidence has not survived. Three position papers are extant, none by a senior councillor, and only one—the anonymous "Device for Alteration of Religion"— suggesting the policy the Queen would follow, namely enacting reform through Parliament at the earliest opportunity. The other two papers simply counseled caution and delay, not a practicable option given the pressure on the Queen and the real possibility of civil violence, perhaps even civil war, in the absence of a clear and determined choice.

It is true that Elizabeth had some gauge of the temper of the Upper House, whose membership was fixed; even so, she may well have been taken aback by the vehemence of the bishops' resistance. The Commons, for their part, were an unknown quantity. J. E. Neale reckoned that at least a quarter of its 404 members would have been "wholeheartedly" sympathetic to the Marian exiles' desire for a thoroughgoing Reformation. This was the origin of the so-called "Puritan choir" —a core of exiles in and around the Commons, and a larger number of nay-saying holdovers from Mary's fractious fourth Parliament—that Neale saw as the foundation of what would be the dominant faction in the parliaments of the next three decades. Once influential, this idea has not withstood scrutiny.[112] On the other hand, there is no doubt that a substantial rapprochement took place between Elizabeth and the leaders of the exile community. The polemics of Knox and Aylmer—essentially an intracommunal debate—may be seen as an attempt to come to terms with the unpalatable reality of a female sovereign who would also have to be accepted as the Erastian leader of the church. The pact between godly ministers and a politique Queen was, however, the product of events in Parliament.

We do not know the religious complexion of the Parliament of 1559. Its most recent student, Norman L. Jones, concedes that the confessional views and (perhaps more importantly) the relative devoutness of the vast majority of the Commons cannot be clearly established, although we may infer by their acts, as Jones does, that most were, or at any rate were willing to be, Protestant.[113] The committed partisans on either side were too few to sway the debate, although once it was joined the Reformers had an edge in the Commons, as conservatives, led by the bishops, did in the Lords. Elizabeth could only gamble that, absent strong passions in the majority, most MPs and temporal lords would welcome a crown initiative to restore something like the pre-Marian religious polity: a comprehensive state-controlled church that would provide latitude for consciences and guarantees for the Henrician land settlement.

In the event, Elizabeth did not offer a bill for the supremacy until February 9, a perilous two and a half weeks into the session. Opinions, if not factions, had formed in this interval, for the bill was vigorously argued for three days before being committed. A second bill, or a set of amendments to the first, was introduced by the crown or from the floor, and became part of the supremacy bill as it was rewritten in committee. The added provisions dealt with uniformity of discipline. The amended bill passed on February 23 after rancorous debate. Jones was inclined to believe that the government introduced the uniformity measures, but even if this were so it only suggests that policy was being made on the fly. Worse was to come, however. The bill was eviscerated in the Lords by the unyielding opposition of the bishops. All reference to divine service was removed, and what remained was a bare acknowledgment, but not a confirmation, of the Queen's claim to the supreme headship of the church.

The Lords' version was worse than no bill at all. Politically, it amounted to a stalemate between the spiritual and temporal estates, the former of which had effectively prevailed in the Upper House as the latter had in the Lower; constitutionally, it dissociated Parliament from any attempt to revive the Henrician church; liturgically, it left England Catholic. The Reformed party in the Commons—as I think we may noncontroversially call those committed to an at least private Protestant worship—was so alarmed that it floated a bill protecting persons using Edwardian rites and ceremonies from prosecution as heretics. Here things might have rested. The bill as it emerged from the Lords had actually been *opposed* by the bishops, who would not credit even the suggestion that the English church could have any head but the Pope. It could thus be represented as a "victory" in the sense that it did not repudiate the Queen's claim. Elizabeth was expected to sign the bill, and to dissolve Parliament. Had she done so, the clerical estate would in essence have prevailed, and the clock would have been set back to 1529. Elizabeth would have been left with an empty title unsupported by Parliament and repudiated by Convocation. The godly party that was willing to tolerate her Erastian pretensions as a means of securing the Gospel would have had no reason to do so if she failed to deliver it. The Henrician Reformation, and the imperial supremacy that was its cornerstone, would have been undone far more thoroughly than Mary could have wished. Even Mary's supremacy had been affirmed by Parliament before she returned to the embrace of Rome, and, technically, she had never resigned it. By failing to reaffirm it unambiguously and to carry out the liturgical reform the Queen had apparently put forward, Parliament would have left the supremacy in a kind of limbo. It is difficult to see how Elizabeth could have regained control of the church under such circumstances, particularly with the handicap of her sex.

Elizabeth firmly grasped the stakes in this, the first and defining crisis of her reign. She did not dissolve Parliament but only dismissed it for Easter, in the meantime staging a disputation at Westminster between Reformed and Catholic partisans that rallied the former and prevented the bishops from consolidating a liturgical victory in the Holy Day celebrations. When the Houses reconvened, she bypassed the mangled bill that had come down from the Lords by introducing a new one, and then yet a third. At the same time, she sent the two bishops who had supported the Catholic position at the Westminster debate, White of Winchester and Watson of Lincoln, to the Tower. This had the salutary effect both of reducing the number of Romanist advocates in the Lords and of reminding the remaining bishops of the fate of Bishop Fisher of Rochester, whom Henry VIII had sent to the block for refusing the Oath of Supremacy. It may also have forestalled an effort by the bishops to pronounce anathema against the Queen at Paul's Cross.

There was muttering in the Commons at the introduction of the third bill, which seemed to indicate a government in disarray. The chief difference in this bill from its predecessors was Elizabeth's assumption of the title of Supreme Governor rather than Supreme Head. This was a victory for the godly party, but also a sop to Catholics. Erastian loyalists complained about the derogation of state authority, but Elizabeth understood the difference between royal style and imperial substance. She could not very well permit her authority to be "amended" in debate; hence the third bill. At the same time, she would enjoy as Governor

> full power and authority . . . to assign, name and authorise . . . such person or persons . . . as your Majesty . . . shall think meet, to exercise . . . all manner of . . . spiritual or ecclesiastical jurisdiction within these your realms . . . and to visit, reform, redress, order, correct and amend all such errors, heresies, schisms, abuses, offences, contempts and enormities whatsoever . . .[114]

The Act of Uniformity (1 Eliz. 1, c. 2), now clearly decoupled from the Act of Supremacy, similarly asserted the Queen's authority over rites, ceremonies, and ornaments. Elizabeth quickly used her powers to clear the episcopal bench, pensioning off those who submitted to the new dispensation although they refused to serve it, and imprisoning those who did not. With little choice, she replaced the nonconforming bishops with a slate heavily weighted toward the godly party.

In retrospect, the resistance of the Marian bishops—as tenacious as it was unexpected—did more than anything else to shape the subsequent character and fortunes of the English church. With the exception of a few principled dissenters, the Anglican episcopate had adjusted itself with equal flexibility to the Erastian order and the Marian restoration. Having adapted itself to

several doctrinal persuasions in a generation and to both confessional extremes in less than a decade, the comprehensive, not to say latitudinarian
church envisaged by Elizabeth would appear to have offered little occasion
for scruple other than, perhaps, the person of its ruler. Had the bishops used
their leverage to shape this church instead of steadfastly opposing it, they
might have outflanked the hotter sort of Protestant to whom their intransigence forced the Queen to turn. With skill they might have returned to a
weakened version of the late Henrician church, notionally schismatic but not
irreparably heterodox.[115] With time, patience, and the long-term tactical agility of someone like Stephen Gardiner, they might have eventually guided
England back to Rome again, as some on the Anglican bench hoped to do
four and a half centuries later. Instead of being content with a return to 1539,
however, they insisted on going back to 1529. Why they chose the latter, far
riskier, and ultimately suicidal course remains one of the enduring questions
of English religious history.

The consequence of the bishops' intransigence was to compel Elizabeth to
construct a bench whose leaders—men such as Sandys and Grindal and
Cox—not only had grave reservations about an Erastian church, let alone
one governed by a woman, but about the episcopal office itself. These
doubters included Matthew Parker, whom Elizabeth finally prevailed on to
accept the archbishopric of Canterbury rather than a prebendship at Cambridge and who faithfully executed her policies while remaining skeptical of
the validity of his office.[116] Not until the effective ascendancy of Whitgift began in 1577 with Grindal's sequestration did the Queen find a cleric wholeheartedly committed both to her supremacy and her ecclesiastical regiment.
That first generation of bishops, however—some of whom remained for
three decades and more—gave church structure and governance a far more
problematic cast than it would otherwise have had. This, in turn, invited a
persistent scrutiny of the church's affairs and performance by Parliament.

The Acts of Supremacy and Uniformity passed in 1559 were both a beginning and an end for Parliament. They marked the end of a thirty-year period
during which the estates had sat more frequently and continually than at
any other comparable point in the surrounding two hundred years, and
when their business had been more largely and consequentially concerned
with the nature of the church and its relation to the state than at any other
time in Parliament's history. This period had witnessed the development of
the royal supremacy, an idea with no indigenous, common law roots but one
derived from the Roman *imperium*, which had grafted itself to native tradition in the notion of the King in Parliament. If the crown had both actually
and symbolically augmented its powers, as the seizure of church lands had
made apparent to everyone in Christendom, the practical necessity of enacting those powers through Parliament had augmented the position of the lat-

ter as well. Within Parliament itself, moreover, the scales of power had been tipped dramatically on behalf of the temporal estates—the peerage and the gentry, recently enriched by the spoil of the church—at the expense of the spiritual estate, which had been correspondingly impoverished, both materially and politically. For a few years under Mary the bishops had recovered ground politically, but with the accession of Elizabeth they were dragged back into harness. From this perspective the Marian bishops' self-immolating resistance to the acts of Supremacy and Uniformity in 1559 may perhaps be better understood. Here was a last opportunity, short of regicide and civil war, to withstand an Erastian, imperial state.

Parliament's revolutionary partnership with the imperial monarchy gave it an unprecedented position. While the beleaguered members of early Stuart parliaments might complain that the privileges of princes grew daily while those of the subject, and of the estates that represented him, were at a stand, the powers of crown and Parliament had grown together during the middle decades of the sixteenth century. Nowhere else in Europe was that the case. When Parliament reaffirmed the royal supremacy over the church in 1559 it was simultaneously asserting its own participation in that supremacy.

What the majority in Parliament hoped in 1559 was that the new religious settlement would hold; what they expected was cogovernance in the church they had jointly constituted with Elizabeth. Critical issues remained to be resolved, most notably the promulgation of a new creed. Other matters had been left at the discretion of the Queen, nominally and temporarily as it was thought: for example, vestments and ornaments. Subsequent parliaments, men thought, would refine what had been done in haste. They did not reckon sufficiently with their Deborah.

Parliament wished, and doubtless expected, to enact the Thirty-Nine Articles that emerged from Convocation in 1563 as the creed of the newly Reformed church, but Elizabeth promulgated them on her own authority alone after personally amending Article 20 and striking Article 29. The amendment to Article 20 seemed anodyne; it stated that "The Church hath power to decree rites or ceremonies, and authority in controversies of faith." This asserted nothing not granted by statute. The words they modified, however— that the church could not ordain anything "contrary to God's word written" —subsumed the critical controversy over whether those rites, ceremonies, and other practices and institutions not commanded in Scripture could be enjoined or even tolerated. For many Reformed consciences strict fidelity to the Word was the mark of a true church, and distinguished it from a false or apostate one (see above, 140-141). Elizabeth's language was not mere boilerplate, therefore, but a strategic intercession that gave her final discretion to direct matters of worship within the church. This power she put to use at once in commanding the use of the cap and surplice in divine service, a practice abhorrent to many of her own bishops as well as to godly ministers and their congregations.

By altering the Articles on her own authority, Elizabeth abolished any notional difference between the supreme governorship she had accepted over the church and the supreme headship her father had enjoyed. In striking Article 29, which dealt with the efficacy of the mass for the reprobate, she assumed not merely a civil jurisdiction but the spiritual authority Henry had claimed as well. Grindal, then Bishop of London, wrote that Convocation had "offered" the Articles to Elizabeth, not presented them, a term implying not only her right to approve or disapprove the Articles as a whole but to modify them.[117] Whether the bishops expected Elizabeth to "offer" such modifications back to them for certification is unclear, but she did not do so. In short, Convocation was not to be a consultative body, but an advisory one. It submitted not ordinances (except insofar as the Queen might permit) but drafts. The enabling authority was Elizabeth's alone. By unilaterally amending the Articles and by promulgating the amended text by decree, she firmly inscribed her supremacy in the constitutions of the church.[118]

Elizabeth's action made the question of parliamentary consent all the more acute. If the Queen's supremacy over the church was absolute, that is, a part of her unquestioned prerogative, then why had she submitted it to Parliament at all, or, having done so, why had she not rested content with the mutilated first bill of 1559 that had acknowledged rather than confirmed her title? Why, too, having decided to adopt the more modest style of Supreme Governor for herself, had she elected to tie both herself and her successors to it by statute? The answer lay, of course, in the predicament that had faced Elizabeth as a female ruler at her accession; that is, in the difference between the suspect and inexperienced queen of 1559 and the confident monarch of 1563. The Erastian church was clearly perceived as a partnership between the Queen and the realm. It was also seen by many of her closest advisers, both clerical and lay, as but halfly Reformed. The strain of conflicting loyalties was, and remained, intense. Parker, at the end of his life, cried out that he cared not a "tippet" for caps and surplices, yet he had deprived scores of able and dedicated ministers for refusing them, a matter he carried on his conscience to his grave.[119] If Convocation could ordain nothing without the Queen, if popish ceremonies were to be retained while exercises with clear scriptural warrant such as prophesying were denied, Parliament was the only recourse of the godly subject.

It was under these circumstances that the confrontations between Elizabeth and her parliaments over religion played themselves out over the next two decades. This drama closely paralleled the struggle to establish the succession through Parliament, and was often inextricable from it. As the House of Commons petitioned the Queen over marriage and the succession in 1566, they also put forward a bill to enact the Thirty-Nine Articles as the law of the land—all of them, apparently, including the one stricken by Elizabeth. It was hurried through the House and dispatched to the Lords, where it had the significant support of the bishops. Elizabeth ordered Bacon to stop further proceedings on the bill as a breach of her prerogative. This put the matter as plainly as could be. Parliament believed it had the right, not to say the duty, to confirm the Articles of the Church as proposed by Convocation. The Queen's authorizing signature pertained to the Act of Parliament, where she concurred in the advice and consent of the realm. Her promulgation of the Articles as Supreme Governor alone was not, in the view of her estates, a sufficient or binding step, but one subject to review by them.

The Queen's isolation in this matter was underscored by the Christmas eve petition of Parker, Young of York, and thirteen other bishops that she allow the bill for confirmation to proceed, and the subsequent draft memorial addressed to her by her chief adviser, Cecil, lamenting that "The bill of religion is stayed, to the comfort of [our?] adversaries." There was even pressure from abroad, where Theodore Beza commented on the general anticipation of parliamentary reforms in the English church.[120]

The act of confirmation was only one of six bills for religion launched in the Parliament of 1566, cataloged by the letter series A-F and referred to as the "Alphabetical" bills. These bills were reintroduced in 1571 following an impassioned sermon by Bishop Sandys, who called for a purge of "all false doctrine[,] . . . idolatry and superstition" from the church. This suggested that the earlier alliance between lay parliamentary reformers and at least some of the bishops still held firm. For its own part, Convocation reaffirmed all Thirty-Nine Articles originally passed and published by it, an act that contested their promulgation in altered form.

The constitutional challenge posed by this front appeared formidable, and the fact that the Alphabetical bills were actually brought forward by the Queen's servant, Thomas Norton, was even more ominous. The front did not hold, however. Some at least of the proponents for a bill of confirmation wished to exclude the Articles enjoining conformity, especially to the Prayer Book. While readily understandable from the standpoint of the godly program as a whole, such a move was tactically disastrous. The bishops could hardly be expected to sponsor and approve one slate of articles in Convocation and another in the House of Lords. Nor were they willing to cede control over the doctrine and discipline of the church to parliamentary laymen, godly or otherwise. For them, Erastian governance meant their leadership in Convocation and Parliament, with the Queen and the laity more or less passively concurring. Though many of them had private doubts about the episcopal office, they had none about their ministry itself. When Elizabeth impeded reform or abused her governorship, they were prepared to use their leverage in Parliament to set the church to rights.[121]

The precarious alliance between godly bishops and MPs was thus premised, at least in the minds of the former, on deference to the cloth. While it might be necessary to leave statutory initiative to the laity, it was only with the tacit reservation that they not usurp clerical authority. That occurring, the bishops could have recourse only to the Supreme Governor. As Peter Wentworth later remembered his passage at arms with the Archbishop of Canterbury in the Parliament of 1571, Parker told the members that they were to "referr your selves wholly to us" regarding the articles of the Church, to which Wentworth replied that "that were but to make yow popes."[122] Parliament had not participated with the Queen in the making of a national church to cede control of it to her bishops.

The Supreme Governor, for her part, was happy to intercede on behalf of her clergy. On May 1, she noted her satisfaction with the proceedings in Convocation concerning the Articles, declaring that it was her intention to have them "executed by the bishops by direction of her highness's regal authority of supremacy of the church of England, and not to have the same dealt in by parliament."[123] Elizabeth would of course in no way have been pleased by Convocation's attempt to restore the Article she had deleted seven years earlier, which plainly defied her command. But she was prepared to overlook this for the moment to deal with the more immediate threat posed by Parliament, which not only challenged her authority but bid fair to divide the church. At issue, finally, was the meaning of the Queen's supremacy and of her sovereignty itself. By declaring her control of the church to be an aspect of the royal prerogative, Elizabeth had defined the supremacy as inherent in the crown as such. What the Act of Supremacy had done was simply to declare this power at the Queen's request and in terms satisfactory to her. It had given Parliament no share in that power, nor any right to deal in religion except at her further request. For Elizabeth, Erastianism meant her governance of the church through her bishops, and the bishops' governance of the laity. This was the notion that would come in time to be expressed as conformity. In 1571, Elizabeth's Archbishop of Canterbury at last embraced it in full. A Queen still wedded to popish ceremonies was exasperating; a Parliament that challenged the ecclesiastical regiment was a menace to all good order in church and state.

Yet Parliament was soon exhorted to make such an attempt, and in terms that brushed aside not only the royal supremacy but the royal authority itself insofar as it contradicted the manifest word of God. The first *Admonition to Parliament*, the work of the godly ministers John Field and Thomas Wilcox, called upon the Parliament of 1572 to hasten the liberation of the English church from the "tyrannous Lordshippe" of clerical impostors from archbishops to archdeacons, whose authority was "forbidden by Christ."[124] The authors did not waste words on the question of where reform properly belonged. Oppression was manifest, and Parliament was a sufficient instrument to redress it:

> Seeing that nothyng in this mortal life is to be more diligently to be soght for, and carefully to be loked unto than the restitution of true religion and reformation of Gods church: it shall be your partes (dearly beloved) in this present Parliament assembled, as much as in you lyeth, to promote the same, and to employ your whole labour and studie; not onely in abandoning al popish ceremonies and regiment, but also in bringing in and placing in Gods church those things only, which the Lord himself in his word commandeth. (8)

Even at a distance of more than four hundred years, the sheer presumption of this statement is extraordinary. This was no petition, but a set of marching orders, made no less peremptory by the tone of clerical condescension in which it was framed. Henry VIII had never been so imperious in delivering his will to a parliament. Scholars have rightly enough preoccupied themselves with Protestant theories of resistance, but such doctrines are finally less impressive than the sense of theological certainty, the indefeasible right not only to speak but to command truth to power on which they rest. It was only in the absence of the appropriate response that resistance need be thought of; it was, that is, a mere corollary of noncompliance with the Word.

The program ordained by the *Admonition* was a godly regime, with bishops and deacons reduced to their functions in the primitive church, "learned & diligent" preachers appointed to every congregation, and discipline supplied by Elders ("Seniors"). Homilies, injunctions, and articles were to be swept away, advowsons and impropriations suppressed, and ecclesiastical courts "plucke[d] downe & utterly overthrow[n]e without hope of restitution" (12–18). Should the MPs fail to enact these reforms forthwith, they would be "without excuse before the majestie of our God, who (for the discharge of our conscience, and manifestation of his truth) hath by us revealed unto you at this present, the sinceritie and simplicitie of his Gospel" (8).

In all of this there is no mention of the Queen or her ministers. This silence speaks a good deal. For the godly, Elizabeth was still to be honored as the Deborah who had defied the popish Antichrist and rescued the Gospel, and still to be prayed for as the ultimate refuge of the kingdom. But her religious proclivities were at this point well known—the cross in her chapel was notorious—and her resistance to further reform was clear. The *Admonition*, with its recital of "Popish Abuses" in worship and governance (20ff.) and its denunciation of prelacy, marked a turning point in relations between the godly and the church; for the first time, the latter was publicly characterized not merely as insufficiently Reformed but as an unworthy vessel. From this point on, religious radicals would look to Parliament for redress of the church until the anti-Puritan legislation of 1593 demonstrated that it, too, was derelict. For those who resisted the temptation of Separatism, the accession of James I offered the hope—far preferable as a practical matter—of an appeal to a god-ly prince. The Millenary Petition presented to James in 1603 was to produce only a further purge of the ministry, but the initial disasters of the Thirty Years War and the rise of an Arminian "faction" in the church of the 1620s cast Parliament once again in the role of a savior, this time for a far broader segment of the population.

The *Admonition's* silence regarding the Queen's authority spoke to another point as well. If for Elizabeth the restoration of her father's church had been a royal act to which Parliament had only given legislative assent, for Field and Wilcox it was rather Parliament that was to "altogether remove whole Antichrist" from the church, "both head body and branch" (19). This was not a dispute about the locus of constitutional authority, nor did Field and Wilcox trouble themselves about how Parliament would win the Queen's consent to any program of church reform, let alone a root and branch one. Any instrument fit for the Lord's work would do; the prophet's role was to proclaim the necessary end, not the contingent means. As for Elizabeth herself, the authors denied "that we meane to take away the authoritie of the civill Magistrate and chief governor, to whom we wish all blessednes, and for the increace of whose godlines we dayly pray." Far from that, she would be "the better obeyed" under the true dispensation and "severe discipline" of Christ (18). The patriarchal, not to say patronizing tone of these comments hardly needs emphasis.

The *Admonition* ends with an address "to the Christian Reader" in which Field and Wilcox apologized for the need to publish anonymously lest they "the more exasperate and provoke them that we deale with" (38). This they accomplished sufficiently; both authors were soon in Newgate Prison, where they received a steady stream of godly well-wishers while their pamphlet, in two further editions, was, as John Whitgift complained, "in every man's hand and mouth."[125] A *Second Admonition* soon followed, whose author or authors have remained unknown.[126] It offered grim warning to Parliament, which had already concluded without accomplishing its prescribed task: "If it were the case of any number, for worldly respectes, this high Court were to provide for it, but being the case of the whole church of Englande, and Irelande, and in deede God his cause, all good conscience shall condemn that Courte, that provideth not for it, but rejecteth it. The scripture is plaine, it shall be easier for Sodom and Gomorrha in the day of judgement, then for such a Court." The author could only ask God's pardon "for the negligence already committed" against his cause; "you have done nothing therein as you ought" (89).

The Admonitions functioned rhetorically on three discrete but interrelated levels. On the plane of prophetic injunction they were addressed to Parliament; on that of polemic, to the clerical establishment; on that of propaganda, to the public at large. In the long run, they were extraordinarily successful on all three fronts. Although the immediate campaign for reform would be frustrated, Parliament would ultimately enact a program whose Presbyterian rigor would exceed even that of the first *Admonition*. The church, stung by the sweeping challenge to its legitimacy from within (Field was a suspended minister), took the bait of controversy, thus affording godly reformers a continuing occasion for debate. Perhaps the most important effect of the tracts, however, was their appeal to public opinion as the judge of last resort. The first *Admonition* had ended with an appeal to the Christian reader; the second began with one to the "Godly" one. Although Parliament remained its putative subject of address, its author confessed that it "cannot chuse I am sure, but to be read of divers, that are not of that honourable assembly at this time." This was plainly intended for the political class from which Parliament was drawn, or at least the sober and God-fearing within it. It suggested the future strategy of trying to return such persons to Parliament that would bear fruit in the 1580s. In a wider sense, however, it was an appeal to a principle of "general consent" (81) in the conduct of the realm's affairs. The consent implied was that of the godly—the principle of election precluded a broadly democratic politics—but it nonetheless suggested a new locus of authority in the body politic, bound only by that special case of conscience known as "revelation." It was a commonplace that the magistrate was bound by the law and will of God, that no discretion was unfettered. What was threatening in the godly challenge to the ecclesiastical establishment and its civil governor was the idea of self-appointed intermediaries who stood between them and the conscientious discharge of their duties, and, where necessary, prescribed those duties to them. The crown had been checked until the advent of the Reformation, at least nominally, by the corporate church; having not only seized control of that church but confirmed its spiritual monopoly over the population at large, it was now confronted by a fractious segment of the laity that claimed supereminent authority over precisely those matters of ecclesiastical dispensation and administration that the crown had taken in hand. From the standpoint of the godly, this was the appropriate exercise of Christian liberty; in the crown's view, it was no less intolerable than the claims of the papacy, and particularly contumacious from subjects. The equation between "Papists" and "Puritans" that was James I's favorite bon mot was thus not merely a means of marginalizing the discourse of the latter but a perception, deeply rooted in his experience of the Scottish Kirk, that the party of the godly would tyrannize over kings as readily as any papal consistory.

Disbeneficed malcontents such as Field were of course as flyspecks compared to the power of the papacy, but they had a constituency, not only
among godly burghers and gentry but within the church where bishops such
as Grindal and Sandys were keenly aware of their compromised position,[127]
and in Parliament as well. J. E. Neale's Puritan "choir" has been reduced to a
few activists trying to simulate an echo chamber by more recent scholars, but
there was sympathy for the godly critique of the church even if it stopped
well short of a willingness to overturn the settlement of 1559 to which many
still in Parliament had been a party. The Commons' remonstrance against
the detention of Walter Strickland in 1571 had not been merely as a matter of
privilege but of conscience, which, as the MP Edward Aglionby said, was
"internal, invisible, and not in the power of the greatest monarch in the
world; in no limits to be straitened, in no bonds to be contained." It was no
accident that Thomas Norton followed Aglionby with a speech urging that
all suspected Papists be required to take an oath of allegiance to Queen and
church.[128] The point was plainly made. Puritans and Papists were not to be
equated but were in fact entirely opposed: the former spoke with the hallowed voice of conscience, the latter to suppress it. Godly speakers, inspired
by the Word, must be permitted to say (within the limits of a subject's loyalty) what they would; Papists must be compelled to say what they should.

Privileging Godly Speech: The Witness of Peter Wentworth

The privilege of godly speech was ringingly asserted on the opening day
of the session of 1576 by Peter Wentworth, member for Tregony,[129] whose
younger brother Paul had made a name for himself in the debates on the
succession a decade earlier. Wentworth's address, long pondered and carefully composed, is one of the central texts of Elizabethan parliamentary history, and one whose implications would overshadow the next two reigns as
well. It demonstrates more fully than any other the indissoluble connection
between godly discourse and the institutional claim of free speech in the
House of Commons, and as such both the speech itself and its consequences
merit careful review.

"I was never of Parliament but the last and the last session," Wentworth
declared (i.e., those of 1571 and 1572, when he defended his cousin Walter
Strickland and clashed with Archbishop Parker), "at both which times I saw
the libertye of free speech, the which is the onely salve to heale all the sores
of this common wealth, soe much and soe many ways infringed and so
many abuses offered to this honourable counsell (whereby the prince and
state are most chiefly mayntained) that my mynde . . . hath not been a little
agreed even of very conscience and love to my prince and state."[130] Conscience and loyalty ("love") are firmly knit together here; the duty a subject
owes his prince is assimilated to the Christian liberty of acting according to

conscience. Wentworth proceeded to offer seven benefits of free speech, the first and foremost, unsurprisingly, being that "all matters that concerne God's honour through free speech shall be propagated here and sett forward and all things that doe hinder it removed, repulsed, and taken away." He argued that the "envious" and the "evill" must be heard out as well, the better to discover their or others' designs—a privilege, perhaps, less of free speech than of self-incrimination. But Wentworth's reasoning was more subtle and complex. The reprobate served the cause of truth even by their wrath, for, he asked, "how can the truth appeare and conquer untill falsehood and all subtillties that should shadow and darken it be found out?" This notion of the truth as disclosed by dialectical argument extended to Westminster the "bracketed" discourse of academic debate in which contending theological positions were deployed under the eye of authority. Such controversy took place within the doctrinal limits of orthodoxy and was stopped if it tested them too closely, as in the debate over the views of Arminius at Cambridge in 1595–1596.[131] The crown wished to police parliamentary speech on the same terms, reserving to itself the right to halt debate whenever it felt the prerogative had been trenched upon or for other matters of state, and the power to punish offending speakers by confinement or other appropriate penalty. Against this position, the House of Commons asserted an equally indefeasible right to police itself, eliding the crown's own interest by insisting that the latter might not take cognizance of proceedings in the House, or indeed even be informed of them, until they were presented in the form of bill, petition, or message—a stance whose manifest impracticality and radical unacceptability did not preclude its repeated affirmation. For Wentworth, however, free speech was the essence of Parliament and Parliament the bulwark of the state, so that "in this House which is tearmed a place of free speech there is nothing soe necessary for the preservacion of the prince and state as free speech, and without it it is a scorne and mockery to call it a parliament house for in truth it is none, but a very schoole of flattery and dissimulacion and soe a fitt place to serve the Devill and his angells in and not to glorifye God and benefitt the comonwealth."

As Wentworth put the honor of God in Parliament before the welfare of the commonwealth not only as a matter of precedence but as a prior condition of the latter, so he justified free speech primarily in terms of truth (the disclosure of God's will) rather than prudence (the perfection of man's). Thus, free speech took on for Wentworth the character of a sacred and absolute value. Free speech was linked to prophecy, and that in turn to the prophesying exercises that Elizabeth was so unadvisedly laboring to suppress. "I will use the words of Eliha [Elihu]," Wentworth declared, invoking Solomon and Isaiah as well, and likening the discourse of Parliament itself, inferentially, to the extended pulpit of godly disputation: "lett it be holden for a principall, Mr. Speaker: that counsell that cometh not together in God's name cannot prosper. For God sayeth, 'When two or three are gathered together in my name there I am in the midst among them'."

Wentworth's challenge to Parliament was to comport itself precisely as such a "counsell," fearing none, yielding to no improper suggestion or intercession, and subordinating itself only to revealed truth. The "two things [that] doe very great hurt in this place," he said, were "rumours and messages," which should be "buryed in Hell." The fact that formal and informal communication between the two houses and the crown was in fact the very means by which Parliament functioned and that the initiative for such communication could not be confined to one party did not occur to Wentworth, or at any rate did not deter him. "[N]oe estate can stand where the prince will not be governed by advice," he declared, in a strong if not peremptory application of the humanist precept of counsel. He might have added—it was the subtext of all discourse of counsel in the last fifty years of the Tudor dynasty—that this was particularly true when the prince was a woman. To be sure, Elizabeth had her own sworn councillors, "And I doubt not," Wentworth allowed, "but that some of her Majestie's counsell have dealt plainely and faithfully with her" in matters pertaining to God's service and to her own and the realm's safety. Their advice, however, had been negated in the previous parliamentary session by "traytors and undermyners." The inference was that only a free Parliament could ensure that the Queen would be well counseled because only through open, unconstrained debate among those chosen for her service by and on behalf of the realm could a completely loyal representation of the public interest be known.

Such a position would be taken by the Long Parliament in the Nineteen Propositions of 1642.[132] Its corollary was that Parliament must meet frequently and regularly. Wentworth confessed that his speech had been prepared two or three years earlier in anticipation of the session that had originally been prorogued to November 1572 but had not in fact been convened until February 1576. The silence enforced on him by this long interregnum could only have made the issue it addressed the more urgent. Not he alone, but the realm itself had been deprived of the right and duty to counsel the Queen. It was not merely the prince who summoned Parliament, nor gave it its commission: "the writt . . . that wee are called up by is chiefly to deale in God's cause, soe that our commission *both from God and our prince* is to deale in God's causes" (emphasis added). Could the prince indefinitely delay such a commission solely at discretion, or because seduced by evil counsel? Had the realm no legitimate recourse under such circumstances, especially when the safety of both prince and commonwealth was manifestly at risk? These questions, implied if not directly posed by Wentworth's speech, were precisely those at issue in the revolutionary crisis of 1640–1642.

Wentworth did not, of course, get to finish the speech in which he defended freedom of speech. He was stopped by the House a bit more than halfway through,[133] long enough for it to have heard that Parliament was a place of prophecy as well as counsel, that God as well as the Queen had an interest in it, and that the conscience and duty of its members were indissolubly connected. Elizabeth confined him in the Tower, though the fiction was carefully maintained that this was "by iudgment of the whole Howse," as was the decision to release him a month later and to restore him to his place.[134]

The episode was not without ramifications. Sir Walter Mildmay, speaking for the crown, sought to differentiate between "liberty of speech, and lycencious speech . . . . which uttereth all impertinently, rashly, arrogantly and immodestly without respect of person, tyme or place." He conceded, however, "that nothing can be well concluded in any councell, but where there is allowed in debating of the cawses brought in deliberacion, libertye and freedom of speech. Otherwise, if in consultacions men be eyther interrupted, or terryfied, so as they cannot, or dare not, speake their opinions freely — like as that councell cannott but be reputed for a servill councell — even so all the proceedinges therein shalbe rather to satisfy the will of a few, then to determyne that which shalbe iust and reasonable."[135] These soothing and temperate words seemed to offer all that could be reasonably desired. What they failed to address, however, was the question of precisely which "cawses" were to be "brought in deliberacion" before Parliament, and by whom. The essential battleground over which the struggle for free speech was to be waged was control of the parliamentary agenda. At least where matters of political or ideological import were at stake, the question was less what particular members had to say than what they had to say it about.

Wentworth, though he offered the conventional submission at the bar when he was readmitted to his seat in the House, remained unrepentant. After the session had ended he offered a version of the questioning in Star Chamber that preceded his confinement in the form of a robust Foxean narrative. His unnamed interrogators apparently included privy councillors who were also members of the House.[136]

As Elton cautions us, Wentworth's account should be read as a polemical performance rather than as a faithful transcript:[137] it was, in fact, an extension of his parliamentary speech, a commentary on it (and the pusillanimity of those who had taken offense at it), and a vindication both of the independence of the House of Commons and of the rights and duties of personal conscience before all other forms of loyalty.[138] Taxed with aspersions against the Queen based on rumor and asked to identify their source, Wentworth answers as the faithful Parliament man, demanding that his examiners define their own positions as well:

Yf your honours aske me as councellors to her Majesty, you shall pardon
me, I will make you no answere; I will not doe such iniurie to the place
from whence I came. For I am now no private person; I am a publicque and
a councellor to the whole state in that place, where it is lawfull for me to
speake my minde freely and not for you (as counsellors) to call me to accompt for any thing that I doe speake in the House. And therefore, if you
aske me as counsellors to her Majesty, you shall pardon me; I will make noe
answere. But if you aske me as committees from the House, I will then willingly make you the best answere I can.

Wentworth is willing, indeed eager to enlarge his own words, but not to
implicate others (he refuses to name names and casuistically turns the question on his interlocutors, forcing them to concede that they too have taken
cognizance of general rumor). He will not speak at all, however, until the
councillors have identified themselves as the examining committee of the
House of Commons—a body to which he is willing to submit his conduct—
rather than as royal officials. By this maneuver he forces them to concede
that their authority as councillors does not reach into the House, where they
themselves are no more than his peers except insofar as they are empowered
by the whole. As a self-governing body whose conduct cannot be examined
except by itself, the House and all its members are not only exempt from
outside scrutiny and judgment, but in this "publicque" capacity superior to
all persons under the prince because it is their duty and prerogative to advise "the whole state," which no other councillors can do. Sir Edward Coke
would attempt, unsuccessfully, to make a more limited claim of independence for the judiciary as chief justice of the Common Pleas and King's Bench,
before casting his lot with Parliament in 1621 as the only institution finally
capable of restraining arbitrary government. Coke's brilliantly successful revival (or reinvention) of Parliament's judicial power of impeachment, the
chief success of his parliamentary career, was implied and foreshadowed in
Wentworth's remarks. If as a member of the High Court of Parliament he
was accountable only to his colleagues because of the supereminent capacity
he shared with them to advise "the whole state," then those colleagues were
a fortiori subject to Parliament in their lesser capacity as privy councillors as
well. The removal by impeachment of councillors or other state servants
guilty of offenses against the public trust as determined by Parliament was
the logical corollary of this view. "Rumors"—the parliamentary code word
for the daily reports of the Commons' debates and activities given by crown
councillors and servants in the House—produced "messages," the term for
royal commands to desist from certain subjects. Restraining the speech of
functionaries outside Parliament was one thing; restricting that of the prince
(or even characterizing it) was another. Taxed with referring to one of the
Queen's messages as "hard," Wentworth upped the ante by calling it

"wicked." Expanding the point, he declared that if any royal message "be against the glory of God, against the prince's safetye or against the libertie of the parlment house whereby the state is maintayned, I neither may nor will hold my peace: I cannot (in soe doing) discharge my conscience, who soever doth send yt."

To borrow Bancroft's later phrase, it would be hard to imagine a more "dangerous position" from the crown's point of view. The Christian's conscience required him to speak when the glory of God was opposed, the subject's conscience when the prince was imperiled (in this case by her own speech), the member's conscience when parliamentary privilege was infringed. These roles were inseparable, for God's glory, the weal of the realm, and the liberties of Parliament were inextricably interwoven. If a common subject could not be denied the exercise of conscience, as Field and Wilcox had exercised theirs in the *Admonition*, how much less could the subject's representative be gainsaid it, especially when the freedom of Parliament on which all else depended was at stake?[139]

Given that the first duty of conscience was to uphold God's glory, the final means of enabling it was to maintain Parliament's privileges, since the safety of the state and the establishment of the church both rested on them. This required a narrative in which Parliament, and specifically the Commons, was responsible for England's deliverances from popery and tyranny. "I have heard it of old parliament men," Wentworth said in his speech, "that the banishment of the Pope and popery and the restoring of true religion had there begining from this Howse, and not from the bishopps, and I have heard that few lawes for religion had their foundacion from them. . . ."[140] This was a riposte not only to Elizabeth's command in 1571 that bills for religion might originate only with the bishops, but with her contention that Parliament had merely given legislative sanction to a church established by the imperial authority of the crown.

Parliament's ultimate responsibility for the state (and the state's church) embraced "the prince's safetye" as well. Such an assertion cut to the heart of the question posed both by Wentworth's speech and his account of his examination, namely the locus of sovereignty itself. If the "state" in its most fundamental sense was the agency charged with the security and defense of the commonweal, then that element within or above it ultimately responsible for the state's own defense, including that of the prince, was of necessity the final authority in the realm. This was most forcibly demonstrated when the prince's perception of her security was at odds with that of this determinative power. In the case at issue, the difference was between Elizabeth's belief that Mary Stuart's continued survival was compatible with her own, and Wentworth's belief—widely shared both by others in Parliament and among the Queen's Council—that it was not.[141] The larger implication was that even in so immediate a matter as the Queen's personal safety, the judgment of Parliament should prevail. This question would be put to the ultimate test during the Civil War when Parliament decided that it was permissible to fire upon the sacred person of a king in order to protect the institutional interest of the crown, and even to separate the king's person and the regal dignity entirely from the state.

If Wentworth's position implied an underlying notion of parliamentary sovereignty, or at least the assumptions on which such a proposition might be based, his reported behavior during his interrogation suggested an even more radical stance. Though his examiners told him he would be held responsible only for the part of his speech he had delivered before being stopped by the House, he insisted on defending the whole of his prepared text. Further, he told them that they were obligated to transmit the entire text to Elizabeth: "Your honours cannot refuse to deliver it to her Majestie for I doe send it to her Majestie as my heart and minde, knowing that it will doe her Majestie good. It will hurt noe man but my selfe" (435).

Wentworth here erected personal conscience into something that rightfully compelled Parliament no less than himself. The test of it — and therefore of the higher loyalty it manifested — was that it would "hurt noe man but my selfe." As Wentworth described his own process of deliberation:

> I will assure your honours that 20 times and more when I walked in my ground when I revolved this speech to prepare it against this day, mine owne fearefull conceipte did say unto me that this speech would carry me to the place whither I shall now goe and feare would have moved me to put it out. Then I weighed whither in conscience and the dutie of a faithfull subject I might keep my selfe out of prison and not to warne my prince from walking in a dangerouse course. My conscience said unto me that I could not be a faithfull subjecte if I did more respect to avoyd my owne danger then my prince's danger. (439)

Wentworth's account casts him in the traditional role of the loyal councillor who respects his prince's interest more than his own, as well as the Foxean one of the willing martyr. What is striking, however, is his insistence that his counsel must be conveyed in full by his "parliamentary" examiners, even though Parliament itself — the authorizing voice of both — had refused him permission to complete his speech, thereby negating it in its entirety as an act of counsel. The terms in which Wentworth has defended the right of free speech in Parliament do not validate the unconditioned right of particular members to say what they please but the body's right as a whole to be heard as the voice of the nation. The particular member, unless authorized by Parliament itself, has no right to be heard at all except in Parliament, and there only insofar as his fellow members are willing to listen to him. By no logic pertaining to parliamentary privilege can Wentworth assert the right to have his personal counsel brought before the Queen, much less to have it delivered through a committee of examiners representing Parliament. Had he acknowledged his examiners in their roles as councillors he would actually have had better grounds for such a claim, for in that case he might have argued that he was appealing from Parliament to the Council. But, as we have seen, Wentworth not only refuses to do this, but insists that he will give account only to his parliamentary colleagues. In effect, he subordinates himself to the House only to demand that it do his bidding.

The contradiction in Wentworth's position between the spokesman for an institutional supremacy who insists that even the Queen's speech must be subordinated to parliamentary procedure and the conscientious individual whose claim of priority for his loyal counsel recognizes no constraint expresses a profound contradiction in the discourse boundaries of late Tudor culture. Wentworth's significance (like that of all truly radical figures) lies in the vehemence with which he exposes this contradiction and the rhetorical energy with which he holds it in tension. His "true reporte" of his examination, while doubtless not devoid of factual content, is structured in the form of a literary dialogue in which he triumphantly holds up both horns of his dilemma as if they were one and vanquishes his interrogators with the force of an argument that overwhelms all resistance: "Surelye wee cannot denye it, you say the truth"; "You have answered us, we are satisfyed" (438, 439).

The Wentworth of the "reporte" is both the stout defender of parliamentary procedure and the irresistible voice of personal conscience, and he can be both because of his underlying conviction that the voice of the House and the voice of conscience must be one. In the last analysis, this position demands the sacralization of Parliament. As the defender of Parliament in an elect nation, Wentworth upheld free speech as the essential vehicle of the subject's political and Christian liberty. These forms of liberty were inseparable, each entailing the other, and in an Erastian commonwealth Parliament was the ultimate guarantor of both. Just as Parliament had reproved and when necessary removed errant kings, so it retained jurisdiction over the temporal church it had established. In moments of crisis, it could even become the direct instrument of God's will for the salvation of church and state alike. This was precisely the situation that appeared to present itself in the late 1620s and early 1640s.

But Wentworth's defense of parliamentary free speech was not and could not be absolute. If as an Erastian constitutionalist he exalted its function in the body politic, as the spokesman of conscience he embodied the revolutionary thrust of Reformation praxis that demanded the primacy of godly inspiration over any formal institution. In submitting himself to his "parliamentary" examiners in the "reporte," he does not mean to be bound by them. It is rather they who must yield to him, and convey *as their own* his speech to the Queen. It is their own not because they have uttered it or because they concur in it but because "counsel" — as Wentworth continues to define what others have adjudged contumacious — can only be transmitted as the act of the entire House. Were Wentworth's interrogators present in their role as councillors, they might offer his speech to the Queen as evidence of this contumacy and, consequently, as grounds for punishment. He has already made clear, however, that he will acknowledge them only as representatives of the House. In that capacity they would have no warrant to transmit his words at all, since by the rule of the House contumacious speeches were not to be published. If, then, the examiners agree to convey his speech to Elizabeth, they are obliged to deliver it as counsel. The fact that Wentworth claims full responsibility (and full liability) for it himself does not make this any less the case.

Of course, all this is purely notional — it exists only in the discourse-world of the "reporte," just as only in that world would Wentworth's examiners suppress their role as interrogators on the Queen's behalf; i.e., as councillors. Wentworth is able to reconcile his personal voice of conscience with the institutional voice of the House only by this rhetorical sleight of hand. In this sense, the "reporte" is a fantasy, although reality piquantly intrudes at the end when Seckford, the Master of Requests, observes that "Mr Wentworth will never acknowledge himself to make a fault nor sey that he is sorrie for any thing that he doth speake; you shall hear none of these things come out of his mouth" (439). This, indeed, has the ring of truth.

In Peter Wentworth as in no other Elizabethan parliamentarian we can see the burden of election as applied to a secular institution. There are two Wentworths speaking to us: the defender of Parliament who uses the rhetoric of humanist counsel and of *dominium politicum et regale* to vindicate its privileges, and the defender of the faith for whom Parliament is, like every other human dispensation, an instrument to be judged by its service to God's cause. For the first Wentworth, Parliament is the ultimate repository of the subject's liberties and therefore of England's special status as a free nation, the land where liberty is best secured and best enjoyed. For the second Wentworth, Parliament has the ultimate temporal responsibility for upholding the true church, and therefore England's special status as an elect nation. These two identities are mutually reinforcing, as political liberty and Christian liberty each reinforce the other. By the same token, though, where Parliament fails to adequately defend one, the other is necessarily weakened; religious liberty cannot consort with political tyranny, and vice versa. The critical importance of Parliament in such a schema suggests something akin to the legal doctrine that the king can do no wrong (though his government may err); namely, that Parliament can counsel no wrong (however its judgment may be temporarily led astray). If, however, Parliament fails to provide proper counsel, especially on spiritual matters and especially after due warning by godly ministers and consciences, this can only be interpreted as a clouding of judgment by a wrathful God. In such a case, it was the duty of godly consciences within Parliament to clear and if need be to compel that judgment, as Wentworth had tried to do in his speech and in the wish fulfillment of his "reporte."

In submitting himself to his parliamentary examiners and to the Queen's judgment, Wentworth affirmed his loyalty as a commonwealthman and as a subject. The discursive limit of conscience was prophecy: the conscientious subject might forewarn, but he could not coerce. The limitation was a practical one, obviously, but it was an ideological one as well. The conscientious subject displayed his sincerity by his loyalty; his willingness to suffer at the hands of his prince, even unto martyrdom, was the best surety for the truth of what he said. It was precisely this, moreover, that distinguished the godly sufferer from those false martyrs, the Jesuit emissaries, of which England was soon to have plentiful example. The Jesuits often died bravely, thus mimicking the true martyrs of Marian times, but only after their treason had been discovered. The quality of conscience was to speak openly, especially when called to a public forum as Peter Wentworth had been; the quality of perfidy was stealth.

Wentworth's conscientious dissent thus remained within a framework that acknowledged the legitimacy of England's constituted order. That acknowledgment, however, was contingent. Implicit in Wentworth's testimony, as in the rhetoric of the *Admonition* that it reflects, is the suggestion that all human institutions may prove broken vessels, even if God has chosen to use them for a time. This too was a conclusion to be made by conscience, although only after the greatest scruple, reflection, and prayer. Such was the conclusion reached by John Lilburne and his Leveller colleagues about the Long Parliament in the 1640s. As with Lilburne, it might be said of Wentworth that his "commitment to complete liberty of conscience . . . was the first and always remained the crux of his conception of liberty."[142] Like Lilburne, too, he was willing, even eager to pay for this commitment with repeated imprisonment, and, after again affirming free speech as the paramount and indefeasible right of Parliament in 1587 and later meddling in the succession question, he would spend the last four years of his life in the Tower, where he died in 1597.

One might argue, as Elton has, that Wentworth was too outré a figure to be representative of the Elizabethan Commons, and that the suspiciously Whiggish ease with which his rhetoric can be assimilated to such figures as Lilburne diminishes his relevance to the 1570s and 1580s. But free speech, as Elton himself concedes, had been a major preoccupation of the parliamentary session of 1572. This was partly owing to the merely conditional grant of it made by Elizabeth in response to the traditional request of the Speaker.[143] "She knoweth," said Lord Keeper Bacon, "that speech fit for the state well placed and used in matters convenient is very necessary, which she graunteth unto yow. But there is a difference betweene staring and stark blinde. Trifling digressions from matters proponed, idle and long discourses her Majestie misliketh and condemneth, wherein she adviseth them to be more wary then they have beene heretofore."[144] In mid-May, "divers" spoke for "the libertie of the House" (Hartley, 327), and there were frequent occasions in which members expressed their determination to speak without let or hindrance, asked favorable construction for their words, or expressed fear of reproach or punishment. Edward Fenner desired "libertie of speech without restraint" (355). Nicholas St. Leger declared that despite the Queen's express wish, "yet my conscience urgeth and pricketh me to speake" in favor of the Commons' bill against Mary Stuart (312). George Greenfield averred that he could not "be scilent" in the face of the kingdom's peril (360). Such protests were, to be sure, in part a rhetorical ploy; they were a way of appealing to the implicit consensus of the House, as well as of deflecting the anticipated displeasure of the Queen or her councillors. Yet neither their sincerity nor the personal and collective anxieties that underlay them should be discounted. When Wentworth made his deeply indiscreet and impolitic speech in 1576, he reminded the Commons of those anxieties, and of the fact that their proximate cause — the continued existence and standing menace of Mary Queen of Scots — remained unredressed. The timing and intemperance of Wentworth's speech transgressed the tacit norms of the House as well as it defied the patience of the Queen, but the matter of it stirred deep emotions and standing frustrations. It was therefore with a sense of relief at the return of a prodigal son, perhaps not untinged with gratitude for someone who had expressed the silent sentiment of the body, that he was received back into the House after his sojourn in the Tower, and, after ritual submission, "restored to his place to the greate contentment of all that were present" (453).

Parliamentary Authority and the Mid-Elizabethan Crisis

If, then, few of Wentworth's colleagues were prepared to emulate his reckless ardor, many shared his sense of embattlement. As the years passed with Mary still protected by Elizabeth's unadvised mercy, an alternate succession still undeclared, and the nation increasingly menaced by Jesuit subversion at home and Spanish aggression abroad, the fabric of English political life was strained to the breaking point. The events of 1584–1587 constituted a kind of rolling coup d'état within the monarchical republic in which royal power was, as in 1640–1642, simultaneously affirmed and constrained. In the latter case, the objective was to remove evil counsel from around the throne; in the former, it was to save Elizabeth from herself. No reader of the

1572 debates can fail to be struck by Parliament's exasperation at the Queen's lagging response to her own transparent peril and its intense frustration when the ostensible business of the session, the provision of political and legal cover for Mary's execution, was balked by her rejection of both bills put up to that end.[145] More than a decade later, the peril had only intensified, and Mary remained alive.

Elizabeth's political isolation at this moment can scarcely be exaggerated. There were no malignant advisers to purge as in 1640; on the contrary, the Queen's councillors, led by Burghley, were in the vanguard of elite and parliamentary agitation. The tripartite rejection of Mary, as a woman, a Scot, and a Catholic, had dire implications for Elizabeth. Mary's wickedness, foreignness, and popery contrasted, of course, with Elizabeth's virtue, Englishness, and piety, and in the fashion dear to the *mentalité* of the epoch the two women were construed as binary opposites. As with all such oppositions, however, a potential identity lurked, particularly since they shared the indelible trait of gender. There are certain questions the historian cannot answer because they do not pass the threshold of debate or even, on some level, of consciousness. One such question Englishmen asked themselves for two decades was why Elizabeth would continue to nourish the viper Mary in her breast. The answers Elizabeth offered—that she was loath to kill a kinswoman and fellow sovereign, and that the justification such an act would provide rebels and assassins in the long run far outweighed any short-term gain in her personal security—were not plausible, or at any rate palatable, to her subjects. Mary, they said, was no sovereign but a deposed tyrant who brazenly claimed not only her own former style but that of the ruler in whose country she had sought refuge, and whose death she openly plotted. The law of England and the law of nations alike condemned her: as Thomas Norton asked pointedly in the debates of 1572, "A common person in warre maie kill a prince that is an ennemie; whie maie not our Queen with iustice kill her, who is in a worse degre than anie ennemie?"[146]

The longer Mary remained alive, the more troubling this question became. If Elizabeth continued to honor the title of someone who claimed her own throne, did she not by implication lend credence to that claim and encourage those who would prosecute it? Her personal inclination to mercy must yield to her manifest duty to secure the realm; under such circumstances, as the bishops told Parliament, a private virtue became a public vice, "*crudelis mise[r]icordis, misericors inobedienta.*" Elizabeth's ambivalence and indecision thus became a willful obstinacy, and that a sin which implicated the entire land:

> The late Scottish Queene hath heaped upp together all the sinnes of the licentious sonnes of David, adulterye, murdere, conspiracye, treasones, and blasphemyes against God also, and if she scape with slight or noe punish-

ment her Majestie oughte in conscience, as also good and faithefull subiectes, to feare that God will reserve her as an instrumente to put her from the royall seat of this kingdome and to plague the unthankefull and noughty subiectes, *quod omen ut Deus avertat precamur.* Shall we thinke that God will not plage it? Surelye our heartes doe greatly feare he will doe it greevouslye.[147]

The accents of Elizabeth's bishops are almost Knoxian, harking back to the polarizing debates of 1558–1559 on the suitability of female sovereigns. Allegiance, even to a virtuous ruler, was contingent on the discharge of fundamental obligations, for, the bishops said, "A prince ought in all conscience before God by all the meanes he can to see to the quietnes, safety and good estat of that people over which God hath appointed him governor."[148] The corollary was clear: a people undefended must defend itself.

It was against this background, and the furor caused by the Jesuit missions, the discovery of another Marian conspiracy, the Throckmorton plot, and the assassination of William the Silent in the Netherlands, that the Bond of Association emerged in 1584. The Bond was drafted by Burghley and Sir Francis Walsingham, Elizabeth's secretary and spymaster, sworn by the Privy Council, and disseminated for elite subscription. It bound by solemn oath those who entered it to pursue to the death all who plotted or abetted "any act, counsel or consent" against the Queen's person, and to refuse allegiance to any intended beneficiary of such acts in the event of her death.[149] Since the Bond lacked any enforcement mechanism it has been taken as a license to vigilantism, but the anarchy it bespoke was within the government itself: a quiet revolution in which the integrity of the crown and the safety of the monarch were asserted (as in the militia debates of 1642) at the expense of actual royal command. The enthusiasm evinced by subscribers suggests that the message was well understood as an attempt to coerce Elizabeth into a final reckoning with Mary by an authorized show of force. With memories of the Catholic earls' rebellion in 1569 still fresh, this loyalist display could hardly have failed to make its point. At the same time, the fact that the county lieutenants were charged with soliciting subscriptions made it a quasi-official muster. In the event, ordinary citizens were permitted to adhere to the Bond, significantly broadening its base while keeping the process under elite control.

As propaganda, the Bond of Association had clear value both in mobilizing the country in a time of crisis and in reassuring it that the government was alert to the need to thwart a Catholic succession. As a political ploy, it daringly challenged Elizabeth's control of Mary's fate by condemning her in advance of any future rebellion and authorizing any sworn member of a national *posse comitatus* to execute justice upon her. As policy and precedent, however, it was too dangerous to stand without statutory definition and constraint. Accordingly, a parliament—already summoned to deal with the general crisis—was offered a bill for the Queen's safety incorporating the Bond.

The conciliar coup had gone too far, however, for the lawyers and country gentlemen in the House of Commons. How, in the absence of due process, were those who executed the Bond to distinguish the innocent from the guilty? For Parliament to enact the Bond as it stood would be an abrogation of law, for, as one member observed, "the worlde might iustlie condemne him and all others of greate wantt in iudgement, who so rashlie would enter into the othe of Assocyation for doeinge of a thinge which afterwarde uppon better advisement thei could not warrantt them selves to doe by lawe." The problem was that many members of Parliament had already taken the oath—the most solemn discursive act available to a private individual—and that to qualify or restrain it might well be construed as violating it. Nor was this simply a conundrum of conscience. The Bond itself stipulated that anyone prescinding from it was to be regarded as included among those against whom it had been formulated. At the same time, its defects and excesses were too patent to be ignored by those whose obligation was to legislate for the realm. Not for the first time, and not for the last, the hasty excogitations of a Council had run up against the sober deliberative responsibility of a Parliament. What made the occasion different was the clash between what many MPs had already done privately and what it was now their duty to do publicly.

The details of this debate need not detain us.[150] The statute that emerged as the Act for the Surety of the Queen's Most Royal Person (27 Eliz., c. 1 [1585]) finessed the problem of reconciling the oath with the act by declaring that the meaning of the former was to be defined and comprehended within the latter. In the process of doing this, the possible succession of James was salvaged from the Bond's affirmation that the collateral as well as intended beneficiaries of any future plot were to be barred from the throne. This entailed an extended discussion of the protocols of monarchical succession as well as a canvassing of possible candidates for it, the matter on which Elizabeth least liked to hear from her subjects. As London's Recorder William Fleetwood observed to Burghley, he had never before heard the *magnalia regni* so bandied about in Parliament.[151] If that was the case, it was Burghley himself who bore much of the responsibility. Nor could Elizabeth silence the debate, since only Parliament could save the Council from the consequences of its action and remove the nearest lineal Protestant candidate for the throne from disqualification by a Catholic plot.

The Queen's role in these events remains less than fully clear. Speaking to the two houses in 1586, she denied any knowledge of the Bond until "a thowsand [of] <u>handes</u> [underlined in original] with many obligacions were shewed mee at Hampton Court, signed and subscribed."[152] This, as Neale remarks, was hardly credible, although his inference that Elizabeth must have been privy to the Bond from the beginning and that "her mind, rather than her Councillors', was reflected in the first draft" of it does not follow either, unless one assumes that the councillors simply overrode her express wishes in the version presented to Parliament. It would seem likelier that the Bond was presented to her as a *fait accompli* by the Council and that she was unable to prevent its dissemination, preferring to work (as she did) through Parliament to mitigate its provisions.[153]

What, then, are we to make of Elizabeth's startling "confession" that she knew nothing of the Bond until it had circulated throughout the country and had been subscribed by the nation's elite? We must not take it any more literally than her auditors presumably did, accustomed as they were to her rhetorical style. What she did was to construe a grave act of conciliar insubordination, not to say insurrection, as a love-gift. In so doing, she was obliged to exaggerate circumstances still further, presenting a picture of herself as ignorant for weeks of a major policy initiative involving virtually the entire structure of government and the responsible elite of the country.

Burghley and his conciliar colleagues were not finished with providing for the realm's safety. The Bond had stipulated who might not succeed Elizabeth in the event of a new plot; it could not provide for the actual succession itself. There were in fact very good reasons for not naming a successor, apart from the Queen's obvious wish to avoid a reversionary interest. It was difficult to imagine those who had sworn themselves to hunt Mary down to the death or who had sought her condemnation in 1572 pledging allegiance to her. To have designated a Protestant heir would have created a new target for assassination, and, in James' case, would have put him in the position of weakening his own blood claim by disavowing his mother's. These reasons were perhaps not compelling, for the need for an acknowledged successor was great. They were sufficient to prevent a name from being formally advanced, however.[154]

Under these circumstances, the possibility of an interregnum had to be faced. To that end, Burghley drafted a contingency plan to govern the realm in the event of Elizabeth's untimely death. A "Grand Regal Council" (*Magnum Consilium Coronae Angliae*), consisting (in various drafts) of the Privy Council, members coopted from the House of Lords, and the four senior judges of the Westminster courts, would temporarily represent the vacant throne and exercise its functions until the last previous Parliament could be recalled to choose a new sovereign. There was evident kinship between this plan and the conciliar regime contemplated by Thomas Starkey in the 1530s, and (since no date of expiration or mechanism for dissolving the Council was provided) it is possible that the new government would have struck a constitutional balance very different from the old. The role of Parliament would also have been significantly altered. No precedent existed for summoning Parliament except by royal writ, let alone for reviving one prorogued or dissolved in a former reign (sitting parliaments were automatically terminated with the death of the monarch). The Grand Council acting as a commission for the crown was a dubious substitute for this authority at best, particularly as the immediate task of Parliament was to be the choice of the ruler. Previous parliaments had ratified royal successions before, but none had ever determined them. Burghley's plan stipulated that no claim to the throne was to be entertained prior to the convening of Parliament. The self-evident purpose of this was to forestall a resort to the sword by contending parties, but the formal separation of the powers of the crown from the person of the ruler had profound implications. Jacobean absolutist theory would claim that monarchy was patriarchally descended from Adam, or, if instituted by popular election, an irrevocable grant of authority to be exercised only by an actual prince. Burghley's draft conceded that it was "very probable" that the realm could not "long endure without a person that by justice ought to be the successor to the Crown shall be known." This awkward passage suggested that monarchy was so entrenched by custom and so intimately connected with the structure of law and government that no other regime was likely to be accepted as legitimate, at least for long. Collinson, who quotes this passage, glosses the phrase "ought to be" as referring to the normative laws of succession.[155] "By justice" would seem to belong to the same phrase as well, but Burghley's subsequent language makes it clear that the determination of the succession would rest with Parliament and be set forth by its authority in the form of an act. "Justice," therefore, refers operationally to Parliament's unfettered act of choice, encompassing the criteria (including blood propinquity, but presumably also a willingness to accept the governorship of the church, and perhaps such factors as age and gender as well) to be applied in making it. Such an ordinance would, moreover, be unique in lacking the royal assent, since the candidate chosen would only be empowered by the act itself. Even to declare the new ruler "acknowledged" rather than "chosen" would hardly obscure the nature of the process, which Burghley, in his own spidery hand, characterized as a "trial" among claimants.[156] The High Court of Parliament would both deliberate the right and of its own authority proclaim it, incorporating for that purpose the powers of the crown which it held in ultimate trust.

Burghley had in mind unique and desperate circumstances, of course. There is nothing to indicate that he wished to alter the established constitutional balance, and if we cannot help seeing the shadow of subsequent events in the Lord Treasurer's design, his own perspective would have been limited by those of 1399, 1485, and 1553. Nonetheless, in dealing with the most vulnerable link in the trinity of "estates" — clergy, laity, and crown[157] — he dis-

covered in Parliament the essential connection between them, the institution
of last appeal. Parliament alone embodied in itself the trinity, and it was, in a
sense, the project of the sixteenth century to discover this. Henry VIII had
anchored the imperial monarchy firmly in Parliament, using it not only to
achieve his reconstruction of the church but to fix the royal succession. At
the same time the clergy had lost status, not to say caste, as a department of
state, and the effort to revive prelacy in the next century would have disastrous consequences. If the church could claim a distinct place in the polity, it
seemed that Parliament—where the bishops sat as Lords Spiritual and alongside which Convocation served—was now the most appropriate locus of
sovereignty.

Thus it was that the formula that Henry had thrown out to describe an aspect of the monarchy had become, in time, descriptive of the state as a whole
and of the commonwealth itself. This was summed up in Sir Thomas Smith's
dictum that "the same may be done by the Parliament of England, which
representeth and hath the power of the whole realm both the head and
body." Nonetheless, it was a moment of considerable significance when in
1585, fresh from devising his scheme for a royal interregnum, Burghley embraced the idea of Parliament as a lawmaking body with three coordinating
elements:

> [T]he Lord Treasurer being the chiefest of the Committees of the Lords [fol-
> lowing a joint conference with members of the Commons], showed unto the
> said Committees of this House, that their Lordships of the Upper House be-
> ing of such quality and calling as they are known to be one Member of the
> Parliament; And also that the Knights, Citizens and Burgesses of the House
> representing the whole Commons of this Realm, are also another Member
> of the same Parliament, and her Majesty the Head; And that of these three
> Estates doth consist the whole Body of the Parliament able to make laws.[158]

Burghley here invoked the familiar trope of the prince as the head of the
body politic and of other elements as members, but by assimilating it to Parliament's distinctive lawmaking activity he subordinated the Queen's role to
the legislative process as a whole. His interest was less (if, essentially, at all)
in the powers of Parliament as such, and more in saving Elizabeth from herself, or, if that could not be done, then in rescuing the commonwealth from a
disputed succession, probable civil war, and possible foreign conquest. This
meant an unusually close collaboration between Parliament and the Council,
but it also meant an emphasis both on law- and policy-making generally as a
consensual activity in which royal recalcitrance in the face of united counsel
could not be indefinitely accepted. What the consequence of such a stalemate
might be was suggested in a comment of Sir Nicholas Bacon that if the realm
remained unsecured then subjects would inevitably be driven to provide for
themselves.[159] The unspoken implication was that the duty to protect the

commonwealth might devolve at that point upon lesser magistrates. Such were the thoughts being harbored by Elizabeth's most senior and loyal lieutenants. To a degree not far short of mutiny, they were acted upon in the mid-1580s. The renewed and ultimately successful campaign to compel Elizabeth's consent to Mary's execution, the interregnum scheme, the Earl of Leicester's unlicensed acceptance of the Governor-Generalship of the United Provinces and the efforts to parlay this into a formal assumption of sovereignty over the Low Countries, all bespoke a determination to impose on the Queen what she would not voluntarily accept, and if need be to proceed without her. It was during this period as well that the young Earl of Essex established himself at Court. Although he soon became Burghley's bitterest rival, the virile and martial values he championed took root in the soil that Burghley had plowed, and the seeds of the actual rebellion he led in 1601 were arguably laid in it.

It is a tribute to Elizabeth's fortitude that she was able to withstand as much of this pressure as she did. She faced down the interregnum scheme with the aid of a prolonged Christmas recess of Parliament in 1584-1585, and sidestepped a compact with the Netherlands. Not until she gave in to the clamor for Mary's head was the pressure relieved, however. This involved concerted action by the entire political establishment, for which Parliament served as the indispensable fulcrum. The session of 1586–1587 opened with a coordinated series of speeches decrying the state of the realm, which was described as in imminent peril of a bloody and all-encompassing destruction of religion, property, and liberty, and the establishment of "a perpetuall tiranny never to bee reformed." Almost fifty-four years later to the day, a similar battery of speeches was delivered to similar effect: England faced foreign subversion on behalf of "absolute monarchy," the overthrow of true religion, and the extirpation of the subject's right. The difference was that the speeches in the first case were offered by the Queen's councillors, appealing to an established consensus, and in the second by a parliamentary opposition aimed at the ministers of Charles I. The constant in both cases was a monarch apparently blind to grave peril.[160]

The councillors' speeches carefully walked the line between the petitionary form of asking that justice be executed on Mary (a rhetorical device that saved the appearances of royal discretion) and the imperative demand that Mary be executed *tout court*. But the Queen's old servant Sir Ralph Sadler, the long-serving Chancellor of the Duchy of Lancaster and a man now in his eightieth year, did not scruple to say openly what Lord Keeper Bacon had suggested privately more than a decade and a half earlier, that if Elizabeth did not act she would lose the allegiance of her subjects: "Yf the Quene's Majesty do not justice upon [Mary], assuredly it wilbe thowght and saide that eyther her Majesty liveth in securety, regardinge the welth nothinge and quiet of this realme and subiectes, or elce plainely that she is afraide to do it."[161] Fear, lassitude, inconstancy: these were the classic vices of woman-hood, the peril of a female ruler. If Elizabeth did not care for her own safety, which was also that of the realm, how long could the realm care for it at the expense of its own? If, whether from perversity or pusillanimity, she contin-ued to nurture that which most endangered her, how indeed was she to be distinguished from it?

The Commons needed little encouragement. Job Throckmorton, in his maiden address to Parliament the next day, echoed Sadler's sentiment that Mary must die if Elizabeth meant "to sitte quietly in her seate." If the Queen could not bring herself to execute justice, Parliament had the right and power to do it of its own authority, for

> Under the warrante of Gode's law, what may not this House doe? I meane the three estates of the lande. To deny the power of this Howse ye knowe is treason: therefore to say that this Howse is not able to cutt of tene such ser-pentes' heades as this is, not be able to reform religion and establish succes-sion, yt is treason; for why? To deny the power of this Howse is treason.

Throckmorton's comments are interesting on several levels. His sweeping assertion that the Lower House could exercise all legitimate powers of gov-ernment, while clearly hotheaded, reflected the growing perception of and resort to the Commons as the primary source of legislative initiative. The fact that he was himself a novice in the House makes the breadth of his claim all the more striking as a reflection, albeit exaggerated, of underlying public sentiment. Catching himself at once, he embraces the "three estates" in-volved in the functions of sovereignty. Throckmorton's impassioned advo-cacy of the Presbyterian bill and book later in the session makes it obvious that he was referring to the new trinity of King, Lords, and Commons rather than to any formulation including the clerical estate. No sooner has he cor-rected his position, however, than he adverts to it again. Twice he declares it to be "treason," a term normally applied to speech or action against the crown,[162] to deny the powers of the Commons, and specifically the suffi-ciency of its authority to sanction Mary, settle religion, and fix the succes-sion—a claim of jurisdiction embracing the courts, the crown, and the Lords. Lest there be any mistaking the point, he reiterates it yet again: "No, I dare not say but that this House can doe all thease, and ought to doe all thease," including its exercise of "absolute power" to dispose of Mary.[163]

We should not parse Throckmorton for a theory of sovereignty, and he concludes, tamely enough, that the House be "suteres" to the Queen to deal finally with Mary. But we should by no means dismiss his speech as mere rhetorical exuberance. That the Commons had the power to reform religion, and, as the representative of the whole realm, to take the initiative in doing so, was a conviction stubbornly held and (until Whitgift's regime got solid

footing) frequently acted upon. Thomas Norton, the crown servant and prototypical Elizabethan man of business, said no less about the succession
when he declared in 1571 "that whosoever shall say the court of Parliament
hath not authoritie to enact and binde the title of the crowne, [is] to be
adiudged a traytor." As for Mary, a Commons delegation told Elizabeth on
November 12, the dilemma she posed was literally forcing Englishmen to
choose between loyalty and conscience, thus stretching not only the bonds of
obedience but the frame of the commonwealth itself to the breaking point:

> Thousandes of all your most loving subiectes of all degrees which have for
> speciall zeale of your safetye made othe before God to pursew to deathe by
> all fforcible and possible meanes, such as she ys by iust sentens now found
> to be, can not save ther othes yf you kepe her alyve. For then eyther we
> must take her lyef from her without your dyrectyon, which wilbe to our ex-
> treame daunger by th'offens of your lawe, or els we must suffer her to lyve
> against our expresse othe, which wilbe to the uttermost perill of our owne
> soule wherwith no act of Parliament or power of man whatsoever can yn
> any wise dispence.[164]

The Bond of Association showed its cash value at this moment, confronting Elizabeth with the fact that she alone stayed the course of justice to
which she had committed herself by statute, thereby encouraging faithful
subjects to entangle themselves in oaths they could neither fulfill nor escape.
Though law might bind civil duty, no statute could repeal an oath, which
was a direct compact with God.[165]

The death of Mary Stuart was a chronicle foretold. In the political world of
the sixteenth century her continued existence was an unacceptable risk, and
would have been so even had she been wholly innocent of the plots hatched
on her behalf. Accordingly, her only safety lay in Elizabeth's death, just as
Elizabeth's only security lay in hers. This equation had been obvious ever
since Mary's flight to England, and it gave privy councillors and backbenchers a community of interest over a decade and a half that had become, by
1586, a unanimous voice of appeal. As the joint petition of the two houses
also presented to Elizabeth on November 12 stiffly declared, unless the sentence of death already pronounced on Mary by the Queen's own tribunal
was executed, "*as now by justyce may and ought to be doon*" [boldface ital-
ics in original], her safety could no longer be guaranteed. The implicit threat
in these words, and the use of the imperative "ought" (inserted, like the entire quoted phrase, in Burghley's own hand), was as close to an ultimatum as
any Tudor sovereign ever received.

The "Chief Authority in the Realm": Parliament in the Late Elizabethan Polity

Mary's execution, over Elizabeth's passive protest, lanced the boil of English politics. It did not, however, mean the end of the Queen's frustration

with the parliamentary session of 1586–1587. Sir Walter Mildmay's call in February for money to put the country on a war footing was the occasion for a major debate on foreign policy. Job Throckmorton again leaped to the fore, and his lengthy address of February 23 is again the fullest surviving text of the discussion. This time, his bluntness landed him in the Tower (and possibly saved his speech for posterity). The professed reason was his disparagement of Mary's son, James VI, but there was plentiful cause otherwise. Throckmorton praised Leicester's initiative in uniting England and the Netherlands; the Dutch, he declared, "desyre even from the bottome of their hartes to lyve under the obeysance of her Majestie before any other prince or potentate of the earth." They were, indeed, precisely the sort of compatriots Englishmen should welcome, for their zeal to true religion was exceeded only by their devotion to their liberties: "It is knowen that upon the infringement of their awntient priviliges, as the bringing in of strangers [another hit at James], or the enforcement of them to the bondage of any foreyne yoke, and such lyke, they are fourthwith discharged of theire feaultye and alleagaunce, and at their libertye make choyce of any other governor whatsoever." Model subjects, to be sure.[166]

The debate over foreign policy that occurred in grand committee the next day was not inaptly described by Vice-Chamberlain Hatton as "such a consultation as the kingdom had not had these hundred years."[167] Dutch sovereignty was the principal issue, but the debate ranged widely over the impending crisis with Spain and the Holy League, and suggestions were freely bruited for intercepting the Spanish treasure fleet and fomenting rebellion in Portugal. As in the case of Mary, the councillors gave the Commons their lead, but the inconclusiveness of the debate and of subsequent drafts for a petition reflected the divisions of the Council itself.[168] Nonetheless, the constitutional precedent was significant. Foreign affairs were, at least in theory, the exclusive prerogative of the crown, and might be discussed only by explicit invitation. Normally such an invitation would proceed through the councillors; normally, as well, the presumption was that the councillors spoke directly for the monarch, and that what was required (if not automatically forthcoming) was support for policies the crown had determined to pursue. To use Parliament as a lever to compel the Queen on a matter about which her councillors were resolved, as had been done regarding Mary, was sufficiently risky; to initiate a debate in the absence of conciliar consensus was a dangerous game indeed, and, in a time of crisis, folly. The weakness of conciliar policymaking was nowhere more visibly on display, and, as the competition for power between councillors of Burghley's generation and those of Hatton's became more acute (with the rise of Essex an additional complication), the weakness of prolonged female rule in a patriarchal order became increasingly transparent. That Elizabeth's prudence was often the wiser course among the headstrong counsels of her male advisers (sovereignty over the Netherlands being a case in point) did not allay the problem, and much of the habitual procrastination that so exasperated them must be considered in the light of a governing style constrained by gender. Elizabeth's agonized reluctance to proceed with Mary's execution, too, must be understood in this context. If that reluctance risked eroding the ideographic distinction between England's Deborah and the Scottish Jezebel (not to mention jeopardizing Elizabeth's life and the realm's safety), the grim determination of a universe of males to shed a sister queen's blood necessarily had a quite different resonance for the only other female monarch in Europe.

The consequences of protracted female rule were felt far beyond the immediate institutions of monarchy. The Queen's councillors had neither need nor notion of Collinson's monarchical republic as far as their ordinary work went. In the long run, however, and in matters of broad policy, a conciliar regime (as I think the mid-Elizabethan polity is better described, at least in its crisis phase) could not avoid appealing to the political nation. This made Parliament more central to the governing mechanism than ever before. From the Bond of Association to the debate over Dutch sovereignty, the Council engaged Parliament in governing over the head of the Queen. The possibilities and liabilities of this kind of politics were displayed in these episodes. A united Council was able to force the issue of Mary's execution with the enthusiastic if sometimes volatile cooperation of Parliament; a divided one churned up an inconclusive debate that revealed the crown's indecision and created a perilous precedent by expanding the discourse boundaries of the Lower House.

That peril was soon apparent. Hardly had the echoes of the Dutch debate died down when Sir Anthony Cope introduced his proposal to void all practices and usages of the existing Church of England and to replace them with the revised Geneva Prayer Book and its incorporated Presbyterian constitution—the Bill and the Book, as it was soon described.[169] As startling and unexpected as the proposal was—Neale's summary comment, "*Tabula rasa*; stark revolution," does not seem too strong[170]—it was the product of long and careful planning and coordination. Once again, too, Job Throckmorton (not yet a guest of the Tower) had a speech prepared. To Throckmorton, the root and branch reform of church government and worship was not a distraction from the necessity of dealing with the crisis of affairs that faced the realm, but its essential accompaniment. That crisis, he said, was the outcome of God's barely restrained wrath against an unreformed church, and it was therefore apparent that "Till this monster of our unworthy ministery bee banished the lande there is no remedy, the prophetes of God have threatened it, it is a case unavoydable: the Church muste needes looke for here-

syes, the prince for treasons, the land for hurleburleyes, the people for destruction."[171]

Throckmorton was plainly under duress, for he began his speech with a
disclaimer that strongly resembled Wentworth's apologia in 1576: "thoughe
fleshe and bloude bidde me be sylent, yet the stearne of my shippe (which is
my conscience) windeth me quite an other waye." He would willingly hold
his peace nonetheless, he said, if those older and wiser than himself would
speak, but "when they that should speake bee muette then burst out they
that should bee stille." It was almost as if members were invited to enter a
trap, "ffor when wee come first into this House there is layed before us a
shew of freedome in our entrye, and yet we fynde by the sequell we are
threatened with bondage before we goe fourth." How could conscience not
be aroused when the Queen's safety was at stake, and how could the most
conscientious not be compelled to speak when the most responsible did not?
Throckmorton likened the situation to that of a minister licensed "to preache
the gospell freely, provided allwayes that he medle neyther with the doc-
tryne of the prophetes nor the apostles." The analogy was not idle. Godly
ministers could not forbear to expound the Word, because this was their
plain errand. Yet the very ecclesiastical licensers who offered them pulpits
lay in wait to suspend or eject them when they performed their duty. Similarly, members of Parliament were called to the service of the commonwealth, and then punished by those who had summoned them for that purpose. The fate of the ministers was readily explained: the government of the
church was unscriptural, and the true exposition of Scripture could not fail
to reveal this. What excuse could then be offered for councillors who forbore
to speak but set snares for those who did? Throckmorton would not charge
them with malice, but dereliction of duty sufficiently condemned them: "To
charge any man in particuler is more I knowe then I have warrant for: but
my hope is those that are religiously wyse will yet be so farre from justifying
them selves in this regard as in the examination of there own hartes betwixt
God and them they will crye out from the depths of theire soules, '*Pec-
cavimus cum patribus nostris*,' it is to trew, o Lord, we have not heerein answered the duty of our callinge."[172]

Throckmorton's complaint is all the more striking when we consider how
forward the councillors *had* been in this Parliament. Less than three weeks
had elapsed since they had finally compassed the execution of Mary, the de-
voutest wish of every Parliament since that of 1571; little more than hours
had passed since they had led the Commons through a debate of unprecedented scope on foreign policy. For Throckmorton, however, all these were
mere preliminaries. It was not enough to foresee threats to Elizabeth's safety
"only for this day, for this weecke, for this yeare," which was the task of
worldly prudence, but to secure it "in continewance," and that could be

done only by reforming the church, the true foundation both of Queen and commonwealth. This was the essence of godly politics, and if few necessarily endorsed the particular prescription on offer, the view that underlay it was broadly shared. As went the church, so went the realm.

Any of the three major speeches Throckmorton delivered in the session of 1586–1587 would normally have been sufficient to send him to the Tower. It speaks to the charged circumstances of the moment that he was able to deliver all three. The councillors, caught off guard by the godly onslaught against the bishops—Mildmay characterized the Bill and the Book as the most radical proposal ever offered in Parliament—scrambled to thwart it. Elizabeth impounded Cope's bill, ordering Speaker Puckering to bring it to her in person for that purpose. The principal contrivers were soon in the Tower. This touched off vigorous debate about whether members could justifiably be imprisoned merely for introducing a bill, and whether Parliament could proceed as a corporate body without its full complement of members. Even prior to the sequestrations, however, Peter Wentworth (soon to join his colleagues in confinement) propounded a highly rhetorical set of questions designed, as he said blandly, to enable each member to "knowe howe farre he may proceede in this honnourable councell in matters that concerne the glorie of God, and our true and loyall service to our prince and state."[173]

Wentworth's first question contains the gravamen of the rest:

> Whether this councell be not a place for anie Member of the same here assembled ffreelie and without controllment of anie person, or dainger of lawe, by bill or speeche to utter anie the greiffes of this common wealth whatsoever touchinge the service of God, the safetie of the prince and this noble realme.

Free speech in Parliament, Wentworth says plainly, relates to all urgent matters of church and state. It inheres in members severally and in the body collectively, for no act or command outside it can restrict it, and no law can be made or applied to its detriment. This is so, as another question stipulates, because no other entity can "make, adde to, or diminishe from" the laws of the realm. In the Lansdowne MS version of the questions, it is stipulated that "free doinges or dealinges" are "graunted to everye on[e] of the Parliament howse by lawe." This is at once a clearer and a vaguer formulation. It suggests that free speech has a specific, recognized basis, but is ultimately a less secure foundation than the broader notion that free speech is constitutive of Parliament, that a parliament is not a parliament without it. Parliament's function is to express and relieve "greiffes," or, as the seventeenth century would more commonly phrase it, grievances, whether by statute or other means. Free speech thus extended both to complaint and remedy; laws, in short, could not be made without it, and laws were the business of Parliament. Nor could a law itself abridge parliamentary free speech, for that would be to undermine the legislative capacity per se, and hence was a contradiction in terms.

What statute itself could not do, no lesser authority could command. It followed from this that as free speech was the precondition of debate within Parliament, confidentiality was the obligation of members outside it: specifically, that it was "against the orders of this councell to make anie secreate or matter of weight which is here in hand knowne to the prince, or anie other, . . . without the consent of the House." The Commons, that is, could request consultation or external counsel (for example, from judges learned in the law), but no advice, much less compulsion, could be obtruded on it.

Since particulars of debate could not be reported outside the House and since when the House did speak, by way of bill or petition, its voice was collective, it followed axiomatically that no member could be censured except by the House itself. This protection of speech applied both "in the Parliament tyme, and aftre," for otherwise the prince could sit on improperly, erroneously, or maliciously reported information until Parliament had dispersed, and then punish individual members at will. No greater offense to the subject could be offered than such postparliamentary retribution, whether by fine, imprisonment, or the imposition of burdensome service. Members chosen to speak in the name of all were penalized without even the right of a private subject to due process of law, although Charles I, the better to publicize the consequences of disloyal conduct, would try Sir John Eliot, Denzil Holles, and Benjamin Valentine in Star Chamber after the breakup of Parliament in 1629. Wentworth himself was, of course, to be a parliamentary martyr, dying in confinement, as did Eliot in 1632.[174]

The only exception Wentworth made in the absolute protection of parliamentary free speech from outside interference was for "trayterous wourds," which category was, of course, defined by statute, and therefore still within the compass of parliamentary authority. The "tale carriar" who breached the confidentiality of debate, however, or indeed anyone else who infringed the liberties of the House, was to be strictly punished by it "as an enymye unto God, the prince and state." This formulation, thrice repeated in the Lansdowne version, signified that the prince no less than the House was abused by any breach of parliamentary privilege. As the Cotton MS version put it, the question was "Whether the prince and state can continewe, stand, and be maintayned without this councell of Parliament, not alteringe the governement of the state." The liberty of Parliament, that of the subject, and the balance of the constitution on which the prince's lawful exercise of power depended, were bound up in an indissoluble whole. A mere whisper at Court, if unexposed and unpunished, was enough to threaten it.

Wentworth also had three questions for the speaker himself in the Cotton version: whether he might interrupt any member while speaking; whether he might adjourn the House without its consent by rising from his place; and whether he had the right to overrule the House in any matter before him, or was himself subject to the rule of the body. By asking Speaker Puckering to read the questions himself, he emphasized his strategic intention to bring the only officer of the House under majority control, for the privy councillors were, as he had pointed out in 1576, only individual members with respect to the whole.[175]

Technically, as we have seen, the Speaker himself was chosen by the House, but in practice he was the crown's nominee, and his choice was ratified by the prince in the formal ceremony of his presentation before the throne. This sequence mimicked the legislative process itself, in which crown bills were preferred by the councillors, passed by the two houses, and assented to by the sovereign. The Speaker thus straddled both institutions; he was the spokesman of the Commons and at least in theory the impartial manager of its debate, while at the same time he was a conduit of crown messages and commands. His discretion in recognizing speakers and his power in interpreting the rules of the House could obviously be used to advance the royal interest, but his credibility with his colleagues depended on maintaining at least the appearance of fairness.[176] It was a fine line to walk, and Wentworth wanted to erase it. Proper counsel, the responsibility of a Parliament, hinged on free speech, and free speech on control of debate by the body, not by a single individual whose powers derived from it. In Wentworth's commonwealth, the Speaker of the House would no longer serve two masters.

Wentworth's questions demonstrate how deeply the Henrician conception of King in Parliament had penetrated the political culture of England, and how easily it could be assimilated to radical ends. The trinity of King, Lords, and Commons it presupposed suggested, for Wentworth, not a pyramid at whose apex the monarch sat, controlling, coordinating, and ultimately giving statutory life to the work of the two houses (which had certainly been Henry's own notion, as it was to be, in more formally absolutist dress, that of James I and Charles I), but rather a horizontal grid whose components possessed independent life and function, and which communicated through formal channels meant to express and maintain the autonomy of each. Wentworth's concerns for the inherent nature of the Commons' liberties, the confidentiality of its debates, and the close control of its presiding officer by the body were thus structurally integrated, and bespoke an overarching conception of the House as a corporate entity which, as the court it claimed to be, made its rules, kept its records, and dealt with its fellows as an equal.

What, then, of the royal component of this troika in Wentworth's scheme? The monarch summoned and dissolved Parliament, although by 1585 the House was claiming the right to adjourn itself. He spoke at the beginning and end of each session, either in person or by representative, expressing his reasons for calling the estates together and approving or taking under further advisement such bills as were presented to him. As matters required it, he might further consult the houses during their session, or they petition him. He might take no cognizance of matters actually before the houses, however, or even receive information about them except by formal communication from the houses themselves. His sole function, then, was to initiate such business as concerned him, and conclude such matters as had concerned the houses. Presumably the interests of the king and those of the houses would overlap if not coincide, but that was not necessarily so. Occasionally a Parliament would sweep aside the royal agenda entirely and substitute its own, as the Merciless Parliament had done in 1388 and the Long Parliament was to do in 1640. In any case, the crown could only urge, not impose its agenda, and it could not prevent the houses from adopting their own, or, at least according to Wentworth, even know its content until it was formally disclosed.

The linchpin of this system was confidentiality; granted that, free speech was entailed, and the Speaker entirely the Commons' creature. By means of it, Wentworth was not merely seeking to widen the boundaries of parliamentary discourse but to eliminate all constraint on it whatever, save the utterance of treason. Under the rubric of "the high service of God, prince, or state," as one of the Cotton questions framed it, it was difficult to imagine a subject that could not be discussed. This included matters of prerogative, or, as James would phrase it, *arcana imperii*. The Commons had debated foreign policy, the succession to the throne, and the religious settlement in 1586-1587. The first two subjects had been raised by privy councillors and only the last from the back benches, but there was no reason in Wentworth why all three could not have arisen from any quarter of the House, and, as Throckmorton had pointed out, all were intimately linked.

Wentworth would have no doubt vigorously rejected the imputation that he aimed at a parity between sovereign and subject. Parliament was a "councell," the king was a ruler. That odd entity the King in Parliament was another matter, however. In its totality it exercised the highest powers of the commonwealth, but as a constituent part of it the king was distinctly limited. In Parliament the king could not know what he otherwise knew, the speech of all his subjects in pulpit, print, and tavern; in Parliament he could not do what he otherwise did, in policing and punishing all such discourse at discretion. The reason for this was that parliamentary discourse was public in a specific, unique, and indivisible way. Members of Parliament were, in their private capacities, subjects liable to the same constraints as any other member of the body politic at large. Within the body of Parliament, however, they had a dual role that distinguished them from all other subjects and even from themselves as private men. First, they spoke for the community—severally for their own constituencies, collectively for the realm as a whole—and as such had privilege in uttering "the greiffes of this common wealth." Secondly, they were called to counsel the prince on affairs of state. In this it was natural that they defer to the privy councillors who ringed the Speaker's chair as they did the throne. The latter presupposed, however, that the councillors would provide appropriate leadership. As Throckmorton remarked, "Such as are nearer than wee by calling, ought of right to be warier then wee in watching; who beinge in place, and having dayly opportunity offered them . . . oughte (in reason) to be the first that shoulde cry out and sett the beacon on fyre them selves."[177] This was too seldom the case; indeed, not only did councillors frequently fail in their duty to advise both the Queen and the House, but they bore responsibility, directly or indirectly, for breaches in the confidentiality of debate. This was a double dereliction, for not only did such councillors fail to hold up the "beacon," they brought reproof on those who did. As Wentworth had remarked in 1576, "I doubt not but that some of her Majestie's counsell have dealt plainely and faithfully with her Majestie . . . if any have, let it be a sure token to her Majestie to know them for approved lovers. And whatsoever they be that did perswade her Majestie soe unkindly to intreat, abuse and oppose her selfe against her nobilitye and people or comend her Majestye for soe doing, let it be a sure token to her Majestye to know them for sure traytors and undermyners of her Majestie's life and safety."[178] When counsel failed the realm was in peril, for, as Wentworth had said as well in 1576, "noe estate can stand where the prince will not be governed by advice,"[179] and advice withheld was as fatal as advice rejected—indeed, more so, for the prince was thereby left to discretion alone. Parliament was essential even when privy councillors did their job, because no particular counsel could replace that of the commonwealth; but when they shirked responsibility, the estates of the realm were the last salvation of the state. What the Privy Council would not do, for whatever reason, it dared not impede the Commons from doing.

In Wentworth and Throckmorton, the humanist theory of counsel—that the prince could not fail to respond to loyal advice—was married to the conviction that the advice that Elizabeth most needed to hear was that her ecclesiastical establishment had to be dismantled if the commonwealth were to survive. It might be thought that the privy councillors had done a very good job of providing leadership in 1586–1587. They had secured the execution of Mary in partnership with the two houses, and had broached the issue of sovereignty over the Netherlands. The former, as Throckmorton conceded, had been a work of note. Without an alteration of church government and a settlement of the succession, however, it would be to no avail: "it was well and worthylie don of her Majestie to execute justice uppon that Guysian impe . . . but yet . . . to reforme the house of God and to settle the crowne to the blisse of posterity shall bee 10 tymes better don." It was well to pursue Ahab and other evildoers, but it was better, and far more critical, to renovate the temple with Josiah.[180]

Wentworth and Throckmorton were not, of course, broadly representative of the Elizabethan House of Commons; they were rather (together with men such as William Strickland, Tristram Pistor, Robert Snagge, George Carleton, Edward Lewkenor, Robert Beale, Anthony Cope, Francis Goodwin, and James Morice) its radical fringe. Synchronically minded historians who proclaim anything outside a functionalist paradigm of the status quo anachronistic, or Foucauldian ones who think that a paradigm retains its integrity until, by some inscrutable process, it metamorphoses overnight into its fully formed successor, will regard such men as marginal and anomalous, and unworthy of much comment.[181] But even in their day they were striking figures who served as lightning rods of the House, articulating sentiments frequently shared if seldom expressed by others. If their demand for a Presbyterian regime was, in the 1580s, a distinctly minority view, their insistence on Parliament's core responsibility for the church struck a far wider chord. In a sense, a modern Parliament and a national church had grown up together, and the power and fortunes of one were bound up with those of the other. These in turn, in the apocalyptic climate of the late sixteenth century, had become the fortunes of England itself under the eye of Providence. There was nothing to suggest that Parliament was an endangered institution under Elizabeth except insofar as England itself was in peril, but in the felt crisis that enveloped both Parliament and the church in the latter 1620s the bond between the two was renewed, with profound consequences. The sense of their mutual dependency and common destiny that Wentworth and Throckmorton had expressed in the 1580s became the text for men like Pym and Eliot, and this time their views were not in the minority.

Wentworth and Throckmorton also bequeathed the House of Commons a tradition of "Country" eloquence. The set-piece speeches of an Elizabethan Parliament were those that came from the throne or, at least presumptively, spoke for it. Bacon, Mildmay, and Hatton were the great orators of the House; they had pride of place, spoke with the voice of authority, and defined both the task of each session at its beginning and its success at the end. Thus it had always been. Lesser crown servants might also speak at length with varying degrees of indulgence; the diarist of the anonymous journal of 2–21 April 1571 observed that Thomas Norton spoke "in his accustomed manner of naturall eloquence" on the subject of free speech but that Sir Francis Knollys "made a longe needles discourse concerninge the subsedy."[182] The diarist found Knollys generally windy,[183] although free speech was apparently a more agreeable subject to him than the subsidy. Eloquence was to some degree a leveler, but debate was generally dominated by officials, and long speeches by backbenchers were rare. The diarist spotted Peter Wentworth as a comer early on, approving his maiden address of April 20 on free speech as "very orderly in many wordes."[184] Wentworth went on to speak "in many wordes" on several memorable occasions, two of which we have noted in detail, and Throckmorton's three major addresses in 1586–1587 were extraordinary not only for their fullness and content but their presumption in coming from a freshman member of the House.[185]

As Wentworth put it in 1572, "he had rather comytt some foly in speech then doe iniury by silence."[186] The true commonwealthman, the true saint (using this term in Michael Walzer's sense)[187] had a duty to speak, especially when those "nearer . . . by calling," as Throckmorton put it, failed to do so. Throckmorton's turn of phrase was indeed telling. Councillors who served the throne were called to their place by their sovereign, but they had a "calling" too in the sense of divinely imposed vocation, for the guidance of England under Providence, the fulfillment of its destiny as an elect nation, was not merely a secular function but one with sacerdotal overtones. The councillors were looked to for leadership because they spoke for the throne, the source of power, privilege, and preferment; but, for godly MPs, they were servants (like the Queen herself) of a higher power too. As such, they were owed deference and respect, but by the same token much was expected of them. This was particularly the case where the cause of God was concerned. Godly MPs may not have been a choir—though they often sang on cue—but by the 1580s they had arrived at a conception of church polity unshakably grounded in Scripture as they interpreted it and therefore presumptively self-evident to all persons of goodwill. It followed that those closest to the Queen had a special responsibility to act in concert with them. When they failed to do so, the "silence" was created which it was the duty of others to fill. This required an eloquence equal to the gravity and consequence of the occasion and capable of persuading—of recalling to duty—not only their fellow backbenchers but great lords of state and even the Queen herself. This was why Wentworth was so anxious that Elizabeth be given the entire text of his 1576 speech. It was a sermon essential for her to read if not to hear.

The eloquence to which godly speakers aspired was not that of the rhetoricians, although rhetoric was a tool that might be put to use, and Wentworth's 1576 speech deploys it with great skill. Rather, they appealed to self-evident truths, brushing aside homiletic or prudential objections ("the king's displeasure is a messenger of death"),[188] and warning of the dire consequences of ignoring revealed will. Throckmorton in particular saw his role in prophetic terms, and he exhorted the Commons to so serve the commonwealth by reform of the church that it might be said forever after "that the holy ghoste him selfe was sure Lord Presydente of this assemblye."[189]

Pari passu, the denial of free speech, particularly in God's service, was a sin against the Holy Ghost: the suppression of conscience. Throckmorton, as we have seen, had likened the restriction of free speech in Parliament to denying preachers access to the Word. In a sense it was an even graver fault, for the "silence" of which Wentworth and Throckmorton complained was doubly compounded: it was the *refusal* to speak on the part of those councillors from whom leadership in God's cause was properly to be expected, and the *denial* of speech to those who in default of their betters were constrained to fill their roles. When preachers were silenced, the laity could hardly take their place; this silence had no remedy, and was therefore an absolute deprivation. When councillors failed to speak in Parliament, however, or at least to speak to the urgent perils of church and state, their dereliction implicated everyone sworn to serve the commonwealth; this was a silence that had to be broken. For those who reproved mere men of the Country who would speak of matters beyond their ken, Throckmorton had a simple reply: "the next [i.e., best] way to put the foole to sylence is fore the wise man to speake in the cause him selfe."[190] For men like Throckmorton, men like Mildmay had only themselves to blame.

The combination of deference and aggression in Wentworth and Throckmorton is characteristic of the godly mind-set of mid-Elizabethan England. Such speakers would for their own part be silent, they suggest, were only others to speak: speak, that is, as they themselves would. The honor of initiating true reform in the church and of replacing popish bishops with pious elders belonged, of precedence if not of right, to the Constantinian emperor. Come what might, however, God's cause would be served, or England pay the forfeit.

The speech of Wentworth and Throckmorton was still inscribed within the forms of parliamentary discourse, of question and petition. Within two years it had given way to the railing satire of the Marprelate tracts, of which Throckmorton has been proposed the author.[191] By 1593 the conformist attack on Separatism eclipsed all else, and the godly found themselves on the defensive, lumped together by now-Lord Keeper Puckering with Papists as sowers of discord and sedition and harassed by the Court of High Commission.[192] The collapse of the movement for godly reform in the latter parliaments of Elizabeth has led some to suggest that its sponsors were an isolated and evanescent faction with little support in the House of Commons. This is a fundamental misreading of the evidence. If only a passionately committed minority shared the zeal of Cope and his colleagues for a Presbyterian polity, there was a much more general constituency for a church that emphasized a learned, preaching ministry, and saw the confessional struggles of the late sixteenth century in eschatological terms. Much the same might be said for many of the councillors themselves, from Burghley on down. Sir Francis

Knollys, the Treasurer of the Household, carried a Commons' petition on religion up to the Lords in December 1586 that included demands for the removal of unqualified ministers and for the restoration of ministers suspended for refusing subscription to the Articles of Religion without reservation or for omitting portions of the Prayer Book. The Lords, for their part, joined themselves "feelingly" with these aims. To an extent this was an exercise—it was clear that Whitgift would scotch the petition—but as an expression of the temper of the House, inclusive of members of the Council, it was significant. This was the "moderate Puritan" program described by Peter Lake, and if we should not mistake its sentiments for those of every member or assume an equal commitment to them among those who did, they suggest an ideological consensus at least acceptable to the majority.[193] Some of that consensus remained a negative one; even when such petitions were no longer preferred in the more repressive climate of the 1590s, anti-papist legislation continued unabated. Throckmorton's vision of an assembly presided over by the Holy Ghost had far deeper resonance for a body that regarded itself as the joint founder and ultimate temporal support of God's church in England than appeared on the surface,[194] and when crisis demanded it, as it did in 1640, it would act on and in a fashion even strive to embody that vision.

The beginnings of Parliament's development as a modern institution were entwined with the issues of religion and the royal succession. Henry VIII's enactment of the Reformation and the successive legitimation, delegitimation, and relegitimation of his offspring by statute had made it a copartner in the reconstruction of the realm and a guarantor of the throne itself. In forging this alliance, Henry had recognized Parliament's indispensability to his designs, but he had gone a step further in assimilating it to his wider conception of imperial monarchy. If King in Parliament had meant for him the monarch in his utmost seat of honor and power, it also meant, for latter observers, an incorporation of the monarchy and the estates in an indissoluble whole that represented the ultimate instrument of sovereignty. This was expressed in the figuration (accepted by Burghley himself, and the Charles I of the 1642 *Answer to the xix Propositions*) of Parliament as an entity composed of King, Lords, and Commons.

Parliament had forestalled Henry's attempt to blur the line between statute and proclamation—the king's power in Parliament and his power out of it—in the 1530s, affirmed its role in the religious settlement of the 1550s and 1560s, and demanded oversight of ecclesiastical governance thereafter. In the crisis of the mid-1580s, Burghley and other councillors had sought a new partnership with Parliament that would have empowered it to recall itself on its own authority in an interregnum and to settle the succession to the throne. By the latter part of the Tudor period, King in Parliament was recognized as the final institution of state, the ultimate incorporation of crown and commonwealth. The principal political commentators of the era, Smith, Harrison, Camden, and William Lambarde, the distinguished antiquarian who described Parliament in the 1590s as the sole body that "delivers laws, that do bind all persons, in all causes, as well ecclesiastical, as temporal," all agreed on this proposition, and no one, apart from Catholic controversialists and religious separatists, dissented from it. The legal scholar and crown servant James Morice declared in his *Readings on the Statute of Westminster the First* (1578) that the power of King in Parliament was of "sovereign rule and . . . chief authority in the realm."[195] If the elements of the mixed polity remained distinct in their function and limited in their discretion—a necessity more urgent than ever if *dominium politicum et regale* was to keep its bounds and King in Parliament not to become the vehicle of either a monarchical or a popular tyranny—it was clear that English political thought already possessed the concept of sovereign power, albeit one embedded in a body that itself presupposed the coordination of independent parts.

The fact that Parliament was summoned irregularly and for relatively short periods—the average length of an Elizabethan session, not counting Christmas or Easter recesses, was just over eleven weeks—did not detract from its constitutional significance, but rather dramatized it. A Parliament was not merely the extension of day-to-day administration, however mundane much of the lesser business it transacted might seem;[196] it was a caesura that marked the years and decades, and whose acts could stamp the centuries. This was not an idea new to the sixteenth century, but one that became more sharply delineated with the development of a formalized legislative procedure (and, with that, a more focused sense of the proper division, articulation, and function of Parliament's distinct parts). The opening ceremonies of a Parliament, which both displayed the hierarchical disjunctions of the body politic and celebrated their unity in the estates of the realm, were, until the great public processions of the Caroline masque, the most impressive manifestations of state apart from coronations and royal funerals.[197]

The convention of Parliament had long been marked by a grand procession. To the public that vied and jostled for a view of the dignitaries, especially the monarch, this was (apart from drawings and prints) the only visual representation of it. A parliament meant brisk trade, of course, and quartering for hundreds of members and their servants. Gossip about its proceedings abounded, ambassadors reported its progress to their governments with varying degrees of accuracy and comprehension, and travelers and correspondents kept the countryside abreast: the walls of Westminster were porous, and Wentworth's strictures presupposed that the king was to be the only interested party in the realm not to know what went on within them. Though individual members could be seen around town, however, the sanctum of Parliament itself was entered only by those invited or summoned to it on specific business. The opening procession, therefore, was the only time when the public at large had symbolic, discursive access to the body that uniquely represented them, even though many of the marchers were not a part of it and though most of those who were, as we shall see, were absent.

The role of the commons in the parliamentary procession was, as on all other ceremonial occasions, strictly prescribed. When in 1559 crowds knelt and hailed the passing Elizabeth with cries of "God save and maintain thee!", they were performing that role in its ideal form, as the unproblematic acknowledgment of power and the unfeigned assertion of loyalty. As in other state processions, however, the commons posed a control problem; enthusiasm might easily shade into unruliness, and the possibility of discordant sentiment, particularly when hurled from the anonymity of a crowd (or, worse, taken up by it) was a standing hazard. In time of plague, the mere presence of the commons could be a threat; the Parliament of 1593 opened without procession for that reason, although that of 1597 attempted to compensate for it with a spectacle of unusual pomp. James I was notoriously averse to crowds, and Charles I even more so. One way to avoid them was to proceed by barge, which offered a majestic but suitably distant glimpse of the royal power: Henry VIII did so in 1529. The commons, however, could not be denied their day, even when the monarch denied herself. In 1586, Elizabeth refused to participate in the parliamentary procession as a means of dissociating herself from the proceedings against Mary, opening it by commission instead. This gesture of personal detachment (and implicit dissent) from the things that would be enacted institutionally in her name was perhaps the most eloquent testimony to the "monarchical republic" of Queen and Council that reached its zenith in the final struggle over Mary.[198]

The extreme awkwardness of the sovereignless procession of 1586 is suggested in the account of it given by the Herald of the House of Lords. When the marchers had made their way from Whitehall to Westminster Abbey, the Dean of Westminster knelt, as he would have in Elizabeth's presence, and recited the Litany and the prayer for her safety. The Bishop of Salisbury delivered the customary sermon, which emphasized the peril of the realm by invasion and the threats to the Queen's person. The two houses having entered the Parliament chamber, Lord Chancellor Bromley

> declared that her Majeste had deputed [her authority?] in her absence for sundery causes respected and by her Majeste's comission for the houldinge of this parlement, and delivering the same unto the Clerk was there redd openly unto those iij named [the Treasurer of the Household, Sir Francis Knollys; the Comptroller, Sir James Croft; and Vice Chamberlain Hatton]. And they imediatly arose and toke theyre place making obeysance to the seat royall. Then the Lord Chancellor cam with reverence to them and

kneled downe to them three and receved the forme of his oration, and so
with obeysance passed by them and went to the usuall place at the barre
behynd the seate on the right hand, and there began his oration for the especiall caulinge therof . . .[199]

The scene had a touch of the eerie, with the throne chair empty and the
Chancellor kneeling before the three councillors of the household who stood
in, like a mock trinity, for the absent sovereign. Such a form might be employed in a minority or for some other exigent reason, but none such was offered: the Queen was absent because she chose to be. Not until Charles I left
London in January 1642 following his failed attempt to arrest five members
of the Commons' leadership did a prince so stiffly turn his back on a parliament. In the immediate context, it was also a kind of rehearsal for what the
self-convened parliament contemplated by Burghley's scheme for an interregnum might have looked like.

There was another and regular "absence" in the opening procession to
Parliament: that of its elected members, the House of Commons. The marchers (state servants, ceremonial attendants, and heralds apart) were those who
occupied their places by prescriptive right—the lords temporal and spiritual.
The procession thus represented the honor elite, those whose position and
authority, whether as peers, bishops,[200] councillors, or judges, derived directly and personally from the prince. It was the "state," the permanent, everyday governance of the realm, as opposed to the "commonwealth," whose
representatives, as yet unsworn, stood, usually in the White Hall or in the
Court of Requests, for the Lord Steward and his deputies to call their roll
and administer the necessary oaths. These neither marched nor heard the
service in the Abbey, but waited "out of all order" and "making strange
noises," as Recorder Fleetwood described them in 1584, in a cold and drafty
room normally used to hear petitions to the crown—a tart reminder that
they, too, were petitioners as well. The Steward's deputies were typically
privy councillors elected to service in the House. Like the Steward himself,
they would have marched in the procession and heard the divine service,
but in their capacity as state servants and only incidentally as MPs.[201]

In the theater of monarchy, the sequestered members thus waited in a
kind of limbo for the archangelic visitation of the Steward, by whose summons they were finally brought to order and guided first to their own chamber (which only now they might rightfully occupy) and then to the Lords'.
The wait could be a long one. The procession to the Abbey was only a few
hundred yards, but in 1597 it was delayed while, for six hours, the Commons
cooled their heels without food, drink, or other provision of nature. Commoners waiting to be touched for the King's Evil could hardly expect worse
usage. When the new-fledged MPs were finally admitted into the splendidly
bedecked Upper chamber, they were confined behind the bar, a grossly in-

adequate space. Many never succeeded in entering at all, or found their places usurped by interlopers. In 1601, the Gentleman Usher who controlled the door failed to open it, leaving the assembled Commons to fume outside. Nor did Jacobean parliaments operate more smoothly.[202]

Such affronts were in part the result of the hurly-burly that attended any large state procession. It is hard to resist the conclusion, however, that a strong element of ritual purification was also in play. Parliament was the only institution above the level of the jury where the "commons" played a significant role in governance, and it was a very significant role indeed. Of course, the men who sat in the Lower House—privy councillors and other crown officials, younger sons of nobility, substantial landowners and merchants, lawyers, and gentlemen—were hardly mere subjects; they were all themselves members of the ruling elite. They were present, however, not in their own capacities, but by virtue of election (or at any rate selection). They were responsible, at least nominally, to the shires or boroughs for which they sat, and they drew their authority from this connection. At the same time, they were contaminated by this very contact. Electors were often (not always) themselves members of local elites, but members represented not only those who had specifically chosen them but the commonalty in general. Representation marked the distinction between responsibility *to* and responsibility *for*. King, Lords, and Commons all shared a responsibility *for* the general welfare, but only the members of the Commons had a responsibility *to* a specific constituency and, in a more extended sense, to the commons as a whole. Representation was thus a kind of derogation, authority being derived from below rather than from above. This paradox was resolved for the institution as a whole by the fact that the prince alone could summon it into being, so that the exercise of the popular franchise, granted initially by royal authority, was triggered only by the royal writ. Nonetheless, the taint persisted for members of the Lower House, and was only negated by the swearing-in ceremony that reconnected them to the fount of all authority and raised them from the status of mere spokesmen or petitioners to that of counselors and legislators. Until such time (and even beyond) they were still merely "commoners" themselves, and made to perform symbolically as such—a jostled and disorderly crowd, not unlike the burlesque representations of the mob in stage play and masque.

The form of the opening procession to Parliament was thus designed to emphasize the power of the king and (secondarily) the hereditary and spiritual elites, while containing the popular element until it could be properly subordinated. It had derived of course from the precedent of medieval times, when the two houses were scarcely yet distinct and the natural focus was on the prince and his retainers. By the end of the sixteenth century, the symbolic valences were quite different. The landed elite that largely composed the

House of Commons were a force of some independence, as well as the effective governors of the countryside both in and out of royal service. If the Lords still took formal precedence, the Commons did the lion's share of Parliament's actual work, legislative and otherwise.[203] The ancient rite of procession was thus what might be called, to borrow modern jargon, a lagging indicator. But there was another way to interpret the Commons' "sequestration" too. It was they, after all, who occupied the halls of Westminster, while the prince and the Lords came to unite with them. Absent prince or lords, it was they who would remain. So it would be in 1642 and 1649. When the breakdown of legitimacy came in the 1640s, when indeed many sought to invent it anew, Parliament proved the indispensable institution, and the House of Commons its core.

CHAPTER 7

Stuart Parliaments and the Crisis of Legitimacy

Parliament and Absolutism

The war parliaments from 1589 to the end of Elizabeth's reign were necessarily preoccupied with the climactic struggle with Spain. In the more conservative temper of the 1590s, the godly effort to reconstruct the church was laid by, and the Church of England got its ideological second wind in the writings of Hooker, Bilson, and others. Elizabeth's last parliaments were by no means docile, however, and serious conflict erupted over the festering issues of purveyance and monopolies in 1597 and 1601. The return of peace — by 1601 the war was essentially over — and the advent of a new dynasty, altered the political landscape. James I found himself confronted by a renewed upsurge of godly activism, while Parliament, still determined to press the unfinished business of the previous reign, faced the daunting constitutional challenge of the Union.

In many respects, the peaceful accession of James was a profound relief. For the first time in fifty-six years England had an adult male sovereign, and one with two male heirs already provided. At thirty-seven, James was mature and experienced, yet young enough to offer the stability of a substantial reign, which he would in fact provide. The dynastic transition had been long planned, for in fact if not in name James had been the heir apparent since the execution of Mary. Administrative continuity was provided by Burghley's son, Sir Robert Cecil, who by his father's death in 1598 had won the decade-long struggle with Essex for control of the Council and succeeded to his father's post as Lord Treasurer. The new King's religious credentials were impeccable, and if godly hopes for structural change were soon rebuffed, James' balanced religious policy, including tacit toleration of godly practice, the promotion of a learned ministry, and defense of the faith abroad, ultimately reconciled all but hardened recusants and those who rejected a comprehensive church on principle.

It was otherwise with Parliament. If James found the English church relatively easy to manage after his often stormy relations with the Scottish Kirk, England's estates, as he soon discovered, were jealous of the privileges they supposed theirs by right, intrusive in matters that pertained solely to the discretion of an absolute monarch, and tightfisted with the bounty that he felt a properly grateful nation owed a just sovereign. Some of the difficulty was discursive. James spoke the language of Continental absolutism (and civil law), one to whose accents Englishmen were unaccustomed. As James repeatedly tried to explain to his new subjects, an absolute king was not an arbitrary ruler, but rather one who, though as God's anointed the source and final locus of all authority, bound himself voluntarily to govern by law in all circumstances where the public weal could be advanced by it. The king's powers were absolute in the sense of being inherent, indefeasible, and inseparable from his person, and superior to all authority, including that of courts and councils, derived from it. James insisted that he had no desire to change English customs and institutions, only that he might do so in theory or in case of necessity (for which he would be, of course, the judge).

Such authority might not, at least on the face of it, seem very different from the powers Henry VIII had claimed for his imperial monarchy. Henry, however, had coupled these powers with their exercise in Parliament, and although he had indulged himself in a ruinous cycle of Continental wars at the end of his reign, he had also presided over the most massive transfer of wealth to elite hands since the Conquest.[1] James, in contrast, had come south to England with high expectations of largesse for his impoverished Court and a jaundiced view of Parliament, which, as he would famously tell the Count of Gondomar, was an institution that should never have been tolerated in a monarchy but that he was now obliged to put up with.[2]

James' remark may have been in part defensive; Gondomar, as the first Spanish envoy received in England for decades, was the representative of a kingdom in which the estates had been put firmly in their place. The King's horizon was Continental, and the Continent did not contain any such bodies as the English Parliament, at least in states with a crowned head.[3] James took cognizance of Parliament as part of the political constellation he had to deal with during his long wait for power in Scotland; he remembered it as the engine that had been used to bring about his mother's death. Cecil and later Bacon explained to him the intricacies of dealing with it. He learned to do so on an instrumental level; he even took a certain pedantic satisfaction in lecturing it on its rights and duties. It is fair to say, however, that he never fully understood its role in English public life, and that what he did understand he did not like. This was not a shortcoming in him; he brought with him a unitary conception of kingship as a set of God-ordained powers and functions that applied universally to all monarchical states, local circumstances notwithstanding. James was not, in his own mind, King of Scotland and King of England, but a King of Britain, and though he might be titularly James VI in one realm and James I in the other, he was not only the same person in both but, *in esse*, the same ruler. This was why, political convenience and economic advantage aside, he was so determined upon the Union. And only Parliament stood in his way.

James' view of kingship was not idiosyncratic but typical of Renaissance political theory, which, unlike the English subset, dealt in typologies rather than custom and usage.[4] Continental discourse was of power and obligation, conceived not in reciprocal but absolute terms. Such discourse was not without influence in England. Charles Merbury, in *A Briefe Discovrse of Royall Monarchie*, made the usual Aristotelian distinction between a "common weale" or rule by "a number of good men . . . of reasonable wealth," an aristocracy consisting of "a few of the best, and choiseste persones," and, most preferable of all, hereditary monarchy, the rule of a single person endowed with authority to provide for the common welfare. Such a person was "to haue . . . that Power, which the Greekes call Akpav exousiav: the Latines MAIESTATEM: Th'Italians SIGNORIA: The Frenchmen SOWERAINETE: That is, Power full and perpetuall ouer all his subiectes in general, and ouer euery one in particular. . . . Neither is he countable of such his gouernement, (saving to God, and his Conscience) else not vnto any other." Merbury explicitly rejected the theory of mixed government that ran through Fortescue, Aylmer, and Smith: "some doe maintaine that a Prince ought to be subiect vnto the states and Peares of his Realme . . . An opinion (if it be not well tempered, and conueniently limited) most preiudiciall vnto th'estate of a MONARCHIE: peruerting, and conuerting the same into a meere ARISTO-CRATIE." Titlès of honor and representative institutions could subsist in a monarchy, but only in subordination to the prince. Thus in all "wel ordained kingdomes" the people had "no other than a voice SUPPLICATIVE," the peers "a voice DELIBERATIVE, and the Prince onely a voice DEFINITIVE." England, Merbury concluded in a more conventional, not to say contradictory strain, was such a kingdom: "our Prince is subiect vnto lawes both ciuill, and common, to customes, priuileges, couenantes, and all kinde of promises, So farre forth as they agreable vnto the law of God . . . wherein we neither diminish the libertie of the subiecte. . . . Neither doe we inlarge to much the Power of the Prince." It was perhaps this last sentiment that induced Thomas Norton, who licensed the book, to describe it as "verie commendable, and safely to be reade to the honour of her Maiestie."[5] The thrust of the book, however, was clearly absolutist, and could almost have been made to order for a Jacobean speech.

Merbury's emphasis on the powers of monarchy was unusual for the 1580s, and no comparable public claims for it were to be made in England until James himself ordered that his *The Trew Law of Free Monarchies* be printed for the edification of his new subjects in 1603.[6] It says something for the paucity of the absolutist case in England that the King was obliged to make it himself, a fact that embarrassed the Bishop of Winchester, James Montagu, when he edited the royal *Workes* for the edition of 1616.[7] The divines who might have helped to make such a case in the Whitgift era were too busy defending the established church, and the grounds they advanced to support it—its continuity through long ages and custom—were not such as to readily translate into an aggressive defense of monarchical authority per se.

The rarity of absolutist argument in the latter part of the sixteenth century is unmysterious. Female rule was not conducive to it. As Merbury himself pointed out, if monarchy was the best of all governments, tyranny was the worst,[8] and the character of the tyrant—arbitrary, inconstant, irrational, and lewd—was drawn, as we have seen, from the stock of female vices. That character was vividly on display on the London stage in the 1590s, and not by accident. As the fifty-year era of gynocracy drew to a close, Englishmen meditated as never before on the dangers of unfettered rule.

At the same time, however, rising figures of the late Elizabethan establishment such as Egerton and Bacon looked forward to the coming reign with a sense that the powers of the monarchy needed reaffirmation. To an extent of course this was opportunistic, but Egerton's support of James' reading of the royal prerogative, particularly as applied to the courts, was grounded in his earlier writings. Similarly, Bacon's zealous prosecution of Essex might seem (as it did to contemporaries) the attempt of an ungrateful client to shuck off a fallen patron, without precluding a sobered assessment on his part of the dangers posed to a weakened crown by an appeal to feudal reaction. This kind of bureaucratic support for monarchy—which linked to Burghley's attempt in the "monarchical republic" to compensate for the defects of female rule—did not necessarily imply an absolutist ideology, but it was certainly compatible with one under the right circumstances. Those circumstances appeared with James.

The King's own initial pronouncements, including his fast-track plans for the Union, his claims to the bounty of his subjects, and his assertion of the right to exercise judicial powers in person, were alarming enough. The appearance in 1607 of *The Interpreter*, a legal dictionary by the civilian John Cowell, created a new flashpoint of controversy. Cowell, a client of Archbishop Bancroft's and the Master of Trinity Hall, Cambridge, was a truculent supporter of high church and absolutist views. It was he who, at Bancroft's request, had urged the case that James might make judicial arbitraments, while scoffing at common law authorities such as Bracton and Littleton who held that the king was subject to the law.

Cowell's entry on Parliament in *The Interpreter* was particularly tendentious. It began with a fairly unexceptionable though subtly weighted description of the body:

> In England we vse [the term] for the assembly of the king and the three estates of the Realme, *videlicet*, the Lords Spirituall, the Lords Temporall, and commons, for the debating of maters touching the common wealth, and especially the making and correcting of lawes, which assembly or court is of all other the highest, and of greatest authoritie.

Unlike Burghley, Cowell did not define a parliamentary trinity of King, Lords, and Commons, but affirmed the old distinction between sovereign and subjects, dividing the latter into the traditional categories of clergy, peers, and commoners. This gave pride of place to the bishops, and emphasized the role of the Upper House, which included the two estates preeminent in dignity. At the same time, Cowell drew out the royalist implications of the Henrician notion of the King in Parliament. The king was part of the "assembly" of the estates, yet clearly apart from it as well. This posed the question—fudged by the newfangled trinity of King, Lords, and Commons—as to where ultimate power in the body lay. Cowell met the issue head-on: "Of these two one must needes be true, that either the king is aboue the Parlament, that is, the positiue lawes of his kingdome, or els that he is not an absolute king."

Cowell does not merely tackle the issue, but sharpens it. Statute law is made by the three estates with the consent of the king, but the king, as the source of all law, must be able to set aside such acts at discretion. This is not to be done lightly, but the power to do it is beyond question: "though it be a mercifull policie, and also a politique mercie (not alterable without great perill) to make lawes by the consent of the whole Realme, because no one part shall haue cause to complaine of a partialitie: yet simply to binde the prince to or by these lawes, weare repugnant to the nature and constitution of an absolute monarchy."[9]

Cowell's shrewdness is evident in this description of absolutist legitimacy. The king has a full and sufficient power to make laws, but the wise ruler will take care that it is not perceived as an arbitrary one; hence he invites the consent of the realm, both as an earnest of his good faith ("a mercifull policie") and as a means of forestalling dissent ("a politique mercie"). Such power, though shared, is nowise alienated or diluted, and can be recuperated at will, if not without "perill." Cowell's description is ultimately one of sovereign discretion, for right is wholly on one side, and mere privilege on the other: the king is the only authorizing agent. As in so much of early modern English thought, the underlying trope of this conception is that of the stage. Like the playwright-director, the ruler apportions the seamless text of his will to "characters" — a nobility, a magistracy, a rabble — and assigns these as speaking parts to actors. The actors are participants in the drama at third hand, being neither the authors of their roles nor (except as permitted) of their speech; yet, although the text is theoretically perfect without them, the play is only performed through them, and once in progress is halted only with difficulty and "perill." The ruler without subjects is a soliloquist, but the ruler with subjects cannot merely ventriloquize: he must, in some sense, persuade others to speak.

The speech of subjects nonetheless remains conditional on the will of the ruler. His superiority to those he governs is demonstrated, in the first place, by his immortality. Under the heading of *king*, Cowell notes that the ruler is always supposed to be of full age and authority: "He is taken as not subiect to death, but is a Corporation in himselfe that liueth euer." For this reason his word in all cases is necessarily conclusive, for as it is the original and perpetually authorizing word of the polity, so it must be the final one. Cowell insists, as in his discussion of Parliament, that the king "is aboue the Law by his absolute power," so that the law, too, is a mortal entity in respect of royal sovereignty, and consequently subordinate to it.[10]

Cowell expatiated further on these points in his discussion of the royal prerogative, which he defined as "that especiall power, preeminence, or priuiledge that the King hath in any kinde, ouer and aboue other persons, and aboue the ordinarie course of the common lawe, in the right of his crowne." Cowell did not make the distinction, common to later royalist discourse, between an "absolute" prerogative in the crown which the king might exercise at discretion and which could not be challenged, and an "ordinary" prerogative (essential to the daily exercise of government) which might be disputed by petition or suit.[11] Rather, he defined it as "all that absolute heighth of power" pertaining to kings that was "subiect only to God."[12] The king might limit himself "of his own benignitie" or by the promise to enforce existing laws in his coronation oath, but such concessions were voluntary and revocable. They could not be a condition of his rule, nor could they modify his absolute discretion to "alter or suspend any particular lawe that seemeth hurtfull to the publike estate." Cowell was particularly concerned to defend James against the notion that his office was constitutionally limited: "Now for those regalities which are of the highest nature," he wrote, ". . . there is not one that belonged to the most absolute prince in the world, which doth not also belong to our king, except the custome of the nations do differ (as indeed they doe) that one thing be in the one accompted a regalitie, that in another is none." Custom, in short, could not constrain authority.

Cowell evidently had England's peculiar institution, Parliament, in mind. It was true that the king made laws with the consent of his three estates, but this could not restrain him, for "he may quash any lawe concluded of by them." In sum, then, he said, "I hold it incontroulable that the king of England is an absolute king."[13]

Cowell's views were clearly tailored to fit James' own. What Parliament might have heard patiently from the King's own mouth, however, they could treat quite differently in a subject's. Cowell's book prudently appeared after the end of the 1607 session, but when the House of Commons reconvened in February 1610 John Hoskins, one of the new generation of lawyer-MPs who were to distinguish themselves in the parliamentary wars of the next two decades, pounced on it as an example of the sycophancy that endangered the King's relations with his subjects.[14] With James trawling for subsidies and Lord Treasurer Salisbury hoping to persuade Parliament to put the King's finances on a permanently secure basis, Cowell was a liability. Accordingly, he was sacrificed—the first of many such sacrifices that James and Charles were compelled to make of those who served as lightning rods for absolutism, or otherwise gave offense in the increasingly tense relations between King and Parliament. When a Commons committee of forty came to the Lords to lodge their complaint against Cowell at the end of February, the Court was already primed to capitulate. Attorney General Hobart, the Commons' spokesman, delivered their charge, and the fine line he walked indicated the terms already negotiated. No exception, he said, should be taken between the common and the civil law, which were "brethren," though "the civil the younger brother." This nod to the primacy of the common law rebuked Cowell while providing cover for other civilians. Hobart also protected the uniquely privileged space of university debate: "To dispute of things in *thesi* we disallow not." Cowell's offense was to speak presumptuously of matters on which he was inexpert and which concerned mysteries of state unfit for public discourse. Nonetheless, as he indicated, the Commons would confine their formal complaint to the book rather than its author—suppression, rather than imprisonment, would suffice.[15]

Salisbury managed to include the King as an offended party by noting that the term "Parliament" on which Cowell had cast aspersion included not only both houses but "the head also"—King in Parliament to the rescue in the approved Burghleyan sense in which the crown enjoyed a kind of parity with the other estates in the business of legislation. Speaking a few days later, he gave this a slightly more politic twist. As Cowell's book "toucheth the whole body," the Lord Treasurer averred, "so it toucheth the head." By leaving the term "body" purposively vague (Parliament? the realm? Parliament as the body of the realm?), the King was construed as both of and above the body politic (however interpreted), united with his subjects both in and out of Parliament yet at the same time *rex solus* in his authority and unanswerable to any earthly judgment.[16]

At this point, Salisbury stopped speaking for himself. When he next reported to the Lords, it was to present the King's own response. James himself had interrogated Cowell, concluding:

> That upon the view of the book and the hearing of the party, he thinketh the book in some things too bold with the common law. Likewise, that he doth in some sort mistake the fundamental constitution of the parliament. That in other high points he doth wade more curiously than standeth with the duty of a subject. If he had seen the book afore the parliament, he would have taken order, as well for the suppression of the book, as to prevent the writing of the like.

James had given satisfaction and reassurance, albeit in notably lukewarm terms — that laconic "in some sort" suggested that Cowell had perhaps gotten some things right. No sooner had he offered these palliatives, however, than he insisted on precisely the description Cowell had given of him, for (Salisbury continued) "there was never a king more unwilling to give the least shadow that the world should think he holdeth not and knoweth not himself to be as absolute a monarch as ever was here": the issue was not the "truth" of what Cowell had said of him but "the apprehension." It was all the more important to defend his regality since "a great enemy," the Pope, had "caluminate[d]" it. After thus implicitly chastising the Commons for giving aid and comfort to that enemy, James concluded by offering assurance that he would suppress Cowell's book and "with his own pen declare his mind not to have any purpose to violate the least of the fundamental law of England."[17]

James was not content to express himself on the nature of monarchy at second hand, and on March 21, 1610, he summoned the two houses to Whitehall to deliver the famous address, of which we have previously taken note, in which he declared "The State of Monarchie" to be "the supremest thing vpon earth" and kings themselves to be "not onely GODS Lieutenants vpon earth" but gods themselves with respect to their subjects, over whom they had the power "of life, and of death." Having far exceeded anything Cowell had had to say, he then applied his customary unguents, distinguishing between what a king might do "in the height of his power" — was the echo of Cowell's phrase merely an accident? — and how he would ordinarily govern in "a Setled state" having "fundamentall Lawes" and established customs.[18]

The King dismissed Cowell himself as a flatterer, for he needed no advice about his powers and had already given his subjects sufficient instruction about them. He added the warning that it was "Sedition" to debate the limits of royal authority. *The Interpreter* was suppressed, as promised, but not disavowed.

James did not forbid all discussions of his authority in his proclamation banning Cowell's book, but confined himself to castigating private individuals who searched into matters beyond their ken: "men in these our dayes doe not spare to wade in all the deepest mysteries that belong to the persons of State or Kings or Princes, that are gods upon Earth. . . . Whereupon it cannot otherwise fall out, but that when men goe out of their element, and meddle with things above their capacitie: themselves shall not only goe astray, but will mislead also divers others." Cowell was thus classed with those who had erred through presumption rather than those who attempted to deliberately mislead:

> he hath fallen in many things to mistake and deceive himselfe: yea, in some poynts very derogatory to the supreme power of this Crowne: In other cases mistaking the true state of the Parliament of this Kingdome, and the fundamentall Constitutions and priviledges thereof: And in some other points speaking unreverently of the Common Law of England, and of the works of some of the most famous and ancient Judges thereof: it being a thing utterly unlawful to any Subject, to speak or write against that lawe under which he liveth, and which we are sworne and resolved to maintaine."[19]

James had carefully enumerated—without actually specifying—the matters at which the Commons had taken offense; he had concluded that in these broad terms Cowell had erred without intending to deceive; he had dissociated him from his patron, Archbishop Bancroft, and distinguished between "persons of State" who might speak for the crown in their institutional capacities and private individuals who might not. It was a calculated performance that offered formal satisfaction but gave little away. Cowell had escaped with a rebuke, far less than John Hayward had paid for writing about the remote days of Henry IV and certainly less than the Elizabethan pamphleteer John Stubbes, whose tract on the Queen's marital status had cost him his right hand. Cowell himself died in 1611, predeceased by Bancroft, who was bruised politically by the episode, as he was to be later in the same year in the battle over prohibitions. Some saw Coke's hand in both matters; the common law, as James had already learned to appreciate, had as resolute a champion as did "free" monarchy.

In political terms, the Cowell affair was a standoff. James had adroitly turned an awkward confrontation into a reaffirmation of his power. The Commons had rebuffed a challenge to their authority (a debate in the Lords, potentially even more damaging, was forestalled by the crown's swift retreat in the Upper House), and had compelled the King to acknowledge the primacy of the common law. If James had narrowed the scope of permissible discourse by declaring discussions of the royal arcana off limits, he had thereby set implicit limits on his own defenders as well. When a short dialogue expounding the duties of subjects to their divinely appointed sovereign, *God and King*, was published in 1615, it was not through the patronage of a surrogate but at the King's express command, and at a time when no Parliament was sitting.

The King did, however, have a forum through which divine right authority was regularly inculcated: the church. Generations had already been indoctrinated in the proper respect due higher powers through the Homily on Obedience, which, first issued in 1547, constituted the most prescriptive statement of a divinely ordained, hierarchical society.[20] This text, revised by Elizabeth, remained unamended under James, but clerics eager for advancement understood the gloss he preferred in characterizing the sacred derivation of monarchy and the duties entailed thereby for the subject. When Samuel Harsnett, Bishop of Chichester, declared that subjects owed tribute to their sovereigns in a sermon at Whitehall in March 1610—a point also advanced by Cowell—the Commons took umbrage. James defused the issue by distinguishing between his subjects' responsibility "in *Abstracto*" and their voluntary discharge of it in Parliament, but it was remembered in the debate over the Great Contract in November by the MP Richard Martin, who adverted to the distinction apparently made by Harsnett between "giving" and "rendering," and grumbled that "the highway to get into a double benefice or to a higher dignity is to tread upon the neck of the common law."[21]

The Apology and Satisfaction

The Commons had already staked out their own ground in June 1604 when, responding to a speech by James (no longer extant) they produced a draft statement of their "ancient and undoubted privileges," the famous Apology and Satisfaction. We can infer the contents of the King's speech, or at least those which caused "grief" in the House, from the subjects particularly in dispute that spring. They included a contested election in Buckinghamshire in which a courtier, Sir John Fortescue, had been returned over the victor at the polls, Sir Francis Goodwin, and grievances about wardship, the royal control over the estates of minors, and purveyance, the levies of goods and services exacted on the King's progresses. These latter, together with complaints about grants of monopoly that had nearly derailed Elizabeth's last parliament in 1601, had been a major theme of recent sessions. All involved aspects of the prerogative, but also the subject's property. All were, directly or indirectly, sources of nonparliamentary revenue.

The Bucks County election case touched the privileges of the Commons most closely. The right to assure proper certification of its members was notionally critical to the House as the constituted body of the realm. Logically it was prior to those rights of free speech and institutional self-discipline for which Peter Wentworth had fought, because such rights, and indeed parliamentary consent itself, were meaningless without the independent judgment of freely chosen representatives. In reality, borough (as opposed to shire) selection was by popular poll of freeholders in only a minority of cases. The crown directed or influenced many nominations, and peers—often councillors—controlled many more. Some town corporations restricted the franchise to themselves. The fact of the matter was that the House of Commons was a body of the propertied elite, composed largely by brokering arrangements that reflected the relative distribution of power among its constituent parts with the haphazard and functionally symbolic participation of selected members of the lower orders: not far unlike the legislative bodies of the formally democratic states of today. Genuine contests could arise from local competition or animosity among the gentry, which could give shire freeholders or borough freemen the casting vote. This did not, however, affect the essential nature of the system, though the size of the electorate and the number of contested elections was rising during our period.

The two major studies of parliamentary recruitment in the early seventeenth century, Derek Hirst's *The Representative of the People?* and Mark Kishlansky's *Parliamentary Selection*, take opposed but not irreconcilable positions on the subject, with Hirst stressing conflict and Kishlansky consensus within the system.[22] Kishlansky's term "selection" does seem appropriate to a process in which the presentation and ratification of candidates was typically, though not certainly, a foregone conclusion. The participation of nonelite elements was not merely token, however, but crucial to the Commons' claim not merely to represent but to *be* the general commons, to personate the realm as a whole. It thus had a key function in legitimating the Commons' self-representation as the prime spokesman of the commonwealth, an image (and the powers associated with it) that it was ultimately to contest with that of the crown.

The Bucks County case, coming on the heels of several other contested returns in late Elizabethan parliaments, involved stiff confrontations with the King, with Chancery, which certified the sheriffs' election writs and thereby exercised the function the Commons claimed as their own, and with the Lords, who unadvisedly yielded to royal pressure and attempted to intervene in the dispute. In the end the Commons seated Goodwin, although the case was neither as unambiguous as Whig scholarship would later have it (local and factional rivalry played the dominant role, rather than a heavy-handed crown attempt to seat a courtier over a commonwealthman), nor the victory as clear-cut (similar disputes continued to be referred to Chancery and other administrative bodies). Nonetheless, the Commons had its way in its first test case with King James, and it would hereafter refer all contested elections to its Committee of Privileges.[23] It also affirmed the larger point that, though its collective writ of summons might come from the King, its actual constitution came from the realm, and that once convened and sworn to the realm's duty, it was the sole and proper judge of the electoral acts that had brought it into being. This sense of institutional autonomy was not new—it was implicit in the very process of legislation, which required the consent of three separate and independent parts—but it was progressively deepened by the development of ever-more precisely articulated me-thods for transacting parliamentary business, including the proliferation of standing committees and the refinement of statutory procedure itself, with its elaborate undergirding of committee work and its three formal readings before the body of each house. It was also to be sharpened by its recurrent jars with the crown over questions increasingly framed in terms of "privilege."[24]

The complaints over wardship and purveyance involved another large issue, the subject's property. These twin grievances had festered under Elizabeth, a notoriously frugal monarch; they took on added urgency with the accession of a spendthrift one in James, who had already, in *The Trew Law of Free Monarchies*, affirmed his right to maintenance at the realm's expense.[25] Wardship and purveyance might seem far afield from a dispute about a shire election, but the authors of the Apology saw them as fundamentally interconnected. They linked, as an indissoluble whole, "the rights and liberties of your subjects of England, and the privileges of this House."[26] The source of this linkage was "inheritance," that is, the secure passage from generation to generation of that in which inalienable possession was to be enjoyed; in a word, property. The issue of wardship was central to such a claim of possession, since it was nothing less than a matter of the "original right in disposing of our children" (229), upon which all society since Adam had been founded. The profit (not to say spoliation) that the crown reaped from the management of wards' estates was placed beside "the great grievance and damage of the subject" caused by the denial of fundamental right, and even the "great contempt and reproach of our nation in foreign countries" for a practice that not only undermined English law but, by inference, the law of nations itself.[27]

The Apology was no less direct on the subject of purveyance: "a general, extreme, unjust, and crying oppression is in cart-takers and purveyors," it declared, "who have rummaged and ransacked since your Majesty's coming-in far more than under any of your royal predecessors" (227). Here, too, the issue was the secure possession of property, the threat to which by arbitrary seizure was regarded as of greater ultimate consequence than the actual depredations themselves. The purveyors' claim to long usage in their traffic—a property claim in its own right—was otiose, the Apology contended, since "They have no prescription, no custom to plead; for there hath not been any Parliament wherein complaint hath not been made and claim of our rights, which doth interrupt [i.e., supersede] prescription." The purveyors' complaint went not to the fact that Parliament wanted to regulate their profession but that it proposed to eliminate it altogether by compounding with the King for the value of the services and revenue derived from their activities. A similar offer had been made to induce James to renounce control of wardship, but in that case no class of livelihood had been affected. The argument of the Apology was thus that the long custom of exacting purveyance had not created a legitimate interest on the part of purveyors because it had been continually contested in Parliament and therefore had never been made good in law. If the right of the subject to be secure from arbitrary seizure was valid, then no right could exist to effect such seizures. The King's own right to avail himself of his subjects' goods while on the road was neither directly questioned nor affirmed. The problem was framed simply in terms of the method of requisition, which fell under the heading of those practices the law called "inconvenient." The solution offered — at first by the crown itself — was to convert the goods so secured into a regular and stipulated revenue. A similar proposal was made with regard to wardship.[28]

The authors of the Apology declared themselves willing to accept such a settlement, but only after recasting it in terms of the ancient formula by which the gracious removal of a grievance was accompanied by a voluntary grant of supply. This was accomplished in a remarkably tortuous passage. The King's councillors had suggested

> a demand of a perpetual yearly revenue in lieu of the taking away of those oppressions [of wardship and purveyance]; unto which composition neither know we well how to yield, being only for justice and due right, which is unsaleable. Neither yet durst we impose it by law upon the people without first acquainting them and having their consents unto it. But if your Majesty might be pleased in your gracious favor to treat of composition with us for some grievance which is by law and just, how ready we should be to take that occasion and colour to supply your Majesty's desire concerning these also which we hold for unjust, should appear, we nothing doubt, to your Majesty's full satisfaction. (228)

The Commons could not, the authors of the Apology said, bargain for the people's right, nor "impose" a settlement on them by statute without first consulting them: as clear a statement of the ideological nexus between electors and elected as one could wish. If, however, James would redress a grievance that had some presumed foundation in law — presumed, at least, by the crown — then the Commons would respond to the removal of practices which they deemed "unjust" by a concrete expression of gratitude that addressed the material interests at stake. In this way, neither side would have to surrender its interpretation of the law, and the fiction that acts of grace and the grants of supply were wholly distinct and voluntary could be maintained. In view of James' oft-repeated complaints that the Commons were excessively "merchantlike" in their dealings with him, this formula seems remarkably sensitive to the need to preserve the appearance that the king's grace and the subject's duty were reciprocal acts of "love" related only by a shared commitment to the general welfare and the maintenance of the commonwealth.[29]

The Apology was much more direct in affirming the inherent rights and privileges of Parliament, which, it stated, was the very right of the subject itself:

The rights and liberties of the Commons of England consisteth chiefly in these three things:

First, That the shires, cities, and boroughs of England, by representation to be present, have free choice of such persons as they shall put in trust to represent them.

Secondly, That the persons chosen, during the time of the Parliament as also of their access and recess, be free from restraint, arrest, and imprisonment.

Thirdly, That in Parliament they may speak freely their consciences without check and controlment, doing the same with due reverence to the Sovereign Court of Parliament, that is, to your Majesty and both the Houses, who all in this case make but one body politic whereof your Highness is the Head. (223–224)

These justly famous words present a quite striking claim. Not only are the rights and privileges of the House of Commons inseparable from those of "the Commons of England" and enjoyed on the same basis, but the first, most essential, and most defining right of Englishmen is to be freely represented in Parliament. This right precedes the right to hold or convey real property, to be secure against arbitrary fine or imprisonment, to be accorded due process, or any other right held to be fundamental; it is the right of rights, the right that guarantees all others. From it the privileges of the House of Commons necessarily follow, to wit, the freedom of its members from "restraint, arrest, and imprisonment," and their freedom to speak "without check or controlment." These privileges are not simply the possession of individual members or of the House as a whole, but of the realm. To deny this is "derogatory in the highest degree to the true dignity, liberty, and authority of your Majesty's High Court of Parliament, *and consequently to the rights of all your Majesty's said subjects and the whole body of this your kingdom*" (221; emphasis added). It is, in short, the greatest offense to the commonwealth that can be offered, an offense that shakes its very foundation.

Some of these words had been spoken before by Peter Wentworth; some could be inferred from the description of Parliament by Sir Thomas Smith and others. As a whole, however, their assertion was startling. Parliament, they said, was the property and possession of "the Commons of England," to whom the "rights of [its] liberties" belonged. Who were "the Commons of England"? The phrase occurs nowhere else in the Apology. When the authors wished to indicate the House of Commons, they referred to "our House of Commons" or "we your poor Commons" or "your Commons in Parliament" or "the Commons" *tout court*. "The Commons of England" could thus designate only the commonwealth itself, the inhabitants of "the shires, cities, and boroughs of England" who, in the immediately subtended clause, were representatively present in Parliament, and had "free choice of such persons as they shall put in trust to represent them." The institution of Parliament, in short, belonged to the people of England. It was not, as Conrad Russell would have it, "an occasional performance," but a permanent possession. It was a possession so fundamental to the commonwealth that the latter could scarcely be imagined without it, since one of the essential attributes of "the Commons of England" was its ability to embody itself in Parliament, to come together by representation in a forum in which its grievances could be aired and remedied, its laws reviewed and amended, and its bounty freely offered.

The rights of the Commons of Parliament were, therefore, part and parcel of the rights of the Commons of England, their "right and due inheritance, no less than our very lands and goods" (221). They could not be "withheld . . . denied, or impaired, but with apparent wrong to the whole state of the realm." On one level, such an assertion did nothing more than state the obvious. The members of the Commons could not claim the privileges they asserted on behalf of themselves as individuals. They could not demand other than as Parliament men that ordinary judgments on debts or warrants against their servants not be executed against them. Nor could they claim, as mere subjects, the right to debate matters of church and state "without check and controlment" other than by themselves, or to share in the sovereign capacity of lawmaking, or freely to relieve the king's wants. These privileges were uniquely reserved to them in their capacity as representatives of the Commons of England, and pertained to them solely in the discharge of that service.

To say that the privileges of the House pertained to its public function was one thing, however; to say that they derived from the Commons of England was another. The formal request made of the king at the beginning of each Parliament for the enjoyment of privilege was, the Apology declared, "an act only of manners" which "doth weaken our right no more than suing to the King for our lands by petition" (ibid.). The king "granted" these privileges because he could not withhold them. They were no property of his, but of his subjects.

To be sure, individual members of the House of Commons had laid claim to their privileges as an institutional right before, and the House had frequently complained of their violation. Never, however, had those privileges been linked so firmly and indissolubly to the property rights of Englishmen. They were not personal, or even corporate, but collective. As such, moreover, they were unique. All other rights in England were specific to individuals, franchises, or corporations. They were rights to exercise certain functions or to conduct certain business or to be exempt from certain burdens or penalties. Even when they were generally shared and assumed, as for example the rights guaranteed in Magna Carta, they pertained severally to individuals, rather than inhering in the community. They were the possession of Englishmen, not of England.

The rights of Parliament alone were different. They did not derive from the body of the commonwealth, but were coextensive with it. If there was an England, there was a Parliament, because the first and most distinguishing characteristic of Englishmen was their right to personate themselves in such a body. It was for this reason, as the Apology makes clear for us, that it was so often claimed that Parliament was a body time out of mind, whose origins were not only untraceable but unthinkable, in the same way that it was absurd to think of a beginning to the people of England. Any attempt to historicize it, as royalist spokesmen (and scholars such as Selden) attempted to do, was on this reading fundamentally to misrepresent it. Like custom itself, it was immemorial not because of the accidental loss of a founding record, but because no such record was in principle recoverable. For this reason, too, the privileges of Parliament could not be said to derive from the commonwealth (as opposed, for example, to proceeding from the king). There was no such rescission, because there was no before from which such an after could have proceeded.

The authors of the Apology did not offer these propositions as a new theory, but as common sense entailed by the nature of a parliament. As J. H. Hexter pointed out in a neglected article, the purpose of the Apology was to state the obvious and incontestable, not the novel and contentious.[30] The committee that framed it was heavily staffed with lawyers and old Parliament hands, including Sir Francis Bacon. It was also very large, consisting of at least seventy-two members: nearly a fifth of the House, and perhaps a half to a third of the number that might be ordinarily present on any given day.[31] We do not know how many actually attended the Committee's meetings, nor who or how many participated in the actual composition of the Apology. We don't know, either, how many among the Committee may have dissented from its conclusions, in part or as a whole. We do know that there was a vigorous and perhaps tumultuous debate when the full House considered the Apology on June 20, 1604, and that it was recommitted.[32] When James prorogued Parliament on July 7 the draft still remained in the Committee, and was rendered moot.

The fact that the Apology was never formally adopted by the House was, for Elton, tantamount to a rejection of it, and Wallace Notestein observed that the text "was such a mélange that it may have pleased neither those who upheld the prerogative nor those who watched over the privileges of Parliament."[33] But of course the Apology did not reemerge from the Committee because James did not permit it to; and if a summer prorogation was in any case due, the fact that it would prevent the most far-reaching statement of privilege ever considered by a House of Commons from returning to the floor would not have been averse to the King.

That the Apology never won the formal endorsement of the House does not diminish its great and justly celebrated constitutional significance. *Pace* Elton, a recommitment is not a rejection. Had the Petition of Right been interrupted during its tortuous two-month gestation in 1628 by a prorogation, would we be justified in saying that the House of Commons had decided after all to make no defense of the right of the subject? We cannot know how the House would have proceeded with the Apology had it been given a further opportunity to deliberate on it, but it seems highly unlikely that it would have made no statement at all. The Committee for the Apology was charged with reviewing, expounding, and justifying the Commons' course of conduct to the King over a more than three-month period. It was, as its original sponsor, Sir Thomas Ridgeway of Devon, propounded it, to be "a Survey of the Proceedings of the House."[34] This is why it was, in Notestein's phrase, a "mélange"; it was meant to be compendious. It was the Committee itself that decided, in the course of producing this Survey, that it would not suffice to write a narrative of events with some contextual explanation, but that it was necessary to express to the new sovereign why the House of Commons had been compelled to act as it did not merely by particular issues and circumstances but by the very nature of a Parliament, and how that nature could not be expressed except in terms of its indubitable and intrinsic privileges.

However the draft Apology might ultimately have been altered, it seems unlikely, then, that the argument of its original authors would have been rejected, namely that the Commons' proceedings could not be expounded without reference to their privileges. It seems even more unlikely that the House would have abandoned the idea of justifying itself to the King entirely, and have simply jettisoned a five thousand word document on which the labor of the best heads in the body had been expended. It should also be remembered that the full House on any given day would not have been more than two or three times the size of the Committee itself, so that a critical mass of votes no less than of argument would have been favorably disposed in the general debate. None of this can be guaranteed, of course; nor need it be. Let us assume that the House would actually have rejected the Apology as a statement of its case, and decided, for one reason or another, not to make that case at all. We would still have in the original draft a re-markably cogent and eloquent statement of the privilege of Parliament and its indissoluble connection to the nation by a not inconsiderable portion of its membership, a statement which by its collective nature alone would have been clear evidence of institutional self-consciousness and concern beyond the isolated statements of a Wentworth or a Throckmorton.

We know more, however. We know that the Apology survived and circu-lated in the form the Committee had left it. We know that at another critical point in the Commons' defense of their liberties, in 1621, the House referred back to it, and that Sir Robert Phelips of Somerset, who had not been a member in 1604, was able to quote it from memory as a document whose ex-istence and argument was clearly known and accepted, at least within the House itself. Sir Edward Coke, who had served in 1604, recalled it as having not only been adopted by the House but presented to the King, an instance of creative (but not deliberate) misremembering. If the Apology had not been adopted in 1604, it clearly expressed the sense of the House in 1621, and of succeeding Stuart parliaments both before and after the Civil War—the Speaker of the Exclusion Parliaments of 1680 and 1681, Sir William Wil-liams, possessed a manuscript copy.[35]

At a minimum, then, we may say that the Apology represented the con-sidered view of a goodly number of the most active and influential members of the House of Commons in 1604, and that seventeen years later it was seen as a fundamental statement of the liberties of the subject in Parliament. If it had not been adopted in 1604, it certainly had been by 1621. The House then restated, by means of Protestation, the Apology's assertion that "the liberties, franchises, privileges, and jurisdictions of Parliament are the ancient and undoubted birthright and inheritance of the subjects of England," and that "every member of the said House [of Parliament] hath . . . freedom from all impeachment, imprisonment, and other molestation (other than by censure of the House itself) for or concerning any speaking, reasoning, or declaring of any matter or matters touching the Parliament or Parliament-business."[36]

With the Protestation, the full House of Commons affirmed what the Committee "to take a Survey of all the Acts and Proceedings of the House . . . and to advise of such Form of Satisfaction to be offered to his Majesty" had asserted in 1604, namely that the privileges of Parliament were the inalien-able possession of the subject. They belonged to him not merely as, in the words of the Apology, his "very lands and goods" did, but in the stronger sense of being a shared and indissoluble part of "the rights and liberties of the whole Commons of [the] realm of England."[37] It was, as the Protestation declared, a *collective* birthright, immemorial and unchallengeable. It was also a birthright that could only be meaningfully enjoyed by being regularly exercised. The privileges of Parliament entailed the calling of parliaments at reasonably frequent intervals and permitting them sufficient time to accomplish their work. The summoning, proroguing, and dissolving of parliaments was at the discretion of the crown, but, like all other aspects of the prerogative, it was a power exercised on behalf of the general welfare. It did not imply the right to call parliaments frivolously or to dissolve them peremptorily. Still less did it imply the right not to call them at all.

The great nineteenth-century scholar Samuel Rawson Gardiner declared that "To understand the Apology is to understand the causes and success of the English Revolution." This is a proposition hardly anyone would accept nowadays without serious qualification, particularly as the very terms *cause*, *success*, and *English Revolution* are themselves so much in dispute.[38] It does not, however, deserve Geoffrey Elton's sneering response: "Here is the full mystical concept: an identifiable single body, 'the Commons', preserving that unity for eighty-four years [i.e., through 1688] on a stand taken from the first."[39] If there was any mysticism in the notion of a House of Commons that persisted as a permanent corporate body defined by a set of "liberties, franchises, privileges, and jurisdictions" that belonged to the body politic as well, it was in the minds of the knights and burgesses of the Commons themselves. They declared it, maintained it, and vindicated it. They did not think of it as mystifying, reifying, or otherwise puffing up themselves, nor as rashly appropriating "Peter Westworth's [sic] extreme doctrine of free speech,"[40] but as stating the obvious. If they had not stated it before, it was perhaps because it had not seemed politic or necessary. Confronted by a foreign king who wished to rush them pell-mell into a transnational union that threatened their laws and institutions and who challenged what they regarded as their intrinsic privileges as Parliament men, they decided to put those privileges on record. They got no further than a committee draft in 1604, but they ratified the essentials of that draft in 1621, and they did not prescind from them. As William Noy, a future Attorney General but in 1621 one of the lawyer MPs in the House, expressed it simply, "we are out of Doubt of the Right of our Privileges."[41]

James I was equally out of doubt, however, about the dependence and subordination of Parliament to royal authority, as of all other institutions in an absolute monarchy. Parliament, he declared to the two houses in 1605:

> is nothing else but the Kings great Councell, which the King doth assemble either vpon occasion of interpreting, or abrogating old Lawes, or making of new, according as ill maners shall deserue, or for the publike punishment of notorious evill doers, or the praise and reward of the vertuous and well deseruers. . . . As to the thing it selfe, It is composed of a Head and a Body:

The Head is the King, the Body are the members of the Parliament. . . . And as to the end for which the Parliament is ordeined, being only for the aduancement of Gods glory, and for the establishment and wealth of the King and his people . . . they are here as sworne Councellours to their King, to giue their best aduise for the furtherance of his Seruice, and the florishing Weale of his Estate.[42]

This was very clear. Parliament was the king's Great Council, called to do him such service as he might require. He bore exactly the same relation to it as he did to the rest of his subjects in general, that is, of a head to a body. The body, as he noted, was divided into an upper house consisting of temporal lords who were "heritable Councellors" and spiritual ones who were "Life Renters," and a lower house composed of members "seruing onely" for particular parliaments. This division was simply internal; it did not create two separate bodies, still less two entities against or within which the king constituted a coordinate third. The king was united with and perpetually present in Parliament in the same way that the natural head and body were knit together as an organic whole, but he was not in any sense contained (still less constrained) by it.

Whether or not James intended a riposte to the Apology, his description of the Commons' membership as the mayflies of a parliamentary day in contrast to the permanent tenure of the Lords was a shrewd hit. In contrast, too, to the Commons' presentation of themselves as faithful representatives of a commonwealth with whom their interests were identical and their relations transparent, he warned them against expressing mere "priuate conceipts" rather than the legitimate grievances of the commonwealth, or so extenuating the latter as to bring government itself into disrepute. They were not, in other words, to "make shew of the quicknesse of their wits here, either in taunting, scoffing, or detracting the Prince or State in any point, or yet in breaking iests vpon their fellowes, for which the Ordinaries or Ale-houses are fitter places." They were to remember, in short, that they were not university undergraduates but members of the King's Great Council.[43]

No doubt some of those already familiar with the notoriously prolix address of their king would have had some difficulty repressing an at least inward protest at these strictures. Nonetheless, the point James tirelessly hammered home was that the members of the Commons—unlike the lords and bishops, who could look on with amusement as their colleagues of the Lower House squirmed at their reproach—were little men come to a great place, and should remember to comport themselves accordingly. From such a standpoint, it was sheer impertinence for the Commons to lay claim to privileges independent of their sovereign, much less to assert that their traditional request for them was merely "an act of manners." No other councillor, not the greatest lord in the land, could speak without being held directly accountable for his tongue, or broach a subject the king had forbidden him. The members of the Commons had a special *duty* to speak the grievances of the commonwealth honestly and forthrightly, and for this reason the *privilege* of free speech was granted them; but to claim that the duty entailed the privilege, and that this in turn entitled the Commons to discuss any matter that struck their fancy, was to make councillors kings: manifestly, an absurd conclusion. It was true, too, that judges of the bench ordinarily had wide latitude in choosing cases, pursuing legal issues, and declaring opinions, and that Parliament was a court. The House of Commons was not in itself such a court, however, as the Apology asserted but James insistently denied, that is, a court of record whose orders and pronouncements had the force of law. Only by statute did Parliament proclaim law, and statutes were petitions given life by the king's assent. Nor, though the Commons were charged with searching out evildoers, could they exercise a court's power to punish them, but must remand them to the king's justice instead.

James, like the Commons, did not regard his views as novel or exceptional. Nor were they; there was little if anything that his Tudor predecessors would have dissented from in them. Elizabeth had never subscribed to Burghley's "monarchical republic" or to his scheme for a royal interregnum, although she no less than her grandfather Henry VII and her half sister Mary had appreciated the use of Parliament in legitimating her rule. By the 1590s her servants had swung back to a more assertively absolutist and imperial conception of the crown. They included men such as Ellesmere and Bacon, who were to play key roles in the Jacobean Court. No doubt these men helped, if not to mold James' views, then certainly to adapt them to the English situation. Factually, moreover, their case was the better grounded. Parliament, as historians versed in new Continental standards of scholarship were beginning to make clear, was neither immemorial nor immutable, but historically based and evolving.[44] The Commons' request for free speech, for example, dated no further back than the speakership of Sir Thomas More in 1523.[45] If they had enjoyed the explicit and intrinsic right of free speech prior to that, why had they then begun to request what they already possessed? Was it merely an access of "manners"?

Such questions increasingly led the Commons back to the Parliament rolls lodged in the Tower of London in search of precedents to support their claims. Sometimes they found or fudged them; sometimes they did not, as in the embarrassing case of Edward Floyd, a Catholic barrister whom the Commons sought to punish for defaming Elizabeth of Bohemia in 1621, only to find no record to support their judicial authority.[46] The Commons' attempt to validate and exert the powers and privileges claimed in the Apology, which continued to the end of the 1620s and set the stage for a revolutionary assumption of sovereignty in the 1640s, was described by Wallace

Notestein in a resonant but somewhat unfortunate phrase as the "winning of the initiative."[47] Notestein put his finger on a real event, but, reading backwards from the Civil War and through the lens of Whig historiography, that very able scholar mistook its tenor. The Apology had complained that "The prerogatives of princes may easily and do daily grow; the privileges of the subject are for the most part at an everlasting stand." This statement, which became one of the tag lines of the parliamentary leadership in the 1620s,[48] makes two distinct assertions: that princes' prerogatives are elastic, and that subjects' privileges are inelastic. The tendency for the former is to grow; the condition of the latter is that, generally speaking, they cannot do so. The implication is that the growth of prerogative is necessarily at the expense of privilege, which, while it cannot expand, is readily contracted. The posture of those who would protect privilege is, therefore, necessarily defensive. To 'win' an 'initiative' would be, contrariwise, to contend for an objective in principle equally elastic for both sides.

This point becomes clearer when we consider the full passage in which our quotation is embedded:

> What cause we your poor Commons have to watch over our privileges is manifest in itself to all men. The prerogatives of princes may easily and do daily grow; the privileges of the subject are for the most part at an everlasting stand. They may be by good providence and care preserved, but being once lost are not recovered but with much disquiet. If good kings were immortal as well as kingdoms, to strive so for privilege were but vanity perhaps and folly; but seeing the same God who in his great mercy hath given us a wise King and religious doth also sometimes permit hypocrites and tyrants in his displeasure and for the sins of the people, from hence hath the desire of rights, liberties, and privileges, both for nobles and commons, had its just original, by which an harmonical and stable State is framed, each member under the Head enjoying that right and performing that duty which for the honour of the Head and happiness of the whole is requisite.[49]

Privilege was thus the stay against tyranny. This was as close as the Commons of our period were to come in suggesting a theory of origins for the exercise of popular and parliamentary rights. Rights were still implicitly conceived as inherent in the people and thus in their representatives, but called forth under particular circumstances. In the time of wicked rulers they were a bulwark; under just ones, they provided a balance.

The awkwardness the Apology's authors felt about grounding privilege in the historical continuum is evident here. Were good kings as immortal as their commonwealths — that is, as immutably and transhistorically constituted — privileges might be superfluous, since grievances, presumably, would be swiftly curbed. In the actual world, however, they were necessary to preserve "an harmonical and stable State" even in the best of times, and, inferentially, to restore one when it was absent. A theory of resistance was embedded here, but well concealed in the pieties about evil rulers sent to punish the people for their "sins." The conventional doctrine of the tyrant-as-scourge was that the people should offer no more than passive resis-tance—prayers, tears, sighs, and at most noncompliance with orders that violated law and conscience—because their suffering was the will of God and their patience in bearing it his required penance. It was not clear how this experience could be the basis for a claim of privilege, let alone the "just original" of it. Were the Apology's authors suggesting that active resistance against a tyrant was justified, or that a preemptive exercise of rights might forestall one? The text is ambiguous on the point, perhaps deliberately. What is clear is that the authors construed privilege in defensive terms. It grew out of danger, and remained embattled. If it was ideally compatible with pre-rogative, the balance was neither easily struck nor readily maintained. Royal power, on the other hand, was inherently expansive: Tudor sovereigns had not idly proclaimed the crown imperial, and a century that had seen the in-corporation of a national church, the absorption of Wales, the pacification of Ireland, and the reduction of a once fiercely independent baronage to a do-mesticated service nobility, had no need to further demonstrate the tendency to monarchical aggrandizement. Faced, moreover, with a seemingly even more dynamic and aggressive dynastic successor, it was no hyperbole to suggest that the prerogative of princes was daily growing: it seemed the bar-est statement of fact.

In an ideally static world—the world of immemorial custom—any altera-tion of established harmony was a breach of the perfected wisdom of the ages and ultimately of divine order itself. That the privileges of the subject were at a stand was just as it should be; they were neither more nor less than what the constitutional balance required. The problem was rather that the prerogatives of princes had exceeded their bounds and were daily exceeding them further. The implication was that they should be cut back down to size. This was a gage thrown at the feet of King James, for whom monarchy, as the source of all civil law and authority, was bounded only by the relented will of the prince. Perhaps it was that above all that persuaded the Commons to send the Apology back to its committee; it was, at any rate, the one that stuck most in the memory of succeeding parliaments as the statement of the case. James would surely have heard it at some point or other: it is hard to imagine that the committee draft did not reach him. The afterlife it enjoyed was arguably even greater than if it had been embodied in a document for-mally approved and presented to him, and hence subject to rebuttal (or, more likely, scathing rejection). It persisted as an echo in the rafters; it be-came at last an accepted wisdom.

The King, the Common Law, and the Ancient Constitution:
The Debates of 1610 and the Petition of Right

Because both James and the Commons started from the shared premise that the proper order of things had been fixed from the beginning, both had a vested interest in defining the original 'scene' of the polity. For James, monarchy was the institution from which all else derived; for the Commons, the commonwealth was grounded in a primordial act of self-recognition by which the people saw themselves as a political entity. Since the efficient causes of this creation scene were veiled (had the monarchy originated in conquest, appeal, or consent? had the people assembled as a whole or in part, spontaneously or at the call of elders?), the first glimpse of the polity would only appear in the form of a settled custom presumed to reflect a basic, antecedent body of rules. This latter was referred to as the ancient constitution or fundamental law of the realm.[50]

The battle over the ancient constitution was joined in Parliament over the course of a wide-ranging series of debates in the spring and summer of 1610 that began, as so many Jacobean wrangles did, with a royal speech. James had unilaterally issued a new Book of Rates for customs duties or impositions two years earlier, having cleared the ground with a decision in the King's Bench that obligingly declared such valuations to be within his discretion.[51] When the Commons objected, he offered, as was his wont, a rebuke, a half concession, and a further assertion of authority. "[T]o dispute what I may do," he told them, ". . . seeing the judges have determined, I will not have you call my prerogative in question." As a gesture of goodwill he would refer any future raise in rates to Parliament, but he would not "tie my prerogative in point of glory" or bind his successors, for "Kings elective as well as successive have ever had power to lay impositions," and, come to that, "a king may have subsidies without parliaments . . . [for] if the king want, he must have it from his subjects for to support his estate and place."[52]

The Commons' response was predictable, and, at this point, well-trodden: "This speeche was so distastfull in some parts thearof to the Howse, as that, the next morning after, they entred into debate thearof, and made choyse of a Committee to devise upon some course to be taken to inform His Majesty how much the liberties of the subjects and the privileges of the parliament was impeached by his inhibition to debate his prerogative."[53] The Committee met at once and, "after large and temperate debate, there being a long and deep silence between every speech," determined to approach James with a Petition of Right declarative of Parliament's rights and privileges. Before that occurred, on July 7, an extraordinary speech by Thomas Hedley, member for Huntington, seconded by those of Nicholas Fuller, James Whitelocke, and others, provided clear linkage between the liberty of the subject, the privilege of Parliament, and the ancient and immemorial constitution of England.

Hedley, speaking in committee on June 28,[54] affirmed "that the parliament hath power over all arts, sciences, mysteries, and professions, practiced in the commonwealth" (172). That included the profession of law and the king's courts, for "the judges of the law . . . are all joined to the parliament" together with "the whole wisdom of the whole realm, the king, his nobilities, clergy and commons" (173).

With this sweeping and summary statement of what after seventy years had become familiar as King in Parliament doctrine, Hedley shifted the rhetorical ground away from the opposition of King *or* Parliament that had governed debate for the previous six years. The King's prerogative and the privilege of Parliament were not in a footrace in which one contestant's leg was bound; rather, Parliament in its most comprehensive sense included both prerogative and privilege, and reconciled whatever differences might momentarily appear between them. Hedley had thereby turned the discussion away from the edgy oppositions of a discourse about sovereignty and back to the more agreeable trope of harmony. That maneuver, however, would not suffice in the face of the King's apparent misconstruction of the constitution; nor, even accepting Hedley's formulation, would it lay to rest the question of sovereign limits as such.

The problem to be negotiated was in essence this: if Parliament were nothing else but the assembled nation, then what if anything could such a body not do? If the common law were construed as the working constitution of the realm, Hedley opined, "then you will say, the parliament, which is nothing else in effect but the mutual consent of the king and people, is that which gives matter and form and all complements to the common law" (173). This, however, would be to subordinate the common law to Parliament, whereas exactly the converse was true, namely that "the parliament hath his power and authority from the common law, and not the common law from the parliament" (174). To be sure, Parliament could amplify or amend the law as occasion required. It could never, however, occupy a transcendent position above it, for "the wisest parliament that ever was could never have made such an excellent law as the common law is" (ibid.). This law was nothing else than "a reasonable usage, throughout the whole realm, approved time out of mind in the king's courts of record which have jurisdiction over the whole kingdom, to be good and profitable to the commonwealth" (175). It was customary, but not bare custom; reasonable, but not mere reason. Here Hedley imported Coke's doctrine of artificial reason, the tried and refined understandings of "many ages together" that made for the perfection of the law: a perfection not immutable and therefore incapable of being adapted to changing circumstances, but one superior to any sovereign or capitulary formulation and so immune to any willful alteration of its established character. Attempts at such alteration, Hedley pointed out, had invariably failed, for the common law — the orderly, processive, cumulative unfolding of a culture's understanding of itself — would not accept anything alien to its essential nature.

The common law was thus construed by Hedley as a living entity, stamped with the very character of the commonwealth it derived from and embodying the perfection of its collective reason, its aspiration through time. This was not unlike the conception of Parliament advanced in the Apology, but pitched upon higher ground. Unlike Parliament, the common law was never out of session, nor dependent on royal discretion. Its antiquity was not subject to dispute, yet it was absolutely contemporary. It was not tied to particular statutes nor limited by general charters, not even the Great Charter itself. Though, as St. German had pointed out, it was best known by the rules and maxims deduced from case law and statute by the learned, it could not be held even to these formulations, which were no more exempt from the test of time than any other statement: "For whatsoever pretended rule or maxim of law, though it be colored or gilt over with precedents and judgments, yet if it will not abide the touchstone of reason and trial of time, it is but counterfeit stuff, and no part of the common law" (178).

If the common law could never be tied to any specific document, formulation, or past judgment, how could it serve to ground the subject's liberty? The ineffability of the law might seem, as Hedley confessed, to cast upon it an "aspersion of levity and change and consequently of uncertainty." He offered three responses to these objections, appealing first to the reflective and contextually sensitive character of common law determination as proof of its superiority to other systems, a process of open-ended discovery as opposed to a peremptory and hidebound application of fixed and inflexible principles: "as restiness in opinion without great reason is properly pertinacity not constancy, so change of opinion upon good grounds is not levity but rather constancy to goodness and reason, and consequently an honor to judgments and judges that impose not upon the first impressions of reason or opinion, but have recourse *ad secundas deliberationes* which always carry with them the reputation of the most approved reason." Secondly, a distinction was to be drawn between "particular cases and judgments," where adjustments in the law were more frequently necessary but less consequential to its structure, and "alterations of general rules," which were "very rare." Thirdly, the absence of prescriptive texts and constitutions was not a weakness but a strength of the law, for "though the common law be no written law, but depends wholly upon reason and custom, yet it is as certain as any written law or human law whatsoever, for as there is more variety and difference of language and speech in the world than of reason and understanding, so there is more doubt and difference in exposition of words than in soundness and consequence of reason" (178–180).

The purpose behind this rather oracular defense was to reinforce the notion of common law discovery as a continuous process of checks and balances. The judgments of lower courts were reviewable at any given point by higher ones, and those of the latter by the highest court, Parliament. Parliament's own judgments, embodied in statutes, were reviewable by subsequent parliaments, and by lower court judges when inconveniences arose.[55] The genius of the common law was that it was incapable of sovereign definition; it escaped all usurpation and survived all error. Such error, Hedley asserted, had been committed in *Bate's Case*, where the King's Bench had found for the King's discretion in setting impositions, and Parliament was now exercising its legitimate function in examining it. He proceeded to do so himself at length, demonstrating by principle, precedent, and statute that impositions, like all other common taxes and charges, were to be set in Parliament, and that the King could no more alter them on his own than he could the laws of the land (181–190).

This discourse took Hedley back to Magna Carta, already enshrined in Coke's *Second Institute* as the proof-text of English liberties.[56] He observed that "cavils" had lately been raised against the Charter to the effect that it was the product of rebellion, "sealed in blood, [and] gotten by force" against a lawful king. In response, he made a shrewd move that was to set the tone, and in some ways the terms of constitutional argument for the next two decades and beyond:

> I will not take upon me to determine within what time a conquered king or his posterity may with force and arms regain his lost kingdom, or if the king never be able or that he or his posterity be utterly extinct, then whether at all, or within what time the conquered subjects may claim or challenge again their ancient laws and liberties. But of this I think there is little question, that if the subjects do obtain a grant of their ancient laws and liberties at the conqueror's hands, though it be first gotten by force, yet if after at several times and in several ages in time of peace it be confirmed by continual consent and oath of king and people and hath so continued and been continually approved for many hundred years, then they will be as firm and strong as any human laws whatsoever. (190)

Hedley's claim—against which Thomas Hobbes was to launch the full force of his argument four decades later—was that Magna Carta had only restored the rights usurped by the Conquest. Those rights were fully embodied in the defeated Saxon line, which as possessing what Hedley called the "honor" and "government" of the realm, were the protectors of its constitution. This line had a prima facie right to recover what had been taken by force, although this right (like any other unenforced claim) might conceivably lapse with time. Were it to do so by extinction of the line then the claim might devolve upon the conquered population or its descendants for some indeterminate but presumably competent period, so that its forcible prosecution would be a justifiable enforcement of right and not an act of willful rebellion. Hedley did not undertake to judge this question dispositively, for to do so would have obliged him to wade deeply into the waters of resistance theory. It was enough for him to suggest that Magna Carta was *arguably* a legitimate act at the time it was forced on King John at Runnymede, for it had incontestably become one in the course of at least thirty solemn confirmations by kings and parliaments.

Hedley's argument left scope for the claim that the people's right, indefeasible even in a succession of reigns and dynasties that suppressed it, could be recovered, in effect, for as long as it was remembered. He himself was content to argue on much narrower grounds. If the circumstances in which Magna Carta had been obtained were to be held suspect, so might the Conquest itself be. This controversy, however, was canceled by the mutual agreement of successive kings and their estates to maintain the Charter as the unaltered pledge of the subject's liberties. The ultimate guarantor of legitimacy was the act of ruler and subject in Parliament, and the repetition of that act "by several parliaments in several kings' times and ages" placed it beyond reasonable question. One Parliament might err in declaring the law, but not many. For his part, Hedley held it as apparent that Magna Carta itself was no new grant or statute, "but a restoring or confirming of the ancient laws and liberties of the kingdom, which by the Conquest had been much impeached and obscured" (i.e., never definitively renounced or taken away) [190]. Even had it been a new foundation, however, its successive confirmations by Parliament made it good: and by its twenty-ninth chapter, which secured all freemen in their goods, it brought all taxation under the purview of Parliament (191–192).

The people's liberty was "ancient," therefore, both in the sense of being immemorial,[57] and of being repeatedly confirmed. It was also validated by the law of nature and the "ancient policy" of the kingdom, for a people whose lands and goods were "in the absolute power" of another would lack vigor in peace and valor in war. England *was* its constitution, Hedley averred, for "it is not the nature of the people or climate . . . that makes . . . difference; but it is the laws, liberties, and government of this realm" (196).

At the same time, Hedley was at pains to rebut any suggestion of incompatibility or conflict between liberty and prerogative. The king's interest and that of the people, rightly understood, could never diverge:

> The felicity and happiness of all kingdoms, but particularly this of ours, resteth as well in the moderate and lawful freedom and liberty of the subjects as in the sovereignty of the king, but in the right composition and mixture of both (which by the common law is excellently performed). This kingdom enjoyeth the blessings and benefits of an absolute monarchy and of a free

estate. . . . Therefore let no man think liberty and sovereignty incompatible, that how much is given to one is taken from the other; but rather like twins, that they have such concordance and coalescence, that one can hardly long subsist without the other. (191)

Hedley's invocation of these well-worn tropes could not conceal the radical nature of his argument. By placing prerogative under the common law, by emphasizing Parliament as the final institutional arbiter of the common law, and by subsuming much of royal authority under the rubric of King in Parliament, he had restricted the discretionary exercise of prerogative considerably indeed. The king, it was true, retained such broad powers as control of the coinage and the making of war and peace, but even here his prerogative was not unfettered and beyond review (183).[58] He could not, for example, debase the coinage without encroaching on the subject's property right, nor could he wage war without parliamentary taxation, as Henry VIII had learned in the 1520s and as Charles I would discover anew in the 1620s.[59] Royal power was thus enmeshed in a web of consent that was no less real for being indirect or post facto. Hedley took a particularly dim view of such revenue enhancements as purveyance, for whereas both the Apology and the Great Contract accepted it as a source of royal income, he declared that it was "no matter of profit to the king if it were not abused" (193).

So great was Hedley's reverence for the subject's property right that he could contend that "the taking away but of [a] small part of a man's wealth is of more consequence in matter of government than the imprisonment of his body for a time," for the former was a capital felony whereas the latter was only an action of trespass, and that to take a man's sustenance was to threaten his life more imperatively than to deprive him of physical liberty (193–194). Echoing Cicero and anticipating Locke, he suggested that political association had originated in the desire to preserve property (192).[60] It followed that the powers of government were ancillary to this purpose, and that if abused they were subject to redress if not recall. The equipoise of liberty and prerogative under the benign auspices of the common law was thus less evenly balanced than might appear; more closely examined, the rights of the subject were primary and indefeasible, whereas those of "absolute" monarchy were conditional upon the discharge of the public trust.[61]

Attorney General Hobart answered Hedley's speech, and, unsurprisingly, took the symmetrically opposite view. All monarchies, he declared, possessed a "*iura majestatis*" or absolute and inherent authority, unless it were specifically limited. This authority included the unfettered right "to make war or peace, to make laws, call or dissolve parliaments, coin, make denizens"; and likewise "to impose." The subject's right, on the other hand, was derivative and conditional, and in all cases where exception was claimed from the prerogative the burden of proof was on the challenger. Thus, English kings had remitted their right to make laws unilaterally, as shown "by the constant course of the common law" and by statute. No such showing could be made in the case of impositions. It was true that Parliament had at times petitioned against particular impositions as a matter of grace, but that only confirmed their general legality. It was true as well that Parliament had occasionally joined the king in laying impositions, but no inference of shared authority could be drawn from that, for "5 or 6 precedents of impositions laid out of parliament are of much more worth." Again, the burden of proof against all exercise of *jura majestatis* rested with the subject, as it should in any alleged shift of authority from its intrinsic and original condition to a subsequent and derivative one. Even if only a single precedent of royal authority remained, no matter how ancient, it was sufficient to establish an undiminished prerogative right, for "intermission loseth the king no right," and no power not formally shared or surrendered could be regarded as alienated from the crown.[62]

Hobart's contention that the king could lose no power once exercised paralleled Hedley's suggestion that the people's right could not be extinguished by the passage of time or the lapse of a dynasty. Such arguments tended to suggest an indefinite regression toward a point of origin, and thus implied an ancestral constitution from which all powers validly derived (or invalidly departed). To lay claim to this point and to define its nature became, increasingly, the focus of seventeenth-century constitutional debate. For the common lawyers who dominated this debate in the House of Commons, the living law was the palimpsest on which the lineaments of the ancestral constitution were to be traced. Thus, said Heneage Finch, in answer to Hobart:

> [P]arliaments are as ancient as the law and a part of the fundamental constitutions of the common law. The courts of justice are as ancient as the law and as the ordinary courts of justice are appointed for their several purposes and one of them subordinate to the other but none more ancient than the other; so the high court of parliament, which is not only an assembly of the great council of the king to advise with him upon the great business of the kingdom but even the highest court of justice and the place appointed to reverse the judgments given in the King's Bench [of which *Bate's Case* was one], cannot in reason be imagined to be of less antiquity than the other courts of justice.[63]

Once again, the subject's right is antecedent, for the king's power never appears except as limited by law. Yet, in the absence of any original contract, was the prerogative not as arguably constitutive of the body politic as the people's liberty, or at least coeval with it? How could it be shown that the former had been empowered or at least limited by the latter, rather than the other way around? James, of course, contended that his powers derived directly from God; that granted, or at least not openly contested, it seemed little less than blasphemy to suggest that they could in any way be legitimately limited except by royal grace. The King solicitously attempted to save his subjects from such a pitfall by ordering them not to discuss the nature of his prerogative at all. A secondary claim was that certain royal powers derived from the law of nations; that is, that they were universally found in all king-doms and were therefore intrinsic to monarchical authority as such. To dis-tinguish such powers which, still in their pristine condition, had not been circumscribed within positive law by act of grace, they were called "indis-putable" or "absolute."

Finch was aware of the prohibitions against discussing the *arcana regis*, but, he said, he owed it to his profession and to "the honor of the common law" to do so:

> I will not deny the distinction of the two powers in the king, a limited power and an absolute, for 9 E.4 gives so much to my Lord Chancellor; but what that absolute power is, is all the question. I say 'tis an absolute power not of will but of reason, not assumed but allowed, not above law but by law. And therefore it is said in 19 H.6 that the law is the most high inheri-tance that the king hath, then the prerogative is not above law. Nay as one says, 'tis the highest prerogative of a king that he cannot do against law . . . to do against law is not a power but an impotency. (234)

As in Hedley's speech of May 18, Finch concedes the existence of an abso-lute prerogative in the crown, but construes it in such a fashion that it cannot be discerned, let alone applied, except in terms of common and statute law. Hedley grants this power a theoretically unbounded character *in esse* but says it cannot be actually known or exercised apart from the law; Finch will not allow even this much, but acknowledges it only through the Edwardian statute that cites it. In effect, the absolute prerogative can claim no notional significance independent of the law, but is wholly its creature.

Finch gives an example of this in treating of the king's prerogative over war and peace. This power is "high and absolute," and yet "the law stands not at a gaze" before it, but defines the difference between wars "foreign and domestical, invasive or defensive," and "doth dispute, try and judge of many accidents and dependancies, which accompany and follow the war in both kinds."[64] The law, in short, empowers the king to initiate and conclude wars at his (presumably advised) discretion, but not to wage them except as prescribed. The scope of discretionary executive authority—which, stripped of its divine right mystifications, is all the absolute prerogative represents— is similarly constrained by law in its other spheres of operation. Absolute or ordinary, however, all prerogative is given by and through the law. Thus, in returning to the vexed question of impositions, Finch asserts that "the law hath not in that point yielded to [the king] an absolute power."[65] The clear implication is that all royal powers are so yielded.

The question that remains, Finch says, "is whether an act of parliament have power to bind the king's prerogative." He concludes that "in all cases where an act of parliament doth concern the particular interest or particular profit of a subject, such an act of parliament will bind the king, not only in such things which the king hath as a great lord, . . . but even in prerogatives regal and incommunicable to subjects." Statute cannot take away that which pertains to the king's regality as such; thus, for example, no act could discharge subjects of their obedience, "for a king cannot be without subjects." Nor can one bind the king in those matters pertaining solely to his personal right or profit, i.e., those in which he can claim the same property right as any of his subjects. The ultimate right is the property right, the right for whose protection power itself exists; and so great is it that the king's own right takes shelter under it. The rule of thumb is, consequently, that the king may act freely in matters assigned him by the law as long as "no man is prejudiced by it . . . but a law which belongs to a common person, be it common law or statute law, the king cannot defeat [i.e., deprive] of common right."[66]

In Finch, the disjunction between the sacred and secular realms is, in terms of governance, as radical as that in Hobbes. *Lex terrae* is the ultimate authority, artificial reason its mode of reckoning, and Parliament its final (though never definitive) court of appeal. The common lawyers' inveterate hostility to all alien forms of jurisdiction, especially ecclesiastical ones, could not be more clearly displayed. Providence might guide history, but not the settlement of estates. A suitably tempered monarchy might be the best of all governments, but divine right was no part of the common law. As Nicholas Fuller put it in a lengthy and imposing speech on June 23, "The common laws of England are the most high inheritance of the kingdom by which both king and people are directed and guided, and . . . without that law there would be neither king nor inheritance in England."[67]

The problem of restraining the king's action remained. Hedley, Finch, Fuller, and others had made the case that England was governed by an ancient constitution expressed in the common law and guaranteed by act and judgment in Parliament. Courts, however, were an uncertain refuge when royal pressure was applied, as *Bate's Case* had demonstrated, and parliaments convened and sat at the king's pleasure alone. When the prince claimed that regal power per se owed nothing to the law and was in large measure unanswerable to it, and when he proceeded to confiscate the subject's property under color of such authority, customary safeguards were inadequate. One response, canvassed in the Commons in 1610, was to call for regular if not annual parliaments, an idea that progressively gathered momentum until it was made law by the Triennial Act of 1641.[68] Greater frequency of parliaments, however, did not necessarily mean better protection for the subject, as the parliaments of the 1620s were to demonstrate. As Fuller said plaintively at the end of his great speech in 1610, "I do earnestly wish from my heart that our gracious sovereign lord, King James, would end this controversy between him and his loving subjects."[69] Fuller meant that he hoped that James would stop quarreling with the law, because neither it nor its defenders in Parliament would recede. Absent this, what was needed was something that would bind the King more closely to parliamentary judgment.

James Whitelocke, a newly seated member for Woodstock at the beginning of a distinguished legal career, provided such a formula in his speech of July 2. Whitelocke grasped the nettle that Hedley had avoided, the question of sovereignty. The law that gave right could not protect it without the power that could abuse it, a paradox inherent in government itself:

> For . . . it will be admitted for a rule, and ground of state, that in every commonwealth and government there be some rights of sovereignty, *jura majestatis*, which regularly and of common right doe belong to the sovereign power of that state; unless custome, or the provisional ordinance of that state, doe otherwise dispose of them; which soveraigne power is *potestas suprema*, a power that can controule all other powers and cannot be controuled but by itself.[70]

To identify the *potestas suprema* would not, Whitelocke contended, endanger the law but protect it, for only when the sovereign power was exercised by hands other than or apart from those to whom the law entrusted it might "the fundamentall law of the realme" be subverted and "a new forme of state and government" erected (481). England's mixed polity, in short, did not depend on an implied system of checks and balances that superstitiously averted its gaze from the Medusa's head of sovereignty, but on a frank recognition that took its precise size and measure. Only by such recognition could Englishmen understand the sort of government they actually had.

That the sovereign power was in the king could not be disputed—in a monarchy, where else was it to be found? The question lay in defining the nature of kingship. For James, starting from the premise of divine right—the suprahistorical, supralegal grant of direct authority to kings by God—kingship was fully and simply identical with the natural person of the monarch. Whitelocke, however, reached back to the medieval distinction between the natural and politic bodies of the king, and to the Henrician doctrine of King in Parliament that Burghley had tweaked in the 1580s. With a nod to Fortescue, he produced a new formula that in effect incorporated the monarchy into Parliament:

> The soveraigne power is agreed to be in the king: but in the king is a twofold power; the one in parliament, as he is assisted with the consent of the whole state; the other out of parliament, as he is sole, and singular, guided

merely by his own will. And if of these two powers in the king one is greater than the other, and can direct and controule the other; that is *suprema potestas*, the soveraigne power, and the other is *subordinata.*—It will then be easily proved, that the power of the king in parliament is greater than his power out of parliament; and doth rule and controule it. (482)

The specific powers Whitelocke assigns to the King in Parliament are the "right of imposing [taxes in general] . . . the power to make lawes; the power of naturalization; the power of erection of arbitrary government: the power to judge without appeale; [and] the power to legitimate" (483). Whitelocke did not admit that *any* powers inhered in the king alone, for doing so would have given him a position outside the law. Rather, he said, there were other powers "of the same nature, that the King may exercise out of parliament, which right is grown unto him in them, more in those others by the use and practice of the common-wealth, as denization, coynage, making warre; which power the king hath time out of minde practised, without the gainsaying and murmuring of his subjects" (ibid.).

The king's powers out of Parliament being "of the same nature" as those exercised in it, they differed only in being assigned him by use and practice, that is, by an immemorial consent silently attested by the absence of controversy at their exercise. These powers were not delegated as such, in which case they would have been revocable at pleasure and the king merely an agent of Parliament. Neither were they inherent in the crown, unique to *rex solus*, but only customary. They happened by ancient usage to be exercised by the king, but there was nothing in their nature that excepted Parliament from them, or prevented a joint exercise with or "in" Parliament. Presumably they had once involved Parliament, for Whitelocke stipulated only that the king *might* exercise them outside the estates. Certainly the power of war required the collaboration if not the consent of Parliament, for without the subject's aid no war could be seriously fought, and, as previous speakers had pointed out, no subject could be compelled to serve overseas against his will.

Whitelocke did not attempt to describe how powers once exercised by the King in Parliament had devolved upon the king alone; it was enough that custom had bestowed them and that long practice had proved them convenient. None of them, however, trenched upon sovereignty, which Whitelocke understood not as a discretionary executive power to be exercised as circumstances dictated but as the power necessary to preserve or rectify the constitutional balance and thereby to protect the overriding social interest of property. This was why the question of impositions cut to the heart of the fundamental laws of the kingdom:

> The question how we have . . . is a question of our very essence . . . whether we have anything or nothing, for if there be a right in the King to alter the propriety of that which is ours without our consent we are but tenants at

will of that which we have. If it be in the King and Parliament then have we proprieties and are tenants at our own wills, and this [is] the very state of the question which is proposed.[71]

The powers to make law and to impose taxes were those that, because they implicated property, defined the difference between freeman and slave. Even the right to declare war did not directly affect property, because, as William Hakewill had observed, the law gave the king no concomitant right to levy taxes, even in case of sudden attack.[72] Nor, Whitelocke noted tartly, could exigency serve as an excuse; the argument that the king must not wait on calling a parliament to obtain provision in an emergency was simply an argument for greater vigilance, and more frequent parliaments.

The notion of a sovereign King in Parliament recombined familiar constitutional elements to produce an elegant formula for restraining monarchical power. Sovereignty remained in the royal office, but not solely in the royal person. At the same time, the king in his natural capacity could not be said to be excluded from any part of it, since his assent was required to give life to all acts of Parliament, which, as Sir Walter Raleigh remarked in *The Prerogative of Parliaments in England*, were "but as empty egg-shells" without it.[73] James himself had conceded the point that monarchs could enjoy their full and absolute powers and yet be restrained. The difference, of course, was that the Jacobean sovereign restrained himself voluntarily, allowing the law but never compelled by it. This was a distinction that even the subtlest argument could not finally bridge. It was also what made subsidy bills different in kind from all others. In all bills but these, the two houses craved the assent of the king. In these alone, although their formal procedure and sequence was—but for the requirement that they originate in the Commons— the same as in all other legislation, with the king's confirmation turning a "gift" into a levy—the effective assent was that of the estates. As Hakewill noted, conceding the tendency of royal power even in a mixed polity to aggrandize itself:

> Is it likely, that if any or all of these Kings [from Henry III on] had thought they had in them any lawfull power by just prerogative to have laid impositions at their pleasure, they would not rather have made use of that, than have taken this course by act of parliament, so full of delay, so prejudiciall to their right, so subject to the pleasure of their people, who never undergoe burdens but with murmuring and much unwillingness? Can there be any thing more hatefull to the high spirit of a king, than to subject himselfe to the pleasure of his people, especially for matter of reliefe, and that by way of prayer, having lawfull power in his hands to relieve himselfe without being beholding to them? (421)

Here spoke the voice of unalloyed candor, if ever it did in the discourse of early modern English legitimacy.

The Commons of 1610 did not permit their grievances to evaporate in speeches or languish in a committee draft. Having framed the debate on impositions in the form of a Petition of Right that served as a direct rebuttal of James' speech of May 21,[74] they summarized the disputes of the session in two further petitions presented to the King on July 7.[75] The Petition affirmed that the Commons fully intended to debate the subject of impositions despite the King's command, and that it was their "ancient, general, and undoubted right" to do so on "all matters which do properly concern the subject and his right or state," for without the free exercise of that right "the essence of the liberty of Parliament is withal dissolved." The Commons declared that they had no intention of reversing the judgment in *Bate's Case* (although they did not waive their right to do so), taking cognizance of it only insofar as "a general conceit is had that the reasons of that judgment may be extended much further, even to the utter ruin of the ancient liberty of this kingdom and of your subjects' right of propriety of their lands and goods." To forbear examining it, however, would be tantamount to "concluding for ever the right of the subject."

While not linking the right of the subject and the privilege of Parliament as imperatively as the Apology had done, the Petition of Right made it clear that without the proper exercise of its privilege the right of the subject would perish. Since the Commons had been given a direct order to desist in their discussion of impositions, they petitioned the King's allowance to continue; but since at the same time they asserted their inalienable right to do so, they laid down a constitutional gauntlet: "We therefore . . . most humbly and instantly beseech your most gracious Majesty that . . . we may, according to the undoubted right and liberty of Parliament, proceed in our intended course." The alternative, it was clear, would be a forced dissolution and with it an end to the King's hopes for supply. King and Commons were to come repeatedly to this impasse in the next two decades.

The Petition of Right asserted the Commons' privilege of free speech and asked for the King's concurrence, a tactic designed to trap him into confirming a binding precedent even as the language of the Petition suggested that none was necessary. James, already a practiced hand at these rhetorical tests, replied with a standard formula of his own, conceding the House its liberties while insisting on his prerogatives.[76] The petitions of ecclesiastical and temporal grievances that followed on July 7 were, in contrast, a double-barreled assault on the King's governance. We have already noted the Commons' complaint against proclamations. To this was added others concerning the abuses of ecclesiastical commissions that poached on civil jurisdictions and violated the common law; the staying of writs; the persistence of injurious monopolies; and, of course, the laying of impositions. The Commons were also dissatisfied with the failure to control Jesuit infiltrators, seminary priests, and recusants, and to curtail ecclesiastical pluralism and nonresidence. They protested as well the deprivation of "divers painful and learned ministers" from the "freehold" of their livings for nonsubscription to Bancroft's canons, whose legality they had challenged since their promulgation in 1604 and 1606.[77]

Many of these grievances were, of course, of long standing; nonetheless, the sheer volume and comprehensiveness of the catalog was a rebuke as such, and the complaints about proclamations, writs, and impositions were all matters of immediate concern. None was more so, however, than impositions, and in the waning days before adjournment—the session had already gone into mid-July, and the grievance petitions had not received a reply—the Commons drafted a bill to deal with them. This was the "Act against Taxes and Impositions upon Merchants and Other Subjects of this Realm or upon Their Wares, Goods or Chattles." It was read, committed,[78] reported, passed, and delivered to the Lords within three days: an emergency speed. It declared that all impositions and other "exactions" imposed without the assent of Parliament were "utterly void in law" and "to none effect," and that any officer attempting to collect them would be deprived of his office "or any the like," and fined the sum of £40.[79] There was no recorded debate. Chancellor Ellesmere, however, left a terse comment on the "pretensed jurisdiction" the Commons had assumed in the bill, and on the "irregular and insolent course" of their proceedings in general.[80]

Why did the Commons rush through the bill on impositions, knowing full well that its chances of becoming law on its own were virtually nil, and that its predictable effect would be to stiffen James' resistance not only on this subject but on all others contained in the petitions of grievances? Perhaps members hoped to use the bill as a bargaining chip in negotiations over subsidies or for the Great Contract, for on the very day it passed the House considered granting the King £200,000 in annual supply; perhaps, too, they felt they could not in the end respond with less than they had done in 1606, when a similar though less stringently worded bill had been introduced.[81] There may be a hint of the Commons' strategy in Sir Edwin Sandys' remark at a conference in the House of Lords as the bill was being delivered there: "In contracts where there is a thing given, there must be security on both sides, from him that buys, from him that sells. . . . I doubt not but we shall have security from his Majesty and his Highness have what he desires."[82]

In the end, the King had little to show for the long investment in his first Parliament, which had blocked the Union with Scotland and was to conclude a few months later by rejecting the Great Contract. From its point of view, the Commons had only with untiring effort beaten back what many regarded as the greatest threat to England's national integrity since the Conquest, and had faced a series of royal claims and actions of dubious legality and dangerous precedent. The Lords, for their part, were soon to be greatly offended when James created a new heritable order of nobility, the baronets, as a financial expedient.[83] Each side, in short, felt abused and beleaguered by the other.

The session of 1610 was in many ways a turning point in the relations between the early Stuarts and their parliaments. The great debate on impositions—which has never fully been explicated, and which we have only sampled—was as remarkable for its manner as for its matter. The lawyer MPs who dominated it, many of whom had argued in *Bate*, *Calvin*, and the other pivotal court cases of the first Stuart decade, spoke with the amplitude and confidence of men used to propounding lengthy, complex arguments before learned audiences. The chief crown spokesmen in the Commons, Bacon and Herbert, were by contrast on the defensive, though no less able in argument. They found themselves at the disadvantage of speaking against, or at least in restraint of the privileges invoked by the court they were addressing. Only a generation before, the privy councillors had still largely set the tone and direction of the House, and "opposition" speakers who challenged the crown's agenda had been rare, except on religious issues. A shift in the climate of the House was discernible in Elizabeth's last parliaments, particularly in the turbulent session of 1601.[84] Notestein's characterization of this shift as a "winning of the initiative" by the House of Commons is, as I have suggested, a misleading although not altogether inapt designation; but what was taking place in this period could with equal justice be described as a loss of initiative by the crown, a point made long ago by David Harris Willson.[85] For Willson, the events of 1610 represented a failure of parliamentary management by James' chief councillor, the Earl of Salisbury, that contrasted lamentably with the efficient style of Burghley. Salisbury was certainly no less astute and conscientious than his father had been, but he had to deal with the provocative and often unpredictable governing style of his Scottish master. Elizabeth had not hesitated to rein in her parliaments and even to dismiss them when they intruded on what she regarded as her prerogative, as in 1566 when the Commons attempted to advise her on the subject of matrimony. Typically, however, she left the management of the houses to her councillors, who for their part used Parliament as a lever to bring her around on key political issues. This tactic worked where there was general elite consensus, as in the 1580s; but that moment, like the half-century reign of a virgin queen itself, was exceptional. When crown policy was forceful but unpopular, the councillors' task was far more challenging, and when it was complicated by a royal tendency toward abrasive and alarming claims of authority, it could become untenable. The result was a perception of the role of counsel very different from that espoused by those sanguine humanists, Elyot and Starkey. In his speech on impositions in 1610, Hakewill wondered how, if kings could levy taxes as they chose, they had not claimed the power previously:

> If perhaps the kings themselves were ignorant of this great prerogative, which cannot be imagined; had they not alwaies about them wise counsellors to assist them, and such as for the better procuring of favor to themselves would not have failed to put them in minde of it? Nay, if they had known any such lawfull prerogative, had they not been bound in conscience so to have done? (421)

The courtier currying favor, not to say the "wise counsellor," was already a well-worn trope of late Renaissance discourse, but Hakewill makes a far more disturbing point: that the counselor of a prince is bound *in conscience* to disclose the full extent of his authority to him when and as he requires it, and to suggest all lawful ways of exercising it. From here it was a short step to the unscrupulous adviser or favorite who offered "new counsels" or "innovations" that sought to stretch royal power beyond its lawful bounds; it was precisely this charge that would be laid against the Duke of Buckingham in the 1620s. The question of false or partisan counsel had already been implicitly joined by 1610, however, for if it was clear, as Hakewill insisted, that new impositions without the consent of Parliament were against the law of the land, then how could the King's councillors argue the contrary without convicting themselves of sophistry and bad faith? The issue was complicated by the fact that Hakewill himself, as he confessed, had originally been "much persuaded" of the validity of the crown's position in *Bate's Case*. He had been disabused only when he further researched the precedents on behalf of the High Court of Parliament itself:

> [B]eing, amongst others, employed by this House to make search in the Exchequer for records, which, by the practise of former ages, might guide our judgments in this weighty point, and having diligently collected the arguments made in the Exchequer, and not only so, but compared my owne collections with reports thereof made by divers of my other friends, and finding that some of the records urged in those arguments were untruly vouched and many misaplyed, I then began to stagger in my opinion, and presently fell to examine the weight of the reasons which had been alleged, which in my poore censure, I found not of strength sufficient, without the concurrence of cleere presidents of former times, to maintaine the judgement given or my opinion grounded thereupon. And therefore, syr, in love to the truth I did forsake my former opinion . . . and so am now become a convert. Those reasons that moved mee . . . I will, with your patience, open unto you, and will therein follow the commandement of Christ to Peter, beeing converted, seeke to convert my brethren. (410–411)

Hakewill's narrative is a fable of the moral enlightenment offered by a rigorous pursuit and application of the law. As in religious revelation, the fundamental unity of the law is not to be grasped in a single vision, but as a progressive unfolding; and as divinity searches out meaning in Scripture, so does artificial reason in the body of the law. In contrast, the pharisaic judges in *Bate's Case* rely — knowingly or not — on a misrepresented record driven to a false conclusion. Hakewill's conversion metaphor is offered, perhaps, in a semi-jocular spirit, but it is the kind of serious jest that gives deeper access to the truth. It also ratifies the superior wisdom and perspicacity of Parliament, which, with its long continuity of judgment, is incomparably superior to what Hedley scornfully called "the reason or opinion of 3 or 4 judges" in an inferior court.[86]

There is a further undertone in Hakewill's redemption story. Although at first led into error, he had persevered with his fellow Parliament men into truth. That truth, being discerned, had led to the judgment embodied in the Commons' declaration in its petition of temporal grievances that "The policy and constitution of this your Majesty's kingdom appropriates unto the kings of this realm, with the assent of parliament, as well the sovereign power of making laws, as that of taxing or imposing upon the subjects' goods or merchandises, wherein they justly have such a propriety, as may not without their consent be altered or charged."[87] This judgment, being that of the whole House, included those of Bacon and Hobart as well, at least in their parliamentary capacities. No one, however, could expect them to act contrary to the King's wishes in their respective roles as his Solicitor and Attorney General. Their unhappy situation was to serve two masters, and their royal one called the final tune. To the extent that they were not only compelled to represent unpopular positions in the House but to enforce them subsequent to parliamentary judgments to the contrary did not only mean that their good faith in the common quest for the truth of the law was suspect. It meant that they were not properly participants in it at all because, unlike Hakewill, they were not free to follow reason and conscience as it led them, to ascend from error to truth. It did not help that when Whitelocke was cited in Star Chamber three years later for a "Contempt of the King's Prerogative," it was Bacon who, as his prosecutor, rhetorically dangled a charge of treason for anyone who suggested, as Whitelocke might be construed to have done, a separation of the King's person from his office.[88]

If there was any precise moment at which the privy councillors lost the House, it was perhaps when it retired into committee on the afternoon of May 22, 1610, to consider the King's speech of the previous day commanding them to forbear further discussion of his prerogative right to lay impositions.[89] It was during this debate that a Petition of Right was propounded. Bacon attempted to forestall it with a speech that was half minatory and half pleading. He stressed his own bona fides ("I was a parliament man when I was but 17 years old")[90], and reminded the House that it had obeyed similar orders from Elizabeth.

At one time such an intervention by a senior councillor might have silenced the House, or at least given it respectful pause. Instead, "divers stood up" to rebut Bacon's argument point by point and to urge the House to "mayntayne [its] liberties and priviledges." A subcommittee was authorized to draft the Petition of Right. The King's spokesmen were appointed to it as a matter of courtesy (and, on this occasion, of cooptation?); but a curious thing happened:

> The King's privy council, Mr. Chancellor of the Exchequer and of the Duchy, Mr. Secretary Herbert and the learned counsel, Mr. Attorney and Solicitor, were appointed subcommittees [i.e., members of the subcommittee]; *but they all went away.* But there were 5 or six and twenty of the subcommittees that stayed and agreed upon the course of the petition . . . (112). [Emphasis added]

But they all went away. . . . Notestein suggests that the councillors may have feared to be associated with the petition. They may also have wished to express their displeasure, and perhaps to intimidate members who had agreed to take part in drafting it. If that was their purpose, we do not know what success they may have had—many members appointed to committees never attended them in any case—but we do know that 25 or 26 "stayed and agreed," and that the petition was ready for the House the next morning. The symbolism of the moment could not have been lost on those who were part of it; it certainly impressed itself on the anonymous diarist who recorded it. Bacon had been a member of the committee that drafted the Apology in 1604, and had done his best to soften if not to scuttle it. This time, he and his colleagues left the field to those who had defied the King's command.[91]

The Addled Parliament

Matters were not improved when James' second Parliament met in 1614. Salisbury's death in 1612 had left a divided Council whose so-called Spanish faction, led by the Catholic Earl of Northampton, opposed the calling of a parliament and did its best to sabotage it.[92] It needed little assistance. The vexed question of impositions at once returned, and this time the Commons were determined to proceed by bill from the outset. The old standard-bearers of the debate in 1610 returned to the lists; Hakewill, recalling his "conversion," again cast the issue in biblical terms, wishing that "his tongue might cleave to the roof of his mouth" if he failed to speak out, while White-locke, undaunted by the attempt to intimidate him in Star Chamber, suggested broadly that the *Bate* judgment smacked of timeserving, and Sir Roger

Owen of Shropshire, another veteran of 1610, flatly denied the King's power to impose.[93]

The Commons were determined this time to make relief from impositions the precondition rather the reward for supplying the King's wants.[94] The rhetoric of harmony had entailed a mystification of the processes by which the "free gift" of the subject was balanced by the king's gracious care in redressing grievances. When illegal taxation itself was the perceived grievance, however, there was no way to maintain the happy fiction, as the events of 1610 had demonstrated. In addition, it was common knowledge that James was canvassing other nonparliamentary ways to raise revenue, employing legal scholars and antiquaries to search the records for precedents.[95] Both sides, it seemed, were backing away from possible compromise. Edward Alford, the member for Colchester, worried that "we shall not part from the King in love," but still insisted on "a deferring of the King's supply."[96] Sir Ralph Winwood, the King's chief spokesman in the House, urged plaintively that "if we would not go directly to grant the King somewhat, yet that we would signify our minds to his Majesty that we intended hereafter to give his Majesty liberally," to which the House tartly replied that "they desired that some of the Privy Council there present would of themselves do that good office" to let the King know that they would act in due time.[97]

Winwood's embarrassment was an augury of far worse to come. The session had been clouded from the beginning by the rumored solicitation of "the principall & most understanding Gentlemen, that were of the last Parliament and are like to bee of this" by offers of place and favor. In an already polarized climate, this was seen not as a ham-handed effort to manage the Commons but as a sinister attempt to manipulate its elections and suborn its leadership. Under the circumstances, the King's councillors were treated with a disdain bordering on contempt, and all efforts to represent the royal position in the House were viewed with suspicion. Matters came to a head when Sir Thomas Parry, the aged Chancellor of the Duchy of Lancaster, was accused of coercing the electors of Stockbridge, which lay within the Duchy. Sir William Walter moved, with gratuitous malice, that Parry "be disabled from this and all other parliaments, which he hopes his age will, of itself, take order with." Sir Francis Bacon tried to rescue his colleague with an almost toadying appeal to the House's better temper:

> Allows the carefulness and earnestness of the House in these misbegotten elections; for whoever enters not well sits not well. . . . Likes the Houses' feeling of their own power, yet proceeding with moderation; speaking sharply, but concluding mercifully.[98]

Bacon's *sub rosa* effort to involve the Lords, like his flattery of the Commons, was to no avail. Sir John Holles observed that Parry was "Not here as a councillor but as a knight of the shire," and therefore under the jursidiction of the House. It is difficult to imagine any Elizabethan councillor being rated in this fashion. Only in 1601, Sir Edward Hoby had been sequestered for affronting the Queen's Vice Chamberlain, Sir Thomas Heneage, an occasion that led her to remark that her councillors were not to be treated as mere "common knights and burgesses of the House."[99] Parry was finally expelled from the House. Bacon's own right to sit in the Commons at all had already been challenged by Sir Roger Owen, who moved that no Attorney General "should at any time be of the House."[100] The question had arisen in 1606 over Hobart, but was then passed over.[101] Now, however, the House decided that no future Attorney should serve, and Owen suggested that the councillors sat in the House at all only as a "courtesy" from the body. One of Bacon's few defenders, Sir Richard Williamson, pointed out that two Solicitors, Onslow and Coke, had served as Speakers, and that as a general principle "Every freeman might be chosen" a member without prejudice. This was a long way indeed from Elizabeth's position that the presence of her councillors in the House was supereminently appropriate because they were permanent advisers, whereas ordinary members were merely chosen for a term. The difference reflected the distinction between the royal conception of Parliament as an extension of the Council table and that now clearly emerging from early Jacobean debate, that members of the House served primarily for their constituencies as senior crown officials could not do. In this we may see the origins of the long dispute about placeholders that vexed the late seventeenth and eighteenth centuries, as well as the increasing determination of the House to set its own agenda and certify its own membership. One argument urged on Bacon's behalf was that he was the bearer of bills of grace, the legislative program offered by the crown at the beginning of a Parliament. This did not sway the House, nor did the implicit (though unspoken) argument that councillors were essential to maintain a "correspondency" between the Commons and the King. To the contrary, removing them would lessen the problem of unauthorized communication that, so bitterly contested by Peter Wentworth, had not ceased to plague the House.[102]

What the Parliament of 1604–1610 had suggested, the Parliament of 1614 confirmed: that the crown had lost control of the House. The Commons had defied or deflected conciliar instruction in the past, as in the battle over proclamations in Henry VIII's parliaments and the debates over marriage and the succession under Elizabeth; now, they simply dismissed it. At the same time, the Council itself was vitiated by personal and policy disputes, a situation reflected not only in the Commons but the Lords. This division had a domino effect, since the Upper House was relied on to act as a brake on the Lower. Instead, a dispute broke out between the houses that threw the often contentious relations among the estates into high relief.

On May 23 the Bishop of Lincoln, Richard Neile, urged the Lords to reject a conference with the Commons on impositions lest they be exposed to "undewtyfull and seditious speches." Neile was reproved by several of his colleagues, but the Lords decided, after much pondering and consultation with the judges (including Coke) who were advisory to them to decline the conference until they had been better counseled. James, regarding this as a vindication of his prerogative, thanked the Upper House. Here were all the elements of a constitutional impasse: the Lords and the Commons at odds, or at least difference, about the powers of the crown; the judges in the middle; and a bishop fanning the flames. To make matters complete, the Commons first learned of Neile's attack from Henry Mervin, a freshman member of the House and a client of the Earl of Nottingham, the senior member of the Howard faction at Court that had opposed the calling of Parliament from the beginning.[103]

The Commons were enraged; one member said that if Neile had been accurately quoted, he deserved to have his head set on Tower Hill. Sir Robert Phelips of Somerset, then in his maiden parliament, worried about the House proceeding merely by "common fame." Were the Commons, having so frequently protested against tale-bearing and rumor, to act on similar information themselves? Phelips concluded, however, that since ecclesiastical courts admitted common fame as a ground of action, turnabout was, in this instance, fair play. Edward Alford, ever cautious, suggested that the House check its own precedents first. How and where to respond posed a conundrum as well. The Lords, it was noted, had permitted bishops to complain directly about the Commons to the King without informing them; why should the House not do likewise?

As several members suggested, Neile, by impugning the loyalty of the House and seeking to divide it from the King, had committed sedition himself. Unless the Commons were to assume jurisdiction over Neile on their own, however, a maneuver of which they did not yet dream, their only recourse was to protest either to the Lords or to the King. Neither avenue was desirable. Those suspected of sowing discord between the houses would be delighted to see the Lower House bringing complaint against the Upper to the Court. If, moreover, the King responded by punishing Neile, what was to prevent the Lords from accusing members of the Commons in the same fashion, thereby giving the King warrant to punish MPs on the basis of common fame? By appealing to the King, the House risked conceding the right of confidentiality and noninterference in its proceedings that the Apology had declared to be the cornerstone of its liberties.[104]

Despite a proffered apology from Neile, the House continued to demand his punishment, agreeing to suspend all other business until the matter was settled—a tactic it was to employ again in 1621 with similarly disastrous re-

sults. James now delivered an ultimatum of his own: that unless Parliament
ceased its wrangling and proceeded at once to grant him supply, he would
dissolve it forthwith. The effect of this was to force the question of impositions to crisis. The threat of dissolution-unless-supply laid bare the harsh political realities behind the subject's ostensibly "free" gift; for James, Parliament was an obstacle course to revenue, and if only obstacles were offered,
there was no point in running the race. For the Commons, on the other hand,
to grant the King supply without resolving the question of impositions
would be tantamount to prescinding from the argument of two bills and a
petition of grievance, accepting the royal position, exposing the subject to
unlimited prerogative taxation, and jeopardizing the future of parliaments.
At the last, both sides sought a face-saving compromise—Sandys proposed,
with some desperation, that the King preside over a joint session of the
houses at which a satisfactory formula might be arrived at—but there was
really no evident way to bridge the ideological gulf between the parties, and
no go-between to patch over the breach of trust. The Lords were at least
temporarily estranged, and their intercession in matters of supply was ill-
received in the best of times. The councillors in the Commons were without
credit in the House, cohesion among themselves, or sufficient influence to
counteract those in the Council who were determined to wreck the session.
Individual efforts at mediation were unavailing. On June 7, Parliament was
dissolved.[105]

The aftermath was bitter. The commission dissolving the estates declared
that as they had been a "Parliamentum . . . inchoatum" so they should be accounted as "nullum Parliamentum"—no Parliament at all.[106] This was an
unprecedented insult. It was also a spiting of the King's own face, for it
killed the bill naturalizing his new son-in-law, the Count Palatine Frederick,
which had passed both houses and required only his assent.[107] Fifteen MPs
were either imprisoned, confined to London, or subjected to other reprisal;
these included such leaders as Sandys, Hakewill, Whitelocke, and Owens.
Others were questioned or ordered to surrender papers. The King's Latin
proclamation was quickly translated into the vernacular of the streets; within
days of its dissolution, the convention of 1614 had gained its permanent sobriquet as the Addled Parliament.[108]

The breakdown of England's central constitutional mechanism was
deeply troubling. Some ascribed the 'addling' of Parliament to the "roaring
boys" in the Commons, others to a sinister faction at Court that, as several
observers in and out of Parliament put it, had "cast bones" to disrupt proceedings.[109] As members trooped home to the forty counties and two hun-
dred-odd boroughs that had returned them—or, in some cases, remained sequestered in London—the shock waves spread across the country. As ill-
omened as the original elections had been, with their rumors of packing and

undertaking, the abrupt dissolution portended far worse. The Tudors had faced rebellion, invasion, and religious revolution, yet the core institutions of government had stood. Now, in a time of relative peace and security, the division between Court and Country — two terms long in use, but only gradually perceived to be in opposition — had suddenly emerged as a glaring fissure in the structure of governance.[110]

In clinical terms, the ones most readily apparent to historians judging events from a perspective of several centuries, the problems of 1610 and 1614 were at bottom monetary ones. Early modern governments were chronically underfunded while facing inflation, an increased demand for services (or at any rate the increased imposition of them), and the ever-escalating costs of defense (or aggression).[111] The English crown suffered particularly from stagnant revenues tied to long-term fixed rates and leases, and the inability to impose direct taxation. When yoked to an unthrifty prince (as any successor to Elizabeth would have seemed), slack administrative and auditing practices (the code for a system of patronage and corruption), and the need to integrate the Courts of two countries, the result could be runaway deficits: by the end of James' reign, an unheard-of £1,000,000.[112] Given this, the problem of financial constraint as an explanatory device for the structural and superstructural crises within the early Stuart state is seductive. It is easy to argue that, but for money, James' high-flown divine right rhetoric would have been of little interest except to ideological taxidermists, and easy to agree with Salisbury that, had the King's finances been put on a secure basis, all would have been well. But the policy of generationally and dynastically successive parliaments in keeping taxation low and the practice of local assessment commissioners in undervaluing such subsidies as they authorized — a practice complained of as far back as the fifteenth century — suggests an ingrained and skeptical prudence about the purposes of government. The French Estates General, a body roughly as old as the English Parliament but one that had long lost the power of the purse, also met in 1614, and though not wholly uncontentious occasioned far fewer broils. An observer witnessing the deliberations of both those ancient assemblies and required to predict which one would not meet again for 175 years would not necessarily have bet against the French. The difference between the two was the power of taxation — a difference appreciated not merely by a few obstructionist lawyers in the House of Commons who either could not or would not acknowledge the funding requirements of a modern state, but also by the 200,000 free-holding, ratepaying electors who stood behind them and comprehended what Henry Ireton would some decades later describe as the permanent interest of the nation.[113]

The one period during which Parliament granted extraordinary levies was that of the war with Spain, which spanned the sessions between 1589 and

1601. Its willingness to do so showed its ability to respond to a genuine crisis and to provide the state with the sinews it needed to defend the country (and to maintain its grip on Ireland). Part at least of the difficulty James faced over supply was the desire to return to normal patterns and levels of taxation, and in the short run at least to recuperate from the burdens of the war years. His desire to enjoy the grandeur he felt appropriate to a Renaissance monarch and to reward needy Scot courtiers drew little sympathy; his pronouncements about the obligation of subjects to relieve their king were still less palatable; and the dispute over impositions brought grants of subsidy effectively to a halt. Yet Parliament had shown its willingness to act when the realm itself was threatened, particularly when the cause of religion was involved. Such circumstances prevailed again after 1618, but instead of a heroic war that vindicated England's position as the champion of Reformed Europe and a naval power to be reckoned with, the result was a comprehensive disaster: defeat at the hands of two traditional rivals; general calamity for the Protestant cause; fears of internal subversion in the church and doubts about the Stuart commitment to true religion, let alone to the role of Constantinian emperor; and what, from Parliament's standpoint, was nothing less than a full-bore assault on the subject's liberty. The consequence of this was a general crisis of legitimacy that set the stage for institutional breakdown and civil war.

The Parliaments of the 1620s

The seven years that elapsed between the Addled Parliament and that of 1621 — the longest interval between sessions in a hundred years[114] — saw major domestic as well as international change. James pressed for additional revenue by new grants of monopoly, a practice bitterly opposed by late Elizabethan parliaments. At the same time he dismissed Coke from the chief justiceship of the King's Bench after having first removed him from the busier Court of Common Pleas. James took the occasion to reaffirm a staunchly *jure divino* view of the relation between a king and his judicial servants:

> Kings are properly Iudges, and Iudgement properly belongs to them from GOD: for Kings sit in the Throne of GOD, and thence all Iudgement is deriued. . . . So this ground I lay, that the seate of Iudgement is properly Gods, and Kings are Gods Viceregents; and by Kings Iudges are deputed vnder them, to beare the burden of gouernement. . . . This I speake, to shew what a neere coniunction that is betweene God and the King vpward; the same coniunction is betweene the King and his Iudges downewards.[115]

Profound changes had also taken place in the royal household. In 1614 James installed a new favorite, George Villiers; by 1618, Villiers had gained an effective monopoly of royal patronage, much of it exercised on behalf of his large and partly Catholic family; by 1621, he had been created Marquis of

Buckingham, making him the senior nobleman in the realm in the absence of a duke, to which honor he would shortly be promoted. The irritation provoked by the sale of baronetcies was thus aggravated by what the peers regarded as the far more palpable insult of the scion of minor gentry being given precedence over the most august peers of the realm.

These were all good reasons for avoiding a Parliament, though the ever-sanguine Bacon had urged one as early as 1615.[116] It is quite conceivable that in the absence of a foreign crisis James would have called no successor to the *parliamentum inchoatum* of 1614, and that the last eleven years of his reign would have been an interregnum as those between 1629 and 1640 were to be in the reign of his son. To be sure, there was no sign of a deliberate buildup of prerogative government such as characterized the Personal Rule of Charles, but the dismissal of Coke, preceded by the famous scene in which James compelled the twelve justices of the courts at Westminster to prostrate themselves before him and vow to favor him in any cause concerning his honor or profit (Coke alone refusing), his above-quoted speech in Star Chamber linking compliance with his interest to obedience to God, and the multiplication of monopolies and so-called projectors—patent-seekers promising wealth to the crown—were all, plausibly, straws in the wind. The veteran Court-watcher John Chamberlain thought so; when James launched a benevolence on behalf of the beleaguered defenders of the Rhenish Palatinate in the fall of 1620, he reported that it had "quite put downe the speach of a parliament for the present, and perhaps the name of yt for hereafter."[117]

A parliament, however, could not be avoided. The Elector Palatine's feckless assumption of the crown of Bohemia, preferred by Protestant noblemen in rebellion against the Holy Roman Emperor Ferdinand II, had set in motion a chain of events that triggered the culminating war in the century-old struggle between Catholic and Protestant in Europe. Pitting the House of Habsburg against the Reformed German states and the Dutch Republic, it produced not only a strategic and dynastic crisis for James but a sharp upsurge in eschatological expectation. Was this, men and women wondered, the final reckoning with the Antichrist, the herald of the last days? Many thought so as the war developed, and the sense that, as Sir Robert Phelips said in 1621, history had reached its 'climacteric'[118] became more pervasive as Protestant losses mounted on the Continent while, by the late 1620s, the word of God seemed to be undermined in its last secure redoubt, the Church of England.

This, then, was the climate and these the circumstances in which Parliament convened in 1621. After the seven years' drought of parliaments, the next seven were to see a virtual deluge—five parliaments in all, the largest concentration since the 1550s. Of these, four would end in violent rupture.

By 1628, Sir Benjamin Rudyard, a veteran of all five, would speak of the "crisis of parliaments," and with it, the crisis of *dominium politicum et regale*.

The parliaments of the 1620s have been treated as a group by Conrad Russell in his *Parliaments and English Politics*, and more recently by Thomas Cogswell in a series of shorter studies. Cogswell refers to them as "war parliaments," and such they were, for, as he points out, the European conflict and the diplomacy that swirled about it were the principal occasion or business of all five. They were also, however, Coke's parliaments, for Coke's election to the Parliament of 1621—his first seat in the Commons since 1593, when he had been Speaker—ushered in a new era of parliamentary jurisdiction, beginning with but hardly limited to the revival of impeachment in 1621 and revolutionizing the work of the House of Lords. It was Coke to whom, in this last chapter of his illustrious career, both houses looked as the oracle of the common law and the champion of the fundamental constitution. The elderly jurist occasionally faltered and even nodded—he was seventy-six by 1628—and he increasingly relied on younger colleagues such as Selden. Nor was he the only or necessarily the chief leader in the House; with veterans such as Sandys, Phelips, Alford, Hakewill, Sir Dudley Digges, and Sir Thomas Wentworth, as well as newcomers including Selden, Rudyard, John Pym, and Sir John Eliot, the parliaments of the 1620s boasted as formidable an array of talent as any in history. But Coke, even in his absence in 1626 when he was pricked for sheriff to keep him out of Parliament, was the indispensable figure, a man whose prestige outweighed that of the entire bench combined and who seemed a living link to Magna Carta itself.[119]

The parliaments of the 1620s, as a group, also mark the beginning of a process more crucial to the shape of the civil war to come than any other. We may describe it as the sanctification of Parliament. Since the Henrician Reformation, Parliament, or in Henry VIII's terms King in Parliament, had assumed a special and implicitly providential role in the grounding, maintenance, and guidance of England's true church. This meant that the Constantinian emperor was present in Parliament, and the effulgence of his office was reflected in it. In a narrower, constitutional sense, Parliament had enacted every structural alteration of religion since Henry's time. Even an apostate ruler like Mary had been obliged to seek parliamentary consent to return to Rome, affirming the principle that the material tenements of the church, no less than any other real property in the kingdom, fell under the ultimate jurisdiction of Parliament. When the care of the church seemed neglected, Parliament had urged its cause, and no session had lacked for religious legislation. The Parliaments of 1621 and 1624 had for the first time made the distressed state of religion abroad their prime focus of concern; those of 1625, 1626, and 1628–1629 were all increasingly engaged by the perceived crypto-Catholic infiltration of the English church itself, even as the international situation worsened.[120] For the first time, too, since 1559 there were doubts about the fidelity of the Constantinian emperor, and, as early as 1623, fears of Charles' apostasy.[121] Under the circumstances, it was natural that hopes for rescuing the church fell on Parliament, and that, gradually, it came to be viewed as the savior of the elect nation as such, and consequently as a divine instrument. This process would be complete by the early 1640s, when the religious—no less than the legal and political—foundations for Parliament's proprietary assumption of sovereignty had been laid. The remainder of our discussion will focus on the three major elements—the crisis of Christendom, the crisis of the constitution, and the crisis of the church— that comprehended what Rudyard referred to as the crisis of parliaments, and whose interaction must structure any coherent narrative of the parliaments of the period.

The Parliament of 1621

The Parliament of 1621 was necessitated by the Spanish invasion of the Lower or Rhenish Palatinate the preceding summer. In launching this attack, Philip III of Spain had significantly widened the war that had begun with the revolt of the Bohemian nobility and the Elector Palatine Frederick's rash assumption of that kingdom's crown. By this act, Philip had made common cause with his cousin, the Emperor Ferdinand, thus linking the two Habsburg crowns in joint military action on the Continent for the first time since their division in 1564 and reviving fears of a Habsburg dominion, or at least condominium in Europe. The Lower Palatinate, moreover, one of the two widely separated provinces that constituted Frederick's own hereditary lands, lay athwart the Flanders Road, crucial to Spain's recovery of the Netherlands. With the expiration of a twelve-year truce with the Dutch imminent, it appeared that the two most important Protestant states on the continent would shortly be under attack. The fact that the Dutch Republic was England's most important trading partner and that Frederick was James' son-in-law—he and Elizabeth, the King's only daughter, had already been compelled to seek refuge in the Netherlands—only compounded England's investment in the gathering struggle. The corantos that streamed in from the Continent painted a picture that grew grimmer from week to week. Short of a threat of direct invasion, England could hardly have faced bleaker prospects.[122]

James, in his opening address to Parliament, acknowledged the troubling interval since it had last been called; its meeting, he noted, had been of "great Expectation." It was now charged with the task of upholding England's honor in the person of his daughter. No mention was made of the country's strategic isolation, or the wider Protestant cause. James had chosen shrewdly in appealing to the chivalry of the houses. Elizabeth of Bohemia, as

Frederick's spouse was known in Reformed circles, was a popular and pathetic figure, a symbol of virtue outraged and prostrate before the Antichrist. At the same time, by focusing on the limited objective of her restoration in the Palatinate, the King kept alive his own hopes for a diplomatic solution to the European crisis by means of rapprochement with Spain.

For its part, the Commons had not forgotten the violation of its privileges in previous sessions or the arrest of the four members in 1614. The King, moreover, had continued to collect impositions, not only at the higher rate established in 1608 but on a vastly greater range of products — more than a thousand in all. Nevertheless, the Commons swiftly voted two subsidies as a "free gift" before presenting grievances, and without making reference to impositions at all. In doing so it seemingly retreated from the ground it had so carefully staked out in 1606 and 1610 and so fiercely defended in 1614. Yet the House had not conceded but only deferred the issue. The King's requests for money in his previous two parliaments had been specifically for the relief of his own wants. To such requests, questions of royal thrift and nonparliamentary levies were germane, as well as the time-honored principle that the king should live on his ordinary revenues. In 1621, however, the honor and defense of the realm were clearly at stake. Parliament had not failed to meet the challenge of the Spanish threat of a generation before; it would not fail now. The King had presented a need but not a policy; the Commons, for its part, would acknowledge the former while it awaited the latter. The veteran councillor Sir Julius Caesar pointed out that two subsidies would hardly suffice to relieve the Palatinate, and asked the Commons to add two fifteens as well. This sum too was grossly inadequate to any sustained military action, and doubtless aroused suspicion: were the councillors understating the necessary amount to collect money to be used for a different purpose?

It was Sir Edward Coke who came up with the renewed formula of the "free gift." The two subsidies were not to be earmarked for any particular purpose, but were simply a token of "Love and Duty" — precisely the rhetoric James favored in describing his subjects' obligation toward him, and that Elizabethan parliaments had employed in their love toasts with the Queen. In doing so, the Commons had put the onus for spending the money on anything other than the Palatinate squarely on the crown. If James truly meant to succor his daughter and son-in-law and to meet the larger Spanish threat, a down payment was at his disposal with an implied promissory note for more. To make the point unequivocally, the House took the unprecedented step of voting that the subsidy might be collected at once, instead of waiting for passage with other bills at the end of the session. Supply would, in this case, not accompany the redress of grievances but deliberately precede it. The Commons thus turned the paucity of their "gift" into a sweeping gesture of good faith.

It was a brilliant maneuver, but one made possible only by the credit of the man who proposed it. When Coke had been removed from the bench in 1616, he seemed destined for the limbo reserved for those who, like Sir Thomas More, had sacrificed power to principle, or at least miscalculated the proportion of the latter tolerable to the preservation of the former. But Coke scrabbled back to royal favor, joining the Council in 1617 just as his great rival Bacon was completing his ascent to the lord chancellorship in succession to Ellesmere. His election to the Commons in 1621 was both a mark of that favor and of the continuing humiliation that was its condition, for Sir Edward, who had been Speaker of the Commons and of counsel to the Lords as the Chief Justice both of Common Pleas and King's Bench, was now returning to the Lower House as a mere member for the remote Cornish borough of Liskeard. His job was no longer to interpret the law but to advance the King's business.

The House received Coke as a privy councillor, that is with some wariness; but he was so solicitous of its privileges and so zealous in prosecuting grievances that even the dour Alford was moved to remark, "That was the first Parliament that he ever saw Councillors of State have such Care of the State."[123] 'Care of State' meant care of the true interests of the state, i.e., removing the projectors and monopolists who wasted the substance of the commonwealth, and, in so doing, starved the crown as well. The plural reference to "Councillors" embraced Sir Lionel Cranfield, the Master of the Wards and soon-to-be Lord Treasurer, whom James had charged with reforming the royal fisc and who eagerly seconded Coke's calls for reform where he did not actually anticipate them.[124] When Coke assumed the chair of the Grand Committee on Grievances, a backbencher's objection to a councillor chairing a committee was brushed away.[125] It was seemingly a far cry from 1614, when the right of councillors to sit in the Commons at all had been challenged.

Coke basked in the general applause of both Court and Commons when he was deputed to bring news of the subsidy grant to James and returned with his sovereign's happy reply. It was a moment of short-lived satisfaction. By the end of Parliament's first month, the Commons were in hot pursuit of monopolists, a trail that led to Bacon, who had certified their patents, and to Buckingham, who controlled access to the Court. The House sought to punish two particularly obnoxious projectors, Sir Francis Michell and Sir Giles Mompesson. As an MP, Mompesson was under the jurisdiction of the House for behavior inside it but not for general public offenses; Michell, a private citizen, was cited for contempt against the House, but also for his conduct as a patentee. The House expelled Mompesson, and sent Michell to the Tower despite Hakewill's warning that precedents for such action were wanting. At the same time, led by Coke, it declared the patents they had held to be a general grievance, thus reversing the judgments of the King's referees.[126]

To have proceeded thus far was dangerous; to take the next step and call to account the referees who had certified the patents, including not only Bacon but also much of the Council and the bench, was to impeach the entire government—a term of art referring not only to a generalized accusation or clamor but to a legal process, long in abeyance, by which the two houses might try and punish lay or clerical officials. The revival and refinement of this process was one of the signal achievements of the parliaments of the 1620s, but what triggered it in 1621 was less a desire to reappropriate old and near-forgotten powers than the need to resolve an immediate crisis. Parliament was a court, but it was by no means clear that the Commons possessed independent judicature beyond its own members. Together with the Lords, however, it was the High Court of the realm, and capable of reviewing the decision of any court or judging any person short of the king himself. That it had not done so recently—the Lords had received no writ of error since 1589, and no case of impeachment had been laid since 1449 or successfully prosecuted since 1397—did not mean that it had renounced the authority to do so; in the world of immemorial custom, a power once exercised could never be lost.[127] Beyond this, it was clear that as a matter of political reality the Commons would require the concurrence of the Lords to proceed against great officers of state. The rift between the Lords and the Commons in 1614 had fatally weakened the latter in its confrontation with the King; it was a mistake that leaders in both houses were determined not to repeat. The crown had often used the Lords as a brake on the Commons in the past and would attempt to do so again, but in 1621 the two houses had a rare community of interest. The Commons hated monopolies and the abuse both of trade and justice they engendered; the Lords were offended at the cheapening of honor by the ennobling of upstart families and the monopolization of favor by a single one. Both grievances led to Buckingham. Neither house could accomplish its goals alone, but jointly their prospects held some promise.

That matters should have come to a head so quickly was the result of unusual circumstances. The swift granting of subsidies had to a certain extent disarmed the King, who could not without ingratitude restrain the pursuit of grievances. The fact that the hunt for monopolists had been spurred on by two royal councillors seemed to give it his blessing, and the blatant thuggery of Michell and Mompesson inflamed an already aroused House. The question of the King's complaisance in the initial stages of judicial rapprochement between the Lords and the Commons remains. Jess Stoddart Flemion suggests that James may have calculated that his prerogative rights were safer in the Upper House, where the Lords would presumably act to restrain the wilder impulses of the Commons. If so, he greatly mistook the temper of the peers, and as greatly underestimated the potential of the resuscitated tool of impeachment.[128]

The emergent scandal meanwhile jumped its firebreaks. From the monopolists themselves it moved on to the referees, and threatened Buckingham directly. On March 10 James came into the Lords to receive the favorite's submission, a carefully staged piece of theater that served to place him under royal protection. At the same time, he challenged the Lords' jurisdiction ("how farre you may punish . . . is a question"), and excoriated the leaders of the Commons: "For though Sir Edward Coke be verie busie and be called the father of the Law and the Commons' howse have divers yonge lawyers in it, yet all is not law that they say. . . . I will give accompt to God and to my people declaratively, and he that will have all doon by parliament is an enemie to monarchie and a traitor to the King of England."[129]

Coke was indeed to be charged with treason and imprisoned for eight months in the Tower after the breakup of Parliament, a life-threatening punishment for a man of his years. James was thus revenged on his renegade councillor, but these were not Henry VIII's days; he dared not create a martyr. The treason charge was dropped, and with his sinuous agility Coke was able to regain the favor or at least the toleration of Buckingham and Prince Charles in 1623–1624. That he was determined to defy prerogative government and vindicate the common law, however, seems to me the only plausible reading of his career in the 1620s. Had James and Charles been able to avoid parliaments in the 1620s, he might have been confined to his writings alone, and unable to affect the course of contemporary events. It is possible that, absent the platform that now only a Parliament could give him, he would have ended as the more or less compliant royal servant he had been in the days of his youth and ambition, and again after his disgrace in 1616. Within a month of the opening of Parliament in 1621, however, he had cast his die, and one can scarcely imagine him not knowing full well what he was doing or what the likely consequences would be. The *parliamentum felix* of 1624, which temporarily allied Coke and other leaders with Charles and Buckingham after the collapse of James' attempt to recover the Palatinate through a treaty with Spain, showed again the different direction relations between crown and Parliament might have taken had there been consensus on a warfaring Protestant policy and some competence in carrying it out. It was not to be, and the road to deadlock resumed.[130]

As Conrad Russell pointed out, Coke never maneuvered directly against Buckingham in 1621 or displayed animus toward him, and the breach between the two men was not irreparable until 1625.[131] With the favorite now shielded, however, and a general assault on the referees undesirable, it was essential to find a scapegoat. Bacon fit the part. Both his eminence and his unpopularity in the Commons, of which he alone seemed unaware, suited him for the role. Coke, seized of the opportunity to bring down the lifelong rival who had been a prime actor in his own fall in 1616, rammed the case home. Bacon became the first major figure to succumb to impeachment, and although James remitted the fine and imprisonment to which he was sentenced and continued to consult him unofficially, his public career was over.[132]

As Coke had defined the impeachment process, the Commons brought an indictment and the Lords acted on it. The procedure was altered and refined throughout the 1620s, with the Commons taking an increasingly active role in the trial proceedings and extending their jurisdiction to clergy as well as the laity. At the same time, the Lords became far more generally active as a court, receiving petitions and issuing writs of error despite their unwieldiness as a body and their dependence on the judges assistant. All was not done by Parliament, but in the middle quarters of the seventeenth century it was more extensively a High Court than it had been at any time since the fourteenth century.[133]

Judicature and Protestant patriotism collided in May 1621 when the Commons sought to punish a Catholic barrister, Edward Floyd, for disparaging remarks about the Elector Palatine and Princess Elizabeth. Though some raised doubts about the jurisdiction of the House, most were closer to Sir Francis Kynaston, who likened Parliament to "the high court of heaven, sitting as angells to iudge the world at the last day." The Commons had finally to defer to the Lords, but the passion aroused by Floyd's case was a reminder of the deep wells of emotion stirred by the plight of the Reformed cause and the King's homeless daughter. A similar wave of feeling swept the House when James abruptly adjourned Parliament for the summer in early June, prompting the Commons to make declaration of their "hartie griefe and sorrow" on behalf of the King's children and the afflicted faithful, and to promise the adventure of "their lyves and fortunes" to recover the Palatinate should diplomacy fail.[134]

Diplomacy did fail, and when Parliament reconvened in late November it heard a frankly negative assessment from the King's peace emissary, Lord Digby. This was followed by a three-day debate, the longest sustained consideration of foreign affairs since the mid-1580s. It was capped when Sir George Goring, a servant of Buckingham, moved to petition James that if Spain would not accede to his "soe iust and reasonable demaundes," he would "not spare to denounce warre" against it or any other power seeking to dispossess his children. The House embraced the idea with alacrity, adding an appeal that marriage negotiations with Spain be broken off and Charles "be happily and timely married to one of our own religion." Only when the councillors belatedly received instructions to oppose the petition did they intervene. Nearly two weeks had passed without the slightest indication that the deliberations of the House did not have the King's blessing and were not indeed part of his strategy for dealing with the Continental crisis. Members were further disconcerted when James, secluded at his hunting retreat in Newmarket, declared that he would not receive, much less respond to, a petition concerning the marriage treaty or disparaging to his fellow monarch, the King of Spain. What had been a question of royal policy now became one of parliamentary privilege. The Commons could not be denied their right to petition, which was the right of the commons of England; nor could they neglect their duty, which was, in words quoted from their writ of summons, to propound, treat, reason, and act upon "the arduous and urgent affairs concerning the King, State, and Defence of the Realm . . ." Until their rights and liberties were vindicated, they said, they could conduct no other business, for their freedom of debate was the ground of all else. As Coke, already the subject of thinly veiled attacks from the Court, put it:

> I will not dispute with my Maister for his words, but when the kinge sayes he can not allowe our liberties of right, this strikes at the roote. Wee serve here for thousands and tenn thousands.[135]

Since James had chosen to speak for himself directly, the Commons *were* in the uncomfortable position of disputing his words. This was particularly the case when, as now, he once again asserted the position that the privileges of the House were a matter of grace and not right. The issues that had called forth the Apology seventeen years earlier and that had been the Tristan chord of Jacobean parliaments, recurrent and forever unresolved—free speech, the right of petition, the confidentiality of debate—were once again in play. This time, however, they touched not only the subject's property but the nation's security, the defense of Christ's religion, and the furtherance of God's cause. Not since the 1580s had constitutional issues been so deeply entwined with religious belief.

Coke himself, of course, was partly responsible for this predicament. The King spoke directly to the House because he had no spokesmen of credit in it, and the man who alone of his Council might have bridged the distance between Newmarket and Westminster was leading the parliamentary opposition. James' control of the Lords had also been weakened by the removal of Bacon, which Coke had finessed. Yet the King's responsibility for the crisis looms large. The Commons had reacted warily to Goring, who had stoked the coals against Floyd the previous spring[136]; as in 1614, there were suspicions of powerful courtiers seeking to divide the houses and break up the parliament. Instead of restraining agents such as Goring and laying out a coherent policy after Digby's address, James had only asked again for financial stopgaps while telling the Commons to defer all grievances until after a Christmas recess. With the King's own personal extravagances unabated, the

Commons grudgingly voted another subsidy.[137] This must have seemed at least a ticket for debate, and when even that was sternly rebuked, the sense of betrayal was strong. Whatever the substantive issues of privilege and prerogative at stake, this was slovenly parliamentary management—unless, as many suspected although none dared say, the King, seduced by Spanish promises, had no intention of bringing Parliament back into session in the new year, and had allowed the enemies of true religion to lure the Commons into a fatal quarrel.[138]

The last two weeks of the Parliament of 1621 make for melancholy reading: messages of increasing asperity from the King and resolutions of increasing despair from the members. Once the debate had turned from the substance of policy to the sterile ground of privilege, nothing could be expected but a repetition of the scenes already enacted in 1604, 1610, and 1614. James continued to insist that parliamentary privilege was grounded, like all subordinate magistracy, in royal favor and consent. The Commons continued to assert that it was an indefeasible right inherent in the fundamental constitution. Both parties were deeply affronted by the other. James told the Commons he could not "endure" their "antimonarchical" expressions, and that their petition had left no point of sovereignty untouched save "the striking of Coin." The Commons contended that, in Hakewill's words, their privileges were "the principall parte of the Lawe of the land" and "the inseparable incidents of a Parliament." Parliaments could no more exist without their privileges than a king without his prerogative; indeed, what was at stake was not king or Parliament, but King in Parliament. As Hakewill put it, "The privileges of this House are the flowers of the Crown, and we shall never sit here again if they be not maintained." This was the final vision of the Jacobean Commons: that parliamentary privilege was the linchpin not only of the liberty of the subject but of the prerogative of the king as well. Rightly understood, rightly exercised, privilege could no more be antithetical to prerogative than to the right of property in any other respect. The subject's own, Parliament's own, the king's own: each form of property was, in its ideal sense, an absolute possession, and the protection of each was the protection of all. This was the sense in which, as Hedley put it in 1610, the king of England was an "absolute" ruler. To be absolute was not to command simply as one wished, but through the law and within one's proper sphere of discretion. And as law itself was the supreme public act, the three estates concurring directly or representatively on behalf of all, so King in Parliament was the sovereign embodiment of the commonwealth.[139]

We shall never sit here again: Hakewill's words had echoed the fear of the entire House. If accommodation could not be reached with the King, if the crown's needs were unmet, the people's grievances unredressed, and yet another parliament sent home with a whipping, there could be scant hope of a successor while James reigned and perhaps after. This had been painful enough to contemplate in 1610 and 1614, but with the King's honor, the realm's safety, and the Reformed cause at stake, the consequences of failure might well be the default of the elect nation itself. So the Commons parsed each successive message from the King for any purchase, any formula on which agreement might be based. They found none, but in their hearts they knew too that any slippery compromise might be worse than nothing. As Conrad Russell put it, "members of the Commons had retreated so far that they could retreat no further. They had abandoned their claims over impositions in 1614. They had abandoned any attempt to advise the King on his foreign policy, or even to ask him what it was." If they could do nothing else, they could still defend their privileges — their and the nation's birthright, and the King's security too. In the Protestation, they did so. James had told them that he "could not allow of the style, [of] calling [privilege] their ancient and undoubted right and inheritance," at least without due acknowledgment of their dependence on royal authority. But that is precisely what they did, declaring without qualification "That the Liberties, Franchises, Priviledges, and Jurisdictions of the Parliament, are the ancient and undoubted Birthright and Inheritance of the Subjects of England." With that they rested. The King ordered the Commons' Journal brought to him and he ripped out the page on which the Protestation had been entered. Two weeks later, after the Christmas recess, he dissolved the Parliament and declared, as in 1614, that it had been no session. In doing so, he gave up the subsidy that had been granted but not yet enacted. The price was paid on both sides.[140]

Refiguring Parliament: Thomas Scott and the Growth of Oppositional Consciousness

The tidings of the next two years were grim. Once again there was a round of punishment for the parliamentary leadership. Sir Edwin Sandys had been already been arrested, and his imprisonment was followed by those of Phelips, Pym, Hakewill, and William Mallory, while several other former MPs were dispatched on uncongenial foreign missions.[141] James launched a new benevolence and ordered a propaganda campaign from the pulpit in support of his efforts to negotiate peace in the Palatinate, but the latter was so unsuccessful that he had to order the clergy to stop questioning matters of state, and even timeservers hardly dared justify him.[142] The fiasco of Charles' and Buckingham's failed attempt to finalize the Spanish marriage treaty in Madrid and the final occupation of the Palatinate by imperial troops in the autumn of 1623 completed the ruin of James' policy.[143]

These years were crucial for the development of an oppositional civic consciousness in England. Not since the reign of Mary had the policy of the crown diverged so egregiously from the sentiment of the nation. There had been pockets of conditional opposition under Elizabeth—opposition to this or that aspect of the Queen's governance within a context of loyalism. Such had been the dissent of godly Protestants and the great majority of Catholics under the Elizabethan church. More specific, situational opposition had also arisen from particular individuals over transitory aspects of policy, such as John Stubbes' tract against the Anjou match, *The Gaping Gulf* (1579). Stubbes, in paying for his temerity with his right hand, had blessed the Queen and affirmed his allegiance. Such dramas of legitimation, provided they were rare, could actually strengthen the regime by inscribing dissent within a wider profession of obedience. But the opposition of the 1620s was more generalized, anxious, and diffuse. James' ecumenicism had never been widely shared or even understood by the majority of his subjects, for whom antipathy to all faiths not their own was axiomatic, and hatred of Spain and Rome the fortieth article of the Anglican formulary.[144] Its secular counterpart, the effort to promote an alliance between England and Spain to keep the religious peace of Europe, was still more baffling. Some attributed it to the King's misguided pacifism, some to the Svengali-like influence of Count Gondomar at Court. On a more popular level, one unfortunate who rashly asserted that if the King were to turn Papist he would slit his throat like a dog paid for the remark with his life. The incident spoke volumes not only for the fear and hatred of popery at large, but for the public perception of royal policy. What king not beguiled would consider entrusting his only son and daughter to the perfidious Spaniard? Catholic polemicists boasted of the coming conversion of Prince Charles, and only the depth of alarm raised by that prospect can explain the spontaneous public rejoicing at his return safe—and unwed—from Madrid. Bonfires lit the road back to London for him, and when he stopped at an inn on his way he was accosted by a woman who, gripping his hand, demanded that he should "never . . . goe againe into Spaine." If ever public sentiment spoke directly to the crown of England, it was on that last leg of Prince Charles' long journey home.[145]

In the absence of a parliament between 1621 and 1624, such sentiment found its most eloquent spokesman in the sermons and screeds of the Norwich minister Thomas Scott, who had served for a time as James' chaplain. Scott had had precursors in John Stubbes and of course in the Admonitions and the Marprelate tracts of the 1570s and 1580s, but his career really anticipated the independent pamphleteers of the 1640s. Like his precursors (and successors), Scott looked to Parliament for the redress of ills, identifying with it to the extent of forging a "speech" by the 1621 MP and military professional Sir Edward Cecil to point out the dangers of the crypto-Catholic doctrine of Arminianism.[146] Scott also promoted the legends of the "patriot" martyrs Essex and Raleigh, both heroes of the war against Spain and the latter seen particularly as a victim of Spanish machinations. These, too, in

Robert, Earle of Essex, His Ghost and *Sir Walter Rawleighs Ghost*, were part of the impersonations he assumed to give his voice resonance and authority, as was his likening of his task to that of the prophet Nehemiah. The very titles of some of his tracts — *Vox Populi, Vox Regis, Vox Dei* — suggests his rhetorical and theatrical pleasure in assuming the parts not only of historical and biblical personages but of the entire discursive range of legitimacy itself. Such acts of dramatic incorporation had their place in the privileged space of stage and pulpit, but in spilling them over into unlicensed and otherwise unfiltered commentary on contested questions of public policy, Scott was creating a new arena of discourse. It was a measure of the times that he was able to do so; *Vox Populi* (1620) went through five editions, and was followed by a *Second Part* (1624).[147]

Parliament nonetheless remained Scott's constant focus. It was, he asserted, only its absence that had compelled him to write, and his *The Belgic Pismire* was dedicated to it. The frequency of parliaments was an index to the health of the state, for "without this Councell the greatest Peere or Officer yea the greatest profest Enginere in State stratagems may easily erre [and] . . . fall into Anarchy or Tyrannie."[148] Scott was careful to limit his admonition to councillors rather than the King, but in *The high-waies of God and the king* (1623) he drew a distinction between the "public" and "private" speech of the ruler that crucially shifted the ground of responsibility from the outer voices of counsel to the inner theater of conscience. The "public" (i.e., public-spirited) voice of the ruler was not merely the product of wise counsel or prudence, but a gift of God who gave him clear sight and which was accordingly to be obeyed by all "for conscience sake," i.e., for the obedience owed not only to the person and office of the ruler but to the divine spirit that spoke through him. This was opposed to the "Spirit of privacie," which Scott described as the "wilfulness" which might overtake "a publique Person, when for his own or peoples sinne he hath lost the publike spirit wherewith God indues Princes." Richard Tuck pointed out the critical significance of Scott's move for English political discourse, since it altered the ground for obedience from the ascribed status of the ruler, which demanded unquestioning compliance, to his performance of "legal and godly actions," which required judgment and consent.[149] In effect, this made every conscience a court of Parliament and every subject a Parliament man. It also fully implicated the commonwealth as a whole in every public action. It is noteworthy that for Scott the prince might lose access to the divine voice not only by his own unworthiness but by that of his subjects. This was rather a different notion from the homiletic commonplace that God might send a wicked ruler to punish the sins of a nation. In Scott's reading, a good ruler could as easily lose his moral compass from the sins of his subjects as they from his. This meant that God's judgment was a perpetually suspended sword over ruler and subject alike, and that the subject could not take refuge in blinkered obedience or, at most, passive resistance. It meant that each subject was compelled to be, in the fullest sense of the word, a citizen. As Conrad Russell observed, such a concept of individual responsibility for the political process was possible only under the presuppositions of a divinely ordained dispensation. Whereas the royalist conception of divine right held by a James I stopped short at the accountability of the prince alone to God's will, however, in Scott's godly, populist version all subjects were equally liable for the execution of God's ordinance, not only on the level of their personal conduct but of their collective praxis. This was a considerable—and fateful—extension of conventional Calvinist resistance theory, which placed responsibility for withstanding illegal commands with the inferior magistrate as a buffer against popular anarchy.[150]

As a practical matter Scott's emphasis on heightened citizen responsibility placed great weight on Parliament as the people's representative and the effective instrument of their overall participation in the political process. It also implied a reconceptualization of Parliament as such. As both supporters and opponents of the King's policies shared to a greater or lesser extent the assumptions of divine right theory, so, too, they had both accepted the Henrician formula of King in Parliament, however they differed as to its interpretation. In Scott's formulation, though, all magistrates were "lesser" in respect of the absolute and unconditioned obligation to obey God's commands; those doing so, whether they wore a crown or not, exercised legitimate authority, while those failing to surrendered it. Parliament could thus exercise a function independent of or even in opposition to the king, not simply as the people's representative but as God's. In this sense Scott went beyond co-ordination theory, which, as developed in the 1640s by Henry Parker, Jeremiah Burroughs, and William Prynne, would argue that Parliament might exercise the royal office which inhered in it in the absence or dereliction of the king.[151] Scott's Parliament, in contrast, was, at least potentially, a divine rather than a constitutional instrument, any or all parts of which, suitably inspired by God's mandate, might exercise sovereign functions. His vision thus took divine right theory beyond the idea of Parliament as a temporary substitute for the king to a vision of it as a quasi-permanent replacement for him, a notion that brought him very close to the position adopted by Levelers such as William Walwyn after the Civil War.[152]

Scott's conception of Parliament was not, of course, incompatible with the notion of King in Parliament, which reinforced while not limiting it. The fact that the royal office participated in Parliament made it, as it were, a default mode for monarchy, as Burghley had suggested in the 1580s. As a Great Council, a High Court, and the co-architect of the Anglican church, however, it was considerably more, while as the popular representative it was linked to the commonwealth in a more comprehensive manner than any institution other than the monarchy could be. If the Constantinian emperor should fail in his duties, a fear entertained not only for James but even before his accession for Charles, the inevitable place to look for the discharge of his office was Parliament. What Scott added to the equation was a far more dynamic relationship between Parliament and its electors. The people could not passively repose their trust in Parliament any more than Parliament could passively submit to the King's interpretation of his responsibility to the law and the church. God held all accountable not only for their duties to each other, but directly to him.

The consequence of this was that parliamentary elections had to be free of corrupt influence so that the relationship between Parliament and the people was transparently expressed in their suffrage. Scott's namesake, Thomas Scott of Canterbury, developed this point along the localist lines first suggested by the anonymous speaker of the Parliament of 1571. "None but an Englishman," he declared, "can, at a generall Councell or Parliament, Civil or sacred, represent England; none but a Kentishman, Kent; [and] None but a Canterburie man Canterburie."[153] Representation had always been critical to legitimation in the theory of *dominium politicum et regale*, but as the early decades of the seventeenth century progressed it had become its crux. There were many reasons for this: the empowerment of the gentry as a political class under the Tudors whose natural focus was Parliament; the general growth of civic consciousness, fed by rising literacy and the proliferation of news sources; the concomitant interest in borough enfranchisement and the extension of voting rights, both as a matter of status and a means of access; the increasing tendency of the House of Commons to connect its new-found role as the guardian of popular liberties with the right to validate its own elections; the polarization of Court and Country, particularly under the regime of Buckingham. But the key ingredient, as the careers of both Thomas Scotts suggest, was a deepened sense of responsibility both for the commonwealth and for God's cause. For Scott of Norwich the war with the Spanish Antichrist took precedence over all else, including constitutional niceties, and if the King would not discharge the role of the Constantinian emperor then a sanctified Parliament must be called upon to do so. For Scott of Canterbury, who sat in the parliaments of 1624 and 1628 and resisted Charles I's Forced Loan, the preservation of liberty at home was no less a part of the struggle against popery than the wars of the Continent. Indeed, they were two faces of the same coin, for, as the latter Scott asserted, "all Juditious puritans [among whom he clearly numbered himself] hold yt Against Conscience to yeald obedience to Tyrannicall and Lawlesse commaunds as of Duety."[154] The command of conscience took precedence over all ordinary deference to authority in the civil no less than the ecclesiastical sphere. It is significant that Scott spoke here not in his role as an MP or a magistrate, but as a godly witness.

"The Only Author of All Grievances": Buckingham
and the Parliaments of the mid-1620s

The parliaments of 1624 and 1625 mark the transition between the reigns of James and Charles. With the prince returned from Spain, the fiasco of his journey overshadowed only by the general rejoicing at its failure, Buckingham had no choice but to embrace the war party.[155] His ability to do so showed where his natural talents lay, and had he confined himself to political management within the context of a "patriot" policy that combined rhetorical commitment to the Protestant cause with strategic alliances and a blue-water naval campaign he might have emerged a hero. But the Duke—as he had now become—was not content with the premature role of an *éminence grise*, nor could he hope to vindicate his new rank and to erase the stigma of the parvenu that still clung to him except by the one sure road to honor, that of military glory. Buckingham has been as unappealing a figure to history as he could be a charming one to contemporaries; his tragedy was not only in the gap between his ambition and his abilities, but in the ghosts of Protestant champions past that continued to haunt him—those raised by Scott of Norwich, Essex and Raleigh, and particularly the figure whose career both he and Charles seemed to have usurped, Henry, Prince of Wales.[156]

The most problematic aspect of Buckingham's position, however, was his dependence on royal favor. Favorites had not been well received historically in England, as the briefest perusal of the stage and chronicle record indicates. Essex was perhaps a partial exception, but his popularity and, more importantly, his posthumous legend lay in his martial prowess and his attempted restoration of traditional aristocratic values. Buckingham had the title of Lord Admiral but no service record, and his jumped-up peerage was an affront not only to the nobility but to commoners such as Scott of Canterbury, who denounced "the plague of sellinge and prostituting of honor" under the Stuarts.[157] With neither merit nor lineage of his own, his only claim to eminence was the favor of two successive kings.

Buckingham was not of course the first favorite of James, though he was to be the last both of James and of Charles. James' predilection for young men was well known, and an early defender of the Stuart regime, Edward Forsett, declared the taking of favorites essential to the health of the sovereign and therefore of the body politic: "The favorites of a Prince may be resembled to the fantasies of the Soule, wherewith he sporteth and delighteth himselfe; which to doe (so the integrity of iudgement, and Maiestie of State be reteyned) is in neither of both reproueable." Such companions were, to the hardworking monarch, "not onely allowable, but plainely necessarie," and should thus not be subject to criticism or "despitefull envying."[158]

Forsett clearly distinguished between the favorite as a boon companion and the state councillor, thus affirming the humanist conception of counsel as the preserve of wisdom, gravitas, and independence of judgment. James himself, as we have seen, had emphasized the difference between his "temporary" councillors in Parliament and his permanent ones at the Council table, bound by oath to put the welfare of king and commonwealth before all private interests. Until about 1618 he had kept his favorites in check politically. Buckingham, however, aspired to the grander position of a Continental-style *valido*, one who could serve as both a social and political intimate and whose glory uniquely reflected that of an absolute monarch. Had not James himself declared that kings had "power to exalt low things, and abase high things, and make of their subiects like men at the Chesse; A pawne to take a Bishop or a Knight, and to cry vp, or cry downe any of their subiects . . . make them beggers, or rich at his pleasure"?[159] James liked to say such things, of course, not as the measure of what he would but of what he could do; yet it was arguable that a potent favorite was not merely an adornment but a logical by-product and essential element of monarchical absolutism. Recent studies have construed the phenomenon of the favorite as structural to early modern monarchy, a point of contact and transition between the royal household and the bureaucratic administration. Less attention has been paid to the idea of the favorite as an alter ego, front man, and idealized self-image of the monarch, whose extravagant lifestyle and monopolization of honor reflected the grandeur of his master, and whose function was thus as much emblematic as practical. Certainly Ben Jonson had caught this latter aspect of the favorite's role in his *Sejanus*.[160]

Whether or not Buckingham conceived his position in ideological terms, he certainly saw himself as the equal of his prominent European counterparts. In describing the Spanish negotiations to Parliament in 1624, he portrayed himself not only as a staunch defender of English interests and parliamentary liberties but as competitively jousting with his chief interlocutor, the Spanish favorite Olivares ("One time I demaunded of Olivares . . . . One day I challenged Olivares").[161] To be a favorite in the ministerial sense meant to control access to and favor from the king, to dominate his Council and bureaucracy, and to be at the center of policy and events. This was asking a great deal of a system, such as England's, that depended on the cooperation of local elites, widely dispersed patronage networks, and shared governance in Parliament. It was not impossible in principle, however, and in 1624 Buckingham seemed to have achieved it; with Charles at his side in their joint relation of the Spanish mission to Parliament and with erstwhile leaders of the opposition such as Phelips, Sandys, Digges, and Southampton angling for favor, he seemed to have triangulated a position of power that embraced the aging King, the callow Prince, and Parliament.

The tenability of Buckingham's position was more apparent than real, however. It depended on a temporary convergence of interest and perception between a distressed Court and an aroused Country, as well as on the uncertain politics of regnal transition. James shrewdly perceived that such "popular" gestures as publicly disclosing the details of a sensitive diplomatic negotiation or stage-managing the impeachment of another crown minister, Cranfield (whose chief sins appear to have been fiscal prudence and political naïveté), would come back to haunt Charles and Buckingham.[162] The other major events of the Parliament of 1624—the passage of an act against monopolies and the provision that the crown render accounts to Parliament of the funds it voted for prosecuting a war with Spain—were clear incursions on the prerogative, even if, as has been lately suggested, the latter was an impolitic concession by the Court itself.[163] When James warned Charles in 1624 that he would live to have his "bellyfull" of parliaments he spoke presciently; but the remark also indicated the degree to which the King's own authority was waning. If James' style of parliamentary management must be rated spotty and episodic at best, by 1624 the initiative was no longer his.[164]

The commitment to embark on war with Spain in 1624 was a decision, essentially, to put the new reign in the hands of Parliament, the only practicable source of funding it. By confiding in Parliament, using it as an instrument to outflank James and break the Spanish party in Court and Council, and accepting parliamentary commissioners to oversee war expenditures, Charles had made it a copartner in policy, not merely an adviser. This required adroit management; instead, Charles ignored even elementary precautions, and squandered much of his political capital within months of his accession in March 1625. No time was permitted to insure the return of councillors to the Parliament called within days of James' death, and those who managed to gain a seat were left without a legislative program or other instruction. Nor had any of the popular leaders of 1624, who had risked capital of their own by supporting the Prince and the Duke, been rewarded with place or favor or even cultivated with an eye toward the future. Charles' ignorance and naïveté were such that he thought he could simply recall the Parliament prorogued the preceding May, unaware that its commission had lapsed with James' demise.[165] One must wonder at the political education he had received.

Even by Jacobean standards, the Parliament of 1625 was a shambles. The circumstances of its summoning were singularly unpropitious. London was ravaged by one of the severest plague outbreaks of the century, and all who could flee the city were doing so. Rumors meanwhile flew of the concessions being made to Catholics in the negotiations for the French match that had succeeded the Spanish one, and was only marginally less unpopular. The talks pushed the opening of Parliament past mid-June, the normal period of a summer recess. Danger and conspiracy overshadowed the session; the hazard and inconvenience of the moment made a convention seem reckless if not punitive. Resentment was only exacerbated when, after a brief pause in July, Parliament was recalled to Oxford for an unprecedented August session.

Charles defended the untimeliness of the sessions by pleading the necessity of the war upon which, as he reminded Parliament, it had encouraged him to embark in 1624. Providing for it was to be the whole of its errand, even though, as Sir Edward Coke pointed out, the commissioners' accounts for current expenditures had not been presented and the grievances of the previous year's Parliament had not been redressed.[166] The Commons responded with a vote of two subsidies, under the circumstances a rebuff;[167] pressed its unwanted petition of grievances as well as a further one requesting enforcement of the penal statutes against recusancy; and, most tellingly, limited the traditional life grant of excise duties known as Tonnage and Poundage to a single year, although the Lords quashed the bill.[168] This last maneuver was clearly an expression of continuing frustration over the Jacobean impositions, which had never ceased to rankle and were considered a major cause of the trade depression that lingered over the decade.[169]

If the Westminster session had been turbulent and distressed, its twelve-day sequel at Oxford was a capital disaster from which the Caroline regime never recovered. The Commons fell at once on the pardon of a Jesuit in Exeter, issued the day after Parliament's adjournment three weeks earlier and with a response to the Commons' petition for enforcement of the recusancy laws still pending. Sir John Eliot, a client of Buckingham's who would soon become his stoutest opponent, captured the mood of the moment:

> The whole House upon the apprehension of these things assumed one face of sorrow. Wonder it wrought in some, fear generally in all. The confusion of their thoughts imposed a silence on their tongues which, having held awhile, thus at length it broke.[170]

No such silence had been seen in the Commons since the last days of the 1621 Parliament, and the reasons were strikingly similar: a suspect royal match; Catholic influence at Court; escalating financial demands in the face of unresolved grievances; a war without a declared enemy. Above all, however, it was speech itself that seemed imperiled, and Coke again took the lead in expressing the sentiment of the House: "That the privilege of the House of Commons was the heartstring of the commonwealth. . . . Many men (and I myself) will speak in parliament that which they dare not speak otherwise." The point needed little emphasis: when men forbore to speak in Parliament itself, the whole realm was struck dumb.[171]

Even at this point the situation might still have been saved by timely compromise, as key members from both houses urged behind the scenes. The King's renewed insistence on immediate supply scotched all hopes for an agreement, however.[172] The Commons had made good-faith grants to the sum of eight subsidies and three fifteenths since 1621, but with no corresponding redress of grievances, no military or diplomatic result, and no hope that further levies would amount to anything but good money thrown after bad. Although Thomas Mallet warned that "Parliaments never breake with the Kinge but they meet with loss," the West Country merchant John Delbridge trenchantly summed up the prospect: "wheras wee returned the last tyme with fastinge and prayer, now wee may retorne with sackclothe and ashes."[173]

It is against this backdrop that we must consider the critical speech of Sir Robert Phelips on August 10. Its most famous line is often quoted: "Wee are the last monarchy in Christendome that retayne our originall rightes and constitutions." Conrad Russell calls this statement a "non sequitur" in the context of the speech as a whole, but it is in fact its logical and inevitable culmination. After taking the House through the previous insistence of Parliament in confirming Magna Carta in 1225 before consenting to supply, impeaching Michael de la Pole in 1387 and William de la Pole in 1450, and condemning Richard II in 1399, he cited the refusal of the French Estates General to ransom John II of France and the Spanish Cortes to levy aids for a war against the Moors until grievances had been redressed. The moral was clear. All free parliaments stood by their own and the subject's right; the loss of the first entailed that of the second; the consequence of such loss was, as the French and Spanish cases showed only too well, prerogative taxation, the oppression of the subject, and the denial of conscience.[174] England stood in danger of all three, for if liberty were to perish religion, already imperiled, would be next to fall. It was no coincidence that the twin bastions of popery, France and Spain, were also the prime examples of arbitrary government, for spiritual and political tyranny were two faces of the same coin. It was nearly too late to save liberty in England, for in failing to protect religion abroad and neglecting it at home the nation had incurred divine wrath; as Phelips had said in a speech five days earlier, the Spanish treaties had been laid on England "for our sins . . . . There have been more assaults upon the liberties of the people, more pressures within this 7 or 8 years than in divers ages. These things argue God to be our enemy, and that we must first make our peace with Him, or else in vain shall we send out armadas or maintain armies abroad." The period cited by Phelips coincided with the outbreak of the Thirty Years War; it was also coterminous with the ascendancy of the Duke of Buckingham.[175]

The attacks on Buckingham at the Oxford session marked the end of the Duke's brief honeymoon with Parliament. Coke openly questioned his fitness for office and even the legality of his appointment as Lord Admiral: "It was never heard that Queen Elizabeth's navy did dance a pavan. . . . If an office be granted to an inexperienced man, it is void." It was not merely a question of ships fitted for battle that idled in port, however. Sir Francis Seymour of Wiltshire pointed to the scandal of the small armada that Sir John Pennington had just turned over to the French with no assurance it would not be used to besiege Huguenot garrisons (as indeed it was) rather than to harry the Spanish coast. Incompetence, profligacy, and monopolization of office were the accusations levied against the Duke in 1625; to these would soon be added the far more dire suspicion of popery.

With all that might have been objected against James I his doctrinal orthodoxy had never been in doubt, at least before 1621. As a controversialist his credentials were impeccable, even if his efforts to promote a rapprochement with Catholicism seemed misguided and his aversion to war made him an uncertain trumpet for the Protestant cause. When he descended from rhetorical exhortations to heal the wounds of Christendom to political and marital alliances with Catholic powers, however, he courted popular resistance. At the same time the doctrines of Arminianism, which had first surfaced in England in the 1590s, were manifestly gaining ground within the English church despite James' own role in condemning them at the Synod of Dort in 1619 and the unquestioned personal orthodoxy of Archbishop Abbot, Bancroft's successor at Canterbury. To a degree this was the result of profound currents within international Calvinism that had begun to undermine the long-standing predestinarian consensus; in part, it reflected the courtship of Catholic powers and the de facto toleration of English Romanism that had followed in its wake. If Catholic practice were to be accorded a protected status at Court, how could the still notionally Reformed doctrine of Arminianism be effectively suppressed? The accommodationist drift of crown policy necessarily exerted an undertow on clerics seeking favor, some of whom perceived Arminianism as a potential *via media* of the future or at least a fashionable trend it would be unwise to dismiss too readily. The future Archbishop William Laud was one such man.[176]

Buckingham's own religious convictions are uncertain, and can perhaps best be described as politique. His carnal relations with James were a scandal to the godly, and his mother's conversion to Catholicism after a disputation in 1622 between Laud and a Jesuit was equally provoking. That same year he patronized an openly Arminian sermon. On the other hand, he had good relations with Abbot, who had sponsored him at Court, and he promoted a minister of impeccably godly credentials, John Preston, thus securing his appointment as chaplain to Prince Charles as well as the coveted mastership of

Emmanuel College, Cambridge. These mixed messages were quite deliberate, and not out of keeping with James' own style of ecclesiastical governance.[177]

The issue of Buckingham's clerical patronage came to a head at the York House conference of February 1626, in which he hosted pro- and anti-Arminian disputants at his London residence for two days of controversy. The origins of this event remain obscure, since it appears to have been at least partly instigated by two godly stalwarts, the Earl of Warwick and Lord Saye and Sele, with the active participation of another, the Earl of Pembroke. Perhaps these peers wanted to flush out Arminians such as Richard Montagu, whose writings had been censured by the parliaments of 1624 and 1625, and John Cosin, Prebend and future Bishop of Durham, who had attacked the "wild conceit of predestination" in a sermon. Perhaps, too, there was a whiff of regency politics in these maneuvers, for the unprepossessing Charles, so lately seen on Buckingham's leading-strings in 1624, seemed hardly in charge of his household, let alone of his kingdom.[178]

For Buckingham, the conference was in part an extension of the theological jousts of which James had been so fond, and as such a statement of his own political coming-of-age. His public repudiation of the Synod of Dort, James' last confessional victory, was framed as an assertion of national pride, but it was also clearly a personal declaration of independence from his late master. If he had measured himself against Olivares during the negotiations for the Spanish match, Cardinal Richelieu seemed to be his model now, a chief minister dominant over both church and state.[179]

Politically, however, the conference was a disaster. The Duke had neither James' learning nor wit, and the appearance of usurping Charles' position as head of the church was ominous. By giving Arminian spokesmen equal voice with defenders of established doctrine in an intramural debate, he drew an imputation of heterodoxy on himself. The rapid rise of the Arminian party thereafter, which the godly equated with popery pure and simple, was consequently laid at his door.[180]

The York House conference could not have been more ill-timed, coming as it did on the heels of a failed naval expedition against Cadiz and coinciding with the first days of a new Parliament. Charles' new tactic for assuring its greater tractability was to prick six opposition leaders for sheriff—Coke, Alford, Phelips, Seymour, Sir Guy Palmes, and Sir Thomas Wentworth—thereby disabling them from service in Parliament, and to pack the Lords with new earls, an admission that the Upper House was now unreliable.[181] Coke fought his exclusion; he secured election for Norfolk, and came before the Council to challenge the requirement that sheriffs remain in their counties.[182] His efforts failed, but so did the King's strategy; new leaders arose to replace the old ones in the Commons, thus undermining the claim that the opposition in the House was merely the work of a few malcontents, while the Lords were more disaffected than ever.

Each house thus brought its own grievances — institutional as well as national — to the session of 1626, and both houses spent a great deal of time on questions of privilege. For the first time in memory, however, the Lords were seen as the prime focus of action. The importance of grievances and the pressure for constituency services gave the Commons the principal impetus for legislation, as did of course their jealously guarded prerogative to initiate money bills. The steadily shrinking legislative agenda of the first two Stuarts further reduced the role of the Lords, for the crown had often found it expedient to introduce its bills in the Upper House.[183] On the other hand, the slow but steady growth in the Lords' business as receivers of judicial petitions and particularly their role as triers of impeachment gave them a new prominence. Impeachment was already coming to serve as a substitute for legislation in remedying grievances, for many of the latter were seen in the increasingly adversarial climate of the 1620s as the result of corruption and incompetence masked behind prerogative, or, worse yet, as "innovation." The latter was an all-purpose category covering malfeasances ranging from extraparliamentary taxation to kneeling at church services. "Innovation" was not novelty; it was the stuff of popish practice and fiscal tyranny, tricked out in the false guise of sanctity and necessity. Bills were effective where the three estates participating in the legislative act were all committed to the remedy proposed; they failed when the goodwill of the sovereign was negated by false counsel. In that case, only the surgical expedient of impeachment remained. Impeachment was the bicameral act of two estates against the third, and in this act, although the Commons retained the initiative of indictment, the Lords alone possessed the judicial authority to prosecute.

As early as 1621, Buckingham had allegedly been characterized as "the only author of all grievances and oppressions whatsoever."[184] If this evaluation was premature, it had become the common wisdom by 1626. The Duke's unpopularity was compounded by the imprisonment of two peers who had run afoul of him, the earls of Arundel and Bristol. Arundel was arguably the premier nobleman in the kingdom before the rise of Buckingham; the Venetian ambassador thought so in 1612. As Earl Marshal, a position formerly held by Essex, he was the steward of English honor.[185] His relations with Buckingham were politic, but he was deeply offended when the favorite succeeded to the only dukedom in the realm, and by 1624 the two men were openly maneuvering against one another in Parliament and on the Council. At Charles' coronation in February 1626, just before the opening of Parliament, the King's barge sailed past the grand reception prepared by Arundel without stopping, an affront clearly arranged by Buckingham. Soon after the Earl was arrested on trumped-up grounds — the marriage of his son without royal permission—a move that deprived him not only of his seat in the Lords but the six proxies sworn to him of their votes as well.[186]

The Lords' Committee for Privileges reported that no peer had ever been imprisoned without trial while Parliament was sitting. Meanwhile, the Earl of Bristol (the former Lord Digby), who had already been confined for two years, found himself charged with treason. Bristol, who had vainly attempted to mediate the crisis of the Palatinate in 1621 and had accompanied Charles and Buckingham to Madrid, was the designated scapegoat for the failed Spanish policy. The plucky Earl responded by accusing the Duke of conspiring with Gondomar to carry the Prince off to Spain, promising his conversion, and concealing his own treason with a false relation to Parliament.[187]

The attacks on Buckingham in 1626 came from several sources and had multiple dimensions, but their common theme was the usurpation of honor, and the consequent disturbance both of the social and constitutional order. Honor was not only the essence of the aristocratic code but the linchpin of the extended hierarchical relations that depended on it and the networks of political, economic, and artistic patronage that grew out of it. Honor justified the hereditary principle as divine right supported the monarchical one, and the crown, as the fountain of honor, was its ultimate repository and guardian. The perversion of honor thus affected the wellsprings of legitimacy. As a masculine ideal, it had suffered under the gynocracy of the last Tudors, and the resulting tensions, barely contained within the Elizabethan cult of chivalry, had come to the fore in the career of Essex. The legacy of Essex, as we have seen, had been an ambiguous one, combining elements of the overmighty subject, the Court favorite, the exemplar of martial prowess, and the Protestant champion. His legend, well cultivated by the 1620s, was softened by the retrospective glow that had settled over Elizabeth's reign and his identification with an aristocratic conciliarism that traded acceptance of modern bureaucratic government for the assured place of the senior peerage around the throne.[188]

Buckingham, in contrast, had none of Essex's advantages. He lacked both his pedigree and his prowess, and he revived rather than allayed gender anxieties. His relations with James were considered corrupt, and his emotional hold on the Prince appeared no less sinister. His wife and mother were Catholic, and his patronage of the Arminians completed the picture. To many he exhibited the classic symptoms of the would-be tyrant, whether in his own person or by association: popery, effeminacy, debauchery. The widespread rumor that he had poisoned James and the scurrility of the popular libels that circulated about him indicated the depth of hostility he had aroused. One by one he had cast off or alienated those who, like Arundel, had attempted to make their peace with him. By 1626 his best hope of avoiding prosecution in the Lords was to pack it with sycophants and to exclude his opponents by preemptive imprisonment.

The attack in the Commons had begun even earlier, with a carefully prepared attack launched against Buckingham by the hitherto obscure Dr. Samuel Turner in March. Turner was a stalking-horse for his patron, the godly Earl of Pembroke, who had been present at the York House conference; within the catalogue of sins he cited was Buckingham's "secret favoring and upholding of recusants" and his family's manifest popery. Turner's speech was immediately circulated in printed copies, and formed the basis of the articles of impeachment brought against the Duke in May.[189]

The rest of Turner's charges concerned Buckingham's mismanagement of the war effort, including the "dishonor" of his not having accompanied the fleet to Cadiz as Lord Admiral; his wasting of the King's treasure; his monopolization of office; and his sale of honors and preferments in church and state. The hit at the Duke's absence at Cadiz was designed to contrast with the martial virtue of the earls of Essex and Nottingham; the latter having been Buckingham's predecessor as Lord Admiral and also the uncle of the imprisoned Arundel.

Charles, with his characteristic tendency to personalize all political disputes, observed that those who attacked Buckingham really aimed at him, adding that his father's judgment was implicated no less than his own.[190] It did not occur to him that the Duke's opponents, whatever their private grievances, might have a larger public interest at heart. To promote men of inferior rank to great place was to beg trouble and insult honor; to place such a man at the center of royal patronage, policy, diplomacy, and command was to ensure disaster. All ills in the state, it was argued, grew from the fact that one man had usurped the perquisites that by rights belonged to the grave, the learned, and the noble. If kings required innocent companionship, as Forsett had said; if they found it convenient to place a single individual between themselves and the importunate suitors who otherwise besieged them; if they came to rely on a particularly trusted minister: all this might for a time be borne, but when the same man discharged these functions across the span of two reigns then constitutional monarchy was at risk.

The Commons had a direct and particular stake in the control of policy, namely its obligation to protect the public purse. The Council of War, called to account for its disbursements of the subsidies granted in 1624, had declined to report, yet the King demanded further supply.[191] The House responded by tabling the subsidy motion until it had been given satisfaction about Buckingham. As Russell points out, this effectively nullified its utility and ensured the dissolution of Parliament.[192] The simplest explanation for why Charles nonetheless permitted the session to continue until mid-June is doubtless the correct one: that with charges and commitments of over

£1,000,000, as Sir John Coke had reported to the House, the King could not dismiss Parliament without aborting his military campaign and abandoning any pretense of participating in the affairs of Europe. Three years later, he would be prepared to do so.[193]

The House was anxious to show itself concerned with the grievances of the Lords as well. Christopher Sherland of Northampton, delivering his portion of the Commons' bill of impeachment against Buckingham to the Lords in May, begged excuse for raising the subject of honor, which belonged properly to their own "higher sphere"; yet, he said, "if well observed," it touched "the commons as directly, if not more nearly, in point of liberty than it does the peers in point of dignity." Honor, he declared, was "above all estimation," "a sublime spiritual inheritance" and "an immediate beam of virtue" emanating from the person in whom it was recognized and the deeds for which he was known. Adopting the divine right rhetoric which, as we have observed with Russell, could serve constitutional as well as absolutist turns, Sherland noted that if kings might be styled gods as Scripture suggested, then "by a good analogy" their peers were to be esteemed "the principalities, powers, and dominions that encompass more nearly the divine Majesty and attend his throne." Like liberty in the commonwealth, honor was inherent in its possessor; and like liberty, it could, in the words of Magna Carta, neither be bought nor sold. Nothing could abuse honor more than to turn it into a commodity, as Buckingham had, and no man of honor could be more abused than to be compelled to purchase that which his own merit might well declare to be his birthright. Sherland even managed to get Buckingham's imputed Arminianism into his argument:

> [It] seems very strange . . . that this great man, who is taken notice to be the principal patron and supporter of a semi-pelagian, semi-popish faction, dangerous to the Church and state, lately set on foot among us that, among other things, hold a modified freedom of will in divine things and a power and liberty in a man to receive or refuse divine grace offered; that this man, I say, should be so incongruous and so far depart from his principles as to deny a man freedom of will in moral things and impose a necessity of receiving the grace of a king in a title of honor whether he would or no.[194]

Honor, liberty, and true religion: all, in Sherland's argument, stood or fell together. Honor was the attestation of virtue; but virtue also coincided with broad acres and ancient lineage, all of which together made up honor's substance. Virtue could reside in anyone of gentle birth ("honesty" or transparency of character and sincerity in dealing was the best that could be expected of the lower orders), but honor represented its full maturity and flowering, including its necessary and inevitable recognition by the sovereign. It was, consequently, transgenerational, an inheritance no less than goods and estates. Pym, in his part of the Commons' relation, elaborated on this theme, which went to the heart of the baronage as a corporate entity in the commonwealth. The Lords were "this High Court of peers," whose very function as receivers and judges of a bill of impeachment made them the ultimate protectors of the realm under the King himself:

> He will not trouble us with recital how ancient, how famous, this degree of barons has been in the western monarchies; he will only say the baronage of England has upheld that dignity and does concern it in a greater height than any other nation.
>
> The Lords are great judges, a court of the last resort. They are great commanders of state, not only for the present but as lawmakers, counselors for the time to come. And this not by delegacy and commission but by birth and inheritance.[195]

Here, from the Commons' spokesmen, was the vindication of the Lords' office as a pillar of the ancient constitution. Institutionally, relations between the two houses involved a continual process of negotiation and accommodation between bodies of different social status and function in which slights and jars were a constant hazard. It is difficult, too, to read Pym's description without thinking forward to the moment, only twenty-three years later, when a House of Commons so largely shaped by his leadership would abolish the upper house as "useless and dangerous."[196] In 1626, however, the description of the Lords' function was sincere in context if fulsome in address. Honor *was* the linchpin of elite values, and the Lords were the living embodiment of it. They shared in the immemorial antiquity of Parliament, not only notionally but in their very bloodlines. This was why James' revival of the noble titles of families such as Arundel's, the Howards, had at first seemed a welcome restoration of honor after the attritions of the Elizabethan years.[197] It was also why the subsequent sales of honor, crudely managed by the Villiers clan, were so profoundly threatening. The advancement of the unworthy and the substitution of cash on the barrel for virtue, merit, and service not only devalued ancient peerages but the honor of gentle status as such, whose place in the social hierarchy was guaranteed by the stability of the system as a whole and cemented by patron-client relationships. Of all the charges against Buckingham, therefore—corruption, extortion, incompetence, mismanagement, monopolization, and even the sensational thirteenth article, delivered by Christopher Wandesford, that the Duke had hastened James' death by illicitly medicating him—the gravest was that he had debased honor.

The awkwardness of the Commons addressing the "higher sphere" of the Lords on the subject of honor was finessed by having the presentation of the indictment reported in the Upper House by the Lords' conference representatives; thus, Sherland's speech was related by the Earl of Devonshire and Pym's by the Earl of Clare. In this way, not only were the peers spared a direct lecture on their dignity by their social inferiors, but the words of the Commons' speakers were transmuted in being repeated and personated by the Lords themselves. This dance of parliamentary etiquette illustrated the proper way of delivering compliment in the bicameral body of a hierarchical system; as a political act in itself, it symbolically restored the proper relation of rank violated by Buckingham and his minions.[198]

The climax of the Commons' presentation was an oration by Sir John Eliot, member for St. Germans, Vice Admiral for Devon, and Buckingham's erstwhile client. Unlike Phelips and the Duke's other temporary allies of 1624, Eliot's association with him preceded his parliamentary service, and he owed both his knighthood and his naval office to him. Such ties of obligation were not easily cast off, even by a man of his famously mercurial temperament, and his defection was all the more striking for its vehemence and bitterness. Eliot had been the first to denounce Buckingham in the Lower House, and remained his most relentless pursuer. In summing up the Commons' case, he offered a classical portrayal of the villainous favorite: "His profuse expenses, his superfluous feasts, his magnificent buildings, his riots, his excesses, what are these but a chronicle of his immense exhausts out of the crown revenues? . . . Of all the precedents I can find none so near resembles him as does Sejanus . . . [his] pride, his high ambition . . . his salaciousness, his neglect of counsels. . . . And does not this man do the like in his whole practice?"[199] Never before, perhaps, had a commoner delivered such a devastating attack on a peer of the realm. And never before had his fellow peers listened so patiently to such a denunciation.[200]

Eliot has been seen as an enigmatic figure, and his ultimate martyrdom— he was briefly imprisoned by Charles after his speech, spent six months in the Gatehouse for rejecting the Forced Loan in 1627, and died in the Tower in 1632 after refusing to acknowledge any jurisdiction over his conduct in Parliament but that of the Commons—made him an icon of Whig historiography. Recent commentators have portrayed a more complex personality. Inevitably, Eliot begs comparison with Peter Wentworth, and his daring, eloquence, and lack of (or disdain for) practical political skills suggests what the Elizabethan radical might have been like in a Stuart setting.[201] Yet what is of particular interest in the context of the attack on Buckingham is Eliot's desertion of a former patron. Bacon had paid a high price for abandoning Essex in 1601, and the profound isolation he found himself in at his fall in 1621 may have been the ultimate measure of it. Eliot, of course, was not deserting a sinking ship as Bacon had done. Buckingham not only had the support of Charles in 1626 but of a substantial band of retainers; indeed, it was one of Eliot's charges that he had "made a party, a party in the court, a party in the country[,] a party almost in all the parts of government both foreign and at home," and that this party, no less than the favorite himself, had isolated the King and denied him faithful counsel.[202]

It may be that Eliot's disaffection stemmed at least in part from his failure to advance in Buckingham's inner circle. In this he would have differed from the other members of Buckingham's parliamentary allies in 1624 only in the prior closeness of his association with the Duke and the vehemence with which he severed his ties. Never before had so powerful a minister so directly organized a group in the Commons, only to desert them as swiftly when his immediate purpose had been accomplished. Phelips' antagonism had been anticipated when he was pricked for sheriff; Eliot, who had labored to reconcile the Duke with the Commons at the Oxford session, was still presumably considered reliable. In assuming the role of "patriot" leader in 1626, he could be seen as vindicating his absent colleagues as well as his own honor, for, having been closer to Buckingham than any of them, he may have felt the need to more openly repudiate him. Nonetheless, in doing so he also broke the cardinal rule of obligation and fidelity that bound all patron-client relationships. The fact that he was not reprehended for this but rather entrusted with the most important role in the Commons' bill of impeachment, that of the final summation, was a testimony not only to his own merits but to the depth of antipathy to Buckingham. If Eliot was performing the office of tribune in his denunciation of the Duke, he was also, by all ordinary standards, practicing that of a turncoat.

Whatever residual guilt or embarrassment Eliot may have suffered over abandoning his former patron, his words showed no sign of it. Rather, they bore all the subtextual marks of a conversion narrative. Beguiled by Buckingham as by Satan's wiles, he had accepted his friendship and favor. Arguably, he had been one of his "party" — that many-headed hydra that had monopolized not only this office or that, but consumed the "whole body of the land." In likening him to Sejanus, he had offered a classical, secular exemplar of wickedness, for the honor of representing the Antichrist belonged to the Church of Rome. As Eliot's rhetoric suggested, however, the image of the tyrant merged with that of universal deceiver: "This only is conceived by us the knights, citizens, and burgesses of the Commons House of parliament: that by him came all our evils. In him we find the causes, on him must be the remedies."[203]

In exposing Buckingham as the source of all evils, Eliot testified to his own salvation. In associating his own testimony with his colleagues, he freed them from the taint of their alliance with the Duke in 1624. Eliot's personal catharsis was that of the House itself, and on that level he was its most appropriate spokesman.

Eliot also reposed the trust of the Commons, and of the kingdom, in the Lords: "[W]e are now addressed to your Lordships in confidence of the justice to which some late examples and your wisdom do invite us. We cannot doubt your Lordships the greatness, the power. The practice of the whole world we know to be all inferior to your greater judgments . . ." He thus rested his and the House's case against Buckingham, confidently expecting "such judgment as his cause merits."[204]

No sooner had the Commons presented their case when Charles descended upon the Upper House to declare himself a "witness" to clear Buckingham of all charges against him, and to announce the arrest of Eliot and Sir Dudley Digges. It was the second time in five years that a king of England had intervened in the Lords on the Duke's behalf. Whereas James had not directly prejudged the case against him in 1621, however, Charles had made it an issue of his personal honor, the honor that trumped everyone else's.

The Commons' consternation was intense. Not since Peter Wentworth's time had members been arrested in the midst of a session. The effect was to throw the House on the defensive as it sought, once again, to vindicate its privileges. The Lords, for their part, remained preoccupied with the case of Bristol and the detention of Arundel. The former was to a degree a means of deferring action on Buckingham, who, pressing the advantage the King had given him, demanded his hearing. The latter was as deep a source of provocation for the Lords as the arrest of Eliot and Digges had been for the Lower House, and on June 2, taking a leaf from the Commons' playbook, they resolved to conduct no further business until Arundel had taken his place among them.[205]

One might argue that in even agreeing to hear the Commons' case against Buckingham from their *rapporteurs* after Charles had pronounced it baseless, the Lords had taken a principled and (for some) personally risky stand on behalf of parliamentary authority. Nonetheless, they had no practical recourse against the Duke as long as the King shielded him, and in returning to the grievances of Bristol and Arundel—both of which centrally involved Buckingham—they chose the better part of valor. The privileges of the Upper House were more easily defended than those of the nation.[206]

Digges and Eliot were released from the Tower after nine days; Arundel returned to the Lords on June 8. The Commons, meanwhile, despairing of an issue in the Lords to their indictment and fearing an imminent dissolution, prepared a Remonstrance against Buckingham. In this they accused him not only of hastening the death of James but of seeking to eliminate parliaments. In the near term at least, it was a self-fulfilling prophecy. Two days later, Charles dissolved Parliament.[207]

In the absence of Parliament, popular discourse took on the task of delegitimating the Duke, in the vernacular as well as the political sense. The rise of the Villiers clan had been accompanied by a steady drumbeat of scurrilous verse, most of it of a graphically sexual character and altogether one of the richest troves of invective in English verse.[208] It gathered force anew after the dissolution of 1626. One poem that commented directly on the breakup of Parliament used the Jacobean simile of the proper relationship of unity and harmony between a "husbandly" king and his "wifely" estates. Buckingham had come between this sanctified relationship on behalf of Spain, sedition, sodomy, and the Devil:

> An art sprung from a blacker seed,
> Then that which he poured in that [reed?]
> > Whom we call Guido Fawkes
> Who if he had fired his vessel
> Of sulfur standing on bare trestle
> > In his sepulchred walks:
> Could not have so dispersed our state
> Nor opened Spain so wide a gate
> > As hath his graceless grace.[209]

The "black" (devilish and sodomizing) seed of the Italianized "Guido" Fawkes, compact of sulfur, gunpowder, and deviant sexuality — a plot to simultaneously poison and explode the body politic — is less threatening than the wiles of Buckingham, who would destroy Parliament as such while (and by) buggering his second king, thus opening the realm to both literal and symbolic assault from the rear. The Duke vaunts the honorific address he commands ("Your Grace"), while lacking precisely the quality it metaphorically implies, i.e., the saving grace of the elect.

Such "rayling and vaunting" verse was the obverse of the elaborate courtesy rituals of hierarchical recognition. It deconstructed with graphic ridicule the circumspect terms in which elite power relations were transacted. Unlike local festivals of misrule in which the lower orders reversed and mimicked everyday authority roles, such ridicule did not reinforce the system of status and command but undermined it. Its presence may be dated back to the Marprelate tracts, when the abuse that had been channeled by Foxe and others against the papal Antichrist was redirected at the established church. In a deeper sense, however, invective was the legacy of the Reformation as such, in which contested legitimacy on the deepest level — that of divine order and judgment — created a world of binary opposition in which authority was defined not as a straightforward relation between the licensed purveyors of command and the obedient subjects of it, but as a perpetual unmasking of false authority that its true source might be known. Marprelate, then, was not so much a point of origin as a watershed, from which attacks on the secular authority linked to the church might flow. These attacks were muted (not absent) in the last decade of Elizabeth's rule, when satire began to flourish in print and on stage as never before, and carried over naturally into the reign of the new, foreign monarch, whose scandal-plagued Court was an inviting target. Alastair Bellany has made a compelling case for the lingering effects of the murder of Sir Thomas Overbury in 1613, a scandal which implicated the Howard clan James had raised to favor.[210] But it was the figure of Buckingham that most conspicuously focused every anxiety of the age: popery, tyranny, and deviance (three interlinked and interchangeable metaphoric clusters); the perversion of honor, hierarchy, and martial virtue; the (presumptive) murder of one king and the seduction of another. No stage personification of Vice could have tapped into more primal levels of fear and disgust.[211]

Parliament, Prerogative Government, and Leighton's Appeal

Both the domestic and international situation deteriorated rapidly after the breakup of the 1626 Parliament. Charles launched first a benevolence and then a so-called Forced Loan, backed by the imprisonment of those who resisted, the billeting of militia on the civilian population (in part a financial expedient, but widely seen as punitive), and the imposition of martial law. In addition, clerics of high church and Arminian leanings were promoted to episcopal vacancies, completing the marginalization of Archbishop Abbot, whose see was to all intents and purposes in reversion to William Laud. The bond between episcopal conformism, Arminian doctrine, and royal autocracy was sealed by Court preachers such as Roger Mainwaring and Robert Sibthorpe, who openly advanced the notion that civil disobedience might entail personal damnation. When five imprisoned loan resisters failed to secure a writ of habeas corpus in the King's Bench to declare the legal grounds of their confinement, it became clear that the courts, too, were no longer to be trusted with the subject's liberties. In all of this the hand of Buckingham was seen, although the Duke, preoccupied with military affairs (and fresh disasters, including the ill-fated assault on the Isle of Rhé), was little in evidence at the Council table or in his new chancellorship at Cambridge University. While he remained "the grievance of grievances," as Coke would call him in 1628, in some respects the situation had gone beyond mere personalities. No such blanket attack on Christian liberty had been seen since the reign of Mary, and no comparable one on civil liberty since the tyranny of Richard III. The removal of one evil counselor, however necessary, would no longer suffice.[212]

The stakes were visible to all. If the Forced Loan were successful—the term, with its grim implication that necessity knew no law, had come from the Council itself—then, as Phelips' correspondent Nathaniel Tompkins put it, "we may forget what the word Parliament means."[213] Charles did raise about £250,000 by this means, as well as lesser amounts from the sale of crown lands and various feudal expedients that looked forward to the fiscal policies of the 1630s, but these sums fell far short of the requirements of what had become a major two-front war.[214] The King had proved that he could raise substantial sums from the country by extraparliamentary means, though not without provoking dogged resistance and perhaps risking rebellion; Parliament had shown that its consent was indispensable to the prosecution of a war. Henry VIII had stood in the same place with his parliaments a century earlier after the failure of the so-called Amicable Grant, except that the pre-Reformation monarchy had no Constantinian duties of religious leadership and pre-Reformation parliaments had no copartnership in church and state such as their successors had asserted. One dynastic war more or less was of limited significance in the life of the nation; to fail the Protestant cause at a time of unprecedented peril was to risk divine wrath, or give proof of having already incurred it. But an even more dire suspicion was abroad: that the Antichrist was actually at work within the commonwealth itself, and that a treacherous favorite, a beguiled king, and an overweening prelacy were his servants.

On the other side of the debate were those who, led by Laud, argued that an extreme faction in the House of Commons lay in wait to assail the King's prerogative in church and state. Laud's counsel was self-interested; Montagu had been impeached in 1626, and there was little doubt that the same fate awaited other clerical defenders of royal authority. The Laudian position, however, represented a growing strain in Court circles that saw Parliament as a popular institution essentially inimical to and perhaps incompatible with monarchy. James himself had set the tone for this, but Elizabethan councillors such as Ellesmere were of similar mind.[215] Parliaments were tolerable only if well bridled, but now they cried "Privilege!" at any restraint, downed their tools, and refused to work. The infection of privilege (and job action) had spread from the Commons to the Lords, while the crown's right to commit dangerous and contumacious persons for reason of state, first challenged by the Commons on behalf of their own members, had been raised by simple commoners themselves in the *Five Knights' Case*. The chief value of Parliament was the revenue it provided; the chief rationale for it was that it was a means by which popular grievances might be vented and the king informed of the state of the realm generally. The revenue was typically insufficient when it was forthcoming at all, however, and the airing of grievances, a noisome affair at best, had become a pretext for attacks on the monarchy. James had never resolved his financial dilemma, and the wars of the 1620s only threw the infirmities of the whole system into stark relief: instead of having direct access to the resources necessary to the conduct of government, the crown was hostage to the whims of a popular democracy. *Dominium politicum et regale* was, in the last analysis, *dominium politicum* without regality in any sense worthy of the name. James had said what Mainwaring and Sibthorpe only repeated, that the people owed their sovereign maintenance by the laws of God. Parliament was only the conduit of that obligation, and if it were for any reason blocked or constricted, the king was free by the law of nature to bypass or dispense with it altogether. Grants, loans, and benevolences were a traditional way of meeting the crown's immediate necessities, and from this perspective the Forced Loan was no different from any other such levy. The only question was whether it was to be, as its predecessors had been, a temporary expedient for or supplement to parliamentary subsidies, or a permanent replacement for them.[216]

This was the argument within the King's Council as it debated the calling of a new parliament over a three-month period from December 1627 to February 1628. Financial necessity and the fear of rebellion settled the question in the end, as it did in 1640. Charles and Buckingham felt honor-bound to pursue their wars. Even if prerogative taxation could keep the government afloat, the resistance it was likely to generate and the repression that it would require would doom the war effort. It was just conceivable that Charles might fight Spain and France, together or successively; it was not possible to do so and fight England as well.

Thus the constitutional moderates on the Council—appealing not to the threat of insurrection but to a rhetoric of unity and harmony—were able to induce Charles to give Parliament a last chance. It was a narrow thing, however, and if the moderates had won the battle, the ideologues had won the war. Even as the writs for Parliament were being sealed, the King was still considering further loans, ship money assessments, excise taxes, and other mulcts. Had they gone forward, they would almost certainly have scuttled the new Parliament. The fact that Charles would still entertain them at this juncture showed that he had already crossed the Rubicon to the Personal Rule, at least intellectually. Parliament would be welcome to do its duty and vote him the monies he required, immediately and unconditionally; he was prepared to collect them in any case.[217]

The Council debate was common knowledge, partly as a result of deliberate leaks by pro-parliamentary councillors which may have included proposals and draft proclamations for new impositions.[218] It was apparent that a battle for the traditional constitution was taking place at the highest levels of government, and that a parliament was its last hope. It was clear as well, at least to the godly, that Christian liberty and the Protestant cause were at stake. John Preston and the future revolutionary Hugh Peter had both preached fire-eating sermons in November 1627 warning of God's judgments, in Preston's case just days before the disaster at Rhé. But the most extraordinary text to emerge from this moment of crisis was Alexander Leighton's *An Appeal to the Parliament, Or Sion's Plea Against the Prelacie* (1628). Leighton, a Scot resident in England, was a throwback to the godly crusaders of Cartwright's day who preached holy war against Spain, denounced episcopacy, and condemned stage plays.[219] His appeal to Parliament to effect true reformation was in the Elizabethan mold too, but with a difference. Addressing the houses, he warned them in verse that:

> Prevailing Prelats strive to quench our Light,
> Except your sacred power quash their might.[220]

Parliament's authority derived not merely from a civil function but a divine commission. It was not the King of England who had summoned it, but the King of Kings:

> As God hath set you forth . . . for this great work of reformacion; so your choyce and place requireth you to bee men of activitie, as the Spirit speaketh, that is inwardly and outwardly compleate with prudence, prowesse, valour and diligence. . . . wee cry to your right Honourable, save us, or wee perish. . . . For Zions sake wee cannot hold our peace.[221]

Leighton assured the houses that as their charge had come from on high, so their powers were plenipotent: "Your priviledges both from divine and humane Laws are both Impregnable and irresistable."[222] This consociation of sacred and secular authority was what marked the Lord's genuine deputies, just as the false claim to it defined prelacy. It was also, however, the nexus of powers that characterized a divine right king. The Presbyterian reformers of Elizabeth's age had exhorted Parliament to the holy work of Reformation, assuming its warrant sufficient within the framework of the Erastian order and the mixed polity of Fortescue and Aylmer. Stuart absolutism, with its claim to direct divine warrant, had called forth in Leighton a symmetrical counterclaim. This was not a full-fledged assertion of parliamentary sovereignty (Leighton had no interest in this), but a particular commission to effect true reformation. It led him, however, to affirm an indefeasible authority in Parliament that extended to secular as well as sacred affairs:

> The Kings royall word; the confirmation of the Lawes, and giving of subsidies, imply a necessity of redresse of grievances, which cannot stand with the dissolving of a Parliament, till reformation be effected; but if the common adversaries should inforce a reformation, because all reformation (if they be well searched) entrencheth upon them; Can it stand with the wisdome, valour, and fidelitie of you, the *great Maisters* of State, to quite the ship, upon the tempestuous hard-blowing of a Babilonish *Euroclydon*? No sure; for as Paule said to the Centurion, and the Souldiers, *Except ye abide in the ship, ye cannot be saved*; So except ye keep the *Ship*, till ye have beaten the *Dunkirkers* of State, neither *King, you* nor *we* can be saved.

It thus stood, and "Your Honours know, that everie dissolution of a Parliament, without reall reformation, is against *right, reason, and record*." Accordingly, Leighton declared, the Court of Parliament must sit as long as it had business to transact, and of this it was necessarily the sole and peremptory judge.[223]

In Leighton's treatise we have, for the first time, all the ingredients of the crisis of 1640. The true church, never firmly planted except by the reformers of Edward's day, had been overwhelmed by prelacy; the monarchy, for its sins of depriving faithful ministers, persecuting the godly, suffering popish relics and liturgy, and above all for tolerating the anti-Christian regime of the bishops, had fallen under its thrall; and Parliament, as the last uncorrupted institution of church and state and the only hope of a perishing nation, was—must be—the instrument of its salvation. Repeatedly, Leighton addresses its members as Josiahs, after the biblical restorer of the temple who, empowered by the Lord, scourged the wicked of his time. This typology would also characterize the discourse of the 1640s.

If the rhetoric of reform in Leighton is familiar, so is the dramaturgy. His story harks back to Bale's *King Johan*, with its devilish prelates, its abused king, and its heaven-sent savior. The difference is that the savior in this case is not a future king, Henry VIII, but a present Parliament. Indeed, Henry figures in Leighton not as a hero but as one in a long line of rulers who had failed to effect a true reformation. It might almost be possible to conclude from the account he offers of the elect nation's religious history that England's sovereigns were obstacles rather than instruments of reform, save for the example of the saintly Edward and to a lesser extent of Elizabeth. Only in Parliament had men of valor always spoken for the true religion; only in Parliament could the uncorrupted voice of the nation still be heard.

It was not enough, however, for the cry of the oppressed to be raised if oppression were not redressed; this was the argument of men such as Sibthorpe and Mainwaring for passive obedience, backed by the scandalous threat of damnation. Accordingly, Leighton's critique entailed Parliament's right to determine the occasion and length of its own sittings that it might persevere until reform had been achieved. As we have noted, the idea of annual parliaments based on ancient custom and precedent had been bruited for a generation or more, but the notion of self-determining ones rested on a claim about their calling to the task of reform and their nature within the polity. It posited further an idea about their centrality within the constitution and their entailed right to the powers necessary to discharge their function within it. This view would be reflected in the Triennial Act of 1641, which provided for the summoning of parliaments at no more than three-year intervals, with or without the royal writ.[224] With the exception of the Caroline interregnum of 1681–1685, no period longer than three years has since passed without a session of Parliament.

Leighton's *Appeal* did more than foreshadow future events, however. It also signified a shift in the locus of divine agency within the elect nation.

Leighton's scathing critique of England's Constaninian emperors brought the complaint of the Elizabethan Presbyterians up to date with a survey of the persecutions of Whitgift and Bancroft and a sharp indictment of James. If he was silent on the subject of Charles, it was because comment was superfluous.

In England's Erastian commonwealth, the only alternative to crown governance of the church was by King in Parliament. Although Leighton's program was focused on godly reform, his emphasis on Parliament's role as a high court and his insistence that its powers encompassed the effectual redress of all grievances clearly suggested a mandate to right the wrongs of church and state alike. This in turn fed into the growing perception that the ills of both were intimately and indissolubly connected.

As a clarion call against prelacy, Leighton's *Appeal* signaled a return to godly militancy and a new phase of resistance to the emerging Laudian regime. It deserves to be read as a third *Admonition*, calling once more on Parliament to complete the task of reform so sadly failed, if not betrayed, by the royal executors of the Constantinian office. Leighton himself, after the loss of his ears and a decade in the Fleet, had the satisfaction of being appointed Keeper of Lambeth House by the Long Parliament, to which he received the keys from Laud himself. He lived long enough to see the beheading of his old nemesis, and the trial of Charles I as well.[225]

The Parliament of 1628: Property, Law, and the Subject's Right

Such triumphs were far beyond the discernible horizon in 1628, however. Only three years earlier, Sir Robert Phelips had spoken of England's Parliament as the last that retained its ancient liberties. Now the question was its survival as such. On March 22, five days after it had convened with a royal demand for an immediate and unconditional grant of subsidies despite the Forced Loan and the continuance of forced billeting, Sir Benjamin Rudyard put the case bluntly: "This is the crisis of parliaments. We shall know by this if parliaments live or die." Rudyard was usually more periphrastic, and Sir Robert Phelips, who followed him, perhaps more accurately restated what his colleague had actually spoken: "It was said by a gentleman below, that ever speaks freely, we must so govern ourselves, *as if* this parliament were the crisis of all parliaments, and *this the last*."[226] Rudyard was suggesting prudence, not panic; but Phelips' emendation of the record conveys an even deeper sense of gravity: what members feared was not whether parliaments would live or die in some unspecified future sense, but, literally, whether the Parliament of 1628 might not be England's last.[227]

That Phelips was present at all was as remarkable as the courageous speech he gave, perhaps the finest of his parliamentary career. Efforts had been made to prevent both his return and that of other stalwarts from previous sessions; the difference between this and former "undertakings" against the parliamentary leadership was that the initiative had come not from royal hardliners but from the Council moderates who had labored to persuade Charles to call another Parliament at all. If the institution were to be saved, men such as Pembroke, Coventry, Edmondes, and Sir John Coke believed, they must reach out to their parliamentary counterparts, men who would not belabor vexed questions of privilege and law but would work to gratify the King and make him, in his own phrase, be "in love with parliaments" again.

The moderates' strategy also included a moratorium on debate about Buckingham, and a swift grant of subsidies. These two points were quickly secured, and Pembroke's client Rudyard, in his "crisis of parliaments" speech, made clear the new parameters of discourse. A successful parliament, and with it the salvation of the institution, would be achieved

> By trusting the King, thereby to breed a trust in him towards us, for without a mutual confidence a good success is not to be expected. By giving the King a large and ample supply . . . for counsel without money is but a speculation. By prostrating our grievances and advices modestly and humbly at his Majesty's feet, for from thence are they likeliest to find a way to his Majesty's heart. By making it appear that whatsoever we shall omit or abate either in substance or circumstance proceeds merely out of a dutiful and awful respect to the King only . . . let our whole labor and endeavor be to get the King on our side, for then we shall obtain whatsoever we can reasonably desire.[228]

Instead of confrontational tactics such as impeachment, Rudyard suggested, Parliament should adopt a politics of supplication and "prostration"; more practically, the Commons had to recognize that an "ample" subsidy, far from being the King's reward or even an incentive for the satisfaction of the subject's grievances, was the precondition for gaining them a hearing at all. Rudyard did observe that the relationship of king and subjects was inherently reciprocal, for "neither can have existence without the other."[229] What the Council moderates suggested, however, was that the definition of "king" and "subject" were being renegotiated.

The limits of the moderates' strategy were soon apparent, however. Sir Peter Heyman introduced a bill to confirm the privileges of Parliament; Sir Francis Seymour, warning against "base flattery," raised the question of counsel again; Sir Thomas Wentworth urged the House to stand by its "ancient sober vital liberties." It was Phelips, however, who set the situation in its direst context. He noted the ancient Roman custom of permitting slaves one day of liberty a year to show the hardness of their lot: "This assembly," he noted, " . . . may hold some resemblance with that." Englishmen were subjects yet, but should they become bondmen—the honeyed way suggested by Rudyard?—they would, unlike those who had lived only as slaves, never wish to remember the liberties they had lost.

Phelips had been one of the most vigorous proponents of the Spanish war, and like many others in and out of Parliament he had seen it in an eschatological framework. Now, however, anti-Christian tyranny was in full cry at home, and foreign entanglement had become its pretext. Spain and France were the lesser threat, one of tactical import merely. England was an island, and though Buckingham had left its coasts dismally vulnerable, no Armada yet loomed. Instead, the nation was menaced from within. The secular turn of Phelips' rhetoric was telling:

> We are not provoked by any, but we have provoked two potent kings, the one too near, who are strongly joined together. The dangers are not chimerical but real. I acknowledge it, but it must be done in a true proportion of our dangers at home. I more fear the violation of public rights at home than a foreign enemy.

The full rhetorical fusion of popery and tyranny that was to be the final consensus of the Parliament of 1628 is still only prospective in Phelips' speech. The intimate relationship of religious and constitutional grievances was plain, but no overarching discourse yet encompassed them. To focus on the violation of liberties, Phelips is still constrained to screen out the eschatological dimension of the war abroad. Similarly, the blessings and rights of a mixed monarchy, though ultimately a gift of God, are still to a degree distinct from the challenges of an elect nation:

> It is well known the people of this state are under no other subjection than what they did voluntarily assent unto by the original contract between King and people, and as many prerogatives and privileges are conferred on the King so there are left to the subject many necessary privileges and liberties, as it appears by the common laws and acts of parliament. This is a right so inherent to us, and so ancient, and confirmed to us by God's word; however two sycophants have said the contrary that abuse the ears of princes, and by this means make subjects less than they ought.

The contract between king and people, a civil compact to be interpreted by civil laws, is guaranteed by the God who offers Christian liberty to all. The "sycophants" who abuse the King—Mainwaring and Sibthorpe are clearly meant—are false clerics, but not yet the agents of an anti-Christian prelacy; the remedy for secular ills does not yet require, as in Leighton, the full-scale renovation of the church.

Phelips deployed all his wonted eloquence to describe the suffering of his countrymen. The warrants of the loan lieutenants were "the strangest engine to rend the liberty of the subject that ever was," and those who executed them "like the Turks who send their Janissar[y], who placeth his halberd at the door and there he is master of the house." Tyranny—the arbitrary seizure of goods and restraint of persons—had, through the ages, a history as old as Haman. The Roman decemvirs who had plundered the provinces of the empire in the pages of Livy and the *poursuivants* of Edward III and Henry VIII were the precursors of the Caroline lieutenancies; English subjects, however, had always defended and recovered their liberties. The question was how to do so now. In the ordinary case, freeborn Englishmen had recourse to the King through his courts of law. That avenue, however, had been blocked by three dire judgments, each exceeding the last in "prejudice" to the subject: *Bate's Case*, twice condemned by Parliament but still cited as the basis for new impositions; *Calvin's Case*, which raised questions about the nature of allegiance and which royalists had interpreted as giving the king final authority over the subject;[230] and, most "fatal" of all, the *Five Knights' Case*:

> I can live though I pay excises and impositions for more than I do, but to have my liberty (which is the soul of my life) taken from me by power, and to be pent up in a jail without remedy by law, and to be so adjudged (shall I perish in jail). Oh improvident ancestors! oh unwise forefathers! to be so curious in providing for the quiet possession of our lands, and the liberties of parliament, and to neglect our persons and bodies, and to let them lie in prison, and that *durant bene placito* remediless. If this be law, what do we talk of our liberties? Why do we trouble ourselves with the dispute of laws, franchises, propriety of goods, and the like? It is the *summa totalis* of all miseries.

Phelips' rhetoric was ironic, for in fact England's forefathers had provided against arbitrary imprisonment in Magna Carta, and Parliament had repeatedly confirmed its principles by statute. Nor had the *Five Knights* judges erected such a power in their decision, although rumor suggested it. What the judges had actually done was to decline to pronounce on the King's discretionary authority, rejecting the plaintiffs' specific suit but not their right to habeas corpus as such. In the eyes of Phelips and his colleagues, however, this was mischief enough. Parliament might confirm Magna Carta as often as it liked, but if the King's ordinary courts would not uphold it in practice it was a dead letter. Such a situation could only encourage a continuing cycle of provocation in which the crown challenged the liberties of the subject to gain a piecemeal judicial validation for absolutism. The Commons had clearly seen *Bate's Case* in this light in 1610, though it mentioned that of *Calvin* only in passing.[231] With Coke's removal from the bench, judicial dependence on the crown increasingly appeared as the weak link in the subject's constitutional protection. In the Parliament of 1621, Edward Alford warned of the danger "that the judges, a fewe persons, dependant and timorous some of them, should judge betweene the king and the state of their liberties." The same Alford also cautioned against inserting the customary reservation exempting "matters of state" from a bill confirming Magna Carta unless the scope of the phrase were defined, for otherwise the House would be actually nullifying the Charter and subjects would henceforward be "Villaines."[232]

If Alford had discerned a trend in 1621, Phelips in 1628 saw a policy. *Bate, Calvin,* and *Darnel* (as the *Five Knights' Case* was also called) were for him signposts on a high road to prerogative government. After a quarter century's experience of the Stuart regime, men such as Phelips, Alford, Coke, Selden, Eliot, and Pym had little doubt of its tendency. The Union project had not been forgotten, and it was this that Phelips had glanced at in citing *Calvin,* which affirmed that all the King's subjects in each of his kingdoms owed him aid and allegiance in his overall sovereign capacity (the principle that enabled Charles to raise English levies against the Scots in 1639). By proclamation, imposition, and canon, first James and then Charles had sought to narrow the scope of statute and common law; through prerogative courts and by the use of the royal dispensing and suspending powers they had attempted to sidestep them. Coke's dismissal in 1616 had been the signal for an effort to not only marginalize but enfeeble the Westminster courts, turning the judges into servants of the royal pleasure. James had not needed a test case after that of *In Commendams* (1616), the suit in which he had forced the judges to prostrate themselves before him, but in the *Five Knights* hearing the crown had found a means not only to indirectly affirm prerogative taxation but to make an even more grievous inroad on the subject's right by discretionary imprisonment without due process of law.

This conspiratorial view was partly at variance with the facts—the crown had actually sought to avoid a legal confrontation over confining the loan resisters, and the judges had given as little legal ground as they could[233]—but it was not wholly unfounded. As we have seen, crown advocates such as Egerton, Bacon, and Caesar, distressed by the "monarchical republic" of Elizabethan days, had begun to make the case for an unfettered prerogative in the 1590s. Their views dovetailed with those of James, who asserted rather than argued royal absolutism and was thus less concerned with building a legal record on controverted points than affirming a set of a priori assumptions, though he clearly recognized the practical utility, and sometimes the necessity, of judicially confirming specific principles. It was therefore a saving of the true, bounded prerogative assumed by defenders of the mixed constitution to read the claims of absolutism in conspiratorial terms, and to suggest that its natural balance was being upset not by a powerful current in the rational-legal bureaucracy of early modern monarchy but by the baneful influence of evil counselors, monopolizing favorites, and grasping clerics. In precisely the same way, the parliamentarians of the 1620s saw Arminian doctrine not as a reactive product of Calvinist orthodoxy but as a stalking-horse for popery.

There was just enough factual support for this view to make it plausible, at least under Charles: the policy disasters wrought by Buckingham were real, and men such as Laud and Neile had begun to wield power in ways that would not have been countenanced under Whitgift and Bancroft. How, though, was Parliament to proceed? The Commons had been compelled to sheathe their most powerful weapon, impeachment, at least as far as Buckingham was concerned: the signals were clear that any attempt to indict the favorite would almost certainly lead to a dissolution. They had only one inducement to offer, the subsidies the King craved. If they could bargain this against a statute or other instrument that would condemn arbitrary taxation, imprisonment, and billeting with explicit penalties, they would have gone as far as their circumstances allowed. Whatever followed, they would have vindicated their liberties, and by committing the King to their course they would have engaged the honor of the three estates.

Phelips rose again to the rhetorical occasion, casting this last accommodation in the tropes of harmony and reconciliation:

> The kings of England were never more glorious than when they trusted their subjects. . . . Let the House consider to prepare our grievances by a committee fit for his Majesty's view not to make a law to give us new liberties but declaratory with restrictive penalties, so as they that violate them, if they will be vile, should fear infamy with men, and then we shall think of such a way to supply as never any king received, and with our monies we shall give our hearts, and give him a new people raised from the dead; then I hope this parliament will be entitled the parliament of wonders . . .[234]

The Commons proceeded to vote Charles five subsidies, but deferred incorporating them into an act.[235] They spent the next several weeks seeking the appropriate vehicle for a confirmation of their liberties acceptable to all parties. The sticking point in the Upper House was the Commons' refusal to incorporate the customary provision saving the king's prerogative into a bill—the issue flagged by Alford in 1621. The Lords' own effort to do so was at once rejected. The lawyers were at close quarters now, and Coke's deconstruction of the Lords' proposal was a particularly masterful piece of dissection.

The Lords' language, which showed the effects of skilled equivocation by their own—that is, the King's—learned counsel, was in effect a restatement of the royal position:

> And as touching his Majesty's royal prerogative, intrinsical to his sovereignty and entrusted him from God *ad communem totius populi salutem, et non ad destructionem*, his Majesty would resolve not to use or divert the same to the prejudice of any his loyal people in [the] propriety of their

goods or liberty of their persons. And in case for the security of his Majesty's royal person, the common safety of his people, or the peaceable government of his kingdom, his Majesty shall find just cause for reason of state to imprison or restrain any man his person, his Majesty would graciously declare that within a convenient time he shall and will express a cause of his commitment or restraint, either general or special, and upon a cause so expressed will leave him immediately to be tried according to the common justice of the kingdom.[236]

The Lords' articles were conveyed by the chief justices, thus pitting Coke against the jurists whose peer he had once been. He glanced at this circumstance wryly: "We see what an advantage they have that are learned in the law in penning articles, above them that are nót, how wise soever." The Commons' resolutions had been "plain and open and clear." The Lords' authors had managed to muddle each one of them, reducing matters of right to matters of grace, and subordinating the common to the martial law. Was the King's prerogative, or any portion of it, "intrinsical"? If so, Coke declared sweepingly, then "all our laws are out." Was the prerogative bestowed by God? Then it was sure that "no law can take it away," and the King's power was accordingly absolute. Such language would annul Magna Carta and all the statutes that had confirmed and explicated it, a thing "our ancestors would never [have] do[ne]." Phelips had stated that the subject needed no new laws and liberties, but only the enforcement of those he already possessed. Coke agreed. It was rather the crown that was bent on innovation, as purposefully expressed by the King's counsel and guilelessly transmitted by the Lords:

> We are now about to declare and we shall now introduce and make a new law, and no king in Christendom claims that law, and it binds the subject where he was never bound. Never yet was any fundamental law shaken but infinite trouble ensued.[237]

Coke concluded by suggesting that if the Lords would "not comply" with the Commons' position, the Lower House would petition the King directly. This was doubtless a bluff, but it showed his sense of position: that the dispute was not between the two houses but between bench and bar. Coke was, in effect, willing to pit his own legal and political prestige against that of the judges. He might lose his case for the present; his confident assertion ("I doubt not our gracious Sovereign will comply with us") was the biggest bluff of all. It was the verdict of history he aimed at, however: "That that I speak is for future times."[238]

Coke was not being quite fair to his judicial colleagues. Justices Hyde and Whitelocke—the James Whitelocke of the 1610 debates—had done what judges ordinarily do when faced with sharply contested constitutional issues in a heated political climate: to wit, as little as possible. As Whitelocke argued in the Lords, the five knights could not be bailed in the absence of a charge without prejudging the crown's action and thereby doing the King injury. Historically, the state had been permitted to arrest persons on a general warrant without an immediate presentment, and there was case law to back the practice up. Since, however, the appellants remained free to sue out "a 2, 3, and 4 writ" for their freedom, the subject's right was equally protected. The judges' elegant solution, with which Whitelocke was evidently pleased, was simply to seal all bids until the nature of the game was known.[239]

The problem was that the prisoners' offense was in fact notorious. As John Guy comments, "If Chief Justice Hyde and his colleagues had allowed themselves to 'know' what everyone else in London knew in 1627, namely that the five knights were in prison for refusing to lend money to the Crown, they would have allowed bail without prejudice to the issue."[240] Whitelocke claimed that this assumption of ignorance was in defense not of the crown's interest but the subject's: "Much spoken that they were committed for a cause illegal. Nothing appeared to us by the record. We are not to take notice otherwise which will be hurtful to the subject."

Whitelocke's apology amounted to a confession that the judges were powerless to redress a manifest but undeclared grievance. That was the function of Parliament. Given that the knights had already been released, their case was moot. The remedy was consequently to be a general one, in the form of a declaration of the law that would restrain all such actions in the future. This could not be done, however, without sharply curtailing if not eliminating the King's power to detain his subjects without express cause. Kings had routinely done such; courts had upheld the practice. Many thought that such a power was essential to ensuring the safety of the realm, and thus, as the Lords had stated, "intrinsical" to the royal prerogative.

From this perspective, the Lords were not being gulled when they sought to save the prerogative, but restating the centrist position staked out, for example, by *Serjeant Browne's Case* (1540), when the Star Chamber judges had affirmed that, while the king was obliged to treat his subjects according to law, his discretion in imprisoning them was not to be questioned. As Guy observes, "the lords [could] not be criticized for trying to plumb the depths of the legal labyrinth without prejudice either to royal prerogative or to the liberty of the subject. . . . [A]t face value, the lords' propositions fairly encapsulated the 'just meridian' between civil liberties and royal prerogative which the peers had sought since the[ir] first conference [with the Commons]."[241] The only apparent way to do so was for the King to agree to express causes of detention at "a convenient time" and to thereupon permit regular judicial process to be exercised.

It was this qualifying phrase on which Selden in particular pounced. As he pointed out, it contradicted rather than confirmed Magna Carta, and gave a new, extralegal power not only to the King and his Council, but to the judges themselves:

> "A convenient time"; but every man was to be delivered by law [in Magna Carta]. If they were so wise then to hold it needless, why is it now necessary? And for convenient time, what is convenient time? Who shall judge of it but the judges? And so they now shall have the power of the lords of the Council. . . . At this little gap every man's liberty may in time go out.[242]

Selden's suspicion of the judges, like Coke's, is striking. They had conveyed the Lords' proposals to the Commons in person, the proposals of which they had been the principal authors and which, as Coke and Selden noted, had in every point loosened and weakened the Commons' language. They had almost certainly been in consultation with Attorney General Heath, who, if not the actual source of the offending phrase about "convenient time," clearly supported the concept. Selden had earlier accused Heath of tampering with the judges' order in the case of the knight he himself had represented, Sir Edmund Hampden, and it was debated then—as it is today—whether Heath had feloniously altered it to make it appear that the judges had entered a judgment rather than an interlocutory order. The question this raised, for Phelips, was whether the judges themselves had colluded in an attempt to pervert the record. "I hope the judges justly refused it," he said, "but if the judges did intend it, we sit not here to answer the trust we are sent for if we present them not to his Majesty to be punished." The Lords themselves were vexed when Justice Hyde declined to discuss the case with them, "we being to give an account only to the King." This remark was complicated when Buckingham revealed that Heath had recast the judges' order at the King's direct command. Hyde relented under pressure and subsequently gave testimony, but Whitelocke neatly encapsulated the dilemma the peers had taken upon themselves in assuming judicial review:

> Is there not a trust to be put to the sovereign power to restrain liberty? Your Lordships may think fit to consider and advise, and we did no more.[243]

The episode of the judges threw Parliament's dilemma into high relief. Though cast in legal language, the *Five Knights' Case* was in essence political. The judges had been asked to cut the Gordian knot of liberty and prerogative; that task, as Whitelocke dryly remarked, was now the Lords'. On neither the legal nor the political level was it welcome to the Upper House. Unlike the Commons, who had in Coke the most eminent jurist and in Selden the ablest legal scholar in the realm, the Lords were dependent on crown servants for advice and expertise insofar as they differed from their junior colleagues. Nor, as the body whose status was most intimately bound up with the prestige of the monarchy, could they be comfortable with a "popular" initiative that, however provoked by circumstances, seemed to curtail critical elements of the crown's authority. It was one thing to restrain the excesses of Caroline government through the ritual sacrifice of ministers and favorites, but quite another to pluck what royalists liked to refer to as the flowers of the crown. The Lords gravitated toward the center under these circumstances, trying to reconcile the liberties of the subject (which were also their own) with the King's just prerogative. What ensued in the next several weeks was, on the Lords' part, a complex effort to triangulate the needs and interests of the three estates.

The Lords had important leverage: there could be no bill without their consent, and, *pace* Coke, no effective petition. Parliament's status as a high court depended on its bicameral unity; the Commons' claim of judicature in their own house was contested, while the preeminence of the Lords had been affirmed in the revival of impeachment and other causes.[244] It may have been with a sense of this that Charles, in early May, abruptly withdrew his previous offer to settle the subject's liberties by bill, a move that narrowed the Commons' scope of action and forced them to fall back on a Petition of Right. Shortly after, the King expressed a view of his prerogative that was clearly incompatible with anything such a petition was likely to contain: "judges have no capacity of judicature nor rules of law to direct and guide their judgements in causes of that transcendent nature, which happening so often, the very intermitting of the constant rules of government for so many ages within this kingdom practised would soon dissolve the very frame and foundation of our monarchy."[245] As Coke and his colleagues appealed to a liberty under the law consecrated by successive ages, so did Charles to an inherent regal power, a *lex coronae* above any *lex terrae* that was within the cognizance of no judge and the purview of no statute. It was this claim that the Lords were still trying to appease, or at least avoid disputing, when they offered new language to the Commons to save the prerogative:

> We present this our humble petition to your Majesty not only with a care of preserving our own liberties, but with a due regard to leave entire that sovereign power wherewith your Majesty is trusted for the protection, safety, and happiness of your people.[246]

This language was much more terse and elliptical. It made no actual reference to the prerogative, "intrinsical" or otherwise. It made no mention of divine right, and was perfectly compatible with a theory that derived the King's power wholly from the consent of the governed. It envisioned no conflict between sovereign authority and the common law, and recognized no exemption from the former on behalf of the latter. The subject's liberty, it suggested, was entire and indefeasible, as was the King's due authority. They were each the undoubted possession of their respective owners.

In some respects the new clause was an implicit restatement of familiar and comfortable clichés. The genius of the constitution was that the subject enjoyed the "best" liberties while the prince had the most perfect preroga-tive. Each upheld the other in a harmonious whole. The subject's liberties made for a free and therefore a brave and prosperous people; the king's power assured their protection and welfare. But in other ways the language was more rigid and troubled, and looked not to the serene pieties of the past but to the confrontations of 1640–1642. The lawyers in the Commons were insisting in 1628, with far more urgency than they had in 1604, 1610, and 1621, that the liberties of the subject were a property right. In the Lords' new clause, the King's authority also appeared as such a right. As each subject en-joyed the right of his own possession side by side with his neighbor, so the king enjoyed his side by side with the people. The king's right was different and unique — it was a *power*, to effect the protection and welfare of the sub-ject — but it was not on that account any the less absolute and secure; that is, it was no less unconditionally a right. If to be an English subject and not a villein was to enjoy certain indisputable liberties, then to be the king of such subjects was to enjoy the certainty of a "sovereign power."

Here was a subtle but critical shift in the discourse of legitimacy, one that suggested the profound difference in style as well as conduct between Jaco-bean and Caroline absolutism. James I had always described himself as a "fa-ther" and "husband" to his people, a strategy that self-consciously reflected the renewal of virility in the English crown with the return of a male sover-eign but also accorded with the King's personal predilections. It would never have occurred to him to have said, as Charles did at the end, that a king and a subject were clean different things. James' was the rhetoric of the paterfa-milias, raised to the uxorious sublime (and reflected in such authors as Robert Filmer); Charles' was that of the dubious and lesser heir, the surviv-ing son whose title, though the first since Henry VIII to be undisputed, was overshadowed not only by a deceased elder sibling but even by a more popular sister.[247] True, Charles lacked the substantial qualification of his fa-ther in the 1620s; he had not produced his own heir. But even after the birth of the future Charles II in 1630 and despite the cult of domesticity he then fostered, the King was an isolated figure, as the equestrian portraits of Van Dyck — studies in psychology as well as emblems of authority — reveal.

Underlying these differences of personal style was a deeper paradigm shift, one that reflected the broader change from a culture of conscience — the common sense of value instilled by God and notionally possessed by all — to one of interest, the idea of value as individually construed and regulated by law. This shift was apparent in England's ever-more litigious courts, in its increasingly market-oriented agriculture,[248] in Charles' own incipient fiscal feudalism with its rack-rent stratagems, and on the concourse of the London stage. What makes Charles so fascinating a transitional figure is that he per-mitted, or required, the monarchy itself to be construed as an interest, while at the same time defining his actions in terms of conscience more than any ruler since Henry VIII, and laying his final appeal, his crown, and his head on a block that, also characteristically, he tried to convert into an altar.[249]

The problem with defining monarchical power in terms of a property right was that it was a right not to be enjoyed in and of itself, as private rights were, but *pro salus populi*, for the benefit of all. The presiding fiction of English law was that this power was so exercised; in the formula cited by the Lords' first version of the saving clause, it was *non ad destructionem*. The events of the previous twelve months, however, had converted this fiction into a fantasy. The Commons' leadership was still willing to credit Charles with good intentions personally, for without that fiction its choice would have been stark indeed. What it was no longer willing to do was trust his judgment. Charles, on the other hand, refused to separate these issues; that is, in practical terms, he was unwilling to allow his authority to be restricted by law. The Lords' second saving clause was an attempt to resolve this impasse by grounding both the royal prerogative and the subject's liberty in an inalienable property right, each absolute in its sphere and neither affecting the other. This was to substitute one fiction for another. Whereas the traditional fiction that the King could do no wrong was merely a normative one, however, the notion that the King's enjoyment of an absolute prerogative was entirely compatible with the subject's enjoyment of his ordinary liberty was contrary to fact. The King's discretionary authority did affect the subject's liberty, since it was precisely over that liberty that it was exercised. The Lords' clause simply mystified this process, and in effect denied it.

From the Commons' point of view, the new clause actually did far worse: it erected a power in the crown that had never existed before, a power without limit or definition. Alford pounced on this point at once:

> Let us look into the words and see what they are. What is "sovereign power"? Bodin says it is that that is free from any condition. By this we shall acknowledge a regal as well as a legal power. Let us give that to the King that the law gives him, and no more.

Pym agreed that the words of the Lords' amendment were unprecedented and dangerous, as did Coke. "This power," Pym said, "seems to be another distinct power from the power of the law. I know how to add 'sovereign' to [the King's] person, but not to his power." This handsome and much-quoted bon mot turned the Lords' phrase back on itself. The word "sovereign" was an appellation for the King in his natural person, either as a noun or as part of an adjectival phrase; it had no meaning in English law apart from that, and could add nothing to the powers the law gave him. Pym dissected too the phrase "leave entire that sovereign power" in which the offending words were embedded. In the passive construction, to "leave entire" was to stand aside from, to refrain from obstructing, diluting, or interfering with. In an active construction, however, it suggested that the people had given sovereign power to be enjoyed by the King. This sounded very much like the familiar royalist theory that the people had made an original and irrevocable grant of sovereign authority to their monarch which now inhered in his office. Pym pointed out that such a thing was impossible, for since no such power existed the people "were never possessed of it" and could not confer it. The only power that did exist was in the law ("All our petition is for the laws of England"), and that power, including the power to make and declare the law itself, had never been ceded by the people, but had always been exercised jointly through Parliament with the king.[250]

Hakewill and Coke spoke to the same effect. "I know the prerogative is part of the law," Sir Edward declared, "but 'sovereign power' is no parliament word in my opinion. It weakens Magna Carta and all other statutes, for they are absolute without any saving of sovereign power; and shall we now add it, we shall weaken the foundations of law, and then the building must needs fall. . . . By implication we give a sovereign power above all these laws."[251]

The thrust of the lawyers' argument was clear. No power existed apart from the laws, and therefore no power could contravene them. The King's authority as such rested in assuring their proper execution. His due prerogative was "part of the law," and wholly contained in it. If certain matters were left to his discretion, they were left there by the law, and this discretion was not arbitrary, but implied counsel by those sworn to his—and therefore the law's—service, and by the estates of the realm. The King had no absolute prerogative at all, if this were taken to mean powers above or indisputable by the law.

Coke brought the hammer of his authority down on the Lords' beleaguered formulation: "We must not admit of it; and to qualify it, it is impossible." With little further discussion, it was rejected outright.[252] As the Commons had refused a saving clause in their previously contemplated bill, so they refused one now in their petition of right. The first clause had been loosely drawn, and was clearly open to objection. The second one was far more tightly crafted but even more broadly unacceptable, since it not only restored to the King a particular power in dispute—that of committing persons without cause shown—but erected, as Pym put it, a generalized power "distinct . . . from the power of the law" itself.[253]

The crown's point man in the Upper House, Lord Keeper Coventry, tried again to rally the Lords behind the saving clause even as Charles, who had first forced the houses to sit through Easter recess and then threatened them with prorogation, insisted that the Lords finish the business of the petition at once in a new attempt to divide them from the Commons. This whiplash strategy, seconded by Buckingham,[254] made Coventry's efforts at persuasion all the more difficult. The Lord Keeper nonetheless attempted to put the most innocent possible construction on the clause. Ironically, the fullest report of his effort is in the report of it that Sir Edward Coke made back to the Commons. In the disputed phrase *leave entire that sovereign power*, Coventry asserted, "the word 'leave' . . . [was] never meant to give or show to the King more than he had before." It was intended not to expand but to narrow and specify the power of the crown, because it "did take away the indefiniteness of 'sovereign power' and reduce it to the King," i.e., to his customary and acknowledged power "to give protection, happiness, and safety to the people." *Sovereign power* was a mere tautology, for "As [the King] was a sovereign he must have power, and his power must be sovereign." Rather than wishing to create new powers, the term had been suggested by the Lords themselves as "milder" and "more easy" than one such as 'prerogative,' about which the Lower House appeared to be so touchy. There was, then, nothing in the Lords' clause that altered in any way the existing frame of the commonwealth. Far from being offered with such a purpose, it had been introduced merely because the words of the petition, having themselves gone beyond previous expositions of the law, required the saving of regal authority to balance them. Such pro forma clauses had often been inserted in statutes and petitions before, and the Commons had declared that they had no intention "to encroach upon [the King's] sovereignty or prerogative"— words they themselves (though Coventry was too politic to point this out) had used interchangeably. Why then, if they wished the King to spell out his repeated verbal assurances of their liberties in writing, should they balk at acknowledging their own former statements?[255]

The Commons parsed these words again in their own chamber, and found in them a world of danger. It was as if the entire constitution of England hung on the phrase that in its entirety read, "to leave entire that sovereign power *wherewith your Majesty is entrusted*" (emphasis added). Trust was, indeed, the nub of the issue, for trust was what Charles had demanded until it had become not the condition of his subjects' obedience but the touchstone of it. The Commons' lawyers would have none of such a trust, that is, of a naked relation between subject and sovereign, but only one mediated by the law. "There is in the King, concerning the statute laws, a trust, but in some there is not," John Glanville said coolly. "There is no trust whatsoever to be above the common law."[256] Robert Mason wondered by whom the King could be said to have been trusted with sovereign power. If it were by God— as the Lords' first saving clause had declared—then the people had no part in it. If it were by right of conquest, they were similarly excluded. If, on the other hand, their trust was entailed, then it was a legal trust by virtue of contract ("*ex pacto*"), the powers referred to could not lie outside the contract, and therefore lay within the law. This meant that the clause was simply otiose. Absolute power could only be derived from an absolute source (God) or an absolute contingency (conquest); if it proceeded from any other source, it could not be absolute. The question was how it should be construed in reference to the petition, which was simply a declaration of the subject's right:

> If it does not refer to the petition, it is merely useless and unnecessary and unbefitting the judgment of this great and grave assembly to add to a petition of this weight. If it has reference unto it, then it destroys not only the strength and virtue of our petition of right, but our rights themselves; for the addition being referred to each part of the petition will necessarily receive this construction: that none ought to be compelled to make any gift, loan, or such like charge without common consent by act of parliament, unless it be by that sovereign power which the King is trusted for the protection, safety, and happiness of his people; that none ought to be compelled to sojourn or billet soldiers unless by the same sovereign power; and so of the rest of the rights contained in the petition. . . . And we may assure ourselves that hereafter all loans, taxes, and billeting will be said to be for the protection, happiness, and safety of the people.[257]

If Charles had made the word "trust" tantamount to obedience, the Commons made it equivalent to consent. Both acknowledged that it was the defining element of a legitimate order, as opposed to a regime based merely on force. For Charles, however, trust began where the laws left off, whereas for the Commons it was a function of the laws themselves. As emphatically and unequivocally as possible, they disavowed any discretion in the King not defined by the law. They did so, moreover, with an extraordinary degree of unanimity and under the intensest political (and, for some, personal) pressure. Not a single member of the leadership suggested compromise with either version of the Lords' saving clause. Some key members of this group—Glanville, Wentworth, Noy, Digges, Littleton, and Seymour—later served the King during the Personal Rule or in the Civil War, just as Whitelocke had chosen to do. Others, such as Phelips and Selden, would make their peace with the Caroline government of the 1630s as best they could. Sitting together in the High Court of Parliament, however, they took their common stand, and the fruit of their labors, the Petition of Right, would as they knew far outlive their personal destinies and the accommodations that opportunity or necessity would later dictate for them. The Petition was famous for what it said, for the liberties it enunciated and secured to the law. But it was equally important for what it refused to say, that there could be any freedom or safety for the subject outside the law.

The Lords were left with the choice of accepting the Commons' petition without a saving clause, rejecting the petition in its absence, or framing a statement of their own. The latter choices were unacceptable. As Pym had pointed out, the liberties of the commons were the Lords' own liberties as well. William Coryton, member for Cornwall, remarked more bluntly: "The Lords, some of them, have been the actors of these loans. I pray God they may consider of it. We are, it may be, at the end of the parliament, then unhappy they are that are the cause of it."[258] The Commons had yoked the petition to the subsidy bill, insisting that it serve for a preface. Without the petition there would be no bill and therefore no supply for the King. This would almost certainly mean the dissolution of the Parliament and the resumption of prerogative taxation. Despite the insistence of the King's party that the Upper House stand fast behind the saving clause and Buckingham's own statement that he would vote against the petition if it lacked it, the Lords were in no position to incur the wrath of the public outside the walls of Westminster. That public was well informed about the proceedings in both houses, and Coryton's remarks, among others, circulated almost as quickly as they were spoken. The great outpouring of joy in the form of bell-ringing, bonfires, and feasting that greeted the final acceptance of the petition on June 7 was an indication of the fervor of popular expectation and the political tension that accompanied it.[259] The body politic was fully engaged in the struggle for the petition, not merely its representatives; and the massive public participation that marked the opening months of the Long Parliament was already being foreshadowed, though organized petitioning and protest still lay in the future.

The Lords, then, were trapped between pressures from above and below. They were not the less irritated by the former than the latter. If a majority of the peers had supported the saving clauses, whether from conviction, interest, or deference to the throne, a vocal minority with ties to the Commons' leadership remained in opposition.[260] The Lords had an equal stake with the Commons in the success—and survival—of Parliament, their own chief institutional base. They were no less irked by the frequent threats of prorogation and dissolution than their colleagues in the Lower House, and they showed this by taking their good time in deliberating and responding to the rejection of the second saving clause despite the King's attempt to impose a twenty-four hour deadline on their proceedings. Finally, most of them had little desire to gratify the Duke of Buckingham, whose personal party in the Upper House had dwindled despite his apparent immunity from direct attack.[261] After several days of tense face-to-face negotiation and behind the scenes accommodation, the Lords yielded to the Commons (who, for their part, accepted two modifications in their own text),[262] and agreed to forward the petition without a saving clause and without a remonstrance of their own. Instead, they appended an innocuous declaration that their intention was "not to lessen or impeach any thing which by the oath of supremacy we have sworn to assist and defend,"[263] a statement which spoke not to the King's power but to the subject's already-sworn obligation. Buckingham, who had threatened to vote against any petition without a saving clause,[264] now expressed his delight with the result and offered to take the petition to Charles personally. The Petition of Right was won.

Charles at once began a rearguard action to nullify the legal and political implications of the Petition. He called the judges privately into consultation, with no other parties present, and asked whether either under existing law or subsequent to the Petition he would be precluded from imprisoning any subject without a concurrently expressed cause, or required to bail him upon request. The occasion, though more narrowly construed and minus ritual prostration, was similar to the one on which his father had demanded of his judicial servants whether they would not consider his honor and profit in their rulings. Substantively, it was a demand for the judgment the judges had assured Parliament they had not given in the *Five Knights' Case*. This time, the judges could not hide behind a veil of ignorance. Adopting the language of the first saving clause, they opined that while "by the general rule of law the cause of commitment . . . ought to be shown," yet "some case *may* require such secrecy that the King *may* commit a subject without showing the cause for a convenient time" (emphasis added). They gave the same response to the query about habeas corpus, and replied to the one about the Petition of Right that, like any law, its particular application could only be defined in practice. Charles took the judges' answers down in his own hand, and compelled them to affix their signatures to his sheet.[265]

The judges doubtless hoped to trade on the ambiguity between the imperative and conditional senses of "may." They had given the King no warrant to withhold cause; they had merely refused to preclude a hypothetical possibility in which prudence or necessity might dictate it. Of course, the whole intent of the Petition of Right was to deny the King any such power, and it was for that reason that the language of "convenient time" now employed by the judges had been rejected. But the Petition was not yet law; the third of the estates had not yet spoken. The King wanted to know whether accepting the Petition would "conclude" him from "committing or restraining a subject for *any* time or cause whatever" without cause shown (emphasis added); the judges answered, clinging as narrowly as possible to Charles' own construction, that "although the petition be granted there is no fear of conclusion as is intimated in the question"—a reply that left open the precise meaning of "conclude," "restrain," "time," and "fear."

Whatever the judges may or may not have wished to obfuscate, Charles now had his own version of the saving clause, and with it the interpretation of the Petition that he desired. The judges had spoken of a "convenient time," but for this Charles himself had substituted "any time"—days, months, or years. The judges made no attempt to modify this formulation, which effectively superseded the one they had adopted in response to the first two questions. The King was still above the law, and the law itself, in the person of the learned judges—those living embodiments of Coke's artificial reason—had told him so.

Charles' next step was to answer the Petition in terms conformable to the judges' reply to his third question. The judges had avoided any positive characterization of the Petition, stating only that its scope and application would be determined in the courts. The King's first answer to the Petition on June 2 in effect reiterated this: "The King willeth that right be done according to the laws and customs of the realm, and that the statutes be put in due execution . . ."[266] This was more than an evasive reply; it was almost a negative one. It made no actual reference to the Petition itself, leaving open for future dispute whether Charles had accepted it, and arguably constituting the first blow in a future court challenge to its legal status. This, too, was consistent with the strategy the King had evolved over the long weeks of debate. After first accepting, indeed promoting the idea of settling the subject's liberty by statute, he had withdrawn his assent when, after the Commons had rejected the Lords' first efforts to water down the text of their bill as well as the first version of the saving clause, it became clear to him that he might face an actual restraint on his authority. The Commons, for their part, prepared the Petition in the form of a bill, giving it the traditional three readings, enrolling it in the statute book, and subsequently treating it as one.[267] Both sides, therefore, maneuvered carefully not only over the text of the Petition but over its precise legal significance. Without the appropriate royal assent, however, it was a document in limbo, of no more force than a protestation. That was the position the Commons found themselves in when, after receiving the King's first reply, they sat confounded in a "great silence."[268]

Several days of public anguish in both houses and intense backstairs negotiation produced a second, grudging reply from the King: "*Soit droit fait comme est desire par le petition.*" This, at least, was the version recorded in the *Proceedings and Debates*.[269] The answer that appears in the *Lords Journal* (3: 844) omits the last three words, as does the official printed version of the Petition of Right, which reads: "*Soit droit fait comme est desire.* Let right be done as is desired."[270] The omission of the final three words might, as the King declared, mean that his new reply was "no more than I granted you in my first answer," since, once again, no specific reference to the thing desired was stated.[271] We cannot be sure what the Commons heard, or thought they heard, because *Proceedings and Debates* is an edited compilation too. Whatever it was, the Commons accepted it with "a great and joyful applause."[272] Coke's gloss on the answer (which also omits the last three words in the *Proceedings and Debates* version, and substitutes "il" for "est"), is instructive:

> I am persuaded his Majesty's meaning was at first to give us as absolute and real an answer as now [this being his politic rejoinder to Charles' asser-

tion that he had given no more in the second answer than in the first], and now it is: *Soit fait droit comme il desire*. If this had been a private bill it is: *Soit fait comme il desire*; if a public, *Le Roy veult*. But the King now says: *Soit droit fait comme ils desire*[nt]. We could never have had a better answer. If we have desired good things, it is granted.[273]

Coke's response suggests a process of negotiation in which a less than 'desiré' but still satisfactory response had been obtained. The Commons wished the Petition to have the status of a public bill, for which the appropriate response, as Arundel pointed out in the Lords when the Petition was first bruited, was "*Le Roy le veult*."[274] What they received was the answer to a private bill or petition, but with the crucial word *droit* inserted. The subject had been granted not some vague assurance that the laws would be executed, but his *right*. It was this word that lit the bonfires and rang the bells throughout London and the kingdom.[275]

The public's joy was short-lived. The houses ordered and Charles consented to the publication of the Petition even before the prorogation of Parliament on June 26. This had never been done before. The King, however, tampered with the text. Both his answers were printed, the rejected as well as the accepted one. In addition, he included his speeches to the houses on June 7 and 26. In the first he had maintained that his prerogative neither had been nor could be infringed by anything his subjects might do. In the second he refused to forbear the collection of Tonnage and Poundage that Parliament had not yet granted him, and denied that to do so would be in violation of the Petition or his own proper authority.[276]

It might be said on Charles' behalf that, as the Petition was an instrument of propaganda no less than a statement of law, he was not unjustified in attempting to state his own side of the case. From his perspective, his first answer to the Petition was as satisfactory as the second, and, as he explicitly stated in granting the latter, offered no more. Both were sovereign utterances, "approved," as he declared, "by the judgment of . . . many wise men."[277] For the King not to enroll both in the official public record would be to imply that the first was defective, if not, as the Commons had suggested, deliberately deceptive. Similarly, the King's explanatory comments might also be considered an essential part of that record, since without them the presence of two answers to a single petition would be confusing to the general public.

The trouble with this defense is that the King had publicly and explicitly agreed in presenting his second answer that it would replace and supersede his first:

> His Majesty, being placed in his royal throne . . . commanded the Clerk [of the Parliaments] to enter in the Journal his former answer unto the said petition [of right] and the request of the Lords and Commons [for a new an-

swer] now to be delivered unto him by the Lord Keeper. And his Majesty did further command the said Clerk to cut off his former answer, which was written under the said petition (*2da Junii*), and to write down his answer which he now delivered unto the same. And accordingly the Clerk did cut off the said former answer which was subscribed to the said petition, in presence of the King, the Lords, and Commons.[278]

The King, in short, *had* entered his first answer in the parliamentary record, thus signifying it as his formal, lawful, sovereign response to the Petition of Right. Then, as a matter of grace, he had removed this answer and replaced it with a second. To remove the first answer was not to repudiate it, since by entering it its full validity had been affirmed. By physically effacing it and putting the second answer in its place, however, Charles had nullified it as a practical instrument. The second answer was now his only answer, and the first one was no longer part of the record. This was the act, and answer, to which the houses responded, and which signified the conclusion of business in the matter of the Petition of Right. It was the form in which the Clerk of the Parliaments, Henry Elsyng, had given the Petition to the King's printer, Bonham Norton, for publication. After 1,500 copies had been printed, Norton was ordered by Attorney General Heath to make "waste paper" of them and to substitute instead "sundry papers with divers hands to them" at the command of the King. This was the edition that appeared at the end of June.[279]

What Charles offered, then, was not a clarification of the Petition of Right, not a "scholarly" edition with all the relevant pronouncements concerning it, nor even a partisan version of it, but a deliberate falsification and misrepresentation of what had actually been done. Sitting in solemn state with the estates of the kingdom, he had dramatically withdrawn his first answer to their petition and razed it from the legal record. Whatever its momentary presence in that record, it was part of it no longer, and was consequently of no effect, standing, or further purpose. To reinstate it was to cloud a sovereign act: in a prince, the most dangerous and destabilizing thing that could be done, as in a subject the most treasonable. Beyond even that, however, Charles had simply broken faith. He had done what he need not have done in coming in person to give his second answer and in staging the removal of his first. That moment was a political compact as well as a legal one, which, had he proceeded in its spirit, might have offered a fresh beginning to the reign. The falsification of the Petition of Right was neither the first nor the last occasion on which Charles I broke faith with his subjects, but it was perhaps the one that was longest and best remembered.[280] It meant, simply, that not even statute made the law safe.

Absolutism had of course its defenders and converts—then and, contextually, now. Conrad Russell has observed that, although the Cokean doctrine that law was the ultimate source of authority has been taken as representing a kind of consensus among the common lawyers of early Stuart England, "In 1628, it was very far from clear that the 'common lawyers' outside the House of Commons were agreed on this interpretation of the common law and of its relationship to the prerogative." The justices, the majorities in the House of Lords who voted for the saving clause (including, in the Earls of Manchester and Marlborough, two former chief justices), as well as the King's legal counsel, were in agreement that the King's prerogative was not simply tied to the law; and, as Attorney-General Heath pointed out, even the lowliest constable could not do his job without a certain latitude. Coke himself was considerably embarrassed when Heath and Solicitor-General Shelton revealed that he had supported discretionary imprisonments both as a jurist and a councillor.[281]

The royalist position was not in fact unreasonable in itself or inconsistent with past practice. As Manchester put it, "that State is happye, where nothinge is lefte to discretion, yett in all places a Latitude is lefte to the Crowne."[282] The problem was that Charles had abused discretion by invoking it to replace regular legal process, and compounded the offense by declaring its discussion out of bounds. The Petition of Right attempted to state the law without debating the prerogative; it did this by construing what the King claimed as his generalized authority in terms of concrete acts by "sundry Commissioners" that violated specific laws, charters, and rights.[283] It was essentially a defensive maneuver that left the question of the prerogative unaddressed, although the Commons' debates made clear their refusal to confirm a discretion above the law. Charles, not the common lawyers, was the one who tried to make the prerogative an issue in the Petition, and this was rightly seen as an attempt to stamp his interpretation of it on the positive law.

The common lawyers in the House were not, then, trying to assert any novel theory of the law in 1628, much less to challenge or divest the King of the powers he rightfully possessed. They were attempting to certify the offenses committed by agents acting in his name by reference to the statutes that forbade them. The lawyers deliberately avoided dealing with the nature and extent of the King's powers as such; they only wanted to state the ways in which they had been abused and to gain surety against similar offenses in the future. Of course, the lawyers assumed certain axioms in their quest. They believed that England was a limited monarchy whose powers were framed by law and exercised by consent. They believed that the common law was uniquely shaped to English circumstances, and that it superseded all other kinds of positive law where those laws clashed with it. They believed that only they, the lawyers, could truly and finally interpret the common law, as the jurisconsults of ancient Rome had interpreted Roman law. These were the ideas of Sir Edward Coke, but they were also the ideas of Christopher St. German and of the lawyers who had sat in Parliament with him a hundred years before.

There was room for discretion in executing the laws, providing that the exercise of that discretion upheld and protected them. The King could suspend or dispense with the laws; he could pardon or reprieve those convicted by them. These powers were entrusted to him, however, so that he might do justice or prevent injustice, not that he might circumvent the laws, which properly bounded him even as he was modifying their operation in a given circumstance. The binding of power by law, the inadmissibility of power beyond law, was the fundamental principle asserted by the tradition of *dominium politicum et regale*. The presence of such abused power was attested by harm. As the King could do no wrong at law, so the law could do no harm. Where harm was present, there law had been infringed. To imprison without cause shown was to do harm, for, as Selden declared, "It is the body and sole distinction of freemen that they cannot be imprisoned at pleasure."[284] A freeman so imprisoned was a contradiction in terms; he became a bondman, and such a person was no longer recognized by the laws of England. He was without the law, in both senses of the term, and no greater harm could be done him: even the taking of his life was not worse.

This was the strong conviction expressed by the lawyers in the House of Commons, and it was by no accident that they expressed it there. Here, in the High Court of Parliament, they practiced a different kind of law than in any inferior court. "I profess though once I was of counsel," said Selden, "though then I spoke for my fee, for the gentlemen in their *habeas corpus*, yet now I speak according to my knowledge and conscience." Even as an attorney defending Sir Edmund Hampden, one of the Five Knights, and arguing on behalf of one man what he now argued on behalf of all, his function was different as his oath was different. He represented no party but the whole commonwealth. Sir Edward Coke, taxed with defending discretionary imprisonment, came as close to admitting the fault of an inferior judge or advocate as he ever would: "Mr. Solicitor, I am afraid, did *simulare*, and God forgive me, I have done so in other courts when I was in his case, but *simulatio*, I must tell you, is a slight passing over of the greatest sin that may be."[285] Rhetorical sleight of hand, and the advocacy it served, had no place in the High Court of Parliament, where law was declared and justice done as it could be done nowhere else.

If the common lawyers in the Parliament of 1628 had no new theory to propound but only, by their lights, an ancient constitution to defend, it would be difficult to overestimate the sense of their responsibility to do so in the body to which they had been called. "I was sent hither and trusted with the lives and liberties of them that sent me," Selden declared. Sir John Eliot went further; the laws themselves, he suggested, were his true constituency:

> The difficulty is great for whom I speak. It is not for myself, that's too narrow; I had rather suffer. It is not for the country for which I serve. It is not for us all and the country which we represent, but for the ancient glory of the ancient laws of England.[286]

The self-conception of the common lawyers (and of country gentlemen such as Eliot who, with perhaps a smattering of the law, conscripted themselves as honorary members of the legal fraternity) as spokesmen of the law was doubtless an inflated, and, as one might argue with Russell, a highly presumptuous one. But it was no less real for that. Its linchpin was the presence of Sir Edward Coke, whose authority had only grown with his exile from the bench and his legendary contests with the crown, and who served as the martyr, oracle, and icon of the law all in one. Did the sitting justices dissent from him, and hold that freemen might, after all, be treated as bondmen for "a convenient time" when necessity of state required it? Coke was, as Phelips called him, the "great *monarcha juris*," whose opinion outweighed all the rest, and even when the inconsistencies of his record were displayed, "we must appeal," Phelips said, "from Sir Edward Coke ill instructed to Sir Edward Coke well instructed"—a monarchical formulation indeed. If the King could do no wrong, neither could Sir Edward Coke.[287]

The lawyers of the House, then, at least in certain moods, regarded themselves as a consecrated elite. Coke, playing the trope of his own martyrdom, remarked at one point that although he was no longer a justice of the King's Bench on earth he hoped that he would be one in heaven. This sounds merely bathetic to a modern ear, but we must remember that in the early seventeenth century positive law on earth was validated by divine law, and consonant with it. For the common lawyers, the common law was God's law in England. In maintaining it they were upholding God's will, upon which both secular and Christian liberty depended. In the High Court of Parliament they were in the temple of the law as its sworn defenders.[288]

The Parliament of 1628: Religion and Liberty

Defending God's law in the common law was a necessary but not a sufficient step if the sphere in which divine command had its most direct application, the maintenance of true religion, were ignored. The notion that secular and Christian liberty were inseparably entwined, long a staple of the godly consensus, was borne home particularly by the perceived link between absolutist politics and Arminian piety. This link became in turn the central heuristic device for explaining England's troubles. The breach of civil law was the consequence of neglecting the welfare of the church and permitting its desecration by popish doctrine and practice. "As we daily see," William

Coryton said, "God is angry with us." Eliot observed that "our turning against heaven has justly caused heaven to cast us down," and even Coke, usually phlegmatic on religious issues, concluded that "God has punished us."[289] Such citations could be multiplied many times over in the parliamentary record. The constitutional emergency precipitated by billeting, martial law, and false imprisonment took immediate precedence, but the crisis in the church was pursued in tandem with it. This was the task of Pym, who had been the first to identify Arminianism as a threat to church and state in the Parliament of 1624 and who now as chair of the Committee for Religion led a fierce counterattack against the perversion of doctrine, the toleration of Papists, and the writings of Court-sponsored clerics, most notably Mainwaring and Sibthorpe but including such old favorites as Montagu and his Arminian bedfellow John Cosin,[290] as well as lesser lights such as Richard Burgess and Thomas Jackson.[291] Mainwaring, a royal chaplain, was actually impeached, making him the first cleric subject to the procedure used against Bacon, Cranfield, and Buckingham.[292] In some respects, obviously, he was a stand-in for the as yet untouchable Duke, but in Pym's comprehensive indictment he incorporated, as Phelips put it, "as many offenses as ever was done by any one man whatsoever." The chief exhibit was Mainwaring's notorious *Religion and Alegiance*, a book of two sermons doubly heinous in that they had been preached in the King's presence before being published to deceive the public at large. Mainwaring's offense too was double, in that he had wilfully distorted Scripture to justify the Forced Loan and to abuse the subject's conscience by threatening resisters with the pains of hell. In this, Pym said, he had done "as much as in him lies . . . to deprive all men of the propriety of their goods," to "infuse" in the King the notion of "an absolute power not bounded by law," to contemn and disparage Parliament, and to set King and subject at odds. All of this might be, and had been said of Buckingham, but the Commons were particularly incensed that a mere cleric should challenge the property rights of his social superiors, and, even more disturbingly, that he should suggest that the divine law could be turned against the common law. Pym, in his charge to the Lords, culled a number of damning passages from *Religion and Alegiance*:

> [I]f any king shall command that which stands not in any opposition to the original laws of God, nature, and nations, and the Gospel (though it not be correspondent in every circumstance to laws national and municipal) no subject may, without hazard of his own damnation in rebelling against God, question or disobey the will and pleasure of the sovereign.

> But, there be pretenders of conscience, against obedience; of religion, against allegiance; of human laws, against divine; of positive, against natural; [and so] of man's wisdom, against the will and wisdom of God; [and] of their own counsel, against the counsel of Solomon.

[W]hat a paradox is this, in the practical observation of human laws, so far
to prefer them in our own practice as to cause them hereby to prejudice and
preponderate divine determinations. . . . In prejudice of which laws of God
and nature, if any man in the world should observe the constitutions of
men, he did sin mortally.[293]

Here, apparently, was a theory hatched in hell, that the common law was
in opposition to what divine law permitted or even required, and that the
name of God be invoked to deny the fundamental liberties of the subject.
This was popery with a vengeance, of which Arminianism was part and parcel but clericalism the essence. Perverting the unquestioned doctrine that divine law stood above human law as its source and measure and that conscience had been implanted to signify it, clericalism asserted that human law
could never be fully congruent with divine intention and that conscience entailed submission to heaven's agents on earth, a divinely anointed king and a
divinely ordained ministry. Clericalism thus appeared in the guise of support for royal absolutism, but its ultimate purpose was an anti-Christian
church that tyrannized over king and subject alike. All false roads led to
Rome.[294]

Doctrinal popery, including its perceived offshoot Arminianism, was the
pernicious claim that the visible church possessed the keys to heaven and
hell. This claim assured the domination of the anti-Christian church. Only
the doctrine of predestination, which excluded the visible church from any
determinative participation in salvation, was proof against the wiles of Babylon, which was why it was the bulwark of both secular and Christian liberty
not only for the godly but for the broad, moderate consensus of the Church
of England. Mainwaring's most scandalous offense was thus in suggesting
that loan resisters incurred the penalty of damnation. If this was not a doctrine of works it came perilously close to one, and it showed how any weakening of predestinarian orthodoxy led speedily to prelacy and autocracy.[295]

In the despairing days between Charles' first and second answers to the
Petition of Right, when Buckingham was at last named as "the grievance of
grievances"[296] and the dissolution of Parliament seemed imminent, religion
came to the fore. Speaking to the motion to lay a charge against the favorite
before the King, Christopher Sherland of Northampton connected popery,
disaster overseas, and oppression at home as evils that emanated from a single source:

All you see tends to innovation, and though the conceptions are Spanish,
yet the issues little better. Disgrace at Ré, Denmark forsaken, Rochelle and
the Protestants not assisted but betrayed. Would not any man think we
sought our own ruin? Are not great papists in favor at court? Are not our
armies full of papists? None so familiar with the greatest next the King [i.e.,
Buckingham] as they. A toleration cannot come in in an instant. Why are

Arminians that have sought the ruin of the Low Countries allowed here? They run in a string with the papists and flatter greatness to oppress the subject.[297]

Sherland's colleagues agreed. Although immediate violations of the law required swiftest redress, the core problem was popery, and its prime sponsor was Buckingham. There was no evil that could not be plausibly ascribed to him. As the master monopolist of all — the one who monopolized royal patronage — he had filled the chief offices of church and state with sycophants and Arminians, and debased the peerage with his kinsmen and dependents, scandalizing honor and spreading the root of popery into Parliament itself. As Lord Admiral he had not only been responsible for the worst naval misadventures since the loss of Dunkirk, but had virtually opened the ports of the kingdom to the foe: "Our enemies," said Sir Robert Mansell, "now come into our harbors, and do survey our rivers, and do understand the secrets of our state." In the same vein, Eliot spoke of "praetorian bands" at the ready, and Benjamin Valentine feared that "this great man has soldiers every place to cut our throats." Most of all, however, whether by design or default, the Duke was the great conduit of Romanism into the kingdom. "If he be no papist," said John Hampden, the future luminary of the Long Parliament, "papists are friends and kindred to him." "What his religion is I know not," Selden said icily, but the consensus was that where there was smoke there was fire, and if no one was willing to openly accuse Buckingham of personal popery, there was general agreement that he had knowingly sponsored Papists and Arminians, given them a public forum, and placed them in positions of trust.[298]

The Remonstrance that the Commons produced in the aftermath of their impassioned debates on Buckingham and the state of the kingdom, and which they duly presented to the King in the presence of the Duke on June 17, was a document unexampled in our period. It has received far less discussion than the Petition of Right,[299] but the Commons considered it no less critical as an exposition of the state of the realm and a discharge of their duty to the subject. It offered an essential context to the Petition, providing, as it were, not only its background but its theory. It has been suggested that the Civil War notion of a "malignant party" of Papists and Arminians was born here,[300] but I would argue rather that the Remonstrance crystallized a sense of conspiracy already largely formed.[301]

If the Petition of Right voiced the secular grievances of the realm and represented the labor and judgment of the lawyers in the House, the Remonstrance expressed the sentiment and worldview of the godly gentry, and particularly of John Pym, whose intellect clearly stamps it. Its first pages deal all but exclusively with the "general fear conceived in your people of secret working and combination to introduce into this kingdom innovation and

change of our holy religion." This theme was linked not only to the toleration of popery but to the deliberate, systematic introduction of a foreign doctrine into the Church of England itself by "the factions of Arminians . . . being Protestants in show but Jesuits in opinion" and "incendiaries of those
states wherein they have gotten any head." Here, plainly, were the "secret
and strange" workings of a general anti-Christian conspiracy whose goal
was nothing less than the "utter expiration" of true religion.[302]

That religion should have had pride of place in the Remonstrance was
readily understandable, since the Petition of Right had dealt with "innovation and change of government" and Charles, by his reply, had "much comforted" the kingdom. The broad allegation of a general conspiracy in the
Remonstrance went far beyond the language of the Petition, however, which
addressed itself to "divers" acts committed by "sundry" individuals and
made no reference to structural "innovation" or "change." The parallelism
between the charge of innovation in religion and innovation in government
was converted in the Remonstrance into the accusation of a comprehensive
intent by "those that . . . contrive to change the frame *both* of religion and
government" (my emphasis).[303]

The Commons had a specific and immediate threat in mind, the presence
of "German horse" around the city. These were the "praetorian bands" of
which Eliot had spoken, and whose purpose was surmised to be a coup
d'état. They were the mercenaries by whom members feared to have their
throats cut, Parliament dissolved in a St. Bartholomew's Day massacre, and
Charles taken prisoner or worse. The King had sent assurance to the contrary, but if anything this only heightened suspicions further.[304] The Commons again professed themselves "comforted" by Charles' words in their
Remonstrance, but unwilling to relinquish the "just cause of fear" the presence of foreign horse inspired: "[T]he bringing in of strangers for aid has
been pernicious to most states where they have been admitted, but to England fatal. . . . [W]e are bold to declare to your Majesty and the whole world
that we hold it far beneath the heart of any free Englishman to think that this
victorious nation should now stand in need of German soldiers to defend
their own King and kingdom" (315).

The German horse were the fulcrum on which the Remonstrance turned,
for it was noted that Buckingham had received an unprecedented standing
commission "to be general of an army within the land in the time of peace,"
i.e., a time without civil hazard. This time had coincided with the rupture of
parliaments, the levying of unauthorized taxes, the discharging of loyal officers and ministers, and the calamities at Cadiz, Rhé, and La Rochelle. All of
these events were associated with Buckingham, and some had formed the
gravamen of the impeachment charges against him in 1626, but, with a mar-
shaling of rhetorical effect, his name was unspoken even as the Homeric

catalog of his sins grew. The Remonstrance added the export of gunpowder, the decay of trade, the vulnerability of the coasts, and the loss of naval command in the Channel, "the regality whereof your Majesty has now in a manner wholly lost," before at last citing Buckingham as "the principal cause" of the "evils and dangers" expressed and calling, in suitably deferential terms, for his removal as an officer, councillor, and companion.

The Petition of Right and the Remonstrance were two differently angled mirrors that reflected the same crisis. The Petition had priority because it was agreed that a restatement of fundamental law to which the King would acknowledge himself bound was of the essence, for without it no common presupposition of discourse was possible. The long process of attaining a satisfactory assent to the Petition, the repeated attempts to introduce a saving clause that would, at least to the Commons' leadership, have to all intents and purposes negated it, and the threat of dissolution if not of a military coup that hung over the proceedings, vitiated any sense of possible agreement even before the Petition was presented to Charles. The inescapable fact of the matter was that the King and the Commons were speaking two different languages, and that those languages—the languages of *dominium politicum et regale* and of royal absolutism—could not be reconciled, at least by those who spoke them. James I had suggested that they could coexist, that an absolute monarch might bind himself to accept constitutional processes without equivocation but also without loss of authority. His son, who combined a rigidly legalistic temperament with a lack of interpersonal skills, insisted on the right to override *dominium politicum* by *dominium regale* under circumstances that were his alone to judge, but which were so frequent as to appear continuous.

This last point is important, because the extent to which Charles deliberately operated a crisis government has not been fully appreciated by historians. The war he cheered on as Crown Prince in 1624 was one he was unprepared to operationally define or wage as King in 1625. The more he blundered and the more military setbacks he suffered, the less willing he was to admit mistakes and change course. Each new attempt to recoup his losses led him deeper into costly adventures no one outside his immediate circle understood and which no modern military or diplomatic historian has been able to rationalize. Each one required as well fresh levies of troops[305] and further infusions of revenue that could not, it seemed, wait upon ordinary constitutional processes. The emergency powers then invoked were defined as inherent in the prerogative, to be wielded at discretion and obeyed on pain of temporal distress and eternal perdition. To impress these powers on the legal record and to stamp them on conscience, judges were intimidated and pulpits abused, and novel doctrine embedded in church and state.

The King explained the necessity for his actions by insisting at each turn that his honor was at stake, an honor apparently indistinguishable from that of his feckless Lord Admiral. When members of the Commons observed bitterly that Charles treated Buckingham as a son, they used more than a figure of speech. With the only heir to the throne, Elizabeth of Bohemia, a penniless exile, the prospect of a coup against the throne was not only a plausible possibility, but, it was feared, already an accomplished fact. This fear had produced the Remonstrance, despite the grudgingly extracted assent to the Petition of Right. The Petition addressed the symptoms of the commonwealth's disease; the Remonstrance exposed its cause. Although the Remonstrance had been prompted only by the King's evasive first reply to the Petition, once introduced its momentum was irreversible. The Commons wanted not only a confirmation of the laws in 1628, but a wholesale reversal of public policy and the removal of the person held principally responsible for it.

It was not the King but the realm that effectively answered the Remonstrance. A London mob assassinated Buckingham's astrologer, Dr. John Lambe, in the waning days of the session, and Buckingham himself was accosted. Predictions of his death freely circulated until, on August 23, John Felton carried out what had become the popular mandate and stabbed him fatally. Felton was a decayed gentleman and a disgruntled client to whom the Duke owed money. But he also regarded himself, at least post factum, as a public avenger, and so he was held to be in the countless toasts that were drunk to him throughout the realm and in the bonfires that celebrated his deed as a providential deliverance. As one woman put it, he was "little David," the defender of the faith and the nation who had slain great Goliath. For his part, Felton cited the Remonstrance in defense of his act. The tyrannicide, he suggested, was the whole realm's act, and he merely its agent. The realm, in turn, embraced him; one versifier likened his sacrifice to that of Christ, and when he showed signs of life after being hanged the woman hired to wrap him in his winding-sheet was cursed when she refused the attempt to revive him. The people's savior was cheated of his resurrection, but the ghost of Felton, like those of Raleigh and Essex, lived on. Despite royalist efforts to blacken his name, it remained a byword for patriotism well into the eighteenth century.[306]

The assassination of Buckingham was the most significant public event in England between the accession of the Stuarts and the attainder of the Earl of Strafford in 1641. It removed the major obstacle to a reconciliation between Charles and his people, and offered a fresh start for the reign. The open question was whether the King would take it. When Eliot likened Buckingham to Sejanus in 1626, Charles famously replied that if the Duke were Sejanus then he must be Tiberius. What the country waited to see after August 1628 was whether he was. The memoirist Lucy Hutchinson, looking back on the abuses of the 1620s, commented that "The whole people were sadly grieved at these misgovernments, and, loath to impute them to the king, cast all the odium on the Duke of Buckingham."[307] The people were "loath," not only because the rhetoric of law and deference said that the king could do no wrong, but because if he did do wrong, not from evil counsel but of set will and purpose, there was no constitutional remedy: the courts were impotent, petition was useless, and counsel mute.

The solution proposed by Parliament in 1628 was twofold: the removal of evil (or complicit) counselors, and an agreement by the King to abide by the rule of law. As we have seen, these remedies were mutually supportive, and they embraced, in effect, both sides of the case. If the "symptom" of the nation's crisis was the violation of law and the "cause" was a scheming favorite, then a reaffirmation of the law, coupled with the removal of the favorite, might suffice to defuse it. In that case, the Remonstrance was the key document of the session. If, however, Buckingham were merely Charles' servant (as both the King and the Duke repeatedly professed), then the Remonstrance was tributary to the Petition after all, and the Petition itself was not an affirmation of law to which both parties unproblematically agreed but a political agreement that bound Charles to a new set of ground rules, however couched in the language of statutory and constitutional consensus. The rhetoric of both documents assumed, of course, the former interpretation. A close reading of text and context, however, suggests that the latter one was strongly entertained even if it could not be openly articulated. The Commons' insistence on getting a direct commitment from Charles in answer to the Petition rather than a vague generality, and making the grant of subsidy conditional on it, has the unmistakable ring of a bargain being struck with the responsible agent. The language of the Remonstrance, in contrast, portrays a fantastic world in which a pious and well-meaning *roi fainéant* is gulled by a rapacious favorite in league with a sinister international conspiracy — almost the plot of *King Johan*. The King is depicted as the fount of "wisdom, goodness, and justice," "a wise and judicious prince . . . above all things desirous of the welfare of your people," and of a true "religious heart." These virtues notwithstanding, he has nonetheless permitted England to become "weakened, impoverished, dishonored, and dejected," and in imminent danger of becoming "the most miserable and contemptible nation in the world." Despite the King's zeal, his Court is a hotbed of popery, his church is riddled with cryptopapists, and faithful ministers are silenced by his own seal. Despite his care for the realm, his coasts have been surrendered to Papist mercenaries from abroad, his forts are decayed and his munitions sold, and his shipping plundered and lost. Despite his acuity of judgment, finally, he is so wholly surrounded by timeservers, sycophants, and malignants that "how your officers and ministers do behave themselves . . .

is scarce possible to be made known unto you but in the parliament." The necessary *politesse* in addressing a sovereign cannot account for this almost schizoid construction. This is language that all but verges on its own negation, and nearly indicts the King for the evils it asks him to redress. Of course it does not do so, for this would cross the line that separates a discourse of legitimacy from one of rebellion; but the very tension it enacts between a "good" king and the bad acts his servants commit in his name makes transparent the implicit condemnation.

Bishop Laud, one of those specifically cited in the Remonstrance, wanted Charles to unmask its language and answer its contumacy. He prepared a draft response which went directly to the contradiction between the rhetorical assertions of the King's care, prudence, and wisdom, and the alleged consequences of his reign:

> In the beginning [the authors of the Remonstrance] call us a good, a just, a wise, a judicious prince. . . . But if we be wise and judicious how comes it to pass we are thus ignorant of imminent dangers, as the same remonstrance would make us? — or led so easily by false shows and pretentions of our ministers? And if we be good and just, how is it that what our wisdom sees amiss in the state, or the ministers of it, is not punished or amended? Be sure it is, and shall be. And we would have not our people only, but the world, know that neither Buckingham nor any man living does or can lead us to or from any action or business of state but as we see cause and reason to move us. And howsoever the intention might be, yet we do much scorn this should be thus unworthily turned upon us.[308]

Laud did not want Charles merely to challenge the premises and rebut the conclusions of the Remonstrance; he also wanted him to 'recall' it — presumably, that is, to remove it from the Commons' Journal as James had done with the Protestation of 1621, and perhaps to emulate his father by casting it into the fire. Clearly, the Bishop of Bath and Wells regarded the Remonstrance as a seditious document that the King could not afford to countenance. We do not know if Charles ever saw Laud's draft. He would certainly have approved it in principle. With the bill for Tonnage and Poundage still pending, however, he contented himself with giving his hand to Buckingham to kiss in the House of Lords, and commenting at the prorogation of Parliament that "For the remonstrance you presented to me I will say to you how pleasing the matter was any man may judge, and as for the words of it, that were such as no wise man will own."[309]

The two-month interval between the prorogation of Parliament and the assassination of Buckingham was of dire portent. The Petition of Right was corruptly printed; Bishop Williams was dismissed from the Council for his support of it; the foreign situation worsened; and Tonnage and Poundage continued to be collected in the absence of parliamentary warrant. Most alarming of all, however, was the raft of new preferments in the church. Several new Arminian or ceremonialist bishops were appointed or promoted, including Neile and Laud, and, perhaps most gallingly, Montagu, arraigned again by Parliament in 1628 and now installed as Bishop of Chichester. Nor was Mainwaring forgotten. Given a royal pardon, he was presented with the rectory of Stamford Rivers, Essex, a living worth four times his meager London benefice of St. Giles-In-the-Fields. Subsequent promotions culminated in his appointment as Bishop of St. David's in 1636, and thus the peer of the Lords who had condemned him.[310]

This, of course, was Charles' real answer to the Remonstrance. Preferment by preferment, the episcopal bench was being given over to the "Arminian party," and Antichrist taking his seat in the bosom of the church. The effect of this on godly opinion can scarcely be overestimated. Parliament in 1628 had lived in fear of an imminent civil coup d'état, and this fear had only grown when Charles secured all the powder in London after proroguing the session;[311] but Laud's promotion to the see of London, the center of godly enterprise, seemed a spiritual coup in fact. Popery was now established in the heart of the kingdom, and the panicked reaction of the Commons to the discovery of an alleged Jesuit cell at Clerkenwell in the session of 1629 showed the depths of their alarm.

If there was any hope for a change in policy after Buckingham's assassination, it was soon dashed. Laud immediately asserted his control as the de facto primate of England. At the same time, the continued collection of Tonnage and Poundage created a crisis in the merchant community as severe as that caused among the gentry by the Forced Loan of the previous year. The Tonnage and Poundage issue was the latest chapter in the two-decade struggle between Parliament and the Stuarts for control of the customs. The Commons were unprepared to authorize collection of Tonnage and Poundage without fixing the rates, and Charles was adamant that, as with all other impositions, such a determination belonged solely to him. The monies involved were not trivial; customs duties were now the largest part of the King's regular income. From the royal point of view, Parliament's grant of Tonnage and Poundage was, as the Commons had said of their traditional request for free speech in the Apology, a matter of form only. Parliament had abdicated its participation in the realm's symbolic acknowledgment of the King's right to his customary revenues—a due part of the ceremony of each new reign—by failing to enact the appropriate statute of Tonnage and Poundage in the Oxford Parliament, and if he graciously permitted it to make amends at a subsequent sitting it was not to be at the cost of tolerating further insults to his prerogative.

From the Commons' perspective, of course, the matter appeared quite differently. Impositions had been the most contested grievance of the previous reign, and a stay or limitation of Tonnage and Poundage was the best means to test a new king's intentions and resolve. That Charles was already demanding new war taxes on top of those already granted in 1624 (and whose disbursement was still unaccounted for) brought the issue to a head. By 1628 the unauthorized collection of Tonnage and Poundage had become the principal complaint of the Petition of Right, taking precedence even over the Forced Loan. In accepting the Petition, Charles had apparently agreed to the necessity, or at least the desirability, of a statutory authorization, despite the caveat that he regarded none of his powers as infringed by it. This placed the onus for prompt action upon the Commons, for if they delayed action while the King forbore to collect his customs they would in effect negate the value of the subsidies they had just granted him. At the same time, however, they had very credible evidence of new plans to raise the rates, not just on Tonnage and Poundage but for customs generally. If, then, the Commons passed a bill for Tonnage and Poundage without regulating the rates themselves, they gave the King carte blanche to do so himself; if they set their own rates, they risked a veto; if they took no action at all, they would appear to be acting in bad faith. Of these alternatives, the first was worst of all; as the member for Bath, Walter Long, put it, "Let us not now grant we know not what."[312]

In the end, the Commons opted to do what they had learned to do best: they remonstrated. The King responded by doing what he did best as well: preempting the presentation of the new remonstrance by a matter of hours, he abruptly prorogued Parliament.

Taken as a financial issue in its largest context, the question of Tonnage and Poundage in early Caroline parliaments may be seen as part of the general effort to rationalize the royal fisc that had begun with the Great Contract. Coke and Phelips had wanted to do this in 1625, making the occasion of the Tonnage and Poundage bill an omnium-gatherum for fixing impositions of all sorts. Coke had continued to insist in 1628 that "The King has no manner of custom but by act of parliament." At the same time, he conceded that Charles could not subsist "if his ordinary revenue do not discharge his ordinary expenses." What he wanted, then, was a broad bill that would stabilize royal finances (pruning what he regarded as superfluous expenses), give security to merchants, and stimulate trade. This was a more modest project than the Great Contract had been, but it was still a substantial initiative. It would make the crown solvent, notionally at any rate, while affirming the principle of taxation by consent of the realm. All parties and institutions would benefit; not least of all, from Sir Edward's perspective, the law.[313]

The accretion of irregular custom charges over several reigns and the uncertainty about their value and incidence made a simple confirmation of Tonnage and Poundage inadequate at this point. Still, a limited bill that would have put the King's collection of imposts on an accepted legal footing was feasible, and the Petition of Right had all but mandated it. It did not come to pass for three reasons, one logistical, another tactical, and the third strategic. Logistically, there was simply not enough time to produce a bill. On June 14, for example, when the Committee for Tonnage and Poundage was scheduled to report, the business of the House included, among other matters, a full-dress debate on the Remonstrance against Buckingham; the approval of charges against Lord Mohun, a newly ennobled client of the Duke, for the oppression and false imprisonment of tin workers; the transmission of the indictment against Mainwaring to the Lords; the report of Christopher Wandesford's committee on Montagu; and Sir Thomas Hoby's report on the presentment of recusants. It was not for another week that the question of Tonnage and Poundage could receive serious debate, and at that point only five days remained to the session.

The tactical problem involved the book of rates. Without an at least temporary agreement to freeze them, any confirmation of Tonnage and Poundage was simply, as Walter Long had observed, a blank check. The Commons were appalled to discover that a courtier (and MP), Sir Edmund Sawyer, had proposed to double the rates by the simple expedient of converting every "1" in the book to "2" by hand. Questioned about this, Sawyer adamantly insisted that he had examined the rates "by the King's command" alone.[314] Rumor had it that Charles and Buckingham had perused them together as well. Under these circumstances, it was essential that Charles personally assure the House that the rates would not be unilaterally altered. Instead, he bluntly confirmed that Sawyer had acted at his behest, and offered no commitment to maintain the existing rates at all.[315]

The strategic problem was, of course, Buckingham. The revenues of Tonnage and Poundage were traditionally dedicated to naval and coastal defense, and, as the Remonstrance observed in detail, the country's ports and seas were in dire condition under the Duke. His removal as Lord Admiral was accordingly the *sine qua non* if these monies too, as Phelips put it, were not to be dissipated "in airy honor."[316] The Commons had yoked the subsidy bill to the Petition of Right, and now they linked the authorization of Tonnage and Poundage to the Remonstrance. When Charles gave his hand to Buckingham in the Lords on June 17, he affirmed his bond with the Duke in the most unambiguous terms and rejected any accommodation that would sacrifice him. That left the Commons with the option of legislating the rates themselves or failing to pass their bill. The consequence of the latter was obvious; "necessity," as Digges glumly put it, would force the King to continue collecting his customs in breach of the Petition of Right. In fact, as the Remonstrance pointed out, the Petition had already been breached, since forced billeting continued in spite of it — an indication, parenthetically, of how closely its execution was being monitored, and of how great was skepticism over the King's intentions.[317] As for fixing the rates, the only way to do so in the time remaining was, as Coke noted sardonically, to adopt Sawyer's method. Accordingly, it petitioned the King to extend the session, or at least to adjourn rather than prorogue it. An adjournment would have enabled it to take up pending business at the point where it had been left; a prorogation would require it to begin de novo. Charles responded with a prorogation.

From one perspective, the debate over Tonnage and Poundage reflected a political impasse between a parliament demanding policy and personnel changes in the crown and a king stiffly resisting them. We must, however, consider the matter in a broader context. As Russell pointed out, the Commons had voted in 1625 to grant Tonnage and Poundage for one year as a stopgap measure when Phelips and Coke were unable to complete work on their reform of the customs, but the Lords failed to act on the measure. Russell noted that "the result of these manoeuvres . . . was not to preserve Parliamentary control of the customs, but almost to bring it to an end," since Charles continued to collect them absent authorization. "For this disastrous muddle," he continues, "the blame must be placed on the plague," for "It was only the plague which made a temporary bill necessary."[318] From whose point of view, however, was this result a "muddle"? It was not, after all, the plague that frustrated a reform of the customs, but Charles' insistence that Parliament sit through it rather than adjourning the session to the fall. Similarly, it was the King's choice to prorogue instead of adjourn Parliament in 1628, thus negating its work on Tonnage and Poundage, and his decision as well to refuse the House the time necessary to bring some form of bill to fruition. It seems reasonable to infer that Charles wished to forestall a bill of Tonnage and Poundage or any other bill Parliament might prefer on customs duties, and that he was content, not to say satisfied, to collect such levies by crown warrant alone. This was not a muddle. It was a clear and consistent policy.[319]

The failure to pass a bill of Tonnage and Poundage in 1628 (or, from a royal perspective, the success in averting one) meant that the King would be in violation of the Petition of Right in continuing to collect it. But Charles had never conceded that his prior collection of it had broken the law, and so he could maintain that in continuing to do so afterwards he was properly exercising his inherent authority. If the Commons wished him to exert that authority with their consent, they must provide it; failing that, he was blameless if he did so in his own fashion. The King emphasized that living up to the Petition of Right was the Commons' responsibility, not his. "I have done my part [in assenting to it]," he told them; "Wherefore, if this parliament have not a happy conclusion, the sin is yours, I am free from it." Instead of confirming his ancient custom, they had drafted a remonstrance with the intent, he said, to "debar me of Tonnage and Poundage, which is a flower of my crown, and without which I neither may nor can subsist."[320] Manifestly, then, the onus for violating the Petition rested with the houses, not with him.

Here was the apparent rub. If the Petition of Right were regarded as a contract between King and Parliament, then from the King's point of view the performance obligation rested exclusively with Parliament, and from Parliament's it rested with the King. Charles had offered his subjects a confirmation of their liberties; instead they had presented him with a catalog of grievances, the remedy for which—the proper provision of his subsidy and custom—lay in their own hands. For Parliament, on the other hand, the Petition was a concrete list of legal violations for which redress was demanded of the appropriate officer. In accepting the Petition with the formula *Let right be done as is desired*, that officer, the King, had undertaken to halt immediately forcible billeting, the confiscation of property, compulsory loans and other forms of unauthorized taxation, unlawful detention, and the suspension of ordinary justice by martial law. Each party to the contract, in short, read it as requiring the other one to act first. Parliament insisted that the King desist from certain actions; the King insisted that Parliament perform them.

Such disputes, in ordinary contracts, are settled by an appeal to a neutral arbiter or court. Between Charles as a sovereign prince and Parliament as high court, however, there was no third party to give legal and binding judgment, and if we regard Parliament and the King as agents in a self-contained system of discourse—as some historians have—then our own ex post facto judgments will be endlessly debatable. Charles had his case, and he has had his defenders. But the Petition of Right was not conceived in a vacuum and it was not received in one. The body of the realm—the thing which the King personated and Parliament represented, which was simultaneously the subject, theater, and audience of their discourse—waited for relief from its oppressions. It saw Parliament as its champion, but it wanted to believe in its King. It greeted the Petition of Right with joy as a herald of reconciliation between King and Parliament as well as a concrete commitment to end martial law, curb the abuses of the soldiery, and return things to their accustomed ways. It longed for the removal of Buckingham as the necessary means to this end, and it greeted the Commons' Remonstrance as its own utterance. It was in no doubt as to the party on whom the burden of execution fell for the restoration of civil justice and order. It did not regard the Petition of Right as a promissory note by Parliament to pour further sums of money into a chimerical war whose object seemed, increasingly, not the King of Spain or the King of France but the people of England themselves. It believed the King had given his pledge, and it waited to see him keep it. The court that judged between King and Parliament in the spring and summer of

1628 was the court of public opinion, and it was clear on whose side it came down.

In what was to have been its parting word, the abortive remonstrance for Tonnage and Poundage, the Commons reminded Charles that as matters stood and in the absence of an authorizing bill, "the receiving of Tonnage and Poundage, and other impositions not granted by Parliament, is a breach of the fundamental liberties of this kingdom, and contrary to your Majesty's royal answer to the . . . Petition of Right."[321] Armed with the Petition and this very direct gloss on it, leading members of the merchant community, including the MP John Rolle, refused to pay Tonnage and Poundage. Resisters' goods were first seized, and then their persons. Although they were granted bail, avoiding a repetition of the *Five Knights' Case*, the Court of the Exchequer upheld the sequestration of the goods, referring all further questions to Parliament.

Perhaps the most dismaying aspect of events in the latter half of 1628 was that Buckingham's removal from the scene had brought about no change in public policy. While thus of immense symbolic importance, the Duke's assassination had little practical consequence. Although the theme of evil counsel would continue to sound (embittered by the defection of one of Parliament's own, Sir Thomas Wentworth, who was reconciled to the Court and elevated to the peerage in July 1628),[322] it too lacked force by itself in the absence of the favorite. If the King were not to be held personally accountable for the actions of his government—that is, if what had been alleged against Buckingham were not to be laid to his charge—then another villain or villains had to be interposed between Charles and the policies carried out in his name.

It might be asked why men did not simply take the King at his word when he insisted, as he did repeatedly, that his servants and councillors were the executors of his will, and that their actions were his own. The answer lay only partly in the powerful inhibitions—legal, religious, cultural, and political—against concluding that a particular king could do wrong, had done wrong, and, unchecked, would continue to do wrong; that is, answered willfully to the name of a tyrant. There was also the practical problem of mounting resistance, assuming that the ideological inhibitions to this, too, could be overcome. There had been no successful rebellion against the crown since 1485, and the favoring conditions of Henry Tudor's insurrection, a disputed succession with a plausible and well-armed pretender on English soil, were absent. Even in the heyday of the medieval baronage, rebellion had often taken decades to mature: twenty years in the cases of Edward II and Richard II, forty in that of Henry III. Nor did noblemen keep private armies at the ready as of yore. The modern barons were deputy lieutenants who trained local militias under royal commissions, not lords with sworn vassals and retainers.[323] The last baronial rebellion, that of the northern earls in 1569, had been an anachronistic exercise in Catholic loyalism and feudal nostalgia, easily suppressed by central authority. The crown had a far more effective monopoly of force than in the early years of Elizabeth, a force it displayed to chilling effect in the collection of the Forced Loan.[324] Even more foreboding than the spectacle of militia units billeted on the local populace, however, was the threat of mercenaries, German, Irish, or other, that so distressed Parliament in 1628. To one's countrymen there was always an appeal, but foreign troops gave no quarter and obeyed whoever paid them. They were also a chilling reminder that England's dynasty was still, after a quarter century, a foreign one. James' march south from Edinburgh in 1603 might have been choreographed as a triumphal progress, but it was still unavoidably a symbolic conquest: so presented, and, despite the theme of a *rex pacificus* that James sought to foster, so received.

The overt power of the crown—its courts and jurisdictions, its ability to impress the bodies of the poor into military servitude, to use those impressed bodies in turn to intimidate their recalcitrant betters through forced billeting, and to consign the latter finally to prison or penury at will—all of this confronted potential resisters with formidable difficulties. Such difficulties were, however, purely negative ones; they were obstacles that could, with sufficient unity and resolve, be overcome. The larger problem was to find a countervailing force, an institution of sufficient authority and regard to serve both as a nucleus for resistance and an alternative source of legitimation. The sole and obvious candidate was Parliament. Politically, it contained the three most serious elements of potential opposition to the Caroline regime: the common lawyers; the godly gentry; and the nobility. None of these elements in themselves provided a viable focus of resistance, but together within the institutional framework of Parliament and as representatives of the commons at large their force was not only combined and augmented but uniquely focused. Without Parliament, the common lawyers could only fight a rearguard action against the rising tide of absolutism and the imposition of a civil law model on England. Within it, they had been able to compel the King to acknowledge the primacy of common law rights and procedures in the Petition of Right. The lawyers' idea of themselves as the guardians of a trust had been only fully realized in the crisis of 1628, but it had expanded there into a sense of almost totalized responsibility for the general welfare. From being the protectors of the common law (progressively identified with the law as a whole), the lawyers had taken upon themselves the function of stewards of the "ancient constitution" and the "fundamental laws," these in turn being identified with the commonwealth itself.

The godly gentry, epitomized by Pym, were a tight-knit community bound by local and regional networks of kinship and ministerial patronage.

If the common lawyers conceived of themselves as speaking for the law as such, the godly gentry were the stalwart defenders of the Calvinist consensus embodied in the national church. They rose as naturally to the defense of that church as the common lawyers did to the law, yet they, too, depended on the forum of Parliament to expose the corruption of Reformed doctrine and practice and to root out its agents. In its absence they would turn to schemes of overseas plantation, hoping to right the foundered ark of the elect nation in the New World while the ministers who were the natural lights of the church sought refuge in private households or with expatriate congregations.

The baronage had once been able to challenge the crown on its own, but its day as an independent actor (or set of actors) was long past. The peers were divided among an increasingly ceremonial Court nobility created under Buckingham's patronage, a service nobility whose status depended on appointment to the Privy Council and the deputy lieutenancies, and an outsider group that contended for favor or nursed its grievances. These categories were shifting and to an extent overlapping, but their organizing principle was proximity or distance from the crown as the acknowledged source and center of power and honor. Older families, particularly excluded ones and those with connections to the godly gentry, were, again, a potential focus of opposition, but the trimming of figures such as Arundel and Pembroke was the measure of aristocratic accommodation to the Court regime. In this as in many other respects, England in the 1620s appeared, on a functionalist analysis, to be conforming itself increasingly to Continental models of centralized monarchy. Only in Parliament did the peers exert authority as an estate, and only there did their political power appear to be waxing rather than waning. But they were not of themselves a sufficiently cohesive interest to resist the crown or to rally the commonwealth at large.

Charles' attraction to Continental styles of monarchy was apparent early, and he showed particular interest in Louis XIII's handling of the French Estates General. The anxiety this provoked was given voice in June 1626 by an MP, George More, who, invoking the familiar trope of English liberty and French subjection, declared that "we were born free and must be free if the King would keep his kingdom." The suggestion that Charles might prove a tyrant was far beyond the pale, and the House sent More to the Tower. It was "not fit," said John Glanville, "for us to hear or for any man to make a possibility that there might be a tyranny in this kingdom." The genie was out of the bottle, however, and the connection between "new counsels," tyranny, and rebellion had been publicly made.[325]

If Charles were susceptible to "tyranny," or at any rate to autocracy, it was evident that Parliament was his chief hindrance. Did he mean, then, to break Parliament to his will, if not to dispense with it altogether? Many observers, foreign and domestic, thought or feared so. Russell has best made the case to the contrary. Although Charles had prorogued Parliament rather than dissolved it, the reasons for bringing it back into session were unpersuasive. The King had already begun to withdraw from his European adventures, a process expedited by the death of Buckingham. Further subsidies were no longer urgent, nor were they likely to be granted except in amounts too trivial to outweigh the political risk. The crown had no urgent legislation to enact. The only pending business of substance was the bill for Tonnage and Poundage, in which the King had shown little interest, if not positive disinterest. The continued collection of the tax in defiance of the Petition of Right was sure to provoke an outcry and a new round of harassment for royal servants, as was the promotion of Laud, Montagu, Mainwaring, and the other Arminian and *jure divino* clerics. Why, then, was Parliament recalled at all? Russell conjectured that

> If a legal grant of Tonnage and Poundage was the only reason Charles had for calling the Parliamentary session of 1629, he may have called it out of inertia. He may have called it in order to keep his word, given in 1628. It is, however, most probable that he called the session because, like other prominent Englishmen of his day, he had a strong attachment to the proper, traditional, and legal way of doing things. A successful Parliament was a symbol, both of his subjects' affection for their King, and of their allegiance. If Charles was still a believer in Parliamentary ways of doing things, the assembly of 1629 needs little explanation. Anyone who wishes to maintain that Charles was a natural enemy to Parliaments must produce a better explanation of the recall of Parliament in 1629 than has yet been heard.[326]

Russell offers no explanation for why Charles prolonged a Parliament that could not possibly be "successful" in his terms, if even loyal, but merely challenges others to do so. The argument from inertia we may lay by as a bagatelle. The notion that Charles may have felt bound by his word must contend with the number of times he had already broken it: in offering Parliament a bill for its liberties and then withdrawing it; in consenting to the Petition of Right and then holding himself unaccountable to its provisions; in agreeing to publish the Petition with the assent the Commons had accepted and then publishing it in altered form. A prorogation was in any event not a promise but a mere statement of royal intentions at the moment; James I had dissolved Parliament after proroguing it in 1622, and Charles was to do the same in 1629. Nor does Russell actually assert that the King was indeed enamored of "the proper, traditional, and legal way of doing things"; to the contrary, he suggests in the same paragraph that by 1628 "Charles had very little use for Parliaments."[327] With this statement, at any rate, one need not take issue.

The most reasonable explanation for the recall of Parliament in 1629 is that Charles needed a dissolution he could justify to the country. He did not have it in June 1628. The Petition of Right had revived hopes, at least momentarily, of a reconciliation between King and Parliament. The prospect that a bill of Tonnage and Poundage might yet be passed would take at least some of the sting out of its continued collection and the consequent violation (as all but the King and his advisers considered it) of the Petition of Right. A premature dissolution would be associated as well with the highly popular Remonstrance against Buckingham. Parliament was the hero of the hour, and it was perhaps for this reason that Charles forbore to confront it directly as Laud, for example, wished him to do. Finally, the prorogation had been hastened by the Commons' pending remonstrance over Tonnage and Poundage, itself prompted by the King's refusal to grant them time to finish their bill. Had Charles dissolved Parliament at that moment, or shortly after, it would have been very difficult for him to pretend that he wished to have any legislation on the subject.

This is not to suggest that Charles intended the 1629 session to fail in any straightforwardly Machiavellian way. If Parliament did his bidding, respected his prerogative in church and state, and accepted governance on his terms, there was no reason why it might not remain as "a symbol, both of subjects' affection for their King, and of their allegiance." If not, however, the onus could be placed on a contentious and obsolescent institution that no longer served the national interest and that, like medieval representative bodies elsewhere, would have shown itself incompatible with the requirements of a modern state. Charles' position was thus fail-safe. Whether Parliament "succeeded" or failed, the result would be to his advantage.

The Session of 1629 and the Breakdown of Legitimacy

The King's opening speech to the session on January 24 called for the immediate passage of a Tonnage and Poundage bill. Past delays were not his fault but that of others, and the bill "would not have been struck on, if men had not imagined that I have taken these duties as appertaining to my hereditary prerogative, in which they are much deceived; for it ever was and still is my meaning, by the gift of my people to enjoy it." Charles had been compelled to collect the duties by "necessity," but he had never claimed them of "right." Having thus settled this "scruple," he expected his subjects to proceed to their "gift" without further loss of time.[328]

Even by the Caroline standard, this speech was disingenuous. In his last address to Parliament on June 26, Charles had described Tonnage and Poundage as "a flower of my crown," a phrase that unambiguously referred to the hereditary prerogative. He now told the houses to remember something other than he had actually said. Not only had they misunderstood him,

Charles insisted, but they had used their own error as a "scruple" to deny him the subject's gift, thus compelling him to collect by necessity that which they had declared it their intention to settle on him by law. Accordingly, it was Parliament, not Charles, who was responsible for the imprisonment of the merchants and the distraint of their goods. This too was disingenuous, since what had prevented the passage of a Tonnage and Poundage bill in 1628 was not the question of whether its collection was a prerogative matter but lack of time to frame a book of rates. Charles not only wanted to persuade the houses that they had heard something other than he had said, but that their misconstruction of his words on June 26 had accounted for their failure to act in the previous three weeks. Cause and effect were thus to run backwards.

The real tactical reason for Charles' haste was to head off the investigation the Commons had already begun on the unauthorized collection of Tonnage and Poundage since the previous session.[329] The status of this collection was of a different nature than it had been prior to June 7, the date the Petition of Right had notionally taken effect. If the King continued to offer a plea of necessity after June 7 as before, it would mean that necessity (interpreted by the King) trumped legality even where a legal remedy was available. That remedy was, of course, the bill for Tonnage and Poundage, which the Commons had undertaken and which Charles had denied them time to complete. If "necessity" had continued in force after June 7, as Digges had warned the Commons it would in the absence of a bill, it was because the King had chosen it. Choice and necessity, however, were logical opposites. The only way the collection of Tonnage and Poundage after June 7 could be reconciled with a claim of necessity was for the Commons to accept Charles' fiction that the blame for not passing a bill was theirs and not his, and the concomitant denial that he had ever claimed Tonnage and Poundage as a matter of right. They would, in short, have to enter his fictive world.

Under these circumstances, then, passing a bill of Tonnage and Poundage would be tantamount to abrogating the Petition of Right. Not only would it mean forgoing the attempt to find and punish those who had collected the new levies in contravention of the Petition (since the royal claim of "necessity" would absolve them), it would mean as well abandoning the merchants who had refused to pay them on the basis of the Petition and had suffered in their goods and persons as a result. It would mean abandoning the country that had supported the merchants and that looked to the Petition to protect it from arbitrary taxation. It would mean severing Parliament from those it represented, and making it the pliant instrument envisioned by Charles I.

The Commons therefore put off the King's demand for an immediate bill, excusing themselves with the bare comment that as a bill of subsidy it was not to be proposed except by the House itself. They proceeded to interrogate and arrest the King's officers, and to seek the restitution of distrained goods. At the same time, however, and with even greater urgency, they opened a broad inquiry into the state of religion. These two issues, Tonnage and Poundage and religion, were to occupy the attention of the House to the virtual exclusion of all other business with the exception of private bills and petitions. The pursuit of Charles' agents was necessitated by their willful breach of the Petition of Right. By continuing to collect Tonnage and Poundage they had defied what King and Parliament had declared to be the law of the land. The Commons could not fail to respond to such defiance without tolerating the usurpation of the crown's authority as well as their own by inferior agents. They knew that in fact these agents had not acted on their own but on the King's authority, because Charles had indicated as much in his speech of January 24. There he had again invoked "necessity" as his and (per corollary) his servants' warrant against the Petition of Right. In pursuing those who had acted on his behalf, the Commons were rejecting the claim of necessity and in effect pleading Charles' own words against him—the words with which he had assented to the Petition of Right. In pronouncing that assent he had committed not only his royal person but the crown he represented and embodied. It was not a conditional assent, or one that could be made with reservation or equivocation. It was not even dependent upon Parliament passing a bill of Tonnage and Poundage, for although that was part of the political bargain the Petition represented, to have admitted such a condition would not only have vitiated the legal standing of the Petition but would have made it hostage to Charles' willingness to grant sufficient time to draft the bill. As we have seen, the Commons complained that they had not been given such time, and Charles had as forcibly rebutted them. Against such a standoff there was no appeal, but whereas Digges (and Wentworth as well) had warned of casting the King back on necessity absent a bill, in January 1629 the House rejected this reasoning. The King's legal obligation to enforce the Petition of Right was binding regardless of (disputed) circumstances.

This was a very tough line indeed, although it is difficult to see at this point how the Commons could have taken another without losing the one victory Parliament had gained for the subject's right. In holding the King strictly to his legal word they denied him the executive discretion that had always accompanied declarations of law, for example in suspending and dispensing from statutes. They made a new and historic distinction between the King's person and his office, a distinction they were to pursue with rigor during the Civil War. Although the monarchy had never been subject to such constraints except in periods of civil war or baronial hegemony, they saw no other way to deal with Charles' abuse of discretion. They had lived in a state of "necessity" with their King for four years. They would do so no longer.

The Commons' investigation of Tonnage and Poundage was inevitably framed in terms of a general inquiry into violations of the Petition of Right and the status of the Petition itself. Selden and Eliot moved immediately for a select committee to examine the circumstances of its printing and to "seek out" all infringements of it. This brought expressions of alarm from those who feared a further concentration of power in the hands of the most radical leadership of the House. The proper forum for such an investigation, Charles Price observed, was the Committee of the Whole for Grievances; the Commons must not "subtract a parliament out of parliament." But Selden and Eliot prevailed, and got their committee. It set to work at once.[330]

For Selden and Eliot, the Petition of Right was to be the template for a grand inquest on the state of the realm and the subject's right. Goods had been seized, Selden said; "Next they will take our arms, and then our legs, and so our lives." Eliot declared that "the Judges, the Councell, Sheriffs Customers, the Attor[ney],[331] and all conspire to trample on the spoiles of the libertie of the sub[ject]s." Sir John Coke rose to take exception to Eliot's words, but instead of demanding that they be withdrawn he merely asked that they be "forborne." Nor apparently did anyone else question them, for Eliot continued to speak without hindrance in the same debate, and added to his contumacy by saying that the King impeded his own business by pestering the House with messages.[332]

Whether or not the Commons fully shared Eliot's sense of a universal conspiracy, no one but the beleaguered Coke was prepared to challenge it. Eliot swept up not only the hapless customs officers on whom the House had discharged its wrath in 1628, but the entire bench, the King's chief legal officer, and his sworn counsel. This embraced all the constitutional elements of mixed monarchy except Parliament itself. It was not merely, however, that these elements were no longer functioning properly—that the courts were unwilling or unable to defend the subject's right, that the humanist ideal of a prince tempered by wise and faithful counselors had collapsed before the temptations of royal *Realpolitik*, and that inferior magistrates, too, had been suborned. Eliot's contention was that the King's judges and officers were actively engaged in an attempt, as Selden had put it, to deprive freeborn Englishmen of their arms, legs, and lives; that the instruments of law and governance had been deliberately perverted to their opposites, anarchy and tyranny; that the sinews of the commonwealth had been turned against itself. The question was how such a thing could have occurred. The usual explanations for misgovernment, ordinary sin, corruption, and sloth, could not account for such systemic inversion. It was as if the old festivals of charivari and misrule that still survived in some quarters had become the order of the day, that the elect nation had become the site of pandemonium.

The simplest explanation for England's crisis was that of classical history and the popular stage: a royal tyrant. Tyrants inevitably corrupted the people and institutions around them, perverting all law and governance. No one, obviously, could publicly call Charles a tyrant—More's indiscretion was still remembered—but we need not entirely doubt Eliot's professions of belief in the King's "goodness and justice."[333] It was only by saving the appearances—by affirming that the King, rightly informed, could do no wrong—that Parliament itself could continue. The alternative was submission or rebellion. The one was moral, and the other material suicide. Parliament did not levy war against Charles in 1642 without having first legally secured itself against dissolution, affirmed its control of the militia, and seized powder and forts from a King who had abandoned his capital. In 1629, the monopoly of force as well as its lawful disposition was the King's. Effective resistance was to all intents and purposes impossible.[334]

There were, then, practical as well as ideological inhibitions against concluding the worst about Charles I. But there was another consideration that gave pause. The notion that Charles was or might become a tyrant was not so much implausible as insufficient. In a field of discourse in which nothing occurred without divine signification, the appearance of a tyrant in the citadel of international Protestantism at the moment of its utmost trial—1629 would mark the high tide of the Counter-Reformation, with imperial armies pushing Catholicism north almost to the Baltic—could not be viewed as an isolated or idiosyncratic event. The fact that popish doctrine and practice was spreading rapidly in England itself under royal patronage made such a conclusion all the more inescapable. Iniquity was at work. Whether Charles was seen as agent or pawn, tyrant or dupe, his regime functionally advanced the dark design of the Antichrist. It had still been possible six months earlier to hope that the site of infection was Buckingham, and that his removal, coupled with a new contract between King and people in the Petition of Right, might right the ship of state and enable Charles to govern tolerably. This was no longer the case. Buckingham was gone and nothing had changed, except for the worse. New culprits were sought, but the malady appeared general. Secular remedies had failed. Again and again in the session of 1628, speakers, not all of them from the "choir" by any means, had warned that God was angry with England. The state would never be reformed unless the church were served first. What a godly minority had once insisted upon in the days of Elizabeth was now the general consensus of the Commons. Then episcopacy had been the enemy, but descried only by the few; now it was Arminianism, and the threat was evident to all those not tainted by it.

The pivotal committee in the Commons of 1629 was thus that for religion, chaired as before by Pym but containing the Erastian Selden and the commonwealthman Eliot as well. Pym's stepbrother, Sir Francis Rous, was also a member of it, and he delivered what was in effect the keynote address of the session in laying out its concerns to the House:

> We have of late entered into consideration of the Petition of Right, and the violation of it, and upon good reason, for it concerns our goods, liberties, and lives; but there is a right of an higher nature that preserves for us far greater things, eternal life, our souls, yea, our God himself; a right of Religion derived to us from the King of Kings, conferred upon us by the King of this Kingdom, enacted by laws in this place, streaming down to us in the blood of the martyrs, and witnessed from Heaven by miracles, even by miraculous deliverances. And this right, in the name of this Nation, I this day claim . . .

Here was the essence of what might be called godly constitutionalism. It was thoroughly conservative in character, deriving Christian liberty from the divine right declension of God as its source, the king as his earthly representative, and Parliament as the popular voice. The precedence of the king in this three-stage process was acknowledged, who in "conferring" true religion acted both as God's deputy and supreme magistrate, while its voluntary reception by the estates was both an enactment of Christian liberty, and, by translation into the positive law of the realm, an affirmation of secular right. The godly community enjoyed, by God's favor and the kingdom's laws, its "goods, liberties, and lives," and the parallel but infinitely higher possession of eternal life, eternal identity, and God himself. These felicities were separate but integrally related; they stood or fell together. The order of precedence and honor, however, was clear. Vigilance for secular liberty was due and appropriate, but futile in and of itself where Christian liberty was undefended by sound doctrine, discipline, and preaching. The disorder of the state, Rous affirmed, only reflected that of the church:

> I desire that we may consider the increase of Arminianism, an error that maketh the grace of God lackey it after the will of man, that maketh the sheep to keep the shepherd, that maketh mortal seed of an immortal God. Yea, I desire that we may look into the belly and bowels of this Trojan horse, to see if there be not men in it ready to open the gates to Romish tyranny and Spanish monarchy. For an Arminian is the spawn of a Papist; and if there come the warmth of favour upon him, you shall see him turn into one of those frogs that rise out of the bottomless pit. And if you mark it well, you shall see an Arminian reaching out his hand to a Papist, a Papist to a Jesuit, a Jesuit gives one hand to the Pope and the other to the King of Spain; and these men having kindled a fire in our neighbour countries, now they have brought over some of it hither, to set on flame this Kingdom also.

Yea let us search further and consider whether these be not the men that break in upon the goods and liberties of this Commonwealth, for by this means they make way for the taking away of our religion.[335]

For Rous, popery and secular tyranny were a closed circuit, each entailing and enabling the other, and both, finally, revealing the Janus face of the anti-Christ. As all liberty was the gift of God, so all tyranny came from the Devil. These antitheses defined the field of discourse; no middle ground was possible. Prudence might dictate whether the struggle against evil be waged by one means or another, but the will to oppose it was constant. In the fire of this vision, the pallid modern notion of "legitimacy" could define only unwavering adherence to God's cause. This had always been the ultimate reference point of post-Henrician England. For those of godly temper it was a reality not merely on the level of ideology but of lived experience. In the crisis of 1628–1629, the godly vision became the presiding one as the general sense of extremity made men susceptible to an apocalyptic interpretation that, resting on shared underlying conventions, provided a comprehensive and integrated explanation of deeply troubling events. In the godly view, Arminianism was simply popery in fresh disguise, the first link in a chain that led hand over hand, in Rous' vivid image, to spiritual tyranny and universal monarchy. In the economy of his vision, the goods and liberties taken from the subject furnished the material and political basis for a totalized oppression that ended, as it had begun, with the usurpation of the church. Like any monocausal view, it brushed aside a world of difference that, under ordinary circumstances, would have commended a more discriminating approach even to those who shared its ultimate eschatological assumptions. The difference in doctrine between a Mainwaring and a Montagu, and between either of them and an Urban VIII, was nugatory, for all shared the same polluted source and all led to the same fatal result. Similarly, those who for reason of state supported a Spanish or a French alliance were equally deceiving, or at best deceived.

There had always been men of Rous' temper in the Commons, but their case had never before been so compelling. Within the framework of Protestant ideology there was no other explanation for the concurrent calamities that had befallen Englishmen—disaster abroad, oppression at home, the breach of law and doctrine—of comparable narrative cogency and of a weight appropriate to the situation. "I am afraid that God sitteth in the council of our enemies against us," Phelips lamented. "I dare boldly say," Sir Walter Erle declared, "never was there . . . a more near conjunction between matter of Religion and matter of State in any Kingdom in the world than there is in this Kingdom at this day." Erle confessed that he had been among those who had agreed to give the subject's liberties pride of place in the previous session, as being most immediately endangered. Civil and spiritual liberty were inextricably linked, but not of equal precedence: " . . . I know full well that the cause of justice is Gods cause as well as the cause of Religion. But what good will those rights and liberties do me, or any man else, that resolves to live and die a Protestant? Nay, what good will they do any man, of what Religion soever he be, that resolves to live and die a freeman and not a slave, if Popery and Arminianism, joining hand in hand as they do, be a means, together with the Romish Hierarchy, to bring in a Spanish tyrany amongst us . . .?"[336] God's cause could be deferred no longer.

Pym may have felt the need to vindicate his Committee, for in a lengthy address he reminded the House of its work in the preceding session: a petition for religion to the King; a bill against recusants; the preferring of charges against Mainwaring, Montagu, and others. These and many previous efforts had been to no avail, for in James' time too, he remembered, there had been "the like gracious answers to Petitions of Religion, and the like Proclamations, the like Declarations, the like commands to put laws in execution against Recusants, and yet little done, being prevented by secret direction and command of some eminent Ministers of State." Pym's foray into Jacobean times was significant, for it cast the shadow of popery back into the previous reign and linked the twin grievances of religion and impositions to the advent of the Stuart dynasty. The questioning of even James' fidelity to the Protestant faith had begun.[337]

By late February, a subcommittee of the Committee for Religion had drafted a new petition to Charles, the Heads and Articles. "Gods religion," it declared, was "in great peril now to be lost." The opposers of true religion were "the mighty and prevalent party" in the church, as evidenced by the spread of Arminian heresy and popish ceremony, the suppression of sound preaching and doctrine, the brazen increase of Papists and Jesuits, and the consequent threat to the peace and security of the King's three realms. As matters stood the Church of England, once the light of the Reformed faith, verged on apostasy and separation from its brethren abroad, themselves "in a great part already ruined, and the rest in the most weak and miserable condition." The unstated but self-evident conclusion was that Christendom itself was in peril.

The Heads and Articles attributed the ills at home to the "unfaithfulness and carelessness" of certain royal ministers. Unlike Buckingham they were not named, though Heath, Sir Richard Weston, the Earl of Dorset, and Dudley Lord Carleton, the newly appointed Secretary of State, were mentioned in debate. Compared to Buckingham, however, these men were all small fry, and Eliot's attempt to promote Weston to the Duke's office as "the great enemy of the Commonwealth" rang particularly hollow.[338] But there was no rhetorical alternative, for if the King were not the victim of apostasy then he was the agent of it, and it was groundless to appeal to him on this or any other subject.

The Committee of the Whole for Merchants faced a similar dilemma in its attempt to punish customs officers for the seizure of goods, particularly those of John Rolle, as a breach both of law and of parliamentary privilege. If their commission had explicitly authorized them to do so the House would be challenging a royal command. To the Committee's relief, Noy discovered that the officers' orders contained no instruction to sequester goods. Its relief was short-lived, however, for the King avowed the officers' actions in their entirety as his own. If the House questioned the legality of his command it challenged him in "Justice and honor." Would it do so?[339]

Those who remembered King James' dictum that he could preside in every court and give law on every issue might have brought it to mind in the confusion that followed this dramatic intervention. Here was the moment that old Parliament hands had dreaded for twenty-five years, when the prerogative of princes that had daily grown finally eclipsed the liberty of the subject.[340] Cries to adjourn were heard. Sir Robert Pye, however, reminded the House that it was still in committee, and that the King's message should be received formally. This had the effect of clearing heads, John Selden's in particular. The question before the House, he said, was the delinquency of the customs officers. It was their act, not the King's, that was under judgment, the King's attempt to vindicate them notwithstanding. As far as that was concerned, "any other Court in Westminster may and ought to proceede, whatsoever comandes is receaved, and we are in this point to consider our previledge to be noe lesse." No intervention could lawfully stay a judicial proceeding; no command within its jurisdiction was exempt from its scrutiny. The King could neither preempt the law nor judge it personally, and his attempt to validate the acts of his servants by taking direct responsibility for them made such acts neither more nor less lawful.[341]

The words of King Charles I and the response of the lawyer John Selden posed the crisis of Stuart legitimacy in its starkest terms. For Charles, there could be no separation of the person of the king from the function of his office, and no separation of both from a command binding on the duty and allegiance of the subject. Final law could reside nowhere else. Hobbes would concur with this, and so would Richard Nixon, who groped for the same idea when he famously said, "When the President does it, that means that it is not illegal." But Charles' assertion was no more descriptive of the polity he governed, a mixed monarchy under the rule of a law defined by no single party, than Nixon's was of his.[342] The King's own words, moreover, belied him. Charles had told Parliament on January 24 that Tonnage and Poundage was not his by law without statutory confirmation, and that although necessity had compelled him to take it he awaited its grant as the free gift of his people. The Court of Exchequer had passed the question of whether the subject's goods might be seized for nonpayment of Tonnage and Poundage to Parliament, as the court of last resort. Yet Charles had not only continued to distrain such goods—an act still arguably justifiable on grounds of necessity—but had claimed that he might do so as a matter of "justice," that is, of settled and indisputable right. This was incoherent, if not dissembling.[343]

Behind the legal morass a political standoff had clearly been reached. The Commons, it was evident, would not pass a bill of Tonnage and Poundage without due punishment for those who had collected it in violation of the Petition of Right and strict security for the future in the form of a parliamentary book of rates, while the King declared himself bound, both as a matter of his prerogative and his honor, to protect the servants who executed his orders. As Charles Price put it ruefully, though Charles was "a gracious King to his people" and the Commons were "good officers and humble to his Majestie," there was no longer a common language between them, for "as if we were charmed wee understand not one another."[344]

The problem with the King's language was that it shifted ground at each occasion. At the least his contradictory statements were irresponsible; at the worst, they suggested, once again, bad faith. In any case they could not be ignored, and in answering Charles' claim that "justice" was inseparable from his person, Selden put forward the counterclaim that no royal command could stay the proceedings of a court or shelter a delinquent. Implicit in this was the contention that the person of the King as such added nothing to the validity of his commands: he was their source, but the law alone was their warrant. If Charles suggested that the ancient fiction that the king could do no wrong be taken for literal fact—that what the king willed must always, insofar as he insisted upon it, be right—Selden replied that the legality of a particular command could never rest with its source alone. This reasoning would be taken to its logical conclusion during the Civil War, when the Long Parliament claimed that the King actually *had* separated himself from his office, whose powers were resumed by the other estates to be exercised in his stead, and finally, with the rejection of all government by a single person, on behalf of the commonwealth.[345]

The Commons' immediate reaction to the King's comments was as tumultuous as any within memory. Cries for adjournment were heard on every side, and Phelips, declaring that "The essential and fundamental liberties of this house is [sic] now before us," suggested that it observe a "fearful silence" for the remainder of the day, the expressive as well as the tactical response when discourse was balked. John Glanville agreed, lamenting that "All ways to reformacions sems now to be stopped." Price averred that "the fate of the Kingdom is in the ballance." Few on that wintry afternoon seem to have doubted it. Most still clung to the rhetoric of evil counselors and

"enemyes to Religion." There was no other conclusion that did not imply rebellion. But the difference between a misled king and an incorrigible one,
even if incorrigible only in his determination to be misled, now seemed
faint.[346]

In the past the Lords had often played a mediating role between crown
and Commons, but communication between the two houses, at least on the
formal level, had been reduced to a trickle of bills. There is no record in 1629
of any joint conferences, in which so much of the drama of the previous session had been played out. Russell speculates that this may have been due in
part to the preoccupation of the Commons with Tonnage and Poundage, a
revenue bill, but the Commons had in fact put by the bill, and the King's
prima facie violation of the Petition of Right certainly concerned both
houses. An alternative explanation might be sought in Christopher Thompson's suggestion that the Commons' leadership was tactically divided, with
Selden and Eliot wishing to pursue the threat to liberty and property and
Pym's circle that of Arminianism. At most, however, this was a difference in
emphasis; the overriding fact about the session of 1629 was the powerful
consensus that the threat to both civil and Christian liberty sprang from a
common source, and that neither issue could be addressed in isolation from
the other.[347] We do know that Charles made a concerted effort to conciliate
key members of the Lords' opposition during the prorogation, notably
Arundel, Bristol, and Archbishop Abbot. This may have succeeded to a degree. Individual lords had more to lose politically than their counterparts in
the Commons. The latter might shelter under their patronage, as Pym and
Rich did under the Earl of Warwick's, and Rudyard under Pembroke's. The
lords had no patron but the King, and with Parliament clearly bound for
shipwreck some would doubtless have considered discretion the better part
of valor. The brevity of the session must be considered as well. Consultation
between the houses normally proceeded with the progress of bills or other
formal business, and the one document the Commons had drafted, the
Heads and Articles, had not yet been seen by the full House. Finally, the
Commons sorely missed the steadying hand and unrivaled prestige of Sir
Edward Coke, whose age and infirmity apparently kept him at home. Especially in conference with the Lords, he was the one member of the Commons
whose stature was comparable to any peer's.[348]

February 23 was a Saturday; on Monday the 25th, Charles adjourned Parliament to the following Saturday, a gesture that suggested further adjournment or worse. The Venetian ambassador reported efforts at compromise
during the week; the failure of these may be reflected in Eliot's attack on
Weston on March 2.[349] Whatever the case, Eliot came that day with a remonstrance, which was put and passed as the Protestation of the House as
Speaker Finch was forcibly kept from reading a new commission of ad-

journment and the doors of the House were bolted. This was insurrection; the House did not, as in 1585 and 1621, stand upon its right to adjourn itself, but commanded the Speaker to do its bidding rather than the King's. The Protestation, too, declared a loyalty beyond the King to the commonwealth itself. Although the second of its articles stated that whoever counseled the taking of Tonnage and Poundage without parliamentary consent was to be reputed a public and capital enemy, the first article, concerning religion, was even more sweeping:

> Whosoever shall bring in innovation of religion, or by favour or countenance seek to extend or introduce Popery or Arminianism, or other opinion disgreeing from the true and orthodox Church, shall be reputed a capital enemy to this Kingdom and Commonwealth.[350]

The broader language was obviously meant to encompass not only councillors and clerics, but any disseminator of false doctrine. Wittingly or unwittingly, however, it did not exclude the King himself from its blanket warrant by any of the covering phrases that might easily have been provided. It said precisely what it said, *Whosoever*, and it addressed itself directly to "this Kingdom and Commonwealth" both as the subject of its address and its surrogate in pursuing to the death any and all who undermined the true church. No such pronouncement had been made since the Bond of Association. The Bond, however, had been instigated by the crown, whatever Elizabeth may have thought of it, and went forward as the word of the three estates; the Protestation was an address to the commons of England by their representatives. To be sure, we must take it as a *cri de coeur* rather than a call to action, but that does not diminish its significance. It silently invoked the Calvinist resistance theory of an appeal to the inferior magistrate and even, in default of all other authority, of the right of the realm as a body to preserve itself.

The Commons did challenge one group to resist: the merchants. In the third and last of the Protestation's articles, it declared that any merchant who voluntarily paid Tonnage and Poundage without parliamentary authorization was to be reputed "a betrayer of the liberties of England, and an enemy to the same." This was an exhortation rather than an appeal to vigilantism; the crucial modifier "capital" was omitted, and the merchants were left with an escape clause. One might say that they were as hardly used by their parliamentary defenders as by their royal assessors, for instead of providing them with the relief they had sought, the Commons had left them as undefended as ever. Not only had they been left to pay an illegal levy on pain of obloquy or to resist on pain of forfeiture and ruin, but the levy itself, unregulated in the absence of a statute, could be raised at will to confiscatory levels. The Petition of Right was a broken reed, and the subject exposed to arbitrary rule.

This stark dénouement suggests the criticism of the Commons' strategy offered by Thompson and Russell. The Commons' decision to punish collectors of Tonnage and Poundage before seeking restitution of distrained goods, it is argued, not only left the merchants without remedy, but provoked a confrontation fatal to the session as a whole. It is difficult to see how the House might have proceeded differently without the loss of its own credit, however. The Commons were not attorneys for the merchants; their client was the commonwealth, and the injury, as in the case of billeting and the Forced Loan, was to the realm as a whole. Nor could passage of the bill of Tonnage and Poundage that Charles repeatedly called for have done any more than to further undermine the Petition of Right and consequently Parliament's legislative authority, for the two houses regarded the Petition as having the force of a statute and had entered it among the statute rolls. To grant Tonnage and Poundage without calling to account those who had collected it in defiance of the Petition of Right would have done what no Parliament had ever done before: to negate a sovereign act not by a statute of repeal but by simple nullification. Nor was Charles willing to allow the Commons to save appearances by accepting a token rebuke to his servants; instead, he forestalled any possible compromise by owning their acts as his. The only choice left to the House was to assert its role in the governance of the realm or to bend its neck to the yoke. Russell's summary judgment that "The Parliament of 1629 brought about its own destruction" is, therefore, unwarrranted except on Caroline assumptions themselves. By any other measure, the responsibility must lie with Charles I.

The King had the last word. On March 2, he had adjourned Parliament to March 10. On that date he dissolved it, issuing a lengthy Declaration to his faithful subjects. As the Commons had attributed the violation of the subject's right to a malignant few, so Charles laid the breakup of Parliament to certain "evil" and "envenomed" spirits who had misled and "distempered" the House of Commons, overcoming the loyal affections of the moderate majority. These spirits had frustrated the collection of the subsidy voted by the majority, first tying it to a bill for the subject's liberty that was used as a pretext to scandalize the government and then delaying it until the military operations it had been meant to succor had collapsed. The King had nonetheless accepted and enrolled the Petition of Right, only to be met by further remonstrances and misrepresentations. Granted another session to complete its work, the Commons, again beguiled, had traduced the King's care and zeal for religion, falsely challenged his right to Tonnage and Poundage, and abused his officers and judges. All this Charles had borne with great patience, preferring injury to himself and his servants to any restriction of free debate. His patience, however, had been in vain; worse, it had encouraged "strange and exorbitant encroachments and usurpations":

We are not ignorant how much that House [of Commons] hath of late years endeavoured to extend their privileges, by setting up general committees for religion, for Courts of Justice, for trade, and the like; a course never heard of until of late: so as, where in former times the Knights and Burgesses were wont to communicate to the House such business as they brought from their countries; now there are so many chairs erected, to make inquiry upon all sorts of men, where complaints of all sorts are entertained, to the unsufferable disturbance and scandal of justice and government, which, having been tolerated awhile by our father and ourself hath daily grown to more and more height; insomuch that young lawyers sitting there take upon them to decry the opinions of the Judges; and some have not doubted to maintain that the resolutions of that House must bind the Judges, a thing never heard of in ages past . . .[351]

Here was the royal riposte to the Commons' claim of "innovation" in church and state. It was not the crown but Parliament, specifically the Lower House, that had erected new jurisdictions and disturbed the proper constitutional balance. Without connective argument, then, Charles had moved from an attack on "evil spirits" within a loyal assembly to one on the House of Commons as an institution; that is, from a body needing only to purge itself of a mischievous minority to one systemically bankrupt, and, in its present form, no longer tolerable. These two narratives were not in principle irreconcilable. The purpose of the Declaration, however, was not logical disputation but propaganda: not the connection between two lines of argument, but the replacement of one by another. An ingenuous but faithful majority was not to be repudiated, and such a fiction was necessary if the link between the King and his faithful subjects at large was to be maintained; an institution infected by faction and popularity might be. Charles emphasized the point by contrasting the incorrigible behavior of the Commons with that of the Lords.[352] It had been his strategy to isolate the Lower House from the Upper; in 1629 it had succeeded, and in 1640 he would appeal overtly to the nobility to detach itself from the leadership of the Commons. The King concluded by again acknowledging the presence of faithful men in the Commons (no longer, however, a majority), and by promising to maintain true religion and the just right of the subject. He was not ready to declare the House of Commons useless and dangerous; it was not necessary to do so. Men could and did read the fate of the oldest institution in the realm between the lines: Sir Simonds D'Ewes, looking back on the end of Charles' third Parliament in 1637, would call it the worst day in five hundred years. He was likening it to the Norman Conquest, and the extinction of ancient English liberty.[353]

D'Ewes' fears were shared by many who, like Phelips, rusticated on their estates in the 1630s and dug in as best they could against prerogative government; by those who, despairing of England, sought to found a new Jerusalem across the sea; and by those who, like Eliot and the others who had defied Charles on March 2—Selden, Strode, Valentine, Hobart, Holles, and Long—languished in prison or other confinement. That those fears were to prove exaggerated does not render them implausible. In the years of Personal Rule the discourse of Parliament was silent, and even discourse about it was muted.[354] Although moderates at Court still discussed another parliament, there is no evidence that Charles himself entertained the thought of one, or reason to doubt the wisdom of the Venetian ambassador's judgment that Parliament would "never reassemble during the present king's life."[355] Not until the guiding principle of the Personal Rule—that never again would royal policy be dictated by financial necessity—at last gave way before the crisis of the first Bishops' War, did Parliament again become a possibility.

Relegitimating the State: The Sanctification of Parliament

When Parliament met at last in 1640, the settled disposition of Caroline government was no longer in doubt. The prolonged detention of former MPs,[356] the silencing of godly ministers and the public reception of papal emissaries, the systematic resort to nonparliamentary taxation backed by fines and imprisonment, the antiespiscopal rising of the Scots Covenanters, and the interregnum of Parliament itself had created a climate in which providential hopes were vested in the summoning of a new parliament. These hopes were temporarily dashed by the failure of the Short Parliament, which showed Charles and his estates as much at loggerheads as ever, but when the King was compelled to call a second parliament in the same year, the balance of power had clearly shifted, and, with the passage of legislation forbidding the dissolution of this parliament without its own consent, its continuation was at least notionally secured.[357]

The unprecedented national focus on Charles' fifth parliament was attested by the hundreds of petitions and addresses that greeted it from all over the country. At first, hopes for it were couched in the traditional terms of reconciliation and harmony. As long as the weakness of Charles' position forced him to accede to the stunning pace of reform that followed its assembly in November 1640—the arrest of his councillors, the attack on his bishops, the triumphant return of silenced ministers and imprisoned MPs—it was possible to imagine the first few months of the Long Parliament as a healthy purge that would leave a chastened king once again on the path of righteousness. One versifier found the sure hand of God in Parliament's return:

> In your recesse how ev'ry heart did pray,
> Praying enquire, enquire with the day

> Of your returne and now you doe fulfill
> Their expectation, and Gods holy will.[358]

The theme of divinely guided reconciliation sounded as well in a prose address, *Englands Glory*. "Blessed be the Lord," it declared, "who hath reduced us to peace and put it into the Kings heart in calling of the happy Assembly of Parliament." Charles' role was thus acknowledged, but for the rest his acquiescence was taken for granted, the author's focus being on Parliament itself, whose "holy Assembly" had as its sole aim "the magnifying of the name of God, the propagation of the Gospel, the purity of Religion, and the just punishment of wickednesse and vice."[359] These functions, normally entrusted to the crown, were now the province of Parliament, the Lord's chosen instrument in the task of national redemption. The author of *Englands Glory* likened its work—as did many other commentators—to that of Hezekiah, the biblical restorer of the temple. For Samuel Fairclough, a Suffolk minister, the members of parliament were as Joshuas, to "extirpate all idolators," and for Richard Ward, minister in Essex, they were in a sense the temple itself, "our Bulwarks, Wals, and Gates, under the Lord; yea, the Hoast of the Lord, and of Gideon his annointed."[360]

Fairclough's sermon was delivered to the House of Commons itself, whose instatement of regular preaching and monthly fasts (belatedly emulated by the House of Lords) effectively supplanted the bishops as representatives of the spiritual estate by godly ministers even before the expulsion of the former from the Lords in February 1642, and testified to the outside world its commitment to the Lord's work.[361] The author of *Englands Glory* praised the Commons for having "opened the mouths of the Ministers that were stopt," and found them "without all doubt . . . filled with the Holy Ghost."[362] Licensed for publication as soon as they were given, the fast sermons served as a crucial link between Parliament and the new public it was trying to forge, and which would follow it into civil war in 1642.

The mutually reinforcing nature of the fast sermons, which elevated both speakers and hearers in the cause of divine service, is well illustrated in *Babylons Downfall*, a sermon preached to the Commons in January 1641 by William Bridge, who had only that month returned from exile in Rotterdam. Reaching out to each individual MP, Bridge exhorted his auditors to see themselves as called and anointed in their task:

> [N]ever did England see a Parliament more fitted for the service and work of God, then this now is. . . . Wherefore then let all those that are of this honourable assembly think; It may be God hath raised mee up to this time, all the while I was at the University, God was laying in of abilities in my education for this occasion; and shall I lose this opportunity, *Opportunitas indicat virum*, opportunity shewes the man, and makes the man, and sometimes hath the casting voyce for mans eternity.[363]

Bridge urged MPs to lay all private interests aside in the great work of reformation, lest "personall sinne should become nationall." In effect, the elect nation had been contracted to Parliament itself, and the stern and unremitting self-examination that typified the godly conscience was now the obligation of all parliament men. God's will could not be done with unclean hands, and a single sinner could retard or perhaps even destroy the work of the House. Thus it was critical that "if there bee ever a drunkard, swearer, adulterer, Sabbath-breaker, or prophane person here, let him labour to get into Christ."[364]

The connection between the individual member, the sanctified House, and the work of reformation was reiterated by Edmund Calamy in his fast sermon of the following December, when the outbreak of rebellion in Ireland and the passage of a Grand Remonstrance detailing the evils of Charles' reign by a deeply divided House had created a far grimmer and more polarized climate. Reformation, he said in terms virtually identical to Bridge's, was both "Personall" and "Nationall," each being understood as a function of the other. Not merely the gross sins cited by Bridge, but even the very smallest ones, gave check to the great cause and merited condign punishment:

> For there is no sinne simply little. There is no little God to sinne against. . . .
> The least offence is committed against an infinite God, and therefore deserves infinite punishment. There was no little price paid for little sins; the least sinne cost the shedding of the bloud of the eternall God.[365]

On the other hand, if members labored to keep themselves personally worthy of the common task, the good effects would be communicated to the nation as a whole:

> If you that are the representative Body of this Nation, as you stand under this relation, be reformed, the Nation it self may be said to be reformed. For you are the Nation representatively, virtually, and eminently; you stand in the place of the whole Nation; and if you stand for Gods cause, the whole Nation doth it in you.[366]

By this synecdoche, Parliament not only assumes responsibility for the general welfare but stands, before God, as the nation itself, its own virtue being the pledge of the whole. This meant maintaining unity of purpose, which, in the face of mounting crisis, entailed more fasting, more prayer, and more repentance—"humiliation," in the preacher's term of art. Such unity was not mere consensus, the politician's task, but solidarity, the product of individual self-perfection and collective self-dedication. It was the unity of every part within the whole, and of the whole in every part. Thus, Calamy offered what he called the picture of a Parliament man:

A Parliament-man must be like *Athanasius*, who was *Magnes* & *Adamas*. A Loadstone, and an Adamant. A Loadstone by his affable carriage, and courteous behavior, drawing all men to the love of him. But in the cause of God he was as an *Adamant*, untameable and unconquerable.[367]

Preaching three months later, in early 1642, Cornelius Burges added touches evocative of Christ to this portrait:

Look upon your selves as *Publike* Persons, that must both bear the sins of others whom you represent, and purge the sins of others, or be them yourselves.[368]

Stephen Marshall, preaching the eulogy of John Pym in December 1643, took him as the ultimate exemplar of the parliament man, who had subordinated all personal interest to the common welfare:

[T]he publike safety was written in His heart, as men report, Queen Mary said, that Callis was in hers: it was His meat and drinke, His worke, His exercise, His recreation, His pleasure, His ambition, His All: What He was, was onely to promote the publike good: in and for this He liv'd, in and by this He died.[369]

As an ideal type, the parliament man was wholly devoted to the public weal in church and state; that is, to the very things whose charge and responsibility had been that of the King. Unlike the King, however, the parliament man (being but one of many, as he was also many in one) had no private estate or interest to uphold, no need of pomp and vainglory, and no spurious "honor" to oppose to the welfare of the nation. Against government by a single person, which always tended to tyranny, the parliament man embodied the republic of virtue, the seamless unity of representer and represented in the immortal commonwealth. As the years of civil war went on, the King came to seem increasingly irrelevant if not hostile to this vision to a significant body of opinion. To call it "republican" in any classical or modern sense would be, however, to mistake its wellspring in the godly pattern of the congregation. Like the congregation of saints, Parliament was composed of those who, feeling themselves individually called (as MPs were, indeed, chosen for the salvation of the realm by their constituents as well as being, in their own persons, the chosen of God), were, corporatively, a sanctified instrument.

While within its walls Parliament's preachers exhorted MPs to the double labor of making themselves worthy parliament men, and, in so doing, of keeping Parliament fit to perform the Lord's work, a rhetoric of praise sounded throughout London's pulpits and in its pamphlet literature. Preaching to the congregation of St. Margaret's, Westminster, John Marston gave thanks for "this blest Parliament," while Samuel Fawcet reproached the Haberdashers' Company for not sufficiently supporting "our Parliament-worthies" in "the great worke of Reformation," and the author of *Englands Doxologie* declared that the MPs were the "Heroes of their Age" and deserved to have their statues "set up in gold."[370] Here the virtue of the MPs was assumed, and they were offered as paragons to inspire the "other" congregations and corporations of the city to contribute their own labors in due proportion. The continued outpouring of petitions, testimonies, and subscriptions from the countryside attested to the aura of faith, hope, and almost millennial expectation that surrounded the Long Parliament in its first months. Whereas only a short time before the monarchy seemed to have usurped, suppressed, or incorporated virtually all other modes of discourse in itself—that of the law courts, rendered docile and subservient; that of the pulpit, haltered by the new conformity; that of the stage, domesticated in the masque; and that of the realm itself, reduced to panegyric—it was now Parliament that spoke for the law, the church, the realm, and even the penitent crown, which, submitting to chastisement and purgation, had offered up its servants for punishment, its policies for correction, and its powers for regulation. The trope of reconciliation that still dominated discourse in the first phase of the English Revolution meant the agreement of the King to the temporary receivership of the Erastian state in Parliament. This was authorized by the fact that both crown and church were, in the persons of the King and of the lords spiritual, inarguably part of Parliament itself. As the preacher Richard Ward reminded the Commons, "the Body of this Land hath but one Head over it, viz. The King," and the representative consisted of "Prince, Peers, and Parliamentaries."[371] While Charles gave nominal consent to the process of reform, his powers could not be regarded as alienated, but instead as exercised within the unity of crown and people in Parliament.

The sanctified Parliament, then, continued to include the sanctified King, both notionally and in carnal fact. With Charles' flight from London in January 1642 and the outbreak of hostilities eight months later, however, the royal body was visibly severed from Parliament, and when the King exposed himself to parliamentary muskets at Edgehill, he in effect defied his adversaries to touch the Lord's anointed. The pamphlet debate that erupted in the wake of Edgehill marked an ideological turning point; if direct resistance could be offered to the King's person, then monarchy itself was no longer to be regarded as consecrated. The parliamentary preacher Jeremiah Burroughs declared the relevant biblical texts to mean "that Kings should not touch people that are Gods anointed," and the author of *A Vindication of Psalme 105.15* similarly glossed them as saying that "Kings ought not to take up Armes against their Subjects."[372] Parliament, representing the people, or the people themselves, in arms for their just liberties and in God's cause, were the hosts of the Lord, the chosen of an elect nation.

The 'heavenly' Parliament sent by God to relieve his people had already been contrasted to the "hellish" parliament of "papists and Brownists" — the latter denoting strict Separatists — that swarmed around London in a tract of 1641, but when Charles called a parliament at Oxford in 1644, the metaphorical antitype took on a new reality. To John Brandon, a self-described soldier and gentleman, this "Anti-Parliament" sat "in councell . . . against God himselfe."[373] For Brandon, the calling of such an assembly revealed the true iniquity of Parliament's foes and the anti-Christian cause they served. It was, he said, no more possible "for two Suns to bee in one Horizon, as two lawfull parliaments at one instant of time in the Kingdome of England." For faithful Englishmen, there was no longer room for doubt about the Caroline monarchy or reason to temporize with it further:

> Sithence it is so that His Majesty and his Queen band themselves together, with popish Rebells and Traitors, with other Incendiaries to this State and Kingdome, against God, the Protestant Religion, the lawfull Parliament of England, the Lawes of the Land, the Liberty of the Subject, let us breake their bonds and cast their cordes from us, and now stand up for the Gospell of Iesus Christ, by standing against those who labour to disinherit us of a faithfull parliament, and of the pure worship of God, and so consequently of God himselfe.[374]

In rejecting Parliament, first by abandoning it in the departure from London, then by taking up arms against it, and finally by erecting a false Parliament in tandem with the false church he had embraced, Charles had shown the colors of the Antichrist. Whether they were truly his own, or whether, as Brandon and others continued to suggest, he was fatally beguiled by his popish Queen, there was no longer any hope of reconciliation or question of unity with a man who had so repeatedly, impenitently, and bloodily broken faith. Legitimacy — the protection of law and liberty, Christian and civil — now rested with Parliament and the "pure worship of God" alone.

Yet Parliament too proved an ultimate disappointment to its godly supporters, persistently scouting accommodation with the King despite his perfidy, seeking to impose new ecclesiastical fetters on religious conscience in concert with the Scottish Kirk, attempting to disband its loyal army after the Civil War while malignants still lurked, and, finally, perpetuating itself as a private interest as its public support waned. It was the agitator Francis White who in 1647 finally declared that Parliament, no less than the King, now meant to keep the nation in "servill bondage," and that the Lord had chosen a new instrument of righteousness. As he wrote publicly to his commander-in-chief, Sir Thomas Fairfax:

> That is properly the highest power that is best able to act, and that only the power of God among men, so long as they doe what is just, and are a terrour to evill workes[;] the Army now at your and his command in all just

things, is the highest power visible in this Kingdome. . . . I affirme as the condition of the Kingdome now is, there is no superintendent authoritie, but what is exercised by the power and force of the Sword.[375]

In retrospect, the sanctification of Parliament—the coalescence of both civil and sacred legitimacy in the representative institution of the realm—was the product of a unique conjuncture of political crisis and millennial expectation. The two houses, and particularly the House of Commons, became invested with the aura that had characterized divine right kingship, and, in Charles' absence, absorbed the charismatic as well as the executive attributes of that kingship one by one. It was, necessarily, a phenomenon of short duration, and when, after the New Model Army briefly assumed the mandate of divine authority, a more plausible assembly of saints, the Barebone's Parliament, was convened, it was rather to be (although for equally complex reasons) a source of embarrassment and derision. Nonetheless, the migration of sacred legitimacy from its original source in divinized, and, latterly, Erastian kingship, was of great significance. It is quite possible that the events of the Civil War would have taken the course they did in any case, given the polarization between Charles I and his ruling elite on matters of taxation, counsel, and worship; but the apocalyptically charged atmosphere that enveloped the Long Parliament from its inception and that had its source in the political struggles of the 1620s gave them a peculiarly intense cast that deepened antagonisms, thwarted compromise, and raised the stakes of legitimation on both sides. It also had a profound and lasting impact on the image of the King, rendering him far more susceptible to the fate that eventually befell him. If Parliament did not long remain an instrument of righteousness, Charles, for those who brought him to trial, was a vessel of wrath, and his death a necessary purgation in the eyes of God. In a very real sense, however, sacred authority did not outlive the death of the once-sacred king. When monarchy was restored in 1660, divinity no longer hedged a king, and its trappings rapidly fell away.[376] A new era had begun, and a new discourse emerged. The uniquely intense moment when civil authority and divine prescription had fused in the apocalyptic energies of the Reformation—the period lived in England between 1529 and the Restoration—had passed. Power began its long travail toward the modern democratic state.

Reference Matter

Abbreviations

AHR	*American Historical Review*
AJLH	*American Journal of Legal History*
APC	*Acts of the Privy Council*
BDBR	Richard L. Greaves and Robert Zaller, eds., *Biographical Dictionary of British Radicals in the Seventeenth Century*, 3 vols.
Bidwell and Jansson, eds., *PP 1626*	William B. Bidwell and Maija Jansson, eds., *Proceedings in Parliament 1626*
BIHR	*Bulletin of the Institute of Historical Research*
BL	British Library
BL Add. MSS.	British Library, Additional Manuscripts
BL Harl. MSS.	British Library, Harleian Manuscripts
CJ	*Journal of the House of Commons*
Collinson, *EPM*	Patrick Collinson, *The Elizabethan Puritan Movement*
Coke, *Reports*	*The Reports of Sir Edward Coke in Thirteen Parts*
CSPD	*Calendar of State Papers Domestic*
CSPV	*Calendar of State Papers Venetian*
DNB	*Dictionary of National Biography*
EcHR	*Economic History Review*
EHR	*English Historical Review*
EETS	*Early English Text Society*

Elton, ed., *TC*	G. R. Elton, ed., *The Tudor Constitution*
ELR	*English Literary Renaissance*
Foster, ed., *PP 1610*	Elizabeth Read Foster, ed., *Proceedings in Parliament, 1610*, 2 vols.
Gardiner, ed., *CDPR*	Samuel Rawson Gardiner, ed., *Constitutional Documents of the Puritan Revolution*
Gardiner, ed., *PD 1610*	Samuel Rawson Gardiner, ed., *Parliamentary Debates in 1610*
Gardiner, ed., *DHC 1625*	Samuel Rawson Gardiner, ed., *Debates in the House of Commons, 1625*
Hartley, ed., *PPE*	T. E. Hartley, ed., *Proceedings in the Parliaments of Elizabeth*, 3 vols.
HJ	*Historical Journal*
HLQ	*Huntington Library Quarterly*
HLRO	House of Lords Record Office, London
HMC	Historical Manuscripts Commission
HR	*Historical Research*
Jansson, ed., *PP 1614*	Maija Jansson, ed., *Proceedings in Parliament 1614 (House of Commons)*
Jansson and Bidwell, eds., *PP 1625*	Maija Jansson and William B. Bidwell, eds., *Proceedings in Parliament 1625*
JBS	*Journal of British Studies*
JEH	*Journal of Ecclesiastical History*
JHI	*Journal of the History of Ideas*
JMH	*Journal of Modern History*
Johnson et al., eds., *CD 1628*	Robert C. Johnson, Mary Frear Keeler, Maija Cole, and William B. Bidwell, eds., *Commons Debates 1628*, 4 vols. [Keeler, Cole, and Bidwell for Vol. IV]
Keeler et al., eds., *LP 1628*	Mary Frear Keeler, Maija Cole, and William B. Bidwell, eds., *Lords Proceedings 1628*
LJ	*Journals of the House of Lords*
McIlwain, ed., *PWJ*	C. H. McIlwain, ed., *The Political Works of James I*
Notestein et al., eds., *CD 1621*	Wallace Notestein, Frances H. Relf, and Hartley Simpson, eds., *Commons Debates 1621*, 7 vols.
Notestein and Relf, eds., *CD 1629*	Wallace Notestein and Frances H. Relf, *Commons Debates 1629*
ODNB	*Oxford Dictionary of National Biography*
PH	*Parliamentary History*
PMLA	*Proceedings of the Modern Language Association*
P&P	*Past and Present*

Relf, ed., *Notes of Debates*	Frances H. Relf, ed., *Notes of Debates in the House of Lords, 1621–1628*
RQ	*Renaissance Quarterly*
Rushworth	John Rushworth, *Historical Collections of Passages of State*, 7 vols. (1659–1701)
Russell, *PEP*	Conrad Russell, *Parliaments and English Politics, 1621–1629*
SCJ	*Sixteenth Century Journal*
SR	*The Statutes of the Realm*, 11 vols. (1810–1828)
ST	W. Cobbett and T. B. Howell, eds., *State Trials*, 33 vols. (1809–1826)
TRHS	*Transactions of the Royal Historical Society*
Zaller, *The Parliament of 1621*	Robert Zaller, *The Parliament of 1621: A Study in Constitutional Conflict*
Zurich Letters	Hastings Robinson, ed., *The Zurich Letters, 1558–1579*, 2 vols.

Notes

Introduction

1. Lawrence Stone, *The Causes of the English Revolution, 1529–1642*, 2d ed., revised (London: Routledge, 1986).

2. Conrad Russell, *The Causes of the English Civil War* (Oxford: The Clarendon Press, 1990), 10.

3. Ibid., 216.

Chapter 1: The Discourse of Monarchy

1. Sir Thomas Elyot, *Four Political Treatises* (Gainesville, FL: Scholars' Facsimiles and Reprints, 1967), 112 (quoting Quintus Curtius).

2. Jasper Ridley, *The Tudor Age* (Woodstock, NY: The Overlook Press, 1990), passim.

3. Julian Cornwall, "English Population in the Early Sixteenth Century," *EcHR*, 2d. ser., 22 (1970): 32–44; E. A. Wrigley and Roger Schofield, *The Population History of England, 1541–1871* (Cambridge: Harvard University Press, 1981). For a broader overview of the significance of demographic factors in early modern revolutions, see Jack A. Goldstone, *Revolution and Rebellion in the Early Modern World* (Berkeley and Los Angeles: University of California Press, 1991).

4. Julian Cornwall, *The Revolt of the Peasantry, 1549* (London: Routledge and Kegan Paul, 1977), 145; Buchanan Sharp, *In Contempt of All Authority: Rural Artisans and Riot in the West of England, 1586–1631* (Berkeley and Los Angeles: University of California Press, 1980); Conrad Russell, *The Fall of the British Monarchies, 1637–1642* (Oxford: The Clarendon Press, 1991); Andy Wood, *Riot, Rebellion and Popular Politics in Early Modern England* (Basingstoke and New York: Palgrave, 2002).

5. Robert Zaller, "What Does the English Revolution Mean? Recent Historiographical Interpretations of Mid-Seventeenth Century England," *Albion* 18 (1986): 617–635; cf. Lawrence Stone, *The Causes of the English Civil War* (London: Routledge, 2d ed., revised, 1986); Conrad Russell, *The Causes of the English Civil War* (Oxford: The Clarendon Press, 1990); Anne Hughes, *The Causes of the English Civil War*, 2d ed. (New York: St. Martin's Press, 1998 [1991]).

6. Richard Lachmann, *From Manor to Market: Structural Change in England, 1536–1640* (Madison: University of Wisconsin Press, 1987), 17.

7. A. L. Beier, *Masterless Men: The Vagrancy Problem in England, 1560–1640* (London: Methuen, 1985).

8. Ernst H. Kantorowicz, *The King's Two Bodies: A Study in Medieval Political Theology* (Princeton: Princeton University Press, 1957).

9. Keith Thomas, *Religion and the Decline of Magic* (New York: Charles Scribner's Sons, 1971), 195; Marc Bloch, *The Royal Touch: Sacred Monarchy and Scrofula,* tr. J. E. Anderson (London: Routledge and Kegan Paul, 1973), 145. See also Frank Barlow, "The King's Evil," *EHR* 95 (1980): 3–27.

10. Percy Ernst Schramm, *A History of the English Coronation* (Oxford: The Clarendon Press, 1937), passim; Cranmer cited at 139. Sir Edward Coke agreed that "coronation was but a royal ornament and outward solemnization of descent": Kantorowicz, op. cit., 317.

11. Bloch, op. cit., 204, 212; Raymond Crawfurd, *The King's Evil* (New York: AMS Press, 1977 [1911]), 112.

12. Frances A. Yates, *Astraea: The Imperial Theme in the Sixteenth Century* (London: Routledge and Kegan Paul, 1975); idem, "Queen Elizabeth as Astraea," *Journal of the Courtauld and Warburg Institutes* 20 (1947): 27–82; Roy Strong, *The Cult of Elizabeth: Elizabethan Portraiture and Pageantry* (London: Thames and Hudson, 1971); John N. King, *Tudor Royal Iconography: Literature and Art in an Age of Religious Crisis* (Princeton: Princeton University Press, 1989).

13. King, op. cit., 126–127, 199, 219.

14. Tessa Watt, *Cheap Print and Popular Piety, 1550–1640* (Cambridge: Cambridge University Press, 1991), 143–144.

15. Gordon Kipling, "Henry VII and the Origins of Tudor Patronage," in Guy Fitch Lytle and Stephen Orgel, eds., *Patronage in the Renaissance* (Princeton: Princeton University Press, 1981), 117–164; quotation at 140.

16. James M. Osborn, ed., *The Quenes Maiesties Passage through the Citie of London to Westminster the Day before her Coronacion* (New Haven: Yale University Press, 1960); C. G. Bayne, "The Coronation of Queen Elizabeth," *EHR* 25 (1910): 650–673; A. L. Rowse, "The Coronation of Queen Elizabeth I," in his *An Elizabethan Garland* (London: Macmillan, 1954); William P. Haugaard, "The Coronation of Elizabeth I," *JEH* 19 (1968): 163–165; David Bergeron, "Elizabeth's Coronation Entry (1559): New Manuscript Evidence," *ELR* 8 (1978): 3–8; Sydney Anglo, *Spectacle, Pageantry, and Early Tu-dor Policy* (Oxford: The Clarendon Press, 1979), 344–359; Richard C. McCoy, "The Wonderfull Spectacle: The Civic Progress of Elizabeth I and the Troublesome Coronation," in Janos M. Bal, ed., *Coronations: Medieval and Early Modern Monarchic Ritual* (Berkeley and Los Angeles: University of California Press, 1990), 217–227; David J. Starkey, "'Continuity' versus 'Change': Historians and English Coronations of the Medieval and Early Modern Periods," idem, 228–245. Cf. Clifford Geertz, "Centers, Kings, and Charisma: Reflections on the Symbolics of Power," in Sean Wilentz, ed., *Rites of Power: Symbolism, Ritual, and Politics Since the Middle Ages* (Philadelphia: University of Pennsylvania Press, 1985), 13–38.

17. Anglo, op. cit., 344, 348, 351, 355–356. The quotation is from Richard Grafton, who designed the pageant.

18. Stephen Orgel, *The Illusion of Power: Political Theater in the English Renaissance* (Berkeley and Los Angeles: University of California Press, 1975); Stephen Greenblatt, *Renaissance Self-Fashioning: From More to Shakespeare* (Chicago: University of Chicago Press, 1980); Walter Cohen, *Drama of a Nation: Public Theater in Renaissance England and Spain* (Ithaca: Cornell University Press, 1985); Timothy Murray, *Theatrical Legitimation: Allegories of Genius in Seventeenth-Century England and France* (Oxford: Oxford University Press, 1987), are among recent discussions.

19. Sir John E. Neale, *Elizabeth I and Her Parliaments,* 2 vols. (London: Jonathan Cape, 1953, 1957), 2: 119.

20. Sir Robert Naunton, *Fragmenta Regalia, or Observations on Queen Elizabeth, Her Times and Favorites*, ed. John S. Cerovski (Washington, D.C.: The Folger Shakespeare Library, 1985), 44, 45; William Camden, *The most renowned and victorious Prince Elizabeth, Late Queen of England*, ed. Wallace T. MacCaffrey (Chicago: University of Chicago Press, 1970), 280–286.

21. Roy Strong, *Henry, Prince of Wales and England's Lost Renaissance* (London: Thames and Hudson, 1986), 151–160.

22. William Hunt, "Spectral Origins of the English Revolution: Legitimation Crisis in Early Stuart England," in Geoff Eley and William Hunt, eds., *Reviving the English Revolution: Reflections and Elaborations on the Work of Christopher Hill* (London: Verso, 1988), 305–332.

23. H. M. Colvin, *The History of the King's Works*, 6 vols. (London: HMSO 1963–1982), 4, Pt. II, 1–367. A convenient summary is printed in David Loades, *The Tudor Court* (Totowa: Barnes and Noble Books, 1987), 193–202.

24. Loades, op. cit., 8.

25. David Starkey et al., *The English Court: From the Wars of the Roses to the Civil War* (London: Longman, 1987), 38.

26. Paul L. Hughes and James F. Larkin, eds., *Tudor Royal Proclamations*. Vol. I: *The Early Tudors (1485–1553)* (New Haven: Yale University Press, 1964), xxi–xliii.

27. Robert Zaller, *The Parliament of 1621: A Study in Constitutional Conflict* (Berkeley and Los Angeles: University of California Press, 1971), 161; see, more generally, David Harris Willson, *Privy Councillors in the House of Commons, 1604–1629* (Minneapolis: University of Minnesota Press, 1940).

28. See the still-classic study by Margaret A. Judson, *The Crisis of the Constitution: An Essay in Constitutional and Political Thought in England, 1603–1645* (New Brunswick: Rutgers University Press, 1949, repr. ed., 1988).

29. Sir Francis Bacon, *The Essayes or Counsels, Civill and Morall*, ed. Michael Kiernan (Cambridge: Harvard University Press, 1985), 64.

30. For Elyot's principal comments on counsel, see Sir Thomas Elyot, *The Boke Named The Gouernour*, ed., Henry Herbert Stephen Croft, 2 vols. (New York: Burt Franklin, 1967 [1531]), 2: 427–448.

31. Sir Philip Sidney, *The Major Works* (Oxford: Oxford University Press, 2002), 67.

32. Richard Marius, *Thomas More: A Biography* (New York: Vintage Books, 1985), 191.

33. Thomas Starkey, *A Dialogue between Pole and Lupset*, ed. T. F. Mayer (London: Royal Historical Society, 4th ser., vol. 37, 1989), 112.

34. Alistair Fox and John Guy, *Reassessing the Henrician Age: Humanism, Politics and Reform 1500–1550* (Oxford: Basil Blackwell, 1986), chapters 1, 6; Thomas F. Mayer, "Faction and Ideology: Thomas Starkey's *Dialogue*," *HJ* 28 (1985): 1–25; cf. G. R. Elton, "Reform by Statute: Thomas Starkey's *Dialogue* and Thomas Cromwell's Policy," *Proceedings of the British Academy* 54 (1968): 165–188.

35. Cf. the argument set out in the (putatively) fourteenth-century *Modus Tenendi Parliamentum*, which suggests that the Steward, the Earl Marshal, and the Constable have the power to convoke a parliamentary commission when the King's peace is "undermined" and the land "afflicted." At one point Starkey suggests that all these officers will be part of his permanent council (166).

36. Kevin Sharpe, "The Earl of Arundel, His Circle and the Opposition to the Duke of Buckingham," in Sharpe, ed., *Faction and Parliament: Essays on Early Stuart History* (Oxford: The Clarendon Press, 1978), 209–244, at 217–218.

37. Michael B. Pulman, *The Elizabethan Privy Council in the 1570s* (Berkeley and Los Angeles: University of California Press, 1971).

38. Starkey, *The English Court*, op. cit.

39. On the authorship of the *Assertion*, see Marius, *Thomas More*, 276–280.

40. Jonathan Goldberg, *James I and the Politics of Literature: Jonson, Shakespeare, Donne, and Their Contemporaries* (Baltimore: The Johns Hopkins University Press, 1983), J. P. Sommerville, *Politics and Ideology in England 1603–1640* (Cambridge: Cam-

bridge University Press, 1986), chapter 1; idem, "James I and the Divine Right of Kings: English Politics and Continental Theory," in Linda Levy Peck, ed., *The Mental World of the Jacobean Court* (Cambridge: Cambridge University Press, 1991), 55–70; idem, *King James VI and I: Political Writings* (Cambridge: Cambridge University Press, 1996), xv–xliv; Jenny Wormald, "James VI and I, *Basilikon Doron,* and *The Trew Law of Free Monarchies*: the Scottish Context and the English Translations," in Peck, op. cit., 36–54: but cf. David Harris Willson, "James I and His Literary Assistants," *HLQ* 8 (1944–1945): 35–57, and James Craigie, "Last Poems of James VI," *Scottish Historical Review* 29 (1950): 134–142.

41. On sixteenth-century iconoclasm see John Phillips, *The Reformation of Images: Destruction of Art in England, 1535–1660* (Berkeley and Los Angeles: University of California Press, 1973); Carlos M. N. Eire, *War Against the Idols: The Reformation of Worship from Erasmus to Calvin* (Cambridge: Cambridge University Press, 1986); Margaret Aston, *England's Iconoclasts: Volume 1, Laws Against Images* (New York: The Clarendon Press, 1988); Eamon Duffy, *The Stripping of the Altars: Traditional Religion in England 1400–1580* (New Haven: Yale University Press, 1993); below, Chapter 2.

42. See the discussion in Phillips, 70–74.

43. The best recent discussion of James' early years and of his conception of king-craft is in Maurice Lee Jr., *Great Britain's Solomon: James VI and I in His Three Kingdoms* (Urbana and Chicago: University of Illinois Press, 1990), chapters 2 and 3; cf. Pauline Croft, *King James* (Houndmills, Basingstoke: Palgrave Macmillan, 2003), chapter 1.

44. C. H. McIlwain, ed., *The Political Works of James I* (Cambridge: Harvard University Press, 1918), 307–308.

45. For a discussion of these documents, see 572ff.

46. Wallace Notestein, Frances Relf, and Hartley Simpson, eds., *Commons Debates 1621,* 7 vols. (New Haven: Yale University Press, 1935), 5: 248.

47. He paid for them with a spell of imprisonment in any case. On Coke's parliamentary career see Stephen D. White, *Sir Edward Coke and 'The Grievances of the Commonwealth'* (Chapel Hill: University of North Carolina Press, 1979), and below, s.v. Coke.

48. Richard C. McCoy, "Gascoigne's *Poemata Castrata*: The Wages of Courtly Success," *Criticism* 27 (1985): 29–54; idem, *The Rites of Knighthood: The Literature and Politics of Elizabethan Chivalry* (Berkeley and Los Angeles: University of California Press, 1989), 43–44, 85–86; Roy Strong, *The Cult of Elizabeth* (London: Thames and Hudson, 1977), 141.

49. McCoy, *Rites of Knighthood,* 28–30; Helen Miller, *Henry VIII and the English Nobility* (Oxford: Basil Blackwell, 1986), 217–220, 227–230; G. W. Bernard, ed., *The Tudor Nobility* (Manchester: Manchester University Press, 1992), 30–34, 58ff.

50. Arthur B. Ferguson, *The Indian Summer of English Chivalry: Studies in the Decline and Transformation of Chivalric Idealism* (Durham: University of North Carolina Press, 1984 [1960]); Dominic Baker-Smith, "'Inglorious glory': 1513 and the Humanist Attack on Chivalry," in Sydney Anglo, ed., *Chivalry in the Renaissance* (Woodbridge, Suffolk: The Boydell Press, 1990), 129–144.

51. Stephen Greenblatt, *Renaissance Self-Fashioning,* op. cit.; Richard Helgerson, *The Elizabethan Prodigals* (Berkeley and Los Angeles: University of California Press, 1976); Louis Adrian Montrose, *The Subject of Elizabeth: Authority, Gender, Representation* (Chicago: University of Chicago Press, 2006).

52. Richard Helgerson, *Forms of Nationhood: The Elizabethan Writing of England* (Chicago: University of Chicago Press, 1992).

53. Graham Parry, *The Golden Age Restor'd: The Culture of the Stuart Court, 1603–42* (New York: St. Martin's Press, 1981), 41.

54. Francis A. Yates, *Theatre of the World* (Chicago: University of Chicago Press, 1969), 85.

55. Ibid., 86. For the association of magic with the stage, see David Woodman, *White Magic and English Renaissance Drama* (Rutherford–Madison–Teaneck, NJ: Fairleigh Dickinson Press, 1973); Charles Nicholl, *The Chemical Theatre* (London: Routledge and

Kegan Paul, 1980); John S. Mebane, *Renaissance Magic and the Return to the Golden Age: The Occult Tradition and Marlowe, Jonson, and Shakespeare* (Lincoln: University of Nebraska Press, 1989); Howard Dobin, *Merlin's Disciples: Prophecy, Poetry, and Power in Renaissance England* (Stanford: Stanford University Press, 1990).

56. Don M. Wolfe et al., eds., *Complete Prose Works of John Milton*, 11 vols. (New Haven: Yale University Press, 1953–1982), 3: 342–343; John Milton, *Political Writings*, ed. Martin Dzelzanis (Cambridge: Cambridge University Press, 1991), 56. For a fuller development of this discussion, see my "The Figure of the Tyrant in English Revolutionary Thought," *JHI* 54 (1993): 585–610.

57. David Norbrook, *Poetry and Politics in the English Renaissance* (London: Routledge and Kegan Paul, 1984), 16–17. See Joseph John Kelly, "Ben Jonson's Politics," *Renaissance and Reformation*, new ser., 7 (1983): 192–215; cf. Annabel Patterson, *Censorship and Interpretation: The Conditions of Writing and Reading in Early Modern England* (Madison: University of Wisconsin Press, 1984), esp. 49–58; Jonathan Dollimore, *Radical Tragedy: Religion, Ideology and Power in the Drama of Shakespeare and His Contemporaries* (Chicago: University of Chicago Press, 1984), 134–138; Jonathan Goldberg, *James I and the Politics of Literature*, passim. Jonson's court entertainments are analyzed in John C. Meagher, *Method and Meaning in Jonson's Masques* (Notre Dame: University of Notre Dame Press, 1966).

58. Kevin Sharpe, *Criticism and Compliment: The Politics of Literature in the England of Charles I* (Cambridge: Cambridge University Press, 1987); cf. Frank Whigham, "Interpretation at Court: Courtesy and the Performer–Author Dialectic," *New Literary History* 14 (1983): 623–639. I have criticized Sharpe's thesis at greater length in a review of *Criticism and Compliment* (*Albion*, 21 [1989]: 115–116).

59. For the increasing dichotomy between the commercial and court stages, see Ira Clark, *Professional Playwrights: Massinger, Ford, Shirley, and Brome* (Lexington: University Press of Kentucky, 1992); cf. Gerald Eades Bentley, *The Profession of Dramatist in Shakespeare's Time, 1590–1642* (Princeton: Princeton University Press, 1971).

60. Graham Parry, *The Seventeenth Century: The Intellectual and Cultural Context of English Literature, 1603–1700* (London: Longman, 1989), 38.

61. John Nichols, ed., *The Progress . . . of Queen Elizabeth*, 3 vols. (London, 1823), 3: 552, quoted in Joel Hurstfield, *Freedom, Corruption, and Government in Elizabethan England* (Cambridge: Harvard University Press, 1937), 137.

62. Denys Hay, *Polydore Vergil: Renaissance Historian and Man of Letters* (Oxford: Oxford University Press, 1952); Richard Koebner, "The Imperial Crown of This Realm: Henry VIII, Constantine, and Polydore Vergil," *BIHR* 26 (1953): 29–52.

63. Cf. Helgerson's discussion of this point in his *Forms of Nationhood*, 131–132.

64. Robert Zaller, "The Concept of Opposition in Early Stuart England," *Albion* 12 (1980): 211–234.

65. Thomas Birch, ed., *The Court and Times of Charles I*, 2 vols. (London: Henry Colburn, 1848), 2: 112.

66. John J. Manning, ed., *The First and Second Parts of John Hayward's The Life and Raigne of King Henrie IIII* (Camden Society, 4th ser., vol. 42 [London: Royal Historical Society, 1991]), 20.

67. Hayward's text dealt only with the first year of Henry IV's reign, although well over half the text was in fact a preface to it, including a detailed account of Richard II's deposition. References to Richard had been stricken from the 1587 edition of Holinshed's *Chronicles*.

68. N. E. McClure, ed., *The Letters of John Chamberlain*, 2 vols. (Philadelphia: American Philosophical Society, 1939), 1: 78.

69. Edward Arber, *A Transcript of the Registers of the Company of Stationers of London 1554–1640*, 5 vols. (London, 1875–1877), 3: 677–678.

70. Manning, op. cit., 21n75; 27n92.

71. Ibid., 28.

72. Ibid., 33.

73. Ibid., 65n1. Manning, 17–34, describes the Hayward affair; see also Margaret Dowling, "Sir John Hayward's Troubles over His *Life of Henry IV*," *The Library*, 4th ser., vol. 11 (1930): 212–224, and Richard Dutton, *Licensing, Censorship and Authority in Early Modern England: Buggeswords* (New York: Palgrave, 2000), chapter 8.

74. D. R. Woolf finds Hayward's text conventional and "quite innocuous" in its treatment of its materials—as if the subject of royal deposition could ever be innocuous in early modern England—and suggests that too much has been made of the affair (op. cit., 107–108). F. J. Levy opines that Hayward's rhetorical justification of the deposition, attributed to Archbishop Arundel but not found in the chronicle literature, was "a trifle too successful" and that Hayward may even "have known that he was treading close to treason," but he concludes nonetheless that "in retrospect it was difficult to see why there was so much excitement" over the incident (*Tudor Historical Thought* [San Marino, CA: The Huntington Library, 1967], 259, 261).

75. *A Conference about the Next Succession to the Crown of England* (1595). Hayward in fact wrote a rebuttal to this pamphlet at James' accession, *An Answer to the First Part of a Certain Conference Concerning Succession* (1603).

76. When the Queen asked Bacon whether there were not places in the book "that might be drawn within the case [i.e., scope] of treason," he answered that "for treason surely I found none, but for fellonie ver many. . . . for [Hayward] had taken most of the sentences of Cornelius Tacitus, and translated them into English, and put them into his text" (*Sir Francis Bacon his Apologie, in Certain Imputations Concerning the Late Earle of Essex* [1604], 34).

77. Chamberlain, op. cit.

78. Quoted in Stephen J. Greenblatt, *Sir Walter Ralegh: The Renaissance Man and His Roles* (New Haven: Yale University Press, 1973), 116.

79. David Harris Willson, *King James VI and I* (New York: Oxford University Press, 1967 [1956]), 222; Maurice Lee Jr., *Great Britain's Solomon*, op. cit., 87.

80. Willson, ibid.

81. Cf. the discussion of this frontispiece in D. R. Woolf, *The Idea of History in Early Stuart England: Erudition, Ideology, and 'The Light of Truth' from the Accession of James I to the Civil War* (Toronto: University of Toronto Press, 1990), 45–46.

82. *The First Part of the History of the World* (1614), in *Works of Sir Walter Ralegh*, 8 vols. (Oxford, 1829), 2: xvi. The modernized spelling has been retained, but punctuation follows the original edition.

83. Ibid., 1: 462–464.

84. Chamberlain, 1: 568. James complained to the Earl of Somerset that Raleigh "speaketh but evil" of "the kings he hates." See C. H. Firth, "Sir Walter Raleigh's *History of the World*," *Proceedings of the British Academy* 8 (1918): 427–446, and John Racin Jr., "The Early Editions of Sir Walter Ralegh's *The History of the World*," *Studies in Bibliography (Virginia)* 17 (1964): 199–209; idem, *Sir Walter Ralegh as Historian* (Salzburg: Universität Salzburg,1974).

85. Woolf, *The Idea of History*, op. cit., 54.

86. W. A. Armstrong, "The Elizabethan Conception of the Tyrant," *Review of English Studies* 22 (1946): 161–181.

87. Robert Cotton and John Heywood [Hayward], *The Histories of the Lives and Reigns of Henry the Third and Henry the Fourth, Kings of England* (London, 1679), 25, 31, 39.

88. Ibid., 4, 6, 8, 23.

89. *Cottoni Posthuma* (1651), sig. A3v, quoted in Kevin Sharpe, *Sir Robert Cotton 1586–1631: History and Politics in Early Modern England* (Oxford: Oxford University Press, 1979), 246.

90. Sharpe, 113–150, 208–218; idem, "The Earl of Arundel, His Circle and the Aristocratic Opposition to the Duke of Buckingham, 1618–1628," in Sharpe, ed., *Faction and Parliament*, op. cit.

91. Sharpe, *Sir Robert Cotton*, 247. For a contrasting interpretation of Cotton's political commitments, see David Berkowitz's article in *BDBR* 1: 179–182.

92. P.R.O., S.P. 16/54/4; Sharpe, *Sir Robert Cotton*, 142.
93. Sharpe, 182–183.

Chapter 2: Sacred Discourse

1. John Bridges, *A Defence of the Government Established in the Churche of Englande for Ecclesiasticall Matters* (London, 1587), 1110.
2. J. E. Booty, ed., *An Apology of the Church of England* (Ithaca: Cornell University Press, 1963 [1561]), 26, 34.
3. Quoted in C. H. Williams, *William Tyndale* (London: Thomas Nelson and Sons, 1969), 25.
4. Gerald T. Sheppard, ed., *The Geneva Bible* (New York: The Pilgrim Press, 1989), 11.
5. R. T. Kendall, *Calvin and English Calvinism to 1649* (Oxford: Oxford University Press, 1979).
6. Patrick Collinson, *The Religion of Protestants: The Church in English Society 1559–1625* (Oxford: The Clarendon Press, 1982), 92, 41; W. H. Frere and C. E. Douglas, eds., *Puritan Manifestoes* (New York: Burt Franklin, 1972 [1907]), 7.
7. Sheppard, op. cit., 8.
8. Ibid., 6; Richard L. Greaves, "Traditionalism and the Seeds of Revolution in the Social Principles of the Geneva Bible," *SCJ* 7 (1976): 94–109; idem, "The Nature and Intellectual Milieu of the Political Principles in the Geneva Bible Marginalia," *Journal of Church and State* 22 (1980): 233–249.
9. These were largely published in the nineteenth century, e.g., Charles Lloyd, ed., *Formularies of Faith Put Forth By Authority During the Reign of Henry VIII* (Oxford: The Clarendon Press, 1856); Joseph Ketley, ed., *The Two Liturgies . . . Set Forth By Authority in the Reign of King Edward VI*, Parker Soc. 29 (Cambridge: Cambridge University Press, 1844); etc.
10. [Thomas Cartwright], "A Second Admonition to the Parliament" (1572), in Frere and Douglas, op. cit., 91.
11. George Carleton, *Tithes Examined and Proved to be Due to the Clergy by a Divine Right* (London, 1606).
12. In Felicity Heal and Rosemary O'Day, eds., *Church and Society in England: Henry VIII to James I* (London: Macmillan, 1977), 107. See also Felicity Heal, *Of Prelates and Princes: A Study of the Economic and Social Position of the Tudor Episcopate* (Cambridge: Cambridge University Press, 1980); Christopher Hill, *Economic Problems of the Church from Whitgift to the Long Parliament* (Oxford: Oxford University Press, 1956); Rosemary O'Day and Felicity Heal, eds., *Princes and Paupers in the English Church* (Leicester: Leicester University Press, 1981).
13. William P. Haugaard, *Elizabeth and the English Reformation: The Struggle for a Stable Settlement* (Cambridge: Cambridge University Press, 1970), 184, 311.
14. On the general question of the significance of gesture, see Jan Bremmer and Herman Roodenburg, eds., *A Cultural History of Gesture* (Ithaca: Cornell University Press, 1992).
15. "A Sermon preached before the Queenes Maiestie the 25. day of February . . ." in Edward Dering, *Workes* (London, 1597), quoted in Patrick Collinson, *Mirror of Elizabethan Puritanism: The Life and Letters of 'Godly Master Dering'* (London: Dr. Williams's Trust, 1964), reprinted in Collinson's *Godly People: Essays on English Protestantism and Puritanism* (London: The Hambledon Press, 1983), 288–324.
16. Patrick Collinson, *Archbishop Grindal 1519–1583: The Struggle for a Reformed Church* (Berkeley and Los Angeles: University of California Press, 1979), 220.
17. Cited in John S. Coolidge, *The Pauline Renaissance in England: Puritanism and the Bible* (Oxford: The Clarendon Press, 1970), xiv.
18. Coolidge, 77.
19. Murray M. Tolmie, *The Triumph of the Saints: The Separate Churches of London, 1616–1649* (Cambridge: Cambridge University Press, 1977), 2.

20. Hastings Robinson, ed., *The Zurich Letters, 1558–1579*, 2 vols. (Cambridge: The Parker Society, 1842), 169, quoted in Coolidge, 44.

21. *Zurich Letters*, quoted in B. R. White, *The English Separatist Tradition: From the Marian Martyrs to the Pilgrim Fathers* (London: Oxford University Press, 1971), 25–26.

22. Laud–Selden–Fairhurst MSS, Lambeth Palace, printed in Stanford E. Lehmberg, "Archbishop Grindal and the Prophesying," *Historical Magazine of the Protestant Episcopal Church* 34 (1965 [87–145]), 93ff.

23. Ibid.

24. The chief account of this meeting, apparently a memorandum by Sir Walter Mildmay, is in Northants. Record Office, F.(M.)P.70.c. It is discussed in Stanford E. Lehmberg, *Sir Walter Mildmay and Tudor Government* (Austin: University of Texas Press, 1964), 148–152.

25. The entire text is reprinted, with an introduction, in Leonard J. Trinterud, ed., *Elizabethan Puritanism* (New York: Library of Protestant Thought, 1971), 191–201.

26. On the date of its composition and its contemporary fame, see Patrick Collinson, "The Downfall of Archbishop Grindal and Its Place in Elizabethan Ecclesiastical and Political History," *Godly People*, 371–398 at 376 and n43.

27. Collinson, *Archbishop Grindal*, 246.

28. Quoted in G. J. R. Parry, *A Protestant Vision: William Harrison and the Reformation of Elizabethan England* (Cambridge: Cambridge University Press, 1987), 247; see Parry's accompanying discussion of the prophetic office.

29. M. St. Clare Byrne, ed., *The Letters of King Henry VIII* (London: Cassell & Co., 1936), 86, quoted in Lacey Baldwin Smith, "A Matter of Conscience," in Theodore K. Rabb and Jerrold E. Seigel, eds., *Action and Conviction in Early Modern Europe: Essays in Memory of E. H. Harbison* (Princeton: Princeton University Press, 1969), 35.

30. *Godly People*, 377ff.

31. John Ayre, ed., *The Sermons of Edwin Sandys . . .* (Cambridge: Cambridge University Press, 1961), 333.

32. Parry, op. cit., 192–195.

33. Quoted in Peter Lake, "Matthew Hutton — A Puritan Bishop?" *History* 64 (1979): 182–204, at 189.

34. *Zurich Letters*, 1: 169.

35. For a comprehensive view, see Patrick Collinson, "Episcopacy and Reform in Later Sixteenth-Century England," *Godly People*, 155–189.

36. Patrick Collinson, *The Elizabethan Puritan Movement* (London: Jonathan Cape, 1967), 201–207.

37. Hugh Trevor-Roper, *Catholics, Anglicans and Puritans: Seventeenth Century Essays* (Chicago: University of Chicago Press, 1988), 48.

38. Peter Lake, *Moderate Puritans and the Elizabethan Church* (Cambridge: Cambridge University Press, 1982), chapter 9. Nicholas Tyacke's views in his study of the growth of English Arminianism are generally supportive of Lake's (*Anti-Calvinists: The Rise of English Arminianism c. 1590–1640* [Oxford: The Clarendon Press, 1987]). On the larger doctrinal context see Kendall, *Calvin and English Calvinism*, op. cit.

39. Tyacke, op. cit., 62ff. John Reynolds led a drive to gain official status for the Lambeth Articles at the Hampton Court Conference in 1604, but James, after some hesitation, rejected the plea.

40. Collinson, *The Religion of Protestants*.

41. Lake, *Anglicans and Puritans*, op. cit., 28–42.

42. Ibid., 119–126; 83.

43. Richard Hooker, *Of the Laws of Ecclesiastical Polity*, ed. Arthur Stephen McGrade (Cambridge: Cambridge University Press, 1989), xv.

44. B. C. Milner, *Calvin's Doctrine of the Church* (Leiden: E. J. Brill, 1990), especially chapter 2; W. D. J. Cargill Thompson, "The Two Regiments: A Study of the Theory of the Development of the Relation of Church and State During the Reformation, with Particular Reference to England" (D. Phil. Thesis, Cambridge University, 1959).

45. Richard Hooker, *Of the Laws of Ecclesiastical Polity*, 2 vols. (London: Dent, 1965), 1: 152–153.

46. Ibid., ed. McGrade (1989), 192, 193, 195.

47. Norman L. Jones, *Faith by Statute: Parliament and the Settlement of Religion, 1559* (London: Royal Historical Society, 1982). The title of Jones' monograph emphasizes the secularizing significance of Parliament's role. John Guy comments as well that the complete absence of clerical consent made "constitutional history" (*Tudor England* [Oxford: Oxford University Press, 1988], 262).

48. Book V, Chapter 11, para. 2 (Morris, 2: 39).

49. Ibid., 41.

50. Ibid., 44.

51. Cited in Lake, *Anglicans and Puritans*, 164.

52. *Laws*, IV, I, 3 (1: 361); quoted in Lake, to whom this discussion is indebted.

53. Ibid., IV, II, 3 (1: 365).

54. Ibid., IV, III, 1 (1: 367); V, XXII, 4, 5 (2: 84, 85).

55. Walter Travers, *A Supplication made to the Privy Counsel* (Oxford: Joseph Barnes, 1612); *A Christian Letter* (1599); see S. J. Knox, *Walter Travers: Paragon of Elizabethan Puritanism* (London: Methuen, 1962), 70–88.

56. Lake, *Anglicans and Puritans*, 196.

57. See, most notably, Patrick McGrath, *Papists and Puritans Under Elizabeth I* (London: Blandford Press, 1967).

58. Christopher Haigh, *English Reformations: Religion, Politics, and Society under the Tudors* (Oxford: The Clarendon Press, 1993), 14.

59. See Jane Facey, "John Foxe and the Defence of the English Church," in Peter Lake and Maria Dowling, eds., *Protestantism and the National Church in Sixteenth Century England* (London: Croom Helm, 1987), 162–192; cf. Lake's own essay, "Presbyterianism, the Idea of a Divine Church and the Argument from Divine Right," ibid., 193–224.

60. Christopher Haigh, ed., *The English Reformation Revised* (Cambridge: Cambridge University Press, 1987), 176.

61. C. G. Bayne, *Anglo–Roman Relations 1558–1565* (Oxford: Oxford University Press, 1913); Peter Holmes, *Resistance and Compromise: The Political Thought of the Elizabethan Catholics* (Cambridge: Cambridge University Press, 1982), 83–89.

62. Christopher Haigh, "The Fall of a Church or the Rise of a Sect? Post-Reformation Catholicism in England," *HJ* 21 (1978): 181–186, at 184–185.

63. Alan Dures, *English Catholicism, 1558–1642: Continuity and Change* (Burnt Mill, Harlow, Essex: Longman, 1983), 91.

64. P.R.O. 12/144/69, unfoliated; calendared in *CSPD 1547–1580*, 691 (December, 1580). The tract has attracted significant modern discussion: Elliot Rose, *Cases of Conscience: Alternatives open to Recusants and Puritans under Elizabeth I and James I* (Cambridge: Cambridge University Press, 1975), 75–81; Holmes, op. cit., 90–94; Alexandra Walsham, *Church Papists: Catholicism, Conformity and Confessional Polemic in Early Modern England* (Woodbridge, Suffolk: The Boydell Press for the Royal Historical Society, 1993), 51–54.

65. P. J. Holmes, ed., *Elizabethan Casuistry* (Catholic Record Society, 1981), 75–76; Walsham, op. cit., 63.

66. Walsham, 82 (quoting Thomas Cooper, *The Cry and Revenge of Blood* [1620]).

67. John Earle, *Earle's Microcosmography*, ed. Alfred S. West (Cambridge: Cambridge University Press, 1897 [1628]).

68. Walsham, 73–74.

69. HMC, *Reports on Manuscripts in Various Collections*, 3: 34–43 at 39, cited in Anthony Pritchard, *Catholic Loyalism in Elizabethan England* (Chapel Hill: University of North Carolina Press, 1979), 52. On the petition, see Roger B. Manning, "Richard Shelley of Warminghurst and the English Catholic Petition for Toleration of 1585," *Recusant History* 6 (1962): 265–274.

70. Holmes, *Elizabethan Casuistry*, chapters 11–14 covers this literature judiciously; see also Thomas H. Clancy, *Papist Pamphleteers: The Allen–Persons Party and the Political Thought of the Counter-Reformation in England, 1572–1615* (Chicago: Loyola University Press, 1964).

71. See, for example, Robert M. Kingdon, "William Allen's Use of Protestant Political Argument," in Charles H. Carter, ed., *From the Renaissance to the Counter-Reformation: Essays in Honor of Garrett Mattingly* (New York: Random House, 1965), 164–178.

72. *A conference about the next succession to the crowne of Ingland . . .* (Antwerp, 1595).

73. The *Memoriall* was unpublished until 1690, but circulated widely in manuscript. On its contents and the controversy it provoked, see Clancy, op. cit.; idem, "Notes on Persons's 'Memorial for the Reformation of England,'" *Recusant History* 5 (1959): 17–34; J. J. Scarisbrick, "Robert Persons's Plan for the 'True' Reformation of England," in Neil McKendrick, ed., *Historical Perspectives: Studies in English Thought and Society in Honour of J. H. Plumb* (London: Europa Publications, 1974), 19–42.

74. Pritchard, op. cit., 196.

75. Holmes, *Elizabethan Casuistry*, 240 n1.

76. Pritchard, 56.

77. HMC, *Misc. Coll.*, 3: 51–58.

78. E.g., Rose and Pritchard.

79. Pritchard, 8.

80. Holmes, Chapter 18. Unlike Appellant writers such as Anthony Copley, however, the Jesuits continued to maintain the validity of the papal deposing power.

81. William Clarke, *A Reply unto a Certain Libel Lately Set Forth by Father Parsons* (1603); Pritchard, 168–170.

82. Elizabeth's death had mooted this particular point, of course, but James I raised it anew when the 1606 Oath of Allegiance demanded that Catholics deny the papal power of deposition.

83. Rose, 102.

84. A. R. Braunmuller, ed., *A Seventeenth-Century Letter Book* (Newark: University of Delaware Press; London and Toronto, Associated University Presses, 1983), 205; also printed in John Strype, *The Life . . . of . . . Whitgift*, 4 vols. (Oxford: The Clarendon Press, 1822), 3: 420–421.

85. Thomas Rogers, *The Faith, Doctrine, and Religion, Professed & protected in the Realme of England . . . Expressed in 39 Articles* (Cambridge, 1607), sig. Qq3.

86. Thomas Rogers, *An Historical Dialogve Tovching Antichrist and Poperie* (London, 1589), sig. A2.

87. Ibid., 34, 38.

88. Rogers, *The Faith, Doctrine, and Religion*, Qq3v.

89. Ibid., Qq4v.

90. Timothy Dwight Bozeman, "Federal Theology and the 'National Covenant': An Elizabethan Case Study," *Church History* 61 (1992): 394–407, at 400.

91. Mark H. Curtis, "The Hampton Court Conference and Its Aftermath," *History* 46 (1961): 1–16; Frederick Shriver, "Hampton Court Revisited: James I and the Puritans," *JEH* 33 (1982): 48–71; Patrick Collinson, "The Jacobean Religious Settlement: The Hampton Court Conference," in Howard Tomlinson, ed., *Before the English Revolution: Essays on Early Stuart Politics and Government* (New York: St. Martin's Press, 1984), 27–51; Tyacke, *Anti-Calvinists*, chapter 1.

92. *BDBR*, 3: 84–85.

93. Rogers, 111.

94. J. Craigie, ed., *The Basilikon Doron of King James VI and I*, 2 vols. (Edinburgh: Scottish Text Society, 1944), 1: 79, quoted in Christopher W. Marsh, *The Family of Love in English Society, 1550–1630* (Cambridge: Cambridge University Press, 1994), 200.

95. *The Diocesans Tryall* (1621), quoted in Kenneth Fincham, *Prelate as Pastor: The Episcopate of James I* (Oxford: The Clarendon Press, 1990), vi.

96. Josias Nichols, *The Plea of the Innocent* (1602), 1–5.

97. Timothy Rogers, *The Roman-Catharist: or The Papist is a Puritan* (London, 1621), 3–7.

98. Ibid., 12ff.

99. Ibid., 37–39.

100. Ibid., 40.

101. Collinson, *EPM*, 84–91; White, *The English Separatist Tradition*, 23–27.

102. Collinson, 89.

103. G. W. Bernard, "The Church of England, c. 1529—c. 1642," *History* 75 (1990): 183–206.

104. Nichols, *The Plea of the Innocent*, 9.

105. George Paule, Whitgift's secretary and biographer, relates how his master pled Grindal's cause until she yielded, saying "That as she had made him an archbishop, so he should die an archbishop." Collinson is properly skeptical of this self–serving tale (*Archbishop Grindal*, 278).

106. Collinson, *EPM*, 316. The myth persisted into the seventeenth century; in a work published in 1653, Edward Leigh's *A Systeme or Body of Divinity*, Elizabeth was said to have attributed the placidity of Suffolk to the effects of good preaching (Paul S. Seaver, "Community Control and Puritan Politics in Elizabethan Suffolk," *Albion* 9 [1977]: 297–315, at 311).

107. As Caroline Bynum has stressed for the medieval period and Debora Kuller Shuger for the early modern one, gender division was much less exclusive, at least on the level of political and religious archetypes, than in modern societies; thus the generalized concept of patriarchal care can be applied to a female ruler such as Elizabeth no less than to males, though obviously not without modification. See Caroline Walker Bynum, *Jesus as Mother: Studies in the Spirituality of the High Middle Ages* (Berkeley and Los Angeles: University of California Press, 1982); Debora Kuller Shuger, *Habits of Thought in the English Renaissance: Religion, Politics, and the Dominant Culture* (Berkeley and Los Angeles: University of California Press, 1990); cf. Susan B. Frye, *Elizabeth I: The Competition for Representation* (Oxford: Oxford University Press, 1993); and, on the theme of patriarchalism generally, Gordon J. Schochet, *Patriarchalism in Political Thought: The Authoritarian Family and Political Speculation and Attitudes Especially in Seventeenth-Century England* (New York: Basic Books, 1975).

108. On Saravia, see J. P. Sommerville, "Richard Hooker, Hadrian Saravia, and the Advent of the Divine Right of Kings," *History of Political Thought* 4 (1983): 229–245.

109. Collinson, *EPM*, 394.

110. *A parte of a register*, cited in Stephen Brachlow, *The Communion of the Saints: Radical Puritan and Separatist Ecclesiology, 1570–1625* (Oxford: Oxford University Press, 1988), 46.

111. *A treatise of reformation without tarying for anie* (1582).

112. White, op. cit., 45.

113. *BDBR* 2: 137–138, 141–142; White, chapter 5.

114. Henry Jacob, *A Defence of the Chvrches and Ministery of Englande* (Middleburg, 1599), 3–11. This was a response to Johnson's own *A Treatise of the Ministery of the Church of Englande* (1595). Johnson published a further response, *An answere to maister H. Iacob his defense* (1600).

115. Johnson himself petitioned James for toleration, leaving however "the suppressing, abolishing or reforming the abuses that we witness against, to his Majesty's discretion" (White, 112).

116. Henry Jacob, *An Attestation of many Learned, Godly, and famous Divines* (1613), 76, 86.

117. Champlin Burrage, *Early English Dissenters*, 2 vols. (Cambridge: Cambridge University Press, 1912), 2: 13–18; White, 30–32.

118. Peter Martyr Vermigli's definition is representative: "Ecclesiastical discipline is nothing else but a power granted to the Church by God, by which the wills and actions of the faithful, are made conformable to the law of God: which is done by doctrine, admonitions, correction, and finally by punishments, and also by excommunica-

Notes to Chapter 2

tion if need require." Cited in Robert M. Kingdon, "Peter Martyr Vermigli and the Marks of the True Church," in F. Forrester Church and Timothy George, eds., *Continuity and Discontinuity in Church History: Essays Presented to George Hunston Williams* (Leiden: E. J. Brill, 1979), 198–214, at 207.

119. On the *notae*, see Paul D. L. Avis, *The Church in the Theology of the Reformers* (London: Marshall, Morgan, and Scott, 1981), Part I; for Beza, ibid., 123–124.

120. Robert Browne, *A Treatise of reformation without tarying for anie*, in Albert Peel and Leland Carlson, eds., *The Writings of Robert Harrison and Robert Browne* (London: George Allen and Unwin, 1953), at 153.

121. Ibid., 152–154.

122. Brachlow, op. cit., 203–204.

123. "Four Causes of Separation," in Leland H. Carlson, ed., *The Writings of Henry Barrow, 1587–1590* (London: George Allen and Unwin, 1962), at 55.

124. Ibid., 109.

125. Leland H. Carlson, ed., *The Writings of John Greenwood and Henry Barrow, 1591–1593* (London: George Allen and Unwin, 1970), 220. The source for this *cri de coeur* was George Paule, Whitgift's secretary and biographer.

126. Ibid., 236.

127. Zaret, *The Heavenly Contract: Ideology and Organization in Pre-Revolutionary Puritanism* (Chicago: University of Chicago Press, 1985), 105.

128. Nichols, 85.

129. On the theme of universal monarchy in the seventeenth century, see particularly the work of Steven Pincus.

130. Avis, op. cit., 17.

131. On Luther's treatment of this problem see W. D. J. Cargill Thompson, "The 'Two Kingdoms' and the 'Two Regiments': Some Problems of Luther's *Zwei-Reiche-Lehre*," in Thompson's *Studies in the Reformation: Luther to Hooker* (London: Athlone Press, 1980). The English treatment of the problem is dealt with in H. F. Woodhouse, *The Doctrine of the Church in Anglican Theology, 1547–1603* (New York: Macmillan, 1954).

132. Tolmie, *The Triumph of the Saints*, op. cit.

133. Smyth denied any link with the Continental Anabaptists, who combined their belief in adult rebaptism with a doctrine of free grace, and, when pressed, conceded that the baptism of an adult believer in a false church might be valid. See W. T. Whitley, ed., *The Works of John Smyth*, 2 vols. (Cambridge: Cambridge University Press, 1915), 2: 332; James Robert Coggins, *John Smyth's Congregation: English Separatism, Mennonite Influence, and the Elect Nation* (Waterloo, Ontario; Scottsdale, PA: Herald Press, 1991), 62–63. Since adult baptisms in non-Anabaptist churches were exceedingly rare and since the believer's condition rather than the church's was the operative factor, this concession was less than substantive.

134. See, e.g., Henoch Clapham, *Error on the Left Hand* (London, 1608); Francis Johnson, *A Brief Treatise conteyning some grounds and reasons, against two errours of the Anabaptists* (Amsterdam, 1609). Smyth and his followers had been part of Johnson's Separatist congregation in Amsterdam.

135. John Robinson, *A Iust and Necessarie Apologie of Certain Christians* (1625), 10.

136. Ibid., 12.

137. Ibid., 13.

138. Ibid., 10. This requirement became a problem for Robinson's church itself when its membership reached some 300.

139. Henry Ainsworth, *A True Confession of the Faith . . . Which Wee . . . Falsely Called Brownists, Doo Hould* (1596), sig. C–Cv. This document is attributed by Brachlow to Francis Johnson.

140. Ainsworth refuses to dignify the Anglican establishment with even the name of a false church, calling it simply "the Antichristian estate."

141. Ainsworth, Cii[v]–iii.

142. Henry Jacob, *A Christian and modest offer of a most indifferent conference . . . betwixt the Prelats, and the late silenced and deprived ministers in England* (Middleburg, 1606), 3.

143. Ibid., 2–3.

144. On relations between the exile churches and the Dutch authorities lay and clerical, see D. Plooj, *The Pilgrim Fathers from a Dutch Point of View* (New York: New York University Press, 1932); Raymond P. Stearns, *Congregationalism in the Dutch Netherlands: The Rise and Fall of the English Congregational Church Classis, 1621–1635* (Chicago: American Society of Church History, 1940); Keith L. Sprunger, *Dutch Puritanism: A History of English and Scottish Churches of the Netherlands in the Sixteenth and Seventeenth Centuries* (Leiden: E. J. Brill, 1982).

145. Article 84 of Smyth's *Confession of Faith* (c. 1612) states that the magistrate ought not "to meddle with religion, or matters of conscience, to force and compel men to this or that form of religion or doctrine; but to leave the Christian religion free to every man's conscience, and to handle only civil transgressions, injuries, and wrongs of men against man" (cited in Leo F. Solt, *Church and State in Early Modern England, 1509–1640* [New York: Oxford University Press, 1990], 146). See also Coggins, *John Smyth's Congregation*, op. cit.; cf. Timothy George, "Between Pacifism and Coercion: The English Baptist Doctrine of Religious Toleration," *Mennonite Quarterly Review* 58 (1984): 30–49.

146. Kingdon, "Peter Martyr," 210.

147. Mary Dewar, ed., *The De Republica Anglorum of Sir Thomas Smith* (Cambridge: Cambridge University Press, 1981). See below, Chapter 3.

148. Sampson Price, *Londons Warning by Laodicea's Luke-warmnesse* (London, 1613), 23, 36.

149. The perplexities of this concept are dealt with in John von Rohr, "Covenant and Assurance in Early English Puritanism," *Church History* 34 (1965): 195–203, and Richard L. Greaves, "The Origins and Early Development of English Covenant Thought," *The Historian* 31 (1968): 21–35.

150. Zaret, op. cit., 139.

151. E. Brooks Holifield, *The Covenant Sealed: The Development of Puritan Sacramental Theology in Old and New England, 1570–1620* (New Haven: Yale University Press, 1974), 64.

152. Collinson, *EPM*, 299.

153. Henry Martyn Dexter, *The Congregationalism of the Last Three Hundred Years* (New York: Harper and Brothers, 1880); F. J. Powicke, *Henry Barrow Separatist (1550?–1593) and the Exiled Church of Amsterdam (1593–1622)* (London: James Clark, 1900); White, *The English Separatist Tradition*; Michael J. Moody, ed., "A Critical Edition of George Johnson's 'A Discourse' " (Ph.D. Diss., Claremont College, 1979); Sprunger, *Dutch Puritanism*. Johnson died in 1618, and most of his congregation perished in a voyage to Virginia the following year. Ainsworth's congregation continued until 1701.

154. *The Communion of Saincts*, 350, 351, 353, 354, 363, 370. Ainsworth conceded that it was improper for females to exercise their gifts in the congregation, but suggested that they might do so in their own company or at home (371).

155. Francis Johnson, *A Short Treatise concerning the exposition of those words of Christ, Tell the Church* (1611).

156. *The Communion of Saincts*, 375, 377–378.

157. *A Defense . . .* (Amsterdam, 1609), 125–128.

158. Ibid., 128–129.

159. *Counterpoyson*, 177.

160. Ibid.

161. David Little, *Religion, Order, and Law: A Study in Pre-Revolutionary England* (New York: Harper Torchbooks, 1969), 72.

162. Ibid. Calvin, of course, did not spare the ministerial rod himself in Geneva, and Little errs, I believe, in suggesting that he conceived of the new order of Christ as

realizable or even seriously approachable under the *saeculum*. In that sense Calvin's thought led not toward revolution but apocalypse. See the following chapter.

163. Brachlow, 162. The term "spiritual lords" as applied to the bishops in the House of Lords was deeply offensive to the godly, for whom the proper honorific for the ministry was "shepherd" or even "servant."

164. *Paralleles, Censures, Observations*, 69.

165. *Counterpoyson*, 177; cf. the *Confession*, art. 34. Johnson's congregation remained without the sacraments during his more than three years of imprisonment.

166. For a summary of opinion about the probable date of Smyth's self-baptism and the chronology of the pamphlet literature that swirled about it, see Coggins, 63–65.

167. White, 126–127.

168. Arminius was particularly unlikely to be regarded as a friend as he and a colleague had long exercised a hostile surveillance on behalf of the Dutch authorities; see Sprunger, 47–48, 54.

169. Quoted in James E. Tull, *Shapers of Baptist Thought* (Macon, GA.: Mercer University Press, 1984), 23.

170. Thomas Helwys, *A Short and Plaine proofe by the Word and Workes of God that Gods decree is not the cause of anye Mans sinne or Condemnation* (1611), sig. B2v, B3.

171. Henry Ainsworth, *A Censure upon a Dialogue of the Anabaptists* (Amsterdam, 1623); John Robinson, *A Defence of the Doctrine Propounded by the Synod at Dort* (Amsterdam, 1624).

172. *A Censure*, 4.

173. The belief in adult baptism as such was not incompatible with Calvinist orthodoxy, of course, as the Particular Baptists, who arose in England in the 1630s in opposition to the original or General Baptists, attested. On the latter, see B. R. White, *A History of the English Baptists, Volume 1: The English Baptists of the Seventeenth Century* (London: The Baptist Historical Society, 1983), chapter 2.

174. Sabine Staresmore, *Certain Notes of M. Henry Aynsworth His Last Sermon . . . Anno 1622* (1630).

175. William Bradshaw, *English Puritanisme* (1640 [1605]), 3, 6, 7.

176. Leonard Busher, *Religion's Peace: A Plea for Liberty of Conscience*, in Edward Bean Underhill, ed., *Tracts on Liberty of Conscience and Persecution 1614–1661* (London: J. Haddon, 1866), 20.

177. *Persecution for Religion Judged and Condemned* (1615), in Underhill, 125, 121.

178. Underhill, 23.

179. Busher, "Certain Reasons Against Persecution," in Underhill, 34.

180. Keith Thomas, "Cases of Conscience in Seventeenth Century England," in John Morrill, Paul Slack, and Daniel Woolf, eds., *Public Duty and Private Conscience in Seventeenth Century England: Essays Presented to G. E. Aylmer* (Oxford: The Clarendon Press, 1993), 29–56. Thomas correctly stresses the crucial nexus between conscience and legitimacy: "The seventeenth century can justly be called an Age of Conscience. . . . For much of the century it was generally believed that conscience, not force of habit or self-interest, was what held together the social and political order" (29).

181. At the same time, the distance traveled from the days of apostolic revelation was also the distance traveled toward the millennium, when special dispensations might again increase. See below.

182. William Perkins, *Works* (2: 171), cited in George L. Mosse, *The Holy Pretence: A Study in Christianity and Reason of State from William Perkins to John Winthrop* (Oxford: Basil Blackwell, 1957), 66.

183. *The Marrow of Sacred Divinity*, cited in Mosse, 86.

184. Underhill, 51.

185. Ibid., 69–70.

186. For an overview, dated but still valuable, see W. K. Jordan, *The Development of Religious Toleration in England . . . 1480–1660*, 4 vols. (Cambridge: Harvard University Press, 1932–1940; repr. ed., Gloucester, MA: Peter Smith, 1965), especially 2: 286–298 for Leonard Busher. For the European context see Joseph Lecler, S. J., *Histoire de la*

Tolérance au siècle de la Reforme, 2 vols. (Paris, 1955), and Henry Kamen, *The Rise of Toleration* (New York and Toronto: McGraw Hill; World University Library, 1967), and, for a recent overview of England, Nicholas Tyacke, "The 'Rise of Puritanism' and the Legalizing of Dissent, 1571–1619," in Ole Peter Grell, Jonathan I. Israel, and Nicholas Tyacke, eds., *From Persecution to Toleration: The Glorious Revolution and Religion in England, 1671–1719* (Oxford: Oxford University Press, 1991), 17–49.

187. Collinson, *The Religion of Protestants*; Haigh, *English Reformations*; but see also Richard L. Greaves, *Society and Religion in Elizabethan England* (Minneapolis: University of Minnesota Press, 1981). The point is not of course novel; as A. G. Dickens wrote in the 1950s, "Anglicanism cannot claim to date, as a spiritual force amongst the people, from the Prayer Book of 1549 or from the Act of Uniformity ten years later; only the age of Hooker saw it develop an appeal upon a national scale, an ethos extending outside a small cultured circle" (A. G. Dickens, *Lollards and Protestants in the Diocese of York 1509–1558* [repr. ed., London: The Hambledon Press, 1982, p. 251]).

188. K. B. McFarlane, *John Wycliffe and the Beginnings of English Nonconformity* (New York: Macmillan, 1953); J. A. F. Thomson, *The Later Lollards, 1514–1520* (London, 1965); Anne Hudson, *The Premature Reformation: Wycliffite Texts and Lollard History* (Oxford: The Clarendon Press, 1988); M. Deansley, *The Lollard Bible and Other Medieval Versions* (Cambridge, 1920); Margaret Aston, "Lollardy and the Reformation: Survival or Revival?", in Aston, *Lollards and Reformers: Images and Literacy in Late Medieval Religion* (London: The Hambledon Press, 1984); A. G. Dickens, "Heresy and the Origins of English Protestantism," in Dickens, *Reformation Studies* (London: The Hambledon Press, 1982), 363–382.

189. Michael R. Watts, *The Dissenters: From the Reformation to the French Revolution* (Oxford: The Clarendon Press, 1978).

190. M. T. Pearse, "Free Will, Dissent, and Henry Hart," *Church History* 58 (1989): 452–459, at 459 and 454.

191. Irvin Buckwalter Horst, *The Radical Brethren: Anabaptism and the English Reformation to 1558* (Nieuwkoop: de Graaf, 1972), 60–62, 78–80, 164–166. For the wider Baptist connection see Claus Peter Clasen, *Anabaptism: A Social History, 1552–1618* (Ithaca: Cornell University Press, 1972). Horst suggests that the English angel of the Bocholt conference, known only as "Henry," may have been Henry Hart, but he adduces no evidence beyond the coincidence of the Christian name.

192. On Barnes and his generation, see William A. Clebsch, *England's Earliest Protestants, 1520–1535* (New Haven: Yale University Press, 1964).

193. Kendall, *Calvin and English Calvinism*; Dewey D. Wallace Jr., *Puritans and Predestination: Grace in English Protestant Theology, 1525–1695* (Chapel Hill: The University of North Carolina Press, 1982). "Calvinism" is used here as a shorthand for predestinarianism, though of course it was a doctrine common to the Rhineland reformers including Zwingli, Oecolampadius, Bucer, and Bullinger. John Patrick Donnelly has argued for Peter Martyr Vermigli as the direct source of the Anglican formulation (*Calvinism and Scholasticism in Vermigli's Doctrine of Man and Grace* [Leiden: E. J. Brill, 1976]); cf. idem, "Italian Influences on the Development of Calvinist Scholasticism," *SCJ* 7 (1976): 81–101.

194. Article Seventeen. The text of the Articles is most conveniently printed (English only) in Gerald Bray, ed., *Documents of the English Reformation* (Minneapolis: Fortress Press, 1994), 284–311. The last article hammers the point home again: "All shall not be saved." Lutheran theology was predestinarian too, of course, and predestinarian elements inhered in the Roman tradition, but the emphasis on predestination in the doctrinal cluster that was given classic expression by Calvin and has come to be known by his name clearly raised it from the status of a consequence of more or less remote interest to that of a foundational premise. Predestination was not new; the idea of it as the keystone of Christian doctrine was.

195. Burrage, *Early English Dissenters*, 2: 1.

196. John Strype, *Ecclesiastical Memorials*, 3 vols. (Oxford: The Clarendon Press, 1822), 2, I, 369.

197. Burrage, 2: 1.

198. In the former tract he writes, "Bretheren, yf ye obeye & be now ledde by the holy spyrit of God, then trulye are ye made the fre sonnes of God, then shal ye also be made perfet and obteyne vyctory agaynst syn, death and hell . . ."

199. Champneys' own treatise of c. 1560 survives in J. A., *An historical narrration . . . concerning God's election* (1631). Robert Crowley, vicar of St. Giles, Cripplegate, attacked it as well in 1566 in his *An apologie or defence of those English writers & preachers which Cerberus . . . chargeth with false doctrine*. On Crowley see J. W. Martin, "Robert Crowley in Two Protestant Churches," in his *Religious Radicals in Tudor England* (London and Ronceverte: The Hambledon Press, 1989), 147–169.

200. *APC* 3: 198–199, 206–207.

201. Aubrey Townshend, ed., *The Writings of John Bradford, M.A.*, 2 vols. (Cambridge: Parker Society, 1848, 1853), contains much of the surviving material; for modern discussions, see Horst, op. cit., 125–128; Martin, 51–55; O. T. Hargrave, "The Freewillers in the English Reformation," *Church History* 37 (1968): 271–280.

202. "The Cause of the Contention in the King's Bench, as Concerning Sects in Religion," in Richard Laurence, ed., *Authentic Documents Relative to the Predestinarian Controversy* (Oxford, 1819): 37–70.

203. Laurence, 65–70.

204. Martin, 63–70, which summarizes the careers of forty-seven known or likely Freewillers.

205. Bradford, 2: 180.

206. Rudolf Otto, *The Idea of the Holy: An Inquiry into the Non-rational Factor in the Idea of the Divine and Its Relation to the Rational*, tr. John W. Harvey (London and New York: Oxford University Press, 1970 [1917]), 5.

207. Cited in Marsh, *The Family of Love*, 23.

208. Printed in Moss, "*Godded with God*," 71, 73, from Folger Shakespeare Library Loseley Ms. L.B. 98.

209. Ibid., 72.

210. Sometime early in Elizabeth's reign, Vitel publicly recanted heretical beliefs at Paul's Cross in London under pressure from Grindal, but they appear to have been Arian rather than specifically Familist. John Rogers described him in *The displaying of an horrible secte . . . naming themselves the Family of Love* (1579) as one "who in king Henrye's raigne, was unconstant, in king Edwardes raigne, a dissembler, and in Queen Maryes raigne a playne Arryan, and now in this our Princes raigne, a chiefe teacher of the Familye of Love" (sig. K3). Christopher Marsh's attempt to trace a clear Familist pedigree in England back to the 1550s through Vitel thus may overstate the case; for a more cautious view, see Felicity Heal, "The Family of Love and the Diocese of Ely," in Derek Baker, ed., *Schism, Heresy, and Religious Protest: Studies in Church History* 9 (Oxford: Basil Blackwell, 1972), 213–222. Heal speculates that during the period between the early 1560s and 1574 "a number of [Familist] converts must have been made, and Vitel must have emerged as the leader of the English movement and translator of the master's works" (216). Her study, which focuses on the emergence of Familist centers in Balsham and on the Isle of Ely, suggests "that they were thoroughly evangelised by preachers of the sect in the 1560s" (217). Specific evidence remains lacking, however, even after Marsh's painstaking investigation of this terrain. The best evidence for a Familist underground in Elizabeth's early reign, other than the singular Guildford deposition, is Vitel's labor in translating a score of H.N.'s works from "Base-almayne"; few authors, and fewer printers, would have undertaken such a project in the absence of a ready audience (and also a secure conduit, since H.N.'s books were of course smuggled into England).

211. Marsh, 57.

212. Marsh, 113.

213. Marsh (103–104) notes that Grindal had treated allegations that a Brighton minister was infected with Familism as a trivial affair in the spring of 1576, and that the minister had boasted of his exoneration by the Archbishop. With Elizabeth anx-

ious to crack down on religious dissidents and already angered by Grindal's failure to suppress prophesyings, the incident may well have undermined his standing further.

214. [Sig.] 4v.

215. Sig. **3v–4r.

216. *The displaying of an horrible secte . . .* , sig. A3.

217. Ibid., L4r–v.

218. Marsh, Chapter 5; John Etherington, *A Brief Discovery of the Blasphemous Doctrine of Familism* (London, 1645 [1623]), 10. Marsh's more imaginative conjectures, such as a covert interest in Familism on the part of Elizabeth herself, carry considerably less plausibility.

219. Marsh, 104–110; Paul L. Hughes and James F. Larkin, eds., *Tudor Royal Proclamations*, 3 vols. (New Haven: Yale University Press, 1964–1969), 2: 475.

220. Goad was Provost of King's College, Cambridge; Greenham, minister at Dry Drayton, was subsequently involved in polemics with the Brownists as well; Fulke, whom we have already met, was the Presbyterian author of *A Brief and Full Declaration Concerning . . . the Discipline and the Reformation of the Church of England* and a prominent antipapal polemicist. Fulke and Goad were both signatories of a 1583 letter to Cartwright urging him to confute the New Testament translation published by the seminary at Rheims "for conscience and country."

221. The examination is printed in Moss, 75–80; see the discussion in Moss, 50–51, Heal, op. cit., 219–220, and Marsh, 106–107.

222. Moss, 76.

223. Ibid., 79–80; cf. Marsh, 37–39. Bourne also signed a brief personal confession and two recantations with other colleagues.

224. Op. cit., 113.

225. Moss, 77; cf. her discussion on p. 51.

226. T. E. Hartley, ed., *Proceedings in the Parliaments of Elizabeth*, 3 vols. (Leicester: Leicester University Press, 1981), 1: 536.

227. W. C. Johnson, "The Family of Love in Stuart Literature: A Chronology of Name-Crossed Lovers," *Journal of Medieval and Renaissance Studies* 7 (1977): 95–112.

228. Marsh, 245–247; David R. Como, *Blown by the Spirit: Puritanism and the Emergence of an Antinomian Undergound in Pre–Civil-War England* (Stanford: Stanford University Press, 2004), 38–53, 167–175, 457–473, and passim. John Evelyn describes a petition from a group of Familists, who described themselves as "a sort of refined *Quakers*" as late as June 1687.

229. Charles Wriothesley, *A Chronicle of England During the Reigns of the Tudors, From A.D. 1485 to 1559*, ed. William Hamilton Douglas, 2 vols. (Camden Society, n.s., vol. 11 (1875–1877), 2: 74–76; Susan Brigden, *London and the Reformation* (Oxford: The Clarendon Press, 1989), 289–290.

230. 26 Henry VIII, c. 1, in G. R. Elton, *The Tudor Constitution: Documents and Commentary* (Cambridge: Cambridge University Press, 1965), 355.

231. Diarmaid MacCulloch, "Henry VIII and the Reform of the Church," in MacCulloch, ed., *The Reign of Henry VIII: Politics, Policy and Piety* (New York: St. Martin's Press, 1995), 178–179.

232. Anne Boleyn introduced Henry to the writings of William Tyndale. On Anne and her Reformed circle, see E. W. Ives, *Anne Boleyn* (Oxford: Basil Blackwell, 1986), and Margaret Dowling, "Anne Boleyn and Reform," *JEH* 35 (1984): 30–45.

233. *Tudor Royal Proclamations* 1: 275–276; Stanford Lehmberg, *The Reformation of Cathedrals: Cathedrals in English Society, 1485–1603* (Princeton: Princeton University Press, 1988), 24–26, 70–72. On the growth of Becket's cult, see Paul A. Brown, "The Development of the Legend of Thomas Beckett" (Ph.D. Diss., University of Pennsylvania, 1930).

234. Peter Happé and John N. King, eds., *The vocacyon of John Bale* (Binghamton, NY: Medieval and Renaissance Texts and Studies, 1990), 49.

235. For example, in Holbein's frontispiece for the Coverdale Bible (1535). The reciprocal motif of the godly minister presenting his own meditations to the king is well

illustrated by the prints of Bale offering his *Illustrium maioris Britanniae scriptorum summarium* (1548) to Edward.

236. Diarmaid MacCulloch, *Suffolk and the Tudors: Politics and Religion in an English County, 1500–1600* (Oxford: The Clarendon Press, 1986), 154–155.

237. Lee Palmer Wandel, *Voracious Idols and Violent Hands: Iconoclasm in Reformation Zurich, Strasbourg, and Basel* (Cambridge: Cambridge University Press, 1995), 62, 125.

238. Carlos M. N. Eire, *War Against the Idols: The Reformation of Worship from Erasmus to Calvin* (Cambridge: Cambridge University Press, 1986), 55–65.

239. G. R. Elton, *Policy and Police: The Enforcement of the Reformation in the Age of Thomas Cromwell* (Cambridge: Cambridge University Press, 1972).

240. *APC* 2: 25.

241. Ibid., 26. In September 1547 the Privy Council was still ordering the punishment of those who had taken down images "havinge non authoritie so to doe," but did not order their reerection (518).

242. Aston, 143.

243. Rex, 124.

244. Ibid., 26.

245. The frontispiece is reproduced in John N. King, *English Reformation Literature: The Tudor Origins of the Protestant Tradition* (Princeton: Princeton University Press, 1982), fig. 2; cf. King's commentary, p. 52.

246. For a full discussion of the iconography of this title page, see Harold R. Willoughby, *The First Authorized English Bible and the Cranmer Preface* (Chicago: University of Chicago Press, 1942), 11–20.

247. Rex, 120, summarizes Henry's various pronouncements on the subject.

248. Cited in Charles C. Butterworth, *The Literary Lineage of the King James Bible, 1340–1611* (Philadelphia: University of Pennsylvania Press, 1941), 138.

249. H. Wheeler Robinson, *The Bible in Its Ancient and English Versions* (Oxford: Oxford University Press, 1940), 180.

250. Christopher Hill, *The English Bible and the Seventeenth-Century Revolution* (London: Penguin, 1993).

251. James F. Mozley, *Coverdale and His Bible* (London: Lutterworth Press, 1953).

252. F. F. Bruce, *The English Bible: A History of Translations from the Earliest English Versions to the New English Bible* (New York: Oxford University Press, 1970), 91.

253. Butterworth, 193.

254. Cf. William Fulke, *A Defence of the Translation of the Translations of the Holy Scriptures into the English Tongue* (London, 1583). Fulke published a *Confutation* of the Rheims (Douai) Bible in 1589.

255. Frere and Douglas, eds., *Puritan Manifestoes*, 91.

256. Hooker, *The Laws of Ecclesiastical Polity*, I.xv.4, cited in John R. Knott Jr., *The Sword and the Spirit: Puritan Responses to the Bible* (Chicago: University of Chicago Press, 1980), 32.

257. H. C. Porter, "The Nose of Wax: Scripture and the Spirit from Erasmus to Milton," *TRHS*, 5th ser., 14 (1964): 155–174.

258. Cited in King, *English Reformation Literature*, 126.

259. Vladimir Solovyov, *Lectures on Divine Humanity*, ed. Boris Jakim, trans. Peter Zouboff (Hudson, NY: Lindisfarne Press, 1995), 17.

260. Hill, *The English Bible*, op. cit., 38.

261. Watt, *Cheap Print and Popular Piety*, op. cit.

262. Cf. the discussion of these woodcuts in King, *English Reformation Literature*, 194–196, 435–437, 439–440.

263. Robin Bruce Barnes, *Prophecy and Gnosis: Apocalypticism in the Wake of the Lutheran Reformation* (Stanford: Stanford University Press, 1988), 14.

264. Cited in Richard Bauckham, *Tudor Apocalypse. Sixteenth Century Apocalypticism, Millenarianism, and the English Reformation: From John Bale to John Foxe and Thomas Brightman* (Appleford, Oxon: The Sutton Courtenay Press, 1975), 121.

265. Bauckham, 48; *A hundred sermons upon the Apocalyps of Jesu Christe* (London, 1561).

266. *An Historical Dialogue touching Antichrist and Poperie*, 90; quoted by Bauckham, 177.

267. Helgerson, *Forms of Nationhood*, 260–264. The image of Elizabeth is reproduced on p. 261.

268. Marvin Arthur Breslow, *A Mirror of England: English Puritan Views of Foreign Nations, 1618–1640* (Cambridge: Harvard University Press, 1970); Carol Z. Wiener, "The Beleaguered Isle: A Study of Elizabethan and Early Jacobean Anti-Catholicism," *P&P* 51 (1971): 27–62.

269. Cited in Markku Peltonen, *Classical Humanism and Republicanism in English Political Thought, 1570–1640* (Cambridge: Cambridge University Press, 1995), 252. Cf. Sir Walter Raleigh, "A Discourse Touching a War with Spain," in *Works*, 8: 299–316.

270. Cited in Katherine R. Firth, *The Apocalyptic Tradition in Reformation Britain, 1530–1645* (Oxford: Oxford University Press, 1979), 89.

271. *The Works of the most High and Mighty Prince James* (London, 1616).

272. Zaller, *The Parliament of 1621*, chapter V; idem, "Interest of State: James I and the Palatinate," *Albion* 6 (1974): 144–175.

273. Helgerson, 283.

274. Yates, *Astraea*, 159–187; Alastair Fowler, *Spenser and the Numbers of Time* (New York: Barnes and Noble, 1964); Daryl J. Gless, *Interpretation and Theology in Spenser* (Cambridge: Cambridge University Press, 1994); Esther Gilman Richey, *The Politics of Revelation in the English Renaissance* (Columbia: University of Missouri Press, 1998), chapter 1; John E. Hankins, "Spenser and the Revelation of St. John," *PMLA* 60 (1945): 364–381; Florence Sandler, "*The Faerie Queene*: An Elizabethan Apocalypse," in C. A. Patrides and Joseph Wittreich, eds., *The Apocalypse in English Renaissance Thought and Literature: Patterns, Antecedents, and Repercussions* (Ithaca: Cornell University Press, 1984), 148–174; Jane Chambers, "Divine Justice, Mercy, and Love: The 'Mutabilitie' Subplot of Spenser's Apocalyptic Theme," *Essays in Literature* 8 (1981): 3–10; John Brittain Prendergast III, "England as a City of God and the Third Troy in *The Faerie Queene*" (Ph.D. Diss., Toronto University, 1976); Carol Ann Stillman, "Spenser's Elect England: Political and Apocalyptic Dimensions of *The Faerie Queene*" (Ph.D. Diss., University of Pennsylvania, 1979); Richard M.Tinsley, "Renaissance Commentaries on the Book of Revelation and Their Influence on Spenser's *Faerie Queene* and d'Aubigné's *Les Tragiques*" (Ph.D. Diss., University of Chicago, 1980).

275. Cited in Bernard Capp, "The Political Dimension of Apocalyptic Thought," in Patrides and Wittreich, 93–124, at 96.

276. Paul Christianson, *Reformers and Babylon: English Apocalyptic Visions from the Reformation to the Eve of the Civil War* (Toronto: University of Toronto Press, 1978), 49–50; Collinson, *Archbishop Grindal*, 177–178.

277. White, *The English Separatist Tradition*, 69.

278. Cited in Christianson, 85.

279. Collinson, *EPM*, 427ff.; Bauckham, 191–204; Alexandra Walsham, "'Frantick Hacket': Prophecy, Sorcery, and the Elizabethan Puritan Movement," *HJ* 41 (1998): 27–66.

280. Susan Doran, "Religion and Politics at the Court of Elizabeth I: The Habsburg Marriage Negotiations of 1559–1567," *EHR* 104 (1989): 908–926.

281. George Gifford, *Sermons Vpon the Whole Booke of the Revelation* (London, 1596), sig. A2r; Bernard R. Capp, *English Almanacs, 1500–1800: Astrology and the Popular Press, 1500–1800* (Ithaca: Cornell University Press, 1979), 168–169.

282. See, e.g., David Owen, *Herod and Pilate Reconciled: Or the Concord of Papist and Puritan . . . for the Coercion, Deposition, and Killing of Kings* (Cambridge, 1610).

283. Thomas Brightman, *A Revelation of the Revelation* (London, 1615), 132.

284. Ibid., 131.

285. Ibid.

286. Ibid., 388, 502–504, 510–511, 524ff.; Firth, op. cit., 170.

287. Brightman, 126.

288. Ibid.

289. Ibid., 124, 127.

290. Cf. the comments in William M. Lamont, *Godly Rule: Politics and Religion, 1603–60* (London: Macmillan, 1969), 49–51.

291. Brightman, 139.

292. Among the antiprelatical tracts printed in the summer of 1641 were two editions of *A Revelation of Mr. Brightman's Revelation: Wherein is shewed how all which Mr. Brightman hath foretold concerning Germany, England and Scotland hath been fulfilled*; cf. *Reverend Mr. Brightman's Judgement on Prophecies* (1643). These works abstracted Brightman, highlighting the more emphatic parts of his commentary. Brightman's complete works were republished in 1644, as well as an edition of his commentary on the Book of Daniel.

293. Brightman, 389.

294. Cf. Michael Walzer, *The Revolution of the Saints* (Cambridge: Harvard University Press, 1965), 292n.

295. Brightman, 616–617, 846.

296. William Stoughton, in *An abstract of certaine acts of parlement* (1584), called for the removal of bishops from the House of Lords. Stoughton sat in the Parliament of 1584–1585. For his career and for these issues generally, see Michael Mendle, *Dangerous Positions: Mixed Government, the Estates of the Realm, and the Answer to the xix propositions* (University, AL: University of Alabama Press, 1985). The closest thing to a millennialist utopia was Johann Andreae's *Christianopolis* (1620), which envisioned a polity in which all barriers to the spiritual life had been removed.

297. *A Key of Knowledge*, 127–129.

298. Cited in Firth, 178; cf. 201–202, and Anthony Milton, *Catholic and Reformed: The Roman and Protestant Churches in English Protestant Thought, 1600–1640* (Cambridge: Cambridge University Press, 1995), 107–110.

299. G. H. Turnbull, *Hartlib, Dury, and Comenius: Gleanings from Hartlib's Papers* (Liverpool: University of Liverpool, 1947); Charles Webster, *The Great Instauration: Science, Medicine, and Reform, 1626–1660* (London: Duckworth, 1975).

300. *The Beloved City, or the Saints Reign on Earth a Thousand Years.*

301. Firth, 223.

302. *The Beloved City*, 37, quoted in Firth, 212.

303. Firth, 221.

304. Christianson, *Reformers and Babylon*, 129; Milton, op. cit., 119.

305. *A Revelation of the Revelation*, 616–617.

306. Firth, 228; Christianson, 111–124.

307. Milton, 123.

308. John Jewel, *An Apology of the Church of England*, op. cit.; Thomas Bilson, *Perpetual government of Christes Church* (London, 1593); George Carleton, *Jurisdiction: regall, episcopall, papall* (London, 1610).

309. Collinson, *The Religion of Protestants*, chapters 1–3. As Collinson points out, the bishops were far more concerned with royal attitudes toward the episcopal bench than with either Roman or godly challenges to its legitimacy.

310. "Bishops," Mede wrote, "are a degree of *Presbyters* of divine ordinance, to be as Heads, Chiefs, and Presidents of their Brethren . . ." (*Discovrses on Sundry Texts of Scripture*, Part I, p. 76, in *The Works of . . . Joseph Mede* [London, 1648]). Laud could hardly have said more.

311. Milton, 116–122.

312. Ibid., 32–33.

313. John Field, *A Caveat for Parsons Howlet* (London, 1581); Thomas Scott, *A Tongue-Combate* (1623). Cf. Peter Lake, "The Significance of the Elizabethan Identification of the Pope as Antichrist," *JEH* 31 (1980): 161–178; Tyacke, *Anti-Calvinists*, passim; Hill, *Antichrist in Seventeenth-Century England* (Oxford: Oxford University Press, 1971), 168–169.

314. Milton, 125. Mede (also known as Mead and Meddus) was also a sophisticated political correspondent whose apocalypticism did not cloud a shrewd and skeptical judgment of contemporary affairs; for this aspect of his career, see David Randall, "Joseph Mead, Novellante: News, Sociability, and Credibility in Early Stuart England," *JBS* 45 (2006): 293–312.

315. William Prynne, *Canterburies Doome* (London, 1644), 551–552.

316. Hill, 37–38; Milton, 125–126; William Scott and James Bliss, eds., *The Works of William Laud*, 7 vols. (Oxford: Oxford University Press, 1847–1860), 6: 577–578.

317. His defense was nonetheless remembered and cited approvingly eighty years later by Prynne (*Canterburies Doome*, 278–279).

318. Tyacke, *Anti-Calvinists*, op. cit., 30–33.

319. Joseph Hall, *Epistles* (London, 1608), 2: 55–56, quoted in Tyacke, 64.

Chapter 3: The Discourse of the Realm

1. Mary Dewar, *Sir Thomas Smith: A Tudor Intellectual in Office* (London: The Athlone Press, 1964), 111.

2. Sir Thomas Smith, *De Republica Anglorum. A Discourse on the Commonwealth of England*, ed. L. Alston (Cambridge: Cambridge University Press, 1906), 142. Subsequent references to this edition will be in the body of the text.

3. Glenn Burgess, *Absolute Monarchy and the Stuart Constitution* (New Haven: Yale University Press, 1996).

4. "The prince whom I now call . . . the Monarch of Englande, King or Queene, hath absolutelie in his power the authoritie of warre and peace, to defie what Prince it shall please him, and to bid him warre, and again to reconcile himselfe and enter into league or truce with him at pleasure or the advice onely of his privie counsell" (58–59).

5. Elton, *TC*, 270.

6. Smith indicates that the party for whom the verdict has been given will customarily stand the jury to dinner: "and this is all that they have for their labour, notwithstanding that they come some xx or xxx or xl miles or more . . . of their own charge" (80).

7. The early modern jury remains remarkably little studied. For an overview, see Thomas Andrew Green, *Verdict According to Conscience: Perspectives on the English Criminal Trial Jury, 1200–1800* (Chicago: University of Chicago Press, 1985), and J. S. Cockburn and Thomas A. Green, eds., *Twelve Men Good and True: The Criminal Trial Jury in England, 1200–1800* (Princeton: Princeton University Press, 1986); the essays by P. G. Lawson and Cockburn cover the mid-Tudor and Jacobean periods.

8. William Harrison, *The Description of England*, ed. Georges Edelen (Ithaca: Cornell University Press, for the Folger Shakespeare Library, 1968), 180.

9. Thomas Harman, *Caveat or Warning for Common Cursitors* (1566), ed. Frederick J. Furnivall (EETS, Ex. Ser., ix, 1869).

10. Ellen Meiskins Wood and Neal Wood, *A Trumpet of Sedition: Political Theory and the Rise of Capitalism, 1509–1688* (New York: New York University Press, 1997): 48–50.

11. Op. cit., 7. All subsequent references are in the body of the text.

12. Harrison himself notes that the "crumbs" of his *Chronology* "fell out very well in the framing" of *The Description* (5). For a full account of the latter, see G. J. R. Parry, *A Protestant Vision: William Harrison and the Reformation of Elizabethan England* (Cambridge: Cambridge University Press, 1987).

13. Georges Edelen, "William Harrison (1535–1593)," *Studies in the Renaissance* 9 (1962): 256–272, at 258–259.

14. Lake, *Moderate Puritans*, op. cit. Lake does not discuss Harrison.

15. The latterly quoted passages closely follow the appendix to Jewel's *Apology* (*Description*, 33 n32).

16. Parry, op. cit., 278, 275.

17. *Illustrium majoris Britanniae scriptorum summarium* (Ipswich, 1548). See Edelen's comprehensive note, *Description* 163 n1.

18. "Times change and we change with them" (proverbial).

19. F. J. Levy, "The Making of Camden's *Britannia*," *Bibliothèque d'humanisme et Renaissance* 26 (1964): 70–97, at 70.

20. T. D. Kendrick, *British Antiquity* (London: Methuen, 1950), 150.

21. Graham Parry, *Trophies of Time: English Antiquarians of the Seventeenth Century* (Oxford: Oxford University Press, 1995), 42.

22. Elton, *TC*, 344.

23. William Camden, *Remains Concerning Britain*, ed. R. D. Dunn (Toronto: University of Toronto Press, 1984), 247. Surrey added: "And as I fought then for him, I will fight for you, when you are established by the said authoritie." On the relationship of the *Remains* to the *Britannia*, see Dunn's introduction, xvi–xix.

24. Ibid., 7.

25. *Britannia*, lxxviii.

26. Helgerson, *Forms of Nationhood*, 114–116.

27. *Remains*, 189; cf. 263.

28. Woolf, *The Idea of History*, op. cit., 117–119; cf. Sharpe, *Cotton*, op. cit., 89–95.

29. William Camden, *The history of . . . Princess Elizabeth*, ed. Wallace T. MacCaffrey (Chicago: University of Chicago Press, 1970), 5.

30. Cited in Woolf, 89. But Daniel was to comment elsewhere that "What chayre soever Monarch sate/ Upon, on Earth, the People was the State" (ibid.).

31. Helgerson, 114.

32. *DNB*, s.v. Wolfe, Reyner or Reginald; *ODNB*; Peter Blayney, *The Bookshops in Paul's Cross Churchyard* (London, 1990).

33. *DNB*; *ODNB*. Holinshed died in April 1582, midway between the first and second editions of the *Chronicles*. The details of his life are scanty, though he claimed a close connection to Lord Burghley.

34. For Stanyhurst, see Colm Lennon, *Richard Stanihurst the Dubliner, 1547–1618* (Blackrock, County Dublin: Irish Academic Press, 1981).

35. On Fleming, see the *DNB*, *ODNB*; Sarah C. Dodson, "Abraham Fleming, Writer and Editor," *University of Texas Studies in English* 34 (1955): 51–66; William E. Miller, "Abraham Fleming, Editor of Shakespeare's Holinshed," *Texas Studies in Language and Literature* 1 (1959): 89–100; Elizabeth Story Donno, "Abraham Fleming: A Learned Corrector in 1586–87," *Studies in Bibliography* 42 (1989): 200–211.

36. For Hooker, a lawyer and MP, see Vernon F. Snow, ed. *Parliament in Elizabethan England: John Hooker's Order and Usage* (New Haven: Yale University Press, 1977).

37. *DNB*, s.v. Thynne; *ODNB*; Joan Evans, *A History of the Society of Antiquaries* (Oxford: Oxford University Press, 1956). A collective study of the authors and editors of the *Chronicles* would be well worth doing. Various other figures were associated with it, notably the famous London chronicler John Stow, who arrogated chief credit for producing the section edition to himself in his *Annals* (1605), though Annabel Patterson's analysis of the evidence does not support this claim (see note 38, next below).

38. On the censor's role in shaping the text, see Anne Castanien, "Censorship and Historiography in Elizabethan England: The Expurgation of Holinshed's *Chronicles*" (Ph.D. Diss., University of California, Davis, 1970), and Annabel Patterson, *Reading Holinshed's Chronicles* (Chicago: University of Chicago Press, 1994).

39. Patterson, op. cit.; see also her "Foul, His Wife, the Mayor, and Foul's Mare: The Power of Anecdote in Tudor History," in Donald R. Kelley and David Harris Sacks, eds., *The Historical Imagination in Early Modern Britain: History, Rhetoric, and Fiction, 1500–1800* (Cambridge: Woodrow Wilson Press and Cambridge University Press, 1997), 159–178, and Richard Helgerson, "Murder in Faversham: Holinshed's Impertinent History," ibid., 133–158. Among earlier studies, see R. Mark Benbow, "The Providential Theory of Historical Causation in Holinshed's *Chronicles*: 1577 and 1587," *Texas Studies in Language and Literature* 1 (1959): 264–276.

40. On the chronicle tradition in Tudor England, see Antonia Gransden, *Historical Writing in England, Vol. II: c. 1307 to the Early Sixteenth Century* (Ithaca: Cornell University Press, 1982); F. J. Levy, *Tudor Historical Thought* (San Marino, CA: Huntington Library, 1967), chapter 5; D. R. Woolf, "Genre into Artifact: The Decline of the English Chronicle in the Sixteenth Century," *SCJ* 19 (1998): 321–354.

41. *Holinshed's Chronicle of England, Scotland, and Ireland*, 6 vols., ed. Henry Ellis (London, 1808; New York, AMS Press, 1976), 3: 57. All references are to the 1587 edition, and are cited in the text.

42. On the Lancastrian legitimation crisis, see Paul Strohm, *England's Empty Throne: Usurpation and the Language of Legitimation, 1399–1422* (New Haven: Yale University Press, 1998).

43. Arthur Ferguson, *The Articulate Citizen and the English Renaissance* (Durham: University of North Carolina Press, 1965).

44. Original text in Richard Sylvester, ed., *The History of King Richard III* (New Haven: Yale University Press, 1976), 70–79.

45. Here is a prime example of the pattern of polyvalent meaning in Holinshed stressed by Patterson, in which the reader is left to judge among various significations, each contributory to the whole but none determinative or prescriptive.

46. Julian H. Franklin, ed. and trans., *Constitutionalism and Resistance in the Sixteenth Century: Three Treatises by Hotman, Beza, and Mornay* (New York: Pegasus, 1969); Donald R. Kelley, *Francois Hotman: A Revolutionary's Ordeal* (Princeton: Princeton University Press, 1973); cf. John Ponet, *A Shorte Treatise of Politike Power* (Strassburg[?], 1556); Donald R. Kelley, "Ideas of Resistance before Elizabeth," in Heather Dubrow and Richard Strier, eds., *The Historical Renaissance: New Essays on Tudor and Stuart Literature and Culture* (Chicago: University of Chicago Press, 1988), 48–76; G. W. Bowler, "English Protestant and Resistance Writings, 1553–1603" (D. Phil. Thesis, University of London, 1981); idem, "'An Axe or an Acte': The Parliament of 1572 and Resistance Theory in Early Elizabethan England," *Canadian Journal of History* 19 (1984): 349–359.

47. J. J. Scarisbrick, *Henry VIII* (London: Eyre and Spottiswood, 1968), 338, cited in G. R. Elton, "Politics and the Pilgrimage of Grace," in Barbara C. Malament, *After the Reformation: Essays in Honor of J. H. Hexter* (Philadelphia: University of Pennsylvania Press, 1980), 25–56, at 30.

48. Elton, 31–37. Lord Darcy and Sir Thomas Percy were among those executed at Tyburn in June 1537.

49. Cf. Margaret Bowker, "Lincolnshire 1536: Heresy, Schism or Religious Discontent," in Derek Baker, ed., *Schism, Heresy and Religious Protest: Studies in Church History* 9 (Oxford: Basil Blackwell, 1972), 195–212; C. S. L. Davies, "Popular Religion and the Pilgrimage of Grace," in Anthony Fletcher and John Stevenson, eds., *Order and Disorder in Early Modern England* (Cambridge: Cambridge University Press, 1985), 58–91; Mervyn E. James, "Obedience and Dissent in Henrician England: The Lincolnshire Rebellion of 1536," in his *Society, Politics and Culture: Studies in Early Modern England* (Cambridge: Cambridge University Press, 1986), 188–269.

50. Frances Rose–Troup, *The Western Rebellion of 1549* (London: Smith, Elder, 1913); Julian Cornwall, *The Revolt of the Peasantry 1549* (Totowa: Rowman and Littlefield, 1977); Stephen K. Land, *Kett's Rebellion: The Norfolk Rising of 1549* (London: Routledge and Kegan Paul, 1977); M. L. Bush, *The Government Policy of Protector Somerset* (London: Edward Arnold, 1979); Joyce Youings, "The South-Western Rebellion of 1549," *Southern History* 1 (1979): 99–122; Barrett L. Beer, *Rebellion and Riot: Popular Disorder in England During the Reign of Edward VI* (Kent, OH: Kent State University Press, 1982); Ethan H. Shagan, "Protector Somerset and the 1549 Rebellions: New Sources and New Perspectives," *EHR* 114 (1999): 34–63; and Shagan's debate with G. W. Bernard and M. L. Bush, *EHR* 115 (2000): 103–133. A new study by Andy Wood is forthcoming.

51. Compare this account with the comment of John Hayward in his contemporaneous description of Kett's Rebellion: "Assuredly the vulgar multitude is not vnfairly termed a beast, with many heads not guided, I will not say with any proportion but

portion of reason, violence and obstinacy like two vntamed horses, draw their desire in a blindefold Carriere. They intend most foolishly what they never put in action, and often act most madly what they never intended, all that they know to doe, is that they know not what to doe, all that they meane to determine proues a determination and meaning to doe nothing" (Barrett L. Beer, ed., *The Life and Raigne of King Edward the Sixth* [Kent, OH: Kent State University Press, 1993], 76). Hayward's text was first published in 1630, but Professor Beer suggests it may have been begun as early as the 1580s.

52. On the siege of Exeter, see Cornwall, op. cit., 98–113, and Wallace T. Mac-Caffrey, *Exeter, 1540–1640: The Growth of an English Town* (Cambridge: Harvard University Press, 1958); Youings, op. cit.; H. M. Speight, "Local Government in the South-Western Rebellion of 1549," *Southern History* 18 (1996): 1–23. Cf. Hayward's account, op. cit., 80, which barely mentions the citizens' determined resistance.

53. On medieval parliamentary petitions and their relation to the legislative process, see A. F. Pollard, *The Evolution of Parliament*, 2d ed. (New York: Russell and Russell, 1964 [1926]); C. H. McIlwain, *The High Court of Parliament and Its Supremacy* (New Haven: Yale University Press, 1963 [1910]); E. B. Fryde and Edward Miller, eds., *Historical Studies of the English Parliament, Vol. I: Origins to 1399* (Cambridge: Cambridge University Press, 1970); Sir Goronwy Edwards, *The Second Century of the English Parliament* (Oxford: The Clarendon Press, 1979); idem, "Some Petitions in Richard II's First Parliament," *BIHR* 26 (1953): 200–213; R. G. Davies and J. H. Denton, eds., *The English Parliament in the Middle Ages* (Manchester: Manchester University Press, 1981); A. R. Myers, *Crown, Household and Parliament in Fifteenth-Century England* (London: The Hambledon Press, 1985); Ronald Bett, *A History of Parliament: The Middle Ages* (London: John Constable, 1989); G. L. Haskins, "The Petitions of Representatives in the Parliaments of Edward I," *EHR* 53 (1938): 1–20; G. L. Harriss, "The Commons Petitions of 1340," *EHR* 78 (1963): 625–654. For petitioning in other courts, see Alan Harding, *The Law Courts of Medieval England* (London: Allen and Unwin, 1973). The monarchy itself encouraged petitions after 1270, with the result that courts and assizes were nearly overwhelmed by them; Richard W. Kaeuper, "Law and Order in Fourteenth-Century England: The Evidence of Special Commissions of Oyer and Terminer," *Speculum* 54 (1979): 734–784. Petitioning was thenceforth an integral part of the constitutional bond between crown and commonwealth in the development of parliamentary government and statute law.

54. Holinshed suggests that the magistrates were also "affected" with the popish ceremonies that the people had been taught to defend (3: 940).

55. For suggestive comments on this point, see Barbara M. Benedict, *Making the Modern Reader: Cultural Mediation in Early Modern Literary Anthologies* (Princeton: Princeton University Press, 1996); Nigel Wheale, *Writing and Society: Print and Politics in Britain, 1590–1660* (London and New York: Routledge, 1999). For seventeenth-century readers of Holinshed, see Patterson, *Reading Holinshed's Chronicles*, chapter 12.

56. Ann Jennalie Cook, *The Privileged Playgoers of Shakespeare's London, 1576–1642* (Princeton: Princeton University Press, 1981); Andrew Gurr, *Playgoing in Shakespeare's London* (Cambridge: Cambridge University Press, 1987); Steven Mullaney, *The Place of the Stage: License, Play, and Power in Renaissance England* (Chicago: University of Chicago Press, 1988).

57. On the general development of an independent–minded civic culture and its impact on legitimation structures, see Phil Withington, *The Politics of Commonwealth: Citizens and Freemen in Early Modern England* (Cambridge: Cambridge University Press, 2005).

Chapter 4: The Discourse of the Law

1. "The Dark Age in English Legal History, 1500–1700," in J. H. Baker, *The Legal Profession and the Common Law: Historical Essays* (London and Ronceverte: The Hambledon Press, 1986), 435–460, at 437.

2. C. L. Kingsford, ed., *Three Fifteenth Century Chronicles* (Westminster: Camden Society, 1880), 96.

3. E. W. Ives, *The Common Lawyers of Pre-Reformation England* (Cambridge: Cambridge University Press, 1983), 7–9, 191; Wilfrid R. Prest, *The Inns of Court under Elizabeth and the Early Stuarts* (Totowa: Rowman and Littlefield, 1972); J. H. Baker, *The Third University of England: The Inns of Court and the Common Law Tradition* (London: Selden Society, 1990); J. G. A. Pocock, *The Ancient Constitution and the Feudal Law*, rev. ed. (Cambridge: Cambridge University Press, 1987).

4. Collinson, *The Religion of Protestants*; Lake, *Moderate Puritans*; Peter White, "The *via media* in the Early Stuart Church," in Kenneth Fincham, ed., *The Early Stuart Church, 1603–1642* (London: Macmillan, 1993), 211–230.

5. Ives, 37, 44; Hughes and Larkin, *Tudor Royal Proclamations*, 1: 408–409; Sir Charles Ogilvie, *The King's Government and the Common Law, 1471–1641* (Oxford: Basil Blackwell, 1958), 20; L. W. Abbott, *Law Reporting in England, 1485–1555* (London: The Athlone Press, 1973) [Dyer cited at p. 3]. Paul Raffield, in *Images and Cultures of Law in Early Modern England: Justice and Political Power, 1558–1660* (Cambridge: Cambridge University Press, 2004), surveys the Inns as a self-contained community.

6. Ogilvie, 24, notes the "sacramental importance" attached to verbal accuracy in common law reporting.

7. Ogilvie, 32; Beresford quoted at 26. William S. Holdsworth's multivolume *A History of English Law* (1922–1952) remains the completest exposition of the common law within the context of the legal system as a whole; cf. his *Historical Introduction to the Land Law* (Oxford: The Clarendon Press, 1927), and T. F. T. Plucknett, *A Concise History of the Common Law*, 5th ed. (Boston: Little, Brown, 1956); S. F. C. Milsom, *Historical Foundations of the Common Law* (London: Butterworths, 1981); A. W. B. Simpson, *A History of the Land Law*, 2d ed. (Oxford: The Clarendon Press, 1986).

8. J. A. Guy, "The Development of Equitable Jurisdiction, 1450–1550," in E. W. Ives and A. H. Manchester, eds., *Law, Litigants and the Legal Profession: Papers Presented to the Fourth British Legal History Conference at the University of Birmingham, 10–13 July 1979* (London: Royal Historical Society, 1979), 80–86; cf. Charles Gray, "The Boundaries of the Equitable Function," *AJLH* 20 (1976): 192–226. Guy makes an important and overlooked point: "The basic truth . . . was that litigants were the most potent force for change in the legal system: they did not care whether their judgements were doctrinally orthodox as long as they met immediate needs and were enforceable" ("Law, Equity, and Conscience in Henrician Juristic Thought," in Alistair Fox and John Guy, *Reassessing the Henrician Age: Humanism, Politics and Reform, 1500–1550* [Oxford: Basil Blackwell, 1986]): 179–198, at 189.

9. John A. Guy, *The Cardinal's Court* (Hassocks: Harvester Press, 1977).

10. Guy, "The Development of Equitable Jurisdictions," 84.

11. T. F. T. Plucknett, "The Place of the Legal Profession in the History of English Law," in Plucknett, *Studies in English Legal History* (London: The Hambledon Press, 1983), 328–340, at 330.

12. Thomas Starkey, *A Dialogue between Pole and Lupset*, ed. T. F. Mayer (Camden Society, 4th ser., Vol. 37 [London: Royal Historical Society, 1989]), 129. Starkey was a member of Pole's circle in Padua in the early 1530s; he presented a part of the *Dialogue* — including the remark quoted — to Cromwell after his appointment as chaplain to Henry VIII in February 1535.

13. Ives, *Common Lawyers*, 224.

14. R. M. Helmholz, "The Early Enforcement of Uses," *Columbia Law Journal* 79 (1979): 1503–1513.

15. 27 Henry VIII, c. 10; E. W. Ives, "The Genesis of the Statute of Uses," *EHR* 82 (1967): 673–697. Ives' discussion, which connects the Dacre case to Henry's overall strategy, supersedes previous accounts. The statute and its drafts are printed in Holdsworth, *History of English Law*, 4: 577–581. See also the overview in A. R. Buck, "The Politics of Land Law in Tudor England, 1529–1640," *Journal of Legal History* 11

(1990): 200–217. For Dacre's case, see J. M. W. Bean, *The Decline of English Feudalism* (Manchester: University of Manchester Press, 1968), 277–284.

16. J. S. Brewer et al., eds, *Letters and Papers, Foreign and Domestic, of the Reign of Henry VIII,* 21 vols.(London: HMSO, 1862–1932), 11: 705 (I), 1246.

17. 32 Henry VIII, c. 1. This legislation was only the centerpiece of an ambitious program of legal reform introduced in the session of 1540, partly by Cromwell and partly by the common lawyers themselves; the latter is conveniently summarized in Stanford E. Lehmberg, *The Later Parliaments of Henry VIII 1536–1547* (Cambridge: Cambridge University Press, 1977), 95–101. Lehmberg suggests that Cromwell had a comprehensive overhaul of the land law in view, but if so its impetus died with him.

18. Stanford E. Lehmberg, *The Reformation Parliament 1529–1536* (Cambridge: Cambridge University Press, 1970).

19. Ralph Houlbrooke, "The Decline of Ecclesiastical Jurisdiction under the Tudors," in Rosemary O'Day and Felicity Heal, eds., *Continuity and Change: Personnel and Administration of the Church of England, 1500–1642* (Leicester: University of Leicester Press, 1976), 239–257; idem, *Church Courts and People During the English Reformation, 1520–1570* (Oxford, 1979); Roland G. Usher, *The Rise and Fall of the High Commission,* rev. ed. (Oxford: The Clarendon Press, 1968 [1913]).

20. By John Guy, in Guy and Fox, *Reassessing the Henrician Age,* 99.

21. On St. German's life and career, see Pearl Hogrefe, "The Life of Christopher St. German," in *The Review of English Studies* 13 (1937): 398–404; Franklin Le Van Baumer, "Christopher St. German: The Political Philosophy of a Tudor Lawyer," *AHR* 42 (1937): 631–651; J. B. Trapp, ed., *The Complete Works of St. Thomas More, Vol. 9: The Apology* (New Haven: Yale University Press, 1979), xli–liv; John Guy, Ralph Keen, Clarence H. Miller, and Ruth McGugan, eds., *The Complete Works of St. Thomas More, Vol. 10: The Debellation of Salem and Bizance* (New Haven: Yale University Press, 1987), xxix–xlvi; R. J. Schoek, "'That Most Erudite of Lawyers,' Christopher St. German," *Journal of the Rocky Mountain Medieval and Renaissance Society* 4 (1983): 197–223; J. A. Guy, *Christopher St. German on Chancery and Statute* (London: Selden Society, 1985), 3–55; idem, "Thomas More and Christopher St. German: The Battle of the Books," in his *Reassessing the Henrician Age,* 100–119; Alan Cromartie, *The Constitutionalist Revolution: An Essay on the History of England, 1450–1642* (Cambridge: Cambridge University Press, 2006), chapter 2.

22. *Doctor and Student,* ed. Plucknett and Barton (London: Selden Society Publications 91, 1974), 7. Subsequent references will be noted in the text.

23. "[It semyth that] yf it were ordayned by statute/ that there should be no remedye vpon suche equyties *nor upon any other matter in conscience whatsoever* in the Chauncerye/ nor in none other place/ but that euery mater shuld be orderyd onely by the rewles and groundes of the common lawe/ *and that there should be no recourse to any remedy outside it* that that statute were agaynst ryght and conscience" (107). This statement has often been taken as a "defense" of equity against the common law; within the larger context of St. German's discussion, however, it is more rightly read as a saving of the common law itself against the inherent limitations of all positive law.

24. Printed in Guy, ed., *St. German on Chancery and Statute,* 99–105, at 105.

25. Ibid., 65–67. Guy puts forward the suggestion that St. German himself may have been the author of the *Replication* (56–62).

26. *A Little Treatise Concerning Writs of Subpoena,* ibid., 106–126, at 124.

27. The extent to which St. German may be regarded as an apologist or propagandist for the Henrician Reformation has been a matter of dispute. G. R. Elton regarded him as an independent voice (*Policy and Police,* 173–174), but, as J. B. Trapp points out, his use of the royal printer Thomas Berthelet suggests a more intimate connection (*More,* 9, lii–liii). St. German's anticlerical tracts were all published anonymously, a distancing device that remained fashionable among commentators on public affairs until the nineteenth century. At a time when all political commentary required coding, whether through genre (allegory, dialogue, historical representation, etc.) or

through the concealment or disguise of the author's identity, ambiguity and indirection was the necessary style of argument. Any other approach risked the lèse-majesté of royal personation. Royal and clerical officials, speaking on behalf of authority, were to a degree exempt from this limitation, but their pronouncements could hardly be described as "commentary." St. German, of course, had no official position, and his age, no less than his apparent inclination, precluded any ambition for one. His was the enviable, but semi–detached role of the senior adviser who remained a private party; his abiding interest was a professional one.

28. *The Treatise Concernynge the Diuision*, in *More*, 9: 175–212, at 191. Further citations are given in the text.

29. *A Lytell Treatise Called the Newe Addicions*, Plucknett, 315–336.

30. Printed in Guy, *St. German on Chancery and Statute*, 127–135.

31. *A dialogue betwixte two englyshe men, wherof one was called Salem, and the other Bizance* (*More*, 10: 332); *Diuision*, 205.

32. *Diuision*, ibid.

33. In March 1531 Henry had intervened in the heresy trial of a preacher, overruling the Archbishop of Canterbury's court (*More*, 9, xxxvi).

34. *More*, 10: xxxix–xl, referencing G. R. Elton, *Studies in Tudor and Stuart Politics and Government*, 3 vols. (Cambridge: Cambridge University Press, 1974–1983), 2: 215–235.

35. *New Addicions*, Plucknett, 317; cited by Guy, *St. German on Chancery and Statute*, 24.

36. *The apologye of syr Thomas More knyght; The debellacyon of Salem and Bizance* (*More*, 9, 10).

37. J. A. Guy, "Henry VIII and the Praemunire Manoeuvres of 1530–1531," *EHR* 97 (1982): 481–503.

38. *The Power of the Clergy*, chapters 5 (sig. B2), 6, 9–10; *The Addicions*, sig. 65v–66.

39. *The Power of the Clergy*, sig. G2; chapter 19.

40. Ibid., Chapter 9, sig. C7.

41. Ibid., D3–D4v.

42. *An Answer*, sig. G5v–6, quoted by Guy, "The Later Career of Christopher St. German," *More*, 10: 403.

43. *The Power of the Clergy*, chapter 6, quoted in *More*, 10: 399.

44. The italicized text is from the original Latin.

45. *More*, 10: 403.

46. On its influence, see William S. Holdsworth, *Some Makers of English Law* (Cambridge: At the Press, 1966), 95ff., and his *Sources and Literature of English Law* (Oxford: Oxford University Press, 1925); cf. S. F. C. Milsom, *Historical Foundations of the Common Law* (London: Butterworths, 1969), 80ff.

47. Simpson, *A History of the Land Law*, op. cit., 164–165.

48. Sir John Davies, *Les Reports des Cases & Matters en Ley, Resolves & Adjudges en les Courts del Roy en Ireland* (London, 1674), quoted in Pocock, *The Ancient Constitution*, 33.

49. Zaller, *The Parliament of 1621*, 69; *BDBR* 1: 156.

50. Abbott, *Law Reporting in England*, op. cit., 226.

51. Ibid., 240–242, 245.

52. J. H. Baker, "Coke's Note-Books and the Sources of His Reports," in his *The Legal Profession and the Common Law*, op. cit., 177–204.

53. On the received tradition of natural law in Coke's time, see Richard Tuck, *Natural Rights Theories: Their Origin and Development* (Cambridge: Cambridge University Press, 1979); Brian Tierney, *The Idea of Natural Rights: Studies on Natural Rights, Natural Law and Church Law, 1150–1625* (Atlanta: Scholars Press, 1997).

54. *The Reports of Sir Edward Coke Knight . . .* (London, 1658), 596–597.

55. Ibid.; idem, xx.

56. McIlwain, ed., *PWJ*, 308.

57. *Reports*, 596.

58. Roland G. Usher, "James I and Sir Edward Coke," *EHR* 18 (1903): 664–675, at 670, 673. James gave a more polished but not essentially different account of his views

in his speech of March 21, 1610 to Parliament: "So in the first originall of Kings . . . their wills . . . serued for Law; Yet how soone Kingdomes began to be setled in ciuilitie and policie, then did Kings set downe their minds by Lawes, which are properly made by the King onely; but at the rogation of the people, the Kings grant being obtained thereunto" (*PWJ*, 309). For a general discussion of James' view of the law, see Louis Knafla, "Britain's Solomon: King James and the Law," in Daniel Fischlin and Mark Fortier, eds., *Royal Subjects: Essays on the Writings of James VI and I* (Detroit: Wayne State University Press, 2002), 235–264; cf. Fortier, "Equity and Ideas: Ellesmere, Coke, and James VI and I," ibid., 265–289; Johann Sommerville, "King James VI and I and John Selden: Two Voices on History and the Constitution," ibid., 290–322. Fortier's comment is judicious: "James most likely understood the English constitution more than he sympathized with it" (280).

59. Cited in Usher, 664.

60. *Fourth Institute* (London, 1817), 70.

61. Evangeline de Villiers, ed., "The Hastings Journal of the Parliament of 1621," *Camden Miscellany* 20 (1953), 27. For the context of the King's speech, see Zaller, *The Parliament of 1621*, chapter II, especially 67–70; cf. Conrad Russell, *Parliaments and English Politics, 1621–1629* (Oxford: Oxford University Press, 1979), 109–112.

62. *First Institute*, 97. Cf. the similar passage in *Calvin's Case*: "for we are but of yesterday, (and therefore had need of the wisdom of those that were before us) and had been ignorant (if we had not received light and knowledge from our forefathers) and our daies upon the earth are but as a shadow, in respect of the old and ancient dayes and times past, wherein the Laws have been by the wisdom of the most excellent men, in many successions of ages, by long and continual experience (the trial of right and truth) fined and refined, which no one man (being of so short a time) albeit he had in his head the wisdom of all the men in the world, in any one age could never have effected or attained unto. And therefore it is *optima regula, qua nulla est verior aut firmior in jure, Neminem oportet esse sapientorum legibus*: no man ought to take upon him to be wiser than the laws" (*Reports*, 586). In reworking this passage for the *Institutes*, Coke sacrificed eloquence to bring out the explicit distinction between artificial and natural reason, creating a Leviathan-like figure to emphasize the absurdity of any single legislator or interpreter.

63. *PWJ*, 309.

64. *The Ancient Constitution*, 35.

65. *PWJ*, 312–313.

66. Coke elaborates this passage in a revealing way in the succeeding paragraph: "I confesse it is a labour of as great pains, as difficulty [to describe the courts]: for as in an high and large building, he that beholds the same after it is finished, and furnished, seeth not the carriages, scaffolding, and other invisible works of labour, industry, and skill in architecture: So he that looketh on a book full of variety of important matter, especially concerning sacred laws, after it is printed and fairly bound and polished, cannot see therein the carriage of the materials, the searching, finding out, perusing, and digesting of authorities in law, rols of parliament, judiciall records, warrants in law, and other invisible works, *tam laboris, quam ingenii*." The message is clear: the house of the law, like the book that describes it, can only be understood by those who have intimately handled its materials.

67. *Fourth Institute*, proeme.

68. Ibid., 78, 81–82.

69. Ibid., 82–84.

70. Lamar Hill, *Bench and Bureaucracy: The Public Career of Sir Julius Caesar, 1580–1636* (Stanford: Stanford University Press, 1988), 51.

71. Bradshaw in his *English Puritanisme* (1605) attacked the oath as "against the very Law of Nature" and "devised by the Antichrist" to cause men to damn their own souls; cited in Stuart Barton Babbage, *Puritanism and Richard Bancroft* (London: SPCK, 1962), 264.

72. Coke, *Second Institute*, 601ff.; Edward Cardwell, ed., *Documentary Annals of the Reformed Church of England*, 2 vols. (Oxford: Oxford University Press, 1839), 2: 82ff.

73. Elton, *TC*, 226–227; Coke, *Fifth Report*, 344–345.

74. *SPD James I*, 14, quoted in Babbage, 265.

75. Coke, *Second Institute*, 604 (Article 6).

76. For local studies, see W. J. Sheils, "'The Right of the Church': The Clergy, Tithes, and the Courts at York," in W. J. Sheils and D. Wood, eds., *The Church and Wealth: Studies in Church History*, 24 (Oxford: Oxford University Press, 1987), 231–255; Helena Hajzyk, "The Church in Lincolnshire, c. 1595 – c. 1640" (D. Phil. Thesis, Cambridge University, 1980).

77. *Second Institute*, 610, 622.

78. Ibid., 609, 610, 614.

79. Louis A. Knafla, *Law and Politics in Jacobean England: The Tracts of Lord Chancellor Ellesmere* (Cambridge: Cambridge University Press, 1977), 155–161; Brian P. Levack, *The Civil Lawyers in England 1603–1641: A Political Study* (Oxford: Oxford University Press, 1973), 72–73, 81–85; Edward Hake, *Epieikeia*, ed. D. E. C. Yale (New Haven: Yale University Press, 1953 [*ante* 1603]). On Bacon's general legal philosophy, see Daniel Coquillette, *Francis Bacon* (Stanford: Stanford University Press, 1992).

80. Coke, *Second Institute*, 609.

81. Ibid., 618, 611.

82. Hill, *Bench and Bureaucracy*, op. cit., 51.

83. Cited in Babbage, 290; emphasis added.

84. Knafla, 140–141.

85. BL Harl. MS 1299, f. 120, "A Conference of the Kinges especiall appointment held . . . on the 23 of May 1611."

86. Knafla, op. cit., 287, 289–290 ("Some Notes and Remembrances, Concerning Prohibitians . . ." [1611]; 297 ("Observacions").

87. Ogilvie, op. cit., 137; Levack, 102; Elton, "Henry VIII's Act of Proclamations," 219, 220. Elton suggests that the government (read: Cromwell) was less sure of its ground than its more confident assertions would indicate.

88. Ogilvie, 138; Wallace Notestein, *The House of Commons, 1604–1610* (New Haven: Yale University Press, 1971), 292–293; Elizabeth Read Foster, *Proceedings in Parliament 1610*, 2 vols. (New Haven: Yale University Press, 1966), 2: 258–263; Levack, 98, 103–106; J. P. Sommerville, *Politics and Ideology in England, 1603–1640* (London: Longman, 1986), 121–127. For Cowell, see below, 566ff.

89. *The Twelfth Part of the Reports of Sir Edward Coke, Kt.* (London, 1656), 74.

90. "The Speech of the Lord Chancellor . . . Touching the *Post-Nati*" (*Calvin's Case*), in Knafla, 207–213, 218–220.

91. The reference is to Coke's commentary on *Bagg's Case*, *Eleventh Report* (1615), ff. 93v–100r.

92. Knafla, 302–303, 307–308; see also Knafla's discussion, 128–133; cf. Paul Birdsall, "'Non Obstante' – A Study of the Dispensing Power of English Kings," in Carl Wittke, ed., *Essays in History and Political Theory in Honor of Charles Howard McIlwain* (Cambridge: Harvard University Press, 1936), 37–76, at 50–55. Birdsall calls Coke "much maligned" in the accusations of antiroyalism leveled at him by Ellesmere and others.

93. *Twelfth Report*, 76.

94. Kevin Sharpe, *The Personal Rule of Charles I* (New Haven: Yale University Press, 1992), 414–417; Paul Slack, *Poverty and Policy in Tudor and Stuart England* (London: Longman, 1988), 142.

95. *CSPD 1611–1618*, 99.

96. Babbage, 292.

97. On the campaign for Coke's dismissal and its broader legal background, see Knafla, 176–181; J. H. Baker, "The Common Lawyers and the Chancery: 1616," in Baker, *The Legal Profession and the Common Law*, op. cit., 205–229; Catherine Drinker Bowen, *The Lion and the Throne: The Life and Times of Sir Edward Coke (1552–1634)* [Boston: Little, Brown, 1957], 325–336. See also G. W. Thomas, "James I, Equity and Lord

Keeper Williams," *EHR* 91 (1976): 506–528. For a contemporary response, see Elizabeth McClure Thomson, ed., *A Selection of the Letters of John Chamberlain Concerning Life in England from 1597 to 1626* (London: Capricorn Books, 1966), 170–176.

98. For a general discussion of the receiving of judicial opinions in England, see Stewart Jay, "Servants of Monarchs and Lords: The Advisory Role of Early English Judges," *AJLH* 38 (1994): 117–196; Jay's discussion of Coke is at 134–140.

99. *Eleventh Report*, 1129.

100. In *Darcy's Case*, Coke concluded that "The Queen was deceived in her grant [of a monopoly for making playing cards], for the Queen as by the preamble appeareth, intended the same to be for the weal publick, and it shall be imployed for the private good of the Patentee . . ." In the *Earl of Devonshire's Case*, he wrote that if a warrant under the privy seal was "founded upon a false suggestion contained in the Privy Seal, by consequence the Privy Seal is utterly void": *Eleventh Report*, 1117; 1120. Cf. Ellesmere's commentary on *Darcy*, which accuses Coke of misrepresenting the judges' opinion and stretching statutory construction to infringe the king's legitimate power (Knafla, 303), and Sir Henry Yelverton's similar critique in BL Stowe MS. 153, f. 40r, also cited by Knafla.

101. James R. Stoner Jr., *Common Law and Liberal Theory: Coke, Hobbes, and the Origins of American Constitutionalism* (Lawrence: University Press of Kansas, 1992), 62.

102. Stephen D. White, *Sir Edward Coke and the 'Grievances of the Commonwealth'* (Durham: University of North Carolina Press, 1979).

103. Stoner, op. cit., ibid.

104. The modern debate on this idea begins of course with Pocock's magisterial *The Ancient Constitution and the Feudal Law* (1957, rev. ed. 1987). It figures importantly in Sommerville's *Politics and Ideology*, which devotes a chapter to it, and in Glenn Burgess' *The Politics of the Ancient Constitution: An Introduction to English Political Thought, 1603–1642* (London: Macmillan, 1992), the controversy about it appears as the defining issue of the period. I have borrowed Burgess' title phrase (though not the assumption behind it) for my own subhead. Paul Christianson has employed the concept extensively in his sensitive discussions of early Stuart English thought; see particularly "Young John Selden and the Ancient Constitution, ca. 1610–1618," *Proceedings of the American Philosophical Society* 128 (1984): 271–315; "Political Thought in Early Stuart England," *HJ* 10 (1987): 955–970; "Royal and Parliamentary Voices on the English Constitution, 1604–1621," in Linda Levy Peck, ed., *The Mental World of the Jacobean Court* (Cambridge: Cambridge University Press, 1991), 71–95, 289–298; "Ancient Constitutions in the Age of Sir Edward Coke and John Selden," in Ellis Sandoz, ed., *The Roots of Liberty: Magna Carta, Ancient Constitution, and the Anglo–American Tradition of Rule of Law* (Columbia: University of Missouri Press, 1993), 89–146, 284–292; and *Discourse on History, Law, and Governance in the Public Career of John Selden, 1610–1635* (Toronto: University of Toronto Press, 1996), passim. For a pre-Pocockian view, in which the "ancient constitution" is conspicuously absent, see J. W. Allen, *English Political Thought 1603–1644* (London: Methuen, 1938).

105. On the distinctions between the king's absolute and ordinary (judiciable) prerogative, see Francis Wormuth, *The Royal Prerogative* (Ithaca: Cornell University Press, 1949); Francis Oakley, "Jacobean Political Theology: The Absolute and Ordinary Powers of the King," *JHI* 29 (1968): 323–346; idem, *Omnipotence, Covenant, and Order* (Ithaca: Cornell University Press, 1984); Sommerville, op. cit., esp. 166–173; Burgess, *The Politics of the Ancient Constitution*, chapter 6.

106. On the general dissemination of Continental thought and scholarly standards in England in this period, see Richard Tuck, *Philosophy and Government, 1572–1651* (Cambridge: Cambridge University Press, 1993). For Gentili, see Gesina H. J. van der Molen, *Alberico Gentili and the Development of International Law: His Work and Times*, 2d ed. (Leyden: A. W. Sijthoff, 1968); for Saravia, J. P. Sommerville, "Richard Hooker, Hadrian Saravia, and the Advent of the Divine Right of Kings," *History of Political Thought* 4 (1983): 229–245; for De Dominis, W. B. Patterson, *King James VI and I and the*

Reunion of Christendom (New York: Cambridge University Press), chapter 7, and Sommerville, *Politics and Ideology*, passim.

107. James Spedding, Robert Leslie Ellis, and Douglas Denon Heath, eds., *The Works of Francis Bacon*, 14 vols. (London, 1857–1874), 7: 415.

108. Spedding, *Works of Bacon*, 7: 327–387; see Coquillette's reading of this text, op. cit., 35–48.

109. Spedding, 358–359; I have quoted the fuller Cambridge MS. Version of the text here.

110. The *locus classicus* of reason of state discourse is Giovanni Botero, *The Reason of State*, trans. P. J. and D. P. Waley, ed. D. P. Waley (London, 1956 [1589]); see also Federico Chabod, *Giovanni Botero* in *Opere II* (Turin, 1967): 269–458; Rodolfo de Mattei, *Il problema della 'ragion di stato' nell'età della Contrariforma* (Milan, 1979); and, for its reception in England, David S. Berkowitz, "Reason of State in England and the Petition of Right," in Roman Schnur, ed., *Staatsrason: Studien zur Geschichte eines politischen Begriffs* (Berlin, 1975), 165–212.

111. Coquillette, 238. The manuscript of the text, discovered in 1980, is at Chatsworth House (Hardwick MS. 51). A translation is provided in Mark S. Neustadt, "The Making of the Instauration: Science, Politics, and Law in the Career of Francis Bacon" (Ph.D. Diss., Johns Hopkins University, 1987). Coquillette suggests that the work, dating to c. 1614, may have circulated in manuscript.

112. *CJ* 1: 171.

113. See, particularly, "A Treatise about the Union of England and Scotland" (Trinity College, Cambridge [R5.15]) and John Russell, "A Treatise of the Happie and Blissed Unioun," in Bruce R. Galloway and Brian P. Levack, eds., *The Jacobean Union: Six Tracts of 1604* (Edinburgh: Scottish History Society, 1985), 39–74, 75–142; John Hayward, *A Treatise of Union of the Two realmes of England and Scotland* (London, 1604); "A Discourse on the Proposed Union between England and Scotland . . .," (BL Harleian MS. 6850, fols. 35–43; PRO, SPD 14/9/37.1; and "Pro Unione" (Gonville and Caius College, Cambridge [MS. 73/40, fols. 183–194]). Scottish advocates of the name change included Sir Thomas Craig, *De Unione Regnorum Britanniae Tractatus*, ed. C. S. Terry (Edinburgh: Scottish Historical Society, 1909); John Gordon, *Ent[Omega]tikon or a Sermon of the Union of Great Brittanie, in antiquitie of language, name[,] religion, and Kingdome* (London, 1604), which offers a cabalistic reading of "Britannia"; and David Hume, *De Unione Insulae Britanniae Tractatus 1* (London, 1605). Gordon's pro–Union treatise, *A Panegyrique of Congratulation for the Concord of the Realmes of Great Britaine in the Unitie of Religion, and under One King* (London, 1603), is notable for seeing in the union the religious fusing of an elect nation; cf. James Maxwell, "Britaines Union in Love," BL Royal MS. 18A.51. Alberico Gentili's "De Unione Regnorum Britanniae," in his *Regales Disputationes Tres* (London, 1605), strongly supports the name change as well as the union in general. Bacon's two treatises in support of the union (and the name change) are in Spedding, 2: 89–99, 217–247. On the persistence of the name of Britain, see Denys Hay, "The Use of the Term 'Great Britain' in the Middle Ages," *Proceedings of the Society of Antiquaries of Scotland* 81 (1958): 55–66.

114. For Sandys' anti-Union activity, see Theodore Rabb, *Jacobean Gentleman: Sir Edwin Sandys, 1561–1629* (Princeton: Princeton University Press, 1998), 76–86, 122–133.

115. On Bacon's activity, see Joel J. Epstein, "Sir Francis Bacon and the Issue of Union, 1603–1608," *HLQ* 33 (1970): 121–132.

116. James Spedding, Robert Leslie Ellis, and Douglas Denon Heath, eds., *The Letters and Life of Francis Bacon*, 7 vols. (London: Longmans, Green, 1861–1874), 3: 197–199; reprinted in Bruce Galloway, *The Union of England and Scotland, 1603–1608* (Edinburgh: John Donald, 1986), 28–29. Galloway's book is the closest study of the union project in James' first parliament; see also the relevant portions of Brian P. Levack, *The Formation of the British State: England, Scotland, and Union, 1603–1707* (Oxford: The Clarendon Press, 1987); Notestein, *The House of Commons, 1604–1610*, op. cit., 78–85, 211–254, 445–446; R. C. Munden, "The Politics of Accession—James I and the Parliament of 1604" (D. Phil. Thesis, East Anglia, 1976); idem, "James I and 'the growth of

mutual distrust': King, Commons, and Reform, 1603–1604," in Sharpe, *Faction and Parliament*, 43–72. On Sandys' role in the union debate, see Theodore K. Rabb, "Sir Edwin Sandys and the Parliament of 1604–10," *AHR* 69 (1976): 646–670; idem, *Jacobean Gentleman*, op. cit.; W. M. Wallace, *Sir Edwin Sandys and the First Parliament of James I* (Philadelphia, 1940).

117. James F. Larkin and Paul L. Hughes, *Stuart Royal Proclamations*, 2 vols. (Oxford: The Clarendon Press, 1973), 1: 94–98.

118. The commission consisted of forty-eight English and thirty-one Scots members, all sympathetic to the cause. After some weeks of debate, in which Bacon took a prominent role, it presented James with an "Instrument" designed to remove legal and commercial barriers between the two realms, and to serve as the basis of the crown's presentation to Parliament. On its work, see Galloway, *The Union of England and Scotland*, chapter 4.

119. Willson, *King James VI and I*, 252.

120. Galloway, *The Union of England and Scotland*, 61; Levack, *The Formation of the British State*, 190; C. V. Wedgwood, "Anglo-Scottish Relations, 1603–1640," *TRHS*, 4th ser., 32 (1950): 31–48, at 33. For an overview of the question of the style during the remainder of the century, see S. T. Bindoff, "The Stuarts and Their Style," *EHR* 60 (1945): 192–216.

121. Galloway, 108.

122. On Sandys' career in general, see Rabb, *Jacobean Gentleman*; on Owen and Wentworth, *BDBR* 2: 284–285, 3: 301–302; *ODNB* (for Owen, s.v. Thomas Owen); William E. Klein, "Ruling Thoughts: The World of Sir Roger Owen of Condover" (Ph.D. Diss., Johns Hopkins University, 1987).

123. Galloway, 107.

124. Ibid., 149.

125. Knafla, 72.

126. Ibid., 244; cf. supra, 230, and Huntington Library Ellesmere MS. 1215, ff. 2r–3v for Ellesmere's views on allegiance.

127. Knafla, 248.

128. Ellesmere himself rejected the two-body analogy, holding that the king's natural body encompassed both his capacities (Knafla, 67).

129. Cf. the discussions in Glenn Burgess, *The Politics of the Ancient Constitution*, passim.; idem, "The Divine Right of Kings Reconsidered," *EHR* 117 (1992): 837–861; James Daly, "The Idea of Absolute Monarchy," *HJ* 21 (1978): 227–250; Robert Eccleshall, *Order and Reason in Politics: Theories of Absolute and Limited Monarchy in Early Modern England* (Oxford: Oxford University Press, 1978); Sommerville, *Politics and Ideology*, chapter 1 and passim. For older views, see J. W. Allen, *English Political Thought*, op. cit., and Margaret A. Judson, *The Crisis of the Constitution: An Essay in Constitutional and Political Thought in England, 1603–1645*, op. cit. Allen declares that, "Put broadly, the claim of the Crown, disputed from 1603 to 1640, was a claim to disregard the law whenever, in the King's judgement, it was best, in the general interest, that this should be done" (13). This, on my understanding, is what a genuinely absolutist theory would *never* claim; the king, unless a tyrant, could never act "outside" the law, which comprehended the cases of necessity that might supersede it in the municipal sense.

130. Knafla, 249.

131. Cf. the argument of Solicitor-General Littleton in the Ship Money case (1637): "The King cannot judge in his own Person, but hath left it to your Lordships, that are sworn to do equal Justice between him and his People; but to say that the King cannot judge himself, I question. Can that be wanting in the Fountain, that issues in the stream? That I utterly deny. Is it not said, *Coram Rege* in the *King's Bench*, and in the *Star-Chamber*, *Coram Conciliis nostris*? This is a new doctrine; and shall not the King judge? . . . Surely he forgot King *James*, who adjudged two cases in the *Star-Chamber*, that of *Bellingham's* and Sir *Thomas Lake's* Case." *ST* 1, col. 553.

132. *ST* 11, col. 79b.

133. Ibid., col. 79b–80a.

134. Ibid., 80a.

135. Ibid., col. 83b.

136. Ibid., col. 80b.

137. McIlwain, ed., *PWJ*, 310.

138. *ST* 11, col. 80a. On the important role of the so–called laws of the Confessor, see Janelle Greenberg, *The Radical Face of the Ancient Constitution: St. Edward's "Laws" in Early Modern Political Thought* (New York: Cambridge University Press, 2001).

139. Linda Van Norden, "The Elizabethan College of Antiquaries" (Ph.D. Diss., University of California, Los Angeles, 1946) and Joan Evans, *A History of the Society of Antiquaries*, op. cit., remain the fullest studies of the Society. For individual members, see James D. Alsop and Wesley M. Stevens, "William Lambarde and the Elizabethan Polity," *Studies in Medieval and Renaissance History*, n.s. (1987): 231–265, and Retha M. Warnicke, *William Lambarde, Elizabethan Antiquary, 1536–1601* (London, 1973); David S. Berkowitz, *John Selden's Formative Years: Politics and Society in Early Seventeenth-Century England*, ed. Maija Jansson (Washington, D.C.: Folger Institute, 1988); Sharpe, *Sir Robert Cotton*, op. cit.; Linda Van Norden, "Sir Henry Spelman on the Chronology of the Elizabethan College of Antiquaries," *HLQ* 13 (1949–1950): 131–160; Parry, *The Trophies of Time*, op. cit., passim. On the close connection between the lawyers and the antiquaries, see R. Schoeck, "The Elizabethan Society of Antiquaries and Men of Law," *Notes and Queries*, n.s. (1954): 417–421.

140. Ethel M. Portal, "The Academ Roial of King James I," *Proceedings of the British Academy* (1915–1916): 189–208; R. W. Caudill, "Some Literary Evidence of the Development of English Virtuoso Interests in the Seventeenth Century" (D. Phil. Thesis, Oxford University, 1975); Rabb, *Jacobean Gentleman*, 302.

141. Edward Forsett, *A Comparative Discourse of the Bodies Natural and Politique* (1606); John Cowell, *The Interpreter* (1607). For brief sketches of both, see Allen, *English Political Thought*, Part III, chapters V and VI (where Cowell is mistakenly referred to as "James"), and, for a more thorough consideration of Cowell's thought, S. B. Chrimes, "The Constitutional Ideas of Dr. John Cowell," *EHR* 64 (1949): 461–487. See also, for both men, *ODNB*. On the backlash to Cowell's book, see Notestein, *The House of Commons, 1604–1610*, 293–297, Sommerville, *Politics and Ideology*, 121–127, and below.

142. On the background to this controversy, see McIlwain, ed., *PWJ*, xxii–xxxiv, and Patterson, *King James VI and I and the Reunion of Christendom*, op. cit., chapter 3. James' voluminous contributions to this controversy include his *Triplici Nodo, Triplex Cuneus, or an Apologie for the Oath of Allegiance, A Premonition to All Most Mightie Monarches, Kings, Free Princes, and States of Christendome*, and *A Defence of the Right of Kings*, in the *Political Works*, 70–268. Numerous other royal spokesmen, including Bacon and John Buckeridge, Bishop of Rochester and James' ablest clerical defender, entered the lists.

143. Berkowitz, *John Selden's Formative Years*, 13–14. The latest study of Selden is Reid Barbour, *John Selden: Measures of the Holy Commonwealth in Seventeenth-Century England* (Toronto: University of Toronto Press, 2003).

144. "The Reverse or Back Face of the English Janus," in *Tracts Written by John Selden*, trans. Redman Westcott [Dr. Adam Littleton] (London, 1683), 8.

145. Samuel Daniel, in his contemporary *Historie of England* (1612), described Britain's leadership as elective from Cassivellaunus (its first historically authenticated ruler) to Edward III; D. R. Woolf, *The Idea of History in Early Stuart England*, 95, 103.

146. Richard T. Vann, "The Free Anglo-Saxons: A Historical Myth," *JHI* 19 (1958): 259–272; Christopher Hill, "The Norman Yoke," in his *Puritanism and Revolution: Studies in Interpretation of the English Revolution of the Seventeenth Century* (London: Secker and Warburg, 1964): 50–122; cf. Stuart Piggott, *Ancient Britons and the Antiquarian Imagination: Ideas from the Renaissance to Regency* (New York: Thames and Hudson, 1989).

147. Op. cit., sig. A3v.

148. *Ioannis Seldeni Ad Fletam Dissertatio*, ed. and trans. David Ogg (Cambridge: Cambridge University Press, 1925), 167; cited in Burgess, *The Politics of the Ancient Constitution*, 64.

149. *Titles of Honor* (London, 1614), 2–3.

150. Ibid., 4–5.

151. Ibid., 14–15; *Jani Anglorum*, 94–99. Selden did not deny that the Norman Conquest had made a significant impact on England; cf. the nuanced discussion in Christianson, *Discourse*, passim.

152. Selden, ed., *De Laudibus Legum Angli*, 20.

153. *Titles of Honor*, 300–301.

154. Ibid., sig. A. The passage is worth quoting in full not only as a defense of Selden's presuming above his own station but as a defense of the scholar's calling: "*If either* Envie *or* Ignorance *question how I, bred from the bottom of Obscuritie, and so farre from Court-Customs, should dare at these* Honors, *let it know, I learn'd long since from a Great Clerk (that* Robert [Grosseteste] *Bishop of* Lincoln *under* Henrie III) *That there was, in* Libraries, *greater aid to the understanding of Honor and Nobilitie, then mongst* Gold *and* Purple outsides."

155. On republicanism and the humanist tradition generally, see Hans Baron, *The Crisis of the Early Italian Renaissance: Civic Humanism and Republican Liberty in an Age of Classicism and Tyranny* (rev. ed., Princeton: Princeton University Press, 1966); Quentin Skinner, *The Foundations of Modern Political Thought*, 2 vols. (Cambridge: Cambridge University Press, 1978); J. G. A. Pocock, *The Machiavellian Moment: Florentine Political Thought and the Atlantic Republican Tradition* (Princeton: Princeton University Press, 1975); Richard Tuck, *Philosophy and Government*, op. cit.; idem, "Humanism and Political Thought," in Anthony Goodman and Angus Mackay, eds., *The Impact of Humanism on Western Thought* (London: Longman, 1990), 43–65; Gisela Bock, Quentin Skinner, and Maurizio Viroli, eds., *Machiavelli and Republicanism* (Cambridge: Cambridge University Press, 1990); and Quentin Skinner and Martin van Gelderen, eds., *Republicanism: A Shared European Heritage* (Cambridge: Cambridge University Press, 2002). On the significance of the Venetian and Dutch republics in Renaissance thought, see William J. Bouwsma, *Venice and the Defense of Republican Liberty* (Berkeley: University of California Press, 1968); E. O. G. Haitsma Mulier, *The Myth of Venice and Dutch Republican Thought in the Seventeenth Century*, trans. G. T. Moran (Assen, 1980); and Martin van Gelderen, *The Political Thought of the Dutch Revolt* (Cambridge: Cambridge University Press, 1992). On English republicanism, Markku Peltonen, *Classical Humanism and Republicanism in English Thought, 1570–1640*, op. cit., is a powerful corrective to the revisionist denigration of the constitutionalist tradition in England; see also the important statement in Patrick Collinson, "The Monarchical Republic of Queen Elizabeth I," *Bulletin of the John Rylands Library* 69 (1987): 394–424, reprinted in his *Elizabethan Essays* (London and Rio Grande, OH: The Hambledon Press, 1994), 31–57. These new perspectives inform David Norbrook's *Writing the English Republic: Poetry, Rhetoric and Politics, 1627–1660* (Cambridge: Cambridge University Press, 1999). Older studies include Zera S. Fink, *The Classical Republicans: An Essay in the Recovery of a Pattern of Thought in Seventeenth-Century England* (Evanston: Northwestern University Press, 1962 [1945]); Donald W. Hanson, *From Kingdom to Commonwealth: The Development of Civic Consciousness in English Political Thought* (Cambridge: Harvard University Press, 1970); Robert Ecclesiall, *Order and Reason in Politics: Theories of Absolute and Limited Monarchy in Early Stuart England*, op. cit.; and Michael Mendle, *Dangerous Positions: Mixed Government, the Estates of the Realm, and the Making of an Answer to the xix propositions*, op. cit. See also the judicious overview in Blair Worden, "English Republicanism," in J. H. Burns, ed., *The Cambridge History of Political Thought, 1450–1700* (Cambridge: Cambridge University Press, 1991), 443–475. For Tacitus, see Kenneth C. Schellhase, *Tacitus in Renaissance Political Thought* (Chicago: University of Chicago Press, 1976); Mary F. Tenney, "Tacitus in the Politics of Early Stuart England," *Classical Journal* 37 (1941): 151–163; Alan T. Bradford, "Stuart Absolutism and the 'Utility' of Tacitus," *HLQ* 46 (1983): 127–155; and David Womersley, "Sir Henry Savile's Transla-

tion of Tacitus and the Political Interpretation of Elizabethan Texts," *The Review of English Studies*, n.s., 42 (1991): 313–342. Tacitus is treated with Cicero and Seneca by J. H. M. Salmon in "Cicero and Tacitus in Seventeenth-Century France," *AHR* 85 (1980): 307–331, and "Stoicism and Roman Example: Seneca and Tacitus in Jacobean England," *JHI* 50 (1989): 199–225. On Seneca's wide influence on Renaissance English culture, see, among others, F. L. Lucas, *Seneca and Elizabethan Tragedy* (Cambridge: Cambridge University Press, 1922); George Williamson, *The Senecan Amble* (Chicago and London: University of Chicago Press, 1951); and Margo Todd, "Seneca and the Protestant Mind: The Influence of Stoicism in Puritan Ethics," *Archiv für Reformationsgeschichte* 75 (1983): 182–199. For Cicero, see Charles Schmitt, *Cicero Scepticus: A Study of the Influence of the Academica in the Renaissance* (The Hague, 1972). The Stoic influence generally is treated in Gerhard Oestreich, *Neostoicism and the Early Modern State*, ed. Birgitta Oestreich and H. G. Koenigsberger, trans. David McLintock (Cambridge: Cambridge University Press, 1982).

156. *Titles of Honor*, 18–19.

157. Ibid., 20.

158. Norbrook, op. cit., 133; ibid., chapter 2, for the significance of Lucan's poem in seventeenth-century English political discourse.

159. *Titles of Honor*, 11.

160. *The History of Britain* [1670] in *The Complete Prose Works of John Milton*, Vol. V, Part I, ed. French Fogle (New Haven: Yale University Press, 1971), c. 450; see the commentary in Nicholas von Maltzahn, *Milton's 'History of Britain': Republican Historiography in the English Revolution* (Oxford: Oxford University Press, 1991).

161. Edward Ayscough's Unionizing history of England and Scotland (1607) had emphasized the barbarism of the early Britons and the civilizing impact of their foreign conquerors, but Ayscough's aim was to reconcile English and Scottish history rather than to relate either to the wider European tradition; on Ayscough, see Woolf, *The Idea of History*, 58–62.

162. Niccolo Machiavelli, *Discourses on Livy*, trans. Julia Conaway Bonadella and Peter Bonadella (New York: Oxford University Press, 1997); Victoria Kahn, "Reduction and the Praise of Disunion in Machiavelli's *Discourses*," *The Journal of Medieval and Renaissance Studies* 18 (1988): 1–19, cited in Norbrook, 97.

163. Cited in Maurizio Viroli, *Machiavelli* (Oxford: Oxford University Press, 1998), 146.

164. *Titles of Honor*, 5.

165. Cited in Felicity Heal and Rosemary O'Day, eds., *Church and Society in England: Henry VIII to James I* (Camden, CT: Archon Books, 1977), 112.

166. Peter Lake, "Presbyterianism, the Idea of a National Church and the Argument from Divine Right," in Peter Lake and Maria Dowling, eds., *Protestantism and the National Church in Sixteenth Century England*, op. cit., 193–224.

167. The émigré churchman Hadrian Saravia, who had already published a defense of *jure divino* episcopacy, took precisely this step in his *De imperandi authoritate* (1593), which contended that kingship had derived by divine decree directly from patriarchal authority, thus bypassing any notion of popular election. Saravia's book was licensed by the Queen's printer, an indication of royal favor (Sommerville, *Politics and Ideology*, 12), and its republication was authorized by James I in 1611. As Richard Tuck points out, Saravian arguments appeared as well in the quasi-official "Bishop Overall's Convocation Book" (1606), which attempted to answer papalist arguments about the limits of royal authority (Tuck, *Philosophy and Government*, 261–262). James refused to license the latter work because it cast doubt on the legitimacy of the Dutch revolt, a good example of ideology deferring to policy.

168. McIlwain, ed., *PWJ*, 308.

169. Lake, "Presbyterianism," 212; Christianson, *Reformers in Babylon*, 63–68. Spelman's volume was not published until 1646.

170. *Historie of Tithes*, Preface; xiv–xv.

171. Ibid., vi.

172. Ibid., 35.
173. Ibid., 39, 43, 51, 29.
174. Ibid., 89–90.
175. Ibid., 154, 157ff., 286–287, 168.
176. Ibid., 150.
177. Ibid., 153.
178. Berkowitz, *John Selden's Formative Years*, 36–39.
179. Berkowitz, 40, 231–292; Christianson, 89, 190–191; Zaller, *The Parliament of 1621*, 139–140; Russell, *PEP*, 122–123. Selden's imprisonment in 1621 was ostensibly for his assistance to the House of Lords in establishing their judicature (though no public charge was expressed), but it is not improbable that the tithes controversy, then still at its height, was a contributing factor.
180. *Titles of Honor*, 2d ed. (London, 1631), 4.
181. As attested by Clarendon (*The History of the Rebellion and Civil Wars in England. . . Also His Life Written by Himself* [Oxford: Oxford University Press, 1843], 923).
182. Sir Frederick Pollock, ed., *Table Talk of John Selden* (London: Quaritch, 1927), 61.
183. Although Selden argued that that freedom could be voluntarily alienated. On the extensive debate over voluntary servitude, see Michael Rosen, *On Voluntary Servitude: False Consciousness and the Theory of Ideology* (Cambridge: Polity Press, 1996).
184. On Selden's conception of natural law, see Tuck, *Natural Rights Theories*, chapter 4; cf. the critique of Tuck's views in Johann P. Sommerville, "John Selden, the Law of Nature, and the Origins of Government," *HJ* 27 (1984): 437–447. The comparison between Erastus and Copernicus (Selden, *Opera Omnia*, ed. David Wilkins, 3 vols. in 6 [London, 1726], I, col. 176) is cited by Tuck, p. 95.
185. *Table Talk*, 61, 60.
186. Ibid., 100.
187. "If the King did not like what the pope would have, hee would forbid his legate to land upon his ground, so that the power was truly then in the King though suffered in the pope." Ibid., 98.
188. Ibid., 100, 102.
189. Tuck, *Natural Rights Theories*, 92ff.
190. *Table Talk*, 60.
191. Tuck, 88.
192. *Table Talk*, 36–37.
193. Ibid., 86.
194. Ibid., 137. "Division" is possibly "decision."
195. Ibid., 85.
196. Ibid., 69, 137.
197. Ibid., 66.

Chapter 5: The Discourse of the Stage

1. F. P. Wilson, *The English Drama, 1485–1585*, ed. G. K. Hunter (New York and Oxford: Oxford University Press, 1969), 55.
2. Greg Walker, *Plays of Persuasion: Drama and Politics at the Court of Henry VIII* (Cambridge: Cambridge University Press, 1991), 20. As Walker points out, Wolsey himself had made sophisticated use of the drama.
3. Ibid., 7.
4. Michael D. Bristol, *Carnival and Theater: Plebeian Culture and the Structure of Authority in Renaissance England* (New York and London: Methuen, 1985), 8, 6.
5. Harold C. Gardiner, *Mysteries End: The Investigation of the Last Days of the Medieval Religious Stage* (New Haven: Yale University Press, 1946).
6. The list is printed in Norman Sanders, Richard Southern, T. W. Craik, and Lois Potter, eds., *The Revels History of Drama in English* (London, 1980), 2: 178.
7. Jesse W. Harris, *John Bale: A Study in the Minor Literature of the Reformation* (Urbana: University of Illinois Press, 1940), 67–74. On the (corrupted) text of the play and

its probable performances, see J. H. Pafford and W. W. Greg, eds., *King Johan by John Bale* (Oxford: The Malone Society, 1931); Walker, *Plays of Perusasion*, 170–174. On the cultural representation of John in general during the sixteenth century, see Carole Levin, *Propaganda and the English Reformation: Heroic and Villainous Images of King John* (Lewiston, ME, and Queenston, Ontario: Edwin Mellen Press, 1988).

8. David Bevington, *Tudor Drama and Politics: A Critical Approach to Topical Meaning* (Cambridge: Harvard University Press, 1968), 98.

9. All textual references are to Barry Adams, ed., *John Bale's King Johan* (San Marino, CA: Huntington Library, 1969).

10. John Bale, *The pageant of Popes* (1574), fol. C4a.

11. *King Johan*, 183–184. In Foxe, Peter appears as a "false counterfeited prophet" and "an idell gadder about."

12. William Tyndale, *The Obedience of a Christen man and How Christen Rulers Ought to Governe* (Antwerp, 1528); J. F. Mozley, *William Tyndale* (London: SPCK, 1937).

13. This is Nobility's speech; Clergy and Civil order too join in praise of Elizabeth (2678–2691).

14. Thora Balslev Blatt, *The Plays of John Bale: A Study of Ideas, Technique and Style* (Copenhagen: Gad, 1968), 84.

15. Edwin Shepard Miller, "The Antiphons in Bale's Cycles of Christ," *Studies in Philology* 48 (1951): 629–638, cited in Blatt, 89.

16. Blatt, 99. Such a figure appears nowhere else in Bale or in the extant drama of the sixteenth century. Blatt argues plausibly that it is a substitution for the prolocutor who is frequently used, and typically in Bale, to introduce plays and point the moral at the end (1115–116).

17. Ibid., 15; James C. Bryant, *Tudor Drama and Religious Controversy* ([Macon, GA] Mercer University Press, 1984), 46. Walker, 210–221, emphasizes Bale's implicit criticism of Henry in *King Johan* in rejecting auricular confession as a chief prop of popery.

18. Blatt, 33.

19. W. W. Greg, ed., *Respublica: An Interlude for Christmas 1553* (London: Oxford University Press for EETS, 1969), ll. 665–671; 1075–1084, 1092–1098.

20. Bevington, *Tudor Drama and Politics*, 117.

21. As James C. Bryant notes, Bale's Henry VIII also fits the pattern of a "male Nemesis," sent (albeit belatedly) to right old wrongs and restore true religion (op. cit., 80).

22. On internal evidence, the play has been attributed to Nicholas Udall (1505–1556), the author of *Ralph Roister Doister*. Udall was favored by Mary although he had Reformed sympathies, a factor that could account for the relatively restrained treatment of Protestant vices in *Respublica*. His authorship remains speculative, however.

23. Wilson, *The English Drama*, 85–101.

24. The touring companies that performed Reformed versions of the mystery and morality plays remained important propagators of Protestant faith and values, however; as the Catholic controversialist Thomas Dorman noted in his *A Proufe of Certeyne Articles* (1564), "Minstrelles and players [are] chief ministres in publishing the nevve ghospell" (quoted in Paul Whitfield White, *Theatre and Reformation: Protestantism, Patronage, and Playing in Tudor England* [Cambridge: Cambridge University Press, 1993], 45).

25. Matthewe Gribalde, *A notable and marvellous Epistle of the famous Doctour, Matthewe Gribalde . . . concernyng the terrible iudgement of God, upon hym that for feare of men, denieth Christ and the knowne verritie: with a Preface of Doctor Calvine*, trans. Edward Aglionby (London, 1570). For the literature on Spera, whose case and example continued to haunt the Protestant imagination down to the eighteenth century, see John Stachniewski, *The Persecutory Imagination: English Puritanism and the Literature of Religious Despair* (Oxford: Clarendon Press, 1991), 37ff. See also the comments in Jonathan Wright, "The World's Worst Worm: Conscience and Conformity during the English Reformation," *SCJ* 30 (1998): 113–133.

26. Nathaniel Woodes, *The Conflict of Conscience* (New York: AMS Reprints, 1970), sig. H4. Note the orthographic play on "whorld," with its triple signification of "whore," "world," and "hurled."

27. Ibid., sig. I4.

28. Ibid., sig. A4v.

29. On this trope in late Tudor culture, see Anthony Esler, *The Aspiring Mind of the Elizabethan Younger Generation* (Durham: University of North Carolina Press, 1966); cf. "Faustus's Rhetoric of Aspiration," in Johannes H. Birringer, *Marlowe's Dr Faustus and Tamberlaine: Theological and Theatrical Perspectives* (Frankfurt am Main: Peter Lang, 1984).

30. Lily B. Campbell was the first to point out the connection in her "Doctor Faustus: A Case of Conscience," *PMLA* 47 (1952): 219–239.

31, The play was retitled *The Tragedie of Ferrex and Porrex* when it was published in 1570, the latter being Gorboduc's sons.

32. John S. Wilks, *The Idea of Conscience in Renaissance Tragedy* (London: Routledge, 1990), 144–145.

33. G. K. Hunter, *Dramatic Identities and Cultural Tradition: Studies in Shakespeare and His Contemporaries* (New York: Barnes and Noble Books, 1978). Perhaps the most judicious description of Marlowe's religious stance is A. D. Nuttall's: "This is a poet of licentious religious imagination" (A. D. Nuttall, *The Alternative Trinity: Gnostic Heresy in Marlowe, Milton, and Blake* [Oxford: Clarendon Press, 1998], 46).

34. *The Plays of Christopher Marlowe*, ed. Leo Kirschbaum (Cleveland: Meridian Books, 1962), p. 343, ll. 15–20. All subsequent references are by line numbers in the text.

35. There has been considerable scholarly debate about the nature of the angels; see, e.g., Paul H. Kocher, *Christopher Marlowe: A Study of His Thought, Character, and Learning* (New York, 1962); Robert Ornstein, "Marlowe and God: The Tragic Theory of *Doctor Faustus*," *PMLA* 83 (1968): 1378–1385; Pauline Honderich, "John Calvin and Doctor Faustus," *Modern Language Review* 68 (1973): 1–13; Joel Altman, *The Tudor Play of Mind* (Berkeley and Los Angeles: University of California Press, 1978); Martha Tuck Rozett, *The Doctrine of Election and the Emergence of Elizabethan Tragedy* (Princeton: Princeton University Press, 1984). It is important to note that Faustus himself takes the visitants as real, i.e., as external to himself, and therefore as proof of his power to summon spirits by pure "aspiration" alone; without casting spells, but merely by reading and concentrating upon his "blasphemous" book, he is immediately attended by presences.

36. Note the Chorus' description of the feast of St. Peter's as "highly solemniz'd" (2.3.25); at 3.1.55 Mephostophilos similarly describes it as a day of "high solemnity," and at 3.1.82 he urges Faustus to "dash the pride of this solemnity."

37. See the discussion of this point in Edward A. Snow, "Marlowe's *Doctor Faustus* and the Ends of Desire," in Harold Bloom, ed., *Christopher Marlowe's Doctor Faustus: Modern Critical Interpretations* (New York: Chelsea House, 1988): 47–75.

38. Cf. Faustus' exclamation at the beginning of 2.1: "Now, Faustus, must thou needs be damn'd, canst thou not be saved!" Faustus (who has not yet signed his pact) is very close here to preferring the certainty of damnation to the doubt of salvation.

39. Pico cited in Barbara Howard Traister, "*Doctor Fautsus*: Masks of Self–Delusion," Bloom, op. cit., 77–92, at 78–79; for Agrippa, see Wilbur Sanders, "Dr. Faustus' Sin," ibid., 27–45, at 31–33. See, more generally, Traister, *Heavenly Necromancers: The Magician in Renaissance Drama* (Columbia: University of Missouri Press, 1984).

40. There is surely erotic significance too in the fact that Faustus consigns his body as well as his soul to Lucifer in the pact he himself composes, as he shortly after reminds Mephistophilos (2.1.129).

41. Hosea 10.8; Luke 23.30; Rev. 6.16.

42. Jonathan Dollimore, in his *Radical Tragedy: Religion, Ideology, and Power in the Drama of Shakespeare and His Contemporaries* (Chicago: University of Chicago Press,

1984), notes the oppressive nature of divinity in *Faustus*; his wider argument that Elizabethan and Jacobean theater contest social power as such is less convincing.

43. In the 1604 text, "a drop, half a drop." Marlowe adds even greater poignancy to this image by inverting it when Faustus, in his final despair, pleads that his soul "be changed into small water-drops/ And fall into the ocean, ne'er [to] be found" (5.2.185–186). The "found" suggests a last prayer for sequestration and personal survival that, as Edward A. Snow suggests, is the necessary converse of a mortal desire for omnipotence.

44. The phrase is Birringer's (Bloom, 103).

45. On Marlowe's transformations of the morality play, see the comments in Edward L. Rocklin, "Marlowe as Experimental Dramatist: The Role of the Audience in *The Jew of Malta*," in Kenneth Friedenreich, Roma Gill, and Constance B. Kuriyama, *"A Poet and a filthy Play-maker": New Essays on Christopher Marlowe* (New York: AMS Press, 1988): 129–142 at 131–132, and references cited.

46. C. L. Barber, *Creating Elizabethan Tragedy: The Theater of Marlowe and Kyd*, ed. Richard P. Wheeler (Chicago: University of Chicago Press, 1988), 15.

47. Ibid., 123.

48. E. M. Albright, *Dramatic Publication in England, 1589–1640* (New York: Gordian Press, 1971 [1927]); G. E. Bentley, *The Profession of Dramatist in Shakespeare's Time, 1590–1642* (Princeton: Princeton University Press, 1971); see also the essays by Richard Dutton, Barbara A. Mowat, and Alexander Leggatt in R. B. Parker and S. B. Zitner, eds., *Elizabethan Theater: Essays in Honor of S. Schoenbaum* (Newark: University of Delaware Press, 1996). As Leggatt points out, Marlowe's *Tamburlaine* was published without authorial attribution, as were the early plays of Shakespeare, but whereas between 1591 and 1600 fifty-five plays were published without attribution, seven with the author's initials only, and twenty-three with his full name, between 1601 and 1610 these proportions were reversed, respectively, to fifty-eight, three, and sixty-five (p. 131). For earlier concepts of authorship, see A. J. Minnis, *Medieval Theory of Authorship* (London: Scolar Press, 1984), and for the modern, deconstructionist view, see Roland Barthes, "The Death of the Author," in *Image–Music–Text*, trans. Stephen Heath (New York: Hill and Wang, 1977), 142–148, and Michel Foucault, "What Is an Author?" in Josue V. Herari, ed., *Textual Strategies: Perspectives in Post–Structuralist Criticism* (Ithaca: Cornell University Press, 1979), 141–160. The collaborative nature of modern screenwriting is in some ways a throwback to the early Elizabethan model.

49. Stephen Greenblatt, *Shakespearean Negotiations: The Circulation of Social Energy in Renaissance England* (Berkeley and Los Angeles: University of California Press, 1988), 133. Cf. Greenblatt's discussion of Marlowe in his *Renaissance Self-Fashioning*, op. cit.

50. *Faustus* was the London stage manager Philip Henslowe's biggest single earner between 1594 and 1597; Alfred Harbage, *Shakespeare's Audience* (New York: Columbia University Press, 1941), Appendix IV.

51. John Melton, *Astrologaster, or, The Figure-Caster* (London, 1620), 31, quoted in G. Blakemore Evans, *Elizabethan–Jacobean Drama: The Theatre in Its Time* (New York: New Amsterdam Books, 1988), 71; E. K. Chambers, *The Elizabethan Stage*, 4 vols. (Oxford: The Clarendon Press, 1923), 3: 423–424.

52. William Empson, *Faustus and the Censor*, ed. John Henry Jones (Oxford: Basil Blackwell, 1987).

53. Richard Dutton, *Mastering the Revels: The Regulation and Censorship of English Renaissance Drama* (Iowa City: Iowa University Press, 1991), 88–89.

54. Janet Clare, *'Art Made tongue–tied by authority': Elizabethan and Jacobean Dramatic Censorship* (Manchester and New York: Manchester University Press, 1990), 27–30, 104–106.

55. Hughes and Larkin, *Tudor Royal Proclamations*, 2: 115–116.

56. Harold C. Gardiner, *Mysteries' End*, op. cit., remains the standard work on the subject.

57. Cited in Clare, 173–174.

58. Janette Dillon, *Theatre, Court, and City, 1595–1610: Drama and Social Space in London* (Cambridge: Cambridge University Press, 2000), 3.

59. David Hickman, "Religious Belief and Pious Practice among London's Elizabethan Elite," *HJ* 42 (1999): 941–960.

60. Dutton, *Mastering the Revels*, 24, 157, 160–161; cf. Philip J. Finkelpearl, "The Role of the Court in the Development of Jacobean Drama," *Criticism* 24 (1982): 138–158.

61. The fullest discussion of this episode is Jerzy Limon, *Dangerous Matter: English Drama and Politics 1623/24* (Cambridge: Cambridge University Press, 1986).

62. Dillon, 3–6; Clare, 24–25; Andrew Gurr, *The Shakespearean Playing Companies* (Oxford: The Clarendon Press, 1996). Robert Greene, John Lyly, and Thomas Nashe were all recruited to produce the anti-Martinist satires.

63. J. W. Lever, *The Tragedy of State: A Study of Jacobean Drama* (London: Methuen, 1987 [1971]).

64. Lever, 19–20. Cf. Kent Cartwright, *Theatre and Humanism: English Drama in the Sixteenth Century* (Cambridge: Cambridge University Press, 1999), and, for the influence of humanism on the older genres, Dorothy H. Brown, *Christian Humanism in Late English Morality Plays* (Gainesville: University Press of Florida, 1999).

65. Thomas Heywood, *If You Know Not Me You Know Nobody*, ed. Madeleine Doran (Oxford: Oxford University Press for the Malone Society, 1935); and see the discussions in Kathleen E. McLuskie, *Dekker and Heywood* (New York: St. Martin's Press, 1994), and Gerald M. Pinciss, *Forbidden Matter: Religion in the Drama of Shakespeare and His Contemporaries* (Newark: University of Delaware Press, 2000), chapter 4.

66. Anthony Munday, *A Second and Third Blast of Retrait from Plaies and Theaters* (New York and London: Garland, 1973 [1580]); Stephen Gosson, *Playes Confuted in fiue Actions* (London, 1582), sig. B.

67. Munday, 79; sig. A2j.

68. Ibid., 1, 62, 73; Gosson, sig. B4.

69. Gosson, sigs. C4, D4v.

70. Munday, 3.

71. There has been much debate over the social composition of the public theater's audience; see, notably, Alfred Harbage, *Shakespeare's Audience* (New York: Columbia University Press, 1941); Anne Jennalie Cook, *The Privileged Playgoers of Shakespeare's London*, op. cit.; Martin Butler, *Theatre and Crisis: 1632–1642*, op. cit.; and Andrew Gurr, *Playgoing in Shakespeare's London* (Cambridge: Cambridge University Press, 1987). The debate is summarized in Dutton, 8–9. Gosson describes the theatrical audience in London as "an assemblie of Tailers, Tinkers, Cordwayners, Saylers, olde Men, young Men, Women, Boyes, Girles, and such like" (*Players Confuted*, sig. D).

72. Munday, "To the Reader," 18; Gosson, sig. B2r–v.

73. Bryan Crockett, *The Play of Paradox: Stage and Sermon in Renaissance England* (Philadelphia: University of Pennsylvania Press, 1995), 6.

74. Martha Tuck Rozett estimates that 88 per cent of English parishes had a preaching minister by 1601 (Rozett, op. cit., 19–20), but offers no evidence, and both Christopher Haigh's study of Lancashire (*Reformation and Resistance in Tudor Lancashire* [Cambridge: Cambridge University Press, 1975]) and Paul Seaver's study of the Puritan lectureships cast serious doubt on this claim. There is no doubt, however, that sermons were widely patronized among godly congregants, that the demand for them was increasing, and that they had become deeply interwoven in the fabric of godly life. I am grateful to Paul Seaver for discussion of this point.

75. Seaver, *The Puritan Lectureships*, op. cit.

76. David Underdown, *Fire from Heaven: Life in an English Town in the Seventeenth Century* (New Haven: Yale University Press, 1992).

77. In this elevated sense, the minister became a prophet, as Gifford, Perkins, Donne, and others argued; for their comments, see Crockett, 9–10.

78. Ibid., 11.

79. Millar MacLure, *The Paul's Cross Sermons*, op. cit.

80. Alexandra Walsham, *Providence in Early Modern England* (Oxford: Oxford University Press, 1999), 134–137.

81. Philip Stubbes, *The Anatomie of Abuses* (New York and London: Garland, 1973 [1583]), "A Preface To the Reader."

82. For Wilson, see G. M. Cameron, *Robert Wilson and the Plays of Shakespeare* (Riverton, New Zealand, 1982); Dutton, 65–73 and passim.

83. On Munday's authorship, see W. W. Greg, ed., *Sir Thomas More* (Oxford: Malone Society Reprints, rev. ed., 1961). Shakespeare has also been suggested as a coauthor: see A. W. Pollard, ed., *Shakespeare's Hand in the Play of Sir Thomas More* (Cambridge: Cambridge University Press, 1923); R. C. Bald, "*The Booke of Sir Thomas More* and Its problems," *Shakespeare Survey* 2 (1949): 44–65; T. H. Howard-Hill, ed., *Shakespeare and Sir Thomas More: Essays on the Play and Its Shakespearean Interest* (Cambridge: Cambridge University Press, 1989); and, more generally, Scott McMillin, *The Elizabethan Theatre and The Book of Sir Thomas More* (Ithaca: Cornell University Press, 1987).

84. Jonas Barish, *The Antitheatrical Prejudice* (Berkeley and Los Angeles: University of California Press, 1981), chapter 3.

85. Dutton, 66.

86. Douglas Bruster, *Drama and the Market in the Age of Shakespeare* (Cambridge: Cambridge University Press, 1992), 3; the first two examples are Bruster's. Cf. Jean-Christophe Agnew, *Worlds Apart: The Market and the Theatre in Anglo-American Thought, 1550–1750* (Cambridge: Cambridge University Press, 1986). Agnew sees the early modern theater as "a proxy form of the new and but partly fathomable relations of a nascent market society" (11), whereas Bruster finds it a sophisticated adjunct of an already developed one. These views are not incompatible; as descriptions of a society in which market norms were both embraced and resisted (and therefore, especially in the City comedies, ripe for satire), they are different perspectives on the same phenomenon.

87. Mullaney, *The Place of the Stage*, op. cit.; Bristol, *Carnival and Theatre*, op. cit.; Collinson, *EPM*; Seaver, *The Puritan Lectureships*.

88. Dutton, 187, 242.

89. S[amuel] Schoenbaum, "*Richard II* and the Realities of Power," in his *Shakespeare and Others* (Washington, D.C. and London: Folger Books / Scolar Press, 1985), 80–96, at 88–89.

90. Glynne Wickham, "The Privy Council Order of 1597 for the Destruction of All London's Theatres," in David Galloway, *The Elizabethan Theatre* (1969), 21–44. Part of Hayward's difficulties lay of course in the references to Richard II in his text.

91. Michael Manheim, *The Weak King Dilemma in the Shakespearean History Play* (Syracuse: Syracuse University Press, 1973), 3.

92. On the subsequent translations of Lucan by Sir Arthur Gorges (1614) and Thomas May (1627), their influence, and their extension in May's *A Continuation of Lucan's Historicall Poem* (1630; 1650), see Norbrook, *Writing the English Revolution*, 23–62, 225–228. May was, of course, Parliament's official historian during the Civil War.

93. Peltonen, *Classical Humanism and Republicanism*, op. cit., 73–102.

94. Dutton, 178; Heinemann, "Political Drama," in A. R. Braunmuller and Michael Hattaway, eds., *The Cambridge Companion to English Renaissance Drama* (Cambridge: Cambridge University Press, 1990), 161–205, at 167.

95. Cited in Claire McEachern, *The Politics of English Nationhood*, op. cit., 85.

96. Cf. Rozett's discussion of *I and II Tamburlaine* in her *The Doctrine of Election*, chapter 5.

97. Edward was likewise depicted in Samuel Rowley's *When You See Me You Know Me* (probably first performed in 1604). For a discussion of both plays see Pinciss, op. cit., chapter 4.

98. *King John*, ed. L. A. Beaurline (Cambridge: Cambridge University Press, 1990).

99. John S. Farmer, ed., *The Troublesome Reign of John, King of England* (Edinburgh and London: The Tudor Facsimile Reprints, 1911 [New York: AMS Reprints, 1970]). All references are to this edition.

100. Phyllis Rackin, "Patriarchal History and Female Subversion in *King John*," in Deborah T. Curren-Aquino, ed., *King John: New Perspectives* (Newark: University of Delaware Press; London and Toronto: Associated University Presses, 1989), 76–90, at 81.

101. Cf. Avi Ehrlich's study, *Hamlet's Absent Father* (Princeton: Princeton University Press, 1977).

102. Michael Manheim, "The Four Voices of the Bastard," in Curren-Aquino, 126–135.

103. On the problem of vagabondage, see, among many studies, Frank Aydelotte, *Elizabethan Rogues and Vagabonds* (Oxford: The Clarendon Press, 1913); John Pound, *Poverty and Vagrancy in Tudor England* (London: Longman, 1971); Peter Clark and Paul Slack, eds., *Crisis and Order in English Towns, 1500–1700* (London: Routledge and Kegan Paul, 1972); Paul A. Slack, "Vagrants and Vagrancy in England, 1598–1664," *EcHR*, 2d ser., 27 (1974): 360–379; idem, *Poverty and Policy in Tudor and Stuart England* (Burnt Mill, Harlow, Essex: Longman, 1988); A. L. Beier, *Masterless Men: The Vagrancy Problem in England, 1560–1640*, op. cit.; Roger B. Manning, *Village Revolts: Social Protest and Popular Disturbances in England, 1509–1640* (Oxford: The Clarendon Press, 1988), chapter 7; Paul Griffiths, Adam Fox, and Steve Hindle, eds., *The Experience of Authority in Early Modern England* (New York: St. Martin's Press, 1995). Hindle has dealt broadly with the management of early modern poverty in *The State and Social Change in Early Modern England, c. 1550–1640* (Houndsmills, Basingstoke: Macmillan, 2000), and *On the Parish? The Micro-Politics of Poor Relief in Rural England, c. 1550–1750* (Oxford: The Clarendon Press, 2004).

104. Rackin, op. cit., 89, n2.

105. Beaurline, ed., *King John*, 42.

106. "Dramatic Perspective in *King John*," *English Studies in Canada* 3 (1977): 1–17, cited in Curren-Aquino, op. cit., 56.

107. As John's fortunes decline steadily in Acts IV and V, the question of the Bastard's continuing loyalty to him must be raised. Unlike the lords who desert John, the Bastard has nothing to offer the invading Dauphin Lewis but himself; having renounced his title and estate, John's recognition of him as a cousin is his only rank. If one wishes to read some vestige of honor into his behavior—and his polyvalent character is put to many uses by Shakespeare—it remains true that his only real option is to attach himself to Prince Henry by a show of fidelity and utility.

108. Rebecca Bushnell, *Tragedies of Tyrants: Political Thought and Theater in the English Renaissance* (Ithaca: Cornell University Press, 1990), 103.

109. For further discussion, see my "Legitimation and Delegitimation in Early Modern Europe: The Case of England," *History of European Ideas* 10 (1989): 641–665, and below, 622–624.

110. Charles R. Forker, ed., *Edward II* (Manchester and New York: Manchester University Press, 1994). All textual references are to this edition.

111. Dating the latter two works, and Marlowe's corpus in general, is notoriously controversial, but whether *Edward II* precedes *The Troublesome Raigne* or *King John* or succeeds them both, the general point is unaffected. Note, too, that Edward's soliloquized defiance comes after he has submitted to Canterbury's authority, and, at least in an aside, admitted it ("It boots me not to threat; I must speak fair. The legate of the pope will be obeyed" [1.4.53–64]), thus inverting the sequence in the *King John* plays.

112. Marlowe has actually degraded Gaveston, who appears in Holinshed as a nobleman, to the status of a member of the lesser gentry; young Mortimer addresses him as "hardly . . . a gentleman by birth" (1.4.29).

113. Cf. Warwick's battle cry, "Saint George for England and the barons' right"—to which the King replies, "Saint George for England and King Edward's right" (3.2.35–36).

114. Cf. 51–52: "Ah, Leicester, weigh how hardly I can brook/ To lose my crown and kingdom without cause."

115. E.g., Eric Sterling, *The Movement Toward Subversion: The English History Play from Skelton to Shakespeare* (Lanham, MD: University Press of America, 1996), 118–119.

116. On the contemporary parallels between Essex and Bolingbrooke, see Barbara Higdon, *The End Crowns All: Closure and Contradiction in Shakespeare's History* (Princeton: Princeton University Press, 1991), 127–130.

117. Moody E. Prior, *The Drama of Power* (Evanston: Northwestern University Press, 1973), 143.

118. F. W. Brownlow, "*Richard II* and the Testing of Legitimacy," in Kirby Farrell, ed., *Critical Essays on Richard II* (New York: G. K. Hall, 1999), 58–80, at 66.

119. All references are to the Arden edition of *King Richard II*, ed. Peter Ure (London and New York: Methuen, 1982).

120. Cf. Heidegger's discussion of the "while" in "The Anaximander Fragment"of his *Early Greek Thinking*, trans. David Farrell Krell and Frank A. Capuzzi (San Francisco: Harper and Row, 1984).

121. Richard calls himself "a subject" at 4.1.307, but only to underline the paradox of his situation. When he calls for a mirror "That it may show me what a face I have/ Since it is bankrupt of majesty" (266–267) and then dashes it to pieces, he expresses the true sense of his condition, that his "glory" and his "face" must vanish together (287–288).

122. York's messenger Berkeley greets Bolingbrooke as "what lord you will" on his entry into England (2.3.76).

123. York also mentions "the prevention of poor Bolingbrooke/ About his marriage" (2.1.167–168), i.e., Richard's intercession to break up Bolingbroke's intended match with the cousin of Charles VI , but there is no further reference to it in the play, though the incident figures prominently in Holinshed and Froissart.

124. Reese, op. cit. For Reese's discussion of majesty, see 104–111, and for his account of *Richard II*, 225–260.

125. See also the extended metaphor of the crown as a well of tears (below).

126. For an overview, see Margot Heinemann, "Political Drama," in Braunmuller and Hattaway, eds., *The Cambridge Companion to English Renaissance Drama*, op. cit., 161–205.

127. All textual references are to Philip J. Ayres, ed., *Sejanus His Fall* (Manchester and New York: Manchester University Press, 1999 [1990]). The editors of the standard edition of Jonson's works estimate that up to a quarter of the text is composed of quotation or paraphrase from his several classical sources (Tacitus, Dio Cassius, and Juvenal for the reign of Tiberius and the career of Sejanus; Seneca, Claudian, Juvenal, Pliny, Lucan, Martial, and Persius for additional material, reflection, and aperçus): C. H. Herford and P. and E. Simpson, eds., *Ben Jonson*, 11 vols. (New Haven: Yale University Press, 1922). Jonson showed off both his considerable erudition and his skill at weaving the sort of composite text a Walter Benjamin would have admired, but he clearly intended the pastiche elements of the play to lend it gravity and authority. For Jonson's own defense of his practice (simultaneously a display of his sources), see Ayres, 51–52 ("To the Readers").

128. David Riggs, *Ben Jonson: A Life* (Cambridge: Harvard University Press, 1989), 105–106. On the history of Jonson's frequent bouts with patrons and censors, see Richard Burt, *Licensed by Authority: Ben Jonson and the Discourses of Censorship* (Ithaca: Cornell University Press, 1993). For a reading of Jonson that stresses his essential conservatism, see Jonathan Goldberg, *James I and the Politics of Literature*, op. cit., 176–186.

129. Samuel Rawson Gardiner, *History of England from the Accession of Elizabeth to the Outbreak of the Civil War, 1603–1642*, 10 vols. (London: Longmans, Green 1905), 6: 103–107; Harold Hulme, *The Life of Sir John Eliot, 1592 to 1632* (New York: New York University Press, 1957); J. N. Ball, "Sir John Eliot and Parliament, 1624–1629," in Sharpe, ed., *Faction and Parliament*, 173–207; Russell, *PEP*, passim.; William B. Bidwell and Maija Jansson, eds., *Proceedings in Parliament 1626*, 4 vols. (New Haven: Yale University Press, 1991), 3: 223.

130. This point eludes Richard Dutton in his otherwise perceptive reading of *Sejanus* (*Ben Jonson: To the First Folio* [Cambridge: Cambridge University Press, 1983], 54–63, at 59 and 62).

131. Ayres, 242n.

132. Cf. Sejanus' assessment: "And there's Arruntius too, he only talks" (2.299).

133. Ayres, 51–52.

134. Albert H. Tricomi, *Anticourt Drama in England, 1603–1642* (Charlottesville: University of Virginia Press, 1989), 75. On what Tricomi calls "tropes of surveillance" in Jonson and Shakespeare, and popular attitudes towards informers generally, see his *Reading Tudor-Stuart Texts Through Cultural Historicism* (Gainesville: University Press of Florida, 1996), chapters 4 and 5.

135. G. K. Hunter, *English Drama, 1586–1642: The Age of Shakespeare* (Oxford: The Clarendon Press, 1997), 527–528.

136. McIlwain, ed., *PWJ*, quoted in Goldberg, *James I and the Politics of Literature*, 84.

137. Ibid.

138. For other Tiberian echoes in James' reign, see Goldberg, 68, 165, 176–177.

139. David Howarth, *Images of Rule: Art and Politics in the English Renaissance, 1485–1649* (Basingstoke and London: Macmillan, 1997), 33.

140. See Howarth's description of Mary's tomb and the relation of its placement to Elizabeth's, 166–170. James' letter of 28 September 1612 to the dean and chapter of Peterborough, from whence Mary's remains were transported, refers carefully (but also cooptively) to "our dear sister, the late Queen Elizabeth," to whom he notes he had already paid ceremonial remembrance (G. P. V. Akrigg, ed., *Letters of King James VI & I* (Berkeley and Los Angeles: University of California Press, 1984), 326–327. James' relation to his absent mother has not received the attention it deserves. For a brief, suggestive account, see Maurice Lee, Jr., *Great Britain's Solomon*, op. cit., 32–34.

141. Graham Parry, *The Golden Age Restor'd*, op. cit., 153; R. Malcolm Smuts, *Court Culture and the Origins of a Royalist Tradition in Early Stuart England* (Philadelphia: University of Pennsylvania Press, 1999 [1987]), 237.

142. Parry, 153–154.

143. For the cycle as a whole, see D. J. Gordon, "Rubens and the Whitehall Ceiling," in Gordon, *The Renaissance Imagination: Essays and Lectures*, ed. Stephen Orgel (Berkeley and Los Angeles: University of California Press, 1975), 24–50; Parry, 32–37.

144. Allardyce Nicoll, *Stuart Masques and the Renaissance Stage* (New York: Benjamin Bloom, 1963 [1938]), 28.

145. Stephen Orgel, *Inigo Jones*, 2 vols. (Berkeley and Los Angeles: University of California Press, 1973), 1: 6–8, 2: 823–826. Cf. the abbreviated discussion in Orgel, *The Illusion of Power* (Berkeley and Los Angeles: University of California Press, 1991 [1975]), 14.

146. Nicoll, 34.

147. James' Queen, Anna of Denmark, often took part in the masques herself from Jonson's *The Masque of Blackness* (1605) on. On the important role Anna played in the development of the Stuart masque, see Leeds Barroll, "The Court of the First Stuart Queen," in Peck, ed., *The Mental World of the Jacobean Court*, op. cit., 191–208; idem, "Inventing the Stuart Masque," in David Bevington and Peter Holbrook, eds., *The Politics of the Stuart Court Masque* (Cambridge: Cambridge University Press, 1998), 121–143. The Queen's presence in the masque, while of considerable representational significance in itself, did not of course carry the same ideological charge as that of the sovereign himself.

148. "An Expostulation with Inigo Jones," most recently printed in Richard Dutton, *Ben Jonson: Authority: Criticism* (New York: St. Martin's Press, 1996), 214–217. For Jonson's quarrel with Jones, see D. J. Gordon, "Poet and Architect: The Intellectual Setting of the Quarrel between Ben Jonson and Inigo Jones," *Journal of the Courtauld and Warburg Institutes* 12 (1949): 152–178, reprinted in Stephen Orgel, ed., *The Renaissance Imagination*, op. cit. On Jonson's changing fortunes as a masque writer at the Jacobean

and Caroline courts, see Leah Marcus, *The Politics of Mirth: Jonson, Herrick, Milton, and the Defense of Old Holiday Pastimes* (Chicago: University of Chicago Press, 1986), 10–19.

149. E. K. Chambers, ed., *Aurelian Townshend's Poems and Masks* (Oxford: The Clarendon Press, 1912), 58–59.

150. Ibid., 65.

151. Alexander B. Grossart, ed., *The Complete Works in Prose and Verse of Samuel Daniel*, 4 vols. (1885), 3: 188–189.

152. Grossart, 3: 43–48.

153. R. Malcolm Smuts, "The Puritan Followers of Henrietta Maria in the 1630s," *EHR* 93 (1978): 24–45.

154. See the essays by Martin Butler, Tom Bishop, and Hugh Craig in David Bevington and Peter Holbrook, eds., *The Politics of the Stuart Court Masque*, op. cit.; cf. Goldberg, op. cit., 123–126.

155. Butler, op. cit., 33.

156. Stephen Orgel, *The Jonsonian Masque* (Cambridge: Harvard University Press, 1965), passim.; Lesley Mickel, *Ben Jonson's Antimasques: A History of Growth and Decline* (Aldershot, Hants., and Burlington, VT: Ashgate, 1999).

157. On the alliance between Charles and Buckingham, see Robert E. Ruigh, *The Parliament of 1624: Politics and Foreign Policy* (Cambridge: Harvard University Press, 1971); S. L. Adams, "Foreign Policy and the Parliaments of 1621 and 1624," in Sharpe, ed., *Faction and Parliament*, 139–171; Cogswell, *The Blessed Revolution*. On *Neptune's Triumph* and other Jonsonian masques of the late Jacobean period, see Sara Pearl, "'Sounding to Present Occasions': Jonson's Masques of 1620–5," in David Lindley, ed., *The Court Masque* (Manchester: Manchester University Press, 1984), 60–77; John Meagher, *Method and Meaning in Jonson's Masques* (Notre Dame: Notre Dame University Press, 1966); M. C. Bradbrook, "Social Change and the Evolution of Ben Jonson's Court Masques," *Studies in the Literary Imagination* 6 (1973): 103–138.

158. Jennifer Chibnell, "'To that secure fix'd state': The Functions of the Caroline Masque Form," in Lindley, op. cit., 78–93.

159. Pearl, op. cit., 72–73.

160. Orgel, *The Jonsonian Masque*, 77–80; Smuts, *Court Culture*, op. cit., 189; Parry, *The Golden Age Restor'd*, chapter 8.

161. Kevin Sharpe, *Criticism and Compliment*, op. cit.; idem, *The Personal Rule of Charles I*, 222–235.

162. Rhodes Dunlap, ed., *The Poems of Thomas Carew, with the Masque Coelum Britannicum* (Oxford: The Clarendon Press, 1964 [1949]), ll. 139–152. Line references in the text are to this edition.

163. Samuel Rawson Gardiner, ed., *The Constitutional Documents of the Puritan Revolution, 1625–1660*, 3rd ed., rev. (Oxford: Oxford University Press, 1979 [1889]), 83.

164. Cf. Sharpe's discussion of *Coelum Britannicum* in *Criticism and Compliment*, 197. As Sharpe notes, Momus does deliver a speech in the bombasticating style of a royal proclamation, and this indeed (as everything Momus says) is intended satirically. But the royal reforms he alludes to in this speech (a tightening of court regulations and residency requirements for the gentry; restrictions on tobacco and alehouses) are "criticized" only in the context of a god of anarchy alarmed by the imposition of order and the restraint of vice. For the rest, "compliment" is still reserved for the court, and "criticism" for the parliamentary lawyers who dare to question royal authority.

165. Orgel, *The Illusion of Power*, 83.

166. Quoted in Barish, *The Antitheatrical Prejudice*, 85. On Prynne's career see William M. Lamont, *Marginal Prynne, 1600–1669* (London: Routledge and Kegan Paul; Toronto: University of Toronto Press, 1963).

167. Bulstrode Whitelocke of the Middle Temple related that it "was hinted at in the Court and by them Intimated to the chief of those Societies that [the offering of a masque] would be well taken from them, and some held it the more seasonable, because this their action would manifest the difference of their opinion, from Mr Prynne's new learning, and serve to confute his *Histrio Mastix* against enterludes."

Stephen Orgel and Roy Strong, *Inigo Jones: The Theater of the Stuart Court*, 2 vols. (Berkeley and Los Angeles: University of California Press, 1973), 2: 539. The cost of the production exceeded £20,000, including a second performance at the Merchant Taylors Hall following that at the Banqueting House "requested" by the Queen. This was vastly more expensive than any other Stuart masque production, and it amounted to a collective fine on the London legal profession. Cf. the discussion in Raffield, *Images and Cultures of Law in Early Modern England*, op. cit., 213–219.

168. *James Shirley* (London: T. Fisher Unwin; New York: Charles Scribner's Sons, n.d. [The Mermaid Series]), 455. All subsequent references in the text are by page numbers.

169. Sharpe, *Criticism and Compliment*, 221; Martin Butler, "Politics and the Masque: *The Triumph of Peace*," *The Seventeenth Century* 2 (1987): 117–141, at 133.

170. See the discussion in Stephen Kogan, *The Hieroglyphic King: Wisdom and Idolatry in the Seventeenth Century*, (Rutherford, NJ: Fairleigh Dickinson University Press; Cranbury, NJ: Associated University Presses, 1986), 142–144.

171. Sharpe offers the most extreme comment on the entire masque: "*The Triumph of Peace* subverts the form of the masque—from the initial procession to the intrusion of the carpenter and painter" (220).

172. Butler, "Politics and the Masque," 129.

173. Justices were ordered to give quarterly reports on alehouses, feared by authorities as a source of vice, disorder, and sedition, in the 1631 *Book of Orders*: Peter Clark, "The Alehouse and the Alternative Society," in D. L. Pennington and Keith Thomas, eds., *Puritans and Revolutionaries: Essays in Seventeenth-Century History Presented to Christopher Hill* (Oxford: Oxford University Press, 1978), 47–72; Sharpe, *The Personal Rule of Charles I*, 482–485, and references cited there.

174. In Philip Massinger's *A New Way to Pay Old Debts*. See R. H. Ball, *The Amazing Career of Sir Giles Overreach* (Princeton: Princeton University Press, 1939); Zaller, *The Parliament of 1621*; Russell, *PEP*; Nancy S. Leonard, "Overreach at Bay: Massinger's *A New Way to Pay Old Debts*," in Douglas Howard, ed., *Philip Massinger: A Critical Reassessment* (Cambridge: Cambridge University Press, 1985); Tricomi, *Anticourt Drama*.

175. Bulstrode Whitelocke, *Memorials of English Affairs*, 4 vols. (Oxford: Oxford University Press, 1853), 1: 18–21; Sharpe, *Criticism and Compliment*, 221–222. Cf. Parry, whose comments (*The Golden Age Restor'd*, 193) emphasize the blurring of criticism by both the form and the occasion of the masque. For background on the production of the masque, see T. Orbison, "The Middle Temple Documents Relating to James Shirley's *Triumph of Peace*," *Malone Society Collections* 12 (1983): 31–84, and Lawrence Venuti, "The Politics of Allusion: The Gentry and Shirley's *Triumph of Peace*," *ELR* 16 (1986): 182–205.

176. W. Knowler, ed., *Strafforde's Letters and Dispatches*, 2 vols. (London, 1739), 1: 177. The Inns were not the only rival centers of wealth to the crown; on the diminishing importance of the court as a center of culture and patronage in London, see R. Malcolm Smuts, *Culture and Power in England, 1585–1685* (New York: St. Martin's Press, 1999), 88, 140.

177. George Parfit, ed., *The Plays of Cyril Tourneur* (Cambridge: Cambridge University Press, 1978). All line references are to this edition. The attribution of this play remains shaky, as Parfit notes (xii–xvii), but for our purposes the text is more important than the auhor, and the name "Tourneur" will do as well as that of Middleton, the most frequently proposed alternative, or of Anonymous.

178. Kenneth Muir, ed., *Thomas Middleton: Three Plays* (London: Dent; Totowa: Rowman and Littlefield, 1975). All line references are to this edition.

179. Elizabeth Hamilton, *Henrietta Maria* (New York: Coward, McCann, and Geoghan, 1976), 142–158; Erica Veevers, *Images of Love and Religion: Queen Henrietta Maria and Court Entertainments* (Cambridge: Cambridge University Press, 1989); Caroline Hibbard, *Charles I and the Popish Plot*, op. cit.

180. Butler, *Theatre and Crisis*, 85. Charles in fact took an active hand in censoring the public theater, as his famous suppression of the lines of Massinger's now-lost *The*

King and the Subject, with their Ricardian allusion to blank charters, indicates. Laud, too, demonstrated his impatience with the public theater, especially as attacks on him grew, and there is some evidence that he was privately scandalized by the masques. See Margot Heinemann, *Puritanism and Theatre: Thomas Middleton and Opposition Drama under the Early Stuarts* (Cambridge: Cambridge University Press, 1980), 220–221, 231.

181. For a particular case study — Middleton's *A Game at Chess* — see Limon, *Dangerous Matter*, op. cit.

182. For a cross–cultural comparison, see Walter Cohen, *Drama of a Nation: Public Theater in Renaissance England and Spain* (Ithaca: Cornell University Press, 1985).

183. Smuts, *Court Culture*, 272.

184. "The King's Answer to the XIX Propositions," in Rushworth, ed., 5: 728–732.

185. Butler, *Theatre and Crisis*, 134.

186. Ibid., Chapter 6.

Chapter 6: The Discourse of Parliament

1. A. F. Pollard, *The Evolution of Parliament* (New York: Russell and Russell, 1964 [1920]), 129; David L. Smith, *The Stuart Parliaments 1603–1689* (London: Edward Arnold, 1999), 6.

2. *CJ* 1: 660.

3. *Letters and Papers, Foreign and Domestic, Henry VIII*, 6: 1381.

4. G. R. Elton, *Reform and Renewal: Thomas Cromwell and the Common Weal* (Cambridge: Cambridge University Press, 1973), 77, 81. Elton's comment in this context that the distinction between private and public acts "is one of the more enduring problems of parliamentary historians" is also pertinent (83).

5. Notably Ian Archer, "The London Lobbies in the Later Sixteenth Century," *HJ* 31 (1988): 17–44, and the several articles by David Dean: "Public or Private? London, Leather and Legislation in Elizabethan England," ibid., 525–548; "London Lobbies and Parliament: The Case of Brewers and Coopers in the Parliament of 1593," *PH* 8 (1989): 341–365; "Parliament and Locality," in D. M. Dean and N. L. Jones, *The Parliaments of Elizabethan England* (Oxford: Basil Blackwell, 1990), 139–162; "Pressure Groups and Lobbies in Elizabethan and Early Jacobean Parliaments," *Parliaments, Estates, and Representation* 11 (1991): 139–152.

6. Paul Birdsall, "'Non Obstante': A Study of the Dispensing Power of English Kings," in Carl Wittke, ed., *Essays in History and Political Theory in Honor of Charles H. McIlwain* (Cambridge: Harvard University Press, 1936), 37–76.

7. McIlwain, ed., *PWJ*, 309.

8. Ibid.

9. Elton, ed., *TC*, 270.

10. Ibid.

11. On their experience in early Stuart parliaments, see David Harris Willson, *Privy Councillors in the House of Commons, 1604–1629* (Minneapolis: University of Minnesota Press, 1940); cf. Russell, *PEP*, passim. On the Elizabethan councillors, see particularly the discussions in J. E. Neale, *The Elizabethan House of Commons* (New Haven: Yale University Press, 1950), and G. R. Elton, *The Parliament of England, 1559–1581* (Cambridge: Cambridge University Press, 1986). On the more general management of business in the Commons by the crown, see the essays by M. A. R. Graves, "The Management of the Elizabethan House of Commons: The Council's 'Men of Business,'" *PH* 2 (1983): 11–38; "The Common Lawyers and the Privy Council's Men-of-Business, 1584–1601," *PH* 8 (1989): 189–215; and "Managing Elizabethan Parliaments," in Dean and Jones, *The Parliaments of Elizabethan England*, 37–63. Cf. Patrick Collinson, "Puritans, Men of Business and Elizabethan Parliaments," *PH* 7 (1988): 187–211, and D. M. Loades, "Politics and the 'Men of Business' in the Tudor Parliaments," *PH* 12 (1993): 73–77.

12. Vernon F. Snow, *Parliament in Elizabethan England: John Hooker's Order and Usage* (New Haven: Yale University Press, 1977), 165–167; Smith, *De Republica Anglorum*, ed. Alston, 53; G. W. Prothero, "The Parliamentary Privilege of Freedom from Arrest and Sir Thomas Shirley's Case, 1604," *EHR* 8 (1893): 733–740; Carl Wittke, "The History of English Parliamentary Privilege," *The Ohio State University Bulletin* 26 (1921): 52–53; J. E. Neale, "The Commons' Privilege of Free Speech in Parliament," in R. W. Seton-Watson, ed., *Tudor Studies* (London: Longmans, Green, 1924), 257–286; A. S. Turberville, "The 'Protection' of Servants and Members of Parliament," *EHR* 42 (1927): 590–600; Johann P. Sommerville, "Parliament, Privilege, and the Liberties of the Subject," in J. H. Hexter, ed., *The Making of Modern Freedom, Vol. 1: Parliament and Liberty from the Reign of Elizabeth to the English Civil War* (Stanford: Stanford University Press, 1992), 56–84, 286–290; David Colclough, *Freedom of Speech in Early Stuart England* (Cambridge: Cambridge University Press, 2005), 120–195.

13. *Ad tractandum et consentiendum pro quibusdam arduis et urgentibus negotiis statum et defensionem regni et ecclesiae Anglicanae tangentibus.*

14. Smith, *The Stuart Parliaments*, 5–6, 9; Michael A. R. Graves, *The Tudor Parliaments: Crown, Lords and Commons,1485–1603* (London and New York: Longman, 1985), 159–160; Jennifer Loach, *Parliament under the Tudors* (Oxford: The Clarendon Press, 1991), 3–4.

15. McIlwain, ed., *PWJ*, 287, 288.

16. Ibid., 289.

17. Snow, *Parliament in Elizabethan England*, 145. Hooker, subsequently one of the editors of the 1587 edition of Holinshed, was Chamberlain of Exeter at the time of composing his tract, and had been MP for Exeter in the Parliament of 1571.

18. BL Cottonian MS. Cleopatra E. VI, fol. 274 (*Letters and Papers . . . Henry VIII*, 5: 721), quoted in Lehmberg, *The Reformation Parliament*, 135.

19. Snow, 145–146. Lord Keeper Puckering told Parliament in 1593 that part of Elizabeth's care for her people had been that she "hath evermore been most loth to call for the assembly of her people in parliament and hath done the same but rarely" (Neale, *The Elizabethan House of Commons*, 381).

20. Ibid.; see also Derek Hirst, *The Representative of the People? Voters and Voting in England under the Early Stuarts* (Cambridge: Cambridge University Press, 1975); John K. Gruenfelder, *Influence in Early Stuart Elections, 1604–1640* (Columbus: Ohio State University Press, 1981); Mark Kishlansky, *Parliamentary Selection* (Cambridge: Cambridge University Press, 1986); Chris R. Kyle, ed., *Parliament, Politics and Elections, 1604–1648* (Cambridge: Cambridge University Press for the Royal Historical Society [Camden Society, 5th ser., vol. 17], 2001).

21. R. W. K. Hinton, "The Decline of Parliamentary Government under Elizabeth I and the Early Stuarts," *Cambridge Historical Journal* 13 (1957): 116–132; Conrad Russell, "Parliamentary History in Perspective, 1604–1629," *History* 61 (1976): 1–27; Kevin Sharpe, "Parliamentary History 1603–1629: In or Out of Perspective?" in Sharpe, ed., *Faction and Parliament*, 1–42.

22. Edward Hall, *Hall's Chronicle* (London, 1889), 784–785, cited in Lehmberg, *The Reformation Parliament*, 140–141.

23. G. Huehns, ed., *Clarendon: Selections from the History of the Rebellion and The Life of Himself* (Oxford: Oxford University Press, 1978 [1935]), 126.

24. Zaller, *The Parliament of 1621*, 137; G. A. Harrison, "Parliaments and Sessions: The Case of 1621," *PH* 12 (1993): 19–28.

25. Even though the power to control its sitting was in the Long Parliament's hands by May 1641, individual members had no more idea than before how long their service would be, and even by midwinter many were restive; few had been perspicuous enough to make long-term housing arrangements in London. See Anthony Fletcher, *The Outbreak of the English Civil War* (London: Edward Arnold, 1985 [corrected edition]), 25.

26. Cited in Conrad Russell, "English Parliaments 1593–1606: One Epoch or Two?" in Dean and Jones, eds., *The Parliaments of Elizabethan England*, 193–213, at 207.

27. Ibid.

28. J. R. Tanner, *Constitutional Documents of the Reign of James I, 1603–1625* (Cambridge: Cambridge University Press, 1961 [1930]), 217–230, at 222. See below, 773 nn23, 26, 29; 774 nn36, 37, 49; 776 nn73, 74; 782 n140.

29. Lehmberg, *The Reformation Parliament*, 253.

30. Elton, ed., *TC*, 344. Elton has discussed the making of the act in detail in "The Evolution of a Reformation Statute," *EHR* 64 (1949): 174–197; cf. Lehmberg's discussion in *The Reformation Parliament*, 163–169, and John Guy's account of the sources of the preamble in Fox and Guy, eds., *Reassessing the Henrician Age*, 151–178.

31. G. R. Elton, "*Lex Terrae Victae*: The Triumph of Parliamentary Common Law in the Sixteenth Century," in Dean and Jones, eds., *The Parliaments of Elizabethan England*, 15–36, at 20–21.

32. Guy, in Fox and Guy, op. cit.

33. Elton, ed., *TC*, 345.

34. Ibid., 351; 352.

35. Ibid., 355.

36. Snow, 134.

37. Lehmberg, *The Reformation Parliament*, 209–211, 240–242; W. Llewelyn Williams, "The Union of England and Wales," *Transactions of the Honorable Society of Cymmrodorion*, 1907–1908, 47–117; William Rees, "The Union of England and Wales," ibid., 27–100.

38. R. B. Merriman, *The Life and Letters of Thomas Cromwell*, 2 vols. (Oxford: The Clarendon Press, 1902), 1: 410.

39. G. R. Elton, "Henry VIII's Act of Proclamations," *EHR* 75 (1960): 208–222, at 220–221.

40. Elton, "Henry VIII's Act of Proclamations," 208–209, summarizes the Whiggish literature.

41. E. R. Adair, "The Statute of Proclamations," *EHR* 32 (1917): 34–46, at 45; Elton, 220; Lehmberg, *The Later Parliaments of Henry VIII*, op. cit., 79.

42. Merriman, op. cit.

43. Adair, 35.

44. Lehmberg, *The Later Parliaments*, 82.

45. James Arthur Miller, ed., *The Letters of Stephen Gardiner* (New York: The Macmillan Co.; Cambridge: Cambridge University Press, 1933), 391; R. W. Heinze, "The Enforcement of Royal Proclamations under the Provisions of the Statute of Proclamations, 1539–1547," in A. J. Slavin, ed., *Tudor Men and Institutions* (Baton Rouge: University of Louisiana Press, 1972): 205–231.

46. Lehmberg, *The Later Parliaments*, 68–74; Glyn Redworth, "A Study in the Formulation of Policy: The Genesis and Evolution of the Act of Six Articles," *JEH* 37 (1986): 42–67; Diarmaid MacCulloch, *Thomas Cranmer: A Life* (New Haven: Yale University Press, 1996), 237–258.

47. This is the full text of Article II; cited in M. L. Bush, "The Act of Proclamations: A Reinterpretation," *AJLH* 27 (1983): 33–53, at 53.

48. MacCullough, op. cit., 244.

49. Bush, 34–35, 48–49.

50. Ibid., 45, 46.

51. Miller, ed., *Gardiner Letters*, 391.

52. Elton, "The Statute of Proclamations," 218.

53. Lehmberg, *The Later Parliaments*, 65–66.

54. Aylmer, *An Haborowe for faithfull and true Subiectes*, sig. H3. As Wilbur K. Jordan pointed out, the lapse of the Statute in 1547 was followed not by a less but a more aggressive use of proclamations under Protector Somerset: "The great majority of them . . . created law at least for the time specified and possessed a kind of legislative character which appears in this reign to have been questioned neither by Parliament nor the courts" (W. K. Jordan, *Edward VI: The Young King. The Protectorship of the Duke of Somerset* [Cambridge: The Belknap Press of Harvard University Press, 1971]), 349.

The Act of 5 and 6 Edward VI, c. 7 actually permitted its repeal and restitution by proclamation, an error not repeated: a proviso in 1586 to the bill to confirm the Oath of Association that would have given Elizabeth power to repeal it by proclamation was rejected as "a dangerous precedent" (Neale, *Elizabeth and Her Parliaments, 1584–1601*, 53).

55. Bush, 51; Elton, "The Statute of Proclamations," 218, 220.

56. Cited in Merriman, *Life and Letters of Thomas Cromwell*, 125n. Merriman himself rejects this interpretation, aligning himself with the view that Cromwell's real aim in the bill "was not to legalize and limit, but to legalize and confirm the power of the Crown." This too is Whiggish, of course; it would not have occurred to either Henry or Cromwell that any royal prerogative needed "legalizing" as such.

57. See above, n. 10.

58. For a vigorous critique of the prevailing orthodoxy and its new historicist out-riders—modified but not in essence challenged by some more recent scholarship—see James Holstun, *Ehud's Dagger: Class Struggle in the English Revolution* (London and New York: Verso, 2000).

59. M. A. R. Graves, "Managing Elizabethan Parliaments," in Dean and Jones, 41.

60. Graves, 50–51; Zaller, *The Parliament of 1621*, chapter II; White, *Sir Edward Coke and the Grievances of the Commonwealth*.

61. Sir Simonds D'Ewes, ed., *The Journals of All the Parliaments During the Reign of Queen Elizabeth* (London, 1682), 633; P. W. Hasler, ed., *The History of Parliament: The House of Commons, 1558–1603* (Leicester: University of Leicester Press, 1981), s.v. Martin; Zaller, 161. For Martin's subsequent career see *BDBR* 2: 221–222, and my article in the *ODNB*. For Hele's subsequent disgrace in Star Chamber, see James S. Cockburn, "The Spoils of Law: The Trial of Sir John Hele, 1604," in Delloyd J. Guth and John W. McKenna, eds., *Tudor Rule and Revolution: Essays for G. R. Elton from His American Friends* (Cambridge: Cambridge University Press, 1982), 309–343.

62. All quotations are from T. E. Hartley, ed., *Proceedings in the Parliaments of Elizabeth. Volume I: 1558–1581* (Leicester: University of Leicester Press, 1981), 225–231.

63. Dean and Jones, 3–4. For Atkins' career, see Neale, *The Elizabethan House of Commons*, 274–281.

64. Hartley, ed., *PPE*, 230; Snow, 42–45.

65. Ellesmere reported with disgust the "popular" speech of Sir John Hare, Clerk of the Court of Wards and member for Morpeth in 1607: "It was said by one of them (a man of great livelihood and ability, and holding a good and gainful place under his Majesty), that they came to deliver grief and sorrow, that the times past were golden days, and the late time a golden time . . . but all was [now] worse and worse . . . [and] it was only the profession of the Gospel which contained and stayed the people" (Foster, ed., *PP 1610* 1: 278).

66. This was true of Henry's final statement of doctrine, the *King's Book* of 1543, although it was technically issued in his own name. *The Homilies of 1547*, as Franklin Le Van Baumer pointed out in *The Early Theory of Tudor Kingship* (New York: Russell and Russell, 1966 [1940], 58), bore the authorization of Edward VI, Protector Somerset, and the Privy Council alone, but the Prayer Book of 1549 was issued solely by Parliament (Jennifer Loach, *Edward VI* [New Haven: Yale University Press, 1999], 47), and subsequent liturgical changes were enacted or confirmed through Parliament.

67. Michael A. R. Graves, *Elizabethan Parliaments 1559–1601*, 2d ed. (Harlow, Essex: Addison Wesley Longman, 1996 [1987]), 40.

68. The first *Admonition* was condemned by proclamation, and all copies ordered to be surrendered (Hughes and Larkin, eds., *Tudor Royal Proclamations*, 2: 375–376); its authors, Field and Wilcox, were imprisoned. The second *Admonition* prompted an official government response, ordered from Whitgift by Archbishop Parker. For a recent discussion, see Michael A. R. Graves, *Thomas Norton: The Parliament Man* (Oxford, and Cambridge, MA: Blackwell, 1994), 299–305.

69. *CJ* 1: 326, 348.

70. Notestein (*The House of Commons, 1604–1610*, 42) suggests that the act referred to is 25 Henry VIII, c. 22.

71. Foster, *PP 1610* 1: 124. The text of the Commons' bill (BL Petyt MSS. 537/18, fols. 101–101v) is given in 124–125n2.

72. Ibid., 125–127.

73. Elton, ed., *TC*, 170–171; idem, *The Parliament of England, 1559–1581*, 272–273; Heinze, "Proclamations and Parliamentary Protest," 239–240. On the contentious session of 1601, see Neale, *Elizabeth and Her Parliaments, 1584–1601*, 369–432, especially 376–388, and David Harris Sacks, "The Countervailing of Benefits: Monopoly, Liberty, and Benevolence in Elizabethan England," in Dale Hoak, ed., *Tudor Political Culture* (Cambridge: Cambridge University Press, 1995), 272–291.

74. *SR* 4: 800; David Dean, *Lawmaking and Society in Late Elizabethan England: The Parliament of England, 1584–1601* (Cambridge: Cambridge University Press, 1996), 210.

75. Proclamations were also used to extend the life of time-specific statutes in the absence of a Parliament to continue them. This, again, was an issue in which the Privy Council might well regard itself as providing a service while Parliament might view it as usurping a privilege. Proclamations could err in citing continuances, as did one in 1562 concerning a prohibition against exporting horses (Elton, *The Parliament of England*, 141n56).

76. *A Treatise of the Office of a Councellor and Principall Secretarie to her Ma[jes]tie*, in Conyers Read, *Mr Secretary Walsingham and the Policy of Queen Elizabeth*, 3 vols. (Oxford: The Clarendon Press, 1925), 1: 423–443, at 439.

77. *Register of the Privy Council of Scotland*, 1st ser., Vol. VII (1604–07), 17; Andrew W. Nicholls, *The Jacobean Union: A Reconsideration of British Civil Policies under the Early Stuarts* (Westport, CT: Greenwood Press, 1999).

78. Samuel Thorne, ed., *A Discourse upon the Exposition and Understanding of Statutes with Sir Thomas Egerton's Additions* (San Marino, CA: Huntington Library, 1942).

79. Foster, *PP 1610* 2: 22 and n49.

80. *CJ* 1: 163, 168, 152, 345; David Harris Willson, ed., *The Parliamentary Diary of Robert Bowyer, 1606–1607* (Minneapolis: University of Minnesota Press, 1931), 265–266.

81. *A Booke of Proclamations, published since the beginning of his Majesty's happy reign over England, etc. until this present moneth of Febr. 3. Anno Dom. 1609* (London, 1609).

82. The phrase appears in a draft document under the heading of "A brief of petitions" (Harl. MS. 6842, fol. 146). The folio is reproduced in Esther S. Cope, "Parliaments and Proclamations 1604–1629" (Ph.D. Diss., Bryn Mawr College, 1968), 75–77.

83. Foster, ed., *PP 1610* 2: 184, 227–228.

84. Ibid., 194–195.

85. Ibid., 1: 130; 2: 253, 273; Samuel Rawson Gardiner, ed., *Parliamentary Debates in 1610* (London: Camden Society, 1st ser., 81, 1861), 123.

86. Foster, ed., *PP 1610* 2: 259.

87. Ibid.; Cowell's *The Interpreter* is the book particularly glanced at.

88. Ibid., 2: 260.

89. *LJ* 2: 659.

90. Harl. MS. 1576, fol. 18; quoted in Cope, op. cit., 78.

91. Edward Nicholas, ed., *Proceedings and Debates in the House of Commons in 1620 and 1621*, 2 vols. (Oxford, 1766), 1: 32; *CD 1621* 3: 324. Cope notes that Alford kept his own "book of proclamations," an annotated collection that dated from Henry VIII's time together with complaints about them (now Harl. MSS. 6800, 6803, 6811, and 7614). John Cramsie has latterly called attention to this important cache (*Kingship and Crown Finance under James VI and I* (Woodbridge, Suffolk, and Rochester, NY: The Royal Historical Society and Boydell Press, 2002), 170n127.

92. Notestein et al., eds., *CD 1621* 2: 120.

93. Ibid., 5: 87.

94. Robert C. Johnson, Mary Frear Keeler, Maija Jansson Cole, and William B. Bidwell, eds., *Proceedings in Parliament 1628*, 6 vols. (New Haven: Yale University Press, 1977–1983), 2: 90. Coryton had resisted the Forced Loan in 1627 and was de-

prived of the vice wardenship of the Stannaries in consequence; the Court attempted to prevent his election to Parliament in 1628 and imprisoned him after the session of 1629 (Russell, *PEP*, 14, 17–18).

95. Johnson et al. eds., *CD 1628* 3: 107, 110.

96. Ibid., 243–244; cf. 258, 264, 270–271, 275. The motion to detach the issue of proclamations from the Remonstrance was made by Sir John Eliot. Sir Thomas Hoby opposed him, but Sir Nathaniel Rich supported Eliot, suggesting that only "new innovations" (i.e., those that could be tied specifically to Buckingham) be included in it.

97. Lehmberg, *The Later Parliaments of Henry VIII*, 72–74; Loach, *Parliament under the Tudors*, 79–80.

98. On the Lords' debate, see MacCulloch, *Thomas Cranmer*, 396–398, 404–408; see also the comments in his *Tudor Church Militant: Edward VI and the Protestant Reformation* (London: Allan Lane / Penguin Press, 1999), 87–89.

99. On the extreme difficulty of reconstructing church finances and recovering even a portion of the church's former treasure, see R. H. Pogson, "Revival and Reform in Mary Tudor's Church: A Question of Money," *JEH* 25 (1974): 249–265, and Thomas F. Mayer, *Reginald Pole: Prince and Prophet* (Cambridge: Cambridge University Press, 2000), chapter 7.

100. MacCulloch, *Tudor Church Militant*; Jennifer Loach, *Parliament and the Crown in the Reign of Mary Tudor* (Oxford: The Clarendon Press, 1986); William P. Haugaard, *Elizabeth and the English Reformation: The Struggle for a Stable Settlement* (Cambridge: Cambridge University Press, 1968).

101. Edward Arber, ed. (New York: AMS Press, 1967 [1878]). All page references are in the text.

102. New York: Da Capo, 1972 (1559). All page references are in the text. Cf. the discussion of these tracts in A. N. McLaren, *Political Culture in the Reign of Elizabeth I: Queen and Commonwealth, 1558–1585* (Cambridge: Cambridge University Press, 1999), 49–69.

103. On the context of the *Blast* and its subsequent polemics, see Patricia-Ann Lee, "'a bodye politique to governe': Aylmer, Knox, and the Debate on Queenship," *Historian* 52 (1990): 242–261; Jane E. Dawson, "The Two John Knoxes: England, Scotland, and the 1558 Tracts," *JEH* 42 (1991): 555–576; Robert M. Healey, "Waiting for Deborah: John Knox and Four Queens," *SCJ* 25 (1994): 371–386; Amanda Shephard, *Gender and Authority in Sixteenth-Century England: The Knox Debate* (Keele: Keele University Press, 1994). Cf. Henry Howard's unpublished treatise, "A Dutiful Defense" (I owe this reference to Richard L. Greaves). For a more general discussion of the problems of female rule in the sixteenth century, see Paula L. Scalinge, "The Scepter or Distaff: The Question of Female Sovereignty, 1516–1607," *Historian* 41 (1978–1979): 59–75, and Constance Jordan, "Women's Rule in Sixteenth-Century British Political Thought," *RQ* 40 (1987): 421–431. On the unease of the courtier poets with female rule under Elizabeth, see Richard A. McCabe, *Spenser's Monstrous Regiment: Elizabeth, Ireland, and the Poetics of Difference* (Oxford: Oxford University Press, 2002). Julia Walker has collected a trove of misogyny in her *Dissing Elizabeth: Negative Representations of Gloriana* (Durham, NC, and London: Duke University Press, 1998). For the perspective of Elizabeth herself, see Carole Levin, Jo Eldridge Charney, and Debra Garrett-Graves, eds., *Elizabeth I: Always Her Own Free Woman* (Aldershot, Hants.; Burlington, Vt.: Ashgate, 2003).

104. The reference was to the loss of Calais in 1558, and with it of England's last Continental foothold. This had providentialist as well as imperial overtones; if the loss of Calais was a punishment for the Marian apostasy, it also cut England off from the Reformed party in Europe. This in turn colored the question of a renewed English presence on the Continent through alliance with or dominion over the United Provinces from the 1580s on. For a thorough discussion, see S. L. Adams, "The Protestant Cause: Religious Alliance with West European Calvinist Communities as a Political Issue in England, 1585–1630" (D. Phil. Thesis, Oxford University, 1973).

105. The legend of Anne as a godly champion and martyr, well established by Aylmer's time, was fixed by Foxe, who declared in the *Actes and Monuments* that "What a zealous defender she was of Christ's gospel all the world doth know, and her acts do and will declare to the world's end" (5: 175). Modern historians have not generally questioned this image; thus E. W. Ives, a recent biographer, concludes that "Anne's central conviction was of the overwhelming importance of the Bible," and characterizes her "brand of reform" as essentially "evangelical" (*Anne Boleyn* [Oxford: Basil Blackwell, 1986], 314); see, too, his "Anne Boleyn and the early Reformation in England: The Contemporary Evidence," *HJ* 37 (1994): 389–400. Retha M. Warnicke, however, challenges Anne's commitment to Protestantism in her *The Rise and Fall of Anne Boleyn: Family Politics at the Court of Henry VIII* (Cambridge: Cambridge University Press, 1993 [1991]), 151–162; cf. Margaret Dowling, "Anne Boleyn and Reform," *JEH* 35 (1984): 30–46.

106. John Ponet, *A Shorte Treatise of politike power, and of the true Obedience which subiectes owe to kynges and other ciuil Gouernours, with an Exhortacion to all true naturall Englishe men* (Strassburg[?], 1556), D7; Christopher Goodman, *How Superior Powers oght to be obeyd of their subiects; and Wherin they may lawfully by Gods Worde be disobeyed and resisted* (Geneva, 1558). On Ponet, see Barbara Peardon, "The Politics of Polemic: John Ponet's *Short Treatise of Politic Power* and Contemporary Circumstances, 1553–1556," *JBS* 20 (1981): 35–49, and Barrett L. Beer, "John Ponet's *Shorte Treatise of Politike Power* reassessed," *SCJ* 21 (1990): 373–383. For a general overview, see Donald R. Kelley, "Ideas of Resistance Before Elizabeth," in Gordon J. Schochet, ed., *Law, Liberty, and the Settlement of Regimes: Proceedings of the Folger Institute Center for the History of Political Thought, Vol. 2* (Washington, D.C.: Folger Shakespeare Library, 1990), 5–28.

107. "An Acte declaring that the Regall Power of the Realm is in the Quenes Majestie as fully and absolutely as euer it was in any of her moste noble Progenitours Kinges of this Realme," HLRO, Original Acts, 1 Mary, sess. 3, 1.

108. William Fleetwood, "Itinerarium at Windsor" (1575), BL Harl. MS. 6234, fols. 20–23v, partially printed in J. D. Alsop, "The Act for the Queen's Regal Power, 1554," *PH* 13 (1994): 261–276, at 275.

109. Ibid., 270.

110. Hartley, ed., *PPE* 1: 34–35. On Bacon, see Robert Tittler, *Nicholas Bacon: The Making of a Tudor Statesman* (Athens, OH: Ohio State University Press, 1976), and Patrick Collinson, "Sir Nicholas Bacon and the Elizabethan *via media*," *HJ* 23 (1980): 255–273. Bacon must have been fond of his description of the "straight line," "pillar," and "buttress," because he recycled the identical passage in his speech opening Parliament in 1571.

111. John Bruce, ed. *Correspondence of Matthew Parker* (Cambridge: Parker Society 1853), 49–62.

112. For criticism of Neale's general thesis, see, e. g., Loach, *Parliament and the Crown in the Reign of Mary Tudor*, chapter 10, and, for specific comments on the "opposition" in the Parliament of 1555, 132–133. Cf. Norman L. Jones, *Faith by Statute: Parliament and the Settlement of Religion 1559* (London: Royal Historical Society, 1982), 186–189; G. R. Elton, "Parliament," in Christopher Haigh, ed., *The Reign of Elizabeth I* (Athens: University of Georgia Press, 1985), 79–100, at 79–84; idem, *The Parliament of England, 1559–1581*, 350–355; and, for a general summary of the debate, Michael A. R. Graves, *Elizabethan Parliaments, 1559–1601*, op. cit., 19–24.

113. Jones, *Faith by Statute*, 70ff.

114. 1 Eliz. I, c. 1, *SR* 4: 351–352. For the three bills, see Jones, 89–144; cf. Neale, "The Elizabethan Acts of Supremacy and Uniformity," *EHR* 65 (1950): 304–332; idem, *Elizabeth and Her Parliaments, 1559–1581*, 51–84; A. G. Dickens, *The English Reformation*, 2d ed. (London: Batsford, 1989 [1964]).

115. Margaret Bowker, "The Supremacy and the Episcopate: the Struggle for Control, 1534–1540," *HJ* 18 (1975): 227–243.

116. *Correspondence of Matthew Parker*, 454.

117. William Nicholson, ed., *The Remains of Edmund Grindal* (Cambridge: Cambridge University Press, 1843), 57.

118. Charles Hardwick, *A History of the Articles of Religion*, 3rd ed. (London, 1895 [1859]); Haugaard, 253–255.

119. *Correspondence of Matthew Parker*, 454.

120. Neale, 166–170.

121. On the self-conception of the bishops in the Elizabethan and Jacobean periods, see Collinson, *The Religion of Protestants*, chapters 1 and 2.

122. Hartley, ed., *PPE* 1: 432. Wentworth had made a note of the episode "two or three yeares" earlier (ibid., 436) in anticipation of the next session, and that in turn as part of the lengthy and famous speech he delivered on 8 February 1576; see below.

123. *CJ* 1: 87.

124. *An Admonition to Parliament*, in W. H. Frere and C. E. Douglas, eds., *Puritan Manifestoes: A Study of the Origin of the Puritan Revolt* (New York: Burt Franklin, 1972 [1907]), 3. Subsequent references are in the text. For the general background, see D. J. McGinn, *The Admonition Controversy* (New Brunswick: Rutgers University Press, 1949). On Field, see Patrick Collinson, "John Field and Elizabethan Puritanism," in S. T. Bindoff, Joel Hurstfield, and C. H. Williams, eds., *Elizabethan Government and Society: Essays Presented to Sir John Neale* (University of London: The Athlone Press, 1961), 127–162, reprinted in his *Godly People: Essays in Protestantism and Puritanism* (London: The Hambledon Press, 1983), 335–370.

125. Collinson, 132; idem, *EPM*, 120.

126. Printed in Frere and Douglas; page references in the text.

127. "The London puritans," remarks Patrick Collinson, "were Grindal's doves . . . or, in brutal modern parlance, his mafia." Field himself was only one of a number of ministers installed personally by Grindal who ran afoul of the hierarchy, and Field himself remembered Grindal's archepiscopate as a halcyon time, its failure to carry out his reform program notwithstanding (Collinson, *Archbishop Grindal*, 169, 287). Sandys, like Grindal, would ignore the Queen's order to suppress prophesying in his diocese of London, though not without support from the Privy Council. Nonetheless, he did not escape godly tongue-lashing in *A friendly caveat to Bishop Sands* (1573).

128. Neale, *Elizabeth I and Her Parliaments, 1559–1581*, 214–215.

129. On Wentworth's background, see J. E. Neale, "Peter Wentworth," *EHR* 39 (1924): 36–54, 175–205, and Hasler, 3: 597–601 (also by Neale). For a more recent view, see Hartley, *Elizabeth's Parliaments*, chapter 7 ("Peter Wentworth Revisited").

130. The speech is in Hartley, ed., *PPE* 1: 425–434.

131. For a thorough discussion, see Peter Lake, *Moderate Puritans and the Anglican Church*, chapter 9, and Nicholas Tyacke, *Anti-Calvinists: The Rise of English Arminianism c. 1590–1640* (Oxford: Oxford University Press, 1987); cf. Peter White, *Predestination, Policy and Polemic: Conflict and Consensus in the English Church from the Reformation to the Civil War* (Cambridge: Cambridge University Press, 1992).

132. On the antecedents of the Nineteen Propositions in Elizabethan Presbyterianism, see Michael Mendle, *Dangerous Positions: Mixed Government, the Estates of the Realm, and the Making of the Answer to the xix propositions* (University, Ala.: University of Alabama Press, 1985), chapter 4.

133. Hartley, ed., *PPE* 1: 430 n45, 476; *CJ* 1: 104.

134. Hartley, ed., *PPE* 1: 452–453.

135. Ibid., 453.

136. For the members of Wentworth's committee, *CJ* 1: 109.

137. Elton, *The Parliament of England, 1559–1581*, 347 n77; cf. Neale, *Elizabeth and Her Parliaments 1559–1581*, 326–329.

138. Hartley, ed., *PPE* 1: 435–439. The fullest extant manuscript, Inner Temple, Petyt 538/17, fols. 251–256, is a copy in two different hands of a lost original.

139. Cf. Wentworth's formulation of this point in the (undelivered) peroration of his speech: "Thus I have holden yow long with my rude speech, the which since it tendeth wholy with pure consciences to seek the advancement of God's glory, our

honourable soveraygne's safety and to the sure defence of this noble ile of England, and all by mayntaining the liberties of this honourable counsell, the fountayne from whence all these doe spring . . ." (Hartley, ed., *PPE* 1: 436).

140. Ibid., 431–432.

141. On proceedings against Mary in the Parliaments of 1571 and 1572, see Neale, *Elizabeth and Her Parliaments, 1559–1581*, 226ff., 247–290, 299, 303ff. Mary was the chief subject of the latter session, and the principal reason for summoning it.

142. John S. Morrill, "John Lilburne," *BDBR* 2: 186–189, at 186.

143. Sir Thomas More, Speaker in 1523, had been the first to make a formal request for freedom of speech, and it had become part of the Speaker's oration at the beginning of Parliament. See John Neale, "The Commons' Privilege of Free Speech in Parliament," in R. W. Seton-Watson, ed., *Tudor Studies*, op. cit.

144. Hartley, ed., *PPE* 1: 341–342.

145. Ibid., 261–418 passim.; Neale, *Elizabeth and Her Parliaments, 1559–1581*, 241–312.

146. Hartley, ed., *PPE* 1: 326.

147. Ibid., 280, 277. Norton, for one, preferred to stay within the framework of English law in judging Mary: "I thinke it our part to do this punishment upon her for treasons sins her cominge into England, and not for her horrible doinges in Scotlande" (326).

148. Ibid.

149. The Bond, its drafts, and relevant correspondence are in PRO SP 12/173 and 176. The most recent treatments of it are in David Cressey, "Binding the Nation: The Bonds of Association, 1584 and 1696," in Guth and McKenna, eds., *Tudor Rule and Revolution*, 217–234, and Edward Vallance, "Loyal or Rebellious? Protestant Association in England 1584–1696," *The Seventeenth Century* 17 (2002): 1–23.

150. For a discussion, see Neale, *Elizabeth and Her Parliaments, 1584–1601*, principally at 16–18, 33–36, and 51–54, and Stanford E. Lehmberg, *Sir Walter Mildmay and Tudor Government* (Austin: University of Texas Press, 1964), 242–244, 250, 256–257. Cf. the briefer comments in Hartley, *Elizabeth's Parliaments*, 67, 68, 74–75, and the summary discussion in Hartley, ed., *PPE* 2: 13. Patrick Collinson also rehearses the episode in "The Monarchical Republic of Queen Elizabeth I," *Godly People*, 48–55. *Pace* Cressy ("Binding the Nation," 225), there is still much work to be done on the parliamentary debates over the Bond. On Burghley's long relationship with the Queen, see Conyers Read's two-volume study, *Mr. Secretary Cecil and Queen Elizabeth* and *Lord Burghley and Queen Elizabeth* (London: Jonathan Cape, 1955, 1960), and Michael A. R. Graves, *Burghley: William Cecil, Lord Burghley* (London and New York: Longman, 1998).

151. Neale, *Elizabeth and Her Parliaments, 1584–1601*, 28.

152. Hartley, ed., *PPE* 2: 252.

153. Neale, *Elizabeth and Her Parliaments, 1584–1601*, 17. If, as Conyers Reads suggests, it was Burghley himself who drafted the face-saving formula that defined the Oath in terms of the Act, then the Queen's advisers may have repented of its harsher consequences. In effect, then, the parliamentary vote was the lifeline that saved them from themselves. Collinson ("Monarchical Republic," 50) quotes a letter from Walsingham to Burghley which seems to support Neale's speculation: "her Majesty would have the matter [of the Bond] carried in such sorte as this course held for her [safety] may seeme to [come more] from the pertyculer care of her well affected subiects then to growe from any publycke directyon" (SP 12/173/88). Collinson opines "that we can substitute for 'her Majesty would' 'we would'." What is on offer here is the even more radical suggestion that Elizabeth's councillors were casually appropriating her name and authority for their own actions even in private correspondence. If this seems strained, however, it is less so than the contrary assumption that the Queen would have encouraged the circulation of a document that consented to Mary's death by lynch law.

154. It was also the case that some of the remoter blood candidates, such as the Earl of Huntington, preferred to let their supporters canvass privately for them. Few

would risk unfavorable odds when opportunity might arise in a situation in which all bets were off.

155. "Monarchical Republic," 54.

156. Huntington Library, MS. EL 1192.

157. The traditional medieval division of estates among *oratores*, *bellatores*, and *laboratores*—those who prayed, those who fought, and those who worked, all under the sovereign eye of monarchy (itself a contested formulation, as the crown's running wars with papal authority and clerical jursidiction demonstrate)—had collapsed with the domestication of the warrior class and its replacement by a service nobility, leaving a bipartite distinction of status (clerical and lay) instead of the tripartite one of function. This left the crown ambiguously situated as a super-estate (having absorbed the military function and created a state church), while at the same time it retained its notional sovereignty over the system as a whole. The "descent" of the monarchy, first into a communitarian trinity (crown, clergy, laity) over which it remained at the same time sovereign and then into a parliamentary one construed as sovereign in itself (in Smith's phrase, the entity that "representeth and hath the power of the whole realme both the head and the bodie," *De Republica Anglorum*, 49), was thus a gradual devolution toward mixed government. The actual principles and features of that government—Fortescue's *dominium politicum et regale*, the Bractonian subordination of power to law, the dispersed authority centers of the political nation—were already long established if continually evolving; but more generalized metaphors govern (and evolve) within a prescribed form too, and the trinitarian metaphor was a powerful way of structuring the perception of early modern society and thereby of affecting its practical performance. In these terms, the at least partial incorporation of the monarchy into a Parliament conceived not merely as an organ of government but, conceptually and authoritatively, as the realm itself, was deeply consequential.

158. D'Ewes, ed., *The Journals of all the Parliaments during the Reign of Queen Elizabeth*, 350.

159. Collinson, "Monarchical Republic," 50.

160. For the speeches of November 3, 1586, see Hartley, ed., *PPE* 2: 214–227 (quotation at 227), and D'Ewes, *Journals*, 408–410; for those of 7 November 1640, Maija Jansson, ed., *Proceedings in the Opening Session of the Long Parliament: House of Commons, Volume 1: 3 November–19 December 1640* (Rochester, NY: University of Rochester Press, 2000), 28–50 passim.

161. Hartley, ed., *PPE* 2: 218; Bodleian Library, Tanner MS. 78. The other conciliar speakers were Sir Christopher Hatton, the Queen's Vice Chamberlain and a leading proponent of the Dutch union; Sir Walter Mildmay, the Chancellor of the Exchequer and the crown's senior spokesman in the House of Commons; and Sir John Wolley, Elizabeth's Latin Secretary. Hartley suggests that "Loveth inseccurety" is a possible reading for "liveth in seccurety," and that "the welth nothinge" may be a mistaken inversion of "nothinge the welth." In any case, Sadler's point is abundantly clear. Neale cites this passage in his summary of the four speeches (*Elizabeth and Her Parliaments, 1584–1601*), 107–109, without, however, remarking on its significance.

162. John Bellamy, *The Tudor Law of Treason: An Introduction* (London: Routledge and Kegan Paul, 1979); on the earlier background, idem, *The Law of Treason in the Later Middle Ages* (Cambridge: Cambridge University Press, 1970). See also G. R. Elton, *Policy and Police* (Cambridge: Cambridge University Press, 1972), especially chapters 6 and 8, and Elton, ed., *TC*, passim.

163. Hartley, ed., *PPE* 2: 228–232 for the entire text of the speech—the only surviving one of the entire debate of November 4 on Mary. The quoted passages are at 232.

164. "Reasons against Mary Queen of Scots delivered to Elizabeth, 12 November 1586." Ibid., 239–243, at 241.

165. For a discussion of this subject and the casuistic literature surrounding it, see David Martin Jones, *Conscience and Allegiance in Seventeenth-Century England: The Political Significance of Oaths and Engagements* (Rochester, NY: University of Rochester Press, 1999).

166. "Job Throckmorton's speech on the Low Countries, 23 February 1587," Hartley, ed., *PPE* 2: 277–289, at 286.

167. Ibid., 300.

168. Ibid., 290–310; Neale, *Elizabeth I and Her Parliaments, 1584–1601,* 166–183.

169. D'Ewes, 410; Hartley, ed., *PPE* 2: 311–319, 332–354; Neale, 146ff.; Collinson, *EPM,* 303–316.

170. Neale, 149.

171. Hartley, ed., *PPE* 2: 318.

172. Ibid., 2: 312, 311, 312.

173. Hartley, *PPE* 2: 320–323 gives both extant versions of the questions. The first, with Wentworth's accompanying oration, propounds eight questions; the second lists ten, but in schematic form and without preface. Neale (*Elizabeth and Her Parliaments, 1584–1601,* 155–156) uses the two versions as complementary, while Hartley (*Elizabeth's Parliaments,* 135ff.) explores the differences in their subject matter and shading. I have preferred the fuller account in BL Cotton MSS. Titus F. I, originally printed in D'Ewes (410–411), supplementing it with the version in BL Landsdowne MS. 105, fol. 182, where a significant distinction appears.

174. Wentworth's last imprisonment was not merely for activity in Parliament but for the publication of a tract dealing with the succession, *A Discourse containing the Author's opinion of the true and lawful successor to her Majesty,* which, as Neale points out, was a statutory crime (*Elizabeth and Her Parliaments, 1584–1601,* 263). For Eliot, see J. N. Ball, "Sir John Eliot and Parliament, 1624–1629," in Sharpe, ed., *Faction and Parliament,* 173–207.

175. Of course, the councillors could supply a visual as opposed to a verbal cue in this instance, particularly since the yea-sayers to a measure were the ones required to rise from their seats and leave the chamber. No doubt it took a certain courage to do so when the councillors sat stolidly in their places. Nonetheless, the principle of one man, one vote applied, so that at least in theory the vote of the lowliest backbencher was equal to that of the greatest minister of state.

176. The Speaker's role is described in Smith, *De Republica Anglorum,* and in Hooker (ed. Snow), *Parliament in Elizabethan England,* 164–171. For modern accounts, see J. E. Neale, *The Elizabethan House of Commons;* Sheila Lambert, "Procedure in the House of Commons in the Early Stuart Period," *EHR* 95 (1980): 753–781, at 774ff.; and David L. Smith, *The Stuart Parliaments,* 68–71 and passim; see also the works cited in Hooker, 164n52. The Speaker's responsibilities included the ceremonial request of the Commons for free speech, free access to the monarch and the House of Lords, freedom from arrests and legal suits during sessions of Parliament (a privilege gradually extended to servants), and the right to correct prejudicial errors and misunderstandings. Perhaps no other function more directly highlighted his role as a "bridge" between crown and Commons.

177. Hartley, ed., *PPE* 1: 312.

178. Ibid., 1: 431.

179. Ibid.

180. Ibid., 2: 313–314.

181. Cf. Elton: "Paul and especially Peter Wentworth have had quite sufficient attention before this to render a lengthy investigation here superfluous" (*The Parliament of England, 1559–1581,* 346).

182. Hartley, ed., *PPE* 1: 213, 202. Thomas Wilson, the Master of Requests, "desired . . . the patience of the House" in a speech on usury in 1571, "first shewinge that in a matter of such waight he could not shortlie speake" (232).

183. Ibid., 204 ("many wordes"); 209 ("a longe speech").

184. Ibid., 237.

185. Patrick Collinson points out that the 40,000–word text on parliamentary supremacy over the church penned in 1584 by Robert Beale, the godly Clerk of the Council (BL Add. MSS. 48,116 [Yelverton Papers, 131], fols. 154–211), is in the form of a speech to the Commons and was presumably intended for actual delivery (*Elizabe-*

than Essays, 81). Neale, who summarizes its contents (*Elizabeth and Her Parliaments, 1584–1601*, 66–68), more cautiously describes it as a "treatise." Perhaps it is best to conceive of it as a speech that morphed into a treatise when it became clear that it was far too long (and dangerous) for utterance. As a draft it doubtless owes something to Wentworth's example, though of course Beale cannot be classed as a "country" speaker in our terms of discussion. His text does show, however, that parliamentary-populist sentiments (as opposed to those of men such as Burghley and Mildmay, for whom Parliament was a tool in their campaign to execute Mary and stabilize the succession) were held with some force even within the inner bureaucratic circle of the court.

186. Hartley, ed., *PPE* 2: 398.

187. Michael Walzer, *The Revolution of the Saints* (Cambridge: Harvard University Press, 1965).

188. Hartley, ed., *PPE* 1: 427 (*Proverbs* 16:14).

189. Ibid., 2: 312. Cf. Peter Mack, *Elizabethan Rhetoric: Theory and Practice* (Cambridge: Cambridge University Press, 2002). Mack remarks of parliamentary disputation that it formed "a deep cultural bulwark against absolutism" (303). In Elizabethan parliaments, where liberty of conscience was so often at issue, it was typically godly conviction that underwrote this; while in early Stuart ones, where matters of property came to the fore, it was an equally intense faith in the common law that did so.

190. Ibid.

191. First by Neale, and, at greater length, in Leland Carlson's *Martin Marprelate, Gentleman: Master Job Throckmorton Laid Open in His Colors* (San Marino, CA: Huntington Library, 1981). If Throckmorton was indeed Martin (a charge brought by contemporaries, and which he denied), his discursive shift from public representative in the House of Commons to pseudonymously scurrilous pamphleteer in the Marprelate tracts would represent the paradigm case of loyalist dissent becoming underground opposition in Elizabethan England.

192. Hartley, ed., *PPE* 3: 17, 30–49; Neale, *Elizabeth and Her Parliaments, 1584–1601*, 267–279; Patrick Collinson, *Elizabethan Essays*, 67–69.

193. Neale, *Elizabeth I and Her Parliaments, 1584–1601*, 60–64; Peter Lake, *Moderate Puritans and the Anglican Church*.

194. Collinson points out that Beale ended his "speech" of 1584 by referring to it as being intended for "the great congregation" (op. cit.; Beale's words refer to *Psalms* 40: 9). For some, at least, Parliament—and particularly the Commons—already appears as a quasi-sacralized body. See below, 700ff.

195. Cited in Jeffrey Goldsworthy, *The Sovereignty of Parliament: History and Philosophy* (Oxford: The Clarendon Press, 1999), 61.

196. Much of that business, both local and personal (communities seeking improvement or relief; companies lobbying for charters and privileges; individuals applying for recovery or changes of legal status), was of course as momentous to those who moved it as great affairs of state were to the commonwealth as a whole, and as contingent on parliamentary action.

197. Royal entries were also occasions of pomp, but they did not involve the attendance of the entire political elite, nor were they necessarily events of political consequence; their symbolic weight was hence lesser.

198. This and succeeding paragraphs are based on Neale, *The Elizabethan House of Commons*; Elizabeth Read Foster, "Staging a Parliament in Early Stuart England," in Peter Clark, Alan G. R. Smith, and Nicholas Tyacke, eds., *The English Commonwealth, 1547–1640: Essays in Politics and Society* (New York: Barnes and Noble, 1979), 129–146; Hartley, ed., *PPE*, passim; David Dean, "Image and Ritual in the Tudor Parliament," in Dale Eugene Hoak, ed., *Tudor Political Culture* (Cambridge: Cambridge University Press, 1995), 243–271; and Henry S. Cobb, "Descriptions of the State Openings of Parliament, 1485–1601," *PH* 18 (1999): 303–315. On Elizabeth's isolation, see Peter Brimacombe, *All the Queen's Men: The World of Elizabeth I* (New York: St. Martin's Press, 2000).

199. Hartley, ed., *PPE* 2: 208–210.

200. In the case of bishops, the royal authority had been nominally shared with the institutional church, but with the Reformation Parliament—or at least its latter sessions—spiritual peers, too, sat solely by virtue of their appointment, or recognition, by the Supreme Head. Bishop Fisher's execution in 1535 had, among other things, served to bring this point home forcibly.

201. Neale, 351, *The Elizabethan House of Commons*. Fleetwood observed the Commons thus when they had reached their own chamber, but doubtless the observation applied *a fortiori* to their sojourn in the Court of Requests.

202. Ibid., 352–353.

203. Hartley (*Elizabeth's Parliaments*, 108) estimates that three-quarters of all Elizabethan bills originated in the Commons, and while private bills amounted to a substantial portion of the legislative product, it is significant that most government bills were introduced in the Commons—an index not only of where the action was but where (despite the Lords' fully coordinate role) the essential element of consent lay. Certainly the Commons jealously guarded their privileges, such as the exclusive right to introduce money bills, and reacted angrily even in cases which concerned the Lords, such as the bill in 1576 to restore Lord Stoughton, when they felt their interests had been slighted (Hartley, ed., *PPE* 1: 457–461 et seq.). They also firmly rejected any attempt to limit their power to initiate legislation, as in the case of the church. Much work has been done on clientage relationships between the Upper House and the Lower, and such relationships were surely important and on occasion critical. The suggestion that the Lords were able to routinely manipulate the Commons through them, or that Parliament is to be seen primarily as a "cockpit" in which conciliar struggles for power were played out, is very wide of the mark. The Council's success in guiding the parliaments of the mid-1580s reflected its unity of purpose and the overwhelming popular sentiment to which it appealed.

Chapter 7: Stuart Parliaments and the Crisis of Legitimacy

1. These events were of course intimately connected. On Henry's boom and bust cycle of warfaring, see Richard Hoyle, "War and Public Finance," in Diarmaid MacCulloch, ed., *The Reign of Henry VIII: Politics, Policy and Piety* (New York: St. Martin's Press, 1995), 75–99, 262–267.

2. Samuel R. Gardiner, *History of England, 1603–1642*, 10 vols.(London: Longmans, Green, 1905), 2: 251. James called the House of Commons "this rotten seed of Egypt" in 1610 (G. P. V. Akrigg, ed., *Letters of King James VI and I* [Berkeley and Los Angeles: University of California Press, 1984], 317).

3. James' view of the Polish state, whose legislature, the *Sjem*, elected its king and whose members each enjoyed a right of veto over all proposed legislation (the *liberum veto*), is not known, but certainly he would not have classed it among the "absolute" monarchies to which he believed himself to belong.

4. Francois Hotman's *Francogallia* (1573), an exposition and close analysis of the French constitution, was a notable exception. Hotman was, of course, concerned to limit the power of the French monarchy.

5. Charles Merbury, *A Briefe Discovrse of Royall Monarchie, as of the Best Common Weale* (New York: Da Capo Press, 1972 [1581]), 7, 40, 43, 44, sig. G3.

6. For a discussion of this event, see Jenny Wormald, "James VI and I, *Basilikon Doron* and *The Trew Law of Free Monarchies*: The Scottish Context and the English Translation," in Linda Levy Peck, ed., *The Mental World of the Jacobean Court* (Cambridge: Cambridge University Press, 1991), 36–54.

7. Johann P. Sommerville, ed., *King James VI and I: Political Writings* (Cambridge: Cambridge University Press, 1996), xix.

8. Merbury, 40.

9. *The Interpreter: or booke containing the significance of words* (New York: Da Capo Press, 1970 [Cambridge, 1607]), sig. Aaa3–3v. On Cowell's thought, see S. B. Chrimes,

"The Constitutional Ideas of Dr. John Cowell," *EHR* 64 (1949): 461–487, and Joan Simon, "Dr. Cowell," *Cambridge Law Journal* 26 (1968): 260–276; for the controversy caused by *The Interpreter*, see Sommerville, *Politics and Ideology in England*, 121–127.

10. Ibid., sig. Qq1.

11. On this point see Francis Oakley, "Jacobean Political Theology: The Absolute and Ordinary Powers of the King," *JHI* 29 (1968): 323–346.

12. Ibid., sig. Ddd3–3v.

13. Qq1; Ddd4. Cowell's use of the word "quash" is evasive: does it refer simply to the king's veto power over proposed legislation, or does it extend to bills already enacted into law by his consent? If to the former, it is certainly a pugnacious description of the formula *le roi s'avisera* by which consent was withheld (not refused); if to the latter, it is obviously a significant enlargement of the generally accepted power of the king to suspend (not "alter") or dispense with the operation of a law for a particular time or in a specific case. For a lawyer, especially one expounding the meaning of legal terminology, Cowell would seem oddly reckless — or purposively vague.

14. *CJ* 1: 399.

15. Elizabeth Read Foster, *Proceedings in Parliament 1610*, 1: 24–25; cf. 183. A flavor of the Commons' prior debate was caught in Sir Ralph Winwood's comment that they "go very near to hang him" (38n1).

16. Ibid., 180, 186.

17. Ibid., 187–188. An embattled Bancroft, Cowell's known patron and *The Interpreter*'s dedicatee, tried to clear himself immediately after but also to complain that Cowell's words had been construed against him and to question whether Parliament had competence to act as a censor: "and if no precedents be, then I think if it shall be thought to appertain to the parliament to examine all books amiss, there will be enough, though they set 7 years together." Ellesmere, however, concluded briefly: "We have heard from the King" (188, 190). Godly victims of Bancroft's sting would doubtless have been amused by his defense of free speech.

18. "A Speech to the Lords and Commons of the Parliament at White–Hall," in McIlwain, ed., *PWJ*, 307, 308, 310, 311.

19. Hughes and Larkin, *Stuart Royal Proclamations*, 1: 243–245.

20. R. B. Bond, ed., *Certain Sermons or Homilies (1547) and A Homily Against Disobedience and Wilful Rebellion (1570)* (Toronto: University of Toronto Press, 1987). The Homilies were the frequent targets of godly reformers who decried them as an evasion of the responsibility to preach the Word. This complaint was not always limited to the learned; at Box in Wiltshire, for example, a weaver and a roughmason denounced the reciting of homilies in 1603 on this ground (Martin Ingram, "Puritans and the Church Courts, 1560–1640," in Christopher Durston and Jacqueline Eales, eds., *The Culture of English Puritanism, 1560–1640* [London: Macmillan, 1996], 58–91, at 85).

21. Rushworth, 1: 442; McIlwain, ed., *PWJ*, 308; Foster, ed., *PP 1610* 2: 328.

22. Derek Hirst, *The Representative of the People? Voters and Voting in England under the Early Stuarts* (Cambridge: Cambridge University Press, 1975); Mark A. Kishlansky, *Parliamentary Selection: Social and Political Choice in Early Modern England* (Cambridge: Cambridge University Press, 1986). See also John K. Gruenfelder, *Influence in Early Stuart Elections, 1604–1640* (Columbus: Ohio State University Press, 1981), and Chris R. Kyle, ed., *Parliaments, Politics and Elections, 1604–1648* (London: Royal Historical Society, 2001). Gruenfelder estimates that roughly a quarter of MPs owed their seats to aristocratic patronage; for examples, see Violet A. Rowe, "The Influence of the Earls of Pembroke on Parliamentary Elections, 1625–41," *EHR* 50 (1935): 242–256; Lawrence Stone, "The Electoral Influence of the Second Earl of Salisbury, 1614–68," *EHR* 71 (1956): 384–400; S. L. Adams, "The Dudley Clientele in the House of Commons, 1559–1586," *PH* 8 (1989): 216–239; and, for a general survey, V. J. Hodges, "The Electoral Influence of the Aristocracy, 1604–41," (Ph.D. Diss., Columbia University, 1977). As Hirst points out, the popular electorate was growing in the seventeenth century, although J. H. Plumb in "The Growth of the Electorate in England from 1600 to 1715,"

(*Past and Present* 45 [1969]): 90–116) sets the increase at a lower rate. For Elizabethan elections, see Neale, *The Elizabethan House of Commons*, which offers a broad overview and several detailed case studies.

23. On the Bucks County Case (aka *Goodwin v. Fortescue*), see, for the traditional Whig view and two modern restatements, J. R. Tanner, ed., *Constitutional Documents of the Reign of James I*, 202–217; Wallace Notestein, *The House of Commons, 1604–1610*, 64–78; and J. H. Hexter, "Parliament, Liberty, and Freedom of Elections," in J. H. Hexter, ed., *The Making of Modern Freedom, Volume I: Parliament and Liberty from the Reign of Elizabeth to the Civil War* (Stanford: Stanford University Press, 1992), 21–55; and cf. Derek Hirst, "Elections and Privileges in the House of Commons in the Early Seventeenth Century: Confrontation or Compromise?", *HJ* 18 (1975): 851–862; R. C. Munden, "The Defeat of Sir John Fortescue: Court Versus Country at the Hustings," *EHR* 93 (1978): 811–816; Linda Levy Peck, "Goodwin v. Fortescue: The Local Context of Parliamentary Controversy," *PH* 3 (1984): 33–56; Eric N. Lindquist, "The Case of Sir Francis Goodwin," *EHR* 104 (1989): 670–677.

24. R. C. Munden, "'All the Privy Councillors Being Members of This House': A Note on the Constitutional Significance of Procedure in the House of Commons, 1589–1614," *PH* 12 (1993): 115–125; cf. Conrad Russell, "English Parliaments 1593–1606: One Epoch or Two?", in Dean and Jones, *The Parliaments of Elizabethan England*, 191–213.

25. On the wardship dispute, see Pauline Croft, "Wardship in the Parliament of 1604," *PH* 2 (1983): 39–48, and, on the Elizabethan background, Joel Hurstfield, *The Queen's Wards: Wardship and Marriage under Elizabeth I* (London: Longmans, Green, 1958). On purveyance, see Croft, "Parliament, Purveyance and the City of London, 1589–1608," *PH* 4 (1985): 9–34; Eric Lindquist, "The King, the People and the House of Commons: The Problem of Early Jacobean Purveyance," *HJ* 31 (1988): 549–570, and, again for the general background, Allegra Woodworth, *Purveyance for the Royal Household in the Reign of Queen Elizabeth* (Philadelphia: American Philosophical Society, 1945).

26. Tanner, 219–230, at 219; subsequent references are in the text. Tanner's text is printed, with some omissions, from William Petyt's *Jus Parliamentarium* (1739): 227–243. On the paleographic and bibliographic record of the Apology—which remains incomplete—see G. R. Elton, "A High Road to Civil War?", in Elton, *Studies in Tudor Politics and Government*, 2: 164–183, at 169–170n3.

27. The Apology also referred to "other burdens" to be removed, such as tenures *in capite* and knight's service; these burdens were, of course, to be multiplied by James' successor.

28. On a practical level these proposals marked the beginning of a long-term effort to consolidate the King's various feudal revenues. They formed the basis of the so-called Great Contract of 1610, by which James would have surrendered these revenues in return for a lump sum payment and an annual income. It failed on the royal side from suspicion of Parliament's intentions, and on the parliamentary side from backbench resistance to the sums involved. The literature on the Great Contract is extensive; see, particularly, Alan G. R. Smith, "Crown, Parliament and Finance: The Great Contract of 1610," in Clark, Smith, and Tyacke, eds., *The English Commonwealth, 1547–1640*, 111–127; Eric Lindquist, "The Failure of the Great Contract," *JMH* 57 (1985): 617–651; and Neil Cuddy, "The Real, Attempted 'Tudor Revolution in Government': Salisbury's Great Contract of 1610," in G. W. Bernard and S. J. Gunn, eds., *Authority and Consent in Tudor England: Essays Presented to C. S. L. Davies* (Aldershot, Hants.: Ashgate, 2002), 249–270. It was not until 1660 that a comprehensive proposal to rationalize royal finances prevailed.

29. Cf. the Apology's discussion of the Bill of Assarts, which dealt with disafforestation. Here the authors conceded that the grievance it addressed "was not unjust in rigour of law," appealing rather to equity to remit it (Tanner, 227). The actions of purveyors were, in contrast, specifically characterized as "unjust."

30. J. H. Hexter, "The Apology," in Richard Ollard and Pamela Tudor-Craig, eds., *For Veronica Wedgwood These: Studies in Seventeenth-Century History* (London: Collins, 1986), 13–44.

31. *CJ* 1: 230b. With the addition of six members, its composition was identical with that of the Committee for Wardships (*CJ* 1: 222). The serjeants-at-law of the House were also attached to the previous committee.

32. Ibid., 243b, 995b. The most detailed narrative of the Apology's course in Parliament is Elton, "A High Road to Civil War?"; cf. Notestein, *The House of Commons 1604–1610*, 125–140.

33. Elton, 176; Notestein, 140.

34. *CJ* 1: 230b.

35. Zaller, *The Parliament of 1621*, 174, 178–183; for Williams, Elton, 175n2. The Clerk of the Commons had begun to transcribe the Apology in his Journal in 1604 but stopped in anticipation of the order to enter it in full, leaving the necessary pages blank.

36. Tanner, 288–289, from Rushworth, 1: 53.

37. Tanner, 221.

38. For a discussion of the subject, see my "What Does the English Revolution Mean? Recent Historiographical Interpretations of Mid–Seventeenth Century England," *Albion* 18 (1986): 617–635, and my review of Alastair MacLachlan, *The Rise and Fall of Revolutionary England: An Essay on the Fabrication of Seventeenth-Century England* (New York: St. Martin's Press, 1996), *Albion* 29 (1997): 291–294.

39. Elton, "A High Road to Civil War?", 170.

40. Ibid.

41. Edward Nicholas, ed., *Proceedings and Debates in the House of Commons in 1620 and 1621*, 2: 354–355, cited in Zaller, *The Parliament of 1621*, 177. Cf. the discussion in David Colclough, *Freedom of Speech in Early Stuart England*, op. cit., 142–145, which stresses the Apology's intention as an act of counsel. For Noy, who retained a reputation for legal integrity even when serving Charles under the Personal Rule, see W. J. Jones, "'The Great Gamaliel of the Law': Mr. Attorney Noy," *HLQ* 40 (1977): 97–126.

42. McIlwain, ed., *PWJ*, 287, 288.

43. Ibid., 288, 314, 289, 290.

44. On the general background of the debate, see E. Evans, "Of the Antiquity of Parliaments in England: Some Elizabethan and Early Stuart Opinion," *History* 23 (1938–1939): 206–221, and Philip Styles, "Politics and Historical Research in the early Seventeenth Century," in Levi Fox, ed., *English Historical Scholarship in the Sixteenth and Seventeenth Centuries* (Oxford: Oxford University Press, 1956), 49–72. For a challenge to the notion of an "immemorial" Parliament, see G. R. Elton, "Arthur Hall, Lord Burghley, and the Antiquity of Parliament," in Elton, *Studies in Tudor and Stuart Politics and Government*, 3: 254–273. The legal scholar Sir John Dodderidge (Doderidge) continued to support immemorialism; see Pauline Croft, "Sir John Doderidge, King James I, and the Antiquity of Parliament," *Parliament, Estates, and Representations* 12 (1992): 95–107.

45. On this episode, see J. E. Neale, "The Commons' Privilege of Free Speech in Parliament," in Seton-Watson, ed., *Tudor Studies*, op. cit.

46. C. H. McIlwain, *Constitutionalism and the Changing World* (Cambridge: Cambridge University Press, 1939), 187–191; Zaller, *The Parliament of 1621*, 104–115; Rabb, *Jacobean Gentleman*, 241–248. The Lords, whose judicial authority had been vindicated in 1621, finally pronounced judgment.

47. Wallace Notestein, "The Winning of the Initiative by the House of Commons," *Proceedings of the British Academy* 11 (1924–1925): 125–175.

48. Russell, *PEP*, 56, 139, 414.

49. Tanner, 222–223.

50. The basic study remains J. W. Gough, *Fundamental Law in English Constitutional History* (Oxford: The Clarendon Press, 1955; corrected edition, 1961); see also Sommerville, *Politics and Ideology*, Chapter 3; J. G. A. Pocock, *The Ancient Constitution and*

the Feudal Law, 2d ed. (Cambridge: Cambridge University Press, 1987 [1957]); Glenn Burgess, *The Politics of the Ancient Constitution: An Introduction to English Political Thought, 1603–1642* (Basingstoke and London: Macmillan, 1992); and William E. Klein, "The Ancient Constitution Revisited," in Nicholas Phillipson and Quentin Skinner, eds., *Political Discourse in Early Modern England* (Cambridge: Cambridge University Press, 1993), 23–44. Pocock calls fundamental law "that most important and elusive of seventeenth-century concepts," but notes that it "was very prevalent indeed" (*The Ancient Constitution*, 48, 51). It was certainly both prevalent in and crucial to the parliamentary debates of 1610.

51. For a recent discussion underscoring the government's careful preparation for this case, see Pauline Croft, "Fresh Light on Bate's Case," *HJ* 30 (1987): 523–539.

52. Foster, ed., *PP 1610* 2: 88–89 (May 21, 1610). This precisely echoed the doctrine of Cowell's *Interpreter* on the duty of subjects to maintain their sovereign, a point singled out in the Commons' debates two months earlier.

53. Samuel Rawson Gardiner, *Parliamentary Debates in 1610* (London: Camden Society, 1862), 36. The joining of "the liberties of the subject and the privileges of the parliament" will be noted. See Gardiner, 36–39, and Foster, ed., *PP 1610* 2: 107–110, for individual responses.

54. Foster, ed., *PP 1610* 2: 170–197; page references in the text.

55. Hedley instanced the reversal of the Statute of Uses in *Chidley's [Chudleigh's] Case*, 31 Eliz., Hil.

56. For the medieval background and the seventeenth-century debate on Magna Carta, see J. C. Holt, *Magna Carta*, 2d ed. (Cambridge: Cambridge University Press, 1992); Faith Thompson, *Magna Carta: Its Role in the Making of the English State, 1300–1629* (Minneapolis: University of Minnesota Press, 1948); and Maurice Ashley, *Magna Carta in the Seventeenth Century* (Charlottesville: University of Virginia Press, 1965).

57. Even granting that the people had not possessed their liberties before 1215, this was close to "immemorial" in the sense that lawyers used the term, i.e., as dating back before 1189, prior to lawbooks and other records. See Alan Wharam, "The 1189 Rule: Fact, Fiction, or Fraud?", *Anglo-American Law Review* 1 (1972): 262–279.

58. Cf. Hedley's speech of 18 May: ". . . as to prerogative though that be such and so large as a parliament cannot make a definition of it and in that respect it may be said [to be] infinite; yet there is no prerogative but *in individuo* is disputable and so may the prerogative in the case in question be disputed and disputed in parliament" (Foster, ed., *PP 1610* 2: 95).

59. G. W. Bernard, *War, Taxation and Rebellion in Early Tudor England: Henry VIII, Wolsey and the Amicable Grant of 1525* (Brighton, Sussex: Harvester Press; New York: St. Martin's Press, 1986); Richard Cust, *The Forced Loan and English Politics, 1626–1628* (Oxford: The Clarendon Press, 1987).

60. Sommerville, *Politics and Ideology*, 106.

61. For other discussion of Hedley's speech, see Pocock, *The Ancient Constitution and the Feudal Law*, 270–273; Glenn Burgess, *The Politics of the Ancient Constitution*, 46–48; and Charles M. Gray, "Parliament, Liberty, and the Law," in Hexter, ed., *Parliament and Liberty*, 155–200, at 188–190.

62. Foster, ed., *PP 1610* 2: 198–201.

63. Ibid., 231. Finch was a member for Rye, and subsequently Speaker of Charles I's first Parliament.

64. Ibid., 235.

65. Ibid., 237.

66. Ibid.

67. Ibid., 151–165, at 151. For commentary on Fuller, see Notestein, *The House of Commons, 1604–1610*, passim; Sommerville, *Politics and Ideology*, passim; Clive Holmes, "Parliament, Liberty, Taxation, and Property," in Hexter, ed., *Parliament and Liberty*, 122–154, at 138ff.; Rabb, *Jacobean Gentleman*, passim. Of course, all acts and laws contrary to the law of God were void, as Fuller pointed out (153); cf. Goldsworthy, *The Sovereignty of Parliament*, 121n316.

68. 16 Car. I, c. 1. See Pauline Croft, "The Debate on Annual Parliaments in the Early Seventeenth Century," *Parliaments, Estates, and Representation* 16 (1996): 163–174; idem, "Annual Parliaments and the Long Parliament," *BIHR* 59 (1986): 155–171.

69. Foster, ed., *PP 1610* 2: 165.

70. *ST*, 2: cols. 477–520, at 482. Subsequent references are in the text.

71. Cited in Notestein, T*he House of Commons 1604-1610*, 561n6.

72. Ibid., 2: 407–476; subsequent references are in the text.

73. Tanner, 265.

74. *CJ* 1: 431–432; Tanner, 245–247.

75. Foster, ed., *PP 1610* 2: 253–271.

76. Ibid., 114–117; Gardiner, ed., *PD 1610*, 42. The latter source reported that "the Howse rested well satisfied" with the King's reply; the former noted only that "a deep and general silence followed."

77. For a summary of the controversy over the canons, see Notestein, *The House of Commons, 1604–1610*, 42–47. The King's replies to the petitions are in *LJ* 2: 658, 659–660.

78. To a subcommittee of the standing Committee on Grievances, composed of Fuller, Sandys, Whitelocke, Nicholas Hyde, Thomas James, "and all that will come"; Notestein, 389.

79. *CJ* 1: 449, 450, 451; Foster, ed., *PP 1610* 2: 410–412.

80. Ibid., 1: 281–282.

81. Ibid., 2: 284–286; *CJ* 1: 451. For the 1606 bill, see Gardiner, ed., *PD 1610*, 162–163. The moment must have been a very tense one, as James openly threatened to dissolve Parliament on the spot if his fiscal demands were not met.

82. Foster, ed., *PP 1610* 1: 143. Sandys noted that the bill on impositions (as well as others) was intended to accompany the petitions. This suggests that the petitions were to serve as preambles to the bills that would be (as that on impositions was) narrowly declarative. This might have reflected legislative economy as well as time pressure; it might also have been a means for the Commons to state their legal and historical case in a form which could stand even if the accompanying legislation did not; or, alternatively, to give the King the option of assenting to the brief without the conclusion, or vice versa. In any case, Ellesmere's comment makes it clear that the King held to his prerogative right to lay impositions (however much he might be prepared to give assurance as to further ones), and was not about to concede it in any negotiation.

83. C. R. Mayes, "The Sale of Peerages in Early Stuart England," *JMH* 29 (1957): 21–37; Lawrence Stone, *The Crisis of the Aristocracy, 1558–1641* (Oxford: Oxford University Press, 1965), 65–128.

84. David Harris Sacks has emphasized the significance of the Parliament of 1601 in his "Parliament, Liberty, and the Commonweal" (Hexter, ed., *Parliament and Liberty*, 85–121), while Clive Holmes concentrates on 1610 in his essay in the same volume. Conrad Russell's "English Parliaments 1593–1606: One Epoch or Two?" applies a narrow lens and finds no substantial change between late Elizabethan parliamentary and early Stuart ones (Dean and Jones, op. cit.). I would contend that it is only by regarding these parliaments as a whole (including the critical session of 1610, which Russell leaves out of his account) that the sea change in relations between crown and Parliament becomes apparent.

85. Willson, *Privy Councillors in the House of Commons, 1604–1629*, op. cit.

86. Foster, ed., *PP 1610* 2: 178.

87. Ibid., 266. This diplomatic formulation, which brings Parliament's assent into play only in a subordinate clause, may reflect Whitelocke's hand as well as his thought. The Commons, having promised not to reverse the judgment in *Bate's Case*, were in a delicate position. They could not enact a statute or use the form of a Petition of Right; to declare impositions a grievance was a more indirect way of pronouncing their own judgment, but still a satisfactory one: as Dudley Carleton pointed out, "we have gained this much, that we now boldly make this matter a grievance, *which we could not have done so long as that judgment in the Exchequer stood for law*" (ibid., 225;

emphasis added). In effect, Parliament was keeping its promise by not directly disputing the judgment in *Bate's Case*, while "discovering" that the law that had been its basis was other than the Exchequer judges had held.

88. *ST* 2: 765–768, at 767: "[I]f a tribunitious popular spirit will go and ask a lawyer, whether the oath and band of allegiance be to the kingdom only, and not to the king, as was Hugh Spenser's Case, and he deliver his opinion as Hugh Spenser did; he will be in Hugh Spenser's danger" (767). Bacon then exempted Whitelocke from such an imputation, but the threat, clearly, was meant to sink in. The Despensers were charged in 1321 with stating that "Homage and oath of allegiance is more by reason of the crown than by reason of the king's person" (*SR* 1: 82). See also Bacon, *Works* 10: 368–380. As Francis Wormuth points out, this was the doctrine ultimately adopted by Parliament in 1642 in defining its powers (*The Origins of Modern Constitutionalism*, 32–40). Whitelocke ultimately made his peace with Bacon, and found the road to preference open. For further discussion of Whitelocke's prosecution, see D. X. Powell, "Why Did James Whitelocke Go to Jail in 1613? Principle and Political Dissent in Jacobean England," *Australian Journal of Law and Society* 11 (1995): 169–190. Bacon was not Whitelocke's only adversary in 1613; Ellsemere and Northampton also supported his prosecution. He did have an important Court protector in Sir Julius Caesar, his uncle. For a full discussion of his career, see Damian X. Powell, *Sir James Whitelocke's Liber Famelicus 1570–1632: Law and Politics in Early Stuart England* (Bern: Peter Lang, 2000).

89. The Committee of the Whole — a procedural device initiated in the Parliament of 1604–1610 and in use by 1606 — enabled the House to constitute itself as a committee. The advantage of such a device was that it enabled the House to choose a chairman who replaced the Speaker (a royal nominee whose position, like that of the councillors, could be an awkward one), and relaxed the rules which limited speakers to a single speech in any given debate. It is significant that no councillor was called to take the chair of such a committee, and that when in 1621 Sir Edward Coke chaired the Commons' Committee for Grievances, it was considered almost a breach of procedure (Notestein et al., eds., *CD 1621* 2: 24). Sir Edwin Sandys, a respected and able figure who had been a vocal opponent of the Union, took the chair on our occasion. Sir Edwin Phelips, a Speaker with little credit in the House, stepped down. The Committee of the Whole was once Exhibit A in the Commons' "winning of the initiative." More recent scholarship has argued that the device was actually suggested by the crown. Whatever its provenance, it was rapidly exploited by those whom James liked to call the popular or factious party in the House. On procedural innovations in the late Elizabethan and early Stuart period, see C. S. Sims, ed., "'Policies in Parliaments': An Early Seventeenth-Century Tractate on House of Commons Procedure," *HLQ* 15 (1951–1952): 45–58; Sheila Lambert, "Procedure in the House of Commons in the Early Stuart Period," *EHR* 95 (1980): 753–781, at 763–767; Mary Freer Keeler, "The Emergence of Standing Committees for Privileges and Returns," *PH* 1 (1982): 25–46; R. C. Munden, "'All the Councillors Being Members of this House': A Note on the Constitutional Significance of Procedure in the House of Commons, 1589–1614," *PH* 12 (1993): 115–125; Chris R. Kyle, "Attendance, Apathy and Order: Parliamentary Committees in Early Stuart England," in Chris R. Kyle and Jason Peacy, eds., *Parliament at Work: Parliamentary Committees, Political Power, and Public Access in Early Modern England* (Rochester, NY: The Boydell Press, 2002), 43–58; idem, "'It will be a scandal to show what we have done with such a number': Committee Attendance Lists," in Kyle, ed., *Parliament, Politics and Elections 1604–1648*, op. cit., 179–235.

90. Actually twenty; Bacon served for Bossiney in the Parliament of 1581.

91. Foster, ed., *PP 1610* 2: 110–113; Gardiner, ed., *PD 1610*, 36–41; Notestein, *The House of Commons, 1604–1610*, 327–331.

92. Linda Levy Peck, *Northampton: Patronage and Policy at the Court of James I* (London: George Allen and Unwin, 1982), 205–212.

93. Maija Jansson, ed., *Proceedings in Parliament 1614 (House of Commons)* [Philadelphia: American Philosophical Society, 1988], 93–97; J. P. Cooper, ed., *Wentworth Papers 1597–1628* (London: Camden Society, 4th ser., vol. 12, 1973), 66–69. Sandys, speaking

two and a half weeks later, had some second thoughts, suggesting that in light of the "misfortune" of the 1610 bill—i.e., its quashing in the Lords—it might be better to proceed at least first by petition (Jansson, 146). His sense of the urgency of the issue was no whit diminished, however, for it reached, he said, "to the foundation of all our interests," and by the same reasoning could empower the King to declare laws on his own and make all subjects "bondmen" (147). The reader of the early Stuart parliamentary record will encounter such dire prophecies with increasing frequency to the end of the 1620s.

94. Jansson, ed., *PP 1614*, 147: "That moved to the committee that the supply might stay till this [impositions] determined; to which most inclined."

95. Kevin Sharpe, *Sir Robert Cotton*, 121–123. James had in addition levied a forced loan on the gentry and merchant communities in 1611, as well as beginning the sale of baronetcies.

96. Jansson, ed., *PP 1614*, 152. Several members expressed irritation that the King had demanded supply at the beginning of Parliament; Sandys "Remember[ed] not in any parliaments for 25 years any mention at a beginning of a parliament of subsidies except one, when *Hannibal ad portas*" (153 and n44). The answer to the vexed scholarly question of whether grievances were held to precede supply or vice versa is that neither were; in the preferred parliamentary metaphor they were "twins" that went forward together (e.g., *CD 1621* 2: 21). By insisting on supply before grievances could even be heard, James broke the implicit compact of "love" between King and Parliament in which subsidy negotiations were shrouded. For James, of course, supply was the unfinished business of the previous Parliament, whereas for the Commons it was the petition and the bill for impositions; thus, the temporal sequence that made for harmony was compromised from the start. Conrad Russell (*The Addled Parliament of 1614: The Limits of Revision* [The Stenton Lecture, University of Reading, 1991]) emphasizes the deep divisions that underlay the positions of both sides in the wake of the failed negotiations of 1610: MPs, he wrote, already suspected that if James had independent supply "he would not need to call Parliaments," whereas the King's distrust of his subjects' willingness to relieve his wants led him "to cling to [the] authority which allowed him to supply himself without their consent" (18, 16).

97. Jansson, ed., *PP 1614*, 158.

98. Ibid., 193 (Walter), 189 (Bacon). The most detailed treatment of the so-called scheme of the "undertakers" to pack Parliament in 1614 is Clayton Roberts and Owen Duncan, "The Parliamentary Undertaking of 1614," *EHR* 93 (1978): 481–498; see also Clayton Roberts, *Schemes and Undertakings: A Study in English Politics in the Seventeenth Century* (Columbus, Ohio: Ohio State University Press, 1985).

99. Ibid., 193; J. E. Neale, *Elizabeth and Her Parliaments, 1584–1601*, 278. At the same time, Elizabeth noted the increasing "irreverence" toward her councillors and rebuked the entire House for it. Ironically, the selfsame Hoby was the next recorded speaker after Holles made his comment; he urged that Parry not be heard in his own defense unless he requested it.

100. Jansson, ed., *PP 1614*, 53. Bacon had succeeded Hobart as Attorney-General in 1613. There was an independent dispute as well over Bacon's eligibility to represent Cambridge, the seat he had chosen over the others for which he had been returned, St. Albans and Ipswich.

101. "[B]y connivancy," as the report from the committee appointed to search precedents on the matter of the Attorney's sitting contended (ibid., 52).

102. Ibid., 52–58; Willson, *Privy Councillors*, 215–217; Thomas L. Moir, *The Addled Parliament of 1614* (Oxford: Oxford University Press, 1958), 85–87.

103. Moir, 116ff.; Jansson, ed., *PP 1614*, 339, 348; *CJ* 1: 496–498; *LJ* 2: 706, 707–708; Rabb, *Jacobean Gentleman*, 195–196; cf. Peck, *Northampton*, 205ff. On Neile, see Andrew Foster, "The Function of a Bishop: The Career of Richard Neile, 1562–1640," in Rosemary O'Day and Felicity Heal, eds., *Continuity and Change: Personnel and Administration of the Church of England, 1500–1642* (Leicester: Leicester University Press, 1976), 33–54.

104. Jansson, ed., *PP 1614*, 340 et seq.; Moir, 116–134, 195–199.

105. *CJ* 1: 501; Jansson, ed., *PP 1614*, 378–445; HMC, *The Manuscripts of His Grace the Duke of Portland*, 10 vols. (London: HMSO, 1891–1931), 9: 135–138; Notestein et al., eds., *CD 1621* 7: 647–656; Moir, 129–145; Rabb, 200–204.

106. *LJ* 2: 717.

107. *CJ* 1: 465; *LJ* 2: 692.

108. HMC, *Portland MSS.*, 9: 138–139; John Bruce, ed., *The Liber Famelicus of James Whitelocke* (London: Camden Society, 1st ser., vol. 70, 1858), 41–43. The imprisoned members were Sir Walter Chute, John Hoskins, Christopher Neville, the son of a peer, and Thomas Wentworth of Oxford.

109. N. E. McClure, ed., *The Letters of John Chamberlain*, 2 vols. (Philadelphia: American Philosophical Society, 1939), 1: 538; *CJ* 1: 500. For a foreign observer's reaction, see *CSPV 1613–1615*, 121–122, 133–135.

110. Perez Zagorin, *Court and Country: The Beginning of the English Revolution* (New York: Atheneum, 1971 [1969]), especially 32–38. For a contemporary example of this usage, see Nicholas Breton, *The Court and the Country* (1618), and, for a case study, my "Edward Alford and the Making of Country Radicalism," *JBS* 22 (1983): 59–79.

111. Richard Bonney, *The European Dynastic States, 1494–1660* (Oxford: Oxford University Press, 1991); Geoffrey Parker, *The Military Revolution: Military Innovation and the Rise of the West, 1500–1800* (Cambridge: Cambridge University Press, 1988).

112. The foundational study of the English fisc in this period remains Frederick C. Dietz, *English Public Finance, 1558–1641* (New York: The Century Company, 1932; reprint, 1964); see also Robert Ashton, "Deficit Finance in the Reign of James I," *EcHR*, 2d ser., 10 (1957–1958), 15–29; Conrad Russell, "Parliament and the King's Finances," in Russell, ed., *The Origins of the English Civil War* (Basingstoke and London: Macmillan, 1973): 91–116; and Michael Braddick, *The Nerves of State: Taxation and the Financing of the English State, 1558–1714* (Manchester: Manchester University Press, 1996). On corruption as a systemic response to underfinancing, see Joel Hurstfield, "Political Corruption in Modern England: The Historian's Problem," *History* 52 (1967): 16–34, and Linda Levy Peck, *Patronage and Corruption in Early Stuart England* (Boston: Unwin Hayman, 1990).

113. On the Estates General as an institution, see J. Russell Major, *Representative Government in Early Modern France* (New Haven: Yale University Press, 1980); for that of 1614, J. Michael Hayden, *France and the Estates General of 1614* (Cambridge: Cambridge University Press, 1974). The declining value of the subsidy is detailed by Roger Schofield, "Taxation and the Political Limits of the Tudor State," in Claire Cross, David Loades, and J. J. Scarisbrick, eds., *Law and Government under the Tudors* (Cambridge: Cambridge University Press, 1988), 227–255, and its effects on the political process are surveyed in Conrad Russell, "Parliament and the King's Finances," and *The Addled Parliament of 1614*, op. cit. See also John Cramsie, "Crown Finance and Reform: The Legacy of the Addled Parliament," in Stephen Clucas and Rosalind Davies, eds., *The Crisis of 1614 and the 'Addled Parliament': Literary and Historical Perspectives* (Aldershot, Hants.: Ashgate, 2002), 39–51. A good overview of the ideological relation between property and taxation is provided by Clive Holmes, "Parliament, Liberty, Taxation, and Property," in J. H. Hexter, ed., *Parliament and Liberty*, 122–154. Per contra, Geoffrey Elton proposed that Parliament had accepted the necessity to supplement royal income on a regular basis in his "Taxation for War and Peace in Early Tudor England," in J. M. Winter, ed., *War and Economic Development: Essays in Memory of David Joslin* (Cambridge: Cambridge University Press, 1975), 33–48, a view developed by J. D. Alsop, "The Theory and Practice of Tudor Taxation," *EHR* 97 (1982): 1–30 and "Innovation in Tudor Taxation," ibid., 99 (1984): 83–93, but contested by G. L. Harriss in several articles: "Medieval Doctrines of Supply, 1610–1629," in Sharpe, ed., *Faction and Parliament*, 73–103; "Thomas Cromwell's 'New' Principle of Taxation," *EHR* 93 (1978): 721–738; and "Theory and Practice of Royal Taxation: Some Observations," *EHR* 97 (1982): 811–819. For an overview of the Tudor period, see Richard Hoyle,

"Crown, Parliament, and Taxation in Sixteenth-Century England," *EHR* 109 (1994): 1174–1196. My views accord with those of Holmes and Harriss.

114. Seven years and nearly four months elapsed between Henry VIII's third and fourth parliaments. Elizabeth called no new parliament between 1572 and 1581, but that of 1572 met again after a lengthy prorogation in 1576. James' assertion that the Addled Parliament was "nullum," i.e., no session at all, would have meant that no valid parliament had sat for more than a decade, a greater interval than that of any Tudor reign. Andrew Thrush emphasizes the King's desire to avoid parliaments in his "The Personal Rule of James I, 1611–1620," in Thomas Cogswell, Richard Cust, and Peter Lake, eds., *Politics, Religion and Popularity in Early Stuart Britain: Essays in Honour of Conrad Russell* (Cambridge: Cambridge University Press, 2002), 84–102.

115. "A Speach in the Starre-Chamber, The XX of Jvne. Anno 1616," McIlwain, ed., *PWJ*, 326–327.

116. Spedding, *Letters and Life*, 5: 176–191.

117. McClure, ed., *Letters of John Chamberlain*, 2: 221.

118. Notestein et al., eds., *CD 1621* 5: 6.

119. Stephen D. White, *Sir Edward Coke and the 'Grievances of the Commonwealth,'* covers Coke's parliamentary career from 1621 to 1628 (Coke did not return to the session of 1629). As White points out, he served as a legal adviser to the Lords in the parliaments between 1593 and 1621, thus maintaining official or unofficial ties to every parliament between 1589 (his first seat in the Commons) and 1628. The connection he had forged with the Lords was especially critical to their acceptance of expanded jurisdiction in the 1620s.

120. Cogswell, *The Blessed Revolution*; S. L. Adams, "Foreign Policy in the Parliaments of 1621 and 1624," in Sharpe, ed., *Faction and Parliament*, 139–171; Tyacke, *Anti–Calvinists*, op. cit.

121. Elisabeth Bourcier, ed., *The Diary of Sir Simonds D'Ewes, 1622–1624* (Paris: Didier, 1974), 121. On the theme of the Constantinian Emperor and the Elect Nation in the early seventeenth century, see Michael McGiffert, "God's Controversy with Jacobean England," *AHR* 88 (1983): 1151–1174, but also McGiffert's partial modification of his views, ibid., 89 (1984): 217–218. I owe the latter reference to Richard L. Greaves.

122. This paragraph summarizes material from my *The Parliament of 1621*, chapter I, and "Interest of State: James I and the Palatinate," *Albion* 6 (1974): 144–175. See also S. L. Adams, "Foreign Policy in the Parliaments of 1621 and 1624," op. cit.; A. W. White, "Suspension of Arms: Anglo–Spanish Mediation, 1621–1625" (Ph.D. diss., Tulane University, 1978); and Brennan C. Pursell, "The Constitutional Causes of the Thirty Years War: Frederick V, the Palatine Crisis, and European Politics" (Ph.D. Diss., Harvard University, 2000). For further background, see, most recently, Ronald Asch, *The Thirty Years War: The Holy Roman Empire and Europe* (New York: St. Martin's Press, 1997), and Geoffrey Parker, ed., *The Thirty Years War*, 2d ed. (London and New York: Routledge, 1997); cf. S. L. Adams, "Spain and the Netherlands? The Dilemma of Early Stuart Foreign Policy," in Howard Tomlinson, ed., *Before the English Civil War: Essays on Early Stuart Politics and Government* (New York: St. Martin's Press, 1983), 79–101. James' role and self-perception as a secular peacemaker is discussed in Malcolm Smuts, "The Making of *Rex Pacificus*: James VI and I and the Problem of Peace in an Age of Religious War," in Daniel Fischlin and Daniel Fortier, eds., *Royal Subjects: Essays on the Writings of James VI and I* (Detroit: Wayne State University Press, 2002), 371–387.

123. Nicholas, ed., *Proceedings and Debates*, 1: 66.

124. For Cranfield's performance in 1621 see Zaller, *The Parliament of 1621*, passim, and Russell, *PEP*, chapter 2; on his wider career, see R. H. Tawney, *Business and Politics under James I: Lionel Cranfield as Merchant and Minister* (Cambridge: Cambridge University Press, 1958); Menna Prestwich, *Cranfield: Politics and Profits under the Early Stuarts* (Oxford: Oxford University Press, 1966); and John Cramsie, for whom Cranfield emerges as the white knight of Jacobean finance (*Kingship and Finance under James VI and I*, chapters 6 and 7).

125. *CD 1621* 2: 24.

126. Colin G. C. Tite, *Impeachment and Parliamentary Judicature in Early Stuart England* (London: Athlone Press of the University Press of London, 1974), 88–95; Zaller, *The Parliament of 1621*, 56–59; Russell, *PEP*, 105–106.

127. J. Stoddart Flemion, "Slow Process, Due Process, and the High Court of Parliament: A Reinterpretation of the Revival of Judicature in the House of Lords in 1621," *HJ* 17 (1974): 3–16, at 8. Thomas Arundel, Archbishop of Canterbury, had been convicted by the two houses in 1397, but Henry VI exiled the Duke of Suffolk in 1449 before judgment was reached. The Commons had forsworn proceeding by writ of error in *Bate's Case*, but in 1621 Coke prevailed on the Lords to revive their use of it (*LJ* 3: 33).

128. Flemion, op. cit., 11–12. Flemion argues, without evidentiary support, that "James became as enthusiastic an advocate of the revival of impeachment as Coke." At most it can be argued that he did not immediately grasp its import; when he did, he moved to quash it (Zaller, *The Parliament of 1621*, 82–83).

129. Evangeline de Villiers, ed., "The Hastings Journal of the Parliament of 1621," *Camden Miscellany*, Vol. 20 (London: Camden Society, 1953), 26–31.

130. For a different perspective, see Stephen White's review of Coke's career, *Sir Edward Coke and the Grievances of the Commonwealth*, 6–10, and Russell, *PEP*, passim; cf. Cogswell, *The Blessed Revolution*, 161–165.

131. Russell, *PEP*, 123.

132. Zaller, *The Parliament of 1621*, 54–90, passim; Tite, op. cit., 110–118 and passim; Jonathan Marwil, *The Trials of Counsel: Francis Bacon in 1621* (Detroit: Wayne State University Press, 1976); Nieves Mathews, *Francis Bacon: The History of a Character Assassination* (New Haven: Yale University Press, 1996); D. X. Powell, "Why Was Sir Francis Bacon Impeached? The Common Lawyers and the Chancery Revisited: 1621," *History* 84 (1996): 511–526; Lisa Jardine and Alan Stewart, *Hostage to Fortune: The Troubled Life of Francis Bacon* (New York: Hill and Wang, 1999). Theodore Rabb's observations (*Jacobean Gentleman*, 223–226) are also suggestive. Russell, in his cursory discussion of Bacon's fall, comments that "the case remains remarkably obscure, but whatever it may be, it cannot be seen as the result of a court–country confrontation" (*PEP*, 113). It seems to me that very nearly the reverse is true.

133. Tite, op. cit.; Flemion, op. cit.; Jesse Stoddart, "Constitutional Crisis in the House of Lords, 1621–1629" (Ph.D. Diss., University of California, Berkeley, 1966); Allen Horstman, "Justice and the Peers: The Judicial Activities of the Seventeenth-Century House of Lords," (Ph.D. Diss., University of California, Berkeley, 1977); idem, "A New *Curia Regis*: The Judicature of the House of Lords in the 1620s," *HJ* 25 (1982): 411–422; Elizabeth Read Foster, *The House of Lords, 1603–1649: Structure, Procedure, and the Nature of Its Business* (Chapel Hill: University of North Carolina Press, 1983); James S. Hart, *Justice Upon Petition: The House of Lords and the Reformation of Justice, 1621–1675* (London: Harper Collins, 1991); Vernon F. Snow, "The Arundel Case, 1626," *The Historian* 26 (1964): 323–349; Harry F. Snapp, "The Impeachment of Roger Maynwaring," *HLQ* 30 (1967): 217–232; William R. Stacy, "Impeachment, Attainder, and the 'Revival' of Parliamentary Judicature under the Early Stuarts," *AJLH* 29 (1985): 40–56.

134. Zaller, *The Parliament of 1621*, 104–115, 136–137; Tite, op. cit., 123–131; cf. Russell, *PEP*, 119–121. For Kynaston's quotation, Notestein et al., eds., *CD 1621* 6: 120; for the Declaration, ibid., 5: 203–204 (reprinted in Zaller, 191).

135. Zaller, *The Parliament of 1621*, chapter V; Thomas Cogswell, "Phaeton's Chariot: The Parliament-Men and the Continental Crisis in 1621," in J. F. Merritt, ed., *The Political World of Thomas Wentworth, Earl of Strafford, 1621–1641* (Cambridge: Cambridge University Press, 1996), 24–46; Brennan C. Pursell, "James I, Gondomar, and the Dissolution of the Parliament of 1621," *History* 88 (2000): 28–45; cf. Conrad Russell, "The Foreign Policy Debate in the House of Commons in 1621," *HJ* 20 (1977): 289–309, reprinted in Russell, *Unrevolutionary England, 1603–1642* (London and Ronceverte: The Hambledon Press, 1990), 59–79, which attempts to decouple the foreign policy de-

bates of December from the free speech crisis. For Coke's speech, *CD 1621* 5: 240, and cf. the version in 6: 240, where Magna Carta is invoked.

136. Notestein et al., eds., *CD 1621* 5: 360; Nicholas, ed., *Proceedings and Debates*, 1: 372.

137. Cogswell, "Phaeton's Chariot," 40, details expenditures in the fall of 1621 on land purchases, gold medals and gilding for the royal barge, jewelry, and a gift to a favored courtier, the Marquis of Hamilton, in all approximately £30,000, or half the value of the Commons' grant.

138. The sinister influence of Count Gondomar, the Spanish ambassador, was a leitmotif of the Parliament, and he was openly cited during the December debates as a sower of division and a "Man of Sin." See Pursell, op. cit., and, for Gondomar's career in England, Charles H. Carter, "Gondomar: Ambassador to James I," *HJ* 3 (1964): 189–208.

139. Nicholas, ed., *Proceedings and Debates*, 2: 339; Notestein et al., eds., *CD 1621* 2: 528; 6: 335; 2: 533 (quoted in Russell, *PEP*, 141); Foster, ed., *PP 1610* 2: 191. Hedley also used the term "absolute" to describe the subject's possession of his land and goods (196). Confusion appears to arise when Hedley also uses the term as a synonym for arbitrary government; the distinction, however, is between an absolute *right* under the law (including the King's prerogative) and an absolute *power* assumed outside the law and exercised without accountability.

140. Nicholas, ed., *Proceedings and Debates* 2: 339; Rushworth, 1: 53; Russell, ibid., Tanner, 295.

141. Zaller, *The Parliament of 1621*, 188–189. On Sandys' confinement and the parliamentary reaction to it, see Rabb, *Jacobean Gentleman*, 260–269; for Phelips, Phelips MSS. 224/87, Somerset Record Office; for Pym, Conrad Russell, "The Parliamentary Career of John Pym," in Russell, *Unrevolutionary England*, 205–228, at 219–220; for Mallory, idem, "The Examination of Mr. Mallory after the Parliament of 1621," ibid., 81–88. Hakewill declared in 1628 that "I was charged with wordes out of the clerkes book" ("Mr. Mallory," 87n1).

142. Rushworth, l: 64–65; Cogswell, *The Blessed Revolution*, 24–34.

143. Samuel Rawson Gardiner, *Prince Charles and the Spanish Marriage, 1617–1623: A Chapter of English History*, 2 vols. (London: Hurst and Blackett, 1869); A. W. White, "Suspension of Arms," op. cit.; Thomas Cogswell, "England and the Spanish Match," in Richard Cust and Anne Hughes, eds., *Conflict in Early Stuart England: Studies in Religion and Politics, 1603–1642* (London and New York: Longman, 1989), 107–133; Brennan C. Pursell, "The End of the Spanish Match," *HJ* 45 (2002): 699–726; Glyn Redworth, *The Prince and the Infanta: The Cultural Politics of the Spanish Match* (New Haven: Yale University Press, 2003).

144. William S. Maltby, *The Black Legend in England: The Development of Anti-Spanish Sentiment, 1558–1660* (Durham, N. C.: Duke University Press, 1971); Carol Z. Wiener, "The Beleaguered Isle: A Study of Elizabethan and Early Jacobean Anti-Catholicism," *P&P* 51 (1971): 27–62; Simon Adams, "The Protestant Cause: Religious Alliance with the West European Calvinist Communities as a Political Issue in England, 1585–1630" (D. Phil. Thesis, Oxford University, 1973); Louis B. Wright, "Propaganda against James I's 'Appeasement' of Spain," *HLQ* 6 (1943): 149–192; Martin Arthur Breslow, *A Mirror of England: English Puritan Views of Foreign Nations, 1618–1640* (Cambridge: Harvard University Press, 1970); Peter Lake, "The Elizabethan Identification of the Pope as Antichrist," *JEH* 21 (1980): 161–178; Robin Clifton, "Fear of Popery," in Conrad Russell, ed., *The Origins of the English Civil War*, (London: Macmillan, 1973), 144–167; Caroline Hibbard, *Charles I and the Popish Plot* (Chapel Hill: University of North Carolina Press, 1983).

145. Cogswell, *The Blessed Revolution*, 6–12; Bourcier, ed., *The Diary of Sir Simonds D'Ewes*, 162.

146. *A Speech Made in the Lower House . . . by Sir Edward Cicill* (1621).

147. *BDBR* 3: 147–148; Peter Clark, "Thomas Scott and the Growth of Urban Opposition to the Early Stuart Regime," *HJ* 21 (1978): 1–26; P. G. Lake, "Constitutional Con-

sensus and the Puritan Opposition in the 1620s: Thomas Scott and the Spanish Match," *HJ* 25 (1982): 805–825. For general background, see Joad Raymond, *Pamphlets and Pamphleteering in Early Modern Britain* (Cambridge: Cambridge University Press, 2003).

148. *Vox Regis* (1624), 18, 68 (cited in Lake, 817).

149. Richard Tuck, "*Power* and *Authority* in Seventeenth-Century England," *HJ* 17 (1974): 43–61, at 49–50.

150. Conrad Russell, "Divine Rights in the Early Seventeenth Century," in John Morrill, Paul Slack, and Daniel Woolf, eds., *Public Duty and Private Conscience: Essays Presented to G. E. Aylmer* (Oxford: The Clarendon Press, 1993), 101–120. Russell does not discuss Scott, but he gets at the essence of his godly *mentalité* when he suggests that "for many, God's sovereignty took up too much room to allow absolute sovereignty to anyone else" (106).

151. On civil war coordination theory, see Corinne Comstock Weston and Janelle Renfrew Greenberg, *Subjects and Sovereigns: The Grand Controversy over Legal Sovereignty in Stuart England* (Cambridge: Cambridge University Press, 1981); chapter 5 treats Prynne. For Parker, see Michael Mendle, *Henry Parker and the English Civil War: The Political Thought of the Public's "Privado"* (Cambridge: Cambridge University Press, 1995); Robert Zaller, "Henry Parker and the Regiment of True Government," *Proceedings of the American Philosophical Society* 135 (1991), 255–285.

152. Jack R. McMichael and Barbara Taft, eds., *The Writings of William Walwyn* (Athens: University of Georgia Press, 1989).

153. Clark, "Thomas Scott and the Growth of Urban Opposition," 16.

154. Ibid., 18. See also Cust, *The Forced Loan and English Politics*, 175–185, for an extensive discussion of Scott's manuscript treatise on the limits of the subject's obedience (Kent Archive Office, Knatchbull MSS. U.951/Z.10).

155. Roger Lockyer, *Buckingham: The Life and Career of George Villiers, Duke of Buckingham, 1592–1628* (London: Longman, 1981); Cogswell, *The Blessed Revolution*, 57–76; Robert E. Ruigh, *The Parliament of 1624: Politics and Foreign Policy* (Cambridge: Harvard University Press, 1971), passim.

156. For the persistence of Henry as an ideal type of Protestant champion-cum-Constantinian Emperor, see William Hunt, "Spectral Origins of the English Revolution," in Geoff Eley and William Hunt, eds., *Reviving the English Revolution* (London: Verso, 1988), 305–332.

157. Clark, 11. On the inflation of honors under James and Charles, see Stone, *Crisis of the Aristocracy*, chapter 3; K. S. van Eerde, "The Sale of the Peerage in Early Stuart England," *JMH* 29 (1957): 137–147; idem, "The Jacobean Baronets," ibid., 33 (1961): 21–37. The number of peers remained virtually flat between 1558 (57) and 1603 (55), a significant decline relative to the general increase in population. Stone regards the early Jacobean creations as a justified compensation for the paucity of Elizabethan ones, and opines that "the peerage in 1615 still retained its full dignity and respect" (103). Instead of leveling off at this point, however, a further forty-five nobles were created between 1615 and 1628, not counting Irish peers (whose numbers rose from 25 in 1603 to 105 by 1641), and the new class of baronets. Baronetcies (hereditary knighthoods) were specifically created as a revenue device in 1611 and marketed at a nominal £1000 per title to status-hungry gentry. This was bad enough, but traditional peerages were soon being hawked as well. Some but not all of the inflation (and corruption) of honor can be laid at the feet of Buckingham and his kin; unsurprisingly, they reaped the full blame, at least publicly. It would be hard to exaggerate the degree of resentment caused by the sale of honors; among Stuart innovations, only those in religious ceremony and doctrine did more to destabilize the consensus of legitimacy.

158. Edward Forsett, *A Comparative Discourse of The Bodies Natural and Politique* (New York: Da Capo Press, 1973 [1606]), 15. Forsett is discussed in J. W. Allen, *English Political Thought 1603–1644* (Hamden, CT: Archon Books, 1967 [1938]), 76–84; Gordon J. Schochet, *Patriarchalism in Political Thought* (New York, 1975); Stephen L. Collins, *From Divine Cosmos to Sovereign State* (Oxford: Oxford University Press, 1989), 109ff.;

and James Daly, *Cosmic Harmony and Political Thinking in Early Stuart England* (Philadelphia: Transactions of the American Historical Society, Vol. 69, Pt. 7 [1979]), 16–17,
18–19. Sommerville (*Politics and Ideology in England, 1603–1640*) gives him scant mention.

159. McIlwain, ed., *PWJ*, 308.

160. Jean Berenger, "Pour une enquête européenne: le problème de ministériat au
XVIIe siecle," *Annales* 29 (1974): 66–92; Elizabeth Marwick, "Favorites in Early Mod-
ern Europe: A Recurring Psychological Role," *Journal of Psychohistory* 10 (1983): 463–
489; Sharon Kettering, "The Historical Development of Political Clientelism," *Journal
of Interdisciplinary History* 18 (1988): 419–447. See also Roger Lockyer, "An English
Valido? Buckingham and James I," in Ollard and Tudor–Craig, eds., *For Veronica
Wedgwood: Thèse*, op., cit., 45–58, and the essays in J. H. Elliott and L. W. B. Brockliss,
The World of the Favourite (New Haven: Yale University Press, 1999). On the favorite as
an aspect of the monarch's conspicuous consumption, see Linda Levy Peck, "'For a
King not to Be Bountiful Were a Fault': Perspectives on Court Patronage in Early Stu-
art England," *JBS* 25 (1986): 31–61. Buckingham's own "conspicuous" collecting on
the art market is noted in R. Malcolm Smuts, "Art and the Material Culture of Majesty," in Smuts, ed., *The Stuart Court and Europe: Essays in Politics and Political Culture*
(Cambridge: Cambridge University Press, 1996), 86–112, at 99–100.

161. David R. Ransome, ed., "The Parliamentary Papers of Nicholas Ferrar, 1624,"
Camden Miscellany 33, Camden Society, 5th ser., Vol. 7 (Cambridge: Royal Historical
Society, 1996), 36.

162. On Cranfield's impeachment, see Tite, 149–172; Prestwich, *Cranfield*, chapter 9;
Ruigh, *The Parliament of 1624*, 316–335, 339–341, and passim; Russell, *PEP*, 198–202;
and Cogswell, *The Blessed Revolution*, 268–273 and passim.

163. Elizabeth Read Foster, "The Procedure of the House of Commons against Patents and Monopolies, 1621–1624," in William Appleman Aitkens and Basil D. Hen-
ning, eds., *Conflict in Stuart England* (London: Jonathan Cape, 1960), 57–85; Chris R.
Kyle, "Lex Loquens: Legislation in the Parliament of 1624" (Ph.D. Diss., University of
Auckland, 1993).

164. On Charles' (misplaced) confidence in his skills as a parliamentary manager,
see Chris R. Kyle, "Prince Charles in the Parliaments of 1621 and 1624," *HJ* 61 (1998):
603–624; cf. the more favorable account in Richard Cust, *Charles I: A Political Life* (London: Pearson Longman, 2005), 38–41.

165. John Hacket, *Scrinia Reserata* (London, 1691), Pt. II, p. 4; Christopher Thompson, "Court Politics and Parliamentary Conflict in 1625," in Cust and Hughes, *Conflict
in Early Stuart England*, 168–192, at 171.

166. Maija Jansson and William B. Bidwell, eds., *Proceedings in Parliament 1625* (New
Haven: Yale University Press, 1987), 375; Samuel Rawson Gardiner, ed., *Debates in the
House of Commons in 1625* (London: Camden Society, n.s., Vol. 6, 1873), 11–12. Coke
gave as an additional reason for not considering new grievances before old ones had
been redressed the danger of infection from complainants, pointing out that the law
courts had recessed their term early for this reason. The risk to the High Court of Parliament was all the more obvious for this.

167. The value of the subsidies was about £140,000; the government's necessities, it
was said, were five times that amount.

168. On the Lords' action, Jansson and Bidwell, eds., *PP 1625*, 372.

169. The issue had nearly flared up anew in 1624, when a speech in defense of impositions by Serjeant Hitcham, the King's counsel, had so incensed the Commons that
they had ordered it razed from their Journal—another striking example of discourtesy
to crown spokesmen in the House. Conrad Russell suggests that the purpose of the
Tonnage and Poundage bill was to augment the King's revenue; it was, however,
quite clearly linked to the general question of impositions (Ruigh, 50 and n.; Russell,
PEP, 198–199, 227–229; Gardiner, ed., *DHC 1625*, 12–13, 43; Jansson and Bidwell, eds.,
PP 1625, 317, 511.

170. Jansson and Bidwell, eds., *PP 1625*, 530. The pardon was unpopular at court as well, where its political ramifications were clearly understood; Russell, *PEP*, 239–240.

171. Jansson and Bidwell, eds., *PP 1625*, 383; cf. Coke's earlier speech at 227.

172. Thompson, "Court Politics and Parliamentary Conflict," 181–184; Lockyer, *Buckingham*, 257–258.

173. Gardiner, ed., *DHC 1625*, 105, 108–109; Jansson and Bidwell, eds., *PP 1625*, 433, 448.

174. Gardiner, ed., *DHC 1625*, 109–110 at 110; Jansson and Bidwell, eds., *PP 1625*, 443–444, 448–449, 556–557; Russell, *PEP*, 250.

175. Jansson and Bidwell, *PP 1625*, 395–397, quoted at 396; 397; 540–543; cf. Gardiner, ed., *DHC 1625*, 80–82.

176. Menna Prestwich, ed., *International Calvinism, 1541–1715* (Oxford: The Clarendon Press, 1986); R. T. Kendall, *Calvin and English Calvinism to 1649*; Peter Lake, "Calvinism and the English Church 1570–1635," *P&P* 114 (1987): 32–76.

177. On the conference see Tyacke, *Anti-Calvinism*, Chapter 7; Barbara Donagan, "The York House Conference Revisited: Laymen, Calvinism and Arminianism," *HR* 44 (1991): 312–330; Lockyer, *Buckingham*, 306–308. For Montagu (or Montague), see J. Macauley, "Richard Montague, Caroline Bishop, 1575–1641" (D. Phil. Thesis, Cambridge University, 1965). Cosin's comment is noted by Tyacke, 119.

178. On Buckingham's clerical patronage, see Lockyer, 19–20, 114–115, 258–259; Cogswell, *The Blessed Revolution*, 93.

179. On Buckingham's relations with Richelieu, see Lockyer, 236–239. Buckingham was certainly aware of the hostility of the French nobility to Richelieu's ascendancy during his visit to France in 1625, though his own experience in 1621 and after could have left him in little need of such instruction. One cannot exclude the perceived benefits to the favorite in publicly presiding over an event that gathered prominent members of the nobility under his aegis.

180. Russell oddly suggests that the conference attracted little attention and was largely ignored by Parliament (*PEP*, 31). The lords who attended it were simultaneously sitting in the upper chamber (Parliament had convened on February 6, and the conference took place on the 11th and 17th). It would have taken an extraordinary feat of personal and political compartmentalization to overlook the significance of the conference for the business at hand in Parliament, or for the lords' colleagues and retainers in the Commons to have similarly passed it by.

181. Gardiner, *History of England*, 6: 33–34; Hirst, *The Representative of the People?*, 77; Russell, *PEP*, 268–269; Holdsworth, *A History of English Law*, 5: 448–449; Myron C. Noonkester, "Charles I and Shrieval Selection, 1625–6," *HR* 44 (1991): 305–311; Cooper, ed., *Wentworth Papers*, 240. Palmes was relatively obscure, but his reference to the execution of two corrupt ministers of Henry VII, Edmund Dudley and Sir Richard Empson, presumably gave sufficient offense (Jansson and Bidwell, eds., *PP 1625*, 451; Gardiner, ed., *DHC 1625*, 112). Palmes had made a critical motion in the debate on referees for monopoly patents in 1621 (Zaller, *The Parliament of 1621*, 65).

182. Russell, *PEP*; White, *Sir Edward Coke and the Grievances of the Commonwealth*, 213.

183. As Elizabeth Read Foster points out, 27 of the 33 public acts passed in 1604 originated in the Commons, and by 1624 the Lords sent not a single public bill to the Lower House, prompting a stinging comment by the diarist Walter Yonge. On the other hand, the Lords initiated 26 of 39 private acts in 1604, suggesting their role as consumers and sponsors of legislation for individual or local beneficiaries (*The House of Lords, 1603–1649*), 201–202.

184. Lockyer, 100–101. The phrase was that of an informant of Buckingham's, and therefore doubtless exaggerated; but the kernel of truth it contained was nonetheless significant.

185. On the Earl Marshal's function, see Richard McCoy, *Rites of Knighthood: The Literature and Politics of English Chivalry* (Berkeley and Los Angeles: University of California Press, 1989), 88–102; and Paul H. Hardacre, "The Earl Marshal, the Heralds,

and the House of Commons, 1604–41," *International Review of Social History* 2 (1975): 106–125.

186. Kevin Sharpe, "The Earl of Arundel, His Circle and the Opposition to the Duke of Buckingham, 1618–1628," in Sharpe, ed., *Faction and Parliament*, 209–244; Snow, "The Arundel Case," op. cit.

187. Samuel Rawson Gardiner, ed., *The Earl of Bristol's Defence of His Negotiations in Spain* (London: Camden Society Miscellany, 6, 1871); *LJ* 3: 176; William B. Bidwell and Maija Jansson, eds., *Proceedings in Parliament 1626*, 4 vols. (New Haven: Yale University Press, 1991), 1: 337–343.

188. On the evolving concept of honor, see Mervyn James, "English Politics and the Concept of Honour, 1485–1642," in James, *Society, Politics, and Culture*, 308–415; and, for an important link between Essex and the aristocratic opposition of the 1620s, Neil Cuddy, "The Conflicting Loyalties of a 'Vulger Counselor': The Third Earl of Southampton," in Morrill, Slack, and Woolf, eds., *Public Duty and Private Conscience in Seventeenth–Century England*, op. cit., 121–150. On the 1620s, see Richard McCoy, "Old English Honour in an Evil Time: Aristocratic Principle in the 1620s," in Smuts, ed., *The Stuart Court and Europe*, 133–155.

189. Bidwell and Jansson, eds., *PP 1626* 2: 261–262, 268; 1: 463–477. Buckingham tried to cultivate (but also to isolate) Pembroke, who opposed the French match as well. Pembroke's laconic comment on the York House conference that no one who had gone into it with one opinion had come out with another has been read as the verdict of a draw, but in the context of his own godly convictions that was hardly the conclusion of an indifferent spectator; it meant that heresy had won official sponsorship, or at least toleration. See Lockyer, 276–277, 306–307. The Duke's agent, Lord Conway, wrote to him after Turner's attack promising to attend the Upper House "and see through whose eyes honor looks and in whose faces envy and unworthiness have fixed . . ." (*PP 1626* 4: 333). Clearly both the source and the ultimately intended arena of the attack had been identified at once.

190. Bidwell and Jansson, eds., *PP 1626* 2: 392–393.

191. Ibid., 230–233, 241–243. The Commons also raised again the grievances of Tonnage and Poundage and pretermitted customs.

192. Russell, *PEP*, 269ff.

193. Charles threatened an early dissolution on March 29 (Bidwell and Jansson, eds., *PP 1626* 2: 394), but did not carry through.

194. Ibid., 1: 445–451, at 448.

195. Ibid., 1: 451. The succession of speeches in the Commons' relation is established by Tite, *Impeachment and Parliamentary Judicature*, 198–199n37.

196. Samuel Rawson Gardiner, ed., *Constitutional Documents of the Puritan Revolution, 1625–1660*, 3rd ed., revised (Oxford: The Clarendon Press, 1979 [1889]), 387–388.

197. See above, n. 157.

198. On compliment as an element of the status system (and as a means of delivering critique), see Kevin Sharpe, *Criticism and Compliment: The Politics of Literature in the England of Charles I* (Cambridge: Cambridge University Press, 1987); on bicameralism, see the chapters by Pauline Croft, I. A. A. Thompson, David Dean, G. W. Harrison, and Ivan Roots in H. W. Blom, W. P. Blockmans, and H. de Schlepper, eds., *Bicameralisme: Tweekamerstelsel vroeger en nu* (The Hague: Sdu Uitgeverij Koninginnegracht, 1992).

199. Bidwell and Jansson, eds., *PP 1626* 3: 220–224.

200. For the protections that hedged a nobleman against attack, see John C. Lassiter, "Defamation of Peers: The Rise and Decline of the Action for Scandalum Magnatum, 1497–1773," *AJLH* 22 (1978): 216–236.

201. The classic Whig biography is John Forster, *Sir John Eliot: A Biography, 1590–1632 [recte 1592]*, 2 vols. (London: Longman, Green, Longman, Roberts, and Green, 1864). More measured is Harold Hulme, *The Life of Sir John Eliot* (New York: New York University Press, 1957); and see A. W. Croesman, "Critics of the Crown" (Ph.D. Thesis, Harvard University, 1976). For Eliot's career in the House, see J. N. Ball, "The

Parliamentary Career of Sir John Eliot" (D. Phil. Thesis, Cambridge University, 1953), and Russell, *PEP*, passim. An excellent brief overview is Wallace MacCaffrey's entry in *BDBR* 1: 245–250.

202. Bidwell and Jansson, eds., *PP 1626* 3: 222.

203. Ibid., 222, 223.

204. Ibid., 223.

205. Ibid., 558–559.

206. On the course of Buckingham's impeachment, which was never formally dropped, see Tite, *Impeachment and Judicature*, chapter 7; J. N. Ball, "The Impeachment of the Duke of Buckingham in 1626," in *Mélanges Antonio Marongiu: Studies Presented to the International Commission for the History of Representative and Parliamentary Institutions* 25 (Palermo: Istituto di Storia Medievale de l'Università di Palermo, 1967); Russell, *PEP*, chapter 5; Lockyer, *Buckingham*, 310–315, 319–330. The Lords' growing interest in their powers was indicated when in 1621 they commissioned a treatise from Selden, *The Priviledges of the Baronage of England When They Sit in Parliament*, published in 1642. On this text see Tite, 32–36.

207. Bidwell and Jansson, eds., *PP 1626* 3: 436–441; 1: 633–635. On the circumstances of the dissolution, see Jess Stoddart Flemion, "The Dissolution of Parliament in 1626: A Revaluation," *EHR* 87 (1972): 784–790. Flemion emphasizes the political importance of Arundel's return, and suggests that his presence (with the proxies he held) may have made Buckingham's impeachment an actual possibility. I remain convinced that Charles' preemptive clearing of the Duke had effectively scotched it, for the Lords would have had to give their sovereign the lie to proceed seriously thereafter, an inconceivable affront to the royal honor. It is nonetheless significant that they heard the Commons' case out at length despite the King's intervention, and that it was still on the table—certainly as an affirmation of the Lords' judicial prerogative, and perhaps as a counter for backstairs negotiation—when Parliament was dissolved on June 15.

208. Many of these were collected in Frederick W. Fairholt, ed., *Poems and Songs Relating to George Villiers, Duke of Buckingham; and His Assassination by John Felton, August 23, 1628* (London, 1850), but a good number more remain in manuscript repositories. On the upsurge of verse libels and popular pamphleteering and their political significance under the early Stuarts, see Raymond, op. cit.; Alastair Bellany, "The Poisoning of Legitimacy? Court Scandal, News Culture and Politics in England, 1603–1660" (Ph.D. Diss., Princeton University, 1995); idem, "'Rayling Rhymes and Vaunting Verse': Libellous Politics in Early Stuart England, 1603–1628," in Kevin Sharpe and Peter Lake, eds., *Culture and Politics in Early Stuart England* (Stanford: Stanford University Press, 1993), 285–310; idem, "Libels in Action: Ritual, Subversion, and the English Literary Underground, 1603–1642," in Tim Harris, ed., *The Politics of the Excluded, c. 1500–1800* (Houndsmill, Basingstoke: Macmillan, 2001); Thomas Cogswell, "Underground Verse and the Transformation of Early Stuart Political Culture," in Susan D. Amussen and Mark Kishlansky, eds., *Political Culture and Cultural Politics in Early Modern England* (Manchester: Manchester University Press, 1995), 277–300; Adam Fox, "Ballads, Libels and Popular Ridicule in Jacobean England," *P&P* 145 (1994): 47–83; idem, "Rumour, News and Popular Political Opposition in Elizabethan and Stuart England," *HJ* 40 (1997): 597–620; David Zaret, *Origins of Democratic Culture: Printing, Petition, and the Public Sphere in early Modern England* (Princeton: Princeton University Press, 2000); Andrew McRae, "The Literary Culture of Early Stuart Libelling," *Modern Philology* 97 (2000): 364–392; idem, *Literature, Satire, and the Early Stuart State* (Cambridge: Cambridge University Press, 2004).

209. Cited in Holstun, *Ehud's Dagger*, 158–159.

210. Austin Bellany, *The Politics of Court Scandal in Early Modern England: News Culture and the Overbury Affair, 1603–1666* (Cambridge: Cambridge University Press, 2002).

211. On the complex relations between fear, disgust, and sexuality, see William Ian Miller, *The Anatomy of Disgust* (Cambridge: Harvard University Press, 1997); cf. Jeffrey Masten, "Is the Fundament a Grave?" in David Hillman and Carla Mazio, eds., *The*

Body in Parts: Fantasies of Corporeality in Early Modern England (New York and London: Routledge, 1997), 129–145.

212. The best general account of the interregnum of 1626–1628 is Cust's *The Forced Loan and English Politics* (for Buckingham's role see particularly the analysis at 43–46; cf. Lockyer, *Buckingham*, chapter 9). See also L. J. Reeve, *Charles I and the Road to Personal Rule* (Cambridge: Cambridge University Press, 1989), and, on the nexus between Arminianism and royal autocracy, Nicholas Tyacke, "Puritanism, Arminianism and Counter-Revolution," in Russell, ed., *The Origins of the English Civil War*, 119–143. The *Five Knights'* (or *Darnel's*) *Case* is summarized and discussed in *ST* 3: 1ff.; see also John Guy, "The Origins of the Petition of Right Reconsidered," *HJ* 25 (1982): 289–312, and, for a revisionist view, Mark Kishlansky, "Tyranny Denied: Charles I, Attorney General Heath, and the Five Knights' Case," *HJ* 42 (1999): 53–83. For Coke's comment, see Robert C. Johnson, Mary Frear Keeler, Maija Jansson, and William B. Bidwell, eds., *Commons Debates 1628*, 6 vols. (New Haven: Yale University Press, 1977–1983), 4: 115, 119, 124, 132. (Vols. 1–4 of this set constitute the *Commons Debates*; Vol. 5 covers the proceedings in the House of Lords; and Vol. 6, *Proceedings in Parliament 1628*, contains appendices and indexes. Vols. 1–4 will be henceforth cited as *CD 1628*; Vol. 5 as *LP 1628*; and Vol. 6 as *PP 1628*.)

213. Cited in Russell, *PEP*, 332.

214. David Smith, *The Stuart Parliaments*, estimates the yield at £240,000; Russell, citing Robert Ashton, gives a figure of £264,000. Richard Cust speculated in *The Forced Loan and English Politics*, 92, that it might have been as high as £267,000, although most recently, in his *Charles I: A Political Life*, he sets it at "over £243,000," thus agreeing with Smith (65). In either case, Cust concludes that the loan was "strikingly successful" (*The Forced Loan*) or "a considerable success" (*Charles I*), in financial terms at least. Nonetheless, it was quite inadequate to fund the war.

215. Richard Cust, "Charles I, the Privy Council and the Parliament of 1628," *TRHS*, 6th ser., Vol. 2 (London, 1992), 25–50, at 27–28.

216. These arguments, repackaged as analysis, form the core of the revisionist case in Elton, Russell, Sharpe, Alsop, and others.

217. On the Council debate, see Cust, *The Forced Loan and English Politics*, 72–85; cf. Russell, *PEP*, 338–340. Cust identifies the moderates as including Pembroke, Sir Thomas Coventry, and Sir Thomas Edmondes, and the anti-Parliament group with Laud, the Earl of Dorset, Sir Edward Conway, and Sir John Savile, with Charles and Buckingham at their head.

218. Keeler et al., eds., *CD 1628* 4: 241–242.

219 *ODNB*; *BDBR* 2: 183–184; Stephen Foster, *Notes from the Caroline Underground: Alexander Leighton, the Puritan Triumvirate, and the Laudian Reaction to Noncomformity* (Hamden, CT: Archon Books, 1978). Leighton had close contacts with London's sectarian fringe, especially the Separatist congregation of Henry Jacob (Foster, 18–19; for Jacob, see Tolmie, *The Triumph of the Saints*, chapter 1 and passim). The *Appeale* was not actually distributed until the breakup of Parliament in 1629, and it is doubtful that any sitting MP saw it (Leighton, *An Epitome or Briefe Discouerie, from the Beginning to the Ending, of the many and Great Troubles that Doctor Leighton Suffered* . . . [London, 1646]), 2, 13, 19.

220. *An Appeale*, frontispiece.

221. Ibid., sig. A3ii, iii, v.

222. Ibid., 344.

223. Ibid., 337, 338.

224. The Triennial Act based itself on legal precedent rather than theological deduction, of course, and it contained no procedure for self-dissolution. The subsequent Act to Prevent Inconveniences . . . by the Untimely Adjourning, Proroguing, or Dissolving This Present Parliament (17 Car. I, c. 7) made a unique exception in that regard but was only, as the Commons declared in the Grand Remonstrance, an attempt to secure the kingdom, and not an effort to take the power of dissolution "out of the Crown" (Gardiner, ed., *CDPR*, 225). The Long Parliament's self-dissolution in 1660 was none-

theless regarded by many as the necessary precondition of the Restoration, and the reaction to the successive prorogations and dissolutions of the parliaments of the Exclusion Crisis made it clear that it was no longer constitutionally permissible to abort parliaments before their work was done. For the prerevolutionary dispensation, see David Harris Willson, "Summoning and Dissolving Parliaments, 1603–1625: The Council's Advice to James I," *AHR* 45 (1939–1940): 279–300.

225. For Leighton's tribulations see his *Epitome*, op. cit.

226. Johnson et al., eds., *CD 1628* 2: 58, 61; emphasis added.

227. This paragraph is based on my "Parliament and the Crisis of European Liberty," in Hexter, ed., *Parliament and Liberty*, 201–224, 309–313, at 219.

228. Johnson et al., eds., *CD 1628* 2: 59. Many copies of Rudyard's speech exist, indicating its wide circulation; see the editors' comment at 58n19.

229. Ibid., 60.

230. For *Bate* and *Calvin*, see above. For a recent discussion of the latter, see Polly J. Price, "Natural Law and Birthright Citizenship in *Calvin's Case*," *Yale Journal of Law and the Humanities* 9 (1997): 73–145.

231. For the latter, see Foster, ed., *PP 1610* 2: 236, 244. Coke, a participant in the *Calvin* decision, analyzed it copiously in his *Reports*, 2: 611–658.

232. Notestein et al., eds., *CD 1621* 5: 195 (cited in Sommerville, *Politics and Ideology in England*, 97); 3: 324. For the context of Alford's latter remark see my "Edward Alford and the Making of Country Radicalism," op. cit., 74.

233. Cust, *The Forced Loan and English Politics*, 60–61.

234. Johnson et al., eds., *CD 1628* 2: 61–64, 68–69.

235. Ibid., 2: 415.

236. Ibid., 3: 345. Petyt MS. 538/7 has a variant, "the cause" for "a cause." The indefinite article would have permitted the King to express the cause only partially, still reserving part of it as "reason of state."

237. *CD 1628* 2: 94, 95. In the same speech Coke expressed skepticism about the meaning of "fundamental" law, sniffing at it as "Holborn Latin." This contradiction may reflect lawyerly concern for the slipperiness of a term that, like "intrinsic" or "absolute," had no firm anchor in the legal record and could be taken in many senses. Coke was prepared (as we see) to use it when it served his own turn or for rhetorical effect—indeed, his whole strategem of contrasting the clarity and candor of the Commons' position with the obfuscation of the Lords' document was itself a rhetorical device. His reservations about removing the debate from the legal to the constitutional realm are nonetheless apparent.

238. Ibid., 96, 94, and cf. the discussion in White, *Sir Edward Coke and the 'Grievances of the Commonwealth,'* 253–256. Selden supported Coke on all points, remarking tersely of the clause on the prerogative that "it is not fit to be had, and therefore not fit to be asked," for it would "destroy our fundamental liberties," a phrase he did not scruple to use. The other speakers in the debate—Sir Francis Nethersole, Noy, Digges, Shervill or Sherfield, Phelips, Ball, Sir Thomas Wentworth, Bankes, Sherland, and Sir John Coke—were less uncompromising, and Nethersole and Coke spoke as councillors. Nethersole called for the reading of that old royal chestnut, the Statute of Proclamations, but Noy brushed the precedent aside (2: 96–99). The firm stand taken by Sir Edward Coke and Selden was essential in saving the day, and as the first speaker Coke's argument was the decisive one. It was an extraordinary display of courage and personal confidence.

239. Keeler et al., eds., *LP 1628*, 219–220.

240. J. A. Guy, "The Origins of the Petition of Right Reconsidered," op. cit., 294.

241. Ibid., 304.

242. Johnson et al., eds., *CD 1628* 2: 97.

243. Guy, op. cit.; Kishlansky, "Tyranny Denied," op. cit.; *CD 1628* 2: 212; *LP 1628*, 214, 226. There was much confusion in both houses over what the judges had actually done. Phelips and others believed they had entered a judgment against the plaintiffs; Charles, as Kishlansky points out, was anxious to know whether they had entered one

for them. Hyde at first described the judges' ruling as a "judgment," but subsequently denied that one had been given.

244. Hart, *Justice Upon Petition*, op. cit., chapter 1. It was Coke himself, of course, who had been primarily responsible for reviving impeachment and thus giving impetus to the development of the Lords' judicature, and Selden who, in response to a commission from the Upper House in 1621, had produced a comprehensive treatise on their privileges (above, n. 205).

245. Russell, *PEP*, 362.

246. Johnson et al., eds., *CD 1628* 3: 452; cf. *LP 1628*, 451.

247. On Charles' relationship with Elizabeth and her personal popularity in England, see Cogswell, *The Blessed Revolution*, passim., and Reeve, *Charles I and the Road to Personal Rule*, passim, especially 223–224, 275, 291.

248. See, among many studies of this development in early modern England, Richard Lachmann, *From Manor to Market: Structural Change in England, 1536–1640* (Madison: University of Wisconsin Press, 1987), and Joan Thirsk, *The Agricultural History of England and Wales, Volume 4, 1500–1640* (Cambridge: Cambridge University Press, 1967). A broader overview is offered in D. C. Coleman, *The Economy of England, 1450–1750* (Oxford: Oxford University Press, 1977); C. G. A. Clay, *Economic Expansion and Social Change: England 1500–1750*, 2 vols. (Cambridge: Cambridge University Press, 1984); and, most recently, Keith Wrightson, *Earthly Necessities: Economic Lives in Early Modern Britain* (New Haven: Yale University Press, 2000).

249. For a discussion of Charles' own rhetorical presentation of conscience, see Kevin Sharpe, "Private Conscience and Public Duty in the Writings of Charles I," *HJ* 40 (1997): 643–665.

250. Cf. the parsing of "leave" and "entire" in Robert Mason's speech of May 22, *CD 1628* 3: 528. Mason, MP for Winchester (and not to be confused with Buckingham's secretary of the same name), contended that "The word 'leave' in a petition is of the same nature as 'saving' in a grant or act of Parliament," and would consequently "imply that something is to be left of what, or with reference to what, we desire." As for a sovereign power "entire," Mason asserted that it was the claim of "a conqueror" restricted by "no new laws."

251. Emphasis added. For the above speeches, *CD 1628* 3: 494–495; cf. 496–497, 501–503, 505, 506–507.

252. Ibid., 495. Phelips, Eliot, and Sir Nathaniel Rich reportedly spoke after Coke, but all to the same effect. Sir Richard Grosvenor's diary gives the phrase attributed to the source known as "Proceedings and Debates" to Rich ("Impossible to qualify this," 503), and other sources attribute the phrase quoted to Pym or Hugh or John Pyne; see the editors' comment (supporting the attribution to Pym) at 494n15. It may be that Rich spoke the phrase more fully recorded as Coke's, or that Grosvenor, in the heat of the scribal moment, misapprehended it; it may be that he merely echoed Coke (all sources agree that he spoke afterwards). Accounts and separates of the debates that circulated at the time must be used with caution, since, apart from their second-hand provenance, the tendency to attribute good lines to popular actors in published texts cannot be overlooked. Such problems have led John Morrill and others to question the use of parliamentary source materials as such. Without recapitulating the debate, one may say that the idea of a perfect record is itself an illusion, and that if Tudor-Stuart historians require such records there will be very little parliamentary history of the period.

253. Ibid., 494.

254. Ibid., 213; *LP 1628*, 489; Frances H. Relf, ed., *Notes of the Debates in the House of Lords, 1621–1628* (London: Camden Society, 3rd ser., Vol. 42, 1929), 192. Alford, characteristically, had protested the Easter sitting as a violation of the Commons' privileges.

255. Johnson et al., eds., *CD 1628* 3: 512–513, 515–516, 517–518, 520, 531, 541. The Commons' statement referred to, delivered by their Speaker, Sir John Finch, at a conference of the houses on May 3, is at 3: 254.

256. Ibid., 527; cf. 536, 539, 549.

257. Ibid., 529; cf. 536, 540, 544, 550.

258. Ibid., 533.

259. Gardiner, *History of England . . . 1603–1642*, 6: 309–310; *PP 1628* 6: 202, 212.

260. Jess Stoddart Flemion estimated that the Court party in the Upper House numbered 84 of the 124 lords temporal and spiritual, including proxies, whereas the "opposition" amounted no more than two dozen ("The Struggle for the Petition of Right in the House of Lords: A Study of an Opposition Party Victory," in Clyve Jones and David Lewis Jones, eds., *Peers, Politics and Power: The House of Lords, 1603–1911* [London and Ronceverte: The Hambledon Press, 1986], 31–48, at 33n9.) Flemion offers no data to support this assertion, nor any list of peers on either side. The argument of her essay is that the opposition gradually won over an amorphous middle group of lords by adroit parliamentary maneuvering, superior argument, and close collaboration with the Commons' leadership. Obviously, the numbers don't add up unless one assumes that a substantial portion of the Court party was detached and ultimately recruited to the opposition. It seems likelier that the core of the Court party, such as the earls of Manchester and Dorset, were a much smaller group, and that many of the peers, such as Pembroke, had diverse and multiple interests that swayed them now one way and now another despite a nominal or politic allegiance to the crown position. The fluidity and frequent confusion of the proceedings in the Upper House over the decisive seven-week period of debate (April 9–May 26) suggests that the Lords felt and responded to many contradictory currents, not the least of which was the desire to maintain the institutional coherence of Parliament and the pressure of public opinion. The concept of the "middle group," first invoked by J. H. Hexter and Valerie Pearl to explain the dynamics of the Long Parliament and then by Christopher Thompson in dealing with the parliaments of the 1620s, appears to me an exhausted one. We need a more flexible account of Stuart political praxis, rather than one that starts from bean-counting. For an extreme example of the latter procedure, see John R. MacCormack, *Revolutionary Politics in the Long Parliament* (Cambridge: Harvard University Press, 1973).

261. Charles raised four new members to the peerage in mid-April in an evident bid to strengthen the Court party in the Lords. One of them, Lord Howard of Escrick, was a nephew of Buckingham's by marriage. The addition of the new peers may have been part of what Joseph Mead (Mede) had in mind when he described "the court faction" in the Lords as "numerous and increasing" on May 3 (Birch, ed., *The Court and Times of Charles the First*, op. cit., 1: 351), but they were also, arguably, a sign of royal insecurity. It is not clear that the elevation of yet another kinsman of Buckingham's would dispose the Lords as a whole more favorably to him, so that the net effect of Charles' maneuver may well have been negative. Lord Howard of Escrick sided with Parliament during the civil war, was one of the handful of peers to support the regicide, and served the Commonwealth: another cautionary note for the bean-counters.

262. One of these, a change in the description of the oaths imposed during the collection of the Forced Loan as "not warrantable by the laws and statutes of this kingdom" instead of "unlawful," was an effort to clear the lords involved in them, both on and off the Council, of culpable wrongdoing. This was not immediately agreed to by the Commons (*CD 1628* 3: 493–494, 497–499, 503–505, 507–508), who, apparently on Selden's motion, at first ordered the original wording to stand. Coke expressed puzzlement at the Lords' request (suspicion of which was doubtless fanned by the fact that Coventry and Heath supported it), but Eliot, who was apparently in the know, declared it to be "in respect of some great officers that may be liable to this word or some other" (505). The concession may well have swayed some votes in the Upper House on behalf of the Petition, and it also served as a face-saving gesture, for the Lords won no other significant revision in the body of the text of the many they had proposed. With this alteration, they could claim authorship of at least one clause in the final product (the language adopted was actually Heath's).

263. Ibid., 3: 533.

264. Ibid., 523, 526, 528 ("a long passionate speech").

265. Keeler et al., eds., *LP 1628*, 46–48. There appear to have been several meetings with the judges between May 26 and 31, and there are copies in other hands as well, including Heath's. Charles maintained that he had proceeded with the advice and cooperation of the Privy Council, and there may have been negotiation between the judges and the legal officers on the text of the answers. It is therefore quite possible that the text in the King's script was an amended version of a verbal consultation that passed back and forth among several hands before receiving final form.

266. Keeler et al., eds., *LP 1628*, 576 (*LJ* 3: 839).

267. Wallace Notestein and Frances Helen Relf, eds., *Commons Debates for 1629* (Minneapolis: University of Minnesota Research Publications in the Social Sciences, 10 [1921]), 4. J. P. Kenyon notes that "There was some doubt at the time [of the Petition's acceptance], and there still is, precisely what the petition was, and whether it was a statute, equivalent to a statute, or superior to one" (Kenyon, ed., *The Stuart Constitution: Documents and Commentary*, 2nd ed. [Cambridge: Cambridge University Press, 1986], 52–53). No one, however, at least on the parliamentary side, took it as inferior to a statute. It was enrolled as such, and it was popularly cited during the Personal Rule, often alongside Magna Carta (Sommerville, *Politics and Ideology*, 213–214; Esther S. Cope, *Politics Without Parliaments 1629–1640* [London: Allen and Unwin, 1987], 75, 96; Maija Jansson, ed., *Two Diaries of the Long Parliament* [Gloucester: Alan Sutton; New York: St. Martin's Press, 1984], 17). In the sense that it was deliberately devised as a statement of fundamental law, it is tempting to see the Petition as a kind of super–statute, and the House of Commons gave great prominence to its violation in the Grand Remonstrance; but it must be remembered that, for the common lawyers, a statute was the ultimate sovereign act, and nothing could exceed it. For a general discussion, see L. J. Reeve, "The Legal Status of the Petition of Right," *HJ* 29 (1986): 257–277, and for the role of the common lawyers in drafting the Petition, Linda S. Popofsky, "Habeas Corpus and the Liberty of the Subject: Legal Arguments for the Petition of Right in the Parliament of 1628," *The Historian* 41 (1979): 257–275.

268. Keeler et al., eds., *CD 1628* 4: 68.

269. Ibid., 182.

270. London, 1628; see *CD 1628* 4: 182n28.

271. Keeler et al., eds., *LP 1628*, 597.

272. Ibid.

273. Keeler et al., eds., *CD 1628* 4: 182; cf. 185: "In a doubtful thing interpretation goes always for the King. But we are here free, there is no doubtfulness nor shadow of ambiguity."

274. Relf, *Notes of Debates*, 170, cited by Elizabeth Read Foster, "Petitions and the Petition of Right," *JBS* 14 (1974): 21–45, at 25. Foster, agreeing with the King, says that "Charles' first answer [to the Petition] was as close to medieval custom as his second." Contemporaries, however, did not agree.

275. As Sir Thomas Myddleton's London agent John Edwards reported, parliamentary fasts and communions were coordinated with those of the London and Westminster churches (*PP 1628*, 205). The King's second answer underwent changes as it was publicly disseminated, too: Sir Francis Nethersole, an MP, reported it to Elizabeth of Bohemia as *"Droit soit fait selon qu'il est desire"* (195).

276. Keeler et al., eds., *LP 1628*, 597; *CD 1628* 4: 480–481; cf. 4: 182, 185, 193, 482, 483–484; *LP 1628* 5: 722–723.

277. *LP 1628*, 597.

278. Ibid., 596.

279. Elizabeth Read Foster, "Printing the Petition of Right," *HLQ* 38 (1974): 81–83; *LP 1628*, 661 (the Lords' order to enroll the Petition of Right with other statutes on the Parliament Roll); Notestein and Relf, eds., *CD 1629*, 4, 5–6, 8–9, 112. For Elsyng's own account, see Bodleian Library Carte MS. 200, fols. 2–50v. Nethersole observed that the printed edition was simply entitled "The Petition" rather than "The Petition of Right,"

suggesting to him not only an effort to deny the Petition the status of a statute but to sow confusion as to whether the petition was of right (i.e., an agreed declaration of law) or of grace (a grant contingent on the pleasure of the King): *PP 1628*, 199.

280. Article 11 of the Grand Remonstrance remembered the episode with special bitterness thirteen years later: "The Petition of Right, which was granted in full Parliament, blasted, with an illegal declaration to make it destructive to itself, to the power of Parliament, to the liberty of the subject, and to that purpose printed with it, and the Petition made of no use . . . " (Gardiner, ed., *CDPR*, 209). The falsification of the Petition raised the specter of the alteration, removal, or destruction of other parts of the statutory record, and thus of the rewriting of the English constitution. With the sealing of other libraries such as Coke's and Cotton's after 1629, the government could plausibly be seen as engaged in such a project.

281. Russell, *PEP*, 363–368 (quote at 363); White, *Sir Edward Coke and the Grievances of the Commonwealth*, 231–234.

282. Relf, ed., *Notes of Debates*, 127; Russell, *PEP*, 365. Cf. Bristol's comment in the same debate: "The matter of the question is the power of the king legally, not his Majesty's power regally" (*LP 1628* 5: 329).

283. Gardiner, ed., *CDPR*, 66–70.

284. Johnson et al., eds., *CD 1628* 2: 151; cf. 149.

285. Ibid., 200; cf. 191.

286. Ibid., 150, 57; cf. 67.

287. Ibid., 2: 212, 218. Coke played on such analogies himself: before one speech he declared that not he but the laws were about to speak, an appropriation of James I's description of himself as *lex loquens*.

288. For a more extended discussion of the common lawyers' ethos in the early seventeenth century, with particular reference to the views of Coke, see Alan Cromartie, "The Constitutionalist Revolution: The Transformation of Political Culture in Early Stuart England," *P&P* 163 (1999): 76–120, and his *The Constitutionalist Revolution*, op. cit.

289. Johnson et al., eds., *CD 1628* 3: 468; 4: 75–76, 119.

290. *DNB*; *ODNB*. Cosin, a protégé of Neile, was prebendary, and, after the Restoration, Bishop of Durham.

291. Burgess, Vicar of Whitney, was accused of "blasphemous speeches," including a reference (which he denied) to "Puritan knaves"; Jackson, a colleague of Montagu's and a member of Neile's circle, was examined for his *Commentaries on the Apostles' Creed*; on his Arminianism, see Tyacke, *Anti-Calvinism*, 66–67, 159–160 (and see also the *DNB* and *ODNB*).

292. An impeachment had been begun against Montagu in 1626, led by Pym, but it was cut short by the dissolution of Parliament. For discussion see Tyacke, *Anti-Calvinism*, 153–157, and Tite, *Impeachment and Judicature*, 207–211.

293. Keeler et al., eds., *CD 1628* 4: 103–110, at 104, 105.

294. For an overview of *jure divino* episcopacy in the early seventeenth century, see William M. Lamont, *Godly Rule: Politics and Religion, 1603–1660* (London: Macmillan, 1969), chapter 3; Sommerville, *Politics and Ideology*, chapter 6; Tyacke, *Anti-Calvinists*, passim; see also Kenneth Fincham, *Prelate as Pastor: The Episcopate of James I* (Oxford: The Clarendon Press, 1990), and the essays in Fincham, ed., *The Early Stuart Church* (Basingstoke and London: Macmillan, 1993).

295. Nicholas Tyacke suggests that there is no "direct evidence" that either Sibthorpe or Mainwaring were doctrinally Arminian, presumably meaning confessional evidence (*Anti-Calvinists*, 159). It seems to me that the political Arminianism of positing a direct relationship between one's acts as a subject and one's prospects in the afterlife comes close enough. Certainly it did for the MPs of 1628.

296. By Sir Edward Coke, *CD 1628* 4: 119.

297. Ibid., 203, 117, 125, 120, 248.

298. Ibid., 120; cf. 125, 130, 132. The Protestation of 1621 was called for in this debate. For Sherland, who had been one of the managers of Buckingham's impeachment in 1626, see *BDBR* 3: 167; *ODNB*.

299. Of modern commentators, Russell, *PEP*, 378–382, and Reeve, *Charles I and the Road to Personal Rule*, 24–31, treat it most fully.

300. Russell, 380; Hillel Schwarz, "Arminianism and the English Parliament, 1624–1629," *JBS* 12 (1973): 41–68, at 66.

301. There was no formal effort to ask the Lords to join in the Remonstrance, which time did not appear to permit. Bristol, however, moved that the Upper House make a remonstrance of its own to apprise Charles of "the true state of his kingdom." The earls of Huntingdon and Essex, as well as Archbishop Abbot, were among the motion's supporters, and a subcommittee was agreed upon in principle to draft it on June 6: *LP 1628*, 587–588, 591–592; Relf, *Notes of Debates in the House of Lords*, 214–216. The next day brought the King's satisfactory answer to the Petition of Right, and there is no record of any further proceeding in the matter.

302. Keeler et al., eds., *CD 1628* 4: 311–318.

303. Ibid., 315.

304. Ibid., 244. Eliot said that, contrary to Charles' "good thoughts," the horse might still be brought "to his prejudice and the prejudice of the kingdom" —as clear an accusation that the King had been beguiled as one could wish.

305. For the brutal methods of raising troops in this period and the appalling standards of their treatment, see Stephen J. Stearns, "Conscription and English Society in the 1620s," *JBS* 11 (1972): 1–23.

306. On Felton's death (and Lambe's), see Holstun, *Ehud's Dagger*, chapter 5; Lockyer, *Buckingham*, 451–454; and Alastair Bellany, *The Death of a Favourite* (Manchester University Press, forthcoming). It has been noted that both Eliot and Felton were clients of Buckingham, and the fact that Felton was imprisoned in the very room where Eliot had once been held suggests that some contemporaries took the same point as well. Though very different in their talents and fortunes, the two men were not far removed in social status; the Earl of Arundel, a kinsman, visited Felton in the Tower and paid his last expenses. Arundel's very public gesture—his wife and his son, Lord Maltrevers, accompanied him—made its own point, not only of family solidarity but of the limits of deference, the reciprocal obligation on which it depended, and the regime of honor that was its essential condition. Buckingham's position made a mockery of honor, for his birth was no better than Eliot's or Felton's, and certainly inferior to Arundel's; his monopoly of patronage crowned and compounded the offense; his abuse of it (he had publicly insulted Felton) was a family disgrace that could not be borne without dishonor. When Felton acknowledged his private grievance as a motive for his act as well as the parliamentary Remonstrance, he was offering not a separate justification for it but an interconnected one. The same affront that had been given the realm had been given him personally, and the private honor that compelled him to seek his own redress was bound up with his sense of his duty as a patriot. Arundel, in discharging his duty to a kinsman, thus demonstrated the proper obligation of a patron and made restitution of Felton's honor. He also thereby embraced Felton's grievance if not his act, and with it the ideological commitment Felton had made to the Remonstrance.

307. *Memoirs of the Life of Colonel Hutchinson*, cited in Holstun, 156.

308. Keeler et al., eds., *PP 1628*, 52–56, at 55.

3098. *CD 1628* 4: 352, 482.

310. For Mainwaring's promotions and subsequent career, see Snapp, op. cit., 230–231. His pardon was reversed by order of Parliament in 1641.

311. Birch, ed., *The Court and Times of Charles the First*, 1: 372, 374–375; Reeve, *Charles I and the Road to Personal Rule*, 33.

312. *CD 1628* 4: 448.

313. For the 1625 bill, see the lucid discussion in Russell, *PEP*, 227–229; *CD 1628* 4: 447, 405 (cf. 413–414).

314. *CD 1628* 4: 393.
315. Ibid., 417, 404n13; *PP 1628,* 119, 198.
316. *CD 1628* 4: 449.
317. Ibid., 449, 314.
318. Russell, *PEP,* 229.
319. Had James I consistently claimed a similar unconditioned authority, it might be argued that Charles was doing no more than his father had. But James had invited Parliament to consider impositions in settling the Great Contract (Foster, ed., *PP 1610* 1: 88–89, 106, 254; 2: 146), and although he no doubt came to regret this he had thereby recognized a legitimate parliamentary interest in the matter. Charles seems to have wished to annul this concession, and to reduce Parliament's interest in the royal fisc solely to its "free" gift of subsidies—a gift which, if not bestowed, would simply be exacted by other means. Such a supposition explains not only why a comprehensive reform of the customs failed in 1625, but also why the stopgap bill in the same session to grant Tonnage and Poundage on a temporary basis died as well. The bill was given a first reading in the Lords, who then, as Russell puts it, "left it to fall asleep." The implication is that the Lords found the bill irregular. Perhaps they did, and perhaps they were told to proceed no further: there is no evidence either way. What is certain is that Charles could have had the bill if he had wished it. A new bill was introduced in 1626, classed as a subsidy bill and tied to the fixing of rates (*PP 1626* 2: 279, 357; 3: 387). Charles, who had ordered the collection of Tonnage and Poundage by privy seal warrant, studiously ignored its progress, until at last the merchant John Rolle, member for Callington, moved a petition to ascertain whether the King would be willing to accept a fixed book of rates and "bind the crown" as his father had offered to do (3: 397). Charles made no response, and Parliament was dissolved a week later.
320. Keeler et al., eds., *CD 1628* 4: 182, 482.
321. Gardiner, *CDPR,* 73.
322. On Wentworth's adherence to the crown, see Perez Zagorin, "Did Wentworth Change Sides?", *EHR* 101 (1986): 149–163, and Richard Cust, "Wentworth's 'Change of Sides' in the 1620s," in Merritt, ed., *The Political World of Thomas Wentworth,* 63–80. On his subsequent role in formulating the politics of the Personal Rule, see idem, Anthony Milton, "Thomas Wentworth and the Political Thought of the Personal Rule," 133–156. See also Reeve's comment, *Charles I and the Road to Personal Rule,* 188.
323. Lindsay Boynton, *The Elizabethan Militia, 1558–1638* (London: Routledge and Kegan Paul; Toronto: University of Toronto Press, 1964). The isolation of the peers is graphically illustrated by the treatment meted out to the Earl of Essex, a loan resister and the son of the Elizabethan favorite. Essex had received early promotion at court— he had been a standard-bearer at Charles I's coronation, and distinguished himself, as his father had done, at Cadiz—but when he refused the loan he was dismissed from his deputy lieutenancy by the King himself, who in the presence of others declared that he was "a willfull younge man." Such shaming of a peer of the realm (Essex was nine years Charles' senior) was unprecedented, and deeply wounding (Vernon F. Snow, *Essex the Rebel* [Lincoln: University of Nebraska Press, 1970]; idem, "Essex and the Aristocratic Opposition to the Early Stuarts," *JMH* 32 (1960): 224–233; Cust, *The Forced Loan and English Politics,* 109).
324. Lois G. Schwoerer, *"No Standing Armies!" The Antiarmy Ideology in Seventeenth-Century England* (Baltimore: The Johns Hopkins Press, 1974), chapter 1.
325. For the episode, *PP 1626* 3: 350, 353–354, 357–360. Only fragments of direct quotation from More's speech survive, but the phrase cited here is given by two sources, Sir John Finch and Sir William Herbert.
326. Russell, *PEP,* 395–396.
327. Ibid., 395.
328. Notestein and Relf, eds., *CD 1629,* 10–11. See also the discussion in Linda S. Popofsky, "The Crisis over Tonnage and Poundage in Parliament in 1629," *P&P* 126 (1990): 44–75.

329. Ibid., 8, 10.

330. Ibid., 4–6.

331. I.e., Heath.

332. *CD 1629*, 5, 112, 113. Charles had called upon the Commons again to pass a bill of Tonnage and Poundage.

333. Ibid., 94.

334. England was to face a similar situation in 1688, with Parliament out of session and Irish troops camped above London. The only solution was to call upon a foreign liberator, William of Orange, who was James II's son-in-law. No such savior was available in 1629.

335. *CD 1629*, 12–13. The variant reading of "countries" for "country" makes more sense in the context of the Thirty Years' War.

336. Ibid., 16; 18–19.

337. Ibid., 65–70.

338. Ibid., 104; cf. 170, 241, 259. Carleton, the confidant of Elizabeth of Bohemia and a member of the godly Barrington circle, was a particularly unlikely agent for the Antichrist.

339. Ibid., 91–92, 167–168, 236–237. Sir John Coke delivered the King's comments.

340. Phelips had recalled the well–worn words of the Apology yet again earlier in the day's debate (*CD 1629*, 230).

341. Ibid., 169, 238.

342. The legal fiction of the king's two bodies, politic and natural, had been gradually extended to cover treasons, a usurpation of his authority anywhere in his kingdom(s) being construed as an attack on his person (see D. Alan Orr, *Treason and the State: Law, Politics, and Ideology in the English Civil War* [Cambridge: Cambridge University Press, 2002]). *Calvin's Case* had established the principle that allegiance to the person of the king transcended the difference of municipal laws between his kingdoms, a position Sir Edward Coke upheld. Neither of these positions entitled the king to rule outside the law. James I had contended that monarchical power was inherently above (not outside) the law because the king was the original lawgiver, and that this necessarily made him its final interpreter. This claim was strenuously resisted by the common lawyers, and was at odds with received descriptions of the constitution such as Sir Thomas Smith's, which tied the laws to the king's politic capacity alone. Charles made no such theoretical claims and typically proceeded only after judicial consultation, but his personalist claim that his command alone shielded his officers was in effect one that he could set aside the law, or, more troubling yet, that such commands *were* the law. This was confused because Charles alternately took the position that his collection of Tonnage and Poundage was an act of necessity and one of right, leaving the source of the authority he claimed in doubt. From either point of view, however, his claim was incompatible with the prevailing common law notion that the king's powers, even in extraordinary circumstances, were circumscribed by law.

343. What Charles had done on February 23 was to revert to his position of the previous June 26, when he declared that Tonnage and Poundage was a flower of the crown. This in turn was a retraction of the pledge he had taken on June 7 in accepting the Petition of Right to "let right be done as is desired." Charles could plead necessity in taking Tonnage and Poundage without parliamentary consent or he could claim prerogative right, but not both. In asserting both by turns he made an accommodation impossible.

344. Notestein and Relf, eds., *CD 1629*, 169.

345. As we have seen, Selden yielded to royal pressure in the 1630s and put his pen at the service of the crown. In 1642, however, he politely but firmly declined an invitation from the Marquis of Hertford to join the King's camp, and his speeches, actions, and writings in the Long Parliament reflect the commitment he had made in 1628–1629; see Richard Tuck, "'The Ancient Law of Freedom': John Selden and the Civil War," in John Morrill, ed., *Reactions to the English Civil War, 1642–1649* (London: Methuen, 1982), 137–161. Tuck, citing the *Table Talk*, notes that Selden does allow for

absolutism where it has been contractually agreed upon in advance. This accords with the emphasis on the historical basis of all political, honorific, and tributary claims in Selden's work. Since, however, absolutism (like all other forms of government) could only be regarded as historically contingent, and since Selden read the English constitution unambiguously as a mixed and limited monarchy, the prohibition on a king as the sole arbiter of his acts was strictly enjoined. Selden insisted on this even in areas normally confided to the king's discretion, as in the case of the militia in 1642. In a system of limited government there could be no unaccountable power as such, a prohibition that, within the contract, *was* absolute. Thus, what looks superficially like a Hobbesian position is in fact an anti-Hobbesian one.

346. *CD 1629*, 168–169, 238. Price was challenged by Secretary Coke for his remark.

347. Russell, *PEP*, 408–409; Christopher Thompson, "The Divided Leadership of the House of Commons in 1629," in Sharpe, ed., *Faction and Parliament*, 245–284.

348. *CJ* 1: 921, which cites Coke's "great age" as the reason for his absence. The House nonetheless sent for him (*CD 1629*, 58). We may assume it would have responded to any hint of duress. John Reeve comments suggestively on the silence of the Lords in 1629 (*Charles I and the Road to Personal Rule*), 80–81.

349. *CSPV 1628–1629*, 579–580; *CD 1629*, 104, 170, 241–242, 259–260.

350. *CD 1629*, 101–102.

351. Gardiner, ed., *CDPR*, 83–99; quotation at 93.

352. Ibid., 96.

353. J. O. Halliwell, ed., *The Autobiography and Correspondence of Sir Simonds D'Ewes*, 2 vols. (London: R. Bentley, 1845), 1: 402. Charles again distinguished between loyal and disloyal MPs in his proclamation for suppressing false rumors about the late Parliament (Larkin, *Stuart Royal Proclamations* 2: 226–228).

354. Esther S. Cope, "Public Images of Parliament during Its Absence," *Legislative Studies Quarterly* 7 (1982): 221–234; idem, *Politics without Parliaments, 1629–1640*, op. cit.; Kevin Sharpe, *The Personal Rule of Charles I*.

355. *CSPV 1628–1629*, 584.

356. Eliot, Selden, Coryton, Denzil Holles, Sir Peter Hayman, Sir Miles Hobart, Walter Long, and Benjamin Valentine, all of whom had been involved in the events of March 2, were imprisoned. Coryton and Hayman made submissions, and, with the intercession of Pembroke and Viscount Dorchester, secured their release although not their freedom. Eliot died in the Tower in 1632, Parliament's first martyr. Strode and Valentine remained in prison until 1640. The legal proceedings against Eliot, Selden, and their colleagues are detailed in L. J. Reeve, "The Arguments in King's Bench Concerning the Imprisonment of John Selden and Other Members of the House of Commons," *JBS* 25 (1986): 264–287; see also his *Charles I and the Road to Personal Rule*, chapter 5. The trial of the imprisoned members was the cause célèbre of 1629, and it was a cause not forgotten; Russell noted that Holles, Long, and Strode "constituted a sort of Martyrs Corner in the House of Commons" in 1642 (Conrad Russell, *The Causes of the English Civil War*, op. cit., 155).

357. An Act to Prevent Inconvenience which May Happen by the Untimely Adjourning, Proroguing, or Dissolving This Present Parliament, 17 Car. I, c. 7, *SR* 5: 103; Gardiner, ed., *CDPR*, 158–159.

358. *Englands reioycing for the Parliaments returne* (London, 1641), 4.

359. *Englands Glory in Her Royall King and Honourable Assembly in the high Court of Parliament* (London, 1641), sig. B.

360. Samuel Fairclough, *The Trovblers Trovbled, or Achan Condemned, and Executed* (London, 1641), 30; Richard Ward, *The Principall Duty of Parliament-Men* (London, 1641), 19.

361. On the genesis of the fast sermons and their antecedents, see John F. Wilson, *Pulpit in Parliament: Puritanism during the English Civil Wars, 1640–1648* (Princeton: Princeton University Press, 1969); see also H. R. Trevor-Roper, "The Fast Sermons of the Long Parliament," in his *Religion, the Reformation and Social Change* (London: Macmillan, 1967), 294–344; and cf. Christopher Durston, "'For the Better Humiliation of

the People': Public Days of Fasting and Thanksgiving during the English Revolution," *The Seventeenth Century* 7 (1992): 129–149. Queen Elizabeth had refused to permit a fast sermon at the opening of Parliament in 1581, but the parliaments of the 1620s had established them, and in 1629 a grudging Charles I permitted the Commons to spend an entire day, February 18, to hear sermons by three ministers. This surely indicated the temper of the House, but regular sermons (and occasional ones after great events) were only institutionalized with the Long Parliament. Wilson distinguishes eight categories of sermons preached to the Long Parliament, of which the monthly fast sermons were only one (43–52).

362. *Englands Glory*, sig. B.

363. William Bridge, *Babylons Downfall* (London, 1641), 21, 22. On Bridge, see *BDBR* 1: 99–100; *ODNB*.

364. Ibid., 22, 23.

365. Edmund Calamy, *Englands Looking-Glasse* (London, 1642), 39, 27–28.

366. Ibid., 45.

367. Ibid., 46.

368. Cornelius Burges, *The Necessity and Benefit of Washing the Heart* (London, 1642), 37.

369. Stephen Marshall, *Threnodia: The Churches Lamentation for The Good man His Losse* (London, 1644), 34–35.

370. John Marston, *A Sermon Preached at St. Margarets in Westminster on Sunday the Sixt of February* (London, 1642), 5; Samuel Fawcet, *A Seasonable Sermon For These Trovblesome Times* (London, 1641), 11; J. L., *Englands Doxologie* (London, 1641), 9.

371. Richard Ward, *The Principall Duty of Parliament-Men* (London, 1641), 21.

372. Jeremiah Burroughs, *The glorious Name of God* (London, 1643), 35; idem, *A Vindication of Psalme 105.15 . . . from some false Glosses lately obtruded on it by Royallists* (London, 1642), sig. A2v. Cf. the fuller discussion of this point in my "Breaking the Vessels: The Desacralization of Monarchy in Early Modern England," *SCJ* 29 (1998): 757–778.

373. *The Hellish Parliament Being a Counter-Parliament To This in England* (London, 1641); John Brandon, *The Oxonian Antipodes, Or, The Oxford Anty-Parliament* (London, 1644), 4. The nomenclature of civil war Separatist groups is discussed in Tolmie, *The Triumph of the Saints*, especially 14–27, and chapters 2 and 3.

374. Brandon, 30–31.

375. Francis White, *The Copy of a Letter* (London, 1647), 5.

376. For a further discussion of this see "Breaking the Vessels," 774–778. Traditional discourse lingered, of course, after 1660, and in France the monarchy remained officially sacred until the Revolution of 1789, as in Russia until 1917. For France, see Jeffrey W. Merrick, *The Desacralization of the French Monarchy in the Eighteenth Century* (Baton Rouge: Louisiana State University Press, 1990), and Susan Dunn, *The Deaths of Louis XVI: Regicide and the French Political Imagination* (Princeton: Princeton University Press, 1994).

Index

Abbot, George, Archbishop of Canterbury, 81, 221, 311, 630, 641, 696, 793 n300

Abbott, L. W., 291

Absolutism, concept of, 225, 322–323, 327–328, 333, 336, 352, 564ff, 591–592; representations of, 461, 464, 470, 476–477; Jacobean and Caroline compared, 656–657; defenders of, 665–666; and clericalism, 670

Act Abolishing Diversity of Opinions, 1539 (Six Articles), 489–492, 498, 506, 507

Act Against Peter's Pence, 486

Act Extinguishing the Authority of the Bishop of Rome (1536), 282, 485

Act for the Queen's Regal Power (1554), 513

Act for the Surety of the Queen's Most Royal Person (1585), 539

Act in Restraint of Appeals (1533), 336, 484–485

Act of Appeals (1533), 244

Act of Supremacy (1534): 200, 282, 473, 486; of 1559: 94, 301, 516–519, 522

Act of Uniformity (1559), 94, 517–519

Act to Prevent . . . Dissolving This Present Parliament (1641), 700, 796 n356

Adair, Edward, 488, 489, 492

Adams, Thomas, 218

Adiaphora, 67, 72, 79; Hooker's conception of, 96

Admonition controversy, 69, 85; Second Admonition, quoted, 195; and Presbyterianism, 498, 499, 522–525; as propaganda, 499; as petition, 522–526; as exercise in conscience, 531, 535; and Thomas Scott, 621

Aglionby, Edward, 526, 748 n25

Agnew, Jean-Christophe, 752 n86

Agrippa, Cornelius, 374

Ainsworth, Henry, 149, 150, 156–160, 163, 165, 723 n138, 724 n152

Alençon, François Hercule, Duke of, 43, 52, 388

Alford, Edward, 504–506, 604, 606, 611, 614, 631, 649–651, 657, 762 n75, 789 n253

Alford, Francis, 496

Allen, J. W., 743 n129

Allen, William, 108–109, 117, 120

Alphabetical Bills, 521

Alsop, James, 513

Alsted, Johann Heinrich, 218, 219–220

Alston, L., 225

Altman, Joel, 372

Alva, Fernando Álvarez de Tolédo y Pimental, Duke of, 115

Ambrose, Bishop of Milan, 73

Ames, William, 166

Amsterdam, Ancient Church of, 155–156

Anabaptism, 51,128, 129, 143, 161, 162, 168–170, 174, 177, 178, 183, 190, 364, 509

Ancient constitution, the, 244, 268, 313ff, 350, 352, 586ff, 636, 667–668, 683; 691, 741 n104

Andrewes, Lancelot, 100, 143, 165, 197

Anglican church, see Church of England

Anglo-Scottish Union, 29, 249, 317ff, 450, 453, 483–484, 502, 513, 599–600, 650, 743 n118

Anna of Denmark, Queen of England, 386, 456, 458–459, 755 n147

331–333, 336, 337, 347–348, 484–487, 518; regnal crises of, 252–253, 264, 501, 538ff; king's two bodies and, 10, 293–294, 320–322, 398, 452, 453, 457, 463, 511, 688, 695, 776 n87, 795 n341; and the law, 279, 282ff; 313ff; as fount of justice, 293; royal style of, 318–320, 331–332, 501, 565; allegiance and, 323–325; represented on stage, 396ff; and "cease of majesty," 405, 432; Court and, 469–470; finances of, 491, 493, 495, 569, 574, 591, 599, 604, 607–610, 620, 641–643, 650, 656, 677ff; female rule and, 508ff; interregnum of, 540–542; role in Parliament, 476–479, 551–552, 567, 583, 619; tyranny and, 437, 566; debated in Parliament, 652ff; as property right, 656–657; monopoly of force, 682–684; desacralized, 704, 706, 797 n375; devolution of, 767 n157. *See also* Absolute prerogative; Absolutism; Forced Loan; Great Contract; *Jure divino*; King's Evil; King in Parliament; Law; Royal coronations; Royal prerogative; Tyranny
Monopolies, 111, 465–466, 471, 501, 504, 572, 598–599, 609, 610, 614–615, 627
Montagu, James, Bishop of Winchester, 566
Montagu, Richard, Bishop of Chichester, 221, 631, 642, 669, 677, 679, 685, 692, 693, 792 nn290 and 291
Morality plays, 356, 367, 368, 373
More, George, 684, 794 n324
More, William, 175
More, Sir Thomas, 23–25, 28, 38, 39, 117, 234, 254, 272, 274, 281, 393, 439, 583, 614, 766 n143
Morice, James, 495, 554, 558
Morrill, John, 789 n251
Munday, Anthony, 388–391
Murton, John, 163, 164
"Mutabilitie," concept of, 224, 236, 252
Myddleton, Sir Thomas, 791 n274
Mystery plays, 357, 364, 385, 388

Napier, John, 206, 215, 219
Naunton, Sir Robert, 17
Neale, Sir John E., 515, 526, 540, 547, 768–769 n185
Neile, Richard, Bishop of Lichfield, 311, 606–607, 651, 677, 792 n290
Nethersole, Sir Francis, 505, 788 n237, 791 n274, 791–792 n278

Neville, Christopher, 778 n107
New Model Army, 706
Nichols, Josias, 128–129, 134, 143
Niclaes, Henrik, 173
Nicodemism, 106, 175
Nicoll, John, 454
Nineteen Propositions, the, 528
Nixon, Richard M., 694
Nobility: domestication of, 7, 20–21, 26, 31, 32, 585, 633, 682–684; and patronage, 33; Cotton's view of, 49; religious divisions of, 81, 82, 108; Camden on, 246; Selden on, 331ff; figured in *King Johan*, 358–363; and Mary, 365; in *Edward II*, 406ff; in *Richard II*, 417ff; and baronets, 600, 610; resentment of Buckingham, 610, 615; Charles I's appeal to, 699; numbers of, 782 n156. *See also* House of Lords
Norbrook, David, 37
Norfolk, Thomas Howard, Duke of, 187, 188, 356
Norman Yoke, the, 284, 330
Northampton, Henry Howard, Earl of, 44, 437, 603, 776 n87
Northern Rebellion [Rising], 76, 115, 211
Norton, Bonham, 665
Norton, Thomas, 369, 495, 496, 498, 521, 526, 537, 545, 554, 565
Notestein, Wallace, 579, 583–584, 600, 603
Nottingham, Charles Howard, Earl of, 606, 634
Novatus, 129
Nowell, Alexander, 237
Noy, William, 463, 465, 466, 581, 660, 694, 773 n41, 788 n237

Oath of Allegiance, 327
Oath of Supremacy, 60–61, 352
Oaths, 12; and Catholics, 123; and the godly, 83, 126; and family of Love, 176; *ex officio*, 300–301, 306; royal oaths, 313, 353; jeopardized by Anglo-Scottish Union, 318; Bond of Association, 538, 539
Occasional conformity, 112, 115, 119
Ogilvie, Sir Charles, 269
Oldcastle, Sir John, 199
Olivares, Gaspar de Guzman, Count of, 626, 631
Onslow, Richard, 478, 605
Orality, 198
Order of Prophecy at Norwich, The, 70, 71

The Discourse of Legitimacy in Early Modern England is a study of the structures of authority in England between the beginning of the English Reformation in 1529 and the outbreak of the civil war of the 1640s. These structures, both secular and sacred, were profoundly affected by the creation of a national Protestant church governed by the crown; by the emerging sense of national consciousness and providential destiny that followed in its wake; by the development of a legal culture that defined and sometimes contested the parameters of authority; by an urban stage that articulated a new civic culture and reflected broad political, social, and religious tensions; and by the growing sophistication and assertiveness of Parliament, the capstone both of elite interest and popular legitimacy, and ultimately the site of resistance to claims of unfettered royal and ecclesiastical power. Together, these elements constituted the discourse of legitimacy through which the daily transactions of power in Tudor and early Stuart England were disputed, mediated, and sometimes resisted. They both expressed and contained the tensions of a rapidly changing society, and were finally the theaters on which its irreconcilable conflicts were enacted as social and political consensus broke down. *The Discourse of Legitimacy* presents a wide-ranging, synoptic view of England's political culture and its conflicts in the crucial period between its two greatest revolutions.